The Standard Israelite National Torah

The Ancient Hebrew Torah

Scribed by YAHUtsadeqnu

𐤁𐤓𐤀𐤔𐤉𐤕.𐤁𐤓𐤀.𐤀𐤋𐤄𐤉𐤌.𐤀𐤕.
𐤄𐤔𐤌𐤉𐤌.𐤅𐤀𐤕.𐤄𐤀𐤓𐤑|

About this scripture

The need for this scripture and Cover design

There is a need for this scripture for
several reasons

1. There are few to no well formatted, well done, easily available, user friendly copies of a Hebraic text fully written in a Paleo Hebrew script which may be purchased for individual usage.
2. It is well known the scripts presently used for the Masoretic text as well as Modern Israeli Hebrew are derivatives of the Aramaic script and are not originally and authentically Hebrew. This scripture provides a view of what the original scripture may have looked like. It also provides a view of what the Masoretic text would look like in an Authentically Hebrew script with punctuation modeled more closely to what it may have looked like or what the punctuation could have been developed to be used as from ancient times as a continued Nation. This is great for

religious and ethnic groups such as (ethnic) Hebrew Israelites/Israelite Hebrews (such as those in the western world) and various other ethnic Hebrews (such as the Lemba, Beta Yisrael, the Igbo, the Ashanti, among many others), various religious Jewish sects, the Hebrew Roots movement, various other Christian groups, various schools of theology, University professors, students, or for personal and family usage.

3. This document may serve as a national text of legislature and historical document completely in the original Hebrew for some Hebraic groups of the lost tribes of Israel (so named above among others) who are seeking national sovereignty especially the Hebrew Israelites of the Americas, Africa, Europe, and Asia or wherever they may have been scattered. Since the Children (Sons) of Israel are an ethnic nationality this book is for them. A product by us and for us.
4. This text may also be useful for those who find fault with the Masoretic pronunciation theory (miqra soferim), the Aramaic script of the Masoretic text, and other Hebraic pronunciation traditions such as Tiberian

and Ashkenatzic. Masoretic traditional pronunciations will for the most part not be used, nor will other traditions be used in pronunciations (if any) in this book. Instead, I use the m'Daber theory of pronunciation which is a pronunciation reconstruction that will be explained outside of this Torah in other future books and videos.

5. For Israelites who will be taking my Israelitish or Shephah Barurah courses.
6. For Morehs, Rabbis, Pastors and other religious teachers and for the everyday individual or professionals such as Linguist (laymen and professional), archaeologist and the like.
7. For those who want to read the Masoretic text in the Ancient script without the vowels, and with or without Qere veKetiv or other tikkunei soferim readings.

The Cover Design

The cover design is based on the on the commands that YHWH gave to decorate the Temple of YHWH and the linen ephod of the priest. The cover has a linen print with gold trimming and the colors that YHWH commanded to be placed in the Temple which were Takelet (around cerulean blue or indigo), Argemen (Purple/di-bromo indigo), and Tola't sheni (scarlet or double dipped crimson). The front cover reads "The Torah of YHWH for/to the Children of Israel" and has below it the ten words or Ten Commandments. The back cover displays the National Israelite flag or the Banner of the Children of Israel with the Shema' above it and below it the verses of Deut 6:5 and 11:1, Leviticus 19:18 and 19:34, then Deut 6:6 and 6:7.

Banner Design

The flag on the back cover I designed to be our (The Children of Israel's) National Flag, it is the new Banner of the Children of Israel (Nes.Beni.Yasher'El). The name of the Banner is YAHUnesnu or YaHuWaH Nesnu (YHWH is our Banner).

We, the children of Israel, should "gather together" under one banner and it will be this one, YHWH willing it. This flag's symbolism is unique and is from YHWH. It contains the colors of YHWH that He commanded us to place in the Temple and of the Lenin Ephods of t5he Priest. Cerulean Blue or indigo, Tyrian purple/dibromo indigo, Crimson/scarlet, and Linen (the border and scroll). It contains upon it, the four most important furniture objects of the Temple. These items were the Alter of Incense with its incense red hot {on the right hand}, the Table of Show Bread with its 12 loaves of unleavened bread (two stacks of 6) its plates, dishes, bowls, and pitchers {center}, and The Manurah with is 22 total bowls, bulbs, and blossoms and 7 flames {on the Left hand have to zoom in to see}. These first three were in the Set Apart place (Holy Place). At the top and center is the "Ark of the Covenant" with its two Karubim and the name and title "YHWH Elohim" as He gave to us to be a memorial for all generations. This item was in The Most Set Apart place (the Holy of Holies) and on the ark is a message in Israelitish (Ancient Israelite Hebrew). The Message says, "Israel is my People (says YHWH and), to you He is calling H'afetsi Bah (My Joy is in Her) and to your land Ba'ulah (Married) and I (YHWH) shall restore to you Shefah Barurah (a pure language/Lip)". All of these items are made to look of the form of pure gold. On the scroll {located at the bottom} it bears the words Torah and Nebi'im (Law and prophets) {on the right hand side of scroll} but on the left hand side it says Katubim (writings). In the Center of the scroll is another message which says Nes.Beni.Yasher'El which means the "Banner or Flag of the Children of Israel." This flag is basically made as a view of the inner part of the Temple of YHWH.

About the Script

The script and font used in this Scripture Is a Paleo Hebrew or Israelitish script in which I have named Shefah Barurah YAHUtsadeqnu. I have synthesized this script to be a compilation, match, and comparative script of various Paleo Hebrew (including Phoenician, Moabite, etc.) text, stela, Ostraca, bullae, scrolls etc. such as The Mesha stela, the Gezer calendar, the signet stamp of King Hezekiah, The Kitef Hinnom silver scrolls, The Kilamuwa stela, the Siloam Inscription, The Ostricon of the house of YHWH, and more. A composite was synthesized by finding the basic forms of each of the 22 alphabets (excluding the ancient letter for "ghain" and the more recent sofit letters) and then formatting each letter into a more uniform, neat, and handsome figure to tie together with a more orderly, clean, and easily discernable appearance in which every letter could be easily differentiated from another yet still retain its true basic and original paleo Hebrew form. If ever there were ever a standard script for The Ancient Israelite dialects of Hebrew and Biblical Hebrew (what I call collectively, Israelitish) I imagine it would be somewhat like this script. Thus, with no conclusive proof of an ancient standard, I call this script the first Israelitish Standard script, or at least the first of this era. The scripts 22 letters from right to left are as follows:

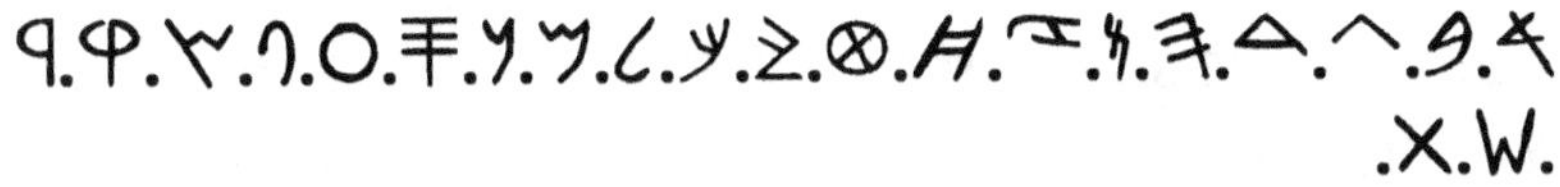

About the numbering system

Because the Arabic numeric symbols used in English are not Hebrew but are associated with being western, and also because gematria can be too complex for some beginners as well as gematria having certain hermeneutical aspects which may distract from the actual message of the text, I have decided to invent a new numbering system.

The numbering system used in this scripture I invented from the first 9 letters of the Hebrew alphabet. This is also another new symbol for the number 0 made from the 1st letter (aleph/elef) and the 12th letter (lamed) combined to form both a word and an acronym, the word being “La” meaning no or not and the phrase being “La ah’ed” meaning “not one”. Thus together it forms a symbol that can be interpreted as meaning "no, not one!" or simply the numeric value of "0".

In Biblical times most numbers were written out as words rather than as written symbols. In the days of the biblical kingdoms of Judah and Israel lines were sometimes used for numbers as seen on the "Ostricon of the House of YHWH" written as a letter shin and 3 diagonal lines to indicate 3 shekels.

Another way in which numbers were indicated were by Hebrew letters as seen on the shekel/shaqel and half shekel coins of the years of the second revolt against Rome (coins of years 67-70 a.d.) when Rome occupied Israel in Judah's latter history before the fall of Jerusalem. This gives us evidence that using letters were an authentically Hebrew way to symbolize numbers and so this adds a layer of validity for this new system. Also, this newly invented system works just like the Arabic numeral system with all numbers going from 1-9 and 0 being added or placed by itself which makes an easier transition from English to Hebrew than gematria does. The only exception is that this new Israelite numeric system works from right to left like the rest of the Hebrew text does.

All together this new Israelitish numeric system makes a new authentically Hebrew system made from the ancient letters

that makes it easy to transition to Hebrew from English, and that does not distract from the message of the text or impede the directional flow of the reader's eye. The numbers of the new system are as follows:
1-9 and 0 from right to left are,

About the book names

Part of the Masoretic scribal duty of fixing the text was to take a solid Hebrew text with no chapter or verse demarcation and to assign "breaks" if you will, into the book. Another such fix, was to name the books of the Torah. When doing this they decided to name the first 5 books, or the Torah, after the first few words of the first verse of each book. In biblical times, however, Ancient Israelites named things by what they did meant what their purpose was for, and so I have proposed several new names based on the central themes of what each book is about. Some of the names have stayed the same and a few of them have changed. Some may, in a way, mirror the meaning of the English names, yet this was not done for that purpose. It is important to say that when writing the names in English I use transliterations of the letters and added vowels based on a reconstruction of the old words by root, and open and closed syllables, (my m'Daber theory of pronunciation) rather than using Masoretic pronunciation. The new names to better reflect the subject matter of each book are as follows:

1. **Safer b'Re'eshit/𐤎𐤐𐤓.𐤁𐤓𐤀𐤔𐤉𐤕 :** Meaning, Book of "In the Beginning" commonly known in English as "Genesis" and in the Masoretic text as "Bereshit".
2. **Safer w'yaA'lu m'Matserim/ 𐤎𐤐𐤓.𐤅𐤉𐤏𐤋𐤅.𐤌𐤌𐤑𐤓𐤉𐤌:** Meaning, Book of "And they came up from Egypt" commonly known in English as "Exodus" and in the Masoretic text as "Shemot"
3. **Safer l'Lewim/𐤎𐤐𐤓.𐤋𐤋𐤅𐤉𐤌 :** Meaning, Book "to the Levites" commonly known in English as "Leviticus" and in the Masoretic text as "Wayiqra".
4. **Safer b'Madaber Seyni/ 𐤎𐤐𐤓.𐤁𐤌𐤃𐤁𐤓.𐤎𐤉𐤍𐤉:** Meaning, Book

of “In the Wilderness of Sinai” commonly known in English as “Numbers” and in the Masoretic text as “Bamidbar” in which I also give this shortened name as “b’Madaber”.

5. **Safer h’Daberim Asher Daber Meshah/ 𐤎𐤐𐤓. 𐤄𐤃𐤁𐤓𐤉𐤌. 𐤀𐤔𐤓. 𐤃𐤁𐤓. 𐤌𐤔𐤄:** Meaning, Book of “ The words that Moses Spoke” commonly known in English as “Deuteronomy” and in the Masoretic text as “Dabarim” in which I also uses as a shortened title “Daberim”.

About the chapters

Because the text can sometimes be confusing for beginners, often seeming to appear backwards or even upside down due to the direction difference and letter orientations of Hebrew opposed to English, all chapters have been formatted to be easy to find for those who may be overwhelmed with the unfamiliarity of the script. Although chapters are referred to as “pereq” or a break in the chapter in some other Hebrew text. However this text, to fit more closely with the concrete nature of the Ancient Israelite people, refers to a chapter as

𐤇𐤋𐤒

or h’aleq. This word means a portion as in a portion of food corresponding to Deuteronomy 8:3 which says, “Man does not live by bread alone but on the every word of YHWH”.

In addition, chapters will be right-aligned, underlined, with the number of the chapter highlighted with black in white colored font, and in a larger font size than the text of the verses for ease of finding. In the following example from right to left the chapter sub heading as Book (b’re’eshit/genesis) is written , the word for chapter,then the number (1) as follows Ex:

𐤁𐤓𐤀𐤔𐤉𐤕.𐤇𐤋𐤒..1.. .

If you notice the number is separated from the rest of the chapter sub heading by four dots, a pair in front and a pair behind the numeral. This is simply to highlight which symbol is the number and is not a form of punctuation that I have come up with. I cannot take credit for this usage, as I've seen it used elsewhere and so why reinvent the wheel.

About the verses

The verses have also been formatted for ease of finding. In this text for all intended purposes and in relation to the context of Deuteronomy 8:3 I refer to a verse as a פת (fet) which means a slice, piece, or morsel so that each chapter may be seen as a portion of food or a bowl and each verse like a spoon full or morsel. All verses are right aligned, with numbers highlighted dark gray , with white colored font, having the two pairs of dots before and after the number to highlight the fact that the number symbol between the two pairs of dots is in fact a number. Words will be separated with single dots and the verse will end with a vertical dash which begins mid-word height and extends below the word (see section about the punctuation and Qere ve Ketiv below). From right to left as follows is this example:

..1..בראשית.ברא.אלהים.את.השמים.ואת.הארץ|

About the (Israelitish) punctuation and Qere ve Ketiv

The punctuation in this book is a composite which is very closely modeled after punctuation found on many Paleo Hebrew stela, scrolls, and ostraca that have been found over the years especially the Mesha stela for its clear indication of quite consistent punctuation. The Mesha stela punctuation has been considered most particularly for its very clear use of a dot to separate each word which I call a "tew dey" meaning mark of sufficiency, which may be seen as a word period.

Another such marking that the stela displays is a vertical line which may be seen at the end of a sentence/verse in which I call a "tew shalem" or mark of completion, which indeed behaves similarly to a period. One other mark which is seen twice on the Stela of King Kilamua and seems to break the document into two paragraphs/sections. This mark appears as two vertical lines along with a perforated horizontal line. Only the two vertical lines will be used in this document as a chapter period.

All other punctuation are modifications of the two previously mentioned to accommodate the usage of chapter, verse, and note punctuation function, which was not available in the days that this style or text was used or written. Since there are various scribal challenges which revolve around Qere ve Ketiv, Qere ve Ketiv and its various forms such as “ketiv ve lo qere”, all forms, in this Torah and the upcoming full Israelitish Tanakh, have been retained, yet separated from the text with quotation which resembles in function a parenthesis. All punctuations are as follows:

.

This small dot is what I call a “tew dey” or mark of sufficiency and is used as a word period and separates words. Ex:

𐤎𐤐𐤓.𐤁𐤓𐤀𐤔𐤉𐤕.

|

This vertical line is what I call “tew shalem” or mark of wholeness/completion and is used as a sentence period. From right to left Deuteronomy 6: 4-5 Ex:

𐤔𐤌𐤏.𐤉𐤔𐤓𐤀𐤋.𐤉𐤄𐤅𐤄.𐤀𐤋𐤄𐤉𐤍𐤅.𐤉𐤄𐤅𐤄.𐤀𐤇𐤃|
𐤅𐤀𐤄𐤁𐤕.𐤀𐤕.𐤉𐤄𐤅𐤄.𐤀𐤋𐤄𐤉𐤊.𐤁𐤊𐤋.𐤋𐤁𐤁𐤊.𐤅𐤁𐤊𐤋
.𐤍𐤐𐤔𐤊.𐤅𐤁𐤊𐤋.𐤌𐤀𐤃𐤊|

..

This is called a when used doubly a "tew m'safer" (mark of a number) is used on each side of a number symbol for separating numbers from the rest of text to show clearly which symbol is the number. Ex:

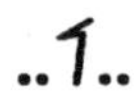

|.

This "tew h'daber" (mark of the word) is used as a quotation mark especially in this text when presenting a shorter name of a book in the book title and is reversed on the other side of what it is encasing. Ex: 

||.

This "tew b'tuk 'hasheb" (mark in the midst of tought) or "tew m'badil beyn 'hasheb" (mark of dividing between thought) is used as a parenthesis especially when denoting Qere, Ketiv ve lo Qere, etc. From right to left Ex 1:

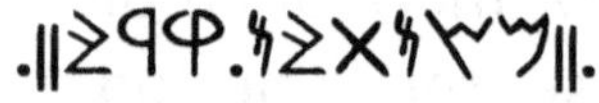

But at the end of a verse appears as Ex 2:

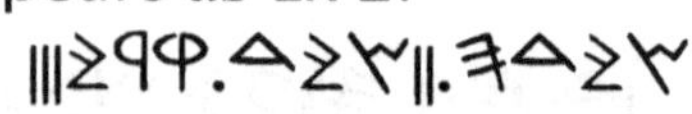

||

This "tew sheba' " (mark of satisfaction) is used as a chapter period/ender and will be used on the end of the last verse of a chapter. Ex: Last verse of the last chapter of genesis, Gen ch 50.

..כו..ויmת.יוסף.בן.מאה.ועשר.שנים.ויחנטו.
אתו.ויישם.בארון.במצרים||

How to Use this Scripture

1. Find books by page number or the large bold underlined font of the book title
2. Find chapters on the right hand side, partly underlined with the number symbol highlighted. It will appear in the order of Book, Chapter, and then chapter number.
3. Find each verse highlighted (either grey or black depending upon the scripture) and aligned on the right hand side, with the number in white color font. Numbers will be in opposite order of English numbers, that is, from right to left for example: the number 18 would appear as “81 or

[1" rather than in the English order as so "18 or 1[".

4. The Qere reading will be put in the Israelitish parenthesis as explained above in the punctuation section. It will list first the reading and then read ≥9φ. The same will be for "Qere ve lo Ketiv". As for "Ketiv ve lo Qere" whenever you see the Israelitish parenthesis the word that is "lo qere" will be the word just before the Israelitish parenthesis. Here is an example with the "lo qere" word underlined and emboldened from right to left ex: .||≥9φ.≮ᒪ5.ϑ≥Xש||.**<u>ﻻ≮</u>**.

<u>Index</u>

This Index will not include page numbers but is based upon the five books and their chapters for the reason that using the new numbering system to number the pages was not feasible with my publishing software and for the fact that most people, when reading or studying scripture, do not use the page numbers anyway but instead use the books and chapters.

1. **Safer b'Re'eshit**
2. **Safer w'yaA'lu m'Matserim**
3. **Safer l'Lewim**
4. **Safer b'Madaber Seyni**
5. **Safer h'Daberim Asher Daber Meshah**

𐤎𐤐𐤓.𐤁𐤓𐤀𐤔𐤉𐤕

𐤁𐤓𐤀𐤔𐤉𐤕.𐤇𐤋𐤒 1

1 𐤁𐤓𐤀𐤔𐤉𐤕.𐤁𐤓𐤀.𐤀𐤋𐤄𐤉𐤌.𐤀𐤕.𐤄𐤔𐤌𐤉𐤌.𐤅𐤀𐤕.𐤄𐤀
𐤓𐤑|
2 𐤅𐤄𐤀𐤓𐤑.𐤄𐤉𐤕𐤄.𐤕𐤄𐤅.𐤅𐤁𐤄𐤅.𐤅𐤇𐤔𐤊.𐤏𐤋.𐤐𐤍𐤉.𐤕𐤄𐤅
𐤌.𐤅𐤓𐤅𐤇.𐤀𐤋𐤄𐤉𐤌.𐤌𐤓𐤇𐤐𐤕.𐤏𐤋.𐤐𐤍𐤉.𐤄𐤌𐤉𐤌|
3 𐤅𐤉𐤀𐤌𐤓.𐤀𐤋𐤄𐤉𐤌.𐤉𐤄𐤉.𐤀𐤅𐤓.𐤅𐤉𐤄𐤉.𐤀𐤅𐤓|
4 𐤅𐤉𐤓𐤀.𐤀𐤋𐤄𐤉𐤌.𐤀𐤕.𐤄𐤀𐤅𐤓.𐤊𐤉.𐤈𐤅𐤁.𐤅𐤉𐤁𐤃𐤋.𐤀𐤋
𐤄𐤉𐤌.𐤁𐤉𐤍.𐤄𐤀𐤅𐤓.𐤅𐤁𐤉𐤍.𐤄𐤇𐤔𐤊|
5 𐤅𐤉𐤒𐤓𐤀.𐤀𐤋𐤄𐤉𐤌.𐤋𐤀𐤅𐤓.𐤉𐤅𐤌.𐤅𐤋𐤇𐤔𐤊.𐤒𐤓𐤀.𐤋𐤉𐤋
𐤄.𐤅𐤉𐤄𐤉.𐤏𐤓𐤁.𐤅𐤉𐤄𐤉.𐤁𐤒𐤓.𐤉𐤅𐤌.𐤀𐤇𐤃|
6 𐤅𐤉𐤀𐤌𐤓.𐤀𐤋𐤄𐤉𐤌.𐤉𐤄𐤉.𐤓𐤒𐤉𐤏.𐤁𐤕𐤅𐤊.𐤄𐤌𐤉𐤌.𐤅𐤉𐤄
𐤉.𐤌𐤁𐤃𐤉𐤋.𐤁𐤉𐤍.𐤌𐤉𐤌.𐤋𐤌𐤉𐤌|
7 𐤅𐤉𐤏𐤔.𐤀𐤋𐤄𐤉𐤌.𐤀𐤕.𐤄𐤓𐤒𐤉𐤏.𐤅𐤉𐤁𐤃𐤋.𐤁𐤉𐤍.𐤄𐤌
𐤉𐤌.𐤀𐤔𐤓.𐤌𐤕𐤇𐤕.𐤋𐤓𐤒𐤉𐤏.𐤅𐤁𐤉𐤍.𐤄𐤌𐤉𐤌.𐤀𐤔𐤓.𐤌𐤏𐤋.
𐤋𐤓𐤒𐤉𐤏.𐤅𐤉𐤄𐤉.𐤊𐤍|
8 𐤅𐤉𐤒𐤓𐤀.𐤀𐤋𐤄𐤉𐤌.𐤋𐤓𐤒𐤉𐤏.𐤔𐤌𐤉𐤌.𐤅𐤉𐤄𐤉.𐤏𐤓𐤁.𐤅𐤉
𐤄𐤉.𐤁𐤒𐤓.𐤉𐤅𐤌.𐤔𐤍𐤉|
9 𐤅𐤉𐤀𐤌𐤓.𐤀𐤋𐤄𐤉𐤌.𐤉𐤒𐤅𐤅.𐤄𐤌𐤉𐤌.𐤌𐤕𐤇𐤕.𐤄𐤔𐤌𐤉𐤌
.𐤀𐤋.𐤌𐤒𐤅𐤌.𐤀𐤇𐤃.𐤅𐤕𐤓𐤀𐤄.𐤄𐤉𐤁𐤔𐤄.𐤅𐤉𐤄𐤉.𐤊𐤍|
10 𐤅𐤉𐤒𐤓𐤀.𐤀𐤋𐤄𐤉𐤌.𐤋𐤉𐤁𐤔𐤄.𐤀𐤓𐤑.𐤅𐤋𐤌𐤒𐤅𐤄.𐤄𐤌𐤉
𐤌.𐤒𐤓𐤀.𐤉𐤌𐤉𐤌.𐤅𐤉𐤓𐤀.𐤀𐤋𐤄𐤉𐤌.𐤊𐤉.𐤈𐤅𐤁|
11 𐤅𐤉𐤀𐤌𐤓.𐤀𐤋𐤄𐤉𐤌.𐤕𐤃𐤔𐤀.𐤄𐤀𐤓𐤑.𐤃𐤔𐤀.𐤏𐤔𐤁.
𐤌𐤆𐤓𐤉𐤏.𐤆𐤓𐤏.𐤏𐤑.𐤐𐤓𐤉.𐤏𐤔𐤄.𐤐𐤓𐤉.𐤋𐤌𐤉𐤍𐤅.𐤀𐤔𐤓.𐤆
𐤓𐤏𐤅.𐤁𐤅.𐤏𐤋.𐤄𐤀𐤓𐤑.𐤅𐤉𐤄𐤉.𐤊𐤍|

𐤉𐤁 𐤅𐤕𐤅𐤑𐤀.𐤄𐤀𐤓𐤑.𐤃𐤔𐤀.𐤏𐤔𐤁.𐤌𐤆𐤓𐤉𐤏.𐤆𐤓𐤏.𐤋
𐤌𐤉𐤍𐤄𐤅.𐤅𐤏𐤑.𐤏𐤔𐤄.𐤐𐤓𐤉.𐤀𐤔𐤓.𐤆𐤓𐤏𐤅.𐤁𐤅.𐤋𐤌𐤉𐤍𐤄𐤅.𐤅𐤉
𐤓𐤀.𐤀𐤋𐤄𐤉𐤌.𐤊𐤉.𐤈𐤅𐤁|
𐤉𐤂 𐤅𐤉𐤄𐤉.𐤏𐤓𐤁.𐤅𐤉𐤄𐤉.𐤁𐤒𐤓.𐤉𐤅𐤌.𐤔𐤋𐤉𐤔𐤉|
𐤉𐤃 𐤅𐤉𐤀𐤌𐤓.𐤀𐤋𐤄𐤉𐤌.𐤉𐤄𐤉.𐤌𐤀𐤓𐤕.𐤁𐤓𐤒𐤉𐤏.𐤄𐤔𐤌𐤉
𐤌.𐤋𐤄𐤁𐤃𐤉𐤋.𐤁𐤉𐤍.𐤄𐤉𐤅𐤌.𐤅𐤁𐤉𐤍.𐤄𐤋𐤉𐤋𐤄.𐤅𐤄𐤉𐤅.𐤋𐤀𐤕𐤕
.𐤅𐤋𐤌𐤅𐤏𐤃𐤉𐤌.𐤅𐤋𐤉𐤌𐤉𐤌.𐤅𐤔𐤍𐤉𐤌|
𐤈𐤅 𐤅𐤄𐤉𐤅.𐤋𐤌𐤀𐤅𐤓𐤕.𐤁𐤓𐤒𐤉𐤏.𐤄𐤔𐤌𐤉𐤌.𐤋𐤄𐤀𐤉𐤓.𐤏𐤋.
𐤄𐤀𐤓𐤑.𐤅𐤉𐤄𐤉.𐤊𐤍|
𐤈𐤆 𐤅𐤉𐤏𐤔.𐤀𐤋𐤄𐤉𐤌.𐤀𐤕.𐤔𐤍𐤉.𐤄𐤌𐤀𐤓𐤕.𐤄𐤂𐤃𐤋𐤉𐤌.
𐤀𐤕.𐤄𐤌𐤀𐤅𐤓.𐤄𐤂𐤃𐤋.𐤋𐤌𐤌𐤔𐤋𐤕.𐤄𐤉𐤅𐤌.𐤅𐤀𐤕.𐤄𐤌𐤀𐤅𐤓.
𐤄𐤒𐤈𐤍.𐤋𐤌𐤌𐤔𐤋𐤕.𐤄𐤋𐤉𐤋𐤄.𐤅𐤀𐤕.𐤄𐤊𐤅𐤊𐤁𐤉𐤌|
𐤉𐤆 𐤅𐤉𐤕𐤍.𐤀𐤕𐤌.𐤀𐤋𐤄𐤉𐤌.𐤁𐤓𐤒𐤉𐤏.𐤄𐤔𐤌𐤉𐤌.𐤋𐤄𐤀𐤉
𐤓.𐤏𐤋.𐤄𐤀𐤓𐤑|
𐤉𐤇 𐤅𐤋𐤌𐤔𐤋.𐤁𐤉𐤅𐤌.𐤅𐤁𐤋𐤉𐤋𐤄.𐤅𐤋𐤄𐤁𐤃𐤉𐤋.𐤁𐤉𐤍.𐤄𐤀𐤅𐤓.
𐤅𐤁𐤉𐤍.𐤄𐤇𐤔𐤊.𐤅𐤉𐤓𐤀.𐤀𐤋𐤄𐤉𐤌.𐤊𐤉.𐤈𐤅𐤁|
𐤉𐤈 𐤅𐤉𐤄𐤉.𐤏𐤓𐤁.𐤅𐤉𐤄𐤉.𐤁𐤒𐤓.𐤉𐤅𐤌.𐤓𐤁𐤉𐤏𐤉|
𐤊 𐤅𐤉𐤀𐤌𐤓.𐤀𐤋𐤄𐤉𐤌.𐤉𐤔𐤓𐤑𐤅.𐤄𐤌𐤉𐤌.𐤔𐤓𐤑.𐤍𐤐𐤔.𐤇
𐤉𐤄.𐤅𐤏𐤅𐤐.𐤉𐤏𐤅𐤐𐤐.𐤏𐤋.𐤄𐤀𐤓𐤑.𐤏𐤋.𐤐𐤍𐤉.𐤓𐤒𐤉𐤏.𐤄𐤔𐤌𐤉
𐤌|
𐤊𐤀 𐤅𐤉𐤁𐤓𐤀.𐤀𐤋𐤄𐤉𐤌.𐤀𐤕.𐤄𐤕𐤍𐤉𐤍𐤌.𐤄𐤂𐤃𐤋𐤉𐤌.𐤅𐤀
𐤕.𐤊𐤋.𐤍𐤐𐤔.𐤄𐤇𐤉𐤄.𐤄𐤓𐤌𐤔𐤕.𐤀𐤔𐤓.𐤔𐤓𐤑𐤅.𐤄𐤌𐤉𐤌.𐤋𐤌
𐤉𐤍𐤄𐤌.𐤅𐤀𐤕.𐤊𐤋.𐤏𐤅𐤐.𐤊𐤍𐤐.𐤋𐤌𐤉𐤍𐤄𐤅.𐤅𐤉𐤓𐤀.𐤀𐤋𐤄𐤉𐤌.𐤊
𐤉.𐤈𐤅𐤁|
𐤊𐤁 𐤅𐤉𐤁𐤓𐤊.𐤀𐤕𐤌.𐤀𐤋𐤄𐤉𐤌.𐤋𐤀𐤌𐤓.𐤐𐤓𐤅.𐤅𐤓𐤁𐤅.𐤅𐤌𐤋𐤀𐤅.
𐤀𐤕.𐤄𐤌𐤉𐤌.𐤁𐤉𐤌𐤉𐤌.𐤅𐤄𐤏𐤅𐤐.𐤉𐤓𐤁.𐤁𐤀𐤓𐤑|
𐤊𐤂 𐤅𐤉𐤄𐤉.𐤏𐤓𐤁.𐤅𐤉𐤄𐤉.𐤁𐤒𐤓.𐤉𐤅𐤌.𐤇𐤌𐤉𐤔𐤉|
𐤊𐤃 𐤅𐤉𐤀𐤌𐤓.𐤀𐤋𐤄𐤉𐤌.𐤕𐤅𐤑𐤀.𐤄𐤀𐤓𐤑.𐤍𐤐𐤔.𐤇𐤉𐤄.𐤋
𐤌𐤉𐤍𐤄.𐤁𐤄𐤌𐤄.𐤅𐤓𐤌𐤔.𐤅𐤇𐤉𐤕𐤅.𐤀𐤓𐤑.𐤋𐤌𐤉𐤍𐤄.𐤅𐤉𐤄𐤉.𐤊
𐤍|

..כה.. 𐤅𐤉𐤏𐤔.𐤀𐤋𐤄𐤉𐤌.𐤀𐤕.𐤇𐤉𐤕.𐤄𐤀𐤓𐤑.𐤋𐤌𐤉𐤍𐤄.𐤅𐤀
𐤕.𐤄𐤁𐤄𐤌𐤄.𐤋𐤌𐤉𐤍𐤄.𐤅𐤀𐤕.𐤊𐤋.𐤓𐤌𐤔.𐤄𐤀𐤃𐤌𐤄.𐤋𐤌𐤉𐤍
𐤄𐤅.𐤅𐤉𐤓𐤀.𐤀𐤋𐤄𐤉𐤌.𐤊𐤉.𐤈𐤅𐤁|

..כו.. 𐤅𐤉𐤀𐤌𐤓.𐤀𐤋𐤄𐤉𐤌.𐤍𐤏𐤔𐤄.𐤀𐤃𐤌.𐤁𐤑𐤋𐤌𐤍𐤅.𐤊𐤃𐤌𐤅
𐤕𐤍𐤅.𐤅𐤉𐤓𐤃𐤅.𐤁𐤃𐤂𐤕.𐤄𐤉𐤌.𐤅𐤁𐤏𐤅𐤐.𐤄𐤔𐤌𐤉𐤌.𐤅𐤁𐤁𐤄𐤌
𐤄.𐤅𐤁𐤊𐤋.𐤄𐤀𐤓𐤑.𐤅𐤁𐤊𐤋.𐤄𐤓𐤌𐤔.𐤄𐤓𐤌𐤔.𐤏𐤋.𐤄𐤀𐤓𐤑|

..כז.. 𐤅𐤉𐤁𐤓𐤀.𐤀𐤋𐤄𐤉𐤌.𐤀𐤕.𐤄𐤀𐤃𐤌.𐤁𐤑𐤋𐤌𐤅.𐤁𐤑𐤋𐤌.
𐤀𐤋𐤄𐤉𐤌.𐤁𐤓𐤀.𐤀𐤕𐤅.𐤆𐤊𐤓.𐤅𐤍𐤒𐤁𐤄.𐤁𐤓𐤀.𐤀𐤕𐤌|

..כח.. 𐤅𐤉𐤁𐤓𐤊.𐤀𐤕𐤌.𐤀𐤋𐤄𐤉𐤌.𐤅𐤉𐤀𐤌𐤓.𐤋𐤄𐤌.𐤀𐤋𐤄𐤉𐤌.𐤐
𐤓𐤅.𐤅𐤓𐤁𐤅.𐤅𐤌𐤋𐤀𐤅.𐤀𐤕.𐤄𐤀𐤓𐤑.𐤅𐤊𐤁𐤔𐤄.𐤅𐤓𐤃𐤅.𐤁𐤃𐤂𐤕.
𐤄𐤉𐤌.𐤅𐤁𐤏𐤅𐤐.𐤄𐤔𐤌𐤉𐤌.𐤅𐤁𐤊𐤋.𐤇𐤉𐤄.𐤄𐤓𐤌𐤔𐤕.𐤏𐤋.𐤄𐤀
𐤓𐤑|

..כט.. 𐤅𐤉𐤀𐤌𐤓.𐤀𐤋𐤄𐤉𐤌.𐤄𐤍𐤄.𐤍𐤕𐤕𐤉.𐤋𐤊𐤌.𐤀𐤕.𐤊𐤋.𐤏
𐤔𐤁.𐤆𐤓𐤏.𐤆𐤓𐤏.𐤀𐤔𐤓.𐤏𐤋.𐤐𐤍𐤉.𐤊𐤋.𐤄𐤀𐤓𐤑.𐤅𐤀𐤕.𐤊𐤋.
𐤄𐤏𐤑.𐤀𐤔𐤓.𐤁𐤅.𐤐𐤓𐤉.𐤏𐤑.𐤆𐤓𐤏.𐤆𐤓𐤏.𐤋𐤊𐤌.𐤉𐤄𐤉𐤄.𐤋
𐤀𐤊𐤋𐤄|

..ל.. 𐤅𐤋𐤊𐤋.𐤇𐤉𐤕.𐤄𐤀𐤓𐤑.𐤅𐤋𐤊𐤋.𐤏𐤅𐤐.𐤄𐤔𐤌𐤉𐤌.𐤅𐤋𐤊𐤋.
𐤓𐤅𐤌𐤔.𐤏𐤋.𐤄𐤀𐤓𐤑.𐤀𐤔𐤓.𐤁𐤅.𐤍𐤐𐤔.𐤇𐤉𐤄.𐤀𐤕.𐤊𐤋.𐤉𐤓𐤒.
𐤏𐤔𐤁.𐤋𐤀𐤊𐤋𐤄.𐤅𐤉𐤄𐤉.𐤊𐤍|

..לא.. 𐤅𐤉𐤓𐤀.𐤀𐤋𐤄𐤉𐤌.𐤀𐤕.𐤊𐤋.𐤀𐤔𐤓.𐤏𐤔𐤄.𐤅𐤄𐤍𐤄.𐤈𐤅𐤁.
𐤌𐤀𐤃.𐤅𐤉𐤄𐤉.𐤏𐤓𐤁.𐤅𐤉𐤄𐤉.𐤁𐤒𐤓.𐤉𐤅𐤌.𐤄𐤔𐤔𐤉||

𐤁𐤓𐤀𐤔𐤉𐤕.𐤇𐤋𐤒 ..ב..

..א.. 𐤅𐤉𐤊𐤋𐤅.𐤄𐤔𐤌𐤉𐤌.𐤅𐤄𐤀𐤓𐤑.𐤅𐤊𐤋.𐤑𐤁𐤀𐤌|

..ב.. 𐤅𐤉𐤊𐤋.𐤀𐤋𐤄𐤉𐤌.𐤁𐤉𐤅𐤌.𐤄𐤔𐤁𐤉𐤏𐤉.𐤌𐤋𐤀𐤊𐤕𐤅.𐤀𐤔𐤓.
𐤏𐤔𐤄.𐤅𐤉𐤔𐤁𐤕.𐤁𐤉𐤅𐤌.𐤄𐤔𐤁𐤉𐤏𐤉.𐤌𐤊𐤋.𐤌𐤋𐤀𐤊𐤕𐤅.𐤀𐤔
𐤓.𐤏𐤔𐤄|

ג 𐤅𐤉𐤁𐤓𐤊.𐤀𐤋𐤄𐤉𐤌.𐤀𐤕.𐤉𐤅𐤌.𐤄𐤔𐤁𐤉𐤏𐤉.𐤅𐤉𐤒𐤃𐤔.𐤀
𐤕𐤅.𐤊𐤉.𐤁𐤅.𐤔𐤁𐤕.𐤌𐤊𐤋.𐤌𐤋𐤀𐤊𐤕𐤅.𐤀𐤔𐤓.𐤁𐤓𐤀.𐤀𐤋𐤄𐤉𐤌.
𐤋𐤏𐤔𐤅𐤕|

ד 𐤀𐤋𐤄.𐤕𐤅𐤋𐤃𐤅𐤕.𐤄𐤔𐤌𐤉𐤌.𐤅𐤄𐤀𐤓𐤑.𐤁𐤄𐤁𐤓𐤀𐤌.𐤁𐤉
𐤅𐤌.𐤏𐤔𐤅𐤕.𐤉𐤄𐤅𐤄.𐤀𐤋𐤄𐤉𐤌.𐤀𐤓𐤑.𐤅𐤔𐤌𐤉𐤌|

ה 𐤅𐤊𐤋.𐤔𐤉𐤇.𐤄𐤔𐤃𐤄.𐤈𐤓𐤌.𐤉𐤄𐤉𐤄.𐤁𐤀𐤓𐤑.𐤅𐤊𐤋.𐤏𐤔
𐤁.𐤄𐤔𐤃𐤄.𐤈𐤓𐤌.𐤉𐤑𐤌𐤇.𐤊𐤉.𐤋𐤀.𐤄𐤌𐤈𐤉𐤓.𐤉𐤄𐤅𐤄.𐤀𐤋
𐤄𐤉𐤌.𐤏𐤋.𐤄𐤀𐤓𐤑.𐤅𐤀𐤃𐤌.𐤀𐤉𐤍.𐤋𐤏𐤁𐤃.𐤀𐤕.𐤄𐤀𐤃𐤌𐤄
|

ו 𐤅𐤀𐤃.𐤉𐤏𐤋𐤄.𐤌𐤍.𐤄𐤀𐤓𐤑.𐤅𐤄𐤔𐤒𐤄.𐤀𐤕.𐤊𐤋.𐤐𐤍𐤉.𐤄
𐤀𐤃𐤌𐤄|

ז 𐤅𐤉𐤉𐤑𐤓.𐤉𐤄𐤅𐤄.𐤀𐤋𐤄𐤉𐤌.𐤀𐤕.𐤄𐤀𐤃𐤌.𐤏𐤐𐤓.𐤌𐤍.𐤄
𐤀𐤃𐤌𐤄.𐤅𐤉𐤐𐤇.𐤁𐤀𐤐𐤉𐤅.𐤍𐤔𐤌𐤕.𐤇𐤉𐤉𐤌.𐤅𐤉𐤄𐤉.𐤄𐤀𐤃𐤌
.𐤋𐤍𐤐𐤔.𐤇𐤉𐤄|

ח 𐤅𐤉𐤈𐤏.𐤉𐤄𐤅𐤄.𐤀𐤋𐤄𐤉𐤌.𐤂𐤍.𐤁𐤏𐤃𐤍.𐤌𐤒𐤃𐤌.𐤅𐤉𐤔
𐤌.𐤔𐤌.𐤀𐤕.𐤄𐤀𐤃𐤌.𐤀𐤔𐤓.𐤉𐤑𐤓|

ט 𐤅𐤉𐤑𐤌𐤇.𐤉𐤄𐤅𐤄.𐤀𐤋𐤄𐤉𐤌.𐤌𐤍.𐤄𐤀𐤃𐤌𐤄.𐤊𐤋.𐤏𐤑.
𐤍𐤇𐤌𐤃.𐤋𐤌𐤓𐤀𐤄.𐤅𐤈𐤅𐤁.𐤋𐤌𐤀𐤊𐤋.𐤅𐤏𐤑.𐤄𐤇𐤉𐤉𐤌.𐤁𐤕𐤅
𐤊.𐤄𐤂𐤍.𐤅𐤏𐤑.𐤄𐤃𐤏𐤕.𐤈𐤅𐤁.𐤅𐤓𐤏|

י 𐤅𐤍𐤄𐤓.𐤉𐤑𐤀.𐤌𐤏𐤃𐤍.𐤋𐤄𐤔𐤒𐤅𐤕.𐤀𐤕.𐤄𐤂𐤍.𐤅𐤌𐤔𐤌
.𐤉𐤐𐤓𐤃.𐤅𐤄𐤉𐤄.𐤋𐤀𐤓𐤁𐤏𐤄.𐤓𐤀𐤔𐤉𐤌|

יא 𐤔𐤌.𐤄𐤀𐤇𐤃.𐤐𐤉𐤔𐤅𐤍.𐤄𐤅𐤀.𐤄𐤎𐤁𐤁.𐤀𐤕.𐤊𐤋.𐤀𐤓𐤑.
𐤄𐤇𐤅𐤉𐤋𐤄.𐤀𐤔𐤓.𐤔𐤌.𐤄𐤆𐤄𐤁|

יב 𐤅𐤆𐤄𐤁.𐤄𐤀𐤓𐤑.𐤄𐤄𐤅𐤀.𐤈𐤅𐤁.𐤔𐤌.𐤄𐤁𐤃𐤋𐤇.𐤅𐤀𐤁𐤍
.𐤄𐤔𐤄𐤌|

יג 𐤅𐤔𐤌.𐤄𐤍𐤄𐤓.𐤄𐤔𐤍𐤉.𐤂𐤉𐤇𐤅𐤍.𐤄𐤅𐤀.𐤄𐤎𐤅𐤁𐤁.𐤀𐤕.
𐤊𐤋.𐤀𐤓𐤑.𐤊𐤅𐤔|

יד 𐤅𐤔𐤌.𐤄𐤍𐤄𐤓.𐤄𐤔𐤋𐤉𐤔𐤉.𐤇𐤃𐤒𐤋.𐤄𐤅𐤀.𐤄𐤄𐤋𐤊.𐤒
𐤃𐤌𐤕.𐤀𐤔𐤅𐤓.𐤅𐤄𐤍𐤄𐤓.𐤄𐤓𐤁𐤉𐤏𐤉.𐤄𐤅𐤀.𐤐𐤓𐤕|

יה 𐤅𐤉𐤒𐤇.𐤉𐤄𐤅𐤄.𐤀𐤋𐤄𐤉𐤌.𐤀𐤕.𐤄𐤀𐤃𐤌.𐤅𐤉𐤍𐤇𐤄𐤅.𐤁
𐤂𐤍.𐤏𐤃𐤍.𐤋𐤏𐤁𐤃𐤄.𐤅𐤋𐤔𐤌𐤓𐤄|

יו ויצו.יהוה.אלהים.על.האדם.לאמר.מכל.
עץ.הגן.אכל.תאכל|
יז ומעץ.הדעת.טוב.ורע.לא.תאכל.ממנו.כי
ביום.אכלך.ממנו.מות.תמות|
יח ויאמר.יהוה.אלהים.לא.טוב.היות.האדם
לבדו.אעשה.לו.עזר.כנגדו|
יט ויצר.יהוה.אלהים.מן.האדמה.כל.חית.
השדה.ואת.כל.עוף.השמים.ויבא.אל.האדם.לראות.מה
יקרא.לו.וכל.אשר.יקרא.לו.האדם.נפ
ש.חיה.הוא.שמו|
כ ויקרא.האדם.שמות.לכל.הבהמה.ולעוף.
השמים.ולכל.חית.השדה.ולאדם.לא.מצא.ע
זר.כנגדו|
כא ויפל.יהוה.אלהים.תרדמה.על.האדם.וי
ישן.ויקח.אחת.מצלעתיו.ויסגר.בשר.תחת
נה|
כב ויבן.יהוה.אלהים.את.הצלע.אשר.לקח.
מן.האדם.לאשה.ויבאה.אל.האדם|
כג ויאמר.האדם.זאת.הפעם.עצם.מעצמי.
ובשר.מבשרי.לזאת.יקרא.אשה.כי.מאיש.לק
חה.זאת|
כד על.כן.יעזב.איש.את.אביו.ואת.אמו.וד
בק.באשתו.והיו.לבשר.אחד|
כה ויהיו.שניהם.ערומים.האדם.ואשתו.ולא
.יתבששו||

בראשית.חלק ג

א והנחש.היה.ערום.מכל.חית.השדה.אשר.
עשה.יהוה.אלהים.ויאמר.אל.האשה.אף.כי.א
מר.אלהים.לא.תאכלו.מכל.עץ.הגן|

𐤁 𐤅𐤕𐤀𐤌𐤓.𐤄𐤀𐤔𐤄.𐤀𐤋.𐤄𐤍𐤇𐤔.𐤌𐤐𐤓𐤉.𐤏𐤑.𐤄𐤂𐤍.𐤍𐤀
𐤊𐤋|
𐤂 𐤅𐤌𐤐𐤓𐤉.𐤄𐤏𐤑.𐤀𐤔𐤓.𐤁𐤕𐤅𐤊.𐤄𐤂𐤍.𐤀𐤌𐤓.𐤀𐤋𐤄𐤉𐤌.𐤋
𐤀.𐤕𐤀𐤊𐤋𐤅.𐤌𐤌𐤍𐤅.𐤅𐤋𐤀.𐤕𐤂𐤏𐤅.𐤁𐤅.𐤐𐤍.𐤕𐤌𐤕𐤅𐤍|
𐤃 𐤅𐤉𐤀𐤌𐤓.𐤄𐤍𐤇𐤔.𐤀𐤋.𐤄𐤀𐤔𐤄.𐤋𐤀.𐤌𐤅𐤕.𐤕𐤌𐤕𐤅𐤍|
𐤄 𐤊𐤉.𐤉𐤃𐤏.𐤀𐤋𐤄𐤉𐤌.𐤊𐤉.𐤁𐤉𐤅𐤌.𐤀𐤊𐤋𐤊𐤌.𐤌𐤌𐤍𐤅.𐤅𐤍𐤐
𐤒𐤇𐤅.𐤏𐤉𐤍𐤉𐤊𐤌.𐤅𐤄𐤉𐤉𐤕𐤌.𐤊𐤀𐤋𐤄𐤉𐤌.𐤉𐤃𐤏𐤉.𐤈𐤅𐤁.𐤅𐤓
𐤏|
𐤅 𐤅𐤕𐤓𐤀.𐤄𐤀𐤔𐤄.𐤊𐤉.𐤈𐤅𐤁.𐤄𐤏𐤑.𐤋𐤌𐤀𐤊𐤋.𐤅𐤊𐤉.𐤕𐤀𐤅
𐤄.𐤄𐤅𐤀.𐤋𐤏𐤉𐤍𐤉𐤌.𐤅𐤍𐤇𐤌𐤃.𐤄𐤏𐤑.𐤋𐤄𐤔𐤊𐤉𐤋.𐤅𐤕𐤒𐤇.
𐤌𐤐𐤓𐤉𐤅.𐤅𐤕𐤀𐤊𐤋.𐤅𐤕𐤕𐤍.𐤂𐤌.𐤋𐤀𐤉𐤔𐤄.𐤏𐤌𐤄.𐤅𐤉𐤀𐤊𐤋|
𐤆 𐤅𐤕𐤐𐤒𐤇𐤍𐤄.𐤏𐤉𐤍𐤉.𐤔𐤍𐤉𐤄𐤌.𐤅𐤉𐤃𐤏𐤅.𐤊𐤉.𐤏𐤉𐤓𐤌𐤌
.𐤄𐤌.𐤅𐤉𐤕𐤐𐤓𐤅.𐤏𐤋𐤄.𐤕𐤀𐤍𐤄.𐤅𐤉𐤏𐤔𐤅.𐤋𐤄𐤌.𐤇𐤂𐤓𐤕|
𐤇 𐤅𐤉𐤔𐤌𐤏𐤅.𐤀𐤕.𐤒𐤅𐤋.𐤉𐤄𐤅𐤄.𐤀𐤋𐤄𐤉𐤌.𐤌𐤕𐤄𐤋𐤊.𐤁𐤂𐤍
.𐤋𐤓𐤅𐤇.𐤄𐤉𐤅𐤌.𐤅𐤉𐤕𐤇𐤁𐤀.𐤄𐤀𐤃𐤌.𐤅𐤀𐤔𐤕𐤅.𐤌𐤐𐤍𐤉.𐤉𐤄𐤅
𐤄.𐤀𐤋𐤄𐤉𐤌.𐤁𐤕𐤅𐤊.𐤏𐤑.𐤄𐤂𐤍|
𐤈 𐤅𐤉𐤒𐤓𐤀.𐤉𐤄𐤅𐤄.𐤀𐤋𐤄𐤉𐤌.𐤀𐤋.𐤄𐤀𐤃𐤌.𐤅𐤉𐤀𐤌𐤓.𐤋𐤅.
𐤀𐤉𐤊𐤄|
𐤉 𐤅𐤉𐤀𐤌𐤓.𐤀𐤕.𐤒𐤋𐤊.𐤔𐤌𐤏𐤕𐤉.𐤁𐤂𐤍.𐤅𐤀𐤉𐤓𐤀.𐤊𐤉.
𐤏𐤉𐤓𐤌.𐤀𐤍𐤊𐤉.𐤅𐤀𐤇𐤁𐤀|
𐤉𐤀 𐤅𐤉𐤀𐤌𐤓.𐤌𐤉.𐤄𐤂𐤉𐤃.𐤋𐤊.𐤊𐤉.𐤏𐤉𐤓𐤌.𐤀𐤕𐤄.𐤄𐤌𐤍.
𐤄𐤏𐤑.𐤀𐤔𐤓.𐤑𐤅𐤉𐤕𐤉𐤊.𐤋𐤁𐤋𐤕𐤉.𐤀𐤊𐤋.𐤌𐤌𐤍𐤅.𐤀𐤊𐤋𐤕|
𐤉𐤁 𐤅𐤉𐤀𐤌𐤓.𐤄𐤀𐤃𐤌.𐤄𐤀𐤔𐤄.𐤀𐤔𐤓.𐤍𐤕𐤕𐤄.𐤏𐤌𐤃𐤉.
𐤄𐤅𐤀.𐤍𐤕𐤍𐤄.𐤋𐤉.𐤌𐤍.𐤄𐤏𐤑.𐤅𐤀𐤊𐤋|
𐤉𐤂 𐤅𐤉𐤀𐤌𐤓.𐤉𐤄𐤅𐤄.𐤀𐤋𐤄𐤉𐤌.𐤋𐤀𐤔𐤄.𐤌𐤄.𐤆𐤀𐤕.𐤏𐤔
𐤉𐤕.𐤅𐤕𐤀𐤌𐤓.𐤄𐤀𐤔𐤄.𐤄𐤍𐤇𐤔.𐤄𐤔𐤉𐤀𐤍𐤉.𐤅𐤀𐤊𐤋|
𐤉𐤃 𐤅𐤉𐤀𐤌𐤓.𐤉𐤄𐤅𐤄.𐤀𐤋𐤄𐤉𐤌.𐤀𐤋.𐤄𐤍𐤇𐤔.𐤊𐤉.𐤏𐤔𐤉𐤕
.𐤆𐤀𐤕.𐤀𐤓𐤅𐤓.𐤀𐤕𐤄.𐤌𐤊𐤋.𐤄𐤁𐤄𐤌𐤄.𐤅𐤌𐤊𐤋.𐤇𐤉𐤕.𐤄𐤔
𐤃𐤄.𐤏𐤋.𐤂𐤇𐤍𐤊.𐤕𐤋𐤊.𐤅𐤏𐤐𐤓.𐤕𐤀𐤊𐤋.𐤊𐤋.𐤉𐤌𐤉.𐤇𐤉𐤉𐤊|

..15.. 𐤅𐤀𐤉𐤁𐤄.𐤀𐤔𐤉𐤕.𐤁𐤉𐤍𐤊.𐤅𐤁𐤉𐤍.𐤄𐤀𐤔𐤄.𐤅𐤁𐤉𐤍.𐤆𐤓
𐤏𐤊.𐤅𐤁𐤉𐤍.𐤆𐤓𐤏𐤄.𐤄𐤅𐤀.𐤉𐤔𐤅𐤐𐤊.𐤓𐤀𐤔.𐤅𐤀𐤕𐤄.𐤕𐤔𐤅𐤐𐤍𐤅
.𐤏𐤒𐤁|

..16.. 𐤀𐤋.𐤄𐤀𐤔𐤄.𐤀𐤌𐤓.𐤄𐤓𐤁𐤄.𐤀𐤓𐤁𐤄.𐤏𐤑𐤁𐤅𐤍𐤊.𐤅𐤄𐤓𐤍
𐤊.𐤁𐤏𐤑𐤁.𐤕𐤋𐤃𐤉.𐤁𐤍𐤉𐤌.𐤅𐤀𐤋.𐤀𐤉𐤔𐤊.𐤕𐤔𐤅𐤒𐤕𐤊.𐤅𐤄𐤅
𐤀.𐤉𐤌𐤔𐤋.𐤁𐤊|

..17.. 𐤅𐤋𐤀𐤃𐤌.𐤀𐤌𐤓.𐤊𐤉.𐤔𐤌𐤏𐤕.𐤋𐤒𐤅𐤋.𐤀𐤔𐤕𐤊.𐤅𐤕𐤀
𐤊𐤋.𐤌𐤍.𐤄𐤏𐤑.𐤀𐤔𐤓.𐤑𐤅𐤉𐤕𐤉𐤊.𐤋𐤀𐤌𐤓.𐤋𐤀.𐤕𐤀𐤊𐤋.𐤌𐤌
𐤍𐤅.𐤀𐤓𐤅𐤓𐤄.𐤄𐤀𐤃𐤌𐤄.𐤁𐤏𐤁𐤅𐤓𐤊.𐤁𐤏𐤑𐤁𐤅𐤍.𐤕𐤀𐤊𐤋𐤍𐤄.𐤊
𐤋.𐤉𐤌𐤉.𐤇𐤉𐤉𐤊|

..18.. 𐤅𐤒𐤅𐤑.𐤅𐤃𐤓𐤃𐤓.𐤕𐤑𐤌𐤉𐤇.𐤋𐤊.𐤅𐤀𐤊𐤋𐤕.𐤀𐤕.𐤏𐤔
𐤁.𐤄𐤔𐤃𐤄|

..19.. 𐤁𐤆𐤏𐤕.𐤀𐤐𐤉𐤊.𐤕𐤀𐤊𐤋.𐤋𐤇𐤌.𐤏𐤃.𐤔𐤅𐤁𐤊.𐤀𐤋.𐤄
𐤀𐤃𐤌𐤄.𐤊𐤉.𐤌𐤌𐤍𐤄.𐤋𐤒𐤇𐤕.𐤊𐤉.𐤏𐤐𐤓.𐤀𐤕𐤄.𐤅𐤀𐤋.𐤏𐤐𐤓
.𐤕𐤔𐤅𐤁|

..20.. 𐤅𐤉𐤒𐤓𐤀.𐤄𐤀𐤃𐤌.𐤔𐤌.𐤀𐤔𐤕𐤅.𐤇𐤅𐤄.𐤊𐤉.𐤄𐤅𐤀.𐤄𐤉
𐤕𐤄.𐤀𐤌.𐤊𐤋.𐤇𐤉|

..21.. 𐤅𐤉𐤏𐤔.𐤉𐤄𐤅𐤄.𐤀𐤋𐤄𐤉𐤌.𐤋𐤀𐤃𐤌.𐤅𐤋𐤀𐤔𐤕𐤅.𐤊𐤕𐤍𐤅
𐤕.𐤏𐤅𐤓.𐤅𐤉𐤋𐤁𐤔𐤌|

..22.. 𐤅𐤉𐤀𐤌𐤓.𐤉𐤄𐤅𐤄.𐤀𐤋𐤄𐤉𐤌.𐤄𐤍.𐤄𐤀𐤃𐤌.𐤄𐤉𐤄.𐤊𐤀
𐤇𐤃.𐤌𐤌𐤍𐤅.𐤋𐤃𐤏𐤕.𐤈𐤅𐤁.𐤅𐤓𐤏.𐤅𐤏𐤕𐤄.𐤐𐤍.𐤉𐤔𐤋𐤇.𐤉𐤃𐤅
.𐤅𐤋𐤒𐤇.𐤂𐤌.𐤌𐤏𐤑.𐤄𐤇𐤉𐤉𐤌.𐤅𐤀𐤊𐤋.𐤅𐤇𐤉.𐤋𐤏𐤋𐤌|

..23.. 𐤅𐤉𐤔𐤋𐤇𐤄𐤅.𐤉𐤄𐤅𐤄.𐤀𐤋𐤄𐤉𐤌.𐤌𐤂𐤍.𐤏𐤃𐤍.𐤋𐤏𐤁𐤃.
𐤀𐤕.𐤄𐤀𐤃𐤌𐤄.𐤀𐤔𐤓.𐤋𐤒𐤇.𐤌𐤔𐤌|

..24.. 𐤅𐤉𐤂𐤓𐤔.𐤀𐤕.𐤄𐤀𐤃𐤌.𐤅𐤉𐤔𐤊𐤍.𐤌𐤒𐤃𐤌.𐤋𐤂𐤍.𐤏
𐤃𐤍.𐤀𐤕.𐤄𐤊𐤓𐤁𐤉𐤌.𐤅𐤀𐤕.𐤋𐤄𐤈.𐤄𐤇𐤓𐤁.𐤄𐤌𐤕𐤄𐤐𐤊𐤕.𐤋
𐤔𐤌𐤓.𐤀𐤕.𐤃𐤓𐤊.𐤏𐤑.𐤄𐤇𐤉𐤉𐤌||

𐤁𐤓𐤀𐤔𐤉𐤕.𐤇𐤋𐤒 ..4..

1 𐤅𐤄𐤀𐤃𐤌.𐤉𐤃𐤏.𐤀𐤕.𐤇𐤅𐤄.𐤀𐤔𐤕𐤅.𐤅𐤕𐤄𐤓.𐤅𐤕𐤋𐤃.𐤀
𐤕.𐤒𐤉𐤍.𐤅𐤕𐤀𐤌𐤓.𐤒𐤍𐤉𐤕𐤉.𐤀𐤉𐤔.𐤀𐤕.𐤉𐤄𐤅𐤄|

2 𐤅𐤕𐤎𐤐.𐤋𐤋𐤃𐤕.𐤀𐤕.𐤀𐤇𐤉𐤅.𐤀𐤕.𐤄𐤁𐤋.𐤅𐤉𐤄𐤉.𐤄𐤁𐤋.𐤓
𐤏𐤄.𐤑𐤀𐤍.𐤅𐤒𐤉𐤍.𐤄𐤉𐤄.𐤏𐤁𐤃.𐤀𐤃𐤌𐤄|

3 𐤅𐤉𐤄𐤉.𐤌𐤒𐤑.𐤉𐤌𐤉𐤌.𐤅𐤉𐤁𐤀.𐤒𐤉𐤍.𐤌𐤐𐤓𐤉.𐤄𐤀𐤃𐤌𐤄
.𐤌𐤍𐤇𐤄.𐤋𐤉𐤄𐤅𐤄|

4 𐤅𐤄𐤁𐤋.𐤄𐤁𐤉𐤀.𐤂𐤌.𐤄𐤅𐤀.𐤌𐤁𐤊𐤓𐤅𐤕.𐤑𐤀𐤍𐤅.𐤅𐤌𐤇𐤋𐤁
𐤄𐤍.𐤅𐤉𐤔𐤏.𐤉𐤄𐤅𐤄.𐤀𐤋.𐤄𐤁𐤋.𐤅𐤀𐤋.𐤌𐤍𐤇𐤕𐤅|

5 𐤅𐤀𐤋.𐤒𐤉𐤍.𐤅𐤀𐤋.𐤌𐤍𐤇𐤕𐤅.𐤋𐤀.𐤔𐤏𐤄.𐤅𐤉𐤇𐤓.𐤋𐤒𐤉𐤍.𐤌
𐤀𐤃.𐤅𐤉𐤐𐤋𐤅.𐤐𐤍𐤉𐤅|

6 𐤅𐤉𐤀𐤌𐤓.𐤉𐤄𐤅𐤄.𐤀𐤋.𐤒𐤉𐤍.𐤋𐤌𐤄.𐤇𐤓𐤄.𐤋𐤊.𐤅𐤋𐤌𐤄.𐤍𐤐
𐤋𐤅.𐤐𐤍𐤉𐤊|

7 𐤄𐤋𐤅𐤀.𐤀𐤌.𐤕𐤉𐤈𐤉𐤁.𐤔𐤀𐤕.𐤅𐤀𐤌.𐤋𐤀.𐤕𐤉𐤈𐤉𐤁.𐤋𐤐
𐤕𐤇.𐤇𐤈𐤀𐤕.𐤓𐤁𐤑.𐤅𐤀𐤋𐤉𐤊.𐤕𐤔𐤅𐤒𐤕𐤅.𐤅𐤀𐤕𐤄.𐤕𐤌𐤔𐤋.
𐤁𐤅|

8 𐤅𐤉𐤀𐤌𐤓.𐤒𐤉𐤍.𐤀𐤋.𐤄𐤁𐤋.𐤀𐤇𐤉𐤅.𐤅𐤉𐤄𐤉.𐤁𐤄𐤉𐤅𐤕𐤌.𐤁
𐤔𐤃𐤄.𐤅𐤉𐤒𐤌.𐤒𐤉𐤍.𐤀𐤋.𐤄𐤁𐤋.𐤀𐤇𐤉𐤅.𐤅𐤉𐤄𐤓𐤂𐤄𐤅|

9 𐤅𐤉𐤀𐤌𐤓.𐤉𐤄𐤅𐤄.𐤀𐤋.𐤒𐤉𐤍.𐤀𐤉.𐤄𐤁𐤋.𐤀𐤇𐤉𐤊.𐤅𐤉𐤀𐤌
𐤓.𐤋𐤀.𐤉𐤃𐤏𐤕𐤉.𐤄𐤔𐤌𐤓.𐤀𐤇𐤉.𐤀𐤍𐤊𐤉|

10 𐤅𐤉𐤀𐤌𐤓.𐤌𐤄.𐤏𐤔𐤉𐤕.𐤒𐤅𐤋.𐤃𐤌𐤉.𐤀𐤇𐤉𐤊.𐤑𐤏𐤒𐤉
𐤌.𐤀𐤋𐤉.𐤌𐤍.𐤄𐤀𐤃𐤌𐤄|

11 𐤅𐤏𐤕𐤄.𐤀𐤓𐤅𐤓.𐤀𐤕𐤄.𐤌𐤍.𐤄𐤀𐤃𐤌𐤄.𐤀𐤔𐤓.𐤐𐤑𐤕𐤄.
𐤀𐤕.𐤐𐤉𐤄.𐤋𐤒𐤇𐤕.𐤀𐤕.𐤃𐤌𐤉.𐤀𐤇𐤉𐤊.𐤌𐤉𐤃𐤊|

12 𐤊𐤉.𐤕𐤏𐤁𐤃.𐤀𐤕.𐤄𐤀𐤃𐤌𐤄.𐤋𐤀.𐤕𐤎𐤐.𐤕𐤕.𐤊𐤇𐤄.
𐤋𐤊.𐤍𐤏.𐤅𐤍𐤃.𐤕𐤄𐤉𐤄.𐤁𐤀𐤓𐤑|

13 𐤅𐤉𐤀𐤌𐤓.𐤒𐤉𐤍.𐤀𐤋.𐤉𐤄𐤅𐤄.𐤂𐤃𐤅𐤋.𐤏𐤅𐤍𐤉.𐤌𐤍𐤔𐤀|

14 𐤄𐤍.𐤂𐤓𐤔𐤕.𐤀𐤕𐤉.𐤄𐤉𐤅𐤌.𐤌𐤏𐤋.𐤐𐤍𐤉.𐤄𐤀𐤃𐤌𐤄.𐤅
𐤌𐤐𐤍𐤉𐤊.𐤀𐤎𐤕𐤓.𐤅𐤄𐤉𐤉𐤕𐤉.𐤍𐤏.𐤅𐤍𐤃.𐤁𐤀𐤓𐤑.𐤅𐤄𐤉𐤄.𐤊𐤋.
𐤌𐤑𐤀𐤉.𐤉𐤄𐤓𐤂𐤍𐤉|

..יה.. 𐤅𐤉𐤀𐤌𐤓.𐤋𐤅.𐤉𐤄𐤅𐤄.𐤋𐤊𐤍.𐤊𐤋.𐤄𐤓𐤂.𐤒𐤉𐤍.𐤔𐤁𐤏𐤕𐤉
𐤌.𐤉𐤒𐤌.𐤅𐤉𐤔𐤌.𐤉𐤄𐤅𐤄.𐤋𐤒𐤉𐤍.𐤀𐤅𐤕.𐤋𐤁𐤋𐤕𐤉.𐤄𐤊𐤅𐤕.𐤀
𐤕𐤅.𐤊𐤋.𐤌𐤑𐤀𐤅|

..יו.. 𐤅𐤉𐤑𐤀.𐤒𐤉𐤍.𐤌𐤋𐤐𐤍𐤉.𐤉𐤄𐤅𐤄.𐤅𐤉𐤔𐤁.𐤁𐤀𐤓𐤑.𐤍𐤅𐤃.
𐤒𐤃𐤌𐤕.𐤏𐤃𐤍|

..יז.. 𐤅𐤉𐤃𐤏.𐤒𐤉𐤍.𐤀𐤕.𐤀𐤔𐤕𐤅.𐤅𐤕𐤄𐤓.𐤅𐤕𐤋𐤃.𐤀𐤕.𐤇𐤍𐤅
𐤊.𐤅𐤉𐤄𐤉.𐤁𐤍𐤄.𐤏𐤉𐤓.𐤅𐤉𐤒𐤓𐤀.𐤔𐤌.𐤄𐤏𐤉𐤓.𐤊𐤔𐤌.𐤁𐤍𐤅.𐤇
𐤍𐤅𐤊|

..יח.. 𐤅𐤉𐤅𐤋𐤃.𐤋𐤇𐤍𐤅𐤊.𐤀𐤕.𐤏𐤉𐤓𐤃.𐤅𐤏𐤉𐤓𐤃.𐤉𐤋𐤃.𐤀𐤕.
𐤌𐤇𐤅𐤉𐤀𐤋.𐤅𐤌𐤇𐤉𐤉𐤀𐤋.𐤉𐤋𐤃.𐤀𐤕.𐤌𐤕𐤅𐤔𐤀𐤋.𐤅𐤌𐤕𐤅𐤔𐤀
𐤋.𐤉𐤋𐤃.𐤀𐤕.𐤋𐤌𐤊|

..יט.. 𐤅𐤉𐤒𐤇.𐤋𐤅.𐤋𐤌𐤊.𐤔𐤕𐤉.𐤍𐤔𐤉𐤌.𐤔𐤌.𐤄𐤀𐤇𐤕.𐤏𐤃
𐤄.𐤅𐤔𐤌.𐤄𐤔𐤍𐤉𐤕.𐤑𐤋𐤄|

..כ.. 𐤅𐤕𐤋𐤃.𐤏𐤃𐤄.𐤀𐤕.𐤉𐤁𐤋.𐤄𐤅𐤀.𐤄𐤉𐤄.𐤀𐤁𐤉.𐤉𐤔𐤁.
𐤀𐤄𐤋.𐤅𐤌𐤒𐤍𐤄|

..כא.. 𐤅𐤔𐤌.𐤀𐤇𐤉𐤅.𐤉𐤅𐤁𐤋.𐤄𐤅𐤀.𐤄𐤉𐤄.𐤀𐤁𐤉.𐤊𐤋.𐤕𐤐𐤔.𐤊
𐤍𐤅𐤓.𐤅𐤏𐤅𐤂𐤁|

..כב.. 𐤅𐤑𐤋𐤄.𐤂𐤌.𐤄𐤅𐤀.𐤉𐤋𐤃𐤄.𐤀𐤕.𐤕𐤅𐤁𐤋.𐤒𐤉𐤍.𐤋𐤈𐤔.
𐤊𐤋.𐤇𐤓𐤔.𐤍𐤇𐤔𐤕.𐤅𐤁𐤓𐤆𐤋.𐤅𐤀𐤇𐤅𐤕.𐤕𐤅𐤁𐤋.𐤒𐤉𐤍.𐤍𐤏𐤌𐤄
|

..כג.. 𐤅𐤉𐤀𐤌𐤓.𐤋𐤌𐤊.𐤋𐤍𐤔𐤉𐤅.𐤏𐤃𐤄.𐤅𐤑𐤋𐤄.𐤔𐤌𐤏𐤍.𐤒𐤅𐤋
𐤉.𐤍𐤔𐤉.𐤋𐤌𐤊.𐤄𐤀𐤆𐤍𐤄.𐤀𐤌𐤓𐤕𐤉.𐤊𐤉.𐤀𐤉𐤔.𐤄𐤓𐤂𐤕𐤉.𐤋
𐤐𐤑𐤏𐤉.𐤅𐤉𐤋𐤃.𐤋𐤇𐤁𐤓𐤕𐤉|

..כד.. 𐤊𐤉.𐤔𐤁𐤏𐤕𐤉𐤌.𐤉𐤒𐤌.𐤒𐤉𐤍.𐤅𐤋𐤌𐤊.𐤔𐤁𐤏𐤉𐤌.𐤅𐤔𐤁
𐤏𐤄|

..כה.. 𐤅𐤉𐤃𐤏.𐤀𐤃𐤌.𐤏𐤅𐤃.𐤀𐤕.𐤀𐤔𐤕𐤅.𐤅𐤕𐤋𐤃.𐤁𐤍.𐤅𐤕𐤒
𐤓𐤀.𐤀𐤕.𐤔𐤌𐤅.𐤔𐤕.𐤊𐤉.𐤔𐤕.𐤋𐤉.𐤀𐤋𐤄𐤉𐤌.𐤆𐤓𐤏.𐤀𐤇𐤓.
𐤕𐤇𐤕.𐤄𐤁𐤋.𐤊𐤉.𐤄𐤓𐤂𐤅.𐤒𐤉𐤍|

..כו.. 𐤅𐤋𐤔𐤕.𐤂𐤌.𐤄𐤅𐤀.𐤉𐤋𐤃.𐤁𐤍.𐤅𐤉𐤒𐤓𐤀.𐤀𐤕.𐤔𐤌𐤅.𐤀𐤍
𐤅𐤔.𐤀𐤆.𐤄𐤅𐤇𐤋.𐤋𐤒𐤓𐤀.𐤁𐤔𐤌.𐤉𐤄𐤅𐤄||

בראשית . חלק ה

א זה . ספר . תולדת . אדם . ביום . ברא . אלהים . א
דם . בדמות . אלהים . עשה . אתו|
ב זכר . ונקבה . בראם . ויברך . אתם . ויקרא . את .
שמם . אדם . ביום . הבראם|
ג ויחי . אדם . שלשים . ומאת . שנה . ויולד . בד
מותו . כצלמו . ויקרא . את . שמו . שת|
ד ויהיו . ימי . אדם . אחרי . הולידו . את . שת . ש
מנה . מאת . שנה . ויולד . בנים . ובנות|
ה ויהיו . כל . ימי . אדם . אשר . חי . תשע . מאות . ש
נה . ושלשים . שנה . וימת|
ו ויחי . שת . חמש . שנים . ומאת . שנה . ויולד . את
. אנוש|
ז ויחי . שת . אחרי . הולידו . את . אנוש . שבע . ש
נים . ושמנה . מאות . שנה . ויולד . בנים . ובנות|
ח ויהיו . כל . ימי . שת . שתים . עשרה . שנה . ותשע
. מאות . שנה . וימת|
ט ויחי . אנוש . תשעים . שנה . ויולד . את . קינן|
י ויחי . אנוש . אחרי . הולידו . את . קינן . חמ
ש . עשרה . שנה . ושמנה . מאות . שנה . ויולד . בנים . ו
בנות|
יא ויהיו . כל . ימי . אנוש . חמש . שנים . ותשע . מא
ות . שנה . וימת|
יב ויחי . קינן . שבעים . שנה . ויולד . את . מהלל
אל|
יג ויחי . קינן . אחרי . הולידו . את . מהללאל . א
רבעים . שנה . ושמנה . מאות . שנה . ויולד . בנים . וב
נות|
יד ויהיו . כל . ימי . קינן . עשר . שנים . ותשע . מא
ות . שנה . וימת|

𐤉𐤄 𐤅𐤉𐤇𐤉.𐤌𐤄𐤋𐤋𐤀𐤋.𐤇𐤌𐤔.𐤔𐤍𐤉𐤌.𐤅𐤔𐤔𐤉𐤌.𐤔𐤍𐤄.𐤅𐤉
𐤅𐤋𐤃.𐤀𐤕.𐤉𐤓𐤃|

𐤉𐤅 𐤅𐤉𐤇𐤉.𐤌𐤄𐤋𐤋𐤀𐤋.𐤀𐤇𐤓𐤉.𐤄𐤅𐤋𐤉𐤃𐤅.𐤀𐤕.𐤉𐤓𐤃.𐤔
𐤋𐤔𐤉𐤌.𐤔𐤍𐤄.𐤅𐤔𐤌𐤍𐤄.𐤌𐤀𐤅𐤕.𐤔𐤍𐤄.𐤅𐤉𐤅𐤋𐤃.𐤁𐤍𐤉𐤌.𐤅𐤁𐤍𐤅
𐤕|

𐤉𐤆 𐤅𐤉𐤄𐤉𐤅.𐤊𐤋.𐤉𐤌𐤉.𐤌𐤄𐤋𐤋𐤀𐤋.𐤇𐤌𐤔.𐤅𐤕𐤔𐤏𐤉𐤌.𐤔
𐤍𐤄.𐤅𐤔𐤌𐤍𐤄.𐤌𐤀𐤅𐤕.𐤔𐤍𐤄.𐤅𐤉𐤌𐤕|

𐤉𐤇 𐤅𐤉𐤇𐤉.𐤉𐤓𐤃.𐤔𐤕𐤉𐤌.𐤅𐤔𐤔𐤉𐤌.𐤔𐤍𐤄.𐤅𐤌𐤀𐤕.𐤔𐤍𐤄.
𐤅𐤉𐤅𐤋𐤃.𐤀𐤕.𐤇𐤍𐤅𐤊|

𐤉𐤈 𐤅𐤉𐤇𐤉.𐤉𐤓𐤃.𐤀𐤇𐤓𐤉.𐤄𐤅𐤋𐤉𐤃𐤅.𐤀𐤕.𐤇𐤍𐤅𐤊.𐤔𐤌𐤍
𐤄.𐤌𐤀𐤅𐤕.𐤔𐤍𐤄.𐤅𐤉𐤅𐤋𐤃.𐤁𐤍𐤉𐤌.𐤅𐤁𐤍𐤅𐤕|

𐤊 𐤅𐤉𐤄𐤉𐤅.𐤊𐤋.𐤉𐤌𐤉.𐤉𐤓𐤃.𐤔𐤕𐤉𐤌.𐤅𐤔𐤔𐤉𐤌.𐤔𐤍𐤄.𐤅
𐤕𐤔𐤏.𐤌𐤀𐤅𐤕.𐤔𐤍𐤄.𐤅𐤉𐤌𐤕|

𐤊𐤀 𐤅𐤉𐤇𐤉.𐤇𐤍𐤅𐤊.𐤇𐤌𐤔.𐤅𐤔𐤔𐤉𐤌.𐤔𐤍𐤄.𐤅𐤉𐤅𐤋𐤃.𐤀𐤕.
𐤌𐤕𐤅𐤔𐤋𐤇|

𐤊𐤁 𐤅𐤉𐤕𐤄𐤋𐤊.𐤇𐤍𐤅𐤊.𐤀𐤕.𐤄𐤀𐤋𐤄𐤉𐤌.𐤀𐤇𐤓𐤉.𐤄𐤅𐤋𐤉
𐤃𐤅.𐤀𐤕.𐤌𐤕𐤅𐤔𐤋𐤇.𐤔𐤋𐤔.𐤌𐤀𐤅𐤕.𐤔𐤍𐤄.𐤅𐤉𐤅𐤋𐤃.𐤁𐤍𐤉𐤌.
𐤅𐤁𐤍𐤅𐤕|

𐤊𐤂 𐤅𐤉𐤄𐤉.𐤊𐤋.𐤉𐤌𐤉.𐤇𐤍𐤅𐤊.𐤇𐤌𐤔.𐤅𐤔𐤔𐤉𐤌.𐤔𐤍𐤄.𐤅𐤔
𐤋𐤔.𐤌𐤀𐤅𐤕.𐤔𐤍𐤄|

𐤊𐤃 𐤅𐤉𐤕𐤄𐤋𐤊.𐤇𐤍𐤅𐤊.𐤀𐤕.𐤄𐤀𐤋𐤄𐤉𐤌.𐤅𐤀𐤉𐤍𐤍𐤅.𐤊𐤉.𐤋
𐤒𐤇.𐤀𐤕𐤅.𐤀𐤋𐤄𐤉𐤌|

𐤊𐤄 𐤅𐤉𐤇𐤉.𐤌𐤕𐤅𐤔𐤋𐤇.𐤔𐤁𐤏.𐤅𐤔𐤌𐤍𐤉𐤌.𐤔𐤍𐤄.𐤅𐤌𐤀𐤕.
𐤔𐤍𐤄.𐤅𐤉𐤅𐤋𐤃.𐤀𐤕.𐤋𐤌𐤊|

𐤊𐤅 𐤅𐤉𐤇𐤉.𐤌𐤕𐤅𐤔𐤋𐤇.𐤀𐤇𐤓𐤉.𐤄𐤅𐤋𐤉𐤃𐤅.𐤀𐤕.𐤋𐤌𐤊.𐤔
𐤕𐤉𐤌.𐤅𐤔𐤌𐤅𐤍𐤉𐤌.𐤔𐤍𐤄.𐤅𐤔𐤁𐤏.𐤌𐤀𐤅𐤕.𐤔𐤍𐤄.𐤅𐤉𐤅𐤋𐤃.𐤁𐤍
𐤉𐤌.𐤅𐤁𐤍𐤅𐤕|

𐤊𐤆 𐤅𐤉𐤄𐤉𐤅.𐤊𐤋.𐤉𐤌𐤉.𐤌𐤕𐤅𐤔𐤋𐤇.𐤕𐤔𐤏.𐤅𐤔𐤔𐤉𐤌.𐤔𐤍
𐤄.𐤅𐤕𐤔𐤏.𐤌𐤀𐤅𐤕.𐤔𐤍𐤄.𐤅𐤉𐤌𐤕|

𐤊𐤇 𐤅𐤉𐤇𐤉.𐤋𐤌𐤊.𐤔𐤕𐤉𐤌.𐤅𐤔𐤌𐤍𐤉𐤌.𐤔𐤍𐤄.𐤅𐤌𐤀𐤕.𐤔𐤍𐤄
.𐤅𐤉𐤅𐤋𐤃.𐤁𐤍|

29 𐤅𐤉𐤒𐤓𐤀.𐤀𐤕.𐤔𐤌𐤅.𐤍𐤇.𐤋𐤀𐤌𐤓.𐤆𐤄.𐤉𐤍𐤇𐤌𐤍𐤅.𐤌𐤌
𐤏𐤔𐤍𐤅.𐤅𐤌𐤏𐤑𐤁𐤅𐤍.𐤉𐤃𐤉𐤍𐤅.𐤌𐤍.𐤄𐤀𐤃𐤌𐤄.𐤀𐤔𐤓.𐤀𐤓𐤓𐤄.
𐤉𐤄𐤅𐤄|

30 𐤅𐤉𐤇𐤉.𐤋𐤌𐤊.𐤀𐤇𐤓𐤉.𐤄𐤅𐤋𐤉𐤃𐤅.𐤀𐤕.𐤍𐤇.𐤇𐤌𐤔.𐤅
𐤕𐤔𐤏𐤉𐤌.𐤔𐤍𐤄.𐤅𐤇𐤌𐤔.𐤌𐤀𐤕.𐤔𐤍𐤄.𐤅𐤉𐤅𐤋𐤃.𐤁𐤍𐤉𐤌.𐤅𐤁𐤍
𐤅𐤕|

31 𐤅𐤉𐤄𐤉.𐤊𐤋.𐤉𐤌𐤉.𐤋𐤌𐤊.𐤔𐤁𐤏.𐤅𐤔𐤁𐤏𐤉𐤌.𐤔𐤍𐤄.𐤅𐤔
𐤁𐤏.𐤌𐤀𐤅𐤕.𐤔𐤍𐤄.𐤅𐤉𐤌𐤕|

32 𐤅𐤉𐤄𐤉.𐤍𐤇.𐤁𐤍.𐤇𐤌𐤔.𐤌𐤀𐤅𐤕.𐤔𐤍𐤄.𐤅𐤉𐤅𐤋𐤃.𐤍𐤇.𐤀
𐤕.𐤔𐤌.𐤀𐤕.𐤇𐤌.𐤅𐤀𐤕.𐤉𐤐𐤕||

𐤁𐤓𐤀𐤔𐤉𐤕.𐤇𐤋𐤒 6

1 𐤅𐤉𐤄𐤉.𐤊𐤉.𐤄𐤇𐤋.𐤄𐤀𐤃𐤌.𐤋𐤓𐤁.𐤏𐤋.𐤐𐤍𐤉.𐤄𐤀𐤃𐤌𐤄.
𐤅𐤁𐤍𐤅𐤕.𐤉𐤋𐤃𐤅.𐤋𐤄𐤌|

2 𐤅𐤉𐤓𐤀𐤅.𐤁𐤍𐤉.𐤄𐤀𐤋𐤄𐤉𐤌.𐤀𐤕.𐤁𐤍𐤅𐤕.𐤄𐤀𐤃𐤌.𐤊𐤉.𐤈
𐤁𐤕.𐤄𐤍𐤄.𐤅𐤉𐤒𐤇𐤅.𐤋𐤄𐤌.𐤍𐤔𐤉𐤌.𐤌𐤊𐤋.𐤀𐤔𐤓.𐤁𐤇𐤓𐤅|

3 𐤅𐤉𐤀𐤌𐤓.𐤉𐤄𐤅𐤄.𐤋𐤀.𐤉𐤃𐤅𐤍.𐤓𐤅𐤇𐤉.𐤁𐤀𐤃𐤌.𐤋𐤏𐤋𐤌.
𐤁𐤔𐤂𐤌.𐤄𐤅𐤀.𐤁𐤔𐤓.𐤅𐤄𐤉𐤅.𐤉𐤌𐤉𐤅.𐤌𐤀𐤄.𐤅𐤏𐤔𐤓𐤉𐤌.𐤔𐤍𐤄|

4 𐤄𐤍𐤐𐤋𐤉𐤌.𐤄𐤉𐤅.𐤁𐤀𐤓𐤑.𐤁𐤉𐤌𐤉𐤌.𐤄𐤄𐤌.𐤅𐤂𐤌.𐤀𐤇𐤓
𐤉.𐤊𐤍.𐤀𐤔𐤓.𐤉𐤁𐤀𐤅.𐤁𐤍𐤉.𐤄𐤀𐤋𐤄𐤉𐤌.𐤀𐤋.𐤁𐤍𐤅𐤕.𐤄𐤀𐤃𐤌.
𐤅𐤉𐤋𐤃𐤅.𐤋𐤄𐤌.𐤄𐤌𐤄.𐤄𐤂𐤁𐤓𐤉𐤌.𐤀𐤔𐤓.𐤌𐤏𐤅𐤋𐤌.𐤀𐤍𐤔𐤉.
𐤄𐤔𐤌|

5 𐤅𐤉𐤓𐤀.𐤉𐤄𐤅𐤄.𐤊𐤉.𐤓𐤁𐤄.𐤓𐤏𐤕.𐤄𐤀𐤃𐤌.𐤁𐤀𐤓𐤑.𐤅𐤊𐤋.
𐤉𐤑𐤓.𐤌𐤇𐤔𐤁𐤕.𐤋𐤁𐤅.𐤓𐤒.𐤓𐤏.𐤊𐤋.𐤄𐤉𐤅𐤌|

6 𐤅𐤉𐤍𐤇𐤌.𐤉𐤄𐤅𐤄.𐤊𐤉.𐤏𐤔𐤄.𐤀𐤕.𐤄𐤀𐤃𐤌.𐤁𐤀𐤓𐤑.𐤅𐤉
𐤕𐤏𐤑𐤁.𐤀𐤋.𐤋𐤁𐤅|

7 𐤅𐤉𐤀𐤌𐤓.𐤉𐤄𐤅𐤄.𐤀𐤌𐤇𐤄.𐤀𐤕.𐤄𐤀𐤃𐤌.𐤀𐤔𐤓.𐤁𐤓𐤀
𐤕𐤉.𐤌𐤏𐤋.𐤐𐤍𐤉.𐤄𐤀𐤃𐤌𐤄.𐤌𐤀𐤃𐤌.𐤏𐤃.𐤁𐤄𐤌𐤄.𐤏𐤃.𐤓
𐤌𐤔.𐤅𐤏𐤃.𐤏𐤅𐤐.𐤄𐤔𐤌𐤉𐤌.𐤊𐤉.𐤍𐤇𐤌𐤕𐤉.𐤊𐤉.𐤏𐤔𐤉𐤕𐤌|

8 𐤅𐤍𐤇.𐤌𐤑𐤀.𐤇𐤍.𐤁𐤏𐤉𐤍𐤉.𐤉𐤄𐤅𐤄|

𐤈 𐤀𐤋𐤄.𐤕𐤅𐤋𐤃𐤕.𐤍𐤇.𐤍𐤇.𐤀𐤉𐤔.𐤑𐤃𐤉𐤒.𐤕𐤌𐤉𐤌.𐤄
𐤉𐤄.𐤁𐤃𐤓𐤕𐤉𐤅.𐤀𐤕.𐤄𐤀𐤋𐤄𐤉𐤌.𐤄𐤕𐤄𐤋𐤊.𐤍𐤇|
𐤉 𐤅𐤉𐤅𐤋𐤃.𐤍𐤇.𐤔𐤋𐤔𐤄.𐤁𐤍𐤉𐤌.𐤀𐤕.𐤔𐤌.𐤀𐤕.𐤇𐤌.𐤅𐤀
𐤕.𐤉𐤐𐤕|
𐤉𐤀 𐤅𐤕𐤔𐤇𐤕.𐤄𐤀𐤓𐤑.𐤋𐤐𐤍𐤉.𐤄𐤀𐤋𐤄𐤉𐤌.𐤅𐤕𐤌𐤋𐤀.𐤄𐤀
𐤓𐤑.𐤇𐤌𐤎|
𐤉𐤁 𐤅𐤉𐤓𐤀.𐤀𐤋𐤄𐤉𐤌.𐤀𐤕.𐤄𐤀𐤓𐤑.𐤅𐤄𐤍𐤄.𐤍𐤔𐤇𐤕𐤄.𐤊𐤉
.𐤄𐤔𐤇𐤉𐤕.𐤊𐤋.𐤁𐤔𐤓.𐤀𐤕.𐤃𐤓𐤊𐤅.𐤏𐤋.𐤄𐤀𐤓𐤑|
𐤉𐤂 𐤅𐤉𐤀𐤌𐤓.𐤀𐤋𐤄𐤉𐤌.𐤋𐤍𐤇.𐤒𐤑.𐤊𐤋.𐤁𐤔𐤓.𐤁𐤀.𐤋𐤐𐤍𐤉.
𐤊𐤉.𐤌𐤋𐤀𐤄.𐤄𐤀𐤓𐤑.𐤇𐤌𐤎.𐤌𐤐𐤍𐤉𐤄𐤌.𐤅𐤄𐤍𐤍𐤉.𐤌𐤔𐤇𐤉𐤕
𐤌.𐤀𐤕.𐤄𐤀𐤓𐤑|
𐤉𐤃 𐤏𐤔𐤄.𐤋𐤊.𐤕𐤁𐤕.𐤏𐤑𐤉.𐤂𐤐𐤓.𐤒𐤍𐤉𐤌.𐤕𐤏𐤔𐤄.𐤀𐤕
.𐤄𐤕𐤁𐤄.𐤅𐤊𐤐𐤓𐤕.𐤀𐤕𐤄.𐤌𐤁𐤉𐤕.𐤅𐤌𐤇𐤅𐤑.𐤁𐤊𐤐𐤓|
𐤈𐤅 𐤅𐤆𐤄.𐤀𐤔𐤓.𐤕𐤏𐤔𐤄.𐤀𐤕𐤄.𐤔𐤋𐤔.𐤌𐤀𐤅𐤕.𐤀𐤌𐤄.𐤀
𐤓𐤊.𐤄𐤕𐤁𐤄.𐤇𐤌𐤔𐤉𐤌.𐤀𐤌𐤄.𐤓𐤇𐤁𐤄.𐤅𐤔𐤋𐤔𐤉𐤌.𐤀𐤌𐤄.
𐤒𐤅𐤌𐤕𐤄|
𐤈𐤆 𐤑𐤄𐤓.𐤕𐤏𐤔𐤄.𐤋𐤕𐤁𐤄.𐤅𐤀𐤋.𐤀𐤌𐤄.𐤕𐤊𐤋𐤍𐤄.𐤌𐤋𐤌
𐤏𐤋𐤄.𐤅𐤐𐤕𐤇.𐤄𐤕𐤁𐤄.𐤁𐤑𐤃𐤄.𐤕𐤔𐤉𐤌.𐤕𐤇𐤕𐤉𐤌.𐤔𐤍𐤉
𐤌.𐤅𐤔𐤋𐤔𐤉𐤌.𐤕𐤏𐤔𐤄|
𐤉𐤆 𐤅𐤀𐤍𐤉.𐤄𐤍𐤍𐤉.𐤌𐤁𐤉𐤀.𐤀𐤕.𐤄𐤌𐤁𐤅𐤋.𐤌𐤉𐤌.𐤏𐤋.𐤄𐤀𐤓
𐤑.𐤋𐤔𐤇𐤕.𐤊𐤋.𐤁𐤔𐤓.𐤀𐤔𐤓.𐤁𐤅.𐤓𐤅𐤇.𐤇𐤉𐤉𐤌.𐤌𐤕𐤇𐤕.𐤄
𐤔𐤌𐤉𐤌.𐤊𐤋.𐤀𐤔𐤓.𐤁𐤀𐤓𐤑.𐤉𐤂𐤅𐤏|
𐤉𐤇 𐤅𐤄𐤒𐤌𐤕𐤉.𐤀𐤕.𐤁𐤓𐤉𐤕𐤉.𐤀𐤕𐤊.𐤅𐤁𐤀𐤕.𐤀𐤋.𐤄𐤕𐤁𐤄
.𐤀𐤕𐤄.𐤅𐤁𐤍𐤉𐤊.𐤅𐤀𐤔𐤕𐤊.𐤅𐤍𐤔𐤉.𐤁𐤍𐤉𐤊.𐤀𐤕𐤊|
𐤉𐤈 𐤅𐤌𐤊𐤋.𐤄𐤇𐤉.𐤌𐤊𐤋.𐤁𐤔𐤓.𐤔𐤍𐤉𐤌.𐤌𐤊𐤋.𐤕𐤁𐤉𐤀.𐤀
𐤋.𐤄𐤕𐤁𐤄.𐤋𐤄𐤇𐤉𐤕.𐤀𐤕𐤊.𐤆𐤊𐤓.𐤅𐤍𐤒𐤁𐤄.𐤉𐤄𐤉𐤅|
𐤊 𐤌𐤄𐤏𐤅𐤐.𐤋𐤌𐤉𐤍𐤄𐤅.𐤅𐤌𐤍.𐤄𐤁𐤄𐤌𐤄.𐤋𐤌𐤉𐤍𐤄.𐤌𐤊𐤋.𐤓
𐤌𐤔.𐤄𐤀𐤃𐤌𐤄.𐤋𐤌𐤉𐤍𐤄𐤅.𐤔𐤍𐤉𐤌.𐤌𐤊𐤋.𐤉𐤁𐤀𐤅.𐤀𐤋𐤉𐤊.𐤋
𐤄𐤇𐤉𐤅𐤕|
𐤊𐤀 𐤅𐤀𐤕𐤄.𐤒𐤇.𐤋𐤊.𐤌𐤊𐤋.𐤌𐤀𐤊𐤋.𐤀𐤔𐤓.𐤉𐤀𐤊𐤋.𐤅𐤀𐤎𐤐
𐤕.𐤀𐤋𐤉𐤊.𐤅𐤄𐤉𐤄.𐤋𐤊.𐤅𐤋𐤄𐤌.𐤋𐤀𐤊𐤋𐤄|

22 𐤅𐤉𐤏𐤔.𐤍𐤇.𐤊𐤊𐤋.𐤀𐤔𐤓.𐤑𐤅𐤄.𐤀𐤕𐤅.𐤀𐤋𐤄𐤉𐤌.𐤊𐤍.
𐤏𐤔𐤄||

7 𐤁𐤓𐤀𐤔𐤉𐤕.𐤇𐤋𐤒

1 𐤅𐤉𐤀𐤌𐤓.𐤉𐤄𐤅𐤄.𐤋𐤍𐤇.𐤁𐤀.𐤀𐤕𐤄.𐤅𐤊𐤋.𐤁𐤉𐤕𐤊.𐤀𐤋.𐤄
𐤕𐤁𐤄.𐤊𐤉.𐤀𐤕𐤊.𐤓𐤀𐤉𐤕𐤉.𐤑𐤃𐤉𐤒.𐤋𐤐𐤍𐤉.𐤁𐤃𐤅𐤓.𐤄𐤆𐤄
|

2 𐤌𐤊𐤋.𐤄𐤁𐤄𐤌𐤄.𐤄𐤈𐤄𐤅𐤓𐤄.𐤕𐤒𐤇.𐤋𐤊.𐤔𐤁𐤏𐤄.𐤔𐤁
𐤏𐤄.𐤀𐤉𐤔.𐤅𐤀𐤔𐤕𐤅.𐤅𐤌𐤍.𐤄𐤁𐤄𐤌𐤄.𐤀𐤔𐤓.𐤋𐤀.𐤈𐤄𐤓𐤄.𐤄𐤅
𐤀.𐤔𐤍𐤉𐤌.𐤀𐤉𐤔.𐤅𐤀𐤔𐤕𐤅|

3 𐤂𐤌.𐤌𐤏𐤅𐤐.𐤄𐤔𐤌𐤉𐤌.𐤔𐤁𐤏𐤄.𐤔𐤁𐤏𐤄.𐤆𐤊𐤓.𐤅𐤍𐤒𐤁
𐤄.𐤋𐤇𐤉𐤅𐤕.𐤆𐤓𐤏.𐤏𐤋.𐤐𐤍𐤉.𐤊𐤋.𐤄𐤀𐤓𐤑|

4 𐤊𐤉.𐤋𐤉𐤌𐤉𐤌.𐤏𐤅𐤃.𐤔𐤁𐤏𐤄.𐤀𐤍𐤊𐤉.𐤌𐤌𐤈𐤉𐤓.𐤏𐤋.𐤄
𐤀𐤓𐤑.𐤀𐤓𐤁𐤏𐤉𐤌.𐤉𐤅𐤌.𐤅𐤀𐤓𐤁𐤏𐤉𐤌.𐤋𐤉𐤋𐤄.𐤅𐤌𐤇𐤉𐤕𐤉.𐤀
𐤕.𐤊𐤋.𐤄𐤉𐤒𐤅𐤌.𐤀𐤔𐤓.𐤏𐤔𐤉𐤕𐤉.𐤌𐤏𐤋.𐤐𐤍𐤉.𐤄𐤀𐤃𐤌𐤄|

5 𐤅𐤉𐤏𐤔.𐤍𐤇.𐤊𐤊𐤋.𐤀𐤔𐤓.𐤑𐤅𐤄𐤅.𐤉𐤄𐤅𐤄|

6 𐤅𐤍𐤇.𐤁𐤍.𐤔𐤔.𐤌𐤀𐤅𐤕.𐤔𐤍𐤄.𐤅𐤄𐤌𐤁𐤅𐤋.𐤄𐤉𐤄.𐤌𐤉𐤌.𐤏𐤋
.𐤄𐤀𐤓𐤑|

7 𐤅𐤉𐤁𐤀.𐤍𐤇.𐤅𐤁𐤍𐤉𐤅.𐤅𐤀𐤔𐤕𐤅.𐤅𐤍𐤔𐤉.𐤁𐤍𐤉𐤅.𐤀𐤕𐤅.𐤀𐤋.
𐤄𐤕𐤁𐤄.𐤌𐤐𐤍𐤉.𐤌𐤉.𐤄𐤌𐤁𐤅𐤋|

8 𐤌𐤍.𐤄𐤁𐤄𐤌𐤄.𐤄𐤈𐤄𐤅𐤓𐤄.𐤅𐤌𐤍.𐤄𐤁𐤄𐤌𐤄.𐤀𐤔𐤓.𐤀𐤉𐤍𐤍
𐤄.𐤈𐤄𐤓𐤄.𐤅𐤌𐤍.𐤄𐤏𐤅𐤐.𐤅𐤊𐤋.𐤀𐤔𐤓.𐤓𐤌𐤔.𐤏𐤋.𐤄𐤀𐤃𐤌𐤄|

9 𐤔𐤍𐤉𐤌.𐤔𐤍𐤉𐤌.𐤁𐤀𐤅.𐤀𐤋.𐤍𐤇.𐤀𐤋.𐤄𐤕𐤁𐤄.𐤆𐤊𐤓.𐤅𐤍
𐤒𐤁𐤄.𐤊𐤀𐤔𐤓.𐤑𐤅𐤄.𐤀𐤋𐤄𐤉𐤌.𐤀𐤕.𐤍𐤇|

10 𐤅𐤉𐤄𐤉.𐤋𐤔𐤁𐤏𐤕.𐤄𐤉𐤌𐤉𐤌.𐤅𐤌𐤉.𐤄𐤌𐤁𐤅𐤋.𐤄𐤉𐤅.𐤏𐤋.
𐤄𐤀𐤓𐤑|

11 𐤁𐤔𐤍𐤕.𐤔𐤔.𐤌𐤀𐤅𐤕.𐤔𐤍𐤄.𐤋𐤇𐤉𐤉.𐤍𐤇.𐤁𐤇𐤃𐤔.𐤄
𐤔𐤍𐤉.𐤁𐤔𐤁𐤏𐤄.𐤏𐤔𐤓.𐤉𐤅𐤌.𐤋𐤇𐤃𐤔.𐤁𐤉𐤅𐤌.𐤄𐤆𐤄.𐤍𐤁𐤒
𐤏𐤅.𐤊𐤋.𐤌𐤏𐤉𐤍𐤕.𐤕𐤄𐤅𐤌.𐤓𐤁𐤄.𐤅𐤀𐤓𐤁𐤕.𐤄𐤔𐤌𐤉𐤌.𐤍𐤐𐤕𐤇
𐤅|

יב ויהי.הגשם.על.הארץ.ארבעים.יום.ואר
בעים.לילה|
יג בעצם.היום.הזה.בא.נח.ושם.וחם.ויפת.
בני.נח.ואשת.נח.ושלשת.נשי.בניו.אתם.אל.ה
תבה|
יד המה.וכל.החיה.למינה.וכל.הבהמה.למי
נה.וכל.הרמש.הרמש.על.הארץ.למינהו.וכל.הע
וף.למינהו.כל.צפור.כל.כנף|
טו ויבאו.אל.נח.אל.התבה.שנים.שנים.מכל.
הבשר.אשר.בו.רוח.חיים|
טז והבאים.זכר.ונקבה.מכל.בשר.באו.כאשר
צוה.אתו.אלהים.ויסגר.יהוה.בעדו|
יז ויהי.המבול.ארבעים.יום.על.הארץ.ויר
בו.המים.וישאו.את.התבה.ותרם.מעל.הארץ|
יח ויגברו.המים.וירבו.מאד.על.הארץ.ותל
ך.התבה.על.פני.המים|
יט והמים.גברו.מאד.מאד.על.הארץ.ויכס
ו.כל.ההרים.הגבהים.אשר.תחת.כל.השמים|
כ חמש.עשרה.אמה.מלמעלה.גברו.המים.ו
יכסו.ההרים|
כא ויגוע.כל.בשר.הרמש.על.הארץ.בעוף.ובב
המה.ובחיה.ובכל.השרץ.השרץ.על.הארץ.וכ
ל.האדם|
כב כל.אשר.נשמת.רוח.חיים.באפיו.מכל.אש
ר.בחרבה.מתו|
כג וימח.את.כל.היקום.אשר.על.פני.האדמ
ה.מאדם.עד.בהמה.עד.רמש.ועוף.השמי
ם.וימחו.מן.הארץ.וישאר.אך.נח.ואשר.אתו.ב
תבה|
כד ויגברו.המים.על.הארץ.חמשים.ומאת.
יום||

בראשית.חלק ח

א ויזכר.אלהים.את.נח.ואת.כל.החיה.ואת.
כל.הבהמה.אשר.אתו.בתבה.ויעבר.אלהים.רו
ח.על.הארץ.וישכו.המים|
ב ויסכרו.מעינת.תהום.וארבת.השמים.ויכל
א.הגשם.מן.השמים|
ג וישבו.המים.מעל.הארץ.הלוך.ושוב.ויחס
רו.המים.מקצה.חמשים.ומאת.יום|
ד ותנח.התבה.בחדש.השביעי.בשבעה.עש
ר.יום.לחדש.על.הרי.אררט|
ה והמים.היו.הלוך.וחסור.עד.החדש.העשי
רי.בעשירי.באחד.לחדש.נראו.ראשי.ההרי
ם|
ו ויהי.מקץ.ארבעים.יום.ויפתח.נח.את.ח
לון.התבה.אשר.עשה|
ז וישלח.את.הערב.ויצא.יצוא.ושוב.עד.י
בשת.המים.מעל.הארץ|
ח וישלח.את.היונה.מאתו.לראות.הקלו.המי
ם.מעל.פני.האדמה|
ט ולא.מצאה.היונה.מנוח.לכף.רגלה.ותשב.
אליו.אל.התבה.כי.מים.על.פני.כל.הארץ.ויש
לח.ידו.ויקחה.ויבא.אתה.אליו.אל.התבה|
י ויחל.עוד.שבעת.ימים.אחרים.ויסף.של
ח.את.היונה.מן.התבה|
יא ותבא.אליו.היונה.לעת.ערב.והנה.עלה.ז
ית.טרף.בפיה.וידע.נח.כי.קלו.המים.מעל.ה
ארץ|
יב וייחל.עוד.שבעת.ימים.אחרים.וישלח.
את.היונה.ולא.יספה.שוב.אליו.עוד|

𐤉𐤂 𐤅𐤉𐤄𐤉.𐤁𐤀𐤇𐤕.𐤅𐤔𐤔.𐤌𐤀𐤅𐤕.𐤔𐤍𐤄.𐤁𐤓𐤀𐤔𐤅𐤍.𐤁𐤀
𐤇𐤃.𐤋𐤇𐤃𐤔.𐤇𐤓𐤁𐤅.𐤄𐤌𐤉𐤌.𐤌𐤏𐤋.𐤄𐤀𐤓𐤑.𐤅𐤉𐤎𐤓.𐤍𐤇.
𐤀𐤕.𐤌𐤊𐤎𐤄.𐤄𐤕𐤁𐤄.𐤅𐤉𐤓𐤀.𐤅𐤄𐤍𐤄.𐤇𐤓𐤁𐤅.𐤐𐤍𐤉.𐤄𐤀𐤃𐤌
𐤄|
𐤉𐤃 𐤅𐤁𐤇𐤃𐤔.𐤄𐤔𐤍𐤉.𐤁𐤔𐤁𐤏𐤄.𐤅𐤏𐤔𐤓𐤉𐤌.𐤉𐤅𐤌.𐤋𐤇
𐤃𐤔.𐤉𐤁𐤔𐤄.𐤄𐤀𐤓𐤑|
𐤈𐤅 𐤅𐤉𐤃𐤁𐤓.𐤀𐤋𐤄𐤉𐤌.𐤀𐤋.𐤍𐤇.𐤋𐤀𐤌𐤓|
𐤈𐤆 𐤑𐤀.𐤌𐤍.𐤄𐤕𐤁𐤄.𐤀𐤕𐤄.𐤅𐤀𐤔𐤕𐤊.𐤅𐤁𐤍𐤉𐤊.𐤅𐤍𐤔𐤉.𐤁𐤍
𐤉𐤊.𐤀𐤕𐤊|
𐤉𐤆 𐤊𐤋.𐤄𐤇𐤉𐤄.𐤀𐤔𐤓.𐤀𐤕𐤊.𐤌𐤊𐤋.𐤁𐤔𐤓.𐤁𐤏𐤅𐤐.𐤅𐤁𐤁𐤄
𐤌𐤄.𐤅𐤁𐤊𐤋.𐤄𐤓𐤌𐤔.𐤄𐤓𐤌𐤔.𐤏𐤋.𐤄𐤀𐤓𐤑.𐤄𐤅𐤑𐤀.||𐤄𐤉𐤑
𐤀.𐤒𐤓𐤉||.𐤀𐤕𐤊.𐤅𐤔𐤓𐤑𐤅.𐤁𐤀𐤓𐤑.𐤅𐤐𐤓𐤅.𐤅𐤓𐤁𐤅.𐤏𐤋.𐤄𐤀𐤓𐤑|
𐤉𐤇 𐤅𐤉𐤑𐤀.𐤍𐤇.𐤅𐤁𐤍𐤉𐤅.𐤅𐤀𐤔𐤕𐤅.𐤅𐤍𐤔𐤉.𐤁𐤍𐤉𐤅.𐤀𐤕𐤅|
𐤉𐤈 𐤊𐤋.𐤄𐤇𐤉𐤄.𐤊𐤋.𐤄𐤓𐤌𐤔.𐤅𐤊𐤋.𐤄𐤏𐤅𐤐.𐤊𐤋.𐤓𐤅𐤌𐤔.𐤏
𐤋.𐤄𐤀𐤓𐤑.𐤋𐤌𐤔𐤐𐤇𐤕𐤉𐤄𐤌.𐤉𐤑𐤀𐤅.𐤌𐤍.𐤄𐤕𐤁𐤄|
𐤊 𐤅𐤉𐤁𐤍.𐤍𐤇.𐤌𐤆𐤁𐤇.𐤋𐤉𐤄𐤅𐤄.𐤅𐤉𐤒𐤇.𐤌𐤊𐤋.𐤄𐤁𐤄𐤌
𐤄.𐤄𐤈𐤄𐤅𐤓𐤄.𐤅𐤌𐤊𐤋.𐤄𐤏𐤅𐤐.𐤄𐤈𐤄𐤓.𐤅𐤉𐤏𐤋.𐤏𐤋𐤕.𐤁𐤌𐤆
𐤁𐤇|
𐤊𐤀 𐤅𐤉𐤓𐤇.𐤉𐤄𐤅𐤄.𐤀𐤕.𐤓𐤉𐤇.𐤄𐤍𐤉𐤇𐤇.𐤅𐤉𐤀𐤌𐤓.𐤉𐤄𐤅
𐤄.𐤀𐤋.𐤋𐤁𐤅.𐤋𐤀.𐤀𐤎𐤐.𐤋𐤒𐤋𐤋.𐤏𐤅𐤃.𐤀𐤕.𐤄𐤀𐤃𐤌𐤄.𐤁𐤏𐤁
𐤅𐤓.𐤄𐤀𐤃𐤌.𐤊𐤉.𐤉𐤑𐤓.𐤋𐤁.𐤄𐤀𐤃𐤌.𐤓𐤏.𐤌𐤍𐤏𐤓𐤉𐤅.𐤅𐤋𐤀.𐤀
𐤎𐤐.𐤏𐤅𐤃.𐤋𐤄𐤊𐤅𐤕.𐤀𐤕.𐤊𐤋.𐤇𐤉.𐤊𐤀𐤔𐤓.𐤏𐤔𐤉𐤕𐤉|
𐤊𐤁 𐤏𐤃.𐤊𐤋.𐤉𐤌𐤉.𐤄𐤀𐤓𐤑.𐤆𐤓𐤏.𐤅𐤒𐤑𐤉𐤓.𐤅𐤒𐤓.𐤅𐤇𐤌.
𐤅𐤒𐤉𐤑.𐤅𐤇𐤓𐤐.𐤅𐤉𐤅𐤌.𐤅𐤋𐤉𐤋𐤄.𐤋𐤀.𐤉𐤔𐤁𐤕𐤅||

𐤁𐤓𐤀𐤔𐤉𐤕.𐤇𐤋𐤒 𐤈

𐤀 𐤅𐤉𐤁𐤓𐤊.𐤀𐤋𐤄𐤉𐤌.𐤀𐤕.𐤍𐤇.𐤅𐤀𐤕.𐤁𐤍𐤉𐤅.𐤅𐤉𐤀𐤌𐤓.𐤋𐤄
𐤌.𐤐𐤓𐤅.𐤅𐤓𐤁𐤅.𐤅𐤌𐤋𐤀𐤅.𐤀𐤕.𐤄𐤀𐤓𐤑|

ב 𐤅𐤌𐤅𐤓𐤀𐤊𐤌.𐤅𐤇𐤕𐤊𐤌.𐤉𐤄𐤉𐤄.𐤏𐤋.𐤊𐤋.𐤇𐤉𐤕.𐤄𐤀𐤓𐤑
.𐤅𐤏𐤋.𐤊𐤋.𐤏𐤅𐤐.𐤄𐤔𐤌𐤉𐤌.𐤁𐤊𐤋.𐤀𐤔𐤓.𐤕𐤓𐤌𐤔.𐤄𐤀𐤃𐤌𐤄.
𐤅𐤁𐤊𐤋.𐤃𐤂𐤉.𐤄𐤉𐤌.𐤁𐤉𐤃𐤊𐤌.𐤍𐤕𐤍𐤅|
ג 𐤊𐤋.𐤓𐤌𐤔.𐤀𐤔𐤓.𐤄𐤅𐤀.𐤇𐤉.𐤋𐤊𐤌.𐤉𐤄𐤉𐤄.𐤋𐤀𐤊𐤋𐤄.𐤊
𐤉𐤓𐤒.𐤏𐤔𐤁.𐤍𐤕𐤕𐤉.𐤋𐤊𐤌.𐤀𐤕.𐤊𐤋|
ד 𐤀𐤊.𐤁𐤔𐤓.𐤁𐤍𐤐𐤔𐤅.𐤃𐤌𐤅.𐤋𐤀.𐤕𐤀𐤊𐤋𐤅|
ה 𐤅𐤀𐤊.𐤀𐤕.𐤃𐤌𐤊𐤌.𐤋𐤍𐤐𐤔𐤕𐤉𐤊𐤌.𐤀𐤃𐤓𐤔.𐤌𐤉𐤃.𐤊𐤋.
𐤇𐤉𐤄.𐤀𐤃𐤓𐤔𐤍𐤅.𐤅𐤌𐤉𐤃.𐤄𐤀𐤃𐤌.𐤌𐤉𐤃.𐤀𐤉𐤔.𐤀𐤇𐤉𐤅.
𐤀𐤃𐤓𐤔.𐤀𐤕.𐤍𐤐𐤔.𐤄𐤀𐤃𐤌|
ו 𐤔𐤐𐤊.𐤃𐤌.𐤄𐤀𐤃𐤌.𐤁𐤀𐤃𐤌.𐤃𐤌𐤅.𐤉𐤔𐤐𐤊.𐤊𐤉.𐤁𐤑𐤋
𐤌.𐤀𐤋𐤄𐤉𐤌.𐤏𐤔𐤄.𐤀𐤕.𐤄𐤀𐤃𐤌|
ז 𐤅𐤀𐤕𐤌.𐤐𐤓𐤅.𐤅𐤓𐤁𐤅.𐤔𐤓𐤑𐤅.𐤁𐤀𐤓𐤑.𐤅𐤓𐤁𐤅.𐤁𐤄|
ח 𐤅𐤉𐤀𐤌𐤓.𐤀𐤋𐤄𐤉𐤌.𐤀𐤋.𐤍𐤇.𐤅𐤀𐤋.𐤁𐤍𐤉𐤅.𐤀𐤕𐤅.𐤋𐤀𐤌𐤓|
ט 𐤅𐤀𐤍𐤉.𐤄𐤍𐤍𐤉.𐤌𐤒𐤉𐤌.𐤀𐤕.𐤁𐤓𐤉𐤕𐤉.𐤀𐤕𐤊𐤌.𐤅𐤀𐤕.
𐤆𐤓𐤏𐤊𐤌.𐤀𐤇𐤓𐤉𐤊𐤌|
י 𐤅𐤀𐤕.𐤊𐤋.𐤍𐤐𐤔.𐤄𐤇𐤉𐤄.𐤀𐤔𐤓.𐤀𐤕𐤊𐤌.𐤁𐤏𐤅𐤐.𐤁𐤁𐤄
𐤌𐤄.𐤅𐤁𐤊𐤋.𐤇𐤉𐤕.𐤄𐤀𐤓𐤑.𐤀𐤕𐤊𐤌.𐤌𐤊𐤋.𐤉𐤑𐤀𐤉.𐤄𐤕𐤁
𐤄.𐤋𐤊𐤋.𐤇𐤉𐤕.𐤄𐤀𐤓𐤑|
יא 𐤅𐤄𐤒𐤌𐤕𐤉.𐤀𐤕.𐤁𐤓𐤉𐤕𐤉.𐤀𐤕𐤊𐤌.𐤅𐤋𐤀.𐤉𐤊𐤓𐤕.𐤊𐤋.
𐤁𐤔𐤓.𐤏𐤅𐤃.𐤌𐤌𐤉.𐤄𐤌𐤁𐤅𐤋.𐤅𐤋𐤀.𐤉𐤄𐤉𐤄.𐤏𐤅𐤃.𐤌𐤁𐤅𐤋.𐤋𐤔
𐤇𐤕.𐤄𐤀𐤓𐤑|
יב 𐤅𐤉𐤀𐤌𐤓.𐤀𐤋𐤄𐤉𐤌.𐤆𐤀𐤕.𐤀𐤅𐤕.𐤄𐤁𐤓𐤉𐤕.𐤀𐤔𐤓.𐤀𐤍
𐤉.𐤍𐤕𐤍.𐤁𐤉𐤍𐤉.𐤅𐤁𐤉𐤍𐤉𐤊𐤌.𐤅𐤁𐤉𐤍.𐤊𐤋.𐤍𐤐𐤔.𐤇𐤉𐤄.𐤀𐤔𐤓.
𐤀𐤕𐤊𐤌.𐤋𐤃𐤓𐤕.𐤏𐤅𐤋𐤌|
יג 𐤀𐤕.𐤒𐤔𐤕𐤉.𐤍𐤕𐤕𐤉.𐤁𐤏𐤍𐤍.𐤅𐤄𐤉𐤕𐤄.𐤋𐤀𐤅𐤕.𐤁𐤓𐤉
𐤕.𐤁𐤉𐤍𐤉.𐤅𐤁𐤉𐤍.𐤄𐤀𐤓𐤑|
יד 𐤅𐤄𐤉𐤄.𐤁𐤏𐤍𐤍𐤉.𐤏𐤍𐤍.𐤏𐤋.𐤄𐤀𐤓𐤑.𐤅𐤍𐤓𐤀𐤕𐤄.𐤄𐤒𐤔𐤕
𐤁𐤏𐤍𐤍|
יה 𐤅𐤆𐤊𐤓𐤕𐤉.𐤀𐤕.𐤁𐤓𐤉𐤕𐤉.𐤀𐤔𐤓.𐤁𐤉𐤍𐤉.𐤅𐤁𐤉𐤍𐤉𐤊𐤌.𐤅
𐤁𐤉𐤍.𐤊𐤋.𐤍𐤐𐤔.𐤇𐤉𐤄.𐤁𐤊𐤋.𐤁𐤔𐤓.𐤅𐤋𐤀.𐤉𐤄𐤉𐤄.𐤏𐤅𐤃.𐤄𐤌
𐤉𐤌.𐤋𐤌𐤁𐤅𐤋.𐤋𐤔𐤇𐤕.𐤊𐤋.𐤁𐤔𐤓|

16 𐤅𐤄𐤉𐤕𐤄.𐤄𐤒𐤔𐤕.𐤁𐤏𐤍𐤍.𐤅𐤓𐤀𐤉𐤕𐤉𐤄.𐤋𐤆𐤊𐤓.𐤁𐤓𐤉
𐤕.𐤏𐤅𐤋𐤌.𐤁𐤉𐤍.𐤀𐤋𐤄𐤉𐤌.𐤅𐤁𐤉𐤍.𐤊𐤋.𐤍𐤐𐤔.𐤇𐤉𐤄.𐤁𐤊𐤋.𐤁𐤔
𐤓.𐤀𐤔𐤓.𐤏𐤋.𐤄𐤀𐤓𐤑|
17 𐤅𐤉𐤀𐤌𐤓.𐤀𐤋𐤄𐤉𐤌.𐤀𐤋.𐤍𐤇.𐤆𐤀𐤕.𐤀𐤅𐤕.𐤄𐤁𐤓𐤉𐤕.
𐤀𐤔𐤓.𐤄𐤒𐤌𐤕𐤉.𐤁𐤉𐤍𐤉.𐤅𐤁𐤉𐤍.𐤊𐤋.𐤁𐤔𐤓.𐤀𐤔𐤓.𐤏𐤋.𐤄𐤀𐤓
𐤑|
18 𐤅𐤉𐤄𐤉𐤅.𐤁𐤍𐤉.𐤍𐤇.𐤄𐤉𐤑𐤀𐤉𐤌.𐤌𐤍.𐤄𐤕𐤁𐤄.𐤔𐤌.𐤅𐤇
𐤌.𐤅𐤉𐤐𐤕.𐤅𐤇𐤌.𐤄𐤅𐤀.𐤀𐤁𐤉.𐤊𐤍𐤏𐤍|
19 𐤔𐤋𐤔𐤄.𐤀𐤋𐤄.𐤁𐤍𐤉.𐤍𐤇.𐤅𐤌𐤀𐤋𐤄.𐤍𐤐𐤑𐤄.𐤊𐤋.𐤄𐤀𐤓
𐤑|
20 𐤅𐤉𐤇𐤋.𐤍𐤇.𐤀𐤉𐤔.𐤄𐤀𐤃𐤌𐤄.𐤅𐤉𐤈𐤏.𐤊𐤓𐤌|
21 𐤅𐤉𐤔𐤕.𐤌𐤍.𐤄𐤉𐤉𐤍.𐤅𐤉𐤔𐤊𐤓.𐤅𐤉𐤕𐤂𐤋.𐤁𐤕𐤅𐤊.𐤀𐤄𐤋𐤄
|
22 𐤅𐤉𐤓𐤀.𐤇𐤌.𐤀𐤁𐤉.𐤊𐤍𐤏𐤍.𐤀𐤕.𐤏𐤓𐤅𐤕.𐤀𐤁𐤉𐤅.𐤅𐤉𐤂
𐤃.𐤋𐤔𐤍𐤉.𐤀𐤇𐤉𐤅.𐤁𐤇𐤅𐤑|
23 𐤅𐤉𐤒𐤇.𐤔𐤌.𐤅𐤉𐤐𐤕.𐤀𐤕.𐤄𐤔𐤌𐤋𐤄.𐤅𐤉𐤔𐤉𐤌𐤅.𐤏𐤋.𐤔
𐤊𐤌.𐤔𐤍𐤉𐤄𐤌.𐤅𐤉𐤋𐤊𐤅.𐤀𐤇𐤓𐤍𐤉𐤕.𐤅𐤉𐤊𐤎𐤅.𐤀𐤕.𐤏𐤓𐤅𐤕.𐤀
𐤁𐤉𐤄𐤌.𐤅𐤐𐤍𐤉𐤄𐤌.𐤀𐤇𐤓𐤍𐤉𐤕.𐤅𐤏𐤓𐤅𐤕.𐤀𐤁𐤉𐤄𐤌.𐤋𐤀.𐤓𐤀𐤅|
24 𐤅𐤉𐤉𐤒𐤑.𐤍𐤇.𐤌𐤉𐤉𐤍𐤅.𐤅𐤉𐤃𐤏.𐤀𐤕.𐤀𐤔𐤓.𐤏𐤔𐤄.𐤋𐤅
.𐤁𐤍𐤅.𐤄𐤒𐤈𐤍|
25 𐤅𐤉𐤀𐤌𐤓.𐤀𐤓𐤅𐤓.𐤊𐤍𐤏𐤍.𐤏𐤁𐤃.𐤏𐤁𐤃𐤉𐤌.𐤉𐤄𐤉𐤄.𐤋
𐤀𐤇𐤉𐤅|
26 𐤅𐤉𐤀𐤌𐤓.𐤁𐤓𐤅𐤊.𐤉𐤄𐤅𐤄.𐤀𐤋𐤄𐤉.𐤔𐤌.𐤅𐤉𐤄𐤉.𐤊𐤍𐤏𐤍.𐤏
𐤁𐤃.𐤋𐤌𐤅|
27 𐤉𐤐𐤕.𐤀𐤋𐤄𐤉𐤌.𐤋𐤉𐤐𐤕.𐤅𐤉𐤔𐤊𐤍.𐤁𐤀𐤄𐤋𐤉.𐤔𐤌.𐤅𐤉𐤄
𐤉.𐤊𐤍𐤏𐤍.𐤏𐤁𐤃.𐤋𐤌𐤅|
28 𐤅𐤉𐤇𐤉.𐤍𐤇.𐤀𐤇𐤓.𐤄𐤌𐤁𐤅𐤋.𐤔𐤋𐤔.𐤌𐤀𐤅𐤕.𐤔𐤍𐤄.𐤅𐤇
𐤌𐤔𐤉𐤌.𐤔𐤍𐤄|
29 𐤅𐤉𐤄𐤉𐤅.𐤊𐤋.𐤉𐤌𐤉.𐤍𐤇.𐤕𐤔𐤏.𐤌𐤀𐤅𐤕.𐤔𐤍𐤄.𐤅𐤇𐤌𐤔
𐤉𐤌.𐤔𐤍𐤄.𐤅𐤉𐤌𐤕||

𐤁𐤓𐤀𐤔𐤉𐤕.𐤇𐤋𐤒 ..י..

..א.. 𐤅𐤀𐤋𐤄.𐤕𐤅𐤋𐤃𐤕.𐤁𐤍𐤉.𐤍𐤇.𐤔𐤌.𐤇𐤌.𐤅𐤉𐤐𐤕.𐤅𐤉𐤅𐤋𐤃𐤅.
𐤋𐤄𐤌.𐤁𐤍𐤉𐤌.𐤀𐤇𐤓.𐤄𐤌𐤁𐤅𐤋|
..ב.. 𐤁𐤍𐤉.𐤉𐤐𐤕.𐤂𐤌𐤓.𐤅𐤌𐤂𐤅𐤂.𐤅𐤌𐤃𐤉.𐤅𐤉𐤅𐤍.𐤅𐤕𐤁𐤋.𐤅𐤌𐤔
𐤊.𐤅𐤕𐤉𐤓𐤎|
..ג.. 𐤅𐤁𐤍𐤉.𐤂𐤌𐤓.𐤀𐤔𐤊𐤍𐤆.𐤅𐤓𐤉𐤐𐤕.𐤅𐤕𐤂𐤓𐤌𐤄|
..ד.. 𐤅𐤁𐤍𐤉.𐤉𐤅𐤍.𐤀𐤋𐤉𐤔𐤄.𐤅𐤕𐤓𐤔𐤉𐤔.𐤊𐤕𐤉𐤌.𐤅𐤃𐤃𐤍𐤉𐤌|
..ה.. 𐤌𐤀𐤋𐤄.𐤍𐤐𐤓𐤃𐤅.𐤀𐤉𐤉.𐤄𐤂𐤅𐤉𐤌.𐤁𐤀𐤓𐤑𐤕𐤌.𐤀𐤉𐤔.𐤋
𐤋𐤔𐤍𐤅.𐤋𐤌𐤔𐤐𐤇𐤕𐤌.𐤁𐤂𐤅𐤉𐤄𐤌|
..ו.. 𐤅𐤁𐤍𐤉.𐤇𐤌.𐤊𐤅𐤔.𐤅𐤌𐤑𐤓𐤉𐤌.𐤅𐤐𐤅𐤈.𐤅𐤊𐤍𐤏𐤍|
..ז.. 𐤅𐤁𐤍𐤉.𐤊𐤅𐤔.𐤎𐤁𐤀.𐤅𐤇𐤅𐤉𐤋𐤄.𐤅𐤎𐤁𐤕𐤄.𐤅𐤓𐤏𐤌𐤄.𐤅𐤎𐤁
𐤕𐤊𐤀.𐤅𐤁𐤍𐤉.𐤓𐤏𐤌𐤄.𐤔𐤁𐤀.𐤅𐤃𐤃𐤍|
..ח.. 𐤅𐤊𐤅𐤔.𐤉𐤋𐤃.𐤀𐤕.𐤍𐤌𐤓𐤃.𐤄𐤅𐤀.𐤄𐤇𐤋.𐤋𐤄𐤉𐤅𐤕.𐤂𐤁𐤓.
𐤁𐤀𐤓𐤑|
..ט.. 𐤄𐤅𐤀.𐤄𐤉𐤄.𐤂𐤁𐤓.𐤑𐤉𐤃.𐤋𐤐𐤍𐤉.𐤉𐤄𐤅𐤄.𐤏𐤋.𐤊𐤍.𐤉𐤀
𐤌𐤓.𐤊𐤍𐤌𐤓𐤃.𐤂𐤁𐤅𐤓.𐤑𐤉𐤃.𐤋𐤐𐤍𐤉.𐤉𐤄𐤅𐤄|
..י.. 𐤅𐤕𐤄𐤉.𐤓𐤀𐤔𐤉𐤕.𐤌𐤌𐤋𐤊𐤕𐤅.𐤁𐤁𐤋.𐤅𐤀𐤓𐤊.𐤅𐤀𐤊𐤃.𐤅
𐤊𐤋𐤍𐤄.𐤁𐤀𐤓𐤑.𐤔𐤍𐤏𐤓|
..יא.. 𐤌𐤍.𐤄𐤀𐤓𐤑.𐤄𐤄𐤅𐤀.𐤉𐤑𐤀.𐤀𐤔𐤅𐤓.𐤅𐤉𐤁𐤍.𐤀𐤕.𐤍𐤉𐤍𐤅
𐤄.𐤅𐤀𐤕.𐤓𐤇𐤁𐤕.𐤏𐤉𐤓.𐤅𐤀𐤕.𐤊𐤋𐤇|
..יב.. 𐤅𐤀𐤕.𐤓𐤎𐤍.𐤁𐤉𐤍.𐤍𐤉𐤍𐤅𐤄.𐤅𐤁𐤉𐤍.𐤊𐤋𐤇.𐤄𐤅𐤀.𐤄𐤏𐤉𐤓.
𐤄𐤂𐤃𐤋𐤄|
..יג.. 𐤅𐤌𐤑𐤓𐤉𐤌.𐤉𐤋𐤃.𐤀𐤕.𐤋𐤅𐤃𐤉𐤌.𐤅𐤀𐤕.𐤏𐤍𐤌𐤉𐤌.𐤅𐤀
𐤕.𐤋𐤄𐤁𐤉𐤌.𐤅𐤀𐤕.𐤍𐤐𐤕𐤇𐤉𐤌|
..יד.. 𐤅𐤀𐤕.𐤐𐤕𐤓𐤎𐤉𐤌.𐤅𐤀𐤕.𐤊𐤎𐤋𐤇𐤉𐤌.𐤀𐤔𐤓.𐤉𐤑𐤀𐤅.𐤌
𐤔𐤌.𐤐𐤋𐤔𐤕𐤉𐤌.𐤅𐤀𐤕.𐤊𐤐𐤕𐤓𐤉𐤌|
..טו.. 𐤅𐤊𐤍𐤏𐤍.𐤉𐤋𐤃.𐤀𐤕.𐤑𐤉𐤃𐤍.𐤁𐤊𐤓𐤅.𐤅𐤀𐤕.𐤇𐤕|
..טז.. 𐤅𐤀𐤕.𐤄𐤉𐤁𐤅𐤎𐤉.𐤅𐤀𐤕.𐤄𐤀𐤌𐤓𐤉.𐤅𐤀𐤕.𐤄𐤂𐤓𐤂𐤔𐤉|
..יז.. 𐤅𐤀𐤕.𐤄𐤇𐤅𐤉.𐤅𐤀𐤕.𐤄𐤏𐤓𐤒𐤉.𐤅𐤀𐤕.𐤄𐤎𐤉𐤍𐤉|

18 ࠅࠀࠕ.ࠄࠀࠓࠅࠃࠉ.ࠅࠀࠕ.ࠄࠑࠌࠓࠉ.ࠅࠀࠕ.ࠄࠇࠌࠕࠉ.ࠅࠀࠇࠓ.ࠍࠐࠑࠅ.ࠌࠔࠐࠇࠅࠕ.ࠄࠊࠍࠏࠍࠉ

19 ࠅࠉࠄࠉ.ࠂࠁࠅࠋ.ࠄࠊࠍࠏࠍࠉ.ࠌࠑࠉࠃࠍ.ࠁࠀࠊࠄ.ࠂࠓࠓࠄ.ࠏࠃ.ࠏࠆࠄ.ࠁࠀࠊࠄ.ࠎࠃࠌࠄ.ࠅࠏࠌࠓࠄ.ࠅࠀࠃࠌࠄ.ࠅࠑࠁࠉࠌ.ࠏࠃ.ࠋࠔࠏ

20 ࠀࠋࠄ.ࠁࠍࠉ.ࠇࠌ.ࠋࠌࠔࠐࠇࠕࠌ.ࠋࠋࠔࠍࠕࠌ.ࠁࠀࠓࠑࠕࠌ.ࠁࠂࠅࠉࠄࠌ

21 ࠅࠋࠔࠌ.ࠉࠋࠃ.ࠂࠌ.ࠄࠅࠀ.ࠀࠁࠉ.ࠊࠋ.ࠁࠍࠉ.ࠏࠁࠓ.ࠀࠇࠉ.ࠉࠐࠕ.ࠄࠂࠃࠅࠋ

22 ࠁࠍࠉ.ࠔࠌ.ࠏࠉࠋࠌ.ࠅࠀࠔࠅࠓ.ࠅࠀࠓࠐࠊࠔࠃ.ࠅࠋࠅࠃ.ࠅࠀࠓࠌ

23 ࠅࠁࠍࠉ.ࠀࠓࠌ.ࠏࠅࠑ.ࠅࠇࠅࠋ.ࠅࠂࠕࠓ.ࠅࠌࠔ

24 ࠅࠀࠓࠐࠊࠔࠃ.ࠉࠋࠃ.ࠀࠕ.ࠔࠋࠇ.ࠅࠔࠋࠇ.ࠉࠋࠃ.ࠀࠕ.ࠏࠁࠓ

25 ࠅࠋࠏࠁࠓ.ࠉࠋࠃ.ࠔࠍࠉ.ࠁࠍࠉࠌ.ࠔࠌ.ࠄࠀࠇࠃ.ࠐࠋࠂ.ࠊࠉ.ࠁࠉࠌࠉࠅ.ࠍࠐࠋࠂࠄ.ࠄࠀࠓࠑ.ࠅࠔࠌ.ࠀࠇࠉࠅ.ࠉࠒࠈࠍ

26 ࠅࠉࠒࠈࠍ.ࠉࠋࠃ.ࠀࠕ.ࠀࠋࠌࠅࠃࠃ.ࠅࠀࠕ.ࠔࠋࠐ.ࠅࠀࠕ.ࠇࠑࠓࠌࠅࠕ.ࠅࠀࠕ.ࠉࠓࠇ

27 ࠅࠀࠕ.ࠄࠃࠅࠓࠌ.ࠅࠀࠕ.ࠀࠅࠆࠋ.ࠅࠀࠕ.ࠃࠒࠋࠄ

28 ࠅࠀࠕ.ࠏࠅࠁࠋ.ࠅࠀࠕ.ࠀࠁࠉࠌࠀࠋ.ࠅࠀࠕ.ࠔࠁࠀ

29 ࠅࠀࠕ.ࠀࠅࠐࠓ.ࠅࠀࠕ.ࠇࠅࠉࠋࠄ.ࠅࠀࠕ.ࠉࠅࠁࠁ.ࠊࠋ.ࠀࠋࠄ.ࠁࠍࠉ.ࠉࠒࠈࠍ

30 ࠅࠉࠄࠉ.ࠌࠅࠔࠁࠌ.ࠌࠌࠔࠀ.ࠁࠀࠊࠄ.ࠎࠐࠓࠄ.ࠄࠓ.ࠄࠒࠃࠌ

31 ࠀࠋࠄ.ࠁࠍࠉ.ࠔࠌ.ࠋࠌࠔࠐࠇࠕࠌ.ࠋࠋࠔࠍࠕࠌ.ࠁࠀࠓࠑࠕࠌ.ࠋࠂࠅࠉࠄࠌ

32 ࠀࠋࠄ.ࠌࠔࠐࠇࠕ.ࠁࠍࠉ.ࠍࠇ.ࠋࠕࠅࠋࠃࠕࠌ.ࠁࠂࠅࠉࠄࠌ.ࠅࠌࠀࠋࠄ.ࠍࠐࠓࠃࠅ.ࠄࠂࠅࠉࠌ.ࠁࠀࠓࠑ.ࠀࠇࠓ.ࠄࠌࠁࠅࠋ

ࠁࠓࠀࠔࠉࠕ.ࠇࠋࠒ 11

א 𐤅𐤉𐤄𐤉.𐤊𐤋.𐤄𐤀𐤓𐤑.𐤔𐤐𐤄.𐤀𐤇𐤕.𐤅𐤃𐤁𐤓𐤉𐤌.𐤀𐤇𐤃𐤉
𐤌|

ב 𐤅𐤉𐤄𐤉.𐤁𐤍𐤎𐤏𐤌.𐤌𐤒𐤃𐤌.𐤅𐤉𐤌𐤑𐤀𐤅.𐤁𐤒𐤏𐤄.𐤁𐤀𐤓𐤑
.𐤔𐤍𐤏𐤓.𐤅𐤉𐤔𐤁𐤅.𐤔𐤌|

ג 𐤅𐤉𐤀𐤌𐤓𐤅.𐤀𐤉𐤔.𐤀𐤋.𐤓𐤏𐤄𐤅.𐤄𐤁𐤄.𐤍𐤋𐤁𐤍𐤄.𐤋𐤁𐤍𐤉𐤌.𐤅
𐤍𐤔𐤓𐤐𐤄.𐤋𐤔𐤓𐤐𐤄.𐤅𐤕𐤄𐤉.𐤋𐤄𐤌.𐤄𐤋𐤁𐤍𐤄.𐤋𐤀𐤁𐤍.𐤅𐤄𐤇𐤌𐤓
.𐤄𐤉𐤄.𐤋𐤄𐤌.𐤋𐤇𐤌𐤓|

ד 𐤅𐤉𐤀𐤌𐤓𐤅.𐤄𐤁𐤄.𐤍𐤁𐤍𐤄.𐤋𐤍𐤅.𐤏𐤉𐤓.𐤅𐤌𐤂𐤃𐤋.𐤅𐤓𐤀𐤔𐤅.
𐤁𐤔𐤌𐤉𐤌.𐤅𐤍𐤏𐤔𐤄.𐤋𐤍𐤅.𐤔𐤌.𐤐𐤍.𐤍𐤐𐤅𐤑.𐤏𐤋.𐤐𐤍𐤉.𐤊𐤋.𐤄𐤀𐤓
𐤑|

ה 𐤅𐤉𐤓𐤃.𐤉𐤄𐤅𐤄.𐤋𐤓𐤀𐤕.𐤀𐤕.𐤄𐤏𐤉𐤓.𐤅𐤀𐤕.𐤄𐤌𐤂𐤃𐤋.
𐤀𐤔𐤓.𐤁𐤍𐤅.𐤁𐤍𐤉.𐤄𐤀𐤃𐤌|

ו 𐤅𐤉𐤀𐤌𐤓.𐤉𐤄𐤅𐤄.𐤄𐤍.𐤏𐤌.𐤀𐤇𐤃.𐤅𐤔𐤐𐤄.𐤀𐤇𐤕.𐤋𐤊𐤋
𐤌.𐤅𐤆𐤄.𐤄𐤇𐤋𐤌.𐤋𐤏𐤔𐤅𐤕.𐤅𐤏𐤕𐤄.𐤋𐤀.𐤉𐤁𐤑𐤓.𐤌𐤄𐤌.𐤊𐤋.
𐤀𐤔𐤓.𐤉𐤆𐤌𐤅.𐤋𐤏𐤔𐤅𐤕|

ז 𐤄𐤁𐤄.𐤍𐤓𐤃𐤄.𐤅𐤍𐤁𐤋𐤄.𐤔𐤌.𐤔𐤐𐤕𐤌.𐤀𐤔𐤓.𐤋𐤀.𐤉𐤔𐤌
𐤏𐤅.𐤀𐤉𐤔.𐤔𐤐𐤕.𐤓𐤏𐤄𐤅|

ח 𐤅𐤉𐤐𐤑.𐤉𐤄𐤅𐤄.𐤀𐤕𐤌.𐤌𐤔𐤌.𐤏𐤋.𐤐𐤍𐤉.𐤊𐤋.𐤄𐤀𐤓𐤑.𐤅𐤉
𐤇𐤃𐤋𐤅.𐤋𐤁𐤍𐤕.𐤄𐤏𐤉𐤓|

ט 𐤏𐤋.𐤊𐤍.𐤒𐤓𐤀.𐤔𐤌𐤄.𐤁𐤁𐤋.𐤊𐤉.𐤔𐤌.𐤁𐤋𐤋.𐤉𐤄𐤅𐤄.𐤔𐤐
𐤕.𐤊𐤋.𐤄𐤀𐤓𐤑.𐤅𐤌𐤔𐤌.𐤄𐤐𐤉𐤑𐤌.𐤉𐤄𐤅𐤄.𐤏𐤋.𐤐𐤍𐤉.𐤊𐤋.𐤄
𐤀𐤓𐤑|

י 𐤀𐤋𐤄.𐤕𐤅𐤋𐤃𐤕.𐤔𐤌.𐤔𐤌.𐤁𐤍.𐤌𐤀𐤕.𐤔𐤍𐤄.𐤅𐤉𐤅𐤋𐤃.
𐤀𐤕.𐤀𐤓𐤐𐤊𐤔𐤃.𐤔𐤍𐤕𐤉𐤌.𐤀𐤇𐤓.𐤄𐤌𐤁𐤅𐤋|

יא 𐤅𐤉𐤇𐤉.𐤔𐤌.𐤀𐤇𐤓𐤉.𐤄𐤅𐤋𐤉𐤃𐤅.𐤀𐤕.𐤀𐤓𐤐𐤊𐤔𐤃.𐤇
𐤌𐤔.𐤌𐤀𐤅𐤕.𐤔𐤍𐤄.𐤅𐤉𐤅𐤋𐤃.𐤁𐤍𐤉𐤌.𐤅𐤁𐤍𐤅𐤕|

יב 𐤅𐤀𐤓𐤐𐤊𐤔𐤃.𐤇𐤉.𐤇𐤌𐤔.𐤅𐤔𐤋𐤔𐤉𐤌.𐤔𐤍𐤄.𐤅𐤉𐤅𐤋𐤃.
𐤀𐤕.𐤔𐤋𐤇|

יג 𐤅𐤉𐤇𐤉.𐤀𐤓𐤐𐤊𐤔𐤃.𐤀𐤇𐤓𐤉.𐤄𐤅𐤋𐤉𐤃𐤅.𐤀𐤕.𐤔𐤋𐤇.
𐤔𐤋𐤔.𐤔𐤍𐤉𐤌.𐤅𐤀𐤓𐤁𐤏.𐤌𐤀𐤅𐤕.𐤔𐤍𐤄.𐤅𐤉𐤅𐤋𐤃.𐤁𐤍𐤉𐤌.𐤅𐤁𐤍
𐤅𐤕|

14 𐤅𐤔𐤋𐤇.𐤇𐤉.𐤔𐤋𐤔𐤉𐤌.𐤔𐤍𐤄.𐤅𐤉𐤅𐤋𐤃.𐤀𐤕.𐤏𐤁𐤓|
15 𐤅𐤉𐤇𐤉.𐤔𐤋𐤇.𐤀𐤇𐤓𐤉.𐤄𐤅𐤋𐤉𐤃𐤅.𐤀𐤕.𐤏𐤁𐤓.𐤔𐤋𐤔.
𐤔𐤍𐤉𐤌.𐤅𐤀𐤓𐤁𐤏.𐤌𐤀𐤅𐤕.𐤔𐤍𐤄.𐤅𐤉𐤅𐤋𐤃.𐤁𐤍𐤉𐤌.𐤅𐤁𐤍𐤅𐤕|
16 𐤅𐤉𐤇𐤉.𐤏𐤁𐤓.𐤀𐤓𐤁𐤏.𐤅𐤔𐤋𐤔𐤉𐤌.𐤔𐤍𐤄.𐤅𐤉𐤅𐤋𐤃.𐤀𐤕.
𐤐𐤋𐤂|
17 𐤅𐤉𐤇𐤉.𐤏𐤁𐤓.𐤀𐤇𐤓𐤉.𐤄𐤅𐤋𐤉𐤃𐤅.𐤀𐤕.𐤐𐤋𐤂.𐤔𐤋𐤔𐤉
𐤌.𐤔𐤍𐤄.𐤅𐤀𐤓𐤁𐤏.𐤌𐤀𐤅𐤕.𐤔𐤍𐤄.𐤅𐤉𐤅𐤋𐤃.𐤁𐤍𐤉𐤌.𐤅𐤁𐤍𐤅𐤕|
18 𐤅𐤉𐤇𐤉.𐤐𐤋𐤂.𐤔𐤋𐤔𐤉𐤌.𐤔𐤍𐤄.𐤅𐤉𐤅𐤋𐤃.𐤀𐤕.𐤓𐤏𐤅|
19 𐤅𐤉𐤇𐤉.𐤐𐤋𐤂.𐤀𐤇𐤓𐤉.𐤄𐤅𐤋𐤉𐤃𐤅.𐤀𐤕.𐤓𐤏𐤅.𐤕𐤔𐤏.
𐤔𐤍𐤉𐤌.𐤅𐤌𐤀𐤕𐤉𐤌.𐤔𐤍𐤄.𐤅𐤉𐤅𐤋𐤃.𐤁𐤍𐤉𐤌.𐤅𐤁𐤍𐤅𐤕|
20 𐤅𐤉𐤇𐤉.𐤓𐤏𐤅.𐤔𐤕𐤉𐤌.𐤅𐤔𐤋𐤔𐤉𐤌.𐤔𐤍𐤄.𐤅𐤉𐤅𐤋𐤃.𐤀𐤕
.𐤔𐤓𐤅𐤂|
21 𐤅𐤉𐤇𐤉.𐤓𐤏𐤅.𐤀𐤇𐤓𐤉.𐤄𐤅𐤋𐤉𐤃𐤅.𐤀𐤕.𐤔𐤓𐤅𐤂.𐤔𐤁𐤏.
𐤔𐤍𐤉𐤌.𐤅𐤌𐤀𐤕𐤉𐤌.𐤔𐤍𐤄.𐤅𐤉𐤅𐤋𐤃.𐤁𐤍𐤉𐤌.𐤅𐤁𐤍𐤅𐤕|
22 𐤅𐤉𐤇𐤉.𐤔𐤓𐤅𐤂.𐤔𐤋𐤔𐤉𐤌.𐤔𐤍𐤄.𐤅𐤉𐤅𐤋𐤃.𐤀𐤕.𐤍𐤇𐤅𐤓|
23 𐤅𐤉𐤇𐤉.𐤔𐤓𐤅𐤂.𐤀𐤇𐤓𐤉.𐤄𐤅𐤋𐤉𐤃𐤅.𐤀𐤕.𐤍𐤇𐤅𐤓.𐤌𐤀
𐤕𐤉𐤌.𐤔𐤍𐤄.𐤅𐤉𐤅𐤋𐤃.𐤁𐤍𐤉𐤌.𐤅𐤁𐤍𐤅𐤕|
24 𐤅𐤉𐤇𐤉.𐤍𐤇𐤅𐤓.𐤕𐤔𐤏.𐤅𐤏𐤔𐤓𐤉𐤌.𐤔𐤍𐤄.𐤅𐤉𐤅𐤋𐤃.𐤀𐤕
.𐤕𐤓𐤇|
25 𐤅𐤉𐤇𐤉.𐤍𐤇𐤅𐤓.𐤀𐤇𐤓𐤉.𐤄𐤅𐤋𐤉𐤃𐤅.𐤀𐤕.𐤕𐤓𐤇.𐤕𐤔𐤏.
𐤏𐤔𐤓𐤄.𐤔𐤍𐤄.𐤅𐤌𐤀𐤕.𐤔𐤍𐤄.𐤅𐤉𐤅𐤋𐤃.𐤁𐤍𐤉𐤌.𐤅𐤁𐤍𐤅𐤕|
26 𐤅𐤉𐤇𐤉.𐤕𐤓𐤇.𐤔𐤁𐤏𐤉𐤌.𐤔𐤍𐤄.𐤅𐤉𐤅𐤋𐤃.𐤀𐤕.𐤀𐤁𐤓𐤌.
𐤀𐤕.𐤍𐤇𐤅𐤓.𐤅𐤀𐤕.𐤄𐤓𐤍|
27 𐤅𐤀𐤋𐤄.𐤕𐤅𐤋𐤃𐤕.𐤕𐤓𐤇.𐤕𐤓𐤇.𐤄𐤅𐤋𐤉𐤃.𐤀𐤕.𐤀𐤁𐤓
𐤌.𐤀𐤕.𐤍𐤇𐤅𐤓.𐤅𐤀𐤕.𐤄𐤓𐤍.𐤅𐤄𐤓𐤍.𐤄𐤅𐤋𐤉𐤃.𐤀𐤕.𐤋𐤅𐤈|
28 𐤅𐤉𐤌𐤕.𐤄𐤓𐤍.𐤏𐤋.𐤐𐤍𐤉.𐤕𐤓𐤇.𐤀𐤁𐤉𐤅.𐤁𐤀𐤓𐤑.𐤌𐤅𐤋𐤃
𐤕𐤅.𐤁𐤀𐤅𐤓.𐤊𐤔𐤃𐤉𐤌|
29 𐤅𐤉𐤒𐤇.𐤀𐤁𐤓𐤌.𐤅𐤍𐤇𐤅𐤓.𐤋𐤄𐤌.𐤍𐤔𐤉𐤌.𐤔𐤌.𐤀𐤔𐤕.
𐤀𐤁𐤓𐤌.𐤔𐤓𐤉.𐤅𐤔𐤌.𐤀𐤔𐤕.𐤍𐤇𐤅𐤓.𐤌𐤋𐤊𐤄.𐤁𐤕.𐤄𐤓𐤍.𐤀𐤁𐤉.
𐤌𐤋𐤊𐤄.𐤅𐤀𐤁𐤉.𐤉𐤎𐤊𐤄|
30 𐤅𐤕𐤄𐤉.𐤔𐤓𐤉.𐤏𐤒𐤓𐤄.𐤀𐤉𐤍.𐤋𐤄.𐤅𐤋𐤃|

לא 𐤅𐤉𐤒𐤇.𐤕𐤓𐤇.𐤀𐤕.𐤀𐤁𐤓𐤌.𐤁𐤍𐤅.𐤅𐤀𐤕.𐤋𐤅𐤈.𐤁𐤍.𐤄𐤓𐤍
.𐤁𐤍.𐤁𐤍𐤅.𐤅𐤀𐤕.𐤔𐤓𐤉.𐤊𐤋𐤕𐤅.𐤀𐤔𐤕.𐤀𐤁𐤓𐤌.𐤁𐤍𐤅.𐤅𐤉𐤑𐤀𐤅.
𐤀𐤕𐤌.𐤌𐤀𐤅𐤓.𐤊𐤔𐤃𐤉𐤌.𐤋𐤋𐤊𐤕.𐤀𐤓𐤑𐤄.𐤊𐤍𐤏𐤍.𐤅𐤉𐤁𐤀𐤅.
𐤏𐤃.𐤇𐤓𐤍.𐤅𐤉𐤔𐤁𐤅.𐤔𐤌|
לב 𐤅𐤉𐤄𐤉𐤅.𐤉𐤌𐤉.𐤕𐤓𐤇.𐤇𐤌𐤔.𐤔𐤍𐤉𐤌.𐤅𐤌𐤀𐤕𐤉𐤌.𐤔𐤍
𐤄.𐤅𐤉𐤌𐤕.𐤕𐤓𐤇.𐤁𐤇𐤓𐤍||

𐤁𐤓𐤀𐤔𐤉𐤕.𐤇𐤋𐤒 יב

א 𐤅𐤉𐤀𐤌𐤓.𐤉𐤄𐤅𐤄.𐤀𐤋.𐤀𐤁𐤓𐤌.𐤋𐤊.𐤋𐤊.𐤌𐤀𐤓𐤑𐤊.𐤅𐤌𐤌𐤅𐤋
𐤃𐤕𐤊.𐤅𐤌𐤁𐤉𐤕.𐤀𐤁𐤉𐤊.𐤀𐤋.𐤄𐤀𐤓𐤑.𐤀𐤔𐤓.𐤀𐤓𐤀𐤊|
ב 𐤅𐤀𐤏𐤔𐤊.𐤋𐤂𐤅𐤉.𐤂𐤃𐤅𐤋.𐤅𐤀𐤁𐤓𐤊𐤊.𐤅𐤀𐤂𐤃𐤋𐤄.𐤔𐤌
𐤊.𐤅𐤄𐤉𐤄.𐤁𐤓𐤊𐤄|
ג 𐤅𐤀𐤁𐤓𐤊𐤄.𐤌𐤁𐤓𐤊𐤉𐤊.𐤅𐤌𐤒𐤋𐤋𐤊.𐤀𐤀𐤓.𐤅𐤍𐤁𐤓𐤊𐤅.𐤁𐤊.
𐤊𐤋.𐤌𐤔𐤐𐤇𐤕.𐤄𐤀𐤃𐤌𐤄|
ד 𐤅𐤉𐤋𐤊.𐤀𐤁𐤓𐤌.𐤊𐤀𐤔𐤓.𐤃𐤁𐤓.𐤀𐤋𐤉𐤅.𐤉𐤄𐤅𐤄.𐤅𐤉𐤋𐤊.𐤀
𐤕𐤅.𐤋𐤅𐤈.𐤅𐤀𐤁𐤓𐤌.𐤁𐤍.𐤇𐤌𐤔.𐤔𐤍𐤉𐤌.𐤅𐤔𐤁𐤏𐤉𐤌.𐤔𐤍𐤄.𐤁
𐤑𐤀𐤕𐤅.𐤌𐤇𐤓𐤍|
ה 𐤅𐤉𐤒𐤇.𐤀𐤁𐤓𐤌.𐤀𐤕.𐤔𐤓𐤉.𐤀𐤔𐤕𐤅.𐤅𐤀𐤕.𐤋𐤅𐤈.𐤁𐤍.𐤀
𐤇𐤉𐤅.𐤅𐤀𐤕.𐤊𐤋.𐤓𐤊𐤅𐤔𐤌.𐤀𐤔𐤓.𐤓𐤊𐤔𐤅.𐤅𐤀𐤕.𐤄𐤍𐤐𐤔.𐤀𐤔𐤓.
𐤏𐤔𐤅.𐤁𐤇𐤓𐤍.𐤅𐤉𐤑𐤀𐤅.𐤋𐤋𐤊𐤕.𐤀𐤓𐤑𐤄.𐤊𐤍𐤏𐤍.𐤅𐤉𐤁𐤀𐤅.𐤀𐤓
𐤑𐤄.𐤊𐤍𐤏𐤍|
ו 𐤅𐤉𐤏𐤁𐤓.𐤀𐤁𐤓𐤌.𐤁𐤀𐤓𐤑.𐤏𐤃.𐤌𐤒𐤅𐤌.𐤔𐤊𐤌.𐤏𐤃.𐤀𐤋
𐤅𐤍.𐤌𐤅𐤓𐤄.𐤅𐤄𐤊𐤍𐤏𐤍𐤉.𐤀𐤆.𐤁𐤀𐤓𐤑|
ז 𐤅𐤉𐤓𐤀.𐤉𐤄𐤅𐤄.𐤀𐤋.𐤀𐤁𐤓𐤌.𐤅𐤉𐤀𐤌𐤓.𐤋𐤆𐤓𐤏𐤊.𐤀𐤕𐤍.
𐤀𐤕.𐤄𐤀𐤓𐤑.𐤄𐤆𐤀𐤕.𐤅𐤉𐤁𐤍.𐤔𐤌.𐤌𐤆𐤁𐤇.𐤋𐤉𐤄𐤅𐤄.𐤄𐤍𐤓
𐤀𐤄.𐤀𐤋𐤉𐤅|
ח 𐤅𐤉𐤏𐤕𐤒.𐤌𐤔𐤌.𐤄𐤄𐤓𐤄.𐤌𐤒𐤃𐤌.𐤋𐤁𐤉𐤕.𐤀𐤋.𐤅𐤉𐤈.𐤀
𐤄𐤋𐤄.𐤁𐤉𐤕.𐤀𐤋.𐤌𐤉𐤌.𐤅𐤄𐤏𐤉.𐤌𐤒𐤃𐤌.𐤅𐤉𐤁𐤍.𐤔𐤌.𐤌𐤆𐤁
𐤇.𐤋𐤉𐤄𐤅𐤄.𐤅𐤉𐤒𐤓𐤀.𐤁𐤔𐤌.𐤉𐤄𐤅𐤄|
ט 𐤅𐤉𐤎𐤏.𐤀𐤁𐤓𐤌.𐤄𐤋𐤅𐤊.𐤅𐤍𐤎𐤅𐤏.𐤄𐤍𐤂𐤁𐤄|

10 𐤅𐤉𐤄𐤉.𐤓𐤏𐤁.𐤁𐤀𐤓𐤑.𐤅𐤉𐤓𐤃.𐤀𐤁𐤓𐤌.𐤌𐤑𐤓𐤉𐤌𐤄.𐤋
𐤂𐤅𐤓.𐤔𐤌.𐤊𐤉.𐤊𐤁𐤃.𐤄𐤓𐤏𐤁.𐤁𐤀𐤓𐤑|
11 𐤅𐤉𐤄𐤉.𐤊𐤀𐤔𐤓.𐤄𐤒𐤓𐤉𐤁.𐤋𐤁𐤅𐤀.𐤌𐤑𐤓𐤉𐤌𐤄.𐤅𐤉𐤀𐤌
𐤓.𐤀𐤋.𐤔𐤓𐤉.𐤀𐤔𐤕𐤅.𐤄𐤍𐤄.𐤍𐤀.𐤉𐤃𐤏𐤕𐤉.𐤊𐤉.𐤀𐤔𐤄.𐤉𐤐𐤕
.𐤌𐤓𐤀𐤄.𐤀𐤕|
12 𐤅𐤄𐤉𐤄.𐤊𐤉.𐤉𐤓𐤀𐤅.𐤀𐤕𐤊.𐤄𐤌𐤑𐤓𐤉𐤌.𐤅𐤀𐤌𐤓𐤅.𐤀𐤔𐤕
𐤅.𐤆𐤀𐤕.𐤅𐤄𐤓𐤂𐤅.𐤀𐤕𐤉.𐤅𐤀𐤕𐤊.𐤉𐤇𐤉𐤅|
13 𐤀𐤌𐤓𐤉.𐤍𐤀.𐤀𐤇𐤕𐤉.𐤀𐤕.𐤋𐤌𐤏𐤍.𐤉𐤉𐤈𐤁.𐤋𐤉.𐤁𐤏𐤁𐤅
𐤓𐤊.𐤅𐤇𐤉𐤕𐤄.𐤍𐤐𐤔𐤉.𐤁𐤂𐤋𐤋𐤊|
14 𐤅𐤉𐤄𐤉.𐤊𐤁𐤅𐤀.𐤀𐤁𐤓𐤌.𐤌𐤑𐤓𐤉𐤌𐤄.𐤅𐤉𐤓𐤀𐤅.𐤄𐤌𐤑𐤓
𐤉𐤌.𐤀𐤕.𐤄𐤀𐤔𐤄.𐤊𐤉.𐤉𐤐𐤄.𐤄𐤅𐤀.𐤌𐤀𐤃|
15 𐤅𐤉𐤓𐤀𐤅.𐤀𐤕𐤄.𐤔𐤓𐤉.𐤐𐤓𐤏𐤄.𐤅𐤉𐤄𐤋𐤋𐤅.𐤀𐤕𐤄.𐤀𐤋.𐤐𐤓
𐤏𐤄.𐤅𐤕𐤒𐤇.𐤄𐤀𐤔𐤄.𐤁𐤉𐤕.𐤐𐤓𐤏𐤄|
16 𐤅𐤋𐤀𐤁𐤓𐤌.𐤄𐤉𐤈𐤉𐤁.𐤁𐤏𐤁𐤅𐤓𐤄.𐤅𐤉𐤄𐤉.𐤋𐤅.𐤑𐤀𐤍.𐤅𐤁
𐤒𐤓.𐤅𐤇𐤌𐤓𐤉𐤌.𐤅𐤏𐤁𐤃𐤉𐤌.𐤅𐤔𐤐𐤇𐤕.𐤅𐤀𐤕𐤍𐤕.𐤅𐤂𐤌𐤋𐤉𐤌|
17 𐤅𐤉𐤍𐤂𐤏.𐤉𐤄𐤅𐤄.𐤀𐤕.𐤐𐤓𐤏𐤄.𐤍𐤂𐤏𐤉𐤌.𐤂𐤃𐤋𐤉𐤌.𐤅
𐤀𐤕.𐤁𐤉𐤕𐤅.𐤏𐤋.𐤃𐤁𐤓.𐤔𐤓𐤉.𐤀𐤔𐤕.𐤀𐤁𐤓𐤌|
18 𐤅𐤉𐤒𐤓𐤀.𐤐𐤓𐤏𐤄.𐤋𐤀𐤁𐤓𐤌.𐤅𐤉𐤀𐤌𐤓.𐤌𐤄.𐤆𐤀𐤕.𐤏𐤔
𐤉𐤕.𐤋𐤉.𐤋𐤌𐤄.𐤋𐤀.𐤄𐤂𐤃𐤕.𐤋𐤉.𐤊𐤉.𐤀𐤔𐤕𐤊.𐤄𐤅𐤀|
19 𐤋𐤌𐤄.𐤀𐤌𐤓𐤕.𐤀𐤇𐤕𐤉.𐤄𐤅𐤀.𐤅𐤀𐤒𐤇.𐤀𐤕𐤄.𐤋𐤉.𐤋
𐤀𐤔𐤄.𐤅𐤏𐤕𐤄.𐤄𐤍𐤄.𐤀𐤔𐤕𐤊.𐤒𐤇.𐤅𐤋𐤊|
20 𐤅𐤉𐤑𐤅.𐤏𐤋𐤉𐤅.𐤐𐤓𐤏𐤄.𐤀𐤍𐤔𐤉𐤌.𐤅𐤉𐤔𐤋𐤇𐤅.𐤀𐤕𐤅.𐤅𐤀
𐤕.𐤀𐤔𐤕𐤅.𐤅𐤀𐤕.𐤊𐤋.𐤀𐤔𐤓.𐤋𐤅||

𐤁𐤓𐤀𐤔𐤉𐤕.𐤇𐤋𐤒 13

1 𐤅𐤉𐤏𐤋.𐤀𐤁𐤓𐤌.𐤌𐤌𐤑𐤓𐤉𐤌.𐤄𐤅𐤀.𐤅𐤀𐤔𐤕𐤅.𐤅𐤊𐤋.𐤀𐤔𐤓.
𐤋𐤅.𐤅𐤋𐤅𐤈.𐤏𐤌𐤅.𐤄𐤍𐤂𐤁𐤄|
2 𐤅𐤀𐤁𐤓𐤌.𐤊𐤁𐤃.𐤌𐤀𐤃.𐤁𐤌𐤒𐤍𐤄.𐤁𐤊𐤎𐤐.𐤅𐤁𐤆𐤄𐤁|

ג 𐤅𐤉𐤋𐤊.𐤋𐤌𐤎𐤏𐤉𐤅.𐤌𐤍𐤂𐤁.𐤅𐤏𐤃.𐤁𐤉𐤕.𐤀𐤋.𐤏𐤃.𐤄𐤌
𐤒𐤅𐤌.𐤀𐤔𐤓.𐤄𐤉𐤄.𐤔𐤌.𐤀𐤄𐤋𐤄.||𐤀𐤄𐤋𐤅.𐤒𐤓𐤉||.𐤁𐤕𐤇𐤋𐤄.
𐤁𐤉𐤍.𐤁𐤉𐤕.𐤀𐤋.𐤅𐤁𐤉𐤍.𐤄𐤏𐤉|
ד 𐤀𐤋.𐤌𐤒𐤅𐤌.𐤄𐤌𐤆𐤁𐤇.𐤀𐤔𐤓.𐤏𐤔𐤄.𐤔𐤌.𐤁𐤓𐤀𐤔𐤍𐤄.
𐤅𐤉𐤒𐤓𐤀.𐤔𐤌.𐤀𐤁𐤓𐤌.𐤁𐤔𐤌.𐤉𐤄𐤅𐤄|
ה 𐤅𐤂𐤌.𐤋𐤋𐤅𐤈.𐤄𐤄𐤋𐤊.𐤀𐤕.𐤀𐤁𐤓𐤌.𐤄𐤉𐤄.𐤑𐤀𐤍.𐤅𐤁𐤒𐤓.
𐤅𐤀𐤄𐤋𐤉𐤌|
ו 𐤅𐤋𐤀.𐤍𐤔𐤀.𐤀𐤕𐤌.𐤄𐤀𐤓𐤑.𐤋𐤔𐤁𐤕.𐤉𐤇𐤃𐤅.𐤊𐤉.𐤄𐤉𐤄
.𐤓𐤊𐤅𐤔𐤌.𐤓𐤁.𐤅𐤋𐤀.𐤉𐤊𐤋𐤅.𐤋𐤔𐤁𐤕.𐤉𐤇𐤃𐤅|
ז 𐤅𐤉𐤄𐤉.𐤓𐤉𐤁.𐤁𐤉𐤍.𐤓𐤏𐤉.𐤌𐤒𐤍𐤄.𐤀𐤁𐤓𐤌.𐤅𐤁𐤉𐤍.𐤓𐤏𐤉.
𐤌𐤒𐤍𐤄.𐤋𐤅𐤈.𐤅𐤄𐤊𐤍𐤏𐤍𐤉.𐤅𐤄𐤐𐤓𐤆𐤉.𐤀𐤆.𐤉𐤔𐤁.𐤁𐤀𐤓𐤑|
ח 𐤅𐤉𐤀𐤌𐤓.𐤀𐤁𐤓𐤌.𐤀𐤋.𐤋𐤅𐤈.𐤀𐤋.𐤍𐤀.𐤕𐤄𐤉.𐤌𐤓𐤉𐤁𐤄.𐤁
𐤉𐤍𐤉.𐤅𐤁𐤉𐤍𐤉𐤊.𐤅𐤁𐤉𐤍.𐤓𐤏𐤉.𐤅𐤁𐤉𐤍.𐤓𐤏𐤉𐤊.𐤊𐤉.𐤀𐤍𐤔𐤉𐤌.
𐤀𐤇𐤉𐤌.𐤀𐤍𐤇𐤍𐤅|
ט 𐤄𐤋𐤀.𐤊𐤋.𐤄𐤀𐤓𐤑.𐤋𐤐𐤍𐤉𐤊.𐤄𐤐𐤓𐤃.𐤍𐤀.𐤌𐤏𐤋𐤉.𐤀𐤌.
𐤄𐤔𐤌𐤀𐤋.𐤅𐤀𐤉𐤌𐤍𐤄.𐤅𐤀𐤌.𐤄𐤉𐤌𐤉𐤍.𐤅𐤀𐤔𐤌𐤀𐤉𐤋𐤄|
י 𐤅𐤉𐤔𐤀.𐤋𐤅𐤈.𐤀𐤕.𐤏𐤉𐤍𐤉𐤅.𐤅𐤉𐤓𐤀.𐤀𐤕.𐤊𐤋.𐤊𐤊𐤓.𐤄𐤉
𐤓𐤃𐤍.𐤊𐤉.𐤊𐤋𐤄.𐤌𐤔𐤒𐤄.𐤋𐤐𐤍𐤉.𐤔𐤇𐤕.𐤉𐤄𐤅𐤄.𐤀𐤕.𐤎𐤃
𐤌.𐤅𐤀𐤕.𐤏𐤌𐤓𐤄.𐤊𐤂𐤍.𐤉𐤄𐤅𐤄.𐤊𐤀𐤓𐤑.𐤌𐤑𐤓𐤉𐤌.𐤁𐤀𐤊𐤄.
𐤑𐤏𐤓|
יא 𐤅𐤉𐤁𐤇𐤓.𐤋𐤅.𐤋𐤅𐤈.𐤀𐤕.𐤊𐤋.𐤊𐤊𐤓.𐤄𐤉𐤓𐤃𐤍.𐤅𐤉𐤎𐤏.𐤋𐤅
𐤈.𐤌𐤒𐤃𐤌.𐤅𐤉𐤐𐤓𐤃𐤅.𐤀𐤉𐤔.𐤌𐤏𐤋.𐤀𐤇𐤉𐤅|
יב 𐤀𐤁𐤓𐤌.𐤉𐤔𐤁.𐤁𐤀𐤓𐤑.𐤊𐤍𐤏𐤍.𐤅𐤋𐤅𐤈.𐤉𐤔𐤁.𐤁𐤏𐤓𐤉.𐤄
𐤊𐤊𐤓.𐤅𐤉𐤀𐤄𐤋.𐤏𐤃.𐤎𐤃𐤌|
יג 𐤅𐤀𐤍𐤔𐤉.𐤎𐤃𐤌.𐤓𐤏𐤉𐤌.𐤅𐤇𐤈𐤀𐤉𐤌.𐤋𐤉𐤄𐤅𐤄.𐤌𐤀𐤃
|
יד 𐤅𐤉𐤄𐤅𐤄.𐤀𐤌𐤓.𐤀𐤋.𐤀𐤁𐤓𐤌.𐤀𐤇𐤓𐤉.𐤄𐤐𐤓𐤃.𐤋𐤅𐤈.𐤌
𐤏𐤌𐤅.𐤔𐤀.𐤍𐤀.𐤏𐤉𐤍𐤉𐤊.𐤅𐤓𐤀𐤄.𐤌𐤍.𐤄𐤌𐤒𐤅𐤌.𐤀𐤔𐤓.𐤀𐤕𐤄.
𐤔𐤌.𐤑𐤐𐤍𐤄.𐤅𐤍𐤂𐤁𐤄.𐤅𐤒𐤃𐤌𐤄.𐤅𐤉𐤌𐤄|
טו 𐤊𐤉.𐤀𐤕.𐤊𐤋.𐤄𐤀𐤓𐤑.𐤀𐤔𐤓.𐤀𐤕𐤄.𐤓𐤀𐤄.𐤋𐤊.𐤀𐤕𐤍𐤍
𐤄.𐤅𐤋𐤆𐤓𐤏𐤊.𐤏𐤃.𐤏𐤅𐤋𐤌|

..𐤉𐤅.. 𐤅𐤔𐤌𐤕𐤉.𐤀𐤕.𐤆𐤓𐤏𐤊.𐤊𐤏𐤐𐤓.𐤄𐤀𐤓𐤑.𐤀𐤔𐤓.𐤀𐤌.𐤉
𐤅𐤊𐤋.𐤀𐤉𐤔.𐤋𐤌𐤍𐤅𐤕.𐤀𐤕.𐤏𐤐𐤓.𐤄𐤀𐤓𐤑.𐤂𐤌.𐤆𐤓𐤏𐤊.𐤉𐤌𐤍
𐤄|

..𐤉𐤆.. 𐤒𐤅𐤌.𐤄𐤕𐤄𐤋𐤊.𐤁𐤀𐤓𐤑.𐤋𐤀𐤓𐤊𐤄.𐤅𐤋𐤓𐤇𐤁𐤄.𐤊𐤉.𐤋
𐤊.𐤀𐤕𐤍𐤍𐤄|

..𐤉𐤇.. 𐤅𐤉𐤀𐤄𐤋.𐤀𐤁𐤓𐤌.𐤅𐤉𐤁𐤀.𐤅𐤉𐤔𐤁.𐤁𐤀𐤋𐤍𐤉.𐤌𐤌𐤓𐤀.𐤀
𐤔𐤓.𐤁𐤇𐤁𐤓𐤅𐤍.𐤅𐤉𐤁𐤍.𐤔𐤌.𐤌𐤆𐤁𐤇.𐤋𐤉𐤄𐤅𐤄||

𐤁𐤓𐤀𐤔𐤉𐤕.𐤇𐤋𐤒 ..𐤉𐤃..

..𐤀.. 𐤅𐤉𐤄𐤉.𐤁𐤉𐤌𐤉.𐤀𐤌𐤓𐤐𐤋.𐤌𐤋𐤊.𐤔𐤍𐤏𐤓.𐤀𐤓𐤉𐤅𐤊.𐤌𐤋𐤊.
𐤀𐤋𐤎𐤓.𐤊𐤃𐤓𐤋𐤏𐤌𐤓.𐤌𐤋𐤊.𐤏𐤉𐤋𐤌.𐤅𐤕𐤃𐤏𐤋.𐤌𐤋𐤊.𐤂𐤅𐤉
𐤌|

..𐤁.. 𐤏𐤔𐤅.𐤌𐤋𐤇𐤌𐤄.𐤀𐤕.𐤁𐤓𐤏.𐤌𐤋𐤊.𐤎𐤃𐤌.𐤅𐤀𐤕.𐤁𐤓𐤔𐤏
𐤌𐤋𐤊.𐤏𐤌𐤓𐤄.𐤔𐤍𐤀𐤁.𐤌𐤋𐤊.𐤀𐤃𐤌𐤄.𐤅𐤔𐤌𐤀𐤁𐤓.𐤌𐤋𐤊.𐤑
𐤁𐤉𐤉𐤌.||𐤑𐤁𐤅𐤉𐤉𐤌.𐤒𐤓𐤉||.𐤅𐤌𐤋𐤊.𐤁𐤋𐤏.𐤄𐤉𐤀.𐤑𐤏𐤓|

..𐤂.. 𐤊𐤋.𐤀𐤋𐤄.𐤇𐤁𐤓𐤅.𐤀𐤋.𐤏𐤌𐤒.𐤄𐤔𐤃𐤉𐤌.𐤄𐤅𐤀.𐤉𐤌.𐤄
𐤌𐤋𐤇|

..𐤃.. 𐤔𐤕𐤉𐤌.𐤏𐤔𐤓𐤄.𐤔𐤍𐤄.𐤏𐤁𐤃𐤅.𐤀𐤕.𐤊𐤃𐤓𐤋𐤏𐤌𐤓.𐤅𐤔
𐤋𐤔.𐤏𐤔𐤓𐤄.𐤔𐤍𐤄.𐤌𐤓𐤃𐤅|

..𐤄.. 𐤅𐤁𐤀𐤓𐤁𐤏.𐤏𐤔𐤓𐤄.𐤔𐤍𐤄.𐤁𐤀.𐤊𐤃𐤓𐤋𐤏𐤌𐤓.𐤅𐤄𐤌𐤋𐤊𐤉
𐤌.𐤀𐤔𐤓.𐤀𐤕𐤅.𐤅𐤉𐤊𐤅.𐤀𐤕.𐤓𐤐𐤀𐤉𐤌.𐤁𐤏𐤔𐤕𐤓𐤕.𐤒𐤓𐤍𐤉𐤌.𐤅
𐤀𐤕.𐤄𐤆𐤅𐤆𐤉𐤌.𐤁𐤄𐤌.𐤅𐤀𐤕.𐤄𐤀𐤉𐤌𐤉𐤌.𐤁𐤔𐤅𐤄.𐤒𐤓𐤉𐤕
𐤉𐤌|

..𐤅.. 𐤅𐤀𐤕.𐤄𐤇𐤓𐤉.𐤁𐤄𐤓𐤓𐤌.𐤔𐤏𐤉𐤓.𐤏𐤃.𐤀𐤉𐤋.𐤐𐤀𐤓𐤍.𐤀
𐤔𐤓.𐤏𐤋.𐤄𐤌𐤃𐤁𐤓|

..𐤆.. 𐤅𐤉𐤔𐤁𐤅.𐤅𐤉𐤁𐤀𐤅.𐤀𐤋.𐤏𐤉𐤍.𐤌𐤔𐤐𐤈.𐤄𐤅𐤀.𐤒𐤃𐤔.𐤅𐤉𐤊
𐤅.𐤀𐤕.𐤊𐤋.𐤔𐤃𐤄.𐤄𐤏𐤌𐤋𐤒𐤉.𐤅𐤂𐤌.𐤀𐤕.𐤄𐤀𐤌𐤓𐤉.𐤄𐤉𐤔
𐤁.𐤁𐤇𐤑𐤑𐤍.𐤕𐤌𐤓|

ח ויצא. מלך. סדם. ומלך. עמרה. ומלך. אדמה. ו
מלך. צביים. ||צבוים. קרי||. ומלך. בלע. הוא. צע
ר. ויערכו. אתם. מלחמה. בעמק. השדים|
ט את. כדרלעמר. מלך. עילם. ותדעל. מלך. גו
ים. ואמרפל. מלך. שנער. ואריוך. מלך. אלסר. ארב
עה. מלכים. את. החמשה|
י ועמק. השדים. בארת. בארת. חמר. וינסו. מ
לך. סדם. ועמרה. ויפלו. שמה. והנשארים. הרה. נ
סו|
יא ויקחו. את. כל. רכש. סדם. ועמרה. ואת. כל. א
כלם. וילכו|
יב ויקחו. את. לוט. ואת. רכשו. בן. אחי. אברם. ו
ילכו. והוא. ישב. בסדם|
יג ויבא. הפליט. ויגד. לאברם. העברי. והוא.
שכן. באלני. ממרא. האמרי. אחי. אשכל. ואחי.
ענר. והם. בעלי. ברית. אברם|
יד וישמע. אברם. כי. נשבה. אחיו. וירק. את.
חניכיו. ילידי. ביתו. שמנה. עשר. ושלש. מאות.
וירדף. עד. דן|
טו ויחלק. עליהם. לילה. הוא. ועבדיו. ויכם. ו
ירדפם. עד. חובה. אשר. משמאל. לדמשק|
טז וישב. את. כל. הרכש. וגם. את. לוט. אחיו. ור
כשו. השיב. וגם. את. הנשים. ואת. העם|
יז ויצא. מלך. סדם. לקראתו. אחרי. שובו. מה
כות. את. כדרלעמר. ואת. המלכים. אשר. אתו. אל
עמק. שוה. הוא. עמק. המלך|
יח ומלכי. צדק. מלך. שלם. הוציא. לחם. ויין.
והוא. כהן. לאל. עליון|
יט ויברכהו. ויאמר. ברוך. אברם. לאל. עליון. ק
נה. שמים. וארץ|

20 וברוך.אל.עליון.אשר.מגן.צריך.בידך.ו
יתן.לו.מעשר.מכל|
21 ויאמר.מלך.סדם.אל.אברם.תן.לי.הנפש.ו
הרכש.קח.לך|
22 ויאמר.אברם.אל.מלך.סדם.הרימתי.ידי
.אל.יהוה.אל.עליון.קנה.שמים.וארץ|
23 אם.מחוט.ועד.שרוך.נעל.ואם.אקח.מכל.
אשר.לך.ולא.תאמר.אני.העשרתי.את.אברם|
24 בלעדי.רק.אשר.אכלו.הנערים.וחלק.ה
אנשים.אשר.הלכו.אתי.ענר.אשכל.וממרא.הם.
יקחו.חלקם| ||

בראשית.חלק 15

1 אחר.הדברים.האלה.היה.דבר.יהוה.אל.א
ברם.במחזה.לאמר.אל.תירא.אברם.אנכי.מג
ן.לך.שכרך.הרבה.מאד|
2 ויאמר.אברם.אדני.יהוה.מה.תתן.לי.ואנכ
י.הולך.ערירי.ובן.משק.ביתי.הוא.דמשק.אל
יעזר|
3 ויאמר.אברם.הן.לי.לא.נתתה.זרע.והנה.ב
ן.ביתי.יורש.אתי|
4 והנה.דבר.יהוה.אליו.לאמר.לא.יירשך.ז
ה.כי.אם.אשר.יצא.ממעיך.הוא.יירשך|
5 ויוצא.אתו.החוצה.ויאמר.הבט.נא.השמי
מה.וספר.הכוכבים.אם.תוכל.לספר.אתם.ויאמר
.לו.כה.יהיה.זרעך|
6 והאמן.ביהוה.ויחשבה.לו.צדקה|
7 ויאמר.אליו.אני.יהוה.אשר.הוצאתיך.מ
אור.כשדים.לתת.לך.את.הארץ.הזאת.לרשת
ה|

ח 𐤅𐤉𐤀𐤌𐤓.𐤀𐤃𐤍𐤉.𐤉𐤄𐤅𐤄.𐤁𐤌𐤄.𐤀𐤃𐤏.𐤊𐤉.𐤀𐤉𐤓𐤔𐤍𐤄

|

ט 𐤅𐤉𐤀𐤌𐤓.𐤀𐤋𐤉𐤅.𐤒𐤇𐤄.𐤋𐤉.𐤏𐤂𐤋𐤄.𐤌𐤔𐤋𐤔𐤕.𐤅𐤏𐤆.

𐤌𐤔𐤋𐤔𐤕.𐤅𐤀𐤉𐤋.𐤌𐤔𐤋𐤔.𐤅𐤕𐤓.𐤅𐤂𐤅𐤆𐤋|

י 𐤅𐤉𐤒𐤇.𐤋𐤅.𐤀𐤕.𐤊𐤋.𐤀𐤋𐤄.𐤅𐤉𐤁𐤕𐤓.𐤀𐤕𐤌.𐤁𐤕𐤅𐤊.𐤅𐤉

𐤕𐤍.𐤀𐤉𐤔.𐤁𐤕𐤓𐤅.𐤋𐤒𐤓𐤀𐤕.𐤓𐤏𐤄𐤅.𐤅𐤀𐤕.𐤄𐤑𐤐𐤓.𐤋𐤀.𐤁𐤕

𐤓|

יא 𐤅𐤉𐤓𐤃.𐤄𐤏𐤉𐤈.𐤏𐤋.𐤄𐤐𐤂𐤓𐤉𐤌.𐤅𐤉𐤔𐤁.𐤀𐤕𐤌.𐤀𐤁𐤓

𐤌|

יב 𐤅𐤉𐤄𐤉.𐤄𐤔𐤌𐤔.𐤋𐤁𐤅𐤀.𐤅𐤕𐤓𐤃𐤌𐤄.𐤍𐤐𐤋𐤄.𐤏𐤋.𐤀𐤁𐤓

𐤌.𐤅𐤄𐤍𐤄.𐤀𐤉𐤌𐤄.𐤇𐤔𐤊𐤄.𐤂𐤃𐤋𐤄.𐤍𐤐𐤋𐤕.𐤏𐤋𐤉𐤅|

יג 𐤅𐤉𐤀𐤌𐤓.𐤋𐤀𐤁𐤓𐤌.𐤉𐤃𐤏.𐤕𐤃𐤏.𐤊𐤉.𐤂𐤓.𐤉𐤄𐤉𐤄.

𐤆𐤓𐤏𐤊.𐤁𐤀𐤓𐤑.𐤋𐤀.𐤋𐤄𐤌.𐤅𐤏𐤁𐤃𐤅𐤌.𐤅𐤏𐤍𐤅.𐤀𐤕𐤌.𐤀𐤓𐤁

𐤏.𐤌𐤀𐤅𐤕.𐤔𐤍𐤄|

יד 𐤅𐤂𐤌.𐤀𐤕.𐤄𐤂𐤅𐤉.𐤀𐤔𐤓.𐤉𐤏𐤁𐤃𐤅.𐤃𐤍.𐤀𐤍𐤊𐤉.𐤅𐤀

𐤇𐤓𐤉.𐤊𐤍.𐤉𐤑𐤀𐤅.𐤁𐤓𐤊𐤔.𐤂𐤃𐤅𐤋|

טו 𐤅𐤀𐤕𐤄.𐤕𐤁𐤅𐤀.𐤀𐤋.𐤀𐤁𐤕𐤉𐤊.𐤁𐤔𐤋𐤅𐤌.𐤕𐤒𐤁𐤓.𐤁𐤔

𐤉𐤁𐤄.𐤈𐤅𐤁𐤄|

טז 𐤅𐤃𐤅𐤓.𐤓𐤁𐤉𐤏𐤉.𐤉𐤔𐤅𐤁𐤅.𐤄𐤍𐤄.𐤊𐤉.𐤋𐤀.𐤔𐤋𐤌.𐤏𐤅𐤍.𐤄

𐤀𐤌𐤓𐤉.𐤏𐤃.𐤄𐤍𐤄|

יז 𐤅𐤉𐤄𐤉.𐤄𐤔𐤌𐤔.𐤁𐤀𐤄.𐤅𐤏𐤋𐤈𐤄.𐤄𐤉𐤄.𐤅𐤄𐤍𐤄.𐤕𐤍𐤅𐤓

.𐤏𐤔𐤍.𐤅𐤋𐤐𐤉𐤃.𐤀𐤔.𐤀𐤔𐤓.𐤏𐤁𐤓.𐤁𐤉𐤍.𐤄𐤂𐤆𐤓𐤉𐤌.𐤄𐤀𐤋

𐤄|

יח 𐤁𐤉𐤅𐤌.𐤄𐤄𐤅𐤀.𐤊𐤓𐤕.𐤉𐤄𐤅𐤄.𐤀𐤕.𐤀𐤁𐤓𐤌.𐤁𐤓𐤉𐤕.𐤋𐤀

𐤌𐤓.𐤋𐤆𐤓𐤏𐤊.𐤍𐤕𐤕𐤉.𐤀𐤕.𐤄𐤀𐤓𐤑.𐤄𐤆𐤀𐤕.𐤌𐤍𐤄𐤓.𐤌𐤑

𐤓𐤉𐤌.𐤏𐤃.𐤄𐤍𐤄𐤓.𐤄𐤂𐤃𐤋.𐤍𐤄𐤓.𐤐𐤓𐤕|

יט 𐤀𐤕.𐤄𐤒𐤉𐤍𐤉.𐤅𐤀𐤕.𐤄𐤒𐤍𐤆𐤉.𐤅𐤀𐤕.𐤄𐤒𐤃𐤌𐤍𐤉|

כ 𐤅𐤀𐤕.𐤄𐤇𐤕𐤉.𐤅𐤀𐤕.𐤄𐤐𐤓𐤆𐤉.𐤅𐤀𐤕.𐤄𐤓𐤐𐤀𐤉𐤌|

כא 𐤅𐤀𐤕.𐤄𐤀𐤌𐤓𐤉.𐤅𐤀𐤕.𐤄𐤊𐤍𐤏𐤍𐤉.𐤅𐤀𐤕.𐤄𐤂𐤓𐤂𐤔𐤉.𐤅

𐤀𐤕.𐤄𐤉𐤁𐤅𐤎𐤉||

𐤁𐤓𐤀𐤔𐤉𐤕.𐤇𐤋𐤒 16

1 𐤅𐤔𐤓𐤉.𐤀𐤔𐤕.𐤀𐤁𐤓𐤌.𐤋𐤀.𐤉𐤋𐤃𐤄.𐤋𐤅.𐤅𐤋𐤄.𐤔𐤐𐤇𐤄.𐤌
𐤑𐤓𐤉𐤕.𐤅𐤔𐤌𐤄.𐤄𐤂𐤓|

2 𐤅𐤕𐤀𐤌𐤓.𐤔𐤓𐤉.𐤀𐤋.𐤀𐤁𐤓𐤌.𐤄𐤍𐤄.𐤍𐤀.𐤏𐤑𐤓𐤍𐤉.𐤉𐤄𐤅
𐤄.𐤌𐤋𐤃𐤕.𐤁𐤀.𐤍𐤀.𐤀𐤋.𐤔𐤐𐤇𐤕𐤉.𐤀𐤅𐤋𐤉.𐤀𐤁𐤍𐤄.𐤌𐤌𐤍𐤄.
𐤅𐤉𐤔𐤌𐤏.𐤀𐤁𐤓𐤌.𐤋𐤒𐤅𐤋.𐤔𐤓𐤉|

3 𐤅𐤕𐤒𐤇.𐤔𐤓𐤉.𐤀𐤔𐤕.𐤀𐤁𐤓𐤌.𐤀𐤕.𐤄𐤂𐤓.𐤄𐤌𐤑𐤓𐤉𐤕.
𐤔𐤐𐤇𐤕𐤄.𐤌𐤒𐤑.𐤏𐤔𐤓.𐤔𐤍𐤉𐤌.𐤋𐤔𐤁𐤕.𐤀𐤁𐤓𐤌.𐤁𐤀𐤓𐤑.
𐤊𐤍𐤏𐤍.𐤅𐤕𐤕𐤍.𐤀𐤕𐤄.𐤋𐤀𐤁𐤓𐤌.𐤀𐤉𐤔𐤄.𐤋𐤅.𐤋𐤀𐤔𐤄|

4 𐤅𐤉𐤁𐤀.𐤀𐤋.𐤄𐤂𐤓.𐤅𐤕𐤄𐤓.𐤅𐤕𐤓𐤀.𐤊𐤉.𐤄𐤓𐤕𐤄.𐤅𐤕𐤒𐤋.
𐤂𐤁𐤓𐤕𐤄.𐤁𐤏𐤉𐤍𐤉𐤄|

5 𐤅𐤕𐤀𐤌𐤓.𐤔𐤓𐤉.𐤀𐤋.𐤀𐤁𐤓𐤌.𐤇𐤌𐤎𐤉.𐤏𐤋𐤉𐤊.𐤀𐤍𐤊𐤉.
𐤍𐤕𐤕𐤉.𐤔𐤐𐤇𐤕𐤉.𐤁𐤇𐤉𐤒𐤊.𐤅𐤕𐤓𐤀.𐤊𐤉.𐤄𐤓𐤕𐤄.𐤅𐤀𐤒𐤋.𐤁
𐤏𐤉𐤍𐤉𐤄.𐤉𐤔𐤐𐤈.𐤉𐤄𐤅𐤄.𐤁𐤉𐤍𐤉.𐤅𐤁𐤉𐤍𐤉𐤊|

6 𐤅𐤉𐤀𐤌𐤓.𐤀𐤁𐤓𐤌.𐤀𐤋.𐤔𐤓𐤉.𐤄𐤍𐤄.𐤔𐤐𐤇𐤕𐤊.𐤁𐤉𐤃𐤊.
𐤏𐤔𐤉.𐤋𐤄.𐤄𐤈𐤅𐤁.𐤁𐤏𐤉𐤍𐤉𐤊.𐤅𐤕𐤏𐤍𐤄.𐤔𐤓𐤉.𐤅𐤕𐤁𐤓𐤇.𐤌𐤐
𐤍𐤉𐤄|

7 𐤅𐤉𐤌𐤑𐤀𐤄.𐤌𐤋𐤀𐤊.𐤉𐤄𐤅𐤄.𐤏𐤋.𐤏𐤉𐤍.𐤄𐤌𐤉𐤌.𐤁𐤌𐤃
𐤁𐤓.𐤏𐤋.𐤄𐤏𐤉𐤍.𐤁𐤃𐤓𐤊.𐤔𐤅𐤓|

8 𐤅𐤉𐤀𐤌𐤓.𐤄𐤂𐤓.𐤔𐤐𐤇𐤕.𐤔𐤓𐤉.𐤀𐤉.𐤌𐤆𐤄.𐤁𐤀𐤕.𐤅𐤀𐤍
𐤄.𐤕𐤋𐤊𐤉.𐤅𐤕𐤀𐤌𐤓.𐤌𐤐𐤍𐤉.𐤔𐤓𐤉.𐤂𐤁𐤓𐤕𐤉.𐤀𐤍𐤊𐤉.𐤁𐤓𐤇
𐤕|

9 𐤅𐤉𐤀𐤌𐤓.𐤋𐤄.𐤌𐤋𐤀𐤊.𐤉𐤄𐤅𐤄.𐤔𐤅𐤁𐤉.𐤀𐤋.𐤂𐤁𐤓𐤕𐤊.
𐤅𐤄𐤕𐤏𐤍𐤉.𐤕𐤇𐤕.𐤉𐤃𐤉𐤄|

10 𐤅𐤉𐤀𐤌𐤓.𐤋𐤄.𐤌𐤋𐤀𐤊.𐤉𐤄𐤅𐤄.𐤄𐤓𐤁𐤄.𐤀𐤓𐤁𐤄.𐤀𐤕.𐤆
𐤓𐤏𐤊.𐤋𐤀.𐤉𐤎𐤐𐤓.𐤌𐤓𐤁|

11 𐤅𐤉𐤀𐤌𐤓.𐤋𐤄.𐤌𐤋𐤀𐤊.𐤉𐤄𐤅𐤄.𐤄𐤍𐤊.𐤄𐤓𐤄.𐤅𐤉𐤋𐤃𐤕.𐤁
𐤍.𐤅𐤒𐤓𐤀𐤕.𐤔𐤌𐤅.𐤉𐤔𐤌𐤏𐤀𐤋.𐤊𐤉.𐤔𐤌𐤏.𐤉𐤄𐤅𐤄.𐤀𐤋.𐤏𐤍𐤉
𐤊|

12 𐤅𐤄𐤅𐤀.𐤉𐤄𐤉𐤄.𐤐𐤓𐤀.𐤀𐤃𐤌.𐤉𐤃𐤅.𐤁𐤊𐤋.𐤅𐤉𐤃.𐤊𐤋.𐤁𐤅.𐤅𐤏𐤋.𐤐𐤍𐤉.𐤊𐤋.𐤀𐤇𐤉𐤅.𐤉𐤔𐤊𐤍|

13 𐤅𐤕𐤒𐤓𐤀.𐤔𐤌.𐤉𐤄𐤅𐤄.𐤄𐤃𐤁𐤓.𐤀𐤋𐤉𐤄.𐤀𐤕𐤄.𐤀𐤋.𐤓𐤀𐤉.𐤊𐤉.𐤀𐤌𐤓𐤄.𐤄𐤂𐤌.𐤄𐤋𐤌.𐤓𐤀𐤉𐤕𐤉.𐤀𐤇𐤓𐤉.𐤓𐤀𐤉|

14 𐤏𐤋.𐤊𐤍.𐤒𐤓𐤀.𐤋𐤁𐤀𐤓.𐤁𐤀𐤓.𐤋𐤇𐤉.𐤓𐤀𐤉.𐤄𐤍𐤄.𐤁𐤉𐤍.𐤒𐤃𐤔.𐤅𐤁𐤉𐤍.𐤁𐤓𐤃|

15 𐤅𐤕𐤋𐤃.𐤄𐤂𐤓.𐤋𐤀𐤁𐤓𐤌.𐤁𐤍.𐤅𐤉𐤒𐤓𐤀.𐤀𐤁𐤓𐤌.𐤔𐤌.𐤁𐤍𐤅.𐤀𐤔𐤓.𐤉𐤋𐤃𐤄.𐤄𐤂𐤓.𐤉𐤔𐤌𐤏𐤀𐤋|

16 𐤅𐤀𐤁𐤓𐤌.𐤁𐤍.𐤔𐤌𐤍𐤉𐤌.𐤔𐤍𐤄.𐤅𐤔𐤔.𐤔𐤍𐤉𐤌.𐤁𐤋𐤃𐤕.𐤄𐤂𐤓.𐤀𐤕.𐤉𐤔𐤌𐤏𐤀𐤋.𐤋𐤀𐤁𐤓𐤌||

17 𐤁𐤓𐤀𐤔𐤉𐤕.𐤇𐤋𐤒

1 𐤅𐤉𐤄𐤉.𐤀𐤁𐤓𐤌.𐤁𐤍.𐤕𐤔𐤏𐤉𐤌.𐤔𐤍𐤄.𐤅𐤕𐤔𐤏.𐤔𐤍𐤉𐤌.𐤅𐤉𐤓𐤀.𐤉𐤄𐤅𐤄.𐤀𐤋.𐤀𐤁𐤓𐤌.𐤅𐤉𐤀𐤌𐤓.𐤀𐤋𐤉𐤅.𐤀𐤍𐤉.𐤀𐤋.𐤔𐤃𐤉.𐤄𐤕𐤄𐤋𐤊.𐤋𐤐𐤍𐤉.𐤅𐤄𐤉𐤄.𐤕𐤌𐤉𐤌|

2 𐤅𐤀𐤕𐤍𐤄.𐤁𐤓𐤉𐤕𐤉.𐤁𐤉𐤍𐤉.𐤅𐤁𐤉𐤍𐤊.𐤅𐤀𐤓𐤁𐤄.𐤀𐤅𐤕𐤊.𐤁𐤌𐤀𐤃.𐤌𐤀𐤃|

3 𐤅𐤉𐤐𐤋.𐤀𐤁𐤓𐤌.𐤏𐤋.𐤐𐤍𐤉𐤅.𐤅𐤉𐤃𐤁𐤓.𐤀𐤕𐤅.𐤀𐤋𐤄𐤉𐤌.𐤋𐤀𐤌𐤓|

4 𐤀𐤍𐤉.𐤄𐤍𐤄.𐤁𐤓𐤉𐤕𐤉.𐤀𐤕𐤊.𐤅𐤄𐤉𐤉𐤕.𐤋𐤀𐤁.𐤄𐤌𐤅𐤍.𐤂𐤅𐤉𐤌|

5 𐤅𐤋𐤀.𐤉𐤒𐤓𐤀.𐤏𐤅𐤃.𐤀𐤕.𐤔𐤌𐤊.𐤀𐤁𐤓𐤌.𐤅𐤄𐤉𐤄.𐤔𐤌𐤊.𐤀𐤁𐤓𐤄𐤌.𐤊𐤉.𐤀𐤁.𐤄𐤌𐤅𐤍.𐤂𐤅𐤉𐤌.𐤍𐤕𐤕𐤉𐤊|

6 𐤅𐤄𐤐𐤓𐤕𐤉.𐤀𐤕𐤊.𐤁𐤌𐤀𐤃.𐤌𐤀𐤃.𐤅𐤍𐤕𐤕𐤉𐤊.𐤋𐤂𐤅𐤉𐤌.𐤅𐤌𐤋𐤊𐤉𐤌.𐤌𐤌𐤊.𐤉𐤑𐤀𐤅|

7 𐤅𐤄𐤒𐤌𐤕𐤉.𐤀𐤕.𐤁𐤓𐤉𐤕𐤉.𐤁𐤉𐤍𐤉.𐤅𐤁𐤉𐤍𐤊.𐤅𐤁𐤉𐤍.𐤆𐤓𐤏𐤊.𐤀𐤇𐤓𐤉𐤊.𐤋𐤃𐤓𐤕𐤌.𐤋𐤁𐤓𐤉𐤕.𐤏𐤅𐤋𐤌.𐤋𐤄𐤉𐤅𐤕.𐤋𐤊.𐤋𐤀𐤋𐤄𐤉𐤌.𐤅𐤋𐤆𐤓𐤏𐤊.𐤀𐤇𐤓𐤉𐤊|

ח 𐤅𐤍𐤕𐤕𐤉.𐤋𐤊.𐤅𐤋𐤆𐤓𐤏𐤊.𐤀𐤇𐤓𐤉𐤊.𐤀𐤕.𐤀𐤓𐤑.𐤌𐤂𐤓𐤉
𐤊.𐤀𐤕.𐤊𐤋.𐤀𐤓𐤑.𐤊𐤍𐤏𐤍.𐤋𐤀𐤇𐤆𐤕.𐤏𐤅𐤋𐤌.𐤅𐤄𐤉𐤉𐤕𐤉.𐤋
𐤄𐤌.𐤋𐤀𐤋𐤄𐤉𐤌|
ט 𐤅𐤉𐤀𐤌𐤓.𐤀𐤋𐤄𐤉𐤌.𐤀𐤋.𐤀𐤁𐤓𐤄𐤌.𐤅𐤀𐤕𐤄.𐤀𐤕.𐤁𐤓𐤉𐤕
𐤉.𐤕𐤔𐤌𐤓.𐤀𐤕𐤄.𐤅𐤆𐤓𐤏𐤊.𐤀𐤇𐤓𐤉𐤊.𐤋𐤃𐤓𐤕𐤌|
י 𐤆𐤀𐤕.𐤁𐤓𐤉𐤕𐤉.𐤀𐤔𐤓.𐤕𐤔𐤌𐤓𐤅.𐤁𐤉𐤍𐤉.𐤅𐤁𐤉𐤍𐤉𐤊𐤌.
𐤅𐤁𐤉𐤍.𐤆𐤓𐤏𐤊.𐤀𐤇𐤓𐤉𐤊.𐤄𐤌𐤅𐤋.𐤋𐤊𐤌.𐤊𐤋.𐤆𐤊𐤓|
יא 𐤅𐤍𐤌𐤋𐤕𐤌.𐤀𐤕.𐤁𐤔𐤓.𐤏𐤓𐤋𐤕𐤊𐤌.𐤅𐤄𐤉𐤄.𐤋𐤀𐤅𐤕.𐤁𐤓
𐤉𐤕.𐤁𐤉𐤍𐤉.𐤅𐤁𐤉𐤍𐤉𐤊𐤌|
יב 𐤅𐤁𐤍.𐤔𐤌𐤍𐤕.𐤉𐤌𐤉𐤌.𐤉𐤌𐤅𐤋.𐤋𐤊𐤌.𐤊𐤋.𐤆𐤊𐤓.𐤋𐤃𐤓𐤕
𐤉𐤊𐤌.𐤉𐤋𐤉𐤃.𐤁𐤉𐤕.𐤅𐤌𐤒𐤍𐤕.𐤊𐤎𐤐.𐤌𐤊𐤋.𐤁𐤍.𐤍𐤊𐤓.𐤀𐤔𐤓.
𐤋𐤀.𐤌𐤆𐤓𐤏𐤊.𐤄𐤅𐤀|
יג 𐤄𐤌𐤅𐤋.𐤉𐤌𐤅𐤋.𐤉𐤋𐤉𐤃.𐤁𐤉𐤕𐤊.𐤅𐤌𐤒𐤍𐤕.𐤊𐤎𐤐𐤊.𐤅𐤄𐤉
𐤕𐤄.𐤁𐤓𐤉𐤕𐤉.𐤁𐤁𐤔𐤓𐤊𐤌.𐤋𐤁𐤓𐤉𐤕.𐤏𐤅𐤋𐤌|
יד 𐤅𐤏𐤓𐤋.𐤆𐤊𐤓.𐤀𐤔𐤓.𐤋𐤀.𐤉𐤌𐤅𐤋.𐤀𐤕.𐤁𐤔𐤓.𐤏𐤓𐤋𐤕𐤅.𐤅
𐤍𐤊𐤓𐤕𐤄.𐤄𐤍𐤐𐤔.𐤄𐤄𐤅𐤀.𐤌𐤏𐤌𐤉𐤄.𐤀𐤕.𐤁𐤓𐤉𐤕𐤉.𐤄𐤐𐤓|
טו 𐤅𐤉𐤀𐤌𐤓.𐤀𐤋𐤄𐤉𐤌.𐤀𐤋.𐤀𐤁𐤓𐤄𐤌.𐤔𐤓𐤉.𐤀𐤔𐤕𐤊.𐤋𐤀.
𐤕𐤒𐤓𐤀.𐤀𐤕.𐤔𐤌𐤄.𐤔𐤓𐤉.𐤊𐤉.𐤔𐤓𐤄.𐤔𐤌𐤄|
טז 𐤅𐤁𐤓𐤊𐤕𐤉.𐤀𐤕𐤄.𐤅𐤂𐤌.𐤍𐤕𐤕𐤉.𐤌𐤌𐤍𐤄.𐤋𐤊.𐤁𐤍.𐤅𐤁𐤓
𐤊𐤕𐤉𐤄.𐤅𐤄𐤉𐤕𐤄.𐤋𐤂𐤅𐤉𐤌.𐤌𐤋𐤊𐤉.𐤏𐤌𐤉𐤌.𐤌𐤌𐤍𐤄.𐤉𐤄𐤉𐤅
|
יז 𐤅𐤉𐤐𐤋.𐤀𐤁𐤓𐤄𐤌.𐤏𐤋.𐤐𐤍𐤉𐤅.𐤅𐤉𐤑𐤇𐤒.𐤅𐤉𐤀𐤌𐤓.𐤁𐤋𐤁
𐤅.𐤄𐤋𐤁𐤍.𐤌𐤀𐤄.𐤔𐤍𐤄.𐤉𐤅𐤋𐤃.𐤅𐤀𐤌.𐤔𐤓𐤄.𐤄𐤁𐤕.𐤕𐤔𐤏𐤉𐤌
𐤔𐤍𐤄.𐤕𐤋𐤃|
יח 𐤅𐤉𐤀𐤌𐤓.𐤀𐤁𐤓𐤄𐤌.𐤀𐤋.𐤄𐤀𐤋𐤄𐤉𐤌.𐤋𐤅.𐤉𐤔𐤌𐤏𐤀𐤋.𐤉
𐤇𐤉𐤄.𐤋𐤐𐤍𐤉𐤊|
יט 𐤅𐤉𐤀𐤌𐤓.𐤀𐤋𐤄𐤉𐤌.𐤀𐤁𐤋.𐤔𐤓𐤄.𐤀𐤔𐤕𐤊.𐤉𐤋𐤃𐤕.𐤋
𐤊.𐤁𐤍.𐤅𐤒𐤓𐤀𐤕.𐤀𐤕.𐤔𐤌𐤅.𐤉𐤑𐤇𐤒.𐤅𐤄𐤒𐤌𐤕𐤉.𐤀𐤕.𐤁𐤓𐤉
𐤕𐤉.𐤀𐤕𐤅.𐤋𐤁𐤓𐤉𐤕.𐤏𐤅𐤋𐤌.𐤋𐤆𐤓𐤏𐤅.𐤀𐤇𐤓𐤉𐤅|

20 ולישמעאל.שמעתיך.הנה.ברכתי.אתו.והפריתי.אתו.והרביתי.אתו.במאד.מאד.שנים.עשר.נשיאם.יוליד.ונתתיו.לגוי.גדול׃

21 ואת.בריתי.אקים.את.יצחק.אשר.תלד.לך.שרה.למועד.הזה.בשנה.האחרת׃

22 ויכל.לדבר.אתו.ויעל.אלהים.מעל.אברהם׃

23 ויקח.אברהם.את.ישמעאל.בנו.ואת.כל.ילידי.ביתו.ואת.כל.מקנת.כספו.כל.זכר.באנשי.בית.אברהם.וימל.את.בשר.ערלתם.בעצם.היום.הזה.כאשר.דבר.אתו.אלהים׃

24 ואברהם.בן.תשעים.ותשע.שנה.בהמלו.בשר.ערלתו׃

25 וישמעאל.בנו.בן.שלש.עשרה.שנה.בהמלו.את.בשר.ערלתו׃

26 בעצם.היום.הזה.נמול.אברהם.וישמעאל.בנו׃

27 וכל.אנשי.ביתו.יליד.בית.ומקנת.כסף.מאת.בן.נכר.נמלו.אתו׃׃

בראשית.חלק 18

1 וירא.אליו.יהוה.באלני.ממרא.והוא.ישב.פתח.האהל.כחם.היום׃

2 וישא.עיניו.וירא.והנה.שלשה.אנשים.נצבים.עליו.וירא.וירץ.לקראתם.מפתח.האהל.וישתחו.ארצה׃

3 ויאמר.אדני.אם.נא.מצאתי.חן.בעיניך.אל.נא.תעבר.מעל.עבדך׃

4 יקח.נא.מעט.מים.ורחצו.רגליכם.והשענו.תחת.העץ׃

ה 𐤅𐤀𐤒𐤇𐤄.𐤐𐤕.𐤋𐤇𐤌.𐤅𐤎𐤏𐤃𐤅.𐤋𐤁𐤊𐤌.𐤀𐤇𐤓.𐤕𐤏𐤁𐤓𐤅
.𐤊𐤉.𐤏𐤋.𐤊𐤍.𐤏𐤁𐤓𐤕𐤌.𐤏𐤋.𐤏𐤁𐤃𐤊𐤌.𐤅𐤉𐤀𐤌𐤓𐤅.𐤊𐤍.𐤕𐤏
𐤔𐤄.𐤊𐤀𐤔𐤓.𐤃𐤁𐤓𐤕|

ו 𐤅𐤉𐤌𐤄𐤓.𐤀𐤁𐤓𐤄𐤌.𐤄𐤀𐤄𐤋𐤄.𐤀𐤋.𐤔𐤓𐤄.𐤅𐤉𐤀𐤌𐤓.𐤌𐤄𐤓
𐤉.𐤔𐤋𐤔.𐤎𐤀𐤉𐤌.𐤒𐤌𐤇.𐤎𐤋𐤕.𐤋𐤅𐤔𐤉.𐤅𐤏𐤔𐤉.𐤏𐤂𐤅𐤕|

ז 𐤅𐤀𐤋.𐤄𐤁𐤒𐤓.𐤓𐤑.𐤀𐤁𐤓𐤄𐤌.𐤅𐤉𐤒𐤇.𐤁𐤍.𐤁𐤒𐤓.𐤓𐤊.𐤅𐤈
𐤅𐤁.𐤅𐤉𐤕𐤍.𐤀𐤋.𐤄𐤍𐤏𐤓.𐤅𐤉𐤌𐤄𐤓.𐤋𐤏𐤔𐤅𐤕.𐤀𐤕𐤅|

ח 𐤅𐤉𐤒𐤇.𐤇𐤌𐤀𐤄.𐤅𐤇𐤋𐤁.𐤅𐤁𐤍.𐤄𐤁𐤒𐤓.𐤀𐤔𐤓.𐤏𐤔𐤄.𐤅𐤉
𐤕𐤍.𐤋𐤐𐤍𐤉𐤄𐤌.𐤅𐤄𐤅𐤀.𐤏𐤌𐤃.𐤏𐤋𐤉𐤄𐤌.𐤕𐤇𐤕.𐤄𐤏𐤑.𐤅𐤉
𐤀𐤊𐤋𐤅|

ט 𐤅𐤉𐤀𐤌𐤓𐤅.𐤀𐤋𐤉𐤅.𐤀𐤉𐤄.𐤔𐤓𐤄.𐤀𐤔𐤕𐤊.𐤅𐤉𐤀𐤌𐤓.𐤄𐤍𐤄
.𐤁𐤀𐤄𐤋|

י 𐤅𐤉𐤀𐤌𐤓.𐤔𐤅𐤁.𐤀𐤔𐤅𐤁.𐤀𐤋𐤉𐤊.𐤊𐤏𐤕.𐤇𐤉𐤄.𐤅𐤄𐤍𐤄.
𐤁𐤍.𐤋𐤔𐤓𐤄.𐤀𐤔𐤕𐤊.𐤅𐤔𐤓𐤄.𐤔𐤌𐤏𐤕.𐤐𐤕𐤇.𐤄𐤀𐤄𐤋.𐤅𐤄𐤅𐤀
.𐤀𐤇𐤓𐤉𐤅|

יא 𐤅𐤀𐤁𐤓𐤄𐤌.𐤅𐤔𐤓𐤄.𐤆𐤒𐤍𐤉𐤌.𐤁𐤀𐤉𐤌.𐤁𐤉𐤌𐤉𐤌.𐤇𐤃
𐤋.𐤋𐤄𐤉𐤅𐤕.𐤋𐤔𐤓𐤄.𐤀𐤓𐤇.𐤊𐤍𐤔𐤉𐤌|

יב 𐤅𐤕𐤑𐤇𐤒.𐤔𐤓𐤄.𐤁𐤒𐤓𐤁𐤄.𐤋𐤀𐤌𐤓.𐤀𐤇𐤓𐤉.𐤁𐤋𐤕𐤉.
𐤄𐤉𐤕𐤄.𐤋𐤉.𐤏𐤃𐤍𐤄.𐤅𐤀𐤃𐤍𐤉.𐤆𐤒𐤍|

יג 𐤅𐤉𐤀𐤌𐤓.𐤉𐤄𐤅𐤄.𐤀𐤋.𐤀𐤁𐤓𐤄𐤌.𐤋𐤌𐤄.𐤆𐤄.𐤑𐤇𐤒𐤄.
𐤔𐤓𐤄.𐤋𐤀𐤌𐤓.𐤄𐤀𐤐.𐤀𐤌𐤍𐤌.𐤀𐤋𐤃.𐤅𐤀𐤍𐤉.𐤆𐤒𐤍𐤕𐤉|

יד 𐤄𐤉𐤐𐤋𐤀.𐤌𐤉𐤄𐤅𐤄.𐤃𐤁𐤓.𐤋𐤌𐤅𐤏𐤃.𐤀𐤔𐤅𐤁.𐤀𐤋𐤉𐤊.
𐤊𐤏𐤕.𐤇𐤉𐤄.𐤅𐤋𐤔𐤓𐤄.𐤁𐤍|

טו 𐤅𐤕𐤊𐤇𐤔.𐤔𐤓𐤄.𐤋𐤀𐤌𐤓.𐤋𐤀.𐤑𐤇𐤒𐤕𐤉.𐤊𐤉.𐤉𐤓𐤀𐤄.
𐤅𐤉𐤀𐤌𐤓.𐤋𐤀.𐤊𐤉.𐤑𐤇𐤒𐤕|

טז 𐤅𐤉𐤒𐤌𐤅.𐤌𐤔𐤌.𐤄𐤀𐤍𐤔𐤉𐤌.𐤅𐤉𐤔𐤒𐤐𐤅.𐤏𐤋.𐤐𐤍𐤉.𐤎𐤃
𐤌.𐤅𐤀𐤁𐤓𐤄𐤌.𐤄𐤋𐤊.𐤏𐤌𐤌.𐤋𐤔𐤋𐤇𐤌|

יז 𐤅𐤉𐤄𐤅𐤄.𐤀𐤌𐤓.𐤄𐤌𐤊𐤎𐤄.𐤀𐤍𐤉.𐤌𐤀𐤁𐤓𐤄𐤌.𐤀𐤔𐤓.𐤀
𐤍𐤉.𐤏𐤔𐤄|

יח 𐤅𐤀𐤁𐤓𐤄𐤌.𐤄𐤉𐤅.𐤉𐤄𐤉𐤄.𐤋𐤂𐤅𐤉.𐤂𐤃𐤅𐤋.𐤅𐤏𐤑𐤅𐤌.𐤅𐤍
𐤁𐤓𐤊𐤅.𐤁𐤅.𐤊𐤋.𐤂𐤅𐤉𐤉.𐤄𐤀𐤓𐤑|

..יט.. כי.ידעתיו.למען.אשר.יצוה.את.בניו.ו
את.ביתו.אחריו.ושמרו.דרך.יהוה.לעשות.צ
דקה.ומשפט.למען.הביא.יהוה.על.אברהם.א
ת.אשר.דבר.עליו|
..כ.. ויאמר.יהוה.זעקת.סדם.ועמרה.כי.רב
ה.וחטאתם.כי.כבדה.מאד|
..כא.. ארדה.נא.ואראה.הכצעקתה.הבאה.אלי.
עשו.כלה.ואם.לא.אדעה|
..כב.. ויפנו.משם.האנשים.וילכו.סדמה.ואברה
ם.עודנו.עמד.לפני.יהוה|
..כג.. ויגש.אברהם.ויאמר.האף.תספה.צדיק.
עם.רשע|
..כד.. אולי.יש.חמשים.צדיקם.בתוך.העיר.ה
אף.תספה.ולא.תשא.למקום.למען.חמשים.הצ
דיקם.אשר.בקרבה|
..כה.. חללה.לך.מעשת.כדבר.הזה.להמית.צד
יק.עם.רשע.והיה.כצדיק.כרשע.חללה.לך.ה
שפט.כל.הארץ.לא.יעשה.משפט|
..כו.. ויאמר.יהוה.אם.אמצא.בסדם.חמשים.
צדיקם.בתוך.העיר.ונשאתי.לכל.המקום.בע
בורם|
..כז.. ויען.אברהם.ויאמר.הנה.נא.הואלתי.לד
בר.אל.אדני.ואנכי.עפר.ואפר|
..כח.. אולי.יחסרון.חמשים.הצדיקם.חמשה.
התשחית.בחמשה.את.כל.העיר.ויאמר.לא.א
שחית.אם.אמצא.שם.ארבעים.וחמשה|
..כט.. ויסף.עוד.לדבר.אליו.ויאמר.אולי.ימצ
און.שם.ארבעים.ויאמר.לא.אעשה.בעבור.הא
רבעים|

𐤋 𐤅𐤉𐤀𐤌𐤓.𐤀𐤋.𐤍𐤀.𐤉𐤇𐤓.𐤋𐤀𐤃𐤍𐤉.𐤅𐤀𐤃𐤁𐤓𐤄.𐤀𐤅𐤋𐤉
𐤉𐤌𐤑𐤀𐤅𐤍.𐤔𐤌.𐤔𐤋𐤔𐤉𐤌.𐤅𐤉𐤀𐤌𐤓.𐤋𐤀.𐤀𐤏𐤔𐤄.𐤀𐤌.𐤀𐤌
𐤑𐤀.𐤔𐤌.𐤔𐤋𐤔𐤉𐤌|

𐤋𐤀 𐤅𐤉𐤀𐤌𐤓.𐤄𐤍𐤄.𐤍𐤀.𐤄𐤅𐤀𐤋𐤕𐤉.𐤋𐤃𐤁𐤓.𐤀𐤋.𐤀𐤃𐤍𐤉.
𐤀𐤅𐤋𐤉.𐤉𐤌𐤑𐤀𐤅𐤍.𐤔𐤌.𐤏𐤔𐤓𐤉𐤌.𐤅𐤉𐤀𐤌𐤓.𐤋𐤀.𐤀𐤔𐤇𐤉𐤕.
𐤁𐤏𐤁𐤅𐤓.𐤄𐤏𐤔𐤓𐤉𐤌|

𐤋𐤁 𐤅𐤉𐤀𐤌𐤓.𐤀𐤋.𐤍𐤀.𐤉𐤇𐤓.𐤋𐤀𐤃𐤍𐤉.𐤅𐤀𐤃𐤁𐤓𐤄.𐤀𐤊.𐤄
𐤐𐤏𐤌.𐤀𐤅𐤋𐤉.𐤉𐤌𐤑𐤀𐤅𐤍.𐤔𐤌.𐤏𐤔𐤓𐤄.𐤅𐤉𐤀𐤌𐤓.𐤋𐤀.𐤀𐤔𐤇
𐤉𐤕.𐤁𐤏𐤁𐤅𐤓.𐤄𐤏𐤔𐤓𐤄|

𐤋𐤂 𐤅𐤉𐤋𐤊.𐤉𐤄𐤅𐤄.𐤊𐤀𐤔𐤓.𐤊𐤋𐤄.𐤋𐤃𐤁𐤓.𐤀𐤋.𐤀𐤁𐤓𐤄𐤌.
𐤅𐤀𐤁𐤓𐤄𐤌.𐤔𐤁.𐤋𐤌𐤒𐤌𐤅||

𐤁𐤓𐤀𐤔𐤉𐤕.𐤇𐤋𐤒 𐤉𐤈

𐤀 𐤅𐤉𐤁𐤀𐤅.𐤔𐤍𐤉.𐤄𐤌𐤋𐤀𐤊𐤉𐤌.𐤎𐤃𐤌𐤄.𐤁𐤏𐤓𐤁.𐤅𐤋𐤅𐤈.𐤉
𐤔𐤁.𐤁𐤔𐤏𐤓.𐤎𐤃𐤌.𐤅𐤉𐤓𐤀.𐤋𐤅𐤈.𐤅𐤉𐤒𐤌.𐤋𐤒𐤓𐤀𐤕𐤌.𐤅𐤉𐤔
𐤕𐤇𐤅.𐤀𐤐𐤉𐤌.𐤀𐤓𐤑𐤄|

𐤁 𐤅𐤉𐤀𐤌𐤓.𐤄𐤍𐤄.𐤍𐤀.𐤀𐤃𐤍𐤉.𐤎𐤅𐤓𐤅.𐤍𐤀.𐤀𐤋.𐤁𐤉𐤕.𐤏𐤁
𐤃𐤊𐤌.𐤅𐤋𐤉𐤍𐤅.𐤅𐤓𐤇𐤑𐤅.𐤓𐤂𐤋𐤉𐤊𐤌.𐤅𐤄𐤔𐤊𐤌𐤕𐤌.𐤅𐤄𐤋𐤊𐤕
𐤌.𐤋𐤃𐤓𐤊𐤊𐤌.𐤅𐤉𐤀𐤌𐤓𐤅.𐤋𐤀.𐤊𐤉.𐤁𐤓𐤇𐤅𐤁.𐤍𐤋𐤉𐤍|

𐤂 𐤅𐤉𐤐𐤑𐤓.𐤁𐤌.𐤌𐤀𐤃.𐤅𐤉𐤎𐤓𐤅.𐤀𐤋𐤉𐤅.𐤅𐤉𐤁𐤀𐤅.𐤀𐤋.𐤁𐤉𐤕
𐤅.𐤅𐤉𐤏𐤔.𐤋𐤄𐤌.𐤌𐤔𐤕𐤄.𐤅𐤌𐤑𐤅𐤕.𐤀𐤐𐤄.𐤅𐤉𐤀𐤊𐤋𐤅|

𐤃 𐤈𐤓𐤌.𐤉𐤔𐤊𐤁𐤅.𐤅𐤀𐤍𐤔𐤉.𐤄𐤏𐤉𐤓.𐤀𐤍𐤔𐤉.𐤎𐤃𐤌.𐤍𐤎𐤁
𐤅.𐤏𐤋.𐤄𐤁𐤉𐤕.𐤌𐤍𐤏𐤓.𐤅𐤏𐤃.𐤆𐤒𐤍.𐤊𐤋.𐤄𐤏𐤌.𐤌𐤒𐤑𐤄|

𐤄 𐤅𐤉𐤒𐤓𐤀𐤅.𐤀𐤋.𐤋𐤅𐤈.𐤅𐤉𐤀𐤌𐤓𐤅.𐤋𐤅.𐤀𐤉𐤄.𐤄𐤀𐤍𐤔𐤉𐤌.𐤀
𐤔𐤓.𐤁𐤀𐤅.𐤀𐤋𐤉𐤊.𐤄𐤋𐤉𐤋𐤄.𐤄𐤅𐤑𐤉𐤀𐤌.𐤀𐤋𐤉𐤍𐤅.𐤅𐤍𐤃𐤏𐤄.
𐤀𐤕𐤌|

𐤅 𐤅𐤉𐤑𐤀.𐤀𐤋𐤄𐤌.𐤋𐤅𐤈.𐤄𐤐𐤕𐤇𐤄.𐤅𐤄𐤃𐤋𐤕.𐤎𐤂𐤓.𐤀𐤇
𐤓𐤉𐤅|

𐤆 𐤅𐤉𐤀𐤌𐤓.𐤀𐤋.𐤍𐤀.𐤀𐤇𐤉.𐤕𐤓𐤏𐤅|

ח 𐤄𐤍𐤄.𐤍𐤀.𐤋𐤉.𐤔𐤕𐤉.𐤁𐤍𐤅𐤕.𐤀𐤔𐤓.𐤋𐤀.𐤉𐤃𐤏𐤅.𐤀𐤉𐤔.
𐤀𐤅𐤑𐤉𐤀𐤄.𐤍𐤀.𐤀𐤕𐤄𐤍.𐤀𐤋𐤉𐤊𐤌.𐤅𐤏𐤔𐤅.𐤋𐤄𐤍.𐤊𐤈𐤅𐤁.𐤁𐤏
𐤉𐤍𐤉𐤊𐤌.𐤓𐤒.𐤋𐤀𐤍𐤔𐤉𐤌.𐤄𐤀𐤋.𐤀𐤋.𐤕𐤏𐤔𐤅.𐤃𐤁𐤓.𐤊𐤉.𐤏𐤋
.𐤊𐤍.𐤁𐤀𐤅.𐤁𐤑𐤋.𐤒𐤓𐤕𐤉|

ט 𐤅𐤉𐤀𐤌𐤓𐤅.𐤂𐤔.𐤄𐤋𐤀𐤄.𐤅𐤉𐤀𐤌𐤓𐤅.𐤄𐤀𐤇𐤃.𐤁𐤀.𐤋𐤂𐤅
𐤓.𐤅𐤉𐤔𐤐𐤈.𐤔𐤐𐤅𐤈.𐤏𐤕𐤄.𐤍𐤓𐤏.𐤋𐤊.𐤌𐤄𐤌.𐤅𐤉𐤐𐤑𐤓𐤅.𐤁𐤀𐤉
𐤔.𐤁𐤋𐤅𐤈.𐤌𐤀𐤃.𐤅𐤉𐤂𐤔𐤅.𐤋𐤔𐤁𐤓.𐤄𐤃𐤋𐤕|

י 𐤅𐤉𐤔𐤋𐤇𐤅.𐤄𐤀𐤍𐤔𐤉𐤌.𐤀𐤕.𐤉𐤃𐤌.𐤅𐤉𐤁𐤉𐤀𐤅.𐤀𐤕.𐤋𐤅
𐤈.𐤀𐤋𐤉𐤄𐤌.𐤄𐤁𐤉𐤕𐤄.𐤅𐤀𐤕.𐤄𐤃𐤋𐤕.𐤎𐤂𐤓𐤅|

יא 𐤅𐤀𐤕.𐤄𐤀𐤍𐤔𐤉𐤌.𐤀𐤔𐤓.𐤐𐤕𐤇.𐤄𐤁𐤉𐤕.𐤄𐤊𐤅.𐤁𐤎𐤍𐤅𐤓
𐤉𐤌.𐤌𐤒𐤈𐤍.𐤅𐤏𐤃.𐤂𐤃𐤅𐤋.𐤅𐤉𐤋𐤀𐤅.𐤋𐤌𐤑𐤀.𐤄𐤐𐤕𐤇|

יב 𐤅𐤉𐤀𐤌𐤓𐤅.𐤄𐤀𐤍𐤔𐤉𐤌.𐤀𐤋.𐤋𐤅𐤈.𐤏𐤃.𐤌𐤉.𐤋𐤊.𐤐𐤄.𐤇
𐤕𐤍.𐤅𐤁𐤍𐤉𐤊.𐤅𐤁𐤍𐤕𐤉𐤊.𐤅𐤊𐤋.𐤀𐤔𐤓.𐤋𐤊.𐤁𐤏𐤉𐤓.𐤄𐤅𐤑𐤀.𐤌𐤍.
𐤄𐤌𐤒𐤅𐤌|

יג 𐤊𐤉.𐤌𐤔𐤇𐤕𐤉𐤌.𐤀𐤍𐤇𐤍𐤅.𐤀𐤕.𐤄𐤌𐤒𐤅𐤌.𐤄𐤆𐤄.𐤊𐤉
.𐤂𐤃𐤋𐤄.𐤑𐤏𐤒𐤕𐤌.𐤀𐤕.𐤐𐤍𐤉.𐤉𐤄𐤅𐤄.𐤅𐤉𐤔𐤋𐤇𐤍𐤅.𐤉𐤄𐤅𐤄
.𐤋𐤔𐤇𐤕𐤄|

יד 𐤅𐤉𐤑𐤀.𐤋𐤅𐤈.𐤅𐤉𐤃𐤁𐤓.𐤀𐤋.𐤇𐤕𐤍𐤉𐤅.𐤋𐤒𐤇𐤉.𐤁𐤍𐤕𐤉
𐤅.𐤅𐤉𐤀𐤌𐤓.𐤒𐤅𐤌𐤅.𐤑𐤀𐤅.𐤌𐤍.𐤄𐤌𐤒𐤅𐤌.𐤄𐤆𐤄.𐤊𐤉.𐤌𐤔𐤇
𐤉𐤕.𐤉𐤄𐤅𐤄.𐤀𐤕.𐤄𐤏𐤉𐤓.𐤅𐤉𐤄𐤉.𐤊𐤌𐤑𐤇𐤒.𐤁𐤏𐤉𐤍𐤉.𐤇𐤕𐤍
𐤉𐤅|

טו 𐤅𐤊𐤌𐤅.𐤄𐤔𐤇𐤓.𐤏𐤋𐤄.𐤅𐤉𐤀𐤉𐤑𐤅.𐤄𐤌𐤋𐤀𐤊𐤉𐤌.𐤁𐤋𐤅
𐤈.𐤋𐤀𐤌𐤓.𐤒𐤅𐤌.𐤒𐤇.𐤀𐤕.𐤀𐤔𐤕𐤊.𐤅𐤀𐤕.𐤔𐤕𐤉.𐤁𐤍𐤕𐤉𐤊.
𐤄𐤍𐤌𐤑𐤀𐤕.𐤐𐤍.𐤕𐤎𐤐𐤄.𐤁𐤏𐤅𐤍.𐤄𐤏𐤉𐤓|

טז 𐤅𐤉𐤕𐤌𐤄𐤌𐤄.𐤅𐤉𐤇𐤆𐤒𐤅.𐤄𐤀𐤍𐤔𐤉𐤌.𐤁𐤉𐤃𐤅.𐤅𐤁𐤉𐤃.
𐤀𐤔𐤕𐤅.𐤅𐤁𐤉𐤃.𐤔𐤕𐤉.𐤁𐤍𐤕𐤉𐤅.𐤁𐤇𐤌𐤋𐤕.𐤉𐤄𐤅𐤄.𐤏𐤋𐤉𐤅.𐤅
𐤉𐤑𐤀𐤄𐤅.𐤅𐤉𐤍𐤇𐤄𐤅.𐤌𐤇𐤅𐤑.𐤋𐤏𐤉𐤓|

יז 𐤅𐤉𐤄𐤉.𐤊𐤄𐤅𐤑𐤉𐤀𐤌.𐤀𐤕𐤌.𐤄𐤇𐤅𐤑𐤄.𐤅𐤉𐤀𐤌𐤓.𐤄𐤌
𐤋𐤈.𐤏𐤋.𐤍𐤐𐤔𐤊.𐤀𐤋.𐤕𐤁𐤉𐤈.𐤀𐤇𐤓𐤉𐤊.𐤅𐤀𐤋.𐤕𐤏𐤌𐤃.𐤁𐤊
𐤋.𐤄𐤊𐤊𐤓.𐤄𐤄𐤓𐤄.𐤄𐤌𐤋𐤈.𐤐𐤍.𐤕𐤎𐤐𐤄|

יח 𐤅𐤉𐤀𐤌𐤓.𐤋𐤅𐤈.𐤀𐤋𐤄𐤌.𐤀𐤋.𐤍𐤀.𐤀𐤃𐤍𐤉|

יט 𐤄𐤍𐤄.𐤍𐤀.𐤌𐤑𐤀.𐤏𐤁𐤃𐤊.𐤇𐤍.𐤁𐤏𐤉𐤍𐤉𐤊.𐤅𐤕𐤂𐤃𐤋
.𐤇𐤎𐤃𐤊.𐤀𐤔𐤓.𐤏𐤔𐤉𐤕.𐤏𐤌𐤃𐤉.𐤋𐤄𐤇𐤉𐤅𐤕.𐤀𐤕.𐤍𐤐𐤔𐤉
.𐤅𐤀𐤍𐤊𐤉.𐤋𐤀.𐤀𐤅𐤊𐤋.𐤋𐤄𐤌𐤋𐤈.𐤄𐤄𐤓𐤄.𐤐𐤍.𐤕𐤃𐤁𐤒𐤍𐤉.𐤄
𐤓𐤏𐤄.𐤅𐤌𐤕𐤉|
כ 𐤄𐤍𐤄.𐤍𐤀.𐤄𐤏𐤉𐤓.𐤄𐤆𐤀𐤕.𐤒𐤓𐤁𐤄.𐤋𐤍𐤅𐤎.𐤔𐤌𐤄.𐤅
𐤄𐤉𐤀.𐤌𐤑𐤏𐤓.𐤀𐤌𐤋𐤈𐤄.𐤍𐤀.𐤔𐤌𐤄.𐤄𐤋𐤀.𐤌𐤑𐤏𐤓.𐤄𐤅𐤀.𐤅
𐤕𐤇𐤉.𐤍𐤐𐤔𐤉|
כא 𐤅𐤉𐤀𐤌𐤓.𐤀𐤋𐤉𐤅.𐤄𐤍𐤄.𐤍𐤔𐤀𐤕𐤉.𐤐𐤍𐤉𐤊.𐤂𐤌.𐤋𐤃𐤁𐤓.
𐤄𐤆𐤄.𐤋𐤁𐤋𐤕𐤉.𐤄𐤐𐤊𐤉.𐤀𐤕.𐤄𐤏𐤉𐤓.𐤀𐤔𐤓.𐤃𐤁𐤓𐤕|
כב 𐤌𐤄𐤓.𐤄𐤌𐤋𐤈.𐤔𐤌𐤄.𐤊𐤉.𐤋𐤀.𐤀𐤅𐤊𐤋.𐤋𐤏𐤔𐤅𐤕.𐤃𐤁
𐤓.𐤏𐤃.𐤁𐤀𐤊.𐤔𐤌𐤄.𐤏𐤋.𐤊𐤍.𐤒𐤓𐤀.𐤔𐤌.𐤄𐤏𐤉𐤓.𐤑𐤅𐤏𐤓|
כג 𐤄𐤔𐤌𐤔.𐤉𐤑𐤀.𐤏𐤋.𐤄𐤀𐤓𐤑.𐤅𐤋𐤅𐤈.𐤁𐤀.𐤑𐤏𐤓𐤄|
כד 𐤅𐤉𐤄𐤅𐤄.𐤄𐤌𐤈𐤉𐤓.𐤏𐤋.𐤎𐤃𐤌.𐤅𐤏𐤋.𐤏𐤌𐤓𐤄.𐤂𐤐𐤓𐤉
𐤕.𐤅𐤀𐤔.𐤌𐤀𐤕.𐤉𐤄𐤅𐤄.𐤌𐤍.𐤄𐤔𐤌𐤉𐤌|
כה 𐤅𐤉𐤄𐤐𐤊.𐤀𐤕.𐤄𐤏𐤓𐤉𐤌.𐤄𐤀𐤋.𐤅𐤀𐤕.𐤊𐤋.𐤄𐤊𐤊𐤓.𐤅𐤀
𐤕.𐤊𐤋.𐤉𐤔𐤁𐤉.𐤄𐤏𐤓𐤉𐤌.𐤅𐤑𐤌𐤇.𐤄𐤀𐤃𐤌𐤄|
כו 𐤅𐤕𐤁𐤈.𐤀𐤔𐤕𐤅.𐤌𐤀𐤇𐤓𐤉𐤅.𐤅𐤕𐤄𐤉.𐤍𐤑𐤉𐤁.𐤌𐤋𐤇|
כז 𐤅𐤉𐤔𐤊𐤌.𐤀𐤁𐤓𐤄𐤌.𐤁𐤁𐤒𐤓.𐤀𐤋.𐤄𐤌𐤒𐤅𐤌.𐤀𐤔𐤓.𐤏𐤌
𐤃.𐤔𐤌.𐤀𐤕.𐤐𐤍𐤉.𐤉𐤄𐤅𐤄|
כח 𐤅𐤉𐤔𐤒𐤐.𐤏𐤋.𐤐𐤍𐤉.𐤎𐤃𐤌.𐤅𐤏𐤌𐤓𐤄.𐤅𐤏𐤋.𐤊𐤋.𐤐𐤍𐤉.𐤀
𐤓𐤑.𐤄𐤊𐤊𐤓.𐤅𐤉𐤓𐤀.𐤅𐤄𐤍𐤄.𐤏𐤋𐤄.𐤒𐤉𐤈𐤓.𐤄𐤀𐤓𐤑.𐤊𐤒𐤉𐤈
𐤓.𐤄𐤊𐤁𐤔𐤍|
כט 𐤅𐤉𐤄𐤉.𐤁𐤔𐤇𐤕.𐤀𐤋𐤄𐤉𐤌.𐤀𐤕.𐤏𐤓𐤉.𐤄𐤊𐤊𐤓.𐤅𐤉𐤆
𐤊𐤓.𐤀𐤋𐤄𐤉𐤌.𐤀𐤕.𐤀𐤁𐤓𐤄𐤌.𐤅𐤉𐤔𐤋𐤇.𐤀𐤕.𐤋𐤅𐤈.𐤌𐤕𐤅𐤊.𐤄
𐤄𐤐𐤊𐤄.𐤁𐤄𐤐𐤊.𐤀𐤕.𐤄𐤏𐤓𐤉𐤌.𐤀𐤔𐤓.𐤉𐤔𐤁.𐤁𐤄𐤍.𐤋𐤅𐤈|
ל 𐤅𐤉𐤏𐤋.𐤋𐤅𐤈.𐤌𐤑𐤅𐤏𐤓.𐤅𐤉𐤔𐤁.𐤁𐤄𐤓.𐤅𐤔𐤕𐤉.𐤁𐤍𐤕𐤉𐤅.
𐤏𐤌𐤅.𐤊𐤉.𐤉𐤓𐤀.𐤋𐤔𐤁𐤕.𐤁𐤑𐤅𐤏𐤓.𐤅𐤉𐤔𐤁.𐤁𐤌𐤏𐤓𐤄.𐤄𐤅𐤀.𐤅
𐤔𐤕𐤉.𐤁𐤍𐤕𐤉𐤅|
לא 𐤅𐤕𐤀𐤌𐤓.𐤄𐤁𐤊𐤉𐤓𐤄.𐤀𐤋.𐤄𐤑𐤏𐤉𐤓𐤄.𐤀𐤁𐤉𐤍𐤅.𐤆𐤒
𐤍.𐤅𐤀𐤉𐤔.𐤀𐤉𐤍.𐤁𐤀𐤓𐤑.𐤋𐤁𐤅𐤀.𐤏𐤋𐤉𐤍𐤅.𐤊𐤃𐤓𐤊.𐤊𐤋.𐤄𐤀𐤓
𐤑|

..𐤋𐤁.. 𐤋𐤊𐤄.𐤍𐤔𐤒𐤄.𐤀𐤕.𐤀𐤁𐤉𐤍𐤅.𐤉𐤉𐤍.𐤅𐤍𐤔𐤊𐤁𐤄.𐤏𐤌𐤅.𐤅
𐤍𐤇𐤉𐤄.𐤌𐤀𐤁𐤉𐤍𐤅.𐤆𐤓𐤏|
..𐤋𐤂.. 𐤅𐤕𐤔𐤒𐤉𐤍.𐤀𐤕.𐤀𐤁𐤉𐤄𐤍.𐤉𐤉𐤍.𐤁𐤋𐤉𐤋𐤄.𐤄𐤅𐤀.𐤅𐤕𐤁
𐤀.𐤄𐤁𐤊𐤉𐤓𐤄.𐤅𐤕𐤔𐤊𐤁.𐤀𐤕.𐤀𐤁𐤉𐤄.𐤅𐤋𐤀.𐤉𐤃𐤏.𐤁𐤔𐤊𐤁
𐤄.𐤅𐤁𐤒𐤅𐤌𐤄|
..𐤋𐤃.. 𐤅𐤉𐤄𐤉.𐤌𐤌𐤇𐤓𐤕.𐤅𐤕𐤀𐤌𐤓.𐤄𐤁𐤊𐤉𐤓𐤄.𐤀𐤋.𐤄𐤑𐤏𐤉
𐤓𐤄.𐤄𐤍.𐤔𐤊𐤁𐤕𐤉.𐤀𐤌𐤔.𐤀𐤕.𐤀𐤁𐤉.𐤍𐤔𐤒𐤍𐤅.𐤉𐤉𐤍.𐤂𐤌.𐤄
𐤋𐤉𐤋𐤄.𐤅𐤁𐤀𐤉.𐤔𐤊𐤁𐤉.𐤏𐤌𐤅.𐤅𐤍𐤇𐤉𐤄.𐤌𐤀𐤁𐤉𐤍𐤅.𐤆𐤓𐤏|
..𐤋𐤄.. 𐤅𐤕𐤔𐤒𐤉𐤍.𐤂𐤌.𐤁𐤋𐤉𐤋𐤄.𐤄𐤄𐤅𐤀.𐤀𐤕.𐤀𐤁𐤉𐤄𐤍.𐤉𐤉
𐤍.𐤅𐤕𐤒𐤌.𐤄𐤑𐤏𐤉𐤓𐤄.𐤅𐤕𐤔𐤊𐤁.𐤏𐤌𐤅.𐤅𐤋𐤀.𐤉𐤃𐤏.𐤁𐤔𐤊𐤁
𐤄.𐤅𐤁𐤒𐤌𐤄|
..𐤋𐤅.. 𐤅𐤕𐤄𐤓𐤉𐤍.𐤔𐤕𐤉.𐤁𐤍𐤅𐤕.𐤋𐤅𐤈.𐤌𐤀𐤁𐤉𐤄𐤍|
..𐤋𐤆.. 𐤅𐤕𐤋𐤃.𐤄𐤁𐤊𐤉𐤓𐤄.𐤁𐤍.𐤅𐤕𐤒𐤓𐤀.𐤔𐤌𐤅.𐤌𐤅𐤀𐤁.𐤄𐤅𐤀
.𐤀𐤁𐤉.𐤌𐤅𐤀𐤁.𐤏𐤃.𐤄𐤉𐤅𐤌|
..𐤋𐤇.. 𐤅𐤄𐤑𐤏𐤉𐤓𐤄.𐤂𐤌.𐤄𐤅𐤀.𐤉𐤋𐤃𐤄.𐤁𐤍.𐤅𐤕𐤒𐤓𐤀.𐤔𐤌𐤅.
𐤁𐤍.𐤏𐤌𐤉.𐤄𐤅𐤀.𐤀𐤁𐤉.𐤁𐤍𐤉.𐤏𐤌𐤅𐤍.𐤏𐤃.𐤄𐤉𐤅𐤌||

𐤁𐤓𐤀𐤔𐤉𐤕.𐤇𐤋𐤒 ..𐤁[illegible]..

..𐤀.. 𐤅𐤉𐤎𐤏.𐤌𐤔𐤌.𐤀𐤁𐤓𐤄𐤌.𐤀𐤓𐤑𐤄.𐤄𐤍𐤂𐤁.𐤅𐤉𐤔𐤁.𐤁𐤉𐤍.
𐤒𐤃𐤔.𐤅𐤁𐤉𐤍.𐤔𐤅𐤓.𐤅𐤉𐤂𐤓.𐤁𐤂𐤓𐤓|
..𐤁.. 𐤅𐤉𐤀𐤌𐤓.𐤀𐤁𐤓𐤄𐤌.𐤀𐤋.𐤔𐤓𐤄.𐤀𐤔𐤕𐤅.𐤀𐤇𐤕𐤉.𐤄𐤅𐤀.𐤅
𐤉𐤔𐤋𐤇.𐤀𐤁𐤉𐤌𐤋𐤊.𐤌𐤋𐤊.𐤂𐤓𐤓.𐤅𐤉𐤒𐤇.𐤀𐤕.𐤔𐤓𐤄|
..𐤂.. 𐤅𐤉𐤁𐤀.𐤀𐤋𐤄𐤉𐤌.𐤀𐤋.𐤀𐤁𐤉𐤌𐤋𐤊.𐤁𐤇𐤋𐤅𐤌.𐤄𐤋𐤉𐤋𐤄.𐤅
𐤉𐤀𐤌𐤓.𐤋𐤅.𐤄𐤍𐤊.𐤌𐤕.𐤏𐤋.𐤄𐤀𐤔𐤄.𐤀𐤔𐤓.𐤋𐤒𐤇𐤕.𐤅𐤄𐤅𐤀.
𐤁𐤏𐤋𐤕.𐤁𐤏𐤋|
..𐤃.. 𐤅𐤀𐤁𐤉𐤌𐤋𐤊.𐤋𐤀.𐤒𐤓𐤁.𐤀𐤋𐤉𐤄.𐤅𐤉𐤀𐤌𐤓.𐤀𐤃𐤍𐤉.𐤄𐤂
𐤅𐤉.𐤂𐤌.𐤑𐤃𐤉𐤒.𐤕𐤄𐤓𐤂|
..𐤄.. 𐤄𐤋𐤀.𐤄𐤅𐤀.𐤀𐤌𐤓.𐤋𐤉.𐤀𐤇𐤕𐤉.𐤄𐤅𐤀.𐤅𐤄𐤉𐤀.𐤂𐤌.𐤄𐤅
𐤀.𐤀𐤌𐤓𐤄.𐤀𐤇𐤉.𐤄𐤅𐤀.𐤁𐤕𐤌.𐤋𐤁𐤁𐤉.𐤅𐤁𐤍𐤒𐤉𐤍.𐤊𐤐𐤉.𐤏𐤔
𐤉𐤕𐤉.𐤆𐤀𐤕|

6 𐤅𐤉𐤀𐤌𐤓.𐤀𐤋𐤉𐤅.𐤄𐤀𐤋𐤄𐤉𐤌.𐤁𐤇𐤋𐤌.𐤂𐤌.𐤀𐤍𐤊𐤉.𐤉𐤃
𐤏𐤕𐤉.𐤊𐤉.𐤁𐤕𐤌.𐤋𐤁𐤁𐤊.𐤏𐤔𐤉𐤕.𐤆𐤀𐤕.𐤅𐤀𐤇𐤔𐤊.𐤂𐤌.
𐤀𐤍𐤊𐤉.𐤀𐤅𐤕𐤊.𐤌𐤇𐤈𐤅.𐤋𐤉.𐤏𐤋.𐤊𐤍.𐤋𐤀.𐤍𐤕𐤕𐤉𐤊.𐤋𐤍𐤂𐤏.
𐤀𐤋𐤉𐤄|

7 𐤅𐤏𐤕𐤄.𐤄𐤔𐤁.𐤀𐤔𐤕.𐤄𐤀𐤉𐤔.𐤊𐤉.𐤍𐤁𐤉𐤀.𐤄𐤅𐤀.𐤅𐤉𐤕
𐤐𐤋𐤋.𐤁𐤏𐤃𐤊.𐤅𐤇𐤉𐤄.𐤅𐤀𐤌.𐤀𐤉𐤍𐤊.𐤌𐤔𐤉𐤁.𐤃𐤏.𐤊𐤉.𐤌𐤅
𐤕.𐤕𐤌𐤅𐤕.𐤀𐤕𐤄.𐤅𐤊𐤋.𐤀𐤔𐤓.𐤋𐤊|

8 𐤅𐤉𐤔𐤊𐤌.𐤀𐤁𐤉𐤌𐤋𐤊.𐤁𐤁𐤒𐤓.𐤅𐤉𐤒𐤓𐤀.𐤋𐤊𐤋.𐤏𐤁𐤃𐤉𐤅.
𐤅𐤉𐤃𐤁𐤓.𐤀𐤕.𐤊𐤋.𐤄𐤃𐤁𐤓𐤉𐤌.𐤄𐤀𐤋𐤄.𐤁𐤀𐤆𐤍𐤉𐤄𐤌.𐤅𐤉𐤉
𐤓𐤀𐤅.𐤄𐤀𐤍𐤔𐤉𐤌.𐤌𐤀𐤃|

9 𐤅𐤉𐤒𐤓𐤀.𐤀𐤁𐤉𐤌𐤋𐤊.𐤋𐤀𐤁𐤓𐤄𐤌.𐤅𐤉𐤀𐤌𐤓.𐤋𐤅.𐤌𐤄.𐤏
𐤔𐤉𐤕.𐤋𐤍𐤅.𐤅𐤌𐤄.𐤇𐤈𐤀𐤕𐤉.𐤋𐤊.𐤊𐤉.𐤄𐤁𐤀𐤕.𐤏𐤋𐤉.𐤅𐤏𐤋.
𐤌𐤌𐤋𐤊𐤕𐤉.𐤇𐤈𐤀𐤄.𐤂𐤃𐤋𐤄.𐤌𐤏𐤔𐤉𐤌.𐤀𐤔𐤓.𐤋𐤀.𐤉𐤏𐤔
𐤅.𐤏𐤔𐤉𐤕.𐤏𐤌𐤃𐤉|

10 𐤅𐤉𐤀𐤌𐤓.𐤀𐤁𐤉𐤌𐤋𐤊.𐤀𐤋.𐤀𐤁𐤓𐤄𐤌.𐤌𐤄.𐤓𐤀𐤉𐤕.𐤊𐤉.
𐤏𐤔𐤉𐤕.𐤀𐤕.𐤄𐤃𐤁𐤓.𐤄𐤆𐤄|

11 𐤅𐤉𐤀𐤌𐤓.𐤀𐤁𐤓𐤄𐤌.𐤊𐤉.𐤀𐤌𐤓𐤕𐤉.𐤓𐤒.𐤀𐤉𐤍.𐤉𐤓𐤀𐤕.
𐤀𐤋𐤄𐤉𐤌.𐤁𐤌𐤒𐤅𐤌.𐤄𐤆𐤄.𐤅𐤄𐤓𐤂𐤅𐤍𐤉.𐤏𐤋.𐤃𐤁𐤓.𐤀𐤔𐤕𐤉|

12 𐤅𐤂𐤌.𐤀𐤌𐤍𐤄.𐤀𐤇𐤕𐤉.𐤁𐤕.𐤀𐤁𐤉.𐤄𐤅𐤀.𐤀𐤊.𐤋𐤀.𐤁𐤕
.𐤀𐤌𐤉.𐤅𐤕𐤄𐤉.𐤋𐤉.𐤋𐤀𐤔𐤄|

13 𐤅𐤉𐤄𐤉.𐤊𐤀𐤔𐤓.𐤄𐤕𐤏𐤅.𐤀𐤕𐤉.𐤀𐤋𐤄𐤉𐤌.𐤌𐤁𐤉𐤕.𐤀𐤁
𐤉.𐤅𐤀𐤌𐤓.𐤋𐤄.𐤆𐤄.𐤇𐤎𐤃𐤊.𐤀𐤔𐤓.𐤕𐤏𐤔𐤉.𐤏𐤌𐤃𐤉.𐤀𐤋.
𐤊𐤋.𐤄𐤌𐤒𐤅𐤌.𐤀𐤔𐤓.𐤍𐤁𐤅𐤀.𐤔𐤌𐤄.𐤀𐤌𐤓𐤉.𐤋𐤉.𐤀𐤇𐤉.𐤄𐤅𐤀|

14 𐤅𐤉𐤒𐤇.𐤀𐤁𐤉𐤌𐤋𐤊.𐤑𐤀𐤍.𐤅𐤁𐤒𐤓.𐤅𐤏𐤁𐤃𐤉𐤌.𐤅𐤔𐤐
𐤇𐤕.𐤅𐤉𐤕𐤍.𐤋𐤀𐤁𐤓𐤄𐤌.𐤅𐤉𐤔𐤁.𐤋𐤅.𐤀𐤕.𐤔𐤓𐤄.𐤀𐤔𐤕𐤅|

15 𐤅𐤉𐤀𐤌𐤓.𐤀𐤁𐤉𐤌𐤋𐤊.𐤄𐤍𐤄.𐤀𐤓𐤑𐤉.𐤋𐤐𐤍𐤉𐤊.𐤁𐤈𐤅𐤁.𐤁
𐤏𐤉𐤍𐤉𐤊.𐤔𐤁|

16 𐤅𐤋𐤔𐤓𐤄.𐤀𐤌𐤓.𐤄𐤍𐤄.𐤍𐤕𐤕𐤉.𐤀𐤋𐤐.𐤊𐤎𐤐.𐤋𐤀𐤇𐤉𐤊.
𐤄𐤍𐤄.𐤄𐤅𐤀.𐤋𐤊.𐤊𐤎𐤅𐤕.𐤏𐤉𐤍𐤉𐤌.𐤋𐤊𐤋.𐤀𐤔𐤓.𐤀𐤕𐤊.𐤅𐤀𐤕.
𐤊𐤋.𐤅𐤍𐤊𐤇𐤕|

..17.. ויתפלל.אברהם.אל.האלהים.וירפא.אלה
ים.את.אבימלך.ואת.אשתו.ואמהתיו.וילדו|
..18.. כי.עצר.עצר.יהוה.בעד.כל.רחם.לבית.
אבימלך.על.דבר.שרה.אשת.אברהם||

בראשית.חלק..21..

..1.. ויהוה.פקד.את.שרה.כאשר.אמר.ויעש.יהו
ה.לשרה.כאשר.דבר|
..2.. ותהר.ותלד.שרה.לאברהם.בן.לזקניו.למו
עד.אשר.דבר.אתו.אלהים|
..3.. ויקרא.אברהם.את.שם.בנו.הנולד.לו.אשר.
ילדה.לו.שרה.יצחק|
..4.. וימל.אברהם.את.יצחק.בנו.בן.שמנת.ימי
ם.כאשר.צוה.אתו.אלהים|
..5.. ואברהם.בן.מאת.שנה.בהולד.לו.את.יצחק
.בנו|
..6.. ותאמר.שרה.צחק.עשה.לי.אלהים.כל.הש
מע.יצחק.לי|
..7.. ותאמר.מי.מלל.לאברהם.היניקה.בנים.ש
רה.כי.ילדתי.בן.לזקניו|
..8.. ויגדל.הילד.ויגמל.ויעש.אברהם.משתה
.גדול.ביום.הגמל.את.יצחק|
..9.. ותרא.שרה.את.בן.הגר.המצרית.אשר.יל
דה.לאברהם.מצחק|
..10.. ותאמר.לאברהם.גרש.האמה.הזאת.ואת.
בנה.כי.לא.יירש.בן.האמה.הזאת.עם.בני.ע
ם.יצחק|
..11.. וירע.הדבר.מאד.בעיני.אברהם.על.אוד
ת.בנו|

יב ויאמר.אלהים.אל.אברהם.אל.ירע.בעיני
ך.על.הנער.ועל.אמתך.כל.אשר.תאמר.אליך.ש
רה.שמע.בקלה.כי.ביצחק.יקרא.לך.זרע|
יג וגם.את.בן.האמה.לגוי.אשימנו.כי.זרע
ך.הוא|
יד וישכם.אברהם.בבקר.ויקח.לחם.וחמת.
מים.ויתן.אל.הגר.שם.על.שכמה.ואת.הילד.ו
ישלחה.ותלך.ותתע.במדבר.באר.שבע|
טו ויכלו.המים.מן.החמת.ותשלך.את.הילד.
תחת.אחד.השיחם|
טז ותלך.ותשב.לה.מנגד.הרחק.כמטחוי.ק
שת.כי.אמרה.אל.אראה.במות.הילד.ותשב.מנ
גד.ותשא.את.קלה.ותבך|
יז וישמע.אלהים.את.קול.הנער.ויקרא.מל
אך.אלהים.אל.הגר.מן.השמים.ויאמר.לה.מה.
לך.הגר.אל.תיראי.כי.שמע.אלהים.אל.קול.ה
נער.באשר.הוא.שם|
יח קומי.שאי.את.הנער.והחזיקי.את.ידך
בו.כי.לגוי.גדול.אשימנו|
יט ויפקח.אלהים.את.עיניה.ותרא.באר.מי
ם.ותלך.ותמלא.את.החמת.מים.ותשק.את.הנע
ר|
כ ויהי.אלהים.את.הנער.ויגדל.וישב.במ
דבר.ויהי.רבה.קשת|
כא וישב.במדבר.פארן.ותקח.לו.אמו.אשה.מ
ארץ.מצרים|
כב ויהי.בעת.ההוא.ויאמר.אבימלך.ופיכל.
שר.צבאו.אל.אברהם.לאמר.אלהים.עמך.בכל.
אשר.אתה.עשה|

..כג..ועתה.השבעה.לי.באלהים.הנה.אם.תשק
ר.לי.ולניני.ולנכדי.כחסד.אשר.עשיתי.עמ
ך.תעשה.עמדי.ועם.הארץ.אשר.גרתה.בה׃
..כד..ויאמר.אברהם.אנכי.אשבע׃
..כה..והוכח.אברהם.את.אבימלך.על.אדות.בא
ר.המים.אשר.גזלו.עבדי.אבימלך׃
..כו..ויאמר.אבימלך.לא.ידעתי.מי.עשה.את.
הדבר.הזה.וגם.אתה.לא.הגדת.לי.וגם.אנ
כי.לא.שמעתי.בלתי.היום׃
..כז..ויקח.אברהם.צאן.ובקר.ויתן.לאבימלך.
ויכרתו.שניהם.ברית׃
..כח..ויצב.אברהם.את.שבע.כבשת.הצאן.לבד
הן׃
..כט..ויאמר.אבימלך.אל.אברהם.מה.הנה.שבע
.כבשת.האלה.אשר.הצבת.לבדנה׃
..ל..ויאמר.כי.את.שבע.כבשת.תקח.מידי.ב
עבור.תהיה.לי.לעדה.כי.חפרתי.את.הבאר.ה
זאת׃
..לא..על.כן.קרא.למקום.ההוא.באר.שבע.כי.ש
ם.נשבעו.שניהם׃
..לב..ויכרתו.ברית.בבאר.שבע.ויקם.אבימלך.
ופיכל.שר.צבאו.וישבו.אל.ארץ.פלשתים׃
..לג..ויטע.אשל.בבאר.שבע.ויקרא.שם.בשם.י
הוה.אל.עולם׃
..לד..ויגר.אברהם.בארץ.פלשתים.ימים.רבי
ם׃׃

..כב..בראשית.חלק

..א..ויהי.אחר.הדברים.האלה.והאלהים.נסה.
את.אברהם.ויאמר.אליו.אברהם.ויאמר.הנני׃

ב 𐤅𐤉𐤀𐤌𐤓.𐤒𐤇.𐤍𐤀.𐤀𐤕.𐤁𐤍𐤊.𐤀𐤕.𐤉𐤇𐤉𐤃𐤊.𐤀𐤔𐤓.𐤀
𐤄𐤁𐤕.𐤀𐤕.𐤉𐤑𐤇𐤒.𐤅𐤋𐤊.𐤋𐤊.𐤀𐤋.𐤀𐤓𐤑.𐤄𐤌𐤓𐤉𐤄.𐤅𐤄𐤏𐤋
𐤄𐤅.𐤔𐤌.𐤋𐤏𐤋𐤄.𐤏𐤋.𐤀𐤇𐤃.𐤄𐤄𐤓𐤉𐤌.𐤀𐤔𐤓.𐤀𐤌𐤓.𐤀𐤋𐤉𐤊
|

ג 𐤅𐤉𐤔𐤊𐤌.𐤀𐤁𐤓𐤄𐤌.𐤁𐤁𐤒𐤓.𐤅𐤉𐤇𐤁𐤔.𐤀𐤕.𐤇𐤌𐤓𐤅.𐤅𐤉
𐤒𐤇.𐤀𐤕.𐤔𐤍𐤉.𐤍𐤏𐤓𐤉𐤅.𐤀𐤕𐤅.𐤅𐤀𐤕.𐤉𐤑𐤇𐤒.𐤁𐤍𐤅.𐤅𐤉𐤁𐤒
𐤏.𐤏𐤑𐤉.𐤏𐤋𐤄.𐤅𐤉𐤒𐤌.𐤅𐤉𐤋𐤊.𐤀𐤋.𐤄𐤌𐤒𐤅𐤌.𐤀𐤔𐤓.𐤀𐤌𐤓.
𐤋𐤅.𐤄𐤀𐤋𐤄𐤉𐤌|

ד 𐤁𐤉𐤅𐤌.𐤄𐤔𐤋𐤉𐤔𐤉.𐤅𐤉𐤔𐤀.𐤀𐤁𐤓𐤄𐤌.𐤀𐤕.𐤏𐤉𐤍𐤉𐤅.𐤅𐤉
𐤓𐤀.𐤀𐤕.𐤄𐤌𐤒𐤅𐤌.𐤌𐤓𐤇𐤒|

ה 𐤅𐤉𐤀𐤌𐤓.𐤀𐤁𐤓𐤄𐤌.𐤀𐤋.𐤍𐤏𐤓𐤉𐤅.𐤔𐤁𐤅.𐤋𐤊𐤌.𐤐𐤄.𐤏𐤌.𐤄
𐤇𐤌𐤅𐤓.𐤅𐤀𐤍𐤉.𐤅𐤄𐤍𐤏𐤓.𐤍𐤋𐤊𐤄.𐤏𐤃.𐤊𐤄.𐤅𐤍𐤔𐤕𐤇𐤅𐤄.𐤅𐤍𐤔
𐤅𐤁𐤄.𐤀𐤋𐤉𐤊𐤌|

ו 𐤅𐤉𐤒𐤇.𐤀𐤁𐤓𐤄𐤌.𐤀𐤕.𐤏𐤑𐤉.𐤄𐤏𐤋𐤄.𐤅𐤉𐤔𐤌.𐤏𐤋.𐤉
𐤑𐤇𐤒.𐤁𐤍𐤅.𐤅𐤉𐤒𐤇.𐤁𐤉𐤃𐤅.𐤀𐤕.𐤄𐤀𐤔.𐤅𐤀𐤕.𐤄𐤌𐤀𐤊𐤋𐤕
.𐤅𐤉𐤋𐤊𐤅.𐤔𐤍𐤉𐤄𐤌.𐤉𐤇𐤃𐤅|

ז 𐤅𐤉𐤀𐤌𐤓.𐤉𐤑𐤇𐤒.𐤀𐤋.𐤀𐤁𐤓𐤄𐤌.𐤀𐤁𐤉𐤅.𐤅𐤉𐤀𐤌𐤓.𐤀𐤁
𐤉.𐤅𐤉𐤀𐤌𐤓.𐤄𐤍𐤍𐤉.𐤁𐤍𐤉.𐤅𐤉𐤀𐤌𐤓.𐤄𐤍𐤄.𐤄𐤀𐤔.𐤅𐤄𐤏𐤑𐤉𐤌.
𐤅𐤀𐤉𐤄.𐤄𐤔𐤄.𐤋𐤏𐤋𐤄|

ח 𐤅𐤉𐤀𐤌𐤓.𐤀𐤁𐤓𐤄𐤌.𐤀𐤋𐤄𐤉𐤌.𐤉𐤓𐤀𐤄.𐤋𐤅.𐤄𐤔𐤄.𐤋𐤏𐤋
𐤄.𐤁𐤍𐤉.𐤅𐤉𐤋𐤊𐤅.𐤔𐤍𐤉𐤄𐤌.𐤉𐤇𐤃𐤅|

ט 𐤅𐤉𐤁𐤀𐤅.𐤀𐤋.𐤄𐤌𐤒𐤅𐤌.𐤀𐤔𐤓.𐤀𐤌𐤓.𐤋𐤅.𐤄𐤀𐤋𐤄𐤉𐤌.𐤅𐤉
𐤁𐤍.𐤔𐤌.𐤀𐤁𐤓𐤄𐤌.𐤀𐤕.𐤄𐤌𐤆𐤁𐤇.𐤅𐤉𐤏𐤓𐤊.𐤀𐤕.𐤄𐤏𐤑𐤉
𐤌.𐤅𐤉𐤏𐤒𐤃.𐤀𐤕.𐤉𐤑𐤇𐤒.𐤁𐤍𐤅.𐤅𐤉𐤔𐤌.𐤀𐤕𐤅.𐤏𐤋.𐤄𐤌𐤆𐤁
𐤇.𐤌𐤌𐤏𐤋.𐤋𐤏𐤑𐤉𐤌|

י 𐤅𐤉𐤔𐤋𐤇.𐤀𐤁𐤓𐤄𐤌.𐤀𐤕.𐤉𐤃𐤅.𐤅𐤉𐤒𐤇.𐤀𐤕.𐤄𐤌𐤀𐤊
𐤋𐤕.𐤋𐤔𐤇𐤈.𐤀𐤕.𐤁𐤍𐤅|

יא 𐤅𐤉𐤒𐤓𐤀.𐤀𐤋𐤉𐤅.𐤌𐤋𐤀𐤊.𐤉𐤄𐤅𐤄.𐤌𐤍.𐤄𐤔𐤌𐤉𐤌.𐤅𐤉𐤀
𐤌𐤓.𐤀𐤁𐤓𐤄𐤌.𐤀𐤁𐤓𐤄𐤌.𐤅𐤉𐤀𐤌𐤓.𐤄𐤍𐤍𐤉|

𐤉𐤁 𐤅𐤉𐤀𐤌𐤓.𐤀𐤋.𐤕𐤔𐤋𐤇.𐤉𐤃𐤊.𐤀𐤋.𐤄𐤍𐤏𐤓.𐤅𐤀𐤋.𐤕𐤏𐤔
.𐤋𐤅.𐤌𐤀𐤅𐤌𐤄.𐤊𐤉.𐤏𐤕𐤄.𐤉𐤃𐤏𐤕𐤉.𐤊𐤉.𐤉𐤓𐤀.𐤀𐤋𐤄𐤉𐤌.𐤀
𐤕𐤄.𐤅𐤋𐤀.𐤇𐤔𐤊𐤕.𐤀𐤕.𐤁𐤍𐤊.𐤀𐤕.𐤉𐤇𐤉𐤃𐤊.𐤌𐤌𐤍𐤉|
𐤉𐤂 𐤅𐤉𐤔𐤀.𐤀𐤁𐤓𐤄𐤌.𐤀𐤕.𐤏𐤉𐤍𐤉𐤅.𐤅𐤉𐤓𐤀.𐤅𐤄𐤍𐤄.𐤀𐤉𐤋.
𐤀𐤇𐤓.𐤍𐤀𐤇𐤆.𐤁𐤎𐤁𐤊.𐤁𐤒𐤓𐤍𐤉𐤅.𐤅𐤉𐤋𐤊.𐤀𐤁𐤓𐤄𐤌.𐤅𐤉𐤒𐤇
.𐤀𐤕.𐤄𐤀𐤉𐤋.𐤅𐤉𐤏𐤋𐤄𐤅.𐤋𐤏𐤋𐤄.𐤕𐤇𐤕.𐤁𐤍𐤅|
𐤉𐤃 𐤅𐤉𐤒𐤓𐤀.𐤀𐤁𐤓𐤄𐤌.𐤔𐤌.𐤄𐤌𐤒𐤅𐤌.𐤄𐤄𐤅𐤀.𐤉𐤄𐤅𐤄.𐤉
𐤓𐤀𐤄.𐤀𐤔𐤓.𐤉𐤀𐤌𐤓.𐤄𐤉𐤅𐤌.𐤁𐤄𐤓.𐤉𐤄𐤅𐤄.𐤉𐤓𐤀𐤄|
𐤈𐤅 𐤅𐤉𐤒𐤓𐤀.𐤌𐤋𐤀𐤊.𐤉𐤄𐤅𐤄.𐤀𐤋.𐤀𐤁𐤓𐤄𐤌.𐤔𐤍𐤉𐤕.𐤌𐤍.𐤄
𐤔𐤌𐤉𐤌|
𐤈𐤆 𐤅𐤉𐤀𐤌𐤓.𐤁𐤉.𐤍𐤔𐤁𐤏𐤕𐤉.𐤍𐤀𐤌.𐤉𐤄𐤅𐤄.𐤊𐤉.𐤉𐤏𐤍.𐤀𐤔
𐤓.𐤏𐤔𐤉𐤕.𐤀𐤕.𐤄𐤃𐤁𐤓.𐤄𐤆𐤄.𐤅𐤋𐤀.𐤇𐤔𐤊𐤕.𐤀𐤕.𐤁𐤍𐤊.
𐤀𐤕.𐤉𐤇𐤉𐤃𐤊|
𐤉𐤆 𐤊𐤉.𐤁𐤓𐤊.𐤀𐤁𐤓𐤊𐤊.𐤅𐤄𐤓𐤁𐤄.𐤀𐤓𐤁𐤄.𐤀𐤕.𐤆𐤓𐤏𐤊.𐤊
𐤊𐤅𐤊𐤁𐤉.𐤄𐤔𐤌𐤉𐤌.𐤅𐤊𐤇𐤅𐤋.𐤀𐤔𐤓.𐤏𐤋.𐤔𐤐𐤕.𐤄𐤉𐤌.𐤅𐤉𐤓𐤔
.𐤆𐤓𐤏𐤊.𐤀𐤕.𐤔𐤏𐤓.𐤀𐤉𐤁𐤉𐤅|
𐤉𐤇 𐤅𐤄𐤕𐤁𐤓𐤊𐤅.𐤁𐤆𐤓𐤏𐤊.𐤊𐤋.𐤂𐤅𐤉𐤉.𐤄𐤀𐤓𐤑.𐤏𐤒𐤁.𐤀
𐤔𐤓.𐤔𐤌𐤏𐤕.𐤁𐤒𐤋𐤉|
𐤉𐤈 𐤅𐤉𐤔𐤁.𐤀𐤁𐤓𐤄𐤌.𐤀𐤋.𐤍𐤏𐤓𐤉𐤅.𐤅𐤉𐤒𐤌𐤅.𐤅𐤉𐤋𐤊𐤅.𐤉𐤇
𐤃𐤅.𐤀𐤋.𐤁𐤀𐤓.𐤔𐤁𐤏.𐤅𐤉𐤔𐤁.𐤀𐤁𐤓𐤄𐤌.𐤁𐤁𐤀𐤓.𐤔𐤁𐤏|
𐤊 𐤅𐤉𐤄𐤉.𐤀𐤇𐤓𐤉.𐤄𐤃𐤁𐤓𐤉𐤌.𐤄𐤀𐤋𐤄.𐤅𐤉𐤂𐤃.𐤋𐤀𐤁𐤓
𐤄𐤌.𐤋𐤀𐤌𐤓.𐤄𐤍𐤄.𐤉𐤋𐤃𐤄.𐤌𐤋𐤊𐤄.𐤂𐤌.𐤄𐤅𐤀.𐤁𐤍𐤉𐤌.𐤋𐤍
𐤇𐤅𐤓.𐤀𐤇𐤉𐤊|
𐤊𐤀 𐤀𐤕.𐤏𐤅𐤑.𐤁𐤊𐤓𐤅.𐤅𐤀𐤕.𐤁𐤅𐤆.𐤀𐤇𐤉𐤅.𐤅𐤀𐤕.𐤒𐤌𐤅𐤀𐤋
.𐤀𐤁𐤉.𐤀𐤓𐤌|
𐤊𐤁 𐤅𐤀𐤕.𐤊𐤔𐤃.𐤅𐤀𐤕.𐤇𐤆𐤅.𐤅𐤀𐤕.𐤐𐤋𐤃𐤔.𐤅𐤀𐤕.𐤉𐤃𐤋
𐤐.𐤅𐤀𐤕.𐤁𐤕𐤅𐤀𐤋|
𐤊𐤂 𐤅𐤁𐤕𐤅𐤀𐤋.𐤉𐤋𐤃.𐤀𐤕.𐤓𐤁𐤒𐤄.𐤔𐤌𐤍𐤄.𐤀𐤋𐤄.𐤉𐤋𐤃
𐤄.𐤌𐤋𐤊𐤄.𐤋𐤍𐤇𐤅𐤓.𐤀𐤇𐤉.𐤀𐤁𐤓𐤄𐤌|
𐤊𐤃 𐤅𐤐𐤉𐤋𐤂𐤔𐤅.𐤅𐤔𐤌𐤄.𐤓𐤀𐤅𐤌𐤄.𐤅𐤕𐤋𐤃.𐤂𐤌.𐤄𐤅𐤀.𐤀
𐤕.𐤈𐤁𐤇.𐤅𐤀𐤕.𐤂𐤇𐤌.𐤅𐤀𐤕.𐤕𐤇𐤔.𐤅𐤀𐤕.𐤌𐤏𐤊𐤄||

𐤁𐤓𐤀𐤔𐤉𐤕.𐤇𐤋𐤒 ..23..

1 𐤅𐤉𐤄𐤉𐤅.𐤇𐤉𐤉.𐤔𐤓𐤄.𐤌𐤀𐤄.𐤔𐤍𐤄.𐤅𐤏𐤔𐤓𐤉𐤌.𐤔𐤍𐤄.𐤅
𐤔𐤁𐤏.𐤔𐤍𐤉𐤌.𐤔𐤍𐤉.𐤇𐤉𐤉.𐤔𐤓𐤄|
2 𐤅𐤕𐤌𐤕.𐤔𐤓𐤄.𐤁𐤒𐤓𐤉𐤕.𐤀𐤓𐤁𐤏.𐤄𐤅𐤀.𐤇𐤁𐤓𐤅𐤍.𐤁𐤀𐤓
𐤑.𐤊𐤍𐤏𐤍.𐤅𐤉𐤁𐤀.𐤀𐤁𐤓𐤄𐤌.𐤋𐤎𐤐𐤃.𐤋𐤔𐤓𐤄.𐤅𐤋𐤁𐤊𐤕𐤄|
3 𐤅𐤉𐤒𐤌.𐤀𐤁𐤓𐤄𐤌.𐤌𐤏𐤋.𐤐𐤍𐤉.𐤌𐤕𐤅.𐤅𐤉𐤃𐤁𐤓.𐤀𐤋.𐤁𐤍𐤉.
𐤇𐤕.𐤋𐤀𐤌𐤓|
4 𐤂𐤓.𐤅𐤕𐤅𐤔𐤁.𐤀𐤍𐤊𐤉.𐤏𐤌𐤊𐤌.𐤕𐤍𐤅.𐤋𐤉.𐤀𐤇𐤆𐤕.𐤒𐤁
𐤓.𐤏𐤌𐤊𐤌.𐤅𐤀𐤒𐤁𐤓𐤄.𐤌𐤕𐤉.𐤌𐤋𐤐𐤍𐤉|
5 𐤅𐤉𐤏𐤍𐤅.𐤁𐤍𐤉.𐤇𐤕.𐤀𐤕.𐤀𐤁𐤓𐤄𐤌.𐤋𐤀𐤌𐤓.𐤋𐤅|
6 𐤔𐤌𐤏𐤍𐤅.𐤀𐤃𐤍𐤉.𐤍𐤔𐤉𐤀.𐤀𐤋𐤄𐤉𐤌.𐤀𐤕𐤄.𐤁𐤕𐤅𐤊𐤍𐤅.𐤁
𐤌𐤁𐤇𐤓.𐤒𐤁𐤓𐤉𐤍𐤅.𐤒𐤁𐤓.𐤀𐤕.𐤌𐤕𐤊.𐤀𐤉𐤔.𐤌𐤌𐤍𐤅.𐤀𐤕.𐤒𐤁
𐤓𐤅.𐤋𐤀.𐤉𐤊𐤋𐤄.𐤌𐤌𐤊.𐤌𐤒𐤁𐤓.𐤌𐤕𐤊|
7 𐤅𐤉𐤒𐤌.𐤀𐤁𐤓𐤄𐤌.𐤅𐤉𐤔𐤕𐤇𐤅.𐤋𐤏𐤌.𐤄𐤀𐤓𐤑.𐤋𐤁𐤍𐤉.𐤇
𐤕|
8 𐤅𐤉𐤃𐤁𐤓.𐤀𐤕𐤌.𐤋𐤀𐤌𐤓.𐤀𐤌.𐤉𐤔.𐤀𐤕.𐤍𐤐𐤔𐤊𐤌.𐤋𐤒𐤁𐤓
𐤀𐤕.𐤌𐤕𐤉.𐤌𐤋𐤐𐤍𐤉.𐤔𐤌𐤏𐤅𐤍𐤉.𐤅𐤐𐤂𐤏𐤅.𐤋𐤉.𐤁𐤏𐤐𐤓𐤅𐤍.𐤁𐤍.
𐤑𐤇𐤓|
9 𐤅𐤉𐤕𐤍.𐤋𐤉.𐤀𐤕.𐤌𐤏𐤓𐤕.𐤄𐤌𐤊𐤐𐤋𐤄.𐤀𐤔𐤓.𐤋𐤅.𐤀𐤔𐤓.𐤁
𐤒𐤑𐤄.𐤔𐤃𐤄𐤅.𐤁𐤊𐤎𐤐.𐤌𐤋𐤀.𐤉𐤕𐤍𐤍𐤄.𐤋𐤉.𐤁𐤕𐤅𐤊𐤊𐤌.𐤋𐤀
𐤇𐤆𐤕.𐤒𐤁𐤓|
10 𐤅𐤏𐤐𐤓𐤅𐤍.𐤉𐤔𐤁.𐤁𐤕𐤅𐤊.𐤁𐤍𐤉.𐤇𐤕.𐤅𐤉𐤏𐤍.𐤏𐤐𐤓𐤅𐤍.𐤄
𐤇𐤕𐤉.𐤀𐤕.𐤀𐤁𐤓𐤄𐤌.𐤁𐤀𐤆𐤍𐤉.𐤁𐤍𐤉.𐤇𐤕.𐤋𐤊𐤋.𐤁𐤀𐤉.𐤔
𐤏𐤓.𐤏𐤉𐤓𐤅.𐤋𐤀𐤌𐤓|
11 𐤋𐤀.𐤀𐤃𐤍𐤉.𐤔𐤌𐤏𐤍𐤉.𐤄𐤔𐤃𐤄.𐤍𐤕𐤕𐤉.𐤋𐤊.𐤅𐤄𐤌𐤏𐤓
𐤄.𐤀𐤔𐤓.𐤁𐤅.𐤋𐤊.𐤍𐤕𐤕𐤉𐤄.𐤋𐤏𐤉𐤍𐤉.𐤁𐤍𐤉.𐤏𐤌𐤉.𐤍𐤕𐤕𐤉𐤄.
𐤋𐤊.𐤒𐤁𐤓.𐤌𐤕𐤊|
12 𐤅𐤉𐤔𐤕𐤇𐤅.𐤀𐤁𐤓𐤄𐤌.𐤋𐤐𐤍𐤉.𐤏𐤌.𐤄𐤀𐤓𐤑|

𐤉𐤂 𐤅𐤉𐤃𐤁𐤓.𐤀𐤋.𐤏𐤐𐤓𐤅𐤍.𐤁𐤀𐤆𐤍𐤉.𐤏𐤌.𐤄𐤀𐤓𐤑.𐤋𐤀𐤌𐤓
.𐤀𐤊.𐤀𐤌.𐤀𐤕𐤄.𐤋𐤅.𐤔𐤌𐤏𐤍𐤉.𐤍𐤕𐤕𐤉.𐤊𐤎𐤐.𐤄𐤔𐤃𐤄.𐤒𐤇
.𐤌𐤌𐤍𐤉.𐤅𐤀𐤒𐤁𐤓𐤄.𐤀𐤕.𐤌𐤕𐤉.𐤔𐤌𐤄|
𐤉𐤃 𐤅𐤉𐤏𐤍.𐤏𐤐𐤓𐤅𐤍.𐤀𐤕.𐤀𐤁𐤓𐤄𐤌.𐤋𐤀𐤌𐤓.𐤋𐤅|
𐤈𐤅 𐤀𐤃𐤍𐤉.𐤔𐤌𐤏𐤍𐤉.𐤀𐤓𐤑.𐤀𐤓𐤁𐤏.𐤌𐤀𐤕.𐤔𐤒𐤋.𐤊𐤎𐤐.
𐤁𐤉𐤍𐤉.𐤅𐤁𐤉𐤍𐤊.𐤌𐤄.𐤄𐤅𐤀.𐤅𐤀𐤕.𐤌𐤕𐤊.𐤒𐤁𐤓|
𐤈𐤆 𐤅𐤉𐤔𐤌𐤏.𐤀𐤁𐤓𐤄𐤌.𐤀𐤋.𐤏𐤐𐤓𐤅𐤍.𐤅𐤉𐤔𐤒𐤋.𐤀𐤁𐤓𐤄𐤌.𐤋
𐤏𐤐𐤓𐤍.𐤀𐤕.𐤄𐤊𐤎𐤐.𐤀𐤔𐤓.𐤃𐤁𐤓.𐤁𐤀𐤆𐤍𐤉.𐤁𐤍𐤉.𐤇𐤕.𐤀𐤓
𐤁𐤏.𐤌𐤀𐤅𐤕.𐤔𐤒𐤋.𐤊𐤎𐤐.𐤏𐤁𐤓.𐤋𐤎𐤇𐤓|
𐤉𐤆 𐤅𐤉𐤒𐤌.𐤔𐤃𐤄.𐤏𐤐𐤓𐤅𐤍.𐤀𐤔𐤓.𐤁𐤌𐤊𐤐𐤋𐤄.𐤀𐤔𐤓.𐤋𐤐𐤍
𐤉.𐤌𐤌𐤓𐤀.𐤄𐤔𐤃𐤄.𐤅𐤄𐤌𐤏𐤓𐤄.𐤀𐤔𐤓.𐤁𐤅.𐤅𐤊𐤋.𐤄𐤏𐤑.𐤀𐤔
𐤓.𐤁𐤔𐤃𐤄.𐤀𐤔𐤓.𐤁𐤊𐤋.𐤂𐤁𐤋𐤅.𐤎𐤁𐤉𐤁|
𐤉𐤇 𐤋𐤀𐤁𐤓𐤄𐤌.𐤋𐤌𐤒𐤍𐤄.𐤋𐤏𐤉𐤍𐤉.𐤁𐤍𐤉.𐤇𐤕.𐤁𐤊𐤋.𐤁𐤀𐤉
.𐤔𐤏𐤓.𐤏𐤉𐤓𐤅|
𐤉𐤈 𐤅𐤀𐤇𐤓𐤉.𐤊𐤍.𐤒𐤁𐤓.𐤀𐤁𐤓𐤄𐤌.𐤀𐤕.𐤔𐤓𐤄.𐤀𐤔𐤕𐤅.𐤀
𐤋.𐤌𐤏𐤓𐤕.𐤔𐤃𐤄.𐤄𐤌𐤊𐤐𐤋𐤄.𐤏𐤋.𐤐𐤍𐤉.𐤌𐤌𐤓𐤀.𐤄𐤅𐤀.𐤇𐤁
𐤓𐤅𐤍.𐤁𐤀𐤓𐤑.𐤊𐤍𐤏𐤍|
𐤊 𐤅𐤉𐤒𐤌.𐤄𐤔𐤃𐤄.𐤅𐤄𐤌𐤏𐤓𐤄.𐤀𐤔𐤓.𐤁𐤅.𐤋𐤀𐤁𐤓𐤄𐤌.𐤋
𐤀𐤇𐤆𐤕.𐤒𐤁𐤓.𐤌𐤀𐤕.𐤁𐤍𐤉.𐤇𐤕||

𐤁𐤓𐤀𐤔𐤉𐤕.𐤇𐤋𐤒 𐤊𐤃

𐤀 𐤅𐤀𐤁𐤓𐤄𐤌.𐤆𐤒𐤍.𐤁𐤀.𐤁𐤉𐤌𐤉𐤌.𐤅𐤉𐤄𐤅𐤄.𐤁𐤓𐤊.𐤀𐤕.𐤀
𐤁𐤓𐤄𐤌.𐤁𐤊𐤋|
𐤁 𐤅𐤉𐤀𐤌𐤓.𐤀𐤁𐤓𐤄𐤌.𐤀𐤋.𐤏𐤁𐤃𐤅.𐤆𐤒𐤍.𐤁𐤉𐤕𐤅.𐤄𐤌𐤔𐤋.
𐤁𐤊𐤋.𐤀𐤔𐤓.𐤋𐤅.𐤔𐤉𐤌.𐤍𐤀.𐤉𐤃𐤊.𐤕𐤇𐤕.𐤉𐤓𐤊𐤉|
𐤂 𐤅𐤀𐤔𐤁𐤉𐤏𐤊.𐤁𐤉𐤄𐤅𐤄.𐤀𐤋𐤄𐤉.𐤄𐤔𐤌𐤉𐤌.𐤅𐤀𐤋𐤄𐤉.𐤄
𐤀𐤓𐤑.𐤀𐤔𐤓.𐤋𐤀.𐤕𐤒𐤇.𐤀𐤔𐤄.𐤋𐤁𐤍𐤉.𐤌𐤁𐤍𐤅𐤕.𐤄𐤊𐤍𐤏𐤍𐤉
.𐤀𐤔𐤓.𐤀𐤍𐤊𐤉.𐤉𐤅𐤔𐤁.𐤁𐤒𐤓𐤁𐤅|
𐤃 𐤊𐤉.𐤀𐤋.𐤀𐤓𐤑𐤉.𐤅𐤀𐤋.𐤌𐤅𐤋𐤃𐤕𐤉.𐤕𐤋𐤊.𐤅𐤋𐤒𐤇𐤕.𐤀
𐤔𐤄.𐤋𐤁𐤍𐤉.𐤋𐤉𐤑𐤇𐤒|

𐤄 𐤅𐤉𐤀𐤌𐤓.𐤀𐤋𐤉𐤅.𐤄𐤏𐤁𐤃.𐤀𐤅𐤋𐤉.𐤋𐤀.𐤕𐤀𐤁𐤄.𐤄𐤀𐤔𐤄.
𐤋𐤋𐤊𐤕.𐤀𐤇𐤓𐤉.𐤀𐤋.𐤄𐤀𐤓𐤑.𐤄𐤆𐤀𐤕.𐤄𐤄𐤔𐤁.𐤀𐤔𐤉𐤁.𐤀
𐤕.𐤁𐤍𐤊.𐤀𐤋.𐤄𐤀𐤓𐤑.𐤀𐤔𐤓.𐤉𐤑𐤀𐤕.𐤌𐤔𐤌|
𐤅 𐤅𐤉𐤀𐤌𐤓.𐤀𐤋𐤉𐤅.𐤀𐤁𐤓𐤄𐤌.𐤄𐤔𐤌𐤓.𐤋𐤊.𐤐𐤍.𐤕𐤔𐤉𐤁.𐤀𐤕
.𐤁𐤍𐤉.𐤔𐤌𐤄|
𐤆 𐤉𐤄𐤅𐤄.𐤀𐤋𐤄𐤉.𐤄𐤔𐤌𐤉𐤌.𐤀𐤔𐤓.𐤋𐤒𐤇𐤍𐤉.𐤌𐤁𐤉𐤕.𐤀
𐤁𐤉.𐤅𐤌𐤀𐤓𐤑.𐤌𐤅𐤋𐤃𐤕𐤉.𐤅𐤀𐤔𐤓.𐤃𐤁𐤓.𐤋𐤉.𐤅𐤀𐤔𐤓.𐤍𐤔𐤁𐤏
.𐤋𐤉.𐤋𐤀𐤌𐤓.𐤋𐤆𐤓𐤏𐤊.𐤀𐤕𐤍.𐤀𐤕.𐤄𐤀𐤓𐤑.𐤄𐤆𐤀𐤕.𐤄𐤅𐤀.
𐤉𐤔𐤋𐤇.𐤌𐤋𐤀𐤊𐤅.𐤋𐤐𐤍𐤉𐤊.𐤅𐤋𐤒𐤇𐤕.𐤀𐤔𐤄.𐤋𐤁𐤍𐤉.𐤌𐤔𐤌|
𐤇 𐤅𐤀𐤌.𐤋𐤀.𐤕𐤀𐤁𐤄.𐤄𐤀𐤔𐤄.𐤋𐤋𐤊𐤕.𐤀𐤇𐤓𐤉𐤊.𐤅𐤍𐤒𐤉𐤕
.𐤌𐤔𐤁𐤏𐤕𐤉.𐤆𐤀𐤕.𐤓𐤒.𐤀𐤕.𐤁𐤍𐤉.𐤋𐤀.𐤕𐤔𐤁.𐤔𐤌𐤄|
𐤈 𐤅𐤉𐤔𐤌.𐤄𐤏𐤁𐤃.𐤀𐤕.𐤉𐤃𐤅.𐤕𐤇𐤕.𐤉𐤓𐤊.𐤀𐤁𐤓𐤄𐤌.𐤀
𐤃𐤍𐤉𐤅.𐤅𐤉𐤔𐤁𐤏.𐤋𐤅.𐤏𐤋.𐤄𐤃𐤁𐤓.𐤄𐤆𐤄|
𐤉 𐤅𐤉𐤒𐤇.𐤄𐤏𐤁𐤃.𐤏𐤔𐤓𐤄.𐤂𐤌𐤋𐤉𐤌.𐤌𐤂𐤌𐤋𐤉.𐤀𐤃
𐤍𐤉𐤅.𐤅𐤉𐤋𐤊.𐤅𐤊𐤋.𐤈𐤅𐤁.𐤀𐤃𐤍𐤉𐤅.𐤁𐤉𐤃𐤅.𐤅𐤉𐤒𐤌.𐤅𐤉𐤋𐤊.𐤀𐤋.
𐤀𐤓𐤌.𐤍𐤄𐤓𐤉𐤌.𐤀𐤋.𐤏𐤉𐤓.𐤍𐤇𐤅𐤓|
𐤉𐤀 𐤅𐤉𐤁𐤓𐤊.𐤄𐤂𐤌𐤋𐤉𐤌.𐤌𐤇𐤅𐤑.𐤋𐤏𐤉𐤓.𐤀𐤋.𐤁𐤀𐤓.𐤄𐤌
𐤉𐤌.𐤋𐤏𐤕.𐤏𐤓𐤁.𐤋𐤏𐤕.𐤑𐤀𐤕.𐤄𐤔𐤀𐤁𐤕|
𐤉𐤁 𐤅𐤉𐤀𐤌𐤓.𐤉𐤄𐤅𐤄.𐤀𐤋𐤄𐤉.𐤀𐤃𐤍𐤉.𐤀𐤁𐤓𐤄𐤌.𐤄𐤒𐤓𐤄.
𐤍𐤀.𐤋𐤐𐤍𐤉.𐤄𐤉𐤅𐤌.𐤅𐤏𐤔𐤄.𐤇𐤎𐤃.𐤏𐤌.𐤀𐤃𐤍𐤉.𐤀𐤁𐤓𐤄𐤌|
𐤉𐤂 𐤄𐤍𐤄.𐤀𐤍𐤊𐤉.𐤍𐤑𐤁.𐤏𐤋.𐤏𐤉𐤍.𐤄𐤌𐤉𐤌.𐤅𐤁𐤍𐤅𐤕.𐤀𐤍𐤔
𐤉.𐤄𐤏𐤉𐤓.𐤉𐤑𐤀𐤕.𐤋𐤔𐤀𐤁.𐤌𐤉𐤌|
𐤉𐤃 𐤅𐤄𐤉𐤄.𐤄𐤍𐤏𐤓𐤄.𐤀𐤔𐤓.𐤀𐤌𐤓.𐤀𐤋𐤉𐤄.𐤄𐤈𐤉.𐤍𐤀.𐤊𐤃
𐤊.𐤅𐤀𐤔𐤕𐤄.𐤅𐤀𐤌𐤓𐤄.𐤔𐤕𐤄.𐤅𐤂𐤌.𐤂𐤌𐤋𐤉𐤊.𐤀𐤔𐤒𐤄.𐤀𐤕
𐤄.𐤄𐤊𐤇𐤕.𐤋𐤏𐤁𐤃𐤊.𐤋𐤉𐤑𐤇𐤒.𐤅𐤁𐤄.𐤀𐤃𐤏.𐤊𐤉.𐤏𐤔𐤉
𐤕.𐤇𐤎𐤃.𐤏𐤌.𐤀𐤃𐤍𐤉|
𐤈𐤅 𐤅𐤉𐤄𐤉.𐤄𐤅𐤀.𐤈𐤓𐤌.𐤊𐤋𐤄.𐤋𐤃𐤁𐤓.𐤅𐤄𐤍𐤄.𐤓𐤁𐤒𐤄.𐤉
𐤑𐤀𐤕.𐤀𐤔𐤓.𐤉𐤋𐤃𐤄.𐤋𐤁𐤕𐤅𐤀𐤋.𐤁𐤍.𐤌𐤋𐤊𐤄.𐤀𐤔𐤕.𐤍𐤇𐤅𐤓
.𐤀𐤇𐤉.𐤀𐤁𐤓𐤄𐤌.𐤅𐤊𐤃𐤄.𐤏𐤋.𐤔𐤊𐤌𐤄|
𐤈𐤆 𐤅𐤄𐤍𐤏𐤓.𐤈𐤁𐤕.𐤌𐤓𐤀𐤄.𐤌𐤀𐤃.𐤁𐤕𐤅𐤋𐤄.𐤅𐤀𐤉𐤔.𐤋𐤀.
𐤉𐤃𐤏𐤄.𐤅𐤕𐤓𐤃.𐤄𐤏𐤉𐤍𐤄.𐤅𐤕𐤌𐤋𐤀.𐤊𐤃𐤄.𐤅𐤕𐤏𐤋|

𐤉𐤆 𐤅𐤉𐤓𐤑.𐤄𐤏𐤁𐤃.𐤋𐤒𐤓𐤀𐤕𐤄.𐤅𐤉𐤀𐤌𐤓.𐤄𐤂𐤌𐤉𐤀𐤉𐤍
𐤉.𐤍𐤀.𐤌𐤏𐤈.𐤌𐤉𐤌.𐤌𐤊𐤃𐤊|
𐤉𐤇 𐤅𐤕𐤀𐤌𐤓.𐤔𐤕𐤄.𐤀𐤃𐤍𐤉.𐤅𐤕𐤌𐤄𐤓.𐤅𐤕𐤓𐤃.𐤊𐤃𐤄.𐤏𐤋
.𐤉𐤃𐤄.𐤅𐤕𐤔𐤒𐤄𐤅|
𐤉𐤈 𐤅𐤕𐤊𐤋.𐤋𐤄𐤔𐤒𐤕𐤅.𐤅𐤕𐤀𐤌𐤓.𐤂𐤌.𐤋𐤂𐤌𐤋𐤉𐤊.𐤀𐤔𐤀
𐤁.𐤏𐤃.𐤀𐤌.𐤊𐤋𐤅.𐤋𐤔𐤕𐤕|
𐤊 𐤅𐤕𐤌𐤄𐤓.𐤅𐤕𐤏𐤓.𐤊𐤃𐤄.𐤀𐤋.𐤄𐤔𐤒𐤕.𐤅𐤕𐤓𐤑.𐤏𐤅𐤃.
𐤀𐤋.𐤄𐤁𐤀𐤓.𐤋𐤔𐤀𐤁.𐤅𐤕𐤔𐤀𐤁.𐤋𐤊𐤋.𐤂𐤌𐤋𐤉𐤅|
𐤊𐤀 𐤅𐤄𐤀𐤉𐤔.𐤌𐤔𐤕𐤀𐤄.𐤋𐤄.𐤌𐤇𐤓𐤉𐤔.𐤋𐤃𐤏𐤕.𐤄𐤄𐤑
𐤋𐤉𐤇.𐤉𐤄𐤅𐤄.𐤃𐤓𐤊𐤅.𐤀𐤌.𐤋𐤀|
𐤊𐤁 𐤅𐤉𐤄𐤉.𐤊𐤀𐤔𐤓.𐤊𐤋𐤅.𐤄𐤂𐤌𐤋𐤉𐤌.𐤋𐤔𐤕𐤅𐤕.𐤅𐤉𐤒𐤇.
𐤄𐤀𐤉𐤔.𐤍𐤆𐤌.𐤆𐤄𐤁.𐤁𐤒𐤏.𐤌𐤔𐤒𐤋𐤅.𐤅𐤔𐤍𐤉.𐤑𐤌𐤉𐤃𐤉𐤌
.𐤏𐤋.𐤉𐤃𐤉𐤄.𐤏𐤔𐤓𐤄.𐤆𐤄𐤁.𐤌𐤔𐤒𐤋𐤌|
𐤊𐤂 𐤅𐤉𐤀𐤌𐤓.𐤁𐤕.𐤌𐤉.𐤀𐤕.𐤄𐤂𐤉𐤃𐤉.𐤍𐤀.𐤋𐤉.𐤄𐤉𐤔.𐤁𐤉
𐤕.𐤀𐤁𐤉𐤊.𐤌𐤒𐤅𐤌.𐤋𐤍𐤅.𐤋𐤋𐤉𐤍|
𐤊𐤃 𐤅𐤕𐤀𐤌𐤓.𐤀𐤋𐤉𐤅.𐤁𐤕.𐤁𐤕𐤅𐤀𐤋.𐤀𐤍𐤊𐤉.𐤁𐤍.𐤌𐤋𐤊𐤄.𐤀
𐤔𐤓.𐤉𐤋𐤃𐤄.𐤋𐤍𐤇𐤅𐤓|
𐤊𐤄 𐤅𐤕𐤀𐤌𐤓.𐤀𐤋𐤉𐤅.𐤂𐤌.𐤕𐤁𐤍.𐤂𐤌.𐤌𐤎𐤐𐤅𐤀.𐤓𐤁.𐤏𐤌𐤍𐤅.
𐤂𐤌.𐤌𐤒𐤅𐤌.𐤋𐤋𐤅𐤍|
𐤊𐤅 𐤅𐤉𐤒𐤃.𐤄𐤀𐤉𐤔.𐤅𐤉𐤔𐤕𐤇𐤅.𐤋𐤉𐤄𐤅𐤄|
𐤊𐤆 𐤅𐤉𐤀𐤌𐤓.𐤁𐤓𐤅𐤊.𐤉𐤄𐤅𐤄.𐤀𐤋𐤄𐤉.𐤀𐤃𐤍𐤉.𐤀𐤁𐤓𐤄𐤌.𐤀
𐤔𐤓.𐤋𐤀.𐤏𐤆𐤁.𐤇𐤎𐤃𐤅.𐤅𐤀𐤌𐤕𐤅.𐤌𐤏𐤌.𐤀𐤃𐤍𐤉.𐤀𐤍𐤊𐤉.𐤁
𐤃𐤓𐤊.𐤍𐤇𐤍𐤉.𐤉𐤄𐤅𐤄.𐤁𐤉𐤕.𐤀𐤇𐤉.𐤀𐤃𐤍𐤉|
𐤊𐤇 𐤅𐤕𐤓𐤑.𐤄𐤍𐤏𐤓.𐤅𐤕𐤂𐤃.𐤋𐤁𐤉𐤕.𐤀𐤌𐤄.𐤊𐤃𐤁𐤓𐤉𐤌.
𐤄𐤀𐤋𐤄|
𐤊𐤈 𐤅𐤋𐤓𐤁𐤒𐤄.𐤀𐤇.𐤅𐤔𐤌𐤅.𐤋𐤁𐤍.𐤅𐤉𐤓𐤑.𐤋𐤁𐤍.𐤀𐤋.𐤄𐤀𐤉
𐤔.𐤄𐤇𐤅𐤑𐤄.𐤀𐤋.𐤄𐤏𐤉𐤍|
𐤋 𐤅𐤉𐤄𐤉.𐤊𐤓𐤀𐤕.𐤀𐤕.𐤄𐤍𐤆𐤌.𐤅𐤀𐤕.𐤄𐤑𐤌𐤉𐤃𐤉𐤌.𐤏
𐤋.𐤉𐤃𐤉.𐤀𐤇𐤕𐤅.𐤅𐤊𐤔𐤌𐤏𐤅.𐤀𐤕.𐤃𐤁𐤓𐤉.𐤓𐤁𐤒𐤄.𐤀𐤇𐤕𐤅.
𐤋𐤀𐤌𐤓.𐤊𐤄.𐤃𐤁𐤓.𐤀𐤋𐤉.𐤄𐤀𐤉𐤔.𐤅𐤉𐤁𐤀.𐤀𐤋.𐤄𐤀𐤉𐤔.𐤅𐤄𐤍
𐤄.𐤏𐤌𐤃.𐤏𐤋.𐤄𐤂𐤌𐤋𐤉𐤌.𐤏𐤋.𐤄𐤏𐤉𐤍|

𐤋𐤀 𐤅𐤉𐤀𐤌𐤓.𐤁𐤅𐤀.𐤁𐤓𐤅𐤊.𐤉𐤄𐤅𐤄.𐤋𐤌𐤄.𐤕𐤏𐤌𐤃.𐤁𐤇𐤅𐤑
.𐤅𐤀𐤍𐤊𐤉.𐤐𐤍𐤉𐤕𐤉.𐤄𐤁𐤉𐤕.𐤅𐤌𐤒𐤅𐤌.𐤋𐤂𐤌𐤋𐤉𐤌|
𐤋𐤁 𐤅𐤉𐤁𐤀.𐤄𐤀𐤉𐤔.𐤄𐤁𐤉𐤕𐤄.𐤅𐤉𐤐𐤕𐤇.𐤄𐤂𐤌𐤋𐤉𐤌.𐤅𐤉
𐤕𐤍.𐤕𐤁𐤍.𐤅𐤌𐤎𐤐𐤅𐤀.𐤋𐤂𐤌𐤋𐤉𐤌.𐤅𐤌𐤉𐤌.𐤋𐤓𐤇𐤑.𐤓𐤂𐤋𐤉𐤅.𐤅
𐤓𐤂𐤋𐤉.𐤄𐤀𐤍𐤔𐤉𐤌.𐤀𐤔𐤓.𐤀𐤕𐤅|
𐤋𐤂 𐤅𐤉𐤉𐤔𐤌.||𐤅𐤉𐤅𐤔𐤌.𐤒𐤓𐤉||.𐤋𐤐𐤍𐤉𐤅.𐤋𐤀𐤊𐤋.𐤅𐤉𐤀𐤌𐤓.𐤋
𐤀.𐤀𐤊𐤋.𐤏𐤃.𐤀𐤌.𐤃𐤁𐤓𐤕𐤉.𐤃𐤁𐤓𐤉.𐤅𐤉𐤀𐤌𐤓.𐤃𐤁𐤓|
𐤋𐤃 𐤅𐤉𐤀𐤌𐤓.𐤏𐤁𐤃.𐤀𐤁𐤓𐤄𐤌.𐤀𐤍𐤊𐤉|
𐤋𐤄 𐤅𐤉𐤄𐤅𐤄.𐤁𐤓𐤊.𐤀𐤕.𐤀𐤃𐤍𐤉.𐤌𐤀𐤃.𐤅𐤉𐤂𐤃𐤋.𐤅𐤉𐤕𐤍.
𐤋𐤅.𐤑𐤀𐤍.𐤅𐤁𐤒𐤓.𐤅𐤊𐤎𐤐.𐤅𐤆𐤄𐤁.𐤅𐤏𐤁𐤃𐤌.𐤅𐤔𐤐𐤇𐤕.𐤅𐤂𐤌
𐤋𐤉𐤌.𐤅𐤇𐤌𐤓𐤉𐤌|
𐤋𐤅 𐤅𐤕𐤋𐤃.𐤔𐤓𐤄.𐤀𐤔𐤕.𐤀𐤃𐤍𐤉.𐤁𐤍.𐤋𐤀𐤃𐤍𐤉.𐤀𐤇𐤓𐤉.
𐤆𐤒𐤍𐤕𐤄.𐤅𐤉𐤕𐤍.𐤋𐤅.𐤀𐤕.𐤊𐤋.𐤀𐤔𐤓.𐤋𐤅|
𐤋𐤆 𐤅𐤉𐤔𐤁𐤏𐤍𐤉.𐤀𐤃𐤍𐤉.𐤋𐤀𐤌𐤓.𐤋𐤀.𐤕𐤒𐤇.𐤀𐤔𐤄.𐤋𐤁
𐤍𐤉.𐤌𐤁𐤍𐤅𐤕.𐤄𐤊𐤍𐤏𐤍𐤉.𐤀𐤔𐤓.𐤀𐤍𐤊𐤉.𐤉𐤔𐤁.𐤁𐤀𐤓𐤑𐤅|
𐤋𐤇 𐤀𐤌.𐤋𐤀.𐤀𐤋.𐤁𐤉𐤕.𐤀𐤁𐤉.𐤕𐤋𐤊.𐤅𐤀𐤋.𐤌𐤔𐤐𐤇𐤕𐤉.𐤅
𐤋𐤒𐤇𐤕.𐤀𐤔𐤄.𐤋𐤁𐤍𐤉|
𐤋𐤈 𐤅𐤀𐤌𐤓.𐤀𐤋.𐤀𐤃𐤍𐤉.𐤀𐤋𐤉.𐤋𐤀.𐤕𐤋𐤊.𐤄𐤀𐤔𐤄.𐤀𐤇
𐤓𐤉|
𐤌 𐤅𐤉𐤀𐤌𐤓.𐤀𐤋𐤉.𐤉𐤄𐤅𐤄.𐤀𐤔𐤓.𐤄𐤕𐤄𐤋𐤊𐤕𐤉.𐤋𐤐𐤍𐤉𐤅.
𐤉𐤔𐤋𐤇.𐤌𐤋𐤀𐤊𐤅.𐤀𐤕𐤊.𐤅𐤄𐤑𐤋𐤉𐤇.𐤃𐤓𐤊𐤊.𐤅𐤋𐤒𐤇𐤕.𐤀
𐤔𐤄.𐤋𐤁𐤍𐤉.𐤌𐤌𐤔𐤐𐤇𐤕𐤉.𐤅𐤌𐤁𐤉𐤕.𐤀𐤁𐤉|
𐤌𐤀 𐤀𐤆.𐤕𐤍𐤒𐤄.𐤌𐤀𐤋𐤕𐤉.𐤊𐤉.𐤕𐤁𐤅𐤀.𐤀𐤋.𐤌𐤔𐤐𐤇𐤕𐤉
.𐤅𐤀𐤌.𐤋𐤀.𐤉𐤕𐤍𐤅.𐤋𐤊.𐤅𐤄𐤉𐤉𐤕.𐤍𐤒𐤉.𐤌𐤀𐤋𐤕𐤉|
𐤌𐤁 𐤅𐤀𐤁𐤀.𐤄𐤉𐤅𐤌.𐤀𐤋.𐤄𐤏𐤉𐤍.𐤅𐤀𐤌𐤓.𐤉𐤄𐤅𐤄.𐤀𐤋𐤄𐤉.
𐤀𐤃𐤍𐤉.𐤀𐤁𐤓𐤄𐤌.𐤀𐤌.𐤉𐤔𐤊.𐤍𐤀.𐤌𐤑𐤋𐤉𐤇.𐤃𐤓𐤊𐤉.𐤀𐤔
𐤓.𐤀𐤍𐤊𐤉.𐤄𐤋𐤊.𐤏𐤋𐤉𐤄|
𐤌𐤂 𐤄𐤍𐤄.𐤀𐤍𐤊𐤉.𐤍𐤑𐤁.𐤏𐤋.𐤏𐤉𐤍.𐤄𐤌𐤉𐤌.𐤅𐤄𐤉𐤄.𐤄𐤏
𐤋𐤌𐤄.𐤄𐤉𐤑𐤀𐤕.𐤋𐤔𐤀𐤁.𐤅𐤀𐤌𐤓𐤕𐤉.𐤀𐤋𐤉𐤄.𐤄𐤔𐤒𐤉𐤍𐤉.𐤍
𐤀.𐤌𐤏𐤈.𐤌𐤉𐤌.𐤌𐤊𐤃𐤊|

..𐤌𐤃.. 𐤅𐤀𐤌𐤓𐤄.𐤀𐤋𐤉.𐤂𐤌.𐤀𐤕𐤄.𐤔𐤕𐤄.𐤅𐤂𐤌.𐤋𐤂𐤌𐤋𐤉
𐤊.𐤀𐤔𐤀𐤁.𐤄𐤅𐤀.𐤄𐤀𐤔𐤄.𐤀𐤔𐤓.𐤄𐤊𐤉𐤇.𐤉𐤄𐤅𐤄.𐤋𐤁𐤍.𐤀
𐤃𐤍𐤉|
..𐤌𐤄.. 𐤀𐤍𐤉.𐤈𐤓𐤌.𐤀𐤊𐤋𐤄.𐤋𐤃𐤁𐤓.𐤀𐤋.𐤋𐤁𐤉.𐤅𐤄𐤍𐤄.𐤓𐤁𐤒
𐤄.𐤉𐤑𐤀𐤕.𐤅𐤊𐤃𐤄.𐤏𐤋.𐤔𐤊𐤌𐤄.𐤅𐤕𐤓𐤃.𐤄𐤏𐤉𐤍𐤄.𐤅𐤕𐤔𐤀
𐤁.𐤅𐤀𐤌𐤓.𐤀𐤋𐤉𐤄.𐤄𐤔𐤒𐤉𐤍𐤉.𐤍𐤀|
..𐤌𐤅.. 𐤅𐤕𐤌𐤄𐤓.𐤅𐤕𐤅𐤓𐤃.𐤊𐤃𐤄.𐤌𐤏𐤋𐤉𐤄.𐤅𐤕𐤀𐤌𐤓.𐤔𐤕𐤄.
𐤅𐤂𐤌.𐤂𐤌𐤋𐤉𐤊.𐤀𐤔𐤒𐤄.𐤅𐤀𐤔𐤕.𐤅𐤂𐤌.𐤄𐤂𐤌𐤋𐤉𐤌.𐤄𐤔
𐤒𐤕𐤄|
..𐤌𐤆.. 𐤅𐤀𐤔𐤀𐤋.𐤀𐤕𐤄.𐤅𐤀𐤌𐤓.𐤁𐤕.𐤌𐤉.𐤀𐤕.𐤅𐤕𐤀𐤌𐤓.𐤁𐤕.
𐤁𐤕𐤅𐤀𐤋.𐤁𐤍.𐤍𐤇𐤅𐤓.𐤀𐤔𐤓.𐤉𐤋𐤃𐤄.𐤋𐤅.𐤌𐤋𐤊𐤄.𐤅𐤀𐤔𐤌.𐤄𐤍
𐤆𐤌.𐤏𐤋.𐤀𐤐𐤄.𐤅𐤄𐤑𐤌𐤉𐤃𐤉𐤌.𐤏𐤋.𐤉𐤃𐤉𐤄|
..𐤌𐤇.. 𐤅𐤀𐤒𐤃.𐤅𐤀𐤔𐤕𐤇𐤅𐤄.𐤋𐤉𐤄𐤅𐤄.𐤅𐤀𐤁𐤓𐤊.𐤀𐤕.𐤉𐤄𐤅𐤄
𐤀𐤋𐤄𐤉.𐤀𐤃𐤍𐤉.𐤀𐤁𐤓𐤄𐤌.𐤀𐤔𐤓.𐤄𐤍𐤇𐤍𐤉.𐤁𐤃𐤓𐤊.𐤀𐤌𐤕.
𐤋𐤒𐤇𐤕.𐤀𐤕.𐤁𐤕.𐤀𐤇𐤉.𐤀𐤃𐤍𐤉.𐤋𐤁𐤍𐤅|
..𐤌𐤈.. 𐤅𐤏𐤕𐤄.𐤀𐤌.𐤉𐤔𐤊𐤌.𐤏𐤔𐤉𐤌.𐤇𐤎𐤃.𐤅𐤀𐤌𐤕.𐤀𐤕.
𐤀𐤃𐤍𐤉.𐤄𐤂𐤉𐤃𐤅.𐤋𐤉.𐤅𐤀𐤌.𐤋𐤀.𐤄𐤂𐤉𐤃𐤅.𐤋𐤉.𐤅𐤀𐤐𐤍𐤄.𐤏
𐤋.𐤉𐤌𐤉𐤍.𐤀𐤅.𐤏𐤋.𐤔𐤌𐤀𐤋|
..𐤍.. 𐤅𐤉𐤏𐤍.𐤋𐤁𐤍.𐤅𐤁𐤕𐤅𐤀𐤋.𐤅𐤉𐤀𐤌𐤓𐤅.𐤌𐤉𐤄𐤅𐤄.𐤉𐤑𐤀.𐤄
𐤃𐤁𐤓.𐤋𐤀.𐤍𐤅𐤊𐤋.𐤃𐤁𐤓.𐤀𐤋𐤉𐤊.𐤓𐤏.𐤀𐤅.𐤈𐤅𐤁|
..𐤍𐤀.. 𐤄𐤍𐤄.𐤓𐤁𐤒𐤄.𐤋𐤐𐤍𐤉𐤊.𐤒𐤇.𐤅𐤋𐤊.𐤅𐤕𐤄𐤉.𐤀𐤔𐤄.𐤋𐤁𐤍.
𐤀𐤃𐤍𐤉𐤊.𐤊𐤀𐤔𐤓.𐤃𐤁𐤓.𐤉𐤄𐤅𐤄|
..𐤍𐤁.. 𐤅𐤉𐤄𐤉.𐤊𐤀𐤔𐤓.𐤔𐤌𐤏.𐤏𐤁𐤃.𐤀𐤁𐤓𐤄𐤌.𐤀𐤕.𐤃𐤁𐤓𐤉
𐤄𐤌.𐤅𐤉𐤔𐤕𐤇𐤅.𐤀𐤓𐤑𐤄.𐤋𐤉𐤄𐤅𐤄|
..𐤍𐤂.. 𐤅𐤉𐤅𐤑𐤀.𐤄𐤏𐤁𐤃.𐤊𐤋𐤉.𐤊𐤎𐤐.𐤅𐤊𐤋𐤉.𐤆𐤄𐤁.𐤅𐤁𐤂𐤃
𐤉𐤌.𐤅𐤉𐤕𐤍.𐤋𐤓𐤁𐤒𐤄.𐤅𐤌𐤂𐤃𐤍𐤕.𐤍𐤕𐤍.𐤋𐤀𐤇𐤉𐤄.𐤅𐤋𐤀𐤌𐤄|
..𐤍𐤃.. 𐤅𐤉𐤀𐤊𐤋𐤅.𐤅𐤉𐤔𐤕𐤅.𐤄𐤅𐤀.𐤅𐤄𐤀𐤍𐤔𐤉𐤌.𐤀𐤔𐤓.𐤏𐤌𐤅.𐤅
𐤉𐤋𐤉𐤍𐤅.𐤅𐤉𐤒𐤅𐤌𐤅.𐤅𐤉𐤀𐤌𐤓.𐤔𐤋𐤇𐤍𐤉.𐤋𐤀𐤃𐤍𐤉|
..𐤍𐤄.. 𐤅𐤉𐤀𐤌𐤓.𐤀𐤇𐤉𐤄.𐤅𐤀𐤌𐤄.𐤕𐤔𐤁.𐤄𐤍𐤏𐤓.𐤀𐤕𐤍𐤅.𐤉𐤌𐤉
𐤌.𐤀𐤅.𐤏𐤔𐤅𐤓.𐤀𐤇𐤓.𐤕𐤋𐤊|

נו ויאמר.אלהם.אל.תאחרו.אתי.ויהוה.הצליח.דרכי.שלחוני.ואלכה.לאדני׃

נז ויאמרו.נקרא.לנער.ונשאלה.את.פיה׃

נח ויקראו.לרבקה.ויאמרו.אליה.התלכי.עם.האיש.הזה.ותאמר.אלך׃

נט וישלחו.את.רבקה.אחתם.ואת.מנקתה.ואת.עבד.אברהם.ואת.אנשיו׃

ס ויברכו.את.רבקה.ויאמרו.לה.אחתנו.את.היי.לאלפי.רבבה.ויירש.זרעך.את.שער.שנאיו׃

סא ותקם.רבקה.ונערתיה.ותרכבנה.על.הגמלים.ותלכנה.אחרי.האיש.ויקח.העבד.את.רבקה.וילך׃

סב ויצחק.בא.מבוא.באר.לחי.ראי.והוא.יושב.בארץ.הנגב׃

סג ויצא.יצחק.לשוח.בשדה.לפנות.ערב.וישא.עיניו.וירא.והנה.גמלים.באים׃

סד ותשא.רבקה.את.עיניה.ותרא.את.יצחק.ותפל.מעל.הגמל׃

סה ותאמר.אל.העבד.מי.האיש.הלזה.ההלך.בשדה.לקראתנו.ויאמר.העבד.הוא.אדני.ותקח.הצעיף.ותתכס׃

סו ויספר.העבד.ליצחק.את.כל.הדברים.אשר.עשה׃

סז ויבאה.יצחק.האהלה.שרה.אמו.ויקח.את.רבקה.ותהי.לו.לאשה.ויאהבה.וינחם.יצחק.אחרי.אמו׃

בראשית.חלק כה

א ויסף.אברהם.ויקח.אשה.ושמה.קטורה׃

𐤁 𐤅𐤕𐤋𐤃.𐤋𐤅.𐤀𐤕.𐤆𐤌𐤓𐤍.𐤅𐤀𐤕.𐤉𐤒𐤔𐤍.𐤅𐤀𐤕.𐤌𐤃𐤍.𐤅𐤀
𐤕.𐤌𐤃𐤉𐤍.𐤅𐤀𐤕.𐤉𐤔𐤁𐤒.𐤅𐤀𐤕.𐤔𐤅𐤇|
𐤂 𐤅𐤉𐤒𐤔𐤍.𐤉𐤋𐤃.𐤀𐤕.𐤔𐤁𐤀.𐤅𐤀𐤕.𐤃𐤃𐤍.𐤅𐤁𐤍𐤉.𐤃𐤃𐤍
.𐤄𐤉𐤅.𐤀𐤔𐤅𐤓𐤌.𐤅𐤋𐤈𐤅𐤔𐤉𐤌.𐤅𐤋𐤀𐤌𐤉𐤌|
𐤃 𐤅𐤁𐤍𐤉.𐤌𐤃𐤉𐤍.𐤏𐤉𐤐𐤄.𐤅𐤏𐤐𐤓.𐤅𐤇𐤍𐤊.𐤅𐤀𐤁𐤉𐤃𐤏.𐤅𐤀𐤋
𐤃𐤏𐤄.𐤊𐤋.𐤀𐤋𐤄.𐤁𐤍𐤉.𐤒𐤈𐤅𐤓𐤄|
𐤄 𐤅𐤉𐤕𐤍.𐤀𐤁𐤓𐤄𐤌.𐤀𐤕.𐤊𐤋.𐤀𐤔𐤓.𐤋𐤅.𐤋𐤉𐤑𐤇𐤒|
𐤅 𐤅𐤋𐤁𐤍𐤉.𐤄𐤐𐤉𐤋𐤂𐤔𐤉𐤌.𐤀𐤔𐤓.𐤋𐤀𐤁𐤓𐤄𐤌.𐤍𐤕𐤍.𐤀𐤁𐤓
𐤄𐤌.𐤌𐤕𐤍𐤕.𐤅𐤉𐤔𐤋𐤇𐤌.𐤌𐤏𐤋.𐤉𐤑𐤇𐤒.𐤁𐤍𐤅.𐤁𐤏𐤅𐤃𐤍𐤅.𐤇
𐤉.𐤒𐤃𐤌𐤄.𐤀𐤋.𐤀𐤓𐤑.𐤒𐤃𐤌|
𐤆 𐤅𐤀𐤋𐤄.𐤉𐤌𐤉.𐤔𐤍𐤉.𐤇𐤉𐤉.𐤀𐤁𐤓𐤄𐤌.𐤀𐤔𐤓.𐤇𐤉.𐤌𐤀𐤕
.𐤔𐤍𐤄.𐤅𐤔𐤁𐤏𐤉𐤌.𐤔𐤍𐤄.𐤅𐤇𐤌𐤔.𐤔𐤍𐤉𐤌|
𐤇 𐤅𐤉𐤂𐤅𐤏.𐤅𐤉𐤌𐤕.𐤀𐤁𐤓𐤄𐤌.𐤁𐤔𐤉𐤁𐤄.𐤈𐤅𐤁𐤄.𐤆𐤒𐤍.𐤅
𐤔𐤁𐤏.𐤅𐤉𐤀𐤎𐤐.𐤀𐤋.𐤏𐤌𐤉𐤅|
𐤈 𐤅𐤉𐤒𐤁𐤓𐤅.𐤀𐤕𐤅.𐤉𐤑𐤇𐤒.𐤅𐤉𐤔𐤌𐤏𐤀𐤋.𐤁𐤍𐤉𐤅.𐤀𐤋.𐤌
𐤏𐤓𐤕.𐤄𐤌𐤊𐤐𐤋𐤄.𐤀𐤋.𐤔𐤃𐤄.𐤏𐤐𐤓𐤍.𐤁𐤍.𐤑𐤇𐤓.𐤄𐤇𐤕𐤉.
𐤀𐤔𐤓.𐤏𐤋.𐤐𐤍𐤉.𐤌𐤌𐤓𐤀|
𐤉 𐤄𐤔𐤃𐤄.𐤀𐤔𐤓.𐤒𐤍𐤄.𐤀𐤁𐤓𐤄𐤌.𐤌𐤀𐤕.𐤁𐤍𐤉.𐤇𐤕.𐤔
𐤌𐤄.𐤒𐤁𐤓.𐤀𐤁𐤓𐤄𐤌.𐤅𐤔𐤓𐤄.𐤀𐤔𐤕𐤅|
𐤉𐤀 𐤅𐤉𐤄𐤉.𐤀𐤇𐤓𐤉.𐤌𐤅𐤕.𐤀𐤁𐤓𐤄𐤌.𐤅𐤉𐤁𐤓𐤊.𐤀𐤋𐤄𐤉𐤌.𐤀
𐤕.𐤉𐤑𐤇𐤒.𐤁𐤍𐤅.𐤅𐤉𐤔𐤁.𐤉𐤑𐤇𐤒.𐤏𐤌.𐤁𐤀𐤓.𐤋𐤇𐤉.𐤓𐤀𐤉|
𐤉𐤁 𐤅𐤀𐤋𐤄.𐤕𐤋𐤃𐤕.𐤉𐤔𐤌𐤏𐤀𐤋.𐤁𐤍.𐤀𐤁𐤓𐤄𐤌.𐤀𐤔𐤓.𐤉𐤋
𐤃𐤄.𐤄𐤂𐤓.𐤄𐤌𐤑𐤓𐤉𐤕.𐤔𐤐𐤇𐤕.𐤔𐤓𐤄.𐤋𐤀𐤁𐤓𐤄𐤌|
𐤉𐤂 𐤅𐤀𐤋𐤄.𐤔𐤌𐤅𐤕.𐤁𐤍𐤉.𐤉𐤔𐤌𐤏𐤀𐤋.𐤁𐤔𐤌𐤕𐤌.𐤋𐤕𐤅𐤋𐤃
𐤕𐤌.𐤁𐤊𐤓.𐤉𐤔𐤌𐤏𐤀𐤋.𐤍𐤁𐤉𐤕.𐤅𐤒𐤃𐤓.𐤅𐤀𐤃𐤁𐤀𐤋.𐤅𐤌𐤁𐤔
𐤌|
𐤉𐤃 𐤅𐤌𐤔𐤌𐤏.𐤅𐤃𐤅𐤌𐤄.𐤅𐤌𐤔𐤀|
𐤈𐤅 𐤇𐤃𐤃.𐤅𐤕𐤉𐤌𐤀.𐤉𐤈𐤅𐤓.𐤍𐤐𐤉𐤔.𐤅𐤒𐤃𐤌𐤄|
𐤈𐤆 𐤀𐤋𐤄.𐤄𐤌.𐤁𐤍𐤉.𐤉𐤔𐤌𐤏𐤀𐤋.𐤅𐤀𐤋𐤄.𐤔𐤌𐤕𐤌.𐤁𐤇𐤑𐤓
𐤉𐤄𐤌.𐤅𐤁𐤈𐤉𐤓𐤕𐤌.𐤔𐤍𐤉𐤌.𐤏𐤔𐤓.𐤍𐤔𐤉𐤀𐤌.𐤋𐤀𐤌𐤕𐤌|

יז 𐤅𐤀𐤋𐤄.𐤔𐤍𐤉.𐤇𐤉𐤉.𐤉𐤔𐤌𐤏𐤀𐤋.𐤌𐤀𐤕.𐤔𐤍𐤄.𐤅𐤔𐤋𐤔
𐤉𐤌.𐤔𐤍𐤄.𐤅𐤔𐤁𐤏.𐤔𐤍𐤉𐤌.𐤅𐤉𐤂𐤅𐤏.𐤅𐤉𐤌𐤕.𐤅𐤉𐤀𐤎𐤐.𐤀𐤋.𐤏
𐤌𐤉𐤅|
יח 𐤅𐤉𐤔𐤊𐤍𐤅.𐤌𐤇𐤅𐤉𐤋𐤄.𐤏𐤃.𐤔𐤅𐤓.𐤀𐤔𐤓.𐤏𐤋.𐤐𐤍𐤉.𐤌𐤑
𐤓𐤉𐤌.𐤁𐤀𐤊𐤄.𐤀𐤔𐤅𐤓𐤄.𐤏𐤋.𐤐𐤍𐤉.𐤊𐤋.𐤀𐤇𐤉𐤅.𐤍𐤐𐤋|
יט 𐤅𐤀𐤋𐤄.𐤕𐤅𐤋𐤃𐤕.𐤉𐤑𐤇𐤒.𐤁𐤍.𐤀𐤁𐤓𐤄𐤌.𐤀𐤁𐤓𐤄𐤌.
𐤄𐤅𐤋𐤉𐤃.𐤀𐤕.𐤉𐤑𐤇𐤒|
כ 𐤅𐤉𐤄𐤉.𐤉𐤑𐤇𐤒.𐤁𐤍.𐤀𐤓𐤁𐤏𐤉𐤌.𐤔𐤍𐤄.𐤁𐤒𐤇𐤕𐤅.𐤀
𐤕.𐤓𐤁𐤒𐤄.𐤁𐤕.𐤁𐤕𐤅𐤀𐤋.𐤄𐤀𐤓𐤌𐤉.𐤌𐤐𐤃𐤍.𐤀𐤓𐤌.𐤀𐤇𐤅𐤕.
𐤋𐤁𐤍.𐤄𐤀𐤓𐤌𐤉.𐤋𐤅.𐤋𐤀𐤔𐤄|
כא 𐤅𐤉𐤏𐤕𐤓.𐤉𐤑𐤇𐤒.𐤋𐤉𐤄𐤅𐤄.𐤋𐤍𐤊𐤇.𐤀𐤔𐤕𐤅.𐤊𐤉.𐤏𐤒
𐤓𐤄.𐤄𐤅𐤀.𐤅𐤉𐤏𐤕𐤓.𐤋𐤅.𐤉𐤄𐤅𐤄.𐤅𐤕𐤄𐤓.𐤓𐤁𐤒𐤄.𐤀𐤔𐤕𐤅|
כב 𐤅𐤉𐤕𐤓𐤑𐤑𐤅.𐤄𐤁𐤍𐤉𐤌.𐤁𐤒𐤓𐤁𐤄.𐤅𐤕𐤀𐤌𐤓.𐤀𐤌.𐤊𐤍.𐤋
𐤌𐤄.𐤆𐤄.𐤀𐤍𐤊𐤉.𐤅𐤕𐤋𐤊.𐤋𐤃𐤓𐤔.𐤀𐤕.𐤉𐤄𐤅𐤄|
כג 𐤅𐤉𐤀𐤌𐤓.𐤉𐤄𐤅𐤄.𐤋𐤄.𐤔𐤍𐤉.𐤂𐤉𐤉𐤌.‖𐤂𐤅𐤉𐤌.𐤒𐤓𐤉‖.
𐤁𐤁𐤈𐤍𐤊.𐤅𐤔𐤍𐤉.𐤋𐤀𐤌𐤉𐤌.𐤌𐤌𐤏𐤉𐤊.𐤉𐤐𐤓𐤃𐤅.𐤅𐤋𐤀𐤌.𐤌𐤋𐤀
𐤌.𐤉𐤀𐤌𐤑.𐤅𐤓𐤁.𐤉𐤏𐤁𐤃.𐤑𐤏𐤉𐤓|
כד 𐤅𐤉𐤌𐤋𐤀𐤅.𐤉𐤌𐤉𐤄.𐤋𐤋𐤃𐤕.𐤅𐤄𐤍𐤄.𐤕𐤅𐤌𐤌.𐤁𐤁𐤈𐤍𐤄|
כה 𐤅𐤉𐤑𐤀.𐤄𐤓𐤀𐤔𐤅𐤍.𐤀𐤃𐤌𐤅𐤍𐤉.𐤊𐤋𐤅.𐤊𐤀𐤃𐤓𐤕.𐤔𐤏𐤓.
𐤅𐤉𐤒𐤓𐤀𐤅.𐤔𐤌𐤅.𐤏𐤔𐤅|
כו 𐤅𐤀𐤇𐤓𐤉.𐤊𐤍.𐤉𐤑𐤀.𐤀𐤇𐤉𐤅.𐤅𐤉𐤃𐤅.𐤀𐤇𐤆𐤕.𐤁𐤏𐤒
𐤁.𐤏𐤔𐤅.𐤅𐤉𐤒𐤓𐤀.𐤔𐤌𐤅.𐤉𐤏𐤒𐤁.𐤅𐤉𐤑𐤇𐤒.𐤁𐤍.𐤔𐤔𐤉𐤌.𐤔
𐤍𐤄.𐤁𐤋𐤃𐤕.𐤀𐤕𐤌|
כז 𐤅𐤉𐤂𐤃𐤋𐤅.𐤄𐤍𐤏𐤓𐤉𐤌.𐤅𐤉𐤄𐤉.𐤏𐤔𐤅.𐤀𐤉𐤔.𐤉𐤃𐤏.
𐤑𐤉𐤃.𐤀𐤉𐤔.𐤔𐤃𐤄.𐤅𐤉𐤏𐤒𐤁.𐤀𐤉𐤔.𐤕𐤌.𐤉𐤔𐤁.𐤀𐤄𐤋𐤉
𐤌|
כח 𐤅𐤉𐤀𐤄𐤁.𐤉𐤑𐤇𐤒.𐤀𐤕.𐤏𐤔𐤅.𐤊𐤉.𐤑𐤉𐤃.𐤁𐤐𐤉𐤅.𐤅𐤓𐤁
𐤒𐤄.𐤀𐤄𐤁𐤕.𐤀𐤕.𐤉𐤏𐤒𐤁|
כט 𐤅𐤉𐤆𐤃.𐤉𐤏𐤒𐤁.𐤍𐤆𐤉𐤃.𐤅𐤉𐤁𐤀.𐤏𐤔𐤅.𐤌𐤍.𐤄𐤔𐤃
𐤄.𐤅𐤄𐤅𐤀.𐤏𐤉𐤐|

..ל..ויאמר.עשו.אל.יעקב.הלעיטני.נא.מן.ה
אדם.האדם.הזה.כי.עיף.אנכי.על.כן.קרא.
שמו.אדום׃
..לא..ויאמר.יעקב.מכרה.כיום.את.בכרתך.לי׃
..לב..ויאמר.עשו.הנה.אנכי.הולך.למות.ולמה.
זה.לי.בכרה׃
..לג..ויאמר.יעקב.השבעה.לי.כיום.וישבע.לו
.וימכר.את.בכרתו.ליעקב׃
..לד..ויעקב.נתן.לעשו.לחם.ונזיד.עדשים.ו
יאכל.וישת.ויקם.וילך.ויבז.עשו.את.הבכרה׃
׃

בראשית.חלק..כו..

..א..ויהי.רעב.בארץ.מלבד.הרעב.הראשון.אש
ר.היה.בימי.אברהם.וילך.יצחק.אל.אבימלך
.מלך.פלשתים.גררה׃
..ב..וירא.אליו.יהוה.ויאמר.אל.תרד.מצרימה.
שכן.בארץ.אשר.אמר.אליך׃
..ג..גור.בארץ.הזאת.ואהיה.עמך.ואברכך.כ
י.לך.ולזרעך.אתן.את.כל.הארצת.האל.והקמ
תי.את.השבעה.אשר.נשבעתי.לאברהם.אביך׃
..ד..והרביתי.את.זרעך.ככוכבי.השמים.ונת
תי.לזרעך.את.כל.הארצת.האל.והתברכו.בז
רעך.כל.גויי.הארץ׃
..ה..עקב.אשר.שמע.אברהם.בקלי.וישמר.משמ
רתי.מצותי.חקותי.ותורתי׃
..ו..וישב.יצחק.בגרר׃
..ז..וישאלו.אנשי.המקום.לאשתו.ויאמר.אחת
י.היא.כי.ירא.לאמר.אשתי.פן.יהרגני.אנשי.
המקום.על.רבקה.כי.טובת.מראה.היא׃

ח 𐤅𐤉𐤄𐤉.𐤊𐤉.𐤀𐤓𐤊𐤅.𐤋𐤅.𐤔𐤌.𐤄𐤉𐤌𐤉𐤌.𐤅𐤉𐤔𐤒𐤐.𐤀𐤁𐤉𐤌
𐤋𐤊.𐤌𐤋𐤊.𐤐𐤋𐤔𐤕𐤉𐤌.𐤁𐤏𐤃.𐤄𐤇𐤋𐤅𐤍.𐤅𐤉𐤓𐤀.𐤅𐤄𐤍𐤄.𐤉𐤑
𐤇𐤒.𐤌𐤑𐤇𐤒.𐤀𐤕.𐤓𐤁𐤒𐤄.𐤀𐤔𐤕𐤅|
ט 𐤅𐤉𐤒𐤓𐤀.𐤀𐤁𐤉𐤌𐤋𐤊.𐤋𐤉𐤑𐤇𐤒.𐤅𐤉𐤀𐤌𐤓.𐤀𐤊.𐤄𐤍𐤄.
𐤀𐤔𐤕𐤊.𐤄𐤅𐤀.𐤅𐤀𐤉𐤊.𐤀𐤌𐤓𐤕.𐤀𐤇𐤕𐤉.𐤄𐤅𐤀.𐤅𐤉𐤀𐤌𐤓.𐤀𐤋
𐤉𐤅.𐤉𐤑𐤇𐤒.𐤊𐤉.𐤀𐤌𐤓𐤕𐤉.𐤐𐤍.𐤀𐤌𐤅𐤕.𐤏𐤋𐤉𐤄|
י 𐤅𐤉𐤀𐤌𐤓.𐤀𐤁𐤉𐤌𐤋𐤊.𐤌𐤄.𐤆𐤀𐤕.𐤏𐤔𐤉𐤕.𐤋𐤍𐤅.𐤊𐤌𐤏
𐤈.𐤔𐤊𐤁.𐤀𐤇𐤃.𐤄𐤏𐤌.𐤀𐤕.𐤀𐤔𐤕𐤊.𐤅𐤄𐤁𐤀𐤕.𐤏𐤋𐤉𐤍𐤅.𐤀
𐤔𐤌|
יא 𐤅𐤉𐤑𐤅.𐤀𐤁𐤉𐤌𐤋𐤊.𐤀𐤕.𐤊𐤋.𐤄𐤏𐤌.𐤋𐤀𐤌𐤓.𐤄𐤍𐤂𐤏.𐤁
𐤀𐤉𐤔.𐤄𐤆𐤄.𐤅𐤁𐤀𐤔𐤕𐤅.𐤌𐤅𐤕.𐤉𐤅𐤌𐤕|
יב 𐤅𐤉𐤆𐤓𐤏.𐤉𐤑𐤇𐤒.𐤁𐤀𐤓𐤑.𐤄𐤄𐤅𐤀.𐤅𐤉𐤌𐤑𐤀.𐤁𐤔𐤍
𐤄.𐤄𐤄𐤅𐤀.𐤌𐤀𐤄.𐤔𐤏𐤓𐤉𐤌.𐤅𐤉𐤁𐤓𐤊𐤄𐤅.𐤉𐤄𐤅𐤄|
יג 𐤅𐤉𐤂𐤃𐤋.𐤄𐤀𐤉𐤔.𐤅𐤉𐤋𐤊.𐤄𐤋𐤅𐤊.𐤅𐤂𐤃𐤋.𐤏𐤃.𐤊𐤉.
𐤂𐤃𐤋.𐤌𐤀𐤃|
יד 𐤅𐤉𐤄𐤉.𐤋𐤅.𐤌𐤒𐤍𐤄.𐤑𐤀𐤍.𐤅𐤌𐤒𐤍𐤄.𐤁𐤒𐤓.𐤅𐤏𐤁𐤃𐤄.
𐤓𐤁𐤄.𐤅𐤉𐤒𐤍𐤀𐤅.𐤀𐤕𐤅.𐤐𐤋𐤔𐤕𐤉𐤌|
טו 𐤅𐤊𐤋.𐤄𐤁𐤀𐤓𐤕.𐤀𐤔𐤓.𐤇𐤐𐤓𐤅.𐤏𐤁𐤃𐤉.𐤀𐤁𐤉𐤅.𐤁𐤉𐤌𐤉.
𐤀𐤁𐤓𐤄𐤌.𐤀𐤁𐤉𐤅.𐤎𐤕𐤌𐤅𐤌.𐤐𐤋𐤔𐤕𐤉𐤌.𐤅𐤉𐤌𐤋𐤀𐤅𐤌.𐤏𐤐𐤓|
טז 𐤅𐤉𐤀𐤌𐤓.𐤀𐤁𐤉𐤌𐤋𐤊.𐤀𐤋.𐤉𐤑𐤇𐤒.𐤋𐤊.𐤌𐤏𐤌𐤍𐤅.𐤊𐤉.
𐤏𐤑𐤌𐤕.𐤌𐤌𐤍𐤅.𐤌𐤀𐤃|
יז 𐤅𐤉𐤋𐤊.𐤌𐤔𐤌.𐤉𐤑𐤇𐤒.𐤅𐤉𐤇𐤍.𐤁𐤍𐤇𐤋.𐤂𐤓𐤓.𐤅𐤉𐤔𐤁.
𐤔𐤌|
יח 𐤅𐤉𐤔𐤁.𐤉𐤑𐤇𐤒.𐤅𐤉𐤇𐤐𐤓.𐤀𐤕.𐤁𐤀𐤓𐤕.𐤄𐤌𐤉𐤌.𐤀𐤔
𐤓.𐤇𐤐𐤓𐤅.𐤁𐤉𐤌𐤉.𐤀𐤁𐤓𐤄𐤌.𐤀𐤁𐤉𐤅.𐤅𐤉𐤎𐤕𐤌𐤅𐤌.𐤐𐤋𐤔𐤕𐤉𐤌.
𐤀𐤇𐤓𐤉.𐤌𐤅𐤕.𐤀𐤁𐤓𐤄𐤌.𐤅𐤉𐤒𐤓𐤀.𐤋𐤄𐤍.𐤔𐤌𐤅𐤕.𐤊𐤔𐤌𐤕.𐤀
𐤔𐤓.𐤒𐤓𐤀.𐤋𐤄𐤍.𐤀𐤁𐤉𐤅|
יט 𐤅𐤉𐤇𐤐𐤓𐤅.𐤏𐤁𐤃𐤉.𐤉𐤑𐤇𐤒.𐤁𐤍𐤇𐤋.𐤅𐤉𐤌𐤑𐤀𐤅.𐤔𐤌
.𐤁𐤀𐤓.𐤌𐤉𐤌.𐤇𐤉𐤉𐤌|

..כ.. 𐤅𐤉𐤓𐤉𐤁𐤅.𐤓𐤏𐤉.𐤂𐤓𐤓.𐤏𐤌.𐤓𐤏𐤉.𐤉𐤑𐤇𐤒.𐤋𐤀𐤌𐤓.𐤋
𐤍𐤅.𐤄𐤌𐤉𐤌.𐤅𐤉𐤒𐤓𐤀.𐤔𐤌.𐤄𐤁𐤀𐤓.𐤏𐤔𐤒.𐤊𐤉.𐤄𐤕𐤏𐤔𐤒𐤅.
𐤏𐤌𐤅|

..כא.. 𐤅𐤉𐤇𐤐𐤓𐤅.𐤁𐤀𐤓.𐤀𐤇𐤓𐤕.𐤅𐤉𐤓𐤉𐤁𐤅.𐤂𐤌.𐤏𐤋𐤉𐤄.𐤅𐤉𐤒
𐤓𐤀.𐤔𐤌𐤄.𐤔𐤈𐤍𐤄|

..כב.. 𐤅𐤉𐤏𐤕𐤒.𐤌𐤔𐤌.𐤅𐤉𐤇𐤐𐤓.𐤁𐤀𐤓.𐤀𐤇𐤓𐤕.𐤅𐤋𐤀.𐤓𐤁𐤅.
𐤏𐤋𐤉𐤄.𐤅𐤉𐤒𐤓𐤀.𐤔𐤌𐤄.𐤓𐤇𐤁𐤅𐤕.𐤅𐤉𐤀𐤌𐤓.𐤊𐤉.𐤏𐤕𐤄.𐤄𐤓
𐤇𐤉𐤁.𐤉𐤄𐤅𐤄.𐤋𐤍𐤅.𐤅𐤐𐤓𐤉𐤍𐤅.𐤁𐤀𐤓𐤑|

..כג.. 𐤅𐤉𐤏𐤋.𐤌𐤔𐤌.𐤁𐤀𐤓.𐤔𐤁𐤏|

..כד.. 𐤅𐤉𐤓𐤀.𐤀𐤋𐤉𐤅.𐤉𐤄𐤅𐤄.𐤁𐤋𐤉𐤋𐤄.𐤄𐤄𐤅𐤀.𐤅𐤉𐤀𐤌𐤓.𐤀𐤍
𐤊𐤉.𐤀𐤋𐤄𐤉.𐤀𐤁𐤓𐤄𐤌.𐤀𐤁𐤉𐤊.𐤀𐤋.𐤕𐤉𐤓𐤀.𐤊𐤉.𐤀𐤕𐤊.𐤀𐤍
𐤊𐤉.𐤅𐤁𐤓𐤊𐤕𐤉𐤊.𐤅𐤄𐤓𐤁𐤉𐤕𐤉.𐤀𐤕.𐤆𐤓𐤏𐤊.𐤁𐤏𐤁𐤅𐤓.𐤀𐤁𐤓
𐤄𐤌.𐤏𐤁𐤃𐤉|

..כה.. 𐤅𐤉𐤁𐤍.𐤔𐤌.𐤌𐤆𐤁𐤇.𐤅𐤉𐤒𐤓𐤀.𐤁𐤔𐤌.𐤉𐤄𐤅𐤄.𐤅𐤉𐤈.𐤔
𐤌.𐤀𐤄𐤋𐤅.𐤅𐤉𐤊𐤓𐤅.𐤔𐤌.𐤏𐤁𐤃𐤉.𐤉𐤑𐤇𐤒.𐤁𐤀𐤓|

..כו.. 𐤅𐤀𐤁𐤉𐤌𐤋𐤊.𐤄𐤋𐤊.𐤀𐤋𐤉𐤅.𐤌𐤂𐤓𐤓.𐤅𐤀𐤇𐤆𐤕.𐤌𐤓𐤏𐤄
𐤅.𐤅𐤐𐤉𐤊𐤋.𐤔𐤓.𐤑𐤁𐤀𐤅|

..כז.. 𐤅𐤉𐤀𐤌𐤓.𐤀𐤋𐤄𐤌.𐤉𐤑𐤇𐤒.𐤌𐤃𐤅𐤏.𐤁𐤀𐤕𐤌.𐤀𐤋𐤉.𐤅
𐤀𐤕𐤌.𐤔𐤍𐤀𐤕𐤌.𐤀𐤕𐤉.𐤅𐤕𐤔𐤋𐤇𐤅𐤍𐤉.𐤌𐤀𐤕𐤊𐤌|

..כח.. 𐤅𐤉𐤀𐤌𐤓𐤅.𐤓𐤀𐤅.𐤓𐤀𐤉𐤍𐤅.𐤊𐤉.𐤄𐤉𐤄.𐤉𐤄𐤅𐤄.𐤏𐤌𐤊.𐤅𐤍
𐤀𐤌𐤓.𐤕𐤄𐤉.𐤍𐤀.𐤀𐤋𐤄.𐤁𐤉𐤍𐤅𐤕𐤉𐤍𐤅.𐤁𐤉𐤍𐤉𐤍𐤅.𐤅𐤁𐤉𐤍𐤊.𐤅𐤍𐤊
𐤓𐤕𐤄.𐤁𐤓𐤉𐤕.𐤏𐤌𐤊|

..כט.. 𐤀𐤌.𐤕𐤏𐤔𐤄.𐤏𐤌𐤍𐤅.𐤓𐤏𐤄.𐤊𐤀𐤔𐤓.𐤋𐤀.𐤍𐤂𐤏𐤍𐤅𐤊.𐤅
𐤊𐤀𐤔𐤓.𐤏𐤔𐤉𐤍𐤅.𐤏𐤌𐤊.𐤓𐤒.𐤈𐤅𐤁.𐤅𐤍𐤔𐤋𐤇𐤊.𐤁𐤔𐤋𐤅𐤌.𐤀𐤕
𐤄.𐤏𐤕𐤄.𐤁𐤓𐤅𐤊.𐤉𐤄𐤅𐤄|

..ל.. 𐤅𐤉𐤏𐤔.𐤋𐤄𐤌.𐤌𐤔𐤕𐤄.𐤅𐤉𐤀𐤊𐤋𐤅.𐤅𐤉𐤔𐤕𐤅|

..לא.. 𐤅𐤉𐤔𐤊𐤉𐤌𐤅.𐤁𐤁𐤒𐤓.𐤅𐤉𐤔𐤁𐤏𐤅.𐤀𐤉𐤔.𐤋𐤀𐤇𐤉𐤅.𐤅𐤉𐤔
𐤋𐤇𐤌.𐤉𐤑𐤇𐤒.𐤅𐤉𐤋𐤊𐤅.𐤌𐤀𐤕𐤅.𐤁𐤔𐤋𐤅𐤌|

..לב.. 𐤅𐤉𐤄𐤉.𐤁𐤉𐤅𐤌.𐤄𐤄𐤅𐤀.𐤅𐤉𐤁𐤀𐤅.𐤏𐤁𐤃𐤉.𐤉𐤑𐤇𐤒.𐤅𐤉
𐤂𐤃𐤅.𐤋𐤅.𐤏𐤋.𐤀𐤃𐤅𐤕.𐤄𐤁𐤀𐤓.𐤀𐤔𐤓.𐤇𐤐𐤓𐤅.𐤅𐤉𐤀𐤌𐤓𐤅.𐤋𐤅.
𐤌𐤑𐤀𐤍𐤅.𐤌𐤉𐤌|

לג ויקרא.אתה.שבעה.על.כן.שם.העיר.באר.
שבע.עד.היום.הזה|
לד ויהי.עשו.בן.ארבעים.שנה.ויקח.אשה.
את.יהודית.בת.בארי.החתי.ואת.בשמת.בת.
אילן.החתי|
לה ותהיין.מרת.רוח.ליצחק.ולרבקה||

בראשית.חלק כז

א ויהי.כי.זקן.יצחק.ותכהין.עיניו.מרא
ת.ויקרא.את.עשו.בנו.הגדל.ויאמר.אליו.בני.
ויאמר.אליו.הנני|
ב ויאמר.הנה.נא.זקנתי.לא.ידעתי.יום.מו
תי|
ג ועתה.שא.נא.כליך.תליך.וקשתך.וצא.הש
דה.וצודה.לי.צידה||.ציד.קרי|||
ד ועשה.לי.מטעמים.כאשר.אהבתי.והביא
ה.לי.ואכלה.בעבור.תברכך.נפשי.בטרם.אמות|
ה ורבקה.שמעת.בדבר.יצחק.אל.עשו.בנו.וי
לך.עשו.השדה.לצוד.ציד.להביא|
ו ורבקה.אמרה.אל.יעקב.בנה.לאמר.הנה.שמ
עתי.את.אביך.מדבר.אל.עשו.אחיך.לאמר|
ז הביאה.לי.ציד.ועשה.לי.מטעמים.ואכל
ה.ואברככה.לפני.יהוה.לפני.מותי|
ח ועתה.בני.שמע.בקלי.לאשר.אני.מצוה.א
תך|
ט לך.נא.אל.הצאן.וקח.לי.משם.שני.גדיי.
עזים.טבים.ואעשה.אתם.מטעמים.לאביך.
כאשר.אהב|
י והבאת.לאביך.ואכל.בעבר.אשר.יברכך.ל
פני.מותו|

11 𐤅𐤉𐤀𐤌𐤓.𐤉𐤏𐤒𐤁.𐤀𐤋.𐤓𐤁𐤒𐤄.𐤀𐤌𐤅.𐤄𐤍.𐤏𐤔𐤅.𐤀𐤇𐤉.
𐤀𐤉𐤔.𐤔𐤏𐤓.𐤅𐤀𐤍𐤊𐤉.𐤀𐤉𐤔.𐤇𐤋𐤒|
12 𐤀𐤅𐤋𐤉.𐤉𐤌𐤔𐤍𐤉.𐤀𐤁𐤉.𐤅𐤄𐤉𐤉𐤕𐤉.𐤁𐤏𐤉𐤍𐤉𐤅.𐤊𐤌𐤕𐤏
𐤕𐤏.𐤅𐤄𐤁𐤀𐤕𐤉.𐤏𐤋𐤉.𐤒𐤋𐤋𐤄.𐤅𐤋𐤀.𐤁𐤓𐤊𐤄|
13 𐤅𐤕𐤀𐤌𐤓.𐤋𐤅.𐤀𐤌𐤅.𐤏𐤋𐤉.𐤒𐤋𐤋𐤕𐤊.𐤁𐤍𐤉.𐤀𐤊.𐤔𐤌𐤏.
𐤁𐤒𐤋𐤉.𐤅𐤋𐤊.𐤒𐤇.𐤋𐤉|
14 𐤅𐤉𐤋𐤊.𐤅𐤉𐤒𐤇.𐤅𐤉𐤁𐤀.𐤋𐤀𐤌𐤅.𐤅𐤕𐤏𐤔.𐤀𐤌𐤅.𐤌𐤈𐤏𐤌
𐤉𐤌.𐤊𐤀𐤔𐤓.𐤀𐤄𐤁.𐤀𐤁𐤉𐤅|
15 𐤅𐤕𐤒𐤇.𐤓𐤁𐤒𐤄.𐤀𐤕.𐤁𐤂𐤃𐤉.𐤏𐤔𐤅.𐤁𐤍𐤄.𐤄𐤂𐤃𐤋.
𐤄𐤇𐤌𐤃𐤕.𐤀𐤔𐤓.𐤀𐤕𐤄.𐤁𐤁𐤉𐤕.𐤅𐤕𐤋𐤁𐤔.𐤀𐤕.𐤉𐤏𐤒𐤁.𐤁
𐤍𐤄.𐤄𐤒𐤈𐤍|
16 𐤅𐤀𐤕.𐤏𐤓𐤕.𐤂𐤃𐤉𐤉.𐤄𐤏𐤆𐤉𐤌.𐤄𐤋𐤁𐤉𐤔𐤄.𐤏𐤋.𐤉
𐤃𐤉𐤅.𐤅𐤏𐤋.𐤇𐤋𐤒𐤕.𐤑𐤅𐤀𐤓𐤉𐤅|
17 𐤅𐤕𐤕𐤍.𐤀𐤕.𐤄𐤌𐤈𐤏𐤌𐤉𐤌.𐤅𐤀𐤕.𐤄𐤋𐤇𐤌.𐤀𐤔𐤓.𐤏𐤔
𐤕𐤄.𐤁𐤉𐤃.𐤉𐤏𐤒𐤁.𐤁𐤍𐤄|
18 𐤅𐤉𐤁𐤀.𐤀𐤋.𐤀𐤁𐤉𐤅.𐤅𐤉𐤀𐤌𐤓.𐤀𐤁𐤉.𐤅𐤉𐤀𐤌𐤓.𐤄𐤍𐤍𐤉.𐤌
𐤉.𐤀𐤕𐤄.𐤁𐤍𐤉|
19 𐤅𐤉𐤀𐤌𐤓.𐤉𐤏𐤒𐤁.𐤀𐤋.𐤀𐤁𐤉𐤅.𐤀𐤍𐤊𐤉.𐤏𐤔𐤅.𐤁𐤊𐤓𐤊.
𐤏𐤔𐤉𐤕𐤉.𐤊𐤀𐤔𐤓.𐤃𐤁𐤓𐤕.𐤀𐤋𐤉.𐤒𐤅𐤌.𐤍𐤀.𐤔𐤁𐤄.𐤅𐤀𐤊𐤋
𐤄.𐤌𐤑𐤉𐤃𐤉.𐤁𐤏𐤁𐤅𐤓.𐤕𐤁𐤓𐤊𐤍𐤉.𐤍𐤐𐤔𐤊|
20 𐤅𐤉𐤀𐤌𐤓.𐤉𐤑𐤇𐤒.𐤀𐤋.𐤁𐤍𐤅.𐤌𐤄.𐤆𐤄.𐤌𐤄𐤓𐤕.𐤋𐤌𐤑
𐤀.𐤁𐤍𐤉.𐤅𐤉𐤀𐤌𐤓.𐤊𐤉.𐤄𐤒𐤓𐤄.𐤉𐤄𐤅𐤄.𐤀𐤋𐤄𐤉𐤊.𐤋𐤐𐤍𐤉|
21 𐤅𐤉𐤀𐤌𐤓.𐤉𐤑𐤇𐤒.𐤀𐤋.𐤉𐤏𐤒𐤁.𐤂𐤔𐤄.𐤍𐤀.𐤅𐤀𐤌𐤔𐤊.
𐤁𐤍𐤉.𐤄𐤀𐤕𐤄.𐤆𐤄.𐤁𐤍𐤉.𐤏𐤔𐤅.𐤀𐤌.𐤋𐤀|
22 𐤅𐤉𐤂𐤔.𐤉𐤏𐤒𐤁.𐤀𐤋.𐤉𐤑𐤇𐤒.𐤀𐤁𐤉𐤅.𐤅𐤉𐤌𐤔𐤄𐤅.𐤅𐤉
𐤀𐤌𐤓.𐤄𐤒𐤋.𐤒𐤅𐤋.𐤉𐤏𐤒𐤁.𐤅𐤄𐤉𐤃𐤉𐤌.𐤉𐤃𐤉.𐤏𐤔𐤅|
23 𐤅𐤋𐤀.𐤄𐤊𐤉𐤓𐤅.𐤊𐤉.𐤄𐤉𐤅.𐤉𐤃𐤉𐤅.𐤊𐤉𐤃𐤉.𐤏𐤔𐤅.𐤀𐤇
𐤉𐤅.𐤔𐤏𐤓𐤕.𐤅𐤉𐤁𐤓𐤊𐤄𐤅|
24 𐤅𐤉𐤀𐤌𐤓.𐤀𐤕𐤄.𐤆𐤄.𐤁𐤍𐤉.𐤏𐤔𐤅.𐤅𐤉𐤀𐤌𐤓.𐤀𐤍𐤉|

כה 𐤅𐤉𐤀𐤌𐤓.𐤄𐤂𐤔𐤄.𐤋𐤉.𐤅𐤀𐤊𐤋𐤄.𐤌𐤑𐤉𐤃.𐤁𐤍𐤉.𐤋𐤌𐤏
𐤍.𐤕𐤁𐤓𐤊𐤊.𐤍𐤐𐤔𐤉.𐤅𐤉𐤂𐤔.𐤋𐤅.𐤅𐤉𐤀𐤊𐤋.𐤅𐤉𐤁𐤀.𐤋𐤅.𐤉𐤉𐤍.𐤅𐤉
𐤔𐤕|

כו 𐤅𐤉𐤀𐤌𐤓.𐤀𐤋𐤉𐤅.𐤉𐤑𐤇𐤒.𐤀𐤁𐤉𐤅.𐤂𐤔𐤄.𐤍𐤀.𐤅𐤔𐤒𐤄.
𐤋𐤉.𐤁𐤍𐤉|

כז 𐤅𐤉𐤂𐤔.𐤅𐤉𐤔𐤒.𐤋𐤅.𐤅𐤉𐤓𐤇.𐤀𐤕.𐤓𐤉𐤇.𐤁𐤂𐤃𐤉𐤅.𐤅𐤉
𐤁𐤓𐤊𐤄𐤅.𐤅𐤉𐤀𐤌𐤓.𐤓𐤀𐤄.𐤓𐤉𐤇.𐤁𐤍𐤉.𐤊𐤓𐤉𐤇.𐤔𐤃𐤄.𐤀𐤔𐤓.
𐤁𐤓𐤊𐤅.𐤉𐤄𐤅𐤄|

כח 𐤅𐤉𐤕𐤍.𐤋𐤊.𐤄𐤀𐤋𐤄𐤉𐤌.𐤌𐤈𐤋.𐤄𐤔𐤌𐤉𐤌.𐤅𐤌𐤔𐤌𐤍𐤉.𐤄
𐤀𐤓𐤑.𐤅𐤓𐤁.𐤃𐤂𐤍.𐤅𐤕𐤉𐤓𐤔|

כט 𐤉𐤏𐤁𐤃𐤅𐤊.𐤏𐤌𐤉𐤌.𐤅𐤉𐤔𐤕𐤇𐤅.‖𐤅𐤉𐤔𐤕𐤇𐤅𐤅.𐤒𐤓𐤉‖.
𐤋𐤊.𐤋𐤀𐤌𐤉𐤌.𐤄𐤅𐤄.𐤂𐤁𐤉𐤓.𐤋𐤀𐤇𐤉𐤊.𐤅𐤉𐤔𐤕𐤇𐤅𐤅.𐤋𐤊.𐤁𐤍
𐤉.𐤀𐤌𐤊.𐤀𐤓𐤓𐤉𐤊.𐤀𐤓𐤅𐤓.𐤅𐤌𐤁𐤓𐤊𐤉𐤊.𐤁𐤓𐤅𐤊|

ל 𐤅𐤉𐤄𐤉.𐤊𐤀𐤔𐤓.𐤊𐤋𐤄.𐤉𐤑𐤇𐤒.𐤋𐤁𐤓𐤊.𐤀𐤕.𐤉𐤏𐤒𐤁
.𐤅𐤉𐤄𐤉.𐤀𐤊.𐤉𐤑𐤀.𐤉𐤑𐤀.𐤉𐤏𐤒𐤁.𐤌𐤀𐤕.𐤐𐤍𐤉.𐤉𐤑𐤇𐤒.
𐤀𐤁𐤉𐤅.𐤅𐤏𐤔𐤅.𐤀𐤇𐤉𐤅.𐤁𐤀.𐤌𐤑𐤉𐤃𐤅|

לא 𐤅𐤉𐤏𐤔.𐤂𐤌.𐤄𐤅𐤀.𐤌𐤈𐤏𐤌𐤉𐤌.𐤅𐤉𐤁𐤀.𐤋𐤀𐤁𐤉𐤅.𐤅𐤉𐤀
𐤌𐤓.𐤋𐤀𐤁𐤉𐤅.𐤉𐤒𐤌.𐤀𐤁𐤉.𐤅𐤉𐤀𐤊𐤋.𐤌𐤑𐤉𐤃.𐤁𐤍𐤅.𐤁𐤏𐤁𐤅𐤓.
𐤕𐤁𐤓𐤊𐤍𐤉.𐤍𐤐𐤔𐤊|

לב 𐤅𐤉𐤀𐤌𐤓.𐤋𐤅.𐤉𐤑𐤇𐤒.𐤀𐤁𐤉𐤅.𐤌𐤉.𐤀𐤕𐤄.𐤅𐤉𐤀𐤌𐤓.𐤀
𐤍𐤉.𐤁𐤍𐤊.𐤁𐤊𐤓𐤊.𐤏𐤔𐤅|

לג 𐤅𐤉𐤇𐤓𐤃.𐤉𐤑𐤇𐤒.𐤇𐤓𐤃𐤄.𐤂𐤃𐤋𐤄.𐤏𐤃.𐤌𐤀𐤃.
𐤅𐤉𐤀𐤌𐤓.𐤌𐤉.𐤀𐤐𐤅𐤀.𐤄𐤅𐤀.𐤄𐤑𐤃.𐤑𐤉𐤃.𐤅𐤉𐤁𐤀.𐤋𐤉.𐤅𐤀𐤊
𐤋.𐤌𐤊𐤋.𐤁𐤈𐤓𐤌.𐤕𐤁𐤅𐤀.𐤅𐤀𐤁𐤓𐤊𐤄𐤅.𐤂𐤌.𐤁𐤓𐤅𐤊.𐤉𐤄𐤉𐤄|

לד 𐤊𐤔𐤌𐤏.𐤏𐤔𐤅.𐤀𐤕.𐤃𐤁𐤓𐤉.𐤀𐤁𐤉𐤅.𐤅𐤉𐤑𐤏𐤒.𐤑𐤏
𐤒𐤄.𐤂𐤃𐤋𐤄.𐤅𐤌𐤓𐤄.𐤏𐤃.𐤌𐤀𐤃.𐤅𐤉𐤀𐤌𐤓.𐤋𐤀𐤁𐤉𐤅.𐤁𐤓𐤊𐤍
𐤉.𐤂𐤌.𐤀𐤍𐤉.𐤀𐤁𐤉|

לה 𐤅𐤉𐤀𐤌𐤓.𐤁𐤀.𐤀𐤇𐤉𐤊.𐤁𐤌𐤓𐤌𐤄.𐤅𐤉𐤒𐤇.𐤁𐤓𐤊𐤕𐤊|

לו 𐤅𐤉𐤀𐤌𐤓.𐤄𐤊𐤉.𐤒𐤓𐤀.𐤔𐤌𐤅.𐤉𐤏𐤒𐤁.𐤅𐤉𐤏𐤒𐤁𐤍𐤉.𐤆
𐤄.𐤐𐤏𐤌𐤉𐤌.𐤀𐤕.𐤁𐤊𐤓𐤕𐤉.𐤋𐤒𐤇.𐤅𐤄𐤍𐤄.𐤏𐤕𐤄.𐤋𐤒𐤇.𐤁𐤓
𐤊𐤕𐤉.𐤅𐤉𐤀𐤌𐤓.𐤄𐤋𐤀.𐤀𐤑𐤋𐤕.𐤋𐤉.𐤁𐤓𐤊𐤄|

..𐤋𐤆.. 𐤅𐤉𐤏𐤍.𐤉𐤑𐤇𐤒.𐤅𐤉𐤀𐤌𐤓.𐤋𐤏𐤔𐤅.𐤄𐤍.𐤂𐤁𐤉𐤓.𐤔𐤌𐤕
𐤉𐤅.𐤋𐤊.𐤅𐤀𐤕.𐤊𐤋.𐤀𐤇𐤉𐤅.𐤍𐤕𐤕𐤉.𐤋𐤅.𐤋𐤏𐤁𐤃𐤉𐤌.𐤅𐤃𐤂𐤍.𐤅
𐤕𐤉𐤓𐤔.𐤎𐤌𐤊𐤕𐤉𐤅.𐤅𐤋𐤊𐤄.𐤀𐤐𐤅𐤀.𐤌𐤄.𐤀𐤏𐤔𐤄.𐤁𐤍𐤉|

..𐤋𐤇.. 𐤅𐤉𐤀𐤌𐤓.𐤏𐤔𐤅.𐤀𐤋.𐤀𐤁𐤉𐤅.𐤄𐤁𐤓𐤊𐤄.𐤀𐤇𐤕.𐤄𐤅𐤀.𐤋
𐤊.𐤀𐤁𐤉.𐤁𐤓𐤊𐤍𐤉.𐤂𐤌.𐤀𐤍𐤉.𐤀𐤁𐤉.𐤅𐤉𐤔𐤀.𐤏𐤔𐤅.𐤒𐤋𐤅.𐤅𐤉𐤁
𐤊|

..𐤋𐤈.. 𐤅𐤉𐤏𐤍.𐤉𐤑𐤇𐤒.𐤀𐤁𐤉𐤅.𐤅𐤉𐤀𐤌𐤓.𐤀𐤋𐤉𐤅.𐤄𐤍𐤄.𐤌𐤔
𐤌𐤍𐤉.𐤄𐤀𐤓𐤑.𐤉𐤄𐤉𐤄.𐤌𐤅𐤔𐤁𐤊.𐤅𐤌𐤈𐤋.𐤄𐤔𐤌𐤉𐤌.𐤌𐤏𐤋|

..𐤌.. 𐤅𐤏𐤋.𐤇𐤓𐤁𐤊.𐤕𐤇𐤉𐤄.𐤅𐤀𐤕.𐤀𐤇𐤉𐤊.𐤕𐤏𐤁𐤃.𐤅𐤄
𐤉𐤄.𐤊𐤀𐤔𐤓.𐤕𐤓𐤉𐤃.𐤅𐤐𐤓𐤒𐤕.𐤏𐤋𐤅.𐤌𐤏𐤋.𐤑𐤅𐤀𐤓𐤊|

..𐤌𐤀.. 𐤅𐤉𐤔𐤈𐤌.𐤏𐤔𐤅.𐤀𐤕.𐤉𐤏𐤒𐤁.𐤏𐤋.𐤄𐤁𐤓𐤊𐤄.𐤀𐤔𐤓.𐤁
𐤓𐤊𐤅.𐤀𐤁𐤉𐤅.𐤅𐤉𐤀𐤌𐤓.𐤏𐤔𐤅.𐤁𐤋𐤁𐤅.𐤉𐤒𐤓𐤁𐤅.𐤉𐤌𐤉.𐤀𐤁𐤋.𐤀
𐤁𐤉.𐤅𐤀𐤄𐤓𐤂𐤄.𐤀𐤕.𐤉𐤏𐤒𐤁.𐤀𐤇𐤉|

..𐤌𐤁.. 𐤅𐤉𐤂𐤃.𐤋𐤓𐤁𐤒𐤄.𐤀𐤕.𐤃𐤁𐤓𐤉.𐤏𐤔𐤅.𐤁𐤍𐤄.𐤄𐤂𐤃
𐤋.𐤅𐤕𐤔𐤋𐤇.𐤅𐤕𐤒𐤓𐤀.𐤋𐤉𐤏𐤒𐤁.𐤁𐤍𐤄.𐤄𐤒𐤈𐤍.𐤅𐤕𐤀𐤌𐤓.𐤀
𐤋𐤉𐤅.𐤄𐤍𐤄.𐤏𐤔𐤅.𐤀𐤇𐤉𐤊.𐤌𐤕𐤍𐤇𐤌.𐤋𐤊.𐤋𐤄𐤓𐤂𐤊|

..𐤌𐤂.. 𐤅𐤏𐤕𐤄.𐤁𐤍𐤉.𐤔𐤌𐤏.𐤁𐤒𐤋𐤉.𐤅𐤒𐤅𐤌.𐤁𐤓𐤇.𐤋𐤊.𐤀𐤋.𐤋
𐤁𐤍.𐤀𐤇𐤉.𐤇𐤓𐤍𐤄|

..𐤌𐤃.. 𐤅𐤉𐤔𐤁𐤕.𐤏𐤌𐤅.𐤉𐤌𐤉𐤌.𐤀𐤇𐤃𐤉𐤌.𐤏𐤃.𐤀𐤔𐤓.𐤕𐤔
𐤅𐤁.𐤇𐤌𐤕.𐤀𐤇𐤉𐤊|

..𐤌𐤄.. 𐤏𐤃.𐤔𐤅𐤁.𐤀𐤐.𐤀𐤇𐤉𐤊.𐤌𐤌𐤊.𐤅𐤔𐤊𐤇.𐤀𐤕.𐤀𐤔𐤓.𐤏
𐤔𐤉𐤕.𐤋𐤅.𐤅𐤔𐤋𐤇𐤕𐤉.𐤅𐤋𐤒𐤇𐤕𐤉𐤊.𐤌𐤔𐤌.𐤋𐤌𐤄.𐤀𐤔𐤊𐤋.
𐤂𐤌.𐤔𐤍𐤉𐤊𐤌.𐤉𐤅𐤌.𐤀𐤇𐤃|

..𐤌𐤅.. 𐤅𐤕𐤀𐤌𐤓.𐤓𐤁𐤒𐤄.𐤀𐤋.𐤉𐤑𐤇𐤒.𐤒𐤑𐤕𐤉.𐤁𐤇𐤉𐤉.𐤌
𐤐𐤍𐤉.𐤁𐤍𐤅𐤕.𐤇𐤕.𐤀𐤌.𐤋𐤒𐤇.𐤉𐤏𐤒𐤁.𐤀𐤔𐤄.𐤌𐤁𐤍𐤅𐤕.𐤇𐤕.
𐤊𐤀𐤋𐤄.𐤌𐤁𐤍𐤅𐤕.𐤄𐤀𐤓𐤑.𐤋𐤌𐤄.𐤋𐤉.𐤇𐤉𐤉𐤌||

𐤁𐤓𐤀𐤔𐤉𐤕.𐤇𐤋𐤒 ..𐤊𐤇..

..𐤀.. 𐤅𐤉𐤒𐤓𐤀.𐤉𐤑𐤇𐤒.𐤀𐤋.𐤉𐤏𐤒𐤁.𐤅𐤉𐤁𐤓𐤊.𐤀𐤕𐤅.𐤅𐤉𐤑𐤅𐤄
𐤅.𐤅𐤉𐤀𐤌𐤓.𐤋𐤅.𐤋𐤀.𐤕𐤒𐤇.𐤀𐤔𐤄.𐤌𐤁𐤍𐤅𐤕.𐤊𐤍𐤏𐤍|

𐤁 𐤒𐤅𐤌.𐤋𐤊.𐤐𐤃𐤍𐤄.𐤀𐤓𐤌.𐤁𐤉𐤕𐤄.𐤁𐤕𐤅𐤀𐤋.𐤀𐤁𐤉.𐤀𐤌𐤊
.𐤅𐤒𐤇.𐤋𐤊.𐤌𐤔𐤌.𐤀𐤔𐤄.𐤌𐤁𐤍𐤅𐤕.𐤋𐤁𐤍.𐤀𐤇𐤉.𐤀𐤌𐤊|
𐤂 𐤅𐤀𐤋.𐤔𐤃𐤉.𐤉𐤁𐤓𐤊.𐤀𐤕𐤊.𐤅𐤉𐤐𐤓𐤊.𐤅𐤉𐤓𐤁𐤊.𐤅𐤄𐤉𐤉𐤕.
𐤋𐤒𐤄𐤋.𐤏𐤌𐤉𐤌|
𐤃 𐤅𐤉𐤕𐤍.𐤋𐤊.𐤀𐤕.𐤁𐤓𐤊𐤕.𐤀𐤁𐤓𐤄𐤌.𐤋𐤊.𐤅𐤋𐤆𐤓𐤏𐤊.𐤀𐤕
𐤊.𐤋𐤓𐤔𐤕𐤊.𐤀𐤕.𐤀𐤓𐤑.𐤌𐤂𐤓𐤉𐤊.𐤀𐤔𐤓.𐤍𐤕𐤍.𐤀𐤋𐤄𐤉𐤌.𐤋
𐤀𐤁𐤓𐤄𐤌|
𐤄 𐤅𐤉𐤔𐤋𐤇.𐤉𐤑𐤇𐤒.𐤀𐤕.𐤉𐤏𐤒𐤁.𐤅𐤉𐤋𐤊.𐤐𐤃𐤍𐤄.𐤀𐤓𐤌.
𐤀𐤋.𐤋𐤁𐤍.𐤁𐤍.𐤁𐤕𐤅𐤀𐤋.𐤄𐤀𐤓𐤌𐤉.𐤀𐤇𐤉.𐤓𐤁𐤒𐤄.𐤀𐤌.𐤉𐤏
𐤒𐤁.𐤅𐤏𐤔𐤅|
𐤅 𐤅𐤉𐤓𐤀.𐤏𐤔𐤅.𐤊𐤉.𐤁𐤓𐤊.𐤉𐤑𐤇𐤒.𐤀𐤕.𐤉𐤏𐤒𐤁.𐤅𐤔𐤋𐤇.
𐤀𐤕𐤅.𐤐𐤃𐤍𐤄.𐤀𐤓𐤌.𐤋𐤒𐤇𐤕.𐤋𐤅.𐤌𐤔𐤌.𐤀𐤔𐤄.𐤁𐤁𐤓𐤊𐤅.𐤀
𐤕𐤅.𐤅𐤉𐤑𐤅.𐤏𐤋𐤉𐤅.𐤋𐤀𐤌𐤓.𐤋𐤀.𐤕𐤒𐤇.𐤀𐤔𐤄.𐤌𐤁𐤍𐤅𐤕.𐤊𐤍𐤏
𐤍|
𐤆 𐤅𐤉𐤔𐤌𐤏.𐤉𐤏𐤒𐤁.𐤀𐤋.𐤀𐤁𐤉𐤅.𐤅𐤀𐤋.𐤀𐤌𐤅.𐤅𐤉𐤋𐤊.𐤐𐤃𐤍
𐤄.𐤀𐤓𐤌|
𐤇 𐤅𐤉𐤓𐤀.𐤏𐤔𐤅.𐤊𐤉.𐤓𐤏𐤅𐤕.𐤁𐤍𐤅𐤕.𐤊𐤍𐤏𐤍.𐤁𐤏𐤉𐤍𐤉.𐤉𐤑
𐤇𐤒.𐤀𐤁𐤉𐤅|
𐤈 𐤅𐤉𐤋𐤊.𐤏𐤔𐤅.𐤀𐤋.𐤉𐤔𐤌𐤏𐤀𐤋.𐤅𐤉𐤒𐤇.𐤀𐤕.𐤌𐤇𐤋𐤕.𐤁
𐤕.𐤉𐤔𐤌𐤏𐤀𐤋.𐤁𐤍.𐤀𐤁𐤓𐤄𐤌.𐤀𐤇𐤅𐤕.𐤍𐤁𐤉𐤅𐤕.𐤏𐤋.𐤍𐤔𐤉𐤅.𐤋
𐤅.𐤋𐤀𐤔𐤄|
𐤉 𐤅𐤉𐤑𐤀.𐤉𐤏𐤒𐤁.𐤌𐤁𐤀𐤓.𐤔𐤁𐤏.𐤅𐤉𐤋𐤊.𐤇𐤓𐤍𐤄|
𐤉𐤀 𐤅𐤉𐤐𐤂𐤏.𐤁𐤌𐤒𐤅𐤌.𐤅𐤉𐤋𐤍.𐤔𐤌.𐤊𐤉.𐤁𐤀.𐤄𐤔𐤌𐤔.𐤅𐤉𐤒
𐤇.𐤌𐤀𐤁𐤍𐤉.𐤄𐤌𐤒𐤅𐤌.𐤅𐤉𐤔𐤌.𐤌𐤓𐤀𐤔𐤕𐤉𐤅.𐤅𐤉𐤔𐤊𐤁.𐤁𐤌𐤒
𐤅𐤌.𐤄𐤄𐤅𐤀|
𐤉𐤁 𐤅𐤉𐤇𐤋𐤌.𐤅𐤄𐤍𐤄.𐤎𐤋𐤌.𐤌𐤑𐤁.𐤀𐤓𐤑𐤄.𐤅𐤓𐤀𐤔𐤅.𐤌𐤂
𐤉𐤏.𐤄𐤔𐤌𐤉𐤌𐤄.𐤅𐤄𐤍𐤄.𐤌𐤋𐤀𐤊𐤉.𐤀𐤋𐤄𐤉𐤌.𐤏𐤋𐤉𐤌.𐤅𐤉𐤓
𐤃𐤉𐤌.𐤁𐤅|
𐤉𐤂 𐤅𐤄𐤍𐤄.𐤉𐤄𐤅𐤄.𐤍𐤑𐤁.𐤏𐤋𐤉𐤅.𐤅𐤉𐤀𐤌𐤓.𐤀𐤍𐤉.𐤉𐤄𐤅𐤄.𐤀
𐤋𐤄𐤉.𐤀𐤁𐤓𐤄𐤌.𐤀𐤁𐤉𐤊.𐤅𐤀𐤋𐤄𐤉.𐤉𐤑𐤇𐤒.𐤄𐤀𐤓𐤑.𐤀𐤔𐤓.
𐤀𐤕𐤄.𐤔𐤊𐤁.𐤏𐤋𐤉𐤄.𐤋𐤊.𐤀𐤕𐤍𐤍𐤄.𐤅𐤋𐤆𐤓𐤏𐤊|

14 והיה.זרעך.כעפר.הארץ.ופרצת.ימה.וק
דמה.וצפנה.ונגבה.ונברכו.בך.כל.משפחת.הא
דמה.ובזרעך|
15 והנה.אנכי.עמך.ושמרתיך.בכל.אשר.תלך.
והשבתיך.אל.האדמה.הזאת.כי.לא.אעזבך.
עד.אשר.אם.עשיתי.את.אשר.דברתי.לך|
16 וייקץ.יעקב.משנתו.ויאמר.אכן.יש.יהו
ה.במקום.הזה.ואנכי.לא.ידעתי|
17 ויירא.ויאמר.מה.נורא.המקום.הזה.אין.
זה.כי.אם.בית.אלהים.וזה.שער.השמים|
18 וישכם.יעקב.בבקר.ויקח.את.האבן.אשר
שם.מראשתיו.וישם.אתה.מצבה.ויצק.שמן.ע
ל.ראשה|
19 ויקרא.את.שם.המקום.ההוא.בית.אל.ואו
לם.לוז.שם.העיר.לראשנה|
20 וידר.יעקב.נדר.לאמר.אם.יהיה.אלהי
ם.עמדי.ושמרני.בדרך.הזה.אשר.אנכי.הולך
.ונתן.לי.לחם.לאכל.ובגד.ללבש|
21 ושבתי.בשלום.אל.בית.אבי.והיה.יהוה.ל
י.לאלהים|
22 והאבן.הזאת.אשר.שמתי.מצבה.יהיה.ב
ית.אלהים.וכל.אשר.תתן.לי.עשר.אעשרנו.לך||

בראשית.חלק 29

1 וישא.יעקב.רגליו.וילך.ארצה.בני.קדם|
2 וירא.והנה.באר.בשדה.והנה.שם.שלשה.ע
דרי.צאן.רבצים.עליה.כי.מן.הבאר.ההוא.י
שקו.העדרים.והאבן.גדלה.על.פי.הבאר|

𐤂 𐤅𐤍𐤀𐤎𐤐𐤅.𐤔𐤌𐤄.𐤊𐤋.𐤄𐤏𐤃𐤓𐤉𐤌.𐤅𐤂𐤋𐤋𐤅.𐤀𐤕.𐤄𐤀𐤁𐤍
.𐤌𐤏𐤋.𐤐𐤉.𐤄𐤁𐤀𐤓.𐤅𐤄𐤔𐤒𐤅.𐤀𐤕.𐤄𐤑𐤀𐤍.𐤅𐤄𐤔𐤉𐤁𐤅.𐤀𐤕.
𐤄𐤀𐤁𐤍.𐤏𐤋.𐤐𐤉.𐤄𐤁𐤀𐤓.𐤋𐤌𐤒𐤌𐤄|
𐤃 𐤅𐤉𐤀𐤌𐤓.𐤋𐤄𐤌.𐤉𐤏𐤒𐤁.𐤀𐤇𐤉.𐤌𐤀𐤉𐤍.𐤀𐤕𐤌.𐤅𐤉𐤀𐤌𐤓
𐤅.𐤌𐤇𐤓𐤍.𐤀𐤍𐤇𐤍𐤅|
𐤄 𐤅𐤉𐤀𐤌𐤓.𐤋𐤄𐤌.𐤄𐤉𐤃𐤏𐤕𐤌.𐤀𐤕.𐤋𐤁𐤍.𐤁𐤍.𐤍𐤇𐤅𐤓.𐤅𐤉𐤀
𐤌𐤓𐤅.𐤉𐤃𐤏𐤍𐤅|
𐤅 𐤅𐤉𐤀𐤌𐤓.𐤋𐤄𐤌.𐤄𐤔𐤋𐤅𐤌.𐤋𐤅.𐤅𐤉𐤀𐤌𐤓𐤅.𐤔𐤋𐤅𐤌.𐤅𐤄𐤍𐤄.𐤓
𐤇𐤋.𐤁𐤕𐤅.𐤁𐤀𐤄.𐤏𐤌.𐤄𐤑𐤀𐤍|
𐤆 𐤅𐤉𐤀𐤌𐤓.𐤄𐤍.𐤏𐤅𐤃.𐤄𐤉𐤅𐤌.𐤂𐤃𐤅𐤋.𐤋𐤀.𐤏𐤕.𐤄𐤀𐤎𐤐.
𐤄𐤌𐤒𐤍𐤄.𐤄𐤔𐤒𐤅.𐤄𐤑𐤀𐤍.𐤅𐤋𐤊𐤅.𐤓𐤏𐤅|
𐤇 𐤅𐤉𐤀𐤌𐤓𐤅.𐤋𐤀.𐤍𐤅𐤊𐤋.𐤏𐤃.𐤀𐤔𐤓.𐤉𐤀𐤎𐤐𐤅.𐤊𐤋.𐤄𐤏𐤃𐤓
𐤉𐤌.𐤅𐤂𐤋𐤋𐤅.𐤀𐤕.𐤄𐤀𐤁𐤍.𐤌𐤏𐤋.𐤐𐤉.𐤄𐤁𐤀𐤓.𐤅𐤄𐤔𐤒𐤉𐤍𐤅.𐤄
𐤑𐤀𐤍|
𐤈 𐤏𐤅𐤃𐤍𐤅.𐤌𐤃𐤁𐤓.𐤏𐤌𐤌.𐤅𐤓𐤇𐤋.𐤁𐤀𐤄.𐤏𐤌.𐤄𐤑𐤀𐤍.𐤀
𐤔𐤓.𐤋𐤀𐤁𐤉𐤄.𐤊𐤉.𐤓𐤏𐤄.𐤄𐤅𐤀|
𐤉 𐤅𐤉𐤄𐤉.𐤊𐤀𐤔𐤓.𐤓𐤀𐤄.𐤉𐤏𐤒𐤁.𐤀𐤕.𐤓𐤇𐤋.𐤁𐤕.𐤋𐤁𐤍.
𐤀𐤇𐤉.𐤀𐤌𐤅.𐤅𐤀𐤕.𐤑𐤀𐤍.𐤋𐤁𐤍.𐤀𐤇𐤉.𐤀𐤌𐤅.𐤅𐤉𐤂𐤔.𐤉𐤏𐤒
𐤁.𐤅𐤉𐤂𐤋.𐤀𐤕.𐤄𐤀𐤁𐤍.𐤌𐤏𐤋.𐤐𐤉.𐤄𐤁𐤀𐤓.𐤅𐤉𐤔𐤒.𐤀𐤕.𐤑𐤀
𐤍.𐤋𐤁𐤍.𐤀𐤇𐤉.𐤀𐤌𐤅|
𐤉𐤀 𐤅𐤉𐤔𐤒.𐤉𐤏𐤒𐤁.𐤋𐤓𐤇𐤋.𐤅𐤉𐤔𐤀.𐤀𐤕.𐤒𐤋𐤅.𐤅𐤉𐤁𐤊|
𐤉𐤁 𐤅𐤉𐤂𐤃.𐤉𐤏𐤒𐤁.𐤋𐤓𐤇𐤋.𐤊𐤉.𐤀𐤇𐤉.𐤀𐤁𐤉𐤄.𐤄𐤅𐤀.𐤅
𐤊𐤉.𐤁𐤍.𐤓𐤁𐤒𐤄.𐤄𐤅𐤀.𐤅𐤕𐤓𐤑.𐤅𐤕𐤂𐤃.𐤋𐤀𐤁𐤉𐤄|
𐤉𐤂 𐤅𐤉𐤄𐤉.𐤊𐤔𐤌𐤏.𐤋𐤁𐤍.𐤀𐤕.𐤔𐤌𐤏.𐤉𐤏𐤒𐤁.𐤁𐤍.𐤀𐤇𐤕
𐤅.𐤅𐤉𐤓𐤑.𐤋𐤒𐤓𐤀𐤕𐤅.𐤅𐤉𐤇𐤁𐤒.𐤋𐤅.𐤅𐤉𐤍𐤔𐤒.𐤋𐤅.𐤅𐤉𐤁𐤉𐤀𐤄𐤅.
𐤀𐤋.𐤁𐤉𐤕𐤅.𐤅𐤉𐤎𐤐𐤓.𐤋𐤋𐤁𐤍.𐤀𐤕.𐤊𐤋.𐤄𐤃𐤁𐤓𐤉𐤌.𐤄𐤀𐤋𐤄|
𐤉𐤃 𐤅𐤉𐤀𐤌𐤓.𐤋𐤅.𐤋𐤁𐤍.𐤀𐤊.𐤏𐤑𐤌𐤉.𐤅𐤁𐤔𐤓𐤉.𐤀𐤕𐤄.𐤅𐤉𐤔
𐤁.𐤏𐤌𐤅.𐤇𐤃𐤔.𐤉𐤌𐤉𐤌|
𐤈𐤅 𐤅𐤉𐤀𐤌𐤓.𐤋𐤁𐤍.𐤋𐤉𐤏𐤒𐤁.𐤄𐤊𐤉.𐤀𐤇𐤉.𐤀𐤕𐤄.𐤅𐤏𐤁𐤃
𐤕𐤍𐤉.𐤇𐤍𐤌.𐤄𐤂𐤉𐤃𐤄.𐤋𐤉.𐤌𐤄.𐤌𐤔𐤊𐤓𐤕𐤊|

..𐤉𐤅.. 𐤅𐤋𐤋𐤁𐤍.𐤔𐤕𐤉.𐤁𐤍𐤅𐤕.𐤔𐤌.𐤄𐤂𐤃𐤋𐤄.𐤋𐤀𐤄.𐤅𐤔𐤌.𐤄
𐤒𐤈𐤍𐤄.𐤓𐤇𐤋|
..𐤉𐤆.. 𐤅𐤏𐤉𐤍𐤉.𐤋𐤀𐤄.𐤓𐤊𐤅𐤕.𐤅𐤓𐤇𐤋.𐤄𐤉𐤕𐤄.𐤉𐤐𐤕.𐤕𐤀𐤓.𐤅
𐤉𐤐𐤕.𐤌𐤓𐤀𐤄|
..𐤉𐤇.. 𐤅𐤉𐤀𐤄𐤁.𐤉𐤏𐤒𐤁.𐤀𐤕.𐤓𐤇𐤋.𐤅𐤉𐤀𐤌𐤓.𐤀𐤏𐤁𐤃𐤊.𐤔
𐤁𐤏.𐤔𐤍𐤉𐤌.𐤁𐤓𐤇𐤋.𐤁𐤕𐤊.𐤄𐤒𐤈𐤍𐤄|
..𐤉𐤈.. 𐤅𐤉𐤀𐤌𐤓.𐤋𐤁𐤍.𐤈𐤅𐤁.𐤕𐤕𐤉.𐤀𐤕𐤄.𐤋𐤊.𐤌𐤕𐤕𐤉.𐤀𐤕
𐤄.𐤋𐤀𐤉𐤔.𐤀𐤇𐤓.𐤔𐤁𐤄.𐤏𐤌𐤃𐤉|
..𐤊.. 𐤅𐤉𐤏𐤁𐤃.𐤉𐤏𐤒𐤁.𐤁𐤓𐤇𐤋.𐤔𐤁𐤏.𐤔𐤍𐤉𐤌.𐤅𐤉𐤄𐤉𐤅.𐤁
𐤏𐤉𐤍𐤉𐤅.𐤊𐤉𐤌𐤉𐤌.𐤀𐤇𐤃𐤉𐤌.𐤁𐤀𐤄𐤁𐤕𐤅.𐤀𐤕𐤄|
..𐤊𐤀.. 𐤅𐤉𐤀𐤌𐤓.𐤉𐤏𐤒𐤁.𐤀𐤋.𐤋𐤁𐤍.𐤄𐤁𐤄.𐤀𐤕.𐤀𐤔𐤕𐤉.𐤊𐤉.
𐤌𐤋𐤀𐤅.𐤉𐤌𐤉.𐤅𐤀𐤁𐤅𐤀𐤄.𐤀𐤋𐤉𐤄|
..𐤊𐤁.. 𐤅𐤉𐤀𐤎𐤐.𐤋𐤁𐤍.𐤀𐤕.𐤊𐤋.𐤀𐤍𐤔𐤉.𐤄𐤌𐤒𐤅𐤌.𐤅𐤉𐤏𐤔.𐤌
𐤔𐤕𐤄|
..𐤊𐤂.. 𐤅𐤉𐤄𐤉.𐤁𐤏𐤓𐤁.𐤅𐤉𐤒𐤇.𐤀𐤕.𐤋𐤀𐤄.𐤁𐤕𐤅.𐤅𐤉𐤁𐤀.𐤀𐤕
𐤄.𐤀𐤋𐤉𐤅.𐤅𐤉𐤁𐤀.𐤀𐤋𐤉𐤄|
..𐤊𐤃.. 𐤅𐤉𐤕𐤍.𐤋𐤁𐤍.𐤋𐤄.𐤀𐤕.𐤆𐤋𐤐𐤄.𐤔𐤐𐤇𐤕𐤅.𐤋𐤋𐤀𐤄.𐤁𐤕
𐤅.𐤔𐤐𐤇𐤄|
..𐤊𐤄.. 𐤅𐤉𐤄𐤉.𐤁𐤁𐤒𐤓.𐤅𐤄𐤍𐤄.𐤄𐤅𐤀.𐤋𐤀𐤄.𐤅𐤉𐤀𐤌𐤓.𐤀𐤋.𐤋𐤁𐤍
.𐤌𐤄.𐤆𐤀𐤕.𐤏𐤔𐤉𐤕.𐤋𐤉.𐤄𐤋𐤀.𐤁𐤓𐤇𐤋.𐤏𐤁𐤃𐤕𐤉.𐤏𐤌𐤊.𐤅
𐤋𐤌𐤄.𐤓𐤌𐤉𐤕𐤍𐤉|
..𐤊𐤅.. 𐤅𐤉𐤀𐤌𐤓.𐤋𐤁𐤍.𐤋𐤀.𐤉𐤏𐤔𐤄.𐤊𐤍.𐤁𐤌𐤒𐤅𐤌𐤍𐤅.𐤋𐤕𐤕.𐤄
𐤑𐤏𐤉𐤓𐤄.𐤋𐤐𐤍𐤉.𐤄𐤁𐤊𐤉𐤓𐤄|
..𐤊𐤆.. 𐤌𐤋𐤀.𐤔𐤁𐤏.𐤆𐤀𐤕.𐤅𐤍𐤕𐤍𐤄.𐤋𐤊.𐤂𐤌.𐤀𐤕.𐤆𐤀𐤕.𐤁
𐤏𐤁𐤃𐤄.𐤀𐤔𐤓.𐤕𐤏𐤁𐤃.𐤏𐤌𐤃𐤉.𐤏𐤅𐤃.𐤔𐤁𐤏.𐤔𐤍𐤉𐤌.𐤀
𐤇𐤓𐤅𐤕|
..𐤊𐤇.. 𐤅𐤉𐤏𐤔.𐤉𐤏𐤒𐤁.𐤊𐤍.𐤅𐤉𐤌𐤋𐤀.𐤔𐤁𐤏.𐤆𐤀𐤕.𐤅𐤉𐤕𐤍.𐤋
𐤅.𐤀𐤕.𐤓𐤇𐤋.𐤁𐤕𐤅.𐤋𐤅.𐤋𐤀𐤔𐤄|
..𐤊𐤈.. 𐤅𐤉𐤕𐤍.𐤋𐤁𐤍.𐤋𐤓𐤇𐤋.𐤁𐤕𐤅.𐤀𐤕.𐤁𐤋𐤄𐤄.𐤔𐤐𐤇𐤕𐤅.𐤋
𐤄.𐤋𐤔𐤐𐤇𐤄|

30 𐤅𐤉𐤁𐤀.𐤂𐤌.𐤀𐤋.𐤓𐤇𐤋.𐤅𐤉𐤀𐤄𐤁.𐤂𐤌.𐤀𐤕.𐤓𐤇𐤋.𐤌𐤋𐤀𐤄.𐤅𐤉𐤏𐤁𐤃.𐤏𐤌𐤅.𐤏𐤅𐤃.𐤔𐤁𐤏.𐤔𐤍𐤉𐤌.𐤀𐤇𐤓𐤅𐤕|

31 𐤅𐤉𐤓𐤀.𐤉𐤄𐤅𐤄.𐤊𐤉.𐤔𐤍𐤅𐤀𐤄.𐤋𐤀𐤄.𐤅𐤉𐤐𐤕𐤇.𐤀𐤕.𐤓𐤇𐤌𐤄.𐤅𐤓𐤇𐤋.𐤏𐤒𐤓𐤄|

32 𐤅𐤕𐤄𐤓.𐤋𐤀𐤄.𐤅𐤕𐤋𐤃.𐤁𐤍.𐤅𐤕𐤒𐤓𐤀.𐤔𐤌𐤅.𐤓𐤀𐤅𐤁𐤍.𐤊𐤉.𐤀𐤌𐤓𐤄.𐤊𐤉.𐤓𐤀𐤄.𐤉𐤄𐤅𐤄.𐤁𐤏𐤍𐤉𐤉.𐤊𐤉.𐤏𐤕𐤄.𐤉𐤀𐤄𐤁𐤍𐤉.𐤀𐤉𐤔𐤉|

33 𐤅𐤕𐤄𐤓.𐤏𐤅𐤃.𐤅𐤕𐤋𐤃.𐤁𐤍.𐤅𐤕𐤀𐤌𐤓.𐤊𐤉.𐤔𐤌𐤏.𐤉𐤄𐤅𐤄.𐤊𐤉.𐤔𐤍𐤅𐤀𐤄.𐤀𐤍𐤊𐤉.𐤅𐤉𐤕𐤍.𐤋𐤉.𐤂𐤌.𐤀𐤕.𐤆𐤄.𐤅𐤕𐤒𐤓𐤀.𐤔𐤌𐤅.𐤔𐤌𐤏𐤅𐤍|

34 𐤅𐤕𐤄𐤓.𐤏𐤅𐤃.𐤅𐤕𐤋𐤃.𐤁𐤍.𐤅𐤕𐤀𐤌𐤓.𐤏𐤕𐤄.𐤄𐤐𐤏𐤌.𐤉𐤋𐤅𐤄.𐤀𐤉𐤔𐤉.𐤀𐤋𐤉.𐤊𐤉.𐤉𐤋𐤃𐤕𐤉.𐤋𐤅.𐤔𐤋𐤔𐤄.𐤁𐤍𐤉𐤌.𐤏𐤋.𐤊𐤍.𐤒𐤓𐤀.𐤔𐤌𐤅.𐤋𐤅𐤉|

35 𐤅𐤕𐤄𐤓.𐤏𐤅𐤃.𐤅𐤕𐤋𐤃.𐤁𐤍.𐤅𐤕𐤀𐤌𐤓.𐤄𐤐𐤏𐤌.𐤀𐤅𐤃𐤄.𐤀𐤕.𐤉𐤄𐤅𐤄.𐤏𐤋.𐤊𐤍.𐤒𐤓𐤀𐤄.𐤔𐤌𐤅.𐤉𐤄𐤅𐤃𐤄.𐤅𐤕𐤏𐤌𐤃.𐤌𐤋𐤃𐤕‖

𐤁𐤓𐤀𐤔𐤉𐤕.𐤇𐤋𐤒 30

1 𐤅𐤕𐤓𐤀.𐤓𐤇𐤋.𐤊𐤉.𐤋𐤀.𐤉𐤋𐤃𐤄.𐤋𐤉𐤏𐤒𐤁.𐤅𐤕𐤒𐤍𐤀.𐤓𐤇𐤋.𐤁𐤀𐤇𐤕𐤄.𐤅𐤕𐤀𐤌𐤓.𐤀𐤋.𐤉𐤏𐤒𐤁.𐤄𐤁𐤄.𐤋𐤉.𐤁𐤍𐤉𐤌.𐤅𐤀𐤌.𐤀𐤉𐤍.𐤌𐤕𐤄.𐤀𐤍𐤊𐤉|

2 𐤅𐤉𐤇𐤓.𐤀𐤐.𐤉𐤏𐤒𐤁.𐤁𐤓𐤇𐤋.𐤅𐤉𐤀𐤌𐤓.𐤄𐤕𐤇𐤕.𐤀𐤋𐤄𐤉𐤌.𐤀𐤍𐤊𐤉.𐤀𐤔𐤓.𐤌𐤍𐤏.𐤌𐤌𐤊.𐤐𐤓𐤉.𐤁𐤈𐤍|

3 𐤅𐤕𐤀𐤌𐤓.𐤄𐤍𐤄.𐤀𐤌𐤕𐤉.𐤁𐤋𐤄𐤄.𐤁𐤀.𐤀𐤋𐤉𐤄.𐤅𐤕𐤋𐤃.𐤏𐤋.𐤁𐤓𐤊𐤉.𐤅𐤀𐤁𐤍𐤄.𐤂𐤌.𐤀𐤍𐤊𐤉.𐤌𐤌𐤍𐤄|

4 𐤅𐤕𐤕𐤍.𐤋𐤅.𐤀𐤕.𐤁𐤋𐤄𐤄.𐤔𐤐𐤇𐤕𐤄.𐤋𐤀𐤔𐤄.𐤅𐤉𐤁𐤀.𐤀𐤋𐤉𐤄.𐤉𐤏𐤒𐤁|

5 𐤅𐤕𐤄𐤓.𐤁𐤋𐤄𐤄.𐤅𐤕𐤋𐤃.𐤋𐤉𐤏𐤒𐤁.𐤁𐤍|

6 𐤅𐤕𐤀𐤌𐤓.𐤓𐤇𐤋.𐤃𐤍𐤍𐤉.𐤀𐤋𐤄𐤉𐤌.𐤅𐤂𐤌.𐤔𐤌𐤏.𐤁𐤒𐤋𐤉.𐤅𐤉𐤕𐤍.𐤋𐤉.𐤁𐤍.𐤏𐤋.𐤊𐤍.𐤒𐤓𐤀𐤄.𐤔𐤌𐤅.𐤃𐤍|

ࠆ ࠅࠕࠄࠓ.ࠏࠅࠃ.ࠅࠕࠋࠃ.ࠁࠋࠄࠄ.ࠔࠐࠇࠕ.ࠓࠇࠋ.ࠁࠍ.ࠔࠍ
ࠉ.ࠋࠉࠏࠒࠁ|
ࠇ ࠅࠕࠀࠌࠓ.ࠓࠇࠋ.ࠍࠐࠕࠅࠋࠉ.ࠀࠋࠄࠉࠌ.ࠍࠐࠕࠋࠕࠉ.ࠏࠌ.ࠀ
ࠇࠕࠉ.ࠂࠌ.ࠉࠊࠋࠕࠉ.ࠅࠕࠒࠓࠀ.ࠔࠌࠅ.ࠍࠐࠕࠋࠉ|
ࠈ ࠅࠕࠓࠀ.ࠋࠀࠄ.ࠊࠉ.ࠏࠌࠃࠄ.ࠌࠋࠃࠕ.ࠅࠕࠒࠇ.ࠀࠕ.ࠆ
ࠋࠐࠄ.ࠔࠐࠇࠕࠄ.ࠅࠕࠕࠍ.ࠀࠕࠄ.ࠋࠉࠏࠒࠁ.ࠋࠀࠔࠄ|
ࠉ ࠅࠕࠋࠃ.ࠆࠋࠐࠄ.ࠔࠐࠇࠕ.ࠋࠀࠄ.ࠋࠉࠏࠒࠁ.ࠁࠍ|
ࠉࠀ ࠅࠕࠀࠌࠓ.ࠋࠀࠄ.ࠁࠂࠃ.||ࠁࠀ.ࠂࠃ.ࠒࠓࠉ||.ࠅࠕࠒࠓࠀ.
ࠀࠕ.ࠔࠌࠅ.ࠂࠃ|
ࠉࠁ ࠅࠕࠋࠃ.ࠆࠋࠐࠄ.ࠔࠐࠇࠕ.ࠋࠀࠄ.ࠁࠍ.ࠔࠍࠉ.ࠋࠉࠏࠒࠁ|
ࠉࠂ ࠅࠕࠀࠌࠓ.ࠋࠀࠄ.ࠁࠀࠔࠓࠉ.ࠊࠉ.ࠀࠔࠓࠅࠍࠉ.ࠁࠍࠅࠕ.ࠅࠕࠒ
ࠓࠀ.ࠀࠕ.ࠔࠌࠅ.ࠀࠔࠓ|
ࠉࠃ ࠅࠉࠋࠊ.ࠓࠀࠅࠁࠍ.ࠁࠉࠌࠉ.ࠒࠑࠉࠓ.ࠇࠈࠉࠌ.ࠅࠉࠌࠑࠀ.
ࠃࠅࠃࠀࠉࠌ.ࠁࠔࠃࠄ.ࠅࠉࠁࠀ.ࠀࠕࠌ.ࠀࠋ.ࠋࠀࠄ.ࠀࠌࠅ.ࠅࠕࠀ
ࠌࠓ.ࠓࠇࠋ.ࠀࠋ.ࠋࠀࠄ.ࠕࠍࠉ.ࠍࠀ.ࠋࠉ.ࠌࠃࠅࠃࠀࠉ.ࠁࠍࠊ|
ࠉࠄ ࠅࠕࠀࠌࠓ.ࠋࠄ.ࠄࠌࠏࠈ.ࠒࠇࠕࠊ.ࠀࠕ.ࠀࠉࠔࠉ.ࠅࠋࠒࠇ
ࠕ.ࠂࠌ.ࠀࠕ.ࠃࠅࠃࠀࠉ.ࠁࠍࠉ.ࠅࠕࠀࠌࠓ.ࠓࠇࠋ.ࠋࠊࠍ.ࠉࠔࠊࠁ.
ࠏࠌࠊ.ࠄࠋࠉࠋࠄ.ࠕࠇࠕ.ࠃࠅࠃࠀࠉ.ࠁࠍࠊ|
ࠉࠅ ࠅࠉࠁࠀ.ࠉࠏࠒࠁ.ࠌࠍ.ࠄࠔࠃࠄ.ࠁࠏࠓࠁ.ࠅࠕࠑࠀ.ࠋࠀࠄ.
ࠋࠒࠓࠀࠕࠅ.ࠅࠕࠀࠌࠓ.ࠀࠋࠉ.ࠕࠁࠅࠀ.ࠊࠉ.ࠔࠊࠓ.ࠔࠊࠓࠕࠉࠊ.ࠁ
ࠃࠅࠃࠀࠉ.ࠁࠍࠉ.ࠅࠉࠔࠊࠁ.ࠏࠌࠄ.ࠁࠋࠉࠋࠄ.ࠄࠅࠀ|
ࠉࠆ ࠅࠉࠔࠌࠏ.ࠀࠋࠄࠉࠌ.ࠀࠋ.ࠋࠀࠄ.ࠅࠕࠄࠓ.ࠅࠕࠋࠃ.ࠋࠉࠏ
ࠒࠁ.ࠁࠍ.ࠇࠌࠉࠔࠉ|
ࠉࠇ ࠅࠕࠀࠌࠓ.ࠋࠀࠄ.ࠍࠕࠍ.ࠀࠋࠄࠉࠌ.ࠔࠊࠓࠉ.ࠀࠔࠓ.ࠍࠕࠕࠉ
.ࠔࠐࠇࠕࠉ.ࠋࠀࠉࠔࠉ.ࠅࠕࠒࠓࠀ.ࠔࠌࠅ.ࠉࠔࠔࠊࠓ|
ࠉࠈ ࠅࠕࠄࠓ.ࠏࠅࠃ.ࠋࠀࠄ.ࠅࠕࠋࠃ.ࠁࠍ.ࠔࠔࠉ.ࠋࠉࠏࠒࠁ|
ࠊ ࠅࠕࠀࠌࠓ.ࠋࠀࠄ.ࠆࠁࠃࠍࠉ.ࠀࠋࠄࠉࠌ.ࠀࠕࠉ.ࠆࠁࠃ.
ࠈࠅࠁ.ࠄࠐࠏࠌ.ࠉࠆࠁࠋࠍࠉ.ࠀࠉࠔࠉ.ࠊࠉ.ࠉࠋࠃࠕࠉ.ࠋࠅ.ࠔࠔࠄ
.ࠁࠍࠉࠌ.ࠅࠕࠒࠓࠀ.ࠀࠕ.ࠔࠌࠅ.ࠆࠁࠋࠅࠍ|
ࠊࠀ ࠅࠀࠇࠓ.ࠉࠋࠃࠄ.ࠁࠕ.ࠅࠕࠒࠓࠀ.ࠀࠕ.ࠔࠌࠄ.ࠃࠉࠍࠄ|

22 𐤅𐤉𐤆𐤊𐤓.𐤀𐤋𐤄𐤉𐤌.𐤀𐤕.𐤓𐤇𐤋.𐤅𐤉𐤔𐤌𐤏.𐤀𐤋𐤉𐤄.𐤀𐤋
𐤄𐤉𐤌.𐤅𐤉𐤐𐤕𐤇.𐤀𐤕.𐤓𐤇𐤌𐤄|
23 𐤅𐤕𐤄𐤓.𐤅𐤕𐤋𐤃.𐤁𐤍.𐤅𐤕𐤀𐤌𐤓.𐤀𐤎𐤐.𐤀𐤋𐤄𐤉𐤌.𐤀𐤕.𐤇
𐤓𐤐𐤕𐤉|
24 𐤅𐤕𐤒𐤓𐤀.𐤀𐤕.𐤔𐤌𐤅.𐤉𐤅𐤎𐤐.𐤋𐤀𐤌𐤓.𐤉𐤎𐤐.𐤉𐤄𐤅𐤄.𐤋𐤉
.𐤁𐤍.𐤀𐤇𐤓|
25 𐤅𐤉𐤄𐤉.𐤊𐤀𐤔𐤓.𐤉𐤋𐤃𐤄.𐤓𐤇𐤋.𐤀𐤕.𐤉𐤅𐤎𐤐.𐤅𐤉𐤀𐤌𐤓.
𐤉𐤏𐤒𐤁.𐤀𐤋.𐤋𐤁𐤍.𐤔𐤋𐤇𐤍𐤉.𐤅𐤀𐤋𐤊𐤄.𐤀𐤋.𐤌𐤒𐤅𐤌𐤉.𐤅𐤋𐤀𐤓
𐤑𐤉|
26 𐤕𐤍𐤄.𐤀𐤕.𐤍𐤔𐤉.𐤅𐤀𐤕.𐤉𐤋𐤃𐤉.𐤀𐤔𐤓.𐤏𐤁𐤃𐤕𐤉.𐤀𐤕
𐤊.𐤁𐤄𐤍.𐤅𐤀𐤋𐤊𐤄.𐤊𐤉.𐤀𐤕𐤄.𐤉𐤃𐤏𐤕.𐤀𐤕.𐤏𐤁𐤃𐤕𐤉.𐤀𐤔
𐤓.𐤏𐤁𐤃𐤕𐤉𐤊|
27 𐤅𐤉𐤀𐤌𐤓.𐤀𐤋𐤉𐤅.𐤋𐤁𐤍.𐤀𐤌.𐤍𐤀.𐤌𐤑𐤀𐤕𐤉.𐤇𐤍.𐤁𐤏𐤉
𐤍𐤉𐤊.𐤍𐤇𐤔𐤕𐤉.𐤅𐤉𐤁𐤓𐤊𐤍𐤉.𐤉𐤄𐤅𐤄.𐤁𐤂𐤋𐤋𐤊|
28 𐤅𐤉𐤀𐤌𐤓.𐤍𐤒𐤁𐤄.𐤔𐤊𐤓𐤊.𐤏𐤋𐤉.𐤅𐤀𐤕𐤍𐤄|
29 𐤅𐤉𐤀𐤌𐤓.𐤀𐤋𐤉𐤅.𐤀𐤕𐤄.𐤉𐤃𐤏𐤕.𐤀𐤕.𐤀𐤔𐤓.𐤏𐤁𐤃
𐤕𐤉𐤊.𐤅𐤀𐤕.𐤀𐤔𐤓.𐤄𐤉𐤄.𐤌𐤒𐤍𐤊.𐤀𐤕𐤉|
30 𐤊𐤉.𐤌𐤏𐤈.𐤀𐤔𐤓.𐤄𐤉𐤄.𐤋𐤊.𐤋𐤐𐤍𐤉.𐤅𐤉𐤐𐤓𐤑.𐤋𐤓𐤁.𐤅
𐤉𐤁𐤓𐤊.𐤉𐤄𐤅𐤄.𐤀𐤕𐤊.𐤋𐤓𐤂𐤋𐤉.𐤅𐤏𐤕𐤄.𐤌𐤕𐤉.𐤀𐤏𐤔𐤄.𐤂
𐤌.𐤀𐤍𐤊𐤉.𐤋𐤁𐤉𐤕𐤉|
31 𐤅𐤉𐤀𐤌𐤓.𐤌𐤄.𐤀𐤕𐤍.𐤋𐤊.𐤅𐤉𐤀𐤌𐤓.𐤉𐤏𐤒𐤁.𐤋𐤀.𐤕𐤕𐤍.
𐤋𐤉.𐤌𐤀𐤅𐤌𐤄.𐤀𐤌.𐤕𐤏𐤔𐤄.𐤋𐤉.𐤄𐤃𐤁𐤓.𐤄𐤆𐤄.𐤀𐤔𐤅𐤁𐤄.
𐤀𐤓𐤏𐤄.𐤑𐤀𐤍𐤊.𐤀𐤔𐤌𐤓|
32 𐤀𐤏𐤁𐤓.𐤁𐤊𐤋.𐤑𐤀𐤍𐤊.𐤄𐤉𐤅𐤌.𐤄𐤎𐤓.𐤌𐤔𐤌.𐤊𐤋.𐤔𐤄.
𐤍𐤒𐤃.𐤅𐤈𐤋𐤅𐤀.𐤅𐤊𐤋.𐤔𐤄.𐤇𐤅𐤌.𐤁𐤊𐤔𐤁𐤉𐤌.𐤅𐤈𐤋𐤅𐤀.𐤅𐤍𐤒
𐤃.𐤁𐤏𐤆𐤉𐤌.𐤅𐤄𐤉𐤄.𐤔𐤊𐤓𐤉|
33 𐤅𐤏𐤍𐤕𐤄.𐤁𐤉.𐤑𐤃𐤒𐤕𐤉.𐤁𐤉𐤅𐤌.𐤌𐤇𐤓.𐤊𐤉.𐤕𐤁𐤅𐤀.
𐤏𐤋.𐤔𐤊𐤓𐤉.𐤋𐤐𐤍𐤉𐤊.𐤊𐤋.𐤀𐤔𐤓.𐤀𐤉𐤍𐤍𐤅.𐤍𐤒𐤃.𐤅𐤈𐤋𐤅𐤀.𐤁
𐤏𐤆𐤉𐤌.𐤅𐤇𐤅𐤌.𐤁𐤊𐤔𐤁𐤉𐤌.𐤂𐤍𐤅𐤁.𐤄𐤅𐤀.𐤀𐤕𐤉|
34 𐤅𐤉𐤀𐤌𐤓.𐤋𐤁𐤍.𐤄𐤍.𐤋𐤅.𐤉𐤄𐤉.𐤊𐤃𐤁𐤓𐤊|

..𐤋𐤄.. 𐤅𐤉𐤎𐤓.𐤁𐤉𐤅𐤌.𐤄𐤄𐤅𐤀.𐤀𐤕.𐤄𐤕𐤉𐤔𐤉𐤌.𐤄𐤏𐤒𐤃𐤉𐤌
.𐤅𐤄𐤈𐤋𐤀𐤉𐤌.𐤅𐤀𐤕.𐤊𐤋.𐤄𐤏𐤆𐤉𐤌.𐤄𐤍𐤒𐤃𐤅𐤕.𐤅𐤄𐤈𐤋𐤀𐤕
.𐤊𐤋.𐤀𐤔𐤓.𐤋𐤁𐤍.𐤁𐤅.𐤅𐤊𐤋.𐤇𐤅𐤌.𐤁𐤊𐤔𐤁𐤉𐤌.𐤅𐤉𐤕𐤍.𐤁𐤉𐤃.𐤁
𐤍𐤉𐤅|

..𐤋𐤅.. 𐤅𐤉𐤔𐤌.𐤃𐤓𐤊.𐤔𐤋𐤔𐤕.𐤉𐤌𐤉𐤌.𐤁𐤉𐤍𐤅.𐤅𐤁𐤉𐤍.𐤉𐤏𐤒𐤁.
𐤅𐤉𐤏𐤒𐤁.𐤓𐤏𐤄.𐤀𐤕.𐤑𐤀𐤍.𐤋𐤁𐤍.𐤄𐤍𐤅𐤕𐤓𐤕|

..𐤋𐤆.. 𐤅𐤉𐤒𐤇.𐤋𐤅.𐤉𐤏𐤒𐤁.𐤌𐤒𐤋.𐤋𐤁𐤍𐤄.𐤋𐤇.𐤅𐤋𐤅𐤆.𐤅𐤏𐤓
𐤌𐤅𐤍.𐤅𐤉𐤐𐤑𐤋.𐤁𐤄𐤍.𐤐𐤑𐤋𐤅𐤕.𐤋𐤁𐤍𐤅𐤕.𐤌𐤇𐤔𐤐.𐤄𐤋𐤁𐤍.𐤀𐤔
𐤓.𐤏𐤋.𐤄𐤌𐤒𐤋𐤅𐤕|

..𐤋𐤇.. 𐤅𐤉𐤑𐤂.𐤀𐤕.𐤄𐤌𐤒𐤋𐤅𐤕.𐤀𐤔𐤓.𐤐𐤑𐤋.𐤁𐤓𐤄𐤈𐤉𐤌.𐤁
𐤔𐤒𐤕𐤅𐤕.𐤄𐤌𐤉𐤌.𐤀𐤔𐤓.𐤕𐤁𐤀𐤍.𐤄𐤑𐤀𐤍.𐤋𐤔𐤕𐤅𐤕.𐤋𐤍𐤊𐤇
.𐤄𐤑𐤀𐤍.𐤅𐤉𐤇𐤌𐤍𐤄.𐤁𐤁𐤀𐤍.𐤋𐤔𐤕𐤅𐤕|

..𐤋𐤈.. 𐤅𐤉𐤇𐤌𐤅.𐤄𐤑𐤀𐤍.𐤀𐤋.𐤄𐤌𐤒𐤋𐤅𐤕.𐤅𐤕𐤋𐤃𐤍.𐤄𐤑𐤀𐤍.
𐤏𐤒𐤃𐤉𐤌.𐤍𐤒𐤃𐤉𐤌.𐤅𐤈𐤋𐤀𐤉𐤌|

..𐤌.. 𐤅𐤄𐤊𐤔𐤁𐤉𐤌.𐤄𐤐𐤓𐤉𐤃.𐤉𐤏𐤒𐤁.𐤅𐤉𐤕𐤍.𐤐𐤍𐤉.𐤄𐤑𐤀
𐤍.𐤀𐤋.𐤏𐤒𐤃.𐤅𐤊𐤋.𐤇𐤅𐤌.𐤁𐤑𐤀𐤍.𐤋𐤁𐤍.𐤅𐤉𐤔𐤕.𐤋𐤅.𐤏𐤃𐤓𐤉
𐤌.𐤋𐤁𐤃𐤅.𐤅𐤋𐤀.𐤔𐤕𐤌.𐤏𐤋.𐤑𐤀𐤍.𐤋𐤁𐤍|

..𐤌𐤀.. 𐤅𐤄𐤉𐤄.𐤁𐤊𐤋.𐤉𐤇𐤌.𐤄𐤑𐤀𐤍.𐤄𐤌𐤒𐤔𐤓𐤅𐤕.𐤅𐤔𐤌.𐤉
𐤏𐤒𐤁.𐤀𐤕.𐤄𐤌𐤒𐤋𐤅𐤕.𐤋𐤏𐤉𐤍𐤉.𐤄𐤑𐤀𐤍.𐤁𐤓𐤄𐤈𐤉𐤌.𐤋𐤉
𐤇𐤌𐤍𐤄.𐤁𐤌𐤒𐤋𐤅𐤕|

..𐤌𐤁.. 𐤅𐤁𐤄𐤏𐤈𐤉𐤐.𐤄𐤑𐤀𐤍.𐤋𐤀.𐤉𐤔𐤉𐤌.𐤅𐤄𐤉𐤄.𐤄𐤏𐤈𐤐𐤉
𐤌.𐤋𐤋𐤁𐤍.𐤅𐤄𐤒𐤔𐤓𐤉𐤌.𐤋𐤉𐤏𐤒𐤁|

..𐤌𐤂.. 𐤅𐤉𐤐𐤓𐤑.𐤄𐤀𐤉𐤔.𐤌𐤀𐤃.𐤌𐤀𐤃.𐤅𐤉𐤄𐤉.𐤋𐤅.𐤑𐤀𐤍.𐤓
𐤁𐤅𐤕.𐤅𐤔𐤐𐤇𐤅𐤕.𐤅𐤏𐤁𐤃𐤉𐤌.𐤅𐤂𐤌𐤋𐤉𐤌.𐤅𐤇𐤌𐤓𐤉𐤌||

𐤁𐤓𐤀𐤔𐤉𐤕.𐤇𐤋𐤒 ..𐤋𐤀..

..𐤀.. 𐤅𐤉𐤔𐤌𐤏.𐤀𐤕.𐤃𐤁𐤓𐤉.𐤁𐤍𐤉.𐤋𐤁𐤍.𐤋𐤀𐤌𐤓.𐤋𐤒𐤇.𐤉𐤏𐤒
𐤁.𐤀𐤕.𐤊𐤋.𐤀𐤔𐤓.𐤋𐤀𐤁𐤉𐤍𐤅.𐤅𐤌𐤀𐤔𐤓.𐤋𐤀𐤁𐤉𐤍𐤅.𐤏𐤔𐤄.𐤀
𐤕.𐤊𐤋.𐤄𐤊𐤁𐤃.𐤄𐤆𐤄|

ב 𐤅𐤉𐤓𐤀.𐤉𐤏𐤒𐤁.𐤀𐤕.𐤐𐤍𐤉.𐤋𐤁𐤍.𐤅𐤄𐤍𐤄.𐤀𐤉𐤍𐤍𐤅.𐤏𐤌𐤅.𐤊
𐤕𐤌𐤅𐤋.𐤔𐤋𐤔𐤅𐤌|

ג 𐤅𐤉𐤀𐤌𐤓.𐤉𐤄𐤅𐤄.𐤀𐤋.𐤉𐤏𐤒𐤁.𐤔𐤅𐤁.𐤀𐤋.𐤀𐤓𐤑.𐤀𐤁𐤅𐤕
𐤉𐤊.𐤅𐤋𐤌𐤅𐤋𐤃𐤕𐤊.𐤅𐤀𐤄𐤉𐤄.𐤏𐤌𐤊|

ד 𐤅𐤉𐤔𐤋𐤇.𐤉𐤏𐤒𐤁.𐤅𐤉𐤒𐤓𐤀.𐤋𐤓𐤇𐤋.𐤅𐤋𐤋𐤀𐤄.𐤄𐤔𐤃𐤄
.𐤀𐤋.𐤑𐤀𐤍𐤅|

ה 𐤅𐤉𐤀𐤌𐤓.𐤋𐤄𐤍.𐤓𐤀𐤄.𐤀𐤍𐤊𐤉.𐤀𐤕.𐤐𐤍𐤉.𐤀𐤁𐤉𐤊𐤍.𐤊𐤉.𐤀
𐤉𐤍𐤍𐤅.𐤀𐤋𐤉.𐤊𐤕𐤌𐤋.𐤔𐤋𐤔𐤌.𐤅𐤀𐤋𐤄𐤉.𐤀𐤁𐤉.𐤄𐤉𐤄.𐤏𐤌𐤃
𐤉|

ו 𐤅𐤀𐤕𐤍𐤄.𐤉𐤃𐤏𐤕𐤍.𐤊𐤉.𐤁𐤊𐤋.𐤊𐤇𐤉.𐤏𐤁𐤃𐤕𐤉.𐤀𐤕.
𐤀𐤁𐤉𐤊𐤍|

ז 𐤅𐤀𐤁𐤉𐤊𐤍.𐤄𐤕𐤋.𐤁𐤉.𐤅𐤄𐤇𐤋𐤐.𐤀𐤕.𐤌𐤔𐤊𐤓𐤕𐤉.𐤏𐤔𐤓
𐤕.𐤌𐤍𐤉𐤌.𐤅𐤋𐤀.𐤍𐤕𐤍𐤅.𐤀𐤋𐤄𐤉𐤌.𐤋𐤄𐤓𐤏.𐤏𐤌𐤃𐤉|

ח 𐤀𐤌.𐤊𐤄.𐤉𐤀𐤌𐤓.𐤍𐤒𐤃𐤉𐤌.𐤉𐤄𐤉𐤄.𐤔𐤊𐤓𐤊.𐤅𐤉𐤋𐤃𐤅.
𐤊𐤋.𐤄𐤑𐤀𐤍.𐤍𐤒𐤃𐤉𐤌.𐤅𐤀𐤌.𐤊𐤄.𐤉𐤀𐤌𐤓.𐤏𐤒𐤃𐤉𐤌.𐤉𐤄𐤉
𐤄.𐤔𐤊𐤓𐤊.𐤅𐤉𐤋𐤃𐤅.𐤊𐤋.𐤄𐤑𐤀𐤍.𐤏𐤒𐤃𐤉𐤌|

ט 𐤅𐤉𐤑𐤋.𐤀𐤋𐤄𐤉𐤌.𐤀𐤕.𐤌𐤒𐤍𐤄.𐤀𐤁𐤉𐤊𐤌.𐤅𐤉𐤕𐤍.𐤋𐤉|

י 𐤅𐤉𐤄𐤉.𐤁𐤏𐤕.𐤉𐤇𐤌.𐤄𐤑𐤀𐤍.𐤅𐤀𐤔𐤀.𐤏𐤉𐤍𐤉.𐤅𐤀𐤓𐤀
.𐤁𐤇𐤋𐤅𐤌.𐤅𐤄𐤍𐤄.𐤄𐤏𐤕𐤃𐤉𐤌.𐤄𐤏𐤋𐤉𐤌.𐤏𐤋.𐤄𐤑𐤀𐤍.𐤏𐤒
𐤃𐤉𐤌.𐤍𐤒𐤃𐤉𐤌.𐤅𐤁𐤓𐤃𐤉𐤌|

יא 𐤅𐤉𐤀𐤌𐤓.𐤀𐤋𐤉.𐤌𐤋𐤀𐤊.𐤄𐤀𐤋𐤄𐤉𐤌.𐤁𐤇𐤋𐤅𐤌.𐤉𐤏𐤒𐤁
.𐤅𐤀𐤌𐤓.𐤄𐤍𐤍𐤉|

יב 𐤅𐤉𐤀𐤌𐤓.𐤔𐤀.𐤍𐤀.𐤏𐤉𐤍𐤉𐤊.𐤅𐤓𐤀𐤄.𐤊𐤋.𐤄𐤏𐤕𐤃𐤉𐤌.
𐤄𐤏𐤋𐤉𐤌.𐤏𐤋.𐤄𐤑𐤀𐤍.𐤏𐤒𐤃𐤉𐤌.𐤍𐤒𐤃𐤉𐤌.𐤅𐤁𐤓𐤃𐤉𐤌.𐤊
𐤉.𐤓𐤀𐤉𐤕𐤉.𐤀𐤕.𐤊𐤋.𐤀𐤔𐤓.𐤋𐤁𐤍.𐤏𐤔𐤄.𐤋𐤊|

יג 𐤀𐤍𐤊𐤉.𐤄𐤀𐤋.𐤁𐤉𐤕.𐤀𐤋.𐤀𐤔𐤓.𐤌𐤔𐤇𐤕.𐤔𐤌.𐤌𐤑𐤁
𐤄.𐤀𐤔𐤓.𐤍𐤃𐤓𐤕.𐤋𐤉.𐤔𐤌.𐤍𐤃𐤓.𐤏𐤕𐤄.𐤒𐤅𐤌.𐤑𐤀.𐤌𐤍.𐤄𐤀
𐤓𐤑.𐤄𐤆𐤀𐤕.𐤅𐤔𐤅𐤁.𐤀𐤋.𐤀𐤓𐤑.𐤌𐤅𐤋𐤃𐤕𐤊|

יד 𐤅𐤕𐤏𐤍.𐤓𐤇𐤋.𐤅𐤋𐤀𐤄.𐤅𐤕𐤀𐤌𐤓𐤍𐤄.𐤋𐤅.𐤄𐤏𐤅𐤃.𐤋𐤍𐤅.𐤇
𐤋𐤒.𐤅𐤍𐤇𐤋𐤄.𐤁𐤁𐤉𐤕.𐤀𐤁𐤉𐤍𐤅|

15 הלוא.נכריות.נחשבנו.לו.כי.מכרנו.ויאכל.
גם.אכול.את.כספנו׃
16 כי.כל.העשר.אשר.הציל.אלהים.מאבינו.
לנו.הוא.ולבנינו.ועתה.כל.אשר.אמר.אלהים.א
ליך.עשה׃
17 ויקם.יעקב.וישא.את.בניו.ואת.נשיו.על
.הגמלים׃
18 וינהג.את.כל.מקנהו.ואת.כל.רכשו.אשר.ר
כש.מקנה.קנינו.אשר.רכש.בפדן.ארם.לבוא.אל
.יצחק.אביו.ארצה.כנען׃
19 ולבן.הלך.לגזז.את.צאנו.ותגנב.רחל.
את.התרפים.אשר.לאביה׃
20 ויגנב.יעקב.את.לב.לבן.הארמי.על.בלי.
הגיד.לו.כי.ברח.הוא׃
21 ויברח.הוא.וכל.אשר.לו.ויקם.ויעבר.את.
הנהר.וישם.את.פניו.הר.הגלעד׃
22 ויגד.ללבן.ביום.השלישי.כי.ברח.יעק
ב׃
23 ויקח.את.אחיו.עמו.וירדף.אחריו.דרך.
שבעת.ימים.וידבק.אתו.בהר.הגלעד׃
24 ויבא.אלהים.אל.לבן.הארמי.בחלם.הלי
לה.ויאמר.לו.השמר.לך.פן.תדבר.עם.יעקב.מט
וב.עד.רע׃
25 וישג.לבן.את.יעקב.ויעקב.תקע.את.אה
לו.בהר.ולבן.תקע.את.אחיו.בהר.הגלעד׃
26 ויאמר.לבן.ליעקב.מה.עשית.ותגנב.את.
לבבי.ותנהג.את.בנתי.כשביות.חרב׃
27 למה.נחבאת.לברח.ותגנב.אתי.ולא.הג
דת.לי.ואשלחך.בשמחה.ובשרים.בתף.ובכנור׃
28 ולא.נטשתני.לנשק.לבני.ולבנתי.עתה.ה
סכלת.עשו׃

כט 𐤉𐤔.𐤋𐤀𐤋.𐤉𐤃𐤉.𐤋𐤏𐤔𐤅𐤕.𐤏𐤌𐤊𐤌.𐤓𐤏.𐤅𐤀𐤋𐤄𐤉.𐤀
𐤁𐤉𐤊𐤌.𐤀𐤌𐤔.𐤀𐤌𐤓.𐤀𐤋𐤉.𐤋𐤀𐤌𐤓.𐤄𐤔𐤌𐤓.𐤋𐤊.𐤌𐤃𐤁𐤓.𐤏
𐤌.𐤉𐤏𐤒𐤁.𐤌𐤈𐤅𐤁.𐤏𐤃.𐤓𐤏|
ל 𐤅𐤏𐤕𐤄.𐤄𐤋𐤊.𐤄𐤋𐤊𐤕.𐤊𐤉.𐤍𐤊𐤎𐤐.𐤍𐤊𐤎𐤐𐤕𐤄.𐤋𐤁𐤉
𐤕.𐤀𐤁𐤉𐤊.𐤋𐤌𐤄.𐤂𐤍𐤁𐤕.𐤀𐤕.𐤀𐤋𐤄𐤉|
לא 𐤅𐤉𐤏𐤍.𐤉𐤏𐤒𐤁.𐤅𐤉𐤀𐤌𐤓.𐤋𐤋𐤁𐤍.𐤊𐤉.𐤉𐤓𐤀𐤕𐤉.𐤊𐤉.𐤀
𐤌𐤓𐤕𐤉.𐤐𐤍.𐤕𐤂𐤆𐤋.𐤀𐤕.𐤁𐤍𐤅𐤕𐤉𐤊.𐤌𐤏𐤌𐤉|
לב 𐤏𐤌.𐤀𐤔𐤓.𐤕𐤌𐤑𐤀.𐤀𐤕.𐤀𐤋𐤄𐤉𐤊.𐤋𐤀.𐤉𐤇𐤉𐤄.𐤍𐤂
𐤃.𐤀𐤇𐤉𐤍𐤅.𐤄𐤊𐤓.𐤋𐤊.𐤌𐤄.𐤏𐤌𐤃𐤉.𐤅𐤒𐤇.𐤋𐤊.𐤅𐤋𐤀.𐤉𐤃
𐤏.𐤉𐤏𐤒𐤁.𐤊𐤉.𐤓𐤇𐤋.𐤂𐤍𐤁𐤕𐤌|
לג 𐤅𐤉𐤁𐤀.𐤋𐤁𐤍.𐤁𐤀𐤄𐤋.𐤉𐤏𐤒𐤁.𐤅𐤁𐤀𐤄𐤋.𐤋𐤀𐤄.𐤅𐤁𐤀𐤄
𐤋.𐤔𐤕𐤉.𐤄𐤀𐤌𐤄𐤕.𐤅𐤋𐤀.𐤌𐤑𐤀.𐤅𐤉𐤑𐤀.𐤌𐤀𐤄𐤋.𐤋𐤀𐤄.𐤅𐤉
𐤁𐤀.𐤁𐤀𐤄𐤋.𐤓𐤇𐤋|
לד 𐤅𐤓𐤇𐤋.𐤋𐤒𐤇𐤄.𐤀𐤕.𐤄𐤕𐤓𐤐𐤉𐤌.𐤅𐤕𐤔𐤌𐤌.𐤁𐤊𐤓.𐤄
𐤂𐤌𐤋.𐤅𐤕𐤔𐤁.𐤏𐤋𐤉𐤄𐤌.𐤅𐤉𐤌𐤔𐤔.𐤋𐤁𐤍.𐤀𐤕.𐤊𐤋.𐤄𐤀𐤄𐤋.𐤅
𐤋𐤀.𐤌𐤑𐤀|
לה 𐤅𐤕𐤀𐤌𐤓.𐤀𐤋.𐤀𐤁𐤉𐤄.𐤀𐤋.𐤉𐤇𐤓.𐤁𐤏𐤉𐤍𐤉.𐤀𐤃𐤍𐤉.𐤊
𐤉.𐤋𐤅𐤀.𐤀𐤅𐤊𐤋.𐤋𐤒𐤅𐤌.𐤌𐤐𐤍𐤉𐤊.𐤊𐤉.𐤃𐤓𐤊.𐤍𐤔𐤉𐤌.𐤋𐤉.𐤅𐤉
𐤇𐤐𐤔.𐤅𐤋𐤀.𐤌𐤑𐤀.𐤀𐤕.𐤄𐤕𐤓𐤐𐤉𐤌|
לו 𐤅𐤉𐤇𐤓.𐤋𐤉𐤏𐤒𐤁.𐤅𐤉𐤓𐤁.𐤁𐤋𐤁𐤍.𐤅𐤉𐤏𐤍.𐤉𐤏𐤒𐤁.𐤅𐤉𐤀
𐤌𐤓.𐤋𐤋𐤁𐤍.𐤌𐤄.𐤐𐤔𐤏𐤉.𐤌𐤄.𐤇𐤈𐤀𐤕𐤉.𐤊𐤉.𐤃𐤋𐤒𐤕.𐤀𐤇
𐤓𐤉|
לז 𐤊𐤉.𐤌𐤔𐤔𐤕.𐤀𐤕.𐤊𐤋.𐤊𐤋𐤉.𐤌𐤄.𐤌𐤑𐤀𐤕.𐤌𐤊𐤋.𐤊
𐤋𐤉.𐤁𐤉𐤕𐤊.𐤔𐤉𐤌.𐤊𐤄.𐤍𐤂𐤃.𐤀𐤇𐤉.𐤅𐤀𐤇𐤉𐤊.𐤅𐤉𐤅𐤊𐤉𐤇𐤅.
𐤁𐤉𐤍.𐤔𐤍𐤉𐤍𐤅|
לח 𐤆𐤄.𐤏𐤔𐤓𐤉𐤌.𐤔𐤍𐤄.𐤀𐤍𐤊𐤉.𐤏𐤌𐤊.𐤓𐤇𐤋𐤉𐤊.𐤅𐤏𐤆
𐤉𐤊.𐤋𐤀.𐤔𐤊𐤋𐤅.𐤅𐤀𐤉𐤋𐤉.𐤑𐤀𐤍𐤊.𐤋𐤀.𐤀𐤊𐤋𐤕𐤉|
לט 𐤈𐤓𐤐𐤄.𐤋𐤀.𐤄𐤁𐤀𐤕𐤉.𐤀𐤋𐤉𐤊.𐤀𐤍𐤊𐤉.𐤀𐤇𐤈𐤍𐤄.𐤌
𐤉𐤃𐤉.𐤕𐤁𐤒𐤔𐤍𐤄.𐤂𐤍𐤁𐤕𐤉.𐤉𐤅𐤌.𐤅𐤂𐤍𐤁𐤕𐤉.𐤋𐤉𐤋𐤄|
מ 𐤄𐤉𐤉𐤕𐤉.𐤁𐤉𐤅𐤌.𐤀𐤊𐤋𐤍𐤉.𐤇𐤓𐤁.𐤅𐤒𐤓𐤇.𐤁𐤋𐤉𐤋𐤄.𐤅
𐤕𐤃𐤃.𐤔𐤍𐤕𐤉.𐤌𐤏𐤉𐤍𐤉|

מא 𐤆𐤄.𐤋𐤉.𐤏𐤔𐤓𐤉𐤌.𐤔𐤍𐤄.𐤁𐤁𐤉𐤕𐤊.𐤏𐤁𐤃𐤕𐤉𐤊.𐤀𐤓
𐤁𐤏.𐤏𐤔𐤓𐤄.𐤔𐤍𐤄.𐤁𐤔𐤕𐤉.𐤁𐤍𐤕𐤉𐤊.𐤅𐤔𐤔.𐤔𐤍𐤉𐤌.𐤁𐤑𐤀
𐤍𐤊.𐤅𐤕𐤇𐤋𐤐.𐤀𐤕.𐤌𐤔𐤊𐤓𐤕𐤉.𐤏𐤔𐤓𐤕.𐤌𐤍𐤉𐤌|

מב 𐤋𐤅𐤋𐤉.𐤀𐤋𐤄𐤉.𐤀𐤁𐤉.𐤀𐤋𐤄𐤉.𐤀𐤁𐤓𐤄𐤌.𐤅𐤐𐤇𐤃.𐤉𐤑
𐤇𐤒.𐤄𐤉𐤄.𐤋𐤉.𐤊𐤉.𐤏𐤕𐤄.𐤓𐤉𐤒𐤌.𐤔𐤋𐤇𐤕𐤍𐤉.𐤀𐤕.𐤏𐤍𐤉
𐤉.𐤅𐤀𐤕.𐤉𐤂𐤉𐤏.𐤊𐤐𐤉.𐤓𐤀𐤄.𐤀𐤋𐤄𐤉𐤌.𐤅𐤉𐤅𐤊𐤇.𐤀𐤌𐤔|

מג 𐤅𐤉𐤏𐤍.𐤋𐤁𐤍.𐤅𐤉𐤀𐤌𐤓.𐤀𐤋.𐤉𐤏𐤒𐤁.𐤄𐤁𐤍𐤅𐤕.𐤁𐤍𐤕𐤉.𐤅
𐤄𐤁𐤍𐤉𐤌.𐤁𐤍𐤉.𐤅𐤄𐤑𐤀𐤍.𐤑𐤀𐤍𐤉.𐤅𐤊𐤋.𐤀𐤔𐤓.𐤀𐤕𐤄.𐤓𐤀𐤄.
𐤋𐤉.𐤄𐤅𐤀.𐤅𐤋𐤁𐤍𐤕𐤉.𐤌𐤄.𐤀𐤏𐤔𐤄.𐤋𐤀𐤋𐤄.𐤄𐤉𐤅𐤌.𐤀𐤅.𐤋𐤁𐤍
𐤉𐤄𐤍.𐤀𐤔𐤓.𐤉𐤋𐤃𐤅|

מד 𐤅𐤏𐤕𐤄.𐤋𐤊𐤄.𐤍𐤊𐤓𐤕𐤄.𐤁𐤓𐤉𐤕.𐤀𐤍𐤉.𐤅𐤀𐤕𐤄.𐤅𐤄𐤉
𐤄.𐤋𐤏𐤃.𐤁𐤉𐤍𐤉.𐤅𐤁𐤉𐤍𐤊|

מה 𐤅𐤉𐤒𐤇.𐤉𐤏𐤒𐤁.𐤀𐤁𐤍.𐤅𐤉𐤓𐤉𐤌𐤄.𐤌𐤑𐤁𐤄|

מו 𐤅𐤉𐤀𐤌𐤓.𐤉𐤏𐤒𐤁.𐤋𐤀𐤇𐤉𐤅.𐤋𐤒𐤈𐤅.𐤀𐤁𐤍𐤉𐤌.𐤅𐤉𐤒𐤇
𐤅.𐤀𐤁𐤍𐤉𐤌.𐤅𐤉𐤏𐤔𐤅.𐤂𐤋.𐤅𐤉𐤀𐤊𐤋𐤅.𐤔𐤌.𐤏𐤋.𐤄𐤂𐤋|

מז 𐤅𐤉𐤒𐤓𐤀.𐤋𐤅.𐤋𐤁𐤍.𐤉𐤂𐤓.𐤔𐤄𐤃𐤅𐤕𐤀.𐤅𐤉𐤏𐤒𐤁.𐤒𐤓
𐤀.𐤋𐤅.𐤂𐤋𐤏𐤃|

מח 𐤅𐤉𐤀𐤌𐤓.𐤋𐤁𐤍.𐤄𐤂𐤋.𐤄𐤆𐤄.𐤏𐤃.𐤁𐤉𐤍𐤉.𐤅𐤁𐤉𐤍𐤊.𐤄
𐤉𐤅𐤌.𐤏𐤋.𐤊𐤍.𐤒𐤓𐤀.𐤔𐤌𐤅.𐤂𐤋𐤏𐤃|

מט 𐤅𐤄𐤌𐤑𐤐𐤄.𐤀𐤔𐤓.𐤀𐤌𐤓.𐤉𐤑𐤐.𐤉𐤄𐤅𐤄.𐤁𐤉𐤍𐤉.𐤅𐤁𐤉
𐤍𐤊.𐤊𐤉.𐤍𐤎𐤕𐤓.𐤀𐤉𐤔.𐤌𐤓𐤏𐤄𐤅|

נ 𐤀𐤌.𐤕𐤏𐤍𐤄.𐤀𐤕.𐤁𐤍𐤕𐤉.𐤅𐤀𐤌.𐤕𐤒𐤇.𐤍𐤔𐤉𐤌.𐤏𐤋.
𐤁𐤍𐤕𐤉.𐤀𐤉𐤍.𐤀𐤉𐤔.𐤏𐤌𐤍𐤅.𐤓𐤀𐤄.𐤀𐤋𐤄𐤉𐤌.𐤏𐤃.𐤁𐤉𐤍𐤉.𐤅
𐤁𐤉𐤍𐤊|

נא 𐤅𐤉𐤀𐤌𐤓.𐤋𐤁𐤍.𐤋𐤉𐤏𐤒𐤁.𐤄𐤍𐤄.𐤄𐤂𐤋.𐤄𐤆𐤄.𐤅𐤄𐤍𐤄.
𐤄𐤌𐤑𐤁𐤄.𐤀𐤔𐤓.𐤉𐤓𐤉𐤕𐤉.𐤁𐤉𐤍𐤉.𐤅𐤁𐤉𐤍𐤊|

נב 𐤏𐤃.𐤄𐤂𐤋.𐤄𐤆𐤄.𐤅𐤏𐤃𐤄.𐤄𐤌𐤑𐤁𐤄.𐤀𐤌.𐤀𐤍𐤉.𐤋
𐤀.𐤀𐤏𐤁𐤓.𐤀𐤋𐤉𐤊.𐤀𐤕.𐤄𐤂𐤋.𐤄𐤆𐤄.𐤅𐤀𐤌.𐤀𐤕𐤄.𐤋𐤀.𐤕
𐤏𐤁𐤓.𐤀𐤋𐤉.𐤀𐤕.𐤄𐤂𐤋.𐤄𐤆𐤄.𐤅𐤀𐤕.𐤄𐤌𐤑𐤁𐤄.𐤄𐤆𐤀𐤕.
𐤋𐤓𐤏𐤄|

..נג.. 𐤀𐤋𐤄𐤉.𐤀𐤁𐤓𐤄𐤌.𐤅𐤀𐤋𐤄𐤉.𐤍𐤇𐤅𐤓.𐤉𐤔𐤐𐤈𐤅.𐤁𐤉𐤍𐤉𐤍𐤅
.𐤀𐤋𐤄𐤉.𐤀𐤁𐤉𐤄𐤌.𐤅𐤉𐤔𐤁𐤏.𐤉𐤏𐤒𐤁.𐤁𐤐𐤇𐤃.𐤀𐤁𐤉𐤅.𐤉𐤑
𐤇𐤒|

..נד.. 𐤅𐤉𐤆𐤁𐤇.𐤉𐤏𐤒𐤁.𐤆𐤁𐤇.𐤁𐤄𐤓.𐤅𐤉𐤒𐤓𐤀.𐤋𐤀𐤇𐤉𐤅.
𐤋𐤀𐤊𐤋.𐤋𐤇𐤌.𐤅𐤉𐤀𐤊𐤋𐤅.𐤋𐤇𐤌.𐤅𐤉𐤋𐤉𐤍𐤅.𐤁𐤄𐤓||

𐤁𐤓𐤀𐤔𐤉𐤕.𐤇𐤋𐤒 ..לב..

..א.. 𐤅𐤉𐤔𐤊𐤌.𐤋𐤁𐤍.𐤁𐤁𐤒𐤓.𐤅𐤉𐤍𐤔𐤒.𐤋𐤁𐤍𐤉𐤅.𐤅𐤋𐤁𐤍𐤅𐤕𐤉𐤅.𐤅
𐤉𐤁𐤓𐤊.𐤀𐤕𐤄𐤌.𐤅𐤉𐤋𐤊.𐤅𐤉𐤔𐤁.𐤋𐤁𐤍.𐤋𐤌𐤒𐤌𐤅|

..ב.. 𐤅𐤉𐤏𐤒𐤁.𐤄𐤋𐤊.𐤋𐤃𐤓𐤊𐤅.𐤅𐤉𐤐𐤂𐤏𐤅.𐤁𐤅.𐤌𐤋𐤀𐤊𐤉.𐤀𐤋
𐤄𐤉𐤌|

..ג.. 𐤅𐤉𐤀𐤌𐤓.𐤉𐤏𐤒𐤁.𐤊𐤀𐤔𐤓.𐤓𐤀𐤌.𐤌𐤇𐤍𐤄.𐤀𐤋𐤄𐤉𐤌.𐤆
𐤄.𐤅𐤉𐤒𐤓𐤀.𐤔𐤌.𐤄𐤌𐤒𐤅𐤌.𐤄𐤄𐤅𐤀.𐤌𐤇𐤍𐤉𐤌|

..ד.. 𐤅𐤉𐤔𐤋𐤇.𐤉𐤏𐤒𐤁.𐤌𐤋𐤀𐤊𐤉𐤌.𐤋𐤐𐤍𐤉𐤅.𐤀𐤋.𐤏𐤔𐤅.𐤀𐤇
𐤉𐤅.𐤀𐤓𐤑𐤄.𐤔𐤏𐤉𐤓.𐤔𐤃𐤄.𐤀𐤃𐤅𐤌|

..ה.. 𐤅𐤉𐤑𐤅.𐤀𐤕𐤌.𐤋𐤀𐤌𐤓.𐤊𐤄.𐤕𐤀𐤌𐤓𐤅𐤍.𐤋𐤀𐤃𐤍𐤉.𐤋𐤏𐤔𐤅.
𐤊𐤄.𐤀𐤌𐤓.𐤏𐤁𐤃𐤊.𐤉𐤏𐤒𐤁.𐤏𐤌.𐤋𐤁𐤍.𐤂𐤓𐤕𐤉.𐤅𐤀𐤇𐤓.𐤏
𐤃.𐤏𐤕𐤄|

..ו.. 𐤅𐤉𐤄𐤉.𐤋𐤉.𐤔𐤅𐤓.𐤅𐤇𐤌𐤅𐤓.𐤑𐤀𐤍.𐤅𐤏𐤁𐤃.𐤅𐤔𐤐𐤇𐤄.𐤅𐤀
𐤔𐤋𐤇𐤄.𐤋𐤄𐤂𐤉𐤃.𐤋𐤀𐤃𐤍𐤉.𐤋𐤌𐤑𐤀.𐤇𐤍.𐤁𐤏𐤉𐤍𐤉𐤊|

..ז.. 𐤅𐤉𐤔𐤁𐤅.𐤄𐤌𐤋𐤀𐤊𐤉𐤌.𐤀𐤋.𐤉𐤏𐤒𐤁.𐤋𐤀𐤌𐤓.𐤁𐤀𐤍𐤅.𐤀𐤋
.𐤀𐤇𐤉𐤊.𐤀𐤋.𐤏𐤔𐤅.𐤅𐤂𐤌.𐤄𐤋𐤊.𐤋𐤒𐤓𐤀𐤕𐤊.𐤅𐤀𐤓𐤁𐤏.𐤌𐤀𐤅
𐤕.𐤀𐤉𐤔.𐤏𐤌𐤅|

..ח.. 𐤅𐤉𐤉𐤓𐤀.𐤉𐤏𐤒𐤁.𐤌𐤀𐤃.𐤅𐤉𐤑𐤓.𐤋𐤅.𐤅𐤉𐤇𐤑.𐤀𐤕.𐤄𐤏
𐤌.𐤀𐤔𐤓.𐤀𐤕𐤅.𐤅𐤀𐤕.𐤄𐤑𐤀𐤍.𐤅𐤀𐤕.𐤄𐤁𐤒𐤓.𐤅𐤄𐤂𐤌𐤋𐤉𐤌.𐤋
𐤔𐤍𐤉.𐤌𐤇𐤍𐤅𐤕|

..ט.. 𐤅𐤉𐤀𐤌𐤓.𐤀𐤌.𐤉𐤁𐤅𐤀.𐤏𐤔𐤅.𐤀𐤋.𐤄𐤌𐤇𐤍𐤄.𐤄𐤀𐤇𐤕.𐤅
𐤄𐤊𐤄𐤅.𐤅𐤄𐤉𐤄.𐤄𐤌𐤇𐤍𐤄.𐤄𐤍𐤔𐤀𐤓.𐤋𐤐𐤋𐤉𐤈𐤄|

10 𐤅𐤉𐤀𐤌𐤓.𐤉𐤏𐤒𐤁.𐤀𐤋𐤄𐤉.𐤀𐤁𐤉.𐤀𐤁𐤓𐤄𐤌.𐤅𐤀𐤋𐤄𐤉.
𐤀𐤁𐤉.𐤉𐤑𐤇𐤒.𐤉𐤄𐤅𐤄.𐤄𐤀𐤌𐤓.𐤀𐤋𐤉.𐤔𐤅𐤁.𐤋𐤀𐤓𐤑𐤊.𐤅𐤋𐤌
𐤅𐤋𐤃𐤕𐤊.𐤅𐤀𐤉𐤈𐤉𐤁𐤄.𐤏𐤌𐤊|
11 𐤒𐤈𐤍𐤕𐤉.𐤌𐤊𐤋.𐤄𐤇𐤎𐤃𐤉𐤌.𐤅𐤌𐤊𐤋.𐤄𐤀𐤌𐤕.𐤀𐤔𐤓.
𐤏𐤔𐤉𐤕.𐤀𐤕.𐤏𐤁𐤃𐤊.𐤊𐤉.𐤁𐤌𐤒𐤋𐤉.𐤏𐤁𐤓𐤕𐤉.𐤀𐤕.𐤄𐤉𐤓
𐤃𐤍.𐤄𐤆𐤄.𐤅𐤏𐤕𐤄.𐤄𐤉𐤉𐤕𐤉.𐤋𐤔𐤍𐤉.𐤌𐤇𐤍𐤅𐤕|
12 𐤄𐤑𐤉𐤋𐤍𐤉.𐤍𐤀.𐤌𐤉𐤃.𐤀𐤇𐤉.𐤌𐤉𐤃.𐤏𐤔𐤅.𐤊𐤉.𐤉𐤓𐤀
.𐤀𐤍𐤊𐤉.𐤀𐤕𐤅.𐤐𐤍.𐤉𐤁𐤅𐤀.𐤅𐤄𐤊𐤍𐤉.𐤀𐤌.𐤏𐤋.𐤁𐤍𐤉𐤌|
13 𐤅𐤀𐤕𐤄.𐤀𐤌𐤓𐤕.𐤄𐤉𐤈𐤁.𐤀𐤉𐤈𐤉𐤁.𐤏𐤌𐤊.𐤅𐤔𐤌𐤕𐤉.
𐤀𐤕.𐤆𐤓𐤏𐤊.𐤊𐤇𐤅𐤋.𐤄𐤉𐤌.𐤀𐤔𐤓.𐤋𐤀.𐤉𐤎𐤐𐤓.𐤌𐤓𐤁|
14 𐤅𐤉𐤋𐤍.𐤔𐤌.𐤁𐤋𐤉𐤋𐤄.𐤄𐤄𐤅𐤀.𐤅𐤉𐤒𐤇.𐤌𐤍.𐤄𐤁𐤀.𐤁𐤉
𐤃𐤅.𐤌𐤍𐤇𐤄.𐤋𐤏𐤔𐤅.𐤀𐤇𐤉𐤅|
15 𐤏𐤆𐤉𐤌.𐤌𐤀𐤕𐤉𐤌.𐤅𐤕𐤉𐤔𐤉𐤌.𐤏𐤔𐤓𐤉𐤌.𐤓𐤇𐤋𐤉𐤌.
𐤌𐤀𐤕𐤉𐤌.𐤅𐤀𐤉𐤋𐤉𐤌.𐤏𐤔𐤓𐤉𐤌|
16 𐤂𐤌𐤋𐤉𐤌.𐤌𐤉𐤍𐤉𐤒𐤅𐤕.𐤅𐤁𐤍𐤉𐤄𐤌.𐤔𐤋𐤔𐤉𐤌.𐤐𐤓𐤅𐤕.𐤀
𐤓𐤁𐤏𐤉𐤌.𐤅𐤐𐤓𐤉𐤌.𐤏𐤔𐤓𐤄.𐤀𐤕𐤍𐤕.𐤏𐤔𐤓𐤉𐤌.𐤅𐤏𐤉𐤓𐤉𐤌.𐤏𐤔
𐤓𐤄|
17 𐤅𐤉𐤕𐤍.𐤁𐤉𐤃.𐤏𐤁𐤃𐤉𐤅.𐤏𐤃𐤓.𐤏𐤃𐤓.𐤋𐤁𐤃𐤅.𐤅𐤉𐤀𐤌
𐤓.𐤀𐤋.𐤏𐤁𐤃𐤉𐤅.𐤏𐤁𐤓𐤅.𐤋𐤐𐤍𐤉.𐤅𐤓𐤅𐤇.𐤕𐤔𐤉𐤌𐤅.𐤁𐤉𐤍.𐤏𐤃𐤓
.𐤅𐤁𐤉𐤍.𐤏𐤃𐤓|
18 𐤅𐤉𐤑𐤅.𐤀𐤕.𐤄𐤓𐤀𐤔𐤅𐤍.𐤋𐤀𐤌𐤓.𐤊𐤉.𐤉𐤐𐤂𐤔𐤊.𐤏𐤔𐤅.
𐤀𐤇𐤉.𐤅𐤔𐤀𐤋𐤊.𐤋𐤀𐤌𐤓.𐤋𐤌𐤉.𐤀𐤕𐤄.𐤅𐤀𐤍𐤄.𐤕𐤋𐤊.𐤅𐤋𐤌𐤉.
𐤀𐤋𐤄.𐤋𐤐𐤍𐤉𐤊|
19 𐤅𐤀𐤌𐤓𐤕.𐤋𐤏𐤁𐤃𐤊.𐤉𐤏𐤒𐤁.𐤌𐤍𐤇𐤄.𐤄𐤉𐤀.𐤔𐤋𐤅𐤇
𐤄.𐤋𐤀𐤃𐤍𐤉.𐤋𐤏𐤔𐤅.𐤅𐤄𐤍𐤄.𐤂𐤌.𐤄𐤅𐤀.𐤀𐤇𐤓𐤉𐤍𐤅|
20 𐤅𐤉𐤑𐤅.𐤂𐤌.𐤀𐤕.𐤄𐤔𐤍𐤉.𐤂𐤌.𐤀𐤕.𐤄𐤔𐤋𐤉𐤔𐤉.𐤂𐤌.
𐤀𐤕.𐤊𐤋.𐤄𐤄𐤋𐤊𐤉𐤌.𐤀𐤇𐤓𐤉.𐤄𐤏𐤃𐤓𐤉𐤌.𐤋𐤀𐤌𐤓.𐤊𐤃𐤁𐤓.
𐤄𐤆𐤄.𐤕𐤃𐤁𐤓𐤅𐤍.𐤀𐤋.𐤏𐤔𐤅.𐤁𐤌𐤑𐤀𐤊𐤌.𐤀𐤕𐤅|
21 𐤅𐤀𐤌𐤓𐤕𐤌.𐤂𐤌.𐤄𐤍𐤄.𐤏𐤁𐤃𐤊.𐤉𐤏𐤒𐤁.𐤀𐤇𐤓𐤉𐤍𐤅.𐤊
𐤉.𐤀𐤌𐤓.𐤀𐤊𐤐𐤓𐤄.𐤐𐤍𐤉𐤅.𐤁𐤌𐤍𐤇𐤄.𐤄𐤄𐤋𐤊𐤕.𐤋𐤐𐤍𐤉𐤅.𐤅𐤀𐤇
𐤓𐤉.𐤊𐤍.𐤀𐤓𐤀𐤄.𐤐𐤍𐤉𐤅.𐤀𐤅𐤋𐤉.𐤉𐤔𐤀.𐤐𐤍𐤉|

..22.. 𐤅𐤕𐤏𐤁𐤓.𐤄𐤌𐤍𐤇𐤄.𐤏𐤋.𐤐𐤍𐤉𐤅.𐤅𐤄𐤅𐤀.𐤋𐤍.𐤁𐤋𐤉𐤋𐤄.𐤄
𐤄𐤅𐤀.𐤁𐤌𐤇𐤍𐤄|
..23.. 𐤅𐤉𐤒𐤌.𐤁𐤋𐤉𐤋𐤄.𐤄𐤅𐤀.𐤅𐤉𐤒𐤇.𐤀𐤕.𐤔𐤕𐤉.𐤍𐤔𐤉𐤅.𐤅
𐤀𐤕.𐤔𐤕𐤉.𐤔𐤐𐤇𐤕𐤉𐤅.𐤅𐤀𐤕.𐤀𐤇𐤃.𐤏𐤔𐤓.𐤉𐤋𐤃𐤉𐤅.𐤅𐤉𐤏
𐤁𐤓.𐤀𐤕.𐤌𐤏𐤁𐤓.𐤉𐤁𐤒|
..24.. 𐤅𐤉𐤒𐤇𐤌.𐤅𐤉𐤏𐤁𐤓𐤌.𐤀𐤕.𐤄𐤍𐤇𐤋.𐤅𐤉𐤏𐤁𐤓.𐤀𐤕.𐤀𐤔
𐤓.𐤋𐤅|
..25.. 𐤅𐤉𐤅𐤕𐤓.𐤉𐤏𐤒𐤁.𐤋𐤁𐤃𐤅.𐤅𐤉𐤀𐤁𐤒.𐤀𐤉𐤔.𐤏𐤌𐤅.𐤏𐤃.
𐤏𐤋𐤅𐤕.𐤄𐤔𐤇𐤓|
..26.. 𐤅𐤉𐤓𐤀.𐤊𐤉.𐤋𐤀.𐤉𐤊𐤋.𐤋𐤅.𐤅𐤉𐤂𐤏.𐤁𐤊𐤐.𐤉𐤓𐤊𐤅.𐤅𐤕𐤒𐤏
.𐤊𐤐.𐤉𐤓𐤊.𐤉𐤏𐤒𐤁.𐤁𐤄𐤀𐤁𐤒𐤅.𐤏𐤌𐤅|
..27.. 𐤅𐤉𐤀𐤌𐤓.𐤔𐤋𐤇𐤍𐤉.𐤊𐤉.𐤏𐤋𐤄.𐤄𐤔𐤇𐤓.𐤅𐤉𐤀𐤌𐤓.𐤋𐤀.
𐤀𐤔𐤋𐤇𐤊.𐤊𐤉.𐤀𐤌.𐤁𐤓𐤊𐤕𐤍𐤉|
..28.. 𐤅𐤉𐤀𐤌𐤓.𐤀𐤋𐤉𐤅.𐤌𐤄.𐤔𐤌𐤊.𐤅𐤉𐤀𐤌𐤓.𐤉𐤏𐤒𐤁|
..29.. 𐤅𐤉𐤀𐤌𐤓.𐤋𐤀.𐤉𐤏𐤒𐤁.𐤉𐤀𐤌𐤓.𐤏𐤅𐤃.𐤔𐤌𐤊.𐤊𐤉.𐤀𐤌
.𐤉𐤔𐤓𐤀𐤋.𐤊𐤉.𐤔𐤓𐤉𐤕.𐤏𐤌.𐤀𐤋𐤄𐤉𐤌.𐤅𐤏𐤌.𐤀𐤍𐤔𐤉𐤌.𐤅𐤕𐤅
𐤊𐤋|
..30.. 𐤅𐤉𐤔𐤀𐤋.𐤉𐤏𐤒𐤁.𐤅𐤉𐤀𐤌𐤓.𐤄𐤂𐤉𐤃𐤄.𐤍𐤀.𐤔𐤌𐤊.𐤅𐤉
𐤀𐤌𐤓.𐤋𐤌𐤄.𐤆𐤄.𐤕𐤔𐤀𐤋.𐤋𐤔𐤌𐤉.𐤅𐤉𐤁𐤓𐤊.𐤀𐤕𐤅.𐤔𐤌|
..31.. 𐤅𐤉𐤒𐤓𐤀.𐤉𐤏𐤒𐤁.𐤔𐤌.𐤄𐤌𐤒𐤅𐤌.𐤐𐤍𐤉𐤀𐤋.𐤊𐤉.𐤓𐤀𐤉
𐤕𐤉.𐤀𐤋𐤄𐤉𐤌.𐤐𐤍𐤉𐤌.𐤀𐤋.𐤐𐤍𐤉𐤌.𐤅𐤕𐤍𐤑𐤋.𐤍𐤐𐤔𐤉|
..32.. 𐤅𐤉𐤆𐤓𐤇.𐤋𐤅.𐤄𐤔𐤌𐤔.𐤊𐤀𐤔𐤓.𐤏𐤁𐤓.𐤀𐤕.𐤐𐤍𐤅𐤀𐤋.𐤅
𐤄𐤅𐤀.𐤑𐤋𐤏.𐤏𐤋.𐤉𐤓𐤊𐤅|
..33.. 𐤏𐤋.𐤊𐤍.𐤋𐤀.𐤉𐤀𐤊𐤋𐤅.𐤁𐤍𐤉.𐤉𐤔𐤓𐤀𐤋.𐤀𐤕.𐤂𐤉𐤃.𐤄
𐤍𐤔𐤄.𐤀𐤔𐤓.𐤏𐤋.𐤊𐤐.𐤄𐤉𐤓𐤊.𐤏𐤃.𐤄𐤉𐤅𐤌.𐤄𐤆𐤄.𐤊𐤉.𐤍𐤂
𐤏.𐤁𐤊𐤐.𐤉𐤓𐤊.𐤉𐤏𐤒𐤁.𐤁𐤂𐤉𐤃.𐤄𐤍𐤔𐤄||

𐤁𐤓𐤀𐤔𐤉𐤕.𐤇𐤋𐤒 ..33..

א 𐤅𐤉𐤔𐤀.𐤉𐤏𐤒𐤁.𐤏𐤉𐤍𐤉𐤅.𐤅𐤉𐤓𐤀.𐤅𐤄𐤍𐤄.𐤏𐤔𐤅.𐤁𐤀.𐤅𐤏
𐤌𐤅.𐤀𐤓𐤁𐤏.𐤌𐤀𐤅𐤕.𐤀𐤉𐤔.𐤅𐤉𐤇𐤑.𐤀𐤕.𐤄𐤉𐤋𐤃𐤉𐤌.𐤏𐤋.𐤋
𐤀𐤄.𐤅𐤏𐤋.𐤓𐤇𐤋.𐤅𐤏𐤋.𐤔𐤕𐤉.𐤄𐤔𐤐𐤇𐤅𐤕|
ב 𐤅𐤉𐤔𐤌.𐤀𐤕.𐤄𐤔𐤐𐤇𐤅𐤕.𐤅𐤀𐤕.𐤉𐤋𐤃𐤉𐤄𐤍.𐤓𐤀𐤔𐤍𐤄.𐤅
𐤀𐤕.𐤋𐤀𐤄.𐤅𐤉𐤋𐤃𐤉𐤄.𐤀𐤇𐤓𐤍𐤉𐤌.𐤅𐤀𐤕.𐤓𐤇𐤋.𐤅𐤀𐤕.𐤉𐤅𐤎
𐤐.𐤀𐤇𐤓𐤍𐤉𐤌|
ג 𐤅𐤄𐤅𐤀.𐤏𐤁𐤓.𐤋𐤐𐤍𐤉𐤄𐤌.𐤅𐤉𐤔𐤕𐤇𐤅.𐤀𐤓𐤑𐤄.𐤔𐤁𐤏.𐤐𐤏
𐤌𐤉𐤌.𐤏𐤃.𐤂𐤔𐤕𐤅.𐤏𐤃.𐤀𐤇𐤉𐤅|
ד 𐤅𐤉𐤓𐤑.𐤏𐤔𐤅.𐤋𐤒𐤓𐤀𐤕𐤅.𐤅𐤉𐤇𐤁𐤒𐤄𐤅.𐤅𐤉𐤐𐤋.𐤏𐤋.𐤑𐤅
𐤀𐤓𐤅.𐤅𐤉𐤔𐤒𐤄𐤅.𐤅𐤉𐤁𐤊𐤅|
ה 𐤅𐤉𐤔𐤀.𐤀𐤕.𐤏𐤉𐤍𐤉𐤅.𐤅𐤉𐤓𐤀.𐤀𐤕.𐤄𐤍𐤔𐤉𐤌.𐤅𐤀𐤕.𐤄𐤉𐤋
𐤃𐤉𐤌.𐤅𐤉𐤀𐤌𐤓.𐤌𐤉.𐤀𐤋𐤄.𐤋𐤊.𐤅𐤉𐤀𐤌𐤓.𐤄𐤉𐤋𐤃𐤉𐤌.𐤀𐤔𐤓.
𐤇𐤍𐤍.𐤀𐤋𐤄𐤉𐤌.𐤀𐤕.𐤏𐤁𐤃𐤊|
ו 𐤅𐤕𐤂𐤔𐤍.𐤄𐤔𐤐𐤇𐤅𐤕.𐤄𐤍𐤄.𐤅𐤉𐤋𐤃𐤉𐤄𐤍.𐤅𐤕𐤔𐤕𐤇𐤅𐤉𐤍
|
ז 𐤅𐤕𐤂𐤔.𐤂𐤌.𐤋𐤀𐤄.𐤅𐤉𐤋𐤃𐤉𐤄.𐤅𐤉𐤔𐤕𐤇𐤅𐤅.𐤅𐤀𐤇𐤓.𐤍
𐤂𐤔.𐤉𐤅𐤎𐤐.𐤅𐤓𐤇𐤋.𐤅𐤉𐤔𐤕𐤇𐤅𐤅|
ח 𐤅𐤉𐤀𐤌𐤓.𐤌𐤉.𐤋𐤊.𐤊𐤋.𐤄𐤌𐤇𐤍𐤄.𐤄𐤆𐤄.𐤀𐤔𐤓.𐤐𐤂𐤔𐤕
𐤉.𐤅𐤉𐤀𐤌𐤓.𐤋𐤌𐤑𐤀.𐤇𐤍.𐤁𐤏𐤉𐤍𐤉.𐤀𐤃𐤍𐤉|
ט 𐤅𐤉𐤀𐤌𐤓.𐤏𐤔𐤅.𐤉𐤔.𐤋𐤉.𐤓𐤁.𐤀𐤇𐤉.𐤉𐤄𐤉.𐤋𐤊.𐤀𐤔𐤓.𐤋
𐤊|
י 𐤅𐤉𐤀𐤌𐤓.𐤉𐤏𐤒𐤁.𐤀𐤋.𐤍𐤀.𐤀𐤌.𐤍𐤀.𐤌𐤑𐤀𐤕𐤉.𐤇𐤍.𐤁
𐤏𐤉𐤍𐤉𐤊.𐤅𐤋𐤒𐤇𐤕.𐤌𐤍𐤇𐤕𐤉.𐤌𐤉𐤃𐤉.𐤊𐤉.𐤏𐤋.𐤊𐤍.𐤓𐤀𐤉𐤕
𐤉.𐤐𐤍𐤉𐤊.𐤊𐤓𐤀𐤕.𐤐𐤍𐤉.𐤀𐤋𐤄𐤉𐤌.𐤅𐤕𐤓𐤑𐤍𐤉|
יא 𐤒𐤇.𐤍𐤀.𐤀𐤕.𐤁𐤓𐤊𐤕𐤉.𐤀𐤔𐤓.𐤄𐤁𐤀𐤕.𐤋𐤊.𐤊𐤉.𐤇𐤍𐤍
𐤉.𐤀𐤋𐤄𐤉𐤌.𐤅𐤊𐤉.𐤉𐤔.𐤋𐤉.𐤊𐤋.𐤅𐤉𐤐𐤑𐤓.𐤁𐤅.𐤅𐤉𐤒𐤇|
יב 𐤅𐤉𐤀𐤌𐤓.𐤍𐤎𐤏𐤄.𐤅𐤍𐤋𐤊𐤄.𐤅𐤀𐤋𐤊𐤄.𐤋𐤍𐤂𐤃𐤊|
יג 𐤅𐤉𐤀𐤌𐤓.𐤀𐤋𐤉𐤅.𐤀𐤃𐤍𐤉.𐤉𐤃𐤏.𐤊𐤉.𐤄𐤉𐤋𐤃𐤉𐤌.𐤓𐤊
𐤉𐤌.𐤅𐤄𐤑𐤀𐤍.𐤅𐤄𐤁𐤒𐤓.𐤏𐤋𐤅𐤕.𐤏𐤋𐤉.𐤅𐤃𐤐𐤒𐤅𐤌.𐤉𐤅𐤌.𐤀𐤇
𐤃.𐤅𐤌𐤕𐤅.𐤊𐤋.𐤄𐤑𐤀𐤍|

יד יעבר.נא.אדני.לפני.עבדו.ואני.אתנהל
ה.לאטי.לרגל.המלאכה.אשר.לפני.ולרגל.היל
דים.עד.אשר.אבא.אל.אדני.שעירה|
טו ויאמר.עשו.אציגה.נא.עמך.מן.העם.אש
ר.אתי.ויאמר.למה.זה.אמצא.חן.בעיני.אדנ
י|
טז וישב.ביום.ההוא.עשו.לדרכו.שעירה|
יז ויעקב.נסע.סכתה.ויבן.לו.בית.ולמקנהו.
עשה.סכת.על.כן.קרא.שם.המקום.סכות|
יח ויבא.יעקב.שלם.עיר.שכם.אשר.בארץ.כ
נען.בבאו.מפדן.ארם.ויחן.את.פני.העיר|
יט ויקן.את.חלקת.השדה.אשר.נטה.שם.א
הלו.מיד.בני.חמור.אבי.שכם.במאה.קשיטה|
כ ויצב.שם.מזבח.ויקרא.לו.אל.אלהי.יש
ראל||

בראשית.חלק לד

א ותצא.דינה.בת.לאה.אשר.ילדה.ליעקב.ל
ראות.בבנות.הארץ|
ב וירא.אתה.שכם.בן.חמור.החוי.נשיא.האר
ץ.ויקח.אתה.וישכב.אתה.ויענה|
ג ותדבק.נפשו.בדינה.בת.יעקב.ויאהב.את
.הנערה.וידבר.על.לב.הנערה|
ד ויאמר.שכם.אל.חמור.אביו.לאמר.קח.לי.
את.הילדה.הזאת.לאשה|
ה ויעקב.שמע.כי.טמא.את.דינה.בתו.ובניו.
היו.את.מקנהו.בשדה.והחרש.יעקב.עד.בא
ם|
ו ויצא.חמור.אבי.שכם.אל.יעקב.לדבר.את
ו|

ז 𐤅𐤁𐤍𐤉.𐤉𐤏𐤒𐤁.𐤁𐤀𐤅.𐤌𐤍.𐤄𐤔𐤃𐤄.𐤊𐤔𐤌𐤏𐤌.𐤅𐤉𐤕𐤏𐤑𐤁𐤅.𐤄𐤀𐤍𐤔𐤉𐤌.𐤅𐤉𐤇𐤓.𐤋𐤄𐤌.𐤌𐤀𐤃.𐤊𐤉.𐤍𐤁𐤋𐤄.𐤏𐤔𐤄.𐤁𐤉𐤔𐤓𐤀𐤋.𐤋𐤔𐤊𐤁.𐤀𐤕.𐤁𐤕.𐤉𐤏𐤒𐤁.𐤅𐤊𐤍.𐤋𐤀.𐤉𐤏𐤔𐤄|

ח 𐤅𐤉𐤃𐤁𐤓.𐤇𐤌𐤅𐤓.𐤀𐤕𐤌.𐤋𐤀𐤌𐤓.𐤔𐤊𐤌.𐤁𐤍𐤉.𐤇𐤔𐤒𐤄.𐤍𐤐𐤔𐤅.𐤁𐤁𐤕𐤊𐤌.𐤕𐤍𐤅.𐤍𐤀.𐤀𐤕𐤄.𐤋𐤅.𐤋𐤀𐤔𐤄|

ט 𐤅𐤄𐤕𐤇𐤕𐤍𐤅.𐤀𐤕𐤍𐤅.𐤁𐤍𐤕𐤉𐤊𐤌.𐤕𐤕𐤍𐤅.𐤋𐤍𐤅.𐤅𐤀𐤕.𐤁𐤍𐤕𐤉𐤍𐤅.𐤕𐤒𐤇𐤅.𐤋𐤊𐤌|

י 𐤅𐤀𐤕𐤍𐤅.𐤕𐤔𐤁𐤅.𐤅𐤄𐤀𐤓𐤑.𐤕𐤄𐤉𐤄.𐤋𐤐𐤍𐤉𐤊𐤌.𐤔𐤁𐤅.𐤅𐤎𐤇𐤓𐤅𐤄.𐤅𐤄𐤀𐤇𐤆𐤅.𐤁𐤄|

יא 𐤅𐤉𐤀𐤌𐤓.𐤔𐤊𐤌.𐤀𐤋.𐤀𐤁𐤉𐤄.𐤅𐤀𐤋.𐤀𐤇𐤉𐤄.𐤀𐤌𐤑𐤀.𐤇𐤍.𐤁𐤏𐤉𐤍𐤉𐤊𐤌.𐤅𐤀𐤔𐤓.𐤕𐤀𐤌𐤓𐤅.𐤀𐤋𐤉.𐤀𐤕𐤍|

יב 𐤄𐤓𐤁𐤅.𐤏𐤋𐤉.𐤌𐤀𐤃.𐤌𐤄𐤓.𐤅𐤌𐤕𐤍.𐤅𐤀𐤕𐤍𐤄.𐤊𐤀𐤔𐤓.𐤕𐤀𐤌𐤓𐤅.𐤀𐤋𐤉.𐤅𐤕𐤍𐤅.𐤋𐤉.𐤀𐤕.𐤄𐤍𐤏𐤓𐤄.𐤋𐤀𐤔𐤄|

יג 𐤅𐤉𐤏𐤍𐤅.𐤁𐤍𐤉.𐤉𐤏𐤒𐤁.𐤀𐤕.𐤔𐤊𐤌.𐤅𐤀𐤕.𐤇𐤌𐤅𐤓.𐤀𐤁𐤉𐤅.𐤁𐤌𐤓𐤌𐤄.𐤅𐤉𐤃𐤁𐤓𐤅.𐤀𐤔𐤓.𐤈𐤌𐤀.𐤀𐤕.𐤃𐤉𐤍𐤄.𐤀𐤇𐤕𐤌|

יד 𐤅𐤉𐤀𐤌𐤓𐤅.𐤀𐤋𐤉𐤄𐤌.𐤋𐤀.𐤍𐤅𐤊𐤋.𐤋𐤏𐤔𐤅𐤕.𐤄𐤃𐤁𐤓.𐤄𐤆𐤄.𐤋𐤕𐤕.𐤀𐤕.𐤀𐤇𐤕𐤍𐤅.𐤋𐤀𐤉𐤔.𐤀𐤔𐤓.𐤋𐤅.𐤏𐤓𐤋𐤄.𐤊𐤉.𐤇𐤓𐤐𐤄.𐤄𐤅𐤀.𐤋𐤍𐤅|

טו 𐤀𐤊.𐤁𐤆𐤀𐤕.𐤍𐤀𐤅𐤕.𐤋𐤊𐤌.𐤀𐤌.𐤕𐤄𐤉𐤅.𐤊𐤌𐤍𐤅.𐤋𐤄𐤌𐤋.𐤋𐤊𐤌.𐤊𐤋.𐤆𐤊𐤓|

טז 𐤅𐤍𐤕𐤍𐤅.𐤀𐤕.𐤁𐤍𐤕𐤉𐤍𐤅.𐤋𐤊𐤌.𐤅𐤀𐤕.𐤁𐤍𐤕𐤉𐤊𐤌.𐤍𐤒𐤇.𐤋𐤍𐤅.𐤅𐤉𐤔𐤁𐤍𐤅.𐤀𐤕𐤊𐤌.𐤅𐤄𐤉𐤉𐤍𐤅.𐤋𐤏𐤌.𐤀𐤇𐤃|

יז 𐤅𐤀𐤌.𐤋𐤀.𐤕𐤔𐤌𐤏𐤅.𐤀𐤋𐤉𐤍𐤅.𐤋𐤄𐤌𐤅𐤋.𐤅𐤋𐤒𐤇𐤍𐤅.𐤀𐤕.𐤁𐤕𐤍𐤅.𐤅𐤄𐤋𐤊𐤍𐤅|

יח 𐤅𐤉𐤉𐤈𐤁𐤅.𐤃𐤁𐤓𐤉𐤄𐤌.𐤁𐤏𐤉𐤍𐤉.𐤇𐤌𐤅𐤓.𐤅𐤁𐤏𐤉𐤍𐤉.𐤔𐤊𐤌.𐤁𐤍.𐤇𐤌𐤅𐤓|

יט 𐤅𐤋𐤀.𐤀𐤇𐤓.𐤄𐤍𐤏𐤓.𐤋𐤏𐤔𐤅𐤕.𐤄𐤃𐤁𐤓.𐤊𐤉.𐤇𐤐𐤑.𐤁𐤁𐤕.𐤉𐤏𐤒𐤁.𐤅𐤄𐤅𐤀.𐤍𐤊𐤁𐤃.𐤌𐤊𐤋.𐤁𐤉𐤕.𐤀𐤁𐤉𐤅|

כ 𐤅𐤉𐤁𐤀.𐤇𐤌𐤅𐤓.𐤅𐤔𐤊𐤌.𐤁𐤍𐤅.𐤀𐤋.𐤔𐤏𐤓.𐤏𐤉𐤓𐤌.𐤅𐤉𐤃𐤁𐤓𐤅.𐤀𐤋.𐤀𐤍𐤔𐤉.𐤏𐤉𐤓𐤌.𐤋𐤀𐤌𐤓|

..𐤊𐤀.. 𐤄𐤀𐤍𐤔𐤉𐤌.𐤄𐤀𐤋𐤄.𐤔𐤋𐤌𐤉𐤌.𐤄𐤌.𐤀𐤕𐤍𐤅.𐤅𐤉𐤔𐤁𐤅.𐤁
𐤀𐤓𐤑.𐤅𐤉𐤎𐤇𐤓𐤅.𐤀𐤕𐤄.𐤅𐤄𐤀𐤓𐤑.𐤄𐤍𐤄.𐤓𐤇𐤁𐤕.𐤉𐤃𐤉𐤌.
𐤋𐤐𐤍𐤉𐤄𐤌.𐤀𐤕.𐤁𐤍𐤕𐤌.𐤍𐤒𐤇.𐤋𐤍𐤅.𐤋𐤍𐤔𐤉𐤌.𐤅𐤀𐤕.𐤁𐤍𐤕𐤉𐤍
𐤅.𐤍𐤕𐤍.𐤋𐤄𐤌|
..𐤊𐤁.. 𐤀𐤊.𐤁𐤆𐤀𐤕.𐤉𐤀𐤕𐤅.𐤋𐤍𐤅.𐤄𐤀𐤍𐤔𐤉𐤌.𐤋𐤔𐤁𐤕.𐤀𐤕𐤍
𐤅.𐤋𐤄𐤉𐤅𐤕.𐤋𐤏𐤌.𐤀𐤇𐤃.𐤁𐤄𐤌𐤅𐤋.𐤋𐤍𐤅.𐤊𐤋.𐤆𐤊𐤓.𐤊𐤀𐤔𐤓.
𐤄𐤌.𐤍𐤌𐤋𐤉𐤌|
..𐤊𐤂.. 𐤌𐤒𐤍𐤉𐤄𐤌.𐤅𐤒𐤍𐤉𐤍𐤌.𐤅𐤊𐤋.𐤁𐤄𐤌𐤕𐤌.𐤄𐤋𐤅𐤀.𐤋𐤍𐤅.𐤄𐤌.
𐤀𐤊.𐤍𐤀𐤅𐤕𐤄.𐤋𐤄𐤌.𐤅𐤉𐤔𐤁𐤅.𐤀𐤕𐤍𐤅|
..𐤊𐤃.. 𐤅𐤉𐤔𐤌𐤏𐤅.𐤀𐤋.𐤇𐤌𐤅𐤓.𐤅𐤀𐤋.𐤔𐤊𐤌.𐤁𐤍𐤅.𐤊𐤋.𐤉𐤑𐤀𐤉
.𐤔𐤏𐤓.𐤏𐤉𐤓𐤅.𐤅𐤉𐤌𐤋𐤅.𐤊𐤋.𐤆𐤊𐤓.𐤊𐤋.𐤉𐤑𐤀𐤉.𐤔𐤏𐤓.𐤏𐤉𐤓𐤅
|
..𐤊𐤄.. 𐤅𐤉𐤄𐤉.𐤁𐤉𐤅𐤌.𐤄𐤔𐤋𐤉𐤔𐤉.𐤁𐤄𐤉𐤅𐤕𐤌.𐤊𐤀𐤁𐤉𐤌.𐤅𐤉
𐤒𐤇𐤅.𐤔𐤍𐤉.𐤁𐤍𐤉.𐤉𐤏𐤒𐤁.𐤔𐤌𐤏𐤅𐤍.𐤅𐤋𐤅𐤉.𐤀𐤇𐤉.𐤃𐤉𐤍𐤄.
𐤀𐤉𐤔.𐤇𐤓𐤁𐤅.𐤅𐤉𐤁𐤀𐤅.𐤏𐤋.𐤄𐤏𐤉𐤓.𐤁𐤈𐤇.𐤅𐤉𐤄𐤓𐤂𐤅.𐤊𐤋.
𐤆𐤊𐤓|
..𐤊𐤅.. 𐤅𐤀𐤕.𐤇𐤌𐤅𐤓.𐤅𐤀𐤕.𐤔𐤊𐤌.𐤁𐤍𐤅.𐤄𐤓𐤂𐤅.𐤋𐤐𐤉.𐤇𐤓𐤁.𐤅𐤉
𐤒𐤇𐤅.𐤀𐤕.𐤃𐤉𐤍𐤄.𐤌𐤁𐤉𐤕.𐤔𐤊𐤌.𐤅𐤉𐤑𐤀𐤅|
..𐤊𐤆.. 𐤁𐤍𐤉.𐤉𐤏𐤒𐤁.𐤁𐤀𐤅.𐤏𐤋.𐤄𐤇𐤋𐤋𐤉𐤌.𐤅𐤉𐤁𐤆𐤅.𐤄𐤏𐤉
𐤓.𐤀𐤔𐤓.𐤈𐤌𐤀𐤅.𐤀𐤇𐤅𐤕𐤌|
..𐤊𐤇.. 𐤀𐤕.𐤑𐤀𐤍𐤌.𐤅𐤀𐤕.𐤁𐤒𐤓𐤌.𐤅𐤀𐤕.𐤇𐤌𐤓𐤉𐤄𐤌.𐤅𐤀𐤕.
𐤀𐤔𐤓.𐤁𐤏𐤉𐤓.𐤅𐤀𐤕.𐤀𐤔𐤓.𐤁𐤔𐤃𐤄.𐤋𐤒𐤇𐤅|
..𐤊𐤈.. 𐤅𐤀𐤕.𐤊𐤋.𐤇𐤉𐤋𐤌.𐤅𐤀𐤕.𐤊𐤋.𐤈𐤐𐤌.𐤅𐤀𐤕.𐤍𐤔𐤉𐤄𐤌.
𐤔𐤁𐤅.𐤅𐤉𐤁𐤆𐤅.𐤅𐤀𐤕.𐤊𐤋.𐤀𐤔𐤓.𐤁𐤁𐤉𐤕|
..𐤋.. 𐤅𐤉𐤀𐤌𐤓.𐤉𐤏𐤒𐤁.𐤀𐤋.𐤔𐤌𐤏𐤅𐤍.𐤅𐤀𐤋.𐤋𐤅𐤉.𐤏𐤊𐤓𐤕𐤌.
𐤀𐤕𐤉.𐤋𐤄𐤁𐤀𐤉𐤔𐤍𐤉.𐤁𐤉𐤅𐤔𐤁.𐤄𐤀𐤓𐤑.𐤁𐤊𐤍𐤏𐤍𐤉.𐤅𐤁𐤐𐤓𐤆
𐤉.𐤅𐤀𐤍𐤉.𐤌𐤕𐤉.𐤌𐤎𐤐𐤓.𐤅𐤍𐤀𐤎𐤐𐤅.𐤏𐤋𐤉.𐤅𐤄𐤊𐤅𐤍𐤉.𐤅𐤍𐤔𐤌𐤃
𐤕𐤉.𐤀𐤍𐤉.𐤅𐤁𐤉𐤕𐤉|
..𐤋𐤀.. 𐤅𐤉𐤀𐤌𐤓𐤅.𐤄𐤊𐤆𐤅𐤍𐤄.𐤉𐤏𐤔𐤄.𐤀𐤕.𐤀𐤇𐤅𐤕𐤍𐤅||

𐤁𐤓𐤀𐤔𐤉𐤕.𐤇𐤋𐤒 ..𐤋𐤄..

1 𐤅𐤉𐤀𐤌𐤓.𐤀𐤋𐤄𐤉𐤌.𐤀𐤋.𐤉𐤏𐤒𐤁.𐤒𐤅𐤌.𐤏𐤋𐤄.𐤁𐤉𐤕.𐤀𐤋
.𐤅𐤔𐤁.𐤔𐤌.𐤅𐤏𐤔𐤄.𐤔𐤌.𐤌𐤆𐤁𐤇.𐤋𐤀𐤋.𐤄𐤍𐤓𐤀𐤄.𐤀𐤋𐤉𐤊.𐤁
𐤁𐤓𐤇𐤊.𐤌𐤐𐤍𐤉.𐤏𐤔𐤅.𐤀𐤇𐤉𐤊|

2 𐤅𐤉𐤀𐤌𐤓.𐤉𐤏𐤒𐤁.𐤀𐤋.𐤁𐤉𐤕𐤅.𐤅𐤀𐤋.𐤊𐤋.𐤀𐤔𐤓.𐤏𐤌𐤅.𐤄
𐤎𐤓𐤅.𐤀𐤕.𐤀𐤋𐤄𐤉.𐤄𐤍𐤊𐤓.𐤀𐤔𐤓.𐤁𐤕𐤊𐤊𐤌.𐤅𐤄𐤈𐤄𐤓𐤅.𐤅𐤄𐤇
𐤋𐤉𐤐𐤅.𐤔𐤌𐤋𐤕𐤉𐤊𐤌|

3 𐤅𐤍𐤒𐤅𐤌𐤄.𐤅𐤍𐤏𐤋𐤄.𐤁𐤉𐤕.𐤀𐤋.𐤅𐤀𐤏𐤔𐤄.𐤔𐤌.𐤌𐤆𐤁𐤇.
𐤋𐤀𐤋.𐤄𐤏𐤍𐤄.𐤀𐤕𐤉.𐤁𐤉𐤅𐤌.𐤑𐤓𐤕𐤉.𐤅𐤉𐤄𐤉.𐤏𐤌𐤃𐤉.𐤁𐤃
𐤓𐤊.𐤀𐤔𐤓.𐤄𐤋𐤊𐤕𐤉|

4 𐤅𐤉𐤕𐤍𐤅.𐤀𐤋.𐤉𐤏𐤒𐤁.𐤀𐤕.𐤊𐤋.𐤀𐤋𐤄𐤉.𐤄𐤍𐤊𐤓.𐤀𐤔𐤓.𐤁
𐤉𐤃𐤌.𐤅𐤀𐤕.𐤄𐤍𐤆𐤌𐤉𐤌.𐤀𐤔𐤓.𐤁𐤀𐤆𐤍𐤉𐤄𐤌.𐤅𐤉𐤈𐤌𐤍.𐤀
𐤕𐤌.𐤉𐤏𐤒𐤁.𐤕𐤇𐤕.𐤄𐤀𐤋𐤄.𐤀𐤔𐤓.𐤏𐤌.𐤔𐤊𐤌|

5 𐤅𐤉𐤎𐤏𐤅.𐤅𐤉𐤄𐤉.𐤇𐤕𐤕.𐤀𐤋𐤄𐤉𐤌.𐤏𐤋.𐤄𐤏𐤓𐤉𐤌.𐤀𐤔𐤓.
𐤎𐤁𐤉𐤁𐤕𐤉𐤄𐤌.𐤅𐤋𐤀.𐤓𐤃𐤐𐤅.𐤀𐤇𐤓𐤉.𐤁𐤍𐤉.𐤉𐤏𐤒𐤁|

6 𐤅𐤉𐤁𐤀.𐤉𐤏𐤒𐤁.𐤋𐤅𐤆𐤄.𐤀𐤔𐤓.𐤁𐤀𐤓𐤑.𐤊𐤍𐤏𐤍.𐤄𐤅𐤀.𐤁
𐤉𐤕.𐤀𐤋.𐤄𐤅𐤀.𐤅𐤊𐤋.𐤄𐤏𐤌.𐤀𐤔𐤓.𐤏𐤌𐤅|

7 𐤅𐤉𐤁𐤍.𐤔𐤌.𐤌𐤆𐤁𐤇.𐤅𐤉𐤒𐤓𐤀.𐤋𐤌𐤒𐤅𐤌.𐤀𐤋.𐤁𐤉𐤕.𐤀𐤋
.𐤊𐤉.𐤔𐤌.𐤍𐤂𐤋𐤅.𐤀𐤋𐤉𐤅.𐤄𐤀𐤋𐤄𐤉𐤌.𐤁𐤁𐤓𐤇𐤅.𐤌𐤐𐤍𐤉.𐤀𐤇
𐤉𐤅|

8 𐤅𐤕𐤌𐤕.𐤃𐤁𐤅𐤓𐤄.𐤌𐤉𐤍𐤒𐤕.𐤓𐤁𐤒𐤄.𐤅𐤕𐤒𐤁𐤓.𐤌𐤕𐤇𐤕.
𐤋𐤁𐤉𐤕.𐤀𐤋.𐤕𐤇𐤕.𐤄𐤀𐤋𐤅𐤍.𐤅𐤉𐤒𐤓𐤀.𐤔𐤌𐤅.𐤀𐤋𐤅𐤍.𐤁𐤊𐤅𐤕|

9 𐤅𐤉𐤓𐤀.𐤀𐤋𐤄𐤉𐤌.𐤀𐤋.𐤉𐤏𐤒𐤁.𐤏𐤅𐤃.𐤁𐤁𐤀𐤅.𐤌𐤐𐤃𐤍.
𐤀𐤓𐤌.𐤅𐤉𐤁𐤓𐤊.𐤀𐤕𐤅|

10 𐤅𐤉𐤀𐤌𐤓.𐤋𐤅.𐤀𐤋𐤄𐤉𐤌.𐤔𐤌𐤊.𐤉𐤏𐤒𐤁.𐤋𐤀.𐤉𐤒𐤓𐤀.𐤔
𐤌𐤊.𐤏𐤅𐤃.𐤉𐤏𐤒𐤁.𐤊𐤉.𐤀𐤌.𐤉𐤔𐤓𐤀𐤋.𐤉𐤄𐤉𐤄.𐤔𐤌𐤊.𐤅𐤉𐤒
𐤓𐤀.𐤀𐤕.𐤔𐤌𐤅.𐤉𐤔𐤓𐤀𐤋|

11 𐤅𐤉𐤀𐤌𐤓.𐤋𐤅.𐤀𐤋𐤄𐤉𐤌.𐤀𐤍𐤉.𐤀𐤋.𐤔𐤃𐤉.𐤐𐤓𐤄.𐤅𐤓𐤁𐤄.
𐤂𐤅𐤉.𐤅𐤒𐤄𐤋.𐤂𐤅𐤉𐤌.𐤉𐤄𐤉𐤄.𐤌𐤌𐤊.𐤅𐤌𐤋𐤊𐤉𐤌.𐤌𐤇𐤋𐤑𐤉
𐤊.𐤉𐤑𐤀𐤅|

..יב.. 𐤅𐤀𐤕.𐤄𐤀𐤓𐤑.𐤀𐤔𐤓.𐤍𐤕𐤕𐤉.𐤋𐤀𐤁𐤓𐤄𐤌.𐤅𐤋𐤉𐤑𐤇𐤒.
𐤋𐤊.𐤀𐤕𐤍𐤍𐤄.𐤅𐤋𐤆𐤓𐤏𐤊.𐤀𐤇𐤓𐤉𐤊.𐤀𐤕𐤍.𐤀𐤕.𐤄𐤀𐤓𐤑|
..יג.. 𐤅𐤉𐤏𐤋.𐤌𐤏𐤋𐤉𐤅.𐤀𐤋𐤄𐤉𐤌.𐤁𐤌𐤒𐤅𐤌.𐤀𐤔𐤓.𐤃𐤁𐤓.𐤀
𐤕𐤅|
..יד.. 𐤅𐤉𐤑𐤁.𐤉𐤏𐤒𐤁.𐤌𐤑𐤁𐤄.𐤁𐤌𐤒𐤅𐤌.𐤀𐤔𐤓.𐤃𐤁𐤓.𐤀𐤕
𐤅.𐤌𐤑𐤁𐤕.𐤀𐤁𐤍.𐤅𐤉𐤎𐤊.𐤏𐤋𐤉𐤄.𐤍𐤎𐤊.𐤅𐤉𐤑𐤒.𐤏𐤋𐤉𐤄.𐤔𐤌
𐤍|
..טו.. 𐤅𐤉𐤒𐤓𐤀.𐤉𐤏𐤒𐤁.𐤀𐤕.𐤔𐤌.𐤄𐤌𐤒𐤅𐤌.𐤀𐤔𐤓.𐤃𐤁𐤓.𐤀
𐤕𐤅.𐤔𐤌.𐤀𐤋𐤄𐤉𐤌.𐤁𐤉𐤕.𐤀𐤋|
..טז.. 𐤅𐤉𐤎𐤏𐤅.𐤌𐤁𐤉𐤕.𐤀𐤋.𐤅𐤉𐤄𐤉.𐤏𐤅𐤃.𐤊𐤁𐤓𐤕.𐤄𐤀𐤓𐤑.𐤋
𐤁𐤅𐤀.𐤀𐤐𐤓𐤕𐤄.𐤅𐤕𐤋𐤃.𐤓𐤇𐤋.𐤅𐤕𐤒𐤔.𐤁𐤋𐤃𐤕𐤄|
..יז.. 𐤅𐤉𐤄𐤉.𐤁𐤄𐤒𐤔𐤕𐤄.𐤁𐤋𐤃𐤕𐤄.𐤅𐤕𐤀𐤌𐤓.𐤋𐤄.𐤄𐤌𐤉𐤋
𐤃𐤕.𐤀𐤋.𐤕𐤉𐤓𐤀𐤉.𐤊𐤉.𐤂𐤌.𐤆𐤄.𐤋𐤊.𐤁𐤍|
..יח.. 𐤅𐤉𐤄𐤉.𐤁𐤑𐤀𐤕.𐤍𐤐𐤔𐤄.𐤊𐤉.𐤌𐤕𐤄.𐤅𐤕𐤒𐤓𐤀.𐤔𐤌𐤅.𐤁
𐤍.𐤀𐤅𐤍𐤉.𐤅𐤀𐤁𐤉𐤅.𐤒𐤓𐤀.𐤋𐤅.𐤁𐤍𐤉𐤌𐤉𐤍|
..יט.. 𐤅𐤕𐤌𐤕.𐤓𐤇𐤋.𐤅𐤕𐤒𐤁𐤓.𐤁𐤃𐤓𐤊.𐤀𐤐𐤓𐤕𐤄.𐤄𐤅𐤀.𐤁𐤉
𐤕.𐤋𐤇𐤌|
..כ.. 𐤅𐤉𐤑𐤁.𐤉𐤏𐤒𐤁.𐤌𐤑𐤁𐤄.𐤏𐤋.𐤒𐤁𐤓𐤕𐤄.𐤄𐤅𐤀.𐤌𐤑𐤁
𐤕.𐤒𐤁𐤓𐤕.𐤓𐤇𐤋.𐤏𐤃.𐤄𐤉𐤅𐤌|
..כא.. 𐤅𐤉𐤎𐤏.𐤉𐤔𐤓𐤀𐤋.𐤅𐤉𐤈.𐤀𐤄𐤋𐤄.𐤌𐤄𐤋𐤀𐤄.𐤋𐤌𐤂𐤃𐤋.
𐤏𐤃𐤓|
..כב.. 𐤅𐤉𐤄𐤉.𐤁𐤔𐤊𐤍.𐤉𐤔𐤓𐤀𐤋.𐤁𐤀𐤓𐤑.𐤄𐤄𐤅𐤀.𐤅𐤉𐤋𐤊.𐤓𐤀𐤅
𐤁𐤍.𐤅𐤉𐤔𐤊𐤁.𐤀𐤕.𐤁𐤋𐤄𐤄.𐤐𐤉𐤋𐤂𐤔.𐤀𐤁𐤉𐤅.𐤅𐤉𐤔𐤌𐤏.𐤉𐤔𐤓
𐤀𐤋.
.𐤅𐤉𐤄𐤉𐤅.𐤁𐤍𐤉.𐤉𐤏𐤒𐤁.𐤔𐤍𐤉𐤌.𐤏𐤔𐤓|
..כג.. 𐤁𐤍𐤉.𐤋𐤀𐤄.𐤁𐤊𐤅𐤓.𐤉𐤏𐤒𐤁.𐤓𐤀𐤅𐤁𐤍.𐤅𐤔𐤌𐤏𐤅𐤍.𐤅𐤋𐤅𐤉.
𐤅𐤉𐤄𐤅𐤃𐤄.𐤅𐤉𐤔𐤔𐤊𐤓.𐤅𐤆𐤁𐤋𐤅𐤍|
..כד.. 𐤁𐤍𐤉.𐤓𐤇𐤋.𐤉𐤅𐤎𐤐.𐤅𐤁𐤍𐤉𐤌𐤍|
..כה.. 𐤅𐤁𐤍𐤉.𐤁𐤋𐤄𐤄.𐤔𐤐𐤇𐤕.𐤓𐤇𐤋.𐤃𐤍.𐤅𐤍𐤐𐤕𐤋𐤉|
..כו.. 𐤅𐤁𐤍𐤉.𐤆𐤋𐤐𐤄.𐤔𐤐𐤇𐤕.𐤋𐤀𐤄.𐤂𐤃.𐤅𐤀𐤔𐤓.𐤀𐤋𐤄.𐤁𐤍
𐤉.𐤉𐤏𐤒𐤁.𐤀𐤔𐤓.𐤉𐤋𐤃.𐤋𐤅.𐤁𐤐𐤃𐤍.𐤀𐤓𐤌|

..כז.. 𐤅𐤉𐤁𐤀.𐤉𐤏𐤒𐤁.𐤀𐤋.𐤉𐤑𐤇𐤒.𐤀𐤁𐤉𐤅.𐤌𐤌𐤓𐤀.𐤒𐤓𐤉
𐤕.𐤄𐤀𐤓𐤁𐤏.𐤄𐤅𐤀.𐤇𐤁𐤓𐤅𐤍.𐤀𐤔𐤓.𐤂𐤓.𐤔𐤌.𐤀𐤁𐤓𐤄𐤌.𐤅𐤉𐤑
𐤇𐤒|

..כח.. 𐤅𐤉𐤄𐤉𐤅.𐤉𐤌𐤉.𐤉𐤑𐤇𐤒.𐤌𐤀𐤕.𐤔𐤍𐤄.𐤅𐤔𐤌𐤍𐤉𐤌.𐤔𐤍
𐤄|

..כט.. 𐤅𐤉𐤂𐤅𐤏.𐤉𐤑𐤇𐤒.𐤅𐤉𐤌𐤕.𐤅𐤉𐤀𐤎𐤐.𐤀𐤋.𐤏𐤌𐤉𐤅.𐤆
𐤒𐤍.𐤅𐤔𐤁𐤏.𐤉𐤌𐤉𐤌.𐤅𐤉𐤒𐤁𐤓𐤅.𐤀𐤕𐤅.𐤏𐤔𐤅.𐤅𐤉𐤏𐤒𐤁.𐤁𐤍𐤉𐤅||

𐤁𐤓𐤀𐤔𐤉𐤕.𐤇𐤋𐤒 ..לו..

..א.. 𐤅𐤀𐤋𐤄.𐤕𐤋𐤃𐤅𐤕.𐤏𐤔𐤅.𐤄𐤅𐤀.𐤀𐤃𐤅𐤌|

..ב.. 𐤏𐤔𐤅.𐤋𐤒𐤇.𐤀𐤕.𐤍𐤔𐤉𐤅.𐤌𐤁𐤍𐤅𐤕.𐤊𐤍𐤏𐤍.𐤀𐤕.𐤏𐤃𐤄.
𐤁𐤕.𐤀𐤉𐤋𐤅𐤍.𐤄𐤇𐤕𐤉.𐤅𐤀𐤕.𐤀𐤄𐤋𐤉𐤁𐤌𐤄.𐤁𐤕.𐤏𐤍𐤄.𐤁𐤕.
𐤑𐤁𐤏𐤅𐤍.𐤄𐤇𐤅𐤉|

..ג.. 𐤅𐤀𐤕.𐤁𐤔𐤌𐤕.𐤁𐤕.𐤉𐤔𐤌𐤏𐤀𐤋.𐤀𐤇𐤅𐤕.𐤍𐤁𐤉𐤅𐤕|

..ד.. 𐤅𐤕𐤋𐤃.𐤏𐤃𐤄.𐤋𐤏𐤔𐤅.𐤀𐤕.𐤀𐤋𐤉𐤐𐤆.𐤅𐤁𐤔𐤌𐤕.𐤉𐤋𐤃
𐤄.𐤀𐤕.𐤓𐤏𐤅𐤀𐤋|

..ה.. 𐤅𐤀𐤄𐤋𐤉𐤁𐤌𐤄.𐤉𐤋𐤃𐤄.𐤀𐤕.𐤉𐤏𐤉𐤔.||𐤉𐤏𐤅𐤔.𐤒𐤓𐤉||.𐤅
𐤀𐤕.𐤉𐤏𐤋𐤌.𐤅𐤀𐤕.𐤒𐤓𐤇.𐤀𐤋𐤄.𐤁𐤍𐤉.𐤏𐤔𐤅.𐤀𐤔𐤓.𐤉𐤋𐤃𐤅.
𐤋𐤅.𐤁𐤀𐤓𐤑.𐤊𐤍𐤏𐤍|

..ו.. 𐤅𐤉𐤒𐤇.𐤏𐤔𐤅.𐤀𐤕.𐤍𐤔𐤉𐤅.𐤅𐤀𐤕.𐤁𐤍𐤉𐤅.𐤅𐤀𐤕.𐤁𐤍𐤕𐤉𐤅.𐤅
𐤀𐤕.𐤊𐤋.𐤍𐤐𐤔𐤅𐤕.𐤁𐤉𐤕𐤅.𐤅𐤀𐤕.𐤌𐤒𐤍𐤄𐤅.𐤅𐤀𐤕.𐤊𐤋.𐤁𐤄𐤌𐤕
𐤅.𐤅𐤀𐤕.𐤊𐤋.𐤒𐤍𐤉𐤍𐤅.𐤀𐤔𐤓.𐤓𐤊𐤔.𐤁𐤀𐤓𐤑.𐤊𐤍𐤏𐤍.𐤅𐤉𐤋𐤊.𐤀
𐤋.𐤀𐤓𐤑.𐤌𐤐𐤍𐤉.𐤉𐤏𐤒𐤁.𐤀𐤇𐤉𐤅|

..ז.. 𐤊𐤉.𐤄𐤉𐤄.𐤓𐤊𐤅𐤔𐤌.𐤓𐤁.𐤌𐤔𐤁𐤕.𐤉𐤇𐤃𐤅.𐤅𐤋𐤀.𐤉𐤊𐤋𐤄
.𐤀𐤓𐤑.𐤌𐤂𐤅𐤓𐤉𐤄𐤌.𐤋𐤔𐤀𐤕.𐤀𐤕𐤌.𐤌𐤐𐤍𐤉.𐤌𐤒𐤍𐤉𐤄𐤌|

..ח.. 𐤅𐤉𐤔𐤁.𐤏𐤔𐤅.𐤁𐤄𐤓.𐤔𐤏𐤉𐤓.𐤏𐤔𐤅.𐤄𐤅𐤀.𐤀𐤃𐤅𐤌|

..ט.. 𐤅𐤀𐤋𐤄.𐤕𐤋𐤃𐤅𐤕.𐤏𐤔𐤅.𐤀𐤁𐤉.𐤀𐤃𐤅𐤌.𐤁𐤄𐤓.𐤔𐤏𐤉𐤓|

..י.. 𐤀𐤋𐤄.𐤔𐤌𐤅𐤕.𐤁𐤍𐤉.𐤏𐤔𐤅.𐤀𐤋𐤉𐤐𐤆.𐤁𐤍.𐤏𐤃𐤄.𐤀𐤔
𐤕.𐤏𐤔𐤅.𐤓𐤏𐤅𐤀𐤋.𐤁𐤍.𐤁𐤔𐤌𐤕.𐤀𐤔𐤕.𐤏𐤔𐤅|

𐤉𐤀 𐤅𐤉𐤄𐤉𐤅.𐤁𐤍𐤉.𐤀𐤋𐤉𐤐𐤆.𐤕𐤉𐤌𐤍.𐤀𐤅𐤌𐤓.𐤑𐤐𐤅.𐤅𐤂𐤏𐤕
𐤌.𐤅𐤒𐤍𐤆|

𐤉𐤁 𐤅𐤕𐤌𐤍𐤏.𐤄𐤉𐤕𐤄.𐤐𐤉𐤋𐤂𐤔.𐤋𐤀𐤋𐤉𐤐𐤆.𐤁𐤍.𐤏𐤔𐤅.𐤅𐤕
𐤋𐤃.𐤋𐤀𐤋𐤉𐤐𐤆.𐤀𐤕.𐤏𐤌𐤋𐤒.𐤀𐤋𐤄.𐤁𐤍𐤉.𐤏𐤃𐤄.𐤀𐤔𐤕.𐤏
𐤔𐤅|

𐤉𐤂 𐤅𐤀𐤋𐤄.𐤁𐤍𐤉.𐤓𐤏𐤅𐤀𐤋.𐤍𐤇𐤕.𐤅𐤆𐤓𐤇.𐤔𐤌𐤄.𐤅𐤌𐤆𐤄.
𐤀𐤋𐤄.𐤄𐤉𐤅.𐤁𐤍𐤉.𐤁𐤔𐤌𐤕.𐤀𐤔𐤕.𐤏𐤔𐤅|

𐤉𐤃 𐤅𐤀𐤋𐤄.𐤄𐤉𐤅.𐤁𐤍𐤉.𐤀𐤄𐤋𐤉𐤁𐤌𐤄.𐤁𐤕.𐤏𐤍𐤄.𐤁𐤕.𐤑𐤁
𐤏𐤅𐤍.𐤀𐤔𐤕.𐤏𐤔𐤅.𐤅𐤕𐤋𐤃.𐤋𐤏𐤔𐤅.𐤀𐤕.𐤉𐤏𐤉𐤔.‖𐤉𐤏𐤅𐤔.𐤒
𐤓𐤉‖.𐤅𐤀𐤕.𐤉𐤏𐤋𐤌.𐤅𐤀𐤕.𐤒𐤓𐤇|

𐤈𐤅 𐤀𐤋𐤄.𐤀𐤋𐤅𐤐𐤉.𐤁𐤍𐤉.𐤏𐤔𐤅.𐤁𐤍𐤉.𐤀𐤋𐤉𐤐𐤆.𐤁𐤊𐤅𐤓.𐤏
𐤔𐤅.𐤀𐤋𐤅𐤐.𐤕𐤉𐤌𐤍.𐤀𐤋𐤅𐤐.𐤀𐤅𐤌𐤓.𐤀𐤋𐤅𐤐.𐤑𐤐𐤅.𐤀𐤋𐤅𐤐.𐤒𐤍𐤆|

𐤈𐤆 𐤀𐤋𐤅𐤐.𐤒𐤓𐤇.𐤀𐤋𐤅𐤐.𐤂𐤏𐤕𐤌.𐤀𐤋𐤅𐤐.𐤏𐤌𐤋𐤒.𐤀𐤋𐤄.
𐤀𐤋𐤅𐤐𐤉.𐤀𐤋𐤉𐤐𐤆.𐤁𐤀𐤓𐤑.𐤀𐤃𐤅𐤌.𐤀𐤋𐤄.𐤁𐤍𐤉.𐤏𐤃𐤄|

𐤉𐤆 𐤅𐤀𐤋𐤄.𐤁𐤍𐤉.𐤓𐤏𐤅𐤀𐤋.𐤁𐤍.𐤏𐤔𐤅.𐤀𐤋𐤅𐤐.𐤍𐤇𐤕.𐤀𐤋𐤅𐤐.
𐤆𐤓𐤇.𐤀𐤋𐤅𐤐.𐤔𐤌𐤄.𐤀𐤋𐤅𐤐.𐤌𐤆𐤄.𐤀𐤋𐤄.𐤀𐤋𐤅𐤐𐤉.𐤓𐤏𐤅𐤀𐤋
.𐤁𐤀𐤓𐤑.𐤀𐤃𐤅𐤌.𐤀𐤋𐤄.𐤁𐤍𐤉.𐤁𐤔𐤌𐤕.𐤀𐤔𐤕.𐤏𐤔𐤅|

𐤉𐤇 𐤅𐤀𐤋𐤄.𐤁𐤍𐤉.𐤀𐤄𐤋𐤉𐤁𐤌𐤄.𐤀𐤔𐤕.𐤏𐤔𐤅.𐤀𐤋𐤅𐤐.𐤉𐤏𐤅
𐤔.𐤀𐤋𐤅𐤐.𐤉𐤏𐤋𐤌.𐤀𐤋𐤅𐤐.𐤒𐤓𐤇.𐤀𐤋𐤄.𐤀𐤋𐤅𐤐𐤉.𐤀𐤄𐤋𐤉𐤁𐤌
𐤄.𐤁𐤕.𐤏𐤍𐤄.𐤀𐤔𐤕.𐤏𐤔𐤅|

𐤉𐤈 𐤀𐤋𐤄.𐤁𐤍𐤉.𐤏𐤔𐤅.𐤅𐤀𐤋𐤄.𐤀𐤋𐤅𐤐𐤉𐤄𐤌.𐤄𐤅𐤀.𐤀𐤃𐤅𐤌|

𐤊 𐤀𐤋𐤄.𐤁𐤍𐤉.𐤔𐤏𐤉𐤓.𐤄𐤇𐤓𐤉.𐤉𐤔𐤁𐤉.𐤄𐤀𐤓𐤑.𐤋𐤅𐤈𐤍.
𐤅𐤔𐤅𐤁𐤋.𐤅𐤑𐤁𐤏𐤅𐤍.𐤅𐤏𐤍𐤄|

𐤊𐤀 𐤅𐤃𐤔𐤅𐤍.𐤅𐤀𐤑𐤓.𐤅𐤃𐤉𐤔𐤍.𐤀𐤋𐤄.𐤀𐤋𐤅𐤐𐤉.𐤄𐤇𐤓𐤉.𐤁𐤍
𐤉.𐤔𐤏𐤉𐤓.𐤁𐤀𐤓𐤑.𐤀𐤃𐤅𐤌|

𐤊𐤁 𐤅𐤉𐤄𐤉𐤅.𐤁𐤍𐤉.𐤋𐤅𐤈𐤍.𐤇𐤓𐤉.𐤅𐤄𐤉𐤌𐤌.𐤅𐤀𐤇𐤅𐤕.𐤋𐤅𐤈𐤍.
𐤕𐤌𐤍𐤏|

𐤊𐤂 𐤅𐤀𐤋𐤄.𐤁𐤍𐤉.𐤔𐤅𐤁𐤋.𐤏𐤋𐤅𐤍.𐤅𐤌𐤍𐤇𐤕.𐤅𐤏𐤉𐤁𐤋.𐤔𐤐𐤅.𐤅
𐤀𐤅𐤍𐤌|

..𐤊𐤃.. 𐤅𐤀𐤋𐤄.𐤁𐤍𐤉.𐤑𐤁𐤏𐤅𐤍.𐤅𐤀𐤉𐤄.𐤅𐤏𐤍𐤄.𐤄𐤅𐤀.𐤏𐤍𐤄.𐤀
𐤔𐤓.𐤌𐤑𐤀.𐤀𐤕.𐤄𐤉𐤌𐤌.𐤁𐤌𐤃𐤁𐤓.𐤁𐤓𐤏𐤕𐤅.𐤀𐤕.𐤄𐤇𐤌𐤓
𐤉𐤌.𐤋𐤑𐤁𐤏𐤅𐤍.𐤀𐤁𐤉𐤅|
..𐤊𐤄.. 𐤅𐤀𐤋𐤄.𐤁𐤍𐤉.𐤏𐤍𐤄.𐤃𐤔𐤍.𐤅𐤀𐤄𐤋𐤉𐤁𐤌𐤄.𐤁𐤕.𐤏𐤍𐤄|
..𐤊𐤅.. 𐤅𐤀𐤋𐤄.𐤁𐤍𐤉.𐤃𐤉𐤔𐤍.𐤇𐤌𐤃𐤍.𐤅𐤀𐤔𐤁𐤍.𐤅𐤉𐤕𐤓𐤍.𐤅𐤊𐤓
𐤍|
..𐤊𐤆.. 𐤀𐤋𐤄.𐤁𐤍𐤉.𐤀𐤑𐤓.𐤁𐤋𐤄𐤍.𐤅𐤆𐤏𐤅𐤍.𐤅𐤏𐤒𐤍|
..𐤊𐤇.. 𐤀𐤋𐤄.𐤁𐤍𐤉.𐤃𐤉𐤔𐤍.𐤏𐤅𐤑.𐤅𐤀𐤓𐤍|
..𐤊𐤈.. 𐤀𐤋𐤄.𐤀𐤋𐤅𐤐𐤉.𐤄𐤇𐤓𐤉.𐤀𐤋𐤅𐤐.𐤋𐤅𐤈𐤍.𐤀𐤋𐤅𐤐.𐤔𐤅𐤁𐤋.
𐤀𐤋𐤅𐤐.𐤑𐤁𐤏𐤅𐤍.𐤀𐤋𐤅𐤐.𐤏𐤍𐤄|
..𐤋.. 𐤀𐤋𐤅𐤐.𐤃𐤔𐤍.𐤀𐤋𐤅𐤐.𐤀𐤑𐤓.𐤀𐤋𐤅𐤐.𐤃𐤉𐤔𐤍.𐤀𐤋𐤄.𐤀
𐤋𐤅𐤐𐤉.𐤄𐤇𐤓𐤉.𐤋𐤀𐤋𐤐𐤉𐤄𐤌.𐤁𐤀𐤓𐤑.𐤔𐤏𐤉𐤓|
..𐤋𐤀.. 𐤅𐤀𐤋𐤄.𐤄𐤌𐤋𐤊𐤉𐤌.𐤀𐤔𐤓.𐤌𐤋𐤊𐤅.𐤁𐤀𐤓𐤑.𐤀𐤃𐤅𐤌.𐤋𐤐
𐤍𐤉.𐤌𐤋𐤊.𐤌𐤋𐤊.𐤋𐤁𐤍𐤉.𐤉𐤔𐤓𐤀𐤋|
..𐤋𐤁.. 𐤅𐤉𐤌𐤋𐤊.𐤁𐤀𐤃𐤅𐤌.𐤁𐤋𐤏.𐤁𐤍.𐤁𐤏𐤅𐤓.𐤅𐤔𐤌.𐤏𐤉𐤓𐤅.𐤃
𐤍𐤄𐤁𐤄|
..𐤋𐤂.. 𐤅𐤉𐤌𐤕.𐤁𐤋𐤏.𐤅𐤉𐤌𐤋𐤊.𐤕𐤇𐤕𐤉𐤅.𐤉𐤅𐤁𐤁.𐤁𐤍.𐤆𐤓𐤇.
𐤌𐤁𐤑𐤓𐤄|
..𐤋𐤃.. 𐤅𐤉𐤌𐤕.𐤉𐤅𐤁𐤁.𐤅𐤉𐤌𐤋𐤊.𐤕𐤇𐤕𐤉𐤅.𐤇𐤔𐤌.𐤌𐤀𐤓𐤑.𐤄
𐤕𐤉𐤌𐤍𐤉|
..𐤋𐤄.. 𐤅𐤉𐤌𐤕.𐤇𐤔𐤌.𐤅𐤉𐤌𐤋𐤊.𐤕𐤇𐤕𐤉𐤅.𐤄𐤃𐤃.𐤁𐤍.𐤁𐤃𐤃
.𐤄𐤌𐤊𐤄.𐤀𐤕.𐤌𐤃𐤉𐤍.𐤁𐤔𐤃𐤄.𐤌𐤅𐤀𐤁.𐤅𐤔𐤌.𐤏𐤉𐤓𐤅.𐤏𐤅𐤉
𐤕|
..𐤋𐤅.. 𐤅𐤉𐤌𐤕.𐤄𐤃𐤃.𐤅𐤉𐤌𐤋𐤊.𐤕𐤇𐤕𐤉𐤅.𐤔𐤌𐤋𐤄.𐤌𐤌𐤔𐤓𐤒
𐤄|
..𐤋𐤆.. 𐤅𐤉𐤌𐤕.𐤔𐤌𐤋𐤄.𐤅𐤉𐤌𐤋𐤊.𐤕𐤇𐤕𐤉𐤅.𐤔𐤀𐤅𐤋.𐤌𐤓𐤇𐤁𐤅
𐤕.𐤄𐤍𐤄𐤓|
..𐤋𐤇.. 𐤅𐤉𐤌𐤕.𐤔𐤀𐤅𐤋.𐤅𐤉𐤌𐤋𐤊.𐤕𐤇𐤕𐤉𐤅.𐤁𐤏𐤋.𐤇𐤍𐤍.𐤁𐤍.𐤏
𐤊𐤁𐤅𐤓|

39 וימת.בעל.חנן.בן.עכבור.וימלך.תחתיו.
הדר.פעו.ושם.עירו.ושם.אשתו.מהיטבאל.בת.
מטרד.בת.מי.זהב|
40 ואלה.שמות.אלופי.עשו.למשפחתם.למק
מתם.בשמתם.אלוף.תמנע.אלוף.עלוה.אלוף.ית
ת|
41 אלוף.אהליבמה.אלוף.אלה.אלוף.פינן|
42 אלוף.קנז.אלוף.תימן.אלוף.מבצר|
43 אלוף.מגדיאל.אלוף.עירם.אלה.אלופי.
אדום.למשבתם.בארץ.אחזתם.הוא.עשו.אבי
.אדום||

בראשית.חלק 37

1 וישב.יעקב.בארץ.מגורי.אביו.בארץ.כנ
ען|
2 אלה.תלדות.יעקב.יוסף.בן.שבע.עשרה.ש
נה.היה.רעה.את.אחיו.בצאן.והוא.נער.את.ב
ני.בלהה.ואת.בני.זלפה.נשי.אביו.ויבא.יוסף.
את.דבתם.רעה.אל.אביהם|
3 וישראל.אהב.את.יוסף.מכל.בניו.כי.בן.ז
קנים.הוא.לו.ועשה.לו.כתנת.פסים|
4 ויראו.אחיו.כי.אתו.אהב.אביהם.מכל.א
חיו.וישנאו.אתו.ולא.יכלו.דברו.לשלם|
5 ויחלם.יוסף.חלום.ויגד.לאחיו.ויוספו.ע
וד.שנא.אתו|
6 ויאמר.אליהם.שמעו.נא.החלום.הזה.אשר.
חלמתי|
7 והנה.אנחנו.מאלמים.אלמים.בתוך.השד
ה.והנה.קמה.אלמתי.וגם.נצבה.והנה.תסבינ
ה.אלמתיכם.ותשתחוין.לאלמתי|

ח 𐤅𐤉𐤀𐤌𐤓𐤅.𐤋𐤅.𐤀𐤇𐤉𐤅.𐤄𐤌𐤋𐤊.𐤕𐤌𐤋𐤊.𐤏𐤋𐤉𐤍𐤅.𐤀𐤌.𐤌𐤔
𐤅𐤋.𐤕𐤌𐤔𐤋.𐤁𐤍𐤅.𐤅𐤉𐤅𐤎𐤐𐤅.𐤏𐤅𐤃.𐤔𐤍𐤀.𐤀𐤕𐤅.𐤏𐤋.𐤇𐤋𐤌𐤕𐤉
𐤅.𐤅𐤏𐤋.𐤃𐤁𐤓𐤉𐤅|
ט 𐤅𐤉𐤇𐤋𐤌.𐤏𐤅𐤃.𐤇𐤋𐤅𐤌.𐤀𐤇𐤓.𐤅𐤉𐤎𐤐𐤓.𐤀𐤕𐤅.𐤋𐤀𐤇𐤉
𐤅.𐤅𐤉𐤀𐤌𐤓.𐤄𐤍𐤄.𐤇𐤋𐤌𐤕𐤉.𐤇𐤋𐤅𐤌.𐤏𐤅𐤃.𐤅𐤄𐤍𐤄.𐤄𐤔𐤌𐤔.𐤅
𐤄𐤉𐤓𐤇.𐤅𐤀𐤇𐤃.𐤏𐤔𐤓.𐤊𐤅𐤊𐤁𐤉𐤌.𐤌𐤔𐤕𐤇𐤅𐤉𐤌.𐤋𐤉|
י 𐤅𐤉𐤎𐤐𐤓.𐤀𐤋.𐤀𐤁𐤉𐤅.𐤅𐤀𐤋.𐤀𐤇𐤉𐤅.𐤅𐤉𐤂𐤏𐤓.𐤁𐤅.𐤀𐤁𐤉
𐤅.𐤅𐤉𐤀𐤌𐤓.𐤋𐤅.𐤌𐤄.𐤄𐤇𐤋𐤅𐤌.𐤄𐤆𐤄.𐤀𐤔𐤓.𐤇𐤋𐤌𐤕.𐤄𐤁𐤅𐤀.
𐤍𐤁𐤅𐤀.𐤀𐤍𐤉.𐤅𐤀𐤌𐤊.𐤅𐤀𐤇𐤉𐤊.𐤋𐤄𐤔𐤕𐤇𐤅𐤕.𐤋𐤊.𐤀𐤓𐤑𐤄|
יא 𐤅𐤉𐤒𐤍𐤀𐤅.𐤁𐤅.𐤀𐤇𐤉𐤅.𐤅𐤀𐤁𐤉𐤅.𐤔𐤌𐤓.𐤀𐤕.𐤄𐤃𐤁𐤓|
יב 𐤅𐤉𐤋𐤊𐤅.𐤀𐤇𐤉𐤅.𐤋𐤓𐤏𐤅𐤕.𐤀𐤕.𐤑𐤀𐤍.𐤀𐤁𐤉𐤄𐤌.𐤁𐤔𐤊
𐤌|
יג 𐤅𐤉𐤀𐤌𐤓.𐤉𐤔𐤓𐤀𐤋.𐤀𐤋.𐤉𐤅𐤎𐤐.𐤄𐤋𐤅𐤀.𐤀𐤇𐤉𐤊.𐤓𐤏𐤉
𐤌.𐤁𐤔𐤊𐤌.𐤋𐤊𐤄.𐤅𐤀𐤔𐤋𐤇𐤊.𐤀𐤋𐤉𐤄𐤌.𐤅𐤉𐤀𐤌𐤓.𐤋𐤅.𐤄𐤍𐤍𐤉|
יד 𐤅𐤉𐤀𐤌𐤓.𐤋𐤅.𐤋𐤊.𐤍𐤀.𐤓𐤀𐤄.𐤀𐤕.𐤔𐤋𐤅𐤌.𐤀𐤇𐤉𐤊.𐤅𐤀
𐤕.𐤔𐤋𐤅𐤌.𐤄𐤑𐤀𐤍.𐤅𐤄𐤔𐤁𐤍𐤉.𐤃𐤁𐤓.𐤅𐤉𐤔𐤋𐤇𐤄𐤅.𐤌𐤏𐤌𐤒.
𐤇𐤁𐤓𐤅𐤍.𐤅𐤉𐤁𐤀.𐤔𐤊𐤌𐤄|
טו 𐤅𐤉𐤌𐤑𐤀𐤄𐤅.𐤀𐤉𐤔.𐤅𐤄𐤍𐤄.𐤕𐤏𐤄.𐤁𐤔𐤃𐤄.𐤅𐤉𐤔𐤀𐤋
𐤄𐤅.𐤄𐤀𐤉𐤔.𐤋𐤀𐤌𐤓.𐤌𐤄.𐤕𐤁𐤒𐤔|
טז 𐤅𐤉𐤀𐤌𐤓.𐤀𐤕.𐤀𐤇𐤉.𐤀𐤍𐤊𐤉.𐤌𐤁𐤒𐤔.𐤄𐤂𐤉𐤃𐤄.𐤍𐤀.
𐤋𐤉.𐤀𐤉𐤐𐤄.𐤄𐤌.𐤓𐤏𐤉𐤌|
יז 𐤅𐤉𐤀𐤌𐤓.𐤄𐤀𐤉𐤔.𐤍𐤎𐤏𐤅.𐤌𐤆𐤄.𐤊𐤉.𐤔𐤌𐤏𐤕𐤉.𐤀𐤌
𐤓𐤉𐤌.𐤍𐤋𐤊𐤄.𐤃𐤕𐤉𐤍𐤄.𐤅𐤉𐤋𐤊.𐤉𐤅𐤎𐤐.𐤀𐤇𐤓.𐤀𐤇𐤉𐤅.𐤅𐤉𐤌
𐤑𐤀𐤌.𐤁𐤃𐤕𐤍|
יח 𐤅𐤉𐤓𐤀𐤅.𐤀𐤕𐤅.𐤌𐤓𐤇𐤒.𐤅𐤁𐤈𐤓𐤌.𐤉𐤒𐤓𐤁.𐤀𐤋𐤉𐤄𐤌.𐤅𐤉
𐤕𐤍𐤊𐤋𐤅.𐤀𐤕𐤅.𐤋𐤄𐤌𐤉𐤕𐤅|
יט 𐤅𐤉𐤀𐤌𐤓𐤅.𐤀𐤉𐤔.𐤀𐤋.𐤀𐤇𐤉𐤅.𐤄𐤍𐤄.𐤁𐤏𐤋.𐤄𐤇𐤋𐤌𐤅
𐤕.𐤄𐤋𐤆𐤄.𐤁𐤀|
כ 𐤅𐤏𐤕𐤄.𐤋𐤊𐤅.𐤅𐤍𐤄𐤓𐤂𐤄𐤅.𐤅𐤍𐤔𐤋𐤊𐤄𐤅.𐤁𐤀𐤇𐤃.𐤄𐤁𐤓
𐤅𐤕.𐤅𐤀𐤌𐤓𐤍𐤅.𐤇𐤉𐤄.𐤓𐤏𐤄.𐤀𐤊𐤋𐤕𐤄𐤅.𐤅𐤍𐤓𐤀𐤄.𐤌𐤄.𐤉𐤄𐤉𐤅.
𐤇𐤋𐤌𐤕𐤉𐤅|

𐤊𐤀 𐤅𐤉𐤔𐤌𐤏.𐤓𐤀𐤅𐤁𐤍.𐤅𐤉𐤑𐤋𐤄𐤅.𐤌𐤉𐤃𐤌.𐤅𐤉𐤀𐤌𐤓.𐤋𐤀.𐤍
𐤊𐤍𐤅.𐤍𐤐𐤔|

𐤊𐤁 𐤅𐤉𐤀𐤌𐤓.𐤀𐤋𐤄𐤌.𐤓𐤀𐤅𐤁𐤍.𐤀𐤋.𐤕𐤔𐤐𐤊𐤅.𐤃𐤌.𐤄𐤔𐤋𐤉
𐤊𐤅.𐤀𐤕𐤅.𐤀𐤋.𐤄𐤁𐤅𐤓.𐤄𐤆𐤄.𐤀𐤔𐤓.𐤁𐤌𐤃𐤁𐤓.𐤅𐤉𐤃.𐤀𐤋.𐤕
𐤔𐤋𐤇𐤅.𐤁𐤅.𐤋𐤌𐤏𐤍.𐤄𐤑𐤉𐤋.𐤀𐤕𐤅.𐤌𐤉𐤃𐤌.𐤋𐤄𐤔𐤉𐤁𐤅.𐤀𐤋.
𐤀𐤁𐤉𐤅|

𐤊𐤂 𐤅𐤉𐤄𐤉.𐤊𐤀𐤔𐤓.𐤁𐤀.𐤉𐤅𐤎𐤐.𐤀𐤋.𐤀𐤇𐤉𐤅.𐤅𐤉𐤐𐤔𐤉𐤈𐤅.
𐤀𐤕.𐤉𐤅𐤎𐤐.𐤀𐤕.𐤊𐤕𐤍𐤕𐤅.𐤀𐤕.𐤊𐤕𐤍𐤕.𐤄𐤐𐤎𐤉𐤌.𐤀𐤔𐤓.𐤏
𐤋𐤉𐤅|

𐤊𐤃 𐤅𐤉𐤒𐤇𐤄𐤅.𐤅𐤉𐤔𐤋𐤊𐤅.𐤀𐤕𐤅.𐤄𐤁𐤓𐤄.𐤅𐤄𐤁𐤅𐤓.𐤓𐤒.𐤀𐤉
𐤍.𐤁𐤅.𐤌𐤉𐤌|

𐤊𐤄 𐤅𐤉𐤔𐤁𐤅.𐤋𐤀𐤊𐤋.𐤋𐤇𐤌.𐤅𐤉𐤔𐤀𐤅.𐤏𐤉𐤍𐤉𐤄𐤌.𐤅𐤉𐤓𐤀𐤅.𐤅
𐤄𐤍𐤄.𐤀𐤓𐤇𐤕.𐤉𐤔𐤌𐤏𐤀𐤋𐤉𐤌.𐤁𐤀𐤄.𐤌𐤂𐤋𐤏𐤃.𐤅𐤂𐤌𐤋𐤉
𐤄𐤌.𐤍𐤔𐤀𐤉𐤌.𐤍𐤊𐤀𐤕.𐤅𐤑𐤓𐤉.𐤅𐤋𐤈.𐤄𐤅𐤋𐤊𐤉𐤌.𐤋𐤄𐤅𐤓𐤉𐤃.
𐤌𐤑𐤓𐤉𐤌𐤄|

𐤊𐤅 𐤅𐤉𐤀𐤌𐤓.𐤉𐤄𐤅𐤃𐤄.𐤀𐤋.𐤀𐤇𐤉𐤅.𐤌𐤄.𐤁𐤑𐤏.𐤊𐤉.𐤍𐤄𐤓
𐤂.𐤀𐤕.𐤀𐤇𐤉𐤍𐤅.𐤅𐤊𐤎𐤉𐤍𐤅.𐤀𐤕.𐤃𐤌𐤅|

𐤊𐤆 𐤋𐤊𐤅.𐤅𐤍𐤌𐤊𐤓𐤍𐤅.𐤋𐤉𐤔𐤌𐤏𐤀𐤋𐤉𐤌.𐤅𐤉𐤃𐤍𐤅.𐤀𐤋.𐤕𐤄𐤉
.𐤁𐤅.𐤊𐤉.𐤀𐤇𐤉𐤍𐤅.𐤁𐤔𐤓𐤍𐤅.𐤄𐤅𐤀.𐤅𐤉𐤔𐤌𐤏𐤅.𐤀𐤇𐤉𐤅|

𐤊𐤇 𐤅𐤉𐤏𐤁𐤓𐤅.𐤀𐤍𐤔𐤉𐤌.𐤌𐤃𐤉𐤍𐤉𐤌.𐤎𐤇𐤓𐤉𐤌.𐤅𐤉𐤌𐤔𐤊𐤅.
𐤅𐤉𐤏𐤋𐤅.𐤀𐤕.𐤉𐤅𐤎𐤐.𐤌𐤍.𐤄𐤁𐤅𐤓.𐤅𐤉𐤌𐤊𐤓𐤅.𐤀𐤕.𐤉𐤅𐤎𐤐.𐤋𐤉𐤔
𐤌𐤏𐤀𐤋𐤉𐤌.𐤁𐤏𐤔𐤓𐤉𐤌.𐤊𐤎𐤐.𐤅𐤉𐤁𐤉𐤀𐤅.𐤀𐤕.𐤉𐤅𐤎𐤐.𐤌𐤑𐤓
𐤉𐤌𐤄|

𐤊𐤈 𐤅𐤉𐤔𐤁.𐤓𐤀𐤅𐤁𐤍.𐤀𐤋.𐤄𐤁𐤅𐤓.𐤅𐤄𐤍𐤄.𐤀𐤉𐤍.𐤉𐤅𐤎𐤐.𐤁𐤁𐤅
𐤓.𐤅𐤉𐤒𐤓𐤏.𐤀𐤕.𐤁𐤂𐤃𐤉𐤅|

𐤋 𐤅𐤉𐤔𐤁.𐤀𐤋.𐤀𐤇𐤉𐤅.𐤅𐤉𐤀𐤌𐤓.𐤄𐤉𐤋𐤃.𐤀𐤉𐤍𐤍𐤅.𐤅𐤀𐤍𐤉
.𐤀𐤍𐤄.𐤀𐤍𐤉.𐤁𐤀|

𐤋𐤀 𐤅𐤉𐤒𐤇𐤅.𐤀𐤕.𐤊𐤕𐤍𐤕.𐤉𐤅𐤎𐤐.𐤅𐤉𐤔𐤇𐤈𐤅.𐤔𐤏𐤉𐤓.𐤏
𐤆𐤉𐤌.𐤅𐤉𐤈𐤁𐤋𐤅.𐤀𐤕.𐤄𐤊𐤕𐤍𐤕.𐤁𐤃𐤌|

𐤋𐤁 𐤅𐤉𐤔𐤋𐤇𐤅.𐤀𐤕.𐤊𐤕𐤍𐤕.𐤄𐤐𐤎𐤉𐤌.𐤅𐤉𐤁𐤉𐤀𐤅.𐤀𐤋.𐤀𐤁𐤉𐤄𐤌.𐤅𐤉𐤀𐤌𐤓𐤅.𐤆𐤀𐤕.𐤌𐤑𐤀𐤍𐤅.𐤄𐤊𐤓.𐤍𐤀.𐤄𐤊𐤕𐤍𐤕.𐤁𐤍𐤊.𐤄𐤅𐤀.𐤀𐤌.𐤋𐤀|

𐤋𐤂 𐤅𐤉𐤊𐤉𐤓𐤄.𐤅𐤉𐤀𐤌𐤓.𐤊𐤕𐤍𐤕.𐤁𐤍𐤉.𐤇𐤉𐤄.𐤓𐤏𐤄.𐤀𐤊𐤋𐤕𐤄𐤅.𐤈𐤓𐤐.𐤈𐤓𐤐.𐤉𐤅𐤎𐤐|

𐤋𐤃 𐤅𐤉𐤒𐤓𐤏.𐤉𐤏𐤒𐤁.𐤔𐤌𐤋𐤕𐤉𐤅.𐤅𐤉𐤔𐤌.𐤔𐤒.𐤁𐤌𐤕𐤍𐤉𐤅.𐤅𐤉𐤕𐤀𐤁𐤋.𐤏𐤋.𐤁𐤍𐤅.𐤉𐤌𐤉𐤌.𐤓𐤁𐤉𐤌|

𐤋𐤄 𐤅𐤉𐤒𐤌𐤅.𐤊𐤋.𐤁𐤍𐤉𐤅.𐤅𐤊𐤋.𐤁𐤍𐤕𐤉𐤅.𐤋𐤍𐤇𐤌𐤅.𐤅𐤉𐤌𐤀𐤍.𐤋𐤄𐤕𐤍𐤇𐤌.𐤅𐤉𐤀𐤌𐤓.𐤊𐤉.𐤀𐤓𐤃.𐤀𐤋.𐤁𐤍𐤉.𐤀𐤁𐤋.𐤔𐤀𐤋𐤄.𐤅𐤉𐤁𐤊.𐤀𐤕𐤅.𐤀𐤁𐤉𐤅|

𐤋𐤅 𐤅𐤄𐤌𐤃𐤍𐤉𐤌.𐤌𐤊𐤓𐤅.𐤀𐤕𐤅.𐤀𐤋.𐤌𐤑𐤓𐤉𐤌.𐤋𐤐𐤅𐤈𐤉𐤐𐤓.𐤎𐤓𐤉𐤎.𐤐𐤓𐤏𐤄.𐤔𐤓.𐤄𐤈𐤁𐤇𐤉𐤌||

𐤁𐤓𐤀𐤔𐤉𐤕.𐤇𐤋𐤒 𐤋𐤇

𐤀 𐤅𐤉𐤄𐤉.𐤁𐤏𐤕.𐤄𐤄𐤅𐤀.𐤅𐤉𐤓𐤃.𐤉𐤄𐤅𐤃𐤄.𐤌𐤀𐤕.𐤀𐤇𐤉𐤅.𐤅𐤉𐤈.𐤏𐤃.𐤀𐤉𐤔.𐤏𐤃𐤋𐤌𐤉.𐤅𐤔𐤌𐤅.𐤇𐤉𐤓𐤄|

𐤁 𐤅𐤉𐤓𐤀.𐤔𐤌.𐤉𐤄𐤅𐤃𐤄.𐤁𐤕.𐤀𐤉𐤔.𐤊𐤍𐤏𐤍𐤉.𐤅𐤔𐤌𐤅.𐤔𐤅𐤏.𐤅𐤉𐤒𐤇𐤄.𐤅𐤉𐤁𐤀.𐤀𐤋𐤉𐤄|

𐤂 𐤅𐤕𐤄𐤓.𐤅𐤕𐤋𐤃.𐤁𐤍.𐤅𐤉𐤒𐤓𐤀.𐤀𐤕.𐤔𐤌𐤅.𐤏𐤓|

𐤃 𐤅𐤕𐤄𐤓.𐤏𐤅𐤃.𐤅𐤕𐤋𐤃.𐤁𐤍.𐤅𐤕𐤒𐤓𐤀.𐤀𐤕.𐤔𐤌𐤅.𐤀𐤅𐤍𐤍|

𐤄 𐤅𐤕𐤎𐤐.𐤏𐤅𐤃.𐤅𐤕𐤋𐤃.𐤁𐤍.𐤅𐤕𐤒𐤓𐤀.𐤀𐤕.𐤔𐤌𐤅.𐤔𐤋𐤄.𐤅𐤄𐤉𐤄.𐤁𐤊𐤆𐤉𐤁.𐤁𐤋𐤃𐤕𐤄.𐤀𐤕𐤅|

𐤅 𐤅𐤉𐤒𐤇.𐤉𐤄𐤅𐤃𐤄.𐤀𐤔𐤄.𐤋𐤏𐤓.𐤁𐤊𐤅𐤓𐤅.𐤅𐤔𐤌𐤄.𐤕𐤌𐤓|

𐤆 𐤅𐤉𐤄𐤉.𐤏𐤓.𐤁𐤊𐤅𐤓.𐤉𐤄𐤅𐤃𐤄.𐤓𐤏.𐤁𐤏𐤉𐤍𐤉.𐤉𐤄𐤅𐤄.𐤅𐤉𐤌𐤕𐤄𐤅.𐤉𐤄𐤅𐤄|

𐤇 𐤅𐤉𐤀𐤌𐤓.𐤉𐤄𐤅𐤃𐤄.𐤋𐤀𐤅𐤍𐤍.𐤁𐤀.𐤀𐤋.𐤀𐤔𐤕.𐤀𐤇𐤉𐤊.𐤅𐤉𐤁𐤌.𐤀𐤕𐤄.𐤅𐤄𐤒𐤌.𐤆𐤓𐤏.𐤋𐤀𐤇𐤉𐤊|

𐤈 𐤅𐤉𐤃𐤏.𐤀𐤅𐤍𐤍.𐤊𐤉.𐤋𐤀.𐤋𐤅.𐤉𐤄𐤉𐤄.𐤄𐤆𐤓𐤏.𐤅𐤄𐤉𐤄.𐤀𐤌.𐤁𐤀.𐤀𐤋.𐤀𐤔𐤕.𐤀𐤇𐤉𐤅.𐤅𐤔𐤇𐤕.𐤀𐤓𐤑𐤄.𐤋𐤁𐤋𐤕𐤉.𐤍𐤕𐤍.𐤆𐤓𐤏.𐤋𐤀𐤇𐤉𐤅|

10 𐤅𐤉𐤓𐤏.𐤁𐤏𐤉𐤍𐤉.𐤉𐤄𐤅𐤄.𐤀𐤔𐤓.𐤏𐤔𐤄.𐤅𐤉𐤌𐤕.𐤂𐤌.𐤀
𐤕𐤅|

11 𐤅𐤉𐤀𐤌𐤓.𐤉𐤄𐤅𐤃𐤄.𐤋𐤕𐤌𐤓.𐤊𐤋𐤕𐤅.𐤔𐤁𐤉.𐤀𐤋𐤌𐤍𐤄.𐤁
𐤉𐤕.𐤀𐤁𐤉𐤊.𐤏𐤃.𐤉𐤂𐤃𐤋.𐤔𐤋𐤄.𐤁𐤍𐤉.𐤊𐤉.𐤀𐤌𐤓.𐤐𐤍.𐤉𐤌𐤅
𐤕.𐤂𐤌.𐤄𐤅𐤀.𐤊𐤀𐤇𐤉𐤅.𐤅𐤕𐤋𐤊.𐤕𐤌𐤓.𐤅𐤕𐤔𐤁.𐤁𐤉𐤕.𐤀𐤁𐤉𐤄
|

12 𐤅𐤉𐤓𐤁𐤅.𐤄𐤉𐤌𐤉𐤌.𐤅𐤕𐤌𐤕.𐤁𐤕.𐤔𐤅𐤏.𐤀𐤔𐤕.𐤉𐤄𐤅𐤃𐤄
.𐤅𐤉𐤍𐤇𐤌.𐤉𐤄𐤅𐤃𐤄.𐤅𐤉𐤏𐤋.𐤏𐤋.𐤂𐤆𐤆𐤉.𐤑𐤀𐤍𐤅.𐤄𐤅𐤀.𐤅
𐤇𐤉𐤓𐤄.𐤓𐤏𐤄𐤅.𐤄𐤏𐤃𐤋𐤌𐤉.𐤕𐤌𐤍𐤕𐤄|

13 𐤅𐤉𐤂𐤃.𐤋𐤕𐤌𐤓.𐤋𐤀𐤌𐤓.𐤄𐤍𐤄.𐤇𐤌𐤉𐤊.𐤏𐤋𐤄.𐤕𐤌𐤍𐤕
𐤄.𐤋𐤂𐤆.𐤑𐤀𐤍𐤅|

14 𐤅𐤕𐤎𐤓.𐤁𐤂𐤃𐤉.𐤀𐤋𐤌𐤍𐤅𐤕𐤄.𐤌𐤏𐤋𐤉𐤄.𐤅𐤕𐤊𐤎.𐤁𐤑
𐤏𐤉𐤐.𐤅𐤕𐤕𐤏𐤋𐤐.𐤅𐤕𐤔𐤁.𐤁𐤐𐤕𐤇.𐤏𐤉𐤍𐤉𐤌.𐤀𐤔𐤓.𐤏𐤋.𐤃𐤓
𐤊.𐤕𐤌𐤍𐤕𐤄.𐤊𐤉.𐤓𐤀𐤕𐤄.𐤊𐤉.𐤂𐤃𐤋.𐤔𐤋𐤄.𐤅𐤄𐤅𐤀.𐤋𐤀.𐤍𐤕
𐤍𐤄.𐤋𐤅.𐤋𐤀𐤔𐤄|

15 𐤅𐤉𐤓𐤀𐤄.𐤉𐤄𐤅𐤃𐤄.𐤅𐤉𐤇𐤔𐤁𐤄.𐤋𐤆𐤅𐤍𐤄.𐤊𐤉.𐤊𐤎𐤕𐤄
.𐤐𐤍𐤉𐤄|

16 𐤅𐤉𐤈.𐤀𐤋𐤉𐤄.𐤀𐤋.𐤄𐤃𐤓𐤊.𐤅𐤉𐤀𐤌𐤓.𐤄𐤁𐤄.𐤍𐤀.𐤀𐤁𐤅
𐤀.𐤀𐤋𐤉𐤊.𐤊𐤉.𐤋𐤀.𐤉𐤃𐤏.𐤊𐤉.𐤊𐤋𐤕𐤅.𐤄𐤅𐤀.𐤅𐤕𐤀𐤌𐤓.𐤌𐤄.
𐤕𐤕𐤍.𐤋𐤉.𐤊𐤉.𐤕𐤁𐤅𐤀.𐤀𐤋𐤉|

17 𐤅𐤉𐤀𐤌𐤓.𐤀𐤍𐤊𐤉.𐤀𐤔𐤋𐤇.𐤂𐤃𐤉.𐤏𐤆𐤉𐤌.𐤌𐤍.𐤄𐤑
𐤀𐤍.𐤅𐤕𐤀𐤌𐤓.𐤀𐤌.𐤕𐤕𐤍.𐤏𐤓𐤁𐤅𐤍.𐤏𐤃.𐤔𐤋𐤇𐤊|

18 𐤅𐤉𐤀𐤌𐤓.𐤌𐤄.𐤄𐤏𐤓𐤁𐤅𐤍.𐤀𐤔𐤓.𐤀𐤕𐤍.𐤋𐤊.𐤅𐤕𐤀𐤌𐤓.𐤇
𐤕𐤌𐤊.𐤅𐤐𐤕𐤉𐤋𐤊.𐤅𐤌𐤈𐤊.𐤀𐤔𐤓.𐤁𐤉𐤃𐤊.𐤅𐤉𐤕𐤍.𐤋𐤄.𐤅𐤉𐤁𐤀.
𐤀𐤋𐤉𐤄.𐤅𐤕𐤄𐤓.𐤋𐤅|

19 𐤅𐤕𐤒𐤌.𐤅𐤕𐤋𐤊.𐤅𐤕𐤎𐤓.𐤑𐤏𐤉𐤐𐤄.𐤌𐤏𐤋𐤉𐤄.𐤅𐤕𐤋𐤁𐤔
.𐤁𐤂𐤃𐤉.𐤀𐤋𐤌𐤍𐤅𐤕𐤄|

20 𐤅𐤉𐤔𐤋𐤇.𐤉𐤄𐤅𐤃𐤄.𐤀𐤕.𐤂𐤃𐤉.𐤄𐤏𐤆𐤉𐤌.𐤁𐤉𐤃.𐤓
𐤏𐤄𐤅.𐤄𐤏𐤃𐤋𐤌𐤉.𐤋𐤒𐤇𐤕.𐤄𐤏𐤓𐤁𐤅𐤍.𐤌𐤉𐤃.𐤄𐤀𐤔𐤄.𐤅𐤋
𐤀.𐤌𐤑𐤀𐤄|

21 𐤅𐤉𐤔𐤀𐤋.𐤀𐤕.𐤀𐤍𐤔𐤉.𐤌𐤒𐤌𐤄.𐤋𐤀𐤌𐤓.𐤀𐤉𐤄.𐤄𐤒𐤃
𐤔𐤄.𐤄𐤅𐤀.𐤁𐤏𐤉𐤍𐤉𐤌.𐤏𐤋.𐤄𐤃𐤓𐤊.𐤅𐤉𐤀𐤌𐤓𐤅.𐤋𐤀.𐤄𐤉𐤕𐤄.
𐤁𐤆𐤄.𐤒𐤃𐤔𐤄|
22 𐤅𐤉𐤔𐤁.𐤀𐤋.𐤉𐤄𐤅𐤃𐤄.𐤅𐤉𐤀𐤌𐤓.𐤋𐤀.𐤌𐤑𐤀𐤕𐤉𐤄.𐤅𐤂
𐤌.𐤀𐤍𐤔𐤉.𐤄𐤌𐤒𐤅𐤌.𐤀𐤌𐤓𐤅.𐤋𐤀.𐤄𐤉𐤕𐤄.𐤁𐤆𐤄.𐤒𐤃𐤔𐤄|
23 𐤅𐤉𐤀𐤌𐤓.𐤉𐤄𐤅𐤃𐤄.𐤕𐤒𐤇.𐤋𐤄.𐤐𐤍.𐤍𐤄𐤉𐤄.𐤋𐤁𐤅𐤆.𐤄
𐤍𐤄.𐤔𐤋𐤇𐤕𐤉.𐤄𐤂𐤃𐤉.𐤄𐤆𐤄.𐤅𐤀𐤕𐤄.𐤋𐤀.𐤌𐤑𐤀𐤕𐤄|
24 𐤅𐤉𐤄𐤉.𐤊𐤌𐤔𐤋𐤔.𐤇𐤃𐤔𐤉𐤌.𐤅𐤉𐤂𐤃.𐤋𐤉𐤄𐤅𐤃𐤄.𐤋
𐤀𐤌𐤓.𐤆𐤍𐤕𐤄.𐤕𐤌𐤓.𐤊𐤋𐤕𐤊.𐤅𐤂𐤌.𐤄𐤍𐤄.𐤄𐤓𐤄.𐤋𐤆𐤍𐤅𐤍𐤉
𐤌.𐤅𐤉𐤀𐤌𐤓.𐤉𐤄𐤅𐤃𐤄.𐤄𐤅𐤑𐤉𐤀𐤅𐤄.𐤅𐤕𐤔𐤓𐤐|
25 𐤄𐤅𐤀.𐤌𐤅𐤑𐤀𐤕.𐤅𐤄𐤉𐤀.𐤔𐤋𐤇𐤄.𐤀𐤋.𐤇𐤌𐤉𐤄.𐤋𐤀𐤌
𐤓.𐤋𐤀𐤉𐤔.𐤀𐤔𐤓.𐤀𐤋𐤄.𐤋𐤅.𐤀𐤍𐤊𐤉.𐤄𐤓𐤄.𐤅𐤕𐤀𐤌𐤓.𐤄𐤊𐤓.𐤍
𐤀.𐤋𐤌𐤉.𐤄𐤇𐤕𐤌𐤕.𐤅𐤄𐤐𐤕𐤉𐤋𐤉𐤌.𐤅𐤄𐤌𐤈𐤄.𐤄𐤀𐤋𐤄|
26 𐤅𐤉𐤊𐤓.𐤉𐤄𐤅𐤃𐤄.𐤅𐤉𐤀𐤌𐤓.𐤑𐤃𐤒𐤄.𐤌𐤌𐤍𐤉.𐤊𐤉.𐤏𐤋.
𐤊𐤍.𐤋𐤀.𐤍𐤕𐤕𐤉𐤄.𐤋𐤔𐤋𐤄.𐤁𐤍𐤉.𐤅𐤋𐤀.𐤉-
𐤎𐤐.𐤏𐤅𐤃.𐤋𐤃𐤏𐤕𐤄|
27 𐤅𐤉𐤄𐤉.𐤁𐤏𐤕.𐤋𐤃𐤕𐤄.𐤅𐤄𐤍𐤄.𐤕𐤀𐤅𐤌𐤉𐤌.𐤁𐤁𐤈𐤍𐤄|
28 𐤅𐤉𐤄𐤉.𐤁𐤋𐤃𐤕𐤄.𐤅𐤉𐤕𐤍.𐤉𐤃.𐤅𐤕𐤒𐤇.𐤄𐤌𐤉𐤋𐤃𐤕.𐤅
𐤕𐤒𐤔𐤓.𐤏𐤋.𐤉𐤃𐤅.𐤔𐤍𐤉.𐤋𐤀𐤌𐤓.𐤆𐤄.𐤉𐤑𐤀.𐤓𐤀𐤔𐤍𐤄|
29 𐤅𐤉𐤄𐤉.𐤊𐤌𐤔𐤉𐤁.𐤉𐤃𐤅.𐤅𐤄𐤍𐤄.𐤉𐤑𐤀.𐤀𐤇𐤉𐤅.𐤅𐤕𐤀
𐤌𐤓.𐤌𐤄.𐤐𐤓𐤑𐤕.𐤏𐤋𐤉𐤊.𐤐𐤓𐤑.𐤅𐤉𐤒𐤓𐤀.𐤔𐤌𐤅.𐤐𐤓𐤑|
30 𐤅𐤀𐤇𐤓.𐤉𐤑𐤀.𐤀𐤇𐤉𐤅.𐤀𐤔𐤓.𐤏𐤋.𐤉𐤃𐤅.𐤄𐤔𐤍𐤉.𐤅𐤉
𐤒𐤓𐤀.𐤔𐤌𐤅.𐤆𐤓𐤇||

𐤁𐤓𐤀𐤔𐤉𐤕.𐤇𐤋𐤒 39

1 𐤅𐤉𐤅𐤎𐤐.𐤄𐤅𐤓𐤃.𐤌𐤑𐤓𐤉𐤌𐤄.𐤅𐤉𐤒𐤍𐤄𐤅.𐤐𐤅𐤈𐤉𐤐𐤓.𐤎𐤓𐤉
𐤎.𐤐𐤓𐤏𐤄.𐤔𐤓.𐤄𐤈𐤁𐤇𐤉𐤌.𐤀𐤉𐤔.𐤌𐤑𐤓𐤉.𐤌𐤉𐤃.𐤄𐤉𐤔𐤌
𐤏𐤀𐤋𐤉𐤌.𐤀𐤔𐤓.𐤄𐤅𐤓𐤃𐤄𐤅.𐤔𐤌𐤄|
2 𐤅𐤉𐤄𐤉.𐤉𐤄𐤅𐤄.𐤀𐤕.𐤉𐤅𐤎𐤐.𐤅𐤉𐤄𐤉.𐤀𐤉𐤔.𐤌𐤑𐤋𐤉𐤇.𐤅𐤉
𐤄𐤉.𐤁𐤁𐤉𐤕.𐤀𐤃𐤍𐤉𐤅.𐤄𐤌𐤑𐤓𐤉|

ג 𐤅𐤉𐤓𐤀.𐤀𐤃𐤍𐤉𐤅.𐤊𐤉.𐤉𐤄𐤅𐤄.𐤀𐤕𐤅.𐤅𐤊𐤋.𐤀𐤔𐤓.𐤄𐤅𐤀.𐤏
𐤔𐤄.𐤉𐤄𐤅𐤄.𐤌𐤑𐤋𐤉𐤇.𐤁𐤉𐤃𐤅

ד 𐤅𐤉𐤌𐤑𐤀.𐤉𐤅𐤎𐤐.𐤇𐤍.𐤁𐤏𐤉𐤍𐤉𐤅.𐤅𐤉𐤔𐤓𐤕.𐤀𐤕𐤅.𐤅𐤉𐤐𐤒
𐤃𐤄𐤅.𐤏𐤋.𐤁𐤉𐤕𐤅.𐤅𐤊𐤋.𐤉𐤔.𐤋𐤅.𐤍𐤕𐤍.𐤁𐤉𐤃𐤅

ה 𐤅𐤉𐤄𐤉.𐤌𐤀𐤆.𐤄𐤐𐤒𐤉𐤃.𐤀𐤕𐤅.𐤁𐤁𐤉𐤕𐤅.𐤅𐤏𐤋.𐤊𐤋.𐤀𐤔
𐤓.𐤉𐤔.𐤋𐤅.𐤅𐤉𐤁𐤓𐤊.𐤉𐤄𐤅𐤄.𐤀𐤕.𐤁𐤉𐤕.𐤄𐤌𐤑𐤓𐤉.𐤁𐤂𐤋𐤋.𐤉𐤅
𐤎𐤐.𐤅𐤉𐤄𐤉.𐤁𐤓𐤊𐤕.𐤉𐤄𐤅𐤄.𐤁𐤊𐤋.𐤀𐤔𐤓.𐤉𐤔.𐤋𐤅.𐤁𐤁𐤉𐤕.𐤅𐤁
𐤔𐤃𐤄

ו 𐤅𐤉𐤏𐤆𐤁.𐤊𐤋.𐤀𐤔𐤓.𐤋𐤅.𐤁𐤉𐤃.𐤉𐤅𐤎𐤐.𐤅𐤋𐤀.𐤉𐤃𐤏.𐤀𐤕
𐤅.𐤌𐤀𐤅𐤌𐤄.𐤊𐤉.𐤀𐤌.𐤄𐤋𐤇𐤌.𐤀𐤔𐤓.𐤄𐤅𐤀.𐤀𐤅𐤊𐤋.𐤅𐤉𐤄𐤉.𐤉𐤅
𐤎𐤐.𐤉𐤐𐤄.𐤕𐤀𐤓.𐤅𐤉𐤐𐤄.𐤌𐤓𐤀𐤄

ז 𐤅𐤉𐤄𐤉.𐤀𐤇𐤓.𐤄𐤃𐤁𐤓𐤉𐤌.𐤄𐤀𐤋𐤄.𐤅𐤕𐤔𐤀.𐤀𐤔𐤕.𐤀
𐤃𐤍𐤉𐤅.𐤀𐤕.𐤏𐤉𐤍𐤉𐤄.𐤀𐤋.𐤉𐤅𐤎𐤐.𐤅𐤕𐤀𐤌𐤓.𐤔𐤊𐤁𐤄.𐤏𐤌𐤉

ח 𐤅𐤉𐤌𐤀𐤍.𐤅𐤉𐤀𐤌𐤓.𐤀𐤋.𐤀𐤔𐤕.𐤀𐤃𐤍𐤉𐤅.𐤄𐤍.𐤀𐤃𐤍𐤉.𐤋
𐤀.𐤉𐤃𐤏.𐤀𐤕𐤉.𐤌𐤄.𐤁𐤁𐤉𐤕.𐤅𐤊𐤋.𐤀𐤔𐤓.𐤉𐤔.𐤋𐤅.𐤍𐤕𐤍.𐤁𐤉
𐤃𐤉

ט 𐤀𐤉𐤍𐤍𐤅.𐤂𐤃𐤅𐤋.𐤁𐤁𐤉𐤕.𐤄𐤆𐤄.𐤌𐤌𐤍𐤉.𐤅𐤋𐤀.𐤇𐤔𐤊.
𐤌𐤌𐤍𐤉.𐤌𐤀𐤅𐤌𐤄.𐤊𐤉.𐤀𐤌.𐤀𐤅𐤕𐤊.𐤁𐤀𐤔𐤓.𐤀𐤕.𐤀𐤔𐤕𐤅.𐤅𐤀
𐤉𐤊.𐤀𐤏𐤔𐤄.𐤄𐤓𐤏𐤄.𐤄𐤂𐤃𐤋𐤄.𐤄𐤆𐤀𐤕.𐤅𐤇𐤈𐤀𐤕𐤉.𐤋
𐤀𐤋𐤄𐤉𐤌

י 𐤅𐤉𐤄𐤉.𐤊𐤃𐤁𐤓𐤄.𐤀𐤋.𐤉𐤅𐤎𐤐.𐤉𐤅𐤌.𐤉𐤅𐤌.𐤅𐤋𐤀.𐤔𐤌𐤏.
𐤀𐤋𐤉𐤄.𐤋𐤔𐤊𐤁.𐤀𐤑𐤋𐤄.𐤋𐤄𐤉𐤅𐤕.𐤏𐤌𐤄

יא 𐤅𐤉𐤄𐤉.𐤊𐤄𐤉𐤅𐤌.𐤄𐤆𐤄.𐤅𐤉𐤁𐤀.𐤄𐤁𐤉𐤕𐤄.𐤋𐤏𐤔𐤅𐤕.
𐤌𐤋𐤀𐤊𐤕𐤅.𐤅𐤀𐤉𐤍.𐤀𐤉𐤔.𐤌𐤀𐤍𐤔𐤉.𐤄𐤁𐤉𐤕.𐤔𐤌.𐤁𐤁𐤉𐤕

יב 𐤅𐤕𐤕𐤐𐤔𐤄𐤅.𐤁𐤁𐤂𐤃𐤅.𐤋𐤀𐤌𐤓.𐤔𐤊𐤁𐤄.𐤏𐤌𐤉.𐤅𐤉𐤏
𐤆𐤁.𐤁𐤂𐤃𐤅.𐤁𐤉𐤃𐤄.𐤅𐤉𐤍𐤎.𐤅𐤉𐤑𐤀.𐤄𐤇𐤅𐤑𐤄

יג 𐤅𐤉𐤄𐤉.𐤊𐤓𐤀𐤅𐤕𐤄.𐤊𐤉.𐤏𐤆𐤁.𐤁𐤂𐤃𐤅.𐤁𐤉𐤃𐤄.𐤅𐤉𐤍
𐤎.𐤄𐤇𐤅𐤑𐤄

יד 𐤅𐤕𐤒𐤓𐤀.𐤋𐤀𐤍𐤔𐤉.𐤁𐤉𐤕𐤄.𐤅𐤕𐤀𐤌𐤓.𐤋𐤄𐤌.𐤋𐤀𐤌𐤓.𐤓
𐤀𐤅.𐤄𐤁𐤉𐤀.𐤋𐤍𐤅.𐤀𐤉𐤔.𐤏𐤁𐤓𐤉.𐤋𐤑𐤇𐤒.𐤁𐤍𐤅.𐤁𐤀.𐤀𐤋𐤉.𐤋
𐤔𐤊𐤁.𐤏𐤌𐤉.𐤅𐤀𐤒𐤓𐤀.𐤁𐤒𐤅𐤋.𐤂𐤃𐤅𐤋

..טו.. ויהי.כשמעו.כי.הרימתי.קולי.ואקרא.וי
עזב.בגדו.אצלי.וינס.ויצא.החוצה|
..טז.. ותנח.בגדו.אצלה.עד.בוא.אדניו.אל.ב
יתו|
..יז.. ותדבר.אליו.כדברים.האלה.לאמר.בא.א
לי.העבד.העברי.אשר.הבאת.לנו.לצחק.בי|
..יח.. ויהי.כהרימי.קולי.ואקרא.ויעזב.בגד
ו.אצלי.וינס.החוצה|
..יט.. ויהי.כשמע.אדניו.את.דברי.אשתו.אש
ר.דברה.אליו.לאמר.כדברים.האלה.עשה.לי.
עבדך.ויחר.אפו|
..כ.. ויקח.אדני.יוסף.אתו.ויתנהו.אל.בית.ה
סהר.מקום.אשר.אסורי.||אסירי.קרי||.המלך.א
סורים.ויהי.שם.בבית.הסהר|
..כא.. ויהי.יהוה.את.יוסף.ויט.אליו.חסד.וית
ן.חנו.בעיני.שר.בית.הסהר|
..כב.. ויתן.שר.בית.הסהר.ביד.יוסף.את.כל.הא
סירם.אשר.בבית.הסהר.ואת.כל.אשר.עשים.ש
ם.הוא.היה.עשה|
..כג.. אין.שר.בית.הסהר.ראה.את.כל.מאומה.ב
ידו.באשר.יהוה.אתו.ואשר.הוא.עשה.יהוה.מ
צליח|

בראשית.חלק ..מ..

..א.. ויהי.אחר.הדברים.האלה.חטאו.משקה.מ
לך.מצרים.והאפה.לאדניהם.למלך.מצרים|
..ב.. ויקצף.פרעה.על.שני.סריסיו.על.שר.המש
קים.ועל.שר.האופים|
..ג.. ויתן.אתם.במשמר.בית.שר.הטבחים.אל.ב
ית.הסהר.מקום.אשר.יוסף.אסור.שם|

𐤃 𐤅𐤉𐤐𐤒𐤃.𐤔𐤓.𐤄𐤈𐤁𐤇𐤉𐤌.𐤀𐤕.𐤉𐤅𐤎𐤐.𐤀𐤕𐤌.𐤅𐤉𐤔𐤓
𐤕.𐤀𐤕𐤌.𐤅𐤉𐤄𐤉𐤅.𐤉𐤌𐤉𐤌.𐤁𐤌𐤔𐤌𐤓|

𐤄 𐤅𐤉𐤇𐤋𐤌𐤅.𐤇𐤋𐤅𐤌.𐤔𐤍𐤉𐤄𐤌.𐤀𐤉𐤔.𐤇𐤋𐤌𐤅.𐤁𐤋𐤉𐤋𐤄.𐤀
𐤇𐤃.𐤀𐤉𐤔.𐤊𐤐𐤕𐤓𐤅𐤍.𐤇𐤋𐤌𐤅.𐤄𐤌𐤔𐤒𐤄.𐤅𐤄𐤀𐤐𐤄.𐤀𐤔𐤓.𐤋
𐤌𐤋𐤊.𐤌𐤑𐤓𐤉𐤌.𐤀𐤔𐤓.𐤀𐤎𐤅𐤓𐤉𐤌.𐤁𐤁𐤉𐤕.𐤄𐤎𐤄𐤓|

𐤅 𐤅𐤉𐤁𐤀.𐤀𐤋𐤉𐤄𐤌.𐤉𐤅𐤎𐤐.𐤁𐤁𐤒𐤓.𐤅𐤉𐤓𐤀.𐤀𐤕𐤌.𐤅𐤄𐤍𐤌.
𐤆𐤏𐤐𐤉𐤌|

𐤆 𐤅𐤉𐤔𐤀𐤋.𐤀𐤕.𐤎𐤓𐤉𐤎𐤉.𐤐𐤓𐤏𐤄.𐤀𐤔𐤓.𐤀𐤕𐤅.𐤁𐤌𐤔𐤌𐤓
𐤁𐤉𐤕.𐤀𐤃𐤍𐤉𐤅.𐤋𐤀𐤌𐤓.𐤌𐤃𐤅𐤏.𐤐𐤍𐤉𐤊𐤌.𐤓𐤏𐤉𐤌.𐤄𐤉𐤅𐤌|

𐤇 𐤅𐤉𐤀𐤌𐤓𐤅.𐤀𐤋𐤉𐤅.𐤇𐤋𐤅𐤌.𐤇𐤋𐤌𐤍𐤅.𐤅𐤐𐤕𐤓.𐤀𐤉𐤍.𐤀𐤕𐤅.𐤅
𐤉𐤀𐤌𐤓.𐤀𐤋𐤄𐤌.𐤉𐤅𐤎𐤐.𐤄𐤋𐤅𐤀.𐤋𐤀𐤋𐤄𐤉𐤌.𐤐𐤕𐤓𐤍𐤉𐤌.𐤎𐤐𐤓
𐤅.𐤍𐤀.𐤋𐤉|

𐤈 𐤅𐤉𐤎𐤐𐤓.𐤔𐤓.𐤄𐤌𐤔𐤒𐤉𐤌.𐤀𐤕.𐤇𐤋𐤌𐤅.𐤋𐤉𐤅𐤎𐤐.𐤅𐤉𐤀𐤌
𐤓.𐤋𐤅.𐤁𐤇𐤋𐤅𐤌𐤉.𐤅𐤄𐤍𐤄.𐤂𐤐𐤍.𐤋𐤐𐤍𐤉|

𐤉 𐤅𐤁𐤂𐤐𐤍.𐤔𐤋𐤔𐤄.𐤔𐤓𐤉𐤂𐤌.𐤅𐤄𐤉𐤀.𐤊𐤐𐤓𐤇𐤕.𐤏𐤋𐤕
𐤄.𐤍𐤑𐤄.𐤄𐤁𐤔𐤉𐤋𐤅.𐤀𐤔𐤊𐤋𐤕𐤉𐤄.𐤏𐤍𐤁𐤉𐤌|

𐤉𐤀 𐤅𐤊𐤅𐤎.𐤐𐤓𐤏𐤄.𐤁𐤉𐤃𐤉.𐤅𐤀𐤒𐤇.𐤀𐤕.𐤄𐤏𐤍𐤁𐤉𐤌.𐤅𐤀
𐤔𐤇𐤈.𐤀𐤕𐤌.𐤀𐤋.𐤊𐤅𐤎.𐤐𐤓𐤏𐤄.𐤅𐤀𐤕𐤍.𐤀𐤕.𐤄𐤊𐤅𐤎.𐤏𐤋.𐤊
𐤐.𐤐𐤓𐤏𐤄|

𐤉𐤁 𐤅𐤉𐤀𐤌𐤓.𐤋𐤅.𐤉𐤅𐤎𐤐.𐤆𐤄.𐤐𐤕𐤓𐤍𐤅.𐤔𐤋𐤔𐤕.𐤄𐤔𐤓𐤂𐤉
𐤌.𐤔𐤋𐤔𐤕.𐤉𐤌𐤉𐤌.𐤄𐤌|

𐤉𐤂 𐤁𐤏𐤅𐤃.𐤔𐤋𐤔𐤕.𐤉𐤌𐤉𐤌.𐤉𐤔𐤀.𐤐𐤓𐤏𐤄.𐤀𐤕.𐤓𐤀𐤔𐤊.
𐤅𐤄𐤔𐤉𐤁𐤊.𐤏𐤋.𐤊𐤍𐤊.𐤅𐤍𐤕𐤕.𐤊𐤅𐤎.𐤐𐤓𐤏𐤄.𐤁𐤉𐤃𐤅.𐤊𐤌𐤔𐤐
𐤈.𐤄𐤓𐤀𐤔𐤅𐤍.𐤀𐤔𐤓.𐤄𐤉𐤉𐤕.𐤌𐤔𐤒𐤄𐤅|

𐤉𐤃 𐤊𐤉.𐤀𐤌.𐤆𐤊𐤓𐤕𐤍𐤉.𐤀𐤕𐤊.𐤊𐤀𐤔𐤓.𐤉𐤉𐤈𐤁.𐤋𐤊.𐤅𐤏
𐤔𐤉𐤕.𐤍𐤀.𐤏𐤌𐤃𐤉.𐤇𐤎𐤃.𐤅𐤄𐤆𐤊𐤓𐤕𐤍𐤉.𐤀𐤋.𐤐𐤓𐤏𐤄.𐤅𐤄
𐤅𐤑𐤀𐤕𐤍𐤉.𐤌𐤍.𐤄𐤁𐤉𐤕.𐤄𐤆𐤄|

𐤈𐤅 𐤊𐤉.𐤂𐤍𐤁.𐤂𐤍𐤁𐤕𐤉.𐤌𐤀𐤓𐤑.𐤄𐤏𐤁𐤓𐤉𐤌.𐤅𐤂𐤌.𐤐𐤄.𐤋
𐤀.𐤏𐤔𐤉𐤕𐤉.𐤌𐤀𐤅𐤌𐤄.𐤊𐤉.𐤔𐤌𐤅.𐤀𐤕𐤉.𐤁𐤁𐤅𐤓|

16 𐤅𐤉𐤓𐤀.𐤔𐤓.𐤄𐤀𐤐𐤉𐤌.𐤊𐤉.𐤈𐤅𐤁.𐤐𐤕𐤓.𐤅𐤉𐤀𐤌𐤓.𐤀𐤋.𐤉𐤅
𐤎𐤐.𐤀𐤐.𐤀𐤍𐤉.𐤁𐤇𐤋𐤅𐤌𐤉.𐤅𐤄𐤍𐤄.𐤔𐤋𐤔𐤄.𐤎𐤋𐤉.𐤇𐤓𐤉.𐤏𐤋.
𐤓𐤀𐤔𐤉|

17 𐤅𐤁𐤎𐤋.𐤄𐤏𐤋𐤉𐤅𐤍.𐤌𐤊𐤋.𐤌𐤀𐤊𐤋.𐤐𐤓𐤏𐤄.𐤌𐤏𐤔𐤄.𐤀𐤐
𐤄.𐤅𐤄𐤏𐤅𐤐.𐤀𐤊𐤋.𐤀𐤕𐤌.𐤌𐤍.𐤄𐤎𐤋.𐤌𐤏𐤋.𐤓𐤀𐤔𐤉|

18 𐤅𐤉𐤏𐤍.𐤉𐤅𐤎𐤐.𐤅𐤉𐤀𐤌𐤓.𐤆𐤄.𐤐𐤕𐤓𐤍𐤅.𐤔𐤋𐤔𐤕.𐤄𐤎𐤋𐤉
𐤌.𐤔𐤋𐤔𐤕.𐤉𐤌𐤉𐤌.𐤄𐤌|

19 𐤁𐤏𐤅𐤃.𐤔𐤋𐤔𐤕.𐤉𐤌𐤉𐤌.𐤉𐤔𐤀.𐤐𐤓𐤏𐤄.𐤀𐤕.𐤓𐤀𐤔𐤊
.𐤌𐤏𐤋𐤉𐤊.𐤅𐤕𐤋𐤄.𐤀𐤅𐤕𐤊.𐤏𐤋.𐤏𐤑.𐤅𐤀𐤊𐤋.𐤄𐤏𐤅𐤐.𐤀𐤕.𐤁𐤔
𐤓𐤊.𐤌𐤏𐤋𐤉𐤊|

20 𐤅𐤉𐤄𐤉.𐤁𐤉𐤅𐤌.𐤄𐤔𐤋𐤉𐤔𐤉.𐤉𐤅𐤌.𐤄𐤋𐤃𐤕.𐤀𐤕.𐤐𐤓𐤏
𐤄.𐤅𐤉𐤏𐤔.𐤌𐤔𐤕𐤄.𐤋𐤊𐤋.𐤏𐤁𐤃𐤉𐤅.𐤅𐤉𐤔𐤀.𐤀𐤕.𐤓𐤀𐤔.𐤔𐤓.
𐤄𐤌𐤔𐤒𐤉𐤌.𐤅𐤀𐤕.𐤓𐤀𐤔.𐤔𐤓.𐤄𐤀𐤐𐤉𐤌.𐤁𐤕𐤅𐤊.𐤏𐤁𐤃𐤉𐤅|

21 𐤅𐤉𐤔𐤁.𐤀𐤕.𐤔𐤓.𐤄𐤌𐤔𐤒𐤉𐤌.𐤏𐤋.𐤌𐤔𐤒𐤄𐤅.𐤅𐤉𐤕𐤍.𐤄
𐤊𐤅𐤎.𐤏𐤋.𐤊𐤐.𐤐𐤓𐤏𐤄|

22 𐤅𐤀𐤕.𐤔𐤓.𐤄𐤀𐤐𐤉𐤌.𐤕𐤋𐤄.𐤊𐤀𐤔𐤓.𐤐𐤕𐤓.𐤋𐤄𐤌.𐤉𐤅𐤎
𐤐|

23 𐤅𐤋𐤀.𐤆𐤊𐤓.𐤔𐤓.𐤄𐤌𐤔𐤒𐤉𐤌.𐤀𐤕.𐤉𐤅𐤎𐤐.𐤅𐤉𐤔𐤊𐤇𐤄
𐤅||

𐤁𐤓𐤀𐤔𐤉𐤕.𐤇𐤋𐤒 41

1 𐤅𐤉𐤄𐤉.𐤌𐤒𐤑.𐤔𐤍𐤕𐤉𐤌.𐤉𐤌𐤉𐤌.𐤅𐤐𐤓𐤏𐤄.𐤇𐤋𐤌.𐤅𐤄𐤍𐤄
.𐤏𐤌𐤃.𐤏𐤋.𐤄𐤉𐤀𐤓|

2 𐤅𐤄𐤍𐤄.𐤌𐤍.𐤄𐤉𐤀𐤓.𐤏𐤋𐤕.𐤔𐤁𐤏.𐤐𐤓𐤅𐤕.𐤉𐤐𐤅𐤕.𐤌𐤓𐤀𐤄.
𐤅𐤁𐤓𐤉𐤀𐤕.𐤁𐤔𐤓.𐤅𐤕𐤓𐤏𐤉𐤍𐤄.𐤁𐤀𐤇𐤅|

3 𐤅𐤄𐤍𐤄.𐤔𐤁𐤏.𐤐𐤓𐤅𐤕.𐤀𐤇𐤓𐤅𐤕.𐤏𐤋𐤅𐤕.𐤀𐤇𐤓𐤉𐤄𐤍.𐤌𐤍.
𐤄𐤉𐤀𐤓.𐤓𐤏𐤅𐤕.𐤌𐤓𐤀𐤄.𐤅𐤃𐤒𐤅𐤕.𐤁𐤔𐤓.𐤅𐤕𐤏𐤌𐤃𐤍𐤄.𐤀𐤑
𐤋.𐤄𐤐𐤓𐤅𐤕.𐤏𐤋.𐤔𐤐𐤕.𐤄𐤉𐤀𐤓|

4 𐤅𐤕𐤀𐤊𐤋𐤍𐤄.𐤄𐤐𐤓𐤅𐤕.𐤄𐤓𐤏𐤅𐤕.𐤄𐤌𐤓𐤀𐤄.𐤅𐤃𐤒𐤕.𐤄𐤁
𐤔𐤓.𐤀𐤕.𐤔𐤁𐤏.𐤄𐤐𐤓𐤅𐤕.𐤉𐤐𐤕.𐤄𐤌𐤓𐤀𐤄.𐤅𐤄𐤁𐤓𐤉𐤀𐤕.𐤅𐤉𐤉
𐤒𐤑.𐤐𐤓𐤏𐤄|

5 𐤅𐤉𐤉𐤔𐤍.𐤅𐤉𐤇𐤋𐤌.𐤔𐤍𐤉𐤕.𐤅𐤄𐤍𐤄.𐤔𐤁𐤏.𐤔𐤁𐤋𐤉𐤌.𐤏𐤋𐤅
𐤕.𐤁𐤒𐤍𐤄.𐤀𐤇𐤃.𐤁𐤓𐤉𐤀𐤅𐤕.𐤅𐤈𐤁𐤅𐤕|

6 𐤅𐤄𐤍𐤄.𐤔𐤁𐤏.𐤔𐤁𐤋𐤉𐤌.𐤃𐤒𐤅𐤕.𐤅𐤔𐤃𐤅𐤐𐤕.𐤒𐤃𐤉𐤌.
𐤑𐤌𐤇𐤅𐤕.𐤀𐤇𐤓𐤉𐤄𐤍|

7 𐤅𐤕𐤁𐤋𐤏𐤍𐤄.𐤄𐤔𐤁𐤋𐤉𐤌.𐤄𐤃𐤒𐤅𐤕.𐤀𐤕.𐤔𐤁𐤏.𐤄𐤔𐤁
𐤋𐤉𐤌.𐤄𐤁𐤓𐤉𐤀𐤅𐤕.𐤅𐤄𐤌𐤋𐤀𐤅𐤕.𐤅𐤉𐤉𐤒𐤑.𐤐𐤓𐤏𐤄.𐤅𐤄𐤍𐤄.
𐤇𐤋𐤅𐤌|

8 𐤅𐤉𐤄𐤉.𐤁𐤁𐤒𐤓.𐤅𐤕𐤐𐤏𐤌.𐤓𐤅𐤇𐤅.𐤅𐤉𐤔𐤋𐤇.𐤅𐤉𐤒𐤓𐤀.𐤀𐤕
.𐤊𐤋.𐤇𐤓𐤈𐤌𐤉.𐤌𐤑𐤓𐤉𐤌.𐤅𐤀𐤕.𐤊𐤋.𐤇𐤊𐤌𐤉𐤄.𐤅𐤉𐤎𐤐𐤓.𐤐𐤓
𐤏𐤄.𐤋𐤄𐤌.𐤀𐤕.𐤇𐤋𐤌𐤅.𐤅𐤀𐤉𐤍.𐤐𐤅𐤕𐤓.𐤀𐤕𐤌.𐤋𐤐𐤓𐤏𐤄|

9 𐤅𐤉𐤃𐤁𐤓.𐤔𐤓.𐤄𐤌𐤔𐤒𐤉𐤌.𐤀𐤕.𐤐𐤓𐤏𐤄.𐤋𐤀𐤌𐤓.𐤀𐤕.
𐤇𐤈𐤀𐤉.𐤀𐤍𐤉.𐤌𐤆𐤊𐤉𐤓.𐤄𐤉𐤅𐤌|

10 𐤐𐤓𐤏𐤄.𐤒𐤑𐤐.𐤏𐤋.𐤏𐤁𐤃𐤉𐤅.𐤅𐤉𐤕𐤍.𐤀𐤕𐤉.𐤁𐤌𐤔𐤌𐤓.
𐤁𐤉𐤕.𐤔𐤓.𐤄𐤈𐤁𐤇𐤉𐤌.𐤀𐤕𐤉.𐤅𐤀𐤕.𐤔𐤓.𐤄𐤀𐤐𐤉𐤌|

11 𐤅𐤍𐤇𐤋𐤌𐤄.𐤇𐤋𐤅𐤌.𐤁𐤋𐤉𐤋𐤄.𐤀𐤇𐤃.𐤀𐤍𐤉.𐤅𐤄𐤅𐤀.𐤀𐤉
𐤔.𐤊𐤐𐤕𐤓𐤅𐤍.𐤇𐤋𐤌𐤅.𐤇𐤋𐤌𐤍𐤅|

12 𐤅𐤔𐤌.𐤀𐤕𐤍𐤅.𐤍𐤏𐤓.𐤏𐤁𐤓𐤉.𐤏𐤁𐤃.𐤋𐤔𐤓.𐤄𐤈𐤁𐤇𐤉𐤌.
𐤅𐤍𐤎𐤐𐤓.𐤋𐤅.𐤅𐤉𐤐𐤕𐤓.𐤋𐤍𐤅.𐤀𐤕.𐤇𐤋𐤌𐤕𐤉𐤍𐤅.𐤀𐤉𐤔.𐤊𐤇𐤋𐤌𐤅.
𐤐𐤕𐤓|

13 𐤅𐤉𐤄𐤉.𐤊𐤀𐤔𐤓.𐤐𐤕𐤓.𐤋𐤍𐤅.𐤊𐤍.𐤄𐤉𐤄.𐤀𐤕𐤉.𐤄𐤔𐤉𐤁.
𐤏𐤋.𐤊𐤍𐤉.𐤅𐤀𐤕𐤅.𐤕𐤋𐤄|

14 𐤅𐤉𐤔𐤋𐤇.𐤐𐤓𐤏𐤄.𐤅𐤉𐤒𐤓𐤀.𐤀𐤕.𐤉𐤅𐤎𐤐.𐤅𐤉𐤓𐤉𐤑𐤄𐤅.
𐤌𐤍.𐤄𐤁𐤅𐤓.𐤅𐤉𐤂𐤋𐤇.𐤅𐤉𐤇𐤋𐤐.𐤔𐤌𐤋𐤕𐤉𐤅.𐤅𐤉𐤁𐤀.𐤀𐤋.𐤐𐤓𐤏
𐤄|

15 𐤅𐤉𐤀𐤌𐤓.𐤐𐤓𐤏𐤄.𐤀𐤋.𐤉𐤅𐤎𐤐.𐤇𐤋𐤅𐤌.𐤇𐤋𐤌𐤕𐤉.𐤅𐤐𐤕𐤓.
𐤀𐤉𐤍.𐤀𐤕𐤅.𐤅𐤀𐤍𐤉.𐤔𐤌𐤏𐤕𐤉.𐤏𐤋𐤉𐤊.𐤋𐤀𐤌𐤓.𐤕𐤔𐤌𐤏.𐤇𐤋
𐤅𐤌.𐤋𐤐𐤕𐤓.𐤀𐤕𐤅|

..יו.. 𐤅𐤉𐤏𐤍.𐤉𐤅𐤎𐤐.𐤀𐤕.𐤐𐤓𐤏𐤄.𐤋𐤀𐤌𐤓.𐤁𐤋𐤏𐤃𐤉.𐤀𐤋𐤄𐤉
𐤌.𐤉𐤏𐤍𐤄.𐤀𐤕.𐤔𐤋𐤅𐤌.𐤐𐤓𐤏𐤄|
..יז.. 𐤅𐤉𐤃𐤁𐤓.𐤐𐤓𐤏𐤄.𐤀𐤋.𐤉𐤅𐤎𐤐.𐤁𐤇𐤋𐤌𐤉.𐤄𐤍𐤍𐤉.𐤏𐤌
𐤃.𐤏𐤋.𐤔𐤐𐤕.𐤄𐤉𐤀𐤓|
..יח.. 𐤅𐤄𐤍𐤄.𐤌𐤍.𐤄𐤉𐤀𐤓.𐤏𐤋𐤕.𐤔𐤁𐤏.𐤐𐤓𐤅𐤕.𐤁𐤓𐤉𐤀𐤅𐤕.𐤁
𐤔𐤓.𐤅𐤉𐤐𐤕.𐤕𐤀𐤓.𐤅𐤕𐤓𐤏𐤉𐤍𐤄.𐤁𐤀𐤇𐤅|
..יט.. 𐤅𐤄𐤍𐤄.𐤔𐤁𐤏.𐤐𐤓𐤅𐤕.𐤀𐤇𐤓𐤅𐤕.𐤏𐤋𐤅𐤕.𐤀𐤇𐤓𐤉𐤄𐤍.
𐤃𐤋𐤅𐤕.𐤅𐤓𐤏𐤅𐤕.𐤕𐤀𐤓.𐤌𐤀𐤃.𐤅𐤓𐤒𐤅𐤕.𐤁𐤔𐤓.𐤋𐤀.𐤓𐤀𐤉𐤕𐤉
.𐤊𐤄𐤍𐤄.𐤁𐤊𐤋.𐤀𐤓𐤑.𐤌𐤑𐤓𐤉𐤌.𐤋𐤓𐤏|
..כ.. 𐤅𐤕𐤀𐤊𐤋𐤍𐤄.𐤄𐤐𐤓𐤅𐤕.𐤄𐤓𐤒𐤅𐤕.𐤅𐤄𐤓𐤏𐤅𐤕.𐤀𐤕.𐤔𐤁
𐤏.𐤄𐤐𐤓𐤅𐤕.𐤄𐤓𐤀𐤔𐤍𐤅𐤕.𐤄𐤁𐤓𐤉𐤀𐤕|
..כא.. 𐤅𐤕𐤁𐤀𐤍𐤄.𐤀𐤋.𐤒𐤓𐤁𐤍𐤄.𐤅𐤋𐤀.𐤍𐤅𐤃𐤏.𐤊𐤉.𐤁𐤀𐤅.𐤀𐤋.
𐤒𐤓𐤁𐤍𐤄.𐤅𐤌𐤓𐤀𐤉𐤄𐤍.𐤓𐤏.𐤊𐤀𐤔𐤓.𐤁𐤕𐤇𐤋𐤄.𐤅𐤀𐤉𐤒𐤑|
..כב.. 𐤅𐤀𐤓𐤀.𐤁𐤇𐤋𐤌𐤉.𐤅𐤄𐤍𐤄.𐤔𐤁𐤏.𐤔𐤁𐤋𐤉𐤌.𐤏𐤋𐤕.𐤁𐤒
𐤍𐤄.𐤀𐤇𐤃.𐤌𐤋𐤀𐤕.𐤅𐤈𐤁𐤅𐤕|
..כג.. 𐤅𐤄𐤍𐤄.𐤔𐤁𐤏.𐤔𐤁𐤋𐤉𐤌.𐤑𐤍𐤌𐤅𐤕.𐤃𐤒𐤅𐤕.𐤔𐤃𐤐𐤅𐤕.
𐤒𐤃𐤉𐤌.𐤑𐤌𐤇𐤅𐤕.𐤀𐤇𐤓𐤉𐤄𐤌|
..כד.. 𐤅𐤕𐤁𐤋𐤏𐤍.𐤄𐤔𐤁𐤋𐤉𐤌.𐤄𐤃𐤒𐤕.𐤀𐤕.𐤔𐤁𐤏.𐤄𐤔𐤁𐤋
𐤉𐤌.𐤄𐤈𐤁𐤅𐤕.𐤅𐤀𐤌𐤓.𐤀𐤋.𐤄𐤇𐤓𐤈𐤌𐤉𐤌.𐤅𐤀𐤉𐤍.𐤌𐤂𐤉𐤃.𐤋
𐤉|
..כה.. 𐤅𐤉𐤀𐤌𐤓.𐤉𐤅𐤎𐤐.𐤀𐤋.𐤐𐤓𐤏𐤄.𐤇𐤋𐤅𐤌.𐤐𐤓𐤏𐤄.𐤀𐤇𐤃.
𐤄𐤅𐤀.𐤀𐤕.𐤀𐤔𐤓.𐤄𐤀𐤋𐤄𐤉𐤌.𐤏𐤔𐤄.𐤄𐤂𐤉𐤃.𐤋𐤐𐤓𐤏𐤄|
..כו.. 𐤔𐤁𐤏.𐤐𐤓𐤕.𐤄𐤈𐤁𐤕.𐤔𐤁𐤏.𐤔𐤍𐤉𐤌.𐤄𐤍𐤄.𐤅𐤔𐤁𐤏.𐤄
𐤔𐤁𐤋𐤉𐤌.𐤄𐤈𐤁𐤕.𐤔𐤁𐤏.𐤔𐤍𐤉𐤌.𐤄𐤍𐤄.𐤇𐤋𐤅𐤌.𐤀𐤇𐤃.𐤄𐤅
𐤀|
..כז.. 𐤅𐤔𐤁𐤏.𐤄𐤐𐤓𐤅𐤕.𐤄𐤓𐤒𐤅𐤕.𐤅𐤄𐤓𐤏𐤕.𐤄𐤏𐤋𐤕.𐤀𐤇𐤓𐤉
𐤄𐤍.𐤔𐤁𐤏.𐤔𐤍𐤉𐤌.𐤄𐤍𐤄.𐤅𐤔𐤁𐤏.𐤄𐤔𐤁𐤋𐤉𐤌.𐤄𐤓𐤒𐤅𐤕.𐤔
𐤃𐤐𐤅𐤕.𐤄𐤒𐤃𐤉𐤌.𐤉𐤄𐤉𐤅.𐤔𐤁𐤏.𐤔𐤍𐤉.𐤓𐤏𐤁|
..כח.. 𐤄𐤅𐤀.𐤄𐤃𐤁𐤓.𐤀𐤔𐤓.𐤃𐤁𐤓𐤕𐤉.𐤀𐤋.𐤐𐤓𐤏𐤄.𐤀𐤔𐤓.𐤄
𐤀𐤋𐤄𐤉𐤌.𐤏𐤔𐤄.𐤄𐤓𐤀𐤄.𐤀𐤕.𐤐𐤓𐤏𐤄|

𐤊𐤈 𐤄𐤍𐤄.𐤔𐤁𐤏.𐤔𐤍𐤉𐤌.𐤁𐤀𐤅𐤕.𐤔𐤁𐤏.𐤂𐤃𐤅𐤋.𐤁𐤊𐤋.𐤀
𐤓𐤑.𐤌𐤑𐤓𐤉𐤌|

𐤋 𐤅𐤒𐤌𐤅.𐤔𐤁𐤏.𐤔𐤍𐤉.𐤓𐤏𐤁.𐤀𐤇𐤓𐤉𐤄𐤍.𐤅𐤍𐤔𐤊𐤇.𐤊𐤋.
𐤄𐤔𐤁𐤏.𐤁𐤀𐤓𐤑.𐤌𐤑𐤓𐤉𐤌.𐤅𐤊𐤋𐤄.𐤄𐤓𐤏𐤁.𐤀𐤕.𐤄𐤀𐤓𐤑|

𐤋𐤀 𐤅𐤋𐤀.𐤉𐤅𐤃𐤏.𐤄𐤔𐤁𐤏.𐤁𐤀𐤓𐤑.𐤌𐤐𐤍𐤉.𐤄𐤓𐤏𐤁.𐤄𐤄𐤅
𐤀.𐤀𐤇𐤓𐤉.𐤊𐤍.𐤊𐤉.𐤊𐤁𐤃.𐤄𐤅𐤀.𐤌𐤀𐤃|

𐤋𐤁 𐤅𐤏𐤋.𐤄𐤔𐤍𐤅𐤕.𐤄𐤇𐤋𐤅𐤌.𐤀𐤋.𐤐𐤓𐤏𐤄.𐤐𐤏𐤌𐤉𐤌.𐤊𐤉.𐤍
𐤊𐤅𐤍.𐤄𐤃𐤁𐤓.𐤌𐤏𐤌.𐤄𐤀𐤋𐤄𐤉𐤌.𐤅𐤌𐤌𐤄𐤓.𐤄𐤀𐤋𐤄𐤉𐤌.𐤋𐤏
𐤔𐤕𐤅|

𐤋𐤂 𐤅𐤏𐤕𐤄.𐤉𐤓𐤀.𐤐𐤓𐤏𐤄.𐤀𐤉𐤔.𐤍𐤁𐤅𐤍.𐤅𐤇𐤊𐤌.𐤅𐤉𐤔𐤉𐤕
𐤄𐤅.𐤏𐤋.𐤀𐤓𐤑.𐤌𐤑𐤓𐤉𐤌|

𐤋𐤃 𐤉𐤏𐤔𐤄.𐤐𐤓𐤏𐤄.𐤅𐤉𐤐𐤒𐤃.𐤐𐤒𐤃𐤉𐤌.𐤏𐤋.𐤄𐤀𐤓𐤑.𐤅
𐤇𐤌𐤔.𐤀𐤕.𐤀𐤓𐤑.𐤌𐤑𐤓𐤉𐤌.𐤁𐤔𐤁𐤏.𐤔𐤍𐤉.𐤄𐤔𐤁𐤏|

𐤋𐤄 𐤅𐤉𐤒𐤁𐤑𐤅.𐤀𐤕.𐤊𐤋.𐤀𐤊𐤋.𐤄𐤔𐤍𐤉𐤌.𐤄𐤈𐤁𐤕.𐤄𐤁𐤀
𐤕.𐤄𐤀𐤋𐤄.𐤅𐤉𐤑𐤁𐤓𐤅.𐤁𐤓.𐤕𐤇𐤕.𐤉𐤃.𐤐𐤓𐤏𐤄.𐤀𐤊𐤋.𐤁𐤏𐤓
𐤉𐤌.𐤅𐤔𐤌𐤓𐤅|

𐤋𐤅 𐤅𐤄𐤉𐤄.𐤄𐤀𐤊𐤋.𐤋𐤐𐤒𐤃𐤅𐤍.𐤋𐤀𐤓𐤑.𐤋𐤔𐤁𐤏.𐤔𐤍𐤉.𐤄
𐤓𐤏𐤁.𐤀𐤔𐤓.𐤕𐤄𐤉𐤉𐤍.𐤁𐤀𐤓𐤑.𐤌𐤑𐤓𐤉𐤌.𐤅𐤋𐤀.𐤕𐤊𐤓𐤕.𐤄𐤀
𐤓𐤑.𐤁𐤓𐤏𐤁|

𐤋𐤆 𐤅𐤉𐤉𐤈𐤁.𐤄𐤃𐤁𐤓.𐤁𐤏𐤉𐤍𐤉.𐤐𐤓𐤏𐤄.𐤅𐤁𐤏𐤉𐤍𐤉.𐤊𐤋.𐤏
𐤁𐤃𐤉𐤅|

𐤋𐤇 𐤅𐤉𐤀𐤌𐤓.𐤐𐤓𐤏𐤄.𐤀𐤋.𐤏𐤁𐤃𐤉𐤅.𐤄𐤍𐤌𐤑𐤀.𐤊𐤆𐤄.𐤀
𐤉𐤔.𐤀𐤔𐤓.𐤓𐤅𐤇.𐤀𐤋𐤄𐤉𐤌.𐤁𐤅|

𐤋𐤈 𐤅𐤉𐤀𐤌𐤓.𐤐𐤓𐤏𐤄.𐤀𐤋.𐤉𐤅𐤎𐤐.𐤀𐤇𐤓𐤉.𐤄𐤅𐤃𐤉𐤏.𐤀𐤋
𐤄𐤉𐤌.𐤀𐤅𐤕𐤊.𐤀𐤕.𐤊𐤋.𐤆𐤀𐤕.𐤀𐤉𐤍.𐤍𐤁𐤅𐤍.𐤅𐤇𐤊𐤌.𐤊𐤌𐤅𐤊|

𐤌 𐤀𐤕𐤄.𐤕𐤄𐤉𐤄.𐤏𐤋.𐤁𐤉𐤕𐤉.𐤅𐤏𐤋.𐤐𐤉𐤊.𐤉𐤔𐤒.𐤊𐤋.
𐤏𐤌𐤉.𐤓𐤒.𐤄𐤊𐤎𐤀.𐤀𐤂𐤃𐤋.𐤌𐤌𐤊|

𐤌𐤀 𐤅𐤉𐤀𐤌𐤓.𐤐𐤓𐤏𐤄.𐤀𐤋.𐤉𐤅𐤎𐤐.𐤓𐤀𐤄.𐤍𐤕𐤕𐤉.𐤀𐤕𐤊.𐤏
𐤋.𐤊𐤋.𐤀𐤓𐤑.𐤌𐤑𐤓𐤉𐤌|

ࠌࠁ ࠅࠉࠎࠓ.ࠐࠓࠏࠄ.ࠀࠕ.ࠈࠁࠏࠕࠅ.ࠌࠏࠋ.ࠉࠃࠅ.ࠅࠉࠕࠍ.ࠀ
ࠕࠄ.ࠏࠋ.ࠉࠃ.ࠉࠅࠎࠐ.ࠅࠉࠋࠁࠔ.ࠀࠕࠅ.ࠁࠂࠃࠉ.ࠔࠔ.ࠅࠉࠔࠌ.
ࠓࠁࠃ.ࠄࠆࠄࠁ.ࠏࠋ.ࠑࠅࠀࠓࠅ|

ࠌࠂ ࠅࠉࠓࠊࠁ.ࠀࠕࠅ.ࠁࠌࠓࠊࠁࠕ.ࠄࠌࠔࠍࠄ.ࠀࠔࠓ.ࠋࠅ.ࠅࠉࠒ
ࠓࠀࠅ.ࠋࠐࠍࠉࠅ.ࠀࠁࠓࠊ.ࠅࠍࠕࠅࠍ.ࠀࠕࠅ.ࠏࠋ.ࠊࠋ.ࠀࠓࠑ.ࠌࠑࠓࠉ
ࠌ|

ࠌࠃ ࠅࠉࠀࠌࠓ.ࠐࠓࠏࠄ.ࠀࠋ.ࠉࠅࠎࠐ.ࠀࠍࠉ.ࠐࠓࠏࠄ.ࠅࠁࠋࠏࠃ
ࠉࠊ.ࠋࠀ.ࠉࠓࠉࠌ.ࠀࠉࠔ.ࠀࠕ.ࠉࠃࠅ.ࠅࠀࠕ.ࠓࠂࠋࠅ.ࠁࠊࠋ.ࠀࠓ
ࠑ.ࠌࠑࠓࠉࠌ|

ࠌࠄ ࠅࠉࠒࠓࠀ.ࠐࠓࠏࠄ.ࠔࠌ.ࠉࠅࠎࠐ.ࠑࠐࠍࠕ.ࠐࠏࠍࠇ.ࠅࠉࠕࠍ.
ࠋࠅ.ࠀࠕ.ࠀࠎࠍࠕ.ࠁࠕ.ࠐࠅࠈࠉ.ࠐࠓࠏ.ࠊࠄࠍ.ࠀࠍ.ࠋࠀࠔࠄ.ࠅࠉࠑ
ࠀ.ࠉࠅࠎࠐ.ࠏࠋ.ࠀࠓࠑ.ࠌࠑࠓࠉࠌ|

ࠌࠅ ࠅࠉࠅࠎࠐ.ࠁࠍ.ࠔࠋࠔࠉࠌ.ࠔࠍࠄ.ࠁࠏࠌࠃࠅ.ࠋࠐࠍࠉ.ࠐࠓࠏࠄ
.ࠌࠋࠊ.ࠌࠑࠓࠉࠌ.ࠅࠉࠑࠀ.ࠉࠅࠎࠐ.ࠌࠋࠐࠍࠉ.ࠐࠓࠏࠄ.ࠅࠉࠏࠁࠓ.
ࠁࠊࠋ.ࠀࠓࠑ.ࠌࠑࠓࠉࠌ|

ࠌࠆ ࠅࠕࠏࠔ.ࠄࠀࠓࠑ.ࠁࠔࠁࠏ.ࠔࠍࠉ.ࠄࠔࠁࠏ.ࠋࠒࠌࠑࠉ
ࠌ|

ࠌࠇ ࠅࠉࠒࠁࠑ.ࠀࠕ.ࠊࠋ.ࠀࠊࠋ.ࠔࠁࠏ.ࠔࠍࠉࠌ.ࠀࠔࠓ.ࠄࠉࠅ.
ࠁࠀࠓࠑ.ࠌࠑࠓࠉࠌ.ࠅࠉࠕࠍ.ࠀࠊࠋ.ࠁࠏࠓࠉࠌ.ࠀࠊࠋ.ࠔࠃࠄ.ࠄ
ࠏࠉࠓ.ࠀࠔࠓ.ࠎࠁࠉࠁࠕࠉࠄ.ࠍࠕࠍ.ࠁࠕࠅࠊࠄ|

ࠌࠈ ࠅࠉࠑࠁࠓ.ࠉࠅࠎࠐ.ࠁࠓ.ࠊࠇࠅࠋ.ࠄࠉࠌ.ࠄࠓࠁࠄ.ࠌࠀࠃ.
ࠏࠃ.ࠊࠉ.ࠇࠃࠋ.ࠋࠎࠐࠓ.ࠊࠉ.ࠀࠉࠍ.ࠌࠎࠐࠓ|

ࠍ ࠅࠋࠉࠅࠎࠐ.ࠉࠋࠃ.ࠔࠍࠉ.ࠁࠍࠉࠌ.ࠁࠈࠓࠌ.ࠕࠁࠅࠀ.ࠔࠍࠕ.
ࠄࠓࠏࠁ.ࠀࠔࠓ.ࠉࠋࠃࠄ.ࠋࠅ.ࠀࠎࠍࠕ.ࠁࠕ.ࠐࠅࠈࠉ.ࠐࠓࠏ.ࠊࠄࠍ.
ࠀࠅࠍ|

ࠍࠀ ࠅࠉࠒࠓࠀ.ࠉࠅࠎࠐ.ࠀࠕ.ࠔࠌ.ࠄࠁࠊࠅࠓ.ࠌࠍࠔࠄ.ࠊࠉ.ࠍࠔࠍ
ࠉ.ࠀࠋࠄࠉࠌ.ࠀࠕ.ࠊࠋ.ࠏࠌࠋࠉ.ࠅࠀࠕ.ࠊࠋ.ࠁࠉࠕ.ࠀࠁࠉ|

ࠍࠁ ࠅࠀࠕ.ࠔࠌ.ࠄࠔࠍࠉ.ࠒࠓࠀ.ࠀࠐࠓࠉࠌ.ࠊࠉ.ࠄࠐࠓࠍࠉ.ࠀࠋ
ࠄࠉࠌ.ࠁࠀࠓࠑ.ࠏࠍࠉࠉ|

ࠍࠂ ࠅࠕࠊࠋࠉࠍࠄ.ࠔࠁࠏ.ࠔࠍࠉ.ࠄࠔࠁࠏ.ࠀࠔࠓ.ࠄࠉࠄ.ࠁࠀࠓ
ࠑ.ࠌࠑࠓࠉࠌ|

𐤍𐤃 𐤅𐤕𐤇𐤋𐤉𐤍𐤄.𐤔𐤁𐤏.𐤔𐤍𐤉.𐤄𐤓𐤏𐤁.𐤋𐤁𐤅𐤀.𐤊𐤀𐤔𐤓.𐤀
𐤌𐤓.𐤉𐤅𐤎𐤐.𐤅𐤉𐤄𐤉.𐤓𐤏𐤁.𐤁𐤊𐤋.𐤄𐤀𐤓𐤑𐤅𐤕.𐤅𐤁𐤊𐤋.𐤀𐤓𐤑.𐤌
𐤑𐤓𐤉𐤌.𐤄𐤉𐤄.𐤋𐤇𐤌|
𐤍𐤄 𐤅𐤕𐤓𐤏𐤁.𐤊𐤋.𐤀𐤓𐤑.𐤌𐤑𐤓𐤉𐤌.𐤅𐤉𐤑𐤏𐤒.𐤄𐤏𐤌.𐤀𐤋.
𐤐𐤓𐤏𐤄.𐤋𐤋𐤇𐤌.𐤅𐤉𐤀𐤌𐤓.𐤐𐤓𐤏𐤄.𐤋𐤊𐤋.𐤌𐤑𐤓𐤉𐤌.𐤋𐤊𐤅.𐤀𐤋.
𐤉𐤅𐤎𐤐.𐤀𐤔𐤓.𐤉𐤀𐤌𐤓.𐤋𐤊𐤌.𐤕𐤏𐤔𐤅|
𐤍𐤅 𐤅𐤄𐤓𐤏𐤁.𐤄𐤉𐤄.𐤏𐤋.𐤊𐤋.𐤐𐤍𐤉.𐤄𐤀𐤓𐤑.𐤅𐤉𐤐𐤕𐤇.𐤉𐤅𐤎
𐤐.𐤀𐤕.𐤊𐤋.𐤀𐤔𐤓.𐤁𐤄𐤌.𐤅𐤉𐤔𐤁𐤓.𐤋𐤌𐤑𐤓𐤉𐤌.𐤅𐤉𐤇𐤆𐤒.𐤄
𐤓𐤏𐤁.𐤁𐤀𐤓𐤑.𐤌𐤑𐤓𐤉𐤌|
𐤍𐤆 𐤅𐤊𐤋.𐤄𐤀𐤓𐤑.𐤁𐤀𐤅.𐤌𐤑𐤓𐤉𐤌𐤄.𐤋𐤔𐤁𐤓.𐤀𐤋.𐤉𐤅𐤎𐤐.
𐤊𐤉.𐤇𐤆𐤒.𐤄𐤓𐤏𐤁.𐤁𐤊𐤋.𐤄𐤀𐤓𐤑||

𐤁𐤓𐤀𐤔𐤉𐤕.𐤇𐤋𐤒 𐤌𐤁

𐤀 𐤅𐤉𐤓𐤀.𐤉𐤏𐤒𐤁.𐤊𐤉.𐤉𐤔.𐤔𐤁𐤓.𐤁𐤌𐤑𐤓𐤉𐤌.𐤅𐤉𐤀𐤌𐤓.𐤉
𐤏𐤒𐤁.𐤋𐤁𐤍𐤉𐤅.𐤋𐤌𐤄.𐤕𐤕𐤓𐤀𐤅|
𐤁 𐤅𐤉𐤀𐤌𐤓.𐤄𐤍𐤄.𐤔𐤌𐤏𐤕𐤉.𐤊𐤉.𐤉𐤔.𐤔𐤁𐤓.𐤁𐤌𐤑𐤓𐤉𐤌.𐤓
𐤃𐤅.𐤔𐤌𐤄.𐤅𐤔𐤁𐤓𐤅.𐤋𐤍𐤅.𐤌𐤔𐤌.𐤅𐤍𐤇𐤉𐤄.𐤅𐤋𐤀.𐤍𐤌𐤅𐤕|
𐤂 𐤅𐤉𐤓𐤃𐤅.𐤀𐤇𐤉.𐤉𐤅𐤎𐤐.𐤏𐤔𐤓𐤄.𐤋𐤔𐤁𐤓.𐤁𐤓.𐤌𐤌𐤑𐤓𐤉𐤌
|
𐤃 𐤅𐤀𐤕.𐤁𐤍𐤉𐤌𐤉𐤍.𐤀𐤇𐤉.𐤉𐤅𐤎𐤐.𐤋𐤀.𐤔𐤋𐤇.𐤉𐤏𐤒𐤁.𐤀
𐤕.𐤀𐤇𐤉𐤅.𐤊𐤉.𐤀𐤌𐤓.𐤐𐤍.𐤉𐤒𐤓𐤀𐤍𐤅.𐤀𐤎𐤅𐤍|
𐤄 𐤅𐤉𐤁𐤀𐤅.𐤁𐤍𐤉.𐤉𐤔𐤓𐤀𐤋.𐤋𐤔𐤁𐤓.𐤁𐤕𐤅𐤊.𐤄𐤁𐤀𐤉𐤌.𐤊𐤉.
𐤄𐤉𐤄.𐤄𐤓𐤏𐤁.𐤁𐤀𐤓𐤑.𐤊𐤍𐤏𐤍|
𐤅 𐤅𐤉𐤅𐤎𐤐.𐤄𐤅𐤀.𐤄𐤔𐤋𐤉𐤈.𐤏𐤋.𐤄𐤀𐤓𐤑.𐤄𐤅𐤀.𐤄𐤌𐤔𐤁𐤉𐤓
𐤋𐤊𐤋.𐤏𐤌.𐤄𐤀𐤓𐤑.𐤅𐤉𐤁𐤀𐤅.𐤀𐤇𐤉.𐤉𐤅𐤎𐤐.𐤅𐤉𐤔𐤕𐤇𐤅𐤅.𐤋𐤅.
𐤀𐤐𐤉𐤌.𐤀𐤓𐤑𐤄|
𐤆 𐤅𐤉𐤓𐤀.𐤉𐤅𐤎𐤐.𐤀𐤕.𐤀𐤇𐤉𐤅.𐤅𐤉𐤊𐤓𐤌.𐤅𐤉𐤕𐤍𐤊𐤓.𐤀𐤋𐤉𐤄
𐤌.𐤅𐤉𐤃𐤁𐤓.𐤀𐤕𐤌.𐤒𐤔𐤅𐤕.𐤅𐤉𐤀𐤌𐤓.𐤀𐤋𐤉𐤄𐤌.𐤌𐤀𐤉𐤍.𐤁𐤀𐤕
𐤌.𐤅𐤉𐤀𐤌𐤓𐤅.𐤌𐤀𐤓𐤑.𐤊𐤍𐤏𐤍.𐤋𐤔𐤁𐤓.𐤀𐤊𐤋|
𐤇 𐤅𐤉𐤊𐤓.𐤉𐤅𐤎𐤐.𐤀𐤕.𐤀𐤇𐤉𐤅.𐤅𐤄𐤌.𐤋𐤀.𐤄𐤊𐤓𐤄𐤅|

ט 𐤅𐤉𐤆𐤊𐤓.𐤉𐤅𐤎𐤐.𐤀𐤕.𐤄𐤇𐤋𐤌𐤅𐤕.𐤀𐤔𐤓.𐤇𐤋𐤌.𐤋𐤄𐤌.𐤅
𐤉𐤀𐤌𐤓.𐤀𐤋𐤄𐤌.𐤌𐤓𐤂𐤋𐤉𐤌.𐤀𐤕𐤌.𐤋𐤓𐤀𐤅𐤕.𐤀𐤕.𐤏𐤓𐤅𐤕.𐤄
𐤀𐤓𐤑.𐤁𐤀𐤕𐤌|
י 𐤅𐤉𐤀𐤌𐤓𐤅.𐤀𐤋𐤉𐤅.𐤋𐤀.𐤀𐤃𐤍𐤉.𐤅𐤏𐤁𐤃𐤉𐤊.𐤁𐤀𐤅.𐤋𐤔
𐤁𐤓.𐤀𐤊𐤋|
יא 𐤊𐤋𐤍𐤅.𐤁𐤍𐤉.𐤀𐤉𐤔.𐤀𐤇𐤃.𐤍𐤇𐤍𐤅.𐤊𐤍𐤉𐤌.𐤀𐤍𐤇𐤍𐤅.𐤋
𐤀.𐤄𐤉𐤅.𐤏𐤁𐤃𐤉𐤊.𐤌𐤓𐤂𐤋𐤉𐤌|
יב 𐤅𐤉𐤀𐤌𐤓.𐤀𐤋𐤄𐤌.𐤋𐤀.𐤊𐤉.𐤏𐤓𐤅𐤕.𐤄𐤀𐤓𐤑.𐤁𐤀𐤕𐤌.𐤋
𐤓𐤀𐤅𐤕|
יג 𐤅𐤉𐤀𐤌𐤓𐤅.𐤔𐤍𐤉𐤌.𐤏𐤔𐤓.𐤏𐤁𐤃𐤉𐤊.𐤀𐤇𐤉𐤌.𐤀𐤍𐤇𐤍𐤅
.𐤁𐤍𐤉.𐤀𐤉𐤔.𐤀𐤇𐤃.𐤁𐤀𐤓𐤑.𐤊𐤍𐤏𐤍.𐤅𐤄𐤍𐤄.𐤄𐤒𐤈𐤍.𐤀𐤕.
𐤀𐤁𐤉𐤍𐤅.𐤄𐤉𐤅𐤌.𐤅𐤄𐤀𐤇𐤃.𐤀𐤉𐤍𐤍𐤅|
יד 𐤅𐤉𐤀𐤌𐤓.𐤀𐤋𐤄𐤌.𐤉𐤅𐤎𐤐.𐤄𐤅𐤀.𐤀𐤔𐤓.𐤃𐤁𐤓𐤕𐤉.𐤀𐤋
𐤊𐤌.𐤋𐤀𐤌𐤓.𐤌𐤓𐤂𐤋𐤉𐤌.𐤀𐤕𐤌|
טו 𐤁𐤆𐤀𐤕.𐤕𐤁𐤇𐤍𐤅.𐤇𐤉.𐤐𐤓𐤏𐤄.𐤀𐤌.𐤕𐤑𐤀𐤅.𐤌𐤆𐤄.
𐤊𐤉.𐤀𐤌.𐤁𐤁𐤅𐤀.𐤀𐤇𐤉𐤊𐤌.𐤄𐤒𐤈𐤍.𐤄𐤍𐤄|
טז 𐤔𐤋𐤇𐤅.𐤌𐤊𐤌.𐤀𐤇𐤃.𐤅𐤉𐤒𐤇.𐤀𐤕.𐤀𐤇𐤉𐤊𐤌.𐤅𐤀𐤕
𐤌.𐤄𐤀𐤎𐤓𐤅.𐤅𐤉𐤁𐤇𐤍𐤅.𐤃𐤁𐤓𐤉𐤊𐤌.𐤄𐤀𐤌𐤕.𐤀𐤕𐤊𐤌.𐤅𐤀𐤌.
𐤋𐤀.𐤇𐤉.𐤐𐤓𐤏𐤄.𐤊𐤉.𐤌𐤓𐤂𐤋𐤉𐤌.𐤀𐤕𐤌|
יז 𐤅𐤉𐤀𐤎𐤐.𐤀𐤕𐤌.𐤀𐤋.𐤌𐤔𐤌𐤓.𐤔𐤋𐤔𐤕.𐤉𐤌𐤉𐤌|
יח 𐤅𐤉𐤀𐤌𐤓.𐤀𐤋𐤄𐤌.𐤉𐤅𐤎𐤐.𐤁𐤉𐤅𐤌.𐤄𐤔𐤋𐤉𐤔𐤉.𐤆𐤀𐤕.
𐤏𐤔𐤅.𐤅𐤇𐤉𐤅.𐤀𐤕.𐤄𐤀𐤋𐤄𐤉𐤌.𐤀𐤍𐤉.𐤉𐤓𐤀|
יט 𐤀𐤌.𐤊𐤍𐤉𐤌.𐤀𐤕𐤌.𐤀𐤇𐤉𐤊𐤌.𐤀𐤇𐤃.𐤉𐤀𐤎𐤓.𐤁𐤁𐤉
𐤕.𐤌𐤔𐤌𐤓𐤊𐤌.𐤅𐤀𐤕𐤌.𐤋𐤊𐤅.𐤄𐤁𐤉𐤀𐤅.𐤔𐤁𐤓.𐤓𐤏𐤁𐤅𐤍.𐤁𐤕𐤉
𐤊𐤌|
כ 𐤅𐤀𐤕.𐤀𐤇𐤉𐤊𐤌.𐤄𐤒𐤈𐤍.𐤕𐤁𐤉𐤀𐤅.𐤀𐤋𐤉.𐤅𐤉𐤀𐤌𐤍𐤅.
𐤃𐤁𐤓𐤉𐤊𐤌.𐤅𐤋𐤀.𐤕𐤌𐤅𐤕𐤅.𐤅𐤉𐤏𐤔𐤅.𐤊𐤍|
כא 𐤅𐤉𐤀𐤌𐤓𐤅.𐤀𐤉𐤔.𐤀𐤋.𐤀𐤇𐤉𐤅.𐤀𐤁𐤋.𐤀𐤔𐤌𐤉𐤌.𐤀𐤍𐤇
𐤍𐤅.𐤏𐤋.𐤀𐤇𐤉𐤍𐤅.𐤀𐤔𐤓.𐤓𐤀𐤉𐤍𐤅.𐤑𐤓𐤕.𐤍𐤐𐤔𐤅.𐤁𐤄𐤕𐤇𐤍𐤍𐤅.
𐤀𐤋𐤉𐤍𐤅.𐤅𐤋𐤀.𐤔𐤌𐤏𐤍𐤅.𐤏𐤋.𐤊𐤍.𐤁𐤀𐤄.𐤀𐤋𐤉𐤍𐤅.𐤄𐤑𐤓𐤄.𐤄
𐤆𐤀𐤕|

22 𐤅𐤉𐤏𐤍.𐤓𐤀𐤅𐤁𐤍.𐤀𐤕𐤌.𐤋𐤀𐤌𐤓.𐤄𐤋𐤅𐤀.𐤀𐤌𐤓𐤕𐤉.𐤀𐤋𐤉
𐤊𐤌.𐤋𐤀𐤌𐤓.𐤀𐤋.𐤕𐤇𐤈𐤀𐤅.𐤁𐤉𐤋𐤃.𐤅𐤋𐤀.𐤔𐤌𐤏𐤕𐤌.𐤅𐤂𐤌.
𐤃𐤌𐤅.𐤄𐤍𐤄.𐤍𐤃𐤓𐤔|
23 𐤅𐤄𐤌.𐤋𐤀.𐤉𐤃𐤏𐤅.𐤊𐤉.𐤔𐤌𐤏.𐤉𐤅𐤎𐤐.𐤊𐤉.𐤄𐤌𐤋𐤉𐤑.
𐤁𐤉𐤍𐤕𐤌|
24 𐤅𐤉𐤎𐤁.𐤌𐤏𐤋𐤉𐤄𐤌.𐤅𐤉𐤁𐤊.𐤅𐤉𐤔𐤁.𐤀𐤋𐤄𐤌.𐤅𐤉𐤃𐤁𐤓.
𐤀𐤋𐤄𐤌.𐤅𐤉𐤒𐤇.𐤌𐤀𐤕𐤌.𐤀𐤕.𐤔𐤌𐤏𐤅𐤍.𐤅𐤉𐤀𐤎𐤓.𐤀𐤕𐤅.𐤋𐤏
𐤉𐤍𐤉𐤄𐤌|
25 𐤅𐤉𐤑𐤅.𐤉𐤅𐤎𐤐.𐤅𐤉𐤌𐤋𐤀𐤅.𐤀𐤕.𐤊𐤋𐤉𐤄𐤌.𐤁𐤓.𐤅𐤋𐤄𐤔𐤉𐤁
.𐤊𐤎𐤐𐤉𐤄𐤌.𐤀𐤉𐤔.𐤀𐤋.𐤔𐤒𐤅.𐤅𐤋𐤕𐤕.𐤋𐤄𐤌.𐤑𐤃𐤄.𐤋𐤃𐤓𐤊
.𐤅𐤉𐤏𐤔.𐤋𐤄𐤌.𐤊𐤍|
26 𐤅𐤉𐤔𐤀𐤅.𐤀𐤕.𐤔𐤁𐤓𐤌.𐤏𐤋.𐤇𐤌𐤓𐤉𐤄𐤌.𐤅𐤉𐤋𐤊𐤅.𐤌𐤔𐤌|
27 𐤅𐤉𐤐𐤕𐤇.𐤄𐤀𐤇𐤃.𐤀𐤕.𐤔𐤒𐤅.𐤋𐤕𐤕.𐤌𐤎𐤐𐤅𐤀.𐤋𐤇
𐤌𐤓𐤅.𐤁𐤌𐤋𐤅𐤍.𐤅𐤉𐤓𐤀.𐤀𐤕.𐤊𐤎𐤐𐤅.𐤅𐤄𐤍𐤄.𐤄𐤅𐤀.𐤁𐤐𐤉.𐤀𐤌𐤕
𐤇𐤕𐤅|
28 𐤅𐤉𐤀𐤌𐤓.𐤀𐤋.𐤀𐤇𐤉𐤅.𐤄𐤅𐤔𐤁.𐤊𐤎𐤐𐤉.𐤅𐤂𐤌.𐤄𐤍𐤄.𐤁
𐤀𐤌𐤕𐤇𐤕𐤉.𐤅𐤉𐤑𐤀.𐤋𐤁𐤌.𐤅𐤉𐤇𐤓𐤃𐤅.𐤀𐤉𐤔.𐤀𐤋.𐤀𐤇𐤉𐤅.
𐤋𐤀𐤌𐤓.𐤌𐤄.𐤆𐤀𐤕.𐤏𐤔𐤄.𐤀𐤋𐤄𐤉𐤌.𐤋𐤍𐤅|
29 𐤅𐤉𐤁𐤀𐤅.𐤀𐤋.𐤉𐤏𐤒𐤁.𐤀𐤁𐤉𐤄𐤌.𐤀𐤓𐤑𐤄.𐤊𐤍𐤏𐤍.𐤅𐤉
𐤂𐤉𐤃𐤅.𐤋𐤅.𐤀𐤕.𐤊𐤋.𐤄𐤒𐤓𐤕.𐤀𐤕𐤌.𐤋𐤀𐤌𐤓|
30 𐤃𐤁𐤓.𐤄𐤀𐤉𐤔.𐤀𐤃𐤍𐤉.𐤄𐤀𐤓𐤑.𐤀𐤕𐤍𐤅.𐤒𐤔𐤅𐤕.𐤅𐤉
𐤕𐤍.𐤀𐤕𐤍𐤅.𐤊𐤌𐤓𐤂𐤋𐤉𐤌.𐤀𐤕.𐤄𐤀𐤓𐤑|
31 𐤅𐤍𐤀𐤌𐤓.𐤀𐤋𐤉𐤅.𐤊𐤍𐤉𐤌.𐤀𐤍𐤇𐤍𐤅.𐤋𐤀.𐤄𐤉𐤉𐤍𐤅.𐤌𐤓𐤂𐤋
𐤉𐤌|
32 𐤔𐤍𐤉𐤌.𐤏𐤔𐤓.𐤀𐤍𐤇𐤍𐤅.𐤀𐤇𐤉𐤌.𐤁𐤍𐤉.𐤀𐤁𐤉𐤍𐤅.𐤄𐤀
𐤇𐤃.𐤀𐤉𐤍𐤍𐤅.𐤅𐤄𐤒𐤈𐤍.𐤄𐤉𐤅𐤌.𐤀𐤕.𐤀𐤁𐤉𐤍𐤅.𐤁𐤀𐤓𐤑.𐤊𐤍𐤏
𐤍|
33 𐤅𐤉𐤀𐤌𐤓.𐤀𐤋𐤉𐤍𐤅.𐤄𐤀𐤉𐤔.𐤀𐤃𐤍𐤉.𐤄𐤀𐤓𐤑.𐤁𐤆𐤀𐤕
.𐤀𐤃𐤏.𐤊𐤉.𐤊𐤍𐤉𐤌.𐤀𐤕𐤌.𐤀𐤇𐤉𐤊𐤌.𐤄𐤀𐤇𐤃.𐤄𐤍𐤉𐤇𐤅.
𐤀𐤕𐤉.𐤅𐤀𐤕.𐤓𐤏𐤁𐤅𐤍.𐤁𐤕𐤉𐤊𐤌.𐤒𐤇𐤅.𐤅𐤋𐤊𐤅|

34 𐤅𐤄𐤁𐤉𐤀𐤅.𐤀𐤕.𐤀𐤇𐤉𐤊𐤌.𐤄𐤒𐤈𐤍.𐤀𐤋𐤉.𐤅𐤀𐤃𐤏𐤄.
𐤊𐤉.𐤋𐤀.𐤌𐤓𐤂𐤋𐤉𐤌.𐤀𐤕𐤌.𐤊𐤉.𐤊𐤍𐤉𐤌.𐤀𐤕𐤌.𐤀𐤕.𐤀𐤇𐤉
𐤊𐤌.𐤀𐤕𐤍.𐤋𐤊𐤌.𐤅𐤀𐤕.𐤄𐤀𐤓𐤑.𐤕𐤎𐤇𐤓𐤅|
35 𐤅𐤉𐤄𐤉.𐤄𐤌.𐤌𐤓𐤉𐤒𐤉𐤌.𐤔𐤒𐤉𐤄𐤌.𐤅𐤄𐤍𐤄.𐤀𐤉𐤔.𐤑𐤓
𐤅𐤓.𐤊𐤎𐤐𐤅.𐤁𐤔𐤒𐤅.𐤅𐤉𐤓𐤀𐤅.𐤀𐤕.𐤑𐤓𐤓𐤅𐤕.𐤊𐤎𐤐𐤉𐤄𐤌.𐤄𐤌𐤄
.𐤅𐤀𐤁𐤉𐤄𐤌.𐤅𐤉𐤉𐤓𐤀𐤅|
36 𐤅𐤉𐤀𐤌𐤓.𐤀𐤋𐤄𐤌.𐤉𐤏𐤒𐤁.𐤀𐤁𐤉𐤄𐤌.𐤀𐤕𐤉.𐤔𐤊𐤋𐤕𐤌
.𐤉𐤅𐤎𐤐.𐤀𐤉𐤍𐤍𐤅.𐤅𐤔𐤌𐤏𐤅𐤍.𐤀𐤉𐤍𐤍𐤅.𐤅𐤀𐤕.𐤁𐤍𐤉𐤌𐤍.𐤕𐤒𐤇𐤅.
𐤏𐤋𐤉.𐤄𐤉𐤅.𐤊𐤋𐤍𐤄|
37 𐤅𐤉𐤀𐤌𐤓.𐤓𐤀𐤅𐤁𐤍.𐤀𐤋.𐤀𐤁𐤉𐤅.𐤋𐤀𐤌𐤓.𐤀𐤕.𐤔𐤍𐤉.𐤁𐤍
𐤉.𐤕𐤌𐤉𐤕.𐤀𐤌.𐤋𐤀.𐤀𐤁𐤉𐤀𐤍𐤅.𐤀𐤋𐤉𐤊.𐤕𐤍𐤄.𐤀𐤕𐤅.𐤏𐤋.𐤉
𐤃𐤉.𐤅𐤀𐤍𐤉.𐤀𐤔𐤉𐤁𐤍𐤅.𐤀𐤋𐤉𐤊|
38 𐤅𐤉𐤀𐤌𐤓.𐤋𐤀.𐤉𐤓𐤃.𐤁𐤍𐤉.𐤏𐤌𐤊𐤌.𐤊𐤉.𐤀𐤇𐤉𐤅.𐤌𐤕.𐤅
𐤄𐤅𐤀.𐤋𐤁𐤃𐤅.𐤍𐤔𐤀𐤓.𐤅𐤒𐤓𐤀𐤄𐤅.𐤀𐤎𐤅𐤍.𐤁𐤃𐤓𐤊.𐤀𐤔𐤓.𐤕𐤋
𐤊𐤅.𐤁𐤄.𐤅𐤄𐤅𐤓𐤃𐤕𐤌.𐤀𐤕.𐤔𐤉𐤁𐤕𐤉.𐤁𐤉𐤂𐤅𐤍.𐤔𐤀𐤅𐤋𐤄||

𐤁𐤓𐤀𐤔𐤉𐤕.𐤇𐤋𐤒 43

1 𐤅𐤄𐤓𐤏𐤁.𐤊𐤁𐤃.𐤁𐤀𐤓𐤑|
2 𐤅𐤉𐤄𐤉.𐤊𐤀𐤔𐤓.𐤊𐤋𐤅.𐤋𐤀𐤊𐤋.𐤀𐤕.𐤄𐤔𐤁𐤓.𐤀𐤔𐤓.𐤄𐤁𐤉
𐤀𐤅.𐤌𐤌𐤑𐤓𐤉𐤌.𐤅𐤉𐤀𐤌𐤓.𐤀𐤋𐤉𐤄𐤌.𐤀𐤁𐤉𐤄𐤌.𐤔𐤁𐤅.𐤔𐤁𐤓𐤅.
𐤋𐤍𐤅.𐤌𐤏𐤈.𐤀𐤊𐤋|
3 𐤅𐤉𐤀𐤌𐤓.𐤀𐤋𐤉𐤅.𐤉𐤄𐤅𐤃𐤄.𐤋𐤀𐤌𐤓.𐤄𐤏𐤃.𐤄𐤏𐤃.𐤁𐤍𐤅.
𐤄𐤀𐤉𐤔.𐤋𐤀𐤌𐤓.𐤋𐤀.𐤕𐤓𐤀𐤅.𐤐𐤍𐤉.𐤁𐤋𐤕𐤉.𐤀𐤇𐤉𐤊𐤌.𐤀𐤕𐤊
𐤌|
4 𐤀𐤌.𐤉𐤔𐤊.𐤌𐤔𐤋𐤇.𐤀𐤕.𐤀𐤇𐤉𐤍𐤅.𐤀𐤕𐤍𐤅.𐤍𐤓𐤃𐤄.𐤅𐤍
𐤔𐤁𐤓𐤄.𐤋𐤊.𐤀𐤊𐤋|
5 𐤅𐤀𐤌.𐤀𐤉𐤍𐤊.𐤌𐤔𐤋𐤇.𐤋𐤀.𐤍𐤓𐤃.𐤊𐤉.𐤄𐤀𐤉𐤔.𐤀𐤌𐤓.𐤀
𐤋𐤉𐤍𐤅.𐤋𐤀.𐤕𐤓𐤀𐤅.𐤐𐤍𐤉.𐤁𐤋𐤕𐤉.𐤀𐤇𐤉𐤊𐤌.𐤀𐤕𐤊𐤌|
6 𐤅𐤉𐤀𐤌𐤓.𐤉𐤔𐤓𐤀𐤋.𐤋𐤌𐤄.𐤄𐤓𐤏𐤕𐤌.𐤋𐤉.𐤋𐤄𐤂𐤉𐤃.𐤋𐤀
𐤉𐤔.𐤄𐤏𐤅𐤃.𐤋𐤊𐤌.𐤀𐤇|

𐤆 𐤅𐤉𐤀𐤌𐤓𐤅.𐤔𐤀𐤅𐤋.𐤔𐤀𐤋.𐤄𐤀𐤉𐤔.𐤋𐤍𐤅.𐤅𐤋𐤌𐤅𐤋𐤃𐤕𐤍𐤅.𐤋
𐤀𐤌𐤓.𐤄𐤏𐤅𐤃.𐤀𐤁𐤉𐤊𐤌.𐤇𐤉.𐤄𐤉𐤔.𐤋𐤊𐤌.𐤀𐤇.𐤅𐤍𐤂𐤃.𐤋𐤅
.𐤏𐤋.𐤐𐤉.𐤄𐤃𐤁𐤓𐤉𐤌.𐤄𐤀𐤋𐤄.𐤄𐤉𐤃𐤅𐤏.𐤍𐤃𐤏.𐤊𐤉.𐤉𐤀𐤌𐤓
.𐤄𐤅𐤓𐤉𐤃𐤅.𐤀𐤕.𐤀𐤇𐤉𐤊𐤌|

𐤇 𐤅𐤉𐤀𐤌𐤓.𐤉𐤄𐤅𐤃𐤄.𐤀𐤋.𐤉𐤔𐤓𐤀𐤋.𐤀𐤁𐤉𐤅.𐤔𐤋𐤇𐤄.𐤄𐤍
𐤏𐤓.𐤀𐤕𐤉.𐤅𐤍𐤒𐤅𐤌𐤄.𐤅𐤍𐤋𐤊𐤄.𐤅𐤍𐤇𐤉𐤄.𐤅𐤋𐤀.𐤍𐤌𐤅𐤕.𐤂𐤌.𐤀
𐤍𐤇𐤍𐤅.𐤂𐤌.𐤀𐤕𐤄.𐤂𐤌.𐤈𐤐𐤍𐤅|

𐤈 𐤀𐤍𐤊𐤉.𐤀𐤏𐤓𐤁𐤍𐤅.𐤌𐤉𐤃𐤉.𐤕𐤁𐤒𐤔𐤍𐤅.𐤀𐤌.𐤋𐤀.𐤄𐤁𐤉
𐤀𐤕𐤉𐤅.𐤀𐤋𐤉𐤊.𐤅𐤄𐤑𐤂𐤕𐤉𐤅.𐤋𐤐𐤍𐤉𐤊.𐤅𐤇𐤈𐤀𐤕𐤉.𐤋𐤊.𐤊𐤋.
𐤄𐤉𐤌𐤉𐤌|

𐤉 𐤊𐤉.𐤋𐤅𐤋𐤀.𐤄𐤕𐤌𐤄𐤌𐤄𐤍𐤅.𐤊𐤉.𐤏𐤕𐤄.𐤔𐤁𐤍𐤅.𐤆𐤄.𐤐
𐤏𐤌𐤉𐤌|

𐤉𐤀 𐤅𐤉𐤀𐤌𐤓.𐤀𐤋𐤄𐤌.𐤉𐤔𐤓𐤀𐤋.𐤀𐤁𐤉𐤄𐤌.𐤀𐤌.𐤊𐤍.𐤀𐤐𐤅𐤀
.𐤆𐤀𐤕.𐤏𐤔𐤅.𐤒𐤇𐤅.𐤌𐤆𐤌𐤓𐤕.𐤄𐤀𐤓𐤑.𐤁𐤊𐤋𐤉𐤊𐤌.𐤅𐤄𐤅𐤓
𐤉𐤃𐤅.𐤋𐤀𐤉𐤔.𐤌𐤍𐤇𐤄.𐤌𐤏𐤈.𐤑𐤓𐤉.𐤅𐤌𐤏𐤈.𐤃𐤁𐤔.𐤍𐤊𐤀
𐤕.𐤅𐤋𐤈.𐤁𐤈𐤍𐤉𐤌.𐤅𐤔𐤒𐤃𐤉𐤌|

𐤉𐤁 𐤅𐤊𐤎𐤐.𐤌𐤔𐤍𐤄.𐤒𐤇𐤅.𐤁𐤉𐤃𐤊𐤌.𐤅𐤀𐤕.𐤄𐤊𐤎𐤐.𐤄𐤌𐤅
𐤔𐤁.𐤁𐤐𐤉.𐤀𐤌𐤕𐤇𐤕𐤉𐤊𐤌.𐤕𐤔𐤉𐤁𐤅.𐤁𐤉𐤃𐤊𐤌.𐤀𐤅𐤋𐤉.𐤌
𐤔𐤂𐤄.𐤄𐤅𐤀|

𐤉𐤂 𐤅𐤀𐤕.𐤀𐤇𐤉𐤊𐤌.𐤒𐤇𐤅.𐤅𐤒𐤅𐤌𐤅.𐤔𐤅𐤁𐤅.𐤀𐤋.𐤄𐤀𐤉𐤔|

𐤉𐤃 𐤅𐤀𐤋.𐤔𐤃𐤉.𐤉𐤕𐤍.𐤋𐤊𐤌.𐤓𐤇𐤌𐤉𐤌.𐤋𐤐𐤍𐤉.𐤄𐤀𐤉𐤔.𐤅
𐤔𐤋𐤇.𐤋𐤊𐤌.𐤀𐤕.𐤀𐤇𐤉𐤊𐤌.𐤀𐤇𐤓.𐤅𐤀𐤕.𐤁𐤍𐤉𐤌𐤉𐤍.𐤅𐤀𐤍𐤉.
𐤊𐤀𐤔𐤓.𐤔𐤊𐤋𐤕𐤉.𐤔𐤊𐤋𐤕𐤉|

𐤉𐤄 𐤅𐤉𐤒𐤇𐤅.𐤄𐤀𐤍𐤔𐤉𐤌.𐤀𐤕.𐤄𐤌𐤍𐤇𐤄.𐤄𐤆𐤀𐤕.𐤅𐤌𐤔𐤍
𐤄.𐤊𐤎𐤐.𐤋𐤒𐤇𐤅.𐤁𐤉𐤃𐤌.𐤅𐤀𐤕.𐤁𐤍𐤉𐤌𐤉𐤍.𐤅𐤉𐤒𐤌𐤅.𐤅𐤉𐤓𐤃𐤅.
𐤌𐤑𐤓𐤉𐤌.𐤅𐤉𐤏𐤌𐤃𐤅.𐤋𐤐𐤍𐤉.𐤉𐤅𐤎𐤐|

𐤉𐤅 𐤅𐤉𐤓𐤀.𐤉𐤅𐤎𐤐.𐤀𐤕𐤌.𐤀𐤕.𐤁𐤍𐤉𐤌𐤉𐤍.𐤅𐤉𐤀𐤌𐤓.𐤋𐤀𐤔𐤓.
𐤏𐤋.𐤁𐤉𐤕𐤅.𐤄𐤁𐤀.𐤀𐤕.𐤄𐤀𐤍𐤔𐤉𐤌.𐤄𐤁𐤉𐤕𐤄.𐤅𐤈𐤁𐤇.𐤈𐤁
𐤇.𐤅𐤄𐤊𐤍.𐤊𐤉.𐤀𐤕𐤉.𐤉𐤀𐤊𐤋𐤅.𐤄𐤀𐤍𐤔𐤉𐤌.𐤁𐤑𐤄𐤓𐤉𐤌|

𐤉𐤆 𐤅𐤉𐤏𐤔.𐤄𐤀𐤉𐤔.𐤊𐤀𐤔𐤓.𐤀𐤌𐤓.𐤉𐤅𐤎𐤐.𐤅𐤉𐤁𐤀.𐤄𐤀𐤉
𐤔.𐤀𐤕.𐤄𐤀𐤍𐤔𐤉𐤌.𐤁𐤉𐤕𐤄.𐤉𐤅𐤎𐤐|

יח 𐤅𐤉𐤉𐤓𐤀𐤅.𐤄𐤀𐤍𐤔𐤉𐤌.𐤊𐤉.𐤄𐤅𐤁𐤀𐤅.𐤁𐤉𐤕.𐤉𐤅𐤎𐤐.𐤅𐤉𐤀
𐤌𐤓𐤅.𐤏𐤋.𐤃𐤁𐤓.𐤄𐤊𐤎𐤐.𐤄𐤔𐤁.𐤁𐤀𐤌𐤕𐤇𐤕𐤉𐤍𐤅.𐤁𐤕𐤇𐤋𐤄
.𐤀𐤍𐤇𐤍𐤅.𐤌𐤅𐤁𐤀𐤉𐤌.𐤋𐤄𐤕𐤂𐤋𐤋.𐤏𐤋𐤉𐤍𐤅.𐤅𐤋𐤄𐤕𐤍𐤐𐤋.𐤏𐤋𐤉
𐤍𐤅.𐤅𐤋𐤒𐤇𐤕.𐤀𐤕𐤍𐤅.𐤋𐤏𐤁𐤃𐤉𐤌.𐤅𐤀𐤕.𐤇𐤌𐤓𐤉𐤍𐤅|
יט 𐤅𐤉𐤂𐤔𐤅.𐤀𐤋.𐤄𐤀𐤉𐤔.𐤀𐤔𐤓.𐤏𐤋.𐤁𐤉𐤕.𐤉𐤅𐤎𐤐.𐤅𐤉𐤃
𐤁𐤓𐤅.𐤀𐤋𐤉𐤅.𐤐𐤕𐤇.𐤄𐤁𐤉𐤕|
כ 𐤅𐤉𐤀𐤌𐤓𐤅.𐤁𐤉.𐤀𐤃𐤍𐤉.𐤉𐤓𐤃.𐤉𐤓𐤃𐤍𐤅.𐤁𐤕𐤇𐤋𐤄.𐤋
𐤔𐤁𐤓.𐤀𐤊𐤋|
כא 𐤅𐤉𐤄𐤉.𐤊𐤉.𐤁𐤀𐤍𐤅.𐤀𐤋.𐤄𐤌𐤋𐤅𐤍.𐤅𐤍𐤐𐤕𐤇𐤄.𐤀𐤕.𐤀𐤌
𐤕𐤇𐤕𐤉𐤍𐤅.𐤅𐤄𐤍𐤄.𐤊𐤎𐤐.𐤀𐤉𐤔.𐤁𐤐𐤉.𐤀𐤌𐤕𐤇𐤕𐤅.𐤊𐤎𐤐𐤍𐤅.
𐤁𐤌𐤔𐤒𐤋𐤅.𐤅𐤍𐤔𐤁.𐤀𐤕𐤅.𐤁𐤉𐤃𐤍𐤅|
כב 𐤅𐤊𐤎𐤐.𐤀𐤇𐤓.𐤄𐤅𐤓𐤃𐤍𐤅.𐤁𐤉𐤃𐤍𐤅.𐤋𐤔𐤁𐤓.𐤀𐤊𐤋.𐤋𐤀.
𐤉𐤃𐤏𐤍𐤅.𐤌𐤉.𐤔𐤌.𐤊𐤎𐤐𐤍𐤅.𐤁𐤀𐤌𐤕𐤇𐤕𐤉𐤍𐤅|
כג 𐤅𐤉𐤀𐤌𐤓.𐤔𐤋𐤅𐤌.𐤋𐤊𐤌.𐤀𐤋.𐤕𐤉𐤓𐤀𐤅.𐤀𐤋𐤄𐤉𐤊𐤌.𐤅𐤀
𐤋𐤄𐤉.𐤀𐤁𐤉𐤊𐤌.𐤍𐤕𐤍.𐤋𐤊𐤌.𐤌𐤈𐤌𐤅𐤍.𐤁𐤀𐤌𐤕𐤇𐤕𐤉𐤊𐤌.𐤊
𐤎𐤐𐤊𐤌.𐤁𐤀.𐤀𐤋𐤉.𐤅𐤉𐤅𐤑𐤀.𐤀𐤋𐤄𐤌.𐤀𐤕.𐤔𐤌𐤏𐤅𐤍|
כד 𐤅𐤉𐤁𐤀.𐤄𐤀𐤉𐤔.𐤀𐤕.𐤄𐤀𐤍𐤔𐤉𐤌.𐤁𐤉𐤕𐤄.𐤉𐤅𐤎𐤐.𐤅𐤉
𐤕𐤍.𐤌𐤉𐤌.𐤅𐤉𐤓𐤇𐤑𐤅.𐤓𐤂𐤋𐤉𐤄𐤌.𐤅𐤉𐤕𐤍.𐤌𐤎𐤐𐤅𐤀.𐤋𐤇𐤌𐤓𐤉
𐤄𐤌|
כה 𐤅𐤉𐤊𐤉𐤍𐤅.𐤀𐤕.𐤄𐤌𐤍𐤇𐤄.𐤏𐤃.𐤁𐤅𐤀.𐤉𐤅𐤎𐤐.𐤁𐤑𐤄𐤓𐤉
𐤌.𐤊𐤉.𐤔𐤌𐤏𐤅.𐤊𐤉.𐤔𐤌.𐤉𐤀𐤊𐤋𐤅.𐤋𐤇𐤌|
כו 𐤅𐤉𐤁𐤀.𐤉𐤅𐤎𐤐.𐤄𐤁𐤉𐤕𐤄.𐤅𐤉𐤁𐤉𐤀𐤅.𐤋𐤅.𐤀𐤕.𐤄𐤌𐤍𐤇𐤄
.𐤀𐤔𐤓.𐤁𐤉𐤃𐤌.𐤄𐤁𐤉𐤕𐤄.𐤅𐤉𐤔𐤕𐤇𐤅𐤅.𐤋𐤅.𐤀𐤓𐤑𐤄|
כז 𐤅𐤉𐤔𐤀𐤋.𐤋𐤄𐤌.𐤋𐤔𐤋𐤅𐤌.𐤅𐤉𐤀𐤌𐤓.𐤄𐤔𐤋𐤅𐤌.𐤀𐤁𐤉𐤊
𐤌.𐤄𐤆𐤒𐤍.𐤀𐤔𐤓.𐤀𐤌𐤓𐤕𐤌.𐤄𐤏𐤅𐤃𐤍𐤅.𐤇𐤉|
כח 𐤅𐤉𐤀𐤌𐤓𐤅.𐤔𐤋𐤅𐤌.𐤋𐤏𐤁𐤃𐤊.𐤋𐤀𐤁𐤉𐤍𐤅.𐤏𐤅𐤃𐤍𐤅.𐤇𐤉.𐤅
𐤉𐤒𐤃𐤅.𐤅𐤉𐤔𐤕𐤇𐤅.||𐤅𐤉𐤔𐤕𐤇𐤅𐤅.𐤒𐤓𐤉|||
כט 𐤅𐤉𐤔𐤀.𐤏𐤉𐤍𐤉𐤅.𐤅𐤉𐤓𐤀.𐤀𐤕.𐤁𐤍𐤉𐤌𐤉𐤍.𐤀𐤇𐤉𐤅.𐤁𐤍.
𐤀𐤌𐤅.𐤅𐤉𐤀𐤌𐤓.𐤄𐤆𐤄.𐤀𐤇𐤉𐤊𐤌.𐤄𐤒𐤈𐤍.𐤀𐤔𐤓.𐤀𐤌𐤓𐤕𐤌.
𐤀𐤋𐤉.𐤅𐤉𐤀𐤌𐤓.𐤀𐤋𐤄𐤉𐤌.𐤉𐤇𐤍𐤊.𐤁𐤍𐤉|

30 𐤅𐤉𐤌𐤄𐤓.𐤉𐤅𐤎𐤐.𐤊𐤉.𐤍𐤊𐤌𐤓𐤅.𐤓𐤇𐤌𐤉𐤅.𐤀𐤋.𐤀𐤇𐤉𐤅.𐤅
𐤉𐤁𐤒𐤔.𐤋𐤁𐤊𐤅𐤕.𐤅𐤉𐤁𐤀.𐤄𐤇𐤃𐤓𐤄.𐤅𐤉𐤁𐤊.𐤔𐤌𐤄|
31 𐤅𐤉𐤓𐤇𐤑.𐤐𐤍𐤉𐤅.𐤅𐤉𐤑𐤀.𐤅𐤉𐤕𐤀𐤐𐤒.𐤅𐤉𐤀𐤌𐤓.𐤔𐤉𐤌𐤅.
𐤋𐤇𐤌|
32 𐤅𐤉𐤔𐤉𐤌𐤅.𐤋𐤅.𐤋𐤁𐤃𐤅.𐤅𐤋𐤄𐤌.𐤋𐤁𐤃𐤌.𐤅𐤋𐤌𐤑𐤓𐤉𐤌.𐤄
𐤀𐤊𐤋𐤉𐤌.𐤀𐤕𐤅.𐤋𐤁𐤃𐤌.𐤊𐤉.𐤋𐤀.𐤉𐤅𐤊𐤋𐤅𐤍.𐤄𐤌𐤑𐤓𐤉𐤌.𐤋𐤀
𐤊𐤋.𐤀𐤕.𐤄𐤏𐤁𐤓𐤉𐤌.𐤋𐤇𐤌.𐤊𐤉.𐤕𐤅𐤏𐤁𐤄.𐤄𐤅𐤀.𐤋𐤌𐤑𐤓𐤉𐤌
|
33 𐤅𐤉𐤔𐤁𐤅.𐤋𐤐𐤍𐤉𐤅.𐤄𐤁𐤊𐤓.𐤊𐤁𐤊𐤓𐤕𐤅.𐤅𐤄𐤑𐤏𐤉𐤓.𐤊𐤑
𐤏𐤓𐤕𐤅.𐤅𐤉𐤕𐤌𐤄𐤅.𐤄𐤀𐤍𐤔𐤉𐤌.𐤀𐤉𐤔.𐤀𐤋.𐤓𐤏𐤄𐤅|
34 𐤅𐤉𐤔𐤀.𐤌𐤔𐤀𐤕.𐤌𐤀𐤕.𐤐𐤍𐤉𐤅.𐤀𐤋𐤄𐤌.𐤅𐤕𐤓𐤁.𐤌𐤔𐤀
𐤕.𐤁𐤍𐤉𐤌𐤍.𐤌𐤌𐤔𐤀𐤕.𐤊𐤋𐤌.𐤇𐤌𐤔.𐤉𐤃𐤅𐤕.𐤅𐤉𐤔𐤕𐤅.𐤅𐤉𐤔
𐤊𐤓𐤅.𐤏𐤌𐤅||

𐤁𐤓𐤀𐤔𐤉𐤕.𐤇𐤋𐤒 44

1 𐤅𐤉𐤑𐤅.𐤀𐤕.𐤀𐤔𐤓.𐤏𐤋.𐤁𐤉𐤕𐤅.𐤋𐤀𐤌𐤓.𐤌𐤋𐤀.𐤀𐤕.𐤀𐤌
𐤕𐤇𐤕.𐤄𐤀𐤍𐤔𐤉𐤌.𐤀𐤊𐤋.𐤊𐤀𐤔𐤓.𐤉𐤅𐤊𐤋𐤅𐤍.𐤔𐤀𐤕.𐤅𐤔𐤉𐤌.
𐤊𐤎𐤐.𐤀𐤉𐤔.𐤁𐤐𐤉.𐤀𐤌𐤕𐤇𐤕𐤅|
2 𐤅𐤀𐤕.𐤂𐤁𐤉𐤏𐤉.𐤂𐤁𐤉𐤏.𐤄𐤊𐤎𐤐.𐤕𐤔𐤉𐤌.𐤁𐤐𐤉.𐤀𐤌𐤕
𐤇𐤕.𐤄𐤒𐤈𐤍.𐤅𐤀𐤕.𐤊𐤎𐤐.𐤔𐤁𐤓𐤅.𐤅𐤉𐤏𐤔.𐤊𐤃𐤁𐤓.𐤉𐤅𐤎𐤐.𐤀
𐤔𐤓.𐤃𐤁𐤓|
3 𐤄𐤁𐤒𐤓.𐤀𐤅𐤓.𐤅𐤄𐤀𐤍𐤔𐤉𐤌.𐤔𐤋𐤇𐤅.𐤄𐤌𐤄.𐤅𐤇𐤌𐤓𐤉𐤄𐤌
|
4 𐤄𐤌.𐤉𐤑𐤀𐤅.𐤀𐤕.𐤄𐤏𐤉𐤓.𐤋𐤀.𐤄𐤓𐤇𐤉𐤒𐤅.𐤅𐤉𐤅𐤎𐤐.𐤀𐤌
𐤓.𐤋𐤀𐤔𐤓.𐤏𐤋.𐤁𐤉𐤕𐤅.𐤒𐤅𐤌.𐤓𐤃𐤐.𐤀𐤇𐤓𐤉.𐤄𐤀𐤍𐤔𐤉𐤌.𐤅𐤄
𐤔𐤂𐤕𐤌.𐤅𐤀𐤌𐤓𐤕.𐤀𐤋𐤄𐤌.𐤋𐤌𐤄.𐤔𐤋𐤌𐤕𐤌.𐤓𐤏𐤄.𐤕𐤇𐤕.
𐤈𐤅𐤁𐤄|
5 𐤄𐤋𐤅𐤀.𐤆𐤄.𐤀𐤔𐤓.𐤉𐤔𐤕𐤄.𐤀𐤃𐤍𐤉.𐤁𐤅.𐤅𐤄𐤅𐤀.𐤍𐤇𐤔.
𐤉𐤍𐤇𐤔.𐤁𐤅.𐤄𐤓𐤏𐤕𐤌.𐤀𐤔𐤓.𐤏𐤔𐤉𐤕𐤌|
6 𐤅𐤉𐤔𐤂𐤌.𐤅𐤉𐤃𐤁𐤓.𐤀𐤋𐤄𐤌.𐤀𐤕.𐤄𐤃𐤁𐤓𐤉𐤌.𐤄𐤀𐤋𐤄|

ז 𐤅𐤉𐤀𐤌𐤓𐤅.𐤀𐤋𐤉𐤅.𐤋𐤌𐤄.𐤉𐤃𐤁𐤓.𐤀𐤃𐤍𐤉.𐤊𐤃𐤁𐤓𐤉𐤌.
𐤄𐤀𐤋𐤄.𐤇𐤋𐤉𐤋𐤄.𐤋𐤏𐤁𐤃𐤉𐤊.𐤌𐤏𐤔𐤅𐤕.𐤊𐤃𐤁𐤓.𐤄𐤆𐤄|
ח 𐤄𐤍.𐤊𐤎𐤐.𐤀𐤔𐤓.𐤌𐤑𐤀𐤍𐤅.𐤁𐤐𐤉.𐤀𐤌𐤕𐤇𐤕𐤉𐤍𐤅.𐤄𐤔𐤉
𐤁𐤍𐤅.𐤀𐤋𐤉𐤊.𐤌𐤀𐤓𐤑.𐤊𐤍𐤏𐤍.𐤅𐤀𐤉𐤊.𐤍𐤂𐤍𐤁.𐤌𐤁𐤉𐤕.𐤀𐤃𐤍
𐤉𐤊.𐤊𐤎𐤐.𐤀𐤅.𐤆𐤄𐤁|
ט 𐤀𐤔𐤓.𐤉𐤌𐤑𐤀.𐤀𐤕𐤅.𐤌𐤏𐤁𐤃𐤉𐤊.𐤅𐤌𐤕.𐤅𐤂𐤌.𐤀𐤍𐤇𐤍
𐤅.𐤍𐤄𐤉𐤄.𐤋𐤀𐤃𐤍𐤉.𐤋𐤏𐤁𐤃𐤉𐤌|
י 𐤅𐤉𐤀𐤌𐤓.𐤂𐤌.𐤏𐤕𐤄.𐤊𐤃𐤁𐤓𐤉𐤊𐤌.𐤊𐤍.𐤄𐤅𐤀.𐤀𐤔𐤓.
𐤉𐤌𐤑𐤀.𐤀𐤕𐤅.𐤉𐤄𐤉𐤄.𐤋𐤉.𐤏𐤁𐤃.𐤅𐤀𐤕𐤌.𐤕𐤄𐤉𐤅.𐤍𐤒𐤉𐤌|
יא 𐤅𐤉𐤌𐤄𐤓𐤅.𐤅𐤉𐤅𐤓𐤃𐤅.𐤀𐤉𐤔.𐤀𐤕.𐤀𐤌𐤕𐤇𐤕𐤅.𐤀𐤓𐤑𐤄.
𐤅𐤉𐤐𐤕𐤇𐤅.𐤀𐤉𐤔.𐤀𐤌𐤕𐤇𐤕𐤅|
יב 𐤅𐤉𐤇𐤐𐤔.𐤁𐤂𐤃𐤅𐤋.𐤄𐤇𐤋.𐤅𐤁𐤒𐤈𐤍.𐤊𐤋𐤄.𐤅𐤉𐤌𐤑𐤀.
𐤄𐤂𐤁𐤉𐤏.𐤁𐤀𐤌𐤕𐤇𐤕.𐤁𐤍𐤉𐤌𐤍|
יג 𐤅𐤉𐤒𐤓𐤏𐤅.𐤔𐤌𐤋𐤕𐤌.𐤅𐤉𐤏𐤌𐤎.𐤀𐤉𐤔.𐤏𐤋.𐤇𐤌𐤓𐤅.𐤅𐤉
𐤔𐤁𐤅.𐤄𐤏𐤉𐤓𐤄|
יד 𐤅𐤉𐤁𐤀.𐤉𐤄𐤅𐤃𐤄.𐤅𐤀𐤇𐤉𐤅.𐤁𐤉𐤕𐤄.𐤉𐤅𐤎𐤐.𐤅𐤄𐤅𐤀.𐤏𐤅
𐤃𐤍𐤅.𐤔𐤌.𐤅𐤉𐤐𐤋𐤅.𐤋𐤐𐤍𐤉𐤅.𐤀𐤓𐤑𐤄|
טו 𐤅𐤉𐤀𐤌𐤓.𐤋𐤄𐤌.𐤉𐤅𐤎𐤐.𐤌𐤄.𐤄𐤌𐤏𐤔𐤄.𐤄𐤆𐤄.𐤀𐤔𐤓.
𐤏𐤔𐤉𐤕𐤌.𐤄𐤋𐤅𐤀.𐤉𐤃𐤏𐤕𐤌.𐤊𐤉.𐤍𐤇𐤔.𐤉𐤍𐤇𐤔.𐤀𐤉𐤔.𐤀
𐤔𐤓.𐤊𐤌𐤍𐤉|
טז 𐤅𐤉𐤀𐤌𐤓.𐤉𐤄𐤅𐤃𐤄.𐤌𐤄.𐤍𐤀𐤌𐤓.𐤋𐤀𐤃𐤍𐤉.𐤌𐤄.𐤍𐤃𐤁𐤓
.𐤅𐤌𐤄.𐤍𐤑𐤈𐤃𐤒.𐤄𐤀𐤋𐤄𐤉𐤌.𐤌𐤑𐤀.𐤀𐤕.𐤏𐤅𐤍.𐤏𐤁𐤃𐤉𐤊.
𐤄𐤍𐤍𐤅.𐤏𐤁𐤃𐤉𐤌.𐤋𐤀𐤃𐤍𐤉.𐤂𐤌.𐤀𐤍𐤇𐤍𐤅.𐤂𐤌.𐤀𐤔𐤓.𐤍𐤌𐤑
𐤀.𐤄𐤂𐤁𐤉𐤏.𐤁𐤉𐤃𐤅|
יז 𐤅𐤉𐤀𐤌𐤓.𐤇𐤋𐤉𐤋𐤄.𐤋𐤉.𐤌𐤏𐤔𐤅𐤕.𐤆𐤀𐤕.𐤄𐤀𐤉𐤔.𐤀
𐤔𐤓.𐤍𐤌𐤑𐤀.𐤄𐤂𐤁𐤉𐤏.𐤁𐤉𐤃𐤅.𐤄𐤅𐤀.𐤉𐤄𐤉𐤄.𐤋𐤉.𐤏𐤁𐤃.𐤅
𐤀𐤕𐤌.𐤏𐤋𐤅.𐤋𐤔𐤋𐤅𐤌.𐤀𐤋.𐤀𐤁𐤉𐤊𐤌|
יח 𐤅𐤉𐤂𐤔.𐤀𐤋𐤉𐤅.𐤉𐤄𐤅𐤃𐤄.𐤅𐤉𐤀𐤌𐤓.𐤁𐤉.𐤀𐤃𐤍𐤉.𐤉𐤃
𐤁𐤓.𐤍𐤀.𐤏𐤁𐤃𐤊.𐤃𐤁𐤓.𐤁𐤀𐤆𐤍𐤉.𐤀𐤃𐤍𐤉.𐤅𐤀𐤋.𐤉𐤇𐤓.𐤀𐤐
𐤊.𐤁𐤏𐤁𐤃𐤊.𐤊𐤉.𐤊𐤌𐤅𐤊.𐤊𐤐𐤓𐤏𐤄|

19 𐤀𐤃𐤍𐤉.𐤔𐤀𐤋.𐤀𐤕.𐤏𐤁𐤃𐤉𐤅.𐤋𐤀𐤌𐤓.𐤄𐤉𐤔.𐤋𐤊𐤌.𐤀𐤁.𐤀𐤅.𐤀𐤇|

20 𐤅𐤍𐤀𐤌𐤓.𐤀𐤋.𐤀𐤃𐤍𐤉.𐤉𐤔.𐤋𐤍𐤅.𐤀𐤁.𐤆𐤒𐤍.𐤅𐤉𐤋𐤃.𐤆𐤒𐤍𐤉𐤌.𐤒𐤈𐤍.𐤅𐤀𐤇𐤉𐤅.𐤌𐤕.𐤅𐤉𐤅𐤕𐤓.𐤄𐤅𐤀.𐤋𐤁𐤃𐤅.𐤋𐤀𐤌𐤅.𐤅𐤀𐤁𐤉𐤅.𐤀𐤄𐤁𐤅|

21 𐤅𐤕𐤀𐤌𐤓.𐤀𐤋.𐤏𐤁𐤃𐤉𐤊.𐤄𐤅𐤓𐤃𐤄𐤅.𐤀𐤋𐤉.𐤅𐤀𐤔𐤉𐤌𐤄.𐤏𐤉𐤍𐤉.𐤏𐤋𐤉𐤅|

22 𐤅𐤍𐤀𐤌𐤓.𐤀𐤋.𐤀𐤃𐤍𐤉.𐤋𐤀.𐤉𐤅𐤊𐤋.𐤄𐤍𐤏𐤓.𐤋𐤏𐤆𐤁.𐤀𐤕.𐤀𐤁𐤉𐤅.𐤅𐤏𐤆𐤁.𐤀𐤕.𐤀𐤁𐤉𐤅.𐤅𐤌𐤕|

23 𐤅𐤕𐤀𐤌𐤓.𐤀𐤋.𐤏𐤁𐤃𐤉𐤊.𐤀𐤌.𐤋𐤀.𐤉𐤓𐤃.𐤀𐤇𐤉𐤊𐤌.𐤄𐤒𐤈𐤍.𐤀𐤕𐤊𐤌.𐤋𐤀.𐤕𐤎𐤐𐤅𐤍.𐤋𐤓𐤀𐤅𐤕.𐤐𐤍𐤉|

24 𐤅𐤉𐤄𐤉.𐤊𐤉.𐤏𐤋𐤉𐤍𐤅.𐤀𐤋.𐤏𐤁𐤃𐤊.𐤀𐤁𐤉.𐤅𐤍𐤂𐤃.𐤋𐤅.𐤀𐤕.𐤃𐤁𐤓𐤉.𐤀𐤃𐤍𐤉|

25 𐤅𐤉𐤀𐤌𐤓.𐤀𐤁𐤉𐤍𐤅.𐤔𐤁𐤅.𐤔𐤁𐤓𐤅.𐤋𐤍𐤅.𐤌𐤏𐤈.𐤀𐤊𐤋|

26 𐤅𐤍𐤀𐤌𐤓.𐤋𐤀.𐤍𐤅𐤊𐤋.𐤋𐤓𐤃𐤕.𐤀𐤌.𐤉𐤔.𐤀𐤇𐤉𐤍𐤅.𐤄𐤒𐤈𐤍.𐤀𐤕𐤍𐤅.𐤅𐤉𐤓𐤃𐤍𐤅.𐤊𐤉.𐤋𐤀.𐤍𐤅𐤊𐤋.𐤋𐤓𐤀𐤅𐤕.𐤐𐤍𐤉.𐤄𐤀𐤉𐤔.𐤅𐤀𐤇𐤉𐤍𐤅.𐤄𐤒𐤈𐤍.𐤀𐤉𐤍𐤍𐤅.𐤀𐤕𐤍𐤅|

27 𐤅𐤉𐤀𐤌𐤓.𐤏𐤁𐤃𐤊.𐤀𐤁𐤉.𐤀𐤋𐤉𐤍𐤅.𐤀𐤕𐤌.𐤉𐤃𐤏𐤕𐤌.𐤊𐤉.𐤔𐤍𐤉𐤌.𐤉𐤋𐤃𐤄.𐤋𐤉.𐤀𐤔𐤕𐤉|

28 𐤅𐤉𐤑𐤀.𐤄𐤀𐤇𐤃.𐤌𐤀𐤕𐤉.𐤅𐤀𐤌𐤓.𐤀𐤊.𐤈𐤓𐤐.𐤈𐤓𐤐.𐤅𐤋𐤀.𐤓𐤀𐤉𐤕𐤉𐤅.𐤏𐤃.𐤄𐤍𐤄|

29 𐤅𐤋𐤒𐤇𐤕𐤌.𐤂𐤌.𐤀𐤕.𐤆𐤄.𐤌𐤏𐤌.𐤐𐤍𐤉.𐤅𐤒𐤓𐤄𐤅.𐤀𐤎𐤅𐤍.𐤅𐤄𐤅𐤓𐤃𐤕𐤌.𐤀𐤕.𐤔𐤉𐤁𐤕𐤉.𐤁𐤓𐤏𐤄.𐤔𐤀𐤋𐤄|

30 𐤅𐤏𐤕𐤄.𐤊𐤁𐤀𐤉.𐤀𐤋.𐤏𐤁𐤃𐤊.𐤀𐤁𐤉.𐤅𐤄𐤍𐤏𐤓.𐤀𐤉𐤍𐤍𐤅.𐤀𐤕𐤍𐤅.𐤅𐤍𐤐𐤔𐤅.𐤒𐤔𐤅𐤓𐤄.𐤁𐤍𐤐𐤔𐤅|

31 𐤅𐤄𐤉𐤄.𐤊𐤓𐤀𐤅𐤕𐤅.𐤊𐤉.𐤀𐤉𐤍.𐤄𐤍𐤏𐤓.𐤅𐤌𐤕.𐤅𐤄𐤅𐤓𐤉𐤃𐤅.𐤏𐤁𐤃𐤉𐤊.𐤀𐤕.𐤔𐤉𐤁𐤕.𐤏𐤁𐤃𐤊.𐤀𐤁𐤉𐤍𐤅.𐤁𐤉𐤂𐤅𐤍.𐤔𐤀𐤋𐤄|

32 𐤊𐤉.𐤏𐤁𐤃𐤊.𐤏𐤓𐤁.𐤀𐤕.𐤄𐤍𐤏𐤓.𐤌𐤏𐤌.𐤀𐤁𐤉.𐤋𐤀𐤌𐤓.𐤀𐤌.𐤋𐤀.𐤀𐤁𐤉𐤀𐤍𐤅.𐤀𐤋𐤉𐤊.𐤅𐤇𐤈𐤀𐤕𐤉.𐤋𐤀𐤁𐤉.𐤊𐤋.𐤄𐤉𐤌𐤉𐤌|

33 ࠅࠏࠕࠄ.ࠉࠔࠁ.ࠍࠀ.ࠏࠁࠃࠊ.ࠕࠇࠕ.ࠄࠍࠏࠓ.ࠏࠁࠃ.ࠋ
ࠀࠃࠍࠉ.ࠅࠄࠍࠏࠓ.ࠉࠏࠋ.ࠏࠌ.ࠀࠇࠉࠅ|
34 ࠊࠉ.ࠀࠉࠊ.ࠀࠏࠋࠄ.ࠀࠋ.ࠀࠁࠉ.ࠅࠄࠍࠏࠓ.ࠀࠉࠍࠍࠅ.ࠀࠕ
ࠉ.ࠐࠍ.ࠀࠓࠀࠄ.ࠁࠓࠏ.ࠀࠔࠓ.ࠉࠌࠑࠀ.ࠀࠕ.ࠀࠁࠉ||

ࠁࠓࠀࠔࠉࠕ.ࠇࠋࠒ 45

1 ࠅࠋࠀ.ࠉࠊࠋ.ࠉࠅࠎࠐ.ࠋࠄࠕࠀࠐࠒ.ࠋࠊࠋ.ࠄࠍࠑࠁࠉࠌ.ࠏࠋࠉࠅ
.ࠅࠉࠒࠓࠀ.ࠄࠅࠑࠉࠀࠅ.ࠊࠋ.ࠀࠉࠔ.ࠌࠏࠋࠉ.ࠅࠋࠀ.ࠏࠌࠃ.ࠀࠉ
ࠔ.ࠀࠕࠅ.ࠁࠄࠕࠅࠃࠏ.ࠉࠅࠎࠐ.ࠀࠋ.ࠀࠇࠉࠅ|
2 ࠅࠉࠕࠍ.ࠀࠕ.ࠒࠋࠅ.ࠁࠁࠊࠉ.ࠅࠉࠔࠌࠏࠅ.ࠌࠑࠓࠉࠌ.ࠅࠉࠔࠌ
ࠏ.ࠁࠉࠕ.ࠐࠓࠏࠄ|
3 ࠅࠉࠀࠌࠓ.ࠉࠅࠎࠐ.ࠀࠋ.ࠀࠇࠉࠅ.ࠀࠍࠉ.ࠉࠅࠎࠐ.ࠄࠏࠅࠃ.ࠀࠁ
ࠉ.ࠇࠉ.ࠅࠋࠀ.ࠉࠊࠋࠅ.ࠀࠇࠉࠅ.ࠋࠏࠍࠅࠕ.ࠀࠕࠅ.ࠊࠉ.ࠍࠁࠄࠋࠅ.ࠌࠐ
ࠍࠉࠅ|
4 ࠅࠉࠀࠌࠓ.ࠉࠅࠎࠐ.ࠀࠋ.ࠀࠇࠉࠅ.ࠂࠔࠅ.ࠍࠀ.ࠀࠋࠉ.ࠅࠉࠂࠔࠅ
.ࠅࠉࠀࠌࠓ.ࠀࠍࠉ.ࠉࠅࠎࠐ.ࠀࠇࠉࠊࠌ.ࠀࠔࠓ.ࠌࠊࠓࠕࠌ.ࠀࠕࠉ.ࠌ
ࠑࠓࠉࠌࠄ|
5 ࠅࠏࠕࠄ.ࠀࠋ.ࠕࠏࠑࠁࠅ.ࠅࠀࠋ.ࠉࠇࠓ.ࠁࠏࠉࠍࠉࠊࠌ.ࠊࠉ.ࠌ
ࠊࠓࠕࠌ.ࠀࠕࠉ.ࠄࠍࠄ.ࠊࠉ.ࠋࠌࠇࠉࠄ.ࠔࠋࠇࠍࠉ.ࠀࠋࠄࠉࠌ.ࠋ
ࠐࠍࠉࠊࠌ|
6 ࠊࠉ.ࠆࠄ.ࠔࠍࠕࠉࠌ.ࠄࠓࠏࠁ.ࠁࠒࠓࠁ.ࠄࠀࠓࠑ.ࠅࠏࠅࠃ.ࠇ
ࠌࠔ.ࠔࠍࠉࠌ.ࠀࠔࠓ.ࠀࠉࠍ.ࠇࠓࠉࠔ.ࠅࠒࠑࠉࠓ|
7 ࠅࠉࠔࠋࠇࠍࠉ.ࠀࠋࠄࠉࠌ.ࠋࠐࠍࠉࠊࠌ.ࠋࠔࠅࠌ.ࠋࠊࠌ.ࠔࠀࠓ
ࠉࠕ.ࠁࠀࠓࠑ.ࠅࠋࠄࠇࠉࠅࠕ.ࠋࠊࠌ.ࠋࠐࠋࠉࠈࠄ.ࠂࠃࠋࠄ|
8 ࠅࠏࠕࠄ.ࠋࠀ.ࠀࠕࠌ.ࠔࠋࠇࠕࠌ.ࠀࠕࠉ.ࠄࠍࠄ.ࠊࠉ.ࠄࠀࠋ
ࠄࠉࠌ.ࠅࠉࠔࠌࠍࠉ.ࠋࠀࠁ.ࠋࠐࠓࠏࠄ.ࠅࠋࠀࠃࠅࠍ.ࠋࠊࠋ.ࠁࠉࠕࠅ.ࠅ
ࠌࠔࠋ.ࠁࠊࠋ.ࠀࠓࠑ.ࠌࠑࠓࠉࠌ|
9 ࠌࠄࠓࠅ.ࠅࠏࠋࠅ.ࠀࠋ.ࠀࠁࠉ.ࠅࠀࠌࠓࠕࠌ.ࠀࠋࠉࠅ.ࠊࠄ.ࠀࠌࠓ.
ࠁࠍࠊ.ࠉࠅࠎࠐ.ࠔࠌࠍࠉ.ࠀࠋࠄࠉࠌ.ࠋࠀࠃࠅࠍ.ࠋࠊࠋ.ࠌࠑࠓࠉࠌ.ࠓ
ࠃࠄ.ࠀࠋࠉ.ࠀࠋ.ࠕࠏࠌࠃ|

10 וישבת.בארץ.גשן.והיית.קרוב.אלי.את
ה.ובניך.ובני.בניך.וצאנך.ובקרך.וכל.אשר.לך|
11 וכלכלתי.אתך.שם.כי.עוד.חמש.שנים.ר
עב.פן.תורש.אתה.וביתך.וכל.אשר.לך|
12 והנה.עיניכם.ראות.ועיני.אחי.בנימין.
כי.פי.המדבר.אליכם|
13 והגדתם.לאבי.את.כל.כבודי.במצרים.ו
את.כל.אשר.ראיתם.ומהרתם.והורדתם.את.אב
י.הנה|
14 ויפל.על.צוארי.בנימן.אחיו.ויבך.ובנימ
ן.בכה.על.צואריו|
15 וינשק.לכל.אחיו.ויבך.עליהם.ואחרי.כן
.דברו.אחיו.אתו|
16 והקל.נשמע.בית.פרעה.לאמר.באו.אחי.יו
סף.וייטב.בעיני.פרעה.ובעיני.עבדיו|
17 ויאמר.פרעה.אל.יוסף.אמר.אל.אחיך.זא
ת.עשו.טענו.את.בעירכם.ולכו.באו.ארצה.כנע
ן|
18 וקחו.את.אביכם.ואת.בתיכם.ובאו.אלי.ו
אתנה.לכם.את.טוב.ארץ.מצרים.ואכלו.את.ח
לב.הארץ|
19 ואתה.צויתה.זאת.עשו.קחו.לכם.מארץ
.מצרים.עגלות.לטפכם.ולנשיכם.ונשאתם.את
.אביכם.ובאתם|
20 ועינכם.אל.תחס.על.כליכם.כי.טוב.כל.
ארץ.מצרים.לכם.הוא|
21 ויעשו.כן.בני.ישראל.ויתן.להם.יוסף.עג
לות.על.פי.פרעה.ויתן.להם.צדה.לדרך|
22 לכלם.נתן.לאיש.חלפות.שמלת.ולבנימן.נ
תן.שלש.מאות.כסף.וחמש.חלפות.שמלת|

..כג..𐤅𐤋𐤀𐤁𐤉𐤅.𐤔𐤋𐤇.𐤊𐤆𐤀𐤕.𐤏𐤔𐤓𐤄.𐤇𐤌𐤓𐤉𐤌.𐤍𐤔𐤀𐤉
𐤌.𐤌𐤈𐤅𐤁.𐤌𐤑𐤓𐤉𐤌.𐤅𐤏𐤔𐤓.𐤀𐤕𐤍𐤕.𐤍𐤔𐤀𐤕.𐤁𐤓.𐤅𐤋𐤇𐤌.𐤅
𐤌𐤆𐤅𐤍.𐤋𐤀𐤁𐤉𐤅.𐤋𐤃𐤓𐤊|
..כד..𐤅𐤉𐤔𐤋𐤇.𐤀𐤕.𐤀𐤇𐤉𐤅.𐤅𐤉𐤋𐤊𐤅.𐤅𐤉𐤀𐤌𐤓.𐤀𐤋𐤄𐤌.𐤀𐤋
.𐤕𐤓𐤂𐤆𐤅.𐤁𐤃𐤓𐤊|
..כה..𐤅𐤉𐤏𐤋𐤅.𐤌𐤌𐤑𐤓𐤉𐤌.𐤅𐤉𐤁𐤀𐤅.𐤀𐤓𐤑.𐤊𐤍𐤏𐤍.𐤀𐤋.𐤉𐤏
𐤒𐤁.𐤀𐤁𐤉𐤄𐤌|
..כו..𐤅𐤉𐤂𐤃𐤅.𐤋𐤅.𐤋𐤀𐤌𐤓.𐤏𐤅𐤃.𐤉𐤅𐤎𐤐.𐤇𐤉.𐤅𐤊𐤉.𐤄𐤅𐤀.𐤌
𐤔𐤋.𐤁𐤊𐤋.𐤀𐤓𐤑.𐤌𐤑𐤓𐤉𐤌.𐤅𐤉𐤐𐤂.𐤋𐤁𐤅.𐤊𐤉.𐤋𐤀.𐤄𐤀𐤌𐤉𐤍.
𐤋𐤄𐤌|
..כז..𐤅𐤉𐤃𐤁𐤓𐤅.𐤀𐤋𐤉𐤅.𐤀𐤕.𐤊𐤋.𐤃𐤁𐤓𐤉.𐤉𐤅𐤎𐤐.𐤀𐤔𐤓.𐤃
𐤁𐤓.𐤀𐤋𐤄𐤌.𐤅𐤉𐤓𐤀.𐤀𐤕.𐤄𐤏𐤂𐤋𐤅𐤕.𐤀𐤔𐤓.𐤔𐤋𐤇.𐤉𐤅𐤎𐤐.𐤋
𐤔𐤀𐤕.𐤀𐤕𐤅.𐤅𐤕𐤇𐤉.𐤓𐤅𐤇.𐤉𐤏𐤒𐤁.𐤀𐤁𐤉𐤄𐤌|
..כח..𐤅𐤉𐤀𐤌𐤓.𐤉𐤔𐤓𐤀𐤋.𐤓𐤁.𐤏𐤅𐤃.𐤉𐤅𐤎𐤐.𐤁𐤍𐤉.𐤇𐤉.𐤀𐤋𐤊
𐤄.𐤅𐤀𐤓𐤀𐤍𐤅.𐤁𐤈𐤓𐤌.𐤀𐤌𐤅𐤕||

𐤁𐤓𐤀𐤔𐤉𐤕.𐤇𐤋𐤒 ..מו..

..א..𐤅𐤉𐤎𐤏.𐤉𐤔𐤓𐤀𐤋.𐤅𐤊𐤋.𐤀𐤔𐤓.𐤋𐤅.𐤅𐤉𐤁𐤀.𐤁𐤀𐤓𐤄.𐤔𐤁𐤏.
𐤅𐤉𐤆𐤁𐤇.𐤆𐤁𐤇𐤉𐤌.𐤋𐤀𐤋𐤄𐤉.𐤀𐤁𐤉𐤅.𐤉𐤑𐤇𐤒|
..ב..𐤅𐤉𐤀𐤌𐤓.𐤀𐤋𐤄𐤉𐤌.𐤋𐤉𐤔𐤓𐤀𐤋.𐤁𐤌𐤓𐤀𐤕.𐤄𐤋𐤉𐤋𐤄.𐤅𐤉
𐤀𐤌𐤓.𐤉𐤏𐤒𐤁.𐤉𐤏𐤒𐤁.𐤅𐤉𐤀𐤌𐤓.𐤄𐤍𐤍𐤉|
..ג..𐤅𐤉𐤀𐤌𐤓.𐤀𐤍𐤊𐤉.𐤄𐤀𐤋.𐤀𐤋𐤄𐤉.𐤀𐤁𐤉𐤊.𐤀𐤋.𐤕𐤉𐤓𐤀.𐤌
𐤓𐤃𐤄.𐤌𐤑𐤓𐤉𐤌𐤄.𐤊𐤉.𐤋𐤂𐤅𐤉.𐤂𐤃𐤅𐤋.𐤀𐤔𐤉𐤌𐤊.𐤔𐤌|
..ד..𐤀𐤍𐤊𐤉.𐤀𐤓𐤃.𐤏𐤌𐤊.𐤌𐤑𐤓𐤉𐤌𐤄.𐤅𐤀𐤍𐤊𐤉.𐤀𐤏𐤋𐤊.𐤂
𐤌.𐤏𐤋𐤄.𐤅𐤉𐤅𐤎𐤐.𐤉𐤔𐤉𐤕.𐤉𐤃𐤅.𐤏𐤋.𐤏𐤉𐤍𐤉𐤊|
..ה..𐤅𐤉𐤒𐤌.𐤉𐤏𐤒𐤁.𐤌𐤁𐤀𐤓.𐤔𐤁𐤏.𐤅𐤉𐤔𐤀𐤅.𐤁𐤍𐤉.𐤉𐤔𐤓𐤀𐤋
.𐤀𐤕.𐤉𐤏𐤒𐤁.𐤀𐤁𐤉𐤄𐤌.𐤅𐤀𐤕.𐤈𐤐𐤌.𐤅𐤀𐤕.𐤍𐤔𐤉𐤄𐤌.𐤁𐤏
𐤂𐤋𐤅𐤕.𐤀𐤔𐤓.𐤔𐤋𐤇.𐤐𐤓𐤏𐤄.𐤋𐤔𐤀𐤕.𐤀𐤕𐤅|

ו 𐤅𐤉𐤒𐤇𐤅.𐤀𐤕.𐤌𐤒𐤍𐤉𐤄𐤌.𐤅𐤀𐤕.𐤓𐤊𐤅𐤔𐤌.𐤀𐤔𐤓.𐤓𐤊𐤔𐤅.
𐤁𐤀𐤓𐤑.𐤊𐤍𐤏𐤍.𐤅𐤉𐤁𐤀𐤅.𐤌𐤑𐤓𐤉𐤌𐤄.𐤉𐤏𐤒𐤁.𐤅𐤊𐤋.𐤆𐤓𐤏𐤅.
𐤀𐤕𐤅|
ז 𐤁𐤍𐤉𐤅.𐤅𐤁𐤍𐤉.𐤁𐤍𐤉𐤅.𐤀𐤕𐤅.𐤁𐤍𐤕𐤉𐤅.𐤅𐤁𐤍𐤅𐤕.𐤁𐤍𐤉𐤅.𐤅𐤊𐤋.
𐤆𐤓𐤏𐤅.𐤄𐤁𐤉𐤀.𐤀𐤕𐤅.𐤌𐤑𐤓𐤉𐤌𐤄|
ח 𐤅𐤀𐤋𐤄.𐤔𐤌𐤅𐤕.𐤁𐤍𐤉.𐤉𐤔𐤓𐤀𐤋.𐤄𐤁𐤀𐤉𐤌.𐤌𐤑𐤓𐤉𐤌𐤄.
𐤉𐤏𐤒𐤁.𐤅𐤁𐤍𐤉𐤅.𐤁𐤊𐤓.𐤉𐤏𐤒𐤁.𐤓𐤀𐤅𐤁𐤍|
ט 𐤅𐤁𐤍𐤉.𐤓𐤀𐤅𐤁𐤍.𐤇𐤍𐤅𐤊.𐤅𐤐𐤋𐤅𐤀.𐤅𐤇𐤑𐤓𐤅𐤍.𐤅𐤊𐤓𐤌𐤉|
י 𐤅𐤁𐤍𐤉.𐤔𐤌𐤏𐤅𐤍.𐤉𐤌𐤅𐤀𐤋.𐤅𐤉𐤌𐤉𐤍.𐤅𐤀𐤄𐤃.𐤅𐤉𐤊𐤉𐤍.𐤅
𐤑𐤇𐤓.𐤅𐤔𐤀𐤅𐤋.𐤁𐤍.𐤄𐤊𐤍𐤏𐤍𐤉𐤕|
יא 𐤅𐤁𐤍𐤉.𐤋𐤅𐤉.𐤂𐤓𐤔𐤅𐤍.𐤒𐤄𐤕.𐤅𐤌𐤓𐤓𐤉|
יב 𐤅𐤁𐤍𐤉.𐤉𐤄𐤅𐤃𐤄.𐤏𐤓.𐤅𐤀𐤅𐤍𐤍.𐤅𐤔𐤋𐤄.𐤅𐤐𐤓𐤑.𐤅𐤆𐤓𐤇.𐤅
𐤉𐤌𐤕.𐤏𐤓.𐤅𐤀𐤅𐤍𐤍.𐤁𐤀𐤓𐤑.𐤊𐤍𐤏𐤍.𐤅𐤉𐤄𐤉𐤅.𐤁𐤍𐤉.𐤐𐤓𐤑.𐤇𐤑
𐤓𐤅𐤍.𐤅𐤇𐤌𐤅𐤋|
יג 𐤅𐤁𐤍𐤉.𐤉𐤔𐤔𐤊𐤓.𐤕𐤅𐤋𐤏.𐤅𐤐𐤅𐤄.𐤅𐤉𐤅𐤁.𐤅𐤔𐤌𐤓𐤅𐤍|
יד 𐤅𐤁𐤍𐤉.𐤆𐤁𐤅𐤋𐤍.𐤎𐤓𐤃.𐤅𐤀𐤋𐤅𐤍.𐤅𐤉𐤇𐤋𐤀𐤋|
טו 𐤀𐤋𐤄.𐤁𐤍𐤉.𐤋𐤀𐤄.𐤀𐤔𐤓.𐤉𐤋𐤃𐤄.𐤋𐤉𐤏𐤒𐤁.𐤁𐤐𐤃𐤍.
𐤀𐤓𐤌.𐤅𐤀𐤕.𐤃𐤉𐤍𐤄.𐤁𐤕𐤅.𐤊𐤋.𐤍𐤐𐤔.𐤁𐤍𐤉𐤅.𐤅𐤁𐤍𐤅𐤕𐤉𐤅.𐤔𐤋𐤔
𐤉𐤌.𐤅𐤔𐤋𐤔|
טז 𐤅𐤁𐤍𐤉.𐤂𐤃.𐤑𐤐𐤉𐤅𐤍.𐤅𐤇𐤂𐤉.𐤔𐤅𐤍𐤉.𐤅𐤀𐤑𐤁𐤍.𐤏𐤓𐤉.𐤅
𐤀𐤓𐤅𐤃𐤉.𐤅𐤀𐤓𐤀𐤋𐤉|
יז 𐤅𐤁𐤍𐤉.𐤀𐤔𐤓.𐤉𐤌𐤍𐤄.𐤅𐤉𐤔𐤅𐤄.𐤅𐤉𐤔𐤅𐤉.𐤅𐤁𐤓𐤉𐤏𐤄.𐤅𐤔
𐤓𐤇.𐤀𐤇𐤕𐤌.𐤅𐤁𐤍𐤉.𐤁𐤓𐤉𐤏𐤄.𐤇𐤁𐤓.𐤅𐤌𐤋𐤊𐤉𐤀𐤋|
יח 𐤀𐤋𐤄.𐤁𐤍𐤉.𐤆𐤋𐤐𐤄.𐤀𐤔𐤓.𐤍𐤕𐤍.𐤋𐤁𐤍.𐤋𐤋𐤀𐤄.𐤁𐤕𐤅.𐤅
𐤕𐤋𐤃.𐤀𐤕.𐤀𐤋𐤄.𐤋𐤉𐤏𐤒𐤁.𐤔𐤔.𐤏𐤔𐤓𐤄.𐤍𐤐𐤔|
יט 𐤁𐤍𐤉.𐤓𐤇𐤋.𐤀𐤔𐤕.𐤉𐤏𐤒𐤁.𐤉𐤅𐤎𐤐.𐤅𐤁𐤍𐤉𐤌𐤍|
כ 𐤅𐤉𐤅𐤋𐤃.𐤋𐤉𐤅𐤎𐤐.𐤁𐤀𐤓𐤑.𐤌𐤑𐤓𐤉𐤌.𐤀𐤔𐤓.𐤉𐤋𐤃𐤄.
𐤋𐤅.𐤀𐤎𐤍𐤕.𐤁𐤕.𐤐𐤅𐤈𐤉.𐤐𐤓𐤏.𐤊𐤄𐤍.𐤀𐤅𐤍.𐤀𐤕.𐤌𐤍𐤔𐤄.𐤅𐤀𐤕.
𐤀𐤐𐤓𐤉𐤌|
כא 𐤅𐤁𐤍𐤉.𐤁𐤍𐤉𐤌𐤍.𐤁𐤋𐤏.𐤅𐤁𐤊𐤓.𐤅𐤀𐤔𐤁𐤋.𐤂𐤓𐤀.𐤅𐤍𐤏𐤌𐤍.
𐤀𐤇𐤉.𐤅𐤓𐤀𐤔.𐤌𐤐𐤉𐤌.𐤅𐤇𐤐𐤉𐤌.𐤅𐤀𐤓𐤃|

..𐤊𐤁.. 𐤀𐤋𐤄.𐤁𐤍𐤉.𐤓𐤇𐤋.𐤀𐤔𐤓.𐤉𐤋𐤃.𐤋𐤉𐤏𐤒𐤁.𐤊𐤋.𐤍𐤐𐤔.
𐤀𐤓𐤁𐤏𐤄.𐤏𐤔𐤓|

..𐤊𐤂.. 𐤅𐤁𐤍𐤉.𐤃𐤍.𐤇𐤔𐤉𐤌|

..𐤊𐤃.. 𐤅𐤁𐤍𐤉.𐤍𐤐𐤕𐤋𐤉.𐤉𐤇𐤑𐤀𐤋.𐤅𐤂𐤅𐤍𐤉.𐤅𐤉𐤑𐤓.𐤅𐤔𐤋𐤌|

..𐤊𐤄.. 𐤀𐤋𐤄.𐤁𐤍𐤉.𐤁𐤋𐤄𐤄.𐤀𐤔𐤓.𐤍𐤕𐤍.𐤋𐤁𐤍.𐤋𐤓𐤇𐤋.𐤁𐤕𐤅.𐤅
𐤕𐤋𐤃.𐤀𐤕.𐤀𐤋𐤄.𐤋𐤉𐤏𐤒𐤁.𐤊𐤋.𐤍𐤐𐤔.𐤔𐤁𐤏𐤄|

..𐤊𐤅.. 𐤊𐤋.𐤄𐤍𐤐𐤔.𐤄𐤁𐤀𐤄.𐤋𐤉𐤏𐤒𐤁.𐤌𐤑𐤓𐤉𐤌𐤄.𐤉𐤑𐤀𐤉.
𐤉𐤓𐤊𐤅.𐤌𐤋𐤁𐤃.𐤍𐤔𐤉.𐤁𐤍𐤉.𐤉𐤏𐤒𐤁.𐤊𐤋.𐤍𐤐𐤔.𐤔𐤔𐤉𐤌.𐤅𐤔
𐤔|

..𐤊𐤆.. 𐤅𐤁𐤍𐤉.𐤉𐤅𐤎𐤐.𐤀𐤔𐤓.𐤉𐤋𐤃.𐤋𐤅.𐤁𐤌𐤑𐤓𐤉𐤌.𐤍𐤐𐤔.𐤔𐤍
𐤉𐤌.𐤊𐤋.𐤄𐤍𐤐𐤔.𐤋𐤁𐤉𐤕.𐤉𐤏𐤒𐤁.𐤄𐤁𐤀𐤄.𐤌𐤑𐤓𐤉𐤌𐤄.𐤔𐤁
𐤏𐤉𐤌|

..𐤊𐤇.. 𐤅𐤀𐤕.𐤉𐤄𐤅𐤃𐤄.𐤔𐤋𐤇.𐤋𐤐𐤍𐤉𐤅.𐤀𐤋.𐤉𐤅𐤎𐤐.𐤋𐤄𐤅𐤓𐤕.𐤋
𐤐𐤍𐤉𐤅.𐤂𐤔𐤍𐤄.𐤅𐤉𐤁𐤀𐤅.𐤀𐤓𐤑𐤄.𐤂𐤔𐤍|

..𐤊𐤈.. 𐤅𐤉𐤀𐤎𐤓.𐤉𐤅𐤎𐤐.𐤌𐤓𐤊𐤁𐤕𐤅.𐤅𐤉𐤏𐤋.𐤋𐤒𐤓𐤀𐤕.𐤉𐤔𐤓𐤀
𐤋.𐤀𐤁𐤉𐤅.𐤂𐤔𐤍𐤄.𐤅𐤉𐤓𐤀.𐤀𐤋𐤉𐤅.𐤅𐤉𐤐𐤋.𐤏𐤋.𐤑𐤅𐤀𐤓𐤉𐤅.𐤅𐤉𐤁
𐤊.𐤏𐤋.𐤑𐤅𐤀𐤓𐤉𐤅.𐤏𐤅𐤃|

..𐤋.. 𐤅𐤉𐤀𐤌𐤓.𐤉𐤔𐤓𐤀𐤋.𐤀𐤋.𐤉𐤅𐤎𐤐.𐤀𐤌𐤅𐤕𐤄.𐤄𐤐𐤏𐤌.𐤀
𐤇𐤓𐤉.𐤓𐤀𐤅𐤕𐤉.𐤀𐤕.𐤐𐤍𐤉𐤊.𐤊𐤉.𐤏𐤅𐤃𐤊.𐤇𐤉|

..𐤋𐤀.. 𐤅𐤉𐤀𐤌𐤓.𐤉𐤅𐤎𐤐.𐤀𐤋.𐤀𐤇𐤉𐤅.𐤅𐤀𐤋.𐤁𐤉𐤕.𐤀𐤁𐤉𐤅.𐤀𐤏
𐤋𐤄.𐤅𐤀𐤂𐤉𐤃𐤄.𐤋𐤐𐤓𐤏𐤄.𐤅𐤀𐤌𐤓𐤄.𐤀𐤋𐤉𐤅.𐤀𐤇𐤉.𐤅𐤁𐤉𐤕.
𐤀𐤁𐤉.𐤀𐤔𐤓.𐤁𐤀𐤓𐤑.𐤊𐤍𐤏𐤍.𐤁𐤀𐤅.𐤀𐤋𐤉|

..𐤋𐤁.. 𐤅𐤄𐤀𐤍𐤔𐤉𐤌.𐤓𐤏𐤉.𐤑𐤀𐤍.𐤊𐤉.𐤀𐤍𐤔𐤉.𐤌𐤒𐤍𐤄.𐤄𐤉𐤅.
𐤅𐤑𐤀𐤍𐤌.𐤅𐤁𐤒𐤓𐤌.𐤅𐤊𐤋.𐤀𐤔𐤓.𐤋𐤄𐤌.𐤄𐤁𐤉𐤀𐤅|

..𐤋𐤂.. 𐤅𐤄𐤉𐤄.𐤊𐤉.𐤉𐤒𐤓𐤀.𐤋𐤊𐤌.𐤐𐤓𐤏𐤄.𐤅𐤀𐤌𐤓.𐤌𐤄.𐤌𐤏𐤔
𐤉𐤊𐤌|

..𐤋𐤃.. 𐤅𐤀𐤌𐤓𐤕𐤌.𐤀𐤍𐤔𐤉.𐤌𐤒𐤍𐤄.𐤄𐤉𐤅.𐤏𐤁𐤃𐤉𐤊.𐤌𐤍𐤏𐤅𐤓
𐤉𐤍𐤅.𐤅𐤏𐤃.𐤏𐤕𐤄.𐤂𐤌.𐤀𐤍𐤇𐤍𐤅.𐤂𐤌.𐤀𐤁𐤕𐤉𐤍𐤅.𐤁𐤏𐤁𐤅𐤓.
𐤕𐤔𐤁𐤅.𐤁𐤀𐤓𐤑.𐤂𐤔𐤍.𐤊𐤉.𐤕𐤅𐤏𐤁𐤕.𐤌𐤑𐤓𐤉𐤌.𐤊𐤋.𐤓𐤏𐤄.
𐤑𐤀𐤍||

𐤁𐤓𐤀𐤔𐤉𐤕.𐤇𐤋𐤒 𐤌𐤆

𐤀 𐤅𐤉𐤁𐤀.𐤉𐤅𐤎𐤐.𐤅𐤉𐤂𐤃.𐤋𐤐𐤓𐤏𐤄.𐤅𐤉𐤀𐤌𐤓.𐤀𐤁𐤉.𐤅𐤀𐤇
𐤉.𐤅𐤑𐤀𐤍𐤌.𐤅𐤁𐤒𐤓𐤌.𐤅𐤊𐤋.𐤀𐤔𐤓.𐤋𐤄𐤌.𐤁𐤀𐤅.𐤌𐤀𐤓𐤑.𐤊𐤍𐤏
𐤍.𐤅𐤄𐤍𐤌.𐤁𐤀𐤓𐤑.𐤂𐤔𐤍|

𐤁 𐤅𐤌𐤒𐤑𐤄.𐤀𐤇𐤉𐤅.𐤋𐤒𐤇.𐤇𐤌𐤔𐤄.𐤀𐤍𐤔𐤉𐤌.𐤅𐤉𐤑𐤂
𐤌.𐤋𐤐𐤍𐤉.𐤐𐤓𐤏𐤄|

𐤂 𐤅𐤉𐤀𐤌𐤓.𐤐𐤓𐤏𐤄.𐤀𐤋.𐤀𐤇𐤉𐤅.𐤌𐤄.𐤌𐤏𐤔𐤉𐤊𐤌.𐤅𐤉𐤀𐤌
𐤓𐤅.𐤀𐤋.𐤐𐤓𐤏𐤄.𐤓𐤏𐤄.𐤑𐤀𐤍.𐤏𐤁𐤃𐤉𐤊.𐤂𐤌.𐤀𐤍𐤇𐤍𐤅.𐤂𐤌.
𐤀𐤁𐤅𐤕𐤉𐤍𐤅|

𐤃 𐤅𐤉𐤀𐤌𐤓𐤅.𐤀𐤋.𐤐𐤓𐤏𐤄.𐤋𐤂𐤅𐤓.𐤁𐤀𐤓𐤑.𐤁𐤀𐤍𐤅.𐤊𐤉.𐤀𐤉
𐤍.𐤌𐤓𐤏𐤄.𐤋𐤑𐤀𐤍.𐤀𐤔𐤓.𐤋𐤏𐤁𐤃𐤉𐤊.𐤊𐤉.𐤊𐤁𐤃.𐤄𐤓𐤏𐤁.𐤁
𐤀𐤓𐤑.𐤊𐤍𐤏𐤍.𐤅𐤏𐤕𐤄.𐤉𐤔𐤁𐤅.𐤍𐤀.𐤏𐤁𐤃𐤉𐤊.𐤁𐤀𐤓𐤑.𐤂𐤔
𐤍|

𐤄 𐤅𐤉𐤀𐤌𐤓.𐤐𐤓𐤏𐤄.𐤀𐤋.𐤉𐤅𐤎𐤐.𐤋𐤀𐤌𐤓.𐤀𐤁𐤉𐤊.𐤅𐤀𐤇𐤉𐤊.
𐤁𐤀𐤅.𐤀𐤋𐤉𐤊|

𐤅 𐤀𐤓𐤑.𐤌𐤑𐤓𐤉𐤌.𐤋𐤐𐤍𐤉𐤊.𐤄𐤅𐤀.𐤁𐤌𐤉𐤈𐤁.𐤄𐤀𐤓𐤑.𐤄𐤅
𐤔𐤁.𐤀𐤕.𐤀𐤁𐤉𐤊.𐤅𐤀𐤕.𐤀𐤇𐤉𐤊.𐤉𐤔𐤁𐤅.𐤁𐤀𐤓𐤑.𐤂𐤔𐤍.𐤅𐤀
𐤌.𐤉𐤃𐤏𐤕.𐤅𐤉𐤔.𐤁𐤌.𐤀𐤍𐤔𐤉.𐤇𐤉𐤋.𐤅𐤔𐤌𐤕𐤌.𐤔𐤓𐤉.𐤌𐤒𐤍
𐤄.𐤏𐤋.𐤀𐤔𐤓.𐤋𐤉|

𐤆 𐤅𐤉𐤁𐤀.𐤉𐤅𐤎𐤐.𐤀𐤕.𐤉𐤏𐤒𐤁.𐤀𐤁𐤉𐤅.𐤅𐤉𐤏𐤌𐤃𐤄𐤅.𐤋𐤐𐤍
𐤉.𐤐𐤓𐤏𐤄.𐤅𐤉𐤁𐤓𐤊.𐤉𐤏𐤒𐤁.𐤀𐤕.𐤐𐤓𐤏𐤄|

𐤇 𐤅𐤉𐤀𐤌𐤓.𐤐𐤓𐤏𐤄.𐤀𐤋.𐤉𐤏𐤒𐤁.𐤊𐤌𐤄.𐤉𐤌𐤉.𐤔𐤍𐤉.𐤇𐤉𐤉
𐤊|

𐤈 𐤅𐤉𐤀𐤌𐤓.𐤉𐤏𐤒𐤁.𐤀𐤋.𐤐𐤓𐤏𐤄.𐤉𐤌𐤉.𐤔𐤍𐤉.𐤌𐤂𐤅𐤓𐤉.𐤔
𐤋𐤔𐤉𐤌.𐤅𐤌𐤀𐤕.𐤔𐤍𐤄.𐤌𐤏𐤈.𐤅𐤓𐤏𐤉𐤌.𐤄𐤉𐤅.𐤉𐤌𐤉.𐤔𐤍𐤉.𐤇
𐤉𐤉.𐤅𐤋𐤀.𐤄𐤔𐤉𐤂𐤅.𐤀𐤕.𐤉𐤌𐤉.𐤔𐤍𐤉.𐤇𐤉𐤉.𐤀𐤁𐤕𐤉.𐤁𐤉𐤌
𐤉.𐤌𐤂𐤅𐤓𐤉𐤄𐤌|

𐤉 𐤅𐤉𐤁𐤓𐤊.𐤉𐤏𐤒𐤁.𐤀𐤕.𐤐𐤓𐤏𐤄.𐤅𐤉𐤑𐤀.𐤌𐤋𐤐𐤍𐤉.𐤐𐤓𐤏
𐤄|

𐤉𐤀 𐤅𐤉𐤅𐤔𐤁.𐤉𐤅𐤎𐤐.𐤀𐤕.𐤀𐤁𐤉𐤅.𐤅𐤀𐤕.𐤀𐤇𐤉𐤅.𐤅𐤉𐤕𐤍.𐤋𐤄
𐤌.𐤀𐤇𐤆𐤄.𐤁𐤀𐤓𐤑.𐤌𐤑𐤓𐤉𐤌.𐤁𐤌𐤉𐤈𐤁.𐤄𐤀𐤓𐤑.𐤁𐤀𐤓𐤑
.𐤓𐤏𐤌𐤎𐤎.𐤊𐤀𐤔𐤓.𐤑𐤅𐤄.𐤐𐤓𐤏𐤄|
𐤉𐤁 𐤅𐤉𐤊𐤋𐤊𐤋.𐤉𐤅𐤎𐤐.𐤀𐤕.𐤀𐤁𐤉𐤅.𐤅𐤀𐤕.𐤀𐤇𐤉𐤅.𐤅𐤀𐤕.𐤊𐤋
.𐤁𐤉𐤕.𐤀𐤁𐤉𐤅.𐤋𐤇𐤌.𐤋𐤐𐤉.𐤄𐤈𐤐|
𐤉𐤂 𐤅𐤋𐤇𐤌.𐤀𐤉𐤍.𐤁𐤊𐤋.𐤄𐤀𐤓𐤑.𐤊𐤉.𐤊𐤁𐤃.𐤄𐤓𐤏𐤁.𐤌𐤀
𐤃.𐤅𐤕𐤋𐤄.𐤀𐤓𐤑.𐤌𐤑𐤓𐤉𐤌.𐤅𐤀𐤓𐤑.𐤊𐤍𐤏𐤍.𐤌𐤐𐤍𐤉.𐤄𐤓𐤏𐤁|
𐤉𐤃 𐤅𐤉𐤋𐤒𐤈.𐤉𐤅𐤎𐤐.𐤀𐤕.𐤊𐤋.𐤄𐤊𐤎𐤐.𐤄𐤍𐤌𐤑𐤀.𐤁𐤀𐤓𐤑
.𐤌𐤑𐤓𐤉𐤌.𐤅𐤁𐤀𐤓𐤑.𐤊𐤍𐤏𐤍.𐤁𐤔𐤁𐤓.𐤀𐤔𐤓.𐤄𐤌.𐤔𐤁𐤓𐤉𐤌.𐤅
𐤉𐤁𐤀.𐤉𐤅𐤎𐤐.𐤀𐤕.𐤄𐤊𐤎𐤐.𐤁𐤉𐤕𐤄.𐤐𐤓𐤏𐤄|
𐤉𐤄 𐤅𐤉𐤕𐤌.𐤄𐤊𐤎𐤐.𐤌𐤀𐤓𐤑.𐤌𐤑𐤓𐤉𐤌.𐤅𐤌𐤀𐤓𐤑.𐤊𐤍𐤏𐤍.𐤅
𐤉𐤁𐤀𐤅.𐤊𐤋.𐤌𐤑𐤓𐤉𐤌.𐤀𐤋.𐤉𐤅𐤎𐤐.𐤋𐤀𐤌𐤓.𐤄𐤁𐤄.𐤋𐤍𐤅.𐤋𐤇𐤌.
𐤅𐤋𐤌𐤄.𐤍𐤌𐤅𐤕.𐤍𐤂𐤃𐤊.𐤊𐤉.𐤀𐤐𐤎.𐤊𐤎𐤐|
𐤉𐤅 𐤅𐤉𐤀𐤌𐤓.𐤉𐤅𐤎𐤐.𐤄𐤁𐤅.𐤌𐤒𐤍𐤉𐤊𐤌.𐤅𐤀𐤕𐤍𐤄.𐤋𐤊𐤌.𐤁𐤌
𐤒𐤍𐤉𐤊𐤌.𐤀𐤌.𐤀𐤐𐤎.𐤊𐤎𐤐|
𐤉𐤆 𐤅𐤉𐤁𐤉𐤀𐤅.𐤀𐤕.𐤌𐤒𐤍𐤉𐤄𐤌.𐤀𐤋.𐤉𐤅𐤎𐤐.𐤅𐤉𐤕𐤍.𐤋𐤄𐤌.
𐤉𐤅𐤎𐤐.𐤋𐤇𐤌.𐤁𐤎𐤅𐤎𐤉𐤌.𐤅𐤁𐤌𐤒𐤍𐤄.𐤄𐤑𐤀𐤍.𐤅𐤁𐤌𐤒𐤍𐤄.𐤄
𐤁𐤒𐤓.𐤅𐤁𐤇𐤌𐤓𐤉𐤌.𐤅𐤉𐤍𐤄𐤋𐤌.𐤁𐤋𐤇𐤌.𐤁𐤊𐤋.𐤌𐤒𐤍𐤄𐤌.𐤁𐤔
𐤍𐤄.𐤄𐤄𐤅𐤀|
𐤉𐤇 𐤅𐤕𐤕𐤌.𐤄𐤔𐤍𐤄.𐤄𐤄𐤅𐤀.𐤅𐤉𐤁𐤀𐤅.𐤀𐤋𐤉𐤅.𐤁𐤔𐤍𐤄.𐤄𐤔𐤍
𐤉𐤕.𐤅𐤉𐤀𐤌𐤓𐤅.𐤋𐤅.𐤋𐤀.𐤍𐤊𐤇𐤃.𐤌𐤀𐤃𐤍𐤉.𐤊𐤉.𐤀𐤌.𐤕𐤌.𐤄
𐤊𐤎𐤐.𐤅𐤌𐤒𐤍𐤄.𐤄𐤁𐤄𐤌𐤄.𐤀𐤋.𐤀𐤃𐤍𐤉.𐤋𐤀.𐤍𐤔𐤀𐤓.𐤋𐤐𐤍𐤉.
𐤀𐤃𐤍𐤉.𐤁𐤋𐤕𐤉.𐤀𐤌.𐤂𐤅𐤉𐤕𐤍𐤅.𐤅𐤀𐤃𐤌𐤕𐤍𐤅|
𐤉𐤈 𐤋𐤌𐤄.𐤍𐤌𐤅𐤕.𐤋𐤏𐤉𐤍𐤉𐤊.𐤂𐤌.𐤀𐤍𐤇𐤍𐤅.𐤂𐤌.𐤀𐤃𐤌𐤕
𐤍𐤅.𐤒𐤍𐤄.𐤀𐤕𐤍𐤅.𐤅𐤀𐤕.𐤀𐤃𐤌𐤕𐤍𐤅.𐤁𐤋𐤇𐤌.𐤅𐤍𐤄𐤉𐤄.𐤀𐤍𐤇𐤍
𐤅.𐤅𐤀𐤃𐤌𐤕𐤍𐤅.𐤏𐤁𐤃𐤉𐤌.𐤋𐤐𐤓𐤏𐤄.𐤅𐤕𐤍.𐤆𐤓𐤏.𐤅𐤍𐤇𐤉𐤄.𐤅𐤋
𐤀.𐤍𐤌𐤅𐤕.𐤅𐤄𐤀𐤃𐤌𐤄.𐤋𐤀.𐤕𐤔𐤌|
𐤊 𐤅𐤉𐤒𐤍.𐤉𐤅𐤎𐤐.𐤀𐤕.𐤊𐤋.𐤀𐤃𐤌𐤕.𐤌𐤑𐤓𐤉𐤌.𐤋𐤐𐤓𐤏𐤄.
𐤊𐤉.𐤌𐤊𐤓𐤅.𐤌𐤑𐤓𐤉𐤌.𐤀𐤉𐤔.𐤔𐤃𐤄𐤅.𐤊𐤉.𐤇𐤆𐤒.𐤏𐤋𐤄𐤌.
𐤄𐤓𐤏𐤁.𐤅𐤕𐤄𐤉.𐤄𐤀𐤓𐤑.𐤋𐤐𐤓𐤏𐤄|

𐤊𐤀 𐤅𐤀𐤕.𐤄𐤏𐤌.𐤄𐤏𐤁𐤉𐤓.𐤀𐤕𐤅.𐤋𐤏𐤓𐤉𐤌.𐤌𐤒𐤑𐤄.𐤂𐤁𐤅
𐤋.𐤌𐤑𐤓𐤉𐤌.𐤅𐤏𐤃.𐤒𐤑𐤄𐤅|

𐤊𐤁 𐤓𐤒.𐤀𐤃𐤌𐤕.𐤄𐤊𐤄𐤍𐤉𐤌.𐤋𐤀.𐤒𐤍𐤄.𐤊𐤉.𐤇𐤒.𐤋𐤊𐤄𐤍
𐤉𐤌.𐤌𐤀𐤕.𐤐𐤓𐤏𐤄.𐤅𐤀𐤊𐤋𐤅.𐤀𐤕.𐤇𐤒𐤌.𐤀𐤔𐤓.𐤍𐤕𐤍.𐤋𐤄𐤌.
𐤐𐤓𐤏𐤄.𐤏𐤋.𐤊𐤍.𐤋𐤀.𐤌𐤊𐤓𐤅.𐤀𐤕.𐤀𐤃𐤌𐤕𐤌|

𐤊𐤂 𐤅𐤉𐤀𐤌𐤓.𐤉𐤅𐤎𐤐.𐤀𐤋.𐤄𐤏𐤌.𐤄𐤍.𐤒𐤍𐤉𐤕𐤉.𐤀𐤕𐤊𐤌.𐤄
𐤉𐤅𐤌.𐤅𐤀𐤕.𐤀𐤃𐤌𐤕𐤊𐤌.𐤋𐤐𐤓𐤏𐤄.𐤄𐤀.𐤋𐤊𐤌.𐤆𐤓𐤏.𐤅𐤆𐤓
𐤏𐤕𐤌.𐤀𐤕.𐤄𐤀𐤃𐤌𐤄|

𐤊𐤃 𐤅𐤄𐤉𐤄.𐤁𐤕𐤁𐤅𐤀𐤕.𐤅𐤍𐤕𐤕𐤌.𐤇𐤌𐤉𐤔𐤉𐤕.𐤋𐤐𐤓𐤏𐤄.𐤅
𐤀𐤓𐤁𐤏.𐤄𐤉𐤃𐤕.𐤉𐤄𐤉𐤄.𐤋𐤊𐤌.𐤋𐤆𐤓𐤏.𐤄𐤔𐤃𐤄.𐤅𐤋𐤀𐤊𐤋
𐤊𐤌.𐤅𐤋𐤀𐤔𐤓.𐤁𐤁𐤕𐤉𐤊𐤌.𐤅𐤋𐤀𐤊𐤋.𐤋𐤈𐤐𐤊𐤌|

𐤊𐤄 𐤅𐤉𐤀𐤌𐤓𐤅.𐤄𐤇𐤉𐤕𐤍𐤅.𐤍𐤌𐤑𐤀.𐤇𐤍.𐤁𐤏𐤉𐤍𐤉.𐤀𐤃𐤍𐤉.
𐤅𐤄𐤉𐤉𐤍𐤅.𐤏𐤁𐤃𐤉𐤌.𐤋𐤐𐤓𐤏𐤄|

𐤊𐤅 𐤅𐤉𐤔𐤌.𐤀𐤕𐤄.𐤉𐤅𐤎𐤐.𐤋𐤇𐤒.𐤏𐤃.𐤄𐤉𐤅𐤌.𐤄𐤆𐤄.𐤏𐤋
.𐤀𐤃𐤌𐤕.𐤌𐤑𐤓𐤉𐤌.𐤋𐤐𐤓𐤏𐤄.𐤋𐤇𐤌𐤔.𐤓𐤒.𐤀𐤃𐤌𐤕.𐤄𐤊𐤄
𐤍𐤉𐤌.𐤋𐤁𐤃𐤌.𐤋𐤀.𐤄𐤉𐤕𐤄.𐤋𐤐𐤓𐤏𐤄|

𐤊𐤆 𐤅𐤉𐤔𐤁.𐤉𐤔𐤓𐤀𐤋.𐤁𐤀𐤓𐤑.𐤌𐤑𐤓𐤉𐤌.𐤁𐤀𐤓𐤑.𐤂𐤔𐤍.𐤅
𐤉𐤀𐤇𐤆𐤅.𐤁𐤄.𐤅𐤉𐤐𐤓𐤅.𐤅𐤉𐤓𐤁𐤅.𐤌𐤀𐤃|

𐤊𐤇 𐤅𐤉𐤇𐤉.𐤉𐤏𐤒𐤁.𐤁𐤀𐤓𐤑.𐤌𐤑𐤓𐤉𐤌.𐤔𐤁𐤏.𐤏𐤔𐤓𐤄.𐤔
𐤍𐤄.𐤅𐤉𐤄𐤉.𐤉𐤌𐤉.𐤉𐤏𐤒𐤁.𐤔𐤍𐤉.𐤇𐤉𐤉𐤅.𐤔𐤁𐤏.𐤔𐤍𐤉𐤌.𐤅𐤀
𐤓𐤁𐤏𐤉𐤌.𐤅𐤌𐤀𐤕.𐤔𐤍𐤄|

𐤊𐤈 𐤅𐤉𐤒𐤓𐤁𐤅.𐤉𐤌𐤉.𐤉𐤔𐤓𐤀𐤋.𐤋𐤌𐤅𐤕.𐤅𐤉𐤒𐤓𐤀.𐤋𐤁𐤍𐤅.𐤋
𐤉𐤅𐤎𐤐.𐤅𐤉𐤀𐤌𐤓.𐤋𐤅.𐤀𐤌.𐤍𐤀.𐤌𐤑𐤀𐤕𐤉.𐤇𐤍.𐤁𐤏𐤉𐤍𐤉𐤊.𐤔𐤉
𐤌.𐤍𐤀.𐤉𐤃𐤊.𐤕𐤇𐤕.𐤉𐤓𐤊𐤉.𐤅𐤏𐤔𐤉𐤕.𐤏𐤌𐤃𐤉.𐤇𐤎𐤃.𐤅𐤀
𐤌𐤕.𐤀𐤋.𐤍𐤀.𐤕𐤒𐤁𐤓𐤍𐤉.𐤁𐤌𐤑𐤓𐤉𐤌|

𐤋 𐤅𐤔𐤊𐤁𐤕𐤉.𐤏𐤌.𐤀𐤁𐤕𐤉.𐤅𐤍𐤔𐤀𐤕𐤍𐤉.𐤌𐤌𐤑𐤓𐤉𐤌.𐤅
𐤒𐤁𐤓𐤕𐤍𐤉.𐤁𐤒𐤁𐤓𐤕𐤌.𐤅𐤉𐤀𐤌𐤓.𐤀𐤍𐤊𐤉.𐤀𐤏𐤔𐤄.𐤊𐤃𐤁𐤓
𐤊|

𐤋𐤀 𐤅𐤉𐤀𐤌𐤓.𐤄𐤔𐤁𐤏𐤄.𐤋𐤉.𐤅𐤉𐤔𐤁𐤏.𐤋𐤅.𐤅𐤉𐤔𐤕𐤇𐤅.𐤉𐤔
𐤓𐤀𐤋.𐤏𐤋.𐤓𐤀𐤔.𐤄𐤌𐤈𐤄||

𐤁𐤓𐤀𐤔𐤉𐤕.𐤇𐤋𐤒 ..מח..

א 𐤅𐤉𐤄𐤉.𐤀𐤇𐤓𐤉.𐤄𐤃𐤁𐤓𐤉𐤌.𐤄𐤀𐤋𐤄.𐤅𐤉𐤀𐤌𐤓.𐤋𐤉𐤅𐤎𐤐.
𐤄𐤍𐤄.𐤀𐤁𐤉𐤊.𐤇𐤋𐤄.𐤅𐤉𐤒𐤇.𐤀𐤕.𐤔𐤍𐤉.𐤁𐤍𐤉𐤅.𐤏𐤌𐤅.𐤀𐤕.
𐤌𐤍𐤔𐤄.𐤅𐤀𐤕.𐤀𐤐𐤓𐤉𐤌|
ב 𐤅𐤉𐤂𐤃.𐤋𐤉𐤏𐤒𐤁.𐤅𐤉𐤀𐤌𐤓.𐤄𐤍𐤄.𐤁𐤍𐤊.𐤉𐤅𐤎𐤐.𐤁𐤀.𐤀𐤋
𐤉𐤊.𐤅𐤉𐤕𐤇𐤆𐤒.𐤉𐤔𐤓𐤀𐤋.𐤅𐤉𐤔𐤁.𐤏𐤋.𐤄𐤌𐤈𐤄|
ג 𐤅𐤉𐤀𐤌𐤓.𐤉𐤏𐤒𐤁.𐤀𐤋.𐤉𐤅𐤎𐤐.𐤀𐤋.𐤔𐤃𐤉.𐤍𐤓𐤀𐤄.𐤀𐤋𐤉.
𐤁𐤋𐤅𐤆.𐤁𐤀𐤓𐤑.𐤊𐤍𐤏𐤍.𐤅𐤉𐤁𐤓𐤊.𐤀𐤕𐤉|
ד 𐤅𐤉𐤀𐤌𐤓.𐤀𐤋𐤉.𐤄𐤍𐤍𐤉.𐤌𐤐𐤓𐤊.𐤅𐤄𐤓𐤁𐤉𐤕𐤊.𐤅𐤍𐤕𐤕𐤉𐤊.
𐤋𐤒𐤄𐤋.𐤏𐤌𐤉𐤌.𐤅𐤍𐤕𐤕𐤉.𐤀𐤕.𐤄𐤀𐤓𐤑.𐤄𐤆𐤀𐤕.𐤋𐤆𐤓𐤏𐤊
.𐤀𐤇𐤓𐤉𐤊.𐤀𐤇𐤆𐤕.𐤏𐤅𐤋𐤌|
ה 𐤅𐤏𐤕𐤄.𐤔𐤍𐤉.𐤁𐤍𐤉𐤊.𐤄𐤍𐤅𐤋𐤃𐤉𐤌.𐤋𐤊.𐤁𐤀𐤓𐤑.𐤌𐤑𐤓𐤉
𐤌.𐤏𐤃.𐤁𐤀𐤉.𐤀𐤋𐤉𐤊.𐤌𐤑𐤓𐤉𐤌𐤄.𐤋𐤉.𐤄𐤌.𐤀𐤐𐤓𐤉𐤌.𐤅𐤌𐤍
𐤔𐤄.𐤊𐤓𐤀𐤅𐤁𐤍.𐤅𐤔𐤌𐤏𐤅𐤍.𐤉𐤄𐤉𐤅.𐤋𐤉|
ו 𐤅𐤌𐤅𐤋𐤃𐤕𐤊.𐤀𐤔𐤓.𐤄𐤅𐤋𐤃𐤕.𐤀𐤇𐤓𐤉𐤄𐤌.𐤋𐤊.𐤉𐤄𐤉𐤅.
𐤏𐤋.𐤔𐤌.𐤀𐤇𐤉𐤄𐤌.𐤉𐤒𐤓𐤀𐤅.𐤁𐤍𐤇𐤋𐤕𐤌|
ז 𐤅𐤀𐤍𐤉.𐤁𐤁𐤀𐤉.𐤌𐤐𐤃𐤍.𐤌𐤕𐤄.𐤏𐤋𐤉.𐤓𐤇𐤋.𐤁𐤀𐤓𐤑.𐤊𐤍
𐤏𐤍.𐤁𐤃𐤓𐤊.𐤁𐤏𐤅𐤃.𐤊𐤁𐤓𐤕.𐤀𐤓𐤑.𐤋𐤁𐤀.𐤀𐤐𐤓𐤕𐤄.𐤅𐤀𐤒𐤁
𐤓𐤄.𐤔𐤌.𐤁𐤃𐤓𐤊.𐤀𐤐𐤓𐤕.𐤄𐤅𐤀.𐤁𐤉𐤕.𐤋𐤇𐤌|
ח 𐤅𐤉𐤓𐤀.𐤉𐤔𐤓𐤀𐤋.𐤀𐤕.𐤁𐤍𐤉.𐤉𐤅𐤎𐤐.𐤅𐤉𐤀𐤌𐤓.𐤌𐤉.𐤀𐤋𐤄|
ט 𐤅𐤉𐤀𐤌𐤓.𐤉𐤅𐤎𐤐.𐤀𐤋.𐤀𐤁𐤉𐤅.𐤁𐤍𐤉.𐤄𐤌.𐤀𐤔𐤓.𐤍𐤕𐤍.𐤋𐤉.
𐤀𐤋𐤄𐤉𐤌.𐤁𐤆𐤄.𐤅𐤉𐤀𐤌𐤓.𐤒𐤇𐤌.𐤍𐤀.𐤀𐤋𐤉.𐤅𐤀𐤁𐤓𐤊𐤌|
י 𐤅𐤏𐤉𐤍𐤉.𐤉𐤔𐤓𐤀𐤋.𐤊𐤁𐤃𐤅.𐤌𐤆𐤒𐤍.𐤋𐤀.𐤉𐤅𐤊𐤋.𐤋𐤓𐤀
𐤅𐤕.𐤅𐤉𐤂𐤔.𐤀𐤕𐤌.𐤀𐤋𐤉𐤅.𐤅𐤉𐤔𐤒.𐤋𐤄𐤌.𐤅𐤉𐤇𐤁𐤒.𐤋𐤄𐤌|
יא 𐤅𐤉𐤀𐤌𐤓.𐤉𐤔𐤓𐤀𐤋.𐤀𐤋.𐤉𐤅𐤎𐤐.𐤓𐤀𐤄.𐤐𐤍𐤉𐤊.𐤋𐤀.𐤐𐤋𐤋
𐤕𐤉.𐤅𐤄𐤍𐤄.𐤄𐤓𐤀𐤄.𐤀𐤕𐤉.𐤀𐤋𐤄𐤉𐤌.𐤂𐤌.𐤀𐤕.𐤆𐤓𐤏𐤊|
יב 𐤅𐤉𐤅𐤑𐤀.𐤉𐤅𐤎𐤐.𐤀𐤕𐤌.𐤌𐤏𐤌.𐤁𐤓𐤊𐤉𐤅.𐤅𐤉𐤔𐤕𐤇𐤅.𐤋
𐤀𐤐𐤉𐤅.𐤀𐤓𐤑𐤄|

..יג.. 𐤅𐤉𐤒𐤇.𐤉𐤅𐤎𐤐.𐤀𐤕.𐤔𐤍𐤉𐤄𐤌.𐤀𐤕.𐤀𐤐𐤓𐤉𐤌.𐤁𐤉𐤌𐤉
𐤍𐤅.𐤌𐤔𐤌𐤀𐤋.𐤉𐤔𐤓𐤀𐤋.𐤅𐤀𐤕.𐤌𐤍𐤔𐤄.𐤁𐤔𐤌𐤀𐤋𐤅.𐤌𐤉𐤌𐤉𐤍.
𐤉𐤔𐤓𐤀𐤋.𐤅𐤉𐤂𐤔.𐤀𐤋𐤉𐤅|

..יד.. 𐤅𐤉𐤔𐤋𐤇.𐤉𐤔𐤓𐤀𐤋.𐤀𐤕.𐤉𐤌𐤉𐤍𐤅.𐤅𐤉𐤔𐤕.𐤏𐤋.𐤓𐤀𐤔.
𐤀𐤐𐤓𐤉𐤌.𐤅𐤄𐤅𐤀.𐤄𐤑𐤏𐤉𐤓.𐤅𐤀𐤕.𐤔𐤌𐤀𐤋𐤅.𐤏𐤋.𐤓𐤀𐤔.𐤌𐤍𐤔
𐤄.𐤔𐤊𐤋.𐤀𐤕.𐤉𐤃𐤉𐤅.𐤊𐤉.𐤌𐤍𐤔𐤄.𐤄𐤁𐤊𐤅𐤓|

..טו.. 𐤅𐤉𐤁𐤓𐤊.𐤀𐤕.𐤉𐤅𐤎𐤐.𐤅𐤉𐤀𐤌𐤓.𐤄𐤀𐤋𐤄𐤉𐤌.𐤀𐤔𐤓.𐤄𐤕𐤄
𐤋𐤊𐤅.𐤀𐤁𐤕𐤉.𐤋𐤐𐤍𐤉𐤅.𐤀𐤁𐤓𐤄𐤌.𐤅𐤉𐤑𐤇𐤒.𐤄𐤀𐤋𐤄𐤉𐤌.𐤄
𐤓𐤏𐤄.𐤀𐤕𐤉.𐤌𐤏𐤅𐤃𐤉.𐤏𐤃.𐤄𐤉𐤅𐤌.𐤄𐤆𐤄|

..טז.. 𐤄𐤌𐤋𐤀𐤊.𐤄𐤂𐤀𐤋.𐤀𐤕𐤉.𐤌𐤊𐤋.𐤓𐤏.𐤉𐤁𐤓𐤊.𐤀𐤕.𐤄𐤍
𐤏𐤓𐤉𐤌.𐤅𐤉𐤒𐤓𐤀.𐤁𐤄𐤌.𐤔𐤌𐤉.𐤅𐤔𐤌.𐤀𐤁𐤕𐤉.𐤀𐤁𐤓𐤄𐤌.𐤅𐤉
𐤑𐤇𐤒.𐤅𐤉𐤃𐤂𐤅.𐤋𐤓𐤁.𐤁𐤒𐤓𐤁.𐤄𐤀𐤓𐤑|

..יז.. 𐤅𐤉𐤓𐤀.𐤉𐤅𐤎𐤐.𐤊𐤉.𐤉𐤔𐤉𐤕.𐤀𐤁𐤉𐤅.𐤉𐤃.𐤉𐤌𐤉𐤍𐤅.𐤏𐤋.
𐤓𐤀𐤔.𐤀𐤐𐤓𐤉𐤌.𐤅𐤉𐤓𐤏.𐤁𐤏𐤉𐤍𐤉𐤅.𐤅𐤉𐤕𐤌𐤊.𐤉𐤃.𐤀𐤁𐤉𐤅.𐤋𐤄
𐤎𐤉𐤓.𐤀𐤕𐤄.𐤌𐤏𐤋.𐤓𐤀𐤔.𐤀𐤐𐤓𐤉𐤌.𐤏𐤋.𐤓𐤀𐤔.𐤌𐤍𐤔𐤄|

..יח.. 𐤅𐤉𐤀𐤌𐤓.𐤉𐤅𐤎𐤐.𐤀𐤋.𐤀𐤁𐤉𐤅.𐤋𐤀.𐤊𐤍.𐤀𐤁𐤉.𐤊𐤉.𐤆𐤄.
𐤄𐤁𐤊𐤓.𐤔𐤉𐤌.𐤉𐤌𐤉𐤍𐤊.𐤏𐤋.𐤓𐤀𐤔𐤅|

..יט.. 𐤅𐤉𐤌𐤀𐤍.𐤀𐤁𐤉𐤅.𐤅𐤉𐤀𐤌𐤓.𐤉𐤃𐤏𐤕𐤉.𐤁𐤍𐤉.𐤉𐤃𐤏𐤕
𐤉.𐤂𐤌.𐤄𐤅𐤀.𐤉𐤄𐤉𐤄.𐤋𐤏𐤌.𐤅𐤂𐤌.𐤄𐤅𐤀.𐤉𐤂𐤃𐤋.𐤅𐤀𐤅𐤋𐤌.
𐤀𐤇𐤉𐤅.𐤄𐤒𐤈𐤍.𐤉𐤂𐤃𐤋.𐤌𐤌𐤍𐤅.𐤅𐤆𐤓𐤏𐤅.𐤉𐤄𐤉𐤄.𐤌𐤋𐤀.𐤄
𐤂𐤅𐤉𐤌|

..כ.. 𐤅𐤉𐤁𐤓𐤊𐤌.𐤁𐤉𐤅𐤌.𐤄𐤄𐤅𐤀.𐤋𐤀𐤌𐤅𐤓.𐤁𐤊.𐤉𐤁𐤓𐤊.𐤉𐤔𐤓
𐤀𐤋.𐤋𐤀𐤌𐤓.𐤉𐤔𐤌𐤊.𐤀𐤋𐤄𐤉𐤌.𐤊𐤀𐤐𐤓𐤉𐤌.𐤅𐤊𐤌𐤍𐤔𐤄.𐤅𐤉𐤔
𐤌.𐤀𐤕.𐤀𐤐𐤓𐤉𐤌.𐤋𐤐𐤍𐤉.𐤌𐤍𐤔𐤄|

..כא.. 𐤅𐤉𐤀𐤌𐤓.𐤉𐤔𐤓𐤀𐤋.𐤀𐤋.𐤉𐤅𐤎𐤐.𐤄𐤍𐤄.𐤀𐤍𐤊𐤉.𐤌𐤕.𐤅𐤄
𐤉𐤄.𐤀𐤋𐤄𐤉𐤌.𐤏𐤌𐤊𐤌.𐤅𐤄𐤔𐤉𐤁.𐤀𐤕𐤊𐤌.𐤀𐤋.𐤀𐤓𐤑.𐤀𐤁𐤕
𐤉𐤊𐤌|

..כב.. 𐤅𐤀𐤍𐤉.𐤍𐤕𐤕𐤉.𐤋𐤊.𐤔𐤊𐤌.𐤀𐤇𐤃.𐤏𐤋.𐤀𐤇𐤉𐤊.𐤀𐤔𐤓
.𐤋𐤒𐤇𐤕𐤉.𐤌𐤉𐤃.𐤄𐤀𐤌𐤓𐤉.𐤁𐤇𐤓𐤁𐤉.𐤅𐤁𐤒𐤔𐤕𐤉||

𐤁𐤓𐤀𐤔𐤉𐤕.𐤇𐤋𐤒 ..מח..

1 𐤅𐤉𐤒𐤓𐤀.𐤉𐤏𐤒𐤁.𐤀𐤋.𐤁𐤍𐤉𐤅.𐤅𐤉𐤀𐤌𐤓.𐤄𐤀𐤎𐤐𐤅.𐤅𐤀𐤂𐤉
𐤃𐤄.𐤋𐤊𐤌.𐤀𐤕.𐤀𐤔𐤓.𐤉𐤒𐤓𐤀.𐤀𐤕𐤊𐤌.𐤁𐤀𐤇𐤓𐤉𐤕.𐤄𐤉𐤌
𐤉𐤌|

2 𐤄𐤒𐤁𐤑𐤅.𐤅𐤔𐤌𐤏𐤅.𐤁𐤍𐤉.𐤉𐤏𐤒𐤁.𐤅𐤔𐤌𐤏𐤅.𐤀𐤋.𐤉𐤔𐤓𐤀
𐤋.𐤀𐤁𐤉𐤊𐤌|

3 𐤓𐤀𐤅𐤁𐤍.𐤁𐤊𐤓𐤉.𐤀𐤕𐤄.𐤊𐤇𐤉.𐤅𐤓𐤀𐤔𐤉𐤕.𐤀𐤅𐤍𐤉.𐤉𐤕𐤓.
𐤔𐤀𐤕.𐤅𐤉𐤕𐤓.𐤏𐤆|

4 𐤐𐤇𐤆.𐤊𐤌𐤉𐤌.𐤀𐤋.𐤕𐤅𐤕𐤓.𐤊𐤉.𐤏𐤋𐤉𐤕.𐤌𐤔𐤊𐤁𐤉.𐤀
𐤁𐤉𐤊.𐤀𐤆.𐤇𐤋𐤋𐤕.𐤉𐤑𐤅𐤏𐤉.𐤏𐤋𐤄|

5 𐤔𐤌𐤏𐤅𐤍.𐤅𐤋𐤅𐤉.𐤀𐤇𐤉𐤌.𐤊𐤋𐤉.𐤇𐤌𐤎.𐤌𐤊𐤓𐤕𐤉𐤄𐤌|

6 𐤁𐤎𐤃𐤌.𐤀𐤋.𐤕𐤁𐤀.𐤍𐤐𐤔𐤉.𐤁𐤒𐤄𐤋𐤌.𐤀𐤋.𐤕𐤇𐤃.𐤊𐤁
𐤃𐤉.𐤊𐤉.𐤁𐤀𐤐𐤌.𐤄𐤓𐤂𐤅.𐤀𐤉𐤔.𐤅𐤁𐤓𐤑𐤍𐤌.𐤏𐤒𐤓𐤅.𐤔𐤅𐤓|

7 𐤀𐤓𐤅𐤓.𐤀𐤐𐤌.𐤊𐤉.𐤏𐤆.𐤅𐤏𐤁𐤓𐤕𐤌.𐤊𐤉.𐤒𐤔𐤕𐤄.𐤀𐤇𐤋
𐤒𐤌.𐤁𐤉𐤏𐤒𐤁.𐤅𐤀𐤐𐤉𐤑𐤌.𐤁𐤉𐤔𐤓𐤀𐤋|

8 𐤉𐤄𐤅𐤃𐤄.𐤀𐤕𐤄.𐤉𐤅𐤃𐤅𐤊.𐤀𐤇𐤉𐤊.𐤉𐤃𐤊.𐤁𐤏𐤓𐤐.𐤀𐤉
𐤁𐤉𐤊.𐤉𐤔𐤕𐤇𐤅𐤅.𐤋𐤊.𐤁𐤍𐤉.𐤀𐤁𐤉𐤊|

9 𐤂𐤅𐤓.𐤀𐤓𐤉𐤄.𐤉𐤄𐤅𐤃𐤄.𐤌𐤈𐤓𐤐.𐤁𐤍𐤉.𐤏𐤋𐤉𐤕.𐤊𐤓𐤏.𐤓
𐤁𐤑.𐤊𐤀𐤓𐤉𐤄.𐤅𐤊𐤋𐤁𐤉𐤀.𐤌𐤉.𐤉𐤒𐤉𐤌𐤍𐤅|

10 𐤋𐤀.𐤉𐤎𐤅𐤓.𐤔𐤁𐤈.𐤌𐤉𐤄𐤅𐤃𐤄.𐤅𐤌𐤇𐤒𐤒.𐤌𐤁𐤉𐤍.𐤓𐤂
𐤋𐤉𐤅.𐤏𐤃.𐤊𐤉.𐤉𐤁𐤀..𐤔𐤉𐤋𐤄.||𐤔𐤉𐤋𐤅.𐤒𐤓𐤉||.𐤅𐤋𐤅.𐤉𐤒𐤄𐤕.
𐤏𐤌𐤉𐤌|

11 𐤀𐤎𐤓𐤉.𐤋𐤂𐤐𐤍.𐤏𐤉𐤓𐤄.||𐤏𐤉𐤓𐤅.𐤒𐤓𐤉||.𐤅𐤋𐤔𐤓𐤒𐤄.𐤁𐤍
𐤉.𐤀𐤕𐤍𐤅.𐤊𐤁𐤎.𐤁𐤉𐤉𐤍.𐤋𐤁𐤔𐤅.𐤅𐤁𐤃𐤌.𐤏𐤍𐤁𐤉𐤌.𐤎𐤅𐤕𐤄.||
𐤎𐤅𐤕𐤅.𐤒𐤓𐤉|||

12 𐤇𐤊𐤋𐤉𐤋𐤉.𐤏𐤉𐤍𐤉𐤌.𐤌𐤉𐤉𐤍.𐤅𐤋𐤁𐤍.𐤔𐤍𐤉𐤌.𐤌𐤇𐤋𐤁|

13 𐤆𐤁𐤅𐤋𐤍.𐤋𐤇𐤅𐤐.𐤉𐤌𐤉𐤌.𐤉𐤔𐤊𐤍.𐤅𐤄𐤅𐤀.𐤋𐤇𐤅𐤐.𐤀𐤍𐤉𐤅
𐤕.𐤅𐤉𐤓𐤊𐤕𐤅.𐤏𐤋.𐤑𐤉𐤃𐤍|

14 𐤉𐤔𐤔𐤊𐤓.𐤇𐤌𐤓.𐤂𐤓𐤌.𐤓𐤁𐤑.𐤁𐤉𐤍.𐤄𐤌𐤔𐤐𐤕𐤉𐤌|

15 𐤅𐤉𐤓𐤀.𐤌𐤍𐤇𐤄.𐤊𐤉.𐤈𐤅𐤁.𐤅𐤀𐤕.𐤄𐤀𐤓𐤑.𐤊𐤉.𐤍𐤏𐤌𐤄.
𐤅𐤉𐤈.𐤔𐤊𐤌𐤅.𐤋𐤎𐤁𐤋.𐤅𐤉𐤄𐤉.𐤋𐤌𐤎.𐤏𐤁𐤃|

טז 𐤃𐤍.𐤉𐤃𐤉𐤍.𐤏𐤌𐤅.𐤊𐤀𐤇𐤃.𐤔𐤁𐤈𐤉.𐤉𐤔𐤓𐤀𐤋𐤟

יז 𐤉𐤄𐤉.𐤃𐤍.𐤍𐤇𐤔.𐤏𐤋𐤉.𐤃𐤓𐤊.𐤔𐤐𐤉𐤐𐤍.𐤏𐤋𐤉.𐤀𐤓𐤇.𐤄𐤍𐤔𐤊.𐤏𐤒𐤁𐤉.𐤎𐤅𐤎.𐤅𐤉𐤐𐤋.𐤓𐤊𐤁𐤅.𐤀𐤇𐤅𐤓𐤟

יח 𐤋𐤉𐤔𐤅𐤏𐤕𐤊.𐤒𐤅𐤉𐤕𐤉.𐤉𐤄𐤅𐤄𐤟

יט 𐤂𐤃.𐤂𐤃𐤅𐤃.𐤉𐤂𐤅𐤃𐤍𐤅.𐤅𐤄𐤅𐤀.𐤉𐤂𐤃.𐤏𐤒𐤁𐤟

כ 𐤌𐤀𐤔𐤓.𐤔𐤌𐤍𐤄.𐤋𐤇𐤌𐤅.𐤅𐤄𐤅𐤀.𐤉𐤕𐤍.𐤌𐤏𐤃𐤍𐤉.𐤌𐤋𐤊𐤟

כא 𐤍𐤐𐤕𐤋𐤉.𐤀𐤉𐤋𐤄.𐤔𐤋𐤇𐤄.𐤄𐤍𐤕𐤍.𐤀𐤌𐤓𐤉.𐤔𐤐𐤓𐤟

כב 𐤁𐤍.𐤐𐤓𐤕.𐤉𐤅𐤎𐤐.𐤁𐤍.𐤐𐤓𐤕.𐤏𐤋𐤉.𐤏𐤉𐤍.𐤁𐤍𐤅𐤕.𐤑𐤏𐤃𐤄.𐤏𐤋𐤉.𐤔𐤅𐤓𐤟

כג 𐤅𐤉𐤌𐤓𐤓𐤄𐤅.𐤅𐤓𐤁𐤅.𐤅𐤉𐤔𐤈𐤌𐤄𐤅.𐤁𐤏𐤋𐤉.𐤇𐤑𐤉𐤌𐤟

כד 𐤅𐤕𐤔𐤁.𐤁𐤀𐤉𐤕𐤍.𐤒𐤔𐤕𐤅.𐤅𐤉𐤐𐤆𐤅.𐤆𐤓𐤏𐤉.𐤉𐤃𐤉𐤅.𐤌𐤉𐤃𐤉.𐤀𐤁𐤉𐤓.𐤉𐤏𐤒𐤁.𐤌𐤔𐤌.𐤓𐤏𐤄.𐤀𐤁𐤍.𐤉𐤔𐤓𐤀𐤋𐤟

כה 𐤌𐤀𐤋.𐤀𐤁𐤉𐤊.𐤅𐤉𐤏𐤆𐤓𐤊.𐤅𐤀𐤕.𐤔𐤃𐤉.𐤅𐤉𐤁𐤓𐤊𐤊.𐤁𐤓𐤊𐤕.𐤔𐤌𐤉𐤌.𐤌𐤏𐤋.𐤁𐤓𐤊𐤕.𐤕𐤄𐤅𐤌.𐤓𐤁𐤑𐤕.𐤕𐤇𐤕.𐤁𐤓𐤊𐤕.𐤔𐤃𐤉𐤌.𐤅𐤓𐤇𐤌𐤟

כו 𐤁𐤓𐤊𐤕.𐤀𐤁𐤉𐤊.𐤂𐤁𐤓𐤅.𐤏𐤋.𐤁𐤓𐤊𐤕.𐤄𐤅𐤓𐤉.𐤏𐤃.𐤕𐤀𐤅𐤕.𐤂𐤁𐤏𐤕.𐤏𐤅𐤋𐤌.𐤕𐤄𐤉𐤉𐤍.𐤋𐤓𐤀𐤔.𐤉𐤅𐤎𐤐.𐤅𐤋𐤒𐤃𐤒𐤃.𐤍𐤆𐤉𐤓.𐤀𐤇𐤉𐤅𐤟

כז 𐤁𐤍𐤉𐤌𐤉𐤍.𐤆𐤀𐤁.𐤉𐤈𐤓𐤐.𐤁𐤁𐤒𐤓.𐤉𐤀𐤊𐤋.𐤏𐤃.𐤅𐤋𐤏𐤓𐤁.𐤉𐤇𐤋𐤒.𐤔𐤋𐤋𐤟

כח 𐤊𐤋.𐤀𐤋𐤄.𐤔𐤁𐤈𐤉.𐤉𐤔𐤓𐤀𐤋.𐤔𐤍𐤉𐤌.𐤏𐤔𐤓.𐤅𐤆𐤀𐤕.𐤀𐤔𐤓.𐤃𐤁𐤓.𐤋𐤄𐤌.𐤀𐤁𐤉𐤄𐤌.𐤅𐤉𐤁𐤓𐤊.𐤀𐤅𐤕𐤌.𐤀𐤉𐤔.𐤀𐤔𐤓.𐤊𐤁𐤓𐤊𐤕𐤅.𐤁𐤓𐤊.𐤀𐤕𐤌𐤟

כט 𐤅𐤉𐤑𐤅.𐤀𐤅𐤕𐤌.𐤅𐤉𐤀𐤌𐤓.𐤀𐤋𐤄𐤌.𐤀𐤍𐤉.𐤍𐤀𐤎𐤐.𐤀𐤋.𐤏𐤌𐤉.𐤒𐤁𐤓𐤅.𐤀𐤕𐤉.𐤀𐤋.𐤀𐤁𐤕𐤉.𐤀𐤋.𐤄𐤌𐤏𐤓𐤄.𐤀𐤔𐤓.𐤁𐤔𐤃𐤄.𐤏𐤐𐤓𐤅𐤍.𐤄𐤇𐤕𐤉𐤟

ל 𐤁𐤌𐤏𐤓𐤄.𐤀𐤔𐤓.𐤁𐤔𐤃𐤄.𐤄𐤌𐤊𐤐𐤋𐤄.𐤀𐤔𐤓.𐤏𐤋.𐤐𐤍𐤉.𐤌𐤌𐤓𐤀.𐤁𐤀𐤓𐤑.𐤊𐤍𐤏𐤍.𐤀𐤔𐤓.𐤒𐤍𐤄.𐤀𐤁𐤓𐤄𐤌.𐤀𐤕.𐤄𐤔𐤃𐤄.𐤌𐤀𐤕.𐤏𐤐𐤓𐤍.𐤄𐤇𐤕𐤉.𐤋𐤀𐤇𐤆𐤕.𐤒𐤁𐤓𐤟

..לא.. 𐤔𐤌𐤄.𐤒𐤁𐤓𐤅.𐤀𐤕.𐤀𐤁𐤓𐤄𐤌.𐤅𐤀𐤕.𐤔𐤓𐤄.𐤀𐤔𐤕𐤅.𐤔
𐤌𐤄.𐤒𐤁𐤓𐤅.𐤀𐤕.𐤉𐤑𐤇𐤒.𐤅𐤀𐤕.𐤓𐤁𐤒𐤄.𐤀𐤔𐤕𐤅.𐤅𐤔𐤌𐤄.𐤒
𐤁𐤓𐤕𐤉.𐤀𐤕.𐤋𐤀𐤄|
..לב.. 𐤌𐤒𐤍𐤄.𐤄𐤔𐤃𐤄.𐤅𐤄𐤌𐤏𐤓𐤄.𐤀𐤔𐤓.𐤁𐤅.𐤌𐤀𐤕.𐤁𐤍𐤉.
𐤇𐤕|
..לג.. 𐤅𐤉𐤊𐤋.𐤉𐤏𐤒𐤁.𐤋𐤑𐤅𐤕.𐤀𐤕.𐤁𐤍𐤉𐤅.𐤅𐤉𐤀𐤎𐤐.𐤓𐤂𐤋𐤉𐤅
.𐤀𐤋.𐤄𐤌𐤈𐤄.𐤅𐤉𐤂𐤅𐤏.𐤅𐤉𐤀𐤎𐤐.𐤀𐤋.𐤏𐤌𐤉𐤅||

𐤁𐤓𐤀𐤔𐤉𐤕.𐤇𐤋𐤒 ..נ..

..א.. 𐤅𐤉𐤐𐤋.𐤉𐤅𐤎𐤐.𐤏𐤋.𐤐𐤍𐤉.𐤀𐤁𐤉𐤅.𐤅𐤉𐤁𐤊.𐤏𐤋𐤉𐤅.𐤅𐤉𐤔𐤒.𐤋
𐤅|
..ב.. 𐤅𐤉𐤑𐤅.𐤉𐤅𐤎𐤐.𐤀𐤕.𐤏𐤁𐤃𐤉𐤅.𐤀𐤕.𐤄𐤓𐤐𐤀𐤉𐤌.𐤋𐤇𐤍𐤈.
𐤀𐤕.𐤀𐤁𐤉𐤅.𐤅𐤉𐤇𐤍𐤈𐤅.𐤄𐤓𐤐𐤀𐤉𐤌.𐤀𐤕.𐤉𐤔𐤓𐤀𐤋|
..ג.. 𐤅𐤉𐤌𐤋𐤀𐤅.𐤋𐤅.𐤀𐤓𐤁𐤏𐤉𐤌.𐤉𐤅𐤌.𐤊𐤉.𐤊𐤍.𐤉𐤌𐤋𐤀𐤅.𐤉𐤌𐤉.
𐤄𐤇𐤍𐤈𐤉𐤌.𐤅𐤉𐤁𐤊𐤅.𐤀𐤕𐤅.𐤌𐤑𐤓𐤉𐤌.𐤔𐤁𐤏𐤉𐤌.𐤉𐤅𐤌|
..ד.. 𐤅𐤉𐤏𐤁𐤓𐤅.𐤉𐤌𐤉.𐤁𐤊𐤉𐤕𐤅.𐤅𐤉𐤃𐤁𐤓.𐤉𐤅𐤎𐤐.𐤀𐤋.𐤁𐤉𐤕.𐤐
𐤓𐤏𐤄.𐤋𐤀𐤌𐤓.𐤀𐤌.𐤍𐤀.𐤌𐤑𐤀𐤕𐤉.𐤇𐤍.𐤁𐤏𐤉𐤍𐤉𐤊𐤌.𐤃𐤁𐤓𐤅
.𐤍𐤀.𐤁𐤀𐤆𐤍𐤉.𐤐𐤓𐤏𐤄.𐤋𐤀𐤌𐤓|
..ה.. 𐤀𐤁𐤉.𐤄𐤔𐤁𐤉𐤏𐤍𐤉.𐤋𐤀𐤌𐤓.𐤄𐤍𐤄.𐤀𐤍𐤊𐤉.𐤌𐤕.𐤁𐤒𐤁𐤓
𐤉.𐤀𐤔𐤓.𐤊𐤓𐤉𐤕𐤉.𐤋𐤉.𐤁𐤀𐤓𐤑.𐤊𐤍𐤏𐤍.𐤔𐤌𐤄.𐤕𐤒𐤁𐤓𐤍𐤉.𐤅
𐤏𐤕𐤄.𐤀𐤏𐤋𐤄.𐤍𐤀.𐤅𐤀𐤒𐤁𐤓𐤄.𐤀𐤕.𐤀𐤁𐤉.𐤅𐤀𐤔𐤅𐤁𐤄|
..ו.. 𐤅𐤉𐤀𐤌𐤓.𐤐𐤓𐤏𐤄.𐤏𐤋𐤄.𐤅𐤒𐤁𐤓.𐤀𐤕.𐤀𐤁𐤉𐤊.𐤊𐤀𐤔𐤓.𐤄
𐤔𐤁𐤉𐤏𐤊|
..ז.. 𐤅𐤉𐤏𐤋.𐤉𐤅𐤎𐤐.𐤋𐤒𐤁𐤓.𐤀𐤕.𐤀𐤁𐤉𐤅.𐤅𐤉𐤏𐤋𐤅.𐤀𐤕𐤅.𐤊𐤋.
𐤏𐤁𐤃𐤉.𐤐𐤓𐤏𐤄.𐤆𐤒𐤍𐤉.𐤁𐤉𐤕𐤅.𐤅𐤊𐤋.𐤆𐤒𐤍𐤉.𐤀𐤓𐤑.𐤌𐤑
𐤓𐤉𐤌|
..ח.. 𐤅𐤊𐤋.𐤁𐤉𐤕.𐤉𐤅𐤎𐤐.𐤅𐤀𐤇𐤉𐤅.𐤅𐤁𐤉𐤕.𐤀𐤁𐤉𐤅.𐤓𐤒.𐤈𐤐𐤌.𐤅
𐤑𐤀𐤍𐤌.𐤅𐤁𐤒𐤓𐤌.𐤏𐤆𐤁𐤅.𐤁𐤀𐤓𐤑.𐤂𐤔𐤍|
..ט.. 𐤅𐤉𐤏𐤋.𐤏𐤌𐤅.𐤂𐤌.𐤓𐤊𐤁.𐤂𐤌.𐤐𐤓𐤔𐤉𐤌.𐤅𐤉𐤄𐤉.𐤄𐤌𐤇𐤍
𐤄.𐤊𐤁𐤃.𐤌𐤀𐤃|

יא 𐤅𐤉𐤁𐤀𐤅.𐤏𐤃.𐤂𐤓𐤍.𐤄𐤀𐤈𐤃.𐤀𐤔𐤓.𐤁𐤏𐤁𐤓.𐤄𐤉𐤓𐤃
𐤍.𐤅𐤉𐤎𐤐𐤃𐤅.𐤔𐤌.𐤌𐤎𐤐𐤃.𐤂𐤃𐤅𐤋.𐤅𐤊𐤁𐤃.𐤌𐤀𐤃.𐤅𐤉𐤏𐤔.
𐤋𐤀𐤁𐤉𐤅.𐤀𐤁𐤋.𐤔𐤁𐤏𐤕.𐤉𐤌𐤉𐤌|
יב 𐤅𐤉𐤓𐤀.𐤉𐤅𐤔𐤁.𐤄𐤀𐤓𐤑.𐤄𐤊𐤍𐤏𐤍𐤉.𐤀𐤕.𐤄𐤀𐤁𐤋.𐤁𐤂𐤓
𐤍.𐤄𐤀𐤈𐤃.𐤅𐤉𐤀𐤌𐤓𐤅.𐤀𐤁𐤋.𐤊𐤁𐤃.𐤆𐤄.𐤋𐤌𐤑𐤓𐤉𐤌.𐤏𐤋.𐤊
𐤍.𐤒𐤓𐤀.𐤔𐤌𐤄.𐤀𐤁𐤋.𐤌𐤑𐤓𐤉𐤌.𐤀𐤔𐤓.𐤁𐤏𐤁𐤓.𐤄𐤉𐤓𐤃𐤍|
יג 𐤅𐤉𐤏𐤔𐤅.𐤁𐤍𐤉𐤅.𐤋𐤅.𐤊𐤍.𐤊𐤀𐤔𐤓.𐤑𐤅𐤌|
יד 𐤅𐤉𐤔𐤀𐤅.𐤀𐤕𐤅.𐤁𐤍𐤉𐤅.𐤀𐤓𐤑𐤄.𐤊𐤍𐤏𐤍.𐤅𐤉𐤒𐤁𐤓𐤅.𐤀𐤕𐤅
.𐤁𐤌𐤏𐤓𐤕.𐤔𐤃𐤄.𐤄𐤌𐤊𐤐𐤋𐤄.𐤀𐤔𐤓.𐤒𐤍𐤄.𐤀𐤁𐤓𐤄𐤌.𐤀𐤕.
𐤄𐤔𐤃𐤄.𐤋𐤀𐤇𐤆𐤕.𐤒𐤁𐤓.𐤌𐤀𐤕.𐤏𐤐𐤓𐤍.𐤄𐤇𐤕𐤉.𐤏𐤋.𐤐𐤍
𐤉.𐤌𐤌𐤓𐤀|
יה 𐤅𐤉𐤔𐤁.𐤉𐤅𐤎𐤐.𐤌𐤑𐤓𐤉𐤌𐤄.𐤄𐤅𐤀.𐤅𐤀𐤇𐤉𐤅.𐤅𐤊𐤋.𐤄𐤏
𐤋𐤉𐤌.𐤀𐤕𐤅.𐤋𐤒𐤁𐤓.𐤀𐤕.𐤀𐤁𐤉𐤅.𐤀𐤇𐤓𐤉.𐤒𐤁𐤓𐤅.𐤀𐤕.𐤀𐤁𐤉
𐤅|
יו 𐤅𐤉𐤓𐤀𐤅.𐤀𐤇𐤉.𐤉𐤅𐤎𐤐.𐤊𐤉.𐤌𐤕.𐤀𐤁𐤉𐤄𐤌.𐤅𐤉𐤀𐤌𐤓𐤅.𐤋
𐤅.𐤉𐤔𐤈𐤌𐤍𐤅.𐤉𐤅𐤎𐤐.𐤅𐤄𐤔𐤁.𐤉𐤔𐤉𐤁.𐤋𐤍𐤅.𐤀𐤕.𐤊𐤋.𐤄𐤓𐤏𐤄.
𐤀𐤔𐤓.𐤂𐤌𐤋𐤍𐤅.𐤀𐤕𐤅|
יז 𐤅𐤉𐤑𐤅𐤅.𐤀𐤋.𐤉𐤅𐤎𐤐.𐤋𐤀𐤌𐤓.𐤀𐤁𐤉𐤊.𐤑𐤅𐤄.𐤋𐤐𐤍𐤉.𐤌𐤅𐤕
𐤅.𐤋𐤀𐤌𐤓|
יח 𐤊𐤄.𐤕𐤀𐤌𐤓𐤅.𐤋𐤉𐤅𐤎𐤐.𐤀𐤍𐤀.𐤔𐤀.𐤍𐤀.𐤐𐤔𐤏.𐤀𐤇𐤉𐤊
.𐤅𐤇𐤈𐤀𐤕𐤌.𐤊𐤉.𐤓𐤏𐤄.𐤂𐤌𐤋𐤅𐤊.𐤅𐤏𐤕𐤄.𐤔𐤀.𐤍𐤀.𐤋𐤐𐤔𐤏.
𐤏𐤁𐤃𐤉.𐤀𐤋𐤄𐤉.𐤀𐤁𐤉𐤊.𐤅𐤉𐤁𐤊.𐤉𐤅𐤎𐤐.𐤁𐤃𐤁𐤓𐤌.𐤀𐤋𐤉𐤅|
יט 𐤅𐤉𐤋𐤊𐤅.𐤂𐤌.𐤀𐤇𐤉𐤅.𐤅𐤉𐤐𐤋𐤅.𐤋𐤐𐤍𐤉𐤅.𐤅𐤉𐤀𐤌𐤓𐤅.𐤄𐤍𐤍𐤅.
𐤋𐤊.𐤋𐤏𐤁𐤃𐤉𐤌|
כ 𐤅𐤉𐤀𐤌𐤓.𐤀𐤋𐤄𐤌.𐤉𐤅𐤎𐤐.𐤀𐤋.𐤕𐤉𐤓𐤀𐤅.𐤊𐤉.𐤄𐤕𐤇𐤕.
𐤀𐤋𐤄𐤉𐤌.𐤀𐤍𐤉|
כא 𐤅𐤀𐤕𐤌.𐤇𐤔𐤁𐤕𐤌.𐤏𐤋𐤉.𐤓𐤏𐤄.𐤀𐤋𐤄𐤉𐤌.𐤇𐤔𐤁𐤄.
𐤋𐤈𐤁𐤄.𐤋𐤌𐤏𐤍.𐤏𐤔𐤄.𐤊𐤉𐤅𐤌.𐤄𐤆𐤄.𐤋𐤄𐤇𐤉𐤕.𐤏𐤌.𐤓𐤁|
כב 𐤅𐤏𐤕𐤄.𐤀𐤋.𐤕𐤉𐤓𐤀𐤅.𐤀𐤍𐤊𐤉.𐤀𐤊𐤋𐤊𐤋.𐤀𐤕𐤊𐤌.𐤅𐤀𐤕
.𐤈𐤐𐤊𐤌.𐤅𐤉𐤍𐤇𐤌.𐤀𐤅𐤕𐤌.𐤅𐤉𐤃𐤁𐤓.𐤏𐤋.𐤋𐤁𐤌|

כב וישב יוסף במצרים הוא ובית אביו ויחי יוסף מאה ועשר שנים |

כג וירא יוסף לאפרים בני שלשים גם בני מכיר בן מנשה ילדו על ברכי יוסף |

כד ויאמר יוסף אל אחיו אנכי מת ואלהים פקד יפקד אתכם והעלה אתכם מן הארץ הזאת אל הארץ אשר נשבע לאברהם ליצחק וליעקב |

כה וישבע יוסף את בני ישראל לאמר פקד יפקד אלהים אתכם והעלתם את עצמתי מזה |

כו וימת יוסף בן מאה ועשר שנים ויחנטו אתו ויישם בארון במצרים ||

𐤎𐤐𐤓.𐤅𐤉𐤏𐤋𐤅.𐤌𐤌𐤑𐤓𐤉𐤌

𐤅𐤉𐤏𐤋𐤅.𐤌𐤌𐤑𐤓𐤉𐤌.𐤇𐤋𐤒 1

1 𐤅𐤀𐤋𐤄.𐤔𐤌𐤅𐤕.𐤁𐤍𐤉.𐤉𐤔𐤓𐤀𐤋.𐤄𐤁𐤀𐤉𐤌.𐤌𐤑𐤓𐤉𐤌𐤄.
𐤀𐤕.𐤉𐤏𐤒𐤁.𐤀𐤉𐤔.𐤅𐤁𐤉𐤕𐤅.𐤁𐤀𐤅|
2 𐤓𐤀𐤅𐤁𐤍.𐤔𐤌𐤏𐤅𐤍.𐤋𐤅𐤉.𐤅𐤉𐤄𐤅𐤃𐤄|
3 𐤉𐤔𐤔𐤊𐤓.𐤆𐤁𐤅𐤋𐤍.𐤅𐤁𐤍𐤉𐤌𐤍|
4 𐤃𐤍.𐤅𐤍𐤐𐤕𐤋𐤉.𐤂𐤃.𐤅𐤀𐤔𐤓|
5 𐤅𐤉𐤄𐤉.𐤊𐤋.𐤍𐤐𐤔.𐤉𐤑𐤀𐤉.𐤉𐤓𐤊.𐤉𐤏𐤒𐤁.𐤔𐤁𐤏𐤉𐤌.𐤍𐤐
𐤔.𐤅𐤉𐤅𐤎𐤐.𐤄𐤉𐤄.𐤁𐤌𐤑𐤓𐤉𐤌|
6 𐤅𐤉𐤌𐤕.𐤉𐤅𐤎𐤐.𐤅𐤊𐤋.𐤀𐤇𐤉𐤅.𐤅𐤊𐤋.𐤄𐤃𐤅𐤓.𐤄𐤄𐤅𐤀|
7 𐤅𐤁𐤍𐤉.𐤉𐤔𐤓𐤀𐤋.𐤐𐤓𐤅.𐤅𐤉𐤔𐤓𐤑𐤅.𐤅𐤉𐤓𐤁𐤅.𐤅𐤉𐤏𐤑𐤌𐤅.𐤁𐤌
𐤀𐤃.𐤌𐤀𐤃.𐤅𐤕𐤌𐤋𐤀.𐤄𐤀𐤓𐤑.𐤀𐤕𐤌|
8 𐤅𐤉𐤒𐤌.𐤌𐤋𐤊.𐤇𐤃𐤔.𐤏𐤋.𐤌𐤑𐤓𐤉𐤌.𐤀𐤔𐤓.𐤋𐤀.𐤉𐤃𐤏.
𐤀𐤕.𐤉𐤅𐤎𐤐|
9 𐤅𐤉𐤀𐤌𐤓.𐤀𐤋.𐤏𐤌𐤅.𐤄𐤍𐤄.𐤏𐤌.𐤁𐤍𐤉.𐤉𐤔𐤓𐤀𐤋.𐤓𐤁.𐤅𐤏
𐤑𐤅𐤌.𐤌𐤌𐤍𐤅|
10 𐤄𐤁𐤄.𐤍𐤕𐤇𐤊𐤌𐤄.𐤋𐤅.𐤐𐤍.𐤉𐤓𐤁𐤄.𐤅𐤄𐤉𐤄.𐤊𐤉.𐤕𐤒𐤓
𐤀𐤍𐤄.𐤌𐤋𐤇𐤌𐤄.𐤅𐤍𐤅𐤎𐤐.𐤂𐤌.𐤄𐤅𐤀.𐤏𐤋.𐤔𐤍𐤀𐤉𐤍𐤅.𐤅𐤍𐤋𐤇𐤌
.𐤁𐤍𐤅.𐤅𐤏𐤋𐤄.𐤌𐤍.𐤄𐤀𐤓𐤑|
11 𐤅𐤉𐤔𐤉𐤌𐤅.𐤏𐤋𐤉𐤅.𐤔𐤓𐤉.𐤌𐤎𐤉𐤌.𐤋𐤌𐤏𐤍.𐤏𐤍𐤕𐤅.𐤁𐤎𐤁
𐤋𐤕𐤌.𐤅𐤉𐤁𐤍.𐤏𐤓𐤉.𐤌𐤎𐤊𐤍𐤅𐤕.𐤋𐤐𐤓𐤏𐤄.𐤀𐤕.𐤐𐤕𐤌.𐤅𐤀𐤕.𐤓
𐤏𐤌𐤎𐤎|
12 𐤅𐤊𐤀𐤔𐤓.𐤉𐤏𐤍𐤅.𐤀𐤕𐤅.𐤊𐤍.𐤉𐤓𐤁𐤄.𐤅𐤊𐤍.𐤉𐤐𐤓𐤑.𐤅𐤉𐤒
𐤑𐤅.𐤌𐤐𐤍𐤉.𐤁𐤍𐤉.𐤉𐤔𐤓𐤀𐤋|
13 𐤅𐤉𐤏𐤁𐤃𐤅.𐤌𐤑𐤓𐤉𐤌.𐤀𐤕.𐤁𐤍𐤉.𐤉𐤔𐤓𐤀𐤋.𐤁𐤐𐤓𐤊|

14 𐤅𐤉𐤌𐤓𐤓𐤅.𐤀𐤕.𐤇𐤉𐤉𐤄𐤌.𐤁𐤏𐤁𐤃𐤄.𐤒𐤔𐤄.𐤁𐤇𐤌𐤓.
𐤅𐤁𐤋𐤁𐤍𐤉𐤌.𐤅𐤁𐤊𐤋.𐤏𐤁𐤃𐤄.𐤁𐤔𐤃𐤄.𐤀𐤕.𐤊𐤋.𐤏𐤁𐤃𐤕𐤌.
𐤀𐤔𐤓.𐤏𐤁𐤃𐤅.𐤁𐤄𐤌.𐤁𐤐𐤓𐤊|

15 𐤅𐤉𐤀𐤌𐤓.𐤌𐤋𐤊.𐤌𐤑𐤓𐤉𐤌.𐤋𐤌𐤉𐤋𐤃𐤕.𐤄𐤏𐤁𐤓𐤉𐤕.𐤀
𐤔𐤓.𐤔𐤌.𐤄𐤀𐤇𐤕.𐤔𐤐𐤓𐤄.𐤅𐤔𐤌.𐤄𐤔𐤍𐤉𐤕.𐤐𐤅𐤏𐤄|

16 𐤅𐤉𐤀𐤌𐤓.𐤁𐤉𐤋𐤃𐤊𐤍.𐤀𐤕.𐤄𐤏𐤁𐤓𐤉𐤅𐤕.𐤅𐤓𐤀𐤉𐤕𐤍.𐤏𐤋.
𐤄𐤀𐤁𐤍𐤉𐤌.𐤀𐤌.𐤁𐤍.𐤄𐤅𐤀.𐤅𐤄𐤌𐤕𐤍.𐤀𐤕𐤅.𐤅𐤀𐤌.𐤁𐤕.𐤄𐤉𐤀.𐤅
𐤇𐤉𐤄|

17 𐤅𐤕𐤉𐤓𐤀𐤍.𐤄𐤌𐤉𐤋𐤃𐤕.𐤀𐤕.𐤄𐤀𐤋𐤄𐤉𐤌.𐤅𐤋𐤀.𐤏𐤔𐤅.
𐤊𐤀𐤔𐤓.𐤃𐤁𐤓.𐤀𐤋𐤉𐤄𐤍.𐤌𐤋𐤊.𐤌𐤑𐤓𐤉𐤌.𐤅𐤕𐤇𐤉𐤉𐤍.𐤀𐤕.𐤄
𐤉𐤋𐤃𐤉𐤌|

18 𐤅𐤉𐤒𐤓𐤀.𐤌𐤋𐤊.𐤌𐤑𐤓𐤉𐤌.𐤋𐤌𐤉𐤋𐤃𐤕.𐤅𐤉𐤀𐤌𐤓.𐤋𐤄𐤍.
𐤌𐤃𐤅𐤏.𐤏𐤔𐤉𐤕𐤍.𐤄𐤃𐤁𐤓.𐤄𐤆𐤄.𐤅𐤕𐤇𐤉𐤉𐤍.𐤀𐤕.𐤄𐤉𐤋
𐤃𐤉𐤌|

19 𐤅𐤕𐤀𐤌𐤓𐤍.𐤄𐤌𐤉𐤋𐤃𐤕.𐤀𐤋.𐤐𐤓𐤏𐤄.𐤊𐤉.𐤋𐤀.𐤊𐤍𐤔𐤉
𐤌.𐤄𐤌𐤑𐤓𐤉𐤕.𐤄𐤏𐤁𐤓𐤉𐤕.𐤊𐤉.𐤇𐤉𐤅𐤕.𐤄𐤍𐤄.𐤁𐤈𐤓𐤌.𐤕𐤁𐤅
𐤀.𐤀𐤋𐤄𐤍.𐤄𐤌𐤉𐤋𐤃𐤕.𐤅𐤉𐤋𐤃𐤅|

20 𐤅𐤉𐤉𐤈𐤁.𐤀𐤋𐤄𐤉𐤌.𐤋𐤌𐤉𐤋𐤃𐤕.𐤅𐤉𐤓𐤁.𐤄𐤏𐤌.𐤅𐤉𐤏
𐤑𐤌𐤅.𐤌𐤀𐤃|

21 𐤅𐤉𐤄𐤉.𐤊𐤉.𐤉𐤓𐤀𐤅.𐤄𐤌𐤉𐤋𐤃𐤕.𐤀𐤕.𐤄𐤀𐤋𐤄𐤉𐤌.𐤅𐤉
𐤏𐤔.𐤋𐤄𐤌.𐤁𐤕𐤉𐤌|

22 𐤅𐤉𐤑𐤅.𐤐𐤓𐤏𐤄.𐤋𐤊𐤋.𐤏𐤌𐤅.𐤋𐤀𐤌𐤓.𐤊𐤋.𐤄𐤁𐤍.𐤄𐤉𐤋𐤅
𐤃.𐤄𐤉𐤀𐤓𐤄.𐤕𐤔𐤋𐤉𐤊𐤄𐤅.𐤅𐤊𐤋.𐤄𐤁𐤕.𐤕𐤇𐤉𐤅𐤍||

2 𐤅𐤉𐤏𐤋𐤅.𐤌𐤌𐤑𐤓𐤉𐤌.𐤇𐤋𐤒

1 𐤅𐤉𐤋𐤊.𐤀𐤉𐤔.𐤌𐤁𐤉𐤕.𐤋𐤅𐤉.𐤅𐤉𐤒𐤇.𐤀𐤕.𐤁𐤕.𐤋𐤅𐤉|

2 𐤅𐤕𐤄𐤓.𐤄𐤀𐤔𐤄.𐤅𐤕𐤋𐤃.𐤁𐤍.𐤅𐤕𐤓𐤀.𐤀𐤕𐤅.𐤊𐤉.𐤈𐤅𐤁.𐤄𐤅
𐤀.𐤅𐤕𐤑𐤐𐤍𐤄𐤅.𐤔𐤋𐤔𐤄.𐤉𐤓𐤇𐤉𐤌|

3 𐤅𐤋𐤀.𐤉𐤊𐤋𐤄.𐤏𐤅𐤃.𐤄𐤑𐤐𐤉𐤍𐤅.𐤅𐤕𐤒𐤇.𐤋𐤅.𐤕𐤁𐤕.𐤂𐤌
𐤀.𐤅𐤕𐤇𐤌𐤓𐤄.𐤁𐤇𐤌𐤓.𐤅𐤁𐤆𐤐𐤕.𐤅𐤕𐤔𐤌.𐤁𐤄.𐤀𐤕.𐤄𐤉𐤋𐤃.
𐤅𐤕𐤔𐤌.𐤁𐤎𐤅𐤐.𐤏𐤋.𐤔𐤐𐤕.𐤄𐤉𐤀𐤓|

4 𐤅𐤕𐤕𐤑𐤁.𐤀𐤇𐤕𐤅.𐤌𐤓𐤇𐤒.𐤋𐤃𐤏𐤄.𐤌𐤄.𐤉𐤏𐤔𐤄.𐤋𐤅|

5 𐤅𐤕𐤓𐤃.𐤁𐤕.𐤐𐤓𐤏𐤄.𐤋𐤓𐤇𐤑.𐤏𐤋.𐤄𐤉𐤀𐤓.𐤅𐤍𐤏𐤓𐤕𐤉𐤄.
𐤄𐤋𐤊𐤕.𐤏𐤋.𐤉𐤃.𐤄𐤉𐤀𐤓.𐤅𐤕𐤓𐤀.𐤀𐤕.𐤄𐤕𐤁𐤄.𐤁𐤕𐤅𐤊.𐤄𐤎
𐤅𐤐.𐤅𐤕𐤔𐤋𐤇.𐤀𐤕.𐤀𐤌𐤕𐤄.𐤅𐤕𐤒𐤇𐤄|

6 𐤅𐤕𐤐𐤕𐤇.𐤅𐤕𐤓𐤀𐤄𐤅.𐤀𐤕.𐤄𐤉𐤋𐤃.𐤅𐤄𐤍𐤄.𐤍𐤏𐤓.𐤁𐤊𐤄.𐤅
𐤕𐤇𐤌𐤋.𐤏𐤋𐤉𐤅.𐤅𐤕𐤀𐤌𐤓.𐤌𐤉𐤋𐤃𐤉.𐤄𐤏𐤁𐤓𐤉𐤌.𐤆𐤄|

7 𐤅𐤕𐤀𐤌𐤓.𐤀𐤇𐤕𐤅.𐤀𐤋.𐤁𐤕.𐤐𐤓𐤏𐤄.𐤄𐤀𐤋𐤊.𐤅𐤒𐤓𐤀𐤕𐤉
𐤋𐤊.𐤀𐤔𐤄.𐤌𐤉𐤍𐤒𐤕.𐤌𐤍.𐤄𐤏𐤁𐤓𐤉𐤕.𐤅𐤕𐤉𐤍𐤒.𐤋𐤊.𐤀𐤕.𐤄
𐤉𐤋𐤃|

8 𐤅𐤕𐤀𐤌𐤓.𐤋𐤄.𐤁𐤕.𐤐𐤓𐤏𐤄.𐤋𐤊𐤉.𐤅𐤕𐤋𐤊.𐤄𐤏𐤋𐤌𐤄.𐤅𐤕
𐤒𐤓𐤀.𐤀𐤕.𐤀𐤌.𐤄𐤉𐤋𐤃|

9 𐤅𐤕𐤀𐤌𐤓.𐤋𐤄.𐤁𐤕.𐤐𐤓𐤏𐤄.𐤄𐤉𐤋𐤉𐤊𐤉.𐤀𐤕.𐤄𐤉𐤋𐤃.𐤄
𐤆𐤄.𐤅𐤄𐤉𐤍𐤒𐤄𐤅.𐤋𐤉.𐤅𐤀𐤍𐤉.𐤀𐤕𐤍.𐤀𐤕.𐤔𐤊𐤓𐤊.𐤅𐤕𐤒𐤇.𐤄
𐤀𐤔𐤄.𐤄𐤉𐤋𐤃.𐤅𐤕𐤍𐤉𐤒𐤄𐤅|

10 𐤅𐤉𐤂𐤃𐤋.𐤄𐤉𐤋𐤃.𐤅𐤕𐤁𐤀𐤄𐤅.𐤋𐤁𐤕.𐤐𐤓𐤏𐤄.𐤅𐤉𐤄𐤉.𐤋
𐤄.𐤋𐤁𐤍.𐤅𐤕𐤒𐤓𐤀.𐤔𐤌𐤅.𐤌𐤔𐤄.𐤅𐤕𐤀𐤌𐤓.𐤊𐤉.𐤌𐤍.𐤄𐤌𐤉𐤌.𐤌
𐤔𐤉𐤕𐤄𐤅|

11 𐤅𐤉𐤄𐤉.𐤁𐤉𐤌𐤉𐤌.𐤄𐤄𐤌.𐤅𐤉𐤂𐤃𐤋.𐤌𐤔𐤄.𐤅𐤉𐤑𐤀.𐤀𐤋.
𐤀𐤇𐤉𐤅.𐤅𐤉𐤓𐤀.𐤁𐤎𐤁𐤋𐤕𐤌.𐤅𐤉𐤓𐤀.𐤀𐤉𐤔.𐤌𐤑𐤓𐤉.𐤌𐤊𐤄.𐤀
𐤉𐤔.𐤏𐤁𐤓𐤉.𐤌𐤀𐤇𐤉𐤅|

12 𐤅𐤉𐤐𐤍.𐤊𐤄.𐤅𐤊𐤄.𐤅𐤉𐤓𐤀.𐤊𐤉.𐤀𐤉𐤍.𐤀𐤉𐤔.𐤅𐤉𐤊.𐤀𐤕.𐤄
𐤌𐤑𐤓𐤉.𐤅𐤉𐤈𐤌𐤍𐤄𐤅.𐤁𐤇𐤅𐤋|

13 𐤅𐤉𐤑𐤀.𐤁𐤉𐤅𐤌.𐤄𐤔𐤍𐤉.𐤅𐤄𐤍𐤄.𐤔𐤍𐤉.𐤀𐤍𐤔𐤉𐤌.𐤏𐤁𐤓
𐤉𐤌.𐤍𐤑𐤉𐤌.𐤅𐤉𐤀𐤌𐤓.𐤋𐤓𐤔𐤏.𐤋𐤌𐤄.𐤕𐤊𐤄.𐤓𐤏𐤊|

14 𐤅𐤉𐤀𐤌𐤓.𐤌𐤉.𐤔𐤌𐤊.𐤋𐤀𐤉𐤔.𐤔𐤓.𐤅𐤔𐤐𐤈.𐤏𐤋𐤉𐤍𐤅.𐤄𐤋
𐤄𐤓𐤂𐤍𐤉.𐤀𐤕𐤄.𐤀𐤌𐤓.𐤊𐤀𐤔𐤓.𐤄𐤓𐤂𐤕.𐤀𐤕.𐤄𐤌𐤑𐤓𐤉.𐤅𐤉
𐤉𐤓𐤀.𐤌𐤔𐤄.𐤅𐤉𐤀𐤌𐤓.𐤀𐤊𐤍.𐤍𐤅𐤃𐤏.𐤄𐤃𐤁𐤓|

יה וישמע.פרעה.את.הדבר.הזה.ויבקש.להרג.את.משה.ויברח.משה.מפני.פרעה.וישב.בארץ.מדין.וישב.על.הבאר|

יו ולכהן.מדין.שבע.בנות.ותבאנה.ותדלנה.ותמלאנה.את.הרהטים.להשקות.צאן.אביהן|

יז ויבאו.הרעים.ויגרשום.ויקם.משה.ויושען.וישק.את.צאנם|

יח ותבאנה.אל.רעואל.אביהן.ויאמר.מדוע.מהרתן.בא.היום|

יט ותאמרן.איש.מצרי.הצילנו.מיד.הרעים.וגם.דלה.דלה.לנו.וישק.את.הצאן|

כ ויאמר.אל.בנתיו.ואיו.למה.זה.עזבתן.את.האיש.קראן.לו.ויאכל.לחם|

כא ויואל.משה.לשבת.את.האיש.ויתן.את.צפרה.בתו.למשה|

כב ותלד.בן.ויקרא.את.שמו.גרשם.כי.אמר.גר.הייתי.בארץ.נכריה|

כג ויהי.בימים.הרבים.ההם.וימת.מלך.מצרים.ויאנחו.בני.ישראל.מן.העבדה.ויזעקו.ותעל.שועתם.אל.האלהים.מן.העבדה|

כד וישמע.אלהים.את.נאקתם.ויזכר.אלהים.את.בריתו.את.אברהם.את.יצחק.ואת.יעקב|

כה וירא.אלהים.את.בני.ישראל.וידע.אלהים||

ויעלו.ממצרים.חלק ג

א ומשה.היה.רעה.את.צאן.יתרו.חתנו.כהן.מדין.וינהג.את.הצאן.אחר.המדבר.ויבא.אל.הר.האלהים.חרבה|

2 𐤅𐤉𐤓𐤀.𐤌𐤋𐤀𐤊.𐤉𐤄𐤅𐤄.𐤀𐤋𐤉𐤅.𐤁𐤋𐤁𐤕.𐤀𐤔.𐤌𐤕𐤅𐤊.𐤄𐤎
𐤍𐤄.𐤅𐤉𐤓𐤀.𐤅𐤄𐤍𐤄.𐤄𐤎𐤍𐤄.𐤁𐤏𐤓.𐤁𐤀𐤔.𐤅𐤄𐤎𐤍𐤄.𐤀𐤉𐤍𐤍𐤅.𐤀
𐤊𐤋|
3 𐤅𐤉𐤀𐤌𐤓.𐤌𐤔𐤄.𐤀𐤎𐤓𐤄.𐤍𐤀.𐤅𐤀𐤓𐤀𐤄.𐤀𐤕.𐤄𐤌𐤓𐤀𐤄.
𐤄𐤂𐤃𐤋.𐤄𐤆𐤄.𐤌𐤃𐤅𐤏.𐤋𐤀.𐤉𐤁𐤏𐤓.𐤄𐤎𐤍𐤄|
4 𐤅𐤉𐤓𐤀.𐤉𐤄𐤅𐤄.𐤊𐤉.𐤎𐤓.𐤋𐤓𐤀𐤅𐤕.𐤅𐤉𐤒𐤓𐤀.𐤀𐤋𐤉𐤅.𐤀𐤋
𐤄𐤉𐤌.𐤌𐤕𐤅𐤊.𐤄𐤎𐤍𐤄.𐤅𐤉𐤀𐤌𐤓.𐤌𐤔𐤄.𐤌𐤔𐤄.𐤅𐤉𐤀𐤌𐤓.𐤄𐤍𐤍
𐤉|
5 𐤅𐤉𐤀𐤌𐤓.𐤀𐤋.𐤕𐤒𐤓𐤁.𐤄𐤋𐤌.𐤔𐤋.𐤍𐤏𐤋𐤉𐤊.𐤌𐤏𐤋.𐤓𐤂𐤋
𐤉𐤊.𐤊𐤉.𐤄𐤌𐤒𐤅𐤌.𐤀𐤔𐤓.𐤀𐤕𐤄.𐤏𐤅𐤌𐤃.𐤏𐤋𐤉𐤅.𐤀𐤃𐤌𐤕.
𐤒𐤃𐤔.𐤄𐤅𐤀|
6 𐤅𐤉𐤀𐤌𐤓.𐤀𐤍𐤊𐤉.𐤀𐤋𐤄𐤉.𐤀𐤁𐤉𐤊.𐤀𐤋𐤄𐤉.𐤀𐤁𐤓𐤄𐤌.𐤀
𐤋𐤄𐤉.𐤉𐤑𐤇𐤒.𐤅𐤀𐤋𐤄𐤉.𐤉𐤏𐤒𐤁.𐤅𐤉𐤎𐤕𐤓.𐤌𐤔𐤄.𐤐𐤍𐤉𐤅.𐤊
𐤉.𐤉𐤓𐤀.𐤌𐤄𐤁𐤉𐤈.𐤀𐤋.𐤄𐤀𐤋𐤄𐤉𐤌|
7 𐤅𐤉𐤀𐤌𐤓.𐤉𐤄𐤅𐤄.𐤓𐤀𐤄.𐤓𐤀𐤉𐤕𐤉.𐤀𐤕.𐤏𐤍𐤉.𐤏𐤌𐤉.𐤀
𐤔𐤓.𐤁𐤌𐤑𐤓𐤉𐤌.𐤅𐤀𐤕.𐤑𐤏𐤒𐤕𐤌.𐤔𐤌𐤏𐤕𐤉.𐤌𐤐𐤍𐤉.𐤍𐤂𐤔
𐤉𐤅.𐤊𐤉.𐤉𐤃𐤏𐤕𐤉.𐤀𐤕.𐤌𐤊𐤀𐤁𐤉𐤅|
8 𐤅𐤀𐤓𐤃.𐤋𐤄𐤑𐤉𐤋𐤅.𐤌𐤉𐤃.𐤌𐤑𐤓𐤉𐤌.𐤅𐤋𐤄𐤏𐤋𐤕𐤅.𐤌𐤍.𐤄
𐤀𐤓𐤑.𐤄𐤄𐤅𐤀.𐤀𐤋.𐤀𐤓𐤑.𐤈𐤅𐤁𐤄.𐤅𐤓𐤇𐤁𐤄.𐤀𐤋.𐤀𐤓𐤑.𐤆𐤁
𐤕.𐤇𐤋𐤁.𐤅𐤃𐤁𐤔.𐤀𐤋.𐤌𐤒𐤅𐤌.𐤄𐤊𐤍𐤏𐤍𐤉.𐤅𐤄𐤇𐤕𐤉.𐤅𐤄𐤀𐤌
𐤓𐤉.𐤅𐤄𐤐𐤓𐤆𐤉.𐤅𐤄𐤇𐤅𐤉.𐤅𐤄𐤉𐤁𐤅𐤎𐤉|
9 𐤅𐤏𐤕𐤄.𐤄𐤍𐤄.𐤑𐤏𐤒𐤕.𐤁𐤍𐤉.𐤉𐤔𐤓𐤀𐤋.𐤁𐤀𐤄.𐤀𐤋𐤉.𐤅
𐤂𐤌.𐤓𐤀𐤉𐤕𐤉.𐤀𐤕.𐤄𐤋𐤇𐤑.𐤀𐤔𐤓.𐤌𐤑𐤓𐤉𐤌.𐤋𐤇𐤑𐤉𐤌.
𐤀𐤕𐤌|
10 𐤅𐤏𐤕𐤄.𐤋𐤊𐤄.𐤅𐤀𐤔𐤋𐤇𐤊.𐤀𐤋.𐤐𐤓𐤏𐤄.𐤅𐤄𐤅𐤑𐤀.𐤀𐤕.
𐤏𐤌𐤉.𐤁𐤍𐤉.𐤉𐤔𐤓𐤀𐤋.𐤌𐤌𐤑𐤓𐤉𐤌|
11 𐤅𐤉𐤀𐤌𐤓.𐤌𐤔𐤄.𐤀𐤋.𐤄𐤀𐤋𐤄𐤉𐤌.𐤌𐤉.𐤀𐤍𐤊𐤉.𐤊𐤉.𐤀𐤋
𐤊.𐤀𐤋.𐤐𐤓𐤏𐤄.𐤅𐤊𐤉.𐤀𐤅𐤑𐤉𐤀.𐤀𐤕.𐤁𐤍𐤉.𐤉𐤔𐤓𐤀𐤋.𐤌𐤌𐤑𐤓
𐤉𐤌|

יב 𐤅𐤉𐤀𐤌𐤓.𐤊𐤉.𐤀𐤄𐤉𐤄.𐤏𐤌𐤊.𐤅𐤆𐤄.𐤋𐤊.𐤄𐤀𐤅𐤕.𐤊𐤉.𐤀𐤍𐤊𐤉.𐤔𐤋𐤇𐤕𐤉𐤊.𐤁𐤄𐤅𐤑𐤉𐤀𐤊.𐤀𐤕.𐤄𐤏𐤌.𐤌𐤌𐤑𐤓𐤉𐤌.𐤕𐤏𐤁𐤃𐤅𐤍.𐤀𐤕.𐤄𐤀𐤋𐤄𐤉𐤌.𐤏𐤋.𐤄𐤄𐤓.𐤄𐤆𐤄|

יג 𐤅𐤉𐤀𐤌𐤓.𐤌𐤔𐤄.𐤀𐤋.𐤄𐤀𐤋𐤄𐤉𐤌.𐤄𐤍𐤄.𐤀𐤍𐤊𐤉.𐤁𐤀.𐤀𐤋.𐤁𐤍𐤉.𐤉𐤔𐤓𐤀𐤋.𐤅𐤀𐤌𐤓𐤕𐤉.𐤋𐤄𐤌.𐤀𐤋𐤄𐤉.𐤀𐤁𐤅𐤕𐤉𐤊𐤌.𐤔𐤋𐤇𐤍𐤉.𐤀𐤋𐤉𐤊𐤌.𐤅𐤀𐤌𐤓𐤅.𐤋𐤉.𐤌𐤄.𐤔𐤌𐤅.𐤌𐤄.𐤀𐤌𐤓.𐤀𐤋𐤄𐤌|

יד 𐤅𐤉𐤀𐤌𐤓.𐤀𐤋𐤄𐤉𐤌.𐤀𐤋.𐤌𐤔𐤄.𐤀𐤄𐤉𐤄.𐤀𐤔𐤓.𐤀𐤄𐤉𐤄.𐤅𐤉𐤀𐤌𐤓.𐤊𐤄.𐤕𐤀𐤌𐤓.𐤋𐤁𐤍𐤉.𐤉𐤔𐤓𐤀𐤋.𐤀𐤄𐤉𐤄.𐤔𐤋𐤇𐤍𐤉.𐤀𐤋𐤉𐤊𐤌|

טו 𐤅𐤉𐤀𐤌𐤓.𐤏𐤅𐤃.𐤀𐤋𐤄𐤉𐤌.𐤀𐤋.𐤌𐤔𐤄.𐤊𐤄.𐤕𐤀𐤌𐤓.𐤀𐤋.𐤁𐤍𐤉.𐤉𐤔𐤓𐤀𐤋.𐤉𐤄𐤅𐤄.𐤀𐤋𐤄𐤉.𐤀𐤁𐤕𐤉𐤊𐤌.𐤀𐤋𐤄𐤉.𐤀𐤁𐤓𐤄𐤌.𐤀𐤋𐤄𐤉.𐤉𐤑𐤇𐤒.𐤅𐤀𐤋𐤄𐤉.𐤉𐤏𐤒𐤁.𐤔𐤋𐤇𐤍𐤉.𐤀𐤋𐤉𐤊𐤌.𐤆𐤄.𐤔𐤌𐤉.𐤋𐤏𐤋𐤌.𐤅𐤆𐤄.𐤆𐤊𐤓𐤉.𐤋𐤃𐤓.𐤃𐤓|

טז 𐤋𐤊.𐤅𐤀𐤎𐤐𐤕.𐤀𐤕.𐤆𐤒𐤍𐤉.𐤉𐤔𐤓𐤀𐤋.𐤅𐤀𐤌𐤓𐤕.𐤀𐤋𐤄𐤌.𐤉𐤄𐤅𐤄.𐤀𐤋𐤄𐤉.𐤀𐤁𐤕𐤉𐤊𐤌.𐤍𐤓𐤀𐤄.𐤀𐤋𐤉.𐤀𐤋𐤄𐤉.𐤀𐤁𐤓𐤄𐤌.𐤉𐤑𐤇𐤒.𐤅𐤉𐤏𐤒𐤁.𐤋𐤀𐤌𐤓.𐤐𐤒𐤃.𐤐𐤒𐤃𐤕𐤉.𐤀𐤕𐤊𐤌.𐤅𐤀𐤕.𐤄𐤏𐤔𐤅𐤉.𐤋𐤊𐤌.𐤁𐤌𐤑𐤓𐤉𐤌|

יז 𐤅𐤀𐤌𐤓.𐤀𐤏𐤋𐤄.𐤀𐤕𐤊𐤌.𐤌𐤏𐤍𐤉.𐤌𐤑𐤓𐤉𐤌.𐤀𐤋.𐤀𐤓𐤑.𐤄𐤊𐤍𐤏𐤍𐤉.𐤅𐤄𐤇𐤕𐤉.𐤅𐤄𐤀𐤌𐤓𐤉.𐤅𐤄𐤐𐤓𐤆𐤉.𐤅𐤄𐤇𐤅𐤉.𐤅𐤄𐤉𐤁𐤅𐤎𐤉.𐤀𐤋.𐤀𐤓𐤑.𐤆𐤁𐤕.𐤇𐤋𐤁.𐤅𐤃𐤁𐤔|

יח 𐤅𐤔𐤌𐤏𐤅.𐤋𐤒𐤋𐤊.𐤅𐤁𐤀𐤕.𐤀𐤕𐤄.𐤅𐤆𐤒𐤍𐤉.𐤉𐤔𐤓𐤀𐤋.𐤀𐤋.𐤌𐤋𐤊.𐤌𐤑𐤓𐤉𐤌.𐤅𐤀𐤌𐤓𐤕𐤌.𐤀𐤋𐤉𐤅.𐤉𐤄𐤅𐤄.𐤀𐤋𐤄𐤉.𐤄𐤏𐤁𐤓𐤉𐤉𐤌.𐤍𐤒𐤓𐤄.𐤏𐤋𐤉𐤍𐤅.𐤅𐤏𐤕𐤄.𐤍𐤋𐤊𐤄.𐤍𐤀.𐤃𐤓𐤊.𐤔𐤋𐤔𐤕.𐤉𐤌𐤉𐤌.𐤁𐤌𐤃𐤁𐤓.𐤅𐤍𐤆𐤁𐤇𐤄.𐤋𐤉𐤄𐤅𐤄.𐤀𐤋𐤄𐤉𐤍𐤅|

יט 𐤅𐤀𐤍𐤉.𐤉𐤃𐤏𐤕𐤉.𐤊𐤉.𐤋𐤀.𐤉𐤕𐤍.𐤀𐤕𐤊𐤌.𐤌𐤋𐤊.𐤌𐤑𐤓𐤉𐤌.𐤋𐤄𐤋𐤊.𐤅𐤋𐤀.𐤁𐤉𐤃.𐤇𐤆𐤒𐤄|

כ 𐤅𐤔𐤋𐤇𐤕𐤉.𐤀𐤕.𐤉𐤃𐤉.𐤅𐤄𐤊𐤉𐤕𐤉.𐤀𐤕.𐤌𐤑𐤓𐤉𐤌.𐤁𐤊𐤋.𐤍𐤐𐤋𐤀𐤕𐤉.𐤀𐤔𐤓.𐤀𐤏𐤔𐤄.𐤁𐤒𐤓𐤁𐤅.𐤅𐤀𐤇𐤓𐤉.𐤊𐤍.𐤉𐤔𐤋𐤇.𐤀𐤕𐤊𐤌|

21 𐤅𐤍𐤕𐤕𐤉.𐤀𐤕.𐤇𐤍.𐤄𐤏𐤌.𐤄𐤆𐤄.𐤁𐤏𐤉𐤍𐤉.𐤌𐤑𐤓𐤉𐤌.
𐤅𐤄𐤉𐤄.𐤊𐤉.𐤕𐤋𐤊𐤅𐤍.𐤋𐤀.𐤕𐤋𐤊𐤅.𐤓𐤉𐤒𐤌|
22 𐤅𐤔𐤀𐤋𐤄.𐤀𐤔𐤄.𐤌𐤔𐤊𐤍𐤕𐤄.𐤅𐤌𐤂𐤓𐤕.𐤁𐤉𐤕𐤄.𐤊𐤋𐤉.
𐤊𐤎𐤐.𐤅𐤊𐤋𐤉.𐤆𐤄𐤁.𐤅𐤔𐤌𐤋𐤕.𐤅𐤔𐤌𐤕𐤌.𐤏𐤋.𐤁𐤍𐤉𐤊𐤌.𐤅𐤏𐤋.
𐤁𐤍𐤕𐤉𐤊𐤌.𐤅𐤍𐤑𐤋𐤕𐤌.𐤀𐤕.𐤌𐤑𐤓𐤉𐤌||

𐤅𐤉𐤏𐤋𐤅.𐤌𐤌𐤑𐤓𐤉𐤌.𐤇𐤋𐤒 ..4..

1 𐤅𐤉𐤏𐤍.𐤌𐤔𐤄.𐤅𐤉𐤀𐤌𐤓.𐤅𐤄𐤍.𐤋𐤀.𐤉𐤀𐤌𐤉𐤍𐤅.𐤋𐤉.𐤅𐤋𐤀.𐤉
𐤔𐤌𐤏𐤅.𐤁𐤒𐤋𐤉.𐤊𐤉.𐤉𐤀𐤌𐤓𐤅.𐤋𐤀.𐤍𐤓𐤀𐤄.𐤀𐤋𐤉𐤊.𐤉𐤄𐤅𐤄|
2 𐤅𐤉𐤀𐤌𐤓.𐤀𐤋𐤉𐤅.𐤉𐤄𐤅𐤄.𐤌𐤆𐤄.‖𐤌𐤄.𐤆𐤄.𐤒𐤓𐤉‖.𐤁𐤉
𐤃𐤊.𐤅𐤉𐤀𐤌𐤓.𐤌𐤈𐤄|
3 𐤅𐤉𐤀𐤌𐤓.𐤄𐤔𐤋𐤉𐤊𐤄𐤅.𐤀𐤓𐤑𐤄.𐤅𐤉𐤔𐤋𐤉𐤊𐤄𐤅.𐤀𐤓𐤑𐤄.
𐤅𐤉𐤄𐤉.𐤋𐤍𐤇𐤔.𐤅𐤉𐤍𐤎.𐤌𐤔𐤄.𐤌𐤐𐤍𐤉𐤅|
4 𐤅𐤉𐤀𐤌𐤓.𐤉𐤄𐤅𐤄.𐤀𐤋.𐤌𐤔𐤄.𐤔𐤋𐤇.𐤉𐤃𐤊.𐤅𐤀𐤇𐤆.𐤁
𐤆𐤍𐤁𐤅.𐤅𐤉𐤔𐤋𐤇.𐤉𐤃𐤅.𐤅𐤉𐤇𐤆𐤒.𐤁𐤅.𐤅𐤉𐤄𐤉.𐤋𐤌𐤈𐤄.𐤁𐤊𐤐
𐤅|
5 𐤋𐤌𐤏𐤍.𐤉𐤀𐤌𐤉𐤍𐤅.𐤊𐤉.𐤍𐤓𐤀𐤄.𐤀𐤋𐤉𐤊.𐤉𐤄𐤅𐤄.𐤀𐤋𐤄𐤉.
𐤀𐤁𐤕𐤌.𐤀𐤋𐤄𐤉.𐤀𐤁𐤓𐤄𐤌.𐤀𐤋𐤄𐤉.𐤉𐤑𐤇𐤒.𐤅𐤀𐤋𐤄𐤉.𐤉𐤏
𐤒𐤁|
6 𐤅𐤉𐤀𐤌𐤓.𐤉𐤄𐤅𐤄.𐤋𐤅.𐤏𐤅𐤃.𐤄𐤁𐤀.𐤍𐤀.𐤉𐤃𐤊.𐤁𐤇𐤉𐤒𐤊.
𐤅𐤉𐤁𐤀.𐤉𐤃𐤅.𐤁𐤇𐤉𐤒𐤅.𐤅𐤉𐤅𐤑𐤀𐤄.𐤅𐤄𐤍𐤄.𐤌𐤑𐤓𐤏𐤕.
𐤊𐤔𐤋𐤂|
7 𐤅𐤉𐤀𐤌𐤓.𐤄𐤔𐤁.𐤉𐤃𐤊.𐤀𐤋.𐤇𐤉𐤒𐤊.𐤅𐤉𐤔𐤁.𐤉𐤃𐤅.𐤀𐤋.
𐤇𐤉𐤒𐤅.𐤅𐤉𐤅𐤑𐤀𐤄.𐤌𐤇𐤉𐤒𐤅.𐤅𐤄𐤍𐤄.𐤔𐤁𐤄.𐤊𐤁𐤔𐤓𐤅|
8 𐤅𐤄𐤉𐤄.𐤀𐤌.𐤋𐤀.𐤉𐤀𐤌𐤉𐤍𐤅.𐤋𐤊.𐤅𐤋𐤀.𐤉𐤔𐤌𐤏𐤅.𐤋𐤒𐤋.𐤄
𐤀𐤕.𐤄𐤓𐤀𐤔𐤅𐤍.𐤅𐤄𐤀𐤌𐤉𐤍𐤅.𐤋𐤒𐤋.𐤄𐤀𐤕.𐤄𐤀𐤇𐤓𐤅𐤍|
9 𐤅𐤄𐤉𐤄.𐤀𐤌.𐤋𐤀.𐤉𐤀𐤌𐤉𐤍𐤅.𐤂𐤌.𐤋𐤔𐤍𐤉.𐤄𐤀𐤕𐤅𐤕.𐤄
𐤀𐤋𐤄.𐤅𐤋𐤀.𐤉𐤔𐤌𐤏𐤅𐤍.𐤋𐤒𐤋𐤊.𐤅𐤋𐤒𐤇𐤕.𐤌𐤌𐤉𐤌𐤉.𐤄𐤉𐤀𐤓
𐤅𐤔𐤐𐤊𐤕.𐤄𐤉𐤁𐤔𐤄.𐤅𐤄𐤉𐤅.𐤄𐤌𐤉𐤌.𐤀𐤔𐤓.𐤕𐤒𐤇.𐤌𐤍.𐤄𐤉
𐤀𐤓.𐤅𐤄𐤉𐤅.𐤋𐤃𐤌.𐤁𐤉𐤁𐤔𐤕|

10 𐤅𐤉𐤀𐤌𐤓.𐤌𐤔𐤄.𐤀𐤋.𐤉𐤄𐤅𐤄.𐤁𐤉.𐤀𐤃𐤍𐤉.𐤋𐤀.𐤀𐤉𐤔.𐤃𐤁𐤓𐤉𐤌.𐤀𐤍𐤊𐤉.𐤂𐤌.𐤌𐤕𐤌𐤅𐤋.𐤂𐤌.𐤌𐤔𐤋𐤔𐤌.𐤂𐤌.𐤌𐤀𐤆.𐤃𐤁𐤓𐤊.𐤀𐤋.𐤏𐤁𐤃𐤊.𐤊𐤉.𐤊𐤁𐤃.𐤐𐤄.𐤅𐤊𐤁𐤃.𐤋𐤔𐤅𐤍.𐤀𐤍𐤊𐤉|

11 𐤅𐤉𐤀𐤌𐤓.𐤉𐤄𐤅𐤄.𐤀𐤋𐤉𐤅.𐤌𐤉.𐤔𐤌.𐤐𐤄.𐤋𐤀𐤃𐤌.𐤀𐤅.𐤌𐤉.𐤉𐤔𐤅𐤌.𐤀𐤋𐤌.𐤀𐤅.𐤇𐤓𐤔.𐤀𐤅.𐤐𐤒𐤇.𐤀𐤅.𐤏𐤅𐤓.𐤄𐤋𐤀.𐤀𐤍𐤊𐤉.𐤉𐤄𐤅𐤄|

12 𐤅𐤏𐤕𐤄.𐤋𐤊.𐤅𐤀𐤍𐤊𐤉.𐤀𐤄𐤉𐤄.𐤏𐤌.𐤐𐤉𐤊.𐤅𐤄𐤅𐤓𐤉𐤕𐤉𐤊.𐤀𐤔𐤓.𐤕𐤃𐤁𐤓|

13 𐤅𐤉𐤀𐤌𐤓.𐤁𐤉.𐤀𐤃𐤍𐤉.𐤔𐤋𐤇.𐤍𐤀.𐤁𐤉𐤃.𐤕𐤔𐤋𐤇|

14 𐤅𐤉𐤇𐤓.𐤀𐤐.𐤉𐤄𐤅𐤄.𐤁𐤌𐤔𐤄.𐤅𐤉𐤀𐤌𐤓.𐤄𐤋𐤀.𐤀𐤄𐤓𐤍.𐤀𐤇𐤉𐤊.𐤄𐤋𐤅𐤉.𐤉𐤃𐤏𐤕𐤉.𐤊𐤉.𐤃𐤁𐤓.𐤉𐤃𐤁𐤓.𐤄𐤅𐤀.𐤅𐤂𐤌.𐤄𐤍𐤄.𐤄𐤅𐤀.𐤉𐤑𐤀.𐤋𐤒𐤓𐤀𐤕𐤊.𐤅𐤓𐤀𐤊.𐤅𐤔𐤌𐤇.𐤁𐤋𐤁𐤅|

15 𐤅𐤃𐤁𐤓𐤕.𐤀𐤋𐤉𐤅.𐤅𐤔𐤌𐤕.𐤀𐤕.𐤄𐤃𐤁𐤓𐤉𐤌.𐤁𐤐𐤉𐤅.𐤅𐤀𐤍𐤊𐤉.𐤀𐤄𐤉𐤄.𐤏𐤌.𐤐𐤉𐤊.𐤅𐤏𐤌.𐤐𐤉𐤄𐤅.𐤅𐤄𐤅𐤓𐤉𐤕𐤉.𐤀𐤕𐤊𐤌.𐤀𐤕.𐤀𐤔𐤓.𐤕𐤏𐤔𐤅𐤍|

16 𐤅𐤃𐤁𐤓.𐤄𐤅𐤀.𐤋𐤊.𐤀𐤋.𐤄𐤏𐤌.𐤅𐤄𐤉𐤄.𐤄𐤅𐤀.𐤉𐤄𐤉𐤄.𐤋𐤊.𐤋𐤐𐤄.𐤅𐤀𐤕𐤄.𐤕𐤄𐤉𐤄.𐤋𐤅.𐤋𐤀𐤋𐤄𐤉𐤌|

17 𐤅𐤀𐤕.𐤄𐤌𐤈𐤄.𐤄𐤆𐤄.𐤕𐤒𐤇.𐤁𐤉𐤃𐤊.𐤀𐤔𐤓.𐤕𐤏𐤔𐤄.𐤁𐤅.𐤀𐤕.𐤄𐤀𐤕𐤕|

18 𐤅𐤉𐤋𐤊.𐤌𐤔𐤄.𐤅𐤉𐤔𐤁.𐤀𐤋.𐤉𐤕𐤓.𐤇𐤕𐤍𐤅.𐤅𐤉𐤀𐤌𐤓.𐤋𐤅.𐤀𐤋𐤊𐤄.𐤍𐤀.𐤅𐤀𐤔𐤅𐤁𐤄.𐤀𐤋.𐤀𐤇𐤉.𐤀𐤔𐤓.𐤁𐤌𐤑𐤓𐤉𐤌.𐤅𐤀𐤓𐤀𐤄.𐤄𐤏𐤅𐤃𐤌.𐤇𐤉𐤉𐤌.𐤅𐤉𐤀𐤌𐤓.𐤉𐤕𐤓𐤅.𐤋𐤌𐤔𐤄.𐤋𐤊.𐤋𐤔𐤋𐤅𐤌|

19 𐤅𐤉𐤀𐤌𐤓.𐤉𐤄𐤅𐤄.𐤀𐤋.𐤌𐤔𐤄.𐤁𐤌𐤃𐤉𐤍.𐤋𐤊.𐤔𐤁.𐤌𐤑𐤓𐤉𐤌.𐤊𐤉.𐤌𐤕𐤅.𐤊𐤋.𐤄𐤀𐤍𐤔𐤉𐤌.𐤄𐤌𐤁𐤒𐤔𐤉𐤌.𐤀𐤕.𐤍𐤐𐤔𐤊|

20 𐤅𐤉𐤒𐤇.𐤌𐤔𐤄.𐤀𐤕.𐤀𐤔𐤕𐤅.𐤅𐤀𐤕.𐤁𐤍𐤉𐤅.𐤅𐤉𐤓𐤊𐤁𐤌.𐤏𐤋.𐤄𐤇𐤌𐤓.𐤅𐤉𐤔𐤁.𐤀𐤓𐤑𐤄.𐤌𐤑𐤓𐤉𐤌.𐤅𐤉𐤒𐤇.𐤌𐤔𐤄.𐤀𐤕.𐤌𐤈𐤄.𐤄𐤀𐤋𐤄𐤉𐤌.𐤁𐤉𐤃𐤅|

21 𐤅𐤉𐤀𐤌𐤓.𐤉𐤄𐤅𐤄.𐤀𐤋.𐤌𐤔𐤄.𐤁𐤋𐤊𐤕𐤊.𐤋𐤔𐤅𐤁.𐤌𐤑𐤓𐤉𐤌𐤄.𐤓𐤀𐤄.𐤊𐤋.𐤄𐤌𐤐𐤕𐤉𐤌.𐤀𐤔𐤓.𐤔𐤌𐤕𐤉.𐤁𐤉𐤃𐤊.𐤅𐤏𐤔𐤉

𐤕𐤌.𐤋𐤐𐤍𐤉.𐤐𐤓𐤏𐤄.𐤅𐤀𐤍𐤉.𐤀𐤇𐤆𐤒.𐤀𐤕.𐤋𐤁𐤅.𐤅𐤋𐤀.𐤉𐤔𐤋𐤇.𐤀𐤕.𐤄𐤏𐤌|

22 𐤅𐤀𐤌𐤓𐤕.𐤀𐤋.𐤐𐤓𐤏𐤄.𐤊𐤄.𐤀𐤌𐤓.𐤉𐤄𐤅𐤄.𐤁𐤍𐤉.𐤁𐤊𐤓𐤉.𐤉𐤔𐤓𐤀𐤋|

23 𐤅𐤀𐤌𐤓.𐤀𐤋𐤉𐤊.𐤔𐤋𐤇.𐤀𐤕.𐤁𐤍𐤉.𐤅𐤉𐤏𐤁𐤃𐤍𐤉.𐤅𐤕𐤌𐤀𐤍.𐤋𐤔𐤋𐤇𐤅.𐤄𐤍𐤄.𐤀𐤍𐤊𐤉.𐤄𐤓𐤂.𐤀𐤕.𐤁𐤍𐤊.𐤁𐤊𐤓𐤊|

24 𐤅𐤉𐤄𐤉.𐤁𐤃𐤓𐤊.𐤁𐤌𐤋𐤅𐤍.𐤅𐤉𐤐𐤂𐤔𐤄𐤅.𐤉𐤄𐤅𐤄.𐤅𐤉𐤁𐤒𐤔.𐤄𐤌𐤉𐤕𐤅|

25 𐤅𐤕𐤒𐤇.𐤑𐤐𐤓𐤄.𐤑𐤓.𐤅𐤕𐤊𐤓𐤕.𐤀𐤕.𐤏𐤓𐤋𐤕.𐤁𐤍𐤄.𐤅𐤕𐤂𐤏.𐤋𐤓𐤂𐤋𐤉𐤅.𐤅𐤕𐤀𐤌𐤓.𐤊𐤉.𐤇𐤕𐤍.𐤃𐤌𐤉𐤌.𐤀𐤕𐤄.𐤋𐤉|

26 𐤅𐤉𐤓𐤐.𐤌𐤌𐤍𐤅.𐤀𐤆.𐤀𐤌𐤓𐤄.𐤇𐤕𐤍.𐤃𐤌𐤉𐤌.𐤋𐤌𐤅𐤋𐤕|

27 𐤅𐤉𐤀𐤌𐤓.𐤉𐤄𐤅𐤄.𐤀𐤋.𐤀𐤄𐤓𐤍.𐤋𐤊.𐤋𐤒𐤓𐤀𐤕.𐤌𐤔𐤄.𐤄𐤌𐤃𐤁𐤓𐤄.𐤅𐤉𐤋𐤊.𐤅𐤉𐤐𐤂𐤔𐤄𐤅.𐤁𐤄𐤓.𐤄𐤀𐤋𐤄𐤉𐤌.𐤅𐤉𐤔𐤒.𐤋𐤅|

28 𐤅𐤉𐤂𐤃.𐤌𐤔𐤄.𐤋𐤀𐤄𐤓𐤍.𐤀𐤕.𐤊𐤋.𐤃𐤁𐤓𐤉.𐤉𐤄𐤅𐤄.𐤀𐤔𐤓.𐤔𐤋𐤇𐤅.𐤅𐤀𐤕.𐤊𐤋.𐤄𐤀𐤕𐤕.𐤀𐤔𐤓.𐤑𐤅𐤄𐤅|

29 𐤅𐤉𐤋𐤊.𐤌𐤔𐤄.𐤅𐤀𐤄𐤓𐤍.𐤅𐤉𐤀𐤎𐤐𐤅.𐤀𐤕.𐤊𐤋.𐤆𐤒𐤍𐤉.𐤁𐤍𐤉.𐤉𐤔𐤓𐤀𐤋|

30 𐤅𐤉𐤃𐤁𐤓.𐤀𐤄𐤓𐤍.𐤀𐤕.𐤊𐤋.𐤄𐤃𐤁𐤓𐤉𐤌.𐤀𐤔𐤓.𐤃𐤁𐤓.𐤉𐤄𐤅𐤄.𐤀𐤋.𐤌𐤔𐤄.𐤅𐤉𐤏𐤔.𐤄𐤀𐤕𐤕.𐤋𐤏𐤉𐤍𐤉.𐤄𐤏𐤌|

31 𐤅𐤉𐤀𐤌𐤍.𐤄𐤏𐤌.𐤅𐤉𐤔𐤌𐤏𐤅.𐤊𐤉.𐤐𐤒𐤃.𐤉𐤄𐤅𐤄.𐤀𐤕.𐤁𐤍𐤉.𐤉𐤔𐤓𐤀𐤋.𐤅𐤊𐤉.𐤓𐤀𐤄.𐤀𐤕.𐤏𐤍𐤉𐤌.𐤅𐤉𐤒𐤃𐤅.𐤅𐤉𐤔𐤕𐤇𐤅𐤅||

𐤅𐤉𐤏𐤋𐤅.𐤌𐤌𐤑𐤓𐤉𐤌.𐤇𐤋𐤒 5

1 𐤅𐤀𐤇𐤓.𐤁𐤀𐤅.𐤌𐤔𐤄.𐤅𐤀𐤄𐤓𐤍.𐤅𐤉𐤀𐤌𐤓𐤅.𐤀𐤋.𐤐𐤓𐤏𐤄.𐤊𐤄.𐤀𐤌𐤓.𐤉𐤄𐤅𐤄.𐤀𐤋𐤄𐤉.𐤉𐤔𐤓𐤀𐤋.𐤔𐤋𐤇.𐤀𐤕.𐤏𐤌𐤉.𐤅𐤉𐤇𐤂𐤅.𐤋𐤉.𐤁𐤌𐤃𐤁𐤓|

ב 𐤅𐤉𐤀𐤌𐤓.𐤐𐤓𐤏𐤄.𐤌𐤉.𐤉𐤄𐤅𐤄.𐤀𐤔𐤓.𐤀𐤔𐤌𐤏.𐤁𐤒𐤋𐤅.𐤋
𐤔𐤋𐤇.𐤀𐤕.𐤉𐤔𐤓𐤀𐤋.𐤋𐤀.𐤉𐤃𐤏𐤕𐤉.𐤀𐤕.𐤉𐤄𐤅𐤄.𐤅𐤂𐤌.𐤀
𐤕.𐤉𐤔𐤓𐤀𐤋.𐤋𐤀.𐤀𐤔𐤋𐤇|

ג 𐤅𐤉𐤀𐤌𐤓𐤅.𐤀𐤋𐤄𐤉.𐤄𐤏𐤁𐤓𐤉𐤌.𐤍𐤒𐤓𐤀.𐤏𐤋𐤉𐤍𐤅.𐤍𐤋𐤊𐤄.
𐤍𐤀.𐤃𐤓𐤊.𐤔𐤋𐤔𐤕.𐤉𐤌𐤉𐤌.𐤁𐤌𐤃𐤁𐤓.𐤅𐤍𐤆𐤁𐤇𐤄.𐤋𐤉𐤄𐤅𐤄.
𐤀𐤋𐤄𐤉𐤍𐤅.𐤐𐤍.𐤉𐤐𐤂𐤏𐤍𐤅.𐤁𐤃𐤁𐤓.𐤀𐤅.𐤁𐤇𐤓𐤁|

ד 𐤅𐤉𐤀𐤌𐤓.𐤀𐤋𐤄𐤌.𐤌𐤋𐤊.𐤌𐤑𐤓𐤉𐤌.𐤋𐤌𐤄.𐤌𐤔𐤄.𐤅𐤀𐤄𐤓
𐤍.𐤕𐤐𐤓𐤉𐤏𐤅.𐤀𐤕.𐤄𐤏𐤌.𐤌𐤌𐤏𐤔𐤉𐤅.𐤋𐤊𐤅.𐤋𐤎𐤁𐤋𐤕𐤉𐤊𐤌|

ה 𐤅𐤉𐤀𐤌𐤓.𐤐𐤓𐤏𐤄.𐤄𐤍.𐤓𐤁𐤉𐤌.𐤏𐤕𐤄.𐤏𐤌.𐤄𐤀𐤓𐤑.𐤅𐤄𐤔
𐤁𐤕𐤌.𐤀𐤕𐤌.𐤌𐤎𐤁𐤋𐤕𐤌|

ו 𐤅𐤉𐤑𐤅.𐤐𐤓𐤏𐤄.𐤁𐤉𐤅𐤌.𐤄𐤄𐤅𐤀.𐤀𐤕.𐤄𐤍𐤂𐤔𐤉𐤌.𐤁𐤏𐤌.𐤅
𐤀𐤕.𐤔𐤈𐤓𐤉𐤅.𐤋𐤀𐤌𐤓|

ז 𐤋𐤀.𐤕𐤀𐤎𐤐𐤅𐤍.𐤋𐤕𐤕.𐤕𐤁𐤍.𐤋𐤏𐤌.𐤋𐤋𐤁𐤍.𐤄𐤋𐤁𐤍𐤉𐤌.𐤊
𐤕𐤌𐤅𐤋.𐤔𐤋𐤔𐤌.𐤄𐤌.𐤉𐤋𐤊𐤅.𐤅𐤒𐤔𐤔𐤅.𐤋𐤄𐤌.𐤕𐤁𐤍|

ח 𐤅𐤀𐤕.𐤌𐤕𐤊𐤍𐤕.𐤄𐤋𐤁𐤍𐤉𐤌.𐤀𐤔𐤓.𐤄𐤌.𐤏𐤔𐤉𐤌.𐤕𐤌𐤅𐤋.
𐤔𐤋𐤔𐤌.𐤕𐤔𐤉𐤌𐤅.𐤏𐤋𐤉𐤄𐤌.𐤋𐤀.𐤕𐤂𐤓𐤏𐤅.𐤌𐤌𐤍𐤅.𐤊𐤉.𐤍𐤓𐤐
𐤉𐤌.𐤄𐤌.𐤏𐤋.𐤊𐤍.𐤄𐤌.𐤑𐤏𐤒𐤉𐤌.𐤋𐤀𐤌𐤓.𐤍𐤋𐤊𐤄.𐤍𐤆𐤁𐤇𐤄
.𐤋𐤀𐤋𐤄𐤉𐤍𐤅|

ט 𐤕𐤊𐤁𐤃.𐤄𐤏𐤁𐤃𐤄.𐤏𐤋.𐤄𐤀𐤍𐤔𐤉𐤌.𐤅𐤉𐤏𐤔𐤅.𐤁𐤄.𐤅𐤀
𐤋.𐤉𐤔𐤏𐤅.𐤁𐤃𐤁𐤓𐤉.𐤔𐤒𐤓|

י 𐤅𐤉𐤑𐤀𐤅.𐤍𐤂𐤔𐤉.𐤄𐤏𐤌.𐤅𐤔𐤈𐤓𐤉𐤅.𐤅𐤉𐤀𐤌𐤓𐤅.𐤀𐤋.𐤄
𐤏𐤌.𐤋𐤀𐤌𐤓.𐤊𐤄.𐤀𐤌𐤓.𐤐𐤓𐤏𐤄.𐤀𐤉𐤍𐤍𐤉.𐤍𐤕𐤍.𐤋𐤊𐤌.𐤕𐤁𐤍|

יא 𐤀𐤕𐤌.𐤋𐤊𐤅.𐤒𐤇𐤅.𐤋𐤊𐤌.𐤕𐤁𐤍.𐤌𐤀𐤔𐤓.𐤕𐤌𐤑𐤀𐤅.𐤊𐤉.
𐤀𐤉𐤍.𐤍𐤂𐤓𐤏.𐤌𐤏𐤁𐤃𐤕𐤊𐤌.𐤃𐤁𐤓|

יב 𐤅𐤉𐤐𐤑.𐤄𐤏𐤌.𐤁𐤊𐤋.𐤀𐤓𐤑.𐤌𐤑𐤓𐤉𐤌.𐤋𐤒𐤔𐤔.𐤒𐤔.𐤋
𐤕𐤁𐤍|

יג 𐤅𐤄𐤍𐤂𐤔𐤉𐤌.𐤀𐤑𐤉𐤌.𐤋𐤀𐤌𐤓.𐤊𐤋𐤅.𐤌𐤏𐤔𐤉𐤊𐤌.𐤃𐤁
𐤓.𐤉𐤅𐤌.𐤁𐤉𐤅𐤌𐤅.𐤊𐤀𐤔𐤓.𐤁𐤄𐤉𐤅𐤕.𐤄𐤕𐤁𐤍|

יד 𐤅𐤉𐤊𐤅.𐤔𐤈𐤓𐤉.𐤁𐤍𐤉.𐤉𐤔𐤓𐤀𐤋.𐤀𐤔𐤓.𐤔𐤌𐤅.𐤏𐤋𐤄𐤌.𐤍
𐤂𐤔𐤉.𐤐𐤓𐤏𐤄.𐤋𐤀𐤌𐤓.𐤌𐤃𐤅𐤏.𐤋𐤀.𐤊𐤋𐤉𐤕𐤌.𐤇𐤒𐤊𐤌.𐤋𐤋
𐤁𐤍.𐤊𐤕𐤌𐤅𐤋.𐤔𐤋𐤔𐤌.𐤂𐤌.𐤕𐤌𐤅𐤋.𐤂𐤌.𐤄𐤉𐤅𐤌|

טו ויבאו.שטרי.בני.ישראל.ויצעקו.אל.פרע
ה.לאמר.למה.תעשה.כה.לעבדיך׃
טז תבן.אין.נתן.לעבדיך.ולבנים.אמרים.לנו
עשו.והנה.עבדיך.מכים.וחטאת.עמך׃
יז ויאמר.נרפים.אתם.נרפים.על.כן.אתם.אמ
רים.נלכה.נזבחה.ליהוה׃
יח ועתה.לכו.עבדו.ותבן.לא.ינתן.לכם.ותכן.
לבנים.תתנו׃
יט ויראו.שטרי.בני.ישראל.אתם.ברע.לאמר
לא.תגרעו.מלבניכם.דבר.יום.ביומו׃
כ ויפגעו.את.משה.ואת.אהרן.נצבים.לקר
אתם.בצאתם.מאת.פרעה׃
כא ויאמרו.אלהם.ירא.יהוה.עליכם.וישפט.
אשר.הבאשתם.את.ריחנו.בעיני.פרעה.ובעינ
י.עבדיו.לתת.חרב.בידם.להרגנו׃
כב וישב.משה.אל.יהוה.ויאמר.אדני.למה.ה
רעתה.לעם.הזה.למה.זה.שלחתני׃
כג ומאז.באתי.אל.פרעה.לדבר.בשמך.הרע.
לעם.הזה.והצל.לא.הצלת.את.עמך׃׃

ויעלו.ממצרים.חלק ו

א ויאמר.יהוה.אל.משה.עתה.תראה.אשר.אע
שה.לפרעה.כי.ביד.חזקה.ישלחם.וביד.ח
זקה.יגרשם.מארצו׃
ב וידבר.אלהים.אל.משה.ויאמר.אליו.אני.י
הוה׃
ג וארא.אל.אברהם.אל.יצחק.ואל.יעקב.בא
ל.שדי.ושמי.יהוה.לא.נודעתי.להם׃
ד וגם.הקמתי.את.בריתי.אתם.לתת.להם.א
ת.ארץ.כנען.את.ארץ.מגריהם.אשר.גרו.בה׃

5 𐤅𐤂𐤌.𐤀𐤍𐤉.𐤔𐤌𐤏𐤕𐤉.𐤀𐤕.𐤍𐤀𐤒𐤕.𐤁𐤍𐤉.𐤉𐤔𐤓𐤀𐤋.𐤀
𐤔𐤓.𐤌𐤑𐤓𐤉𐤌.𐤌𐤏𐤁𐤃𐤉𐤌.𐤀𐤕𐤌.𐤅𐤀𐤆𐤊𐤓.𐤀𐤕.𐤁𐤓𐤉𐤕𐤉|
6 𐤋𐤊𐤍.𐤀𐤌𐤓.𐤋𐤁𐤍𐤉.𐤉𐤔𐤓𐤀𐤋.𐤀𐤍𐤉.𐤉𐤄𐤅𐤄.𐤅𐤄𐤅𐤑𐤀𐤕𐤉
.𐤀𐤕𐤊𐤌.𐤌𐤕𐤇𐤕.𐤎𐤁𐤋𐤕.𐤌𐤑𐤓𐤉𐤌.𐤅𐤄𐤑𐤋𐤕𐤉.𐤀𐤕𐤊𐤌.
𐤌𐤏𐤁𐤃𐤕𐤌.𐤅𐤂𐤀𐤋𐤕𐤉.𐤀𐤕𐤊𐤌.𐤁𐤆𐤓𐤅𐤏.𐤍𐤈𐤅𐤉𐤄.𐤅𐤁𐤔
𐤐𐤈𐤉𐤌.𐤂𐤃𐤋𐤉𐤌|
7 𐤅𐤋𐤒𐤇𐤕𐤉.𐤀𐤕𐤊𐤌.𐤋𐤉.𐤋𐤏𐤌.𐤅𐤄𐤉𐤉𐤕𐤉.𐤋𐤊𐤌.𐤋𐤀𐤋
𐤄𐤉𐤌.𐤅𐤉𐤃𐤏𐤕𐤌.𐤊𐤉.𐤀𐤍𐤉.𐤉𐤄𐤅𐤄.𐤀𐤋𐤄𐤉𐤊𐤌.𐤄𐤌𐤅𐤑𐤉
𐤀.𐤀𐤕𐤊𐤌.𐤌𐤕𐤇𐤕.𐤎𐤁𐤋𐤅𐤕.𐤌𐤑𐤓𐤉𐤌|
8 𐤅𐤄𐤁𐤀𐤕𐤉.𐤀𐤕𐤊𐤌.𐤀𐤋.𐤄𐤀𐤓𐤑.𐤀𐤔𐤓.𐤍𐤔𐤀𐤕𐤉.𐤀𐤕
.𐤉𐤃𐤉.𐤋𐤕𐤕.𐤀𐤕𐤄.𐤋𐤀𐤁𐤓𐤄𐤌.𐤋𐤉𐤑𐤇𐤒.𐤅𐤋𐤉𐤏𐤒𐤁.𐤅𐤍
𐤕𐤕𐤉.𐤀𐤕𐤄.𐤋𐤊𐤌.𐤌𐤅𐤓𐤔𐤄.𐤀𐤍𐤉.𐤉𐤄𐤅𐤄|
9 𐤅𐤉𐤃𐤁𐤓.𐤌𐤔𐤄.𐤊𐤍.𐤀𐤋.𐤁𐤍𐤉.𐤉𐤔𐤓𐤀𐤋.𐤅𐤋𐤀.𐤔𐤌𐤏𐤅.
𐤀𐤋.𐤌𐤔𐤄.𐤌𐤒𐤑𐤓.𐤓𐤅𐤇.𐤅𐤌𐤏𐤁𐤃𐤄.𐤒𐤔𐤄|
10 𐤅𐤉𐤃𐤁𐤓.𐤉𐤄𐤅𐤄.𐤀𐤋.𐤌𐤔𐤄.𐤋𐤀𐤌𐤓|
11 𐤁𐤀.𐤃𐤁𐤓.𐤀𐤋.𐤐𐤓𐤏𐤄.𐤌𐤋𐤊.𐤌𐤑𐤓𐤉𐤌.𐤅𐤉𐤔𐤋𐤇.𐤀
𐤕.𐤁𐤍𐤉.𐤉𐤔𐤓𐤀𐤋.𐤌𐤀𐤓𐤑𐤅|
12 𐤅𐤉𐤃𐤁𐤓.𐤌𐤔𐤄.𐤋𐤐𐤍𐤉.𐤉𐤄𐤅𐤄.𐤋𐤀𐤌𐤓.𐤄𐤍.𐤁𐤍𐤉.𐤉𐤔
𐤓𐤀𐤋.𐤋𐤀.𐤔𐤌𐤏𐤅.𐤀𐤋𐤉.𐤅𐤀𐤉𐤊.𐤉𐤔𐤌𐤏𐤍𐤉.𐤐𐤓𐤏𐤄.𐤅𐤀𐤍𐤉.
𐤏𐤓𐤋.𐤔𐤐𐤕𐤉𐤌|
13 𐤅𐤉𐤃𐤁𐤓.𐤉𐤄𐤅𐤄.𐤀𐤋.𐤌𐤔𐤄.𐤅𐤀𐤋.𐤀𐤄𐤓𐤍.𐤅𐤉𐤑𐤅𐤌.𐤀
𐤋.𐤁𐤍𐤉.𐤉𐤔𐤓𐤀𐤋.𐤅𐤀𐤋.𐤐𐤓𐤏𐤄.𐤌𐤋𐤊.𐤌𐤑𐤓𐤉𐤌.𐤋𐤄𐤅𐤑𐤉𐤀.
𐤀𐤕.𐤁𐤍𐤉.𐤉𐤔𐤓𐤀𐤋.𐤌𐤀𐤓𐤑.𐤌𐤑𐤓𐤉𐤌|
14 𐤀𐤋𐤄.𐤓𐤀𐤔𐤉.𐤁𐤉𐤕.𐤀𐤁𐤕𐤌.𐤁𐤍𐤉.𐤓𐤀𐤅𐤁𐤍.𐤁𐤊𐤓.𐤉
𐤔𐤓𐤀𐤋.𐤇𐤍𐤅𐤊.𐤅𐤐𐤋𐤅𐤀.𐤇𐤑𐤓𐤅𐤍.𐤅𐤊𐤓𐤌𐤉.𐤀𐤋𐤄.𐤌𐤔𐤐𐤇𐤕.
𐤓𐤀𐤅𐤁𐤍|
15 𐤅𐤁𐤍𐤉.𐤔𐤌𐤏𐤅𐤍.𐤉𐤌𐤅𐤀𐤋.𐤅𐤉𐤌𐤉𐤍.𐤅𐤀𐤄𐤃.𐤅𐤉𐤊𐤉𐤍.𐤅
𐤑𐤇𐤓.𐤅𐤔𐤀𐤅𐤋.𐤁𐤍.𐤄𐤊𐤍𐤏𐤍𐤉𐤕.𐤀𐤋𐤄.𐤌𐤔𐤐𐤇𐤕.𐤔𐤌𐤏𐤅𐤍
|

טז 𐤅𐤀𐤋𐤄.𐤔𐤌𐤅𐤕.𐤁𐤍𐤉.𐤋𐤅𐤉.𐤋𐤕𐤋𐤃𐤕𐤌.𐤂𐤓𐤔𐤅𐤍.𐤅𐤒𐤄
𐤕.𐤅𐤌𐤓𐤓𐤉.𐤅𐤔𐤍𐤉.𐤇𐤉𐤉.𐤋𐤅𐤉.𐤔𐤁𐤏.𐤅𐤔𐤋𐤔𐤉𐤌.𐤅𐤌𐤀𐤕.𐤔
𐤍𐤄|
יז 𐤁𐤍𐤉.𐤂𐤓𐤔𐤅𐤍.𐤋𐤁𐤍𐤉.𐤅𐤔𐤌𐤏𐤉.𐤋𐤌𐤔𐤐𐤇𐤕𐤌|
יח 𐤅𐤁𐤍𐤉.𐤒𐤄𐤕.𐤏𐤌𐤓𐤌.𐤅𐤉𐤑𐤄𐤓.𐤅𐤇𐤁𐤓𐤅𐤍.𐤅𐤏𐤆𐤉𐤀𐤋.
𐤅𐤔𐤍𐤉.𐤇𐤉𐤉.𐤒𐤄𐤕.𐤔𐤋𐤔.𐤅𐤔𐤋𐤔𐤉𐤌.𐤅𐤌𐤀𐤕.𐤔𐤍𐤄|
יט 𐤅𐤁𐤍𐤉.𐤌𐤓𐤓𐤉.𐤌𐤇𐤋𐤉.𐤅𐤌𐤅𐤔𐤉.𐤀𐤋𐤄.𐤌𐤔𐤐𐤇𐤕.𐤄𐤋
𐤅𐤉.𐤋𐤕𐤋𐤃𐤕𐤌|
כ 𐤅𐤉𐤒𐤇.𐤏𐤌𐤓𐤌.𐤀𐤕.𐤉𐤅𐤊𐤁𐤃.𐤃𐤃𐤕𐤅.𐤋𐤅.𐤋𐤀𐤔𐤄.
𐤅𐤕𐤋𐤃.𐤋𐤅.𐤀𐤕.𐤀𐤄𐤓𐤍.𐤅𐤀𐤕.𐤌𐤔𐤄.𐤅𐤔𐤍𐤉.𐤇𐤉𐤉.𐤏𐤌𐤓𐤌.
𐤔𐤁𐤏.𐤅𐤔𐤋𐤔𐤉𐤌.𐤅𐤌𐤀𐤕.𐤔𐤍𐤄|
כא 𐤅𐤁𐤍𐤉.𐤉𐤑𐤄𐤓.𐤒𐤓𐤇.𐤅𐤍𐤐𐤂.𐤅𐤆𐤊𐤓𐤉|
כב 𐤅𐤁𐤍𐤉.𐤏𐤆𐤉𐤀𐤋.𐤌𐤉𐤔𐤀𐤋.𐤅𐤀𐤋𐤑𐤐𐤍.𐤅𐤎𐤕𐤓𐤉|
כג 𐤅𐤉𐤒𐤇.𐤀𐤄𐤓𐤍.𐤀𐤕.𐤀𐤋𐤉𐤔𐤁𐤏.𐤁𐤕.𐤏𐤌𐤉𐤍𐤃𐤁.𐤀
𐤇𐤅𐤕.𐤍𐤇𐤔𐤅𐤍.𐤋𐤅.𐤋𐤀𐤔𐤄.𐤅𐤕𐤋𐤃.𐤋𐤅.𐤀𐤕.𐤍𐤃𐤁.𐤅𐤀𐤕.𐤀
𐤁𐤉𐤄𐤅𐤀.𐤀𐤕.𐤀𐤋𐤏𐤆𐤓.𐤅𐤀𐤕.𐤀𐤉𐤕𐤌𐤓|
כד 𐤅𐤁𐤍𐤉.𐤒𐤓𐤇.𐤀𐤎𐤉𐤓.𐤅𐤀𐤋𐤒𐤍𐤄.𐤅𐤀𐤁𐤉𐤀𐤎𐤐.𐤀𐤋𐤄.
𐤌𐤔𐤐𐤇𐤕.𐤄𐤒𐤓𐤇𐤉|
כה 𐤅𐤀𐤋𐤏𐤆𐤓.𐤁𐤍.𐤀𐤄𐤓𐤍.𐤋𐤒𐤇.𐤋𐤅.𐤌𐤁𐤍𐤅𐤕.𐤐𐤅𐤈𐤉𐤀𐤋.
𐤋𐤅.𐤋𐤀𐤔𐤄.𐤅𐤕𐤋𐤃.𐤋𐤅.𐤀𐤕.𐤐𐤉𐤍𐤇𐤎.𐤀𐤋𐤄.𐤓𐤀𐤔𐤉.𐤀𐤁𐤅
𐤕.𐤄𐤋𐤅𐤉𐤌.𐤋𐤌𐤔𐤐𐤇𐤕𐤌|
כו 𐤄𐤅𐤀.𐤀𐤄𐤓𐤍.𐤅𐤌𐤔𐤄.𐤀𐤔𐤓.𐤀𐤌𐤓.𐤉𐤄𐤅𐤄.𐤋𐤄𐤌.𐤄𐤅
𐤑𐤉𐤀𐤅.𐤀𐤕.𐤁𐤍𐤉.𐤉𐤔𐤓𐤀𐤋.𐤌𐤀𐤓𐤑.𐤌𐤑𐤓𐤉𐤌.𐤏𐤋.𐤑𐤁𐤀
𐤕𐤌|
כז 𐤄𐤌.𐤄𐤌𐤃𐤁𐤓𐤉𐤌.𐤀𐤋.𐤐𐤓𐤏𐤄.𐤌𐤋𐤊.𐤌𐤑𐤓𐤉𐤌.𐤋𐤄𐤅
𐤑𐤉𐤀.𐤀𐤕.𐤁𐤍𐤉.𐤉𐤔𐤓𐤀𐤋.𐤌𐤌𐤑𐤓𐤉𐤌.𐤄𐤅𐤀.𐤌𐤔𐤄.𐤅𐤀𐤄𐤓
𐤍|
כח 𐤅𐤉𐤄𐤉.𐤁𐤉𐤅𐤌.𐤃𐤁𐤓.𐤉𐤄𐤅𐤄.𐤀𐤋.𐤌𐤔𐤄.𐤁𐤀𐤓𐤑.𐤌𐤑
𐤓𐤉𐤌|

..𐤊𐤈.. 𐤅𐤉𐤃𐤁𐤓.𐤉𐤄𐤅𐤄.𐤀𐤋.𐤌𐤔𐤄.𐤋𐤀𐤌𐤓.𐤀𐤍𐤉.𐤉𐤄𐤅𐤄.𐤃
𐤁𐤓.𐤀𐤋.𐤐𐤓𐤏𐤄.𐤌𐤋𐤊.𐤌𐤑𐤓𐤉𐤌.𐤀𐤕.𐤊𐤋.𐤀𐤔𐤓.𐤀𐤍𐤉.𐤃𐤁
𐤓.𐤀𐤋𐤉𐤊|
..𐤋.. 𐤅𐤉𐤀𐤌𐤓.𐤌𐤔𐤄.𐤋𐤐𐤍𐤉.𐤉𐤄𐤅𐤄.𐤄𐤍.𐤀𐤍𐤉.𐤏𐤓𐤋.𐤔𐤐𐤕
𐤉𐤌.𐤅𐤀𐤉𐤊.𐤉𐤔𐤌𐤏.𐤀𐤋𐤉.𐤐𐤓𐤏𐤄||

𐤅𐤉𐤏𐤋𐤅.𐤌𐤌𐤑𐤓𐤉𐤌.𐤇𐤋𐤒 ..𐤆..

..𐤀.. 𐤅𐤉𐤀𐤌𐤓.𐤉𐤄𐤅𐤄.𐤀𐤋.𐤌𐤔𐤄.𐤓𐤀𐤄.𐤍𐤕𐤕𐤉𐤊.𐤀𐤋𐤄𐤉𐤌.
𐤋𐤐𐤓𐤏𐤄.𐤅𐤀𐤄𐤓𐤍.𐤀𐤇𐤉𐤊.𐤉𐤄𐤉𐤄.𐤍𐤁𐤉𐤀𐤊|
..𐤁.. 𐤀𐤕𐤄.𐤕𐤃𐤁𐤓.𐤀𐤕.𐤊𐤋.𐤀𐤔𐤓.𐤀𐤑𐤅𐤊.𐤅𐤀𐤄𐤓𐤍.𐤀𐤇𐤉
𐤊.𐤉𐤃𐤁𐤓.𐤀𐤋.𐤐𐤓𐤏𐤄.𐤅𐤔𐤋𐤇.𐤀𐤕.𐤁𐤍𐤉.𐤉𐤔𐤓𐤀𐤋.𐤌𐤀𐤓
𐤑𐤅|
..𐤂.. 𐤅𐤀𐤍𐤉.𐤀𐤒𐤔𐤄.𐤀𐤕.𐤋𐤁.𐤐𐤓𐤏𐤄.𐤅𐤄𐤓𐤁𐤉𐤕𐤉.𐤀𐤕.𐤀
𐤕𐤕𐤉.𐤅𐤀𐤕.𐤌𐤅𐤐𐤕𐤉.𐤁𐤀𐤓𐤑.𐤌𐤑𐤓𐤉𐤌|
..𐤃.. 𐤅𐤋𐤀.𐤉𐤔𐤌𐤏.𐤀𐤋𐤊𐤌.𐤐𐤓𐤏𐤄.𐤅𐤍𐤕𐤕𐤉.𐤀𐤕.𐤉𐤃𐤉.𐤁
𐤌𐤑𐤓𐤉𐤌.𐤅𐤄𐤅𐤑𐤀𐤕𐤉.𐤀𐤕.𐤑𐤁𐤀𐤕𐤉.𐤀𐤕.𐤏𐤌𐤉.𐤁𐤍𐤉.𐤉
𐤔𐤓𐤀𐤋.𐤌𐤀𐤓𐤑.𐤌𐤑𐤓𐤉𐤌.𐤁𐤔𐤐𐤈𐤉𐤌.𐤂𐤃𐤋𐤉𐤌|
..𐤄.. 𐤅𐤉𐤃𐤏𐤅.𐤌𐤑𐤓𐤉𐤌.𐤊𐤉.𐤀𐤍𐤉.𐤉𐤄𐤅𐤄.𐤁𐤍𐤈𐤕𐤉.𐤀𐤕.𐤉
𐤃𐤉.𐤏𐤋.𐤌𐤑𐤓𐤉𐤌.𐤅𐤄𐤅𐤑𐤀𐤕𐤉.𐤀𐤕.𐤁𐤍𐤉.𐤉𐤔𐤓𐤀𐤋.𐤌𐤕𐤅
𐤊𐤌|
..𐤅.. 𐤅𐤉𐤏𐤔.𐤌𐤔𐤄.𐤅𐤀𐤄𐤓𐤍.𐤊𐤀𐤔𐤓.𐤑𐤅𐤄.𐤉𐤄𐤅𐤄.𐤀𐤕𐤌.𐤊
𐤍.𐤏𐤔𐤅|
..𐤆.. 𐤅𐤌𐤔𐤄.𐤁𐤍.𐤔𐤌𐤍𐤉𐤌.𐤔𐤍𐤄.𐤅𐤀𐤄𐤓𐤍.𐤁𐤍.𐤔𐤋𐤔.𐤅𐤔𐤌𐤍
𐤉𐤌.𐤔𐤍𐤄.𐤁𐤃𐤁𐤓𐤌.𐤀𐤋.𐤐𐤓𐤏𐤄|
..𐤇.. 𐤅𐤉𐤀𐤌𐤓.𐤉𐤄𐤅𐤄.𐤀𐤋.𐤌𐤔𐤄.𐤅𐤀𐤋.𐤀𐤄𐤓𐤍.𐤋𐤀𐤌𐤓|
..𐤈.. 𐤊𐤉.𐤉𐤃𐤁𐤓.𐤀𐤋𐤊𐤌.𐤐𐤓𐤏𐤄.𐤋𐤀𐤌𐤓.𐤕𐤍𐤅.𐤋𐤊𐤌.𐤌𐤅𐤐
𐤕.𐤅𐤀𐤌𐤓𐤕.𐤀𐤋.𐤀𐤄𐤓𐤍.𐤒𐤇.𐤀𐤕.𐤌𐤈𐤊.𐤅𐤄𐤔𐤋𐤊.𐤋𐤐𐤍𐤉.𐤐
𐤓𐤏𐤄.𐤉𐤄𐤉.𐤋𐤕𐤍𐤉𐤍|

10 𐤅𐤉𐤁𐤀.𐤌𐤔𐤄.𐤅𐤀𐤄𐤓𐤍.𐤀𐤋.𐤐𐤓𐤏𐤄.𐤅𐤉𐤏𐤔𐤅.𐤊𐤍.𐤊𐤀
𐤔𐤓.𐤑𐤅𐤄.𐤉𐤄𐤅𐤄.𐤅𐤉𐤔𐤋𐤊.𐤀𐤄𐤓𐤍.𐤀𐤕.𐤌𐤈𐤄𐤅.𐤋𐤐𐤍𐤉.𐤐𐤓
𐤏𐤄.𐤅𐤋𐤐𐤍𐤉.𐤏𐤁𐤃𐤉𐤅.𐤅𐤉𐤄𐤉.𐤋𐤕𐤍𐤉𐤍|

11 𐤅𐤉𐤒𐤓𐤀.𐤂𐤌.𐤐𐤓𐤏𐤄.𐤋𐤇𐤊𐤌𐤉𐤌.𐤅𐤋𐤌𐤊𐤔𐤐𐤉𐤌.𐤅𐤉
𐤏𐤔𐤅.𐤂𐤌.𐤄𐤌.𐤇𐤓𐤈𐤌𐤉.𐤌𐤑𐤓𐤉𐤌.𐤁𐤋𐤄𐤈𐤉𐤄𐤌.𐤊𐤍|

12 𐤅𐤉𐤔𐤋𐤉𐤊𐤅.𐤀𐤉𐤔.𐤌𐤈𐤄𐤅.𐤅𐤉𐤄𐤉𐤅.𐤋𐤕𐤍𐤉𐤍𐤌.𐤅𐤉𐤁𐤋
𐤏.𐤌𐤈𐤄.𐤀𐤄𐤓𐤍.𐤀𐤕.𐤌𐤈𐤕𐤌|

13 𐤅𐤉𐤇𐤆𐤒.𐤋𐤁.𐤐𐤓𐤏𐤄.𐤅𐤋𐤀.𐤔𐤌𐤏.𐤀𐤋𐤄𐤌.𐤊𐤀𐤔𐤓.
𐤃𐤁𐤓.𐤉𐤄𐤅𐤄|

14 𐤅𐤉𐤀𐤌𐤓.𐤉𐤄𐤅𐤄.𐤀𐤋.𐤌𐤔𐤄.𐤊𐤁𐤃.𐤋𐤁.𐤐𐤓𐤏𐤄.𐤌𐤀𐤍
𐤋𐤔𐤋𐤇.𐤄𐤏𐤌|

15 𐤋𐤊.𐤀𐤋.𐤐𐤓𐤏𐤄.𐤁𐤁𐤒𐤓.𐤄𐤍𐤄.𐤉𐤑𐤀.𐤄𐤌𐤉𐤌𐤄.𐤅𐤍𐤑
𐤁𐤕.𐤋𐤒𐤓𐤀𐤕𐤅.𐤏𐤋.𐤔𐤐𐤕.𐤄𐤉𐤀𐤓.𐤅𐤄𐤌𐤈𐤄.𐤀𐤔𐤓.𐤍𐤄𐤐𐤊.
𐤋𐤍𐤇𐤔.𐤕𐤒𐤇.𐤁𐤉𐤃𐤊|

16 𐤅𐤀𐤌𐤓𐤕.𐤀𐤋𐤉𐤅.𐤉𐤄𐤅𐤄.𐤀𐤋𐤄𐤉.𐤄𐤏𐤁𐤓𐤉𐤌.𐤔𐤋𐤇𐤍
𐤉.𐤀𐤋𐤉𐤊.𐤋𐤀𐤌𐤓.𐤔𐤋𐤇.𐤀𐤕.𐤏𐤌𐤉.𐤅𐤉𐤏𐤁𐤃𐤍𐤉.𐤁𐤌𐤃𐤁
𐤓.𐤅𐤄𐤍𐤄.𐤋𐤀.𐤔𐤌𐤏𐤕.𐤏𐤃.𐤊𐤄|

17 𐤊𐤄.𐤀𐤌𐤓.𐤉𐤄𐤅𐤄.𐤁𐤆𐤀𐤕.𐤕𐤃𐤏.𐤊𐤉.𐤀𐤍𐤉.𐤉𐤄𐤅𐤄
.𐤄𐤍𐤄.𐤀𐤍𐤊𐤉.𐤌𐤊𐤄.𐤁𐤌𐤈𐤄.𐤀𐤔𐤓.𐤁𐤉𐤃𐤉.𐤏𐤋.𐤄𐤌𐤉𐤌.
𐤀𐤔𐤓.𐤁𐤉𐤀𐤓.𐤅𐤍𐤄𐤐𐤊𐤅.𐤋𐤃𐤌|

18 𐤅𐤄𐤃𐤂𐤄.𐤀𐤔𐤓.𐤁𐤉𐤀𐤓.𐤕𐤌𐤅𐤕.𐤅𐤁𐤀𐤔.𐤄𐤉𐤀𐤓.𐤅𐤍𐤋
𐤀𐤅.𐤌𐤑𐤓𐤉𐤌.𐤋𐤔𐤕𐤅𐤕.𐤌𐤉𐤌.𐤌𐤍.𐤄𐤉𐤀𐤓|

19 𐤅𐤉𐤀𐤌𐤓.𐤉𐤄𐤅𐤄.𐤀𐤋.𐤌𐤔𐤄.𐤀𐤌𐤓.𐤀𐤋.𐤀𐤄𐤓𐤍.𐤒𐤇.
𐤌𐤈𐤊.𐤅𐤍𐤈𐤄.𐤉𐤃𐤊.𐤏𐤋.𐤌𐤉𐤌𐤉.𐤌𐤑𐤓𐤉𐤌.𐤏𐤋.𐤍𐤄𐤓𐤕𐤌.
𐤏𐤋.𐤉𐤀𐤓𐤉𐤄𐤌.𐤅𐤏𐤋.𐤀𐤂𐤌𐤉𐤄𐤌.𐤅𐤏𐤋.𐤊𐤋.𐤌𐤒𐤅𐤄.𐤌𐤉𐤌
𐤉𐤄𐤌.𐤅𐤉𐤄𐤉𐤅.𐤃𐤌.𐤅𐤄𐤉𐤄.𐤃𐤌.𐤁𐤊𐤋.𐤀𐤓𐤑.𐤌𐤑𐤓𐤉𐤌.𐤅𐤁
𐤏𐤑𐤉𐤌.𐤅𐤁𐤀𐤁𐤍𐤉𐤌|

20 𐤅𐤉𐤏𐤔𐤅.𐤊𐤍.𐤌𐤔𐤄.𐤅𐤀𐤄𐤓𐤍.𐤊𐤀𐤔𐤓.𐤑𐤅𐤄.𐤉𐤄𐤅𐤄.𐤅
𐤉𐤓𐤌.𐤁𐤌𐤈𐤄.𐤅𐤉𐤊.𐤀𐤕.𐤄𐤌𐤉𐤌.𐤀𐤔𐤓.𐤁𐤉𐤀𐤓.𐤋𐤏𐤉𐤍𐤉.𐤐
𐤓𐤏𐤄.𐤅𐤋𐤏𐤉𐤍𐤉.𐤏𐤁𐤃𐤉𐤅.𐤅𐤉𐤄𐤐𐤊𐤅.𐤊𐤋.𐤄𐤌𐤉𐤌.𐤀𐤔𐤓.𐤁
𐤉𐤀𐤓.𐤋𐤃𐤌|

כא 𐤅𐤄𐤃𐤂𐤄.𐤀𐤔𐤓.𐤁𐤉𐤀𐤓.𐤌𐤕𐤄.𐤅𐤉𐤁𐤀𐤔.𐤄𐤉𐤀𐤓.𐤅𐤋𐤀.𐤉𐤊𐤋𐤅.𐤌𐤑𐤓𐤉𐤌.𐤋𐤔𐤕𐤅𐤕.𐤌𐤉𐤌.𐤌𐤍.𐤄𐤉𐤀𐤓.𐤅𐤉𐤄𐤉.𐤄𐤃𐤌.𐤁𐤊𐤋.𐤀𐤓𐤑.𐤌𐤑𐤓𐤉𐤌|

כב 𐤅𐤉𐤏𐤔𐤅.𐤊𐤍.𐤇𐤓𐤈𐤌𐤉.𐤌𐤑𐤓𐤉𐤌.𐤁𐤋𐤈𐤉𐤄𐤌.𐤅𐤉𐤇𐤆𐤒.𐤋𐤁.𐤐𐤓𐤏𐤄.𐤅𐤋𐤀.𐤔𐤌𐤏.𐤀𐤋𐤄𐤌.𐤊𐤀𐤔𐤓.𐤃𐤁𐤓.𐤉𐤄𐤅𐤄|

כג 𐤅𐤉𐤐𐤍.𐤐𐤓𐤏𐤄.𐤅𐤉𐤁𐤀.𐤀𐤋.𐤁𐤉𐤕𐤅.𐤅𐤋𐤀.𐤔𐤕.𐤋𐤁𐤅.𐤂𐤌.𐤋𐤆𐤀𐤕|

כד 𐤅𐤉𐤇𐤐𐤓𐤅.𐤊𐤋.𐤌𐤑𐤓𐤉𐤌.𐤎𐤁𐤉𐤁𐤕.𐤄𐤉𐤀𐤓.𐤌𐤉𐤌.𐤋𐤔𐤕𐤅𐤕.𐤊𐤉.𐤋𐤀.𐤉𐤊𐤋𐤅.𐤋𐤔𐤕𐤕.𐤌𐤌𐤉𐤌𐤉.𐤄𐤉𐤀𐤓|

כה 𐤅𐤉𐤌𐤋𐤀.𐤔𐤁𐤏𐤕.𐤉𐤌𐤉𐤌.𐤀𐤇𐤓𐤉.𐤄𐤊𐤅𐤕.𐤉𐤄𐤅𐤄.𐤀𐤕.𐤄𐤉𐤀𐤓|

כו 𐤅𐤉𐤀𐤌𐤓.𐤉𐤄𐤅𐤄.𐤀𐤋.𐤌𐤔𐤄.𐤁𐤀.𐤀𐤋.𐤐𐤓𐤏𐤄.𐤅𐤀𐤌𐤓𐤕.𐤀𐤋𐤉𐤅.𐤊𐤄.𐤀𐤌𐤓.𐤉𐤄𐤅𐤄.𐤔𐤋𐤇.𐤀𐤕.𐤏𐤌𐤉.𐤅𐤉𐤏𐤁𐤃𐤍𐤉|

כז 𐤅𐤀𐤌.𐤌𐤀𐤍.𐤀𐤕𐤄.𐤋𐤔𐤋𐤇.𐤄𐤍𐤄.𐤀𐤍𐤊𐤉.𐤍𐤂𐤐.𐤀𐤕.𐤊𐤋.𐤂𐤁𐤅𐤋𐤊.𐤁𐤑𐤐𐤓𐤃𐤏𐤉𐤌|

כח 𐤅𐤔𐤓𐤑.𐤄𐤉𐤀𐤓.𐤑𐤐𐤓𐤃𐤏𐤉𐤌.𐤅𐤏𐤋𐤅.𐤅𐤁𐤀𐤅.𐤁𐤁𐤉𐤕𐤊.𐤅𐤁𐤇𐤃𐤓.𐤌𐤔𐤊𐤁𐤊.𐤅𐤏𐤋.𐤌𐤈𐤕𐤊.𐤅𐤁𐤁𐤉𐤕.𐤏𐤁𐤃𐤉𐤊.𐤅𐤁𐤏𐤌𐤊.𐤅𐤁𐤕𐤍𐤅𐤓𐤉𐤊.𐤅𐤁𐤌𐤔𐤀𐤓𐤅𐤕𐤉𐤊|

כט 𐤅𐤁𐤊𐤄.𐤅𐤁𐤏𐤌𐤊.𐤅𐤁𐤊𐤋.𐤏𐤁𐤃𐤉𐤊.𐤉𐤏𐤋𐤅.𐤄𐤑𐤐𐤓𐤃𐤏𐤉𐤌||

𐤅𐤉𐤏𐤋𐤅.𐤌𐤌𐤑𐤓𐤉𐤌.𐤇𐤋𐤒 ח

א 𐤅𐤉𐤀𐤌𐤓.𐤉𐤄𐤅𐤄.𐤀𐤋.𐤌𐤔𐤄.𐤀𐤌𐤓.𐤀𐤋.𐤀𐤄𐤓𐤍.𐤍𐤈𐤄.𐤀𐤕.𐤉𐤃𐤊.𐤁𐤌𐤈𐤊.𐤏𐤋.𐤄𐤍𐤄𐤓𐤕.𐤏𐤋.𐤄𐤉𐤀𐤓𐤉𐤌.𐤅𐤏𐤋.𐤄𐤀𐤂𐤌𐤉𐤌.𐤅𐤄𐤏𐤋.𐤀𐤕.𐤄𐤑𐤐𐤓𐤃𐤏𐤉𐤌.𐤏𐤋.𐤀𐤓𐤑.𐤌𐤑𐤓𐤉𐤌|

ב 𐤅𐤉𐤈.𐤀𐤄𐤓𐤍.𐤀𐤕.𐤉𐤃𐤅.𐤏𐤋.𐤌𐤉𐤌𐤉.𐤌𐤑𐤓𐤉𐤌.𐤅𐤕𐤏𐤋.𐤄𐤑𐤐𐤓𐤃𐤏.𐤅𐤕𐤊𐤎.𐤀𐤕.𐤀𐤓𐤑.𐤌𐤑𐤓𐤉𐤌|

3 𐤅𐤉𐤏𐤔𐤅.𐤊𐤍.𐤄𐤇𐤓𐤈𐤌𐤉𐤌.𐤁𐤋𐤈𐤉𐤄𐤌.𐤅𐤉𐤏𐤋𐤅.𐤀𐤕.
𐤄𐤑𐤐𐤓𐤃𐤏𐤉𐤌.𐤏𐤋.𐤀𐤓𐤑.𐤌𐤑𐤓𐤉𐤌|

4 𐤅𐤉𐤒𐤓𐤀.𐤐𐤓𐤏𐤄.𐤋𐤌𐤔𐤄.𐤅𐤋𐤀𐤄𐤓𐤍.𐤅𐤉𐤀𐤌𐤓.𐤄𐤏𐤕𐤉
𐤓𐤅.𐤀𐤋.𐤉𐤄𐤅𐤄.𐤅𐤉𐤎𐤓.𐤄𐤑𐤐𐤓𐤃𐤏𐤉𐤌.𐤌𐤌𐤍𐤉.𐤅𐤌𐤏𐤌𐤉.𐤅
𐤀𐤔𐤋𐤇𐤄.𐤀𐤕.𐤄𐤏𐤌.𐤅𐤉𐤆𐤁𐤇𐤅.𐤋𐤉𐤄𐤅𐤄|

5 𐤅𐤉𐤀𐤌𐤓.𐤌𐤔𐤄.𐤋𐤐𐤓𐤏𐤄.𐤄𐤕𐤐𐤀𐤓.𐤏𐤋𐤉.𐤋𐤌𐤕𐤉.𐤀𐤏
𐤕𐤉𐤓.𐤋𐤊.𐤅𐤋𐤏𐤁𐤃𐤉𐤊.𐤅𐤋𐤏𐤌𐤊.𐤋𐤄𐤊𐤓𐤉𐤕.𐤄𐤑𐤐𐤓𐤃𐤏𐤉
𐤌.𐤌𐤌𐤊.𐤅𐤌𐤁𐤕𐤉𐤊.𐤓𐤒.𐤁𐤉𐤀𐤓.𐤕𐤔𐤀𐤓𐤍𐤄|

6 𐤅𐤉𐤀𐤌𐤓.𐤋𐤌𐤇𐤓.𐤅𐤉𐤀𐤌𐤓.𐤊𐤃𐤁𐤓𐤊.𐤋𐤌𐤏𐤍.𐤕𐤃𐤏.𐤊
𐤉.𐤀𐤉𐤍.𐤊𐤉𐤄𐤅𐤄.𐤀𐤋𐤄𐤉𐤍𐤅|

7 𐤅𐤎𐤓𐤅.𐤄𐤑𐤐𐤓𐤃𐤏𐤉𐤌.𐤌𐤌𐤊.𐤅𐤌𐤁𐤕𐤉𐤊.𐤅𐤌𐤏𐤁𐤃𐤉𐤊
𐤅𐤌𐤏𐤌𐤊.𐤓𐤒.𐤁𐤉𐤀𐤓.𐤕𐤔𐤀𐤓𐤍𐤄|

8 𐤅𐤉𐤑𐤀.𐤌𐤔𐤄.𐤅𐤀𐤄𐤓𐤍.𐤌𐤏𐤌.𐤐𐤓𐤏𐤄.𐤅𐤉𐤑𐤏𐤒.𐤌𐤔𐤄
𐤀𐤋.𐤉𐤄𐤅𐤄.𐤏𐤋.𐤃𐤁𐤓.𐤄𐤑𐤐𐤓𐤃𐤏𐤉𐤌.𐤀𐤔𐤓.𐤔𐤌.𐤋𐤐𐤓𐤏
𐤄|

9 𐤅𐤉𐤏𐤔.𐤉𐤄𐤅𐤄.𐤊𐤃𐤁𐤓.𐤌𐤔𐤄.𐤅𐤉𐤌𐤕𐤅.𐤄𐤑𐤐𐤓𐤃𐤏𐤉
𐤌.𐤌𐤍.𐤄𐤁𐤕𐤉𐤌.𐤌𐤍.𐤄𐤇𐤑𐤓𐤕.𐤅𐤌𐤍.𐤄𐤔𐤃𐤕|

10 𐤅𐤉𐤑𐤁𐤓𐤅.𐤀𐤕𐤌.𐤇𐤌𐤓𐤌.𐤇𐤌𐤓𐤌.𐤅𐤕𐤁𐤀𐤔.𐤄𐤀𐤓𐤑|

11 𐤅𐤉𐤓𐤀.𐤐𐤓𐤏𐤄.𐤊𐤉.𐤄𐤉𐤕𐤄.𐤄𐤓𐤅𐤇𐤄.𐤅𐤄𐤊𐤁𐤃.𐤀𐤕.
𐤋𐤁𐤅.𐤅𐤋𐤀.𐤔𐤌𐤏.𐤀𐤋𐤄𐤌.𐤊𐤀𐤔𐤓.𐤃𐤁𐤓.𐤉𐤄𐤅𐤄|

12 𐤅𐤉𐤀𐤌𐤓.𐤉𐤄𐤅𐤄.𐤀𐤋.𐤌𐤔𐤄.𐤀𐤌𐤓.𐤀𐤋.𐤀𐤄𐤓𐤍.𐤍𐤈𐤄.
𐤀𐤕.𐤌𐤈𐤊.𐤅𐤄𐤊.𐤀𐤕.𐤏𐤐𐤓.𐤄𐤀𐤓𐤑.𐤅𐤄𐤉𐤄.𐤋𐤊𐤍𐤌.
𐤁𐤊𐤋.𐤀𐤓𐤑.𐤌𐤑𐤓𐤉𐤌|

13 𐤅𐤉𐤏𐤔𐤅.𐤊𐤍.𐤅𐤉𐤈.𐤀𐤄𐤓𐤍.𐤀𐤕.𐤉𐤃𐤅.𐤁𐤌𐤈𐤄𐤅.𐤅𐤉𐤊.
𐤀𐤕.𐤏𐤐𐤓.𐤄𐤀𐤓𐤑.𐤅𐤕𐤄𐤉.𐤄𐤊𐤍𐤌.𐤁𐤀𐤃𐤌.𐤅𐤁𐤁𐤄𐤌𐤄.𐤊
𐤋.𐤏𐤐𐤓.𐤄𐤀𐤓𐤑.𐤄𐤉𐤄.𐤊𐤍𐤉𐤌.𐤁𐤊𐤋.𐤀𐤓𐤑.𐤌𐤑𐤓𐤉𐤌|

14 𐤅𐤉𐤏𐤔𐤅.𐤊𐤍.𐤄𐤇𐤓𐤈𐤌𐤉𐤌.𐤁𐤋𐤈𐤉𐤄𐤌.𐤋𐤄𐤅𐤑𐤉𐤀.
𐤀𐤕.𐤄𐤊𐤍𐤉𐤌.𐤅𐤋𐤀.𐤉𐤊𐤋𐤅.𐤅𐤕𐤄𐤉.𐤄𐤊𐤍𐤌.𐤁𐤀𐤃𐤌.𐤅𐤁𐤁𐤄
𐤌𐤄|

טו 𐤅𐤉𐤀𐤌𐤓𐤅.𐤄𐤇𐤓𐤈𐤌𐤉𐤌.𐤀𐤋.𐤐𐤓𐤏𐤄.𐤀𐤑𐤁𐤏.𐤀𐤋𐤄
𐤉𐤌.𐤄𐤅𐤀.𐤅𐤉𐤇𐤆𐤒.𐤋𐤁.𐤐𐤓𐤏𐤄.𐤅𐤋𐤀.𐤔𐤌𐤏.𐤀𐤋𐤄𐤌.𐤊𐤀
𐤔𐤓.𐤃𐤁𐤓.𐤉𐤄𐤅𐤄|

טז 𐤅𐤉𐤀𐤌𐤓.𐤉𐤄𐤅𐤄.𐤀𐤋.𐤌𐤔𐤄.𐤄𐤔𐤊𐤌.𐤁𐤁𐤒𐤓.𐤅𐤄𐤕𐤉
𐤑𐤁.𐤋𐤐𐤍𐤉.𐤐𐤓𐤏𐤄.𐤄𐤍𐤄.𐤉𐤅𐤑𐤀.𐤄𐤌𐤉𐤌𐤄.𐤅𐤀𐤌𐤓𐤕.𐤀𐤋
𐤉𐤅.𐤊𐤄.𐤀𐤌𐤓.𐤉𐤄𐤅𐤄.𐤔𐤋𐤇.𐤏𐤌𐤉.𐤅𐤉𐤏𐤁𐤃𐤍𐤉|

יז 𐤊𐤉.𐤀𐤌.𐤀𐤉𐤍𐤊.𐤌𐤔𐤋𐤇.𐤀𐤕.𐤏𐤌𐤉.𐤄𐤍𐤍𐤉.𐤌𐤔𐤋𐤉
𐤇.𐤁𐤊.𐤅𐤁𐤏𐤁𐤃𐤉𐤊.𐤅𐤁𐤏𐤌𐤊.𐤅𐤁𐤁𐤕𐤉𐤊.𐤀𐤕.𐤄𐤏𐤓𐤁.𐤅𐤌𐤋
𐤀𐤅.𐤁𐤕𐤉.𐤌𐤑𐤓𐤉𐤌.𐤀𐤕.𐤄𐤏𐤓𐤁.𐤅𐤂𐤌.𐤄𐤀𐤃𐤌𐤄.𐤀𐤔𐤓.
𐤄𐤌.𐤏𐤋𐤉𐤄|

יח 𐤅𐤄𐤐𐤋𐤉𐤕𐤉.𐤁𐤉𐤅𐤌.𐤄𐤄𐤅𐤀.𐤀𐤕.𐤀𐤓𐤑.𐤂𐤔𐤍.𐤀𐤔𐤓.
𐤏𐤌𐤉.𐤏𐤌𐤃.𐤏𐤋𐤉𐤄.𐤋𐤁𐤋𐤕𐤉.𐤄𐤉𐤅𐤕.𐤔𐤌.𐤏𐤓𐤁.𐤋𐤌𐤏𐤍.
𐤕𐤃𐤏.𐤊𐤉.𐤀𐤍𐤉.𐤉𐤄𐤅𐤄.𐤁𐤒𐤓𐤁.𐤄𐤀𐤓𐤑|

יט 𐤅𐤔𐤌𐤕𐤉.𐤐𐤃𐤕.𐤁𐤉𐤍.𐤏𐤌𐤉.𐤅𐤁𐤉𐤍.𐤏𐤌𐤊.𐤋𐤌𐤇𐤓.𐤉
𐤄𐤉𐤄.𐤄𐤀𐤕.𐤄𐤆𐤄|

כ 𐤅𐤉𐤏𐤔.𐤉𐤄𐤅𐤄.𐤊𐤍.𐤅𐤉𐤁𐤀.𐤏𐤓𐤁.𐤊𐤁𐤃.𐤁𐤉𐤕𐤄.𐤐𐤓
𐤏𐤄.𐤅𐤁𐤉𐤕.𐤏𐤁𐤃𐤉𐤅.𐤅𐤁𐤊𐤋.𐤀𐤓𐤑.𐤌𐤑𐤓𐤉𐤌.𐤕𐤔𐤇𐤕.𐤄
𐤀𐤓𐤑.𐤌𐤐𐤍𐤉.𐤄𐤏𐤓𐤁|

כא 𐤅𐤉𐤒𐤓𐤀.𐤐𐤓𐤏𐤄.𐤀𐤋.𐤌𐤔𐤄.𐤅𐤋𐤀𐤄𐤓𐤍.𐤅𐤉𐤀𐤌𐤓.𐤋𐤊𐤅.
𐤆𐤁𐤇𐤅.𐤋𐤀𐤋𐤄𐤉𐤊𐤌.𐤁𐤀𐤓𐤑|

כב 𐤅𐤉𐤀𐤌𐤓.𐤌𐤔𐤄.𐤋𐤀.𐤍𐤊𐤅𐤍.𐤋𐤏𐤔𐤅𐤕.𐤊𐤍.𐤊𐤉.𐤕𐤅𐤏𐤁
𐤕.𐤌𐤑𐤓𐤉𐤌.𐤍𐤆𐤁𐤇.𐤋𐤉𐤄𐤅𐤄.𐤀𐤋𐤄𐤉𐤍𐤅.𐤄𐤍.𐤍𐤆𐤁𐤇.𐤀𐤕
.𐤕𐤅𐤏𐤁𐤕.𐤌𐤑𐤓𐤉𐤌.𐤋𐤏𐤉𐤍𐤉𐤄𐤌.𐤅𐤋𐤀.𐤉𐤎𐤒𐤋𐤍𐤅|

כג 𐤃𐤓𐤊.𐤔𐤋𐤔𐤕.𐤉𐤌𐤉𐤌.𐤍𐤋𐤊.𐤁𐤌𐤃𐤁𐤓.𐤅𐤆𐤁𐤇𐤍𐤅.𐤋
𐤉𐤄𐤅𐤄.𐤀𐤋𐤄𐤉𐤍𐤅.𐤊𐤀𐤔𐤓.𐤉𐤀𐤌𐤓.𐤀𐤋𐤉𐤍𐤅|

כד 𐤅𐤉𐤀𐤌𐤓.𐤐𐤓𐤏𐤄.𐤀𐤍𐤊𐤉.𐤀𐤔𐤋𐤇.𐤀𐤕𐤊𐤌.𐤅𐤆𐤁𐤇
𐤕𐤌.𐤋𐤉𐤄𐤅𐤄.𐤀𐤋𐤄𐤉𐤊𐤌.𐤁𐤌𐤃𐤁𐤓.𐤓𐤒.𐤄𐤓𐤇𐤒.𐤋𐤀.𐤕𐤓
𐤇𐤉𐤒𐤅.𐤋𐤋𐤊𐤕.𐤄𐤏𐤕𐤉𐤓𐤅.𐤁𐤏𐤃𐤉|

כה 𐤅𐤉𐤀𐤌𐤓.𐤌𐤔𐤄.𐤄𐤍𐤄.𐤀𐤍𐤊𐤉.𐤉𐤅𐤑𐤀.𐤌𐤏𐤌𐤊.𐤅𐤄𐤏
𐤕𐤓𐤕𐤉.𐤀𐤋.𐤉𐤄𐤅𐤄.𐤅𐤎𐤓.𐤄𐤏𐤓𐤁.𐤌𐤐𐤓𐤏𐤄.𐤌𐤏𐤁𐤃𐤉𐤅.𐤅𐤌

𐤏𐤌𐤅.𐤌𐤇𐤓.𐤓𐤒.𐤀𐤋.𐤉𐤎𐤐.𐤐𐤓𐤏𐤄.𐤄𐤕𐤋.𐤋𐤁𐤋𐤕𐤉.𐤔𐤋𐤇.
𐤀𐤕.𐤄𐤏𐤌.𐤋𐤆𐤁𐤇.𐤋𐤉𐤄𐤅𐤄|
26 𐤅𐤉𐤑𐤀.𐤌𐤔𐤄.𐤌𐤏𐤌.𐤐𐤓𐤏𐤄.𐤅𐤉𐤏𐤕𐤓.𐤀𐤋.𐤉𐤄𐤅𐤄|
27 𐤅𐤉𐤏𐤔.𐤉𐤄𐤅𐤄.𐤊𐤃𐤁𐤓.𐤌𐤔𐤄.𐤅𐤉𐤎𐤓.𐤄𐤏𐤓𐤁.𐤌𐤐𐤓
𐤏𐤄.𐤌𐤏𐤁𐤃𐤉𐤅.𐤅𐤌𐤏𐤌𐤅.𐤋𐤀.𐤍𐤔𐤀𐤓.𐤀𐤇𐤃|
28 𐤅𐤉𐤊𐤁𐤃.𐤐𐤓𐤏𐤄.𐤀𐤕.𐤋𐤁𐤅.𐤂𐤌.𐤁𐤐𐤏𐤌.𐤄𐤆𐤀𐤕.𐤅𐤋
𐤀.𐤔𐤋𐤇.𐤀𐤕.𐤄𐤏𐤌||

𐤅𐤉𐤏𐤋𐤅.𐤌𐤌𐤑𐤓𐤉𐤌.𐤇𐤋𐤒 𐤈

1 𐤅𐤉𐤀𐤌𐤓.𐤉𐤄𐤅𐤄.𐤀𐤋.𐤌𐤔𐤄.𐤁𐤀.𐤀𐤋.𐤐𐤓𐤏𐤄.𐤅𐤃𐤁𐤓𐤕.
𐤀𐤋𐤉𐤅.𐤊𐤄.𐤀𐤌𐤓.𐤉𐤄𐤅𐤄.𐤀𐤋𐤄𐤉.𐤄𐤏𐤁𐤓𐤉𐤌.𐤔𐤋𐤇.𐤀𐤕.
𐤏𐤌𐤉.𐤅𐤉𐤏𐤁𐤃𐤍𐤉|
2 𐤊𐤉.𐤀𐤌.𐤌𐤀𐤍.𐤀𐤕𐤄.𐤋𐤔𐤋𐤇.𐤅𐤏𐤅𐤃𐤊.𐤌𐤇𐤆𐤉𐤒.𐤁
𐤌|
3 𐤄𐤍𐤄.𐤉𐤃.𐤉𐤄𐤅𐤄.𐤄𐤅𐤉𐤄.𐤁𐤌𐤒𐤍𐤊.𐤀𐤔𐤓.𐤁𐤔𐤃𐤄.𐤁
𐤎𐤅𐤎𐤉𐤌.𐤁𐤇𐤌𐤓𐤉𐤌.𐤁𐤂𐤌𐤋𐤉𐤌.𐤁𐤁𐤒𐤓.𐤅𐤁𐤑𐤀𐤍.𐤃𐤁𐤓.
𐤊𐤁𐤃.𐤌𐤀𐤃|
4 𐤅𐤄𐤐𐤋𐤄.𐤉𐤄𐤅𐤄.𐤁𐤉𐤍.𐤌𐤒𐤍𐤄.𐤉𐤔𐤓𐤀𐤋.𐤅𐤁𐤉𐤍.𐤌𐤒
𐤍𐤄.𐤌𐤑𐤓𐤉𐤌.𐤅𐤋𐤀.𐤉𐤌𐤅𐤕.𐤌𐤊𐤋.𐤋𐤁𐤍𐤉.𐤉𐤔𐤓𐤀𐤋.𐤃𐤁𐤓|
5 𐤅𐤉𐤔𐤌.𐤉𐤄𐤅𐤄.𐤌𐤅𐤏𐤃.𐤋𐤀𐤌𐤓.𐤌𐤇𐤓.𐤉𐤏𐤔𐤄.𐤉𐤄𐤅𐤄.
𐤄𐤃𐤁𐤓.𐤄𐤆𐤄.𐤁𐤀𐤓𐤑|
6 𐤅𐤉𐤏𐤔.𐤉𐤄𐤅𐤄.𐤀𐤕.𐤄𐤃𐤁𐤓.𐤄𐤆𐤄.𐤌𐤌𐤇𐤓𐤕.𐤅𐤉𐤌𐤕.
𐤊𐤋.𐤌𐤒𐤍𐤄.𐤌𐤑𐤓𐤉𐤌.𐤅𐤌𐤌𐤒𐤍𐤄.𐤁𐤍𐤉.𐤉𐤔𐤓𐤀𐤋.𐤋𐤀.𐤌𐤕.
𐤀𐤇𐤃|
7 𐤅𐤉𐤔𐤋𐤇.𐤐𐤓𐤏𐤄.𐤅𐤄𐤍𐤄.𐤋𐤀.𐤌𐤕.𐤌𐤌𐤒𐤍𐤄.𐤉𐤔𐤓𐤀𐤋.
𐤏𐤃.𐤀𐤇𐤃.𐤅𐤉𐤊𐤁𐤃.𐤋𐤁.𐤐𐤓𐤏𐤄.𐤅𐤋𐤀.𐤔𐤋𐤇.𐤀𐤕.𐤄𐤏𐤌
|
8 𐤅𐤉𐤀𐤌𐤓.𐤉𐤄𐤅𐤄.𐤀𐤋.𐤌𐤔𐤄.𐤅𐤀𐤋.𐤀𐤄𐤓𐤍.𐤒𐤇𐤅.𐤋𐤊𐤌.
𐤌𐤋𐤀.𐤇𐤐𐤍𐤉𐤊𐤌.𐤐𐤉𐤇.𐤊𐤁𐤔𐤍.𐤅𐤆𐤓𐤒𐤅.𐤌𐤔𐤄.𐤄𐤔𐤌𐤉𐤌
𐤄.𐤋𐤏𐤉𐤍𐤉.𐤐𐤓𐤏𐤄|

ט 𐤅𐤄𐤉𐤄.𐤋𐤀𐤁𐤒.𐤏𐤋.𐤊𐤋.𐤀𐤓𐤑.𐤌𐤑𐤓𐤉𐤌.𐤅𐤄𐤉𐤄.𐤏𐤋.
𐤄𐤀𐤃𐤌.𐤅𐤏𐤋.𐤄𐤁𐤄𐤌𐤄.𐤋𐤔𐤇𐤉𐤍.𐤐𐤓𐤇.𐤀𐤁𐤏𐤁𐤏𐤕.𐤁𐤊
𐤋.𐤀𐤓𐤑.𐤌𐤑𐤓𐤉𐤌|

י 𐤅𐤉𐤒𐤇𐤅.𐤀𐤕.𐤐𐤉𐤇.𐤄𐤊𐤁𐤔𐤍.𐤅𐤉𐤏𐤌𐤃𐤅.𐤋𐤐𐤍𐤉.𐤐𐤓
𐤏𐤄.𐤅𐤉𐤆𐤓𐤒.𐤀𐤕𐤅.𐤌𐤔𐤄.𐤄𐤔𐤌𐤉𐤌𐤄.𐤅𐤉𐤄𐤉.𐤔𐤇𐤉𐤍.𐤀
𐤁𐤏𐤁𐤏𐤕.𐤐𐤓𐤇.𐤁𐤀𐤃𐤌.𐤅𐤁𐤁𐤄𐤌𐤄|

יא 𐤅𐤋𐤀.𐤉𐤊𐤋𐤅.𐤄𐤇𐤓𐤈𐤌𐤉𐤌.𐤋𐤏𐤌𐤃.𐤋𐤐𐤍𐤉.𐤌𐤔𐤄.𐤌𐤐
𐤍𐤉.𐤄𐤔𐤇𐤉𐤍.𐤊𐤉.𐤄𐤉𐤄.𐤄𐤔𐤇𐤉𐤍.𐤁𐤇𐤓𐤈𐤌𐤌.𐤅𐤁𐤊𐤋.𐤌
𐤑𐤓𐤉𐤌|

יב 𐤅𐤉𐤇𐤆𐤒.𐤉𐤄𐤅𐤄.𐤀𐤕.𐤋𐤁.𐤐𐤓𐤏𐤄.𐤅𐤋𐤀.𐤔𐤌𐤏.𐤀𐤋
𐤄𐤌.𐤊𐤀𐤔𐤓.𐤃𐤁𐤓.𐤉𐤄𐤅𐤄.𐤀𐤋.𐤌𐤔𐤄|

יג 𐤅𐤉𐤀𐤌𐤓.𐤉𐤄𐤅𐤄.𐤀𐤋.𐤌𐤔𐤄.𐤄𐤔𐤊𐤌.𐤁𐤁𐤒𐤓.𐤅𐤄𐤕𐤉
𐤑𐤁.𐤋𐤐𐤍𐤉.𐤐𐤓𐤏𐤄.𐤅𐤀𐤌𐤓𐤕.𐤀𐤋𐤉𐤅.𐤊𐤄.𐤀𐤌𐤓.𐤉𐤄𐤅𐤄.𐤀𐤋
𐤄𐤉.𐤄𐤏𐤁𐤓𐤉𐤌.𐤔𐤋𐤇.𐤀𐤕.𐤏𐤌𐤉.𐤅𐤉𐤏𐤁𐤃𐤍𐤉|

יד 𐤊𐤉.𐤁𐤐𐤏𐤌.𐤄𐤆𐤀𐤕.𐤀𐤍𐤉.𐤔𐤋𐤇.𐤀𐤕.𐤊𐤋.𐤌𐤂𐤐𐤕
𐤉.𐤀𐤋.𐤋𐤁𐤊.𐤅𐤁𐤏𐤁𐤃𐤉𐤊.𐤅𐤁𐤏𐤌𐤊.𐤁𐤏𐤁𐤅𐤓.𐤕𐤃𐤏.𐤊𐤉.𐤀
𐤉𐤍.𐤊𐤌𐤍𐤉.𐤁𐤊𐤋.𐤄𐤀𐤓𐤑|

טו 𐤊𐤉.𐤏𐤕𐤄.𐤔𐤋𐤇𐤕𐤉.𐤀𐤕.𐤉𐤃𐤉.𐤅𐤀𐤊.𐤀𐤅𐤕𐤊.𐤅𐤀𐤕.
𐤏𐤌𐤊.𐤁𐤃𐤁𐤓.𐤅𐤕𐤊𐤇𐤃.𐤌𐤍.𐤄𐤀𐤓𐤑|

טז 𐤅𐤀𐤅𐤋𐤌.𐤁𐤏𐤁𐤅𐤓.𐤆𐤀𐤕.𐤄𐤏𐤌𐤃𐤕𐤉𐤊.𐤁𐤏𐤁𐤅𐤓.𐤄𐤓
𐤀𐤕𐤊.𐤀𐤕.𐤊𐤇𐤉.𐤅𐤋𐤌𐤏𐤍.𐤎𐤐𐤓.𐤔𐤌𐤉.𐤁𐤊𐤋.𐤄𐤀𐤓𐤑|

יז 𐤏𐤅𐤃𐤊.𐤌𐤎𐤕𐤅𐤋𐤋.𐤁𐤏𐤌𐤉.𐤋𐤁𐤋𐤕𐤉.𐤔𐤋𐤇𐤌|

יח 𐤄𐤍𐤍𐤉.𐤌𐤌𐤈𐤉𐤓.𐤊𐤏𐤕.𐤌𐤇𐤓.𐤁𐤓𐤃.𐤊𐤁𐤃.𐤌𐤀𐤃.
𐤀𐤔𐤓.𐤋𐤀.𐤄𐤉𐤄.𐤊𐤌𐤄𐤅.𐤁𐤌𐤑𐤓𐤉𐤌.𐤋𐤌𐤍.𐤄𐤉𐤅𐤌.𐤄𐤅𐤎𐤃
𐤄.𐤅𐤏𐤃.𐤏𐤕𐤄|

יט 𐤅𐤏𐤕𐤄.𐤔𐤋𐤇.𐤄𐤏𐤆.𐤀𐤕.𐤌𐤒𐤍𐤊.𐤅𐤀𐤕.𐤊𐤋.𐤀𐤔𐤓.
𐤋𐤊.𐤁𐤔𐤃𐤄.𐤊𐤋.𐤄𐤀𐤃𐤌.𐤅𐤄𐤁𐤄𐤌𐤄.𐤀𐤔𐤓.𐤉𐤌𐤑𐤀.𐤁𐤔
𐤃𐤄.𐤅𐤋𐤀.𐤉𐤀𐤎𐤐.𐤄𐤁𐤉𐤕𐤄.𐤅𐤉𐤓𐤃.𐤏𐤋𐤄𐤌.𐤄𐤁𐤓𐤃.𐤅𐤌
𐤕𐤅|

כ 𐤄𐤉𐤓𐤀.𐤀𐤕.𐤃𐤁𐤓.𐤉𐤄𐤅𐤄.𐤌𐤏𐤁𐤃𐤉.𐤐𐤓𐤏𐤄.𐤄𐤍𐤉
𐤎.𐤀𐤕.𐤏𐤁𐤃𐤉𐤅.𐤅𐤀𐤕.𐤌𐤒𐤍𐤄𐤅.𐤀𐤋.𐤄𐤁𐤕𐤉𐤌|

𐤊𐤀 𐤅𐤀𐤔𐤓.𐤋𐤀.𐤔𐤌.𐤋𐤁𐤅.𐤀𐤋.𐤃𐤁𐤓.𐤉𐤄𐤅𐤄.𐤅𐤉𐤏𐤆𐤁.𐤀
𐤕.𐤏𐤁𐤃𐤉𐤅.𐤅𐤀𐤕.𐤌𐤒𐤍𐤄𐤅.𐤁𐤔𐤃𐤄|
𐤊𐤁 𐤅𐤉𐤀𐤌𐤓.𐤉𐤄𐤅𐤄.𐤀𐤋.𐤌𐤔𐤄.𐤍𐤈𐤄.𐤀𐤕.𐤉𐤃𐤊.𐤏𐤋.𐤄
𐤔𐤌𐤉𐤌.𐤅𐤉𐤄𐤉.𐤁𐤓𐤃.𐤁𐤊𐤋.𐤀𐤓𐤑.𐤌𐤑𐤓𐤉𐤌.𐤏𐤋.𐤄𐤀𐤃𐤌
.𐤅𐤏𐤋.𐤄𐤁𐤄𐤌𐤄.𐤅𐤏𐤋.𐤊𐤋.𐤏𐤔𐤁.𐤄𐤔𐤃𐤄.𐤁𐤀𐤓𐤑.𐤌𐤑𐤓𐤉
𐤌|
𐤊𐤂 𐤅𐤉𐤈.𐤌𐤔𐤄.𐤀𐤕.𐤌𐤈𐤄𐤅.𐤏𐤋.𐤄𐤔𐤌𐤉𐤌.𐤅𐤉𐤄𐤅𐤄.𐤍𐤕
𐤍.𐤒𐤋𐤕.𐤅𐤁𐤓𐤃.𐤅𐤕𐤄𐤋𐤊.𐤀𐤔.𐤀𐤓𐤑𐤄.𐤅𐤉𐤌𐤈𐤓.𐤉𐤄𐤅𐤄.𐤁
𐤓𐤃.𐤏𐤋.𐤀𐤓𐤑.𐤌𐤑𐤓𐤉𐤌|
𐤊𐤃 𐤅𐤉𐤄𐤉.𐤁𐤓𐤃.𐤅𐤀𐤔.𐤌𐤕𐤋𐤒𐤇𐤕.𐤁𐤕𐤅𐤊.𐤄𐤁𐤓𐤃.𐤊
𐤁𐤃.𐤌𐤀𐤃.𐤀𐤔𐤓.𐤋𐤀.𐤄𐤉𐤄.𐤊𐤌𐤄𐤅.𐤁𐤊𐤋.𐤀𐤓𐤑.𐤌𐤑𐤓𐤉
𐤌.𐤌𐤀𐤆.𐤄𐤉𐤕𐤄.𐤋𐤂𐤅𐤉|
𐤊𐤄 𐤅𐤉𐤊.𐤄𐤁𐤓𐤃.𐤁𐤊𐤋.𐤀𐤓𐤑.𐤌𐤑𐤓𐤉𐤌.𐤀𐤕.𐤊𐤋.𐤀𐤔𐤓.
𐤁𐤔𐤃𐤄.𐤌𐤀𐤃𐤌.𐤅𐤏𐤃.𐤁𐤄𐤌𐤄.𐤅𐤀𐤕.𐤊𐤋.𐤏𐤔𐤁.𐤄𐤔𐤃
𐤄.𐤄𐤊𐤄.𐤄𐤁𐤓𐤃.𐤅𐤀𐤕.𐤊𐤋.𐤏𐤑.𐤄𐤔𐤃𐤄.𐤔𐤁𐤓|
𐤊𐤅 𐤓𐤒.𐤁𐤀𐤓𐤑.𐤂𐤔𐤍.𐤀𐤔𐤓.𐤔𐤌.𐤁𐤍𐤉.𐤉𐤔𐤓𐤀𐤋.𐤋𐤀.𐤄
𐤉𐤄.𐤁𐤓𐤃|
𐤊𐤆 𐤅𐤉𐤔𐤋𐤇.𐤐𐤓𐤏𐤄.𐤅𐤉𐤒𐤓𐤀.𐤋𐤌𐤔𐤄.𐤅𐤋𐤀𐤄𐤓𐤍.𐤅𐤉𐤀
𐤌𐤓.𐤀𐤋𐤄𐤌.𐤇𐤈𐤀𐤕𐤉.𐤄𐤐𐤏𐤌.𐤉𐤄𐤅𐤄.𐤄𐤑𐤃𐤉𐤒.𐤅𐤀𐤍𐤉.
𐤅𐤏𐤌𐤉.𐤄𐤓𐤔𐤏𐤉𐤌|
𐤊𐤇 𐤄𐤏𐤕𐤉𐤓𐤅.𐤀𐤋.𐤉𐤄𐤅𐤄.𐤅𐤓𐤁.𐤌𐤄𐤉𐤕.𐤒𐤋𐤕.𐤀𐤋𐤄𐤉𐤌
.𐤅𐤁𐤓𐤃.𐤅𐤀𐤔𐤋𐤇𐤄.𐤀𐤕𐤊𐤌.𐤅𐤋𐤀.𐤕𐤎𐤐𐤅𐤍.𐤋𐤏𐤌𐤃|
𐤊𐤈 𐤅𐤉𐤀𐤌𐤓.𐤀𐤋𐤉𐤅.𐤌𐤔𐤄.𐤊𐤑𐤀𐤕𐤉.𐤀𐤕.𐤄𐤏𐤉𐤓.𐤀𐤐
𐤓𐤔.𐤀𐤕.𐤊𐤐𐤉.𐤀𐤋.𐤉𐤄𐤅𐤄.𐤄𐤒𐤋𐤅𐤕.𐤉𐤇𐤃𐤋𐤅𐤍.𐤅𐤄𐤁𐤓𐤃.
𐤋𐤀.𐤉𐤄𐤉𐤄.𐤏𐤅𐤃.𐤋𐤌𐤏𐤍.𐤕𐤃𐤏.𐤊𐤉.𐤋𐤉𐤄𐤅𐤄.𐤄𐤀𐤓𐤑|
𐤋 𐤅𐤀𐤕𐤄.𐤅𐤏𐤁𐤃𐤉𐤊.𐤉𐤃𐤏𐤕𐤉.𐤊𐤉.𐤈𐤓𐤌.𐤕𐤉𐤓𐤀𐤅𐤍.
𐤌𐤐𐤍𐤉.𐤉𐤄𐤅𐤄.𐤀𐤋𐤄𐤉𐤌|
𐤋𐤀 𐤅𐤄𐤐𐤔𐤕𐤄.𐤅𐤄𐤔𐤏𐤓𐤄.𐤍𐤊𐤕𐤄.𐤊𐤉.𐤄𐤔𐤏𐤓𐤄.𐤀𐤁𐤉
𐤁.𐤅𐤄𐤐𐤔𐤕𐤄.𐤂𐤁𐤏𐤋|
𐤋𐤁 𐤅𐤄𐤇𐤈𐤄.𐤅𐤄𐤊𐤎𐤌𐤕.𐤋𐤀.𐤍𐤊𐤅.𐤊𐤉.𐤀𐤐𐤉𐤋𐤕.𐤄𐤍𐤄|

..לג.. ויצא.משה.מעם.פרעה.את.העיר.ויפרש.
כפיו.אל.יהוה.ויחדלו.הקלות.והברד.ומטר.ל
א.נתך.ארצה|
..לד.. וירא.פרעה.כי.חדל.המטר.והברד.והקל
ת.ויסף.לחטא.ויכבד.לבו.הוא.ועבדיו|
..לה.. ויחזק.לב.פרעה.ולא.שלח.את.בני.ישר
אל.כאשר.דבר.יהוה.ביד.משה||

..יא.. ויעלו.ממצרים.חלק

..א.. ויאמר.יהוה.אל.משה.בא.אל.פרעה.כי.אני.
הכבדתי.את.לבו.ואת.לב.עבדיו.למען.שתי.
אתתי.אלה.בקרבו|
..ב.. ולמען.תספר.באזני.בנך.ובן.בנך.את.אשר.
התעללתי.במצרים.ואת.אתתי.אשר.שמתי.ב
ם.וידעתם.כי.אני.יהוה|
..ג.. ויבא.משה.ואהרן.אל.פרעה.ויאמרו.אליו.כ
ה.אמר.יהוה.אלהי.העברים.עד.מתי.מאנת.ל
ענת.מפני.שלח.עמי.ויעבדני|
..ד.. כי.אם.מאן.אתה.לשלח.את.עמי.הנני.מב
יא.מחר.ארבה.בגבלך|
..ה.. וכסה.את.עין.הארץ.ולא.יוכל.לראת.את.ה
ארץ.ואכל.את.יתר.הפלטה.הנשארת.לכם.מן.
הברד.ואכל.את.כל.העץ.הצמח.לכם.מן.השד
ה|
..ו.. ומלאו.בתיך.ובתי.כל.עבדיך.ובתי.כל.מצ
רים.אשר.לא.ראו.אבתיך.ואבות.אבתיך.מיום.
היותם.על.האדמה.עד.היום.הזה.ויפן.ויצ
א.מעם.פרעה|
..ז.. ויאמרו.עבדי.פרעה.אליו.עד.מתי.יהיה
.זה.לנו.למוקש.שלח.את.האנשים.ויעבדו.א

𐤕.𐤉𐤄𐤅𐤄.𐤀𐤋𐤄𐤉𐤄𐤌.𐤄𐤈𐤓𐤌.𐤕𐤃𐤏.𐤊𐤉.𐤀𐤁𐤃𐤄.𐤌𐤑𐤓
𐤉𐤌|
ח 𐤅𐤉𐤅𐤔𐤁.𐤀𐤕.𐤌𐤔𐤄.𐤅𐤀𐤕.𐤀𐤄𐤓𐤍.𐤀𐤋.𐤐𐤓𐤏𐤄.𐤅𐤉𐤀𐤌𐤓
𐤀𐤋𐤄𐤌.𐤋𐤊𐤅.𐤏𐤁𐤃𐤅.𐤀𐤕.𐤉𐤄𐤅𐤄.𐤀𐤋𐤄𐤉𐤊𐤌.𐤌𐤉.𐤅𐤌𐤉.𐤄
𐤄𐤋𐤊𐤉𐤌|
ט 𐤅𐤉𐤀𐤌𐤓.𐤌𐤔𐤄.𐤁𐤍𐤏𐤓𐤉𐤍𐤅.𐤅𐤁𐤆𐤒𐤍𐤉𐤍𐤅.𐤍𐤋𐤊.𐤁𐤁𐤍𐤉
𐤍𐤅.𐤅𐤁𐤁𐤍𐤅𐤕𐤍𐤅.𐤁𐤑𐤀𐤍𐤍𐤅.𐤅𐤁𐤁𐤒𐤓𐤍𐤅.𐤍𐤋𐤊.𐤊𐤉.𐤇𐤂.𐤉𐤄𐤅
𐤄.𐤋𐤍𐤅|
י 𐤅𐤉𐤀𐤌𐤓.𐤀𐤋𐤄𐤌.𐤉𐤄𐤉.𐤊𐤍.𐤉𐤄𐤅𐤄.𐤏𐤌𐤊𐤌.𐤊𐤀𐤔𐤓.
𐤀𐤔𐤋𐤇.𐤀𐤕𐤊𐤌.𐤅𐤀𐤕.𐤈𐤐𐤊𐤌.𐤓𐤀𐤅.𐤊𐤉.𐤓𐤏𐤄.𐤍𐤂𐤃.𐤐𐤍
𐤉𐤊𐤌|
יא 𐤋𐤀.𐤊𐤍.𐤋𐤊𐤅.𐤍𐤀.𐤄𐤂𐤁𐤓𐤉𐤌.𐤅𐤏𐤁𐤃𐤅.𐤀𐤕.𐤉𐤄𐤅𐤄.𐤊
𐤉.𐤀𐤕𐤄.𐤀𐤕𐤌.𐤌𐤁𐤒𐤔𐤉𐤌.𐤅𐤉𐤂𐤓𐤔.𐤀𐤕𐤌.𐤌𐤀𐤕.𐤐𐤍𐤉.𐤐
𐤓𐤏𐤄|
יב 𐤅𐤉𐤀𐤌𐤓.𐤉𐤄𐤅𐤄.𐤀𐤋.𐤌𐤔𐤄.𐤍𐤈𐤄.𐤉𐤃𐤊.𐤏𐤋.𐤀𐤓𐤑.
𐤌𐤑𐤓𐤉𐤌.𐤁𐤀𐤓𐤁𐤄.𐤅𐤉𐤏𐤋.𐤏𐤋.𐤀𐤓𐤑.𐤌𐤑𐤓𐤉𐤌.𐤅𐤉𐤀𐤊𐤋.
𐤀𐤕.𐤊𐤋.𐤏𐤔𐤁.𐤄𐤀𐤓𐤑.𐤀𐤕.𐤊𐤋.𐤀𐤔𐤓.𐤄𐤔𐤀𐤉𐤓.𐤄𐤁𐤓𐤃|
יג 𐤅𐤉𐤈.𐤌𐤔𐤄.𐤀𐤕.𐤌𐤈𐤄𐤅.𐤏𐤋.𐤀𐤓𐤑.𐤌𐤑𐤓𐤉𐤌.𐤅𐤉𐤄𐤅
𐤄.𐤍𐤄𐤂.𐤓𐤅𐤇.𐤒𐤃𐤉𐤌.𐤁𐤀𐤓𐤑.𐤊𐤋.𐤄𐤉𐤅𐤌.𐤄𐤄𐤅𐤀.𐤅𐤊𐤋.
𐤄𐤋𐤉𐤋𐤄.𐤄𐤁𐤒𐤓.𐤄𐤉𐤄.𐤅𐤓𐤅𐤇.𐤄𐤒𐤃𐤉𐤌.𐤍𐤔𐤀.𐤀𐤕.𐤄𐤀
𐤓𐤁𐤄|
יד 𐤅𐤉𐤏𐤋.𐤄𐤀𐤓𐤁𐤄.𐤏𐤋.𐤊𐤋.𐤀𐤓𐤑.𐤌𐤑𐤓𐤉𐤌.𐤅𐤉𐤍𐤇.𐤁
𐤊𐤋.𐤂𐤁𐤅𐤋.𐤌𐤑𐤓𐤉𐤌.𐤊𐤁𐤃.𐤌𐤀𐤃.𐤋𐤐𐤍𐤉𐤅.𐤋𐤀.𐤄𐤉𐤄.𐤊𐤍.
𐤀𐤓𐤁𐤄.𐤊𐤌𐤄𐤅.𐤅𐤀𐤇𐤓𐤉𐤅.𐤋𐤀.𐤉𐤄𐤉𐤄.𐤊𐤍|
טו 𐤅𐤉𐤊𐤎.𐤀𐤕.𐤏𐤉𐤍.𐤊𐤋.𐤄𐤀𐤓𐤑.𐤅𐤕𐤇𐤔𐤊.𐤄𐤀𐤓𐤑.𐤅𐤉
𐤀𐤊𐤋.𐤀𐤕.𐤊𐤋.𐤏𐤔𐤁.𐤄𐤀𐤓𐤑.𐤅𐤀𐤕.𐤊𐤋.𐤐𐤓𐤉.𐤄𐤏𐤑.𐤀𐤔
𐤓.𐤄𐤅𐤕𐤉𐤓.𐤄𐤁𐤓𐤃.𐤅𐤋𐤀.𐤍𐤅𐤕𐤓.𐤊𐤋.𐤉𐤓𐤒.𐤁𐤏𐤑.𐤅𐤁𐤏𐤔𐤁.
𐤄𐤔𐤃𐤄.𐤁𐤊𐤋.𐤀𐤓𐤑.𐤌𐤑𐤓𐤉𐤌|
טז 𐤅𐤉𐤌𐤄𐤓.𐤐𐤓𐤏𐤄.𐤋𐤒𐤓𐤀.𐤋𐤌𐤔𐤄.𐤅𐤋𐤀𐤄𐤓𐤍.𐤅𐤉𐤀𐤌𐤓.
𐤇𐤈𐤀𐤕𐤉.𐤋𐤉𐤄𐤅𐤄.𐤀𐤋𐤄𐤉𐤊𐤌.𐤅𐤋𐤊𐤌|

17 𐤅𐤏𐤕𐤄.𐤔𐤀.𐤍𐤀.𐤇𐤈𐤀𐤕𐤉.𐤀𐤊.𐤄𐤐𐤏𐤌.𐤅𐤄𐤏𐤕𐤉𐤓
𐤅.𐤋𐤉𐤄𐤅𐤄.𐤀𐤋𐤄𐤉𐤊𐤌.𐤅𐤉𐤎𐤓.𐤌𐤏𐤋𐤉.𐤓𐤒.𐤀𐤕.𐤄𐤌𐤅𐤕.𐤄
𐤆𐤄|
18 𐤅𐤉𐤑𐤀.𐤌𐤏𐤌.𐤐𐤓𐤏𐤄.𐤅𐤉𐤏𐤕𐤓.𐤀𐤋.𐤉𐤄𐤅𐤄|
19 𐤅𐤉𐤄𐤐𐤊.𐤉𐤄𐤅𐤄.𐤓𐤅𐤇.𐤉𐤌.𐤇𐤆𐤒.𐤌𐤀𐤃.𐤅𐤉𐤔𐤀.𐤀
𐤕.𐤄𐤀𐤓𐤁𐤄.𐤅𐤉𐤕𐤒𐤏𐤄𐤅.𐤉𐤌𐤄.𐤎𐤅𐤐.𐤋𐤀.𐤍𐤔𐤀𐤓.𐤀𐤓𐤁𐤄.
𐤀𐤇𐤃.𐤁𐤊𐤋.𐤂𐤁𐤅𐤋.𐤌𐤑𐤓𐤉𐤌|
20 𐤅𐤉𐤇𐤆𐤒.𐤉𐤄𐤅𐤄.𐤀𐤕.𐤋𐤁.𐤐𐤓𐤏𐤄.𐤅𐤋𐤀.𐤔𐤋𐤇.𐤀𐤕.
𐤁𐤍𐤉.𐤉𐤔𐤓𐤀𐤋|
21 𐤅𐤉𐤀𐤌𐤓.𐤉𐤄𐤅𐤄.𐤀𐤋.𐤌𐤔𐤄.𐤍𐤈𐤄.𐤉𐤃𐤊.𐤏𐤋.𐤄𐤔𐤌𐤉𐤌
𐤅𐤉𐤄𐤉.𐤇𐤔𐤊.𐤏𐤋.𐤀𐤓𐤑.𐤌𐤑𐤓𐤉𐤌.𐤅𐤉𐤌𐤔.𐤇𐤔𐤊|
22 𐤅𐤉𐤈.𐤌𐤔𐤄.𐤀𐤕.𐤉𐤃𐤅.𐤏𐤋.𐤄𐤔𐤌𐤉𐤌.𐤅𐤉𐤄𐤉.𐤇𐤔𐤊
.𐤀𐤐𐤋𐤄.𐤁𐤊𐤋.𐤀𐤓𐤑.𐤌𐤑𐤓𐤉𐤌.𐤔𐤋𐤔𐤕.𐤉𐤌𐤉𐤌|
23 𐤋𐤀.𐤓𐤀𐤅.𐤀𐤉𐤔.𐤀𐤕.𐤀𐤇𐤉𐤅.𐤅𐤋𐤀.𐤒𐤌𐤅.𐤀𐤉𐤔.𐤌𐤕
𐤇𐤕𐤉𐤅.𐤔𐤋𐤔𐤕.𐤉𐤌𐤉𐤌.𐤅𐤋𐤊𐤋.𐤁𐤍𐤉.𐤉𐤔𐤓𐤀𐤋.𐤄𐤉𐤄.𐤀𐤅𐤓.
𐤁𐤌𐤅𐤔𐤁𐤕𐤌|
24 𐤅𐤉𐤒𐤓𐤀.𐤐𐤓𐤏𐤄.𐤀𐤋.𐤌𐤔𐤄.𐤅𐤉𐤀𐤌𐤓.𐤋𐤊𐤅.𐤏𐤁𐤃𐤅.
𐤀𐤕.𐤉𐤄𐤅𐤄.𐤓𐤒.𐤑𐤀𐤍𐤊𐤌.𐤅𐤁𐤒𐤓𐤊𐤌.𐤉𐤑𐤂.𐤂𐤌.𐤈𐤐𐤊𐤌
.𐤉𐤋𐤊.𐤏𐤌𐤊𐤌|
25 𐤅𐤉𐤀𐤌𐤓.𐤌𐤔𐤄.𐤂𐤌.𐤀𐤕𐤄.𐤕𐤕𐤍.𐤁𐤉𐤃𐤍𐤅.𐤆𐤁𐤇𐤉
𐤌.𐤅𐤏𐤋𐤕.𐤅𐤏𐤔𐤉𐤍𐤅.𐤋𐤉𐤄𐤅𐤄.𐤀𐤋𐤄𐤉𐤍𐤅|
26 𐤅𐤂𐤌.𐤌𐤒𐤍𐤍𐤅.𐤉𐤋𐤊.𐤏𐤌𐤍𐤅.𐤋𐤀.𐤕𐤔𐤀𐤓.𐤐𐤓𐤎𐤄.𐤊𐤉.
𐤌𐤌𐤍𐤅.𐤍𐤒𐤇.𐤋𐤏𐤁𐤃.𐤀𐤕.𐤉𐤄𐤅𐤄.𐤀𐤋𐤄𐤉𐤍𐤅.𐤅𐤀𐤍𐤇𐤍𐤅.𐤋
𐤀.𐤍𐤃𐤏.𐤌𐤄.𐤍𐤏𐤁𐤃.𐤀𐤕.𐤉𐤄𐤅𐤄.𐤏𐤃.𐤁𐤀𐤍𐤅.𐤔𐤌𐤄|
27 𐤅𐤉𐤇𐤆𐤒.𐤉𐤄𐤅𐤄.𐤀𐤕.𐤋𐤁.𐤐𐤓𐤏𐤄.𐤅𐤋𐤀.𐤀𐤁𐤄.𐤋𐤔
𐤋𐤇𐤌|
28 𐤅𐤉𐤀𐤌𐤓.𐤋𐤅.𐤐𐤓𐤏𐤄.𐤋𐤊.𐤌𐤏𐤋𐤉.𐤄𐤔𐤌𐤓.𐤋𐤊.𐤀𐤋.𐤕𐤎
𐤐.𐤓𐤀𐤅𐤕.𐤐𐤍𐤉.𐤊𐤉.𐤁𐤉𐤅𐤌.𐤓𐤀𐤕𐤊.𐤐𐤍𐤉.𐤕𐤌𐤅𐤕|
29 𐤅𐤉𐤀𐤌𐤓.𐤌𐤔𐤄.𐤊𐤍.𐤃𐤁𐤓𐤕.𐤋𐤀.𐤀𐤎𐤐.𐤏𐤅𐤃.𐤓𐤀𐤅
𐤕.𐤐𐤍𐤉𐤊||

𐤅𐤉𐤏𐤋𐤅.𐤌𐤌𐤑𐤓𐤉𐤌.𐤇𐤋𐤒 11

1 𐤅𐤉𐤀𐤌𐤓.𐤉𐤄𐤅𐤄.𐤀𐤋.𐤌𐤔𐤄.𐤏𐤅𐤃.𐤍𐤂𐤏.𐤀𐤇𐤃.𐤀𐤁𐤉
𐤀.𐤏𐤋.𐤐𐤓𐤏𐤄.𐤅𐤏𐤋.𐤌𐤑𐤓𐤉𐤌.𐤀𐤇𐤓𐤉.𐤊𐤍.𐤉𐤔𐤋𐤇.𐤀𐤕𐤊
𐤌.𐤌𐤆𐤄.𐤊𐤔𐤋𐤇𐤅.𐤊𐤋𐤄.𐤂𐤓𐤔.𐤉𐤂𐤓𐤔.𐤀𐤕𐤊𐤌.𐤌𐤆𐤄|

2 𐤃𐤁𐤓.𐤍𐤀.𐤁𐤀𐤆𐤍𐤉.𐤄𐤏𐤌.𐤅𐤉𐤔𐤀𐤋𐤅.𐤀𐤉𐤔.𐤌𐤀𐤕.𐤓
𐤏𐤄𐤅.𐤅𐤀𐤔𐤄.𐤌𐤀𐤕.𐤓𐤏𐤅𐤕𐤄.𐤊𐤋𐤉.𐤊𐤎𐤐.𐤅𐤊𐤋𐤉.𐤆𐤄𐤁|

3 𐤅𐤉𐤕𐤍.𐤉𐤄𐤅𐤄.𐤀𐤕.𐤇𐤍.𐤄𐤏𐤌.𐤁𐤏𐤉𐤍𐤉.𐤌𐤑𐤓𐤉𐤌.𐤂
𐤌.𐤄𐤀𐤉𐤔.𐤌𐤔𐤄.𐤂𐤃𐤅𐤋.𐤌𐤀𐤃.𐤁𐤀𐤓𐤑.𐤌𐤑𐤓𐤉𐤌.𐤁𐤏𐤉
𐤍𐤉.𐤏𐤁𐤃𐤉.𐤐𐤓𐤏𐤄.𐤅𐤁𐤏𐤉𐤍𐤉.𐤄𐤏𐤌|

4 𐤅𐤉𐤀𐤌𐤓.𐤌𐤔𐤄.𐤊𐤄.𐤀𐤌𐤓.𐤉𐤄𐤅𐤄.𐤊𐤇𐤑𐤕.𐤄𐤋𐤉𐤋𐤄.
𐤀𐤍𐤉.𐤉𐤅𐤑𐤀.𐤁𐤕𐤅𐤊.𐤌𐤑𐤓𐤉𐤌|

5 𐤅𐤌𐤕.𐤊𐤋.𐤁𐤊𐤅𐤓.𐤁𐤀𐤓𐤑.𐤌𐤑𐤓𐤉𐤌.𐤌𐤁𐤊𐤅𐤓.𐤐𐤓𐤏𐤄.𐤄
𐤉𐤔𐤁.𐤏𐤋.𐤊𐤎𐤀𐤅.𐤏𐤃.𐤁𐤊𐤅𐤓.𐤄𐤔𐤐𐤇𐤄.𐤀𐤔𐤓.𐤀𐤇𐤓.𐤄𐤓
𐤇𐤉𐤌.𐤅𐤊𐤋.𐤁𐤊𐤅𐤓.𐤁𐤄𐤌𐤄|

6 𐤅𐤄𐤉𐤕𐤄.𐤑𐤏𐤒𐤄.𐤂𐤃𐤋𐤄.𐤁𐤊𐤋.𐤀𐤓𐤑.𐤌𐤑𐤓𐤉𐤌.𐤀
𐤔𐤓.𐤊𐤌𐤄𐤅.𐤋𐤀.𐤍𐤄𐤉𐤕𐤄.𐤅𐤊𐤌𐤄𐤅.𐤋𐤀.𐤕𐤎𐤐|

7 𐤅𐤋𐤊𐤋.𐤁𐤍𐤉.𐤉𐤔𐤓𐤀𐤋.𐤋𐤀.𐤉𐤇𐤓𐤑.𐤊𐤋𐤁.𐤋𐤔𐤍𐤅.𐤋𐤌𐤀
𐤉𐤔.𐤅𐤏𐤃.𐤁𐤄𐤌𐤄.𐤋𐤌𐤏𐤍.𐤕𐤃𐤏𐤅𐤍.𐤀𐤔𐤓.𐤉𐤐𐤋𐤄.𐤉𐤄𐤅𐤄.
𐤁𐤉𐤍.𐤌𐤑𐤓𐤉𐤌.𐤅𐤁𐤉𐤍.𐤉𐤔𐤓𐤀𐤋|

8 𐤅𐤉𐤓𐤃𐤅.𐤊𐤋.𐤏𐤁𐤃𐤉𐤊.𐤀𐤋𐤄.𐤀𐤋𐤉.𐤅𐤄𐤔𐤕𐤇𐤅𐤅.𐤋𐤉.𐤋
𐤀𐤌𐤓.𐤑𐤀.𐤀𐤕𐤄.𐤅𐤊𐤋.𐤄𐤏𐤌.𐤀𐤔𐤓.𐤁𐤓𐤂𐤋𐤉𐤊.𐤅𐤀𐤇𐤓𐤉.
𐤊𐤍.𐤀𐤑𐤀.𐤅𐤉𐤑𐤀.𐤌𐤏𐤌.𐤐𐤓𐤏𐤄.𐤁𐤇𐤓𐤉.𐤀𐤐|

9 𐤅𐤉𐤀𐤌𐤓.𐤉𐤄𐤅𐤄.𐤀𐤋.𐤌𐤔𐤄.𐤋𐤀.𐤉𐤔𐤌𐤏.𐤀𐤋𐤉𐤊𐤌.𐤐𐤓
𐤏𐤄.𐤋𐤌𐤏𐤍.𐤓𐤁𐤅𐤕.𐤌𐤅𐤐𐤕𐤉.𐤁𐤀𐤓𐤑.𐤌𐤑𐤓𐤉𐤌|

10 𐤅𐤌𐤔𐤄.𐤅𐤀𐤄𐤓𐤍.𐤏𐤔𐤅.𐤀𐤕.𐤊𐤋.𐤄𐤌𐤐𐤕𐤉𐤌.𐤄𐤀𐤋𐤄.
𐤋𐤐𐤍𐤉.𐤐𐤓𐤏𐤄.𐤅𐤉𐤇𐤆𐤒.𐤉𐤄𐤅𐤄.𐤀𐤕.𐤋𐤁.𐤐𐤓𐤏𐤄.𐤅𐤋𐤀.𐤔𐤋
𐤇.𐤀𐤕.𐤁𐤍𐤉.𐤉𐤔𐤓𐤀𐤋.𐤌𐤀𐤓𐤑𐤅||

𐤅𐤉𐤏𐤋𐤅.𐤌𐤌𐤑𐤓𐤉𐤌.𐤇𐤋𐤒 12

1 𐤅𐤉𐤀𐤌𐤓.𐤉𐤄𐤅𐤄.𐤀𐤋.𐤌𐤔𐤄.𐤅𐤀𐤋.𐤀𐤄𐤓𐤍.𐤁𐤀𐤓𐤑.𐤌𐤑
𐤓𐤉𐤌.𐤋𐤀𐤌𐤓|
2 𐤄𐤇𐤃𐤔.𐤄𐤆𐤄.𐤋𐤊𐤌.𐤓𐤀𐤔.𐤇𐤃𐤔𐤉𐤌.𐤓𐤀𐤔𐤅𐤍.𐤄𐤅
𐤀.𐤋𐤊𐤌.𐤋𐤇𐤃𐤔𐤉.𐤄𐤔𐤍𐤄|
3 𐤃𐤁𐤓𐤅.𐤀𐤋.𐤊𐤋.𐤏𐤃𐤕.𐤉𐤔𐤓𐤀𐤋.𐤋𐤀𐤌𐤓.𐤁𐤏𐤔𐤓.𐤋𐤇
𐤃𐤔.𐤄𐤆𐤄.𐤅𐤉𐤒𐤇𐤅.𐤋𐤄𐤌.𐤀𐤉𐤔.𐤔𐤄.𐤋𐤁𐤉𐤕.𐤀𐤁𐤕.𐤔
𐤄.𐤋𐤁𐤉𐤕|
4 𐤅𐤀𐤌.𐤉𐤌𐤏𐤈.𐤄𐤁𐤉𐤕.𐤌𐤄𐤉𐤕.𐤌𐤔𐤄.𐤅𐤋𐤒𐤇.𐤄𐤅𐤀.𐤅
𐤔𐤊𐤍𐤅.𐤄𐤒𐤓𐤁.𐤀𐤋.𐤁𐤉𐤕𐤅.𐤁𐤌𐤊𐤎𐤕.𐤍𐤐𐤔𐤕.𐤀𐤉𐤔.𐤋𐤐𐤉.
𐤀𐤊𐤋𐤅.𐤕𐤊𐤎𐤅.𐤏𐤋.𐤄𐤔𐤄|
5 𐤔𐤄.𐤕𐤌𐤉𐤌.𐤆𐤊𐤓.𐤁𐤍.𐤔𐤍𐤄.𐤉𐤄𐤉𐤄.𐤋𐤊𐤌.𐤌𐤍.𐤄𐤊𐤁
𐤔𐤉𐤌.𐤅𐤌𐤍.𐤄𐤏𐤆𐤉𐤌.𐤕𐤒𐤇𐤅|
6 𐤅𐤄𐤉𐤄.𐤋𐤊𐤌.𐤋𐤌𐤔𐤌𐤓𐤕.𐤏𐤃.𐤀𐤓𐤁𐤏𐤄.𐤏𐤔𐤓.𐤉𐤅𐤌.𐤋
𐤇𐤃𐤔.𐤄𐤆𐤄.𐤅𐤔𐤇𐤈𐤅.𐤀𐤕𐤅.𐤊𐤋.𐤒𐤄𐤋.𐤏𐤃𐤕.𐤉𐤔𐤓𐤀𐤋
.𐤁𐤉𐤍.𐤄𐤏𐤓𐤁𐤉𐤌|
7 𐤅𐤋𐤒𐤇𐤅.𐤌𐤍.𐤄𐤃𐤌.𐤅𐤍𐤕𐤍𐤅.𐤏𐤋.𐤔𐤕𐤉.𐤄𐤌𐤆𐤅𐤆𐤕.𐤅
𐤏𐤋.𐤄𐤌𐤔𐤒𐤅𐤐.𐤏𐤋.𐤄𐤁𐤕𐤉𐤌.𐤀𐤔𐤓.𐤉𐤀𐤊𐤋𐤅.𐤀𐤕𐤅.𐤁𐤄𐤌|
8 𐤅𐤀𐤊𐤋𐤅.𐤀𐤕.𐤄𐤁𐤔𐤓.𐤁𐤋𐤉𐤋𐤄.𐤄𐤆𐤄.𐤑𐤋𐤉.𐤀𐤔.𐤅𐤌
𐤑𐤅𐤕.𐤏𐤋.𐤌𐤓𐤓𐤉𐤌.𐤉𐤀𐤊𐤋𐤄𐤅|
9 𐤀𐤋.𐤕𐤀𐤊𐤋𐤅.𐤌𐤌𐤍𐤅.𐤍𐤀.𐤅𐤁𐤔𐤋.𐤌𐤁𐤔𐤋.𐤁𐤌𐤉𐤌.𐤊𐤉.
𐤀𐤌.𐤑𐤋𐤉.𐤀𐤔.𐤓𐤀𐤔𐤅.𐤏𐤋.𐤊𐤓𐤏𐤉𐤅.𐤅𐤏𐤋.𐤒𐤓𐤁𐤅|
10 𐤅𐤋𐤀.𐤕𐤅𐤕𐤉𐤓𐤅.𐤌𐤌𐤍𐤅.𐤏𐤃.𐤁𐤒𐤓.𐤅𐤄𐤍𐤕𐤓.𐤌𐤌𐤍𐤅.𐤏
𐤃.𐤁𐤒𐤓.𐤁𐤀𐤔.𐤕𐤔𐤓𐤐𐤅|
11 𐤅𐤊𐤊𐤄.𐤕𐤀𐤊𐤋𐤅.𐤀𐤕𐤅.𐤌𐤕𐤍𐤉𐤊𐤌.𐤇𐤂𐤓𐤉𐤌.𐤍𐤏𐤋𐤉
𐤊𐤌.𐤁𐤓𐤂𐤋𐤉𐤊𐤌.𐤅𐤌𐤒𐤋𐤊𐤌.𐤁𐤉𐤃𐤊𐤌.𐤅𐤀𐤊𐤋𐤕𐤌.𐤀𐤕𐤅.
𐤁𐤇𐤐𐤆𐤅𐤍.𐤐𐤎𐤇.𐤄𐤅𐤀.𐤋𐤉𐤄𐤅𐤄|
12 𐤅𐤏𐤁𐤓𐤕𐤉.𐤁𐤀𐤓𐤑.𐤌𐤑𐤓𐤉𐤌.𐤁𐤋𐤉𐤋𐤄.𐤄𐤆𐤄.𐤅𐤄𐤊
𐤉𐤕𐤉.𐤊𐤋.𐤁𐤊𐤅𐤓.𐤁𐤀𐤓𐤑.𐤌𐤑𐤓𐤉𐤌.𐤌𐤀𐤃𐤌.𐤅𐤏𐤃.𐤁𐤄𐤌
𐤄.𐤅𐤁𐤊𐤋.𐤀𐤋𐤄𐤉.𐤌𐤑𐤓𐤉𐤌.𐤀𐤏𐤔𐤄.𐤔𐤐𐤈𐤉𐤌.𐤀𐤍𐤉.𐤉𐤄𐤅
𐤄|

𐤉𐤂 𐤅𐤄𐤉𐤄.𐤄𐤃𐤌.𐤋𐤊𐤌.𐤋𐤀𐤕.𐤏𐤋.𐤄𐤁𐤕𐤉𐤌.𐤀𐤔𐤓.𐤀𐤕
𐤌.𐤔𐤌.𐤅𐤓𐤀𐤉𐤕𐤉.𐤀𐤕.𐤄𐤃𐤌.𐤅𐤐𐤎𐤇𐤕𐤉.𐤏𐤋𐤊𐤌.𐤅𐤋𐤀.𐤉
𐤄𐤉𐤄.𐤁𐤊𐤌.𐤍𐤂𐤐.𐤋𐤌𐤔𐤇𐤉𐤕.𐤁𐤄𐤊𐤕𐤉.𐤁𐤀𐤓𐤑.𐤌𐤑𐤓𐤉
𐤌|
𐤉𐤃 𐤅𐤄𐤉𐤄.𐤄𐤉𐤅𐤌.𐤄𐤆𐤄.𐤋𐤊𐤌.𐤋𐤆𐤊𐤓𐤅𐤍.𐤅𐤇𐤂𐤕𐤌.𐤀
𐤕𐤅.𐤇𐤂.𐤋𐤉𐤄𐤅𐤄.𐤋𐤃𐤓𐤕𐤉𐤊𐤌.𐤇𐤒𐤕.𐤏𐤅𐤋𐤌.𐤕𐤇𐤂𐤄𐤅|
𐤈𐤅 𐤔𐤁𐤏𐤕.𐤉𐤌𐤉𐤌.𐤌𐤑𐤅𐤕.𐤕𐤀𐤊𐤋𐤅.𐤀𐤊.𐤁𐤉𐤅𐤌.𐤄𐤓𐤀
𐤔𐤅𐤍.𐤕𐤔𐤁𐤉𐤕𐤅.𐤔𐤀𐤓.𐤌𐤁𐤕𐤉𐤊𐤌.𐤊𐤉.𐤊𐤋.𐤀𐤊𐤋.𐤇𐤌𐤑.𐤅
𐤍𐤊𐤓𐤕𐤄.𐤄𐤍𐤐𐤔.𐤄𐤄𐤅𐤀.𐤌𐤉𐤔𐤓𐤀𐤋.𐤌𐤉𐤅𐤌.𐤄𐤓𐤀𐤔𐤍.𐤏𐤃
.𐤉𐤅𐤌.𐤄𐤔𐤁𐤏𐤉|
𐤈𐤆 𐤅𐤁𐤉𐤅𐤌.𐤄𐤓𐤀𐤔𐤅𐤍.𐤌𐤒𐤓𐤀.𐤒𐤃𐤔.𐤅𐤁𐤉𐤅𐤌.𐤄𐤔𐤁𐤉
𐤏𐤉.𐤌𐤒𐤓𐤀.𐤒𐤃𐤔.𐤉𐤄𐤉𐤄.𐤋𐤊𐤌.𐤊𐤋.𐤌𐤋𐤀𐤊𐤄.𐤋𐤀.𐤉𐤏
𐤔𐤄.𐤁𐤄𐤌.𐤀𐤊.𐤀𐤔𐤓.𐤉𐤀𐤊𐤋.𐤋𐤊𐤋.𐤍𐤐𐤔.𐤄𐤅𐤀.𐤋𐤁𐤃𐤅.𐤉
𐤏𐤔𐤄.𐤋𐤊𐤌|
𐤉𐤆 𐤅𐤔𐤌𐤓𐤕𐤌.𐤀𐤕.𐤄𐤌𐤑𐤅𐤕.𐤊𐤉.𐤁𐤏𐤑𐤌.𐤄𐤉𐤅𐤌.𐤄𐤆
𐤄.𐤄𐤅𐤑𐤀𐤕𐤉.𐤀𐤕.𐤑𐤁𐤀𐤅𐤕𐤉𐤊𐤌.𐤌𐤀𐤓𐤑.𐤌𐤑𐤓𐤉𐤌.𐤅𐤔
𐤌𐤓𐤕𐤌.𐤀𐤕.𐤄𐤉𐤅𐤌.𐤄𐤆𐤄.𐤋𐤃𐤓𐤕𐤉𐤊𐤌.𐤇𐤒𐤕.𐤏𐤅𐤋𐤌|
𐤉𐤇 𐤁𐤓𐤀𐤔𐤍.𐤁𐤀𐤓𐤁𐤏𐤄.𐤏𐤔𐤓.𐤉𐤅𐤌.𐤋𐤇𐤃𐤔.𐤁𐤏𐤓𐤁.𐤕
𐤀𐤊𐤋𐤅.𐤌𐤑𐤅𐤕.𐤏𐤃.𐤉𐤅𐤌.𐤄𐤀𐤇𐤃.𐤅𐤏𐤔𐤓𐤉𐤌.𐤋𐤇𐤃𐤔.𐤁
𐤏𐤓𐤁|
𐤉𐤈 𐤔𐤁𐤏𐤕.𐤉𐤌𐤉𐤌.𐤔𐤀𐤓.𐤋𐤀.𐤉𐤌𐤑𐤀.𐤁𐤁𐤕𐤉𐤊𐤌.𐤊
𐤉.𐤊𐤋.𐤀𐤊𐤋.𐤌𐤇𐤌𐤑𐤕.𐤅𐤍𐤊𐤓𐤕𐤄.𐤄𐤍𐤐𐤔.𐤄𐤄𐤅𐤀.𐤌𐤏𐤃
𐤕.𐤉𐤔𐤓𐤀𐤋.𐤁𐤂𐤓.𐤅𐤁𐤀𐤆𐤓𐤇.𐤄𐤀𐤓𐤑|
𐤊 𐤊𐤋.𐤌𐤇𐤌𐤑𐤕.𐤋𐤀.𐤕𐤀𐤊𐤋𐤅.𐤁𐤊𐤋.𐤌𐤅𐤔𐤁𐤕𐤉𐤊𐤌.
𐤕𐤀𐤊𐤋𐤅.𐤌𐤑𐤅𐤕|
𐤊𐤀 𐤅𐤉𐤒𐤓𐤀.𐤌𐤔𐤄.𐤋𐤊𐤋.𐤆𐤒𐤍𐤉.𐤉𐤔𐤓𐤀𐤋.𐤅𐤉𐤀𐤌𐤓.𐤀𐤋
𐤄𐤌.𐤌𐤔𐤊𐤅.𐤅𐤒𐤇𐤅.𐤋𐤊𐤌.𐤑𐤀𐤍.𐤋𐤌𐤔𐤐𐤇𐤕𐤉𐤊𐤌.𐤅𐤔𐤇𐤈
𐤅.𐤄𐤐𐤎𐤇|
𐤊𐤁 𐤅𐤋𐤒𐤇𐤕𐤌.𐤀𐤂𐤃𐤕.𐤀𐤆𐤅𐤁.𐤅𐤈𐤁𐤋𐤕𐤌.𐤁𐤃𐤌.𐤀
𐤔𐤓.𐤁𐤎𐤐.𐤅𐤄𐤂𐤏𐤕𐤌.𐤀𐤋.𐤄𐤌𐤔𐤒𐤅𐤐.𐤅𐤀𐤋.𐤔𐤕𐤉.𐤄𐤌𐤆𐤅

𐤆𐤕.𐤌𐤍.𐤄𐤃𐤌.𐤀𐤔𐤓.𐤁𐤎𐤐.𐤅𐤀𐤕𐤌.𐤋𐤀.𐤕𐤑𐤀𐤅.𐤀𐤉𐤔.𐤌
𐤐𐤕𐤇.𐤁𐤉𐤕𐤅.𐤏𐤃.𐤁𐤒𐤓|
𐤊𐤂 𐤅𐤏𐤁𐤓.𐤉𐤄𐤅𐤄.𐤋𐤍𐤂𐤐.𐤀𐤕.𐤌𐤑𐤓𐤉𐤌.𐤅𐤓𐤀𐤄.𐤀𐤕.𐤄
𐤃𐤌.𐤏𐤋.𐤄𐤌𐤔𐤒𐤅𐤐.𐤅𐤏𐤋.𐤔𐤕𐤉.𐤄𐤌𐤆𐤅𐤆𐤕.𐤅𐤐𐤎𐤇.𐤉𐤄
𐤅𐤄.𐤏𐤋.𐤄𐤐𐤕𐤇.𐤅𐤋𐤀.𐤉𐤕𐤍.𐤄𐤌𐤔𐤇𐤉𐤕.𐤋𐤁𐤀.𐤀𐤋.𐤁𐤕𐤉
𐤊𐤌.𐤋𐤍𐤂𐤐|
𐤊𐤃 𐤅𐤔𐤌𐤓𐤕𐤌.𐤀𐤕.𐤄𐤃𐤁𐤓.𐤄𐤆𐤄.𐤋𐤇𐤒.𐤋𐤊.𐤅𐤋𐤁𐤍𐤉
𐤊.𐤏𐤃.𐤏𐤅𐤋𐤌|
𐤊𐤄 𐤅𐤄𐤉𐤄.𐤊𐤉.𐤕𐤁𐤀𐤅.𐤀𐤋.𐤄𐤀𐤓𐤑.𐤀𐤔𐤓.𐤉𐤕𐤍.𐤉𐤄𐤅𐤄.
𐤋𐤊𐤌.𐤊𐤀𐤔𐤓.𐤃𐤁𐤓.𐤅𐤔𐤌𐤓𐤕𐤌.𐤀𐤕.𐤄𐤏𐤁𐤃𐤄.𐤄𐤆𐤀𐤕|
𐤊𐤅 𐤅𐤄𐤉𐤄.𐤊𐤉.𐤉𐤀𐤌𐤓𐤅.𐤀𐤋𐤉𐤊𐤌.𐤁𐤍𐤉𐤊𐤌.𐤌𐤄.𐤄𐤏𐤁𐤃
𐤄.𐤄𐤆𐤀𐤕.𐤋𐤊𐤌|
𐤊𐤆 𐤅𐤀𐤌𐤓𐤕𐤌.𐤆𐤁𐤇.𐤐𐤎𐤇.𐤄𐤅𐤀.𐤋𐤉𐤄𐤅𐤄.𐤀𐤔𐤓.𐤐𐤎
𐤇.𐤏𐤋.𐤁𐤕𐤉.𐤁𐤍𐤉.𐤉𐤔𐤓𐤀𐤋.𐤁𐤌𐤑𐤓𐤉𐤌.𐤁𐤍𐤂𐤐𐤅.𐤀𐤕.𐤌
𐤑𐤓𐤉𐤌.𐤅𐤀𐤕.𐤁𐤕𐤉𐤍𐤅.𐤄𐤑𐤉𐤋.𐤅𐤉𐤒𐤃.𐤄𐤏𐤌.𐤅𐤉𐤔𐤕𐤇𐤅𐤅|
𐤊𐤇 𐤅𐤉𐤋𐤊𐤅.𐤅𐤉𐤏𐤔𐤅.𐤁𐤍𐤉.𐤉𐤔𐤓𐤀𐤋.𐤊𐤀𐤔𐤓.𐤑𐤅𐤄.𐤉𐤄𐤅
𐤄.𐤀𐤕.𐤌𐤔𐤄.𐤅𐤀𐤄𐤓𐤍.𐤊𐤍.𐤏𐤔𐤅|
𐤊𐤈 𐤅𐤉𐤄𐤉.𐤁𐤇𐤑𐤉.𐤄𐤋𐤉𐤋𐤄.𐤅𐤉𐤄𐤅𐤄.𐤄𐤊𐤄.𐤊𐤋.𐤁𐤊𐤅𐤓
𐤁𐤀𐤓𐤑.𐤌𐤑𐤓𐤉𐤌.𐤌𐤁𐤊𐤓.𐤐𐤓𐤏𐤄.𐤄𐤉𐤔𐤁.𐤏𐤋.𐤊𐤎𐤀𐤅.𐤏
𐤃.𐤁𐤊𐤅𐤓.𐤄𐤔𐤁𐤉.𐤀𐤔𐤓.𐤁𐤁𐤉𐤕.𐤄𐤁𐤅𐤓.𐤅𐤊𐤋.𐤁𐤊𐤅𐤓.𐤁𐤄𐤌
𐤄|
𐤋 𐤅𐤉𐤒𐤌.𐤐𐤓𐤏𐤄.𐤋𐤉𐤋𐤄.𐤄𐤅𐤀.𐤅𐤊𐤋.𐤏𐤁𐤃𐤉𐤅.𐤅𐤊𐤋.𐤌
𐤑𐤓𐤉𐤌.𐤅𐤕𐤄𐤉.𐤑𐤏𐤒𐤄.𐤂𐤃𐤋𐤄.𐤁𐤌𐤑𐤓𐤉𐤌.𐤊𐤉.𐤀𐤉𐤍.
𐤁𐤉𐤕.𐤀𐤔𐤓.𐤀𐤉𐤍.𐤔𐤌.𐤌𐤕|
𐤋𐤀 𐤅𐤉𐤒𐤓𐤀.𐤋𐤌𐤔𐤄.𐤅𐤋𐤀𐤄𐤓𐤍.𐤋𐤉𐤋𐤄.𐤅𐤉𐤀𐤌𐤓.𐤒𐤅𐤌𐤅.
𐤑𐤀𐤅.𐤌𐤕𐤅𐤊.𐤏𐤌𐤉.𐤂𐤌.𐤀𐤕𐤌.𐤂𐤌.𐤁𐤍𐤉.𐤉𐤔𐤓𐤀𐤋.𐤅𐤋𐤊𐤅.
𐤏𐤁𐤃𐤅.𐤀𐤕.𐤉𐤄𐤅𐤄.𐤊𐤃𐤁𐤓𐤊𐤌|
𐤋𐤁 𐤂𐤌.𐤑𐤀𐤍𐤊𐤌.𐤂𐤌.𐤁𐤒𐤓𐤊𐤌.𐤒𐤇𐤅.𐤊𐤀𐤔𐤓.𐤃𐤁𐤓
𐤕𐤌.𐤅𐤋𐤊𐤅.𐤅𐤁𐤓𐤊𐤕𐤌.𐤂𐤌.𐤀𐤕𐤉|
𐤋𐤂 𐤅𐤕𐤇𐤆𐤒.𐤌𐤑𐤓𐤉𐤌.𐤏𐤋.𐤄𐤏𐤌.𐤋𐤌𐤄𐤓.𐤋𐤔𐤋𐤇𐤌.
𐤌𐤍.𐤄𐤀𐤓𐤑.𐤊𐤉.𐤀𐤌𐤓𐤅.𐤊𐤋𐤍𐤅.𐤌𐤕𐤉𐤌|

𐤋𐤃 𐤅𐤉𐤔𐤀.𐤄𐤏𐤌.𐤀𐤕.𐤁𐤑𐤒𐤅.𐤈𐤓𐤌.𐤉𐤇𐤌𐤑.𐤌𐤔𐤀𐤓
𐤕𐤌.𐤑𐤓𐤓𐤕.𐤁𐤔𐤌𐤋𐤕𐤌.𐤏𐤋.𐤔𐤊𐤌𐤌|
𐤋𐤄 𐤅𐤁𐤍𐤉.𐤉𐤔𐤓𐤀𐤋.𐤏𐤔𐤅.𐤊𐤃𐤁𐤓.𐤌𐤔𐤄.𐤅𐤉𐤔𐤀𐤋𐤅.𐤌𐤌
𐤑𐤓𐤉𐤌.𐤊𐤋𐤉.𐤊𐤎𐤐.𐤅𐤊𐤋𐤉.𐤆𐤄𐤁.𐤅𐤔𐤌𐤋𐤕|
𐤋𐤅 𐤅𐤉𐤄𐤅𐤄.𐤍𐤕𐤍.𐤀𐤕.𐤇𐤍.𐤄𐤏𐤌.𐤁𐤏𐤉𐤍𐤉.𐤌𐤑𐤓𐤉𐤌.𐤅𐤉
𐤔𐤀𐤋𐤅𐤌.𐤅𐤉𐤍𐤑𐤋𐤅.𐤀𐤕.𐤌𐤑𐤓𐤉𐤌|
𐤋𐤆 𐤅𐤉𐤎𐤏𐤅.𐤁𐤍𐤉.𐤉𐤔𐤓𐤀𐤋.𐤌𐤓𐤏𐤌𐤎𐤎.𐤎𐤊𐤕𐤄.𐤊𐤔𐤔
.𐤌𐤀𐤅𐤕.𐤀𐤋𐤐.𐤓𐤂𐤋𐤉.𐤄𐤂𐤁𐤓𐤉𐤌.𐤋𐤁𐤃.𐤌𐤈𐤐|
𐤋𐤇 𐤅𐤂𐤌.𐤏𐤓𐤁.𐤓𐤁.𐤏𐤋𐤄.𐤀𐤕𐤌.𐤅𐤑𐤀𐤍.𐤅𐤁𐤒𐤓.𐤌𐤒𐤍𐤄.
𐤊𐤁𐤃.𐤌𐤀𐤃|
𐤋𐤈 𐤅𐤉𐤀𐤐𐤅.𐤀𐤕.𐤄𐤁𐤑𐤒.𐤀𐤔𐤓.𐤄𐤅𐤑𐤉𐤀𐤅.𐤌𐤌𐤑𐤓𐤉𐤌
.𐤏𐤂𐤕.𐤌𐤑𐤅𐤕.𐤊𐤉.𐤋𐤀.𐤇𐤌𐤑.𐤊𐤉.𐤂𐤓𐤔𐤅.𐤌𐤌𐤑𐤓𐤉𐤌.𐤅
𐤋𐤀.𐤉𐤊𐤋𐤅.𐤋𐤄𐤕𐤌𐤄𐤌𐤄.𐤅𐤂𐤌.𐤑𐤃𐤄.𐤋𐤀.𐤏𐤔𐤅.𐤋𐤄𐤌|
𐤌 𐤅𐤌𐤅𐤔𐤁.𐤁𐤍𐤉.𐤉𐤔𐤓𐤀𐤋.𐤀𐤔𐤓.𐤉𐤔𐤁𐤅.𐤁𐤌𐤑𐤓𐤉𐤌.
𐤔𐤋𐤔𐤉𐤌.𐤔𐤍𐤄.𐤅𐤀𐤓𐤁𐤏.𐤌𐤀𐤅𐤕.𐤔𐤍𐤄|
𐤌𐤀 𐤅𐤉𐤄𐤉.𐤌𐤒𐤑.𐤔𐤋𐤔𐤉𐤌.𐤔𐤍𐤄.𐤅𐤀𐤓𐤁𐤏.𐤌𐤀𐤅𐤕.𐤔𐤍
𐤄.𐤅𐤉𐤄𐤉.𐤁𐤏𐤑𐤌.𐤄𐤉𐤅𐤌.𐤄𐤆𐤄.𐤉𐤑𐤀𐤅.𐤊𐤋.𐤑𐤁𐤀𐤅𐤕.𐤉
𐤄𐤅𐤄.𐤌𐤀𐤓𐤑.𐤌𐤑𐤓𐤉𐤌|
𐤌𐤁 𐤋𐤉𐤋.𐤔𐤌𐤓𐤉𐤌.𐤄𐤅𐤀.𐤋𐤉𐤄𐤅𐤄.𐤋𐤄𐤅𐤑𐤉𐤀𐤌.𐤌𐤀𐤓
𐤑.𐤌𐤑𐤓𐤉𐤌.𐤄𐤅𐤀.𐤄𐤋𐤉𐤋𐤄.𐤄𐤆𐤄.𐤋𐤉𐤄𐤅𐤄.𐤔𐤌𐤓𐤉𐤌.𐤋
𐤊𐤋.𐤁𐤍𐤉.𐤉𐤔𐤓𐤀𐤋.𐤋𐤃𐤓𐤕𐤌|
𐤌𐤂 𐤅𐤉𐤀𐤌𐤓.𐤉𐤄𐤅𐤄.𐤀𐤋.𐤌𐤔𐤄.𐤅𐤀𐤄𐤓𐤍.𐤆𐤀𐤕.𐤇𐤒𐤕.
𐤄𐤐𐤎𐤇.𐤊𐤋.𐤁𐤍.𐤍𐤊𐤓.𐤋𐤀.𐤉𐤀𐤊𐤋.𐤁𐤅|
𐤌𐤃 𐤅𐤊𐤋.𐤏𐤁𐤃.𐤀𐤉𐤔.𐤌𐤒𐤍𐤕.𐤊𐤎𐤐.𐤅𐤌𐤋𐤕𐤄.𐤀𐤕𐤅.𐤀
𐤆.𐤉𐤀𐤊𐤋.𐤁𐤅|
𐤌𐤄 𐤕𐤅𐤔𐤁.𐤅𐤔𐤊𐤉𐤓.𐤋𐤀.𐤉𐤀𐤊𐤋.𐤁𐤅|
𐤌𐤅 𐤁𐤁𐤉𐤕.𐤀𐤇𐤃.𐤉𐤀𐤊𐤋.𐤋𐤀.𐤕𐤅𐤑𐤉𐤀.𐤌𐤍.𐤄𐤁𐤉𐤕.
𐤌𐤍.𐤄𐤁𐤔𐤓.𐤇𐤅𐤑𐤄.𐤅𐤏𐤑𐤌.𐤋𐤀.𐤕𐤔𐤁𐤓𐤅.𐤁𐤅|
𐤌𐤆 𐤊𐤋.𐤏𐤃𐤕.𐤉𐤔𐤓𐤀𐤋.𐤉𐤏𐤔𐤅.𐤀𐤕𐤅|

מח וכי.יגור.אתך.גר.ועשה.פסח.ליהוה.המ
ול.לו.כל.זכר.ואז.יקרב.לעשתו.והיה.כאזר
ח.הארץ.וכל.ערל.לא.יאכל.בו|
מט תורה.אחת.יהיה.לאזרח.ולגר.הגר.ב
תוככם|
נ ויעשו.כל.בני.ישראל.כאשר.צוה.יהוה.א
ת.משה.ואת.אהרן.כן.עשו|
נא ויהי.בעצם.היום.הזה.הוציא.יהוה.את
.בני.ישראל.מארץ.מצרים.על.צבאתם||

ויעלו.ממצרים.חלק יג

א וידבר.יהוה.אל.משה.לאמר|
ב קדש.לי.כל.בכור.פטר.כל.רחם.בבני.ישרא
ל.באדם.ובבהמה.לי.הוא|
ג ויאמר.משה.אל.העם.זכור.את.היום.הזה
.אשר.יצאתם.ממצרים.מבית.עבדים.כי.בח
זק.יד.הוציא.יהוה.אתכם.מזה.ולא.יאכל.
חמץ|
ד היום.אתם.יצאים.בחדש.האביב|
ה והיה.כי.יביאך.יהוה.אל.ארץ.הכנעני.וה
חתי.והאמרי.והחוי.והיבוסי.אשר.נשבע.לא
בתיך.לתת.לך.ארץ.זבת.חלב.ודבש.ועבדת.
את.העבדה.הזאת.בחדש.הזה|
ו שבעת.ימים.תאכל.מצת.וביום.השביעי.
חג.ליהוה|
ז מצות.יאכל.את.שבעת.הימים.ולא.יראה.
לך.חמץ.ולא.יראה.לך.שאר.בכל.גבלך|
ח והגדת.לבנך.ביום.ההוא.לאמר.בעבור.זה
.עשה.יהוה.לי.בצאתי.ממצרים|

𐤈 𐤅𐤄𐤉𐤄.𐤋𐤊.𐤋𐤀𐤅𐤕.𐤏𐤋.𐤉𐤃𐤊.𐤅𐤋𐤆𐤊𐤓𐤅𐤍.𐤁𐤉𐤍.𐤏𐤉𐤍
𐤉𐤊.𐤋𐤌𐤏𐤍.𐤕𐤄𐤉𐤄.𐤕𐤅𐤓𐤕.𐤉𐤄𐤅𐤄.𐤁𐤐𐤉𐤊.𐤊𐤉.𐤁𐤉𐤃.𐤇
𐤆𐤒𐤄.𐤄𐤅𐤑𐤀𐤊.𐤉𐤄𐤅𐤄.𐤌𐤌𐤑𐤓𐤉𐤌|

𐤉 𐤅𐤔𐤌𐤓𐤕.𐤀𐤕.𐤄𐤇𐤒𐤄.𐤄𐤆𐤀𐤕.𐤋𐤌𐤅𐤏𐤃𐤄.𐤌𐤉𐤌
𐤉𐤌.𐤉𐤌𐤉𐤌𐤄|

𐤉𐤀 𐤅𐤄𐤉𐤄.𐤊𐤉.𐤉𐤁𐤀𐤊.𐤉𐤄𐤅𐤄.𐤀𐤋.𐤀𐤓𐤑.𐤄𐤊𐤍𐤏𐤍𐤉.𐤊
𐤀𐤔𐤓.𐤍𐤔𐤁𐤏.𐤋𐤊.𐤅𐤋𐤀𐤁𐤕𐤉𐤊.𐤅𐤍𐤕𐤍𐤄.𐤋𐤊|

𐤉𐤁 𐤅𐤄𐤏𐤁𐤓𐤕.𐤊𐤋.𐤐𐤈𐤓.𐤓𐤇𐤌.𐤋𐤉𐤄𐤅𐤄.𐤅𐤊𐤋.𐤐𐤈𐤓.𐤔𐤂
𐤓.𐤁𐤄𐤌𐤄.𐤀𐤔𐤓.𐤉𐤄𐤉𐤄.𐤋𐤊.𐤄𐤆𐤊𐤓𐤉𐤌.𐤋𐤉𐤄𐤅𐤄|

𐤉𐤂 𐤅𐤊𐤋.𐤐𐤈𐤓.𐤇𐤌𐤓.𐤕𐤐𐤃𐤄.𐤁𐤔𐤄.𐤅𐤀𐤌.𐤋𐤀.𐤕𐤐𐤃𐤄.
𐤅𐤏𐤓𐤐𐤕𐤅.𐤅𐤊𐤋.𐤁𐤊𐤅𐤓.𐤀𐤃𐤌.𐤁𐤁𐤍𐤉𐤊.𐤕𐤐𐤃𐤄|

𐤉𐤃 𐤅𐤄𐤉𐤄.𐤊𐤉.𐤉𐤔𐤀𐤋𐤊.𐤁𐤍𐤊.𐤌𐤇𐤓.𐤋𐤀𐤌𐤓.𐤌𐤄.𐤆𐤀
𐤕.𐤅𐤀𐤌𐤓𐤕.𐤀𐤋𐤉𐤅.𐤁𐤇𐤆𐤒.𐤉𐤃.𐤄𐤅𐤑𐤉𐤀𐤍𐤅.𐤉𐤄𐤅𐤄.𐤌𐤌
𐤑𐤓𐤉𐤌.𐤌𐤁𐤉𐤕.𐤏𐤁𐤃𐤉𐤌|

𐤈𐤅 𐤅𐤉𐤄𐤉.𐤊𐤉.𐤄𐤒𐤔𐤄.𐤐𐤓𐤏𐤄.𐤋𐤔𐤋𐤇𐤍𐤅.𐤅𐤉𐤄𐤓𐤂.𐤉𐤄
𐤅𐤄.𐤊𐤋.𐤁𐤊𐤅𐤓.𐤁𐤀𐤓𐤑.𐤌𐤑𐤓𐤉𐤌.𐤌𐤁𐤊𐤓.𐤀𐤃𐤌.𐤅𐤏𐤃.𐤁𐤊
𐤅𐤓.𐤁𐤄𐤌𐤄.𐤏𐤋.𐤊𐤍.𐤀𐤍𐤉.𐤆𐤁𐤇.𐤋𐤉𐤄𐤅𐤄.𐤊𐤋.𐤐𐤈𐤓.𐤓𐤇𐤌
.𐤄𐤆𐤊𐤓𐤉𐤌.𐤅𐤊𐤋.𐤁𐤊𐤅𐤓.𐤁𐤍𐤉.𐤀𐤐𐤃𐤄|

𐤈𐤆 𐤅𐤄𐤉𐤄.𐤋𐤀𐤅𐤕.𐤏𐤋.𐤉𐤃𐤊𐤄.𐤅𐤋𐤈𐤅𐤈𐤐𐤕.𐤁𐤉𐤍.𐤏𐤉𐤍
𐤉𐤊.𐤊𐤉.𐤁𐤇𐤆𐤒.𐤉𐤃.𐤄𐤅𐤑𐤉𐤀𐤍𐤅.𐤉𐤄𐤅𐤄.𐤌𐤌𐤑𐤓𐤉𐤌|

𐤉𐤆 𐤅𐤉𐤄𐤉.𐤁𐤔𐤋𐤇.𐤐𐤓𐤏𐤄.𐤀𐤕.𐤄𐤏𐤌.𐤅𐤋𐤀.𐤍𐤇𐤌.𐤀𐤋
𐤄𐤉𐤌.𐤃𐤓𐤊.𐤀𐤓𐤑.𐤐𐤋𐤔𐤕𐤉𐤌.𐤊𐤉.𐤒𐤓𐤅𐤁.𐤄𐤅𐤀.𐤊𐤉.𐤀𐤌𐤓
𐤀𐤋𐤄𐤉𐤌.𐤐𐤍.𐤉𐤍𐤇𐤌.𐤄𐤏𐤌.𐤁𐤓𐤀𐤕𐤌.𐤌𐤋𐤇𐤌𐤄.𐤅𐤔𐤁𐤅.𐤌
𐤑𐤓𐤉𐤌𐤄|

𐤉𐤇 𐤅𐤉𐤎𐤁.𐤀𐤋𐤄𐤉𐤌.𐤀𐤕.𐤄𐤏𐤌.𐤃𐤓𐤊.𐤄𐤌𐤃𐤁𐤓.𐤉𐤌.𐤎
𐤅𐤐.𐤅𐤇𐤌𐤔𐤉𐤌.𐤏𐤋𐤅.𐤁𐤍𐤉.𐤉𐤔𐤓𐤀𐤋.𐤌𐤀𐤓𐤑.𐤌𐤑𐤓𐤉𐤌|

𐤉𐤈 𐤅𐤉𐤒𐤇.𐤌𐤔𐤄.𐤀𐤕.𐤏𐤑𐤌𐤅𐤕.𐤉𐤅𐤎𐤐.𐤏𐤌𐤅.𐤊𐤉.𐤄𐤔
𐤁𐤏.𐤄𐤔𐤁𐤉𐤏.𐤀𐤕.𐤁𐤍𐤉.𐤉𐤔𐤓𐤀𐤋.𐤋𐤀𐤌𐤓.𐤐𐤒𐤃.𐤉𐤐𐤒𐤃
.𐤀𐤋𐤄𐤉𐤌.𐤀𐤕𐤊𐤌.𐤅𐤄𐤏𐤋𐤉𐤕𐤌.𐤀𐤕.𐤏𐤑𐤌𐤕𐤉.𐤌𐤆𐤄.𐤀
𐤕𐤊𐤌|

20 𐤅𐤉𐤎𐤏𐤅.𐤌𐤎𐤊𐤕.𐤅𐤉𐤇𐤍𐤅.𐤁𐤀𐤕𐤌.𐤁𐤒𐤑𐤄.𐤄𐤌𐤃𐤁
𐤓|

21 𐤅𐤉𐤄𐤅𐤄.𐤄𐤋𐤊.𐤋𐤐𐤍𐤉𐤄𐤌.𐤉𐤅𐤌𐤌.𐤁𐤏𐤌𐤅𐤃.𐤏𐤍𐤍.𐤋𐤍
𐤇𐤕𐤌.𐤄𐤃𐤓𐤊.𐤅𐤋𐤉𐤋𐤄.𐤁𐤏𐤌𐤅𐤃.𐤀𐤔.𐤋𐤄𐤀𐤉𐤓.𐤋𐤄𐤌.𐤋𐤋
𐤊𐤕.𐤉𐤅𐤌𐤌.𐤅𐤋𐤉𐤋𐤄|

22 𐤋𐤀.𐤉𐤌𐤉𐤔.𐤏𐤌𐤅𐤃.𐤄𐤏𐤍𐤍.𐤉𐤅𐤌𐤌.𐤅𐤏𐤌𐤅𐤃.𐤄𐤀𐤔.
𐤋𐤉𐤋𐤄.𐤋𐤐𐤍𐤉.𐤄𐤏𐤌||

𐤅𐤉𐤏𐤋𐤅.𐤌𐤌𐤑𐤓𐤉𐤌.𐤇𐤋𐤒 14

1 𐤅𐤉𐤃𐤁𐤓.𐤉𐤄𐤅𐤄.𐤀𐤋.𐤌𐤔𐤄.𐤋𐤀𐤌𐤓|

2 𐤃𐤁𐤓.𐤀𐤋.𐤁𐤍𐤉.𐤉𐤔𐤓𐤀𐤋.𐤅𐤉𐤔𐤁𐤅.𐤅𐤉𐤇𐤍𐤅.𐤋𐤐𐤍𐤉.𐤐𐤉.
𐤄𐤇𐤉𐤓𐤕.𐤁𐤉𐤍.𐤌𐤂𐤃𐤋.𐤅𐤁𐤉𐤍.𐤄𐤉𐤌.𐤋𐤐𐤍𐤉.𐤁𐤏𐤋.𐤑𐤐𐤍.𐤍
𐤊𐤇𐤅.𐤕𐤇𐤍𐤅.𐤏𐤋.𐤄𐤉𐤌|

3 𐤅𐤀𐤌𐤓.𐤐𐤓𐤏𐤄.𐤋𐤁𐤍𐤉.𐤉𐤔𐤓𐤀𐤋.𐤍𐤁𐤊𐤉𐤌.𐤄𐤌.𐤁𐤀𐤓𐤑
.𐤎𐤂𐤓.𐤏𐤋𐤉𐤄𐤌.𐤄𐤌𐤃𐤁𐤓|

4 𐤅𐤇𐤆𐤒𐤕𐤉.𐤀𐤕.𐤋𐤁.𐤐𐤓𐤏𐤄.𐤅𐤓𐤃𐤐.𐤀𐤇𐤓𐤉𐤄𐤌.𐤅𐤀
𐤊𐤁𐤃𐤄.𐤁𐤐𐤓𐤏𐤄.𐤅𐤁𐤊𐤋.𐤇𐤉𐤋𐤅.𐤅𐤉𐤃𐤏𐤅.𐤌𐤑𐤓𐤉𐤌.𐤊𐤉.
𐤀𐤍𐤉.𐤉𐤄𐤅𐤄.𐤅𐤉𐤏𐤔𐤅.𐤊𐤍|

5 𐤅𐤉𐤂𐤃.𐤋𐤌𐤋𐤊.𐤌𐤑𐤓𐤉𐤌.𐤊𐤉.𐤁𐤓𐤇.𐤄𐤏𐤌.𐤅𐤉𐤄𐤐𐤊.𐤋
𐤁𐤁.𐤐𐤓𐤏𐤄.𐤅𐤏𐤁𐤃𐤉𐤅.𐤀𐤋.𐤄𐤏𐤌.𐤅𐤉𐤀𐤌𐤓𐤅.𐤌𐤄.𐤆𐤀𐤕.𐤏
𐤔𐤉𐤍𐤅.𐤊𐤉.𐤔𐤋𐤇𐤍𐤅.𐤀𐤕.𐤉𐤔𐤓𐤀𐤋.𐤌𐤏𐤁𐤃𐤍𐤅|

6 𐤅𐤉𐤀𐤎𐤓.𐤀𐤕.𐤓𐤊𐤁𐤅.𐤅𐤀𐤕.𐤏𐤌𐤅.𐤋𐤒𐤇.𐤏𐤌𐤅|

7 𐤅𐤉𐤒𐤇.𐤔𐤔.𐤌𐤀𐤅𐤕.𐤓𐤊𐤁.𐤁𐤇𐤅𐤓.𐤅𐤊𐤋.𐤓𐤊𐤁.𐤌𐤑𐤓𐤉
𐤅𐤔𐤋𐤔𐤌.𐤏𐤋.𐤊𐤋𐤅|

8 𐤅𐤉𐤇𐤆𐤒.𐤉𐤄𐤅𐤄.𐤀𐤕.𐤋𐤁.𐤐𐤓𐤏𐤄.𐤌𐤋𐤊.𐤌𐤑𐤓𐤉𐤌.𐤅𐤉𐤓𐤃𐤐.𐤀𐤇𐤓𐤉.𐤁𐤍𐤉
𐤉𐤔𐤓𐤀𐤋.𐤅𐤁𐤍𐤉.𐤉𐤔𐤓𐤀𐤋.𐤉𐤑𐤀𐤉𐤌.
𐤁𐤉𐤃.𐤓𐤌𐤄|

9 𐤅𐤉𐤓𐤃𐤐𐤅.𐤌𐤑𐤓𐤉𐤌.𐤀𐤇𐤓𐤉𐤄𐤌.𐤅𐤉𐤔𐤉𐤂𐤅.𐤀𐤅𐤕𐤌.
𐤇𐤍𐤉𐤌.𐤏𐤋.𐤄𐤉𐤌.𐤊𐤋.𐤎𐤅𐤎.𐤓𐤊𐤁.𐤐𐤓𐤏𐤄.𐤅𐤐𐤓𐤔𐤉𐤅.𐤅𐤇𐤉
𐤋𐤅.𐤏𐤋.𐤐𐤉.𐤄𐤇𐤉𐤓𐤕.𐤋𐤐𐤍𐤉.𐤁𐤏𐤋.𐤑𐤐𐤍|

10 ופרעה.הקריב.וישאו.בני.ישראל.את.עי
ניהם.והנה.מצרים.נסע.אחריהם.וייראו.מא
ד.ויצעקו.בני.ישראל.אל.יהוה|
11 ויאמרו.אל.משה.המבלי.אין.קברים.במצ
רים.לקחתנו.למות.במדבר.מה.זאת.עשית.לנ
ו.להוציאנו.ממצרים|
12 הלא.זה.הדבר.אשר.דברנו.אליך.במצרי
ם.לאמר.חדל.ממנו.ונעבדה.את.מצרים.כי.ט
וב.לנו.עבד.את.מצרים.ממתנו.במדבר|
13 ויאמר.משה.אל.העם.אל.תיראו.התיצבו.
וראו.את.ישועת.יהוה.אשר.יעשה.לכם.היום.
כי.אשר.ראיתם.את.מצרים.היום.לא.תספו.ל
ראתם.עוד.עד.עולם|
14 יהוה.ילחם.לכם.ואתם.תחרישון|
15 ויאמר.יהוה.אל.משה.מה.תצעק.אלי.דב
ר.אל.בני.ישראל.ויסעו|
16 ואתה.הרם.את.מטך.ונטה.את.ידך.על.הי
ם.ובקעהו.ויבאו.בני.ישראל.בתוך.הים.ביבש
ה|
17 ואני.הנני.מחזק.את.לב.מצרים.ויבאו.
אחריהם.ואכבדה.בפרעה.ובכל.חילו.ברכבו.ובפ
רשיו|
18 וידעו.מצרים.כי.אני.יהוה.בהכבדי.ב
פרעה.ברכבו.ובפרשיו|
19 ויסע.מלאך.האלהים.ההלך.לפני.מחנה.יש
ראל.וילך.מאחריהם.ויסע.עמוד.הענן.מפ
ניהם.ויעמד.מאחריהם|
20 ויבא.בין.מחנה.מצרים.ובין.מחנה.ישר
אל.ויהי.הענן.והחשך.ויאר.את.הלילה.ולא.ק
רב.זה.אל.זה.כל.הלילה|

כא ויט.משה.את.ידו.על.הים.ויולך.יהוה.א
ת.הים.ברוח.קדים.עזה.כל.הלילה.וישם.א
ת.הים.לחרבה.ויבקעו.המים|
כב ויבאו.בני.ישראל.בתוך.הים.ביבשה.והמ
ים.להם.חמה.מימינם.ומשמאלם|
כג וירדפו.מצרים.ויבאו.אחריהם.כל.סוס.
פרעה.רכבו.ופרשיו.אל.תוך.הים|
כד ויהי.באשמרת.הבקר.וישקף.יהוה.אל.מ
חנה.מצרים.בעמוד.אש.וענן.ויהם.את.מחנה
.מצרים|
כה ויסר.את.אפן.מרכבתיו.וינהגהו.בכבדת
.ויאמר.מצרים.אנוסה.מפני.ישראל.כי.יהוה.
נלחם.להם.במצרים|
כו ויאמר.יהוה.אל.משה.נטה.את.ידך.על.ה
ים.וישבו.המים.על.מצרים.על.רכבו.ועל.פרש
יו|
כז ויט.משה.את.ידו.על.הים.וישב.הים.לפ
נות.בקר.לאיתנו.ומצרים.נסים.לקראתו.וינע
ר.יהוה.את.מצרים.בתוך.הים|
כח וישבו.המים.ויכסו.את.הרכב.ואת.הפרשי
ם.לכל.חיל.פרעה.הבאים.אחריהם.בים.לא.נ
שאר.בהם.עד.אחד|
כט ובני.ישראל.הלכו.ביבשה.בתוך.הים.וה
מים.להם.חמה.מימינם.ומשמאלם|
ל ויושע.יהוה.ביום.ההוא.את.ישראל.מי
ד.מצרים.וירא.ישראל.את.מצרים.מת.על.שפ
ת.הים|
לא וירא.ישראל.את.היד.הגדלה.אשר.עש
ה.יהוה.במצרים.וייראו.העם.את.יהוה.ויאמ
ינו.ביהוה.ובמשה.עבדו||

𐤅𐤉𐤏𐤋𐤅.𐤌𐤌𐤑𐤓𐤉𐤌.𐤇𐤋𐤒 ..15..

..1.. 𐤀𐤆.𐤉𐤔𐤉𐤓.𐤌𐤔𐤄.𐤅𐤁𐤍𐤉.𐤉𐤔𐤓𐤀𐤋.𐤀𐤕.𐤄𐤔𐤉𐤓𐤄.𐤄
𐤆𐤀𐤕.𐤋𐤉𐤄𐤅𐤄.𐤅𐤉𐤀𐤌𐤓𐤅.𐤋𐤀𐤌𐤓.𐤀𐤔𐤉𐤓𐤄.𐤋𐤉𐤄𐤅𐤄.𐤊𐤉.
𐤂𐤀𐤄.𐤂𐤀𐤄.𐤎𐤅𐤎.𐤅𐤓𐤊𐤁𐤅.𐤓𐤌𐤄.𐤁𐤉𐤌|

..2.. 𐤏𐤆𐤉.𐤅𐤆𐤌𐤓𐤕.𐤉𐤄.𐤅𐤉𐤄𐤉.𐤋𐤉.𐤋𐤉𐤔𐤅𐤏𐤄.𐤆𐤄.𐤀𐤋
𐤉.𐤅𐤀𐤍𐤅𐤄𐤅.𐤀𐤋𐤄𐤉.𐤀𐤁𐤉.𐤅𐤀𐤓𐤌𐤌𐤍𐤄𐤅|

..3.. 𐤉𐤄𐤅𐤄.𐤀𐤉𐤔.𐤌𐤋𐤇𐤌𐤄.𐤉𐤄𐤅𐤄.𐤔𐤌𐤅|

..4.. 𐤌𐤓𐤊𐤁𐤕.𐤐𐤓𐤏𐤄.𐤅𐤇𐤉𐤋𐤅.𐤉𐤓𐤄.𐤁𐤉𐤌.𐤅𐤌𐤁𐤇𐤓.𐤔𐤋𐤔
𐤉𐤅.𐤈𐤁𐤏𐤅.𐤁𐤉𐤌.𐤎𐤅𐤐|

..5.. 𐤕𐤄𐤌𐤕.𐤉𐤊𐤎𐤉𐤌𐤅.𐤉𐤓𐤃𐤅.𐤁𐤌𐤑𐤅𐤋𐤕.𐤊𐤌𐤅.𐤀𐤁𐤍|

..6.. 𐤉𐤌𐤉𐤍𐤊.𐤉𐤄𐤅𐤄.𐤍𐤀𐤃𐤓𐤉.𐤁𐤊𐤇.𐤉𐤌𐤉𐤍𐤊.𐤉𐤄𐤅𐤄.𐤕𐤓
𐤏𐤑.𐤀𐤅𐤉𐤁|

..7.. 𐤅𐤁𐤓𐤁.𐤂𐤀𐤅𐤍𐤊.𐤕𐤄𐤓𐤎.𐤒𐤌𐤉𐤊.𐤕𐤔𐤋𐤇.𐤇𐤓𐤍𐤊.𐤉𐤀
𐤊𐤋𐤌𐤅.𐤊𐤒𐤔|

..8.. 𐤅𐤁𐤓𐤅𐤇.𐤀𐤐𐤉𐤊.𐤍𐤏𐤓𐤌𐤅.𐤌𐤉𐤌.𐤍𐤑𐤁𐤅.𐤊𐤌𐤅.𐤍𐤃.𐤍𐤆𐤋
𐤉𐤌.𐤒𐤐𐤀𐤅.𐤕𐤄𐤌𐤕.𐤁𐤋𐤁.𐤉𐤌|

..9.. 𐤀𐤌𐤓.𐤀𐤅𐤉𐤁.𐤀𐤓𐤃𐤐.𐤀𐤔𐤉𐤂.𐤀𐤇𐤋𐤒.𐤔𐤋𐤋.𐤕𐤌𐤋
𐤀𐤌𐤅.𐤍𐤐𐤔𐤉.𐤀𐤓𐤉𐤒.𐤇𐤓𐤁𐤉.𐤕𐤅𐤓𐤉𐤔𐤌𐤅.𐤉𐤃𐤉|

..10.. 𐤍𐤔𐤐𐤕.𐤁𐤓𐤅𐤇𐤊.𐤊𐤎𐤌𐤅.𐤉𐤌.𐤑𐤋𐤋𐤅.𐤊𐤏𐤅𐤐𐤓𐤕.𐤁𐤌𐤉
𐤌.𐤀𐤃𐤉𐤓𐤉𐤌|

..11.. 𐤌𐤉.𐤊𐤌𐤊𐤄.𐤁𐤀𐤋𐤌.𐤉𐤄𐤅𐤄.𐤌𐤉.𐤊𐤌𐤊𐤄.𐤍𐤀𐤃𐤓.𐤁
𐤒𐤃𐤔.𐤍𐤅𐤓𐤀.𐤕𐤄𐤋𐤕.𐤏𐤔𐤄.𐤐𐤋𐤀|

..12.. 𐤍𐤈𐤉𐤕.𐤉𐤌𐤉𐤍𐤊.𐤕𐤁𐤋𐤏𐤌𐤅.𐤀𐤓𐤑|

..13.. 𐤍𐤇𐤉𐤕.𐤁𐤇𐤎𐤃𐤊.𐤏𐤌.𐤆𐤅.𐤂𐤀𐤋𐤕.𐤍𐤄𐤋𐤕.𐤁𐤏𐤆
𐤊.𐤀𐤋.𐤍𐤅𐤄.𐤒𐤃𐤔𐤊|

..14.. 𐤔𐤌𐤏𐤅.𐤏𐤌𐤉𐤌.𐤉𐤓𐤂𐤆𐤅𐤍.𐤇𐤉𐤋.𐤀𐤇𐤆.𐤉𐤔𐤁𐤉.𐤐
𐤋𐤔𐤕|

..15.. 𐤀𐤆.𐤍𐤁𐤄𐤋𐤅.𐤀𐤋𐤅𐤐𐤉.𐤀𐤃𐤅𐤌.𐤀𐤉𐤋𐤉.𐤌𐤅𐤀𐤁.𐤉𐤀𐤇
𐤆𐤌𐤅.𐤓𐤏𐤃.𐤍𐤌𐤂𐤅.𐤊𐤋.𐤉𐤔𐤁𐤉.𐤊𐤍𐤏𐤍|

𐤉𐤅 𐤕𐤐𐤋.𐤏𐤋𐤉𐤄𐤌.𐤀𐤉𐤌𐤕𐤄.𐤅𐤐𐤇𐤃.𐤁𐤂𐤃𐤋.𐤆𐤓𐤅𐤏𐤊
.𐤉𐤃𐤌𐤅.𐤊𐤀𐤁𐤍.𐤏𐤃.𐤉𐤏𐤁𐤓.𐤏𐤌𐤊.𐤉𐤄𐤅𐤄.𐤏𐤃.𐤉𐤏𐤁𐤓.
𐤏𐤌.𐤆𐤅.𐤒𐤍𐤉𐤕|
𐤉𐤆 𐤕𐤁𐤀𐤌𐤅.𐤅𐤕𐤈𐤏𐤌𐤅.𐤁𐤄𐤓.𐤍𐤇𐤋𐤕𐤊.𐤌𐤊𐤅𐤍.𐤋𐤔𐤁𐤕
𐤊.𐤐𐤏𐤋𐤕.𐤉𐤄𐤅𐤄.𐤌𐤒𐤃𐤔.𐤀𐤃𐤍𐤉.𐤊𐤅𐤍𐤍𐤅.𐤉𐤃𐤉𐤊|
𐤉𐤇 𐤉𐤄𐤅𐤄.𐤉𐤌𐤋𐤊.𐤋𐤏𐤋𐤌.𐤅𐤏𐤃|
𐤉𐤈 𐤊𐤉.𐤁𐤀.𐤎𐤅𐤎.𐤐𐤓𐤏𐤄.𐤁𐤓𐤊𐤁𐤅.𐤅𐤁𐤐𐤓𐤔𐤉𐤅.𐤁𐤉𐤌.𐤅𐤉
𐤔𐤁.𐤉𐤄𐤅𐤄.𐤏𐤋𐤉𐤄𐤌.𐤀𐤕.𐤌𐤉.𐤄𐤉𐤌.𐤅𐤁𐤍𐤉.𐤉𐤔𐤓𐤀𐤋.𐤄𐤋𐤊
𐤅.𐤁𐤉𐤁𐤔𐤄.𐤁𐤕𐤅𐤊.𐤄𐤉𐤌|
𐤊 𐤅𐤕𐤒𐤇.𐤌𐤓𐤉𐤌.𐤄𐤍𐤁𐤉𐤀𐤄.𐤀𐤇𐤅𐤕.𐤀𐤄𐤓𐤍.𐤀𐤕.𐤄
𐤕𐤐.𐤁𐤉𐤃𐤄.𐤅𐤕𐤑𐤀𐤍.𐤊𐤋.𐤄𐤍𐤔𐤉𐤌.𐤀𐤇𐤓𐤉𐤄.𐤁𐤕𐤐𐤉𐤌.𐤅
𐤁𐤌𐤇𐤋𐤕|
𐤊𐤀 𐤅𐤕𐤏𐤍.𐤋𐤄𐤌.𐤌𐤓𐤉𐤌.𐤔𐤉𐤓𐤅.𐤋𐤉𐤄𐤅𐤄.𐤊𐤉.𐤂𐤀𐤄.𐤂
𐤀𐤄.𐤎𐤅𐤎.𐤅𐤓𐤊𐤁𐤅.𐤓𐤌𐤄.𐤁𐤉𐤌|
𐤊𐤁 𐤅𐤉𐤎𐤏.𐤌𐤔𐤄.𐤀𐤕.𐤉𐤔𐤓𐤀𐤋.𐤌𐤉𐤌.𐤎𐤅𐤐.𐤅𐤉𐤑𐤀𐤅.𐤀
𐤋.𐤌𐤃𐤁𐤓.𐤔𐤅𐤓.𐤅𐤉𐤋𐤊𐤅.𐤔𐤋𐤔𐤕.𐤉𐤌𐤉𐤌.𐤁𐤌𐤃𐤁𐤓.𐤅𐤋𐤀.𐤌
𐤑𐤀𐤅.𐤌𐤉𐤌|
𐤊𐤂 𐤅𐤉𐤁𐤀𐤅.𐤌𐤓𐤕𐤄.𐤅𐤋𐤀.𐤉𐤊𐤋𐤅.𐤋𐤔𐤕𐤕.𐤌𐤉𐤌.𐤌𐤌𐤓𐤄.
𐤊𐤉.𐤌𐤓𐤉𐤌.𐤄𐤌.𐤏𐤋.𐤊𐤍.𐤒𐤓𐤀.𐤔𐤌𐤄.𐤌𐤓𐤄|
𐤊𐤃 𐤅𐤉𐤋𐤍𐤅.𐤄𐤏𐤌.𐤏𐤋.𐤌𐤔𐤄.𐤋𐤀𐤌𐤓.𐤌𐤄.𐤍𐤔𐤕𐤄|
𐤊𐤄 𐤅𐤉𐤑𐤏𐤒.𐤀𐤋.𐤉𐤄𐤅𐤄.𐤅𐤉𐤅𐤓𐤄𐤅.𐤏𐤑.𐤅𐤉𐤔𐤋𐤊
.𐤀𐤋.𐤄𐤌𐤉𐤌.𐤅𐤉𐤌𐤕𐤒𐤅.𐤄𐤌𐤉𐤌.𐤔𐤌.𐤔𐤌.𐤋𐤅.𐤇𐤒.𐤅𐤌𐤔𐤐
𐤈.𐤅𐤔𐤌.𐤍𐤎𐤄𐤅|
𐤊𐤅 𐤅𐤉𐤀𐤌𐤓.𐤀𐤌.𐤔𐤌𐤅𐤏.𐤕𐤔𐤌𐤏.𐤋𐤒𐤅𐤋.𐤉𐤄𐤅𐤄.𐤀𐤋𐤄𐤉
𐤊.𐤅𐤄𐤉𐤔𐤓.𐤁𐤏𐤉𐤍𐤉𐤅.𐤕𐤏𐤔𐤄.𐤅𐤄𐤀𐤆𐤍𐤕.𐤋𐤌𐤑𐤅𐤕𐤉𐤅.𐤅
𐤔𐤌𐤓𐤕.𐤊𐤋.𐤇𐤒𐤉𐤅.𐤊𐤋.𐤄𐤌𐤇𐤋𐤄.𐤀𐤔𐤓.𐤔𐤌𐤕𐤉.𐤁𐤌𐤑𐤓
𐤉𐤌.𐤋𐤀.𐤀𐤔𐤉𐤌.𐤏𐤋𐤉𐤊.𐤊𐤉.𐤀𐤍𐤉.𐤉𐤄𐤅𐤄.𐤓𐤐𐤀𐤊|
𐤊𐤆 𐤅𐤉𐤁𐤀𐤅.𐤀𐤉𐤋𐤌𐤄.𐤅𐤔𐤌.𐤔𐤕𐤉𐤌.𐤏𐤔𐤓𐤄.𐤏𐤉𐤍𐤕.𐤌
𐤉𐤌.𐤅𐤔𐤁𐤏𐤉𐤌.𐤕𐤌𐤓𐤉𐤌.𐤅𐤉𐤇𐤍𐤅.𐤔𐤌.𐤏𐤋.𐤄𐤌𐤉𐤌||

𐤉𐤅 𐤅𐤉𐤏𐤋𐤅.𐤌𐤌𐤑𐤓𐤉𐤌.𐤇𐤋𐤒

1 𐤅𐤉𐤎𐤏𐤅.𐤌𐤀𐤉𐤋𐤌.𐤅𐤉𐤁𐤀𐤅.𐤊𐤋.𐤏𐤃𐤕.𐤁𐤍𐤉.𐤉𐤔𐤓𐤀𐤋.
𐤀𐤋.𐤌𐤃𐤁𐤓.𐤎𐤉𐤍.𐤀𐤔𐤓.𐤁𐤉𐤍.𐤀𐤉𐤋𐤌.𐤅𐤁𐤉𐤍.𐤎𐤉𐤍𐤉.𐤁𐤇
𐤌𐤔𐤄.𐤏𐤔𐤓.𐤉𐤅𐤌.𐤋𐤇𐤃𐤔.𐤄𐤔𐤍𐤉.𐤋𐤑𐤀𐤕𐤌.𐤌𐤀𐤓𐤑.𐤌
𐤑𐤓𐤉𐤌|
2 𐤅𐤉𐤋𐤉𐤍𐤅.||𐤅𐤉𐤋𐤅𐤍𐤅.𐤒𐤓𐤉||.𐤊𐤋.𐤏𐤃𐤕.𐤁𐤍𐤉.𐤉𐤔𐤓𐤀𐤋.𐤏
𐤋.𐤌𐤔𐤄.𐤅𐤏𐤋.𐤀𐤄𐤓𐤍.𐤁𐤌𐤃𐤁𐤓|
3 𐤅𐤉𐤀𐤌𐤓𐤅.𐤀𐤋𐤄𐤌.𐤁𐤍𐤉.𐤉𐤔𐤓𐤀𐤋.𐤌𐤉.𐤉𐤕𐤍.𐤌𐤅𐤕𐤍𐤅.𐤁
𐤉𐤃.𐤉𐤄𐤅𐤄.𐤁𐤀𐤓𐤑.𐤌𐤑𐤓𐤉𐤌.𐤁𐤔𐤁𐤕𐤍𐤅.𐤏𐤋.𐤎𐤉𐤓.𐤄𐤁𐤔
𐤓.𐤁𐤀𐤊𐤋𐤍𐤅.𐤋𐤇𐤌.𐤋𐤔𐤁𐤏.𐤊𐤉.𐤄𐤅𐤑𐤀𐤕𐤌.𐤀𐤕𐤍𐤅.𐤀𐤋.𐤄
𐤌𐤃𐤁𐤓.𐤄𐤆𐤄.𐤋𐤄𐤌𐤉𐤕.𐤀𐤕.𐤊𐤋.𐤄𐤒𐤄𐤋.𐤄𐤆𐤄.𐤁𐤓𐤏𐤁|
4 𐤅𐤉𐤀𐤌𐤓.𐤉𐤄𐤅𐤄.𐤀𐤋.𐤌𐤔𐤄.𐤄𐤍𐤍𐤉.𐤌𐤌𐤈𐤉𐤓.𐤋𐤊𐤌.𐤋
𐤇𐤌.𐤌𐤍.𐤄𐤔𐤌𐤉𐤌.𐤅𐤉𐤑𐤀.𐤄𐤏𐤌.𐤅𐤋𐤒𐤈𐤅.𐤃𐤁𐤓.𐤉𐤅𐤌.𐤁𐤉
𐤅𐤌𐤅.𐤋𐤌𐤏𐤍.𐤀𐤍𐤎𐤍𐤅.𐤄𐤉𐤋𐤊.𐤁𐤕𐤅𐤓𐤕𐤉.𐤀𐤌.𐤋𐤀|
5 𐤅𐤄𐤉𐤄.𐤁𐤉𐤅𐤌.𐤄𐤔𐤔𐤉.𐤅𐤄𐤊𐤉𐤍𐤅.𐤀𐤕.𐤀𐤔𐤓.𐤉𐤁𐤉𐤀𐤅.𐤅
𐤄𐤉𐤄.𐤌𐤔𐤍𐤄.𐤏𐤋.𐤀𐤔𐤓.𐤉𐤋𐤒𐤈𐤅.𐤉𐤅𐤌.𐤉𐤅𐤌|
6 𐤅𐤉𐤀𐤌𐤓.𐤌𐤔𐤄.𐤅𐤀𐤄𐤓𐤍.𐤀𐤋.𐤊𐤋.𐤁𐤍𐤉.𐤉𐤔𐤓𐤀𐤋.𐤏𐤓𐤁.
𐤅𐤉𐤃𐤏𐤕𐤌.𐤊𐤉.𐤉𐤄𐤅𐤄.𐤄𐤅𐤑𐤉𐤀.𐤀𐤕𐤊𐤌.𐤌𐤀𐤓𐤑.𐤌𐤑𐤓
𐤉𐤌|
7 𐤅𐤁𐤒𐤓.𐤅𐤓𐤀𐤉𐤕𐤌.𐤀𐤕.𐤊𐤁𐤅𐤃.𐤉𐤄𐤅𐤄.𐤁𐤔𐤌𐤏𐤅.𐤀𐤕.
𐤕𐤋𐤍𐤕𐤉𐤊𐤌.𐤏𐤋.𐤉𐤄𐤅𐤄.𐤅𐤍𐤇𐤍𐤅.𐤌𐤄.𐤊𐤉.𐤕𐤋𐤅𐤍𐤅.||𐤕𐤋𐤉𐤍𐤅
.𐤒𐤓𐤉||.𐤏𐤋𐤉𐤍𐤅|
8 𐤅𐤉𐤀𐤌𐤓.𐤌𐤔𐤄.𐤁𐤕𐤕.𐤉𐤄𐤅𐤄.𐤋𐤊𐤌.𐤁𐤏𐤓𐤁.𐤁𐤔𐤓.𐤋𐤀
𐤊𐤋.𐤅𐤋𐤇𐤌.𐤁𐤁𐤒𐤓.𐤋𐤔𐤁𐤏.𐤁𐤔𐤌𐤏.𐤉𐤄𐤅𐤄.𐤀𐤕.𐤕𐤋𐤍𐤕𐤉
𐤊𐤌.𐤀𐤔𐤓.𐤀𐤕𐤌.𐤌𐤋𐤉𐤍𐤌.𐤏𐤋𐤉𐤅.𐤅𐤍𐤇𐤍𐤅.𐤌𐤄.𐤋𐤀.𐤏𐤋𐤉𐤍𐤅
.𐤕𐤋𐤍𐤕𐤉𐤊𐤌.𐤊𐤉.𐤏𐤋.𐤉𐤄𐤅𐤄|
9 𐤅𐤉𐤀𐤌𐤓.𐤌𐤔𐤄.𐤀𐤋.𐤀𐤄𐤓𐤍.𐤀𐤌𐤓.𐤀𐤋.𐤊𐤋.𐤏𐤃𐤕.𐤁𐤍
𐤉.𐤉𐤔𐤓𐤀𐤋.𐤒𐤓𐤁𐤅.𐤋𐤐𐤍𐤉.𐤉𐤄𐤅𐤄.𐤊𐤉.𐤔𐤌𐤏.𐤀𐤕.𐤕𐤋𐤍𐤕𐤉
𐤊𐤌|

10 𐤅𐤉𐤄𐤉.𐤊𐤃𐤁𐤓.𐤀𐤄𐤓𐤍.𐤀𐤋.𐤊𐤋.𐤏𐤃𐤕.𐤁𐤍𐤉.𐤉𐤔𐤓𐤀
𐤋.𐤅𐤉𐤐𐤍𐤅.𐤀𐤋.𐤄𐤌𐤃𐤁𐤓.𐤅𐤄𐤍𐤄.𐤊𐤁𐤅𐤃.𐤉𐤄𐤅𐤄.𐤍𐤓𐤀𐤄.𐤁𐤏
𐤍𐤍|

11 𐤅𐤉𐤃𐤁𐤓.𐤉𐤄𐤅𐤄.𐤀𐤋.𐤌𐤔𐤄.𐤋𐤀𐤌𐤓|

12 𐤔𐤌𐤏𐤕𐤉.𐤀𐤕.𐤕𐤋𐤅𐤍𐤕.𐤁𐤍𐤉.𐤉𐤔𐤓𐤀𐤋.𐤃𐤁𐤓.𐤀𐤋𐤄
𐤌.𐤋𐤀𐤌𐤓.𐤁𐤉𐤍.𐤄𐤏𐤓𐤁𐤉𐤌.𐤕𐤀𐤊𐤋𐤅.𐤁𐤔𐤓.𐤅𐤁𐤁𐤒𐤓.𐤕𐤔𐤁
𐤏𐤅.𐤋𐤇𐤌.𐤅𐤉𐤃𐤏𐤕𐤌.𐤊𐤉.𐤀𐤍𐤉.𐤉𐤄𐤅𐤄.𐤀𐤋𐤄𐤉𐤊𐤌|

13 𐤅𐤉𐤄𐤉.𐤁𐤏𐤓𐤁.𐤅𐤕𐤏𐤋.𐤄𐤔𐤋𐤅.𐤅𐤕𐤊𐤎.𐤀𐤕.𐤄𐤌𐤇𐤍𐤄
.𐤅𐤁𐤁𐤒𐤓.𐤄𐤉𐤕𐤄.𐤔𐤊𐤁𐤕.𐤄𐤈𐤋.𐤎𐤁𐤉𐤁.𐤋𐤌𐤇𐤍𐤄|

14 𐤅𐤕𐤏𐤋.𐤔𐤊𐤁𐤕.𐤄𐤈𐤋.𐤅𐤄𐤍𐤄.𐤏𐤋.𐤐𐤍𐤉.𐤄𐤌𐤃𐤁𐤓.
𐤃𐤒.𐤌𐤇𐤎𐤐𐤎.𐤃𐤒.𐤊𐤊𐤐𐤓.𐤏𐤋.𐤄𐤀𐤓𐤑|

15 𐤅𐤉𐤓𐤀𐤅.𐤁𐤍𐤉.𐤉𐤔𐤓𐤀𐤋.𐤅𐤉𐤀𐤌𐤓𐤅.𐤀𐤉𐤔.𐤀𐤋.𐤀𐤇𐤉𐤅.
𐤌𐤍.𐤄𐤅𐤀.𐤊𐤉.𐤋𐤀.𐤉𐤃𐤏𐤅.𐤌𐤄.𐤄𐤅𐤀.𐤅𐤉𐤀𐤌𐤓.𐤌𐤔𐤄.𐤀𐤋𐤄
𐤌.𐤄𐤅𐤀.𐤄𐤋𐤇𐤌.𐤀𐤔𐤓.𐤍𐤕𐤍.𐤉𐤄𐤅𐤄.𐤋𐤊𐤌.𐤋𐤀𐤊𐤋𐤄|

16 𐤆𐤄.𐤄𐤃𐤁𐤓.𐤀𐤔𐤓.𐤑𐤅𐤄.𐤉𐤄𐤅𐤄.𐤋𐤒𐤈𐤅.𐤌𐤌𐤍𐤅.𐤀𐤉
𐤔.𐤋𐤐𐤉.𐤀𐤊𐤋𐤅.𐤏𐤌𐤓.𐤋𐤂𐤋𐤂𐤋𐤕.𐤌𐤎𐤐𐤓.𐤍𐤐𐤔𐤕𐤉𐤊𐤌.𐤀
𐤉𐤔.𐤋𐤀𐤔𐤓.𐤁𐤀𐤄𐤋𐤅.𐤕𐤒𐤇𐤅|

17 𐤅𐤉𐤏𐤔𐤅.𐤊𐤍.𐤁𐤍𐤉.𐤉𐤔𐤓𐤀𐤋.𐤅𐤉𐤋𐤒𐤈𐤅.𐤄𐤌𐤓𐤁𐤄.𐤅𐤄
𐤌𐤌𐤏𐤉𐤈|

18 𐤅𐤉𐤌𐤃𐤅.𐤁𐤏𐤌𐤓.𐤅𐤋𐤀.𐤄𐤏𐤃𐤉𐤐.𐤄𐤌𐤓𐤁𐤄.𐤅𐤄𐤌𐤌𐤏
𐤉𐤈.𐤋𐤀.𐤄𐤇𐤎𐤉𐤓.𐤀𐤉𐤔.𐤋𐤐𐤉.𐤀𐤊𐤋𐤅.𐤋𐤒𐤈𐤅|

19 𐤅𐤉𐤀𐤌𐤓.𐤌𐤔𐤄.𐤀𐤋𐤄𐤌.𐤀𐤉𐤔.𐤀𐤋.𐤉𐤅𐤕𐤓.𐤌𐤌𐤍𐤅.𐤏
𐤃.𐤁𐤒𐤓|

20 𐤅𐤋𐤀.𐤔𐤌𐤏𐤅.𐤀𐤋.𐤌𐤔𐤄.𐤅𐤉𐤅𐤕𐤓𐤅.𐤀𐤍𐤔𐤉𐤌.𐤌𐤌𐤍𐤅.
𐤏𐤃.𐤁𐤒𐤓.𐤅𐤉𐤓𐤌.𐤕𐤅𐤋𐤏𐤉𐤌.𐤅𐤉𐤁𐤀𐤔.𐤅𐤉𐤒𐤑𐤐.𐤏𐤋𐤄𐤌.
𐤌𐤔𐤄|

21 𐤅𐤉𐤋𐤒𐤈𐤅.𐤀𐤕𐤅.𐤁𐤁𐤒𐤓.𐤁𐤁𐤒𐤓.𐤀𐤉𐤔.𐤊𐤐𐤉.𐤀𐤊𐤋𐤅.𐤅
𐤇𐤌.𐤄𐤔𐤌𐤔.𐤅𐤍𐤌𐤎|

22 𐤅𐤉𐤄𐤉.𐤁𐤉𐤅𐤌.𐤄𐤔𐤔𐤉.𐤋𐤒𐤈𐤅.𐤋𐤇𐤌.𐤌𐤔𐤍𐤄.𐤔𐤍𐤉.
𐤄𐤏𐤌𐤓.𐤋𐤀𐤇𐤃.𐤅𐤉𐤁𐤀𐤅.𐤊𐤋.𐤍𐤔𐤉𐤀𐤉.𐤄𐤏𐤃𐤄.𐤅𐤉𐤂𐤉
𐤃𐤅.𐤋𐤌𐤔𐤄|

..𐤊𐤂.. 𐤅𐤉𐤀𐤌𐤓.𐤀𐤋𐤄𐤌.𐤄𐤅𐤀.𐤀𐤔𐤓.𐤃𐤁𐤓.𐤉𐤄𐤅𐤄.𐤔𐤁𐤕𐤅𐤍
.𐤔𐤁𐤕.𐤒𐤃𐤔.𐤋𐤉𐤄𐤅𐤄.𐤌𐤇𐤓.𐤀𐤕.𐤀𐤔𐤓.𐤕𐤀𐤐𐤅.𐤀𐤐𐤅.𐤅𐤀
𐤕.𐤀𐤔𐤓.𐤕𐤁𐤔𐤋𐤅.𐤁𐤔𐤋𐤅.𐤅𐤀𐤕.𐤊𐤋.𐤄𐤏𐤃𐤐.𐤄𐤍𐤉𐤇𐤅.𐤋𐤊
𐤌.𐤋𐤌𐤔𐤌𐤓𐤕.𐤏𐤃.𐤄𐤁𐤒𐤓|
..𐤊𐤃.. 𐤅𐤉𐤍𐤉𐤇𐤅.𐤀𐤕𐤅.𐤏𐤃.𐤄𐤁𐤒𐤓.𐤊𐤀𐤔𐤓.𐤑𐤅𐤄.𐤌𐤔𐤄.𐤅
𐤋𐤀.𐤄𐤁𐤀𐤉𐤔.𐤅𐤓𐤌𐤄.𐤋𐤀.𐤄𐤉𐤕𐤄.𐤁𐤅|
..𐤊𐤄.. 𐤅𐤉𐤀𐤌𐤓.𐤌𐤔𐤄.𐤀𐤊𐤋𐤄𐤅.𐤄𐤉𐤅𐤌.𐤊𐤉.𐤔𐤁𐤕.𐤄𐤉𐤅𐤌.𐤋
𐤉𐤄𐤅𐤄.𐤄𐤉𐤅𐤌.𐤋𐤀.𐤕𐤌𐤑𐤀𐤄𐤅.𐤁𐤔𐤃𐤄|
..𐤊𐤅.. 𐤔𐤔𐤕.𐤉𐤌𐤉𐤌.𐤕𐤋𐤒𐤈𐤄𐤅.𐤅𐤁𐤉𐤅𐤌.𐤄𐤔𐤁𐤉𐤏𐤉.𐤔𐤁
𐤕.𐤋𐤀.𐤉𐤄𐤉𐤄.𐤁𐤅|
..𐤊𐤆.. 𐤅𐤉𐤄𐤉.𐤁𐤉𐤅𐤌.𐤄𐤔𐤁𐤉𐤏𐤉.𐤉𐤑𐤀𐤅.𐤌𐤍.𐤄𐤏𐤌.𐤋𐤋𐤒
𐤈.𐤅𐤋𐤀.𐤌𐤑𐤀𐤅|
..𐤊𐤇.. 𐤅𐤉𐤀𐤌𐤓.𐤉𐤄𐤅𐤄.𐤀𐤋.𐤌𐤔𐤄.𐤏𐤃.𐤀𐤍𐤄.𐤌𐤀𐤍𐤕𐤌.𐤋
𐤔𐤌𐤓.𐤌𐤑𐤅𐤕𐤉.𐤅𐤕𐤅𐤓𐤕𐤉|
..𐤊𐤈.. 𐤓𐤀𐤅.𐤊𐤉.𐤉𐤄𐤅𐤄.𐤍𐤕𐤍.𐤋𐤊𐤌.𐤄𐤔𐤁𐤕.𐤏𐤋.𐤊𐤍.𐤄𐤅𐤀.
𐤍𐤕𐤍.𐤋𐤊𐤌.𐤁𐤉𐤅𐤌.𐤄𐤔𐤔𐤉.𐤋𐤇𐤌.𐤉𐤅𐤌𐤉𐤌.𐤔𐤁𐤅.𐤀𐤉𐤔.𐤕
𐤇𐤕𐤉𐤅.𐤀𐤋.𐤉𐤑𐤀.𐤀𐤉𐤔.𐤌𐤌𐤒𐤌𐤅.𐤁𐤉𐤅𐤌.𐤄𐤔𐤁𐤉𐤏𐤉|
..𐤋.. 𐤅𐤉𐤔𐤁𐤕𐤅.𐤄𐤏𐤌.𐤁𐤉𐤅𐤌.𐤄𐤔𐤁𐤏𐤉|
..𐤋𐤀.. 𐤅𐤉𐤒𐤓𐤀𐤅.𐤁𐤉𐤕.𐤉𐤔𐤓𐤀𐤋.𐤀𐤕.𐤔𐤌𐤅.𐤌𐤍.𐤅𐤄𐤅𐤀.𐤊𐤆
𐤓𐤏.𐤂𐤃.𐤋𐤁𐤍.𐤅𐤈𐤏𐤌𐤅.𐤊𐤑𐤐𐤉𐤇𐤕.𐤁𐤃𐤁𐤔|
..𐤋𐤁.. 𐤅𐤉𐤀𐤌𐤓.𐤌𐤔𐤄.𐤆𐤄.𐤄𐤃𐤁𐤓.𐤀𐤔𐤓.𐤑𐤅𐤄.𐤉𐤄𐤅𐤄.𐤌
𐤋𐤀.𐤄𐤏𐤌𐤓.𐤌𐤌𐤍𐤅.𐤋𐤌𐤔𐤌𐤓𐤕.𐤋𐤃𐤓𐤕𐤉𐤊𐤌.𐤋𐤌𐤏𐤍.𐤉𐤓𐤀
𐤅.𐤀𐤕.𐤄𐤋𐤇𐤌.𐤀𐤔𐤓.𐤄𐤀𐤊𐤋𐤕𐤉.𐤀𐤕𐤊𐤌.𐤁𐤌𐤃𐤁𐤓.𐤁𐤄𐤅
𐤑𐤉𐤀𐤉.𐤀𐤕𐤊𐤌.𐤌𐤀𐤓𐤑.𐤌𐤑𐤓𐤉𐤌|
..𐤋𐤂.. 𐤅𐤉𐤀𐤌𐤓.𐤌𐤔𐤄.𐤀𐤋.𐤀𐤄𐤓𐤍.𐤒𐤇.𐤑𐤍𐤑𐤍𐤕.𐤀𐤇𐤕.𐤅
𐤕𐤍.𐤔𐤌𐤄.𐤌𐤋𐤀.𐤄𐤏𐤌𐤓.𐤌𐤍.𐤅𐤄𐤍𐤇.𐤀𐤕𐤅.𐤋𐤐𐤍𐤉.𐤉𐤄𐤅𐤄.𐤋
𐤌𐤔𐤌𐤓𐤕.𐤋𐤃𐤓𐤕𐤉𐤊𐤌|
..𐤋𐤃.. 𐤊𐤀𐤔𐤓.𐤑𐤅𐤄.𐤉𐤄𐤅𐤄.𐤀𐤋.𐤌𐤔𐤄.𐤅𐤉𐤍𐤉𐤇𐤄𐤅.𐤀𐤄𐤓
𐤍.𐤋𐤐𐤍𐤉.𐤄𐤏𐤃𐤕.𐤋𐤌𐤔𐤌𐤓𐤕|

לה 𐤅𐤁𐤍𐤉.𐤉𐤔𐤓𐤀𐤋.𐤀𐤊𐤋𐤅.𐤀𐤕.𐤄𐤌𐤍.𐤀𐤓𐤁𐤏𐤉𐤌.𐤔𐤍𐤄.
𐤏𐤃.𐤁𐤀𐤌.𐤀𐤋.𐤀𐤓𐤑.𐤍𐤅𐤔𐤁𐤕.𐤀𐤕.𐤄𐤌𐤍.𐤀𐤊𐤋𐤅.𐤏𐤃.𐤁
𐤀𐤌.𐤀𐤋.𐤒𐤑𐤄.𐤀𐤓𐤑.𐤊𐤍𐤏𐤍|

לו 𐤅𐤄𐤏𐤌𐤓.𐤏𐤔𐤓𐤉𐤕.𐤄𐤀𐤉𐤐𐤄.𐤄𐤅𐤀||

𐤅𐤉𐤏𐤋𐤅.𐤌𐤌𐤑𐤓𐤉𐤌.𐤇𐤋𐤒 יז

א 𐤅𐤉𐤎𐤏𐤅.𐤊𐤋.𐤏𐤃𐤕.𐤁𐤍𐤉.𐤉𐤔𐤓𐤀𐤋.𐤌𐤌𐤃𐤁𐤓.𐤎𐤉𐤍.𐤋
𐤌𐤎𐤏𐤉𐤄𐤌.𐤏𐤋.𐤐𐤉.𐤉𐤄𐤅𐤄.𐤅𐤉𐤇𐤍𐤅.𐤁𐤓𐤐𐤉𐤃𐤉𐤌.𐤅𐤀𐤉𐤍.
𐤌𐤉𐤌.𐤋𐤔𐤕𐤕.𐤄𐤏𐤌|

ב 𐤅𐤉𐤓𐤁.𐤄𐤏𐤌.𐤏𐤌.𐤌𐤔𐤄.𐤅𐤉𐤀𐤌𐤓𐤅.𐤕𐤍𐤅.𐤋𐤍𐤅.𐤌𐤉𐤌.𐤅𐤍
𐤔𐤕𐤄.𐤅𐤉𐤀𐤌𐤓.𐤋𐤄𐤌.𐤌𐤔𐤄.𐤌𐤄.𐤕𐤓𐤉𐤁𐤅𐤍.𐤏𐤌𐤃𐤉.𐤌𐤄.
𐤕𐤍𐤎𐤅𐤍.𐤀𐤕.𐤉𐤄𐤅𐤄|

ג 𐤅𐤉𐤑𐤌𐤀.𐤔𐤌.𐤄𐤏𐤌.𐤋𐤌𐤉𐤌.𐤅𐤉𐤋𐤍.𐤄𐤏𐤌.𐤏𐤋.𐤌𐤔𐤄.
𐤅𐤉𐤀𐤌𐤓.𐤋𐤌𐤄.𐤆𐤄.𐤄𐤏𐤋𐤉𐤕𐤍𐤅.𐤌𐤌𐤑𐤓𐤉𐤌.𐤋𐤄𐤌𐤉𐤕.𐤀
𐤕𐤉.𐤅𐤀𐤕.𐤁𐤍𐤉.𐤅𐤀𐤕.𐤌𐤒𐤍𐤉.𐤁𐤑𐤌𐤀|

ד 𐤅𐤉𐤑𐤏𐤒.𐤌𐤔𐤄.𐤀𐤋.𐤉𐤄𐤅𐤄.𐤋𐤀𐤌𐤓.𐤌𐤄.𐤀𐤏𐤔𐤄.𐤋
𐤏𐤌.𐤄𐤆𐤄.𐤏𐤅𐤃.𐤌𐤏𐤈.𐤅𐤎𐤒𐤋𐤍𐤉|

ה 𐤅𐤉𐤀𐤌𐤓.𐤉𐤄𐤅𐤄.𐤀𐤋.𐤌𐤔𐤄.𐤏𐤁𐤓.𐤋𐤐𐤍𐤉.𐤄𐤏𐤌.𐤅𐤒𐤇.
𐤀𐤕𐤊.𐤌𐤆𐤒𐤍𐤉.𐤉𐤔𐤓𐤀𐤋.𐤅𐤌𐤈𐤊.𐤀𐤔𐤓.𐤄𐤊𐤉𐤕.𐤁𐤅.𐤀𐤕.
𐤄𐤉𐤀𐤓.𐤒𐤇.𐤁𐤉𐤃𐤊.𐤅𐤄𐤋𐤊𐤕|

ו 𐤄𐤍𐤍𐤉.𐤏𐤌𐤃.𐤋𐤐𐤍𐤉𐤊.𐤔𐤌.𐤏𐤋.𐤄𐤑𐤅𐤓.𐤁𐤇𐤓𐤁.𐤅𐤄𐤊
𐤉𐤕.𐤁𐤑𐤅𐤓.𐤅𐤉𐤑𐤀𐤅.𐤌𐤌𐤍𐤅.𐤌𐤉𐤌.𐤅𐤔𐤕𐤄.𐤄𐤏𐤌.𐤅𐤉𐤏𐤔.𐤊
𐤍.𐤌𐤔𐤄.𐤋𐤏𐤉𐤍𐤉.𐤆𐤒𐤍𐤉.𐤉𐤔𐤓𐤀𐤋|

ז 𐤅𐤉𐤒𐤓𐤀.𐤔𐤌.𐤄𐤌𐤒𐤅𐤌.𐤌𐤎𐤄.𐤅𐤌𐤓𐤉𐤁𐤄.𐤏𐤋.𐤓𐤉𐤁.𐤁
𐤍𐤉.𐤉𐤔𐤓𐤀𐤋.𐤅𐤏𐤋.𐤍𐤎𐤕𐤌.𐤀𐤕.𐤉𐤄𐤅𐤄.𐤋𐤀𐤌𐤓.𐤄𐤉𐤔.𐤉𐤄𐤅
𐤄.𐤁𐤒𐤓𐤁𐤍𐤅.𐤀𐤌.𐤀𐤉𐤍|

ח 𐤅𐤉𐤁𐤀.𐤏𐤌𐤋𐤒.𐤅𐤉𐤋𐤇𐤌.𐤏𐤌.𐤉𐤔𐤓𐤀𐤋.𐤁𐤓𐤐𐤉𐤃𐤌|

ט 𐤅𐤉𐤀𐤌𐤓.𐤌𐤔𐤄.𐤀𐤋.𐤉𐤄𐤅𐤔𐤏.𐤁𐤇𐤓.𐤋𐤍𐤅.𐤀𐤍𐤔𐤉𐤌.𐤅
𐤑𐤀.𐤄𐤋𐤇𐤌.𐤁𐤏𐤌𐤋𐤒.𐤌𐤇𐤓.𐤀𐤍𐤊𐤉.𐤍𐤑𐤁.𐤏𐤋.𐤓𐤀𐤔.𐤄
𐤂𐤁𐤏𐤄.𐤅𐤌𐤈𐤄.𐤄𐤀𐤋𐤄𐤉𐤌.𐤁𐤉𐤃𐤉|

10 𐤅𐤉𐤏𐤔.𐤉𐤄𐤅𐤔𐤏.𐤊𐤀𐤔𐤓.𐤀𐤌𐤓.𐤋𐤅.𐤌𐤔𐤄.𐤋𐤄𐤋𐤇𐤌.
𐤁𐤏𐤌𐤋𐤒.𐤅𐤌𐤔𐤄.𐤀𐤄𐤓𐤍.𐤅𐤇𐤅𐤓.𐤏𐤋𐤅.𐤓𐤀𐤔.𐤄𐤂𐤁𐤏𐤄|
11 𐤅𐤄𐤉𐤄.𐤊𐤀𐤔𐤓.𐤉𐤓𐤉𐤌.𐤌𐤔𐤄.𐤉𐤃𐤅.𐤅𐤂𐤁𐤓.𐤉𐤔𐤓𐤀𐤋
.𐤅𐤊𐤀𐤔𐤓.𐤉𐤍𐤉𐤇.𐤉𐤃𐤅.𐤅𐤂𐤁𐤓.𐤏𐤌𐤋𐤒|
12 𐤅𐤉𐤃𐤉.𐤌𐤔𐤄.𐤊𐤁𐤃𐤉𐤌.𐤅𐤉𐤒𐤇𐤅.𐤀𐤁𐤍.𐤅𐤉𐤔𐤉𐤌𐤅.𐤕
𐤇𐤕𐤉𐤅.𐤅𐤉𐤔𐤁.𐤏𐤋𐤉𐤄.𐤅𐤀𐤄𐤓𐤍.𐤅𐤇𐤅𐤓.𐤕𐤌𐤊𐤅.𐤁𐤉𐤃𐤉𐤅.𐤌
𐤆𐤄.𐤀𐤇𐤃.𐤅𐤌𐤆𐤄.𐤀𐤇𐤃.𐤅𐤉𐤄𐤉.𐤉𐤃𐤉𐤅.𐤀𐤌𐤅𐤍𐤄.𐤏𐤃
.𐤁𐤀.𐤄𐤔𐤌𐤔|
13 𐤅𐤉𐤇𐤋𐤔.𐤉𐤄𐤅𐤔𐤏.𐤀𐤕.𐤏𐤌𐤋𐤒.𐤅𐤀𐤕.𐤏𐤌𐤅.𐤋𐤐𐤉.𐤇
𐤓𐤁|
14 𐤅𐤉𐤀𐤌𐤓.𐤉𐤄𐤅𐤄.𐤀𐤋.𐤌𐤔𐤄.𐤊𐤕𐤁.𐤆𐤀𐤕.𐤆𐤊𐤓𐤅𐤍.
𐤁𐤎𐤐𐤓.𐤅𐤔𐤉𐤌.𐤁𐤀𐤆𐤍𐤉.𐤉𐤄𐤅𐤔𐤏.𐤊𐤉.𐤌𐤇𐤄.𐤀𐤌𐤇𐤄.𐤀
𐤕.𐤆𐤊𐤓.𐤏𐤌𐤋𐤒.𐤌𐤕𐤇𐤕.𐤄𐤔𐤌𐤉𐤌|
15 𐤅𐤉𐤁𐤍.𐤌𐤔𐤄.𐤌𐤆𐤁𐤇.𐤅𐤉𐤒𐤓𐤀.𐤔𐤌𐤅.𐤉𐤄𐤅𐤄.𐤍𐤎𐤉|
16 𐤅𐤉𐤀𐤌𐤓.𐤊𐤉.𐤉𐤃.𐤏𐤋.𐤊𐤎.𐤉𐤄.𐤌𐤋𐤇𐤌𐤄.𐤋𐤉𐤄𐤅𐤄.
𐤁𐤏𐤌𐤋𐤒.𐤌𐤃𐤓.𐤃𐤓||

𐤅𐤉𐤏𐤋𐤅.𐤌𐤌𐤑𐤓𐤉𐤌.𐤇𐤋𐤒 18

1 𐤅𐤉𐤔𐤌𐤏.𐤉𐤕𐤓𐤅.𐤊𐤄𐤍.𐤌𐤃𐤉𐤍.𐤇𐤕𐤍.𐤌𐤔𐤄.𐤀𐤕.𐤊𐤋.
𐤀𐤔𐤓.𐤏𐤔𐤄.𐤀𐤋𐤄𐤉𐤌.𐤋𐤌𐤔𐤄.𐤅𐤋𐤉𐤔𐤓𐤀𐤋.𐤏𐤌𐤅.𐤊𐤉.𐤄𐤅
𐤑𐤉𐤀.𐤉𐤄𐤅𐤄.𐤀𐤕.𐤉𐤔𐤓𐤀𐤋.𐤌𐤌𐤑𐤓𐤉𐤌|
2 𐤅𐤉𐤒𐤇.𐤉𐤕𐤓𐤅.𐤇𐤕𐤍.𐤌𐤔𐤄.𐤀𐤕.𐤑𐤐𐤓𐤄.𐤀𐤔𐤕.𐤌𐤔
𐤄.𐤀𐤇𐤓.𐤔𐤋𐤅𐤇𐤉𐤄|
3 𐤅𐤀𐤕.𐤔𐤍𐤉.𐤁𐤍𐤉𐤄.𐤀𐤔𐤓.𐤔𐤌.𐤄𐤀𐤇𐤃.𐤂𐤓𐤔𐤌.𐤊𐤉.
𐤀𐤌𐤓.𐤂𐤓.𐤄𐤉𐤉𐤕𐤉.𐤁𐤀𐤓𐤑.𐤍𐤊𐤓𐤉𐤄|
4 𐤅𐤔𐤌.𐤄𐤀𐤇𐤃.𐤀𐤋𐤉𐤏𐤆𐤓.𐤊𐤉.𐤀𐤋𐤄𐤉.𐤀𐤁𐤉.𐤁𐤏𐤆
𐤓𐤉.𐤅𐤉𐤑𐤋𐤍𐤉.𐤌𐤇𐤓𐤁.𐤐𐤓𐤏𐤄|
5 𐤅𐤉𐤁𐤀.𐤉𐤕𐤓𐤅.𐤇𐤕𐤍.𐤌𐤔𐤄.𐤅𐤁𐤍𐤉𐤅.𐤅𐤀𐤔𐤕𐤅.𐤀𐤋.𐤌𐤔
𐤄.𐤀𐤋.𐤄𐤌𐤃𐤁𐤓.𐤀𐤔𐤓.𐤄𐤅𐤀.𐤇𐤍𐤄.𐤔𐤌.𐤄𐤓.𐤄𐤀𐤋𐤄𐤉𐤌|

𐤅 𐤅𐤉𐤀𐤌𐤓.𐤀𐤋.𐤌𐤔𐤄.𐤀𐤍𐤉.𐤇𐤕𐤍𐤊.𐤉𐤕𐤓𐤅.𐤁𐤀.𐤀𐤋𐤉𐤊.𐤅
𐤀𐤔𐤕𐤊.𐤅𐤔𐤍𐤉.𐤁𐤍𐤉𐤄.𐤏𐤌𐤄|
𐤆 𐤅𐤉𐤑𐤀.𐤌𐤔𐤄.𐤋𐤒𐤓𐤀𐤕.𐤇𐤕𐤍𐤅.𐤅𐤉𐤔𐤕𐤇𐤅.𐤅𐤉𐤔𐤒.𐤋
𐤅.𐤅𐤉𐤔𐤀𐤋𐤅.𐤀𐤉𐤔.𐤋𐤓𐤏𐤄𐤅.𐤋𐤔𐤋𐤅𐤌.𐤅𐤉𐤁𐤀𐤅.𐤄𐤀𐤄𐤋𐤄|
𐤇 𐤅𐤉𐤎𐤐𐤓.𐤌𐤔𐤄.𐤋𐤇𐤕𐤍𐤅.𐤀𐤕.𐤊𐤋.𐤀𐤔𐤓.𐤏𐤔𐤄.𐤉𐤄𐤅𐤄.
𐤋𐤐𐤓𐤏𐤄.𐤅𐤋𐤌𐤑𐤓𐤉𐤌.𐤏𐤋.𐤀𐤅𐤃𐤕.𐤉𐤔𐤓𐤀𐤋.𐤀𐤕.𐤊𐤋.𐤄𐤕
𐤋𐤀𐤄.𐤀𐤔𐤓.𐤌𐤑𐤀𐤕𐤌.𐤁𐤃𐤓𐤊.𐤅𐤉𐤑𐤋𐤌.𐤉𐤄𐤅𐤄|
𐤈 𐤅𐤉𐤇𐤃.𐤉𐤕𐤓𐤅.𐤏𐤋.𐤊𐤋.𐤄𐤈𐤅𐤁𐤄.𐤀𐤔𐤓.𐤏𐤔𐤄.𐤉𐤄𐤅
𐤄.𐤋𐤉𐤔𐤓𐤀𐤋.𐤀𐤔𐤓.𐤄𐤑𐤉𐤋𐤅.𐤌𐤉𐤃.𐤌𐤑𐤓𐤉𐤌|
𐤉 𐤅𐤉𐤀𐤌𐤓.𐤉𐤕𐤓𐤅.𐤁𐤓𐤅𐤊.𐤉𐤄𐤅𐤄.𐤀𐤔𐤓.𐤄𐤑𐤉𐤋.𐤀𐤕𐤊
𐤌.𐤌𐤉𐤃.𐤌𐤑𐤓𐤉𐤌.𐤅𐤌𐤉𐤃.𐤐𐤓𐤏𐤄.𐤀𐤔𐤓.𐤄𐤑𐤉𐤋.𐤀𐤕.𐤄
𐤏𐤌.𐤌𐤕𐤇𐤕.𐤉𐤃.𐤌𐤑𐤓𐤉𐤌|
𐤉𐤀 𐤏𐤕𐤄.𐤉𐤃𐤏𐤕𐤉.𐤊𐤉.𐤂𐤃𐤅𐤋.𐤉𐤄𐤅𐤄.𐤌𐤊𐤋.𐤄𐤀𐤋𐤄
𐤉𐤌.𐤊𐤉.𐤁𐤃𐤁𐤓.𐤀𐤔𐤓.𐤆𐤃𐤅.𐤏𐤋𐤉𐤄𐤌|
𐤉𐤁 𐤅𐤉𐤒𐤇.𐤉𐤕𐤓𐤅.𐤇𐤕𐤍.𐤌𐤔𐤄.𐤏𐤋𐤄.𐤅𐤆𐤁𐤇𐤉𐤌.𐤋𐤀𐤋
𐤄𐤉𐤌.𐤅𐤉𐤁𐤀.𐤀𐤄𐤓𐤍.𐤅𐤊𐤋.𐤆𐤒𐤍𐤉.𐤉𐤔𐤓𐤀𐤋.𐤋𐤀𐤊𐤋.𐤋𐤇𐤌
.𐤏𐤌.𐤇𐤕𐤍.𐤌𐤔𐤄.𐤋𐤐𐤍𐤉.𐤄𐤀𐤋𐤄𐤉𐤌|
𐤉𐤂 𐤅𐤉𐤄𐤉.𐤌𐤌𐤇𐤓𐤕.𐤅𐤉𐤔𐤁.𐤌𐤔𐤄.𐤋𐤔𐤐𐤈.𐤀𐤕.𐤄𐤏𐤌.
𐤅𐤉𐤏𐤌𐤃.𐤄𐤏𐤌.𐤏𐤋.𐤌𐤔𐤄.𐤌𐤍.𐤄𐤁𐤒𐤓.𐤏𐤃.𐤄𐤏𐤓𐤁|
𐤉𐤃 𐤅𐤉𐤓𐤀.𐤇𐤕𐤍.𐤌𐤔𐤄.𐤀𐤕.𐤊𐤋.𐤀𐤔𐤓.𐤄𐤅𐤀.𐤏𐤔𐤄.𐤋
𐤏𐤌.𐤅𐤉𐤀𐤌𐤓.𐤌𐤄.𐤄𐤃𐤁𐤓.𐤄𐤆𐤄.𐤀𐤔𐤓.𐤀𐤕𐤄.𐤏𐤔𐤄.𐤋𐤏
𐤌.𐤌𐤃𐤅𐤏.𐤀𐤕𐤄.𐤉𐤅𐤔𐤁.𐤋𐤁𐤃𐤊.𐤅𐤊𐤋.𐤄𐤏𐤌.𐤍𐤑𐤁.𐤏𐤋𐤉
𐤊.𐤌𐤍.𐤁𐤒𐤓.𐤏𐤃.𐤏𐤓𐤁|
𐤈𐤅 𐤅𐤉𐤀𐤌𐤓.𐤌𐤔𐤄.𐤋𐤇𐤕𐤍𐤅.𐤊𐤉.𐤉𐤁𐤀.𐤀𐤋𐤉.𐤄𐤏𐤌.𐤋𐤃
𐤓𐤔.𐤀𐤋𐤄𐤉𐤌|
𐤈𐤆 𐤊𐤉.𐤉𐤄𐤉𐤄.𐤋𐤄𐤌.𐤃𐤁𐤓.𐤁𐤀.𐤀𐤋𐤉.𐤅𐤔𐤐𐤈𐤕𐤉.𐤁𐤉𐤍.
𐤀𐤉𐤔.𐤅𐤁𐤉𐤍.𐤓𐤏𐤄𐤅.𐤅𐤄𐤅𐤃𐤏𐤕𐤉.𐤀𐤕.𐤇𐤒𐤉.𐤄𐤀𐤋𐤄𐤉𐤌.
𐤅𐤀𐤕.𐤕𐤅𐤓𐤕𐤉𐤅|
𐤉𐤆 𐤅𐤉𐤀𐤌𐤓.𐤇𐤕𐤍.𐤌𐤔𐤄.𐤀𐤋𐤉𐤅.𐤋𐤀.𐤈𐤅𐤁.𐤄𐤃𐤁𐤓.𐤀𐤔
𐤓.𐤀𐤕𐤄.𐤏𐤔𐤄|

יח נבל.תבל.גם.אתה.גם.העם.הזה.אשר.ע
מך.כי.כבד.ממך.הדבר.לא.תוכל.עשהו.לבדך|
יט עתה.שמע.בקלי.איעצך.ויהי.אלהים.
עמך.היה.אתה.לעם.מול.האלהים.והבאת.את
ה.את.הדברים.אל.האלהים|
כ והזהרתה.אתהם.את.החקים.ואת.התור
ת.והודעת.להם.את.הדרך.ילכו.בה.ואת.המע
שה.אשר.יעשון|
כא ואתה.תחזה.מכל.העם.אנשי.חיל.יראי
אלהים.אנשי.אמת.שנאי.בצע.ושמת.עלהם.
שרי.אלפים.שרי.מאות.שרי.חמשים.ושרי.עש
רת|
כב ושפטו.את.העם.בכל.עת.והיה.כל.הדבר.
הגדל.יביאו.אליך.וכל.הדבר.הקטן.ישפטו.
הם.והקל.מעליך.ונשאו.אתך|
כג אם.את.הדבר.הזה.תעשה.וצוך.אלהים.
ויכלת.עמד.וגם.כל.העם.הזה.על.מקמו.יבא
.בשלום|
כד וישמע.משה.לקול.חתנו.ויעש.כל.אשר.א
מר|
כה ויבחר.משה.אנשי.חיל.מכל.ישראל.ויתן
אתם.ראשים.על.העם.שרי.אלפים.שרי.מאות.
שרי.חמשים.ושרי.עשרת|
כו ושפטו.את.העם.בכל.עת.את.הדבר.הקש
ה.יביאון.אל.משה.וכל.הדבר.הקטן.ישפוטו.
הם|
כז וישלח.משה.את.חתנו.וילך.לו.אל.ארצו||

ויעלו.ממצרים.חלק יט

א 𐤁𐤇𐤃𐤔.𐤄𐤔𐤋𐤉𐤔𐤉.𐤋𐤑𐤀𐤕.𐤁𐤍𐤉.𐤉𐤔𐤓𐤀𐤋.𐤌𐤀𐤓𐤑
.𐤌𐤑𐤓𐤉𐤌.𐤁𐤉𐤅𐤌.𐤄𐤆𐤄.𐤁𐤀𐤅.𐤌𐤃𐤁𐤓.𐤎𐤉𐤍𐤉|

ב 𐤅𐤉𐤎𐤏𐤅.𐤌𐤓𐤐𐤉𐤃𐤉𐤌.𐤅𐤉𐤁𐤀𐤅.𐤌𐤃𐤁𐤓.𐤎𐤉𐤍𐤉.𐤅𐤉𐤇𐤍𐤅
.𐤁𐤌𐤃𐤁𐤓.𐤅𐤉𐤇𐤍.𐤔𐤌.𐤉𐤔𐤓𐤀𐤋.𐤍𐤂𐤃.𐤄𐤄𐤓|

ג 𐤅𐤌𐤔𐤄.𐤏𐤋𐤄.𐤀𐤋.𐤄𐤀𐤋𐤄𐤉𐤌.𐤅𐤉𐤒𐤓𐤀.𐤀𐤋𐤉𐤅.𐤉𐤄𐤅𐤄
.𐤌𐤍.𐤄𐤄𐤓.𐤋𐤀𐤌𐤓.𐤊𐤄.𐤕𐤀𐤌𐤓.𐤋𐤁𐤉𐤕.𐤉𐤏𐤒𐤁.𐤅𐤕𐤂𐤉𐤃.
𐤋𐤁𐤍𐤉.𐤉𐤔𐤓𐤀𐤋|

ד 𐤀𐤕𐤌.𐤓𐤀𐤉𐤕𐤌.𐤀𐤔𐤓.𐤏𐤔𐤉𐤕𐤉.𐤋𐤌𐤑𐤓𐤉𐤌.𐤅𐤀𐤔𐤀
.𐤀𐤕𐤊𐤌.𐤏𐤋.𐤊𐤍𐤐𐤉.𐤍𐤔𐤓𐤉𐤌.𐤅𐤀𐤁𐤀.𐤀𐤕𐤊𐤌.𐤀𐤋𐤉|

ה 𐤅𐤏𐤕𐤄.𐤀𐤌.𐤔𐤌𐤅𐤏.𐤕𐤔𐤌𐤏𐤅.𐤁𐤒𐤋𐤉.𐤅𐤔𐤌𐤓𐤕𐤌.𐤀𐤕
.𐤁𐤓𐤉𐤕𐤉.𐤅𐤄𐤉𐤉𐤕𐤌.𐤋𐤉.𐤎𐤂𐤋𐤄.𐤌𐤊𐤋.𐤄𐤏𐤌𐤉𐤌.𐤊𐤉.𐤋𐤉
.𐤊𐤋.𐤄𐤀𐤓𐤑|

ו 𐤅𐤀𐤕𐤌.𐤕𐤄𐤉𐤅.𐤋𐤉.𐤌𐤌𐤋𐤊𐤕.𐤊𐤄𐤍𐤉𐤌.𐤅𐤂𐤅𐤉.𐤒𐤃𐤔
.𐤀𐤋𐤄.𐤄𐤃𐤁𐤓𐤉𐤌.𐤀𐤔𐤓.𐤕𐤃𐤁𐤓.𐤀𐤋.𐤁𐤍𐤉.𐤉𐤔𐤓𐤀𐤋|

ז 𐤅𐤉𐤁𐤀.𐤌𐤔𐤄.𐤅𐤉𐤒𐤓𐤀.𐤋𐤆𐤒𐤍𐤉.𐤄𐤏𐤌.𐤅𐤉𐤔𐤌.𐤋𐤐𐤍
𐤉𐤄𐤌.𐤀𐤕.𐤊𐤋.𐤄𐤃𐤁𐤓𐤉𐤌.𐤄𐤀𐤋𐤄.𐤀𐤔𐤓.𐤑𐤅𐤄𐤅.𐤉𐤄𐤅𐤄|

ח 𐤅𐤉𐤏𐤍𐤅.𐤊𐤋.𐤄𐤏𐤌.𐤉𐤇𐤃𐤅.𐤅𐤉𐤀𐤌𐤓𐤅.𐤊𐤋.𐤀𐤔𐤓.𐤃𐤁𐤓.
𐤉𐤄𐤅𐤄.𐤍𐤏𐤔𐤄.𐤅𐤉𐤔𐤁.𐤌𐤔𐤄.𐤀𐤕.𐤃𐤁𐤓𐤉.𐤄𐤏𐤌.𐤀𐤋.𐤉𐤄
𐤅𐤄|

ט 𐤅𐤉𐤀𐤌𐤓.𐤉𐤄𐤅𐤄.𐤀𐤋.𐤌𐤔𐤄.𐤄𐤍𐤄.𐤀𐤍𐤊𐤉.𐤁𐤀.𐤀𐤋𐤉𐤊
.𐤁𐤏𐤁.𐤄𐤏𐤍𐤍.𐤁𐤏𐤁𐤅𐤓.𐤉𐤔𐤌𐤏.𐤄𐤏𐤌.𐤁𐤃𐤁𐤓𐤉.𐤏𐤌𐤊.𐤅
𐤂𐤌.𐤁𐤊.𐤉𐤀𐤌𐤉𐤍𐤅.𐤋𐤏𐤅𐤋𐤌.𐤅𐤉𐤂𐤃.𐤌𐤔𐤄.𐤀𐤕.𐤃𐤁𐤓𐤉.
𐤄𐤏𐤌.𐤀𐤋.𐤉𐤄𐤅𐤄|

י 𐤅𐤉𐤀𐤌𐤓.𐤉𐤄𐤅𐤄.𐤀𐤋.𐤌𐤔𐤄.𐤋𐤊.𐤀𐤋.𐤄𐤏𐤌.𐤅𐤒𐤃𐤔
𐤕𐤌.𐤄𐤉𐤅𐤌.𐤅𐤌𐤇𐤓.𐤅𐤊𐤁𐤎𐤅.𐤔𐤌𐤋𐤕𐤌|

יא 𐤅𐤄𐤉𐤅.𐤍𐤊𐤍𐤉𐤌.𐤋𐤉𐤅𐤌.𐤄𐤔𐤋𐤉𐤔𐤉.𐤊𐤉.𐤁𐤉𐤅𐤌.𐤄𐤔𐤋
𐤉𐤔𐤉.𐤉𐤓𐤃.𐤉𐤄𐤅𐤄.𐤋𐤏𐤉𐤍𐤉.𐤊𐤋.𐤄𐤏𐤌.𐤏𐤋.𐤄𐤓.𐤎𐤉𐤍𐤉|

יב 𐤅𐤄𐤂𐤁𐤋𐤕.𐤀𐤕.𐤄𐤏𐤌.𐤎𐤁𐤉𐤁.𐤋𐤀𐤌𐤓.𐤄𐤔𐤌𐤓𐤅.𐤋𐤊
𐤌.𐤏𐤋𐤅𐤕.𐤁𐤄𐤓.𐤅𐤍𐤂𐤏.𐤁𐤒𐤑𐤄𐤅.𐤊𐤋.𐤄𐤍𐤂𐤏.𐤁𐤄𐤓.𐤌𐤅𐤕.
𐤉𐤅𐤌𐤕|

𐤉𐤂 𐤋𐤀.𐤕𐤂𐤏.𐤁𐤅.𐤉𐤃.𐤊𐤉.𐤎𐤒𐤅𐤋.𐤉𐤎𐤒𐤋.𐤀𐤅.𐤉𐤓𐤄.𐤉
𐤉𐤓𐤄.𐤀𐤌.𐤁𐤄𐤌𐤄.𐤀𐤌.𐤀𐤉𐤔.𐤋𐤀.𐤉𐤇𐤉𐤄.𐤁𐤌𐤔𐤊.𐤄𐤉𐤁
𐤋.𐤄𐤌𐤄.𐤉𐤏𐤋𐤅.𐤁𐤄𐤓|

𐤉𐤃 𐤅𐤉𐤓𐤃.𐤌𐤔𐤄.𐤌𐤍.𐤄𐤄𐤓.𐤀𐤋.𐤄𐤏𐤌.𐤅𐤉𐤒𐤃𐤔.𐤀𐤕.
𐤄𐤏𐤌.𐤅𐤉𐤊𐤁𐤎𐤅.𐤔𐤌𐤋𐤕𐤌|

𐤈𐤅 𐤅𐤉𐤀𐤌𐤓.𐤀𐤋.𐤄𐤏𐤌.𐤄𐤉𐤅.𐤍𐤊𐤍𐤉𐤌.𐤋𐤔𐤋𐤔𐤕.𐤉𐤌𐤉𐤌.
𐤀𐤋.𐤕𐤂𐤔𐤅.𐤀𐤋.𐤀𐤔𐤄|

𐤈𐤆 𐤅𐤉𐤄𐤉.𐤁𐤉𐤅𐤌.𐤄𐤔𐤋𐤉𐤔𐤉.𐤁𐤄𐤉𐤕.𐤄𐤁𐤒𐤓.𐤅𐤉𐤄𐤉.𐤒
𐤋𐤕.𐤅𐤁𐤓𐤒𐤉𐤌.𐤅𐤏𐤍𐤍.𐤊𐤁𐤃.𐤏𐤋.𐤄𐤄𐤓.𐤅𐤒𐤋.𐤔𐤐𐤓.𐤇𐤆𐤒.
𐤌𐤀𐤃.𐤅𐤉𐤇𐤓𐤃.𐤊𐤋.𐤄𐤏𐤌.𐤀𐤔𐤓.𐤁𐤌𐤇𐤍𐤄|

𐤉𐤆 𐤅𐤉𐤅𐤑𐤀.𐤌𐤔𐤄.𐤀𐤕.𐤄𐤏𐤌.𐤋𐤒𐤓𐤀𐤕.𐤄𐤀𐤋𐤄𐤉𐤌.𐤌
𐤍.𐤄𐤌𐤇𐤍𐤄.𐤅𐤉𐤕𐤉𐤑𐤁𐤅.𐤁𐤕𐤇𐤕𐤉𐤕.𐤄𐤄𐤓|

𐤉𐤇 𐤅𐤄𐤓.𐤎𐤉𐤍𐤉.𐤏𐤔𐤍.𐤊𐤋𐤅.𐤌𐤐𐤍𐤉.𐤀𐤔𐤓.𐤉𐤓𐤃.𐤏𐤋𐤉𐤅.
𐤉𐤄𐤅𐤄.𐤁𐤀𐤔.𐤅𐤉𐤏𐤋.𐤏𐤔𐤍𐤅.𐤊𐤏𐤔𐤍.𐤄𐤊𐤁𐤔𐤍.𐤅𐤉𐤇𐤓𐤃.
𐤊𐤋.𐤄𐤄𐤓.𐤌𐤀𐤃|

𐤉𐤈 𐤅𐤉𐤄𐤉.𐤒𐤅𐤋.𐤄𐤔𐤐𐤓.𐤄𐤅𐤋𐤊.𐤅𐤇𐤆𐤒.𐤌𐤀𐤃.𐤌𐤔𐤄.
𐤉𐤃𐤁𐤓.𐤅𐤄𐤀𐤋𐤄𐤉𐤌.𐤉𐤏𐤍𐤍𐤅.𐤁𐤒𐤅𐤋|

𐤊 𐤅𐤉𐤓𐤃.𐤉𐤄𐤅𐤄.𐤏𐤋.𐤄𐤓.𐤎𐤉𐤍𐤉.𐤀𐤋.𐤓𐤀𐤔.𐤄𐤄𐤓.𐤅𐤉
𐤒𐤓𐤀.𐤉𐤄𐤅𐤄.𐤋𐤌𐤔𐤄.𐤀𐤋.𐤓𐤀𐤔.𐤄𐤄𐤓.𐤅𐤉𐤏𐤋.𐤌𐤔𐤄|

𐤊𐤀 𐤅𐤉𐤀𐤌𐤓.𐤉𐤄𐤅𐤄.𐤀𐤋.𐤌𐤔𐤄.𐤓𐤃.𐤄𐤏𐤃.𐤁𐤏𐤌.𐤐𐤍.𐤉
𐤄𐤓𐤎𐤅.𐤀𐤋.𐤉𐤄𐤅𐤄.𐤋𐤓𐤀𐤅𐤕.𐤅𐤍𐤐𐤋.𐤌𐤌𐤍𐤅.𐤓𐤁|

𐤊𐤁 𐤅𐤂𐤌.𐤄𐤊𐤄𐤍𐤉𐤌.𐤄𐤍𐤂𐤔𐤉𐤌.𐤀𐤋.𐤉𐤄𐤅𐤄.𐤉𐤕𐤒𐤃
𐤔𐤅.𐤐𐤍.𐤉𐤐𐤓𐤑.𐤁𐤄𐤌.𐤉𐤄𐤅𐤄|

𐤊𐤂 𐤅𐤉𐤀𐤌𐤓.𐤌𐤔𐤄.𐤀𐤋.𐤉𐤄𐤅𐤄.𐤋𐤀.𐤉𐤅𐤊𐤋.𐤄𐤏𐤌.𐤋𐤏𐤋
𐤕.𐤀𐤋.𐤄𐤓.𐤎𐤉𐤍𐤉.𐤊𐤉.𐤀𐤕𐤄.𐤄𐤏𐤃𐤕𐤄.𐤁𐤍𐤅.𐤋𐤀𐤌𐤓.𐤄
𐤂𐤁𐤋.𐤀𐤕.𐤄𐤄𐤓.𐤅𐤒𐤃𐤔𐤕𐤅|

𐤊𐤃 𐤅𐤉𐤀𐤌𐤓.𐤀𐤋𐤉𐤅.𐤉𐤄𐤅𐤄.𐤋𐤊.𐤓𐤃.𐤅𐤏𐤋𐤉𐤕.𐤀𐤕𐤄.𐤅𐤀
𐤄𐤓𐤍.𐤏𐤌𐤊.𐤅𐤄𐤊𐤄𐤍𐤉𐤌.𐤅𐤄𐤏𐤌.𐤀𐤋.𐤉𐤄𐤓𐤎𐤅.𐤋𐤏𐤋𐤕.𐤀𐤋.
𐤉𐤄𐤅𐤄.𐤐𐤍.𐤉𐤐𐤓𐤑.𐤁𐤌|

𐤊𐤄 𐤅𐤉𐤓𐤃.𐤌𐤔𐤄.𐤀𐤋.𐤄𐤏𐤌.𐤅𐤉𐤀𐤌𐤓.𐤀𐤋𐤄𐤌||

𐤅𐤉𐤏𐤋𐤅.𐤌𐤌𐤑𐤓𐤉𐤌.𐤇𐤋𐤒 ..20..

1 𐤅𐤉𐤃𐤁𐤓.𐤀𐤋𐤄𐤉𐤌.𐤀𐤕.𐤊𐤋.𐤄𐤃𐤁𐤓𐤉𐤌.𐤄𐤀𐤋𐤄.𐤋𐤀
𐤌𐤓|
2 𐤀𐤍𐤊𐤉.𐤉𐤄𐤅𐤄.𐤀𐤋𐤄𐤉𐤊.𐤀𐤔𐤓.𐤄𐤅𐤑𐤀𐤕𐤉𐤊.𐤌𐤀𐤓𐤑.
𐤌𐤑𐤓𐤉𐤌.𐤌𐤁𐤉𐤕.𐤏𐤁𐤃𐤉𐤌|
3 𐤋𐤀.𐤉𐤄𐤉𐤄.𐤋𐤊.𐤀𐤋𐤄𐤉𐤌.𐤀𐤇𐤓𐤉𐤌.𐤏𐤋.𐤐𐤍𐤉|
4 𐤋𐤀.𐤕𐤏𐤔𐤄.𐤋𐤊.𐤐𐤎𐤋.𐤅𐤊𐤋.𐤕𐤌𐤅𐤍𐤄.𐤀𐤔𐤓.𐤁𐤔𐤌𐤉𐤌
.𐤌𐤌𐤏𐤋.𐤅𐤀𐤔𐤓.𐤁𐤀𐤓𐤑.𐤌𐤕𐤇𐤕.𐤅𐤀𐤔𐤓.𐤁𐤌𐤉𐤌.𐤌𐤕𐤇𐤕
.𐤋𐤀𐤓𐤑|
5 𐤋𐤀.𐤕𐤔𐤕𐤇𐤅𐤄.𐤋𐤄𐤌.𐤅𐤋𐤀.𐤕𐤏𐤁𐤃𐤌.𐤊𐤉.𐤀𐤍𐤊𐤉.𐤉
𐤄𐤅𐤄.𐤀𐤋𐤄𐤉𐤊.𐤀𐤋.𐤒𐤍𐤀.𐤐𐤒𐤃.𐤏𐤅𐤍.𐤀𐤁𐤕.𐤏𐤋.𐤁𐤍𐤉𐤌.
𐤏𐤋.𐤔𐤋𐤔𐤉𐤌.𐤅𐤏𐤋.𐤓𐤁𐤏𐤉𐤌.𐤋𐤔𐤍𐤀𐤉|
6 𐤅𐤏𐤔𐤄.𐤇𐤎𐤃.𐤋𐤀𐤋𐤐𐤉𐤌.𐤋𐤀𐤄𐤁𐤉.𐤅𐤋𐤔𐤌𐤓𐤉.𐤌𐤑𐤅
𐤕𐤉|
7 𐤋𐤀.𐤕𐤔𐤀.𐤀𐤕.𐤔𐤌.𐤉𐤄𐤅𐤄.𐤀𐤋𐤄𐤉𐤊.𐤋𐤔𐤅𐤀.𐤊𐤉.𐤋
𐤀.𐤉𐤍𐤒𐤄.𐤉𐤄𐤅𐤄.𐤀𐤕.𐤀𐤔𐤓.𐤉𐤔𐤀.𐤀𐤕.𐤔𐤌𐤅.𐤋𐤔𐤅𐤀|
8 𐤆𐤊𐤅𐤓.𐤀𐤕.𐤉𐤅𐤌.𐤄𐤔𐤁𐤕.𐤋𐤒𐤃𐤔𐤅|
9 𐤔𐤔𐤕.𐤉𐤌𐤉𐤌.𐤕𐤏𐤁𐤃.𐤅𐤏𐤔𐤉𐤕.𐤊𐤋.𐤌𐤋𐤀𐤊𐤕𐤊|
10 𐤅𐤉𐤅𐤌.𐤄𐤔𐤁𐤉𐤏𐤉.𐤔𐤁𐤕.𐤋𐤉𐤄𐤅𐤄.𐤀𐤋𐤄𐤉𐤊.𐤋𐤀.𐤕
𐤏𐤔𐤄.𐤊𐤋.𐤌𐤋𐤀𐤊𐤄.𐤀𐤕𐤄.𐤅𐤁𐤍𐤊.𐤅𐤁𐤕𐤊.𐤏𐤁𐤃𐤊.𐤅𐤀𐤌𐤕
𐤊.𐤅𐤁𐤄𐤌𐤕𐤊.𐤅𐤂𐤓𐤊.𐤀𐤔𐤓.𐤁𐤔𐤏𐤓𐤉𐤊|
11 𐤊𐤉.𐤔𐤔𐤕.𐤉𐤌𐤉𐤌.𐤏𐤔𐤄.𐤉𐤄𐤅𐤄.𐤀𐤕.𐤄𐤔𐤌𐤉𐤌.𐤅𐤀
𐤕.𐤄𐤀𐤓𐤑.𐤀𐤕.𐤄𐤉𐤌.𐤅𐤀𐤕.𐤊𐤋.𐤀𐤔𐤓.𐤁𐤌.𐤅𐤉𐤍𐤇.𐤁𐤉𐤅𐤌.
𐤄𐤔𐤁𐤉𐤏𐤉.𐤏𐤋.𐤊𐤍.𐤁𐤓𐤊.𐤉𐤄𐤅𐤄.𐤀𐤕.𐤉𐤅𐤌.𐤄𐤔𐤁𐤕.𐤅𐤉𐤒
𐤃𐤔𐤄𐤅|
12 𐤊𐤁𐤃.𐤀𐤕.𐤀𐤁𐤉𐤊.𐤅𐤀𐤕.𐤀𐤌𐤊.𐤋𐤌𐤏𐤍.𐤉𐤀𐤓𐤊𐤅𐤍.𐤉
𐤌𐤉𐤊.𐤏𐤋.𐤄𐤀𐤃𐤌𐤄.𐤀𐤔𐤓.𐤉𐤄𐤅𐤄.𐤀𐤋𐤄𐤉𐤊.𐤍𐤕𐤍.𐤋𐤊|
13 𐤋𐤀.𐤕𐤓𐤑𐤇|
14 𐤋𐤀.𐤕𐤍𐤀𐤐|
15 𐤋𐤀.𐤕𐤂𐤍𐤁|

..16.. לא.תענה.ברעך.עד.שקר|

..17.. לא.תחמד.בית.רעך.לא.תחמד.אשת.רעך.ועבדו.ואמתו.ושורו.וחמרו.וכל.אשר.לרעך|

..18.. וכל.העם.ראים.את.הקולת.ואת.הלפידם.ואת.קול.השפר.ואת.ההר.עשן.וירא.העם.וינעו.ויעמדו.מרחק|

..19.. ויאמרו.אל.משה.דבר.אתה.עמנו.ונשמעה.ואל.ידבר.עמנו.אלהים.פן.נמות|

..20.. ויאמר.משה.אל.העם.אל.תיראו.כי.לבעבור.נסות.אתכם.בא.האלהים.ובעבור.תהיה.יראתו.על.פניכם.לבלתי.תחטאו|

..21.. ויעמד.העם.מרחק.ומשה.נגש.אל.הערפל.אשר.שם.האלהים|

..22.. ויאמר.יהוה.אל.משה.כה.תאמר.אל.בני.ישראל.אתם.ראיתם.כי.מן.השמים.דברתי.עמכם|

..23.. לא.תעשון.אתי.אלהי.כסף.ואלהי.זהב.לא.תעשו.לכם|

..24.. מזבח.אדמה.תעשה.לי.וזבחת.עליו.את.עלתיך.ואת.שלמיך.את.צאנך.ואת.בקרך.בכל.המקום.אשר.אזכיר.את.שמי.אבוא.אליך.וברכתיך|

..25.. ואם.מזבח.אבנים.תעשה.לי.לא.תבנה.אתהן.גזית.כי.חרבך.הנפת.עליה.ותחללה|

..26.. ולא.תעלה.במעלת.על.מזבחי.אשר.לא.תגלה.ערותך.עליו||

ויעלו.ממצרים.חלק ..21..

..1.. ואלה.המשפטים.אשר.תשים.לפניהם|

ב כי.תקנה.עבד.עברי.שש.שנים.יעבד.ובשבעת.יצא.לחפשי.חנם|

ג אם.בגפו.יבא.בגפו.יצא.אם.בעל.אשה.הוא.ויצאה.אשתו.עמו|

ד אם.אדניו.יתן.לו.אשה.וילדה.לו.בנים.או.בנות.האשה.וילדיה.תהיה.לאדניה.והוא.יצא.בגפו|

ה ואם.אמר.יאמר.העבד.אהבתי.את.אדני.את.אשתי.ואת.בני.לא.אצא.חפשי|

ו והגישו.אדניו.אל.האלהים.והגישו.אל.הדלת.או.אל.המזוזה.ורצע.אדניו.את.אזנו.במרצע.ועבדו.לעלם|

ז וכי.ימכר.איש.את.בתו.לאמה.לא.תצא.כצאת.העבדים|

ח אם.רעה.בעיני.אדניה.אשר.לא.||לו.קרי||.יעדה.והפדה.לעם.נכרי.לא.ימשל.למכרה.בבגדו.בה|

ט ואם.לבנו.ייעדנה.כמשפט.הבנות.יעשה.לה|

י אם.אחרת.יקח.לו.שארה.כסותה.וענתה.לא.יגרע|

יא ואם.שלש.אלה.לא.יעשה.לה.ויצאה.חנם.אין.כסף|

יב מכה.איש.ומת.מות.יומת|

יג ואשר.לא.צדה.והאלהים.אנה.לידו.ושמתי.לך.מקום.אשר.ינוס.שמה|

יד וכי.יזד.איש.על.רעהו.להרגו.בערמה.מעם.מזבחי.תקחנו.למות|

טו ומכה.אביו.ואמו.מות.יומת|

טז וגנב.איש.ומכרו.ונמצא.בידו.מות.יומת|

יז ומקלל.אביו.ואמו.מות.יומת|

18 𐤅𐤊𐤉.𐤉𐤓𐤉𐤁𐤍.𐤀𐤍𐤔𐤉𐤌.𐤅𐤄𐤊𐤄.𐤀𐤉𐤔.𐤀𐤕.𐤓𐤏𐤄𐤅.𐤁
𐤀𐤁𐤍.𐤀𐤅.𐤁𐤀𐤂𐤓𐤐.𐤅𐤋𐤀.𐤉𐤌𐤅𐤕.𐤅𐤍𐤐𐤋.𐤋𐤌𐤔𐤊𐤁|
19 𐤀𐤌.𐤉𐤒𐤅𐤌.𐤅𐤄𐤕𐤄𐤋𐤊.𐤁𐤇𐤅𐤑.𐤏𐤋.𐤌𐤔𐤏𐤍𐤕𐤅.𐤅𐤍
𐤒𐤄.𐤄𐤌𐤊𐤄.𐤓𐤒.𐤔𐤁𐤕𐤅.𐤉𐤕𐤍.𐤅𐤓𐤐𐤀.𐤉𐤓𐤐𐤀|
20 𐤅𐤊𐤉.𐤉𐤊𐤄.𐤀𐤉𐤔.𐤀𐤕.𐤏𐤁𐤃𐤅.𐤀𐤅.𐤀𐤕.𐤀𐤌𐤕𐤅.𐤁𐤔
𐤁𐤈.𐤅𐤌𐤕.𐤕𐤇𐤕.𐤉𐤃𐤅.𐤍𐤒𐤌.𐤉𐤍𐤒𐤌|
21 𐤀𐤊.𐤀𐤌.𐤉𐤅𐤌.𐤀𐤅.𐤉𐤅𐤌𐤉𐤌.𐤉𐤏𐤌𐤃.𐤋𐤀.𐤉𐤒𐤌.𐤊𐤉.
𐤊𐤎𐤐𐤅.𐤄𐤅𐤀|
22 𐤅𐤊𐤉.𐤉𐤍𐤑𐤅.𐤀𐤍𐤔𐤉𐤌.𐤅𐤍𐤂𐤐𐤅.𐤀𐤔𐤄.𐤄𐤓𐤄.𐤅𐤉𐤑𐤀𐤅.
𐤉𐤋𐤃𐤉𐤄.𐤅𐤋𐤀.𐤉𐤄𐤉𐤄.𐤀𐤎𐤅𐤍.𐤏𐤍𐤅𐤔.𐤉𐤏𐤍𐤔.𐤊𐤀𐤔𐤓.𐤉
𐤔𐤉𐤕.𐤏𐤋𐤉𐤅.𐤁𐤏𐤋.𐤄𐤀𐤔𐤄.𐤅𐤍𐤕𐤍.𐤁𐤐𐤋𐤋𐤉𐤌|
23 𐤅𐤀𐤌.𐤀𐤎𐤅𐤍.𐤉𐤄𐤉𐤄.𐤅𐤍𐤕𐤕𐤄.𐤍𐤐𐤔.𐤕𐤇𐤕.𐤍𐤐𐤔|
24 𐤏𐤉𐤍.𐤕𐤇𐤕.𐤏𐤉𐤍.𐤔𐤍.𐤕𐤇𐤕.𐤔𐤍.𐤉𐤃.𐤕𐤇𐤕.𐤉𐤃
.𐤓𐤂𐤋.𐤕𐤇𐤕.𐤓𐤂𐤋|
25 𐤊𐤅𐤉𐤄.𐤕𐤇𐤕.𐤊𐤅𐤉𐤄.𐤐𐤑𐤏.𐤕𐤇𐤕.𐤐𐤑𐤏.𐤇𐤁𐤅𐤓𐤄.
𐤕𐤇𐤕.𐤇𐤁𐤅𐤓𐤄|
26 𐤅𐤊𐤉.𐤉𐤊𐤄.𐤀𐤉𐤔.𐤀𐤕.𐤏𐤉𐤍.𐤏𐤁𐤃𐤅.𐤀𐤅.𐤀𐤕.𐤏𐤉𐤍.
𐤀𐤌𐤕𐤅.𐤅𐤔𐤇𐤕𐤄.𐤋𐤇𐤐𐤔𐤉.𐤉𐤔𐤋𐤇𐤍𐤅.𐤕𐤇𐤕.𐤏𐤉𐤍𐤅|
27 𐤅𐤀𐤌.𐤔𐤍.𐤏𐤁𐤃𐤅.𐤀𐤅.𐤔𐤍.𐤀𐤌𐤕𐤅.𐤉𐤐𐤉𐤋.𐤋𐤇𐤐𐤔𐤉.
𐤉𐤔𐤋𐤇𐤍𐤅.𐤕𐤇𐤕.𐤔𐤍𐤅|
28 𐤅𐤊𐤉.𐤉𐤂𐤇.𐤔𐤅𐤓.𐤀𐤕.𐤀𐤉𐤔.𐤀𐤅.𐤀𐤕.𐤀𐤔𐤄.𐤅𐤌𐤕.
𐤎𐤒𐤅𐤋.𐤉𐤎𐤒𐤋.𐤄𐤔𐤅𐤓.𐤅𐤋𐤀.𐤉𐤀𐤊𐤋.𐤀𐤕.𐤁𐤔𐤓𐤅.𐤅𐤁𐤏𐤋.𐤄
𐤔𐤅𐤓.𐤍𐤒𐤉|
29 𐤅𐤀𐤌.𐤔𐤅𐤓.𐤍𐤂𐤇.𐤄𐤅𐤀.𐤌𐤕𐤌𐤋.𐤔𐤋𐤔𐤌.𐤅𐤄𐤅𐤏𐤃.𐤁
𐤁𐤏𐤋𐤉𐤅.𐤅𐤋𐤀.𐤉𐤔𐤌𐤓𐤍𐤅.𐤅𐤄𐤌𐤉𐤕.𐤀𐤉𐤔.𐤀𐤅.𐤀𐤔𐤄.𐤄𐤔𐤅𐤓
.𐤉𐤎𐤒𐤋.𐤅𐤂𐤌.𐤁𐤏𐤋𐤉𐤅.𐤉𐤅𐤌𐤕|
30 𐤀𐤌.𐤊𐤐𐤓.𐤉𐤅𐤔𐤕.𐤏𐤋𐤉𐤅.𐤅𐤍𐤕𐤍.𐤐𐤃𐤉𐤅𐤍.𐤍𐤐𐤔𐤅.𐤊𐤊𐤋.
𐤀𐤔𐤓.𐤉𐤅𐤔𐤕.𐤏𐤋𐤉𐤅|
31 𐤀𐤅.𐤁𐤍.𐤉𐤂𐤇.𐤀𐤅.𐤁𐤕.𐤉𐤂𐤇.𐤊𐤌𐤔𐤐𐤈.𐤄𐤆𐤄.𐤉𐤏
𐤔𐤄.𐤋𐤅|

..32.. 𐤀𐤌.𐤏𐤁𐤃.𐤉𐤂𐤇.𐤄𐤔𐤅𐤓.𐤀𐤅.𐤀𐤌𐤄.𐤊𐤎𐤐.𐤔𐤋𐤔𐤉
𐤌.𐤔𐤒𐤋𐤉𐤌.𐤉𐤕𐤍.𐤋𐤀𐤃𐤍𐤉𐤅.𐤅𐤄𐤔𐤅𐤓.𐤉𐤎𐤒𐤋|
..33.. 𐤅𐤊𐤉.𐤉𐤐𐤕𐤇.𐤀𐤉𐤔.𐤁𐤅𐤓.𐤀𐤅.𐤊𐤉.𐤉𐤊𐤓𐤄.𐤀𐤉𐤔.𐤁𐤓.
𐤅𐤋𐤀.𐤉𐤊𐤎𐤍𐤅.𐤅𐤍𐤐𐤋.𐤔𐤌𐤄.𐤔𐤅𐤓.𐤀𐤅.𐤇𐤌𐤅𐤓|
..34.. 𐤁𐤏𐤋.𐤄𐤁𐤅𐤓.𐤉𐤔𐤋𐤌.𐤊𐤎𐤐.𐤉𐤔𐤉𐤁.𐤋𐤁𐤏𐤋𐤉𐤅.𐤅𐤄𐤌
𐤕.𐤉𐤄𐤉𐤄.𐤋𐤅|
..35.. 𐤅𐤊𐤉.𐤉𐤂𐤐.𐤔𐤅𐤓.𐤀𐤉𐤔.𐤀𐤕.𐤔𐤅𐤓.𐤓𐤏𐤄𐤅.𐤅𐤌𐤕.𐤅𐤌𐤊
𐤓𐤅.𐤀𐤕.𐤄𐤔𐤅𐤓.𐤄𐤇𐤉.𐤅𐤇𐤑𐤅.𐤀𐤕.𐤊𐤎𐤐𐤅.𐤅𐤂𐤌.𐤀𐤕.𐤄𐤌
𐤕.𐤉𐤇𐤑𐤅𐤍|
..36.. 𐤀𐤅.𐤍𐤅𐤃𐤏.𐤊𐤉.𐤔𐤅𐤓.𐤍𐤂𐤇.𐤄𐤅𐤀.𐤌𐤕𐤌𐤅𐤋.𐤔𐤋𐤔𐤌.𐤅
𐤋𐤀.𐤉𐤔𐤌𐤓𐤍𐤅.𐤁𐤏𐤋𐤉𐤅.𐤔𐤋𐤌.𐤉𐤔𐤋𐤌.𐤔𐤅𐤓.𐤕𐤇𐤕.𐤄𐤔𐤅𐤓.
𐤅𐤄𐤌𐤕.𐤉𐤄𐤉𐤄.𐤋𐤅|
..37.. 𐤊𐤉.𐤉𐤂𐤍𐤁.𐤀𐤉𐤔.𐤔𐤅𐤓.𐤀𐤅.𐤔𐤄.𐤅𐤈𐤁𐤇𐤅.𐤀𐤅.𐤌𐤊𐤓
𐤅.𐤇𐤌𐤔𐤄.𐤁𐤒𐤓.𐤉𐤔𐤋𐤌.𐤕𐤇𐤕.𐤄𐤔𐤅𐤓.𐤅𐤀𐤓𐤁𐤏.𐤑𐤀𐤍.𐤕
𐤇𐤕.𐤄𐤔𐤄||

𐤅𐤉𐤏𐤋𐤅.𐤌𐤌𐤑𐤓𐤉𐤌.𐤇𐤋𐤒 ..22..

..1.. 𐤀𐤌.𐤁𐤌𐤇𐤕𐤓𐤕.𐤉𐤌𐤑𐤀.𐤄𐤂𐤍𐤁.𐤅𐤄𐤊𐤄.𐤅𐤌𐤕.𐤀𐤉𐤍.
𐤋𐤅.𐤃𐤌𐤉𐤌|
..2.. 𐤀𐤌.𐤆𐤓𐤇𐤄.𐤄𐤔𐤌𐤔.𐤏𐤋𐤉𐤅.𐤃𐤌𐤉𐤌.𐤋𐤅.𐤔𐤋𐤌.𐤉𐤔𐤋
𐤌.𐤀𐤌.𐤀𐤉𐤍.𐤋𐤅.𐤅𐤍𐤌𐤊𐤓.𐤁𐤂𐤍𐤁𐤕𐤅|
..3.. 𐤀𐤌.𐤄𐤌𐤑𐤀.𐤕𐤌𐤑𐤀.𐤁𐤉𐤃𐤅.𐤄𐤂𐤍𐤁𐤄.𐤌𐤔𐤅𐤓.𐤏𐤃.
𐤇𐤌𐤅𐤓.𐤏𐤃.𐤔𐤄.𐤇𐤉𐤉𐤌.𐤔𐤍𐤉𐤌.𐤉𐤔𐤋𐤌|
..4.. 𐤊𐤉.𐤉𐤁𐤏𐤓.𐤀𐤉𐤔.𐤔𐤃𐤄.𐤀𐤅.𐤊𐤓𐤌.𐤅𐤔𐤋𐤇.𐤀𐤕.𐤁𐤏
𐤉𐤓𐤄.||𐤁𐤏𐤉𐤓𐤅.𐤒𐤓𐤉||.𐤅𐤁𐤏𐤓.𐤁𐤔𐤃𐤄.𐤀𐤇𐤓.𐤌𐤉𐤈𐤁.𐤔
𐤃𐤄𐤅.𐤅𐤌𐤉𐤈𐤁.𐤊𐤓𐤌𐤅.𐤉𐤔𐤋𐤌|
..5.. 𐤊𐤉.𐤕𐤑𐤀.𐤀𐤔.𐤅𐤌𐤑𐤀𐤄.𐤒𐤑𐤉𐤌.𐤅𐤍𐤀𐤊𐤋.𐤂𐤃𐤉𐤔.
𐤀𐤅.𐤄𐤒𐤌𐤄.𐤀𐤅.𐤄𐤔𐤃𐤄.𐤔𐤋𐤌.𐤉𐤔𐤋𐤌.𐤄𐤌𐤁𐤏𐤓.𐤀𐤕.𐤄
𐤁𐤏𐤓𐤄|

𐤅 𐤊𐤉.𐤉𐤕𐤍.𐤀𐤉𐤔.𐤀𐤋.𐤓𐤏𐤄𐤅.𐤊𐤎𐤐.𐤀𐤅.𐤊𐤋𐤉𐤌.𐤋𐤔𐤌𐤓.
𐤅𐤂𐤍𐤁.𐤌𐤁𐤉𐤕.𐤄𐤀𐤉𐤔.𐤀𐤌.𐤉𐤌𐤑𐤀.𐤄𐤂𐤍𐤁.𐤉𐤔𐤋𐤌.𐤔𐤍
𐤉𐤌|
𐤆 𐤀𐤌.𐤋𐤀.𐤉𐤌𐤑𐤀.𐤄𐤂𐤍𐤁.𐤅𐤍𐤒𐤓𐤁.𐤁𐤏𐤋.𐤄𐤁𐤉𐤕.𐤀𐤋.
𐤄𐤀𐤋𐤄𐤉𐤌.𐤀𐤌.𐤋𐤀.𐤔𐤋𐤇.𐤉𐤃𐤅.𐤁𐤌𐤋𐤀𐤊𐤕.𐤓𐤏𐤄𐤅|
𐤇 𐤏𐤋.𐤊𐤋.𐤃𐤁𐤓.𐤐𐤔𐤏.𐤏𐤋.𐤔𐤅𐤓.𐤏𐤋.𐤇𐤌𐤅𐤓.𐤏𐤋.𐤔𐤄.𐤏
𐤋.𐤔𐤋𐤌𐤄.𐤏𐤋.𐤊𐤋.𐤀𐤁𐤃𐤄.𐤀𐤔𐤓.𐤉𐤀𐤌𐤓.𐤊𐤉.𐤄𐤅𐤀.𐤆𐤄.
𐤏𐤃.𐤄𐤀𐤋𐤄𐤉𐤌.𐤉𐤁𐤀.𐤃𐤁𐤓.𐤔𐤍𐤉𐤄𐤌.𐤀𐤔𐤓.𐤉𐤓𐤔𐤉𐤏𐤍.
𐤀𐤋𐤄𐤉𐤌.𐤉𐤔𐤋𐤌.𐤔𐤍𐤉𐤌.𐤋𐤓𐤏𐤄𐤅|
𐤈 𐤊𐤉.𐤉𐤕𐤍.𐤀𐤉𐤔.𐤀𐤋.𐤓𐤏𐤄𐤅.𐤇𐤌𐤅𐤓.𐤀𐤅.𐤔𐤅𐤓.𐤀𐤅.𐤔𐤄
.𐤅𐤊𐤋.𐤁𐤄𐤌𐤄.𐤋𐤔𐤌𐤓.𐤅𐤌𐤕.𐤀𐤅.𐤍𐤔𐤁𐤓.𐤀𐤅.𐤍𐤔𐤁𐤄.𐤀𐤉𐤍.𐤓
𐤀𐤄|
𐤉 𐤔𐤁𐤏𐤕.𐤉𐤄𐤅𐤄.𐤕𐤄𐤉𐤄.𐤁𐤉𐤍.𐤔𐤍𐤉𐤄𐤌.𐤀𐤌.𐤋𐤀.𐤔
𐤋𐤇.𐤉𐤃𐤅.𐤁𐤌𐤋𐤀𐤊𐤕.𐤓𐤏𐤄𐤅.𐤅𐤋𐤒𐤇.𐤁𐤏𐤋𐤉𐤅.𐤅𐤋𐤀.𐤉𐤔𐤋
𐤌|
𐤉𐤀 𐤅𐤀𐤌.𐤂𐤍𐤁.𐤉𐤂𐤍𐤁.𐤌𐤏𐤌𐤅.𐤉𐤔𐤋𐤌.𐤋𐤁𐤏𐤋𐤉𐤅|
𐤉𐤁 𐤀𐤌.𐤈𐤓𐤐.𐤉𐤈𐤓𐤐.𐤉𐤁𐤀𐤄𐤅.𐤏𐤃.𐤄𐤈𐤓𐤐𐤄.𐤋𐤀.𐤉𐤔𐤋
𐤌|
𐤉𐤂 𐤅𐤊𐤉.𐤉𐤔𐤀𐤋.𐤀𐤉𐤔.𐤌𐤏𐤌.𐤓𐤏𐤄𐤅.𐤅𐤍𐤔𐤁𐤓.𐤀𐤅.𐤌𐤕.
𐤁𐤏𐤋𐤉𐤅.𐤀𐤉𐤍.𐤏𐤌𐤅.𐤔𐤋𐤌.𐤉𐤔𐤋𐤌|
𐤉𐤃 𐤀𐤌.𐤁𐤏𐤋𐤉𐤅.𐤏𐤌𐤅.𐤋𐤀.𐤉𐤔𐤋𐤌.𐤀𐤌.𐤔𐤊𐤉𐤓.𐤄𐤅𐤀.𐤁
𐤀.𐤁𐤔𐤊𐤓𐤅|
𐤈𐤅 𐤅𐤊𐤉.𐤉𐤐𐤕𐤄.𐤀𐤉𐤔.𐤁𐤕𐤅𐤋𐤄.𐤀𐤔𐤓.𐤋𐤀.𐤀𐤓𐤔𐤄.𐤅𐤔
𐤊𐤁.𐤏𐤌𐤄.𐤌𐤄𐤓.𐤉𐤌𐤄𐤓𐤍𐤄.𐤋𐤅.𐤋𐤀𐤔𐤄|
𐤈𐤆 𐤀𐤌.𐤌𐤀𐤍.𐤉𐤌𐤀𐤍.𐤀𐤁𐤉𐤄.𐤋𐤕𐤕𐤄.𐤋𐤅.𐤊𐤎𐤐.𐤉𐤔𐤒𐤋.
𐤊𐤌𐤄𐤓.𐤄𐤁𐤕𐤅𐤋𐤕|
𐤉𐤆 𐤌𐤊𐤔𐤐𐤄.𐤋𐤀.𐤕𐤇𐤉𐤄|
𐤉𐤇 𐤊𐤋.𐤔𐤊𐤁.𐤏𐤌.𐤁𐤄𐤌𐤄.𐤌𐤅𐤕.𐤉𐤅𐤌𐤕|
𐤉𐤈 𐤆𐤁𐤇.𐤋𐤀𐤋𐤄𐤉𐤌.𐤉𐤇𐤓𐤌.𐤁𐤋𐤕𐤉.𐤋𐤉𐤄𐤅𐤄.𐤋𐤁𐤃𐤅|
𐤊 𐤅𐤂𐤓.𐤋𐤀.𐤕𐤅𐤍𐤄.𐤅𐤋𐤀.𐤕𐤋𐤇𐤑𐤍𐤅.𐤊𐤉.𐤂𐤓𐤉𐤌.𐤄𐤉𐤉
𐤕𐤌.𐤁𐤀𐤓𐤑.𐤌𐤑𐤓𐤉𐤌|

..𐤊𐤀.. 𐤊𐤋.𐤀𐤋𐤌𐤍𐤄.𐤅𐤉𐤕𐤅𐤌.𐤋𐤀.𐤕𐤏𐤍𐤅𐤍|
..𐤊𐤁.. 𐤀𐤌.𐤏𐤍𐤄.𐤕𐤏𐤍𐤄.𐤀𐤕𐤅.𐤊𐤉.𐤀𐤌.𐤑𐤏𐤒.𐤉𐤑𐤏𐤒.
𐤀𐤋𐤉.𐤔𐤌𐤏.𐤀𐤔𐤌𐤏.𐤑𐤏𐤒𐤕𐤅|
..𐤊𐤂.. 𐤅𐤇𐤓𐤄.𐤀𐤐𐤉.𐤅𐤄𐤓𐤂𐤕𐤉.𐤀𐤕𐤊𐤌.𐤁𐤇𐤓𐤁.𐤅𐤄𐤉𐤅.𐤍𐤔
𐤉𐤊𐤌.𐤀𐤋𐤌𐤍𐤅𐤕.𐤅𐤁𐤍𐤉𐤊𐤌.𐤉𐤕𐤌𐤉𐤌|
..𐤊𐤃.. 𐤀𐤌.𐤊𐤎𐤐.𐤕𐤋𐤅𐤄.𐤀𐤕.𐤏𐤌𐤉.𐤀𐤕.𐤄𐤏𐤍𐤉.𐤏𐤌𐤊.𐤋
𐤀.𐤕𐤄𐤉𐤄.𐤋𐤅.𐤊𐤍𐤔𐤄.𐤋𐤀.𐤕𐤔𐤉𐤌𐤅𐤍.𐤏𐤋𐤉𐤅.𐤍𐤔𐤊|
..𐤊𐤄.. 𐤀𐤌.𐤇𐤁𐤋.𐤕𐤇𐤁𐤋.𐤔𐤋𐤌𐤕.𐤓𐤏𐤊.𐤏𐤃.𐤁𐤀.𐤄𐤔𐤌𐤔
.𐤕𐤔𐤉𐤁𐤍𐤅.𐤋𐤅|
..𐤊𐤅.. 𐤊𐤉.𐤄𐤅𐤀.𐤊𐤎𐤅𐤕𐤄.||𐤊𐤎𐤅𐤕𐤅.𐤒𐤓𐤉||.𐤋𐤁𐤃𐤄.𐤄𐤅𐤀.
𐤔𐤌𐤋𐤕𐤅.𐤋𐤏𐤓𐤅.𐤁𐤌𐤄.𐤉𐤔𐤊𐤁.𐤅𐤄𐤉𐤄.𐤊𐤉.𐤉𐤑𐤏𐤒.𐤀𐤋𐤉.
𐤅𐤔𐤌𐤏𐤕𐤉.𐤊𐤉.𐤇𐤍𐤅𐤍.𐤀𐤍𐤉|
..𐤊𐤆.. 𐤀𐤋𐤄𐤉𐤌.𐤋𐤀.𐤕𐤒𐤋𐤋.𐤅𐤍𐤔𐤉𐤀.𐤁𐤏𐤌𐤊.𐤋𐤀.𐤕𐤀𐤓|
..𐤊𐤇.. 𐤌𐤋𐤀𐤕𐤊.𐤅𐤃𐤌𐤏𐤊.𐤋𐤀.𐤕𐤀𐤇𐤓.𐤁𐤊𐤅𐤓.𐤁𐤍𐤉𐤊.𐤕𐤕
𐤍.𐤋𐤉|
..𐤊𐤈.. 𐤊𐤍.𐤕𐤏𐤔𐤄.𐤋𐤔𐤓𐤊.𐤋𐤑𐤀𐤍𐤊.𐤔𐤁𐤏𐤕.𐤉𐤌𐤉𐤌.𐤉𐤄
𐤉𐤄.𐤏𐤌.𐤀𐤌𐤅.𐤁𐤉𐤅𐤌.𐤄𐤔𐤌𐤉𐤍𐤉.𐤕𐤕𐤍𐤅.𐤋𐤉|
..𐤋.. 𐤅𐤀𐤍𐤔𐤉.𐤒𐤃𐤔.𐤕𐤄𐤉𐤅𐤍.𐤋𐤉.𐤅𐤁𐤔𐤓.𐤁𐤔𐤃𐤄.𐤈𐤓𐤐
𐤄.𐤋𐤀.𐤕𐤀𐤊𐤋𐤅.𐤋𐤊𐤋𐤁.𐤕𐤔𐤋𐤊𐤅𐤍.𐤀𐤕𐤅||

𐤅𐤉𐤏𐤋𐤅.𐤌𐤌𐤑𐤓𐤉𐤌.𐤇𐤋𐤒..𐤊𐤂..

..𐤀.. 𐤋𐤀.𐤕𐤔𐤀.𐤔𐤌𐤏.𐤔𐤅𐤀.𐤀𐤋.𐤕𐤔𐤕.𐤉𐤃𐤊.𐤏𐤌.𐤓𐤔𐤏.
𐤋𐤄𐤉𐤕.𐤏𐤃.𐤇𐤌𐤎|
..𐤁.. 𐤋𐤀.𐤕𐤄𐤉𐤄.𐤀𐤇𐤓𐤉.𐤓𐤁𐤉𐤌.𐤋𐤓𐤏𐤕.𐤅𐤋𐤀.𐤕𐤏𐤍𐤄.𐤏𐤋
.𐤓𐤁.𐤋𐤍𐤈𐤕.𐤀𐤇𐤓𐤉.𐤓𐤁𐤉𐤌.𐤋𐤄𐤈𐤕|
..𐤂.. 𐤅𐤃𐤋.𐤋𐤀.𐤕𐤄𐤃𐤓.𐤁𐤓𐤉𐤁𐤅|
..𐤃.. 𐤊𐤉.𐤕𐤐𐤂𐤏.𐤔𐤅𐤓.𐤀𐤉𐤁𐤊.𐤀𐤅.𐤇𐤌𐤓𐤅.𐤕𐤏𐤄.𐤄𐤔𐤁.𐤕
𐤔𐤉𐤁𐤍𐤅.𐤋𐤅|
..𐤄.. 𐤊𐤉.𐤕𐤓𐤀𐤄.𐤇𐤌𐤅𐤓.𐤔𐤍𐤀𐤊.𐤓𐤁𐤑.𐤕𐤇𐤕.𐤌𐤔𐤀𐤅.𐤅𐤇
𐤃𐤋𐤕.𐤌𐤏𐤆𐤁.𐤋𐤅.𐤏𐤆𐤁.𐤕𐤏𐤆𐤁.𐤏𐤌𐤅|

ו 𐤋𐤀.𐤕𐤈𐤄.𐤌𐤔𐤐𐤈.𐤀𐤁𐤉𐤍𐤊.𐤁𐤓𐤉𐤁𐤅|
ז 𐤌𐤃𐤁𐤓.𐤔𐤒𐤓.𐤕𐤓𐤇𐤒.𐤅𐤍𐤒𐤉.𐤅𐤑𐤃𐤉𐤒.𐤀𐤋.𐤕𐤄𐤓
𐤂.𐤊𐤉.𐤋𐤀.𐤀𐤑𐤃𐤉𐤒.𐤓𐤔𐤏|
ח 𐤅𐤔𐤇𐤃.𐤋𐤀.𐤕𐤒𐤇.𐤊𐤉.𐤄𐤔𐤇𐤃.𐤉𐤏𐤅𐤓.𐤐𐤒𐤇𐤉𐤌.𐤅
𐤉𐤎𐤋𐤐.𐤃𐤁𐤓𐤉.𐤑𐤃𐤉𐤒𐤉𐤌|
ט 𐤅𐤂𐤓.𐤋𐤀.𐤕𐤋𐤇𐤑.𐤅𐤀𐤕𐤌.𐤉𐤃𐤏𐤕𐤌.𐤀𐤕.𐤍𐤐𐤔.𐤄𐤂
𐤓.𐤊𐤉.𐤂𐤓𐤉𐤌.𐤄𐤉𐤉𐤕𐤌.𐤁𐤀𐤓𐤑.𐤌𐤑𐤓𐤉𐤌|
י 𐤅𐤔𐤔.𐤔𐤍𐤉𐤌.𐤕𐤆𐤓𐤏.𐤀𐤕.𐤀𐤓𐤑𐤊.𐤅𐤀𐤎𐤐𐤕.𐤀𐤕.
𐤕𐤁𐤅𐤀𐤕𐤄|
יא 𐤅𐤄𐤔𐤁𐤉𐤏𐤕.𐤕𐤔𐤌𐤈𐤍𐤄.𐤅𐤍𐤈𐤔𐤕𐤄.𐤅𐤀𐤊𐤋𐤅.𐤀𐤁𐤉𐤍
𐤉.𐤏𐤌𐤊.𐤅𐤉𐤕𐤓𐤌.𐤕𐤀𐤊𐤋.𐤇𐤉𐤕.𐤄𐤔𐤃𐤄.𐤊𐤍.𐤕𐤏𐤔𐤄.𐤋
𐤊𐤓𐤌𐤊.𐤋𐤆𐤉𐤕𐤊|
יב 𐤔𐤔𐤕.𐤉𐤌𐤉𐤌.𐤕𐤏𐤔𐤄.𐤌𐤏𐤔𐤉𐤊.𐤅𐤁𐤉𐤅𐤌.𐤄𐤔𐤁𐤉
𐤏𐤉.𐤕𐤔𐤁𐤕.𐤋𐤌𐤏𐤍.𐤉𐤍𐤅𐤇.𐤔𐤅𐤓𐤊.𐤅𐤇𐤌𐤓𐤊.𐤅𐤉𐤍𐤐𐤔.𐤁𐤍.
𐤀𐤌𐤕𐤊.𐤅𐤄𐤂𐤓|
יג 𐤅𐤁𐤊𐤋.𐤀𐤔𐤓.𐤀𐤌𐤓𐤕𐤉.𐤀𐤋𐤉𐤊𐤌.𐤕𐤔𐤌𐤓𐤅.𐤅𐤔𐤌.𐤀𐤋
𐤄𐤉𐤌.𐤀𐤇𐤓𐤉𐤌.𐤋𐤀.𐤕𐤆𐤊𐤉𐤓𐤅.𐤋𐤀.𐤉𐤔𐤌𐤏.𐤏𐤋.𐤐𐤉𐤊|
יד 𐤔𐤋𐤔.𐤓𐤂𐤋𐤉𐤌.𐤕𐤇𐤂.𐤋𐤉.𐤁𐤔𐤍𐤄|
טו 𐤀𐤕.𐤇𐤂.𐤄𐤌𐤑𐤅𐤕.𐤕𐤔𐤌𐤓.𐤔𐤁𐤏𐤕.𐤉𐤌𐤉𐤌.𐤕𐤀𐤊
𐤋.𐤌𐤑𐤅𐤕.𐤊𐤀𐤔𐤓.𐤑𐤅𐤉𐤕𐤊.𐤋𐤌𐤅𐤏𐤃.𐤇𐤃𐤔.𐤄𐤀𐤁𐤉𐤁.𐤊
𐤉.𐤁𐤅.𐤉𐤑𐤀𐤕.𐤌𐤌𐤑𐤓𐤉𐤌.𐤅𐤋𐤀.𐤉𐤓𐤀𐤅.𐤐𐤍𐤉.𐤓𐤉𐤒𐤌|
טז 𐤅𐤇𐤂.𐤄𐤒𐤑𐤉𐤓.𐤁𐤊𐤅𐤓𐤉.𐤌𐤏𐤔𐤉𐤊.𐤀𐤔𐤓.𐤕𐤆𐤓𐤏.
𐤁𐤔𐤃𐤄.𐤅𐤇𐤂.𐤄𐤀𐤎𐤐.𐤁𐤑𐤀𐤕.𐤄𐤔𐤍𐤄.𐤁𐤀𐤎𐤐𐤊.𐤀𐤕.𐤌
𐤏𐤔𐤉𐤊.𐤌𐤍.𐤄𐤔𐤃𐤄|
יז 𐤔𐤋𐤔.𐤐𐤏𐤌𐤉𐤌.𐤁𐤔𐤍𐤄.𐤉𐤓𐤀𐤄.𐤊𐤋.𐤆𐤊𐤅𐤓𐤊.𐤀𐤋.𐤐
𐤍𐤉.𐤄𐤀𐤃𐤍.𐤉𐤄𐤅𐤄|
יח 𐤋𐤀.𐤕𐤆𐤁𐤇.𐤏𐤋.𐤇𐤌𐤑.𐤃𐤌.𐤆𐤁𐤇𐤉.𐤅𐤋𐤀.𐤉𐤋𐤉𐤍.
𐤇𐤋𐤁.𐤇𐤂𐤉.𐤏𐤃.𐤁𐤒𐤓|
יט 𐤓𐤀𐤔𐤉𐤕.𐤁𐤊𐤅𐤓𐤉.𐤀𐤃𐤌𐤕𐤊.𐤕𐤁𐤉𐤀.𐤁𐤉𐤕.𐤉𐤄𐤅𐤄
.𐤀𐤋𐤄𐤉𐤊.𐤋𐤀.𐤕𐤁𐤔𐤋.𐤂𐤃𐤉.𐤁𐤇𐤋𐤁.𐤀𐤌𐤅|

20 𐤄𐤍𐤄.𐤀𐤍𐤊𐤉.𐤔𐤋𐤇.𐤌𐤋𐤀𐤊.𐤋𐤐𐤍𐤉𐤊.𐤋𐤔𐤌𐤓𐤊.𐤁𐤃
𐤓𐤊.𐤅𐤋𐤄𐤁𐤉𐤀𐤊.𐤀𐤋.𐤄𐤌𐤒𐤅𐤌.𐤀𐤔𐤓.𐤄𐤊𐤍𐤕𐤉|
21 𐤄𐤔𐤌𐤓.𐤌𐤐𐤍𐤉𐤅.𐤅𐤔𐤌𐤏.𐤁𐤒𐤋𐤅.𐤀𐤋.𐤕𐤌𐤓.𐤁𐤅.𐤊𐤉.𐤋
𐤀.𐤉𐤔𐤀.𐤋𐤐𐤔𐤏𐤊𐤌.𐤊𐤉.𐤔𐤌𐤉.𐤁𐤒𐤓𐤁𐤅|
22 𐤊𐤉.𐤀𐤌.𐤔𐤌𐤏.𐤕𐤔𐤌𐤏.𐤁𐤒𐤋𐤅.𐤅𐤏𐤔𐤉𐤕.𐤊𐤋.𐤀𐤔𐤓.
𐤀𐤃𐤁𐤓.𐤅𐤀𐤉𐤁𐤕𐤉.𐤀𐤕.𐤀𐤉𐤁𐤉𐤊.𐤅𐤑𐤓𐤕𐤉.𐤀𐤕.𐤑𐤓𐤓𐤉𐤊|
23 𐤊𐤉.𐤉𐤋𐤊.𐤌𐤋𐤀𐤊𐤉.𐤋𐤐𐤍𐤉𐤊.𐤅𐤄𐤁𐤉𐤀𐤊.𐤀𐤋.𐤄𐤀𐤌𐤓
𐤉.𐤅𐤄𐤇𐤕𐤉.𐤅𐤄𐤐𐤓𐤆𐤉.𐤅𐤄𐤊𐤍𐤏𐤍𐤉.𐤄𐤇𐤅𐤉.𐤅𐤄𐤉𐤁𐤅𐤎𐤉.𐤅
𐤄𐤊𐤇𐤃𐤕𐤉𐤅|
24 𐤋𐤀.𐤕𐤔𐤕𐤇𐤅𐤄.𐤋𐤀𐤋𐤄𐤉𐤄𐤌.𐤅𐤋𐤀.𐤕𐤏𐤁𐤃𐤌.𐤅𐤋𐤀
.𐤕𐤏𐤔𐤄.𐤊𐤌𐤏𐤔𐤉𐤄𐤌.𐤊𐤉.𐤄𐤓𐤎.𐤕𐤄𐤓𐤎𐤌.𐤅𐤔𐤁𐤓.𐤕𐤔𐤁
𐤓.𐤌𐤑𐤁𐤕𐤉𐤄𐤌|
25 𐤅𐤏𐤁𐤃𐤕𐤌.𐤀𐤕.𐤉𐤄𐤅𐤄.𐤀𐤋𐤄𐤉𐤊𐤌.𐤅𐤁𐤓𐤊.𐤀𐤕.𐤋𐤇
𐤌𐤊.𐤅𐤀𐤕.𐤌𐤉𐤌𐤉𐤊.𐤅𐤄𐤎𐤓𐤕𐤉.𐤌𐤇𐤋𐤄.𐤌𐤒𐤓𐤁𐤊|
26 𐤋𐤀.𐤕𐤄𐤉𐤄.𐤌𐤔𐤊𐤋𐤄.𐤅𐤏𐤒𐤓𐤄.𐤁𐤀𐤓𐤑𐤊.𐤀𐤕.𐤌𐤎
𐤐𐤓.𐤉𐤌𐤉𐤊.𐤀𐤌𐤋𐤀|
27 𐤀𐤕.𐤀𐤉𐤌𐤕𐤉.𐤀𐤔𐤋𐤇.𐤋𐤐𐤍𐤉𐤊.𐤅𐤄𐤌𐤕𐤉.𐤀𐤕.𐤊𐤋.
𐤄𐤏𐤌.𐤀𐤔𐤓.𐤕𐤁𐤀.𐤁𐤄𐤌.𐤅𐤍𐤕𐤕𐤉.𐤀𐤕.𐤊𐤋.𐤀𐤉𐤁𐤉𐤊.𐤀𐤋
𐤉𐤊.𐤏𐤓𐤐|
28 𐤅𐤔𐤋𐤇𐤕𐤉.𐤀𐤕.𐤄𐤑𐤓𐤏𐤄.𐤋𐤐𐤍𐤉𐤊.𐤅𐤂𐤓𐤔𐤄.𐤀𐤕.
𐤄𐤇𐤅𐤉.𐤀𐤕.𐤄𐤊𐤍𐤏𐤍𐤉.𐤅𐤀𐤕.𐤄𐤇𐤕𐤉.𐤌𐤋𐤐𐤍𐤉𐤊|
29 𐤋𐤀.𐤀𐤂𐤓𐤔𐤍𐤅.𐤌𐤐𐤍𐤉𐤊.𐤁𐤔𐤍𐤄.𐤀𐤇𐤕.𐤐𐤍.𐤕𐤄𐤉𐤄.
𐤄𐤀𐤓𐤑.𐤔𐤌𐤌𐤄.𐤅𐤓𐤁𐤄.𐤏𐤋𐤉𐤊.𐤇𐤉𐤕.𐤄𐤔𐤃𐤄|
30 𐤌𐤏𐤈.𐤌𐤏𐤈.𐤀𐤂𐤓𐤔𐤍𐤅.𐤌𐤐𐤍𐤉𐤊.𐤏𐤃.𐤀𐤔𐤓.𐤕𐤐𐤓
𐤄.𐤅𐤍𐤇𐤋𐤕.𐤀𐤕.𐤄𐤀𐤓𐤑|
31 𐤅𐤔𐤕𐤉.𐤀𐤕.𐤂𐤁𐤋𐤊.𐤌𐤉𐤌.𐤎𐤅𐤐.𐤅𐤏𐤃.𐤉𐤌.𐤐𐤋𐤔𐤕𐤉
𐤌.𐤅𐤌𐤌𐤃𐤁𐤓.𐤏𐤃.𐤄𐤍𐤄𐤓.𐤊𐤉.𐤀𐤕𐤍.𐤁𐤉𐤃𐤊𐤌.𐤀𐤕.𐤉𐤔
𐤁𐤉.𐤄𐤀𐤓𐤑.𐤅𐤂𐤓𐤔𐤕𐤌𐤅.𐤌𐤐𐤍𐤉𐤊|
32 𐤋𐤀.𐤕𐤊𐤓𐤕.𐤋𐤄𐤌.𐤅𐤋𐤀𐤋𐤄𐤉𐤄𐤌.𐤁𐤓𐤉𐤕|
33 𐤋𐤀.𐤉𐤔𐤁𐤅.𐤁𐤀𐤓𐤑𐤊.𐤐𐤍.𐤉𐤇𐤈𐤉𐤀𐤅.𐤀𐤕𐤊.𐤋𐤉.𐤊𐤉
.𐤕𐤏𐤁𐤃.𐤀𐤕.𐤀𐤋𐤄𐤉𐤄𐤌.𐤊𐤉.𐤉𐤄𐤉𐤄.𐤋𐤊.𐤋𐤌𐤅𐤒𐤔||

𐤅𐤉𐤏𐤋𐤅.𐤌𐤌𐤑𐤓𐤉𐤌.𐤇𐤋𐤒 24

1 𐤅𐤀𐤋.𐤌𐤔𐤄.𐤀𐤌𐤓.𐤏𐤋𐤄.𐤀𐤋.𐤉𐤄𐤅𐤄.𐤀𐤕𐤄.𐤅𐤀𐤄𐤓𐤍.𐤍
𐤃𐤁.𐤅𐤀𐤁𐤉𐤄𐤅𐤀.𐤅𐤔𐤁𐤏𐤉𐤌.𐤌𐤆𐤒𐤍𐤉.𐤉𐤔𐤓𐤀𐤋.𐤅𐤄𐤔𐤕
𐤇𐤅𐤉𐤕𐤌.𐤌𐤓𐤇𐤒|

2 𐤅𐤍𐤂𐤔.𐤌𐤔𐤄.𐤋𐤁𐤃𐤅.𐤀𐤋.𐤉𐤄𐤅𐤄.𐤅𐤄𐤌.𐤋𐤀.𐤉𐤂𐤔𐤅.𐤅
𐤄𐤏𐤌.𐤋𐤀.𐤉𐤏𐤋𐤅.𐤏𐤌𐤅|

3 𐤅𐤉𐤁𐤀.𐤌𐤔𐤄.𐤅𐤉𐤎𐤐𐤓.𐤋𐤏𐤌.𐤀𐤕.𐤊𐤋.𐤃𐤁𐤓𐤉.𐤉𐤄𐤅𐤄.
𐤅𐤀𐤕.𐤊𐤋.𐤄𐤌𐤔𐤐𐤈𐤉𐤌.𐤅𐤉𐤏𐤍.𐤊𐤋.𐤄𐤏𐤌.𐤒𐤅𐤋.𐤀𐤇𐤃.𐤅𐤉
𐤀𐤌𐤓𐤅.𐤊𐤋.𐤄𐤃𐤁𐤓𐤉𐤌.𐤀𐤔𐤓.𐤃𐤁𐤓.𐤉𐤄𐤅𐤄.𐤍𐤏𐤔𐤄|

4 𐤅𐤉𐤊𐤕𐤁.𐤌𐤔𐤄.𐤀𐤕.𐤊𐤋.𐤃𐤁𐤓𐤉.𐤉𐤄𐤅𐤄.𐤅𐤉𐤔𐤊𐤌.𐤁
𐤁𐤒𐤓.𐤅𐤉𐤁𐤍.𐤌𐤆𐤁𐤇.𐤕𐤇𐤕.𐤄𐤄𐤓.𐤅𐤔𐤕𐤉𐤌.𐤏𐤔𐤓𐤄.𐤌𐤑
𐤁𐤄.𐤋𐤔𐤍𐤉𐤌.𐤏𐤔𐤓.𐤔𐤁𐤈𐤉.𐤉𐤔𐤓𐤀𐤋|

5 𐤅𐤉𐤔𐤋𐤇.𐤀𐤕.𐤍𐤏𐤓𐤉.𐤁𐤍𐤉.𐤉𐤔𐤓𐤀𐤋.𐤅𐤉𐤏𐤋𐤅.𐤏𐤋𐤕.𐤅𐤉
𐤆𐤁𐤇𐤅.𐤆𐤁𐤇𐤉𐤌.𐤔𐤋𐤌𐤉𐤌.𐤋𐤉𐤄𐤅𐤄.𐤐𐤓𐤉𐤌|

6 𐤅𐤉𐤒𐤇.𐤌𐤔𐤄.𐤇𐤑𐤉.𐤄𐤃𐤌.𐤅𐤉𐤔𐤌.𐤁𐤀𐤂𐤍𐤕.𐤅𐤇𐤑
𐤉.𐤄𐤃𐤌.𐤆𐤓𐤒.𐤏𐤋.𐤄𐤌𐤆𐤁𐤇|

7 𐤅𐤉𐤒𐤇.𐤎𐤐𐤓.𐤄𐤁𐤓𐤉𐤕.𐤅𐤉𐤒𐤓𐤀.𐤁𐤀𐤆𐤍𐤉.𐤄𐤏𐤌.𐤅𐤉
𐤀𐤌𐤓𐤅.𐤊𐤋.𐤀𐤔𐤓.𐤃𐤁𐤓.𐤉𐤄𐤅𐤄.𐤍𐤏𐤔𐤄.𐤅𐤍𐤔𐤌𐤏|

8 𐤅𐤉𐤒𐤇.𐤌𐤔𐤄.𐤀𐤕.𐤄𐤃𐤌.𐤅𐤉𐤆𐤓𐤒.𐤏𐤋.𐤄𐤏𐤌.𐤅𐤉𐤀
𐤌𐤓.𐤄𐤍𐤄.𐤃𐤌.𐤄𐤁𐤓𐤉𐤕.𐤀𐤔𐤓.𐤊𐤓𐤕.𐤉𐤄𐤅𐤄.𐤏𐤌𐤊𐤌.𐤏𐤋.
𐤊𐤋.𐤄𐤃𐤁𐤓𐤉𐤌.𐤄𐤀𐤋𐤄|

9 𐤅𐤉𐤏𐤋.𐤌𐤔𐤄.𐤅𐤀𐤄𐤓𐤍.𐤍𐤃𐤁.𐤅𐤀𐤁𐤉𐤄𐤅𐤀.𐤅𐤔𐤁𐤏𐤉𐤌.
𐤌𐤆𐤒𐤍𐤉.𐤉𐤔𐤓𐤀𐤋|

10 𐤅𐤉𐤓𐤀𐤅.𐤀𐤕.𐤀𐤋𐤄𐤉.𐤉𐤔𐤓𐤀𐤋.𐤅𐤕𐤇𐤕.𐤓𐤂𐤋𐤉𐤅.𐤊𐤌
𐤏𐤔𐤄.𐤋𐤁𐤍𐤕.𐤄𐤎𐤐𐤉𐤓.𐤅𐤊𐤏𐤑𐤌.𐤄𐤔𐤌𐤉𐤌.𐤋𐤈𐤄𐤓|

11 𐤅𐤀𐤋.𐤀𐤑𐤉𐤋𐤉.𐤁𐤍𐤉.𐤉𐤔𐤓𐤀𐤋.𐤋𐤀.𐤔𐤋𐤇.𐤉𐤃𐤅.𐤅𐤉
𐤇𐤆𐤅.𐤀𐤕.𐤄𐤀𐤋𐤄𐤉𐤌.𐤅𐤉𐤀𐤊𐤋𐤅.𐤅𐤉𐤔𐤕𐤅|

יב 𐤅𐤉𐤀𐤌𐤓.𐤉𐤄𐤅𐤄.𐤀𐤋.𐤌𐤔𐤄.𐤏𐤋𐤄.𐤀𐤋𐤉.𐤄𐤄𐤓𐤄.𐤅𐤄
𐤉𐤄.𐤔𐤌.𐤅𐤀𐤕𐤍𐤄.𐤋𐤊.𐤀𐤕.𐤋𐤇𐤕.𐤄𐤀𐤁𐤍.𐤅𐤄𐤕𐤅𐤓𐤄.𐤅𐤄𐤌
𐤑𐤅𐤄.𐤀𐤔𐤓.𐤊𐤕𐤁𐤕𐤉.𐤋𐤄𐤅𐤓𐤕𐤌|

יג 𐤅𐤉𐤒𐤌.𐤌𐤔𐤄.𐤅𐤉𐤄𐤅𐤔𐤏.𐤌𐤔𐤓𐤕𐤅.𐤅𐤉𐤏𐤋.𐤌𐤔𐤄.𐤀𐤋
.𐤄𐤓.𐤄𐤀𐤋𐤄𐤉𐤌|

יד 𐤅𐤀𐤋.𐤄𐤆𐤒𐤍𐤉𐤌.𐤀𐤌𐤓.𐤔𐤁𐤅.𐤋𐤍𐤅.𐤁𐤆𐤄.𐤏𐤃.𐤀𐤔
𐤓.𐤍𐤔𐤅𐤁.𐤀𐤋𐤉𐤊𐤌.𐤅𐤄𐤍𐤄.𐤀𐤄𐤓𐤍.𐤅𐤇𐤅𐤓.𐤏𐤌𐤊𐤌.𐤌𐤉.𐤁𐤏
𐤋.𐤃𐤁𐤓𐤉𐤌.𐤉𐤂𐤔.𐤀𐤋𐤄𐤌|

יה 𐤅𐤉𐤏𐤋.𐤌𐤔𐤄.𐤀𐤋.𐤄𐤄𐤓.𐤅𐤉𐤊𐤎.𐤄𐤏𐤍𐤍.𐤀𐤕.𐤄𐤄𐤓|

יו 𐤅𐤉𐤔𐤊𐤍.𐤊𐤁𐤅𐤃.𐤉𐤄𐤅𐤄.𐤏𐤋.𐤄𐤓.𐤎𐤉𐤍𐤉.𐤅𐤉𐤊𐤎𐤄𐤅.𐤄
𐤏𐤍𐤍.𐤔𐤔𐤕.𐤉𐤌𐤉𐤌.𐤅𐤉𐤒𐤓𐤀.𐤀𐤋.𐤌𐤔𐤄.𐤁𐤉𐤅𐤌.𐤄𐤔𐤁𐤉𐤏
𐤉.𐤌𐤕𐤅𐤊.𐤄𐤏𐤍𐤍|

יז 𐤅𐤌𐤓𐤀𐤄.𐤊𐤁𐤅𐤃.𐤉𐤄𐤅𐤄.𐤊𐤀𐤔.𐤀𐤊𐤋𐤕.𐤁𐤓𐤀𐤔.𐤄𐤄
𐤓.𐤋𐤏𐤉𐤍𐤉.𐤁𐤍𐤉.𐤉𐤔𐤓𐤀𐤋|

יח 𐤅𐤉𐤁𐤀.𐤌𐤔𐤄.𐤁𐤕𐤅𐤊.𐤄𐤏𐤍𐤍.𐤅𐤉𐤏𐤋.𐤀𐤋.𐤄𐤄𐤓.𐤅𐤉𐤄
𐤉.𐤌𐤔𐤄.𐤁𐤄𐤓.𐤀𐤓𐤁𐤏𐤉𐤌.𐤉𐤅𐤌.𐤅𐤀𐤓𐤁𐤏𐤉𐤌.𐤋𐤉𐤋𐤄||

𐤅𐤉𐤏𐤋𐤅.𐤌𐤌𐤑𐤓𐤉𐤌.𐤇𐤋𐤒 כה

א 𐤅𐤉𐤃𐤁𐤓.𐤉𐤄𐤅𐤄.𐤀𐤋.𐤌𐤔𐤄.𐤋𐤀𐤌𐤓|

ב 𐤃𐤁𐤓.𐤀𐤋.𐤁𐤍𐤉.𐤉𐤔𐤓𐤀𐤋.𐤅𐤉𐤒𐤇𐤅.𐤋𐤉.𐤕𐤓𐤅𐤌𐤄.𐤌𐤀
𐤕.𐤊𐤋.𐤀𐤉𐤔.𐤀𐤔𐤓.𐤉𐤃𐤁𐤍𐤅.𐤋𐤁𐤅.𐤕𐤒𐤇𐤅.𐤀𐤕.𐤕𐤓𐤅𐤌𐤕𐤉|

ג 𐤅𐤆𐤀𐤕.𐤄𐤕𐤓𐤅𐤌𐤄.𐤀𐤔𐤓.𐤕𐤒𐤇𐤅.𐤌𐤀𐤕𐤌.𐤆𐤄𐤁.𐤅𐤊
𐤎𐤐.𐤅𐤍𐤇𐤔𐤕|

ד 𐤅𐤕𐤊𐤋𐤕.𐤅𐤀𐤓𐤂𐤌𐤍.𐤅𐤕𐤅𐤋𐤏𐤕.𐤔𐤍𐤉.𐤅𐤔𐤔.𐤅𐤏𐤆𐤉𐤌|

ה 𐤅𐤏𐤓𐤕.𐤀𐤉𐤋𐤌.𐤌𐤀𐤃𐤌𐤉𐤌.𐤅𐤏𐤓𐤕.𐤕𐤇𐤔𐤉𐤌.𐤅𐤏𐤑𐤉
.𐤔𐤈𐤉𐤌|

ו 𐤔𐤌𐤍.𐤋𐤌𐤀𐤓.𐤁𐤔𐤌𐤉𐤌.𐤋𐤔𐤌𐤍.𐤄𐤌𐤔𐤇𐤄.𐤅𐤋𐤒𐤈𐤓𐤕.
𐤄𐤎𐤌𐤉𐤌|

ז 𐤀𐤁𐤍𐤉.𐤔𐤄𐤌.𐤅𐤀𐤁𐤍𐤉.𐤌𐤋𐤀𐤉𐤌.𐤋𐤀𐤐𐤃.𐤅𐤋𐤇𐤔𐤍|

ח 𐤅𐤏𐤔𐤅.𐤋𐤉.𐤌𐤒𐤃𐤔.𐤅𐤔𐤊𐤍𐤕𐤉.𐤁𐤕𐤅𐤊𐤌|

9 ࠊࠊࠋ.ࠀࠔࠓ.ࠀࠍࠉ.ࠌࠓࠀࠄ.ࠀࠅࠕࠊ.ࠀࠕ.ࠕࠁࠍࠉࠕ.ࠄࠌ
ࠔࠊࠍ.ࠅࠀࠕ.ࠕࠁࠍࠉࠕ.ࠊࠋ.ࠊࠋࠉࠅ.ࠅࠊࠍ.ࠕࠏࠔࠅ|
10 ࠅࠏࠔࠅ.ࠀࠓࠅࠍ.ࠏࠑࠉ.ࠔࠈࠉࠌ.ࠀࠌࠕࠉࠌ.ࠅࠇࠑࠉ.ࠀࠓ
ࠊࠅ.ࠅࠀࠌࠄ.ࠅࠇࠑࠉ.ࠓࠇࠁࠅ.ࠅࠀࠌࠄ.ࠅࠇࠑࠉ.ࠒࠌࠕࠅ|
11 ࠅࠑࠐࠉࠕ.ࠀࠕࠅ.ࠆࠄࠁ.ࠈࠄࠅࠓ.ࠌࠁࠉࠕ.ࠅࠌࠇࠅࠑ.ࠕࠑ
ࠐࠍࠅ.ࠅࠏࠔࠉࠕ.ࠏࠋࠉࠅ.ࠆࠓ.ࠆࠄࠁ.ࠎࠁࠉࠁ|
12 ࠅࠉࠑࠒࠕ.ࠋࠅ.ࠀࠓࠁࠏ.ࠈࠁࠏࠕ.ࠆࠄࠁ.ࠅࠍࠕࠕࠄ.ࠏࠋ.
ࠀࠓࠁࠏ.ࠐࠏࠌࠕࠉࠅ.ࠅࠔࠕࠉ.ࠈࠁࠏࠕ.ࠏࠋ.ࠑࠋࠏࠅ.ࠄࠀࠇࠕ.ࠅ
ࠔࠕࠉ.ࠈࠁࠏࠕ.ࠏࠋ.ࠑࠋࠏࠅ.ࠄࠔࠍࠉࠕ|
13 ࠅࠏࠔࠉࠕ.ࠁࠃࠉ.ࠏࠑࠉ.ࠔࠈࠉࠌ.ࠅࠑࠐࠉࠕ.ࠀࠕࠌ.ࠆ
ࠄࠁ|
14 ࠅࠄࠁࠀࠕ.ࠀࠕ.ࠄࠁࠃࠉࠌ.ࠁࠈࠁࠏࠕ.ࠏࠋ.ࠑࠋࠏࠕ.ࠄ
ࠀࠓࠍ.ࠋࠔࠀࠕ.ࠀࠕ.ࠄࠀࠓࠍ.ࠁࠄࠌ|
15 ࠁࠈࠁࠏࠕ.ࠄࠀࠓࠍ.ࠉࠄࠉࠅ.ࠄࠁࠃࠉࠌ.ࠋࠀ.ࠉࠎࠓࠅ.ࠌࠌࠍ
ࠅ|
16 ࠅࠍࠕࠕ.ࠀࠋ.ࠄࠀࠓࠍ.ࠀࠕ.ࠄࠏࠃࠕ.ࠀࠔࠓ.ࠀࠕࠍ.ࠀࠋࠉ
ࠊ|
17 ࠅࠏࠔࠉࠕ.ࠊࠐࠓࠕ.ࠆࠄࠁ.ࠈࠄࠅࠓ.ࠀࠌࠕࠉࠌ.ࠅࠇࠑࠉ.
ࠀࠓࠊࠄ.ࠅࠀࠌࠄ.ࠅࠇࠑࠉ.ࠓࠇࠁࠄ|
18 ࠅࠏࠔࠉࠕ.ࠔࠍࠉࠌ.ࠊࠓࠁࠉࠌ.ࠆࠄࠁ.ࠌࠒࠔࠄ.ࠕࠏࠔࠄ.
ࠀࠕࠌ.ࠌࠔࠍࠉ.ࠒࠑࠅࠕ.ࠄࠊࠐࠓࠕ|
19 ࠅࠏࠔࠄ.ࠊࠓࠅࠁ.ࠀࠇࠃ.ࠌࠒࠑࠄ.ࠌࠆࠄ.ࠅࠊࠓࠅࠁ.ࠀࠇ
ࠃ.ࠌࠒࠑࠄ.ࠌࠆࠄ.ࠌࠍ.ࠄࠊࠐࠓࠕ.ࠕࠏࠔࠅ.ࠀࠕ.ࠄࠊࠓࠁࠉࠌ.
ࠏࠋ.ࠔࠍࠉ.ࠒࠑࠅࠕࠉࠅ|
20 ࠅࠄࠉࠅ.ࠄࠊࠓࠁࠉࠌ.ࠐࠓࠔࠉ.ࠊࠍࠐࠉࠌ.ࠋࠌࠏࠋࠄ.ࠎࠊࠊࠉ
ࠌ.ࠁࠊࠍࠐࠉࠄࠌ.ࠏࠋ.ࠄࠊࠐࠓࠕ.ࠅࠐࠍࠉࠄࠌ.ࠀࠉࠔ.ࠀࠋ.ࠀࠇࠉࠅ
.ࠀࠋ.ࠄࠊࠐࠓࠕ.ࠉࠄࠉࠅ.ࠐࠍࠉ.ࠄࠊࠓࠁࠉࠌ|
21 ࠅࠍࠕࠕ.ࠀࠕ.ࠄࠊࠐࠓࠕ.ࠏࠋ.ࠄࠀࠓࠍ.ࠌࠋࠌࠏࠋࠄ.ࠅࠀࠋ.ࠄ
ࠀࠓࠍ.ࠕࠕࠍ.ࠀࠕ.ࠄࠏࠃࠕ.ࠀࠔࠓ.ࠀࠕࠍ.ࠀࠋࠉࠊ|

𐤊𐤁 𐤅𐤍𐤅𐤏𐤃𐤕𐤉.𐤋𐤊.𐤔𐤌.𐤅𐤃𐤁𐤓𐤕𐤉.𐤀𐤕𐤊.𐤌𐤏𐤋.𐤄𐤊𐤐𐤓
𐤕.𐤌𐤁𐤉𐤍.𐤔𐤍𐤉.𐤄𐤊𐤓𐤁𐤉𐤌.𐤀𐤔𐤓.𐤏𐤋.𐤀𐤓𐤍.𐤄𐤏𐤃𐤕.𐤀𐤕.
𐤊𐤋.𐤀𐤔𐤓.𐤀𐤑𐤅𐤄.𐤀𐤅𐤕𐤊.𐤀𐤋.𐤁𐤍𐤉.𐤉𐤔𐤓𐤀𐤋
𐤊𐤂 𐤅𐤏𐤔𐤉𐤕.𐤔𐤋𐤇𐤍.𐤏𐤑𐤉.𐤔𐤈𐤉𐤌.𐤀𐤌𐤕𐤉𐤌.𐤀𐤓𐤊𐤅.
𐤅𐤀𐤌𐤄.𐤓𐤇𐤁𐤅.𐤅𐤀𐤌𐤄.𐤅𐤇𐤑𐤉.𐤒𐤌𐤕𐤅
𐤊𐤃 𐤅𐤑𐤐𐤉𐤕.𐤀𐤕𐤅.𐤆𐤄𐤁.𐤈𐤄𐤅𐤓.𐤅𐤏𐤔𐤉𐤕.𐤋𐤅.𐤆𐤓.𐤆
𐤄𐤁.𐤎𐤁𐤉𐤁
𐤊𐤄 𐤅𐤏𐤔𐤉𐤕.𐤋𐤅.𐤌𐤎𐤂𐤓𐤕.𐤈𐤐𐤇.𐤎𐤁𐤉𐤁.𐤅𐤏𐤔𐤉𐤕.𐤆𐤓
.𐤆𐤄𐤁.𐤋𐤌𐤎𐤂𐤓𐤕𐤅.𐤎𐤁𐤉𐤁
𐤊𐤅 𐤅𐤏𐤔𐤉𐤕.𐤋𐤅.𐤀𐤓𐤁𐤏.𐤈𐤁𐤏𐤕.𐤆𐤄𐤁.𐤅𐤍𐤕𐤕.𐤀𐤕.𐤄
𐤈𐤁𐤏𐤕.𐤏𐤋.𐤀𐤓𐤁𐤏.𐤄𐤐𐤀𐤕.𐤀𐤔𐤓.𐤋𐤀𐤓𐤁𐤏.𐤓𐤂𐤋𐤉𐤅
𐤊𐤆 𐤋𐤏𐤌𐤕.𐤄𐤌𐤎𐤂𐤓𐤕.𐤕𐤄𐤉𐤉𐤍.𐤄𐤈𐤁𐤏𐤕.𐤋𐤁𐤕𐤉𐤌.
𐤋𐤁𐤃𐤉𐤌.𐤋𐤔𐤀𐤕.𐤀𐤕.𐤄𐤔𐤋𐤇𐤍
𐤊𐤇 𐤅𐤏𐤔𐤉𐤕.𐤀𐤕.𐤄𐤁𐤃𐤉𐤌.𐤏𐤑𐤉.𐤔𐤈𐤉𐤌.𐤅𐤑𐤐𐤉𐤕.
𐤀𐤕𐤌.𐤆𐤄𐤁.𐤅𐤍𐤔𐤀.𐤁𐤌.𐤀𐤕.𐤄𐤔𐤋𐤇𐤍
𐤊𐤈 𐤅𐤏𐤔𐤉𐤕.𐤒𐤏𐤓𐤕𐤉𐤅.𐤅𐤊𐤐𐤕𐤉𐤅.𐤅𐤒𐤔𐤅𐤕𐤉𐤅.𐤅𐤌𐤍𐤒𐤉
𐤕𐤉𐤅.𐤀𐤔𐤓.𐤉𐤎𐤊.𐤁𐤄𐤍.𐤆𐤄𐤁.𐤈𐤄𐤅𐤓.𐤕𐤏𐤔𐤄.𐤀𐤕𐤌
𐤋 𐤅𐤍𐤕𐤕.𐤏𐤋.𐤄𐤔𐤋𐤇𐤍.𐤋𐤇𐤌.𐤐𐤍𐤉𐤌.𐤋𐤐𐤍𐤉.𐤕𐤌𐤉𐤃
𐤋𐤀 𐤅𐤏𐤔𐤉𐤕.𐤌𐤍𐤓𐤕.𐤆𐤄𐤁.𐤈𐤄𐤅𐤓.𐤌𐤒𐤔𐤄.𐤕𐤏𐤔𐤄.𐤄
𐤌𐤍𐤅𐤓𐤄.𐤉𐤓𐤊𐤄.𐤅𐤒𐤍𐤄.𐤂𐤁𐤉𐤏𐤉𐤄.𐤊𐤐𐤕𐤓𐤉𐤄.𐤅𐤐𐤓𐤇𐤉𐤄.
𐤌𐤌𐤍𐤄.𐤉𐤄𐤉𐤅
𐤋𐤁 𐤅𐤔𐤔𐤄.𐤒𐤍𐤉𐤌.𐤉𐤑𐤀𐤉𐤌.𐤌𐤑𐤃𐤉𐤄.𐤔𐤋𐤔𐤄.𐤒𐤍𐤉
.𐤌𐤍𐤓𐤄.𐤌𐤑𐤃𐤄.𐤄𐤀𐤇𐤃.𐤅𐤔𐤋𐤔𐤄.𐤒𐤍𐤉.𐤌𐤍𐤓𐤄.𐤌𐤑𐤃
𐤄.𐤄𐤔𐤍𐤉
𐤋𐤂 𐤔𐤋𐤔𐤄.𐤂𐤁𐤏𐤉𐤌.𐤌𐤔𐤒𐤃𐤉𐤌.𐤁𐤒𐤍𐤄.𐤄𐤀𐤇𐤃.
𐤊𐤐𐤕𐤓.𐤅𐤐𐤓𐤇.𐤅𐤔𐤋𐤔𐤄.𐤂𐤁𐤏𐤉𐤌.𐤌𐤔𐤒𐤃𐤉𐤌.𐤁𐤒𐤍𐤄.𐤄
𐤀𐤇𐤃.𐤊𐤐𐤕𐤓.𐤅𐤐𐤓𐤇.𐤊𐤍.𐤋𐤔𐤔𐤕.𐤄𐤒𐤍𐤉𐤌.𐤄𐤉𐤑𐤀𐤉𐤌.
𐤌𐤍.𐤄𐤌𐤍𐤓𐤄
𐤋𐤃 𐤅𐤁𐤌𐤍𐤓𐤄.𐤀𐤓𐤁𐤏𐤄.𐤂𐤁𐤏𐤉𐤌.𐤌𐤔𐤒𐤃𐤉𐤌.𐤊𐤐𐤕𐤓
𐤉𐤄.𐤅𐤐𐤓𐤇𐤉𐤄

לה 𐤅𐤊𐤐𐤕𐤓.𐤕𐤇𐤕.𐤔𐤍𐤉.𐤄𐤒𐤍𐤉𐤌.𐤌𐤌𐤍𐤄.𐤅𐤊𐤐𐤕𐤓.𐤕
𐤇𐤕.𐤔𐤍𐤉.𐤄𐤒𐤍𐤉𐤌.𐤌𐤌𐤍𐤄.𐤅𐤊𐤐𐤕𐤓.𐤕𐤇𐤕.𐤔𐤍𐤉.𐤄𐤒𐤍𐤉
𐤌.𐤌𐤌𐤍𐤄.𐤋𐤔𐤔𐤕.𐤄𐤒𐤍𐤉𐤌.𐤄𐤉𐤑𐤀𐤉𐤌.𐤌𐤍.𐤄𐤌𐤍𐤓𐤄|
לו 𐤊𐤐𐤕𐤓𐤉𐤄𐤌.𐤅𐤒𐤍𐤕𐤌.𐤌𐤌𐤍𐤄.𐤉𐤄𐤉𐤅.𐤊𐤋𐤄.𐤌𐤒𐤔𐤄
.𐤀𐤇𐤕.𐤆𐤄𐤁.𐤈𐤄𐤅𐤓|
לז 𐤅𐤏𐤔𐤉𐤕.𐤀𐤕.𐤍𐤓𐤕𐤉𐤄.𐤔𐤁𐤏𐤄.𐤅𐤄𐤏𐤋𐤄.𐤀𐤕.𐤍𐤓
𐤕𐤉𐤄.𐤅𐤄𐤀𐤉𐤓.𐤏𐤋.𐤏𐤁𐤓.𐤐𐤍𐤉𐤄|
לח 𐤅𐤌𐤋𐤒𐤇𐤉𐤄.𐤅𐤌𐤇𐤕𐤕𐤉𐤄.𐤆𐤄𐤁.𐤈𐤄𐤅𐤓|
לט 𐤊𐤊𐤓.𐤆𐤄𐤁.𐤈𐤄𐤅𐤓.𐤉𐤏𐤔𐤄.𐤀𐤕𐤄.𐤀𐤕.𐤊𐤋.𐤄𐤊𐤋
𐤉𐤌.𐤄𐤀𐤋𐤄|
מ 𐤅𐤓𐤀𐤄.𐤅𐤏𐤔𐤄.𐤁𐤕𐤁𐤍𐤉𐤕𐤌.𐤀𐤔𐤓.𐤀𐤕𐤄.𐤌𐤓𐤀𐤄.
𐤁𐤄𐤓||

𐤅𐤉𐤏𐤋𐤅.𐤌𐤌𐤑𐤓𐤉𐤌.𐤇𐤋𐤒 כו

א 𐤅𐤀𐤕.𐤄𐤌𐤔𐤊𐤍.𐤕𐤏𐤔𐤄.𐤏𐤔𐤓.𐤉𐤓𐤉𐤏𐤕.𐤔𐤔.𐤌𐤔𐤆
𐤓.𐤅𐤕𐤊𐤋𐤕.𐤅𐤀𐤓𐤂𐤌𐤍.𐤅𐤕𐤋𐤏𐤕.𐤔𐤍𐤉.𐤊𐤓𐤁𐤉𐤌.𐤌𐤏𐤔𐤄.
𐤇𐤔𐤁.𐤕𐤏𐤔𐤄.𐤀𐤕𐤌|
ב 𐤀𐤓𐤊.𐤄𐤉𐤓𐤉𐤏𐤄.𐤄𐤀𐤇𐤕.𐤔𐤌𐤍𐤄.𐤅𐤏𐤔𐤓𐤉𐤌.𐤁𐤀𐤌
𐤄.𐤅𐤓𐤇𐤁.𐤀𐤓𐤁𐤏.𐤁𐤀𐤌𐤄.𐤄𐤉𐤓𐤉𐤏𐤄.𐤄𐤀𐤇𐤕.𐤌𐤃𐤄.𐤀
𐤇𐤕.𐤋𐤊𐤋.𐤄𐤉𐤓𐤉𐤏𐤕|
ג 𐤇𐤌𐤔.𐤄𐤉𐤓𐤉𐤏𐤕.𐤕𐤄𐤉𐤉𐤍.𐤇𐤁𐤓𐤕.𐤀𐤔𐤄.𐤀𐤋.𐤀𐤇
𐤕𐤄.𐤅𐤇𐤌𐤔.𐤉𐤓𐤉𐤏𐤕.𐤇𐤁𐤓𐤕.𐤀𐤔𐤄.𐤀𐤋.𐤀𐤇𐤕𐤄|
ד 𐤅𐤏𐤔𐤉𐤕.𐤋𐤋𐤀𐤕.𐤕𐤊𐤋𐤕.𐤏𐤋.𐤔𐤐𐤕.𐤄𐤉𐤓𐤉𐤏𐤄.𐤄𐤀
𐤇𐤕.𐤌𐤒𐤑𐤄.𐤁𐤇𐤁𐤓𐤕.𐤅𐤊𐤍.𐤕𐤏𐤔𐤄.𐤁𐤔𐤐𐤕.𐤄𐤉𐤓𐤉𐤏𐤄
.𐤄𐤒𐤉𐤑𐤅𐤍𐤄.𐤁𐤌𐤇𐤁𐤓𐤕.𐤄𐤔𐤍𐤉𐤕|
ה 𐤇𐤌𐤔𐤉𐤌.𐤋𐤋𐤀𐤕.𐤕𐤏𐤔𐤄.𐤁𐤉𐤓𐤉𐤏𐤄.𐤄𐤀𐤇𐤕.𐤅𐤇
𐤌𐤔𐤉𐤌.𐤋𐤋𐤀𐤕.𐤕𐤏𐤔𐤄.𐤁𐤒𐤑𐤄.𐤄𐤉𐤓𐤉𐤏𐤄.𐤀𐤔𐤓.𐤁𐤌
𐤇𐤁𐤓𐤕.𐤄𐤔𐤍𐤉𐤕.𐤌𐤒𐤁𐤉𐤋𐤕.𐤄𐤋𐤋𐤀𐤕.𐤀𐤔𐤄.𐤀𐤋.𐤀𐤇
𐤕𐤄|

ו 𐤅𐤏𐤔𐤉𐤕.𐤇𐤌𐤔𐤉𐤌.𐤒𐤓𐤎𐤉.𐤆𐤄𐤁.𐤅𐤇𐤁𐤓𐤕.𐤀𐤕.𐤄𐤉𐤓𐤉𐤏𐤕.𐤀𐤔𐤄.𐤀𐤋.𐤀𐤇𐤕𐤄.𐤁𐤒𐤓𐤎𐤉𐤌.𐤅𐤄𐤉𐤄.𐤄𐤌𐤔𐤊𐤍.𐤀𐤇𐤃|

ז 𐤅𐤏𐤔𐤉𐤕.𐤉𐤓𐤉𐤏𐤕.𐤏𐤆𐤉𐤌.𐤋𐤀𐤄𐤋.𐤏𐤋.𐤄𐤌𐤔𐤊𐤍.𐤏𐤔𐤕𐤉.𐤏𐤔𐤓𐤄.𐤉𐤓𐤉𐤏𐤕.𐤕𐤏𐤔𐤄.𐤀𐤕𐤌|

ח 𐤀𐤓𐤊.𐤄𐤉𐤓𐤉𐤏𐤄.𐤄𐤀𐤇𐤕.𐤔𐤋𐤔𐤉𐤌.𐤁𐤀𐤌𐤄.𐤅𐤓𐤇𐤁.𐤀𐤓𐤁𐤏.𐤁𐤀𐤌𐤄.𐤄𐤉𐤓𐤉𐤏𐤄.𐤄𐤀𐤇𐤕.𐤌𐤃𐤄.𐤀𐤇𐤕.𐤋𐤏𐤔𐤕𐤉.𐤏𐤔𐤓𐤄.𐤉𐤓𐤉𐤏𐤕|

ט 𐤅𐤇𐤁𐤓𐤕.𐤀𐤕.𐤇𐤌𐤔.𐤄𐤉𐤓𐤉𐤏𐤕.𐤋𐤁𐤃.𐤅𐤀𐤕.𐤔𐤔.𐤄𐤉𐤓𐤉𐤏𐤕.𐤋𐤁𐤃.𐤅𐤊𐤐𐤋𐤕.𐤀𐤕.𐤄𐤉𐤓𐤉𐤏𐤄.𐤄𐤔𐤔𐤉𐤕.𐤀𐤋.𐤌𐤅𐤋.𐤐𐤍𐤉.𐤄𐤀𐤄𐤋|

י 𐤅𐤏𐤔𐤉𐤕.𐤇𐤌𐤔𐤉𐤌.𐤋𐤋𐤀𐤕.𐤏𐤋.𐤔𐤐𐤕.𐤄𐤉𐤓𐤉𐤏𐤄.𐤄𐤀𐤇𐤕.𐤄𐤒𐤉𐤑𐤍𐤄.𐤁𐤇𐤁𐤓𐤕.𐤅𐤇𐤌𐤔𐤉𐤌.𐤋𐤋𐤀𐤕.𐤏𐤋.𐤔𐤐𐤕.𐤄𐤉𐤓𐤉𐤏𐤄.𐤄𐤇𐤁𐤓𐤕.𐤄𐤔𐤍𐤉𐤕|

יא 𐤅𐤏𐤔𐤉𐤕.𐤒𐤓𐤎𐤉.𐤍𐤇𐤔𐤕.𐤇𐤌𐤔𐤉𐤌.𐤅𐤄𐤁𐤀𐤕.𐤀𐤕.𐤄𐤒𐤓𐤎𐤉𐤌.𐤁𐤋𐤋𐤀𐤕.𐤅𐤇𐤁𐤓𐤕.𐤀𐤕.𐤄𐤀𐤄𐤋.𐤅𐤄𐤉𐤄.𐤀𐤇𐤃|

יב 𐤅𐤎𐤓𐤇.𐤄𐤏𐤃𐤐.𐤁𐤉𐤓𐤉𐤏𐤕.𐤄𐤀𐤄𐤋.𐤇𐤑𐤉.𐤄𐤉𐤓𐤉𐤏𐤄.𐤄𐤏𐤃𐤐𐤕.𐤕𐤎𐤓𐤇.𐤏𐤋.𐤀𐤇𐤓𐤉.𐤄𐤌𐤔𐤊𐤍|

יג 𐤅𐤄𐤀𐤌𐤄.𐤌𐤆𐤄.𐤅𐤄𐤀𐤌𐤄.𐤌𐤆𐤄.𐤁𐤏𐤃𐤐.𐤁𐤀𐤓𐤊.𐤉𐤓𐤉𐤏𐤕.𐤄𐤀𐤄𐤋.𐤉𐤄𐤉𐤄.𐤎𐤓𐤅𐤇.𐤏𐤋.𐤑𐤃𐤉.𐤄𐤌𐤔𐤊𐤍.𐤌𐤆𐤄.𐤅𐤌𐤆𐤄.𐤋𐤊𐤎𐤕𐤅|

יד 𐤅𐤏𐤔𐤉𐤕.𐤌𐤊𐤎𐤄.𐤋𐤀𐤄𐤋.𐤏𐤓𐤕.𐤀𐤉𐤋𐤌.𐤌𐤀𐤃𐤌𐤉𐤌.𐤅𐤌𐤊𐤎𐤄.𐤏𐤓𐤕.𐤕𐤇𐤔𐤉𐤌.𐤌𐤋𐤌𐤏𐤋𐤄|

טו 𐤅𐤏𐤔𐤉𐤕.𐤀𐤕.𐤄𐤒𐤓𐤔𐤉𐤌.𐤋𐤌𐤔𐤊𐤍.𐤏𐤑𐤉.𐤔𐤈𐤉𐤌.𐤏𐤌𐤃𐤉𐤌|

טז 𐤏𐤔𐤓.𐤀𐤌𐤅𐤕.𐤀𐤓𐤊.𐤄𐤒𐤓𐤔.𐤅𐤀𐤌𐤄.𐤅𐤇𐤑𐤉.𐤄𐤀𐤌𐤄.𐤓𐤇𐤁.𐤄𐤒𐤓𐤔.𐤄𐤀𐤇𐤃|

יז 𐤔𐤕𐤉.𐤉𐤃𐤅𐤕.𐤋𐤒𐤓𐤔.𐤄𐤀𐤇𐤃.𐤌𐤔𐤋𐤁𐤕.𐤀𐤔𐤄.𐤀𐤋.𐤀𐤇𐤕𐤄.𐤊𐤍.𐤕𐤏𐤔𐤄.𐤋𐤊𐤋.𐤒𐤓𐤔𐤉.𐤄𐤌𐤔𐤊𐤍|

𐤉𐤇 𐤅𐤏𐤔𐤉𐤕.𐤀𐤕.𐤄𐤒𐤓𐤔𐤉𐤌.𐤋𐤌𐤔𐤊𐤍.𐤏𐤔𐤓𐤉𐤌.𐤒𐤓𐤔
𐤋𐤐𐤀𐤕.𐤍𐤂𐤁𐤄.𐤕𐤉𐤌𐤍𐤄|

𐤉𐤈 𐤅𐤀𐤓𐤁𐤏𐤉𐤌.𐤀𐤃𐤍𐤉.𐤊𐤎𐤐.𐤕𐤏𐤔𐤄.𐤕𐤇𐤕.𐤏𐤔𐤓𐤉
𐤌.𐤄𐤒𐤓𐤔.𐤔𐤍𐤉.𐤀𐤃𐤍𐤉𐤌.𐤕𐤇𐤕.𐤄𐤒𐤓𐤔.𐤄𐤀𐤇𐤃.𐤋𐤔
𐤕𐤉.𐤉𐤃𐤕𐤉𐤅.𐤅𐤔𐤍𐤉.𐤀𐤃𐤍𐤉𐤌.𐤕𐤇𐤕.𐤄𐤒𐤓𐤔.𐤄𐤀𐤇𐤃.
𐤋𐤔𐤕𐤉.𐤉𐤃𐤕𐤉𐤅|

𐤊 𐤅𐤋𐤑𐤋𐤏.𐤄𐤌𐤔𐤊𐤍.𐤄𐤔𐤍𐤉𐤕.𐤋𐤐𐤀𐤕.𐤑𐤐𐤅𐤍.𐤏𐤔𐤓𐤉
𐤌.𐤒𐤓𐤔|

𐤊𐤀 𐤅𐤀𐤓𐤁𐤏𐤉𐤌.𐤀𐤃𐤍𐤉𐤄𐤌.𐤊𐤎𐤐.𐤔𐤍𐤉.𐤀𐤃𐤍𐤉𐤌.𐤕𐤇
𐤕.𐤄𐤒𐤓𐤔.𐤄𐤀𐤇𐤃.𐤅𐤔𐤍𐤉.𐤀𐤃𐤍𐤉𐤌.𐤕𐤇𐤕.𐤄𐤒𐤓𐤔.𐤄
𐤀𐤇𐤃|

𐤊𐤁 𐤅𐤋𐤉𐤓𐤊𐤕𐤉.𐤄𐤌𐤔𐤊𐤍.𐤉𐤌𐤄.𐤕𐤏𐤔𐤄.𐤔𐤔𐤄.𐤒𐤓𐤔𐤉
𐤌|

𐤊𐤂 𐤅𐤔𐤍𐤉.𐤒𐤓𐤔𐤉𐤌.𐤕𐤏𐤔𐤄.𐤋𐤌𐤒𐤑𐤏𐤕.𐤄𐤌𐤔𐤊𐤍.𐤁
𐤉𐤓𐤊𐤕𐤉𐤌|

𐤊𐤃 𐤅𐤉𐤄𐤉𐤅.𐤕𐤀𐤌𐤉𐤌.𐤌𐤋𐤌𐤈𐤄.𐤅𐤉𐤇𐤃𐤅.𐤉𐤄𐤉𐤅.𐤕𐤌𐤉
𐤌.𐤏𐤋.𐤓𐤀𐤔𐤅.𐤀𐤋.𐤄𐤈𐤁𐤏𐤕.𐤄𐤀𐤇𐤕.𐤊𐤍.𐤉𐤄𐤉𐤄.𐤋𐤔𐤍𐤉
𐤄𐤌.𐤋𐤔𐤍𐤉.𐤄𐤌𐤒𐤑𐤏𐤕.𐤉𐤄𐤉𐤅|

𐤊𐤄 𐤅𐤄𐤉𐤅.𐤔𐤌𐤍𐤄.𐤒𐤓𐤔𐤉𐤌.𐤅𐤀𐤃𐤍𐤉𐤄𐤌.𐤊𐤎𐤐.𐤔𐤔𐤄.
𐤏𐤔𐤓.𐤀𐤃𐤍𐤉𐤌.𐤔𐤍𐤉.𐤀𐤃𐤍𐤉𐤌.𐤕𐤇𐤕.𐤄𐤒𐤓𐤔.𐤄𐤀𐤇𐤃
.𐤅𐤔𐤍𐤉.𐤀𐤃𐤍𐤉𐤌.𐤕𐤇𐤕.𐤄𐤒𐤓𐤔.𐤄𐤀𐤇𐤃|

𐤊𐤅 𐤅𐤏𐤔𐤉𐤕.𐤁𐤓𐤉𐤇𐤌.𐤏𐤑𐤉.𐤔𐤈𐤉𐤌.𐤇𐤌𐤔𐤄.𐤋𐤒𐤓𐤔
𐤉.𐤑𐤋𐤏.𐤄𐤌𐤔𐤊𐤍.𐤄𐤀𐤇𐤃|

𐤊𐤆 𐤅𐤇𐤌𐤔𐤄.𐤁𐤓𐤉𐤇𐤌.𐤋𐤒𐤓𐤔𐤉.𐤑𐤋𐤏.𐤄𐤌𐤔𐤊𐤍.𐤄𐤔
𐤍𐤉𐤕.𐤅𐤇𐤌𐤔𐤄.𐤁𐤓𐤉𐤇𐤌.𐤋𐤒𐤓𐤔𐤉.𐤑𐤋𐤏.𐤄𐤌𐤔𐤊𐤍.𐤋𐤉𐤓
𐤊𐤕𐤉𐤌.𐤉𐤌𐤄|

𐤊𐤇 𐤅𐤄𐤁𐤓𐤉𐤇.𐤄𐤕𐤉𐤊𐤍.𐤁𐤕𐤅𐤊.𐤄𐤒𐤓𐤔𐤉𐤌.𐤌𐤁𐤓𐤇.𐤌𐤍
.𐤄𐤒𐤑𐤄.𐤀𐤋.𐤄𐤒𐤑𐤄|

𐤊𐤈 𐤅𐤀𐤕.𐤄𐤒𐤓𐤔𐤉𐤌.𐤕𐤑𐤐𐤄.𐤆𐤄𐤁.𐤅𐤀𐤕.𐤈𐤁𐤏𐤕𐤉
𐤄𐤌.𐤕𐤏𐤔𐤄.𐤆𐤄𐤁.𐤁𐤕𐤉𐤌.𐤋𐤁𐤓𐤉𐤇𐤌.𐤅𐤑𐤐𐤉𐤕.𐤀𐤕.𐤄
𐤁𐤓𐤉𐤇𐤌.𐤆𐤄𐤁|

30 והקמת.את.המשכן.כמשפטו.אשר.הראית.בהר|

31 ועשית.פרכת.תכלת.וארגמן.ותולעת.שני.ושש.משזר.מעשה.חשב.יעשה.אתה.כרבים|

32 ונתתה.אתה.על.ארבעה.עמודי.שטים.מצפים.זהב.וויהם.זהב.על.ארבעה.אדני.כסף|

33 ונתתה.את.הפרכת.תחת.הקרסים.והבאת.שמה.מבית.לפרכת.את.ארון.העדות.והבדילה.הפרכת.לכם.בין.הקדש.ובין.קדש.הקדשים|

34 ונתת.את.הכפרת.על.ארון.העדת.בקדש.הקדשים|

35 ושמת.את.השלחן.מחוץ.לפרכת.ואת.המנרה.נכח.השלחן.על.צלע.המשכן.תימנה.והשלחן.תתן.על.צלע.צפון|

36 ועשית.מסך.לפתח.האהל.תכלת.וארגמן.ותולעת.שני.ושש.משזר.מעשה.רקם|

37 ועשית.למסך.חמשה.עמודי.שטים.וצפית.אתם.זהב.וויהם.זהב.ויצקת.להם.חמשה.אדני.נחשת||

ויעלו.ממצרים.חלק 27

1 ועשית.את.המזבח.עצי.שטים.חמש.אמות.ארך.וחמש.אמות.רחב.רבוע.יהיה.המזבח.ושלש.אמות.קמתו|

2 ועשית.קרנתיו.על.ארבע.פנתיו.ממנו.תהיין.קרנתיו.וצפית.אתו.נחשת|

3 ועשית.סירתיו.לדשנו.ויעיו.ומזרקתיו.ומזלגתיו.ומחתתיו.לכל.כליו.תעשה.נחשת|

𐤃 𐤅𐤏𐤔𐤉𐤕.𐤋𐤅.𐤌𐤊𐤁𐤓.𐤌𐤏𐤔𐤄.𐤓𐤔𐤕.𐤍𐤇𐤔𐤕.𐤅𐤏𐤔𐤉
𐤕.𐤏𐤋.𐤄𐤓𐤔𐤕.𐤀𐤓𐤁𐤏.𐤈𐤁𐤏𐤕.𐤍𐤇𐤔𐤕.𐤏𐤋.𐤀𐤓𐤁𐤏.𐤒
𐤑𐤅𐤕𐤉𐤅|
𐤄 𐤅𐤍𐤕𐤕𐤄.𐤀𐤕𐤄.𐤕𐤇𐤕.𐤊𐤓𐤊𐤁.𐤄𐤌𐤆𐤁𐤇.𐤌𐤋𐤌𐤈𐤄.𐤅
𐤄𐤉𐤕𐤄.𐤄𐤓𐤔𐤕.𐤏𐤃.𐤇𐤑𐤉.𐤄𐤌𐤆𐤁𐤇|
𐤅 𐤅𐤏𐤔𐤉𐤕.𐤁𐤃𐤉𐤌.𐤋𐤌𐤆𐤁𐤇.𐤁𐤃𐤉.𐤏𐤑𐤉.𐤔𐤈𐤉𐤌.𐤅
𐤑𐤐𐤉𐤕.𐤀𐤕𐤌.𐤍𐤇𐤔𐤕|
𐤆 𐤅𐤄𐤅𐤁𐤀.𐤀𐤕.𐤁𐤃𐤉𐤅.𐤁𐤈𐤁𐤏𐤕.𐤅𐤄𐤉𐤅.𐤄𐤁𐤃𐤉𐤌.𐤏𐤋.
𐤔𐤕𐤉.𐤑𐤋𐤏𐤕.𐤄𐤌𐤆𐤁𐤇.𐤁𐤔𐤀𐤕.𐤀𐤕𐤅|
𐤇 𐤍𐤁𐤅𐤁.𐤋𐤇𐤕.𐤕𐤏𐤔𐤄.𐤀𐤕𐤅.𐤊𐤀𐤔𐤓.𐤄𐤓𐤀𐤄.𐤀𐤕𐤊.𐤁
𐤄𐤓.𐤊𐤍.𐤉𐤏𐤔𐤅|
𐤈 𐤅𐤏𐤔𐤉𐤕.𐤀𐤕.𐤇𐤑𐤓.𐤄𐤌𐤔𐤊𐤍.𐤋𐤐𐤀𐤕.𐤍𐤂𐤁.𐤕𐤉𐤌𐤍
𐤄.𐤒𐤋𐤏𐤉𐤌.𐤋𐤇𐤑𐤓.𐤔𐤔.𐤌𐤔𐤆𐤓.𐤌𐤀𐤄.𐤁𐤀𐤌𐤄.𐤀𐤓𐤊.𐤋
𐤐𐤀𐤄.𐤄𐤀𐤇𐤕|
𐤉 𐤅𐤏𐤌𐤃𐤉𐤅.𐤏𐤔𐤓𐤉𐤌.𐤅𐤀𐤃𐤍𐤉𐤄𐤌.𐤏𐤔𐤓𐤉𐤌.𐤍𐤇𐤔
𐤕.𐤅𐤅𐤉.𐤄𐤏𐤌𐤃𐤉𐤌.𐤅𐤇𐤔𐤒𐤉𐤄𐤌.𐤊𐤎𐤐|
𐤉𐤀 𐤅𐤊𐤍.𐤋𐤐𐤀𐤕.𐤑𐤐𐤅𐤍.𐤁𐤀𐤓𐤊.𐤒𐤋𐤏𐤉𐤌.𐤌𐤀𐤄.𐤀𐤓𐤊.𐤅
𐤏𐤌𐤃𐤅.||𐤅𐤏𐤌𐤅𐤃𐤉𐤅.𐤒𐤓𐤉||.𐤏𐤔𐤓𐤉𐤌.𐤅𐤀𐤃𐤍𐤉𐤄𐤌.𐤏𐤔𐤓
𐤉𐤌.𐤍𐤇𐤔𐤕.𐤅𐤅𐤉.𐤄𐤏𐤌𐤃𐤉𐤌.𐤅𐤇𐤔𐤒𐤉𐤄𐤌.𐤊𐤎𐤐|
𐤉𐤁 𐤅𐤓𐤇𐤁.𐤄𐤇𐤑𐤓.𐤋𐤐𐤀𐤕.𐤉𐤌.𐤒𐤋𐤏𐤉𐤌.𐤇𐤌𐤔𐤉𐤌.𐤀
𐤌𐤄.𐤏𐤌𐤃𐤉𐤄𐤌.𐤏𐤔𐤓𐤄.𐤅𐤀𐤃𐤍𐤉𐤄𐤌.𐤏𐤔𐤓𐤄|
𐤉𐤂 𐤅𐤓𐤇𐤁.𐤄𐤇𐤑𐤓.𐤋𐤐𐤀𐤕.𐤒𐤃𐤌𐤄.𐤌𐤆𐤓𐤇𐤄.𐤇𐤌𐤔
𐤉𐤌.𐤀𐤌𐤄|
𐤉𐤃 𐤅𐤇𐤌𐤔.𐤏𐤔𐤓𐤄.𐤀𐤌𐤄.𐤒𐤋𐤏𐤉𐤌.𐤋𐤊𐤕𐤐.𐤏𐤌𐤃𐤉𐤄
𐤌.𐤔𐤋𐤔𐤄.𐤅𐤀𐤃𐤍𐤉𐤄𐤌.𐤔𐤋𐤔𐤄|
𐤈𐤅 𐤅𐤋𐤊𐤕𐤐.𐤄𐤔𐤍𐤉𐤕.𐤇𐤌𐤔.𐤏𐤔𐤓𐤄.𐤒𐤋𐤏𐤉𐤌.𐤏𐤌𐤃
𐤉𐤄𐤌.𐤔𐤋𐤔𐤄.𐤅𐤀𐤃𐤍𐤉𐤄𐤌.𐤔𐤋𐤔𐤄|
𐤈𐤆 𐤅𐤋𐤔𐤏𐤓.𐤄𐤇𐤑𐤓.𐤌𐤎𐤊.𐤏𐤔𐤓𐤉𐤌.𐤀𐤌𐤄.𐤕𐤊𐤋𐤕.𐤅𐤀
𐤓𐤂𐤌𐤍.𐤅𐤕𐤅𐤋𐤏𐤕.𐤔𐤍𐤉.𐤅𐤔𐤔.𐤌𐤔𐤆𐤓.𐤌𐤏𐤔𐤄.𐤓𐤒𐤌.𐤏𐤌
𐤃𐤉𐤄𐤌.𐤀𐤓𐤁𐤏𐤄.𐤅𐤀𐤃𐤍𐤉𐤄𐤌.𐤀𐤓𐤁𐤏𐤄|

יז כל.עמודי.החצר.סביב.מחשקים.כסף.ו
ויהם.כסף.ואדניהם.נחשת׃
יח ארך.החצר.מאה.באמה.ורחב.חמשים.ב
חמשים.וקמה.חמש.אמות.שש.משזר.ואדני
הם.נחשת׃
יט לכל.כלי.המשכן.בכל.עבדתו.וכל.יתדת
יו.וכל.יתדת.החצר.נחשת׃
כ ואתה.תצוה.את.בני.ישראל.ויקחו.אלי
ך.שמן.זית.זך.כתית.למאור.להעלת.נר.תמי
ד׃
כא באהל.מועד.מחוץ.לפרכת.אשר.על.העד
ת.יערכו.אתו.אהרן.ובניו.מערב.עד.בקר.לפני.
יהוה.חקת.עולם.לדרתם.מאת.בני.ישראל׃׃

ויעלו.ממצרים.חלק כח

א ואתה.הקרב.אליך.את.אהרן.אחיך.ואת.בנ
יו.אתו.מתוך.בני.ישראל.לכהנו.לי.אהרן.נדב.
ואביהוא.אלעזר.ואיתמר.בני.אהרן׃
ב ועשית.בגדי.קדש.לאהרן.אחיך.לכבוד
.ולתפארת׃
ג ואתה.תדבר.אל.כל.חכמי.לב.אשר.מלאתי
ו.רוח.חכמה.ועשו.את.בגדי.אהרן.לקדשו.ל
כהנו.לי׃
ד ואלה.הבגדים.אשר.יעשו.חשן.ואפוד.ומ
עיל.וכתנת.תשבץ.מצנפת.ואבנט.ועשו.בגד
י.קדש.לאהרן.אחיך.ולבניו.לכהנו.לי׃
ה והם.יקחו.את.הזהב.ואת.התכלת.ואת.הא
רגמן.ואת.תולעת.השני.ואת.השש׃
ו ועשו.את.האפד.זהב.תכלת.וארגמן.תולע
ת.שני.ושש.משזר.מעשה.חשב׃

ז 𐤔𐤕𐤉.𐤊𐤕𐤐𐤕.𐤇𐤁𐤓𐤕.𐤉𐤄𐤉𐤄.𐤋𐤅.𐤀𐤋.𐤔𐤍𐤉.𐤒𐤑𐤅𐤕
𐤉𐤅.𐤅𐤇𐤁𐤓|

ח 𐤅𐤇𐤔𐤁.𐤀𐤐𐤃𐤕𐤅.𐤀𐤔𐤓.𐤏𐤋𐤉𐤅.𐤊𐤌𐤏𐤔𐤄𐤅.𐤌𐤌𐤍𐤅.𐤉𐤄
𐤉𐤄.𐤆𐤄𐤁.𐤕𐤊𐤋𐤕.𐤅𐤀𐤓𐤂𐤌𐤍.𐤅𐤕𐤅𐤋𐤏𐤕.𐤔𐤍𐤉.𐤅𐤔𐤔.𐤌𐤔
𐤆𐤓|

ט 𐤅𐤋𐤒𐤇𐤕.𐤀𐤕.𐤔𐤕𐤉.𐤀𐤁𐤍𐤉.𐤔𐤄𐤌.𐤅𐤐𐤕𐤇𐤕.𐤏𐤋𐤉𐤄
𐤌.𐤔𐤌𐤅𐤕.𐤁𐤍𐤉.𐤉𐤔𐤓𐤀𐤋|

י 𐤔𐤔𐤄.𐤌𐤔𐤌𐤕𐤌.𐤏𐤋.𐤄𐤀𐤁𐤍.𐤄𐤀𐤇𐤕.𐤅𐤀𐤕.𐤔𐤌𐤅
𐤕.𐤄𐤔𐤔𐤄.𐤄𐤍𐤅𐤕𐤓𐤉𐤌.𐤏𐤋.𐤄𐤀𐤁𐤍.𐤄𐤔𐤍𐤉𐤕.𐤊𐤕𐤅𐤋𐤃𐤕
𐤌|

יא 𐤌𐤏𐤔𐤄.𐤇𐤓𐤔.𐤀𐤁𐤍.𐤐𐤕𐤅𐤇𐤉.𐤇𐤕𐤌.𐤕𐤐𐤕𐤇.𐤀𐤕.
𐤔𐤕𐤉.𐤄𐤀𐤁𐤍𐤉𐤌.𐤏𐤋.𐤔𐤌𐤕.𐤁𐤍𐤉.𐤉𐤔𐤓𐤀𐤋.𐤌𐤎𐤁𐤕.𐤌𐤔
𐤁𐤑𐤅𐤕.𐤆𐤄𐤁.𐤕𐤏𐤔𐤄.𐤀𐤕𐤌|

יב 𐤅𐤔𐤌𐤕.𐤀𐤕.𐤔𐤕𐤉.𐤄𐤀𐤁𐤍𐤉𐤌.𐤏𐤋.𐤊𐤕𐤐𐤕.𐤄𐤀𐤐𐤃.
𐤀𐤁𐤍𐤉.𐤆𐤊𐤓𐤍.𐤋𐤁𐤍𐤉.𐤉𐤔𐤓𐤀𐤋.𐤅𐤍𐤔𐤀.𐤀𐤄𐤓𐤍.𐤀𐤕.𐤔𐤌𐤅
𐤕𐤌.𐤋𐤐𐤍𐤉.𐤉𐤄𐤅𐤄.𐤏𐤋.𐤔𐤕𐤉.𐤊𐤕𐤐𐤉𐤅.𐤋𐤆𐤊𐤓𐤍|

יג 𐤅𐤏𐤔𐤉𐤕.𐤌𐤔𐤁𐤑𐤕.𐤆𐤄𐤁|

יד 𐤅𐤔𐤕𐤉.𐤔𐤓𐤔𐤓𐤕.𐤆𐤄𐤁.𐤈𐤄𐤅𐤓.𐤌𐤂𐤁𐤋𐤕.𐤕𐤏𐤔𐤄.
𐤀𐤕𐤌.𐤌𐤏𐤔𐤄.𐤏𐤁𐤕.𐤅𐤍𐤕𐤕𐤄.𐤀𐤕.𐤔𐤓𐤔𐤓𐤕.𐤄𐤏𐤁𐤕𐤕.
𐤏𐤋.𐤄𐤌𐤔𐤁𐤑𐤕|

טו 𐤅𐤏𐤔𐤉𐤕.𐤇𐤔𐤍.𐤌𐤔𐤐𐤈.𐤌𐤏𐤔𐤄.𐤇𐤔𐤁.𐤊𐤌𐤏𐤔𐤄.
𐤀𐤐𐤃.𐤕𐤏𐤔𐤍𐤅.𐤆𐤄𐤁.𐤕𐤊𐤋𐤕.𐤅𐤀𐤓𐤂𐤌𐤍.𐤅𐤕𐤅𐤋𐤏𐤕.𐤔𐤍𐤉
.𐤅𐤔𐤔.𐤌𐤔𐤆𐤓.𐤕𐤏𐤔𐤄.𐤀𐤕𐤅|

טז 𐤓𐤁𐤅𐤏.𐤉𐤄𐤉𐤄.𐤊𐤐𐤅𐤋.𐤆𐤓𐤕.𐤀𐤓𐤊𐤅.𐤅𐤆𐤓𐤕.𐤓𐤇𐤁𐤅|

יז 𐤅𐤌𐤋𐤀𐤕.𐤁𐤅.𐤌𐤋𐤀𐤕.𐤀𐤁𐤍.𐤀𐤓𐤁𐤏𐤄.𐤈𐤅𐤓𐤉𐤌.𐤀𐤁𐤍.
𐤈𐤅𐤓.𐤀𐤃𐤌.𐤐𐤈𐤃𐤄.𐤅𐤁𐤓𐤒𐤕.𐤄𐤈𐤅𐤓.𐤄𐤀𐤇𐤃|

יח 𐤅𐤄𐤈𐤅𐤓.𐤄𐤔𐤍𐤉.𐤍𐤐𐤊.𐤎𐤐𐤉𐤓.𐤅𐤉𐤄𐤋𐤌|

יט 𐤅𐤄𐤈𐤅𐤓.𐤄𐤔𐤋𐤉𐤔𐤉.𐤋𐤔𐤌.𐤔𐤁𐤅.𐤅𐤀𐤇𐤋𐤌𐤄|

כ 𐤅𐤄𐤈𐤅𐤓.𐤄𐤓𐤁𐤉𐤏𐤉.𐤕𐤓𐤔𐤉𐤔.𐤅𐤔𐤄𐤌.𐤅𐤉𐤔𐤐𐤄.𐤌𐤔
𐤁𐤑𐤉𐤌.𐤆𐤄𐤁.𐤉𐤄𐤉𐤅.𐤁𐤌𐤋𐤅𐤀𐤕𐤌|

𐤊𐤀 𐤅𐤄𐤀𐤁𐤍𐤉𐤌.𐤕𐤄𐤉𐤉𐤍.𐤏𐤋.𐤔𐤌𐤕.𐤁𐤍𐤉.𐤉𐤔𐤓𐤀𐤋.𐤔
𐤕𐤉𐤌.𐤏𐤔𐤓𐤄.𐤏𐤋.𐤔𐤌𐤕𐤌.𐤐𐤕𐤅𐤇𐤉.𐤇𐤅𐤕𐤌.𐤀𐤉𐤔.𐤏𐤋.
𐤔𐤌𐤅.𐤕𐤄𐤉𐤉𐤍.𐤋𐤔𐤍𐤉.𐤏𐤔𐤓.𐤔𐤁𐤈|
𐤊𐤁 𐤅𐤏𐤔𐤉𐤕.𐤏𐤋.𐤄𐤇𐤔𐤍.𐤔𐤓𐤔𐤕.𐤂𐤁𐤋𐤕.𐤌𐤏𐤔𐤄.𐤏
𐤁𐤕.𐤆𐤄𐤁.𐤈𐤄𐤅𐤓|
𐤊𐤂 𐤅𐤏𐤔𐤉𐤕.𐤏𐤋.𐤄𐤇𐤔𐤍.𐤔𐤕𐤉.𐤈𐤁𐤏𐤅𐤕.𐤆𐤄𐤁.𐤅𐤍𐤕
𐤕.𐤀𐤕.𐤔𐤕𐤉.𐤄𐤈𐤁𐤏𐤅𐤕.𐤏𐤋.𐤔𐤍𐤉.𐤒𐤑𐤅𐤕.𐤄𐤇𐤔𐤍|
𐤊𐤃 𐤅𐤍𐤕𐤕𐤄.𐤀𐤕.𐤔𐤕𐤉.𐤏𐤁𐤕𐤕.𐤄𐤆𐤄𐤁.𐤏𐤋.𐤔𐤕𐤉.𐤄
𐤈𐤁𐤏𐤕.𐤀𐤋.𐤒𐤑𐤅𐤕.𐤄𐤇𐤔𐤍|
𐤊𐤄 𐤅𐤀𐤕.𐤔𐤕𐤉.𐤒𐤑𐤅𐤕.𐤔𐤕𐤉.𐤄𐤏𐤁𐤕𐤕.𐤕𐤕𐤍.𐤏𐤋.𐤔
𐤕𐤉.𐤄𐤌𐤔𐤁𐤑𐤅𐤕.𐤅𐤍𐤕𐤕𐤄.𐤏𐤋.𐤊𐤕𐤐𐤅𐤕.𐤄𐤀𐤐𐤃.𐤀𐤋.𐤌𐤅
𐤋.𐤐𐤍𐤉𐤅|
𐤊𐤅 𐤅𐤏𐤔𐤉𐤕.𐤔𐤕𐤉.𐤈𐤁𐤏𐤅𐤕.𐤆𐤄𐤁.𐤅𐤔𐤌𐤕.𐤀𐤕𐤌.𐤏𐤋.
𐤔𐤍𐤉.𐤒𐤑𐤅𐤕.𐤄𐤇𐤔𐤍.𐤏𐤋.𐤔𐤐𐤕𐤅.𐤀𐤔𐤓.𐤀𐤋.𐤏𐤁𐤓.𐤄𐤀𐤐
𐤃.𐤁𐤉𐤕𐤄|
𐤊𐤆 𐤅𐤏𐤔𐤉𐤕.𐤔𐤕𐤉.𐤈𐤁𐤏𐤅𐤕.𐤆𐤄𐤁.𐤅𐤍𐤕𐤕𐤄.𐤀𐤕𐤌.𐤏
𐤋.𐤔𐤕𐤉.𐤊𐤕𐤐𐤅𐤕.𐤄𐤀𐤐𐤅𐤃.𐤌𐤋𐤌𐤈𐤄.𐤌𐤌𐤅𐤋.𐤐𐤍𐤉𐤅.𐤋𐤏𐤌
𐤕.𐤌𐤇𐤁𐤓𐤕𐤅.𐤌𐤌𐤏𐤋.𐤋𐤇𐤔𐤁.𐤄𐤀𐤐𐤅𐤃|
𐤊𐤇 𐤅𐤉𐤓𐤊𐤎𐤅.𐤀𐤕.𐤄𐤇𐤔𐤍.𐤌𐤈𐤁𐤏𐤕𐤅||𐤌𐤈𐤁𐤏𐤕𐤉𐤅.𐤒
𐤓𐤉||.𐤀𐤋.𐤈𐤁𐤏𐤕.𐤄𐤀𐤐𐤃.𐤁𐤐𐤕𐤉𐤋.𐤕𐤊𐤋𐤕.𐤋𐤄𐤉𐤅𐤕.𐤏𐤋.
𐤇𐤔𐤁.𐤄𐤀𐤐𐤅𐤃.𐤅𐤋𐤀.𐤉𐤆𐤇.𐤄𐤇𐤔𐤍.𐤌𐤏𐤋.𐤄𐤀𐤐𐤅𐤃|
𐤊𐤈 𐤅𐤍𐤔𐤀.𐤀𐤄𐤓𐤍.𐤀𐤕.𐤔𐤌𐤅𐤕.𐤁𐤍𐤉.𐤉𐤔𐤓𐤀𐤋.𐤁𐤇𐤔𐤍.
𐤄𐤌𐤔𐤐𐤈.𐤏𐤋.𐤋𐤁𐤅.𐤁𐤁𐤀𐤅.𐤀𐤋.𐤄𐤒𐤃𐤔.𐤋𐤆𐤊𐤓𐤍.𐤋𐤐𐤍𐤉.
𐤉𐤄𐤅𐤄.𐤕𐤌𐤉𐤃|
𐤋 𐤅𐤍𐤕𐤕.𐤀𐤋.𐤇𐤔𐤍.𐤄𐤌𐤔𐤐𐤈.𐤀𐤕.𐤄𐤀𐤅𐤓𐤉𐤌.𐤅𐤀𐤕.
𐤄𐤕𐤌𐤉𐤌.𐤅𐤄𐤉𐤅.𐤏𐤋.𐤋𐤁.𐤀𐤄𐤓𐤍.𐤁𐤁𐤀𐤅.𐤋𐤐𐤍𐤉.𐤉𐤄𐤅𐤄.𐤅𐤍
𐤔𐤀.𐤀𐤄𐤓𐤍.𐤀𐤕.𐤌𐤔𐤐𐤈.𐤁𐤍𐤉.𐤉𐤔𐤓𐤀𐤋.𐤏𐤋.𐤋𐤁𐤅.𐤋𐤐𐤍𐤉.
𐤉𐤄𐤅𐤄.𐤕𐤌𐤉𐤃|
𐤋𐤀 𐤅𐤏𐤔𐤉𐤕.𐤀𐤕.𐤌𐤏𐤉𐤋.𐤄𐤀𐤐𐤅𐤃.𐤊𐤋𐤉𐤋.𐤕𐤊𐤋𐤕|
𐤋𐤁 𐤅𐤄𐤉𐤄.𐤐𐤉.𐤓𐤀𐤔𐤅.𐤁𐤕𐤅𐤊𐤅.𐤔𐤐𐤄.𐤉𐤄𐤉𐤄.𐤋𐤐𐤉𐤅.𐤎𐤁
𐤉𐤁.𐤌𐤏𐤔𐤄.𐤀𐤓𐤂.𐤊𐤐𐤉.𐤕𐤇𐤓𐤀.𐤉𐤄𐤉𐤄.𐤋𐤅.𐤋𐤀.𐤉𐤒𐤓𐤏|

..𐤋𐤂.. 𐤅𐤏𐤔𐤉𐤕.𐤏𐤋.𐤔𐤅𐤋𐤉𐤅.𐤓𐤌𐤍𐤉.𐤕𐤊𐤋𐤕.𐤅𐤀𐤓𐤂𐤌𐤍.𐤅𐤕
𐤅𐤋𐤏𐤕.𐤔𐤍𐤉.𐤏𐤋.𐤔𐤅𐤋𐤉𐤅.𐤎𐤁𐤉𐤁.𐤅𐤐𐤏𐤌𐤍𐤉.𐤆𐤄𐤁.𐤁𐤕𐤅𐤊
𐤌.𐤎𐤁𐤉𐤁|
..𐤋𐤃.. 𐤐𐤏𐤌𐤍.𐤆𐤄𐤁.𐤅𐤓𐤌𐤅𐤍.𐤐𐤏𐤌𐤍.𐤆𐤄𐤁.𐤅𐤓𐤌𐤅𐤍.𐤏𐤋.𐤔𐤅
𐤋𐤉.𐤄𐤌𐤏𐤉𐤋.𐤎𐤁𐤉𐤁|
..𐤋𐤄.. 𐤅𐤄𐤉𐤄.𐤏𐤋.𐤀𐤄𐤓𐤍.𐤋𐤔𐤓𐤕.𐤅𐤍𐤔𐤌𐤏.𐤒𐤅𐤋𐤅.𐤁𐤁𐤀𐤅.𐤀
𐤋.𐤄𐤒𐤃𐤔.𐤋𐤐𐤍𐤉.𐤉𐤄𐤅𐤄.𐤅𐤁𐤑𐤀𐤕𐤅.𐤅𐤋𐤀.𐤉𐤌𐤅𐤕|
..𐤋𐤅.. 𐤅𐤏𐤔𐤉𐤕.𐤑𐤉𐤑.𐤆𐤄𐤁.𐤈𐤄𐤅𐤓.𐤅𐤐𐤕𐤇𐤕.𐤏𐤋𐤉𐤅.𐤐𐤕
𐤅𐤇𐤉.𐤇𐤕𐤌.𐤒𐤃𐤔.𐤋𐤉𐤄𐤅𐤄|
..𐤋𐤆.. 𐤅𐤔𐤌𐤕.𐤀𐤕𐤅.𐤏𐤋.𐤐𐤕𐤉𐤋.𐤕𐤊𐤋𐤕.𐤅𐤄𐤉𐤄.𐤏𐤋.𐤄𐤌
𐤑𐤍𐤐𐤕.𐤀𐤋.𐤌𐤅𐤋.𐤐𐤍𐤉.𐤄𐤌𐤑𐤍𐤐𐤕.𐤉𐤄𐤉𐤄|
..𐤋𐤇.. 𐤅𐤄𐤉𐤄.𐤏𐤋.𐤌𐤑𐤇.𐤀𐤄𐤓𐤍.𐤅𐤍𐤔𐤀.𐤀𐤄𐤓𐤍.𐤀𐤕.𐤏𐤅𐤍.
𐤄𐤒𐤃𐤔𐤉𐤌.𐤀𐤔𐤓.𐤉𐤒𐤃𐤉𐤔𐤅.𐤁𐤍𐤉.𐤉𐤔𐤓𐤀𐤋.𐤋𐤊𐤋.𐤌𐤕𐤍
𐤕.𐤒𐤃𐤔𐤉𐤄𐤌.𐤅𐤄𐤉𐤄.𐤏𐤋.𐤌𐤑𐤇𐤅.𐤕𐤌𐤉𐤃.𐤋𐤓𐤑𐤅𐤍.𐤋𐤄
𐤌.𐤋𐤐𐤍𐤉.𐤉𐤄𐤅𐤄|
..𐤋𐤈.. 𐤅𐤔𐤁𐤑𐤕.𐤄𐤊𐤕𐤍𐤕.𐤔𐤔.𐤅𐤏𐤔𐤉𐤕.𐤌𐤑𐤍𐤐𐤕.𐤔𐤔.𐤅
𐤀𐤁𐤍𐤈.𐤕𐤏𐤔𐤄.𐤌𐤏𐤔𐤄.𐤓𐤒𐤌|
..𐤌.. 𐤅𐤋𐤁𐤍𐤉.𐤀𐤄𐤓𐤍.𐤕𐤏𐤔𐤄.𐤊𐤕𐤍𐤕.𐤅𐤏𐤔𐤉𐤕.𐤋𐤄𐤌.𐤀
𐤁𐤍𐤈𐤉𐤌.𐤅𐤌𐤂𐤁𐤏𐤅𐤕.𐤕𐤏𐤔𐤄.𐤋𐤄𐤌.𐤋𐤊𐤁𐤅𐤃.𐤅𐤋𐤕𐤐𐤀𐤓
𐤕|
..𐤌𐤀.. 𐤅𐤄𐤋𐤁𐤔𐤕.𐤀𐤕𐤌.𐤀𐤕.𐤀𐤄𐤓𐤍.𐤀𐤇𐤉𐤊.𐤅𐤀𐤕.𐤁𐤍𐤉𐤅.
𐤀𐤕𐤅.𐤅𐤌𐤔𐤇𐤕.𐤀𐤕𐤌.𐤅𐤌𐤋𐤀𐤕.𐤀𐤕.𐤉𐤃𐤌.𐤅𐤒𐤃𐤔𐤕.𐤀
𐤕𐤌.𐤅𐤊𐤄𐤍𐤅.𐤋𐤉|
..𐤌𐤁.. 𐤅𐤏𐤔𐤄.𐤋𐤄𐤌.𐤌𐤊𐤍𐤎𐤉.𐤁𐤃.𐤋𐤊𐤎𐤅𐤕.𐤁𐤔𐤓.𐤏𐤓𐤅𐤄.
𐤌𐤌𐤕𐤍𐤉𐤌.𐤅𐤏𐤃.𐤉𐤓𐤊𐤉𐤌.𐤉𐤄𐤉𐤅|
..𐤌𐤂.. 𐤅𐤄𐤉𐤅.𐤏𐤋.𐤀𐤄𐤓𐤍.𐤅𐤏𐤋.𐤁𐤍𐤉𐤅.𐤁𐤁𐤀𐤌.𐤀𐤋.𐤀𐤄𐤋.𐤌
𐤅𐤏𐤃.𐤀𐤅.𐤁𐤂𐤔𐤕𐤌.𐤀𐤋.𐤄𐤌𐤆𐤁𐤇.𐤋𐤔𐤓𐤕.𐤁𐤒𐤃𐤔.𐤅
𐤋𐤀.𐤉𐤔𐤀𐤅.𐤏𐤅𐤍.𐤅𐤌𐤕𐤅.𐤇𐤒𐤕.𐤏𐤅𐤋𐤌.𐤋𐤅.𐤅𐤋𐤆𐤓𐤏𐤅.𐤀𐤇𐤓
𐤉𐤅||

𐤅𐤉𐤏𐤋𐤅.𐤌𐤌𐤑𐤓𐤉𐤌.𐤇𐤋𐤒 ..𐤊𐤈..

א 𐤅𐤆𐤄.𐤄𐤃𐤁𐤓.𐤀𐤔𐤓.𐤕𐤏𐤔𐤄.𐤋𐤄𐤌.𐤋𐤒𐤃𐤔.𐤀𐤕𐤌.𐤋
𐤊𐤄𐤍.𐤋𐤉.𐤋𐤒𐤇.𐤐𐤓.𐤀𐤇𐤃.𐤁𐤍.𐤁𐤒𐤓.𐤅𐤀𐤉𐤋𐤌.𐤔𐤍𐤉𐤌.𐤕
𐤌𐤉𐤌𐤌|
ב 𐤅𐤋𐤇𐤌.𐤌𐤑𐤅𐤕.𐤅𐤇𐤋𐤕.𐤌𐤑𐤕.𐤁𐤋𐤅𐤋𐤕.𐤁𐤔𐤌𐤍.𐤅𐤓𐤒𐤉
𐤒𐤉.𐤌𐤑𐤅𐤕.𐤌𐤔𐤇𐤉𐤌.𐤁𐤔𐤌𐤍.𐤎𐤋𐤕.𐤇𐤈𐤉𐤌.𐤕𐤏𐤔𐤄.𐤀
𐤕𐤌|
ג 𐤅𐤍𐤕𐤕.𐤀𐤅𐤕𐤌.𐤏𐤋.𐤎𐤋.𐤀𐤇𐤃.𐤅𐤄𐤒𐤓𐤁𐤕.𐤀𐤕𐤌.𐤁𐤎
𐤋.𐤅𐤀𐤕.𐤄𐤐𐤓.𐤅𐤀𐤕.𐤔𐤍𐤉.𐤄𐤀𐤉𐤋𐤌|
ד 𐤅𐤀𐤕.𐤀𐤄𐤓𐤍.𐤅𐤀𐤕.𐤁𐤍𐤉𐤅.𐤕𐤒𐤓𐤉𐤁.𐤀𐤋.𐤐𐤕𐤇.𐤀𐤄𐤋.
𐤌𐤅𐤏𐤃.𐤅𐤓𐤇𐤑𐤕.𐤀𐤕𐤌.𐤁𐤌𐤉𐤌|
ה 𐤅𐤋𐤒𐤇𐤕.𐤀𐤕.𐤄𐤁𐤂𐤃𐤉𐤌.𐤅𐤄𐤋𐤁𐤔𐤕.𐤀𐤕.𐤀𐤄𐤓𐤍.𐤀
𐤕.𐤄𐤊𐤕𐤍𐤕.𐤅𐤀𐤕.𐤌𐤏𐤉𐤋.𐤄𐤀𐤐𐤃.𐤅𐤀𐤕.𐤄𐤀𐤐𐤃.𐤄
𐤇𐤔𐤍.𐤅𐤀𐤐𐤃𐤕.𐤋𐤅.𐤁𐤇𐤔𐤁.𐤄𐤀𐤐𐤃|
ו 𐤅𐤔𐤌𐤕.𐤄𐤌𐤑𐤍𐤐𐤕.𐤏𐤋.𐤓𐤀𐤔𐤅.𐤅𐤍𐤕𐤕.𐤀𐤕.𐤍𐤆𐤓.𐤄𐤒
𐤃𐤔.𐤏𐤋.𐤄𐤌𐤑𐤍𐤐𐤕|
ז 𐤅𐤋𐤒𐤇𐤕.𐤀𐤕.𐤔𐤌𐤍.𐤄𐤌𐤔𐤇𐤄.𐤅𐤉𐤑𐤒𐤕.𐤏𐤋.𐤓𐤀𐤔
𐤅.𐤅𐤌𐤔𐤇𐤕.𐤀𐤕𐤅|
ח 𐤅𐤀𐤕.𐤁𐤍𐤉𐤅.𐤕𐤒𐤓𐤉𐤁.𐤅𐤄𐤋𐤁𐤔𐤕𐤌.𐤊𐤕𐤍𐤕|
ט 𐤅𐤇𐤂𐤓𐤕.𐤀𐤕𐤌.𐤀𐤁𐤍𐤈.𐤀𐤄𐤓𐤍.𐤅𐤁𐤍𐤉𐤅.𐤅𐤇𐤁𐤔𐤕.𐤋
𐤄𐤌.𐤌𐤂𐤁𐤏𐤕.𐤅𐤄𐤉𐤕𐤄.𐤋𐤄𐤌.𐤊𐤄𐤍𐤄.𐤋𐤇𐤒𐤕.𐤏𐤅𐤋𐤌.𐤅
𐤌𐤋𐤀𐤕.𐤉𐤃.𐤀𐤄𐤓𐤍.𐤅𐤉𐤃.𐤁𐤍𐤉𐤅|
י 𐤅𐤄𐤒𐤓𐤁𐤕.𐤀𐤕.𐤄𐤐𐤓.𐤋𐤐𐤍𐤉.𐤀𐤄𐤋.𐤌𐤅𐤏𐤃.𐤅𐤎𐤌𐤊.
𐤀𐤄𐤓𐤍.𐤅𐤁𐤍𐤉𐤅.𐤀𐤕.𐤉𐤃𐤉𐤄𐤌.𐤏𐤋.𐤓𐤀𐤔.𐤄𐤐𐤓|
יא 𐤅𐤔𐤇𐤈𐤕.𐤀𐤕.𐤄𐤐𐤓.𐤋𐤐𐤍𐤉.𐤉𐤄𐤅𐤄.𐤐𐤕𐤇.𐤀𐤄𐤋.𐤌𐤅
𐤏𐤃|
יב 𐤅𐤋𐤒𐤇𐤕.𐤌𐤃𐤌.𐤄𐤐𐤓.𐤅𐤍𐤕𐤕𐤄.𐤏𐤋.𐤒𐤓𐤍𐤕.𐤄𐤌𐤆𐤁
𐤇.𐤁𐤀𐤑𐤁𐤏𐤊.𐤅𐤀𐤕.𐤊𐤋.𐤄𐤃𐤌.𐤕𐤔𐤐𐤊.𐤀𐤋.𐤉𐤎𐤅𐤃.𐤄𐤌
𐤆𐤁𐤇|

..𐤉𐤂.. 𐤅𐤋𐤒𐤇𐤕.𐤀𐤕.𐤊𐤋.𐤄𐤇𐤋𐤁.𐤄𐤌𐤊𐤎𐤄.𐤀𐤕.𐤄𐤒𐤓𐤁.𐤅
𐤀𐤕.𐤄𐤉𐤕𐤓𐤕.𐤏𐤋.𐤄𐤊𐤁𐤃.𐤅𐤀𐤕.𐤔𐤕𐤉.𐤄𐤊𐤋𐤉𐤕.𐤅𐤀𐤕.
𐤄𐤇𐤋𐤁.𐤀𐤔𐤓.𐤏𐤋𐤉𐤄𐤍.𐤅𐤄𐤒𐤈𐤓𐤕.𐤄𐤌𐤆𐤁𐤇𐤄|
..𐤉𐤃.. 𐤅𐤀𐤕.𐤁𐤔𐤓.𐤄𐤐𐤓.𐤅𐤀𐤕.𐤏𐤓𐤅.𐤅𐤀𐤕.𐤐𐤓𐤔𐤅.𐤕𐤔𐤓𐤐.𐤁
𐤀𐤔.𐤌𐤇𐤅𐤑.𐤋𐤌𐤇𐤍𐤄.𐤇𐤈𐤀𐤕.𐤄𐤅𐤀|
..𐤉𐤄.. 𐤅𐤀𐤕.𐤄𐤀𐤉𐤋.𐤀𐤇𐤃.𐤕𐤒𐤇.𐤅𐤎𐤌𐤊𐤅.𐤀𐤄𐤓𐤍.𐤅𐤁𐤍
𐤉𐤅.𐤀𐤕.𐤉𐤃𐤉𐤄𐤌.𐤏𐤋.𐤓𐤀𐤔.𐤄𐤀𐤉𐤋|
..𐤉𐤅.. 𐤅𐤔𐤇𐤈𐤕.𐤀𐤕.𐤄𐤀𐤉𐤋.𐤅𐤋𐤒𐤇𐤕.𐤀𐤕.𐤃𐤌𐤅.𐤅𐤆𐤓𐤒
𐤕.𐤏𐤋.𐤄𐤌𐤆𐤁𐤇.𐤎𐤁𐤉𐤁|
..𐤉𐤆.. 𐤅𐤀𐤕.𐤄𐤀𐤉𐤋.𐤕𐤍𐤕𐤇.𐤋𐤍𐤕𐤇𐤉𐤅.𐤅𐤓𐤇𐤑𐤕.𐤒𐤓𐤁𐤅.𐤅
𐤊𐤓𐤏𐤉𐤅.𐤅𐤍𐤕𐤕.𐤏𐤋.𐤍𐤕𐤇𐤉𐤅.𐤅𐤏𐤋.𐤓𐤀𐤔𐤅|
..𐤉𐤇.. 𐤅𐤄𐤒𐤈𐤓𐤕.𐤀𐤕.𐤊𐤋.𐤄𐤀𐤉𐤋.𐤄𐤌𐤆𐤁𐤇𐤄.𐤏𐤋𐤄.𐤄𐤅
𐤀.𐤋𐤉𐤄𐤅𐤄.𐤓𐤉𐤇.𐤍𐤉𐤇𐤅𐤇.𐤀𐤔𐤄.𐤋𐤉𐤄𐤅𐤄.𐤄𐤅𐤀|
..𐤉𐤈.. 𐤅𐤋𐤒𐤇𐤕.𐤀𐤕.𐤄𐤀𐤉𐤋.𐤄𐤔𐤍𐤉.𐤅𐤎𐤌𐤊.𐤀𐤄𐤓𐤍.𐤅𐤁𐤍𐤉
𐤅.𐤀𐤕.𐤉𐤃𐤉𐤄𐤌.𐤏𐤋.𐤓𐤀𐤔.𐤄𐤀𐤉𐤋|
..𐤊.. 𐤅𐤔𐤇𐤈𐤕.𐤀𐤕.𐤄𐤀𐤉𐤋.𐤅𐤋𐤒𐤇𐤕.𐤌𐤃𐤌𐤅.𐤅𐤍𐤕𐤕𐤄.
𐤏𐤋.𐤕𐤍𐤅𐤊.𐤀𐤆𐤍.𐤀𐤄𐤓𐤍.𐤅𐤏𐤋.𐤕𐤍𐤅𐤊.𐤀𐤆𐤍.𐤁𐤍𐤉𐤅.𐤄𐤉𐤌𐤍
𐤉𐤕.𐤅𐤏𐤋.𐤁𐤄𐤍.𐤉𐤃𐤌.𐤄𐤉𐤌𐤍𐤉𐤕.𐤅𐤏𐤋.𐤁𐤄𐤍.𐤓𐤂𐤋𐤌.𐤄𐤉
𐤌𐤍𐤉𐤕.𐤅𐤆𐤓𐤒𐤕.𐤀𐤕.𐤄𐤃𐤌.𐤏𐤋.𐤄𐤌𐤆𐤁𐤇.𐤎𐤁𐤉𐤁|
..𐤊𐤀.. 𐤅𐤋𐤒𐤇𐤕.𐤌𐤍.𐤄𐤃𐤌.𐤀𐤔𐤓.𐤏𐤋.𐤄𐤌𐤆𐤁𐤇.𐤅𐤌𐤔𐤌𐤍.
𐤄𐤌𐤔𐤇𐤄.𐤅𐤄𐤆𐤉𐤕.𐤏𐤋.𐤀𐤄𐤓𐤍.𐤅𐤏𐤋.𐤁𐤂𐤃𐤉𐤅.𐤅𐤏𐤋.𐤁𐤍
𐤉𐤅.𐤅𐤏𐤋.𐤁𐤂𐤃𐤉.𐤁𐤍𐤉𐤅.𐤀𐤕𐤅.𐤅𐤒𐤃𐤔.𐤄𐤅𐤀.𐤅𐤁𐤂𐤃𐤉𐤅.𐤅
𐤁𐤍𐤉𐤅.𐤅𐤁𐤂𐤃𐤉.𐤁𐤍𐤉𐤅.𐤀𐤕𐤅|
..𐤊𐤁.. 𐤅𐤋𐤒𐤇𐤕.𐤌𐤍.𐤄𐤀𐤉𐤋.𐤄𐤇𐤋𐤁.𐤅𐤄𐤀𐤋𐤉𐤄.𐤅𐤀𐤕.𐤄𐤇
𐤋𐤁.𐤄𐤌𐤊𐤎𐤄.𐤀𐤕.𐤄𐤒𐤓𐤁.𐤅𐤀𐤕.𐤉𐤕𐤓𐤕.𐤄𐤊𐤁𐤃.𐤅𐤀𐤕.
𐤔𐤕𐤉.𐤄𐤊𐤋𐤉𐤕.𐤅𐤀𐤕.𐤄𐤇𐤋𐤁.𐤀𐤔𐤓.𐤏𐤋𐤄𐤍.𐤅𐤀𐤕.𐤔𐤅𐤒.
𐤄𐤉𐤌𐤉𐤍.𐤊𐤉.𐤀𐤉𐤋.𐤌𐤋𐤀𐤉𐤌.𐤄𐤅𐤀|
..𐤊𐤂.. 𐤅𐤊𐤊𐤓.𐤋𐤇𐤌.𐤀𐤇𐤕.𐤅𐤇𐤋𐤕.𐤋𐤇𐤌.𐤔𐤌𐤍.𐤀𐤇𐤕.𐤅𐤓
𐤒𐤉𐤒.𐤀𐤇𐤃.𐤌𐤎𐤋.𐤄𐤌𐤑𐤅𐤕.𐤀𐤔𐤓.𐤋𐤐𐤍𐤉.𐤉𐤄𐤅𐤄|
..𐤊𐤃.. 𐤅𐤔𐤌𐤕.𐤄𐤊𐤋.𐤏𐤋.𐤊𐤐𐤉.𐤀𐤄𐤓𐤍.𐤅𐤏𐤋.𐤊𐤐𐤉.𐤁𐤍𐤉𐤅.𐤅
𐤄𐤍𐤐𐤕.𐤀𐤕𐤌.𐤕𐤍𐤅𐤐𐤄.𐤋𐤐𐤍𐤉.𐤉𐤄𐤅𐤄|

𐤊𐤄 𐤅𐤋𐤒𐤇𐤕.𐤀𐤕𐤌.𐤌𐤉𐤃𐤌.𐤅𐤄𐤒𐤈𐤓𐤕.𐤄𐤌𐤆𐤁𐤇𐤄.
𐤏𐤋.𐤄𐤏𐤋𐤄.𐤋𐤓𐤉𐤇.𐤍𐤉𐤇𐤅𐤇.𐤋𐤐𐤍𐤉.𐤉𐤄𐤅𐤄.𐤀𐤔𐤄.𐤄𐤅𐤀.
𐤋𐤉𐤄𐤅𐤄|

𐤊𐤅 𐤅𐤋𐤒𐤇𐤕.𐤀𐤕.𐤄𐤇𐤆𐤄.𐤌𐤀𐤉𐤋.𐤄𐤌𐤋𐤀𐤉𐤌.𐤀𐤔𐤓.𐤋
𐤀𐤄𐤓𐤍.𐤅𐤄𐤍𐤐𐤕.𐤀𐤕𐤅.𐤕𐤍𐤅𐤐𐤄.𐤋𐤐𐤍𐤉.𐤉𐤄𐤅𐤄.𐤅𐤄𐤉𐤄.𐤋𐤊.𐤋
𐤌𐤍𐤄|

𐤊𐤆 𐤅𐤒𐤃𐤔𐤕.𐤀𐤕.𐤇𐤆𐤄.𐤄𐤕𐤍𐤅𐤐𐤄.𐤅𐤀𐤕.𐤔𐤅𐤒.𐤄𐤕𐤓
𐤅𐤌𐤄.𐤀𐤔𐤓.𐤄𐤅𐤍𐤐.𐤅𐤀𐤔𐤓.𐤄𐤅𐤓𐤌.𐤌𐤀𐤉𐤋.𐤄𐤌𐤋𐤀𐤉𐤌.𐤌𐤀
𐤔𐤓.𐤋𐤀𐤄𐤓𐤍.𐤅𐤌𐤀𐤔𐤓.𐤋𐤁𐤍𐤉𐤅|

𐤊𐤇 𐤅𐤄𐤉𐤄.𐤋𐤀𐤄𐤓𐤍.𐤅𐤋𐤁𐤍𐤉𐤅.𐤋𐤇𐤒.𐤏𐤅𐤋𐤌.𐤌𐤀𐤕.𐤁𐤍𐤉.
𐤉𐤔𐤓𐤀𐤋.𐤊𐤉.𐤕𐤓𐤅𐤌𐤄.𐤄𐤅𐤀.𐤅𐤕𐤓𐤅𐤌𐤄.𐤉𐤄𐤉𐤄.𐤌𐤀𐤕.𐤁𐤍
𐤉.𐤉𐤔𐤓𐤀𐤋.𐤌𐤆𐤁𐤇𐤉.𐤔𐤋𐤌𐤉𐤄𐤌.𐤕𐤓𐤅𐤌𐤕𐤌.𐤋𐤉𐤄𐤅𐤄|

𐤊𐤈 𐤅𐤁𐤂𐤃𐤉.𐤄𐤒𐤃𐤔.𐤀𐤔𐤓.𐤋𐤀𐤄𐤓𐤍.𐤉𐤄𐤉𐤅.𐤋𐤁𐤍𐤉𐤅.
𐤀𐤇𐤓𐤉𐤅.𐤋𐤌𐤔𐤇𐤄.𐤁𐤄𐤌.𐤅𐤋𐤌𐤋𐤀.𐤁𐤌.𐤀𐤕.𐤉𐤃𐤌|

𐤋 𐤔𐤁𐤏𐤕.𐤉𐤌𐤉𐤌.𐤉𐤋𐤁𐤔𐤌.𐤄𐤊𐤄𐤍.𐤕𐤇𐤕𐤉𐤅.𐤌𐤁𐤍𐤉
𐤅.𐤀𐤔𐤓.𐤉𐤁𐤀.𐤀𐤋.𐤀𐤄𐤋.𐤌𐤅𐤏𐤃.𐤋𐤔𐤓𐤕.𐤁𐤒𐤃𐤔|

𐤋𐤀 𐤅𐤀𐤕.𐤀𐤉𐤋.𐤄𐤌𐤋𐤀𐤉𐤌.𐤕𐤒𐤇.𐤅𐤁𐤔𐤋𐤕.𐤀𐤕.𐤁𐤔𐤓𐤅
.𐤁𐤌𐤒𐤌.𐤒𐤃𐤔|

𐤋𐤁 𐤅𐤀𐤊𐤋.𐤀𐤄𐤓𐤍.𐤅𐤁𐤍𐤉𐤅.𐤀𐤕.𐤁𐤔𐤓.𐤄𐤀𐤉𐤋.𐤅𐤀𐤕.𐤄𐤋
𐤇𐤌.𐤀𐤔𐤓.𐤁𐤎𐤋.𐤐𐤕𐤇.𐤀𐤄𐤋.𐤌𐤅𐤏𐤃|

𐤋𐤂 𐤅𐤀𐤊𐤋𐤅.𐤀𐤕𐤌.𐤀𐤔𐤓.𐤊𐤐𐤓.𐤁𐤄𐤌.𐤋𐤌𐤋𐤀.𐤀𐤕.𐤉𐤃
𐤌.𐤋𐤒𐤃𐤔.𐤀𐤕𐤌.𐤅𐤆𐤓.𐤋𐤀.𐤉𐤀𐤊𐤋.𐤊𐤉.𐤒𐤃𐤔.𐤄𐤌|

𐤋𐤃 𐤅𐤀𐤌.𐤉𐤅𐤕𐤓.𐤌𐤁𐤔𐤓.𐤄𐤌𐤋𐤀𐤉𐤌.𐤅𐤌𐤍.𐤄𐤋𐤇𐤌.𐤏𐤃
.𐤄𐤁𐤒𐤓.𐤅𐤔𐤓𐤐𐤕.𐤀𐤕.𐤄𐤍𐤅𐤕𐤓.𐤁𐤀𐤔.𐤋𐤀.𐤉𐤀𐤊𐤋.𐤊𐤉.𐤒
𐤃𐤔.𐤄𐤅𐤀|

𐤋𐤄 𐤅𐤏𐤔𐤉𐤕.𐤋𐤀𐤄𐤓𐤍.𐤅𐤋𐤁𐤍𐤉𐤅.𐤊𐤊𐤄.𐤊𐤊𐤋.𐤀𐤔𐤓.𐤑𐤅𐤉
𐤕𐤉.𐤀𐤕𐤊𐤄.𐤔𐤁𐤏𐤕.𐤉𐤌𐤉𐤌.𐤕𐤌𐤋𐤀.𐤉𐤃𐤌|

𐤋𐤅 𐤅𐤐𐤓.𐤇𐤈𐤀𐤕.𐤕𐤏𐤔𐤄.𐤋𐤉𐤅𐤌.𐤏𐤋.𐤄𐤊𐤐𐤓𐤉𐤌.𐤅𐤇𐤈
𐤀𐤕.𐤏𐤋.𐤄𐤌𐤆𐤁𐤇.𐤁𐤊𐤐𐤓𐤊.𐤏𐤋𐤉𐤅.𐤅𐤌𐤔𐤇𐤕.𐤀𐤕𐤅.𐤋𐤒
𐤃𐤔𐤅|

37 ࠔࠁࠏࠕ.ࠉࠌࠉࠌ.ࠕࠊࠐࠓ.ࠏࠋ.ࠄࠌࠆࠁࠇ.ࠅࠒࠃࠔࠕ.
ࠀࠕࠅ.ࠅࠄࠉࠄ.ࠄࠌࠆࠁࠇ.ࠒࠃࠔ.ࠒࠃࠔࠉࠌ.ࠊࠋ.ࠄࠍࠂࠏ.
ࠁࠌࠆࠁࠇ.ࠉࠒࠃࠔ|
38 ࠅࠆࠄ.ࠀࠔࠓ.ࠕࠏࠔࠄ.ࠏࠋ.ࠄࠌࠆࠁࠇ.ࠊࠁࠔࠉࠌ.ࠁࠍ
ࠉ.ࠔࠍࠄ.ࠔࠍࠉࠌ.ࠋࠉࠅࠌ.ࠕࠌࠉࠃ|
39 ࠀࠕ.ࠄࠊࠁࠔ.ࠄࠀࠇࠃ.ࠕࠏࠔࠄ.ࠁࠁࠒࠓ.ࠅࠀࠕ.ࠄࠊ
ࠁࠔ.ࠄࠔࠍࠉ.ࠕࠏࠔࠄ.ࠁࠉࠍ.ࠄࠏࠓࠁࠉࠌ|
40 ࠅࠏࠔࠓࠍ.ࠎࠋࠕ.ࠁࠋࠅࠋ.ࠁࠔࠌࠍ.ࠊࠕࠉࠕ.ࠓࠁࠏ.ࠄࠄࠉࠍ
.ࠅࠍࠎࠊ.ࠓࠁࠏࠉࠕ.ࠄࠄࠉࠍ.ࠉࠉࠍ.ࠋࠊࠁࠔ.ࠄࠀࠇࠃ|
41 ࠅࠀࠕ.ࠄࠊࠁࠔ.ࠄࠔࠍࠉ.ࠕࠏࠔࠄ.ࠁࠉࠍ.ࠄࠏࠓࠁࠉࠌ.ࠊ
ࠌࠍࠇࠕ.ࠄࠁࠒࠓ.ࠅࠊࠍࠎࠊࠄ.ࠕࠏࠔࠄ.ࠋࠄ.ࠋࠓࠉࠇ.ࠍࠉࠇࠇ.
ࠀࠔࠄ.ࠋࠉࠄࠅࠄ|
42 ࠏࠋࠕ.ࠕࠌࠉࠃ.ࠋࠃࠓࠕࠉࠊࠌ.ࠐࠕࠇ.ࠀࠄࠋ.ࠌࠅࠏࠃ.
ࠋࠐࠍࠉ.ࠉࠄࠅࠄ.ࠀࠔࠓ.ࠀࠅࠏࠃ.ࠋࠊࠌ.ࠔࠌࠄ.ࠋࠃࠁࠓ.ࠀࠋࠉࠊ.
ࠔࠌ|
43 ࠅࠍࠏࠃࠕࠉ.ࠔࠌࠄ.ࠋࠁࠍࠉ.ࠉࠔࠓࠀࠋ.ࠅࠍࠒࠃࠔ.ࠁࠊࠁ
ࠃࠉ|
44 ࠅࠒࠃࠔࠕࠉ.ࠀࠕ.ࠀࠄࠋ.ࠌࠅࠏࠃ.ࠅࠀࠕ.ࠄࠌࠆࠁࠇ.ࠅ
ࠀࠕ.ࠀࠄࠓࠍ.ࠅࠀࠕ.ࠁࠍࠉࠅ.ࠀࠒࠃࠔ.ࠋࠊࠄࠍ.ࠋࠉ|
45 ࠅࠔࠊࠍࠕࠉ.ࠁࠕࠅࠊ.ࠁࠍࠉ.ࠉࠔࠓࠀࠋ.ࠅࠄࠉࠉࠕࠉ.ࠋࠄࠌ.
ࠋࠀࠋࠄࠉࠌ|
46 ࠅࠉࠃࠏࠅ.ࠊࠉ.ࠀࠍࠉ.ࠉࠄࠅࠄ.ࠀࠋࠄࠉࠄࠌ.ࠀࠔࠓ.ࠄࠅࠑ
ࠀࠕࠉ.ࠀࠕࠌ.ࠌࠀࠓࠑ.ࠌࠑࠓࠉࠌ.ࠋࠔࠊࠍࠉ.ࠁࠕࠅࠊࠌ.ࠀࠍࠉ.
ࠉࠄࠅࠄ.ࠀࠋࠄࠉࠄࠌ||

ࠅࠉࠏࠋࠅ.ࠌࠌࠑࠓࠉࠌ.ࠇࠋࠒ 30

1 ࠅࠏࠔࠉࠕ.ࠌࠆࠁࠇ.ࠌࠒࠈࠓ.ࠒࠈࠓࠕ.ࠏࠑࠉ.ࠔࠈࠉࠌ.
ࠕࠏࠔࠄ.ࠀࠕࠅ|
2 ࠀࠌࠄ.ࠀࠓࠊࠅ.ࠅࠀࠌࠄ.ࠓࠇࠁࠅ.ࠓࠁࠅࠏ.ࠉࠄࠉࠄ.ࠅࠀࠌࠕࠉ
ࠌ.ࠒࠌࠕࠅ.ࠌࠌࠍࠅ.ࠒࠓࠍࠕࠉࠅ|

3 𐤅𐤑𐤐𐤉𐤕.𐤀𐤕𐤅.𐤆𐤄𐤁.𐤈𐤄𐤅𐤓.𐤀𐤕.𐤂𐤂𐤅.𐤅𐤀𐤕.𐤒𐤉𐤓
𐤕𐤉𐤅.𐤎𐤁𐤉𐤁.𐤅𐤀𐤕.𐤒𐤓𐤍𐤕𐤉𐤅.𐤅𐤏𐤔𐤉𐤕.𐤋𐤅.𐤆𐤓.𐤆𐤄𐤁.𐤎
𐤁𐤉𐤁|
4 𐤅𐤔𐤕𐤉.𐤈𐤁𐤏𐤕.𐤆𐤄𐤁.𐤕𐤏𐤔𐤄.𐤋𐤅.𐤌𐤕𐤇𐤕.𐤋𐤆𐤓𐤅.
𐤏𐤋.𐤔𐤕𐤉.𐤑𐤋𐤏𐤕𐤉𐤅.𐤕𐤏𐤔𐤄.𐤏𐤋.𐤔𐤍𐤉.𐤑𐤃𐤉𐤅.𐤅𐤄𐤉𐤄.
𐤋𐤁𐤕𐤉𐤌.𐤋𐤁𐤃𐤉𐤌.𐤋𐤔𐤀𐤕.𐤀𐤕𐤅.𐤁𐤄𐤌𐤄|
5 𐤅𐤏𐤔𐤉𐤕.𐤀𐤕.𐤄𐤁𐤃𐤉𐤌.𐤏𐤑𐤉.𐤔𐤈𐤉𐤌.𐤅𐤑𐤐𐤉𐤕.𐤀
𐤕𐤌.𐤆𐤄𐤁|
6 𐤅𐤍𐤕𐤕𐤄.𐤀𐤕𐤅.𐤋𐤐𐤍𐤉.𐤄𐤐𐤓𐤊𐤕.𐤀𐤔𐤓.𐤏𐤋.𐤀𐤓𐤍.𐤄𐤏𐤃
𐤕.𐤋𐤐𐤍𐤉.𐤄𐤊𐤐𐤓𐤕.𐤀𐤔𐤓.𐤏𐤋.𐤄𐤏𐤃𐤕.𐤀𐤔𐤓.𐤀𐤅𐤏𐤃.𐤋𐤊.
𐤔𐤌𐤄|
7 𐤅𐤄𐤒𐤈𐤉𐤓.𐤏𐤋𐤉𐤅.𐤀𐤄𐤓𐤍.𐤒𐤈𐤓𐤕.𐤎𐤌𐤉𐤌.𐤁𐤁𐤒𐤓.𐤁
𐤁𐤒𐤓.𐤁𐤄𐤉𐤈𐤉𐤁𐤅.𐤀𐤕.𐤄𐤍𐤓𐤕.𐤉𐤒𐤈𐤉𐤓𐤍𐤄|
8 𐤅𐤁𐤄𐤏𐤋𐤕.𐤀𐤄𐤓𐤍.𐤀𐤕.𐤄𐤍𐤓𐤕.𐤁𐤉𐤍.𐤄𐤏𐤓𐤁𐤉𐤌.𐤉𐤒
𐤈𐤉𐤓𐤍𐤄.𐤒𐤈𐤓𐤕.𐤕𐤌𐤉𐤃.𐤋𐤐𐤍𐤉.𐤉𐤄𐤅𐤄.𐤋𐤃𐤓𐤕𐤉𐤊𐤌|
9 𐤋𐤀.𐤕𐤏𐤋𐤅.𐤏𐤋𐤉𐤅.𐤒𐤈𐤓𐤕.𐤆𐤓𐤄.𐤅𐤏𐤋𐤄.𐤅𐤌𐤍𐤇𐤄.𐤅
𐤍𐤎𐤊.𐤋𐤀.𐤕𐤎𐤊𐤅.𐤏𐤋𐤉𐤅|
10 𐤅𐤊𐤐𐤓.𐤀𐤄𐤓𐤍.𐤏𐤋.𐤒𐤓𐤍𐤕𐤉𐤅.𐤀𐤇𐤕.𐤁𐤔𐤍𐤄.𐤌𐤃𐤌.
𐤇𐤈𐤀𐤕.𐤄𐤊𐤐𐤓𐤉𐤌.𐤀𐤇𐤕.𐤁𐤔𐤍𐤄.𐤉𐤊𐤐𐤓.𐤏𐤋𐤉𐤅.𐤋𐤃𐤓𐤕
𐤉𐤊𐤌.𐤒𐤃𐤔.𐤒𐤃𐤔𐤉𐤌.𐤄𐤅𐤀.𐤋𐤉𐤄𐤅𐤄|
11 𐤅𐤉𐤃𐤁𐤓.𐤉𐤄𐤅𐤄.𐤀𐤋.𐤌𐤔𐤄.𐤋𐤀𐤌𐤓|
12 𐤊𐤉.𐤕𐤔𐤀.𐤀𐤕.𐤓𐤀𐤔.𐤁𐤍𐤉.𐤉𐤔𐤓𐤀𐤋.𐤋𐤐𐤒𐤃𐤉𐤄𐤌.
𐤅𐤍𐤕𐤍𐤅.𐤀𐤉𐤔.𐤊𐤐𐤓.𐤍𐤐𐤔𐤅.𐤋𐤉𐤄𐤅𐤄.𐤁𐤐𐤒𐤃.𐤀𐤕𐤌.𐤅𐤋𐤀.𐤉
𐤄𐤉𐤄.𐤁𐤄𐤌.𐤍𐤂𐤐.𐤁𐤐𐤒𐤃.𐤀𐤕𐤌|
13 𐤆𐤄.𐤉𐤕𐤍𐤅.𐤊𐤋.𐤄𐤏𐤁𐤓.𐤏𐤋.𐤄𐤐𐤒𐤃𐤉𐤌.𐤌𐤇𐤑𐤉𐤕
.𐤄𐤔𐤒𐤋.𐤁𐤔𐤒𐤋.𐤄𐤒𐤃𐤔.𐤏𐤔𐤓𐤉𐤌.𐤂𐤓𐤄.𐤄𐤔𐤒𐤋.𐤌𐤇
𐤑𐤉𐤕.𐤄𐤔𐤒𐤋.𐤕𐤓𐤅𐤌𐤄.𐤋𐤉𐤄𐤅𐤄|
14 𐤊𐤋.𐤄𐤏𐤁𐤓.𐤏𐤋.𐤄𐤐𐤒𐤃𐤉𐤌.𐤌𐤁𐤍.𐤏𐤔𐤓𐤉𐤌.𐤔𐤍𐤄.
𐤅𐤌𐤏𐤋𐤄.𐤉𐤕𐤍.𐤕𐤓𐤅𐤌𐤕.𐤉𐤄𐤅𐤄|

𐤈𐤅 𐤄𐤏𐤔𐤉𐤓.𐤋𐤀.𐤉𐤓𐤁𐤄.𐤅𐤄𐤃𐤋.𐤋𐤀.𐤉𐤌𐤏𐤉𐤈.𐤌𐤌𐤇
𐤑𐤉𐤕.𐤄𐤔𐤒𐤋.𐤋𐤕𐤕.𐤀𐤕.𐤕𐤓𐤅𐤌𐤕.𐤉𐤄𐤅𐤄.𐤋𐤊𐤐𐤓.𐤏𐤋.𐤍𐤐
𐤔𐤕𐤉𐤊𐤌|

𐤈𐤆 𐤅𐤋𐤒𐤇𐤕.𐤀𐤕.𐤊𐤎𐤐.𐤄𐤊𐤐𐤓𐤉𐤌.𐤌𐤀𐤕.𐤁𐤍𐤉.𐤉𐤔𐤓𐤀
𐤋.𐤅𐤍𐤕𐤕.𐤀𐤕𐤅.𐤏𐤋.𐤏𐤁𐤃𐤕.𐤀𐤄𐤋.𐤌𐤅𐤏𐤃.𐤅𐤄𐤉𐤄.𐤋𐤁𐤍𐤉.
𐤉𐤔𐤓𐤀𐤋.𐤋𐤆𐤊𐤓𐤅𐤍.𐤋𐤐𐤍𐤉.𐤉𐤄𐤅𐤄.𐤋𐤊𐤐𐤓.𐤏𐤋.𐤍𐤐𐤔𐤕𐤉𐤊𐤌
|

𐤉𐤆 𐤅𐤉𐤃𐤁𐤓.𐤉𐤄𐤅𐤄.𐤀𐤋.𐤌𐤔𐤄.𐤋𐤀𐤌𐤓|

𐤉𐤇 𐤅𐤏𐤔𐤉𐤕.𐤊𐤉𐤅𐤓.𐤍𐤇𐤔𐤕.𐤅𐤊𐤍𐤅.𐤍𐤇𐤔𐤕.𐤋𐤓𐤇𐤑𐤄.𐤅
𐤍𐤕𐤕.𐤀𐤕𐤅.𐤁𐤉𐤍.𐤀𐤄𐤋.𐤌𐤅𐤏𐤃.𐤅𐤁𐤉𐤍.𐤄𐤌𐤆𐤁𐤇.𐤅𐤍𐤕𐤕.
𐤔𐤌𐤄.𐤌𐤉𐤌|

𐤉𐤈 𐤅𐤓𐤇𐤑𐤅.𐤀𐤄𐤓𐤍.𐤅𐤁𐤍𐤉𐤅.𐤌𐤌𐤍𐤅.𐤀𐤕.𐤉𐤃𐤉𐤄𐤌.𐤅𐤀𐤕
.𐤓𐤂𐤋𐤉𐤄𐤌|

𐤊 𐤁𐤁𐤀𐤌.𐤀𐤋.𐤀𐤄𐤋.𐤌𐤅𐤏𐤃.𐤉𐤓𐤇𐤑𐤅.𐤌𐤉𐤌.𐤅𐤋𐤀.𐤉
𐤌𐤕𐤅.𐤀𐤅.𐤁𐤂𐤔𐤕𐤌.𐤀𐤋.𐤄𐤌𐤆𐤁𐤇.𐤋𐤔𐤓𐤕.𐤋𐤄𐤒𐤈𐤉𐤓.𐤀
𐤔𐤄.𐤋𐤉𐤄𐤅𐤄|

𐤊𐤀 𐤅𐤓𐤇𐤑𐤅.𐤉𐤃𐤉𐤄𐤌.𐤅𐤓𐤂𐤋𐤉𐤄𐤌.𐤅𐤋𐤀.𐤉𐤌𐤕𐤅.𐤅𐤄𐤉𐤕
𐤄.𐤋𐤄𐤌.𐤇𐤒.𐤏𐤅𐤋𐤌.𐤋𐤅.𐤅𐤋𐤆𐤓𐤏𐤅.𐤋𐤃𐤓𐤕𐤌|

𐤊𐤁 𐤅𐤉𐤃𐤁𐤓.𐤉𐤄𐤅𐤄.𐤀𐤋.𐤌𐤔𐤄.𐤋𐤀𐤌𐤓|

𐤊𐤂 𐤅𐤀𐤕𐤄.𐤒𐤇.𐤋𐤊.𐤁𐤔𐤌𐤉𐤌.𐤓𐤀𐤔.𐤌𐤓.𐤃𐤓𐤅𐤓.𐤇𐤌𐤔
𐤌𐤀𐤅𐤕.𐤅𐤒𐤍𐤌𐤍.𐤁𐤔𐤌.𐤌𐤇𐤑𐤉𐤕𐤅.𐤇𐤌𐤔𐤉𐤌.𐤅𐤌𐤀𐤕𐤉𐤌.
𐤅𐤒𐤍𐤄.𐤁𐤔𐤌.𐤇𐤌𐤔𐤉𐤌.𐤅𐤌𐤀𐤕𐤉𐤌|

𐤊𐤃 𐤅𐤒𐤃𐤄.𐤇𐤌𐤔.𐤌𐤀𐤅𐤕.𐤁𐤔𐤒𐤋.𐤄𐤒𐤃𐤔.𐤅𐤔𐤌𐤍.𐤆
𐤉𐤕.𐤄𐤉𐤍|

𐤊𐤄 𐤅𐤏𐤔𐤉𐤕.𐤀𐤕𐤅.𐤔𐤌𐤍.𐤌𐤔𐤇𐤕.𐤒𐤃𐤔.𐤓𐤒𐤇.𐤌𐤓𐤒
𐤇𐤕.𐤌𐤏𐤔𐤄.𐤓𐤒𐤇.𐤔𐤌𐤍.𐤌𐤔𐤇𐤕.𐤒𐤃𐤔.𐤉𐤄𐤉𐤄|

𐤊𐤅 𐤅𐤌𐤔𐤇𐤕.𐤁𐤅.𐤀𐤕.𐤀𐤄𐤋.𐤌𐤅𐤏𐤃.𐤅𐤀𐤕.𐤀𐤓𐤅𐤍.𐤄𐤏𐤃
𐤕|

𐤊𐤆 𐤅𐤀𐤕.𐤄𐤔𐤋𐤇𐤍.𐤅𐤀𐤕.𐤊𐤋.𐤊𐤋𐤉𐤅.𐤅𐤀𐤕.𐤄𐤌𐤍𐤓𐤄.𐤅𐤀
𐤕.𐤊𐤋𐤉𐤄.𐤅𐤀𐤕.𐤌𐤆𐤁𐤇.𐤄𐤒𐤈𐤓𐤕|

..𐤊𐤇.. 𐤅𐤀𐤕.𐤌𐤆𐤁𐤇.𐤄𐤏𐤋𐤄.𐤅𐤀𐤕.𐤊𐤋.𐤊𐤋𐤉𐤅.𐤅𐤀𐤕.𐤄𐤊𐤉
𐤓.𐤅𐤀𐤕.𐤊𐤍𐤅|
..𐤊𐤈.. 𐤅𐤒𐤃𐤔𐤕.𐤀𐤕𐤌.𐤅𐤄𐤉𐤅.𐤒𐤃𐤔.𐤒𐤃𐤔𐤉𐤌.𐤊𐤋.𐤄𐤍
𐤂𐤏.𐤁𐤄𐤌.𐤉𐤒𐤃𐤔|
..𐤋.. 𐤅𐤀𐤕.𐤀𐤄𐤓𐤍.𐤅𐤀𐤕.𐤁𐤍𐤉𐤅.𐤕𐤌𐤔𐤇.𐤅𐤒𐤃𐤔𐤕.𐤀𐤕
𐤌.𐤋𐤊𐤄𐤍.𐤋𐤉|
..𐤋𐤀.. 𐤅𐤀𐤋.𐤁𐤍𐤉.𐤉𐤔𐤓𐤀𐤋.𐤕𐤃𐤁𐤓.𐤋𐤀𐤌𐤓.𐤔𐤌𐤍.𐤌𐤔𐤇𐤕.
𐤒𐤃𐤔.𐤉𐤄𐤉𐤄.𐤆𐤄.𐤋𐤉.𐤋𐤃𐤓𐤕𐤉𐤊𐤌|
..𐤋𐤁.. 𐤏𐤋.𐤁𐤔𐤓.𐤀𐤃𐤌.𐤋𐤀.𐤉𐤉𐤎𐤊.𐤅𐤁𐤌𐤕𐤊𐤍𐤕𐤅.𐤋𐤀.𐤕
𐤏𐤔𐤅.𐤊𐤌𐤄𐤅.𐤒𐤃𐤔.𐤄𐤅𐤀.𐤒𐤃𐤔.𐤉𐤄𐤉𐤄.𐤋𐤊𐤌|
..𐤋𐤂.. 𐤀𐤉𐤔.𐤀𐤔𐤓.𐤉𐤓𐤒𐤇.𐤊𐤌𐤄𐤅.𐤅𐤀𐤔𐤓.𐤉𐤕𐤍.𐤌𐤌𐤍𐤅.𐤏
𐤋.𐤆𐤓.𐤅𐤍𐤊𐤓𐤕.𐤌𐤏𐤌𐤉𐤅|
..𐤋𐤃.. 𐤅𐤉𐤀𐤌𐤓.𐤉𐤄𐤅𐤄.𐤀𐤋.𐤌𐤔𐤄.𐤒𐤇.𐤋𐤊.𐤎𐤌𐤉𐤌.𐤍𐤈𐤐.
𐤅𐤔𐤇𐤋𐤕.𐤅𐤇𐤋𐤁𐤍𐤄.𐤎𐤌𐤉𐤌.𐤅𐤋𐤁𐤍𐤄.𐤆𐤊𐤄.𐤁𐤃.𐤁𐤁𐤃.𐤉
𐤄𐤉𐤄|
..𐤋𐤄.. 𐤅𐤏𐤔𐤉𐤕.𐤀𐤕𐤄.𐤒𐤈𐤓𐤕.𐤓𐤒𐤇.𐤌𐤏𐤔𐤄.𐤓𐤅𐤒𐤇.𐤌
𐤌𐤋𐤇.𐤈𐤄𐤅𐤓.𐤒𐤃𐤔|
..𐤋𐤅.. 𐤅𐤔𐤇𐤒𐤕.𐤌𐤌𐤍𐤄.𐤄𐤃𐤒.𐤅𐤍𐤕𐤕𐤄.𐤌𐤌𐤍𐤄.𐤋𐤐𐤍𐤉.𐤄
𐤏𐤃𐤕.𐤁𐤀𐤄𐤋.𐤌𐤅𐤏𐤃.𐤀𐤔𐤓.𐤀𐤅𐤏𐤃.𐤋𐤊.𐤔𐤌𐤄.𐤒𐤃𐤔.
𐤒𐤃𐤔𐤉𐤌.𐤕𐤄𐤉𐤄.𐤋𐤊𐤌|
..𐤋𐤆.. 𐤅𐤄𐤒𐤈𐤓𐤕.𐤀𐤔𐤓.𐤕𐤏𐤔𐤄.𐤁𐤌𐤕𐤊𐤍𐤕𐤄.𐤋𐤀.𐤕𐤏
𐤔𐤅.𐤋𐤊𐤌.𐤒𐤃𐤔.𐤕𐤄𐤉𐤄.𐤋𐤊.𐤋𐤉𐤄𐤅𐤄|
..𐤋𐤇.. 𐤀𐤉𐤔.𐤀𐤔𐤓.𐤉𐤏𐤔𐤄.𐤊𐤌𐤅𐤄.𐤋𐤄𐤓𐤉𐤇.𐤁𐤄.𐤅𐤍𐤊𐤓𐤕.
𐤌𐤏𐤌𐤉𐤅||

𐤅𐤉𐤏𐤋𐤅.𐤌𐤌𐤑𐤓𐤉𐤌.𐤇𐤋𐤒 ..𐤋𐤀..

..𐤀.. 𐤅𐤉𐤃𐤁𐤓.𐤉𐤄𐤅𐤄.𐤀𐤋.𐤌𐤔𐤄.𐤋𐤀𐤌𐤓|
..𐤁.. 𐤓𐤀𐤄.𐤒𐤓𐤀𐤕𐤉.𐤁𐤔𐤌.𐤁𐤑𐤋𐤀𐤋.𐤁𐤍.𐤀𐤅𐤓𐤉.𐤁𐤍.𐤇𐤅𐤓.
𐤋𐤌𐤈𐤄.𐤉𐤄𐤅𐤃𐤄|

3 𐤅𐤀𐤌𐤋𐤀.𐤀𐤕𐤅.𐤓𐤅𐤇.𐤀𐤋𐤄𐤉𐤌.𐤁𐤇𐤊𐤌𐤄.𐤅𐤁𐤕𐤁𐤅𐤍𐤄.
𐤅𐤁𐤃𐤏𐤕.𐤅𐤁𐤊𐤋.𐤌𐤋𐤀𐤊𐤄|
4 𐤋𐤇𐤔𐤁.𐤌𐤇𐤔𐤁𐤕.𐤋𐤏𐤔𐤅𐤕.𐤁𐤆𐤄𐤁.𐤅𐤁𐤊𐤎𐤐.𐤅𐤁𐤍
𐤇𐤔𐤕|
5 𐤅𐤁𐤇𐤓𐤔𐤕.𐤀𐤁𐤍.𐤋𐤌𐤋𐤀𐤕.𐤅𐤁𐤇𐤓𐤔𐤕.𐤏𐤑.𐤋𐤏𐤔𐤅𐤕.
𐤁𐤊𐤋.𐤌𐤋𐤀𐤊𐤄|
6 𐤅𐤀𐤍𐤉.𐤄𐤍𐤄.𐤍𐤕𐤕𐤉.𐤀𐤕𐤅.𐤀𐤕.𐤀𐤄𐤋𐤉𐤀𐤁.𐤁𐤍.𐤀𐤇𐤉
𐤎𐤌𐤊.𐤋𐤌𐤈𐤄.𐤃𐤍.𐤅𐤁𐤋𐤁.𐤊𐤋.𐤇𐤊𐤌.𐤋𐤁.𐤍𐤕𐤕𐤉.𐤇𐤊𐤌𐤄.
𐤅𐤏𐤔𐤅.𐤀𐤕.𐤊𐤋.𐤀𐤔𐤓.𐤑𐤅𐤉𐤕𐤊|
7 𐤀𐤕.𐤀𐤄𐤋.𐤌𐤅𐤏𐤃.𐤅𐤀𐤕.𐤄𐤀𐤓𐤍.𐤋𐤏𐤃𐤕.𐤅𐤀𐤕.𐤄𐤊𐤐
𐤓𐤕.𐤀𐤔𐤓.𐤏𐤋𐤉𐤅.𐤅𐤀𐤕.𐤊𐤋.𐤊𐤋𐤉.𐤄𐤀𐤄𐤋|
8 𐤅𐤀𐤕.𐤄𐤔𐤋𐤇𐤍.𐤅𐤀𐤕.𐤊𐤋𐤉𐤅.𐤅𐤀𐤕.𐤄𐤌𐤍𐤓𐤄.𐤄𐤈𐤄𐤓𐤄
.𐤅𐤀𐤕.𐤊𐤋.𐤊𐤋𐤉𐤄.𐤅𐤀𐤕.𐤌𐤆𐤁𐤇.𐤄𐤒𐤈𐤓𐤕|
9 𐤅𐤀𐤕.𐤌𐤆𐤁𐤇.𐤄𐤏𐤋𐤄.𐤅𐤀𐤕.𐤊𐤋.𐤊𐤋𐤉𐤅.𐤅𐤀𐤕.𐤄𐤊𐤉𐤅
𐤓.𐤅𐤀𐤕.𐤊𐤍𐤅|
10 𐤅𐤀𐤕.𐤁𐤂𐤃𐤉.𐤄𐤔𐤓𐤃.𐤅𐤀𐤕.𐤁𐤂𐤃𐤉.𐤄𐤒𐤃𐤔.𐤋
𐤀𐤄𐤓𐤍.𐤄𐤊𐤄𐤍.𐤅𐤀𐤕.𐤁𐤂𐤃𐤉.𐤁𐤍𐤉𐤅.𐤋𐤊𐤄𐤍|
11 𐤅𐤀𐤕.𐤔𐤌𐤍.𐤄𐤌𐤔𐤇𐤄.𐤅𐤀𐤕.𐤒𐤈𐤓𐤕.𐤄𐤎𐤌𐤉𐤌.𐤋𐤒
𐤃𐤔.𐤊𐤊𐤋.𐤀𐤔𐤓.𐤑𐤅𐤉𐤕𐤊.𐤉𐤏𐤔𐤅|
12 𐤅𐤉𐤀𐤌𐤓.𐤉𐤄𐤅𐤄.𐤀𐤋.𐤌𐤔𐤄.𐤋𐤀𐤌𐤓|
13 𐤅𐤀𐤕𐤄.𐤃𐤁𐤓.𐤀𐤋.𐤁𐤍𐤉.𐤉𐤔𐤓𐤀𐤋.𐤋𐤀𐤌𐤓.𐤀𐤊.𐤀𐤕.
𐤔𐤁𐤕𐤕𐤉.𐤕𐤔𐤌𐤓𐤅.𐤊𐤉.𐤀𐤅𐤕.𐤄𐤅𐤀.𐤁𐤉𐤍𐤉.𐤅𐤁𐤉𐤍𐤉𐤊𐤌.𐤋
𐤃𐤓𐤕𐤉𐤊𐤌.𐤋𐤃𐤏𐤕.𐤊𐤉.𐤀𐤍𐤉.𐤉𐤄𐤅𐤄.𐤌𐤒𐤃𐤔𐤊𐤌|
14 𐤅𐤔𐤌𐤓𐤕𐤌.𐤀𐤕.𐤄𐤔𐤁𐤕.𐤊𐤉.𐤒𐤃𐤔.𐤄𐤅𐤀.𐤋𐤊𐤌.𐤌
𐤇𐤋𐤋𐤉𐤄.𐤌𐤅𐤕.𐤉𐤅𐤌𐤕.𐤊𐤉.𐤊𐤋.𐤄𐤏𐤔𐤄.𐤁𐤄.𐤌𐤋𐤀𐤊𐤄.𐤅𐤍
𐤊𐤓𐤕𐤄.𐤄𐤍𐤐𐤔.𐤄𐤄𐤅𐤀.𐤌𐤒𐤓𐤁.𐤏𐤌𐤉𐤄|
15 𐤔𐤔𐤕.𐤉𐤌𐤉𐤌.𐤉𐤏𐤔𐤄.𐤌𐤋𐤀𐤊𐤄.𐤅𐤁𐤉𐤅𐤌.𐤄𐤔𐤁𐤉𐤏
𐤉.𐤔𐤁𐤕.𐤔𐤁𐤕𐤅𐤍.𐤒𐤃𐤔.𐤋𐤉𐤄𐤅𐤄.𐤊𐤋.𐤄𐤏𐤔𐤄.𐤌𐤋𐤀𐤊𐤄.
𐤁𐤉𐤅𐤌.𐤄𐤔𐤁𐤕.𐤌𐤅𐤕.𐤉𐤅𐤌𐤕|
16 𐤅𐤔𐤌𐤓𐤅.𐤁𐤍𐤉.𐤉𐤔𐤓𐤀𐤋.𐤀𐤕.𐤄𐤔𐤁𐤕.𐤋𐤏𐤔𐤅𐤕.𐤀𐤕.
𐤄𐤔𐤁𐤕.𐤋𐤃𐤓𐤕𐤌.𐤁𐤓𐤉𐤕.𐤏𐤅𐤋𐤌|

..𐤉𐤆.. 𐤁𐤉𐤍𐤉.𐤅𐤁𐤉𐤍.𐤁𐤍𐤉.𐤉𐤔𐤓𐤀𐤋.𐤀𐤅𐤕.𐤄𐤅𐤀.𐤋𐤏𐤋𐤌.𐤊𐤉
.𐤔𐤔𐤕.𐤉𐤌𐤉𐤌.𐤏𐤔𐤄.𐤉𐤄𐤅𐤄.𐤀𐤕.𐤄𐤔𐤌𐤉𐤌.𐤅𐤀𐤕.𐤄𐤀𐤓
𐤑.𐤅𐤁𐤉𐤅𐤌.𐤄𐤔𐤁𐤉𐤏𐤉.𐤔𐤁𐤕.𐤅𐤉𐤍𐤐𐤔|
..𐤉𐤇.. 𐤅𐤉𐤕𐤍.𐤀𐤋.𐤌𐤔𐤄.𐤊𐤊𐤋𐤕𐤅.𐤋𐤃𐤁𐤓.𐤀𐤕𐤅.𐤁𐤄𐤓.𐤎𐤉𐤍
𐤉.𐤔𐤍𐤉.𐤋𐤇𐤕.𐤄𐤏𐤃𐤕.𐤋𐤇𐤕.𐤀𐤁𐤍.𐤊𐤕𐤁𐤉𐤌.𐤁𐤀𐤑𐤁𐤏.
𐤀𐤋𐤄𐤉𐤌||

𐤅𐤉𐤏𐤋𐤅.𐤌𐤌𐤑𐤓𐤉𐤌.𐤇𐤋𐤒 ..𐤋𐤁..

..𐤀.. 𐤅𐤉𐤓𐤀.𐤄𐤏𐤌.𐤊𐤉.𐤁𐤔𐤔.𐤌𐤔𐤄.𐤋𐤓𐤃𐤕.𐤌𐤍.𐤄𐤄𐤓.𐤅𐤉
𐤒𐤄𐤋.𐤄𐤏𐤌.𐤏𐤋.𐤀𐤄𐤓𐤍.𐤅𐤉𐤀𐤌𐤓𐤅.𐤀𐤋𐤉𐤅.𐤒𐤅𐤌.𐤏𐤔𐤄.𐤋𐤍
𐤅.𐤀𐤋𐤄𐤉𐤌.𐤀𐤔𐤓.𐤉𐤋𐤊𐤅.𐤋𐤐𐤍𐤉𐤍𐤅.𐤊𐤉.𐤆𐤄.𐤌𐤔𐤄.𐤄𐤀𐤉
𐤔.𐤀𐤔𐤓.𐤄𐤏𐤋𐤍𐤅.𐤌𐤀𐤓𐤑.𐤌𐤑𐤓𐤉𐤌.𐤋𐤀.𐤉𐤃𐤏𐤍𐤅.𐤌𐤄.𐤄
𐤉𐤄.𐤋𐤅|
..𐤁.. 𐤅𐤉𐤀𐤌𐤓.𐤀𐤋𐤄𐤌.𐤀𐤄𐤓𐤍.𐤐𐤓𐤒𐤅.𐤍𐤆𐤌𐤉.𐤄𐤆𐤄𐤁.𐤀𐤔
𐤓.𐤁𐤀𐤆𐤍𐤉.𐤍𐤔𐤉𐤊𐤌.𐤁𐤍𐤉𐤊𐤌.𐤅𐤁𐤍𐤕𐤉𐤊𐤌.𐤅𐤄𐤁𐤉𐤀𐤅.𐤀𐤋
𐤉|
..𐤂.. 𐤅𐤉𐤕𐤐𐤓𐤒𐤅.𐤊𐤋.𐤄𐤏𐤌.𐤀𐤕.𐤍𐤆𐤌𐤉.𐤄𐤆𐤄𐤁.𐤀𐤔𐤓.𐤁
𐤀𐤆𐤍𐤉𐤄𐤌.𐤅𐤉𐤁𐤉𐤀𐤅.𐤀𐤋.𐤀𐤄𐤓𐤍|
..𐤃.. 𐤅𐤉𐤒𐤇.𐤌𐤉𐤃𐤌.𐤅𐤉𐤑𐤓.𐤀𐤕𐤅.𐤁𐤇𐤓𐤈.𐤅𐤉𐤏𐤔𐤄𐤅.𐤏
𐤂𐤋.𐤌𐤎𐤊𐤄.𐤅𐤉𐤀𐤌𐤓𐤅.𐤀𐤋𐤄.𐤀𐤋𐤄𐤉𐤊.𐤉𐤔𐤓𐤀𐤋.𐤀𐤔𐤓.𐤄
𐤏𐤋𐤅𐤊.𐤌𐤀𐤓𐤑.𐤌𐤑𐤓𐤉𐤌|
..𐤄.. 𐤅𐤉𐤓𐤀.𐤀𐤄𐤓𐤍.𐤅𐤉𐤁𐤍.𐤌𐤆𐤁𐤇.𐤋𐤐𐤍𐤉𐤅.𐤅𐤉𐤒𐤓𐤀.𐤀𐤄𐤓𐤍
.𐤅𐤉𐤀𐤌𐤓.𐤇𐤂.𐤋𐤉𐤄𐤅𐤄.𐤌𐤇𐤓|
..𐤅.. 𐤅𐤉𐤔𐤊𐤉𐤌𐤅.𐤌𐤌𐤇𐤓𐤕.𐤅𐤉𐤏𐤋𐤅.𐤏𐤋𐤕.𐤅𐤉𐤂𐤔𐤅.𐤔𐤋𐤌𐤉
𐤌.𐤅𐤉𐤔𐤁.𐤄𐤏𐤌.𐤋𐤀𐤊𐤋.𐤅𐤔𐤕𐤅.𐤅𐤉𐤒𐤌𐤅.𐤋𐤑𐤇𐤒|
..𐤆.. 𐤅𐤉𐤃𐤁𐤓.𐤉𐤄𐤅𐤄.𐤀𐤋.𐤌𐤔𐤄.𐤋𐤊.𐤓𐤃.𐤊𐤉.𐤔𐤇𐤕.𐤏𐤌
𐤊.𐤀𐤔𐤓.𐤄𐤏𐤋𐤉𐤕.𐤌𐤀𐤓𐤑.𐤌𐤑𐤓𐤉𐤌|
..𐤇.. 𐤎𐤓𐤅.𐤌𐤄𐤓.𐤌𐤍.𐤄𐤃𐤓𐤊.𐤀𐤔𐤓.𐤑𐤅𐤉𐤕𐤌.𐤏𐤔𐤅.𐤋𐤄𐤌.
𐤏𐤂𐤋.𐤌𐤎𐤊𐤄.𐤅𐤉𐤔𐤕𐤇𐤅𐤅.𐤋𐤅.𐤅𐤉𐤆𐤁𐤇𐤅.𐤋𐤅.𐤅𐤉𐤀𐤌𐤓𐤅.𐤀
𐤋𐤄.𐤀𐤋𐤄𐤉𐤊.𐤉𐤔𐤓𐤀𐤋.𐤀𐤔𐤓.𐤄𐤏𐤋𐤅𐤊.𐤌𐤀𐤓𐤑.𐤌𐤑𐤓𐤉𐤌|

𐤈 𐤅𐤉𐤀𐤌𐤓.𐤉𐤄𐤅𐤄.𐤀𐤋.𐤌𐤔𐤄.𐤓𐤀𐤉𐤕𐤉.𐤀𐤕.𐤄𐤏𐤌.𐤄
𐤆𐤄.𐤅𐤄𐤍𐤄.𐤏𐤌.𐤒𐤔𐤄.𐤏𐤓𐤐.𐤄𐤅𐤀|
𐤉 𐤅𐤏𐤕𐤄.𐤄𐤍𐤉𐤇𐤄.𐤋𐤉.𐤅𐤉𐤇𐤓.𐤀𐤐𐤉.𐤁𐤄𐤌.𐤅𐤀𐤊𐤋𐤌.𐤅
𐤀𐤏𐤔𐤄.𐤀𐤅𐤕𐤊.𐤋𐤂𐤅𐤉.𐤂𐤃𐤅𐤋|
𐤉𐤀 𐤅𐤉𐤇𐤋.𐤌𐤔𐤄.𐤀𐤕.𐤐𐤍𐤉.𐤉𐤄𐤅𐤄.𐤀𐤋𐤄𐤉𐤅.𐤅𐤉𐤀𐤌𐤓.𐤋
𐤌𐤄.𐤉𐤄𐤅𐤄.𐤉𐤇𐤓𐤄.𐤀𐤐𐤊.𐤁𐤏𐤌𐤊.𐤀𐤔𐤓.𐤄𐤅𐤑𐤀𐤕.𐤌𐤀𐤓
𐤑.𐤌𐤑𐤓𐤉𐤌.𐤁𐤊𐤇.𐤂𐤃𐤅𐤋.𐤅𐤁𐤉𐤃.𐤇𐤆𐤒𐤄|
𐤉𐤁 𐤋𐤌𐤄.𐤉𐤀𐤌𐤓𐤅.𐤌𐤑𐤓𐤉𐤌.𐤋𐤀𐤌𐤓.𐤁𐤓𐤏𐤄.𐤄𐤅𐤑𐤉𐤀𐤌
.𐤋𐤄𐤓𐤂.𐤀𐤕𐤌.𐤁𐤄𐤓𐤉𐤌.𐤅𐤋𐤊𐤋𐤕𐤌.𐤌𐤏𐤋.𐤐𐤍𐤉.𐤄𐤀𐤃𐤌𐤄
.𐤔𐤅𐤁.𐤌𐤇𐤓𐤅𐤍.𐤀𐤐𐤊.𐤅𐤄𐤍𐤇𐤌.𐤏𐤋.𐤄𐤓𐤏𐤄.𐤋𐤏𐤌𐤊|
𐤉𐤂 𐤆𐤊𐤓.𐤋𐤀𐤁𐤓𐤄𐤌.𐤋𐤉𐤑𐤇𐤒.𐤅𐤋𐤉𐤔𐤓𐤀𐤋.𐤏𐤁𐤃𐤉𐤊.
𐤀𐤔𐤓.𐤍𐤔𐤁𐤏𐤕.𐤋𐤄𐤌.𐤁𐤊.𐤅𐤕𐤃𐤁𐤓.𐤀𐤋𐤄𐤌.𐤀𐤓𐤁𐤄.𐤀𐤕.
𐤆𐤓𐤏𐤊𐤌.𐤊𐤊𐤅𐤊𐤁𐤉.𐤄𐤔𐤌𐤉𐤌.𐤅𐤊𐤋.𐤄𐤀𐤓𐤑.𐤄𐤆𐤀𐤕.𐤀
𐤔𐤓.𐤀𐤌𐤓𐤕𐤉.𐤀𐤕𐤍.𐤋𐤆𐤓𐤏𐤊𐤌.𐤅𐤍𐤇𐤋𐤅.𐤋𐤏𐤋𐤌|
𐤉𐤃 𐤅𐤉𐤍𐤇𐤌.𐤉𐤄𐤅𐤄.𐤏𐤋.𐤄𐤓𐤏𐤄.𐤀𐤔𐤓.𐤃𐤁𐤓.𐤋𐤏𐤔𐤅𐤕.
𐤋𐤏𐤌𐤅|
𐤉𐤄 𐤅𐤉𐤐𐤍.𐤅𐤉𐤓𐤃.𐤌𐤔𐤄.𐤌𐤍.𐤄𐤄𐤓.𐤅𐤔𐤍𐤉.𐤋𐤇𐤕.𐤄𐤏𐤃
𐤕.𐤁𐤉𐤃𐤅.𐤋𐤇𐤕.𐤊𐤕𐤁𐤉𐤌.𐤌𐤔𐤍𐤉.𐤏𐤁𐤓𐤉𐤄𐤌.𐤌𐤆𐤄.𐤅𐤌
𐤆𐤄.𐤄𐤌.𐤊𐤕𐤁𐤉𐤌|
𐤉𐤅 𐤅𐤄𐤋𐤇𐤕.𐤌𐤏𐤔𐤄.𐤀𐤋𐤄𐤉𐤌.𐤄𐤌𐤄.𐤅𐤄𐤌𐤊𐤕𐤁.𐤌𐤊𐤕
𐤁.𐤀𐤋𐤄𐤉𐤌.𐤄𐤅𐤀.𐤇𐤓𐤅𐤕.𐤏𐤋.𐤄𐤋𐤇𐤕|
𐤉𐤆 𐤅𐤉𐤔𐤌𐤏.𐤉𐤄𐤅𐤔𐤏.𐤀𐤕.𐤒𐤅𐤋.𐤄𐤏𐤌.𐤁𐤓𐤏𐤄.𐤅𐤉𐤀𐤌
𐤓.𐤀𐤋.𐤌𐤔𐤄.𐤒𐤅𐤋.𐤌𐤋𐤇𐤌𐤄.𐤁𐤌𐤇𐤍𐤄|
𐤉𐤇 𐤅𐤉𐤀𐤌𐤓.𐤀𐤉𐤍.𐤒𐤅𐤋.𐤏𐤍𐤅𐤕.𐤂𐤁𐤅𐤓𐤄.𐤅𐤀𐤉𐤍.𐤒𐤅𐤋.𐤏𐤍
𐤅𐤕.𐤇𐤋𐤅𐤔𐤄.𐤒𐤅𐤋.𐤏𐤍𐤅𐤕.𐤀𐤍𐤊𐤉.𐤔𐤌𐤏|
𐤉𐤈 𐤅𐤉𐤄𐤉.𐤊𐤀𐤔𐤓.𐤒𐤓𐤁.𐤀𐤋.𐤄𐤌𐤇𐤍𐤄.𐤅𐤉𐤓𐤀.𐤀𐤕.𐤄
𐤏𐤂𐤋.𐤅𐤌𐤇𐤋𐤕.𐤅𐤉𐤇𐤓.𐤀𐤐.𐤌𐤔𐤄.𐤅𐤉𐤔𐤋𐤊.𐤌𐤉𐤃𐤅.||𐤌𐤉
𐤃𐤉𐤅.𐤒𐤓𐤉||.𐤀𐤕.𐤄𐤋𐤇𐤕.𐤅𐤉𐤔𐤁𐤓.𐤀𐤕𐤌.𐤕𐤇𐤕.𐤄𐤄𐤓|
𐤊 𐤅𐤉𐤒𐤇.𐤀𐤕.𐤄𐤏𐤂𐤋.𐤀𐤔𐤓.𐤏𐤔𐤅.𐤅𐤉𐤔𐤓𐤐.𐤁𐤀𐤔.𐤅
𐤉𐤈𐤇𐤍.𐤏𐤃.𐤀𐤔𐤓.𐤃𐤒.𐤅𐤉𐤆𐤓.𐤏𐤋.𐤐𐤍𐤉.𐤄𐤌𐤉𐤌.𐤅𐤉𐤔𐤒
.𐤀𐤕.𐤁𐤍𐤉.𐤉𐤔𐤓𐤀𐤋|

𐤊𐤀 𐤅𐤉𐤀𐤌𐤓.𐤌𐤔𐤄.𐤀𐤋.𐤀𐤄𐤓𐤍.𐤌𐤄.𐤏𐤔𐤄.𐤋𐤊.𐤄𐤏𐤌.𐤄
𐤆𐤄.𐤊𐤉.𐤄𐤁𐤀𐤕.𐤏𐤋𐤉𐤅.𐤇𐤈𐤀𐤄.𐤂𐤃𐤋𐤄|
𐤊𐤁 𐤅𐤉𐤀𐤌𐤓.𐤀𐤄𐤓𐤍.𐤀𐤋.𐤉𐤇𐤓.𐤀𐤐.𐤀𐤃𐤍𐤉.𐤀𐤕𐤄.𐤉𐤃
𐤏𐤕.𐤀𐤕.𐤄𐤏𐤌.𐤊𐤉.𐤁𐤓𐤏.𐤄𐤅𐤀|
𐤊𐤂 𐤅𐤉𐤀𐤌𐤓𐤅.𐤋𐤉.𐤏𐤔𐤄.𐤋𐤍𐤅.𐤀𐤋𐤄𐤉𐤌.𐤀𐤔𐤓.𐤉𐤋𐤊𐤅.𐤋𐤐
𐤍𐤉𐤍𐤅.𐤊𐤉.𐤆𐤄.𐤌𐤔𐤄.𐤄𐤀𐤉𐤔.𐤀𐤔𐤓.𐤄𐤏𐤋𐤍𐤅.𐤌𐤀𐤓𐤑.𐤌
𐤑𐤓𐤉𐤌.𐤋𐤀.𐤉𐤃𐤏𐤍𐤅.𐤌𐤄.𐤄𐤉𐤄.𐤋𐤅|
𐤊𐤃 𐤅𐤀𐤌𐤓.𐤋𐤄𐤌.𐤋𐤌𐤉.𐤆𐤄𐤁.𐤄𐤕𐤐𐤓𐤒𐤅.𐤅𐤉𐤕𐤍𐤅.𐤋𐤉.𐤅
𐤀𐤔𐤋𐤊𐤄𐤅.𐤁𐤀𐤔.𐤅𐤉𐤑𐤀.𐤄𐤏𐤂𐤋.𐤄𐤆𐤄|
𐤊𐤄 𐤅𐤉𐤓𐤀.𐤌𐤔𐤄.𐤀𐤕.𐤄𐤏𐤌.𐤊𐤉.𐤐𐤓𐤏.𐤄𐤅𐤀.𐤊𐤉.𐤐𐤓𐤏𐤄
.𐤀𐤄𐤓𐤍.𐤋𐤔𐤌𐤑𐤄.𐤁𐤒𐤌𐤉𐤄𐤌|
𐤊𐤅 𐤅𐤉𐤏𐤌𐤃.𐤌𐤔𐤄.𐤁𐤔𐤏𐤓.𐤄𐤌𐤇𐤍𐤄.𐤅𐤉𐤀𐤌𐤓.𐤌𐤉.𐤋𐤉
𐤄𐤅𐤄.𐤀𐤋𐤉.𐤅𐤉𐤀𐤎𐤐𐤅.𐤀𐤋𐤉𐤅.𐤊𐤋.𐤁𐤍𐤉.𐤋𐤅𐤉|
𐤊𐤆 𐤅𐤉𐤀𐤌𐤓.𐤋𐤄𐤌.𐤊𐤄.𐤀𐤌𐤓.𐤉𐤄𐤅𐤄.𐤀𐤋𐤄𐤉.𐤉𐤔𐤓𐤀𐤋.
𐤔𐤉𐤌𐤅.𐤀𐤉𐤔.𐤇𐤓𐤁𐤅.𐤏𐤋.𐤉𐤓𐤊𐤅.𐤏𐤁𐤓𐤅.𐤅𐤔𐤅𐤁𐤅.𐤌𐤔𐤏𐤓.𐤋
𐤔𐤏𐤓.𐤁𐤌𐤇𐤍𐤄.𐤅𐤄𐤓𐤂𐤅.𐤀𐤉𐤔.𐤀𐤕.𐤀𐤇𐤉𐤅.𐤅𐤀𐤉𐤔.𐤀𐤕.
𐤓𐤏𐤄𐤅.𐤅𐤀𐤉𐤔.𐤀𐤕.𐤒𐤓𐤁𐤅|
𐤊𐤇 𐤅𐤉𐤏𐤔𐤅.𐤁𐤍𐤉.𐤋𐤅𐤉.𐤊𐤃𐤁𐤓.𐤌𐤔𐤄.𐤅𐤉𐤐𐤋.𐤌𐤍.𐤄𐤏𐤌.
𐤁𐤉𐤅𐤌.𐤄𐤄𐤅𐤀.𐤊𐤔𐤋𐤔𐤕.𐤀𐤋𐤐𐤉.𐤀𐤉𐤔|
𐤊𐤈 𐤅𐤉𐤀𐤌𐤓.𐤌𐤔𐤄.𐤌𐤋𐤀𐤅.𐤉𐤃𐤊𐤌.𐤄𐤉𐤅𐤌.𐤋𐤉𐤄𐤅𐤄.𐤊
𐤉.𐤀𐤉𐤔.𐤁𐤁𐤍𐤅.𐤅𐤁𐤀𐤇𐤉𐤅.𐤅𐤋𐤕𐤕.𐤏𐤋𐤉𐤊𐤌.𐤄𐤉𐤅𐤌.𐤁𐤓𐤊𐤄
|
𐤋 𐤅𐤉𐤄𐤉.𐤌𐤌𐤇𐤓𐤕.𐤅𐤉𐤀𐤌𐤓.𐤌𐤔𐤄.𐤀𐤋.𐤄𐤏𐤌.𐤀𐤕𐤌.
𐤇𐤈𐤀𐤕𐤌.𐤇𐤈𐤀𐤄.𐤂𐤃𐤋𐤄.𐤅𐤏𐤕𐤄.𐤀𐤏𐤋𐤄.𐤀𐤋.𐤉𐤄𐤅𐤄
.𐤀𐤅𐤋𐤉.𐤀𐤊𐤐𐤓𐤄.𐤁𐤏𐤃.𐤇𐤈𐤀𐤕𐤊𐤌|
𐤋𐤀 𐤅𐤉𐤔𐤁.𐤌𐤔𐤄.𐤀𐤋.𐤉𐤄𐤅𐤄.𐤅𐤉𐤀𐤌𐤓.𐤀𐤍𐤀.𐤇𐤈𐤀.𐤄
𐤏𐤌.𐤄𐤆𐤄.𐤇𐤈𐤀𐤄.𐤂𐤃𐤋𐤄.𐤅𐤉𐤏𐤔𐤅.𐤋𐤄𐤌.𐤀𐤋𐤄𐤉.𐤆
𐤄𐤁|
𐤋𐤁 𐤅𐤏𐤕𐤄.𐤀𐤌.𐤕𐤔𐤀.𐤇𐤈𐤀𐤕𐤌.𐤅𐤀𐤌.𐤀𐤉𐤍.𐤌𐤇𐤍𐤉.𐤍
𐤀.𐤌𐤎𐤐𐤓𐤊.𐤀𐤔𐤓.𐤊𐤕𐤁𐤕|

..𐤋𐤂.. 𐤅𐤉𐤀𐤌𐤓.𐤉𐤄𐤅𐤄.𐤀𐤋.𐤌𐤔𐤄.𐤌𐤉.𐤀𐤔𐤓.𐤇𐤈𐤀.𐤋𐤉.𐤀
𐤌𐤇𐤍𐤅.𐤌𐤎𐤐𐤓𐤉|
..𐤋𐤃.. 𐤅𐤏𐤕𐤄.𐤋𐤊.𐤍𐤇𐤄.𐤀𐤕.𐤄𐤏𐤌.𐤀𐤋.𐤀𐤔𐤓.𐤃𐤁𐤓𐤕𐤉.
𐤋𐤊.𐤄𐤍𐤄.𐤌𐤋𐤀𐤊𐤉.𐤉𐤋𐤊.𐤋𐤐𐤍𐤉𐤊.𐤅𐤁𐤉𐤅𐤌.𐤐𐤒𐤃𐤉.𐤅𐤐𐤒𐤃
𐤕𐤉.𐤏𐤋𐤉𐤄𐤌.𐤇𐤈𐤀𐤕𐤌|
..𐤋𐤄.. 𐤅𐤉𐤂𐤐.𐤉𐤄𐤅𐤄.𐤀𐤕.𐤄𐤏𐤌.𐤏𐤋.𐤀𐤔𐤓.𐤏𐤔𐤅.𐤀𐤕.𐤄𐤏
𐤂𐤋.𐤀𐤔𐤓.𐤏𐤔𐤄.𐤀𐤄𐤓𐤍||

𐤅𐤉𐤏𐤋𐤅.𐤌𐤌𐤑𐤓𐤉𐤌.𐤇𐤋𐤒 ..𐤋𐤂..

..𐤀.. 𐤅𐤉𐤃𐤁𐤓.𐤉𐤄𐤅𐤄.𐤀𐤋.𐤌𐤔𐤄.𐤋𐤊.𐤏𐤋𐤄.𐤌𐤆𐤄.𐤀𐤕𐤄.𐤅
𐤄𐤏𐤌.𐤀𐤔𐤓.𐤄𐤏𐤋𐤉𐤕.𐤌𐤀𐤓𐤑.𐤌𐤑𐤓𐤉𐤌.𐤀𐤋.𐤄𐤀𐤓𐤑.𐤀
𐤔𐤓.𐤍𐤔𐤁𐤏𐤕𐤉.𐤋𐤀𐤁𐤓𐤄𐤌.𐤋𐤉𐤑𐤇𐤒.𐤅𐤋𐤉𐤏𐤒𐤁.𐤋𐤀𐤌𐤓.
𐤋𐤆𐤓𐤏𐤊.𐤀𐤕𐤍𐤍𐤄|
..𐤁.. 𐤅𐤔𐤋𐤇𐤕𐤉.𐤋𐤐𐤍𐤉𐤊.𐤌𐤋𐤀𐤊.𐤅𐤂𐤓𐤔𐤕𐤉.𐤀𐤕.𐤄𐤊𐤍𐤏𐤍
𐤉.𐤄𐤀𐤌𐤓𐤉.𐤅𐤄𐤇𐤕𐤉.𐤅𐤄𐤐𐤓𐤆𐤉.𐤄𐤇𐤅𐤉.𐤅𐤄𐤉𐤁𐤅𐤎𐤉|
..𐤂.. 𐤀𐤋.𐤀𐤓𐤑.𐤆𐤁𐤕.𐤇𐤋𐤁.𐤅𐤃𐤁𐤔.𐤊𐤉.𐤋𐤀.𐤀𐤏𐤋𐤄.𐤁𐤒
𐤓𐤁𐤊.𐤊𐤉.𐤏𐤌.𐤒𐤔𐤄.𐤏𐤓𐤐.𐤀𐤕𐤄.𐤐𐤍.𐤀𐤊𐤋𐤊.𐤁𐤃𐤓𐤊|
..𐤃.. 𐤅𐤉𐤔𐤌𐤏.𐤄𐤏𐤌.𐤀𐤕.𐤄𐤃𐤁𐤓.𐤄𐤓𐤏.𐤄𐤆𐤄.𐤅𐤉𐤕𐤀𐤁
𐤋𐤅.𐤅𐤋𐤀.𐤔𐤕𐤅.𐤀𐤉𐤔.𐤏𐤃𐤉𐤅.𐤏𐤋𐤉𐤅|
..𐤄.. 𐤅𐤉𐤀𐤌𐤓.𐤉𐤄𐤅𐤄.𐤀𐤋.𐤌𐤔𐤄.𐤀𐤌𐤓.𐤀𐤋.𐤁𐤍𐤉.𐤉𐤔𐤓𐤀𐤋.
𐤀𐤕𐤌.𐤏𐤌.𐤒𐤔𐤄.𐤏𐤓𐤐.𐤓𐤂𐤏.𐤀𐤇𐤃.𐤀𐤏𐤋𐤄.𐤁𐤒𐤓𐤁𐤊.𐤅
𐤊𐤋𐤉𐤕𐤉𐤊.𐤅𐤏𐤕𐤄.𐤄𐤅𐤓𐤃.𐤏𐤃𐤉𐤊.𐤌𐤏𐤋𐤉𐤊.𐤅𐤀𐤃𐤏𐤄.
𐤌𐤄.𐤀𐤏𐤔𐤄.𐤋𐤊|
..𐤅.. 𐤅𐤉𐤕𐤍𐤑𐤋𐤅.𐤁𐤍𐤉.𐤉𐤔𐤓𐤀𐤋.𐤀𐤕.𐤏𐤃𐤉𐤌.𐤌𐤄𐤓.𐤇𐤅𐤓𐤁|
..𐤆.. 𐤅𐤌𐤔𐤄.𐤉𐤒𐤇.𐤀𐤕.𐤄𐤀𐤄𐤋.𐤅𐤍𐤈𐤄.𐤋𐤅.𐤌𐤇𐤅𐤑.𐤋𐤌𐤇
𐤍𐤄.𐤄𐤓𐤇𐤒.𐤌𐤍.𐤄𐤌𐤇𐤍𐤄.𐤅𐤒𐤓𐤀.𐤋𐤅.𐤀𐤄𐤋.𐤌𐤅𐤏𐤃.𐤅𐤄𐤉
𐤄.𐤊𐤋.𐤌𐤁𐤒𐤔.𐤉𐤄𐤅𐤄.𐤉𐤑𐤀.𐤀𐤋.𐤀𐤄𐤋.𐤌𐤅𐤏𐤃.𐤀𐤔𐤓.𐤌
𐤇𐤅𐤑.𐤋𐤌𐤇𐤍𐤄|

ח והיה.כצאת.משה.אל.האהל.יקומו.כל.הע
ם.ונצבו.איש.פתח.אהלו.והביטו.אחרי.משה.
עד.באו.האהלה׃
ט והיה.כבא.משה.האהלה.ירד.עמוד.הענן
.ועמד.פתח.האהל.ודבר.עם.משה׃
י וראה.כל.העם.את.עמוד.הענן.עמד.פתח
.האהל.וקם.כל.העם.והשתחוו.איש.פתח.אהלו
׃
יא ודבר.יהוה.אל.משה.פנים.אל.פנים.כאשר.
ידבר.איש.אל.רעהו.ושב.אל.המחנה.ומשרתו.
יהושע.בן.נון.נער.לא.ימיש.מתוך.האהל׃
יב ויאמר.משה.אל.יהוה.ראה.אתה.אמר.אלי
.העל.את.העם.הזה.ואתה.לא.הודעתני.את.
אשר.תשלח.עמי.ואתה.אמרת.ידעתיך.בשם.ו
גם.מצאת.חן.בעיני׃
יג ועתה.אם.נא.מצאתי.חן.בעיניך.הודענ
י.נא.את.דרכך.ואדעך.למען.אמצא.חן.בעינ
יך.וראה.כי.עמך.הגוי.הזה׃
יד ויאמר.פני.ילכו.והנחתי.לך׃
טו ויאמר.אליו.אם.אין.פניך.הלכים.אל.תע
לנו.מזה׃
טז ובמה.יודע.אפוא.כי.מצאתי.חן.בעיני
ך.אני.ועמך.הלוא.בלכתך.עמנו.ונפלינו.אני.ו
עמך.מכל.העם.אשר.על.פני.האדמה׃
יז ויאמר.יהוה.אל.משה.גם.את.הדבר.הז
ה.אשר.דברת.אעשה.כי.מצאת.חן.בעיני.וא
דעך.בשם׃
יח ויאמר.הראני.נא.את.כבדך׃
יט ויאמר.אני.אעביר.כל.טובי.על.פניך.וק
ראתי.בשם.יהוה.לפניך.וחנתי.את.אשר.אחן.
ורחמתי.את.אשר.ארחם׃

20 𐤅𐤉𐤀𐤌𐤓.𐤋𐤀.𐤕𐤅𐤊𐤋.𐤋𐤓𐤀𐤕.𐤀𐤕.𐤐𐤍𐤉.𐤊𐤉.𐤋𐤀.𐤉𐤓
𐤀𐤍𐤉.𐤄𐤀𐤃𐤌.𐤅𐤇𐤉|
21 𐤅𐤉𐤀𐤌𐤓.𐤉𐤄𐤅𐤄.𐤄𐤍𐤄.𐤌𐤒𐤅𐤌.𐤀𐤕𐤉.𐤅𐤍𐤑𐤁𐤕.𐤏𐤋.𐤄
𐤑𐤅𐤓|
22 𐤅𐤄𐤉𐤄.𐤁𐤏𐤁𐤓.𐤊𐤁𐤃𐤉.𐤅𐤔𐤌𐤕𐤉𐤊.𐤁𐤍𐤒𐤓𐤕.𐤄𐤑𐤅𐤓
.𐤅𐤔𐤊𐤕𐤉.𐤊𐤐𐤉.𐤏𐤋𐤉𐤊.𐤏𐤃.𐤏𐤁𐤓𐤉|
23 𐤅𐤄𐤎𐤓𐤕𐤉.𐤀𐤕.𐤊𐤐𐤉.𐤅𐤓𐤀𐤉𐤕.𐤀𐤕.𐤀𐤇𐤓𐤉.𐤅𐤐𐤍𐤉.𐤋
𐤀.𐤉𐤓𐤀𐤅||

𐤅𐤉𐤏𐤋𐤅.𐤌𐤌𐤑𐤓𐤉𐤌.𐤇𐤋𐤒 34

1 𐤅𐤉𐤀𐤌𐤓.𐤉𐤄𐤅𐤄.𐤀𐤋.𐤌𐤔𐤄.𐤐𐤎𐤋.𐤋𐤊.𐤔𐤍𐤉.𐤋𐤇𐤕.𐤀𐤁
𐤍𐤉𐤌.𐤊𐤓𐤀𐤔𐤍𐤉𐤌.𐤅𐤊𐤕𐤁𐤕𐤉.𐤏𐤋.𐤄𐤋𐤇𐤕.𐤀𐤕.𐤄𐤃𐤁𐤓𐤉
𐤌.𐤀𐤔𐤓.𐤄𐤉𐤅.𐤏𐤋.𐤄𐤋𐤇𐤕.𐤄𐤓𐤀𐤔𐤍𐤉𐤌.𐤀𐤔𐤓.𐤔𐤁𐤓𐤕|
2 𐤅𐤄𐤉𐤄.𐤍𐤊𐤅𐤍.𐤋𐤁𐤒𐤓.𐤅𐤏𐤋𐤉𐤕.𐤁𐤁𐤒𐤓.𐤀𐤋.𐤄𐤓.𐤎𐤉𐤍𐤉
.𐤅𐤍𐤑𐤁𐤕.𐤋𐤉.𐤔𐤌.𐤏𐤋.𐤓𐤀𐤔.𐤄𐤄𐤓|
3 𐤅𐤀𐤉𐤔.𐤋𐤀.𐤉𐤏𐤋𐤄.𐤏𐤌𐤊.𐤅𐤂𐤌.𐤀𐤉𐤔.𐤀𐤋.𐤉𐤓𐤀.𐤁𐤊
𐤋.𐤄𐤄𐤓.𐤂𐤌.𐤄𐤑𐤀𐤍.𐤅𐤄𐤁𐤒𐤓.𐤀𐤋.𐤉𐤓𐤏𐤅.𐤀𐤋.𐤌𐤅𐤋.𐤄𐤄𐤓.
𐤄𐤄𐤅𐤀|
4 𐤅𐤉𐤐𐤎𐤋.𐤔𐤍𐤉.𐤋𐤇𐤕.𐤀𐤁𐤍𐤉𐤌.𐤊𐤓𐤀𐤔𐤍𐤉𐤌.𐤅𐤉𐤔𐤊𐤌.
𐤌𐤔𐤄.𐤁𐤁𐤒𐤓.𐤅𐤉𐤏𐤋.𐤀𐤋.𐤄𐤓.𐤎𐤉𐤍𐤉.𐤊𐤀𐤔𐤓.𐤑𐤅𐤄.𐤉𐤄𐤅
𐤄.𐤀𐤕𐤅.𐤅𐤉𐤒𐤇.𐤁𐤉𐤃𐤅.𐤔𐤍𐤉.𐤋𐤇𐤕.𐤀𐤁𐤍𐤉𐤌|
5 𐤅𐤉𐤓𐤃.𐤉𐤄𐤅𐤄.𐤁𐤏𐤍𐤍.𐤅𐤉𐤕𐤉𐤑𐤁.𐤏𐤌𐤅.𐤔𐤌.𐤅𐤉𐤒𐤓𐤀.
𐤁𐤔𐤌.𐤉𐤄𐤅𐤄|
6 𐤅𐤉𐤏𐤁𐤓.𐤉𐤄𐤅𐤄.𐤏𐤋.𐤐𐤍𐤉𐤅.𐤅𐤉𐤒𐤓𐤀.𐤉𐤄𐤅𐤄.𐤉𐤄𐤅𐤄.𐤀
𐤋.𐤓𐤇𐤅𐤌.𐤅𐤇𐤍𐤅𐤍.𐤀𐤓𐤊.𐤀𐤐𐤉𐤌.𐤅𐤓𐤁.𐤇𐤎𐤃.𐤅𐤀𐤌𐤕|
7 𐤍𐤑𐤓.𐤇𐤎𐤃.𐤋𐤀𐤋𐤐𐤉𐤌.𐤍𐤔𐤀.𐤏𐤅𐤍.𐤅𐤐𐤔𐤏.𐤅𐤇𐤈𐤀𐤄
.𐤅𐤍𐤒𐤄.𐤋𐤀.𐤉𐤍𐤒𐤄.𐤐𐤒𐤃.𐤏𐤅𐤍.𐤀𐤁𐤅𐤕.𐤏𐤋.𐤁𐤍𐤉𐤌.𐤅𐤏𐤋.
𐤁𐤍𐤉.𐤁𐤍𐤉𐤌.𐤏𐤋.𐤔𐤋𐤔𐤉𐤌.𐤅𐤏𐤋.𐤓𐤁𐤏𐤉𐤌|
8 𐤅𐤉𐤌𐤄𐤓.𐤌𐤔𐤄.𐤅𐤉𐤒𐤃.𐤀𐤓𐤑𐤄.𐤅𐤉𐤔𐤕𐤇𐤅|

ט 𐤅𐤉𐤀𐤌𐤓.𐤀𐤌.𐤍𐤀.𐤌𐤑𐤀𐤕𐤉.𐤇𐤍.𐤁𐤏𐤉𐤍𐤉𐤊.𐤀𐤃𐤍𐤉.
𐤉𐤋𐤊.𐤍𐤀.𐤀𐤃𐤍𐤉.𐤁𐤒𐤓𐤁𐤍𐤅.𐤊𐤉.𐤏𐤌.𐤒𐤔𐤄.𐤏𐤓𐤐.𐤄𐤅𐤀.𐤅
𐤎𐤋𐤇𐤕.𐤋𐤏𐤅𐤍𐤍𐤅.𐤅𐤋𐤇𐤈𐤀𐤕𐤍𐤅.𐤅𐤍𐤇𐤋𐤕𐤍𐤅|
י 𐤅𐤉𐤀𐤌𐤓.𐤄𐤍𐤄.𐤀𐤍𐤊𐤉.𐤊𐤓𐤕.𐤁𐤓𐤉𐤕.𐤍𐤂𐤃.𐤊𐤋.𐤏𐤌
𐤊.𐤀𐤏𐤔𐤄.𐤍𐤐𐤋𐤀𐤕.𐤀𐤔𐤓.𐤋𐤀.𐤍𐤁𐤓𐤀𐤅.𐤁𐤊𐤋.𐤄𐤀𐤓𐤑.𐤅𐤁
𐤊𐤋.𐤄𐤂𐤅𐤉𐤌.𐤅𐤓𐤀𐤄.𐤊𐤋.𐤄𐤏𐤌.𐤀𐤔𐤓.𐤀𐤕𐤄.𐤁𐤒𐤓𐤁𐤅.𐤀
𐤕.𐤌𐤏𐤔𐤄.𐤉𐤄𐤅𐤄.𐤊𐤉.𐤍𐤅𐤓𐤀.𐤄𐤅𐤀.𐤀𐤔𐤓.𐤀𐤍𐤉.𐤏𐤔𐤄.𐤏
𐤌𐤊|
יא 𐤔𐤌𐤓.𐤋𐤊.𐤀𐤕.𐤀𐤔𐤓.𐤀𐤍𐤊𐤉.𐤌𐤑𐤅𐤊.𐤄𐤉𐤅𐤌.𐤄𐤍𐤍𐤉.
𐤂𐤓𐤔.𐤌𐤐𐤍𐤉𐤊.𐤀𐤕.𐤄𐤀𐤌𐤓𐤉.𐤅𐤄𐤊𐤍𐤏𐤍𐤉.𐤅𐤄𐤇𐤕𐤉.𐤅𐤄𐤐
𐤓𐤆𐤉.𐤅𐤄𐤇𐤅𐤉.𐤅𐤄𐤉𐤁𐤅𐤎𐤉|
יב 𐤄𐤔𐤌𐤓.𐤋𐤊.𐤐𐤍.𐤕𐤊𐤓𐤕.𐤁𐤓𐤉𐤕.𐤋𐤉𐤅𐤔𐤁.𐤄𐤀𐤓𐤑.𐤀
𐤔𐤓.𐤀𐤕𐤄.𐤁𐤀.𐤏𐤋𐤉𐤄.𐤐𐤍.𐤉𐤄𐤉𐤄.𐤋𐤌𐤅𐤒𐤔.𐤁𐤒𐤓𐤁𐤊|
יג 𐤊𐤉.𐤀𐤕.𐤌𐤆𐤁𐤇𐤕𐤌.𐤕𐤕𐤑𐤅𐤍.𐤅𐤀𐤕.𐤌𐤑𐤁𐤕𐤌.𐤕
𐤔𐤁𐤓𐤅𐤍.𐤅𐤀𐤕.𐤀𐤔𐤓𐤉𐤅.𐤕𐤊𐤓𐤕𐤅𐤍|
יד 𐤊𐤉.𐤋𐤀.𐤕𐤔𐤕𐤇𐤅𐤄.𐤋𐤀𐤋.𐤀𐤇𐤓.𐤊𐤉.𐤉𐤄𐤅𐤄.𐤒𐤍𐤀.
𐤔𐤌𐤅.𐤀𐤋.𐤒𐤍𐤀.𐤄𐤅𐤀|
טו 𐤐𐤍.𐤕𐤊𐤓𐤕.𐤁𐤓𐤉𐤕.𐤋𐤉𐤅𐤔𐤁.𐤄𐤀𐤓𐤑.𐤅𐤆𐤍𐤅.𐤀𐤇𐤓𐤉.
𐤀𐤋𐤄𐤉𐤄𐤌.𐤅𐤆𐤁𐤇𐤅.𐤋𐤀𐤋𐤄𐤉𐤄𐤌.𐤅𐤒𐤓𐤀.𐤋𐤊.𐤅𐤀𐤊𐤋𐤕.𐤌
𐤆𐤁𐤇𐤅|
טז 𐤅𐤋𐤒𐤇𐤕.𐤌𐤁𐤍𐤕𐤉𐤅.𐤋𐤁𐤍𐤉𐤊.𐤅𐤄𐤆𐤍𐤅.𐤁𐤍𐤕𐤉𐤅.𐤀𐤇𐤓𐤉.
𐤀𐤋𐤄𐤉𐤄𐤍.𐤅𐤄𐤆𐤍𐤅.𐤀𐤕.𐤁𐤍𐤉𐤊.𐤀𐤇𐤓𐤉.𐤀𐤋𐤄𐤉𐤄𐤍|
יז 𐤀𐤋𐤄𐤉.𐤌𐤎𐤊𐤄.𐤋𐤀.𐤕𐤏𐤔𐤄.𐤋𐤊|
יח 𐤀𐤕.𐤇𐤂.𐤄𐤌𐤑𐤅𐤕.𐤕𐤔𐤌𐤓.𐤔𐤁𐤏𐤕.𐤉𐤌𐤉𐤌.𐤕𐤀𐤊
𐤋.𐤌𐤑𐤅𐤕.𐤊𐤀𐤔𐤓.𐤑𐤅𐤉𐤕𐤊.𐤋𐤌𐤅𐤏𐤃.𐤇𐤃𐤔.𐤄𐤀𐤁𐤉𐤁.𐤊𐤉
.𐤁𐤇𐤃𐤔.𐤄𐤀𐤁𐤉𐤁.𐤉𐤑𐤀𐤕.𐤌𐤌𐤑𐤓𐤉𐤌|
יט 𐤊𐤋.𐤐𐤈𐤓.𐤓𐤇𐤌.𐤋𐤉.𐤅𐤊𐤋.𐤌𐤒𐤍𐤊.𐤕𐤆𐤊𐤓.𐤐𐤈𐤓.𐤔𐤅
𐤓.𐤅𐤔𐤄|
כ 𐤅𐤐𐤈𐤓.𐤇𐤌𐤅𐤓.𐤕𐤐𐤃𐤄.𐤁𐤔𐤄.𐤅𐤀𐤌.𐤋𐤀.𐤕𐤐𐤃𐤄.𐤅𐤏
𐤓𐤐𐤕𐤅.𐤊𐤋.𐤁𐤊𐤅𐤓.𐤁𐤍𐤉𐤊.𐤕𐤐𐤃𐤄.𐤅𐤋𐤀.𐤉𐤓𐤀𐤅.𐤐𐤍𐤉.𐤓𐤉𐤒
𐤌|

..𐤊𐤀.. 𐤔𐤔𐤕.𐤉𐤌𐤉𐤌.𐤕𐤏𐤁𐤃.𐤅𐤁𐤉𐤅𐤌.𐤄𐤔𐤁𐤉𐤏𐤉.𐤕𐤔𐤁
𐤕.𐤁𐤇𐤓𐤉𐤔.𐤅𐤁𐤒𐤑𐤉𐤓.𐤕𐤔𐤁𐤕|
..𐤊𐤁.. 𐤅𐤇𐤂.𐤔𐤁𐤏𐤕.𐤕𐤏𐤔𐤄.𐤋𐤊.𐤁𐤊𐤅𐤓𐤉.𐤒𐤑𐤉𐤓.𐤇𐤈𐤉
𐤌.𐤅𐤇𐤂.𐤄𐤀𐤎𐤉𐤐.𐤕𐤒𐤅𐤐𐤕.𐤄𐤔𐤍𐤄|
..𐤊𐤂.. 𐤔𐤋𐤔.𐤐𐤏𐤌𐤉𐤌.𐤁𐤔𐤍𐤄.𐤉𐤓𐤀𐤄.𐤊𐤋.𐤆𐤊𐤅𐤓𐤊.𐤀𐤕.𐤐
𐤍𐤉.𐤄𐤀𐤃𐤍.𐤉𐤄𐤅𐤄.𐤀𐤋𐤄𐤉.𐤉𐤔𐤓𐤀𐤋|
..𐤊𐤃.. 𐤊𐤉.𐤀𐤅𐤓𐤉𐤔.𐤂𐤅𐤉𐤌.𐤌𐤐𐤍𐤉𐤊.𐤅𐤄𐤓𐤇𐤁𐤕𐤉.𐤀𐤕.𐤂
𐤁𐤅𐤋𐤊.𐤅𐤋𐤀.𐤉𐤇𐤌𐤃.𐤀𐤉𐤔.𐤀𐤕.𐤀𐤓𐤑𐤊.𐤁𐤏𐤋𐤕𐤊.𐤋𐤓𐤀𐤅
𐤕.𐤀𐤕.𐤐𐤍𐤉.𐤉𐤄𐤅𐤄.𐤀𐤋𐤄𐤉𐤊.𐤔𐤋𐤔.𐤐𐤏𐤌𐤉𐤌.𐤁𐤔𐤍𐤄|
..𐤊𐤄.. 𐤋𐤀.𐤕𐤔𐤇𐤈.𐤏𐤋.𐤇𐤌𐤑.𐤃𐤌.𐤆𐤁𐤇𐤉.𐤅𐤋𐤀.𐤉𐤋𐤉𐤍.
𐤋𐤁𐤒𐤓.𐤆𐤁𐤇.𐤇𐤂.𐤄𐤐𐤎𐤇|
..𐤊𐤅.. 𐤓𐤀𐤔𐤉𐤕.𐤁𐤊𐤅𐤓𐤉.𐤀𐤃𐤌𐤕𐤊.𐤕𐤁𐤉𐤀.𐤁𐤉𐤕.𐤉𐤄𐤅𐤄.
𐤀𐤋𐤄𐤉𐤊.𐤋𐤀.𐤕𐤁𐤔𐤋.𐤂𐤃𐤉.𐤁𐤇𐤋𐤁.𐤀𐤌𐤅|
..𐤊𐤆.. 𐤅𐤉𐤀𐤌𐤓.𐤉𐤄𐤅𐤄.𐤀𐤋.𐤌𐤔𐤄.𐤊𐤕𐤁.𐤋𐤊.𐤀𐤕.𐤄𐤃𐤁𐤓
𐤉𐤌.𐤄𐤀𐤋𐤄.𐤊𐤉.𐤏𐤋.𐤐𐤉.𐤄𐤃𐤁𐤓𐤉𐤌.𐤄𐤀𐤋𐤄.𐤊𐤓𐤕𐤉.𐤀𐤕
𐤊.𐤁𐤓𐤉𐤕.𐤅𐤀𐤕.𐤉𐤔𐤓𐤀𐤋|
..𐤊𐤇.. 𐤅𐤉𐤄𐤉.𐤔𐤌.𐤏𐤌.𐤉𐤄𐤅𐤄.𐤀𐤓𐤁𐤏𐤉𐤌.𐤉𐤅𐤌.𐤅𐤀𐤓𐤁𐤏𐤉
𐤌.𐤋𐤉𐤋𐤄.𐤋𐤇𐤌.𐤋𐤀.𐤀𐤊𐤋.𐤅𐤌𐤉𐤌.𐤋𐤀.𐤔𐤕𐤄.𐤅𐤉𐤊𐤕𐤁.𐤏
𐤋.𐤄𐤋𐤇𐤕.𐤀𐤕.𐤃𐤁𐤓𐤉.𐤄𐤁𐤓𐤉𐤕.𐤏𐤔𐤓𐤕.𐤄𐤃𐤁𐤓𐤉𐤌|
..𐤊𐤈.. 𐤅𐤉𐤄𐤉.𐤁𐤓𐤃𐤕.𐤌𐤔𐤄.𐤌𐤄𐤓.𐤎𐤉𐤍𐤉.𐤅𐤔𐤍𐤉.𐤋𐤇𐤕.
𐤄𐤏𐤃𐤕.𐤁𐤉𐤃.𐤌𐤔𐤄.𐤁𐤓𐤃𐤕𐤅.𐤌𐤍.𐤄𐤄𐤓.𐤅𐤌𐤔𐤄.𐤋𐤀.𐤉
𐤃𐤏.𐤊𐤉.𐤒𐤓𐤍.𐤏𐤅𐤓.𐤐𐤍𐤉𐤅.𐤁𐤃𐤁𐤓𐤅.𐤀𐤕𐤅|
..𐤋.. 𐤅𐤉𐤓𐤀.𐤀𐤄𐤓𐤍.𐤅𐤊𐤋.𐤁𐤍𐤉.𐤉𐤔𐤓𐤀𐤋.𐤀𐤕.𐤌𐤔𐤄.𐤅𐤄𐤍
𐤄.𐤒𐤓𐤍.𐤏𐤅𐤓.𐤐𐤍𐤉𐤅.𐤅𐤉𐤉𐤓𐤀𐤅.𐤌𐤂𐤔𐤕.𐤀𐤋𐤉𐤅|
..𐤋𐤀.. 𐤅𐤉𐤒𐤓𐤀.𐤀𐤋𐤄𐤌.𐤌𐤔𐤄.𐤅𐤉𐤔𐤁𐤅.𐤀𐤋𐤉𐤅.𐤀𐤄𐤓𐤍.𐤅𐤊𐤋.
𐤄𐤍𐤔𐤀𐤉𐤌.𐤁𐤏𐤃𐤄.𐤅𐤉𐤃𐤁𐤓.𐤌𐤔𐤄.𐤀𐤋𐤄𐤌|
..𐤋𐤁.. 𐤅𐤀𐤇𐤓𐤉.𐤊𐤍.𐤍𐤂𐤔𐤅.𐤊𐤋.𐤁𐤍𐤉.𐤉𐤔𐤓𐤀𐤋.𐤅𐤉𐤑𐤅𐤌.𐤀
𐤕.𐤊𐤋.𐤀𐤔𐤓.𐤃𐤁𐤓.𐤉𐤄𐤅𐤄.𐤀𐤕𐤅.𐤁𐤄𐤓.𐤎𐤉𐤍𐤉|
..𐤋𐤂.. 𐤅𐤉𐤊𐤋.𐤌𐤔𐤄.𐤌𐤃𐤁𐤓.𐤀𐤕𐤌.𐤅𐤉𐤕𐤍.𐤏𐤋.𐤐𐤍𐤉𐤅.𐤌𐤎𐤅
𐤄|

𐤋𐤃 𐤅𐤁𐤁𐤀.𐤌𐤔𐤄.𐤋𐤐𐤍𐤉.𐤉𐤄𐤅𐤄.𐤋𐤃𐤁𐤓.𐤀𐤕𐤅.𐤉𐤎𐤉𐤓.
𐤀𐤕.𐤄𐤌𐤎𐤅𐤄.𐤏𐤃.𐤑𐤀𐤕𐤅.𐤅𐤉𐤑𐤀.𐤅𐤃𐤁𐤓.𐤀𐤋.𐤁𐤍𐤉.𐤉𐤔
𐤓𐤀𐤋.𐤀𐤕.𐤀𐤔𐤓.𐤉𐤑𐤅𐤄|
𐤋𐤄 𐤅𐤓𐤀𐤅.𐤁𐤍𐤉.𐤉𐤔𐤓𐤀𐤋.𐤀𐤕.𐤐𐤍𐤉.𐤌𐤔𐤄.𐤊𐤉.𐤒𐤓𐤍.𐤏𐤅
𐤓.𐤐𐤍𐤉.𐤌𐤔𐤄.𐤅𐤄𐤔𐤉𐤁.𐤌𐤔𐤄.𐤀𐤕.𐤄𐤌𐤎𐤅𐤄.𐤏𐤋.𐤐𐤍𐤉𐤅.𐤏
𐤃.𐤁𐤀𐤅.𐤋𐤃𐤁𐤓.𐤀𐤕𐤅||

𐤅𐤉𐤏𐤋𐤅.𐤌𐤌𐤑𐤓𐤉𐤌.𐤇𐤋𐤒 𐤋𐤄

𐤀 𐤅𐤉𐤒𐤄𐤋.𐤌𐤔𐤄.𐤀𐤕.𐤊𐤋.𐤏𐤃𐤕.𐤁𐤍𐤉.𐤉𐤔𐤓𐤀𐤋.𐤅𐤉𐤀
𐤌𐤓.𐤀𐤋𐤄𐤌.𐤀𐤋𐤄.𐤄𐤃𐤁𐤓𐤉𐤌.𐤀𐤔𐤓.𐤑𐤅𐤄.𐤉𐤄𐤅𐤄.𐤋𐤏𐤔
𐤕.𐤀𐤕𐤌|
𐤁 𐤔𐤔𐤕.𐤉𐤌𐤉𐤌.𐤕𐤏𐤔𐤄.𐤌𐤋𐤀𐤊𐤄.𐤅𐤁𐤉𐤅𐤌.𐤄𐤔𐤁𐤉𐤏
𐤉.𐤉𐤄𐤉𐤄.𐤋𐤊𐤌.𐤒𐤃𐤔.𐤔𐤁𐤕.𐤔𐤁𐤕𐤅𐤍.𐤋𐤉𐤄𐤅𐤄.𐤊𐤋.𐤄𐤏
𐤔𐤄.𐤁𐤅.𐤌𐤋𐤀𐤊𐤄.𐤉𐤅𐤌𐤕|
𐤂 𐤋𐤀.𐤕𐤁𐤏𐤓𐤅.𐤀𐤔.𐤁𐤊𐤋.𐤌𐤔𐤁𐤕𐤉𐤊𐤌.𐤁𐤉𐤅𐤌.𐤄𐤔𐤁𐤕
|
𐤃 𐤅𐤉𐤀𐤌𐤓.𐤌𐤔𐤄.𐤀𐤋.𐤊𐤋.𐤏𐤃𐤕.𐤁𐤍𐤉.𐤉𐤔𐤓𐤀𐤋.𐤋𐤀𐤌
𐤓.𐤆𐤄.𐤄𐤃𐤁𐤓.𐤀𐤔𐤓.𐤑𐤅𐤄.𐤉𐤄𐤅𐤄.𐤋𐤀𐤌𐤓|
𐤄 𐤒𐤇𐤅.𐤌𐤀𐤕𐤊𐤌.𐤕𐤓𐤅𐤌𐤄.𐤋𐤉𐤄𐤅𐤄.𐤊𐤋.𐤍𐤃𐤉𐤁.𐤋𐤁𐤅.𐤉
𐤁𐤉𐤀𐤄.𐤀𐤕.𐤕𐤓𐤅𐤌𐤕.𐤉𐤄𐤅𐤄.𐤆𐤄𐤁.𐤅𐤊𐤎𐤐.𐤅𐤍𐤇𐤔𐤕|
𐤅 𐤅𐤕𐤊𐤋𐤕.𐤅𐤀𐤓𐤂𐤌𐤍.𐤅𐤕𐤅𐤋𐤏𐤕.𐤔𐤍𐤉.𐤅𐤔𐤔.𐤅𐤏𐤆𐤉𐤌|
𐤆 𐤅𐤏𐤓𐤕.𐤀𐤉𐤋𐤌.𐤌𐤀𐤃𐤌𐤉𐤌.𐤅𐤏𐤓𐤕.𐤕𐤇𐤔𐤉𐤌.𐤅𐤏𐤑
𐤉.𐤔𐤈𐤉𐤌|
𐤇 𐤅𐤔𐤌𐤍.𐤋𐤌𐤀𐤓.𐤅𐤁𐤔𐤌𐤉𐤌.𐤋𐤔𐤌𐤍.𐤄𐤌𐤔𐤇𐤄.𐤅𐤋𐤒𐤈
𐤓𐤕.𐤄𐤎𐤌𐤉𐤌|
𐤈 𐤅𐤀𐤁𐤍𐤉.𐤔𐤄𐤌.𐤅𐤀𐤁𐤍𐤉.𐤌𐤋𐤀𐤉𐤌.𐤋𐤀𐤐𐤃.𐤅𐤋𐤇𐤔𐤍|
𐤉 𐤅𐤊𐤋.𐤇𐤊𐤌.𐤋𐤁.𐤁𐤊𐤌.𐤉𐤁𐤀𐤅.𐤅𐤉𐤏𐤔𐤅.𐤀𐤕.𐤊𐤋.𐤀𐤔
𐤓.𐤑𐤅𐤄.𐤉𐤄𐤅𐤄|

11 𐤀𐤕.𐤄𐤌𐤔𐤊𐤍.𐤀𐤕.𐤀𐤄𐤋𐤅.𐤅𐤀𐤕.𐤌𐤊𐤎𐤄𐤅.𐤀𐤕.𐤒𐤓
𐤎𐤉𐤅.𐤅𐤀𐤕.𐤒𐤓𐤔𐤉𐤅.𐤀𐤕.𐤁𐤓𐤉𐤇𐤅.𐤀𐤕.𐤏𐤌𐤃𐤉𐤅.𐤅𐤀𐤕.𐤀
𐤃𐤍𐤉𐤅|

12 𐤀𐤕.𐤄𐤀𐤓𐤍.𐤅𐤀𐤕.𐤁𐤃𐤉𐤅.𐤀𐤕.𐤄𐤊𐤐𐤓𐤕.𐤅𐤀𐤕.𐤐𐤓𐤊
𐤕.𐤄𐤌𐤎𐤊|

13 𐤀𐤕.𐤄𐤔𐤋𐤇𐤍.𐤅𐤀𐤕.𐤁𐤃𐤉𐤅.𐤅𐤀𐤕.𐤊𐤋.𐤊𐤋𐤉𐤅.𐤅𐤀𐤕.
𐤋𐤇𐤌.𐤄𐤐𐤍𐤉𐤌|

14 𐤅𐤀𐤕.𐤌𐤍𐤓𐤕.𐤄𐤌𐤀𐤅𐤓.𐤅𐤀𐤕.𐤊𐤋𐤉𐤄.𐤅𐤀𐤕.𐤍𐤓𐤕𐤉𐤄.
𐤅𐤀𐤕.𐤔𐤌𐤍.𐤄𐤌𐤀𐤅𐤓|

15 𐤅𐤀𐤕.𐤌𐤆𐤁𐤇.𐤄𐤒𐤈𐤓𐤕.𐤅𐤀𐤕.𐤁𐤃𐤉𐤅.𐤅𐤀𐤕.𐤔𐤌𐤍.
𐤄𐤌𐤔𐤇𐤄.𐤅𐤀𐤕.𐤒𐤈𐤓𐤕.𐤄𐤎𐤌𐤉𐤌.𐤅𐤀𐤕.𐤌𐤎𐤊.𐤄𐤐𐤕𐤇.
𐤋𐤐𐤕𐤇.𐤄𐤌𐤔𐤊𐤍|

16 𐤀𐤕.𐤌𐤆𐤁𐤇.𐤄𐤏𐤋𐤄.𐤅𐤀𐤕.𐤌𐤊𐤁𐤓.𐤄𐤍𐤇𐤔𐤕.𐤀𐤔𐤓
.𐤋𐤅.𐤀𐤕.𐤁𐤃𐤉𐤅.𐤅𐤀𐤕.𐤊𐤋.𐤊𐤋𐤉𐤅.𐤀𐤕.𐤄𐤊𐤉𐤓.𐤅𐤀𐤕.𐤊𐤍𐤅|

17 𐤀𐤕.𐤒𐤋𐤏𐤉.𐤄𐤇𐤑𐤓.𐤀𐤕.𐤏𐤌𐤃𐤉𐤅.𐤅𐤀𐤕.𐤀𐤃𐤍𐤉
𐤄.𐤅𐤀𐤕.𐤌𐤎𐤊.𐤔𐤏𐤓.𐤄𐤇𐤑𐤓|

18 𐤀𐤕.𐤉𐤕𐤃𐤕.𐤄𐤌𐤔𐤊𐤍.𐤅𐤀𐤕.𐤉𐤕𐤃𐤕.𐤄𐤇𐤑𐤓.𐤅𐤀
𐤕.𐤌𐤉𐤕𐤓𐤉𐤄𐤌|

19 𐤀𐤕.𐤁𐤂𐤃𐤉.𐤄𐤔𐤓𐤃.𐤋𐤔𐤓𐤕.𐤁𐤒𐤃𐤔.𐤀𐤕.𐤁𐤂
𐤃𐤉.𐤄𐤒𐤃𐤔.𐤋𐤀𐤄𐤓𐤍.𐤄𐤊𐤄𐤍.𐤅𐤀𐤕.𐤁𐤂𐤃𐤉.𐤁𐤍𐤉𐤅.𐤋𐤊
𐤄𐤍|

20 𐤅𐤉𐤑𐤀𐤅.𐤊𐤋.𐤏𐤃𐤕.𐤁𐤍𐤉.𐤉𐤔𐤓𐤀𐤋.𐤌𐤋𐤐𐤍𐤉.𐤌𐤔𐤄|

21 𐤅𐤉𐤁𐤀𐤅.𐤊𐤋.𐤀𐤉𐤔.𐤀𐤔𐤓.𐤍𐤔𐤀𐤅.𐤋𐤁𐤅.𐤅𐤊𐤋.𐤀𐤔𐤓.𐤍
𐤃𐤁𐤄.𐤓𐤅𐤇𐤅.𐤀𐤕𐤅.𐤄𐤁𐤉𐤀𐤅.𐤀𐤕.𐤕𐤓𐤅𐤌𐤕.𐤉𐤄𐤅𐤄.𐤋𐤌𐤋𐤀
𐤊𐤕.𐤀𐤄𐤋.𐤌𐤅𐤏𐤃.𐤅𐤋𐤊𐤋.𐤏𐤁𐤃𐤕𐤅.𐤅𐤋𐤁𐤂𐤃𐤉.𐤄𐤒𐤃𐤔|

22 𐤅𐤉𐤁𐤀𐤅.𐤄𐤀𐤍𐤔𐤉𐤌.𐤏𐤋.𐤄𐤍𐤔𐤉𐤌.𐤊𐤋.𐤍𐤃𐤉𐤁.𐤋𐤁.
𐤄𐤁𐤉𐤀𐤅.𐤇𐤇.𐤅𐤍𐤆𐤌.𐤅𐤈𐤁𐤏𐤕.𐤅𐤊𐤅𐤌𐤆.𐤊𐤋.𐤊𐤋𐤉.𐤆𐤄𐤁
.𐤅𐤊𐤋.𐤀𐤉𐤔.𐤀𐤔𐤓.𐤄𐤍𐤉𐤐.𐤕𐤍𐤅𐤐𐤕.𐤆𐤄𐤁.𐤋𐤉𐤄𐤅𐤄|

23 𐤅𐤊𐤋.𐤀𐤉𐤔.𐤀𐤔𐤓.𐤍𐤌𐤑𐤀.𐤀𐤕𐤅.𐤕𐤊𐤋𐤕.𐤅𐤀𐤓𐤂𐤌𐤍.
𐤅𐤕𐤅𐤋𐤏𐤕.𐤔𐤍𐤉.𐤅𐤔𐤔.𐤅𐤏𐤆𐤉𐤌.𐤅𐤏𐤓𐤕.𐤀𐤉𐤋𐤌.𐤌𐤀𐤃𐤌𐤉
𐤌.𐤅𐤏𐤓𐤕.𐤕𐤇𐤔𐤉𐤌.𐤄𐤁𐤉𐤀𐤅|

..24.. 𐤊𐤋.𐤌𐤓𐤉𐤌.𐤕𐤓𐤅𐤌𐤕.𐤊𐤎𐤐.𐤅𐤍𐤇𐤔𐤕.𐤄𐤁𐤉𐤀𐤅.𐤀𐤕.
𐤕𐤓𐤅𐤌𐤕.𐤉𐤄𐤅𐤄.𐤅𐤊𐤋.𐤀𐤔𐤓.𐤍𐤌𐤑𐤀.𐤀𐤕𐤅.𐤏𐤑𐤉.𐤔𐤈𐤉𐤌.
𐤋𐤊𐤋.𐤌𐤋𐤀𐤊𐤕.𐤄𐤏𐤁𐤃𐤄.𐤄𐤁𐤉𐤀𐤅|
..25.. 𐤅𐤊𐤋.𐤀𐤔𐤄.𐤇𐤊𐤌𐤕.𐤋𐤁.𐤁𐤉𐤃𐤉𐤄.𐤈𐤅𐤅.𐤅𐤉𐤁𐤉𐤀𐤅.𐤌
𐤈𐤅𐤄.𐤀𐤕.𐤄𐤕𐤊𐤋𐤕.𐤅𐤀𐤕.𐤄𐤀𐤓𐤂𐤌𐤍.𐤀𐤕.𐤕𐤅𐤋𐤏𐤕.𐤄𐤔
𐤍𐤉.𐤅𐤀𐤕.𐤄𐤔𐤔|
..26.. 𐤅𐤊𐤋.𐤄𐤍𐤔𐤉𐤌.𐤀𐤔𐤓.𐤍𐤔𐤀.𐤋𐤁𐤍.𐤀𐤕𐤍𐤄.𐤁𐤇𐤊𐤌𐤄.
𐤈𐤅𐤅.𐤀𐤕.𐤄𐤏𐤆𐤉𐤌|
..27.. 𐤅𐤄𐤍𐤔𐤀𐤌.𐤄𐤁𐤉𐤀𐤅.𐤀𐤕.𐤀𐤁𐤍𐤉.𐤄𐤔𐤄𐤌.𐤅𐤀𐤕.𐤀𐤁
𐤍𐤉.𐤄𐤌𐤋𐤀𐤉𐤌.𐤋𐤀𐤐𐤅𐤃.𐤅𐤋𐤇𐤔𐤍|
..28.. 𐤅𐤀𐤕.𐤄𐤁𐤔𐤌.𐤅𐤀𐤕.𐤄𐤔𐤌𐤍.𐤋𐤌𐤀𐤅𐤓.𐤅𐤋𐤔𐤌𐤍.𐤄𐤌𐤔
𐤇𐤄.𐤅𐤋𐤒𐤈𐤓𐤕.𐤄𐤎𐤌𐤉𐤌|
..29.. 𐤊𐤋.𐤀𐤉𐤔.𐤅𐤀𐤔𐤄.𐤀𐤔𐤓.𐤍𐤃𐤁.𐤋𐤁𐤌.𐤀𐤕𐤌.𐤋𐤄𐤁𐤉
𐤀.𐤋𐤊𐤋.𐤄𐤌𐤋𐤀𐤊𐤄.𐤀𐤔𐤓.𐤑𐤅𐤄.𐤉𐤄𐤅𐤄.𐤋𐤏𐤔𐤅𐤕.𐤁𐤉𐤃.
𐤌𐤔𐤄.𐤄𐤁𐤉𐤀𐤅.𐤁𐤍𐤉.𐤉𐤔𐤓𐤀𐤋.𐤍𐤃𐤁𐤄.𐤋𐤉𐤄𐤅𐤄|
..30.. 𐤅𐤉𐤀𐤌𐤓.𐤌𐤔𐤄.𐤀𐤋.𐤁𐤍𐤉.𐤉𐤔𐤓𐤀𐤋.𐤓𐤀𐤅.𐤒𐤓𐤀.𐤉𐤄𐤅
𐤄.𐤁𐤔𐤌.𐤁𐤑𐤋𐤀𐤋.𐤁𐤍.𐤀𐤅𐤓𐤉.𐤁𐤍.𐤇𐤅𐤓.𐤋𐤌𐤈𐤄.𐤉𐤄𐤅𐤃𐤄|
..31.. 𐤅𐤉𐤌𐤋𐤀.𐤀𐤕𐤅.𐤓𐤅𐤇.𐤀𐤋𐤄𐤉𐤌.𐤁𐤇𐤊𐤌𐤄.𐤁𐤕𐤁𐤅𐤍𐤄.
𐤅𐤁𐤃𐤏𐤕.𐤅𐤁𐤊𐤋.𐤌𐤋𐤀𐤊𐤄|
..32.. 𐤅𐤋𐤇𐤔𐤁.𐤌𐤇𐤔𐤁𐤕.𐤋𐤏𐤔𐤕.𐤁𐤆𐤄𐤁.𐤅𐤁𐤊𐤎𐤐.𐤅𐤁𐤍
𐤇𐤔𐤕|
..33.. 𐤅𐤁𐤇𐤓𐤔𐤕.𐤀𐤁𐤍.𐤋𐤌𐤋𐤀𐤕.𐤅𐤁𐤇𐤓𐤔𐤕.𐤏𐤑.𐤋𐤏𐤔𐤅
𐤕.𐤁𐤊𐤋.𐤌𐤋𐤀𐤊𐤕.𐤌𐤇𐤔𐤁𐤕|
..34.. 𐤅𐤋𐤄𐤅𐤓𐤕.𐤍𐤕𐤍.𐤁𐤋𐤁𐤅.𐤄𐤅𐤀.𐤅𐤀𐤄𐤋𐤉𐤀𐤁.𐤁𐤍.𐤀𐤇𐤉
𐤎𐤌𐤊.𐤋𐤌𐤈𐤄.𐤃𐤍|
..35.. 𐤌𐤋𐤀.𐤀𐤕𐤌.𐤇𐤊𐤌𐤕.𐤋𐤁.𐤋𐤏𐤔𐤅𐤕.𐤊𐤋.𐤌𐤋𐤀𐤊𐤕.
𐤇𐤓𐤔.𐤅𐤇𐤔𐤁.𐤅𐤓𐤒𐤌.𐤁𐤕𐤊𐤋𐤕.𐤅𐤁𐤀𐤓𐤂𐤌𐤍.𐤁𐤕𐤅𐤋𐤏𐤕.𐤄
𐤔𐤍𐤉.𐤅𐤁𐤔𐤔.𐤅𐤀𐤓𐤂.𐤏𐤔𐤉.𐤊𐤋.𐤌𐤋𐤀𐤊𐤄.𐤅𐤇𐤔𐤁𐤉.𐤌𐤇
𐤔𐤁𐤕||

𐤅𐤉𐤏𐤋𐤅.𐤌𐤌𐤑𐤓𐤉𐤌.𐤇𐤋𐤒 ..36..

1 𐤅𐤏𐤔𐤄.𐤁𐤑𐤋𐤀𐤋.𐤅𐤀𐤄𐤋𐤉𐤀𐤁.𐤅𐤊𐤋.𐤀𐤉𐤔.𐤇𐤊𐤌.𐤋𐤁.
𐤀𐤔𐤓.𐤍𐤕𐤍.𐤉𐤄𐤅𐤄.𐤇𐤊𐤌𐤄.𐤅𐤕𐤁𐤅𐤍𐤄.𐤁𐤄𐤌𐤄.𐤋𐤃𐤏𐤕.𐤋
𐤏𐤔𐤕.𐤀𐤕.𐤊𐤋.𐤌𐤋𐤀𐤊𐤕.𐤏𐤁𐤃𐤕.𐤄𐤒𐤃𐤔.𐤋𐤊𐤋.𐤀𐤔𐤓.
𐤑𐤅𐤄.𐤉𐤄𐤅𐤄|

2 𐤅𐤉𐤒𐤓𐤀.𐤌𐤔𐤄.𐤀𐤋.𐤁𐤑𐤋𐤀𐤋.𐤅𐤀𐤋.𐤀𐤄𐤋𐤉𐤀𐤁.𐤅𐤀𐤋.
𐤊𐤋.𐤀𐤉𐤔.𐤇𐤊𐤌.𐤋𐤁.𐤀𐤔𐤓.𐤍𐤕𐤍.𐤉𐤄𐤅𐤄.𐤇𐤊𐤌𐤄.𐤁𐤋𐤁𐤅.
𐤊𐤋.𐤀𐤔𐤓.𐤍𐤔𐤀𐤅.𐤋𐤁𐤅.𐤋𐤒𐤓𐤁𐤄.𐤀𐤋.𐤄𐤌𐤋𐤀𐤊𐤄.𐤋𐤏𐤔𐤕.
𐤀𐤕𐤄|

3 𐤅𐤉𐤒𐤇𐤅.𐤌𐤋𐤐𐤍𐤉.𐤌𐤔𐤄.𐤀𐤕.𐤊𐤋.𐤄𐤕𐤓𐤅𐤌𐤄.𐤀𐤔𐤓.𐤄
𐤁𐤉𐤀𐤅.𐤁𐤍𐤉.𐤉𐤔𐤓𐤀𐤋.𐤋𐤌𐤋𐤀𐤊𐤕.𐤏𐤁𐤃𐤕.𐤄𐤒𐤃𐤔.𐤋𐤏
𐤔𐤕.𐤀𐤕𐤄.𐤅𐤄𐤌.𐤄𐤁𐤉𐤀𐤅.𐤀𐤋𐤉𐤅.𐤏𐤅𐤃.𐤍𐤃𐤁𐤄.𐤁𐤁𐤒𐤓.𐤁
𐤁𐤒𐤓|

4 𐤅𐤉𐤁𐤀𐤅.𐤊𐤋.𐤄𐤇𐤊𐤌𐤉𐤌.𐤄𐤏𐤔𐤉𐤌.𐤀𐤕.𐤊𐤋.𐤌𐤋𐤀𐤊
𐤕.𐤄𐤒𐤃𐤔.𐤀𐤉𐤔.𐤀𐤉𐤔.𐤌𐤌𐤋𐤀𐤊𐤕𐤅.𐤀𐤔𐤓.𐤄𐤌𐤄.𐤏𐤔𐤉
𐤌|

5 𐤅𐤉𐤀𐤌𐤓𐤅.𐤀𐤋.𐤌𐤔𐤄.𐤋𐤀𐤌𐤓.𐤌𐤓𐤁𐤉𐤌.𐤄𐤏𐤌.𐤋𐤄𐤁𐤉𐤀
.𐤌𐤃𐤉.𐤄𐤏𐤁𐤃𐤄.𐤋𐤌𐤋𐤀𐤊𐤄.𐤀𐤔𐤓.𐤑𐤅𐤄.𐤉𐤄𐤅𐤄.𐤋𐤏𐤔
𐤕.𐤀𐤕𐤄|

6 𐤅𐤉𐤑𐤅.𐤌𐤔𐤄.𐤅𐤉𐤏𐤁𐤉𐤓𐤅.𐤒𐤅𐤋.𐤁𐤌𐤇𐤍𐤄.𐤋𐤀𐤌𐤓.𐤀𐤉
𐤔.𐤅𐤀𐤔𐤄.𐤀𐤋.𐤉𐤏𐤔𐤅.𐤏𐤅𐤃.𐤌𐤋𐤀𐤊𐤄.𐤋𐤕𐤓𐤅𐤌𐤕.𐤄𐤒𐤃
𐤔.𐤅𐤉𐤊𐤋𐤀.𐤄𐤏𐤌.𐤌𐤄𐤁𐤉𐤀|

7 𐤅𐤄𐤌𐤋𐤀𐤊𐤄.𐤄𐤉𐤕𐤄.𐤃𐤉𐤌.𐤋𐤊𐤋.𐤄𐤌𐤋𐤀𐤊𐤄.𐤋𐤏𐤔
𐤅𐤕.𐤀𐤕𐤄.𐤅𐤄𐤅𐤕𐤓|

8 𐤅𐤉𐤏𐤔𐤅.𐤊𐤋.𐤇𐤊𐤌.𐤋𐤁.𐤁𐤏𐤔𐤉.𐤄𐤌𐤋𐤀𐤊𐤄.𐤀𐤕.𐤄𐤌
𐤔𐤊𐤍.𐤏𐤔𐤓.𐤉𐤓𐤉𐤏𐤕.𐤔𐤔.𐤌𐤔𐤆𐤓.𐤅𐤕𐤊𐤋𐤕.𐤅𐤀𐤓𐤂𐤌𐤍.𐤅
𐤕𐤅𐤋𐤏𐤕.𐤔𐤍𐤉.𐤊𐤓𐤁𐤉𐤌.𐤌𐤏𐤔𐤄.𐤇𐤔𐤁.𐤏𐤔𐤄.𐤀𐤕𐤌|

9 𐤀𐤓𐤊.𐤄𐤉𐤓𐤉𐤏𐤄.𐤄𐤀𐤇𐤕.𐤔𐤌𐤍𐤄.𐤅𐤏𐤔𐤓𐤉𐤌.𐤁𐤀𐤌
𐤄.𐤅𐤓𐤇𐤁.𐤀𐤓𐤁𐤏.𐤁𐤀𐤌𐤄.𐤄𐤉𐤓𐤉𐤏𐤄.𐤄𐤀𐤇𐤕.𐤌𐤃𐤄.𐤀
𐤇𐤕.𐤋𐤊𐤋.𐤄𐤉𐤓𐤉𐤏𐤕|

10 ויחבר.את.חמש.היריעת.אחת.אל.אחת.
וחמש.יריעת.חבר.אחת.אל.אחת׃
11 ויעש.ללאת.תכלת.על.שפת.היריעה.הא
חת.מקצה.במחברת.כן.עשה.בשפת.היריעה.
הקיצונה.במחברת.השנית׃
12 חמשים.ללאת.עשה.ביריעה.האחת.וחמ
שים.ללאת.עשה.בקצה.היריעה.אשר.במחב
רת.השנית.מקבילת.הללאת.אחת.אל.אחת׃
13 ויעש.חמשים.קרסי.זהב.ויחבר.את.הי
ריעת.אחת.אל.אחת.בקרסים.ויהי.המשכן.א
חד׃
14 ויעש.יריעת.עזים.לאהל.על.המשכן.ע
שתי.עשרה.יריעת.עשה.אתם׃
15 ארך.היריעה.האחת.שלשים.באמה.וארב
ע.אמות.רחב.היריעה.האחת.מדה.אחת.לע
שתי.עשרה.יריעת׃
16 ויחבר.את.חמש.היריעת.לבד.ואת.שש.ה
יריעת.לבד׃
17 ויעש.ללאת.חמשים.על.שפת.היריעה.ה
קיצנה.במחברת.וחמשים.ללאת.עשה.על.שפ
ת.היריעה.החברת.השנית׃
18 ויעש.קרסי.נחשת.חמשים.לחבר.את.הא
הל.להית.אחד׃
19 ויעש.מכסה.לאהל.ערת.אילם.מאדמים.
ומכסה.ערת.תחשים.מלמעלה׃
20 ויעש.את.הקרשים.למשכן.עצי.שטים.
עמדים׃
21 עשר.אמת.ארך.הקרש.ואמה.וחצי.האמה.
רחב.הקרש.האחד׃
22 שתי.ידת.לקרש.האחד.משלבת.אחת.א
ל.אחת.כן.עשה.לכל.קרשי.המשכן׃

כג ויעש.את.הקרשים.למשכן.עשרים.קרשי
ם.לפאת.נגב.תימנה|
כד וארבעים.אדני.כסף.עשה.תחת.עשרים
.הקרשים.שני.אדנים.תחת.הקרש.האחד.ל
שתי.ידתיו.ושני.אדנים.תחת.הקרש.האח
ד.לשתי.ידתיו|
כה ולצלע.המשכן.השנית.לפאת.צפון.עשה.
עשרים.קרשים|
כו וארבעים.אדניהם.כסף.שני.אדנים.תח
ת.הקרש.האחד.ושני.אדנים.תחת.הקרש.ה
אחד|
כז ולירכתי.המשכן.ימה.עשה.ששה.קרשי
ם|
כח ושני.קרשים.עשה.למקצעת.המשכן.ביר
כתים|
כט והיו.תואמם.מלמטה.ויחדו.יהיו.תמים
.אל.ראשו.אל.הטבעת.האחת.כן.עשה.לשניה
ם.לשני.המקצעת|
ל והיו.שמנה.קרשים.ואדניהם.כסף.ששה.
עשר.אדנים.שני.אדנים.שני.אדנים.תחת.
הקרש.האחד|
לא ויעש.בריחי.עצי.שטים.חמשה.לקרשי
.צלע.המשכן.האחת|
לב וחמשה.בריחם.לקרשי.צלע.המשכן.הש
נית.וחמשה.בריחם.לקרשי.המשכן.לירכתי
ם.ימה|
לג ויעש.את.הבריח.התיכן.לברח.בתוך.ה
קרשים.מן.הקצה.אל.הקצה|
לד ואת.הקרשים.צפה.זהב.ואת.טבעתם.ע
שה.זהב.בתים.לבריחם.ויצף.את.הבריחם.
זהב|

𐤋𐤄 𐤅𐤉𐤏𐤔.𐤀𐤕.𐤄𐤐𐤓𐤊𐤕.𐤕𐤊𐤋𐤕.𐤅𐤀𐤓𐤂𐤌𐤍.𐤅𐤕𐤅𐤋𐤏𐤕.
𐤔𐤍𐤉.𐤅𐤔𐤔.𐤌𐤔𐤆𐤓.𐤌𐤏𐤔𐤄.𐤇𐤔𐤁.𐤏𐤔𐤄.𐤀𐤕𐤄.𐤊𐤓𐤁𐤉
𐤌|

𐤋𐤅 𐤅𐤉𐤏𐤔.𐤋𐤄.𐤀𐤓𐤁𐤏𐤄.𐤏𐤌𐤅𐤃𐤉.𐤔𐤈𐤉𐤌.𐤅𐤉𐤑𐤐𐤌.
𐤆𐤄𐤁.𐤅𐤅𐤉𐤄𐤌.𐤆𐤄𐤁.𐤅𐤉𐤑𐤒.𐤋𐤄𐤌.𐤀𐤓𐤁𐤏𐤄.𐤀𐤃𐤍𐤉.𐤊
𐤎𐤐|

𐤋𐤆 𐤅𐤉𐤏𐤔.𐤌𐤎𐤊.𐤋𐤐𐤕𐤇.𐤄𐤀𐤄𐤋.𐤕𐤊𐤋𐤕.𐤅𐤀𐤓𐤂𐤌𐤍.𐤅
𐤕𐤅𐤋𐤏𐤕.𐤔𐤍𐤉.𐤅𐤔𐤔.𐤌𐤔𐤆𐤓.𐤌𐤏𐤔𐤄.𐤓𐤒𐤌|

𐤋𐤇 𐤅𐤀𐤕.𐤏𐤌𐤅𐤃𐤉𐤅.𐤇𐤌𐤔𐤄.𐤅𐤀𐤕.𐤅𐤅𐤉𐤄𐤌.𐤅𐤑𐤐𐤄.𐤓𐤀
𐤔𐤉𐤄𐤌.𐤅𐤇𐤔𐤒𐤉𐤄𐤌.𐤆𐤄𐤁.𐤅𐤀𐤃𐤍𐤉𐤄𐤌.𐤇𐤌𐤔𐤄.𐤍𐤇
𐤔𐤕||

𐤅𐤉𐤏𐤋𐤅.𐤌𐤌𐤑𐤓𐤉𐤌.𐤇𐤋𐤒 𐤋𐤆

𐤀 𐤅𐤉𐤏𐤔.𐤁𐤑𐤋𐤀𐤋.𐤀𐤕.𐤄𐤀𐤓𐤍.𐤏𐤑𐤉.𐤔𐤈𐤉𐤌.𐤀𐤌𐤕𐤉
𐤌.𐤅𐤇𐤑𐤉.𐤀𐤓𐤊𐤅.𐤅𐤀𐤌𐤄.𐤅𐤇𐤑𐤉.𐤓𐤇𐤁𐤅.𐤅𐤀𐤌𐤄.𐤅𐤇𐤑𐤉.
𐤒𐤌𐤕𐤅|

𐤁 𐤅𐤉𐤑𐤐𐤄𐤅.𐤆𐤄𐤁.𐤈𐤄𐤅𐤓.𐤌𐤁𐤉𐤕.𐤅𐤌𐤇𐤅𐤑.𐤅𐤉𐤏𐤔.𐤋𐤅.
𐤆𐤓.𐤆𐤄𐤁.𐤎𐤁𐤉𐤁|

𐤂 𐤅𐤉𐤑𐤒.𐤋𐤅.𐤀𐤓𐤁𐤏.𐤈𐤁𐤏𐤕.𐤆𐤄𐤁.𐤏𐤋.𐤀𐤓𐤁𐤏.𐤐𐤏𐤌
𐤕𐤉𐤅.𐤅𐤔𐤕𐤉.𐤈𐤁𐤏𐤕.𐤏𐤋.𐤑𐤋𐤏𐤅.𐤄𐤀𐤇𐤕.𐤅𐤔𐤕𐤉.𐤈𐤁𐤏
𐤅𐤕.𐤏𐤋.𐤑𐤋𐤏𐤅.𐤄𐤔𐤍𐤉𐤕|

𐤃 𐤅𐤉𐤏𐤔.𐤁𐤃𐤉.𐤏𐤑𐤉.𐤔𐤈𐤉𐤌.𐤅𐤉𐤑𐤐.𐤀𐤕𐤌.𐤆𐤄𐤁|

𐤄 𐤅𐤉𐤁𐤀.𐤀𐤕.𐤄𐤁𐤃𐤉𐤌.𐤁𐤈𐤁𐤏𐤕.𐤏𐤋.𐤑𐤋𐤏𐤕.𐤄𐤀𐤓𐤍
.𐤋𐤔𐤀𐤕.𐤀𐤕.𐤄𐤀𐤓𐤍|

𐤅 𐤅𐤉𐤏𐤔.𐤊𐤐𐤓𐤕.𐤆𐤄𐤁.𐤈𐤄𐤅𐤓.𐤀𐤌𐤕𐤉𐤌.𐤅𐤇𐤑𐤉.𐤀𐤓𐤊
𐤄.𐤅𐤀𐤌𐤄.𐤅𐤇𐤑𐤉.𐤓𐤇𐤁𐤄|

𐤆 𐤅𐤉𐤏𐤔.𐤔𐤍𐤉.𐤊𐤓𐤁𐤉𐤌.𐤆𐤄𐤁.𐤌𐤒𐤔𐤄.𐤏𐤔𐤄.𐤀𐤕𐤌.
𐤌𐤔𐤍𐤉.𐤒𐤑𐤅𐤕.𐤄𐤊𐤐𐤓𐤕|

8 𐤊𐤓𐤅𐤁.𐤀𐤇𐤃.𐤌𐤒𐤑𐤄.𐤌𐤆𐤄.𐤅𐤊𐤓𐤅𐤁.𐤀𐤇𐤃.𐤌𐤒𐤑
𐤄.𐤌𐤆𐤄.𐤌𐤍.𐤄𐤊𐤐𐤓𐤕.𐤏𐤔𐤄.𐤀𐤕.𐤄𐤊𐤓𐤁𐤉𐤌.𐤌𐤔𐤍𐤉.𐤒
𐤑𐤅𐤅𐤕𐤅.||𐤒𐤑𐤅𐤕𐤉𐤅.𐤒𐤓𐤉|||

9 𐤅𐤉𐤄𐤉𐤅.𐤄𐤊𐤓𐤁𐤉𐤌.𐤐𐤓𐤔𐤉.𐤊𐤍𐤐𐤉𐤌.𐤋𐤌𐤏𐤋𐤄.𐤎𐤊𐤊
𐤉𐤌.𐤁𐤊𐤍𐤐𐤉𐤄𐤌.𐤏𐤋.𐤄𐤊𐤐𐤓𐤕.𐤅𐤐𐤍𐤉𐤄𐤌.𐤀𐤉𐤔.𐤀𐤋.𐤀𐤇
𐤉𐤅.𐤀𐤋.𐤄𐤊𐤐𐤓𐤕.𐤄𐤉𐤅.𐤐𐤍𐤉.𐤄𐤊𐤓𐤁𐤉𐤌|

10 𐤅𐤉𐤏𐤔.𐤀𐤕.𐤄𐤔𐤋𐤇𐤍.𐤏𐤑𐤉.𐤔𐤈𐤉𐤌.𐤀𐤌𐤕𐤉𐤌.𐤀
𐤓𐤊𐤅.𐤅𐤀𐤌𐤄.𐤓𐤇𐤁𐤅.𐤅𐤀𐤌𐤄.𐤅𐤇𐤑𐤉.𐤒𐤌𐤕𐤅|

11 𐤅𐤉𐤑𐤐.𐤀𐤕𐤅.𐤆𐤄𐤁.𐤈𐤄𐤅𐤓.𐤅𐤉𐤏𐤔.𐤋𐤅.𐤆𐤓.𐤆𐤄𐤁.𐤎
𐤁𐤉𐤁|

12 𐤅𐤉𐤏𐤔.𐤋𐤅.𐤌𐤎𐤂𐤓𐤕.𐤈𐤐𐤇.𐤎𐤁𐤉𐤁.𐤅𐤉𐤏𐤔.𐤆𐤓.𐤆
𐤄𐤁.𐤋𐤌𐤎𐤂𐤓𐤕𐤅.𐤎𐤁𐤉𐤁|

13 𐤅𐤉𐤑𐤒.𐤋𐤅.𐤀𐤓𐤁𐤏.𐤈𐤁𐤏𐤕.𐤆𐤄𐤁.𐤅𐤉𐤕𐤍.𐤀𐤕.𐤄𐤈
𐤁𐤏𐤕.𐤏𐤋.𐤀𐤓𐤁𐤏.𐤄𐤐𐤀𐤕.𐤀𐤔𐤓.𐤋𐤀𐤓𐤁𐤏.𐤓𐤂𐤋𐤉𐤅|

14 𐤋𐤏𐤌𐤕.𐤄𐤌𐤎𐤂𐤓𐤕.𐤄𐤉𐤅.𐤄𐤈𐤁𐤏𐤕.𐤁𐤕𐤉𐤌.𐤋𐤁𐤃
𐤉𐤌.𐤋𐤔𐤀𐤕.𐤀𐤕.𐤄𐤔𐤋𐤇𐤍|

15 𐤅𐤉𐤏𐤔.𐤀𐤕.𐤄𐤁𐤃𐤉𐤌.𐤏𐤑𐤉.𐤔𐤈𐤉𐤌.𐤅𐤉𐤑𐤐.𐤀𐤕𐤌
.𐤆𐤄𐤁.𐤋𐤔𐤀𐤕.𐤀𐤕.𐤄𐤔𐤋𐤇𐤍|

16 𐤅𐤉𐤏𐤔.𐤀𐤕.𐤄𐤊𐤋𐤉𐤌.𐤀𐤔𐤓.𐤏𐤋.𐤄𐤔𐤋𐤇𐤍.𐤀𐤕.𐤒𐤏
𐤓𐤕𐤉𐤅.𐤅𐤀𐤕.𐤊𐤐𐤕𐤉𐤅.𐤅𐤀𐤕.𐤌𐤍𐤒𐤉𐤕𐤉𐤅.𐤅𐤀𐤕.𐤄𐤒𐤔𐤅𐤕.𐤀
𐤔𐤓.𐤉𐤎𐤊.𐤁𐤄𐤍.𐤆𐤄𐤁.𐤈𐤄𐤅𐤓|

17 𐤅𐤉𐤏𐤔.𐤀𐤕.𐤄𐤌𐤍𐤓𐤄.𐤆𐤄𐤁.𐤈𐤄𐤅𐤓.𐤌𐤒𐤔𐤄.𐤏𐤔𐤄
.𐤀𐤕.𐤄𐤌𐤍𐤓𐤄.𐤉𐤓𐤊𐤄.𐤅𐤒𐤍𐤄.𐤂𐤁𐤉𐤏𐤉𐤄.𐤊𐤐𐤕𐤓𐤉𐤄.𐤅𐤐𐤓
𐤇𐤉𐤄.𐤌𐤌𐤍𐤄.𐤄𐤉𐤅|

18 𐤅𐤔𐤔𐤄.𐤒𐤍𐤉𐤌.𐤉𐤑𐤀𐤉𐤌.𐤌𐤑𐤃𐤉𐤄.𐤔𐤋𐤔𐤄.𐤒𐤍𐤉.
𐤌𐤍𐤓𐤄.𐤌𐤑𐤃𐤄.𐤄𐤀𐤇𐤃.𐤅𐤔𐤋𐤔𐤄.𐤒𐤍𐤉.𐤌𐤍𐤓𐤄.𐤌𐤑𐤃
𐤄.𐤄𐤔𐤍𐤉|

19 𐤔𐤋𐤔𐤄.𐤂𐤁𐤏𐤉𐤌.𐤌𐤔𐤒𐤃𐤉𐤌.𐤁𐤒𐤍𐤄.𐤄𐤀𐤇𐤃.
𐤊𐤐𐤕𐤓.𐤅𐤐𐤓𐤇.𐤅𐤔𐤋𐤔𐤄.𐤂𐤁𐤏𐤉𐤌.𐤌𐤔𐤒𐤃𐤉𐤌.𐤁𐤒𐤍𐤄.
𐤀𐤇𐤃.𐤊𐤐𐤕𐤓.𐤅𐤐𐤓𐤇.𐤊𐤍.𐤋𐤔𐤔𐤕.𐤄𐤒𐤍𐤉𐤌.𐤄𐤉𐤑𐤀𐤉𐤌.
𐤌𐤍.𐤄𐤌𐤍𐤓𐤄|

20 𐤅𐤁𐤌𐤍𐤓𐤄.𐤀𐤓𐤁𐤏𐤄.𐤂𐤁𐤏𐤉𐤌.𐤌𐤔𐤒𐤃𐤉𐤌.𐤊𐤐𐤕𐤓
𐤉𐤄.𐤅𐤐𐤓𐤇𐤉𐤄|

21 𐤅𐤊𐤐𐤕𐤓.𐤕𐤇𐤕.𐤔𐤍𐤉.𐤄𐤒𐤍𐤉𐤌.𐤌𐤌𐤍𐤄.𐤅𐤊𐤐𐤕𐤓.𐤕𐤇
𐤕.𐤔𐤍𐤉.𐤄𐤒𐤍𐤉𐤌.𐤌𐤌𐤍𐤄.𐤅𐤊𐤐𐤕𐤓.𐤕𐤇𐤕.𐤔𐤍𐤉.𐤄𐤒𐤍𐤉𐤌.
𐤌𐤌𐤍𐤄.𐤋𐤔𐤔𐤕.𐤄𐤒𐤍𐤉𐤌.𐤄𐤉𐤑𐤀𐤉𐤌.𐤌𐤌𐤍𐤄|

22 𐤊𐤐𐤕𐤓𐤉𐤄𐤌.𐤅𐤒𐤍𐤕𐤌.𐤌𐤌𐤍𐤄.𐤄𐤉𐤅.𐤊𐤋𐤄.𐤌𐤒𐤔𐤄.
𐤀𐤇𐤕.𐤆𐤄𐤁.𐤈𐤄𐤅𐤓|

23 𐤅𐤉𐤏𐤔.𐤀𐤕.𐤍𐤓𐤕𐤉𐤄.𐤔𐤁𐤏𐤄.𐤅𐤌𐤋𐤒𐤇𐤉𐤄.𐤅𐤌𐤇𐤕
𐤕𐤉𐤄.𐤆𐤄𐤁.𐤈𐤄𐤅𐤓|

24 𐤊𐤊𐤓.𐤆𐤄𐤁.𐤈𐤄𐤅𐤓.𐤏𐤔𐤄.𐤀𐤕𐤄.𐤅𐤀𐤕.𐤊𐤋.𐤊𐤋𐤉𐤄
|

25 𐤅𐤉𐤏𐤔.𐤀𐤕.𐤌𐤆𐤁𐤇.𐤄𐤒𐤈𐤓𐤕.𐤏𐤑𐤉.𐤔𐤈𐤉𐤌.𐤀𐤌
𐤄.𐤀𐤓𐤊𐤅.𐤅𐤀𐤌𐤄.𐤓𐤇𐤁𐤅.𐤓𐤁𐤅𐤏.𐤅𐤀𐤌𐤕𐤉𐤌.𐤒𐤌𐤕𐤅.𐤌𐤌𐤍𐤅.
𐤄𐤉𐤅.𐤒𐤓𐤍𐤕𐤉𐤅|

26 𐤅𐤉𐤑𐤐.𐤀𐤕𐤅.𐤆𐤄𐤁.𐤈𐤄𐤅𐤓.𐤀𐤕.𐤂𐤂𐤅.𐤅𐤀𐤕.𐤒𐤉𐤓𐤕
𐤉𐤅.𐤎𐤁𐤉𐤁.𐤅𐤀𐤕.𐤒𐤓𐤍𐤕𐤉𐤅.𐤅𐤉𐤏𐤔.𐤋𐤅.𐤆𐤓.𐤆𐤄𐤁.𐤎𐤁𐤉𐤁|

27 𐤅𐤔𐤕𐤉.𐤈𐤁𐤏𐤕.𐤆𐤄𐤁.𐤏𐤔𐤄.𐤋𐤅.𐤌𐤕𐤇𐤕.𐤋𐤆𐤓𐤅.
𐤏𐤋.𐤔𐤕𐤉.𐤑𐤋𐤏𐤕𐤉𐤅.𐤏𐤋.𐤔𐤍𐤉.𐤑𐤃𐤉𐤅.𐤋𐤁𐤕𐤉𐤌.𐤋𐤁𐤃
𐤉𐤌.𐤋𐤔𐤀𐤕.𐤀𐤕𐤅.𐤁𐤄𐤌|

28 𐤅𐤉𐤏𐤔.𐤀𐤕.𐤄𐤁𐤃𐤉𐤌.𐤏𐤑𐤉.𐤔𐤈𐤉𐤌.𐤅𐤉𐤑𐤐.𐤀𐤕
𐤌.𐤆𐤄𐤁|

29 𐤅𐤉𐤏𐤔.𐤀𐤕.𐤔𐤌𐤍.𐤄𐤌𐤔𐤇𐤄.𐤒𐤃𐤔.𐤅𐤀𐤕.𐤒𐤈𐤓𐤕
.𐤄𐤎𐤌𐤉𐤌.𐤈𐤄𐤅𐤓.𐤌𐤏𐤔𐤄.𐤓𐤒𐤇||

38 𐤅𐤉𐤏𐤋𐤅.𐤌𐤌𐤑𐤓𐤉𐤌.𐤇𐤋𐤒

1 𐤅𐤉𐤏𐤔.𐤀𐤕.𐤌𐤆𐤁𐤇.𐤄𐤏𐤋𐤄.𐤏𐤑𐤉.𐤔𐤈𐤉𐤌.𐤇𐤌𐤔.
𐤀𐤌𐤅𐤕.𐤀𐤓𐤊𐤅.𐤅𐤇𐤌𐤔.𐤀𐤌𐤅𐤕.𐤓𐤇𐤁𐤅.𐤓𐤁𐤅𐤏.𐤅𐤔𐤋𐤔.𐤀𐤌𐤅
𐤕.𐤒𐤌𐤕𐤅|

2 𐤅𐤉𐤏𐤔.𐤒𐤓𐤍𐤕𐤉𐤅.𐤏𐤋.𐤀𐤓𐤁𐤏.𐤐𐤍𐤕𐤉𐤅.𐤌𐤌𐤍𐤅.𐤄𐤉𐤅.𐤒
𐤓𐤍𐤕𐤉𐤅.𐤅𐤉𐤑𐤐.𐤀𐤕𐤅.𐤍𐤇𐤔𐤕|

ג 𐤅𐤉𐤏𐤔.𐤀𐤕.𐤊𐤋.𐤊𐤋𐤉.𐤄𐤌𐤆𐤁𐤇.𐤀𐤕.𐤄𐤎𐤉𐤓𐤕.𐤅𐤀
𐤕.𐤄𐤉𐤏𐤉𐤌.𐤅𐤀𐤕.𐤄𐤌𐤆𐤓𐤒𐤕.𐤀𐤕.𐤄𐤌𐤆𐤋𐤂𐤕.𐤅𐤀𐤕.𐤄
𐤌𐤇𐤕𐤕.𐤊𐤋.𐤊𐤋𐤉𐤅.𐤏𐤔𐤄.𐤍𐤇𐤔𐤕|
ד 𐤅𐤉𐤏𐤔.𐤋𐤌𐤆𐤁𐤇.𐤌𐤊𐤁𐤓.𐤌𐤏𐤔𐤄.𐤓𐤔𐤕.𐤍𐤇𐤔𐤕.𐤕
𐤇𐤕.𐤊𐤓𐤊𐤁𐤅.𐤌𐤋𐤌𐤈𐤄.𐤏𐤃.𐤇𐤑𐤉𐤅|
ה 𐤅𐤉𐤑𐤒.𐤀𐤓𐤁𐤏.𐤈𐤁𐤏𐤕.𐤁𐤀𐤓𐤁𐤏.𐤄𐤒𐤑𐤅𐤕.𐤋𐤌𐤊𐤁𐤓
.𐤄𐤍𐤇𐤔𐤕.𐤁𐤕𐤉𐤌.𐤋𐤁𐤃𐤉𐤌|
ו 𐤅𐤉𐤏𐤔.𐤀𐤕.𐤄𐤁𐤃𐤉𐤌.𐤏𐤑𐤉.𐤔𐤈𐤉𐤌.𐤅𐤉𐤑𐤐.𐤀𐤕𐤌.
𐤍𐤇𐤔𐤕|
ז 𐤅𐤉𐤁𐤀.𐤀𐤕.𐤄𐤁𐤃𐤉𐤌.𐤁𐤈𐤁𐤏𐤕.𐤏𐤋.𐤑𐤋𐤏𐤕.𐤄𐤌𐤆
𐤁𐤇.𐤋𐤔𐤀𐤕.𐤀𐤕𐤅.𐤁𐤄𐤌.𐤍𐤁𐤅𐤁.𐤋𐤇𐤕.𐤏𐤔𐤄.𐤀𐤕𐤅|
ח 𐤅𐤉𐤏𐤔.𐤀𐤕.𐤄𐤊𐤉𐤅𐤓.𐤍𐤇𐤔𐤕.𐤅𐤀𐤕.𐤊𐤍𐤅.𐤍𐤇𐤔𐤕.𐤁𐤌
𐤓𐤀𐤕.𐤄𐤑𐤁𐤀𐤕.𐤀𐤔𐤓.𐤑𐤁𐤀𐤅.𐤐𐤕𐤇.𐤀𐤄𐤋.𐤌𐤅𐤏𐤃|
ט 𐤅𐤉𐤏𐤔.𐤀𐤕.𐤄𐤇𐤑𐤓.𐤋𐤐𐤀𐤕.𐤍𐤂𐤁.𐤕𐤉𐤌𐤍𐤄.𐤒𐤋𐤏𐤉
.𐤄𐤇𐤑𐤓.𐤔𐤔.𐤌𐤔𐤆𐤓.𐤌𐤀𐤄.𐤁𐤀𐤌𐤄|
י 𐤏𐤌𐤅𐤃𐤉𐤄𐤌.𐤏𐤔𐤓𐤉𐤌.𐤅𐤀𐤃𐤍𐤉𐤄𐤌.𐤏𐤔𐤓𐤉𐤌.𐤍𐤇
𐤔𐤕.𐤅𐤅𐤉.𐤄𐤏𐤌𐤅𐤃𐤉𐤌.𐤅𐤇𐤔𐤒𐤉𐤄𐤌.𐤊𐤎𐤐|
יא 𐤅𐤋𐤐𐤀𐤕.𐤑𐤐𐤅𐤍.𐤌𐤀𐤄.𐤁𐤀𐤌𐤄.𐤏𐤌𐤅𐤃𐤉𐤄𐤌.𐤏𐤔𐤓𐤉
𐤌.𐤅𐤀𐤃𐤍𐤉𐤄𐤌.𐤏𐤔𐤓𐤉𐤌.𐤍𐤇𐤔𐤕.𐤅𐤅𐤉.𐤄𐤏𐤌𐤅𐤃𐤉𐤌.𐤅𐤇
𐤔𐤒𐤉𐤄𐤌.𐤊𐤎𐤐|
יב 𐤅𐤋𐤐𐤀𐤕.𐤉𐤌.𐤒𐤋𐤏𐤉𐤌.𐤇𐤌𐤔𐤉𐤌.𐤁𐤀𐤌𐤄.𐤏𐤌𐤅𐤃𐤉
𐤄𐤌.𐤏𐤔𐤓𐤄.𐤅𐤀𐤃𐤍𐤉𐤄𐤌.𐤏𐤔𐤓𐤄.𐤅𐤅𐤉.𐤄𐤏𐤌𐤃𐤉𐤌.𐤅𐤇𐤔
𐤅𐤒𐤉𐤄𐤌.𐤊𐤎𐤐|
יג 𐤅𐤋𐤐𐤀𐤕.𐤒𐤃𐤌𐤄.𐤌𐤆𐤓𐤇𐤄.𐤇𐤌𐤔𐤉𐤌.𐤀𐤌𐤄|
יד 𐤒𐤋𐤏𐤉𐤌.𐤇𐤌𐤔.𐤏𐤔𐤓𐤄.𐤀𐤌𐤄.𐤀𐤋.𐤄𐤊𐤕𐤐.𐤏𐤌𐤅
𐤃𐤉𐤄𐤌.𐤔𐤋𐤔𐤄.𐤅𐤀𐤃𐤍𐤉𐤄𐤌.𐤔𐤋𐤔𐤄|
יה 𐤅𐤋𐤊𐤕𐤐.𐤄𐤔𐤍𐤉𐤕.𐤌𐤆𐤄.𐤅𐤌𐤆𐤄.𐤋𐤔𐤏𐤓.𐤄𐤇𐤑𐤓.
𐤒𐤋𐤏𐤉𐤌.𐤇𐤌𐤔.𐤏𐤔𐤓𐤄.𐤀𐤌𐤄.𐤏𐤌𐤃𐤉𐤄𐤌.𐤔𐤋𐤔𐤄.𐤅𐤀
𐤃𐤍𐤉𐤄𐤌.𐤔𐤋𐤔𐤄|
יו 𐤊𐤋.𐤒𐤋𐤏𐤉.𐤄𐤇𐤑𐤓.𐤎𐤁𐤉𐤁.𐤔𐤔.𐤌𐤔𐤆𐤓|

𐤉𐤆 𐤅𐤄𐤀𐤃𐤍𐤉𐤌.𐤋𐤏𐤌𐤃𐤉𐤌.𐤍𐤇𐤔𐤕.𐤅𐤅𐤉.𐤄𐤏𐤌𐤅𐤃𐤉
𐤌.𐤅𐤇𐤔𐤅𐤒𐤉𐤄𐤌.𐤊𐤎𐤐.𐤅𐤑𐤐𐤅𐤉.𐤓𐤀𐤔𐤉𐤄𐤌.𐤊𐤎𐤐.𐤅𐤄𐤌.𐤌
𐤇𐤔𐤒𐤉𐤌.𐤊𐤎𐤐.𐤊𐤋.𐤏𐤌𐤃𐤉.𐤄𐤇𐤑𐤓|

𐤉𐤇 𐤅𐤌𐤎𐤊.𐤔𐤏𐤓.𐤄𐤇𐤑𐤓.𐤌𐤏𐤔𐤄.𐤓𐤒𐤌.𐤕𐤊𐤋𐤕.𐤅𐤀𐤓
𐤂𐤌𐤍.𐤅𐤕𐤅𐤋𐤏𐤕.𐤔𐤍𐤉.𐤅𐤔𐤔.𐤌𐤔𐤆𐤓.𐤅𐤏𐤔𐤓𐤉𐤌.𐤀𐤌𐤄.𐤀
𐤓𐤊.𐤅𐤒𐤅𐤌𐤄.𐤁𐤓𐤇𐤁.𐤇𐤌𐤔.𐤀𐤌𐤅𐤕.𐤋𐤏𐤌𐤕.𐤒𐤋𐤏𐤉.𐤄𐤇
𐤑𐤓|

𐤉𐤈 𐤅𐤏𐤌𐤃𐤉𐤄𐤌.𐤀𐤓𐤁𐤏𐤄.𐤅𐤀𐤃𐤍𐤉𐤄𐤌.𐤀𐤓𐤁𐤏𐤄.𐤍𐤇
𐤔𐤕.𐤅𐤅𐤉𐤄𐤌.𐤊𐤎𐤐.𐤅𐤑𐤐𐤅𐤉.𐤓𐤀𐤔𐤉𐤄𐤌.𐤅𐤇𐤔𐤒𐤉𐤄𐤌.𐤊𐤎
𐤐|

𐤊 𐤅𐤊𐤋.𐤄𐤉𐤕𐤃𐤕.𐤋𐤌𐤔𐤊𐤍.𐤅𐤋𐤇𐤑𐤓.𐤎𐤁𐤉𐤁.𐤍𐤇𐤔𐤕|

𐤊𐤀 𐤀𐤋𐤄.𐤐𐤒𐤅𐤃𐤉.𐤄𐤌𐤔𐤊𐤍.𐤌𐤔𐤊𐤍.𐤄𐤏𐤃𐤕.𐤀𐤔𐤓.𐤐
𐤒𐤃.𐤏𐤋.𐤐𐤉.𐤌𐤔𐤄.𐤏𐤁𐤃𐤕.𐤄𐤋𐤅𐤉𐤌.𐤁𐤉𐤃.𐤀𐤉𐤕𐤌𐤓.𐤁
𐤍.𐤀𐤄𐤓𐤍.𐤄𐤊𐤄𐤍|

𐤊𐤁 𐤅𐤁𐤑𐤋𐤀𐤋.𐤁𐤍.𐤀𐤅𐤓𐤉.𐤁𐤍.𐤇𐤅𐤓.𐤋𐤌𐤈𐤄.𐤉𐤄𐤅𐤃𐤄.𐤏
𐤔𐤄.𐤀𐤕.𐤊𐤋.𐤀𐤔𐤓.𐤑𐤅𐤄.𐤉𐤄𐤅𐤄.𐤀𐤕.𐤌𐤔𐤄|

𐤊𐤂 𐤅𐤀𐤕𐤅.𐤀𐤄𐤋𐤉𐤀𐤁.𐤁𐤍.𐤀𐤇𐤉𐤎𐤌𐤊.𐤋𐤌𐤈𐤄.𐤃𐤍.𐤇
𐤓𐤔.𐤅𐤇𐤔𐤁.𐤅𐤓𐤒𐤌.𐤁𐤕𐤊𐤋𐤕.𐤅𐤁𐤀𐤓𐤂𐤌𐤍.𐤅𐤁𐤕𐤅𐤋𐤏𐤕.𐤄
𐤔𐤍𐤉.𐤅𐤁𐤔𐤔|

𐤊𐤃 𐤊𐤋.𐤄𐤆𐤄𐤁.𐤄𐤏𐤔𐤅𐤉.𐤋𐤌𐤋𐤀𐤊𐤄.𐤁𐤊𐤋.𐤌𐤋𐤀𐤊𐤕.
𐤄𐤒𐤃𐤔.𐤅𐤉𐤄𐤉.𐤆𐤄𐤁.𐤄𐤕𐤍𐤅𐤐𐤄.𐤕𐤔𐤏.𐤅𐤏𐤔𐤓𐤉𐤌.𐤊𐤊𐤓
.𐤅𐤔𐤁𐤏.𐤌𐤀𐤅𐤕.𐤅𐤔𐤋𐤔𐤉𐤌.𐤔𐤒𐤋.𐤁𐤔𐤒𐤋.𐤄𐤒𐤃𐤔|

𐤊𐤄 𐤅𐤊𐤎𐤐.𐤐𐤒𐤅𐤃𐤉.𐤄𐤏𐤃𐤄.𐤌𐤀𐤕.𐤊𐤊𐤓.𐤅𐤀𐤋𐤐.𐤅𐤔𐤁
𐤏.𐤌𐤀𐤅𐤕.𐤅𐤇𐤌𐤔𐤄.𐤅𐤔𐤁𐤏𐤉𐤌.𐤔𐤒𐤋.𐤁𐤔𐤒𐤋.𐤄𐤒𐤃𐤔|

𐤊𐤅 𐤁𐤒𐤏.𐤋𐤂𐤋𐤂𐤋𐤕.𐤌𐤇𐤑𐤉𐤕.𐤄𐤔𐤒𐤋.𐤁𐤔𐤒𐤋.𐤄𐤒
𐤃𐤔.𐤋𐤊𐤋.𐤄𐤏𐤁𐤓.𐤏𐤋.𐤄𐤐𐤒𐤃𐤉𐤌.𐤌𐤁𐤍.𐤏𐤔𐤓𐤉𐤌.𐤔𐤍𐤄.
𐤅𐤌𐤏𐤋𐤄.𐤋𐤔𐤔.𐤌𐤀𐤅𐤕.𐤀𐤋𐤐.𐤅𐤔𐤋𐤔𐤕.𐤀𐤋𐤐𐤉𐤌.𐤅𐤇𐤌𐤔.
𐤌𐤀𐤅𐤕.𐤅𐤇𐤌𐤔𐤉𐤌|

𐤊𐤆 𐤅𐤉𐤄𐤉.𐤌𐤀𐤕.𐤊𐤊𐤓.𐤄𐤊𐤎𐤐.𐤋𐤑𐤒𐤕.𐤀𐤕.𐤀𐤃𐤍𐤉.
𐤄𐤒𐤃𐤔.𐤅𐤀𐤕.𐤀𐤃𐤍𐤉.𐤄𐤐𐤓𐤊𐤕.𐤌𐤀𐤕.𐤀𐤃𐤍𐤉𐤌.𐤋𐤌𐤀
𐤕.𐤄𐤊𐤊𐤓.𐤊𐤊𐤓.𐤋𐤀𐤃𐤍|

כח ואת האלף ושבע המאות וחמשה ושבעים עשה ווים לעמודים וצפה ראשיהם וחשק אתם|

כט ונחשת התנופה שבעים ככר ואלפים וארבע מאות שקל|

ל ויעש בה את אדני פתח אהל מועד ואת מזבח הנחשת ואת מכבר הנחשת אשר לו ואת כל כלי המזבח|

לא ואת אדני החצר סביב ואת אדני שער החצר ואת כל יתדת המשכן ואת כל יתדת החצר סביב||

לט ויעלו ממצרים חלק

א ומן התכלת והארגמן ותולעת השני עשו בגדי שרד לשרת בקדש ויעשו את בגדי הקדש אשר לאהרן כאשר צוה יהוה את משה|

ב ויעש את האפד זהב תכלת וארגמן ותולעת שני ושש משזר|

ג וירקעו את פחי הזהב וקצץ פתילם לעשות בתוך התכלת ובתוך הארגמן ובתוך תולעת השני ובתוך השש מעשה חשב|

ד כתפת עשו לו חברת על שני קצוותו ||קצותיו קרי|| חבר|

ה וחשב אפדתו אשר עליו ממנו הוא כמעשהו זהב תכלת וארגמן ותולעת שני ושש משזר כאשר צוה יהוה את משה|

ו ויעשו את אבני השהם מסבת משבצת זהב מפתחת פתוחי חותם על שמות בני ישראל|

ז וישם אתם על כתפת האפד אבני זכרון לבני ישראל כאשר צוה יהוה את משה|

ח 𐤅𐤉𐤏𐤔.𐤀𐤕.𐤄𐤇𐤔𐤍.𐤌𐤏𐤔𐤄.𐤇𐤔𐤁.𐤊𐤌𐤏𐤔𐤄.𐤀𐤐
𐤃.𐤆𐤄𐤁.𐤕𐤊𐤋𐤕.𐤅𐤀𐤓𐤂𐤌𐤍.𐤅𐤕𐤅𐤋𐤏𐤕.𐤔𐤍𐤉.𐤅𐤔𐤔.𐤌𐤔
𐤆𐤓

ט 𐤓𐤁𐤅𐤏.𐤄𐤉𐤄.𐤊𐤐𐤅𐤋.𐤏𐤔𐤅.𐤀𐤕.𐤄𐤇𐤔𐤍.𐤆𐤓𐤕.𐤀𐤓𐤊𐤅
.𐤅𐤆𐤓𐤕.𐤓𐤇𐤁𐤅.𐤊𐤐𐤅𐤋

י 𐤅𐤉𐤌𐤋𐤀𐤅.𐤁𐤅.𐤀𐤓𐤁𐤏𐤄.𐤈𐤅𐤓𐤉.𐤀𐤁𐤍.𐤈𐤅𐤓.𐤀𐤃𐤌.𐤐
𐤈𐤃𐤄.𐤅𐤁𐤓𐤒𐤕.𐤄𐤈𐤅𐤓.𐤄𐤀𐤇𐤃

יא 𐤅𐤄𐤈𐤅𐤓.𐤄𐤔𐤍𐤉.𐤍𐤐𐤊.𐤎𐤐𐤉𐤓.𐤅𐤉𐤄𐤋𐤌

יב 𐤅𐤄𐤈𐤅𐤓.𐤄𐤔𐤋𐤉𐤔𐤉.𐤋𐤔𐤌.𐤔𐤁𐤅.𐤅𐤀𐤇𐤋𐤌𐤄

יג 𐤅𐤄𐤈𐤅𐤓.𐤄𐤓𐤁𐤉𐤏𐤉.𐤕𐤓𐤔𐤉𐤔.𐤔𐤄𐤌.𐤅𐤉𐤔𐤐𐤄.𐤌𐤅𐤎
𐤁𐤕.𐤌𐤔𐤁𐤑𐤅𐤕.𐤆𐤄𐤁.𐤁𐤌𐤋𐤀𐤕𐤌

יד 𐤅𐤄𐤀𐤁𐤍𐤉𐤌.𐤏𐤋.𐤔𐤌𐤕.𐤁𐤍𐤉.𐤉𐤔𐤓𐤀𐤋.𐤄𐤍𐤄.𐤔𐤕𐤉
𐤌.𐤏𐤔𐤓𐤄.𐤏𐤋.𐤔𐤌𐤕𐤌.𐤐𐤕𐤅𐤇𐤉.𐤇𐤕𐤌.𐤀𐤉𐤔.𐤏𐤋.𐤔𐤌𐤅.
𐤋𐤔𐤍𐤉𐤌.𐤏𐤔𐤓.𐤔𐤁𐤈

טו 𐤅𐤉𐤏𐤔𐤅.𐤏𐤋.𐤄𐤇𐤔𐤍.𐤔𐤓𐤔𐤓𐤕.𐤂𐤁𐤋𐤕.𐤌𐤏𐤔𐤄.𐤏
𐤁𐤕.𐤆𐤄𐤁.𐤈𐤄𐤅𐤓

טז 𐤅𐤉𐤏𐤔𐤅.𐤔𐤕𐤉.𐤌𐤔𐤁𐤑𐤕.𐤆𐤄𐤁.𐤅𐤔𐤕𐤉.𐤈𐤁𐤏𐤕.𐤆
𐤄𐤁.𐤅𐤉𐤕𐤍𐤅.𐤀𐤕.𐤔𐤕𐤉.𐤄𐤈𐤁𐤏𐤕.𐤏𐤋.𐤔𐤍𐤉.𐤒𐤑𐤅𐤕.𐤄𐤇
𐤔𐤍

יז 𐤅𐤉𐤕𐤍𐤅.𐤔𐤕𐤉.𐤄𐤏𐤁𐤕𐤕.𐤄𐤆𐤄𐤁.𐤏𐤋.𐤔𐤕𐤉.𐤄𐤈𐤁
𐤏𐤕.𐤏𐤋.𐤒𐤑𐤅𐤕.𐤄𐤇𐤔𐤍

יח 𐤅𐤀𐤕.𐤔𐤕𐤉.𐤒𐤑𐤅𐤕.𐤔𐤕𐤉.𐤄𐤏𐤁𐤕𐤕.𐤍𐤕𐤍𐤅.𐤏𐤋.𐤔
𐤕𐤉.𐤄𐤌𐤔𐤁𐤑𐤕.𐤅𐤉𐤕𐤍𐤌.𐤏𐤋.𐤊𐤕𐤐𐤕.𐤄𐤀𐤐𐤃.𐤀𐤋.𐤌𐤅𐤋.
𐤐𐤍𐤉𐤅

יט 𐤅𐤉𐤏𐤔𐤅.𐤔𐤕𐤉.𐤈𐤁𐤏𐤕.𐤆𐤄𐤁.𐤅𐤉𐤔𐤉𐤌𐤅.𐤏𐤋.𐤔𐤍𐤉
.𐤒𐤑𐤅𐤕.𐤄𐤇𐤔𐤍.𐤏𐤋.𐤔𐤐𐤕𐤅.𐤀𐤔𐤓.𐤀𐤋.𐤏𐤁𐤓.𐤄𐤀𐤐𐤃.𐤁
𐤉𐤕𐤄

כ 𐤅𐤉𐤏𐤔𐤅.𐤔𐤕𐤉.𐤈𐤁𐤏𐤕.𐤆𐤄𐤁.𐤅𐤉𐤕𐤍𐤌.𐤏𐤋.𐤔𐤕𐤉.
𐤊𐤕𐤐𐤕.𐤄𐤀𐤐𐤃.𐤌𐤋𐤌𐤈𐤄.𐤌𐤌𐤅𐤋.𐤐𐤍𐤉𐤅.𐤋𐤏𐤌𐤕.𐤌𐤇𐤁𐤓
𐤕𐤅.𐤌𐤌𐤏𐤋.𐤋𐤇𐤔𐤁.𐤄𐤀𐤐𐤃

21 𐤅𐤉𐤓𐤊𐤎𐤅.𐤀𐤕.𐤄𐤇𐤔𐤍.𐤌𐤈𐤁𐤏𐤕𐤉𐤅.𐤀𐤋.𐤈𐤁𐤏𐤕.𐤄
𐤀𐤐𐤃.𐤁𐤐𐤕𐤉𐤋.𐤕𐤊𐤋𐤕.𐤋𐤄𐤉𐤕.𐤏𐤋.𐤇𐤔𐤁.𐤄𐤀𐤐𐤃.𐤅𐤋𐤀.
𐤉𐤆𐤇.𐤄𐤇𐤔𐤍.𐤌𐤏𐤋.𐤄𐤀𐤐𐤃.𐤊𐤀𐤔𐤓.𐤑𐤅𐤄.𐤉𐤄𐤅𐤄.𐤀𐤕.
𐤌𐤔𐤄|

22 𐤅𐤉𐤏𐤔.𐤀𐤕.𐤌𐤏𐤉𐤋.𐤄𐤀𐤐𐤃.𐤌𐤏𐤔𐤄.𐤀𐤓𐤂.𐤊𐤋𐤉𐤋
.𐤕𐤊𐤋𐤕|

23 𐤅𐤐𐤉.𐤄𐤌𐤏𐤉𐤋.𐤁𐤕𐤅𐤊𐤅.𐤊𐤐𐤉.𐤕𐤇𐤓𐤀.𐤔𐤐𐤄.𐤋𐤐𐤉𐤅.
𐤎𐤁𐤉𐤁.𐤋𐤀.𐤉𐤒𐤓𐤏|

24 𐤅𐤉𐤏𐤔𐤅.𐤏𐤋.𐤔𐤅𐤋𐤉.𐤄𐤌𐤏𐤉𐤋.𐤓𐤌𐤅𐤍𐤉.𐤕𐤊𐤋𐤕.𐤅𐤀𐤓
𐤂𐤌𐤍.𐤅𐤕𐤅𐤋𐤏𐤕.𐤔𐤍𐤉.𐤌𐤔𐤆𐤓|

25 𐤅𐤉𐤏𐤔𐤅.𐤐𐤏𐤌𐤍𐤉.𐤆𐤄𐤁.𐤈𐤄𐤅𐤓.𐤅𐤉𐤕𐤍𐤅.𐤀𐤕.𐤄𐤐𐤏
𐤌𐤍𐤉𐤌.𐤁𐤕𐤅𐤊.𐤄𐤓𐤌𐤍𐤉𐤌.𐤏𐤋.𐤔𐤅𐤋𐤉.𐤄𐤌𐤏𐤉𐤋.𐤎𐤁𐤉𐤁.𐤁
𐤕𐤅𐤊.𐤄𐤓𐤌𐤍𐤉𐤌|

26 𐤐𐤏𐤌𐤍.𐤅𐤓𐤌𐤍.𐤐𐤏𐤌𐤍.𐤅𐤓𐤌𐤍.𐤏𐤋.𐤔𐤅𐤋𐤉.𐤄𐤌𐤏𐤉𐤋.𐤎
𐤁𐤉𐤁.𐤋𐤔𐤓𐤕.𐤊𐤀𐤔𐤓.𐤑𐤅𐤄.𐤉𐤄𐤅𐤄.𐤀𐤕.𐤌𐤔𐤄|

27 𐤅𐤉𐤏𐤔𐤅.𐤀𐤕.𐤄𐤊𐤕𐤍𐤕.𐤔𐤔.𐤌𐤏𐤔𐤄.𐤀𐤓𐤂.𐤋𐤀𐤄𐤓
𐤍.𐤅𐤋𐤁𐤍𐤉𐤅|

28 𐤅𐤀𐤕.𐤄𐤌𐤑𐤍𐤐𐤕.𐤔𐤔.𐤅𐤀𐤕.𐤐𐤀𐤓𐤉.𐤄𐤌𐤂𐤁𐤏𐤕.𐤔
𐤔.𐤅𐤀𐤕.𐤌𐤊𐤍𐤎𐤉.𐤄𐤁𐤃.𐤔𐤔.𐤌𐤔𐤆𐤓|

29 𐤅𐤀𐤕.𐤄𐤀𐤁𐤍𐤈.𐤔𐤔.𐤌𐤔𐤆𐤓.𐤅𐤕𐤊𐤋𐤕.𐤅𐤀𐤓𐤂𐤌𐤍.𐤅
𐤕𐤅𐤋𐤏𐤕.𐤔𐤍𐤉.𐤌𐤏𐤔𐤄.𐤓𐤒𐤌.𐤊𐤀𐤔𐤓.𐤑𐤅𐤄.𐤉𐤄𐤅𐤄.𐤀𐤕.
𐤌𐤔𐤄|

30 𐤅𐤉𐤏𐤔𐤅.𐤀𐤕.𐤑𐤉𐤑.𐤍𐤆𐤓.𐤄𐤒𐤃𐤔.𐤆𐤄𐤁.𐤈𐤄𐤅𐤓.
𐤅𐤉𐤊𐤕𐤁𐤅.𐤏𐤋𐤉𐤅.𐤌𐤊𐤕𐤁.𐤐𐤕𐤅𐤇𐤉.𐤇𐤅𐤕𐤌.𐤒𐤃𐤔.𐤋𐤉𐤄𐤅
𐤄|

31 𐤅𐤉𐤕𐤍𐤅.𐤏𐤋𐤉𐤅.𐤐𐤕𐤉𐤋.𐤕𐤊𐤋𐤕.𐤋𐤕𐤕.𐤏𐤋.𐤄𐤌𐤑𐤍𐤐
𐤕.𐤌𐤋𐤌𐤏𐤋𐤄.𐤊𐤀𐤔𐤓.𐤑𐤅𐤄.𐤉𐤄𐤅𐤄.𐤀𐤕.𐤌𐤔𐤄|

32 𐤅𐤕𐤊𐤋.𐤊𐤋.𐤏𐤁𐤃𐤕.𐤌𐤔𐤊𐤍.𐤀𐤄𐤋.𐤌𐤅𐤏𐤃.𐤅𐤉𐤏𐤔𐤅.
𐤁𐤍𐤉.𐤉𐤔𐤓𐤀𐤋.𐤊𐤊𐤋.𐤀𐤔𐤓.𐤑𐤅𐤄.𐤉𐤄𐤅𐤄.𐤀𐤕.𐤌𐤔𐤄.𐤊𐤍.
𐤏𐤔𐤅|

𐤋𐤂 𐤅𐤉𐤁𐤉𐤀𐤅.𐤀𐤕.𐤄𐤌𐤔𐤊𐤍.𐤀𐤋.𐤌𐤔𐤄.𐤀𐤕.𐤄𐤀𐤄𐤋.𐤅
𐤀𐤕.𐤊𐤋.𐤊𐤋𐤉𐤅.𐤒𐤓𐤎𐤉𐤅.𐤒𐤓𐤔𐤉𐤅.𐤁𐤓𐤉𐤇𐤅.‖𐤁𐤓𐤉𐤇𐤉𐤅.𐤒
𐤓𐤉‖.𐤅𐤏𐤌𐤃𐤉𐤅.𐤅𐤀𐤃𐤍𐤉𐤅|

𐤋𐤃 𐤅𐤀𐤕.𐤌𐤊𐤎𐤄.𐤏𐤅𐤓𐤕.𐤄𐤀𐤉𐤋𐤌.𐤄𐤌𐤀𐤃𐤌𐤉𐤌.𐤅𐤀
𐤕.𐤌𐤊𐤎𐤄.𐤏𐤓𐤕.𐤄𐤕𐤇𐤔𐤉𐤌.𐤅𐤀𐤕.𐤐𐤓𐤊𐤕.𐤄𐤌𐤎𐤊|

𐤋𐤄 𐤀𐤕.𐤀𐤓𐤍.𐤄𐤏𐤃𐤕.𐤅𐤀𐤕.𐤁𐤃𐤉𐤅.𐤅𐤀𐤕.𐤄𐤊𐤐𐤓𐤕|

𐤋𐤅 𐤀𐤕.𐤄𐤔𐤋𐤇𐤍.𐤀𐤕.𐤊𐤋.𐤊𐤋𐤉𐤅.𐤅𐤀𐤕.𐤋𐤇𐤌.𐤄𐤐𐤍𐤉𐤌|

𐤋𐤆 𐤀𐤕.𐤄𐤌𐤍𐤓𐤄.𐤄𐤈𐤄𐤓𐤄.𐤀𐤕.𐤍𐤓𐤕𐤉𐤄.𐤍𐤓𐤕.𐤄𐤌𐤏
𐤓𐤊𐤄.𐤅𐤀𐤕.𐤊𐤋.𐤊𐤋𐤉𐤄.𐤅𐤀𐤕.𐤔𐤌𐤍.𐤄𐤌𐤀𐤅𐤓|

𐤋𐤇 𐤅𐤀𐤕.𐤌𐤆𐤁𐤇.𐤄𐤆𐤄𐤁.𐤅𐤀𐤕.𐤔𐤌𐤍.𐤄𐤌𐤔𐤇𐤄.𐤅𐤀
𐤕.𐤒𐤈𐤓𐤕.𐤄𐤎𐤌𐤉𐤌.𐤅𐤀𐤕.𐤌𐤎𐤊.𐤐𐤕𐤇.𐤄𐤀𐤄𐤋|

𐤋𐤈 𐤀𐤕.𐤌𐤆𐤁𐤇.𐤄𐤍𐤇𐤔𐤕.𐤅𐤀𐤕.𐤌𐤊𐤁𐤓.𐤄𐤍𐤇𐤔𐤕.
𐤀𐤔𐤓.𐤋𐤅.𐤀𐤕.𐤁𐤃𐤉𐤅.𐤅𐤀𐤕.𐤊𐤋.𐤊𐤋𐤉𐤅.𐤀𐤕.𐤄𐤊𐤉𐤓.𐤅𐤀𐤕.
𐤊𐤍𐤅|

𐤌 𐤀𐤕.𐤒𐤋𐤏𐤉.𐤄𐤇𐤑𐤓.𐤀𐤕.𐤏𐤌𐤃𐤉𐤄.𐤅𐤀𐤕.𐤀𐤃𐤍
𐤉𐤄.𐤅𐤀𐤕.𐤄𐤌𐤎𐤊.𐤋𐤔𐤏𐤓.𐤄𐤇𐤑𐤓.𐤀𐤕.𐤌𐤉𐤕𐤓𐤉𐤅.𐤅𐤉𐤕
𐤃𐤕𐤉𐤄.𐤅𐤀𐤕.𐤊𐤋.𐤊𐤋𐤉.𐤏𐤁𐤃𐤕.𐤄𐤌𐤔𐤊𐤍.𐤋𐤀𐤄𐤋.𐤌𐤅𐤏
𐤃|

𐤌𐤀 𐤀𐤕.𐤁𐤂𐤃𐤉.𐤄𐤔𐤓𐤃.𐤋𐤔𐤓𐤕.𐤁𐤒𐤃𐤔.𐤀𐤕.𐤁𐤂
𐤃𐤉.𐤄𐤒𐤃𐤔.𐤋𐤀𐤄𐤓𐤍.𐤄𐤊𐤄𐤍.𐤅𐤀𐤕.𐤁𐤂𐤃𐤉.𐤁𐤍𐤉𐤅.𐤋𐤊
𐤄𐤍|

𐤌𐤁 𐤊𐤊𐤋.𐤀𐤔𐤓.𐤑𐤅𐤄.𐤉𐤄𐤅𐤄.𐤀𐤕.𐤌𐤔𐤄.𐤊𐤍.𐤏𐤔𐤅.𐤁𐤍
𐤉.𐤉𐤔𐤓𐤀𐤋.𐤀𐤕.𐤊𐤋.𐤄𐤏𐤁𐤃𐤄|

𐤌𐤂 𐤅𐤉𐤓𐤀.𐤌𐤔𐤄.𐤀𐤕.𐤊𐤋.𐤄𐤌𐤋𐤀𐤊𐤄.𐤅𐤄𐤍𐤄.𐤏𐤔𐤅.𐤀
𐤕𐤄.𐤊𐤀𐤔𐤓.𐤑𐤅𐤄.𐤉𐤄𐤅𐤄.𐤊𐤍.𐤏𐤔𐤅.𐤅𐤉𐤁𐤓𐤊.𐤀𐤕𐤌.𐤌𐤔𐤄|
|

𐤅𐤉𐤏𐤋𐤅.𐤌𐤌𐤑𐤓𐤉𐤌.𐤇𐤋𐤒 𐤌

𐤀 𐤅𐤉𐤃𐤁𐤓.𐤉𐤄𐤅𐤄.𐤀𐤋.𐤌𐤔𐤄.𐤋𐤀𐤌𐤓|

2 𐤁𐤉𐤅𐤌.𐤄𐤇𐤃𐤔.𐤄𐤓𐤀𐤔𐤅𐤍.𐤁𐤀𐤇𐤃.𐤋𐤇𐤃𐤔.𐤕𐤒𐤉
𐤌.𐤀𐤕.𐤌𐤔𐤊𐤍.𐤀𐤄𐤋.𐤌𐤅𐤏𐤃|
3 𐤅𐤔𐤌𐤕.𐤔𐤌.𐤀𐤕.𐤀𐤓𐤅𐤍.𐤄𐤏𐤃𐤅𐤕.𐤅𐤎𐤊𐤕.𐤏𐤋.𐤄𐤀𐤓𐤍
.𐤀𐤕.𐤄𐤐𐤓𐤊𐤕|
4 𐤅𐤄𐤁𐤀𐤕.𐤀𐤕.𐤄𐤔𐤋𐤇𐤍.𐤅𐤏𐤓𐤊𐤕.𐤀𐤕.𐤏𐤓𐤊𐤅.𐤅𐤄𐤁𐤀
𐤕.𐤀𐤕.𐤄𐤌𐤍𐤓𐤄.𐤅𐤄𐤏𐤋𐤉𐤕.𐤀𐤕.𐤍𐤓𐤕𐤉𐤄|
5 𐤅𐤍𐤕𐤕𐤄.𐤀𐤕.𐤌𐤆𐤁𐤇.𐤄𐤆𐤄𐤁.𐤋𐤒𐤈𐤓𐤕.𐤋𐤐𐤍𐤉.𐤀𐤓𐤅
𐤍.𐤄𐤏𐤃𐤕.𐤅𐤔𐤌𐤕.𐤀𐤕.𐤌𐤎𐤊.𐤄𐤐𐤕𐤇.𐤋𐤌𐤔𐤊𐤍|
6 𐤅𐤍𐤕𐤕𐤄.𐤀𐤕.𐤌𐤆𐤁𐤇.𐤄𐤏𐤋𐤄.𐤋𐤐𐤍𐤉.𐤐𐤕𐤇.𐤌𐤔𐤊𐤍.
𐤀𐤄𐤋.𐤌𐤅𐤏𐤃|
7 𐤅𐤍𐤕𐤕.𐤀𐤕.𐤄𐤊𐤉𐤓.𐤁𐤉𐤍.𐤀𐤄𐤋.𐤌𐤅𐤏𐤃.𐤅𐤁𐤉𐤍.𐤄𐤌𐤆
𐤁𐤇.𐤅𐤍𐤕𐤕.𐤔𐤌.𐤌𐤉𐤌|
8 𐤅𐤔𐤌𐤕.𐤀𐤕.𐤄𐤇𐤑𐤓.𐤎𐤁𐤉𐤁.𐤅𐤍𐤕𐤕.𐤀𐤕.𐤌𐤎𐤊.𐤔𐤏𐤓
.𐤄𐤇𐤑𐤓|
9 𐤅𐤋𐤒𐤇𐤕.𐤀𐤕.𐤔𐤌𐤍.𐤄𐤌𐤔𐤇𐤄.𐤅𐤌𐤔𐤇𐤕.𐤀𐤕.𐤄𐤌
𐤔𐤊𐤍.𐤅𐤀𐤕.𐤊𐤋.𐤀𐤔𐤓.𐤁𐤅.𐤅𐤒𐤃𐤔𐤕.𐤀𐤕𐤅.𐤅𐤀𐤕.𐤊𐤋.𐤊𐤋𐤉
𐤅.𐤅𐤄𐤉𐤄.𐤒𐤃𐤔|
10 𐤅𐤌𐤔𐤇𐤕.𐤀𐤕.𐤌𐤆𐤁𐤇.𐤄𐤏𐤋𐤄.𐤅𐤀𐤕.𐤊𐤋.𐤊𐤋𐤉𐤅.𐤅
𐤒𐤃𐤔𐤕.𐤀𐤕.𐤄𐤌𐤆𐤁𐤇.𐤅𐤄𐤉𐤄.𐤄𐤌𐤆𐤁𐤇.𐤒𐤃𐤔.𐤒𐤃
𐤔𐤉𐤌|
11 𐤅𐤌𐤔𐤇𐤕.𐤀𐤕.𐤄𐤊𐤉𐤓.𐤅𐤀𐤕.𐤊𐤍𐤅.𐤅𐤒𐤃𐤔𐤕.𐤀𐤕𐤅|
12 𐤅𐤄𐤒𐤓𐤁𐤕.𐤀𐤕.𐤀𐤄𐤓𐤍.𐤅𐤀𐤕.𐤁𐤍𐤉𐤅.𐤀𐤋.𐤐𐤕𐤇.𐤀𐤄𐤋
.𐤌𐤅𐤏𐤃.𐤅𐤓𐤇𐤑𐤕.𐤀𐤕𐤌.𐤁𐤌𐤉𐤌|
13 𐤅𐤄𐤋𐤁𐤔𐤕.𐤀𐤕.𐤀𐤄𐤓𐤍.𐤀𐤕.𐤁𐤂𐤃𐤉.𐤄𐤒𐤃𐤔.𐤅𐤌
𐤔𐤇𐤕.𐤀𐤕𐤅.𐤅𐤒𐤃𐤔𐤕.𐤀𐤕𐤅.𐤅𐤊𐤄𐤍.𐤋𐤉|
14 𐤅𐤀𐤕.𐤁𐤍𐤉𐤅.𐤕𐤒𐤓𐤉𐤁.𐤅𐤄𐤋𐤁𐤔𐤕.𐤀𐤕𐤌.𐤊𐤕𐤍𐤕|
15 𐤅𐤌𐤔𐤇𐤕.𐤀𐤕𐤌.𐤊𐤀𐤔𐤓.𐤌𐤔𐤇𐤕.𐤀𐤕.𐤀𐤁𐤉𐤄𐤌.𐤅𐤊
𐤄𐤍𐤅.𐤋𐤉.𐤅𐤄𐤉𐤕𐤄.𐤋𐤄𐤉𐤕.𐤋𐤄𐤌.𐤌𐤔𐤇𐤕𐤌.𐤋𐤊𐤄𐤍𐤕.𐤏𐤅𐤋
𐤌.𐤋𐤃𐤓𐤕𐤌|
16 𐤅𐤉𐤏𐤔.𐤌𐤔𐤄.𐤊𐤊𐤋.𐤀𐤔𐤓.𐤑𐤅𐤄.𐤉𐤄𐤅𐤄.𐤀𐤕𐤅.𐤊𐤍.𐤏
𐤔𐤄|

יז ויהי.בחדש.הראשון.בשנה.השנית.באח
ד.לחדש.הוקם.המשכן|
יח ויקם.משה.את.המשכן.ויתן.את.אדניו.ו
ישם.את.קרשיו.ויתן.את.בריחיו.ויקם.את.ע
מודיו|
יט ויפרש.את.האהל.על.המשכן.וישם.את.מ
כסה.האהל.עליו.מלמעלה.כאשר.צוה.יהוה.א
ת.משה|
כ ויקח.ויתן.את.העדת.אל.הארן.וישם.א
ת.הבדים.על.הארן.ויתן.את.הכפרת.על.הארן
.מלמעלה|
כא ויבא.את.הארן.אל.המשכן.וישם.את.פרכ
ת.המסך.ויסך.על.ארון.העדות.כאשר.צוה.יה
וה.את.משה|
כב ויתן.את.השלחן.באהל.מועד.על.ירך.המ
שכן.צפנה.מחוץ.לפרכת|
כג ויערך.עליו.ערך.לחם.לפני.יהוה.כאשר.
צוה.יהוה.את.משה|
כד וישם.את.המנרה.באהל.מועד.נכח.השל
חן.על.ירך.המשכן.נגבה|
כה ויעל.הנרת.לפני.יהוה.כאשר.צוה.יהוה.
את.משה|
כו וישם.את.מזבח.הזהב.באהל.מועד.לפנ
י.הפרכת|
כז ויקטר.עליו.קטרת.סמים.כאשר.צוה.יה
וה.את.משה|
כח וישם.את.מסך.הפתח.למשכן|
כט ואת.מזבח.העלה.שם.פתח.משכן.אהל.מ
ועד.ויעל.עליו.את.העלה.ואת.המנחה.כאשר
.צוה.יהוה.את.משה|

ל וישם.את.הכיר.בין.אהל.מועד.ובין.המ
זבח.ויתן.שמה.מים.לרחצה|
לא ורחצו.ממנו.משה.ואהרן.ובניו.את.ידיה
ם.ואת.רגליהם|
לב בבאם.אל.אהל.מועד.ובקרבתם.אל.המז
בח.ירחצו.כאשר.צוה.יהוה.את.משה|
לג ויקם.את.החצר.סביב.למשכן.ולמזבח.
ויתן.את.מסך.שער.החצר.ויכל.משה.את.המל
אכה|
לד ויכס.הענן.את.אהל.מועד.וכבוד.יהוה.
מלא.את.המשכן|
לה ולא.יכל.משה.לבוא.אל.אהל.מועד.כי.שכ
ן.עליו.הענן.וכבוד.יהוה.מלא.את.המשכן|
לו ובהעלות.הענן.מעל.המשכן.יסעו.בני.י
שראל.בכל.מסעיהם|
לז ואם.לא.יעלה.הענן.ולא.יסעו.עד.יום.ה
עלתו|
לח כי.ענן.יהוה.על.המשכן.יומם.ואש.תהי
ה.לילה.בו.לעיני.כל.בית.ישראל.בכל.מסעי
הם||

ספר.ללוים

ללוים.חלק 1

1 ויקרא.אל.משה.וידבר.יהוה.אליו.מאהל.מ
ועד.לאמר|
2 דבר.אל.בני.ישראל.ואמרת.אלהם.אדם.כ
י.יקריב.מכם.קרבן.ליהוה.מן.הבהמה.מן.הב
קר.ומן.הצאן.תקריבו.את.קרבנכם|
3 אם.עלה.קרבנו.מן.הבקר.זכר.תמים.יקרי
בנו.אל.פתח.אהל.מועד.יקריב.אתו.לרצנו.לפ
ני.יהוה|
4 וסמך.ידו.על.ראש.העלה.ונרצה.לו.לכפר.
עליו|
5 ושחט.את.בן.הבקר.לפני.יהוה.והקריבו.ב
ני.אהרן.הכהנים.את.הדם.וזרקו.את.הדם.ע
ל.המזבח.סביב.אשר.פתח.אהל.מועד|
6 והפשיט.את.העלה.ונתח.אתה.לנתחיה|
7 ונתנו.בני.אהרן.הכהן.אש.על.המזבח.וע
רכו.עצים.על.האש|

8 𐤅𐤏𐤓𐤊𐤅.𐤁𐤍𐤉.𐤀𐤄𐤓𐤍.𐤄𐤊𐤄𐤍𐤉𐤌.𐤀𐤕.𐤄𐤍𐤕𐤇𐤉𐤌.𐤀𐤕
.𐤄𐤓𐤀𐤔.𐤅𐤀𐤕.𐤄𐤐𐤃𐤓.𐤏𐤋.𐤄𐤏𐤑𐤉𐤌.𐤀𐤔𐤓.𐤏𐤋.𐤄𐤀𐤔.𐤀
𐤔𐤓.𐤏𐤋.𐤄𐤌𐤆𐤁𐤇|
9 𐤅𐤒𐤓𐤁𐤅.𐤅𐤊𐤓𐤏𐤉𐤅.𐤉𐤓𐤇𐤑.𐤁𐤌𐤉𐤌.𐤅𐤄𐤒𐤈𐤉𐤓.𐤄𐤊𐤄
𐤍.𐤀𐤕.𐤄𐤊𐤋.𐤄𐤌𐤆𐤁𐤇𐤄.𐤏𐤋𐤄.𐤀𐤔𐤄.𐤓𐤉𐤇.𐤍𐤉𐤇𐤅𐤇.𐤋
𐤉𐤄𐤅𐤄|
10 𐤅𐤀𐤌.𐤌𐤍.𐤄𐤑𐤀𐤍.𐤒𐤓𐤁𐤍𐤅.𐤌𐤍.𐤄𐤊𐤔𐤁𐤉𐤌.𐤀𐤅.𐤌𐤍.𐤄
𐤏𐤆𐤉𐤌.𐤋𐤏𐤋𐤄.𐤆𐤊𐤓.𐤕𐤌𐤉𐤌.𐤉𐤒𐤓𐤉𐤁𐤍𐤅|
11 𐤅𐤔𐤇𐤈.𐤀𐤕𐤅.𐤏𐤋.𐤉𐤓𐤊.𐤄𐤌𐤆𐤁𐤇.𐤑𐤐𐤍𐤄.𐤋𐤐𐤍𐤉.𐤉
𐤄𐤅𐤄.𐤅𐤆𐤓𐤒𐤅.𐤁𐤍𐤉.𐤀𐤄𐤓𐤍.𐤄𐤊𐤄𐤍𐤉𐤌.𐤀𐤕.𐤃𐤌𐤅.𐤏𐤋.𐤄
𐤌𐤆𐤁𐤇.𐤎𐤁𐤉𐤁|
12 𐤅𐤍𐤕𐤇.𐤀𐤕𐤅.𐤋𐤍𐤕𐤇𐤉𐤅.𐤅𐤀𐤕.𐤓𐤀𐤔𐤅.𐤅𐤀𐤕.𐤐𐤃𐤓𐤅.𐤅
𐤏𐤓𐤊.𐤄𐤊𐤄𐤍.𐤀𐤕𐤌.𐤏𐤋.𐤄𐤏𐤑𐤉𐤌.𐤀𐤔𐤓.𐤏𐤋.𐤄𐤀𐤔.𐤀𐤔
𐤓.𐤏𐤋.𐤄𐤌𐤆𐤁𐤇|
13 𐤅𐤄𐤒𐤓𐤁.𐤅𐤄𐤊𐤓𐤏𐤉𐤌.𐤉𐤓𐤇𐤑.𐤁𐤌𐤉𐤌.𐤅𐤄𐤒𐤓𐤉𐤁.𐤄
𐤊𐤄𐤍.𐤀𐤕.𐤄𐤊𐤋.𐤅𐤄𐤒𐤈𐤉𐤓.𐤄𐤌𐤆𐤁𐤇𐤄.𐤏𐤋𐤄.𐤄𐤅𐤀.𐤀
𐤔𐤄.𐤓𐤉𐤇.𐤍𐤉𐤇𐤇.𐤋𐤉𐤄𐤅𐤄|
14 𐤅𐤀𐤌.𐤌𐤍.𐤄𐤏𐤅𐤐.𐤏𐤋𐤄.𐤒𐤓𐤁𐤍𐤅.𐤋𐤉𐤄𐤅𐤄.𐤅𐤄𐤒𐤓𐤉𐤁.
𐤌𐤍.𐤄𐤕𐤓𐤉𐤌.𐤀𐤅.𐤌𐤍.𐤁𐤍𐤉.𐤄𐤉𐤅𐤍𐤄.𐤀𐤕.𐤒𐤓𐤁𐤍𐤅|
15 𐤅𐤄𐤒𐤓𐤉𐤁𐤅.𐤄𐤊𐤄𐤍.𐤀𐤋.𐤄𐤌𐤆𐤁𐤇.𐤅𐤌𐤋𐤒.𐤀𐤕.𐤓
𐤀𐤔𐤅.𐤅𐤄𐤒𐤈𐤉𐤓.𐤄𐤌𐤆𐤁𐤇𐤄.𐤅𐤍𐤌𐤑𐤄.𐤃𐤌𐤅.𐤏𐤋.𐤒𐤉𐤓.𐤄
𐤌𐤆𐤁𐤇|
16 𐤅𐤄𐤎𐤉𐤓.𐤀𐤕.𐤌𐤓𐤀𐤕𐤅.𐤁𐤍𐤑𐤕𐤄.𐤅𐤄𐤔𐤋𐤉𐤊.𐤀𐤕𐤄.
𐤀𐤑𐤋.𐤄𐤌𐤆𐤁𐤇.𐤒𐤃𐤌𐤄.𐤀𐤋.𐤌𐤒𐤅𐤌.𐤄𐤃𐤔𐤍|
17 𐤅𐤔𐤎𐤏.𐤀𐤕𐤅.𐤁𐤊𐤍𐤐𐤉𐤅.𐤋𐤀.𐤉𐤁𐤃𐤉𐤋.𐤅𐤄𐤒𐤈𐤉𐤓.𐤀
𐤕𐤅.𐤄𐤊𐤄𐤍.𐤄𐤌𐤆𐤁𐤇𐤄.𐤏𐤋.𐤄𐤏𐤑𐤉𐤌.𐤀𐤔𐤓.𐤏𐤋.𐤄𐤀𐤔.
𐤏𐤋𐤄.𐤄𐤅𐤀.𐤀𐤔𐤄.𐤓𐤉𐤇.𐤍𐤉𐤇𐤇.𐤋𐤉𐤄𐤅𐤄||

2 𐤋𐤋𐤅𐤉𐤌.𐤇𐤋𐤒

1 𐤅𐤍𐤐𐤔.𐤊𐤉.𐤕𐤒𐤓𐤉𐤁.𐤒𐤓𐤁𐤍.𐤌𐤍𐤇𐤄.𐤋𐤉𐤄𐤅𐤄.𐤎𐤋𐤕.𐤉
𐤄𐤉𐤄.𐤒𐤓𐤁𐤍𐤅.𐤅𐤉𐤑𐤒.𐤏𐤋𐤉𐤄.𐤔𐤌𐤍.𐤅𐤍𐤕𐤍.𐤏𐤋𐤉𐤄.𐤋𐤁𐤍𐤄
|

2 𐤅𐤄𐤁𐤉𐤀𐤄.𐤀𐤋.𐤁𐤍𐤉.𐤀𐤄𐤓𐤍.𐤄𐤊𐤄𐤍𐤉𐤌.𐤅𐤒𐤌𐤑.𐤌𐤔
𐤌.𐤌𐤋𐤀.𐤒𐤌𐤑𐤅.𐤌𐤎𐤋𐤕𐤄.𐤅𐤌𐤔𐤌𐤍𐤄.𐤏𐤋.𐤊𐤋.𐤋𐤁𐤍𐤕𐤄.𐤅
𐤄𐤒𐤈𐤉𐤓.𐤄𐤊𐤄𐤍.𐤀𐤕.𐤀𐤆𐤊𐤓𐤕𐤄.𐤄𐤌𐤆𐤁𐤇𐤄.𐤀𐤔𐤄.𐤓
𐤉𐤇.𐤍𐤉𐤇𐤇.𐤋𐤉𐤄𐤅𐤄|

3 𐤅𐤄𐤍𐤅𐤕𐤓𐤕.𐤌𐤍.𐤄𐤌𐤍𐤇𐤄.𐤋𐤀𐤄𐤓𐤍.𐤅𐤋𐤁𐤍𐤉𐤅.𐤒𐤃𐤔.
𐤒𐤃𐤔𐤉𐤌.𐤌𐤀𐤔𐤉.𐤉𐤄𐤅𐤄|

4 𐤅𐤊𐤉.𐤕𐤒𐤓𐤁.𐤒𐤓𐤁𐤍.𐤌𐤍𐤇𐤄.𐤌𐤀𐤐𐤄.𐤕𐤍𐤅𐤓.𐤎𐤋𐤕.𐤇
𐤋𐤅𐤕.𐤌𐤑𐤕.𐤁𐤋𐤅𐤋𐤕.𐤁𐤔𐤌𐤍.𐤅𐤓𐤒𐤉𐤒𐤉.𐤌𐤑𐤅𐤕.𐤌𐤔𐤇𐤉𐤌
.𐤁𐤔𐤌𐤍|

5 𐤅𐤀𐤌.𐤌𐤍𐤇𐤄.𐤏𐤋.𐤄𐤌𐤇𐤁𐤕.𐤒𐤓𐤁𐤍𐤊.𐤎𐤋𐤕.𐤁𐤋𐤅𐤋𐤄.
𐤁𐤔𐤌𐤍.𐤌𐤑𐤄.𐤕𐤄𐤉𐤄|

6 𐤅𐤐𐤕𐤅𐤕.𐤀𐤕𐤄.𐤐𐤕𐤉𐤌.𐤅𐤉𐤑𐤒𐤕.𐤏𐤋𐤉𐤄.𐤔𐤌𐤍.𐤌𐤍𐤇𐤄
.𐤄𐤅𐤀|

7 𐤅𐤀𐤌.𐤌𐤍𐤇𐤕.𐤌𐤓𐤇𐤔𐤕.𐤒𐤓𐤁𐤍𐤊.𐤎𐤋𐤕.𐤁𐤔𐤌𐤍.𐤕𐤏
𐤔𐤄|

8 𐤅𐤄𐤁𐤀𐤕.𐤀𐤕.𐤄𐤌𐤍𐤇𐤄.𐤀𐤔𐤓.𐤉𐤏𐤔𐤄.𐤌𐤀𐤋𐤄.𐤋𐤉𐤄
𐤅𐤄.𐤅𐤄𐤒𐤓𐤉𐤁𐤄.𐤀𐤋.𐤄𐤊𐤄𐤍.𐤅𐤄𐤂𐤉𐤔𐤄.𐤀𐤋.𐤄𐤌𐤆𐤁𐤇|

9 𐤅𐤄𐤓𐤉𐤌.𐤄𐤊𐤄𐤍.𐤌𐤍.𐤄𐤌𐤍𐤇𐤄.𐤀𐤕.𐤀𐤆𐤊𐤓𐤕𐤄.𐤅𐤄
𐤒𐤈𐤉𐤓.𐤄𐤌𐤆𐤁𐤇𐤄.𐤀𐤔𐤄.𐤓𐤉𐤇.𐤍𐤉𐤇𐤇.𐤋𐤉𐤄𐤅𐤄|

10 𐤅𐤄𐤍𐤅𐤕𐤓𐤕.𐤌𐤍.𐤄𐤌𐤍𐤇𐤄.𐤋𐤀𐤄𐤓𐤍.𐤅𐤋𐤁𐤍𐤉𐤅.𐤒𐤃𐤔.
𐤒𐤃𐤔𐤉𐤌.𐤌𐤀𐤔𐤉.𐤉𐤄𐤅𐤄|

11 𐤊𐤋.𐤄𐤌𐤍𐤇𐤄.𐤀𐤔𐤓.𐤕𐤒𐤓𐤉𐤁𐤅.𐤋𐤉𐤄𐤅𐤄.𐤋𐤀.𐤕𐤏𐤔
𐤄.𐤇𐤌𐤑.𐤊𐤉.𐤊𐤋.𐤔𐤀𐤓.𐤅𐤊𐤋.𐤃𐤁𐤔.𐤋𐤀.𐤕𐤒𐤈𐤉𐤓𐤅.𐤌𐤌𐤍
𐤅.𐤀𐤔𐤄.𐤋𐤉𐤄𐤅𐤄|

12 𐤒𐤓𐤁𐤍.𐤓𐤀𐤔𐤉𐤕.𐤕𐤒𐤓𐤉𐤁𐤅.𐤀𐤕𐤌.𐤋𐤉𐤄𐤅𐤄.𐤅𐤀𐤋.𐤄
𐤌𐤆𐤁𐤇.𐤋𐤀.𐤉𐤏𐤋𐤅.𐤋𐤓𐤉𐤇.𐤍𐤉𐤇𐤇|

יג וכל.קרבן.מנחתך.במלח.תמלח.ולא.תשבית.מלח.ברית.אלהיך.מעל.מנחתך.על.כל.קרבנך.תקריב.מלח|

יד ואם.תקריב.מנחת.בכורים.ליהוה.אביב.קלוי.באש.גרש.כרמל.תקריב.את.מנחת.בכוריך|

יה ונתת.עליה.שמן.ושמת.עליה.לבנה.מנחה.הוא|

יו והקטיר.הכהן.את.אזכרתה.מגרשה.ומשמנה.על.כל.לבנתה.אשה.ליהוה||

ללוים.חלק ג

א ואם.זבח.שלמים.קרבנו.אם.מן.הבקר.הוא.מקריב.אם.זכר.אם.נקבה.תמים.יקריבנו.לפני.יהוה|

ב וסמך.ידו.על.ראש.קרבנו.ושחטו.פתח.אהל.מועד.וזרקו.בני.אהרן.הכהנים.את.הדם.על.המזבח.סביב|

ג והקריב.מזבח.השלמים.אשה.ליהוה.את.החלב.המכסה.את.הקרב.ואת.כל.החלב.אשר.על.הקרב|

ד ואת.שתי.הכלית.ואת.החלב.אשר.עלהן.אשר.על.הכסלים.ואת.היתרת.על.הכבד.על.הכלית.יסירנה|

ה והקטירו.אתו.בני.אהרן.המזבחה.על.העלה.אשר.על.העצים.אשר.על.האש.אשה.ריח.ניחח.ליהוה|

ו ואם.מן.הצאן.קרבנו.לזבח.שלמים.ליהוה.זכר.או.נקבה.תמים.יקריבנו|

ז 𐤀𐤌.𐤊𐤔𐤁.𐤄𐤅𐤀.𐤌𐤒𐤓𐤉𐤁.𐤀𐤕.𐤒𐤓𐤁𐤍𐤅.𐤅𐤄𐤒𐤓𐤉𐤁.𐤀
𐤕𐤅.𐤋𐤐𐤍𐤉.𐤉𐤄𐤅𐤄|
ח 𐤅𐤎𐤌𐤊.𐤀𐤕.𐤉𐤃𐤅.𐤏𐤋.𐤓𐤀𐤔.𐤒𐤓𐤁𐤍𐤅.𐤅𐤔𐤇𐤈.𐤀𐤕𐤅.𐤋
𐤐𐤍𐤉.𐤀𐤄𐤋.𐤌𐤅𐤏𐤃.𐤅𐤆𐤓𐤒𐤅.𐤁𐤍𐤉.𐤀𐤄𐤓𐤍.𐤀𐤕.𐤃𐤌𐤅.𐤏𐤋.
𐤄𐤌𐤆𐤁𐤇.𐤎𐤁𐤉𐤁|
ט 𐤅𐤄𐤒𐤓𐤉𐤁.𐤌𐤆𐤁𐤇.𐤄𐤔𐤋𐤌𐤉𐤌.𐤀𐤔𐤄.𐤋𐤉𐤄𐤅𐤄.𐤇𐤋
𐤁𐤅.𐤄𐤀𐤋𐤉𐤄.𐤕𐤌𐤉𐤌𐤄.𐤋𐤏𐤌𐤕.𐤄𐤏𐤑𐤄.𐤉𐤎𐤉𐤓𐤍𐤄.𐤅𐤀𐤕
.𐤄𐤇𐤋𐤁.𐤄𐤌𐤊𐤎𐤄.𐤀𐤕.𐤄𐤒𐤓𐤁.𐤅𐤀𐤕.𐤊𐤋.𐤄𐤇𐤋𐤁.𐤀𐤔𐤓.
𐤏𐤋.𐤄𐤒𐤓𐤁|
י 𐤅𐤀𐤕.𐤔𐤕𐤉.𐤄𐤊𐤋𐤉𐤕.𐤅𐤀𐤕.𐤄𐤇𐤋𐤁.𐤀𐤔𐤓.𐤏𐤋𐤄𐤍.
𐤀𐤔𐤓.𐤏𐤋.𐤄𐤊𐤎𐤋𐤉𐤌.𐤅𐤀𐤕.𐤄𐤉𐤕𐤓𐤕.𐤏𐤋.𐤄𐤊𐤁𐤃.𐤏𐤋.𐤄
𐤊𐤋𐤉𐤕.𐤉𐤎𐤉𐤓𐤍𐤄|
יא 𐤅𐤄𐤒𐤈𐤉𐤓𐤅.𐤄𐤊𐤄𐤍.𐤄𐤌𐤆𐤁𐤇𐤄.𐤋𐤇𐤌.𐤀𐤔𐤄.𐤋𐤉
𐤄𐤅𐤄|
יב 𐤅𐤀𐤌.𐤏𐤆.𐤒𐤓𐤁𐤍𐤅.𐤅𐤄𐤒𐤓𐤉𐤁𐤅.𐤋𐤐𐤍𐤉.𐤉𐤄𐤅𐤄|
יג 𐤅𐤎𐤌𐤊.𐤀𐤕.𐤉𐤃𐤅.𐤏𐤋.𐤓𐤀𐤔𐤅.𐤅𐤔𐤇𐤈.𐤀𐤕𐤅.𐤋𐤐𐤍𐤉.
𐤀𐤄𐤋.𐤌𐤅𐤏𐤃.𐤅𐤆𐤓𐤒𐤅.𐤁𐤍𐤉.𐤀𐤄𐤓𐤍.𐤀𐤕.𐤃𐤌𐤅.𐤏𐤋.𐤄𐤌
𐤆𐤁𐤇.𐤎𐤁𐤉𐤁|
יד 𐤅𐤄𐤒𐤓𐤉𐤁.𐤌𐤌𐤍𐤅.𐤒𐤓𐤁𐤍𐤅.𐤀𐤔𐤄.𐤋𐤉𐤄𐤅𐤄.𐤀𐤕.𐤄𐤇
𐤋𐤁.𐤄𐤌𐤊𐤎𐤄.𐤀𐤕.𐤄𐤒𐤓𐤁.𐤅𐤀𐤕.𐤊𐤋.𐤄𐤇𐤋𐤁.𐤀𐤔𐤓.𐤏𐤋.
𐤄𐤒𐤓𐤁|
טו 𐤅𐤀𐤕.𐤔𐤕𐤉.𐤄𐤊𐤋𐤉𐤕.𐤅𐤀𐤕.𐤄𐤇𐤋𐤁.𐤀𐤔𐤓.𐤏𐤋𐤄𐤍.
𐤀𐤔𐤓.𐤏𐤋.𐤄𐤊𐤎𐤋𐤉𐤌.𐤅𐤀𐤕.𐤄𐤉𐤕𐤓𐤕.𐤏𐤋.𐤄𐤊𐤁𐤃.𐤏𐤋.𐤄
𐤊𐤋𐤉𐤕.𐤉𐤎𐤉𐤓𐤍𐤄|
טז 𐤅𐤄𐤒𐤈𐤉𐤓𐤌.𐤄𐤊𐤄𐤍.𐤄𐤌𐤆𐤁𐤇𐤄.𐤋𐤇𐤌.𐤀𐤔𐤄.𐤋𐤓
𐤉𐤇.𐤍𐤉𐤇𐤇.𐤊𐤋.𐤇𐤋𐤁.𐤋𐤉𐤄𐤅𐤄|
יז 𐤇𐤒𐤕.𐤏𐤅𐤋𐤌.𐤋𐤃𐤓𐤕𐤉𐤊𐤌.𐤁𐤊𐤋.𐤌𐤅𐤔𐤁𐤕𐤉𐤊𐤌.𐤊
𐤋.𐤇𐤋𐤁.𐤅𐤊𐤋.𐤃𐤌.𐤋𐤀.𐤕𐤀𐤊𐤋𐤅||

𐤋𐤋𐤅𐤉𐤌.𐤇𐤋𐤒 ד

1 𐤅𐤉𐤃𐤁𐤓.𐤉𐤄𐤅𐤄.𐤀𐤋.𐤌𐤔𐤄.𐤋𐤀𐤌𐤓|
2 𐤃𐤁𐤓.𐤀𐤋.𐤁𐤍𐤉.𐤉𐤔𐤓𐤀𐤋.𐤋𐤀𐤌𐤓.𐤍𐤐𐤔.𐤊𐤉.𐤕𐤇𐤈𐤀.
𐤁𐤔𐤂𐤂𐤄.𐤌𐤊𐤋.𐤌𐤑𐤅𐤕.𐤉𐤄𐤅𐤄.𐤀𐤔𐤓.𐤋𐤀.𐤕𐤏𐤔𐤉𐤍𐤄.𐤅
𐤏𐤔𐤄.𐤌𐤀𐤇𐤕.𐤌𐤄𐤍𐤄|
3 𐤀𐤌.𐤄𐤊𐤄𐤍.𐤄𐤌𐤔𐤉𐤇.𐤉𐤇𐤈𐤀.𐤋𐤀𐤔𐤌𐤕.𐤄𐤏𐤌.𐤅𐤄
𐤒𐤓𐤉𐤁.𐤏𐤋.𐤇𐤈𐤀𐤕𐤅.𐤀𐤔𐤓.𐤇𐤈𐤀.𐤐𐤓.𐤁𐤍.𐤁𐤒𐤓.𐤕𐤌𐤉𐤌
.𐤋𐤉𐤄𐤅𐤄.𐤋𐤇𐤈𐤀𐤕|
4 𐤅𐤄𐤁𐤉𐤀.𐤀𐤕.𐤄𐤐𐤓.𐤀𐤋.𐤐𐤕𐤇.𐤀𐤄𐤋.𐤌𐤅𐤏𐤃.𐤋𐤐𐤍𐤉.
𐤉𐤄𐤅𐤄.𐤅𐤎𐤌𐤊.𐤀𐤕.𐤉𐤃𐤅.𐤏𐤋.𐤓𐤀𐤔.𐤄𐤐𐤓.𐤅𐤔𐤇𐤈.𐤀𐤕.𐤄
𐤐𐤓.𐤋𐤐𐤍𐤉.𐤉𐤄𐤅𐤄|
5 𐤅𐤋𐤒𐤇.𐤄𐤊𐤄𐤍.𐤄𐤌𐤔𐤉𐤇.𐤌𐤃𐤌.𐤄𐤐𐤓.𐤅𐤄𐤁𐤉𐤀.𐤀𐤕𐤅
.𐤀𐤋.𐤀𐤄𐤋.𐤌𐤅𐤏𐤃|
6 𐤅𐤈𐤁𐤋.𐤄𐤊𐤄𐤍.𐤀𐤕.𐤀𐤑𐤁𐤏𐤅.𐤁𐤃𐤌.𐤅𐤄𐤆𐤄.𐤌𐤍.𐤄𐤃
𐤌.𐤔𐤁𐤏.𐤐𐤏𐤌𐤉𐤌.𐤋𐤐𐤍𐤉.𐤉𐤄𐤅𐤄.𐤀𐤕.𐤐𐤍𐤉.𐤐𐤓𐤊𐤕.𐤄𐤒𐤃
𐤔|
7 𐤅𐤍𐤕𐤍.𐤄𐤊𐤄𐤍.𐤌𐤍.𐤄𐤃𐤌.𐤏𐤋.𐤒𐤓𐤍𐤅𐤕.𐤌𐤆𐤁𐤇.𐤒𐤈
𐤓𐤕.𐤄𐤎𐤌𐤉𐤌.𐤋𐤐𐤍𐤉.𐤉𐤄𐤅𐤄.𐤀𐤔𐤓.𐤁𐤀𐤄𐤋.𐤌𐤅𐤏𐤃.𐤅𐤀𐤕.
𐤊𐤋.𐤃𐤌.𐤄𐤐𐤓.𐤉𐤔𐤐𐤊.𐤀𐤋.𐤉𐤎𐤅𐤃.𐤌𐤆𐤁𐤇.𐤄𐤏𐤋𐤄.𐤀𐤔
𐤓.𐤐𐤕𐤇.𐤀𐤄𐤋.𐤌𐤅𐤏𐤃|
8 𐤅𐤀𐤕.𐤊𐤋.𐤇𐤋𐤁.𐤐𐤓.𐤄𐤇𐤈𐤀𐤕.𐤉𐤓𐤉𐤌.𐤌𐤌𐤍𐤅.𐤀𐤕.𐤄
𐤇𐤋𐤁.𐤄𐤌𐤊𐤎𐤄.𐤏𐤋.𐤄𐤒𐤓𐤁.𐤅𐤀𐤕.𐤊𐤋.𐤄𐤇𐤋𐤁.𐤀𐤔𐤓.𐤏𐤋
.𐤄𐤒𐤓𐤁|
9 𐤅𐤀𐤕.𐤔𐤕𐤉.𐤄𐤊𐤋𐤉𐤕.𐤅𐤀𐤕.𐤄𐤇𐤋𐤁.𐤀𐤔𐤓.𐤏𐤋𐤉𐤄𐤍.
𐤀𐤔𐤓.𐤏𐤋.𐤄𐤊𐤎𐤋𐤉𐤌.𐤅𐤀𐤕.𐤄𐤉𐤕𐤓𐤕.𐤏𐤋.𐤄𐤊𐤁𐤃.𐤏𐤋.𐤄
𐤊𐤋𐤉𐤅𐤕.𐤉𐤎𐤉𐤓𐤍𐤄|
10 𐤊𐤀𐤔𐤓.𐤉𐤅𐤓𐤌.𐤌𐤔𐤅𐤓.𐤆𐤁𐤇.𐤄𐤔𐤋𐤌𐤉𐤌.𐤅𐤄𐤒𐤈𐤉
𐤓𐤌.𐤄𐤊𐤄𐤍.𐤏𐤋.𐤌𐤆𐤁𐤇.𐤄𐤏𐤋𐤄|
11 𐤅𐤀𐤕.𐤏𐤅𐤓.𐤄𐤐𐤓.𐤅𐤀𐤕.𐤊𐤋.𐤁𐤔𐤓𐤅.𐤏𐤋.𐤓𐤀𐤔𐤅.𐤅𐤏𐤋.𐤊
𐤓𐤏𐤉𐤅.𐤅𐤒𐤓𐤁𐤅.𐤅𐤐𐤓𐤔𐤅|

..𐤉𐤁.. 𐤅𐤄𐤅𐤑𐤉𐤀.𐤀𐤕.𐤊𐤋.𐤄𐤐𐤓.𐤀𐤋.𐤌𐤇𐤅𐤑.𐤋𐤌𐤇𐤍𐤄.𐤀𐤋.
𐤌𐤒𐤅𐤌.𐤈𐤄𐤅𐤓.𐤀𐤋.𐤔𐤐𐤊.𐤄𐤃𐤔𐤍.𐤅𐤔𐤓𐤐.𐤀𐤕𐤅.𐤏𐤋.𐤏𐤑𐤉
𐤌.𐤁𐤀𐤔.𐤏𐤋.𐤔𐤐𐤊.𐤄𐤃𐤔𐤍.𐤉𐤔𐤓𐤐|

..𐤉𐤂.. 𐤅𐤀𐤌.𐤊𐤋.𐤏𐤃𐤕.𐤉𐤔𐤓𐤀𐤋.𐤉𐤔𐤂𐤅.𐤅𐤍𐤏𐤋𐤌.𐤃𐤁𐤓.𐤌
𐤏𐤉𐤍𐤉.𐤄𐤒𐤄𐤋.𐤅𐤏𐤔𐤅.𐤀𐤇𐤕.𐤌𐤊𐤋.𐤌𐤑𐤅𐤕.𐤉𐤄𐤅𐤄.𐤀𐤔𐤓
.𐤋𐤀.𐤕𐤏𐤔𐤉𐤍𐤄.𐤅𐤀𐤔𐤌𐤅|

..𐤉𐤃.. 𐤅𐤍𐤅𐤃𐤏𐤄.𐤄𐤇𐤈𐤀𐤕.𐤀𐤔𐤓.𐤇𐤈𐤀𐤅.𐤏𐤋𐤉𐤄.𐤅𐤄𐤒
𐤓𐤉𐤁𐤅.𐤄𐤒𐤄𐤋.𐤐𐤓.𐤁𐤍.𐤁𐤒𐤓.𐤋𐤇𐤈𐤀𐤕.𐤅𐤄𐤁𐤉𐤀𐤅.𐤀𐤕𐤅.𐤋
𐤐𐤍𐤉.𐤀𐤄𐤋.𐤌𐤅𐤏𐤃|

..𐤉𐤄.. 𐤅𐤎𐤌𐤊𐤅.𐤆𐤒𐤍𐤉.𐤄𐤏𐤃𐤄.𐤀𐤕.𐤉𐤃𐤉𐤄𐤌.𐤏𐤋.𐤓𐤀𐤔
.𐤄𐤐𐤓.𐤋𐤐𐤍𐤉.𐤉𐤄𐤅𐤄.𐤅𐤔𐤇𐤈.𐤀𐤕.𐤄𐤐𐤓.𐤋𐤐𐤍𐤉.𐤉𐤄𐤅𐤄|

..𐤉𐤅.. 𐤅𐤄𐤁𐤉𐤀.𐤄𐤊𐤄𐤍.𐤄𐤌𐤔𐤉𐤇.𐤌𐤃𐤌.𐤄𐤐𐤓.𐤀𐤋.𐤀𐤄𐤋.
𐤌𐤅𐤏𐤃|

..𐤉𐤆.. 𐤅𐤈𐤁𐤋.𐤄𐤊𐤄𐤍.𐤀𐤑𐤁𐤏𐤅.𐤌𐤍.𐤄𐤃𐤌.𐤅𐤄𐤆𐤄.𐤔𐤁𐤏.
𐤐𐤏𐤌𐤉𐤌.𐤋𐤐𐤍𐤉.𐤉𐤄𐤅𐤄.𐤀𐤕.𐤐𐤍𐤉.𐤄𐤐𐤓𐤊𐤕|

..𐤉𐤇.. 𐤅𐤌𐤍.𐤄𐤃𐤌.𐤉𐤕𐤍.𐤏𐤋.𐤒𐤓𐤍𐤕.𐤄𐤌𐤆𐤁𐤇.𐤀𐤔𐤓.𐤋𐤐𐤍
𐤉.𐤉𐤄𐤅𐤄.𐤀𐤔𐤓.𐤁𐤀𐤄𐤋.𐤌𐤅𐤏𐤃.𐤅𐤀𐤕.𐤊𐤋.𐤄𐤃𐤌.𐤉𐤔𐤐𐤊.
𐤀𐤋.𐤉𐤎𐤅𐤃.𐤌𐤆𐤁𐤇.𐤄𐤏𐤋𐤄.𐤀𐤔𐤓.𐤐𐤕𐤇.𐤀𐤄𐤋.𐤌𐤅𐤏𐤃|

..𐤉𐤈.. 𐤅𐤀𐤕.𐤊𐤋.𐤇𐤋𐤁𐤅.𐤉𐤓𐤉𐤌.𐤌𐤌𐤍𐤅.𐤅𐤄𐤒𐤈𐤉𐤓.𐤄𐤌𐤆𐤁
𐤇𐤄|

..𐤊.. 𐤅𐤏𐤔𐤄.𐤋𐤐𐤓.𐤊𐤀𐤔𐤓.𐤏𐤔𐤄.𐤋𐤐𐤓.𐤄𐤇𐤈𐤀𐤕.𐤊𐤍.𐤉
𐤏𐤔𐤄.𐤋𐤅.𐤅𐤊𐤐𐤓.𐤏𐤋𐤄𐤌.𐤄𐤊𐤄𐤍.𐤅𐤍𐤎𐤋𐤇.𐤋𐤄𐤌|

..𐤊𐤀.. 𐤅𐤄𐤅𐤑𐤉𐤀.𐤀𐤕.𐤄𐤐𐤓.𐤀𐤋.𐤌𐤇𐤅𐤑.𐤋𐤌𐤇𐤍𐤄.𐤅𐤔𐤓𐤐.
𐤀𐤕𐤅.𐤊𐤀𐤔𐤓.𐤔𐤓𐤐.𐤀𐤕.𐤄𐤐𐤓.𐤄𐤓𐤀𐤔𐤅𐤍.𐤇𐤈𐤀𐤕.𐤄𐤒𐤄
𐤋.𐤄𐤅𐤀|

..𐤊𐤁.. 𐤀𐤔𐤓.𐤍𐤔𐤉𐤀.𐤉𐤇𐤈𐤀.𐤅𐤏𐤔𐤄.𐤀𐤇𐤕.𐤌𐤊𐤋.𐤌𐤑𐤅
𐤕.𐤉𐤄𐤅𐤄.𐤀𐤋𐤄𐤉𐤅.𐤀𐤔𐤓.𐤋𐤀.𐤕𐤏𐤔𐤉𐤍𐤄.𐤁𐤔𐤂𐤂𐤄.𐤅𐤀
𐤔𐤌|

..𐤊𐤂.. 𐤀𐤅.𐤄𐤅𐤃𐤏.𐤀𐤋𐤉𐤅.𐤇𐤈𐤀𐤕𐤅.𐤀𐤔𐤓.𐤇𐤈𐤀.𐤁𐤄.𐤅𐤄
𐤁𐤉𐤀.𐤀𐤕.𐤒𐤓𐤁𐤍𐤅.𐤔𐤏𐤉𐤓.𐤏𐤆𐤉𐤌.𐤆𐤊𐤓.𐤕𐤌𐤉𐤌|

..𐤊𐤃.. 𐤅𐤎𐤌𐤊.𐤉𐤃𐤅.𐤏𐤋.𐤓𐤀𐤔.𐤄𐤔𐤏𐤉𐤓.𐤅𐤔𐤇𐤈.𐤀𐤕𐤅.𐤁
𐤌𐤒𐤅𐤌.𐤀𐤔𐤓.𐤉𐤔𐤇𐤈.𐤀𐤕.𐤄𐤏𐤋𐤄.𐤋𐤐𐤍𐤉.𐤉𐤄𐤅𐤄.𐤇𐤈𐤀
𐤕.𐤄𐤅𐤀|

..𐤊𐤄.. 𐤅𐤋𐤒𐤇.𐤄𐤊𐤄𐤍.𐤌𐤃𐤌.𐤄𐤇𐤈𐤀𐤕.𐤁𐤀𐤑𐤁𐤏𐤅.𐤅𐤍𐤕𐤍
.𐤏𐤋.𐤒𐤓𐤍𐤕.𐤌𐤆𐤁𐤇.𐤄𐤏𐤋𐤄.𐤅𐤀𐤕.𐤃𐤌𐤅.𐤉𐤔𐤐𐤊.𐤀𐤋.𐤉
𐤎𐤅𐤃.𐤌𐤆𐤁𐤇.𐤄𐤏𐤋𐤄|

..𐤊𐤅.. 𐤅𐤀𐤕.𐤊𐤋.𐤇𐤋𐤁𐤅.𐤉𐤒𐤈𐤉𐤓.𐤄𐤌𐤆𐤁𐤇𐤄.𐤊𐤇𐤋𐤁.𐤆
𐤁𐤇.𐤄𐤔𐤋𐤌𐤉𐤌.𐤅𐤊𐤐𐤓.𐤏𐤋𐤉𐤅.𐤄𐤊𐤄𐤍.𐤌𐤇𐤈𐤀𐤕𐤅.𐤅𐤍𐤎𐤋
𐤇.𐤋𐤅|

..𐤊𐤆.. 𐤅𐤀𐤌.𐤍𐤐𐤔.𐤀𐤇𐤕.𐤕𐤇𐤈𐤀.𐤁𐤔𐤂𐤂𐤄.𐤌𐤏𐤌.𐤄𐤀
𐤓𐤑.𐤁𐤏𐤔𐤕𐤄.𐤀𐤇𐤕.𐤌𐤌𐤑𐤅𐤕.𐤉𐤄𐤅𐤄.𐤀𐤔𐤓.𐤋𐤀.𐤕𐤏𐤔
𐤉𐤍𐤄.𐤅𐤀𐤔𐤌|

..𐤊𐤇.. 𐤀𐤅.𐤄𐤅𐤃𐤏.𐤀𐤋𐤉𐤅.𐤇𐤈𐤀𐤕𐤅.𐤀𐤔𐤓.𐤇𐤈𐤀.𐤅𐤄𐤁𐤉𐤀
.𐤒𐤓𐤁𐤍𐤅.𐤔𐤏𐤉𐤓𐤕.𐤏𐤆𐤉𐤌.𐤕𐤌𐤉𐤌𐤄.𐤍𐤒𐤁𐤄.𐤏𐤋.𐤇𐤈𐤀
𐤕𐤅.𐤀𐤔𐤓.𐤇𐤈𐤀|

..𐤊𐤈.. 𐤅𐤎𐤌𐤊.𐤀𐤕.𐤉𐤃𐤅.𐤏𐤋.𐤓𐤀𐤔.𐤄𐤇𐤈𐤀𐤕.𐤅𐤔𐤇𐤈.𐤀
𐤕.𐤄𐤇𐤈𐤀𐤕.𐤁𐤌𐤒𐤅𐤌.𐤄𐤏𐤋𐤄|

..𐤋.. 𐤅𐤋𐤒𐤇.𐤄𐤊𐤄𐤍.𐤌𐤃𐤌𐤄.𐤁𐤀𐤑𐤁𐤏𐤅.𐤅𐤍𐤕𐤍.𐤏𐤋.𐤒𐤓
𐤍𐤕.𐤌𐤆𐤁𐤇.𐤄𐤏𐤋𐤄.𐤅𐤀𐤕.𐤊𐤋.𐤃𐤌𐤄.𐤉𐤔𐤐𐤊.𐤀𐤋.𐤉𐤎𐤅
𐤃.𐤄𐤌𐤆𐤁𐤇|

..𐤋𐤀.. 𐤅𐤀𐤕.𐤊𐤋.𐤇𐤋𐤁𐤄.𐤉𐤎𐤉𐤓.𐤊𐤀𐤔𐤓.𐤄𐤅𐤎𐤓.𐤇𐤋𐤁.𐤌𐤏
𐤋.𐤆𐤁𐤇.𐤄𐤔𐤋𐤌𐤉𐤌.𐤅𐤄𐤒𐤈𐤉𐤓.𐤄𐤊𐤄𐤍.𐤄𐤌𐤆𐤁𐤇𐤄.𐤋𐤓
𐤉𐤇.𐤍𐤉𐤇𐤇.𐤋𐤉𐤄𐤅𐤄.𐤅𐤊𐤐𐤓.𐤏𐤋𐤉𐤅.𐤄𐤊𐤄𐤍.𐤅𐤍𐤎𐤋𐤇.𐤋𐤅|

..𐤋𐤁.. 𐤅𐤀𐤌.𐤊𐤁𐤔.𐤉𐤁𐤉𐤀.𐤒𐤓𐤁𐤍𐤅.𐤋𐤇𐤈𐤀𐤕.𐤍𐤒𐤁𐤄.𐤕𐤌
𐤉𐤌𐤄.𐤉𐤁𐤉𐤀𐤍𐤄|

..𐤋𐤂.. 𐤅𐤎𐤌𐤊.𐤀𐤕.𐤉𐤃𐤅.𐤏𐤋.𐤓𐤀𐤔.𐤄𐤇𐤈𐤀𐤕.𐤅𐤔𐤇𐤈.𐤀
𐤕𐤄.𐤋𐤇𐤈𐤀𐤕.𐤁𐤌𐤒𐤅𐤌.𐤀𐤔𐤓.𐤉𐤔𐤇𐤈.𐤀𐤕.𐤄𐤏𐤋𐤄|

..𐤋𐤃.. 𐤅𐤋𐤒𐤇.𐤄𐤊𐤄𐤍.𐤌𐤃𐤌.𐤄𐤇𐤈𐤀𐤕.𐤁𐤀𐤑𐤁𐤏𐤅.𐤅𐤍𐤕
𐤍.𐤏𐤋.𐤒𐤓𐤍𐤕.𐤌𐤆𐤁𐤇.𐤄𐤏𐤋𐤄.𐤅𐤀𐤕.𐤊𐤋.𐤃𐤌𐤄.𐤉𐤔𐤐𐤊.
𐤀𐤋.𐤉𐤎𐤅𐤃.𐤄𐤌𐤆𐤁𐤇|

לה 𐤅𐤀𐤕.𐤊𐤋.𐤇𐤋𐤁𐤄.𐤉𐤎𐤉𐤓.𐤊𐤀𐤔𐤓.𐤉𐤅𐤎𐤓.𐤇𐤋𐤁.𐤄𐤊
𐤔𐤁.𐤌𐤆𐤁𐤇.𐤄𐤔𐤋𐤌𐤉𐤌.𐤅𐤄𐤒𐤈𐤉𐤓.𐤄𐤊𐤄𐤍.𐤀𐤕𐤌.𐤄𐤌
𐤆𐤁𐤇𐤄.𐤏𐤋.𐤀𐤔𐤉.𐤉𐤄𐤅𐤄.𐤅𐤊𐤐𐤓.𐤏𐤋𐤉𐤅.𐤄𐤊𐤄𐤍.𐤏𐤋.𐤇
𐤈𐤀𐤕𐤅.𐤀𐤔𐤓.𐤇𐤈𐤀.𐤅𐤍𐤎𐤋𐤇.𐤋𐤅||

𐤋𐤋𐤅𐤉𐤌.𐤇𐤋𐤒 ה

א 𐤅𐤍𐤐𐤔.𐤊𐤉.𐤕𐤇𐤈𐤀.𐤅𐤔𐤌𐤏𐤄.𐤒𐤅𐤋.𐤀𐤋𐤄.𐤅𐤄𐤅𐤀.𐤏𐤃
.𐤀𐤅.𐤓𐤀𐤄.𐤀𐤅.𐤉𐤃𐤏.𐤀𐤌.𐤋𐤅𐤀.𐤉𐤂𐤉𐤃.𐤅𐤍𐤔𐤀.𐤏𐤅𐤍𐤅|

ב 𐤀𐤅.𐤍𐤐𐤔.𐤀𐤔𐤓.𐤕𐤂𐤏.𐤁𐤊𐤋.𐤃𐤁𐤓.𐤈𐤌𐤀.𐤀𐤅.𐤁𐤍𐤁𐤋
𐤕.𐤇𐤉𐤄.𐤈𐤌𐤀𐤄.𐤀𐤅.𐤁𐤍𐤁𐤋𐤕.𐤁𐤄𐤌𐤄.𐤈𐤌𐤀𐤄.𐤀𐤅.𐤁𐤍𐤁
𐤋𐤕.𐤔𐤓𐤑.𐤈𐤌𐤀.𐤅𐤍𐤏𐤋𐤌.𐤌𐤌𐤍𐤅.𐤅𐤄𐤅𐤀.𐤈𐤌𐤀.𐤅𐤀𐤔𐤌|

ג 𐤀𐤅.𐤊𐤉.𐤉𐤂𐤏.𐤁𐤈𐤌𐤀𐤕.𐤀𐤃𐤌.𐤋𐤊𐤋.𐤈𐤌𐤀𐤕𐤅.𐤀𐤔
𐤓.𐤉𐤈𐤌𐤀.𐤁𐤄.𐤅𐤍𐤏𐤋𐤌.𐤌𐤌𐤍𐤅.𐤅𐤄𐤅𐤀.𐤉𐤃𐤏.𐤅𐤀𐤔𐤌|

ד 𐤀𐤅.𐤍𐤐𐤔.𐤊𐤉.𐤕𐤔𐤁𐤏.𐤋𐤁𐤈𐤀.𐤁𐤔𐤐𐤕𐤉𐤌.𐤋𐤄𐤓𐤏.𐤀
𐤅.𐤋𐤄𐤉𐤈𐤉𐤁.𐤋𐤊𐤋.𐤀𐤔𐤓.𐤉𐤁𐤈𐤀.𐤄𐤀𐤃𐤌.𐤁𐤔𐤁𐤏𐤄.𐤅𐤍𐤏
𐤋𐤌.𐤌𐤌𐤍𐤅.𐤅𐤄𐤅𐤀.𐤉𐤃𐤏.𐤅𐤀𐤔𐤌.𐤋𐤀𐤇𐤕.𐤌𐤀𐤋𐤄|

ה 𐤅𐤄𐤉𐤄.𐤊𐤉.𐤉𐤀𐤔𐤌.𐤋𐤀𐤇𐤕.𐤌𐤀𐤋𐤄.𐤅𐤄𐤕𐤅𐤃𐤄.𐤀𐤔
𐤓.𐤇𐤈𐤀.𐤏𐤋𐤉𐤄|

ו 𐤅𐤄𐤁𐤉𐤀.𐤀𐤕.𐤀𐤔𐤌𐤅.𐤋𐤉𐤄𐤅𐤄.𐤏𐤋.𐤇𐤈𐤀𐤕𐤅.𐤀𐤔𐤓.
𐤇𐤈𐤀.𐤍𐤒𐤁𐤄.𐤌𐤍.𐤄𐤑𐤀𐤍.𐤊𐤔𐤁𐤄.𐤀𐤅.𐤔𐤏𐤉𐤓𐤕.𐤏𐤆𐤉
𐤌.𐤋𐤇𐤈𐤀𐤕.𐤅𐤊𐤐𐤓.𐤏𐤋𐤉𐤅.𐤄𐤊𐤄𐤍.𐤌𐤇𐤈𐤀𐤕𐤅|

ז 𐤅𐤀𐤌.𐤋𐤀.𐤕𐤂𐤉𐤏.𐤉𐤃𐤅.𐤃𐤉.𐤔𐤄.𐤅𐤄𐤁𐤉𐤀.𐤀𐤕.𐤀𐤔
𐤌𐤅.𐤀𐤔𐤓.𐤇𐤈𐤀.𐤔𐤕𐤉.𐤕𐤓𐤉𐤌.𐤀𐤅.𐤔𐤍𐤉.𐤁𐤍𐤉.𐤉𐤅𐤍𐤄.𐤋𐤉
𐤄𐤅𐤄.𐤀𐤇𐤃.𐤋𐤇𐤈𐤀𐤕.𐤅𐤀𐤇𐤃.𐤋𐤏𐤋𐤄|

ח 𐤅𐤄𐤁𐤉𐤀.𐤀𐤕𐤌.𐤀𐤋.𐤄𐤊𐤄𐤍.𐤅𐤄𐤒𐤓𐤉𐤁.𐤀𐤕.𐤀𐤔𐤓.𐤋
𐤇𐤈𐤀𐤕.𐤓𐤀𐤔𐤅𐤍𐤄.𐤅𐤌𐤋𐤒.𐤀𐤕.𐤓𐤀𐤔𐤅.𐤌𐤌𐤅𐤋.𐤏𐤓𐤐𐤅.𐤅𐤋𐤀
.𐤉𐤁𐤃𐤉𐤋|

ט 𐤅𐤄𐤆𐤄.𐤌𐤃𐤌.𐤄𐤇𐤈𐤀𐤕.𐤏𐤋.𐤒𐤉𐤓.𐤄𐤌𐤆𐤁𐤇.𐤅𐤄
𐤍𐤔𐤀𐤓.𐤁𐤃𐤌.𐤉𐤌𐤑𐤄.𐤀𐤋.𐤉𐤎𐤅𐤃.𐤄𐤌𐤆𐤁𐤇.𐤇𐤈𐤀𐤕.
𐤄𐤅𐤀|

10 𐤅𐤀𐤕.𐤄𐤔𐤍𐤉.𐤉𐤏𐤔𐤄.𐤏𐤋𐤄.𐤊𐤌𐤔𐤐𐤈.𐤅𐤊𐤐𐤓.𐤏𐤋𐤉𐤅
.𐤄𐤊𐤄𐤍.𐤌𐤇𐤈𐤀𐤕𐤅.𐤀𐤔𐤓.𐤇𐤈𐤀.𐤅𐤍𐤎𐤋𐤇.𐤋𐤅|
11 𐤅𐤀𐤌.𐤋𐤀.𐤕𐤔𐤉𐤂.𐤉𐤃𐤅.𐤋𐤔𐤕𐤉.𐤕𐤓𐤉𐤌.𐤀𐤅.𐤋𐤔𐤍𐤉.
𐤁𐤍𐤉.𐤉𐤅𐤍𐤄.𐤅𐤄𐤁𐤉𐤀.𐤀𐤕.𐤒𐤓𐤁𐤍𐤅.𐤀𐤔𐤓.𐤇𐤈𐤀.𐤏𐤔𐤉𐤓𐤕
.𐤄𐤀𐤐𐤄.𐤎𐤋𐤕.𐤋𐤇𐤈𐤀𐤕.𐤋𐤀.𐤉𐤔𐤉𐤌.𐤏𐤋𐤉𐤄.𐤔𐤌𐤍.𐤅𐤋𐤀
𐤉𐤕𐤍.𐤏𐤋𐤉𐤄.𐤋𐤁𐤍𐤄.𐤊𐤉.𐤇𐤈𐤀𐤕.𐤄𐤅𐤀|
12 𐤅𐤄𐤁𐤉𐤀𐤄.𐤀𐤋.𐤄𐤊𐤄𐤍.𐤅𐤒𐤌𐤑.𐤄𐤊𐤄𐤍.𐤌𐤌𐤍𐤄.𐤌𐤋𐤅
𐤀.𐤒𐤌𐤑𐤅.𐤀𐤕.𐤀𐤆𐤊𐤓𐤕𐤄.𐤅𐤄𐤒𐤈𐤉𐤓.𐤄𐤌𐤆𐤁𐤇𐤄.𐤏𐤋.
𐤀𐤔𐤉.𐤉𐤄𐤅𐤄.𐤇𐤈𐤀𐤕.𐤄𐤅𐤀|
13 𐤅𐤊𐤐𐤓.𐤏𐤋𐤉𐤅.𐤄𐤊𐤄𐤍.𐤏𐤋.𐤇𐤈𐤀𐤕𐤅.𐤀𐤔𐤓.𐤇𐤈𐤀.𐤌
𐤀𐤇𐤕.𐤌𐤀𐤋𐤄.𐤅𐤍𐤎𐤋𐤇.𐤋𐤅.𐤅𐤄𐤉𐤕𐤄.𐤋𐤊𐤄𐤍.𐤊𐤌𐤍𐤇𐤄|
14 𐤅𐤉𐤃𐤁𐤓.𐤉𐤄𐤅𐤄.𐤀𐤋.𐤌𐤔𐤄.𐤋𐤀𐤌𐤓|
15 𐤍𐤐𐤔.𐤊𐤉.𐤕𐤌𐤏𐤋.𐤌𐤏𐤋.𐤅𐤇𐤈𐤀𐤄.𐤁𐤔𐤂𐤂𐤄.𐤌𐤒
𐤃𐤔𐤉.𐤉𐤄𐤅𐤄.𐤅𐤄𐤁𐤉𐤀.𐤀𐤕.𐤀𐤔𐤌𐤅.𐤋𐤉𐤄𐤅𐤄.𐤀𐤉𐤋.𐤕𐤌𐤉
𐤌.𐤌𐤍.𐤄𐤑𐤀𐤍.𐤁𐤏𐤓𐤊𐤊.𐤊𐤎𐤐.𐤔𐤒𐤋𐤉𐤌.𐤁𐤔𐤒𐤋.𐤄𐤒𐤃
𐤔.𐤋𐤀𐤔𐤌|
16 𐤅𐤀𐤕.𐤀𐤔𐤓.𐤇𐤈𐤀.𐤌𐤍.𐤄𐤒𐤃𐤔.𐤉𐤔𐤋𐤌.𐤅𐤀𐤕.𐤇𐤌
𐤉𐤔𐤕𐤅.𐤉𐤅𐤎𐤐.𐤏𐤋𐤉𐤅.𐤅𐤍𐤕𐤍.𐤀𐤕𐤅.𐤋𐤊𐤄𐤍.𐤅𐤄𐤊𐤄𐤍.𐤉𐤊𐤐𐤓.
𐤏𐤋𐤉𐤅.𐤁𐤀𐤉𐤋.𐤄𐤀𐤔𐤌.𐤅𐤍𐤎𐤋𐤇.𐤋𐤅|
17 𐤅𐤀𐤌.𐤍𐤐𐤔.𐤊𐤉.𐤕𐤇𐤈𐤀.𐤅𐤏𐤔𐤕𐤄.𐤀𐤇𐤕.𐤌𐤊𐤋.𐤌
𐤑𐤅𐤕.𐤉𐤄𐤅𐤄.𐤀𐤔𐤓.𐤋𐤀.𐤕𐤏𐤔𐤉𐤍𐤄.𐤅𐤋𐤀.𐤉𐤃𐤏.𐤅𐤀𐤔𐤌.𐤅
𐤍𐤔𐤀.𐤏𐤅𐤍𐤅|
18 𐤅𐤄𐤁𐤉𐤀.𐤀𐤉𐤋.𐤕𐤌𐤉𐤌.𐤌𐤍.𐤄𐤑𐤀𐤍.𐤁𐤏𐤓𐤊𐤊.𐤋𐤀𐤔
𐤌.𐤀𐤋.𐤄𐤊𐤄𐤍.𐤅𐤊𐤐𐤓.𐤏𐤋𐤉𐤅.𐤄𐤊𐤄𐤍.𐤏𐤋.𐤔𐤂𐤂𐤕𐤅.𐤀𐤔𐤓.
𐤔𐤂𐤂.𐤅𐤄𐤅𐤀.𐤋𐤀.𐤉𐤃𐤏.𐤅𐤍𐤎𐤋𐤇.𐤋𐤅|
19 𐤀𐤔𐤌.𐤄𐤅𐤀.𐤀𐤔𐤌.𐤀𐤔𐤌.𐤋𐤉𐤄𐤅𐤄|
20 𐤅𐤉𐤃𐤁𐤓.𐤉𐤄𐤅𐤄.𐤀𐤋.𐤌𐤔𐤄.𐤋𐤀𐤌𐤓|
21 𐤍𐤐𐤔.𐤊𐤉.𐤕𐤇𐤈𐤀.𐤅𐤌𐤏𐤋𐤄.𐤌𐤏𐤋.𐤁𐤉𐤄𐤅𐤄.𐤅𐤊𐤇𐤔.
𐤁𐤏𐤌𐤉𐤕𐤅.𐤁𐤐𐤒𐤃𐤅𐤍.𐤀𐤅.𐤁𐤕𐤔𐤅𐤌𐤕.𐤉𐤃.𐤀𐤅.𐤁𐤂𐤆𐤋.𐤀
𐤅.𐤏𐤔𐤒.𐤀𐤕.𐤏𐤌𐤉𐤕𐤅|

𐤊𐤁 𐤀𐤅.𐤌𐤑𐤀.𐤀𐤁𐤃𐤄.𐤅𐤊𐤇𐤔.𐤁𐤄.𐤅𐤍𐤔𐤁𐤏.𐤏𐤋.𐤔𐤒𐤓
𐤏𐤋.𐤀𐤇𐤕.𐤌𐤊𐤋.𐤀𐤔𐤓.𐤉𐤏𐤔𐤄.𐤄𐤀𐤃𐤌.𐤋𐤇𐤈𐤀.𐤁𐤄𐤍
𐤄|

𐤊𐤂 𐤅𐤄𐤉𐤄.𐤊𐤉.𐤉𐤇𐤈𐤀.𐤅𐤀𐤔𐤌.𐤅𐤄𐤔𐤉𐤁.𐤀𐤕.𐤄𐤂𐤆𐤋
𐤄.𐤀𐤔𐤓.𐤂𐤆𐤋.𐤀𐤅.𐤀𐤕.𐤄𐤏𐤔𐤒.𐤀𐤔𐤓.𐤏𐤔𐤒.𐤀𐤅.𐤀𐤕.
𐤄𐤐𐤒𐤃𐤅𐤍.𐤀𐤔𐤓.𐤄𐤐𐤒𐤃.𐤀𐤕𐤅.𐤀𐤅.𐤀𐤕.𐤄𐤀𐤁𐤃𐤄.𐤀𐤔𐤓
.𐤌𐤑𐤀|

𐤊𐤃 𐤀𐤅.𐤌𐤊𐤋.𐤀𐤔𐤓.𐤉𐤔𐤁𐤏.𐤏𐤋𐤉𐤅.𐤋𐤔𐤒𐤓.𐤅𐤔𐤋𐤌.𐤀𐤕
𐤅.𐤁𐤓𐤀𐤔𐤅.𐤅𐤇𐤌𐤔𐤕𐤉𐤅.𐤉𐤎𐤐.𐤏𐤋𐤉𐤅.𐤋𐤀𐤔𐤓.𐤄𐤅𐤀.𐤋𐤅.𐤉𐤕
𐤍𐤍𐤅.𐤁𐤉𐤅𐤌.𐤀𐤔𐤌𐤕𐤅|

𐤊𐤄 𐤅𐤀𐤕.𐤀𐤔𐤌𐤅.𐤉𐤁𐤉𐤀.𐤋𐤉𐤄𐤅𐤄.𐤀𐤉𐤋.𐤕𐤌𐤉𐤌.𐤌𐤍.𐤄
𐤑𐤀𐤍.𐤁𐤏𐤓𐤊𐤊.𐤋𐤀𐤔𐤌.𐤀𐤋.𐤄𐤊𐤄𐤍|

𐤊𐤅 𐤅𐤊𐤐𐤓.𐤏𐤋𐤉𐤅.𐤄𐤊𐤄𐤍.𐤋𐤐𐤍𐤉.𐤉𐤄𐤅𐤄.𐤅𐤍𐤎𐤋𐤇.𐤋𐤅.𐤏𐤋.
𐤀𐤇𐤕.𐤌𐤊𐤋.𐤀𐤔𐤓.𐤉𐤏𐤔𐤄.𐤋𐤀𐤔𐤌𐤄.𐤁𐤄||

𐤅 𐤋𐤋𐤅𐤉𐤌.𐤇𐤋𐤒

𐤀 𐤅𐤉𐤃𐤁𐤓.𐤉𐤄𐤅𐤄.𐤀𐤋.𐤌𐤔𐤄.𐤋𐤀𐤌𐤓|

𐤁 𐤑𐤅.𐤀𐤕.𐤀𐤄𐤓𐤍.𐤅𐤀𐤕.𐤁𐤍𐤉𐤅.𐤋𐤀𐤌𐤓.𐤆𐤀𐤕.𐤕𐤅𐤓𐤕.𐤄
𐤏𐤋𐤄.𐤄𐤅𐤀.𐤄𐤏𐤋𐤄.𐤏𐤋.𐤌𐤅𐤒𐤃𐤄.𐤏𐤋.𐤄𐤌𐤆𐤁𐤇.𐤊𐤋.𐤄
𐤋𐤉𐤋𐤄.𐤏𐤃.𐤄𐤁𐤒𐤓.𐤅𐤀𐤔.𐤄𐤌𐤆𐤁𐤇.𐤕𐤅𐤒𐤃.𐤁𐤅|

𐤂 𐤅𐤋𐤁𐤔.𐤄𐤊𐤄𐤍.𐤌𐤃𐤅.𐤁𐤃.𐤅𐤌𐤊𐤍𐤎𐤉.𐤁𐤃.𐤉𐤋𐤁𐤔.𐤏𐤋
.𐤁𐤔𐤓𐤅.𐤅𐤄𐤓𐤉𐤌.𐤀𐤕.𐤄𐤃𐤔𐤍.𐤀𐤔𐤓.𐤕𐤀𐤊𐤋.𐤄𐤀𐤔.𐤀𐤕.
𐤄𐤏𐤋𐤄.𐤏𐤋.𐤄𐤌𐤆𐤁𐤇.𐤅𐤔𐤌𐤅.𐤀𐤑𐤋.𐤄𐤌𐤆𐤁𐤇|

𐤃 𐤅𐤐𐤔𐤈.𐤀𐤕.𐤁𐤂𐤃𐤉𐤅.𐤅𐤋𐤁𐤔.𐤁𐤂𐤃𐤉𐤌.𐤀𐤇𐤓𐤉𐤌.𐤅
𐤄𐤅𐤑𐤉𐤀.𐤀𐤕.𐤄𐤃𐤔𐤍.𐤀𐤋.𐤌𐤇𐤅𐤑.𐤋𐤌𐤇𐤍𐤄.𐤀𐤋.𐤌𐤒𐤅𐤌
.𐤈𐤄𐤅𐤓|

𐤄 𐤅𐤄𐤀𐤔.𐤏𐤋.𐤄𐤌𐤆𐤁𐤇.𐤕𐤅𐤒𐤃.𐤁𐤅.𐤋𐤀.𐤕𐤊𐤁𐤄.𐤅𐤁𐤏
𐤓.𐤏𐤋𐤉𐤄.𐤄𐤊𐤄𐤍.𐤏𐤑𐤉𐤌.𐤁𐤁𐤒𐤓.𐤁𐤁𐤒𐤓.𐤅𐤏𐤓𐤊.𐤏𐤋𐤉𐤄.
𐤄𐤏𐤋𐤄.𐤅𐤄𐤒𐤈𐤉𐤓.𐤏𐤋𐤉𐤄.𐤇𐤋𐤁𐤉.𐤄𐤔𐤋𐤌𐤉𐤌|

𐤅 𐤀𐤔.𐤕𐤌𐤉𐤃.𐤕𐤅𐤒𐤃.𐤏𐤋.𐤄𐤌𐤆𐤁𐤇.𐤋𐤀.𐤕𐤊𐤁𐤄|

ז 𐤅𐤆𐤀𐤕.𐤕𐤅𐤓𐤕.𐤄𐤌𐤍𐤇𐤄.𐤄𐤒𐤓𐤁.𐤀𐤕𐤄.𐤁𐤍𐤉.𐤀𐤄𐤓
𐤍.𐤋𐤐𐤍𐤉.𐤉𐤄𐤅𐤄.𐤀𐤋.𐤐𐤍𐤉.𐤄𐤌𐤆𐤁𐤇|
ח 𐤅𐤄𐤓𐤉𐤌.𐤌𐤌𐤍𐤅.𐤁𐤒𐤌𐤑𐤅.𐤌𐤎𐤋𐤕.𐤄𐤌𐤍𐤇𐤄.𐤅𐤌𐤔𐤌𐤍
𐤄.𐤅𐤀𐤕.𐤊𐤋.𐤄𐤋𐤁𐤍𐤄.𐤀𐤔𐤓.𐤏𐤋.𐤄𐤌𐤍𐤇𐤄.𐤅𐤄𐤒𐤈𐤉𐤓.𐤄
𐤌𐤆𐤁𐤇.𐤓𐤉𐤇.𐤍𐤉𐤇𐤇.𐤀𐤆𐤊𐤓𐤕𐤄.𐤋𐤉𐤄𐤅𐤄|
ט 𐤅𐤄𐤍𐤅𐤕𐤓𐤕.𐤌𐤌𐤍𐤄.𐤉𐤀𐤊𐤋𐤅.𐤀𐤄𐤓𐤍.𐤅𐤁𐤍𐤉𐤅.𐤌𐤑𐤅𐤕.
𐤕𐤀𐤊𐤋.𐤁𐤌𐤒𐤅𐤌.𐤒𐤃𐤔.𐤁𐤇𐤑𐤓.𐤀𐤄𐤋.𐤌𐤅𐤏𐤃.𐤉𐤀𐤊𐤋𐤅
𐤄|
י 𐤋𐤀.𐤕𐤀𐤐𐤄.𐤇𐤌𐤑.𐤇𐤋𐤒𐤌.𐤍𐤕𐤕𐤉.𐤀𐤕𐤄.𐤌𐤀𐤔𐤉
.𐤒𐤃𐤔.𐤒𐤃𐤔𐤉𐤌.𐤄𐤅𐤀.𐤊𐤇𐤈𐤀𐤕.𐤅𐤊𐤀𐤔𐤌|
יא 𐤊𐤋.𐤆𐤊𐤓.𐤁𐤁𐤍𐤉.𐤀𐤄𐤓𐤍.𐤉𐤀𐤊𐤋𐤍𐤄.𐤇𐤒.𐤏𐤅𐤋𐤌.𐤋
𐤃𐤓𐤕𐤉𐤊𐤌.𐤌𐤀𐤔𐤉.𐤉𐤄𐤅𐤄.𐤊𐤋.𐤀𐤔𐤓.𐤉𐤂𐤏.𐤁𐤄𐤌.𐤉𐤒
𐤃𐤔|
יב 𐤅𐤉𐤃𐤁𐤓.𐤉𐤄𐤅𐤄.𐤀𐤋.𐤌𐤔𐤄.𐤋𐤀𐤌𐤓|
יג 𐤆𐤄.𐤒𐤓𐤁𐤍.𐤀𐤄𐤓𐤍.𐤅𐤁𐤍𐤉𐤅.𐤀𐤔𐤓.𐤉𐤒𐤓𐤉𐤁𐤅.𐤋𐤉𐤄𐤅
𐤄.𐤁𐤉𐤅𐤌.𐤄𐤌𐤔𐤇.𐤀𐤕𐤅.𐤏𐤔𐤉𐤓𐤕.𐤄𐤀𐤐𐤄.𐤎𐤋𐤕.𐤌𐤍𐤇𐤄.
𐤕𐤌𐤉𐤃.𐤌𐤇𐤑𐤉𐤕𐤄.𐤁𐤁𐤒𐤓.𐤅𐤌𐤇𐤑𐤉𐤕𐤄.𐤁𐤏𐤓𐤁|
יד 𐤏𐤋.𐤌𐤇𐤁𐤕.𐤁𐤔𐤌𐤍.𐤕𐤏𐤔𐤄.𐤌𐤓𐤁𐤊𐤕.𐤕𐤁𐤉𐤀𐤍𐤄.
𐤕𐤐𐤉𐤍𐤉.𐤌𐤍𐤇𐤕.𐤐𐤕𐤉𐤌.𐤕𐤒𐤓𐤉𐤁.𐤓𐤉𐤇.𐤍𐤉𐤇𐤇.𐤋𐤉𐤄𐤅
𐤄|
טו 𐤅𐤄𐤊𐤄𐤍.𐤄𐤌𐤔𐤉𐤇.𐤕𐤇𐤕𐤉𐤅.𐤌𐤁𐤍𐤉𐤅.𐤉𐤏𐤔𐤄.𐤀𐤕
𐤄.𐤇𐤒.𐤏𐤅𐤋𐤌.𐤋𐤉𐤄𐤅𐤄.𐤊𐤋𐤉𐤋.𐤕𐤒𐤈𐤓|
טז 𐤅𐤊𐤋.𐤌𐤍𐤇𐤕.𐤊𐤄𐤍.𐤊𐤋𐤉𐤋.𐤕𐤄𐤉𐤄.𐤋𐤀.𐤕𐤀𐤊𐤋|
יז 𐤅𐤉𐤃𐤁𐤓.𐤉𐤄𐤅𐤄.𐤀𐤋.𐤌𐤔𐤄.𐤋𐤀𐤌𐤓|
יח 𐤃𐤁𐤓.𐤀𐤋.𐤀𐤄𐤓𐤍.𐤅𐤀𐤋.𐤁𐤍𐤉𐤅.𐤋𐤀𐤌𐤓.𐤆𐤀𐤕.𐤕𐤅𐤓𐤕.
𐤄𐤇𐤈𐤀𐤕.𐤁𐤌𐤒𐤅𐤌.𐤀𐤔𐤓.𐤕𐤔𐤇𐤈.𐤄𐤏𐤋𐤄.𐤕𐤔𐤇𐤈.𐤄
𐤇𐤈𐤀𐤕.𐤋𐤐𐤍𐤉.𐤉𐤄𐤅𐤄.𐤒𐤃𐤔.𐤒𐤃𐤔𐤉𐤌.𐤄𐤅𐤀|
יט 𐤄𐤊𐤄𐤍.𐤄𐤌𐤇𐤈𐤀.𐤀𐤕𐤄.𐤉𐤀𐤊𐤋𐤍𐤄.𐤁𐤌𐤒𐤅𐤌.𐤒
𐤃𐤔.𐤕𐤀𐤊𐤋.𐤁𐤇𐤑𐤓.𐤀𐤄𐤋.𐤌𐤅𐤏𐤃|

20 𐤊𐤋.𐤀𐤔𐤓.𐤉𐤂𐤏.𐤁𐤁𐤔𐤓𐤄.𐤉𐤒𐤃𐤔.𐤅𐤀𐤔𐤓.𐤉𐤆𐤄.
𐤌𐤃𐤌𐤄.𐤏𐤋.𐤄𐤁𐤂𐤃.𐤀𐤔𐤓.𐤉𐤆𐤄.𐤏𐤋𐤉𐤄.𐤕𐤊𐤁𐤎.𐤁𐤌
𐤒𐤅𐤌.𐤒𐤃𐤔|
21 𐤅𐤊𐤋𐤉.𐤇𐤓𐤔.𐤀𐤔𐤓.𐤕𐤁𐤔𐤋.𐤁𐤅.𐤉𐤔𐤁𐤓.𐤅𐤀𐤌.𐤁𐤊𐤋𐤉
.𐤍𐤇𐤔𐤕.𐤁𐤔𐤋𐤄.𐤅𐤌𐤓𐤒.𐤅𐤔𐤈𐤐.𐤁𐤌𐤉𐤌|
22 𐤊𐤋.𐤆𐤊𐤓.𐤁𐤊𐤄𐤍𐤉𐤌.𐤉𐤀𐤊𐤋.𐤀𐤕𐤄.𐤒𐤃𐤔.𐤒𐤃𐤔
𐤉𐤌.𐤄𐤅𐤀|
23 𐤅𐤊𐤋.𐤇𐤈𐤀𐤕.𐤀𐤔𐤓.𐤉𐤅𐤁𐤀.𐤌𐤃𐤌𐤄.𐤀𐤋.𐤀𐤄𐤋.𐤌𐤅
𐤏𐤃.𐤋𐤊𐤐𐤓.𐤁𐤒𐤃𐤔.𐤋𐤀.𐤕𐤀𐤊𐤋.𐤁𐤀𐤔.𐤕𐤔𐤓𐤐||

7 𐤋𐤋𐤅𐤉𐤌.𐤇𐤋𐤒

1 𐤅𐤆𐤀𐤕.𐤕𐤅𐤓𐤕.𐤄𐤀𐤔𐤌.𐤒𐤃𐤔.𐤒𐤃𐤔𐤉𐤌.𐤄𐤅𐤀|
2 𐤁𐤌𐤒𐤅𐤌.𐤀𐤔𐤓.𐤉𐤔𐤇𐤈𐤅.𐤀𐤕.𐤄𐤏𐤋𐤄.𐤉𐤔𐤇𐤈𐤅.𐤀𐤕
.𐤄𐤀𐤔𐤌.𐤅𐤀𐤕.𐤃𐤌𐤅.𐤉𐤆𐤓𐤒.𐤏𐤋.𐤄𐤌𐤆𐤁𐤇.𐤎𐤁𐤉𐤁|
3 𐤅𐤀𐤕.𐤊𐤋.𐤇𐤋𐤁𐤅.𐤉𐤒𐤓𐤉𐤁.𐤌𐤌𐤍𐤅.𐤀𐤕.𐤄𐤀𐤋𐤉𐤄.𐤅𐤀
𐤕.𐤄𐤇𐤋𐤁.𐤄𐤌𐤊𐤎𐤄.𐤀𐤕.𐤄𐤒𐤓𐤁|
4 𐤅𐤀𐤕.𐤔𐤕𐤉.𐤄𐤊𐤋𐤉𐤕.𐤅𐤀𐤕.𐤄𐤇𐤋𐤁.𐤀𐤔𐤓.𐤏𐤋𐤉𐤄𐤍.
𐤀𐤔𐤓.𐤏𐤋.𐤄𐤊𐤎𐤋𐤉𐤌.𐤅𐤀𐤕.𐤄𐤉𐤕𐤓𐤕.𐤏𐤋.𐤄𐤊𐤁𐤃.𐤏𐤋.𐤄
𐤊𐤋𐤉𐤕.𐤉𐤎𐤉𐤓𐤍𐤄|
5 𐤅𐤄𐤒𐤈𐤉𐤓.𐤀𐤕𐤌.𐤄𐤊𐤄𐤍.𐤄𐤌𐤆𐤁𐤇𐤄.𐤀𐤔𐤄.𐤋𐤉𐤄𐤅
𐤄.𐤀𐤔𐤌.𐤄𐤅𐤀|
6 𐤊𐤋.𐤆𐤊𐤓.𐤁𐤊𐤄𐤍𐤉𐤌.𐤉𐤀𐤊𐤋𐤍𐤅.𐤁𐤌𐤒𐤅𐤌.𐤒𐤃𐤅𐤔.𐤉𐤀
𐤊𐤋.𐤒𐤃𐤔.𐤒𐤃𐤔𐤉𐤌.𐤄𐤅𐤀|
7 𐤊𐤇𐤈𐤀𐤕.𐤊𐤀𐤔𐤌.𐤕𐤅𐤓𐤄.𐤀𐤇𐤕.𐤋𐤄𐤌.𐤄𐤊𐤄𐤍.𐤀𐤔
𐤓.𐤉𐤊𐤐𐤓.𐤁𐤅.𐤋𐤅.𐤉𐤄𐤉𐤄|
8 𐤅𐤄𐤊𐤄𐤍.𐤄𐤌𐤒𐤓𐤉𐤁.𐤀𐤕.𐤏𐤋𐤕.𐤀𐤉𐤔.𐤏𐤅𐤓.𐤄𐤏𐤋𐤄.
𐤀𐤔𐤓.𐤄𐤒𐤓𐤉𐤁.𐤋𐤊𐤄𐤍.𐤋𐤅.𐤉𐤄𐤉𐤄|
9 𐤅𐤊𐤋.𐤌𐤍𐤇𐤄.𐤀𐤔𐤓.𐤕𐤀𐤐𐤄.𐤁𐤕𐤍𐤅𐤓.𐤅𐤊𐤋.𐤍𐤏𐤔𐤄.𐤁
𐤌𐤓𐤇𐤔𐤕.𐤅𐤏𐤋.𐤌𐤇𐤁𐤕.𐤋𐤊𐤄𐤍.𐤄𐤌𐤒𐤓𐤉𐤁.𐤀𐤕𐤄.𐤋𐤅.𐤕
𐤄𐤉𐤄|

10 𐤅𐤊𐤋.𐤌𐤍𐤇𐤄.𐤁𐤋𐤅𐤋𐤄.𐤁𐤔𐤌𐤍.𐤅𐤇𐤓𐤁𐤄.𐤋𐤊𐤋.𐤁𐤍𐤉.
𐤀𐤄𐤓𐤍.𐤕𐤄𐤉𐤄.𐤀𐤉𐤔.𐤊𐤀𐤇𐤉𐤅|
11 𐤅𐤆𐤀𐤕.𐤕𐤅𐤓𐤕.𐤆𐤁𐤇.𐤄𐤔𐤋𐤌𐤉𐤌.𐤀𐤔𐤓.𐤉𐤒𐤓𐤉𐤁.
𐤋𐤉𐤄𐤅𐤄|
12 𐤀𐤌.𐤏𐤋.𐤕𐤅𐤃𐤄.𐤉𐤒𐤓𐤉𐤁𐤍𐤅.𐤅𐤄𐤒𐤓𐤉𐤁.𐤏𐤋.𐤆𐤁𐤇.
𐤄𐤕𐤅𐤃𐤄.𐤇𐤋𐤅𐤕.𐤌𐤑𐤅𐤕.𐤁𐤋𐤅𐤋𐤕.𐤁𐤔𐤌𐤍.𐤅𐤓𐤒𐤉𐤒𐤉.𐤌𐤑
𐤅𐤕.𐤌𐤔𐤇𐤉𐤌.𐤁𐤔𐤌𐤍.𐤅𐤎𐤋𐤕.𐤌𐤓𐤁𐤊𐤕.𐤇𐤋𐤕.𐤁𐤋𐤅𐤋𐤕.𐤁
𐤔𐤌𐤍|
13 𐤏𐤋.𐤇𐤋𐤕.𐤋𐤇𐤌.𐤇𐤌𐤑.𐤉𐤒𐤓𐤉𐤁.𐤒𐤓𐤁𐤍𐤅.𐤏𐤋.𐤆𐤁
𐤇.𐤕𐤅𐤃𐤕.𐤔𐤋𐤌𐤉𐤅|
14 𐤅𐤄𐤒𐤓𐤉𐤁.𐤌𐤌𐤍𐤅.𐤀𐤇𐤃.𐤌𐤊𐤋.𐤒𐤓𐤁𐤍.𐤕𐤓𐤅𐤌𐤄.𐤋𐤉
𐤄𐤅𐤄.𐤋𐤊𐤄𐤍.𐤄𐤆𐤓𐤒.𐤀𐤕.𐤃𐤌.𐤄𐤔𐤋𐤌𐤉𐤌.𐤋𐤅.𐤉𐤄𐤉𐤄|
15 𐤅𐤁𐤔𐤓.𐤆𐤁𐤇.𐤕𐤅𐤃𐤕.𐤔𐤋𐤌𐤉𐤅.𐤁𐤉𐤅𐤌.𐤒𐤓𐤁𐤍𐤅.𐤉𐤀
𐤊𐤋.𐤋𐤀.𐤉𐤍𐤉𐤇.𐤌𐤌𐤍𐤅.𐤏𐤃.𐤁𐤒𐤓|
16 𐤅𐤀𐤌.𐤍𐤃𐤓.𐤀𐤅.𐤍𐤃𐤁𐤄.𐤆𐤁𐤇.𐤒𐤓𐤁𐤍𐤅.𐤁𐤉𐤅𐤌.𐤄𐤒𐤓
𐤉𐤁𐤅.𐤀𐤕.𐤆𐤁𐤇𐤅.𐤉𐤀𐤊𐤋.𐤅𐤌𐤌𐤇𐤓𐤕.𐤅𐤄𐤍𐤅𐤕𐤓.𐤌𐤌𐤍𐤅.𐤉𐤀
𐤊𐤋|
17 𐤅𐤄𐤍𐤅𐤕𐤓.𐤌𐤁𐤔𐤓.𐤄𐤆𐤁𐤇.𐤁𐤉𐤅𐤌.𐤄𐤔𐤋𐤉𐤔𐤉.𐤁𐤀
𐤔.𐤉𐤔𐤓𐤐|
18 𐤅𐤀𐤌.𐤄𐤀𐤊𐤋.𐤉𐤀𐤊𐤋.𐤌𐤁𐤔𐤓.𐤆𐤁𐤇.𐤔𐤋𐤌𐤉𐤅.𐤁𐤉𐤅
𐤌.𐤄𐤔𐤋𐤉𐤔𐤉.𐤋𐤀.𐤉𐤓𐤑𐤄.𐤄𐤌𐤒𐤓𐤉𐤁.𐤀𐤕𐤅.𐤋𐤀.𐤉𐤇𐤔𐤁.
𐤋𐤅.𐤐𐤂𐤅𐤋.𐤉𐤄𐤉𐤄.𐤅𐤄𐤍𐤐𐤔.𐤄𐤀𐤊𐤋𐤕.𐤌𐤌𐤍𐤅.𐤏𐤅𐤍𐤄.𐤕𐤔𐤀|
19 𐤅𐤄𐤁𐤔𐤓.𐤀𐤔𐤓.𐤉𐤂𐤏.𐤁𐤊𐤋.𐤈𐤌𐤀.𐤋𐤀.𐤉𐤀𐤊𐤋.𐤁𐤀
𐤔.𐤉𐤔𐤓𐤐.𐤅𐤄𐤁𐤔𐤓.𐤊𐤋.𐤈𐤄𐤅𐤓.𐤉𐤀𐤊𐤋.𐤁𐤔𐤓|
20 𐤅𐤄𐤍𐤐𐤔.𐤀𐤔𐤓.𐤕𐤀𐤊𐤋.𐤁𐤔𐤓.𐤌𐤆𐤁𐤇.𐤄𐤔𐤋𐤌𐤉𐤌.
𐤀𐤔𐤓.𐤋𐤉𐤄𐤅𐤄.𐤅𐤈𐤌𐤀𐤕𐤅.𐤏𐤋𐤉𐤅.𐤅𐤍𐤊𐤓𐤕𐤄.𐤄𐤍𐤐𐤔.𐤄𐤄𐤅
𐤀.𐤌𐤏𐤌𐤉𐤄|
21 𐤅𐤍𐤐𐤔.𐤊𐤉.𐤕𐤂𐤏.𐤁𐤊𐤋.𐤈𐤌𐤀.𐤁𐤈𐤌𐤀𐤕.𐤀𐤃𐤌.𐤀𐤅
.𐤁𐤁𐤄𐤌𐤄.𐤈𐤌𐤀𐤄.𐤀𐤅.𐤁𐤊𐤋.𐤔𐤒𐤑.𐤈𐤌𐤀.𐤅𐤀𐤊𐤋.𐤌𐤁𐤔𐤓
.𐤆𐤁𐤇.𐤄𐤔𐤋𐤌𐤉𐤌.𐤀𐤔𐤓.𐤋𐤉𐤄𐤅𐤄.𐤅𐤍𐤊𐤓𐤕𐤄.𐤄𐤍𐤐𐤔.𐤄𐤄
𐤅𐤀.𐤌𐤏𐤌𐤉𐤄|

𐤊𐤁 𐤅𐤉𐤃𐤁𐤓.𐤉𐤄𐤅𐤄.𐤀𐤋.𐤌𐤔𐤄.𐤋𐤀𐤌𐤓|
𐤊𐤂 𐤃𐤁𐤓.𐤀𐤋.𐤁𐤍𐤉.𐤉𐤔𐤓𐤀𐤋.𐤋𐤀𐤌𐤓.𐤊𐤋.𐤇𐤋𐤁.𐤔𐤅𐤓.𐤅
𐤊𐤔𐤁.𐤅𐤏𐤆.𐤋𐤀.𐤕𐤀𐤊𐤋𐤅|
𐤊𐤃 𐤅𐤇𐤋𐤁.𐤍𐤁𐤋𐤄.𐤅𐤇𐤋𐤁.𐤈𐤓𐤐𐤄.𐤉𐤏𐤔𐤄.𐤋𐤊𐤋.𐤌𐤋𐤀
𐤊𐤄.𐤅𐤀𐤊𐤋.𐤋𐤀.𐤕𐤀𐤊𐤋𐤄𐤅|
𐤊𐤄 𐤊𐤉.𐤊𐤋.𐤀𐤊𐤋.𐤇𐤋𐤁.𐤌𐤍.𐤄𐤁𐤄𐤌𐤄.𐤀𐤔𐤓.𐤉𐤒𐤓𐤉𐤁.
𐤌𐤌𐤍𐤄.𐤀𐤔𐤄.𐤋𐤉𐤄𐤅𐤄.𐤅𐤍𐤊𐤓𐤕𐤄.𐤄𐤍𐤐𐤔.𐤄𐤀𐤊𐤋𐤕.𐤌𐤏𐤌
𐤉𐤄|
𐤊𐤅 𐤅𐤊𐤋.𐤃𐤌.𐤋𐤀.𐤕𐤀𐤊𐤋𐤅.𐤁𐤊𐤋.𐤌𐤅𐤔𐤁𐤕𐤉𐤊𐤌.𐤋𐤏𐤅𐤐.𐤅
𐤋𐤁𐤄𐤌𐤄|
𐤊𐤆 𐤊𐤋.𐤍𐤐𐤔.𐤀𐤔𐤓.𐤕𐤀𐤊𐤋.𐤊𐤋.𐤃𐤌.𐤅𐤍𐤊𐤓𐤕𐤄.𐤄𐤍𐤐𐤔.
𐤄𐤄𐤅𐤀.𐤌𐤏𐤌𐤉𐤄|
𐤊𐤇 𐤅𐤉𐤃𐤁𐤓.𐤉𐤄𐤅𐤄.𐤀𐤋.𐤌𐤔𐤄.𐤋𐤀𐤌𐤓|
𐤊𐤈 𐤃𐤁𐤓.𐤀𐤋.𐤁𐤍𐤉.𐤉𐤔𐤓𐤀𐤋.𐤋𐤀𐤌𐤓.𐤄𐤌𐤒𐤓𐤉𐤁.𐤀𐤕.
𐤆𐤁𐤇.𐤔𐤋𐤌𐤉𐤅.𐤋𐤉𐤄𐤅𐤄.𐤉𐤁𐤉𐤀.𐤀𐤕.𐤒𐤓𐤁𐤍𐤅.𐤋𐤉𐤄𐤅𐤄.𐤌
𐤆𐤁𐤇.𐤔𐤋𐤌𐤉𐤅|
𐤋 𐤉𐤃𐤉𐤅.𐤕𐤁𐤉𐤀𐤉𐤍𐤄.𐤀𐤕.𐤀𐤔𐤉.𐤉𐤄𐤅𐤄.𐤀𐤕.𐤄𐤇𐤋
𐤁.𐤏𐤋.𐤄𐤇𐤆𐤄.𐤉𐤁𐤉𐤀𐤍𐤅.𐤀𐤕.𐤄𐤇𐤆𐤄.𐤋𐤄𐤍𐤉𐤐.𐤀𐤕𐤅.
𐤕𐤍𐤅𐤐𐤄.𐤋𐤐𐤍𐤉.𐤉𐤄𐤅𐤄|
𐤋𐤀 𐤅𐤄𐤒𐤈𐤉𐤓.𐤄𐤊𐤄𐤍.𐤀𐤕.𐤄𐤇𐤋𐤁.𐤄𐤌𐤆𐤁𐤇𐤄.𐤅𐤄𐤉
𐤄.𐤄𐤇𐤆𐤄.𐤋𐤀𐤄𐤓𐤍.𐤅𐤋𐤁𐤍𐤉𐤅|
𐤋𐤁 𐤅𐤀𐤕.𐤔𐤅𐤒.𐤄𐤉𐤌𐤉𐤍.𐤕𐤕𐤍𐤅.𐤕𐤓𐤅𐤌𐤄.𐤋𐤊𐤄𐤍.𐤌𐤆𐤁
𐤇𐤉.𐤔𐤋𐤌𐤉𐤊𐤌|
𐤋𐤂 𐤄𐤌𐤒𐤓𐤉𐤁.𐤀𐤕.𐤃𐤌.𐤄𐤔𐤋𐤌𐤉𐤌.𐤅𐤀𐤕.𐤄𐤇𐤋𐤁.𐤌
𐤁𐤍𐤉.𐤀𐤄𐤓𐤍.𐤋𐤅.𐤕𐤄𐤉𐤄.𐤔𐤅𐤒.𐤄𐤉𐤌𐤉𐤍.𐤋𐤌𐤍𐤄|
𐤋𐤃 𐤊𐤉.𐤀𐤕.𐤇𐤆𐤄.𐤄𐤕𐤍𐤅𐤐𐤄.𐤅𐤀𐤕.𐤔𐤅𐤒.𐤄𐤕𐤓𐤅𐤌𐤄.
𐤋𐤒𐤇𐤕𐤉.𐤌𐤀𐤕.𐤁𐤍𐤉.𐤉𐤔𐤓𐤀𐤋.𐤌𐤆𐤁𐤇𐤉.𐤔𐤋𐤌𐤉𐤊𐤌.𐤅
𐤀𐤕𐤍.𐤀𐤕𐤌.𐤋𐤀𐤄𐤓𐤍.𐤄𐤊𐤄𐤍.𐤅𐤋𐤁𐤍𐤉𐤅.𐤋𐤇𐤒.𐤏𐤅𐤋𐤌.𐤌𐤀
𐤕.𐤁𐤍𐤉.𐤉𐤔𐤓𐤀𐤋|
𐤋𐤄 𐤆𐤀𐤕.𐤌𐤔𐤇𐤕.𐤀𐤄𐤓𐤍.𐤅𐤌𐤔𐤇𐤕.𐤁𐤍𐤉𐤅.𐤌𐤀𐤔𐤉.𐤉
𐤄𐤅𐤄.𐤁𐤉𐤅𐤌.𐤄𐤒𐤓𐤉𐤁.𐤀𐤕𐤌.𐤋𐤊𐤄𐤍.𐤋𐤉𐤄𐤅𐤄|

לו אשר.צוה.יהוה.לתת.להם.ביום.משחו.את
ם.מאת.בני.ישראל.חקת.עולם.לדרתם|
לז זאת.התורה.לעלה.למנחה.ולחטאת.ולא
שם.ולמלואים.ולזבח.השלמים|
לח אשר.צוה.יהוה.את.משה.בהר.סיני.ביום
.צותו.את.בני.ישראל.להקריב.את.קרבניהם.
ליהוה.במדבר.סיני||

ללוים.חלק ח

א וידבר.יהוה.אל.משה.לאמר|
ב קח.את.אהרן.ואת.בניו.אתו.ואת.הבגדי
ם.ואת.שמן.המשחה.ואת.פר.החטאת.ואת.שני
.האילים.ואת.סל.המצות|
ג ואת.כל.העדה.הקהל.אל.פתח.אהל.מועד|
ד ויעש.משה.כאשר.צוה.יהוה.אתו.ותקהל.
העדה.אל.פתח.אהל.מועד|
ה ויאמר.משה.אל.העדה.זה.הדבר.אשר.צו
ה.יהוה.לעשות|
ו ויקרב.משה.את.אהרן.ואת.בניו.וירחץ.את
ם.במים|
ז ויתן.עליו.את.הכתנת.ויחגר.אתו.באבנ
ט.וילבש.אתו.את.המעיל.ויתן.עליו.את.האפ
ד.ויחגר.אתו.בחשב.האפד.ויאפד.לו.בו|
ח וישם.עליו.את.החשן.ויתן.אל.החשן.את.
האורים.ואת.התמים|
ט וישם.את.המצנפת.על.ראשו.וישם.על.המ
צנפת.אל.מול.פניו.את.ציץ.הזהב.נזר.הקד
ש.כאשר.צוה.יהוה.את.משה|
י ויקח.משה.את.שמן.המשחה.וימשח.את.
המשכן.ואת.כל.אשר.בו.ויקדש.אתם|

𐤉𐤀 𐤅𐤉𐤆.𐤌𐤌𐤍𐤅.𐤏𐤋.𐤄𐤌𐤆𐤁𐤇.𐤔𐤁𐤏.𐤐𐤏𐤌𐤉𐤌.𐤅𐤉𐤌𐤔𐤇.𐤀𐤕.𐤄𐤌𐤆𐤁𐤇.𐤅𐤀𐤕.𐤊𐤋.𐤊𐤋𐤉𐤅.𐤅𐤀𐤕.𐤄𐤊𐤉𐤓.𐤅𐤀𐤕.𐤊𐤍𐤅.𐤋𐤒𐤃𐤔𐤌|

𐤉𐤁 𐤅𐤉𐤑𐤒.𐤌𐤔𐤌𐤍.𐤄𐤌𐤔𐤇𐤄.𐤏𐤋.𐤓𐤀𐤔.𐤀𐤄𐤓𐤍.𐤅𐤉𐤌𐤔𐤇.𐤀𐤕𐤅.𐤋𐤒𐤃𐤔𐤅|

𐤉𐤂 𐤅𐤉𐤒𐤓𐤁.𐤌𐤔𐤄.𐤀𐤕.𐤁𐤍𐤉.𐤀𐤄𐤓𐤍.𐤅𐤉𐤋𐤁𐤔𐤌.𐤊𐤕𐤍𐤕.𐤅𐤉𐤇𐤂𐤓.𐤀𐤕𐤌.𐤀𐤁𐤍𐤈.𐤅𐤉𐤇𐤁𐤔.𐤋𐤄𐤌.𐤌𐤂𐤁𐤏𐤅𐤕.𐤊𐤀𐤔𐤓.𐤑𐤅𐤄.𐤉𐤄𐤅𐤄.𐤀𐤕.𐤌𐤔𐤄|

𐤉𐤃 𐤅𐤉𐤂𐤔.𐤀𐤕.𐤐𐤓.𐤄𐤇𐤈𐤀𐤕.𐤅𐤉𐤎𐤌𐤊𐤅.𐤀𐤄𐤓𐤍.𐤅𐤁𐤍𐤉𐤅.𐤀𐤕.𐤉𐤃𐤉𐤄𐤌.𐤏𐤋.𐤓𐤀𐤔.𐤐𐤓.𐤄𐤇𐤈𐤀𐤕|

𐤈𐤅 𐤅𐤉𐤔𐤇𐤈.𐤅𐤉𐤒𐤇.𐤌𐤔𐤄.𐤀𐤕.𐤄𐤃𐤌.𐤅𐤉𐤕𐤍.𐤏𐤋.𐤒𐤓𐤍𐤅𐤕.𐤄𐤌𐤆𐤁𐤇.𐤎𐤁𐤉𐤁.𐤁𐤀𐤑𐤁𐤏𐤅.𐤅𐤉𐤇𐤈𐤀.𐤀𐤕.𐤄𐤌𐤆𐤁𐤇.𐤅𐤀𐤕.𐤄𐤃𐤌.𐤉𐤑𐤒.𐤀𐤋.𐤉𐤎𐤅𐤃.𐤄𐤌𐤆𐤁𐤇.𐤅𐤉𐤒𐤃𐤔𐤄𐤅.𐤋𐤊𐤐𐤓.𐤏𐤋𐤉𐤅|

𐤈𐤆 𐤅𐤉𐤒𐤇.𐤀𐤕.𐤊𐤋.𐤄𐤇𐤋𐤁.𐤀𐤔𐤓.𐤏𐤋.𐤄𐤒𐤓𐤁.𐤅𐤀𐤕.𐤉𐤕𐤓𐤕.𐤄𐤊𐤁𐤃.𐤅𐤀𐤕.𐤔𐤕𐤉.𐤄𐤊𐤋𐤉𐤕.𐤅𐤀𐤕.𐤇𐤋𐤁𐤄𐤍.𐤅𐤉𐤒𐤈𐤓.𐤌𐤔𐤄.𐤄𐤌𐤆𐤁𐤇𐤄|

𐤉𐤆 𐤅𐤀𐤕.𐤄𐤐𐤓.𐤅𐤀𐤕.𐤏𐤓𐤅.𐤅𐤀𐤕.𐤁𐤔𐤓𐤅.𐤅𐤀𐤕.𐤐𐤓𐤔𐤅.𐤔𐤓𐤐.𐤁𐤀𐤔.𐤌𐤇𐤅𐤑.𐤋𐤌𐤇𐤍𐤄.𐤊𐤀𐤔𐤓.𐤑𐤅𐤄.𐤉𐤄𐤅𐤄.𐤀𐤕.𐤌𐤔𐤄|

𐤉𐤇 𐤅𐤉𐤒𐤓𐤁.𐤀𐤕.𐤀𐤉𐤋.𐤄𐤏𐤋𐤄.𐤅𐤉𐤎𐤌𐤊𐤅.𐤀𐤄𐤓𐤍.𐤅𐤁𐤍𐤉𐤅.𐤀𐤕.𐤉𐤃𐤉𐤄𐤌.𐤏𐤋.𐤓𐤀𐤔.𐤄𐤀𐤉𐤋|

𐤉𐤈 𐤅𐤉𐤔𐤇𐤈.𐤅𐤉𐤆𐤓𐤒.𐤌𐤔𐤄.𐤀𐤕.𐤄𐤃𐤌.𐤏𐤋.𐤄𐤌𐤆𐤁𐤇.𐤎𐤁𐤉𐤁|

𐤊 𐤅𐤀𐤕.𐤄𐤀𐤉𐤋.𐤍𐤕𐤇.𐤋𐤍𐤕𐤇𐤉𐤅.𐤅𐤉𐤒𐤈𐤓.𐤌𐤔𐤄.𐤀𐤕.𐤄𐤓𐤀𐤔.𐤅𐤀𐤕.𐤄𐤍𐤕𐤇𐤉𐤌.𐤅𐤀𐤕.𐤄𐤐𐤃𐤓|

𐤊𐤀 𐤅𐤀𐤕.𐤄𐤒𐤓𐤁.𐤅𐤀𐤕.𐤄𐤊𐤓𐤏𐤉𐤌.𐤓𐤇𐤑.𐤁𐤌𐤉𐤌.𐤅𐤉𐤒𐤈𐤓.𐤌𐤔𐤄.𐤀𐤕.𐤊𐤋.𐤄𐤀𐤉𐤋.𐤄𐤌𐤆𐤁𐤇𐤄.𐤏𐤋𐤄.𐤄𐤅𐤀.𐤋𐤓𐤉𐤇.𐤍𐤉𐤇𐤇.𐤀𐤔𐤄.𐤄𐤅𐤀.𐤋𐤉𐤄𐤅𐤄.𐤊𐤀𐤔𐤓.𐤑𐤅𐤄.𐤉𐤄𐤅𐤄.𐤀𐤕.𐤌𐤔𐤄|

𐤊𐤁 𐤅𐤉𐤒𐤓𐤁.𐤀𐤕.𐤄𐤀𐤉𐤋.𐤄𐤔𐤍𐤉.𐤀𐤉𐤋.𐤄𐤌𐤋𐤀𐤉𐤌.𐤅𐤉
𐤎𐤌𐤊𐤅.𐤀𐤄𐤓𐤍.𐤅𐤁𐤍𐤉𐤅.𐤀𐤕.𐤉𐤃𐤉𐤄𐤌.𐤏𐤋.𐤓𐤀𐤔.𐤄𐤀𐤉𐤋|

𐤊𐤂 𐤅𐤉𐤔𐤇𐤈.𐤅𐤉𐤒𐤇.𐤌𐤔𐤄.𐤌𐤃𐤌𐤅.𐤅𐤉𐤕𐤍.𐤏𐤋.𐤕𐤍𐤅𐤊.
𐤀𐤆𐤍.𐤀𐤄𐤓𐤍.𐤄𐤉𐤌𐤍𐤉𐤕.𐤅𐤏𐤋.𐤁𐤄𐤍.𐤉𐤃𐤅.𐤄𐤉𐤌𐤍𐤉𐤕.𐤅𐤏
𐤋.𐤁𐤄𐤍.𐤓𐤂𐤋𐤅.𐤄𐤉𐤌𐤍𐤉𐤕|

𐤊𐤃 𐤅𐤉𐤒𐤓𐤁.𐤀𐤕.𐤁𐤍𐤉.𐤀𐤄𐤓𐤍.𐤅𐤉𐤕𐤍.𐤌𐤔𐤄.𐤌𐤍.𐤄𐤃𐤌.
𐤏𐤋.𐤕𐤍𐤅𐤊.𐤀𐤆𐤍𐤌.𐤄𐤉𐤌𐤍𐤉𐤕.𐤅𐤏𐤋.𐤁𐤄𐤍.𐤉𐤃𐤌.𐤄𐤉𐤌𐤍𐤉
𐤕.𐤅𐤏𐤋.𐤁𐤄𐤍.𐤓𐤂𐤋𐤌.𐤄𐤉𐤌𐤍𐤉𐤕.𐤅𐤉𐤆𐤓𐤒.𐤌𐤔𐤄.𐤀𐤕.𐤄
𐤃𐤌.𐤏𐤋.𐤄𐤌𐤆𐤁𐤇.𐤎𐤁𐤉𐤁|

𐤊𐤄 𐤅𐤉𐤒𐤇.𐤀𐤕.𐤄𐤇𐤋𐤁.𐤅𐤀𐤕.𐤄𐤀𐤋𐤉𐤄.𐤅𐤀𐤕.𐤊𐤋.𐤄𐤇
𐤋𐤁.𐤀𐤔𐤓.𐤏𐤋.𐤄𐤒𐤓𐤁.𐤅𐤀𐤕.𐤉𐤕𐤓𐤕.𐤄𐤊𐤁𐤃.𐤅𐤀𐤕.𐤔𐤕𐤉.
𐤄𐤊𐤋𐤉𐤕.𐤅𐤀𐤕.𐤇𐤋𐤁𐤄𐤍.𐤅𐤀𐤕.𐤔𐤅𐤒.𐤄𐤉𐤌𐤉𐤍|

𐤊𐤅 𐤅𐤌𐤎𐤋.𐤄𐤌𐤑𐤅𐤕.𐤀𐤔𐤓.𐤋𐤐𐤍𐤉.𐤉𐤄𐤅𐤄.𐤋𐤒𐤇.𐤇𐤋𐤕.
𐤌𐤑𐤄.𐤀𐤇𐤕.𐤅𐤇𐤋𐤕.𐤋𐤇𐤌.𐤔𐤌𐤍.𐤀𐤇𐤕.𐤅𐤓𐤒𐤉𐤒.𐤀𐤇
𐤃.𐤅𐤉𐤔𐤌.𐤏𐤋.𐤄𐤇𐤋𐤁𐤉𐤌.𐤅𐤏𐤋.𐤔𐤅𐤒.𐤄𐤉𐤌𐤉𐤍|

𐤊𐤆 𐤅𐤉𐤕𐤍.𐤀𐤕.𐤄𐤊𐤋.𐤏𐤋.𐤊𐤐𐤉.𐤀𐤄𐤓𐤍.𐤅𐤏𐤋.𐤊𐤐𐤉.𐤁𐤍𐤉
𐤅.𐤅𐤉𐤍𐤐.𐤀𐤕𐤌.𐤕𐤍𐤅𐤐𐤄.𐤋𐤐𐤍𐤉.𐤉𐤄𐤅𐤄|

𐤊𐤇 𐤅𐤉𐤒𐤇.𐤌𐤔𐤄.𐤀𐤕𐤌.𐤌𐤏𐤋.𐤊𐤐𐤉𐤄𐤌.𐤅𐤉𐤒𐤈𐤓.𐤄𐤌
𐤆𐤁𐤇𐤄.𐤏𐤋.𐤄𐤏𐤋𐤄.𐤌𐤋𐤀𐤉𐤌.𐤄𐤌.𐤋𐤓𐤉𐤇.𐤍𐤉𐤇𐤇.𐤀𐤔
𐤄.𐤄𐤅𐤀.𐤋𐤉𐤄𐤅𐤄|

𐤊𐤈 𐤅𐤉𐤒𐤇.𐤌𐤔𐤄.𐤀𐤕.𐤄𐤇𐤆𐤄.𐤅𐤉𐤍𐤐𐤄𐤅.𐤕𐤍𐤅𐤐𐤄.𐤋
𐤐𐤍𐤉.𐤉𐤄𐤅𐤄.𐤌𐤀𐤉𐤋.𐤄𐤌𐤋𐤀𐤉𐤌.𐤋𐤌𐤔𐤄.𐤄𐤉𐤄.𐤋𐤌𐤍𐤄.𐤊
𐤀𐤔𐤓.𐤑𐤅𐤄.𐤉𐤄𐤅𐤄.𐤀𐤕.𐤌𐤔𐤄|

𐤋 𐤅𐤉𐤒𐤇.𐤌𐤔𐤄.𐤌𐤔𐤌𐤍.𐤄𐤌𐤔𐤇𐤄.𐤅𐤌𐤍.𐤄𐤃𐤌.𐤀𐤔
𐤓.𐤏𐤋.𐤄𐤌𐤆𐤁𐤇.𐤅𐤉𐤆.𐤏𐤋.𐤀𐤄𐤓𐤍.𐤏𐤋.𐤁𐤂𐤃𐤉𐤅.𐤅𐤏𐤋.𐤁
𐤍𐤉𐤅.𐤅𐤏𐤋.𐤁𐤂𐤃𐤉.𐤁𐤍𐤉𐤅.𐤀𐤕𐤅.𐤅𐤉𐤒𐤃𐤔.𐤀𐤕.𐤀𐤄𐤓𐤍.𐤀
𐤕.𐤁𐤂𐤃𐤉𐤅.𐤅𐤀𐤕.𐤁𐤍𐤉𐤅.𐤅𐤀𐤕.𐤁𐤂𐤃𐤉.𐤁𐤍𐤉𐤅.𐤀𐤕𐤅|

𐤋𐤀 𐤅𐤉𐤀𐤌𐤓.𐤌𐤔𐤄.𐤀𐤋.𐤀𐤄𐤓𐤍.𐤅𐤀𐤋.𐤁𐤍𐤉𐤅.𐤁𐤔𐤋𐤅.𐤀𐤕.
𐤄𐤁𐤔𐤓.𐤐𐤕𐤇.𐤀𐤄𐤋.𐤌𐤅𐤏𐤃.𐤅𐤔𐤌.𐤕𐤀𐤊𐤋𐤅.𐤀𐤕𐤅.𐤅𐤀𐤕.𐤄
𐤋𐤇𐤌.𐤀𐤔𐤓.𐤁𐤎𐤋.𐤄𐤌𐤋𐤀𐤉𐤌.𐤊𐤀𐤔𐤓.𐤑𐤅𐤉𐤕𐤉.𐤋𐤀𐤌𐤓.
𐤀𐤄𐤓𐤍.𐤅𐤁𐤍𐤉𐤅.𐤉𐤀𐤊𐤋𐤄𐤅|

לב והנותר.בבשר.ובלחם.באש.תשרפו|

לג ומפתח.אהל.מועד.לא.תצאו.שבעת.ימי
ם.עד.יום.מלאת.ימי.מלאיכם.כי.שבעת.ימי
ם.ימלא.את.ידכם|

לד כאשר.עשה.ביום.הזה.צוה.יהוה.לעש
ת.לכפר.עליכם|

לה ופתח.אהל.מועד.תשבו.יומם.ולילה.שבע
ת.ימים.ושמרתם.את.משמרת.יהוה.ולא.תמותו
.כי.כן.צויתי|

לו ויעש.אהרן.ובניו.את.כל.הדברים.אשר.
צוה.יהוה.ביד.משה||

ט ללוים.חלק

א ויהי.ביום.השמיני.קרא.משה.לאהרן.ולבנ
יו.ולזקני.ישראל|

ב ויאמר.אל.אהרן.קח.לך.עגל.בן.בקר.לחט
את.ואיל.לעלה.תמימם.והקרב.לפני.יהוה|

ג ואל.בני.ישראל.תדבר.לאמר.קחו.שעיר.ע
זים.לחטאת.ועגל.וכבש.בני.שנה.תמימם.ל
עלה|

ד ושור.ואיל.לשלמים.לזבח.לפני.יהוה.ומנ
חה.בלולה.בשמן.כי.היום.יהוה.נראה.אליכם|

ה ויקחו.את.אשר.צוה.משה.אל.פני.אהל.מוע
ד.ויקרבו.כל.העדה.ויעמדו.לפני.יהוה|

ו ויאמר.משה.זה.הדבר.אשר.צוה.יהוה.תע
שו.וירא.אליכם.כבוד.יהוה|

ז ויאמר.משה.אל.אהרן.קרב.אל.המזבח.וע
שה.את.חטאתך.ואת.עלתך.וכפר.בעדך.ובעד
.העם.ועשה.את.קרבן.העם.וכפר.בעדם.כאשר.
צוה.יהוה|

8 𐤅𐤉𐤒𐤓𐤁.𐤀𐤄𐤓𐤍.𐤀𐤋.𐤄𐤌𐤆𐤁𐤇.𐤅𐤉𐤔𐤇𐤈.𐤀𐤕.𐤏𐤂𐤋
𐤄𐤇𐤈𐤀𐤕.𐤀𐤔𐤓.𐤋𐤅|

9 𐤅𐤉𐤒𐤓𐤁𐤅.𐤁𐤍𐤉.𐤀𐤄𐤓𐤍.𐤀𐤕.𐤄𐤃𐤌.𐤀𐤋𐤉𐤅.𐤅𐤉𐤈𐤁𐤋.𐤀
𐤑𐤁𐤏𐤅.𐤁𐤃𐤌.𐤅𐤉𐤕𐤍.𐤏𐤋.𐤒𐤓𐤍𐤅𐤕.𐤄𐤌𐤆𐤁𐤇.𐤅𐤀𐤕.𐤄𐤃
𐤌.𐤉𐤑𐤒.𐤀𐤋.𐤉𐤎𐤅𐤃.𐤄𐤌𐤆𐤁𐤇|

10 𐤅𐤀𐤕.𐤄𐤇𐤋𐤁.𐤅𐤀𐤕.𐤄𐤊𐤋𐤉𐤕.𐤅𐤀𐤕.𐤄𐤉𐤕𐤓𐤕.𐤌𐤍.𐤄
𐤊𐤁𐤃.𐤌𐤍.𐤄𐤇𐤈𐤀𐤕.𐤄𐤒𐤈𐤉𐤓.𐤄𐤌𐤆𐤁𐤇𐤄.𐤊𐤀𐤔𐤓.𐤑𐤅
𐤄.𐤉𐤄𐤅𐤄.𐤀𐤕.𐤌𐤔𐤄|

11 𐤅𐤀𐤕.𐤄𐤁𐤔𐤓.𐤅𐤀𐤕.𐤄𐤏𐤅𐤓.𐤔𐤓𐤐.𐤁𐤀𐤔.𐤌𐤇𐤅𐤑.𐤋𐤌
𐤇𐤍𐤄|

12 𐤅𐤉𐤔𐤇𐤈.𐤀𐤕.𐤄𐤏𐤋𐤄.𐤅𐤉𐤌𐤑𐤀𐤅.𐤁𐤍𐤉.𐤀𐤄𐤓𐤍.𐤀𐤋
𐤉𐤅.𐤀𐤕.𐤄𐤃𐤌.𐤅𐤉𐤆𐤓𐤒𐤄𐤅.𐤏𐤋.𐤄𐤌𐤆𐤁𐤇.𐤎𐤁𐤉𐤁|

13 𐤅𐤀𐤕.𐤄𐤏𐤋𐤄.𐤄𐤌𐤑𐤉𐤀𐤅.𐤀𐤋𐤉𐤅.𐤋𐤍𐤕𐤇𐤉𐤄.𐤅𐤀𐤕.
𐤄𐤓𐤀𐤔.𐤅𐤉𐤒𐤈𐤓.𐤏𐤋.𐤄𐤌𐤆𐤁𐤇|

14 𐤅𐤉𐤓𐤇𐤑.𐤀𐤕.𐤄𐤒𐤓𐤁.𐤅𐤀𐤕.𐤄𐤊𐤓𐤏𐤉𐤌.𐤅𐤉𐤒𐤈𐤓.
𐤏𐤋.𐤄𐤏𐤋𐤄.𐤄𐤌𐤆𐤁𐤇𐤄|

15 𐤅𐤉𐤒𐤓𐤁.𐤀𐤕.𐤒𐤓𐤁𐤍.𐤄𐤏𐤌.𐤅𐤉𐤒𐤇.𐤀𐤕.𐤔𐤏𐤉𐤓.𐤄
𐤇𐤈𐤀𐤕.𐤀𐤔𐤓.𐤋𐤏𐤌.𐤅𐤉𐤔𐤇𐤈𐤄𐤅.𐤅𐤉𐤇𐤈𐤀𐤄𐤅.𐤊𐤓𐤀𐤔𐤅
𐤍|

16 𐤅𐤉𐤒𐤓𐤁.𐤀𐤕.𐤄𐤏𐤋𐤄.𐤅𐤉𐤏𐤔𐤄.𐤊𐤌𐤔𐤐𐤈|

17 𐤅𐤉𐤒𐤓𐤁.𐤀𐤕.𐤄𐤌𐤍𐤇𐤄.𐤅𐤉𐤌𐤋𐤀.𐤊𐤐𐤅.𐤌𐤌𐤍𐤄.𐤅𐤉𐤒
𐤈𐤓.𐤏𐤋.𐤄𐤌𐤆𐤁𐤇.𐤌𐤋𐤁𐤃.𐤏𐤋𐤕.𐤄𐤁𐤒𐤓|

18 𐤅𐤉𐤔𐤇𐤈.𐤀𐤕.𐤄𐤔𐤅𐤓.𐤅𐤀𐤕.𐤄𐤀𐤉𐤋.𐤆𐤁𐤇.𐤄𐤔𐤋𐤌
𐤉𐤌.𐤀𐤔𐤓.𐤋𐤏𐤌.𐤅𐤉𐤌𐤑𐤀𐤅.𐤁𐤍𐤉.𐤀𐤄𐤓𐤍.𐤀𐤕.𐤄𐤃𐤌.𐤀𐤋
𐤉𐤅.𐤅𐤉𐤆𐤓𐤒𐤄𐤅.𐤏𐤋.𐤄𐤌𐤆𐤁𐤇.𐤎𐤁𐤉𐤁|

19 𐤅𐤀𐤕.𐤄𐤇𐤋𐤁𐤉𐤌.𐤌𐤍.𐤄𐤔𐤅𐤓.𐤅𐤌𐤍.𐤄𐤀𐤉𐤋.𐤄𐤀𐤋𐤉𐤄
.𐤅𐤄𐤌𐤊𐤎𐤄.𐤅𐤄𐤊𐤋𐤉𐤕.𐤅𐤉𐤕𐤓𐤕.𐤄𐤊𐤁𐤃|

20 𐤅𐤉𐤔𐤉𐤌𐤅.𐤀𐤕.𐤄𐤇𐤋𐤁𐤉𐤌.𐤏𐤋.𐤄𐤇𐤆𐤅𐤕.𐤅𐤉𐤒𐤈𐤓.
𐤄𐤇𐤋𐤁𐤉𐤌.𐤄𐤌𐤆𐤁𐤇𐤄|

21 𐤅𐤀𐤕.𐤄𐤇𐤆𐤅𐤕.𐤅𐤀𐤕.𐤔𐤅𐤒.𐤄𐤉𐤌𐤉𐤍.𐤄𐤍𐤉𐤐.𐤀𐤄𐤓𐤍
.𐤕𐤍𐤅𐤐𐤄.𐤋𐤐𐤍𐤉.𐤉𐤄𐤅𐤄.𐤊𐤀𐤔𐤓.𐤑𐤅𐤄.𐤌𐤔𐤄|

22 𐤅𐤉𐤔𐤀.𐤀𐤄𐤓𐤍.𐤀𐤕.𐤉𐤃𐤅.‖𐤉𐤃𐤉𐤅.𐤒𐤓𐤉‖.𐤀𐤋.𐤄𐤏𐤌
.𐤅𐤉𐤁𐤓𐤊𐤌.𐤅𐤉𐤓𐤃.𐤌𐤏𐤔𐤕.𐤄𐤇𐤈𐤀𐤕.𐤅𐤄𐤏𐤋𐤄.𐤅𐤄𐤔𐤋𐤌
𐤉𐤌|

23 𐤅𐤉𐤁𐤀.𐤌𐤔𐤄.𐤅𐤀𐤄𐤓𐤍.𐤀𐤋.𐤀𐤄𐤋.𐤌𐤅𐤏𐤃.𐤅𐤉𐤑𐤀𐤅.𐤅
𐤉𐤁𐤓𐤊𐤅.𐤀𐤕.𐤄𐤏𐤌.𐤅𐤉𐤓𐤀.𐤊𐤁𐤅𐤃.𐤉𐤄𐤅𐤄.𐤀𐤋.𐤊𐤋.𐤄𐤏𐤌|

24 𐤅𐤕𐤑𐤀.𐤀𐤔.𐤌𐤋𐤐𐤍𐤉.𐤉𐤄𐤅𐤄.𐤅𐤕𐤀𐤊𐤋.𐤏𐤋.𐤄𐤌𐤆𐤁
𐤇.𐤀𐤕.𐤄𐤏𐤋𐤄.𐤅𐤀𐤕.𐤄𐤇𐤋𐤁𐤉𐤌.𐤅𐤉𐤓𐤀.𐤊𐤋.𐤄𐤏𐤌.𐤅𐤉𐤓𐤍
𐤅.𐤅𐤉𐤐𐤋𐤅.𐤏𐤋.𐤐𐤍𐤉𐤄𐤌‖

𐤋𐤋𐤅𐤉𐤌.𐤇𐤋𐤒 10

1 𐤅𐤉𐤒𐤇𐤅.𐤁𐤍𐤉.𐤀𐤄𐤓𐤍.𐤍𐤃𐤁.𐤅𐤀𐤁𐤉𐤄𐤅𐤀.𐤀𐤉𐤔.𐤌𐤇𐤕
𐤕𐤅.𐤅𐤉𐤕𐤍𐤅.𐤁𐤄𐤍.𐤀𐤔.𐤅𐤉𐤔𐤉𐤌𐤅.𐤏𐤋𐤉𐤄.𐤒𐤈𐤓𐤕.𐤅𐤉𐤒𐤓𐤁
𐤅.𐤋𐤐𐤍𐤉.𐤉𐤄𐤅𐤄.𐤀𐤔.𐤆𐤓𐤄.𐤀𐤔𐤓.𐤋𐤀.𐤑𐤅𐤄.𐤀𐤕𐤌|

2 𐤅𐤕𐤑𐤀.𐤀𐤔.𐤌𐤋𐤐𐤍𐤉.𐤉𐤄𐤅𐤄.𐤅𐤕𐤀𐤊𐤋.𐤀𐤅𐤕𐤌.𐤅𐤉𐤌𐤕
𐤅.𐤋𐤐𐤍𐤉.𐤉𐤄𐤅𐤄|

3 𐤅𐤉𐤀𐤌𐤓.𐤌𐤔𐤄.𐤀𐤋.𐤀𐤄𐤓𐤍.𐤄𐤅𐤀.𐤀𐤔𐤓.𐤃𐤁𐤓.𐤉𐤄𐤅𐤄.
𐤋𐤀𐤌𐤓.𐤁𐤒𐤓𐤁𐤉.𐤀𐤒𐤃𐤔.𐤅𐤏𐤋.𐤐𐤍𐤉.𐤊𐤋.𐤄𐤏𐤌.𐤀𐤊𐤁𐤃.
𐤅𐤉𐤃𐤌.𐤀𐤄𐤓𐤍|

4 𐤅𐤉𐤒𐤓𐤀.𐤌𐤔𐤄.𐤀𐤋.𐤌𐤉𐤔𐤀𐤋.𐤅𐤀𐤋.𐤀𐤋𐤑𐤐𐤍.𐤁𐤍𐤉.𐤏
𐤆𐤉𐤀𐤋.𐤃𐤃.𐤀𐤄𐤓𐤍.𐤅𐤉𐤀𐤌𐤓.𐤀𐤋𐤄𐤌.𐤒𐤓𐤁𐤅.𐤔𐤀𐤅.𐤀𐤕.
𐤀𐤇𐤉𐤊𐤌.𐤌𐤀𐤕.𐤐𐤍𐤉.𐤄𐤒𐤃𐤔.𐤀𐤋.𐤌𐤇𐤅𐤑.𐤋𐤌𐤇𐤍𐤄|

5 𐤅𐤉𐤒𐤓𐤁𐤅.𐤅𐤉𐤔𐤀𐤌.𐤁𐤊𐤕𐤍𐤕𐤌.𐤀𐤋.𐤌𐤇𐤅𐤑.𐤋𐤌𐤇𐤍𐤄.
𐤊𐤀𐤔𐤓.𐤃𐤁𐤓.𐤌𐤔𐤄|

6 𐤅𐤉𐤀𐤌𐤓.𐤌𐤔𐤄.𐤀𐤋.𐤀𐤄𐤓𐤍.𐤅𐤋𐤀𐤋𐤏𐤆𐤓.𐤅𐤋𐤀𐤉𐤕𐤌𐤓.
𐤁𐤍𐤉𐤅.𐤓𐤀𐤔𐤉𐤊𐤌.𐤀𐤋.𐤕𐤐𐤓𐤏𐤅.𐤅𐤁𐤂𐤃𐤉𐤊𐤌.𐤋𐤀.𐤕𐤐𐤓𐤌𐤅
.𐤅𐤋𐤀.𐤕𐤌𐤕𐤅.𐤅𐤏𐤋.𐤊𐤋.𐤄𐤏𐤃𐤄.𐤉𐤒𐤑𐤐.𐤅𐤀𐤇𐤉𐤊𐤌.𐤊𐤋.
𐤁𐤉𐤕.𐤉𐤔𐤓𐤀𐤋.𐤉𐤁𐤊𐤅.𐤀𐤕.𐤄𐤔𐤓𐤐𐤄.𐤀𐤔𐤓.𐤔𐤓𐤐.𐤉𐤄𐤅𐤄|

7 𐤅𐤌𐤐𐤕𐤇.𐤀𐤄𐤋.𐤌𐤅𐤏𐤃.𐤋𐤀.𐤕𐤑𐤀𐤅.𐤐𐤍.𐤕𐤌𐤕𐤅.𐤊𐤉.
𐤔𐤌𐤍.𐤌𐤔𐤇𐤕.𐤉𐤄𐤅𐤄.𐤏𐤋𐤉𐤊𐤌.𐤅𐤉𐤏𐤔𐤅.𐤊𐤃𐤁𐤓.𐤌𐤔𐤄|

8 𐤅𐤉𐤃𐤁𐤓.𐤉𐤄𐤅𐤄.𐤀𐤋.𐤀𐤄𐤓𐤍.𐤋𐤀𐤌𐤓|

ט 𐤉𐤉𐤍.𐤅𐤔𐤊𐤓.𐤀𐤋.𐤕𐤔𐤕.𐤀𐤕𐤄.𐤅𐤁𐤍𐤉𐤊.𐤀𐤕𐤊.𐤁𐤁𐤀𐤊
𐤌.𐤀𐤋.𐤀𐤄𐤋.𐤌𐤅𐤏𐤃.𐤅𐤋𐤀.𐤕𐤌𐤕𐤅.𐤇𐤒𐤕.𐤏𐤅𐤋𐤌.𐤋𐤃𐤓𐤕
𐤉𐤊𐤌|
י 𐤅𐤋𐤄𐤁𐤃𐤉𐤋.𐤁𐤉𐤍.𐤄𐤒𐤃𐤔.𐤅𐤁𐤉𐤍.𐤄𐤇𐤋.𐤅𐤁𐤉𐤍.𐤄𐤈
𐤌𐤀.𐤅𐤁𐤉𐤍.𐤄𐤈𐤄𐤅𐤓|
יא 𐤅𐤋𐤄𐤅𐤓𐤕.𐤀𐤕.𐤁𐤍𐤉.𐤉𐤔𐤓𐤀𐤋.𐤀𐤕.𐤊𐤋.𐤄𐤇𐤒𐤉𐤌.𐤀
𐤔𐤓.𐤃𐤁𐤓.𐤉𐤄𐤅𐤄.𐤀𐤋𐤉𐤄𐤌.𐤁𐤉𐤃.𐤌𐤔𐤄|
יב 𐤅𐤉𐤃𐤁𐤓.𐤌𐤔𐤄.𐤀𐤋.𐤀𐤄𐤓𐤍.𐤅𐤀𐤋.𐤀𐤋𐤏𐤆𐤓.𐤅𐤀𐤋.𐤀
𐤉𐤕𐤌𐤓.𐤁𐤍𐤉𐤅.𐤄𐤍𐤅𐤕𐤓𐤉𐤌.𐤒𐤇𐤅.𐤀𐤕.𐤄𐤌𐤍𐤇𐤄.𐤄𐤍𐤅𐤕𐤓𐤕
𐤌𐤀𐤔𐤉.𐤉𐤄𐤅𐤄.𐤅𐤀𐤊𐤋𐤅𐤄.𐤌𐤑𐤅𐤕.𐤀𐤑𐤋.𐤄𐤌𐤆𐤁𐤇.𐤊𐤉.
𐤒𐤃𐤔.𐤒𐤃𐤔𐤉𐤌.𐤄𐤅𐤀|
יג 𐤅𐤀𐤊𐤋𐤕𐤌.𐤀𐤕𐤄.𐤁𐤌𐤒𐤅𐤌.𐤒𐤃𐤔.𐤊𐤉.𐤇𐤒𐤊.𐤅𐤇
𐤒.𐤁𐤍𐤉𐤊.𐤄𐤅𐤀.𐤌𐤀𐤔𐤉.𐤉𐤄𐤅𐤄.𐤊𐤉.𐤊𐤍.𐤑𐤅𐤉𐤕𐤉|
יד 𐤅𐤀𐤕.𐤇𐤆𐤄.𐤄𐤕𐤍𐤅𐤐𐤄.𐤅𐤀𐤕.𐤔𐤅𐤒.𐤄𐤕𐤓𐤅𐤌𐤄.𐤕𐤀
𐤊𐤋𐤅.𐤁𐤌𐤒𐤅𐤌.𐤈𐤄𐤅𐤓.𐤀𐤕𐤄.𐤅𐤁𐤍𐤉𐤊.𐤅𐤁𐤍𐤕𐤉𐤊.𐤀𐤕𐤊.𐤊𐤉
.𐤇𐤒𐤊.𐤅𐤇𐤒.𐤁𐤍𐤉𐤊.𐤍𐤕𐤍𐤅.𐤌𐤆𐤁𐤇𐤉.𐤔𐤋𐤌𐤉.𐤁𐤍𐤉.𐤉𐤔𐤓
𐤀𐤋|
טו 𐤔𐤅𐤒.𐤄𐤕𐤓𐤅𐤌𐤄.𐤅𐤇𐤆𐤄.𐤄𐤕𐤍𐤅𐤐𐤄.𐤏𐤋.𐤀𐤔𐤉.𐤄𐤇
𐤋𐤁𐤉𐤌.𐤉𐤁𐤉𐤀𐤅.𐤋𐤄𐤍𐤉𐤐.𐤕𐤍𐤅𐤐𐤄.𐤋𐤐𐤍𐤉.𐤉𐤄𐤅𐤄.𐤅𐤄𐤉𐤄.𐤋
𐤊.𐤅𐤋𐤁𐤍𐤉𐤊.𐤀𐤕𐤊.𐤋𐤇𐤒.𐤏𐤅𐤋𐤌.𐤊𐤀𐤔𐤓.𐤑𐤅𐤄.𐤉𐤄𐤅𐤄|
טז 𐤅𐤀𐤕.𐤔𐤏𐤉𐤓.𐤄𐤇𐤈𐤀𐤕.𐤃𐤓𐤔.𐤃𐤓𐤔.𐤌𐤔𐤄.𐤅𐤄𐤍𐤄
.𐤔𐤓𐤐.𐤅𐤉𐤒𐤑𐤐.𐤏𐤋.𐤀𐤋𐤏𐤆𐤓.𐤅𐤏𐤋.𐤀𐤉𐤕𐤌𐤓.𐤁𐤍𐤉.𐤀𐤄𐤓
𐤍.𐤄𐤍𐤅𐤕𐤓𐤌.𐤋𐤀𐤌𐤓|
יז 𐤌𐤃𐤅𐤏.𐤋𐤀.𐤀𐤊𐤋𐤕𐤌.𐤀𐤕.𐤄𐤇𐤈𐤀𐤕.𐤁𐤌𐤒𐤅𐤌.𐤄
𐤒𐤃𐤔.𐤊𐤉.𐤒𐤃𐤔.𐤒𐤃𐤔𐤉𐤌.𐤄𐤅𐤀.𐤅𐤀𐤕𐤄.𐤍𐤕𐤍.𐤋𐤊𐤌.𐤋
𐤔𐤀𐤕.𐤀𐤕.𐤏𐤅𐤍.𐤄𐤏𐤃𐤄.𐤋𐤊𐤐𐤓.𐤏𐤋𐤉𐤄𐤌.𐤋𐤐𐤍𐤉.𐤉𐤄𐤅𐤄|
יח 𐤄𐤍.𐤋𐤀.𐤄𐤅𐤁𐤀.𐤀𐤕.𐤃𐤌𐤄.𐤀𐤋.𐤄𐤒𐤃𐤔.𐤐𐤍𐤉𐤌𐤄.
𐤀𐤊𐤅𐤋.𐤕𐤀𐤊𐤋𐤅.𐤀𐤕𐤄.𐤁𐤒𐤃𐤔.𐤊𐤀𐤔𐤓.𐤑𐤅𐤉𐤕𐤉|
יט 𐤅𐤉𐤃𐤁𐤓.𐤀𐤄𐤓𐤍.𐤀𐤋.𐤌𐤔𐤄.𐤄𐤍.𐤄𐤉𐤅𐤌.𐤄𐤒𐤓𐤉𐤁𐤅.
𐤀𐤕.𐤇𐤈𐤀𐤕𐤌.𐤅𐤀𐤕.𐤏𐤋𐤕𐤌.𐤋𐤐𐤍𐤉.𐤉𐤄𐤅𐤄.𐤅𐤕𐤒𐤓𐤀𐤍𐤄.

אתי.כאלה.ואכלתי.חטאת.היום.הייטב.בעיני.יהוה|

..כ..וישמע.משה.וייטב.בעיניו||

..יא.. ללוים.חלק

..א..וידבר.יהוה.אל.משה.ואל.אהרן.לאמר.אלהם|

..ב..דברו.אל.בני.ישראל.לאמר.זאת.החיה.אשר.תאכלו.מכל.הבהמה.אשר.על.הארץ|

..ג..כל.מפרסת.פרסה.ושסעת.שסע.פרסת.מעלת.גרה.בבהמה.אתה.תאכלו|

..ד..אך.את.זה.לא.תאכלו.ממעלי.הגרה.וממפריסי.הפרסה.את.הגמל.כי.מעלה.גרה.הוא.ופרסה.איננו.מפריס.טמא.הוא.לכם|

..ה..ואת.השפן.כי.מעלה.גרה.הוא.ופרסה.לא.יפריס.טמא.הוא.לכם|

..ו..ואת.הארנבת.כי.מעלת.גרה.הוא.ופרסה.לא.הפריסה.טמאה.הוא.לכם|

..ז..ואת.החזיר.כי.מפריס.פרסה.הוא.ושסע.שסע.פרסה.והוא.גרה.לא.יגר.טמא.הוא.לכם|

..ח..מבשרם.לא.תאכלו.ובנבלתם.לא.תגעו.טמאים.הם.לכם|

..ט..את.זה.תאכלו.מכל.אשר.במים.כל.אשר.לו.סנפיר.וקשקשת.במים.בימים.ובנחלים.אתם.תאכלו|

..י..וכל.אשר.אין.לו.סנפיר.וקשקשת.בימים.ובנחלים.מכל.שרץ.המים.ומכל.נפש.החיה.אשר.במים.שקץ.הם.לכם|

..יא..ושקץ.יהיו.לכם.מבשרם.לא.תאכלו.ואת.נבלתם.תשקצו|

יב 𐤊𐤋.𐤀𐤔𐤓.𐤀𐤉𐤍.𐤋𐤅.𐤎𐤍𐤐𐤉𐤓.𐤅𐤒𐤔𐤒𐤔𐤕.𐤁𐤌𐤉𐤌.𐤔𐤒𐤑.𐤄𐤅𐤀.𐤋𐤊𐤌|

יג 𐤅𐤀𐤕.𐤀𐤋𐤄.𐤕𐤔𐤒𐤑𐤅.𐤌𐤍.𐤄𐤏𐤅𐤐.𐤋𐤀.𐤉𐤀𐤊𐤋𐤅.𐤔𐤒𐤑.𐤄𐤌.𐤀𐤕.𐤄𐤍𐤔𐤓.𐤅𐤀𐤕.𐤄𐤐𐤓𐤎.𐤅𐤀𐤕.𐤄𐤏𐤆𐤍𐤉𐤄|

יד 𐤅𐤀𐤕.𐤄𐤃𐤀𐤄.𐤅𐤀𐤕.𐤄𐤀𐤉𐤄.𐤋𐤌𐤉𐤍𐤄|

טו 𐤀𐤕.𐤊𐤋.𐤏𐤓𐤁.𐤋𐤌𐤉𐤍𐤅|

טז 𐤅𐤀𐤕.𐤁𐤕.𐤄𐤉𐤏𐤍𐤄.𐤅𐤀𐤕.𐤄𐤕𐤇𐤌𐤎.𐤅𐤀𐤕.𐤄𐤔𐤇𐤐.𐤅𐤀𐤕.𐤄𐤍𐤑.𐤋𐤌𐤉𐤍𐤄𐤅|

יז 𐤅𐤀𐤕.𐤄𐤊𐤅𐤎.𐤅𐤀𐤕.𐤄𐤔𐤋𐤊.𐤅𐤀𐤕.𐤄𐤉𐤍𐤔𐤅𐤐|

יח 𐤅𐤀𐤕.𐤄𐤕𐤍𐤔𐤌𐤕.𐤅𐤀𐤕.𐤄𐤒𐤀𐤕.𐤅𐤀𐤕.𐤄𐤓𐤇𐤌|

יט 𐤅𐤀𐤕.𐤄𐤇𐤎𐤉𐤃𐤄.𐤄𐤀𐤍𐤐𐤄.𐤋𐤌𐤉𐤍𐤄.𐤅𐤀𐤕.𐤄𐤃𐤅𐤊𐤉𐤐𐤕.𐤅𐤀𐤕.𐤄𐤏𐤈𐤋𐤐|

כ 𐤊𐤋.𐤔𐤓𐤑.𐤄𐤏𐤅𐤐.𐤄𐤄𐤋𐤊.𐤏𐤋.𐤀𐤓𐤁𐤏.𐤔𐤒𐤑.𐤄𐤅𐤀.𐤋𐤊𐤌|

כא 𐤀𐤊.𐤀𐤕.𐤆𐤄.𐤕𐤀𐤊𐤋𐤅.𐤌𐤊𐤋.𐤔𐤓𐤑.𐤄𐤏𐤅𐤐.𐤄𐤄𐤋𐤊.𐤏𐤋.𐤀𐤓𐤁𐤏.𐤀𐤔𐤓.𐤋𐤀.||𐤋𐤅.𐤒𐤓𐤉||.𐤊𐤓𐤏𐤉𐤌.𐤌𐤌𐤏𐤋.𐤋𐤓𐤂𐤋𐤉𐤅.𐤋𐤍𐤕𐤓.𐤁𐤄𐤍.𐤏𐤋.𐤄𐤀𐤓𐤑|

כב 𐤀𐤕.𐤀𐤋𐤄.𐤌𐤄𐤌.𐤕𐤀𐤊𐤋𐤅.𐤀𐤕.𐤄𐤀𐤓𐤁𐤄.𐤋𐤌𐤉𐤍𐤅.𐤅𐤀𐤕.𐤄𐤎𐤋𐤏𐤌.𐤋𐤌𐤉𐤍𐤄𐤅.𐤅𐤀𐤕.𐤄𐤇𐤓𐤂𐤋.𐤋𐤌𐤉𐤍𐤄𐤅.𐤅𐤀𐤕.𐤄𐤇𐤂𐤁.𐤋𐤌𐤉𐤍𐤄𐤅|

כג 𐤅𐤊𐤋.𐤔𐤓𐤑.𐤄𐤏𐤅𐤐.𐤀𐤔𐤓.𐤋𐤅.𐤀𐤓𐤁𐤏.𐤓𐤂𐤋𐤉𐤌.𐤔𐤒𐤑.𐤄𐤅𐤀.𐤋𐤊𐤌|

כד 𐤅𐤋𐤀𐤋𐤄.𐤕𐤈𐤌𐤀𐤅.𐤊𐤋.𐤄𐤍𐤂𐤏.𐤁𐤍𐤁𐤋𐤕𐤌.𐤉𐤈𐤌𐤀.𐤏𐤃.𐤄𐤏𐤓𐤁|

כה 𐤅𐤊𐤋.𐤄𐤍𐤔𐤀.𐤌𐤍𐤁𐤋𐤕𐤌.𐤉𐤊𐤁𐤎.𐤁𐤂𐤃𐤉𐤅.𐤅𐤈𐤌𐤀.𐤏𐤃.𐤄𐤏𐤓𐤁|

כו 𐤋𐤊𐤋.𐤄𐤁𐤄𐤌𐤄.𐤀𐤔𐤓.𐤄𐤅𐤀.𐤌𐤐𐤓𐤎𐤕.𐤐𐤓𐤎𐤄.𐤅𐤔𐤎𐤏.𐤀𐤉𐤍𐤍𐤄.𐤔𐤎𐤏𐤕.𐤅𐤂𐤓𐤄.𐤀𐤉𐤍𐤍𐤄.𐤌𐤏𐤋𐤄.𐤈𐤌𐤀𐤉𐤌.𐤄𐤌.𐤋𐤊𐤌.𐤊𐤋.𐤄𐤍𐤂𐤏.𐤁𐤄𐤌.𐤉𐤈𐤌𐤀|

𐤊𐤆 𐤅𐤊𐤋.𐤄𐤅𐤋𐤊.𐤏𐤋.𐤊𐤐𐤉𐤅.𐤁𐤊𐤋.𐤄𐤇𐤉𐤄.𐤄𐤄𐤋𐤊𐤕.𐤏
𐤋.𐤀𐤓𐤁𐤏.𐤈𐤌𐤀𐤉𐤌.𐤄𐤌.𐤋𐤊𐤌.𐤊𐤋.𐤄𐤍𐤂𐤏.𐤁𐤍𐤁𐤋𐤕𐤌.𐤉
𐤈𐤌𐤀.𐤏𐤃.𐤄𐤏𐤓𐤁|
𐤊𐤇 𐤅𐤄𐤍𐤔𐤀.𐤀𐤕.𐤍𐤁𐤋𐤕𐤌.𐤉𐤊𐤁𐤎.𐤁𐤂𐤃𐤉𐤅.𐤅𐤈𐤌𐤀.𐤏
𐤃.𐤄𐤏𐤓𐤁.𐤈𐤌𐤀𐤉𐤌.𐤄𐤌𐤄.𐤋𐤊𐤌|
𐤊𐤈 𐤅𐤆𐤄.𐤋𐤊𐤌.𐤄𐤈𐤌𐤀.𐤁𐤔𐤓𐤑.𐤄𐤔𐤓𐤑.𐤏𐤋.𐤄𐤀𐤓𐤑
.𐤄𐤇𐤋𐤃.𐤅𐤄𐤏𐤊𐤁𐤓.𐤅𐤄𐤑𐤁.𐤋𐤌𐤉𐤍𐤄𐤅|
𐤋 𐤅𐤄𐤀𐤍𐤒𐤄.𐤅𐤄𐤊𐤇.𐤅𐤄𐤋𐤈𐤀𐤄.𐤅𐤄𐤇𐤌𐤈.𐤅𐤄𐤕𐤍𐤔
𐤌𐤕|
𐤋𐤀 𐤀𐤋𐤄.𐤄𐤈𐤌𐤀𐤉𐤌.𐤋𐤊𐤌.𐤁𐤊𐤋.𐤄𐤔𐤓𐤑.𐤊𐤋.𐤄𐤍𐤂𐤏
.𐤁𐤄𐤌.𐤁𐤌𐤕𐤌.𐤉𐤈𐤌𐤀.𐤏𐤃.𐤄𐤏𐤓𐤁|
𐤋𐤁 𐤅𐤊𐤋.𐤀𐤔𐤓.𐤉𐤐𐤋.𐤏𐤋𐤉𐤅.𐤌𐤄𐤌.𐤁𐤌𐤕𐤌.𐤉𐤈𐤌𐤀.𐤌𐤊
𐤋.𐤊𐤋𐤉.𐤏𐤑.𐤀𐤅.𐤁𐤂𐤃.𐤀𐤅.𐤏𐤅𐤓.𐤀𐤅.𐤔𐤒.𐤊𐤋.𐤊𐤋𐤉.𐤀𐤔𐤓
.𐤉𐤏𐤔𐤄.𐤌𐤋𐤀𐤊𐤄.𐤁𐤄𐤌.𐤁𐤌𐤉𐤌.𐤉𐤅𐤁𐤀.𐤅𐤈𐤌𐤀.𐤏𐤃.𐤄
𐤏𐤓𐤁.𐤅𐤈𐤄𐤓|
𐤋𐤂 𐤅𐤊𐤋.𐤊𐤋𐤉.𐤇𐤓𐤔.𐤀𐤔𐤓.𐤉𐤐𐤋.𐤌𐤄𐤌.𐤀𐤋.𐤕𐤅𐤊𐤅.𐤊𐤋.
𐤀𐤔𐤓.𐤁𐤕𐤅𐤊𐤅.𐤉𐤈𐤌𐤀.𐤅𐤀𐤕𐤅.𐤕𐤔𐤁𐤓𐤅|
𐤋𐤃 𐤌𐤊𐤋.𐤄𐤀𐤊𐤋.𐤀𐤔𐤓.𐤉𐤀𐤊𐤋.𐤀𐤔𐤓.𐤉𐤁𐤅𐤀.𐤏𐤋𐤉𐤅.𐤌
𐤉𐤌.𐤉𐤈𐤌𐤀.𐤅𐤊𐤋.𐤌𐤔𐤒𐤄.𐤀𐤔𐤓.𐤉𐤔𐤕𐤄.𐤁𐤊𐤋.𐤊𐤋𐤉.𐤉𐤈
𐤌𐤀|
𐤋𐤄 𐤅𐤊𐤋.𐤀𐤔𐤓.𐤉𐤐𐤋.𐤌𐤍𐤁𐤋𐤕𐤌.𐤏𐤋𐤉𐤅.𐤉𐤈𐤌𐤀.𐤕𐤍𐤅𐤓.𐤅
𐤊𐤉𐤓𐤉𐤌.𐤉𐤕𐤑.𐤈𐤌𐤀𐤉𐤌.𐤄𐤌.𐤅𐤈𐤌𐤀𐤉𐤌.𐤉𐤄𐤉𐤅.𐤋𐤊𐤌|
𐤋𐤅 𐤀𐤊.𐤌𐤏𐤉𐤍.𐤅𐤁𐤅𐤓.𐤌𐤒𐤅𐤄.𐤌𐤉𐤌.𐤉𐤄𐤉𐤄.𐤈𐤄𐤅𐤓.𐤅𐤍
𐤂𐤏.𐤁𐤍𐤁𐤋𐤕𐤌.𐤉𐤈𐤌𐤀|
𐤋𐤆 𐤅𐤊𐤉.𐤉𐤐𐤋.𐤌𐤍𐤁𐤋𐤕𐤌.𐤏𐤋.𐤊𐤋.𐤆𐤓𐤏.𐤆𐤓𐤅𐤏.𐤀𐤔𐤓.
𐤉𐤆𐤓𐤏.𐤈𐤄𐤅𐤓.𐤄𐤅𐤀|
𐤋𐤇 𐤅𐤊𐤉.𐤉𐤕𐤍.𐤌𐤉𐤌.𐤏𐤋.𐤆𐤓𐤏.𐤅𐤍𐤐𐤋.𐤌𐤍𐤁𐤋𐤕𐤌.𐤏𐤋𐤉𐤅
.𐤈𐤌𐤀.𐤄𐤅𐤀.𐤋𐤊𐤌|
𐤋𐤈 𐤅𐤊𐤉.𐤉𐤌𐤅𐤕.𐤌𐤍.𐤄𐤁𐤄𐤌𐤄.𐤀𐤔𐤓.𐤄𐤉𐤀.𐤋𐤊𐤌.𐤋𐤀
𐤊𐤋𐤄.𐤄𐤍𐤂𐤏.𐤁𐤍𐤁𐤋𐤕𐤄.𐤉𐤈𐤌𐤀.𐤏𐤃.𐤄𐤏𐤓𐤁|

מ 𐤅𐤄𐤀𐤊𐤋.𐤌𐤍𐤁𐤋𐤕𐤄.𐤉𐤊𐤁𐤎.𐤁𐤂𐤃𐤉𐤅.𐤅𐤈𐤌𐤀.𐤏
𐤃.𐤄𐤏𐤓𐤁.𐤅𐤄𐤍𐤔𐤀.𐤀𐤕.𐤍𐤁𐤋𐤕𐤄.𐤉𐤊𐤁𐤎.𐤁𐤂𐤃𐤉𐤅.𐤅𐤈
𐤌𐤀.𐤏𐤃.𐤄𐤏𐤓𐤁|
מא 𐤅𐤊𐤋.𐤄𐤔𐤓𐤑.𐤄𐤔𐤓𐤑.𐤏𐤋.𐤄𐤀𐤓𐤑.𐤔𐤒𐤑.𐤄𐤅𐤀.𐤋
𐤀.𐤉𐤀𐤊𐤋|
מב 𐤊𐤋.𐤄𐤅𐤋𐤊.𐤏𐤋.𐤂𐤇𐤅𐤍.𐤅𐤊𐤋.𐤄𐤅𐤋𐤊.𐤏𐤋.𐤀𐤓𐤁𐤏.𐤏
𐤃.𐤊𐤋.𐤌𐤓𐤁𐤄.𐤓𐤂𐤋𐤉𐤌.𐤋𐤊𐤋.𐤄𐤔𐤓𐤑.𐤄𐤔𐤓𐤑.𐤏𐤋.𐤄𐤀𐤓
𐤑.𐤋𐤀.𐤕𐤀𐤊𐤋𐤅𐤌.𐤊𐤉.𐤔𐤒𐤑.𐤄𐤌|
מג 𐤀𐤋.𐤕𐤔𐤒𐤑𐤅.𐤀𐤕.𐤍𐤐𐤔𐤕𐤉𐤊𐤌.𐤁𐤊𐤋.𐤄𐤔𐤓𐤑.𐤄
𐤔𐤓𐤑.𐤅𐤋𐤀.𐤕𐤈𐤌𐤀𐤅.𐤁𐤄𐤌.𐤅𐤍𐤈𐤌𐤕𐤌.𐤁𐤌|
מד 𐤊𐤉.𐤀𐤍𐤉.𐤉𐤄𐤅𐤄.𐤀𐤋𐤄𐤉𐤊𐤌.𐤅𐤄𐤕𐤒𐤃𐤔𐤕𐤌.𐤅𐤄
𐤉𐤉𐤕𐤌.𐤒𐤃𐤔𐤉𐤌.𐤊𐤉.𐤒𐤃𐤅𐤔.𐤀𐤍𐤉.𐤅𐤋𐤀.𐤕𐤈𐤌𐤀𐤅.𐤀𐤕
.𐤍𐤐𐤔𐤕𐤉𐤊𐤌.𐤁𐤊𐤋.𐤄𐤔𐤓𐤑.𐤄𐤓𐤌𐤔.𐤏𐤋.𐤄𐤀𐤓𐤑|
מה 𐤊𐤉.𐤀𐤍𐤉.𐤉𐤄𐤅𐤄.𐤄𐤌𐤏𐤋𐤄.𐤀𐤕𐤊𐤌.𐤌𐤀𐤓𐤑.𐤌𐤑𐤓
𐤉𐤌.𐤋𐤄𐤉𐤕.𐤋𐤊𐤌.𐤋𐤀𐤋𐤄𐤉𐤌.𐤅𐤄𐤉𐤉𐤕𐤌.𐤒𐤃𐤔𐤉𐤌.𐤊𐤉.
𐤒𐤃𐤅𐤔.𐤀𐤍𐤉|
מו 𐤆𐤀𐤕.𐤕𐤅𐤓𐤕.𐤄𐤁𐤄𐤌𐤄.𐤅𐤄𐤏𐤅𐤐.𐤅𐤊𐤋.𐤍𐤐𐤔.𐤄𐤇𐤉
𐤄.𐤄𐤓𐤌𐤔𐤕.𐤁𐤌𐤉𐤌.𐤅𐤋𐤊𐤋.𐤍𐤐𐤔.𐤄𐤔𐤓𐤑𐤕.𐤏𐤋.𐤄𐤀𐤓𐤑|
מז 𐤋𐤄𐤁𐤃𐤉𐤋.𐤁𐤉𐤍.𐤄𐤈𐤌𐤀.𐤅𐤁𐤉𐤍.𐤄𐤈𐤄𐤓.𐤅𐤁𐤉𐤍.𐤄
𐤇𐤉𐤄.𐤄𐤍𐤀𐤊𐤋𐤕.𐤅𐤁𐤉𐤍.𐤄𐤇𐤉𐤄.𐤀𐤔𐤓.𐤋𐤀.𐤕𐤀𐤊𐤋||

𐤋𐤋𐤅𐤉𐤌.𐤇𐤋𐤒 יב

א 𐤅𐤉𐤃𐤁𐤓.𐤉𐤄𐤅𐤄.𐤀𐤋.𐤌𐤔𐤄.𐤋𐤀𐤌𐤓|
ב 𐤃𐤁𐤓.𐤀𐤋.𐤁𐤍𐤉.𐤉𐤔𐤓𐤀𐤋.𐤋𐤀𐤌𐤓.𐤀𐤔𐤄.𐤊𐤉.𐤕𐤆𐤓𐤉
𐤏.𐤅𐤉𐤋𐤃𐤄.𐤆𐤊𐤓.𐤅𐤈𐤌𐤀𐤄.𐤔𐤁𐤏𐤕.𐤉𐤌𐤉𐤌.𐤊𐤉𐤌𐤉.𐤍𐤃
𐤕.𐤃𐤅𐤕𐤄.𐤕𐤈𐤌𐤀|
ג 𐤅𐤁𐤉𐤅𐤌.𐤄𐤔𐤌𐤉𐤍𐤉.𐤉𐤌𐤅𐤋.𐤁𐤔𐤓.𐤏𐤓𐤋𐤕𐤅|
ד 𐤅𐤔𐤋𐤔𐤉𐤌.𐤉𐤅𐤌.𐤅𐤔𐤋𐤔𐤕.𐤉𐤌𐤉𐤌.𐤕𐤔𐤁.𐤁𐤃𐤌𐤉.𐤈
𐤄𐤓𐤄.𐤁𐤊𐤋.𐤒𐤃𐤔.𐤋𐤀.𐤕𐤂𐤏.𐤅𐤀𐤋.𐤄𐤌𐤒𐤃𐤔.𐤋𐤀.𐤕𐤁
𐤀.𐤏𐤃.𐤌𐤋𐤀𐤕.𐤉𐤌𐤉.𐤈𐤄𐤓𐤄|

𐤄 𐤅𐤀𐤌.𐤍𐤒𐤁𐤄.𐤕𐤋𐤃.𐤅𐤈𐤌𐤀𐤄.𐤔𐤁𐤏𐤉𐤌.𐤊𐤍𐤃𐤕𐤄.𐤅
𐤔𐤔𐤉𐤌.𐤉𐤅𐤌.𐤅𐤔𐤔𐤕.𐤉𐤌𐤉𐤌.𐤕𐤔𐤁.𐤏𐤋.𐤃𐤌𐤉.𐤈𐤄𐤓𐤄|

𐤅 𐤅𐤁𐤌𐤋𐤀𐤕.𐤉𐤌𐤉.𐤈𐤄𐤓𐤄.𐤋𐤁𐤍.𐤀𐤅.𐤋𐤁𐤕.𐤕𐤁𐤉𐤀.𐤊𐤁
𐤔.𐤁𐤍.𐤔𐤍𐤕𐤅.𐤋𐤏𐤋𐤄.𐤅𐤁𐤍.𐤉𐤅𐤍𐤄.𐤀𐤅.𐤕𐤓.𐤋𐤇𐤈𐤀𐤕.𐤀𐤋.𐤐
𐤕𐤇.𐤀𐤄𐤋.𐤌𐤅𐤏𐤃.𐤀𐤋.𐤄𐤊𐤄𐤍|

𐤆 𐤅𐤄𐤒𐤓𐤉𐤁𐤅.𐤋𐤐𐤍𐤉.𐤉𐤄𐤅𐤄.𐤅𐤊𐤐𐤓.𐤏𐤋𐤉𐤄.𐤅𐤈𐤄𐤓𐤄.𐤌
𐤌𐤒𐤓.𐤃𐤌𐤉𐤄.𐤆𐤀𐤕.𐤕𐤅𐤓𐤕.𐤄𐤉𐤋𐤃𐤕.𐤋𐤆𐤊𐤓.𐤀𐤅.𐤋𐤍𐤒
𐤁𐤄|

𐤇 𐤅𐤀𐤌.𐤋𐤀.𐤕𐤌𐤑𐤀.𐤉𐤃𐤄.𐤃𐤉.𐤔𐤄.𐤅𐤋𐤒𐤇𐤄.𐤔𐤕𐤉.
𐤕𐤓𐤉𐤌.𐤀𐤅.𐤔𐤍𐤉.𐤁𐤍𐤉.𐤉𐤅𐤍𐤄.𐤀𐤇𐤃.𐤋𐤏𐤋𐤄.𐤅𐤀𐤇𐤃.𐤋
𐤇𐤈𐤀𐤕.𐤅𐤊𐤐𐤓.𐤏𐤋𐤉𐤄.𐤄𐤊𐤄𐤍.𐤅𐤈𐤄𐤓𐤄||

𐤋𐤋𐤅𐤉𐤌.𐤇𐤋𐤒 𐤉𐤂

𐤀 𐤅𐤉𐤃𐤁𐤓.𐤉𐤄𐤅𐤄.𐤀𐤋.𐤌𐤔𐤄.𐤅𐤀𐤋.𐤀𐤄𐤓𐤍.𐤋𐤀𐤌𐤓|

𐤁 𐤀𐤃𐤌.𐤊𐤉.𐤉𐤄𐤉𐤄.𐤁𐤏𐤅𐤓.𐤁𐤔𐤓𐤅.𐤔𐤀𐤕.𐤀𐤅.𐤎𐤐𐤇𐤕.
𐤀𐤅.𐤁𐤄𐤓𐤕.𐤅𐤄𐤉𐤄.𐤁𐤏𐤅𐤓.𐤁𐤔𐤓𐤅.𐤋𐤍𐤂𐤏.𐤑𐤓𐤏𐤕.𐤅𐤄𐤅𐤁𐤀
.𐤀𐤋.𐤀𐤄𐤓𐤍.𐤄𐤊𐤄𐤍.𐤀𐤅.𐤀𐤋.𐤀𐤇𐤃.𐤌𐤁𐤍𐤉𐤅.𐤄𐤊𐤄𐤍𐤉𐤌|

𐤂 𐤅𐤓𐤀𐤄.𐤄𐤊𐤄𐤍.𐤀𐤕.𐤄𐤍𐤂𐤏.𐤁𐤏𐤅𐤓.𐤄𐤁𐤔𐤓.𐤅𐤔𐤏𐤓.𐤁
𐤍𐤂𐤏.𐤄𐤐𐤊.𐤋𐤁𐤍.𐤅𐤌𐤓𐤀𐤄.𐤄𐤍𐤂𐤏.𐤏𐤌𐤒.𐤌𐤏𐤅𐤓.𐤁𐤔𐤓𐤅.𐤍
𐤂𐤏.𐤑𐤓𐤏𐤕.𐤄𐤅𐤀.𐤅𐤓𐤀𐤄𐤅.𐤄𐤊𐤄𐤍.𐤅𐤈𐤌𐤀.𐤀𐤕𐤅|

𐤃 𐤅𐤀𐤌.𐤁𐤄𐤓𐤕.𐤋𐤁𐤍𐤄.𐤄𐤅𐤀.𐤁𐤏𐤅𐤓.𐤁𐤔𐤓𐤅.𐤅𐤏𐤌𐤒.𐤀𐤉
𐤍.𐤌𐤓𐤀𐤄.𐤌𐤍.𐤄𐤏𐤅𐤓.𐤅𐤔𐤏𐤓𐤄.𐤋𐤀.𐤄𐤐𐤊.𐤋𐤁𐤍.𐤅𐤄𐤎𐤂𐤉𐤓.
𐤄𐤊𐤄𐤍.𐤀𐤕.𐤄𐤍𐤂𐤏.𐤔𐤁𐤏𐤕.𐤉𐤌𐤉𐤌|

𐤄 𐤅𐤓𐤀𐤄𐤅.𐤄𐤊𐤄𐤍.𐤁𐤉𐤅𐤌.𐤄𐤔𐤁𐤉𐤏𐤉.𐤅𐤄𐤍𐤄.𐤄𐤍𐤂𐤏.𐤏
𐤌𐤃.𐤁𐤏𐤉𐤍𐤉𐤅.𐤋𐤀.𐤐𐤔𐤄.𐤄𐤍𐤂𐤏.𐤁𐤏𐤅𐤓.𐤅𐤄𐤎𐤂𐤉𐤓𐤅.𐤄𐤊
𐤄𐤍.𐤔𐤁𐤏𐤕.𐤉𐤌𐤉𐤌.𐤔𐤍𐤉𐤕|

𐤅 𐤅𐤓𐤀𐤄.𐤄𐤊𐤄𐤍.𐤀𐤕𐤅.𐤁𐤉𐤅𐤌.𐤄𐤔𐤁𐤉𐤏𐤉.𐤔𐤍𐤉𐤕.𐤅𐤄𐤍
𐤄.𐤊𐤄𐤄.𐤄𐤍𐤂𐤏.𐤅𐤋𐤀.𐤐𐤔𐤄.𐤄𐤍𐤂𐤏.𐤁𐤏𐤅𐤓.𐤅𐤈𐤄𐤓𐤅.𐤄𐤊
𐤄𐤍.𐤌𐤎𐤐𐤇𐤕.𐤄𐤉𐤀.𐤅𐤊𐤁𐤎.𐤁𐤂𐤃𐤉𐤅.𐤅𐤈𐤄𐤓|

ז 𐤅𐤀𐤌.𐤐𐤔𐤄.𐤕𐤐𐤔𐤄.𐤄𐤌𐤎𐤐𐤇𐤕.𐤁𐤏𐤅𐤓.𐤀𐤇𐤓𐤉.𐤄𐤓
𐤀𐤕𐤅.𐤀𐤋.𐤄𐤊𐤄𐤍.𐤋𐤈𐤄𐤓𐤕𐤅.𐤅𐤍𐤓𐤀𐤄.𐤔𐤍𐤉𐤕.𐤀𐤋.𐤄𐤊𐤄𐤍|
ח 𐤅𐤓𐤀𐤄.𐤄𐤊𐤄𐤍.𐤅𐤄𐤍𐤄.𐤐𐤔𐤕𐤄.𐤄𐤌𐤎𐤐𐤇𐤕.𐤁𐤏𐤅𐤓.𐤅𐤈
𐤌𐤀𐤅.𐤄𐤊𐤄𐤍.𐤑𐤓𐤏𐤕.𐤄𐤅𐤀|
ט 𐤍𐤂𐤏.𐤑𐤓𐤏𐤕.𐤊𐤉.𐤕𐤄𐤉𐤄.𐤁𐤀𐤃𐤌.𐤅𐤄𐤅𐤁𐤀.𐤀𐤋.𐤄
𐤊𐤄𐤍|
י 𐤅𐤓𐤀𐤄.𐤄𐤊𐤄𐤍.𐤅𐤄𐤍𐤄.𐤔𐤀𐤕.𐤋𐤁𐤍𐤄.𐤁𐤏𐤅𐤓.𐤅𐤄𐤉𐤀.
𐤄𐤐𐤊𐤄.𐤔𐤏𐤓.𐤋𐤁𐤍.𐤅𐤌𐤇𐤉𐤕.𐤁𐤔𐤓.𐤇𐤉.𐤁𐤔𐤀𐤕|
יא 𐤑𐤓𐤏𐤕.𐤍𐤅𐤔𐤍𐤕.𐤄𐤅𐤀.𐤁𐤏𐤅𐤓.𐤁𐤔𐤓𐤅.𐤅𐤈𐤌𐤀𐤅.𐤄𐤊𐤄
𐤍.𐤋𐤀.𐤉𐤎𐤂𐤓𐤍𐤅.𐤊𐤉.𐤈𐤌𐤀.𐤄𐤅𐤀|
יב 𐤅𐤀𐤌.𐤐𐤓𐤅𐤇.𐤕𐤐𐤓𐤇.𐤄𐤑𐤓𐤏𐤕.𐤁𐤏𐤅𐤓.𐤅𐤊𐤎𐤕𐤄.𐤄
𐤑𐤓𐤏𐤕.𐤀𐤕.𐤊𐤋.𐤏𐤅𐤓.𐤄𐤍𐤂𐤏.𐤌𐤓𐤀𐤔𐤅.𐤅𐤏𐤃.𐤓𐤂𐤋𐤉𐤅.𐤋
𐤊𐤋.𐤌𐤓𐤀𐤄.𐤏𐤉𐤍𐤉.𐤄𐤊𐤄𐤍|
יג 𐤅𐤓𐤀𐤄.𐤄𐤊𐤄𐤍.𐤅𐤄𐤍𐤄.𐤊𐤎𐤕𐤄.𐤄𐤑𐤓𐤏𐤕.𐤀𐤕.𐤊𐤋.
𐤁𐤔𐤓𐤅.𐤅𐤈𐤄𐤓.𐤀𐤕.𐤄𐤍𐤂𐤏.𐤊𐤋𐤅.𐤄𐤐𐤊.𐤋𐤁𐤍.𐤈𐤄𐤅𐤓.𐤄𐤅𐤀|
יד 𐤅𐤁𐤉𐤅𐤌.𐤄𐤓𐤀𐤅𐤕.𐤁𐤅.𐤁𐤔𐤓.𐤇𐤉.𐤉𐤈𐤌𐤀|
טו 𐤅𐤓𐤀𐤄.𐤄𐤊𐤄𐤍.𐤀𐤕.𐤄𐤁𐤔𐤓.𐤄𐤇𐤉.𐤅𐤈𐤌𐤀𐤅.𐤄𐤁𐤔𐤓.
𐤄𐤇𐤉.𐤈𐤌𐤀.𐤄𐤅𐤀.𐤑𐤓𐤏𐤕.𐤄𐤅𐤀|
טז 𐤀𐤅.𐤊𐤉.𐤉𐤔𐤅𐤁.𐤄𐤁𐤔𐤓.𐤄𐤇𐤉.𐤅𐤍𐤄𐤐𐤊.𐤋𐤋𐤁𐤍.𐤅𐤁𐤀.
𐤀𐤋.𐤄𐤊𐤄𐤍|
יז 𐤅𐤓𐤀𐤄𐤅.𐤄𐤊𐤄𐤍.𐤅𐤄𐤍𐤄.𐤍𐤄𐤐𐤊.𐤄𐤍𐤂𐤏.𐤋𐤋𐤁𐤍.𐤅𐤈𐤄
𐤓.𐤄𐤊𐤄𐤍.𐤀𐤕.𐤄𐤍𐤂𐤏.𐤈𐤄𐤅𐤓.𐤄𐤅𐤀|
יח 𐤅𐤁𐤔𐤓.𐤊𐤉.𐤉𐤄𐤉𐤄.𐤁𐤅.𐤁𐤏𐤓𐤅.𐤔𐤇𐤉𐤍.𐤅𐤍𐤓𐤐𐤀|
יט 𐤅𐤄𐤉𐤄.𐤁𐤌𐤒𐤅𐤌.𐤄𐤔𐤇𐤉𐤍.𐤔𐤀𐤕.𐤋𐤁𐤍𐤄.𐤀𐤅.𐤁𐤄𐤓
𐤕.𐤋𐤁𐤍𐤄.𐤀𐤃𐤌𐤃𐤌𐤕.𐤅𐤍𐤓𐤀𐤄.𐤀𐤋.𐤄𐤊𐤄𐤍|
כ 𐤅𐤓𐤀𐤄.𐤄𐤊𐤄𐤍.𐤅𐤄𐤍𐤄.𐤌𐤓𐤀𐤄.𐤔𐤐𐤋.𐤌𐤍.𐤄𐤏𐤅𐤓.𐤅𐤔
𐤏𐤓𐤄.𐤄𐤐𐤊.𐤋𐤁𐤍.𐤅𐤈𐤌𐤀𐤅.𐤄𐤊𐤄𐤍.𐤍𐤂𐤏.𐤑𐤓𐤏𐤕.𐤄𐤅𐤀.𐤁
𐤔𐤇𐤉𐤍.𐤐𐤓𐤇𐤄|
כא 𐤅𐤀𐤌.𐤉𐤓𐤀𐤍𐤄.𐤄𐤊𐤄𐤍.𐤅𐤄𐤍𐤄.𐤀𐤉𐤍.𐤁𐤄.𐤔𐤏𐤓.𐤋𐤁𐤍.
𐤅𐤔𐤐𐤋𐤄.𐤀𐤉𐤍𐤍𐤄.𐤌𐤍.𐤄𐤏𐤅𐤓.𐤅𐤄𐤉𐤀.𐤊𐤄𐤄.𐤅𐤄𐤎𐤂𐤉𐤓𐤅.𐤄
𐤊𐤄𐤍.𐤔𐤁𐤏𐤕.𐤉𐤌𐤉𐤌|

𐤊𐤁 𐤅𐤀𐤌.𐤐𐤔𐤄.𐤕𐤐𐤔𐤄.𐤁𐤏𐤅𐤓.𐤅𐤈𐤌𐤀.𐤄𐤊𐤄𐤍.𐤀𐤕𐤅.𐤍
𐤂𐤏.𐤄𐤅𐤀|

𐤊𐤂 𐤅𐤀𐤌.𐤕𐤇𐤕𐤉𐤄.𐤕𐤏𐤌𐤃.𐤄𐤁𐤄𐤓𐤕.𐤋𐤀.𐤐𐤔𐤕𐤄.𐤑
𐤓𐤁𐤕.𐤄𐤔𐤇𐤉𐤍.𐤄𐤅𐤀.𐤅𐤈𐤄𐤓𐤅.𐤄𐤊𐤄𐤍|

𐤊𐤃 𐤀𐤅.𐤁𐤔𐤓.𐤊𐤉.𐤉𐤄𐤉𐤄.𐤁𐤏𐤓𐤅.𐤌𐤊𐤅𐤕.𐤀𐤔.𐤅𐤄𐤉𐤕𐤄.
𐤌𐤇𐤉𐤕.𐤄𐤌𐤊𐤅𐤄.𐤁𐤄𐤓𐤕.𐤋𐤁𐤍𐤄.𐤀𐤃𐤌𐤃𐤌𐤕.𐤀𐤅.𐤋𐤁𐤍𐤄
|

𐤊𐤄 𐤅𐤓𐤀𐤄.𐤀𐤕𐤄.𐤄𐤊𐤄𐤍.𐤅𐤄𐤍𐤄.𐤍𐤄𐤐𐤊.𐤔𐤏𐤓.𐤋𐤁𐤍.𐤁𐤁
𐤄𐤓𐤕.𐤅𐤌𐤓𐤀𐤄.𐤏𐤌𐤒.𐤌𐤍.𐤄𐤏𐤅𐤓.𐤑𐤓𐤏𐤕.𐤄𐤅𐤀.𐤁𐤌𐤊𐤅𐤄.
𐤐𐤓𐤇𐤄.𐤅𐤈𐤌𐤀.𐤀𐤕𐤅.𐤄𐤊𐤄𐤍.𐤍𐤂𐤏.𐤑𐤓𐤏𐤕.𐤄𐤅𐤀|

𐤊𐤅 𐤅𐤀𐤌.𐤉𐤓𐤀𐤍𐤄.𐤄𐤊𐤄𐤍.𐤅𐤄𐤍𐤄.𐤀𐤉𐤍.𐤁𐤁𐤄𐤓𐤕.𐤔𐤏𐤓.
𐤋𐤁𐤍.𐤅𐤔𐤐𐤋𐤄.𐤀𐤉𐤍𐤍𐤄.𐤌𐤍.𐤄𐤏𐤅𐤓.𐤅𐤄𐤅𐤀.𐤊𐤄𐤄.𐤅𐤄𐤎𐤂𐤉
𐤓𐤅.𐤄𐤊𐤄𐤍.𐤔𐤁𐤏𐤕.𐤉𐤌𐤉𐤌|

𐤊𐤆 𐤅𐤄𐤓𐤀𐤄𐤅.𐤄𐤊𐤄𐤍.𐤁𐤉𐤅𐤌.𐤄𐤔𐤁𐤉𐤏𐤉.𐤀𐤌.𐤐𐤔𐤄.𐤕𐤐
𐤔𐤄.𐤁𐤏𐤅𐤓.𐤅𐤈𐤌𐤀.𐤄𐤊𐤄𐤍.𐤀𐤕𐤅.𐤍𐤂𐤏.𐤑𐤓𐤏𐤕.𐤄𐤅𐤀|

𐤊𐤇 𐤅𐤀𐤌.𐤕𐤇𐤕𐤉𐤄.𐤕𐤏𐤌𐤃.𐤄𐤁𐤄𐤓𐤕.𐤋𐤀.𐤐𐤔𐤕𐤄.𐤁
𐤏𐤅𐤓.𐤅𐤄𐤅𐤀.𐤊𐤄𐤄.𐤔𐤀𐤕.𐤄𐤌𐤊𐤅𐤄.𐤄𐤅𐤀.𐤅𐤈𐤄𐤓𐤅.𐤄𐤊𐤄𐤍.
𐤊𐤉.𐤑𐤓𐤁𐤕.𐤄𐤌𐤊𐤅𐤄.𐤄𐤅𐤀|

𐤊𐤈 𐤅𐤀𐤉𐤔.𐤀𐤅.𐤀𐤔𐤄.𐤊𐤉.𐤉𐤄𐤉𐤄.𐤁𐤅.𐤍𐤂𐤏.𐤁𐤓𐤀𐤔.𐤀
𐤅.𐤁𐤆𐤒𐤍|

𐤋 𐤅𐤓𐤀𐤄.𐤄𐤊𐤄𐤍.𐤀𐤕.𐤄𐤍𐤂𐤏.𐤅𐤄𐤍𐤄.𐤌𐤓𐤀𐤄𐤅.𐤏𐤌𐤒
.𐤌𐤍.𐤄𐤏𐤅𐤓.𐤅𐤁𐤅.𐤔𐤏𐤓.𐤑𐤄𐤁.𐤃𐤒.𐤅𐤈𐤌𐤀.𐤀𐤕𐤅.𐤄𐤊𐤄𐤍.𐤍
𐤕𐤒.𐤄𐤅𐤀.𐤑𐤓𐤏𐤕.𐤄𐤓𐤀𐤔.𐤀𐤅.𐤄𐤆𐤒𐤍.𐤄𐤅𐤀|

𐤋𐤀 𐤅𐤊𐤉.𐤉𐤓𐤀𐤄.𐤄𐤊𐤄𐤍.𐤀𐤕.𐤍𐤂𐤏.𐤄𐤍𐤕𐤒.𐤅𐤄𐤍𐤄.𐤀𐤉
𐤍.𐤌𐤓𐤀𐤄𐤅.𐤏𐤌𐤒.𐤌𐤍.𐤄𐤏𐤅𐤓.𐤅𐤔𐤏𐤓.𐤔𐤇𐤓.𐤀𐤉𐤍.𐤁𐤅.𐤅𐤄𐤎
𐤂𐤉𐤓.𐤄𐤊𐤄𐤍.𐤀𐤕.𐤍𐤂𐤏.𐤄𐤍𐤕𐤒.𐤔𐤁𐤏𐤕.𐤉𐤌𐤉𐤌|

𐤋𐤁 𐤅𐤓𐤀𐤄.𐤄𐤊𐤄𐤍.𐤀𐤕.𐤄𐤍𐤂𐤏.𐤁𐤉𐤅𐤌.𐤄𐤔𐤁𐤉𐤏𐤉.𐤅𐤄
𐤍𐤄.𐤋𐤀.𐤐𐤔𐤄.𐤄𐤍𐤕𐤒.𐤅𐤋𐤀.𐤄𐤉𐤄.𐤁𐤅.𐤔𐤏𐤓.𐤑𐤄𐤁.𐤅𐤌𐤓𐤀
𐤄.𐤄𐤍𐤕𐤒.𐤀𐤉𐤍.𐤏𐤌𐤒.𐤌𐤍.𐤄𐤏𐤅𐤓|

𐤋𐤂 𐤅𐤄𐤕𐤂𐤋𐤇.𐤅𐤀𐤕.𐤄𐤍𐤕𐤒.𐤋𐤀.𐤉𐤂𐤋𐤇.𐤅𐤄𐤎𐤂𐤉𐤓.
𐤄𐤊𐤄𐤍.𐤀𐤕.𐤄𐤍𐤕𐤒.𐤔𐤁𐤏𐤕.𐤉𐤌𐤉𐤌.𐤔𐤍𐤉𐤕|

..𐤋𐤃.. 𐤅𐤓𐤀𐤄.𐤄𐤊𐤄𐤍.𐤀𐤕.𐤄𐤍𐤕𐤒.𐤁𐤉𐤅𐤌.𐤄𐤔𐤁𐤉𐤏𐤉.𐤅𐤄
𐤍𐤄.𐤋𐤀.𐤐𐤔𐤄.𐤄𐤍𐤕𐤒.𐤁𐤏𐤅𐤓.𐤅𐤌𐤓𐤀𐤄𐤅.𐤀𐤉𐤍𐤍𐤅.𐤏𐤌𐤒.𐤌𐤍
.𐤄𐤏𐤅𐤓.𐤅𐤈𐤄𐤓.𐤀𐤕𐤅.𐤄𐤊𐤄𐤍.𐤅𐤊𐤁𐤎.𐤁𐤂𐤃𐤉𐤅.𐤅𐤈𐤄𐤓|
..𐤋𐤄.. 𐤅𐤀𐤌.𐤐𐤔𐤄.𐤉𐤐𐤔𐤄.𐤄𐤍𐤕𐤒.𐤁𐤏𐤅𐤓.𐤀𐤇𐤓𐤉.𐤈𐤄𐤓𐤕
𐤅|
..𐤋𐤅.. 𐤅𐤓𐤀𐤄𐤅.𐤄𐤊𐤄𐤍.𐤅𐤄𐤍𐤄.𐤐𐤔𐤄.𐤄𐤍𐤕𐤒.𐤁𐤏𐤅𐤓.𐤋𐤀.𐤉
𐤁𐤒𐤓.𐤄𐤊𐤄𐤍.𐤋𐤔𐤏𐤓.𐤄𐤑𐤄𐤁.𐤈𐤌𐤀.𐤄𐤅𐤀|
..𐤋𐤆.. 𐤅𐤀𐤌.𐤁𐤏𐤉𐤍𐤉𐤅.𐤏𐤌𐤃.𐤄𐤍𐤕𐤒.𐤅𐤔𐤏𐤓.𐤔𐤇𐤓.𐤑𐤌
𐤇.𐤁𐤅.𐤍𐤓𐤐𐤀.𐤄𐤍𐤕𐤒.𐤈𐤄𐤅𐤓.𐤄𐤅𐤀.𐤅𐤈𐤄𐤓𐤅.𐤄𐤊𐤄𐤍|
..𐤋𐤇.. 𐤅𐤀𐤉𐤔.𐤀𐤅.𐤀𐤔𐤄.𐤊𐤉.𐤉𐤄𐤉𐤄.𐤁𐤏𐤅𐤓.𐤁𐤔𐤓𐤌.𐤁𐤄𐤓
𐤕.𐤁𐤄𐤓𐤕.𐤋𐤁𐤍𐤕|
..𐤋𐤈.. 𐤅𐤓𐤀𐤄.𐤄𐤊𐤄𐤍.𐤅𐤄𐤍𐤄.𐤁𐤏𐤅𐤓.𐤁𐤔𐤓𐤌.𐤁𐤄𐤓𐤕.𐤊𐤄𐤅
𐤕.𐤋𐤁𐤍𐤕.𐤁𐤄𐤒.𐤄𐤅𐤀.𐤐𐤓𐤇.𐤁𐤏𐤅𐤓.𐤈𐤄𐤅𐤓.𐤄𐤅𐤀|
..𐤌.. 𐤅𐤀𐤉𐤔.𐤊𐤉.𐤉𐤌𐤓𐤈.𐤓𐤀𐤔𐤅.𐤒𐤓𐤇.𐤄𐤅𐤀.𐤈𐤄𐤅𐤓.𐤄𐤅
𐤀|
..𐤌𐤀.. 𐤅𐤀𐤌.𐤌𐤐𐤀𐤕.𐤐𐤍𐤉𐤅.𐤉𐤌𐤓𐤈.𐤓𐤀𐤔𐤅.𐤂𐤁𐤇.𐤄𐤅𐤀.𐤈
𐤄𐤅𐤓.𐤄𐤅𐤀|
..𐤌𐤁.. 𐤅𐤊𐤉.𐤉𐤄𐤉𐤄.𐤁𐤒𐤓𐤇𐤕.𐤀𐤅.𐤁𐤂𐤁𐤇𐤕.𐤍𐤂𐤏.𐤋𐤁𐤍.
𐤀𐤃𐤌𐤃𐤌.𐤑𐤓𐤏𐤕.𐤐𐤓𐤇𐤕.𐤄𐤅𐤀.𐤁𐤒𐤓𐤇𐤕𐤅.𐤀𐤅.𐤁𐤂𐤁
𐤇𐤕𐤅|
..𐤌𐤂.. 𐤅𐤓𐤀𐤄.𐤀𐤕𐤅.𐤄𐤊𐤄𐤍.𐤅𐤄𐤍𐤄.𐤔𐤀𐤕.𐤄𐤍𐤂𐤏.𐤋𐤁𐤍𐤄.
𐤀𐤃𐤌𐤃𐤌𐤕.𐤁𐤒𐤓𐤇𐤕𐤅.𐤀𐤅.𐤁𐤂𐤁𐤇𐤕𐤅.𐤊𐤌𐤓𐤀𐤄.𐤑𐤓𐤏
𐤕.𐤏𐤅𐤓.𐤁𐤔𐤓|
..𐤌𐤃.. 𐤀𐤉𐤔.𐤑𐤓𐤅𐤏.𐤄𐤅𐤀.𐤈𐤌𐤀.𐤄𐤅𐤀.𐤈𐤌𐤀.𐤉𐤈𐤌𐤀𐤍𐤅.
𐤄𐤊𐤄𐤍.𐤁𐤓𐤀𐤔𐤅.𐤍𐤂𐤏𐤅|
..𐤌𐤄.. 𐤅𐤄𐤑𐤓𐤅𐤏.𐤀𐤔𐤓.𐤁𐤅.𐤄𐤍𐤂𐤏.𐤁𐤂𐤃𐤉𐤅.𐤉𐤄𐤉𐤅.𐤐𐤓𐤌
𐤉𐤌.𐤅𐤓𐤀𐤔𐤅.𐤉𐤄𐤉𐤄.𐤐𐤓𐤅𐤏.𐤅𐤏𐤋.𐤔𐤐𐤌.𐤉𐤏𐤈𐤄.𐤅𐤈𐤌𐤀.𐤈
𐤌𐤀.𐤉𐤒𐤓𐤀|
..𐤌𐤅.. 𐤊𐤋.𐤉𐤌𐤉.𐤀𐤔𐤓.𐤄𐤍𐤂𐤏.𐤁𐤅.𐤉𐤈𐤌𐤀.𐤈𐤌𐤀.𐤄𐤅𐤀.𐤁
𐤃𐤃.𐤉𐤔𐤁.𐤌𐤇𐤅𐤑.𐤋𐤌𐤇𐤍𐤄.𐤌𐤅𐤔𐤁𐤅|

𐤌𐤆 𐤅𐤄𐤁𐤂𐤃.𐤊𐤉.𐤉𐤄𐤉𐤄.𐤁𐤅.𐤍𐤂𐤏.𐤑𐤓𐤏𐤕.𐤁𐤁𐤂𐤃
.𐤑𐤌𐤓.𐤀𐤅.𐤁𐤁𐤂𐤃.𐤐𐤔𐤕𐤉𐤌|
𐤌𐤇 𐤀𐤅.𐤁𐤔𐤕𐤉.𐤀𐤅.𐤁𐤏𐤓𐤁.𐤋𐤐𐤔𐤕𐤉𐤌.𐤅𐤋𐤑𐤌𐤓.𐤀𐤅.𐤁
𐤏𐤅𐤓.𐤀𐤅.𐤁𐤊𐤋.𐤌𐤋𐤀𐤊𐤕.𐤏𐤅𐤓|
𐤌𐤈 𐤅𐤄𐤉𐤄.𐤄𐤍𐤂𐤏.𐤉𐤓𐤒𐤓𐤒.𐤀𐤅.𐤀𐤃𐤌𐤃𐤌.𐤁𐤁𐤂𐤃
.𐤀𐤅.𐤁𐤏𐤅𐤓.𐤀𐤅.𐤁𐤔𐤕𐤉.𐤀𐤅.𐤁𐤏𐤓𐤁.𐤀𐤅.𐤁𐤊𐤋.𐤊𐤋𐤉.𐤏𐤅𐤓.𐤍
𐤂𐤏.𐤑𐤓𐤏𐤕.𐤄𐤅𐤀.𐤅𐤄𐤓𐤀𐤄.𐤀𐤕.𐤄𐤊𐤄𐤍|
𐤍 𐤅𐤓𐤀𐤄.𐤄𐤊𐤄𐤍.𐤀𐤕.𐤄𐤍𐤂𐤏.𐤅𐤄𐤎𐤂𐤉𐤓.𐤀𐤕.𐤄𐤍𐤂
𐤏.𐤔𐤁𐤏𐤕.𐤉𐤌𐤉𐤌|
𐤍𐤀 𐤅𐤓𐤀𐤄.𐤀𐤕.𐤄𐤍𐤂𐤏.𐤁𐤉𐤅𐤌.𐤄𐤔𐤁𐤉𐤏𐤉.𐤊𐤉.𐤐𐤔𐤄.𐤄
𐤍𐤂𐤏.𐤁𐤁𐤂𐤃.𐤀𐤅.𐤁𐤔𐤕𐤉.𐤀𐤅.𐤁𐤏𐤓𐤁.𐤀𐤅.𐤁𐤏𐤅𐤓.𐤋𐤊𐤋.𐤀
𐤔𐤓.𐤉𐤏𐤔𐤄.𐤄𐤏𐤅𐤓.𐤋𐤌𐤋𐤀𐤊𐤄.𐤑𐤓𐤏𐤕.𐤌𐤌𐤀𐤓𐤕.𐤄𐤍𐤂
𐤏.𐤈𐤌𐤀.𐤄𐤅𐤀|
𐤍𐤁 𐤅𐤔𐤓𐤐.𐤀𐤕.𐤄𐤁𐤂𐤃.𐤀𐤅.𐤀𐤕.𐤄𐤔𐤕𐤉.𐤀𐤅.𐤀𐤕.𐤄𐤏
𐤓𐤁.𐤁𐤑𐤌𐤓.𐤀𐤅.𐤁𐤐𐤔𐤕𐤉𐤌.𐤀𐤅.𐤀𐤕.𐤊𐤋.𐤊𐤋𐤉.𐤄𐤏𐤅𐤓.𐤀𐤔
𐤓.𐤉𐤄𐤉𐤄.𐤁𐤅.𐤄𐤍𐤂𐤏.𐤊𐤉.𐤑𐤓𐤏𐤕.𐤌𐤌𐤀𐤓𐤕.𐤄𐤅𐤀.𐤁𐤀𐤔.
𐤕𐤔𐤓𐤐|
𐤍𐤂 𐤅𐤀𐤌.𐤉𐤓𐤀𐤄.𐤄𐤊𐤄𐤍.𐤅𐤄𐤍𐤄.𐤋𐤀.𐤐𐤔𐤄.𐤄𐤍𐤂𐤏.𐤁𐤁
𐤂𐤃.𐤀𐤅.𐤁𐤔𐤕𐤉.𐤀𐤅.𐤁𐤏𐤓𐤁.𐤀𐤅.𐤁𐤊𐤋.𐤊𐤋𐤉.𐤏𐤅𐤓|
𐤍𐤃 𐤅𐤑𐤅𐤄.𐤄𐤊𐤄𐤍.𐤅𐤊𐤁𐤎𐤅.𐤀𐤕.𐤀𐤔𐤓.𐤁𐤅.𐤄𐤍𐤂𐤏.𐤅𐤄𐤎
𐤂𐤉𐤓𐤅.𐤔𐤁𐤏𐤕.𐤉𐤌𐤉𐤌.𐤔𐤍𐤉𐤕|
𐤍𐤄 𐤅𐤓𐤀𐤄.𐤄𐤊𐤄𐤍.𐤀𐤇𐤓𐤉.𐤄𐤊𐤁𐤎.𐤀𐤕.𐤄𐤍𐤂𐤏.𐤅𐤄𐤍𐤄.
𐤋𐤀.𐤄𐤐𐤊.𐤄𐤍𐤂𐤏.𐤀𐤕.𐤏𐤉𐤍𐤅.𐤅𐤄𐤍𐤂𐤏.𐤋𐤀.𐤐𐤔𐤄.𐤈𐤌𐤀.
𐤄𐤅𐤀.𐤁𐤀𐤔.𐤕𐤔𐤓𐤐𐤍𐤅.𐤐𐤇𐤕𐤕.𐤄𐤅𐤀.𐤁𐤒𐤓𐤇𐤕𐤅.𐤀𐤅.𐤁𐤂
𐤁𐤇𐤕𐤅|
𐤍𐤅 𐤅𐤀𐤌.𐤓𐤀𐤄.𐤄𐤊𐤄𐤍.𐤅𐤄𐤍𐤄.𐤊𐤄𐤄.𐤄𐤍𐤂𐤏.𐤀𐤇𐤓𐤉.𐤄
𐤊𐤁𐤎.𐤀𐤕𐤅.𐤅𐤒𐤓𐤏.𐤀𐤕𐤅.𐤌𐤍.𐤄𐤁𐤂𐤃.𐤀𐤅.𐤌𐤍.𐤄𐤏𐤅𐤓.𐤀𐤅.
𐤌𐤍.𐤄𐤔𐤕𐤉.𐤀𐤅.𐤌𐤍.𐤄𐤏𐤓𐤁|
𐤍𐤆 𐤅𐤀𐤌.𐤕𐤓𐤀𐤄.𐤏𐤅𐤃.𐤁𐤁𐤂𐤃.𐤀𐤅.𐤁𐤔𐤕𐤉.𐤀𐤅.𐤁𐤏𐤓
𐤁.𐤀𐤅.𐤁𐤊𐤋.𐤊𐤋𐤉.𐤏𐤅𐤓.𐤐𐤓𐤇𐤕.𐤄𐤅𐤀.𐤁𐤀𐤔.𐤕𐤔𐤓𐤐𐤍𐤅.𐤀𐤕
.𐤀𐤔𐤓.𐤁𐤅.𐤄𐤍𐤂𐤏|

נח 𐤅𐤄𐤁𐤂𐤃.𐤀𐤅.𐤄𐤔𐤕𐤉.𐤀𐤅.𐤄𐤏𐤓𐤁.𐤀𐤅.𐤊𐤋.𐤊𐤋𐤉.𐤄
𐤏𐤅𐤓.𐤀𐤔𐤓.𐤕𐤊𐤁𐤎.𐤅𐤎𐤓.𐤌𐤄𐤌.𐤄𐤍𐤂𐤏.𐤅𐤊𐤁𐤎.𐤔𐤍𐤉𐤕.𐤅
𐤈𐤄𐤓|
נט 𐤆𐤀𐤕.𐤕𐤅𐤓𐤕.𐤍𐤂𐤏.𐤑𐤓𐤏𐤕.𐤁𐤂𐤃.𐤄𐤑𐤌𐤓.𐤀𐤅.
𐤄𐤐𐤔𐤕𐤉𐤌.𐤀𐤅.𐤄𐤔𐤕𐤉.𐤀𐤅.𐤄𐤏𐤓𐤁.𐤀𐤅.𐤊𐤋.𐤊𐤋𐤉.𐤏𐤅𐤓.𐤋
𐤈𐤄𐤓𐤅.𐤀𐤅.𐤋𐤈𐤌𐤀𐤅||

𐤋𐤋𐤅𐤉𐤌.𐤇𐤋𐤒 יד

א 𐤅𐤉𐤃𐤁𐤓.𐤉𐤄𐤅𐤄.𐤀𐤋.𐤌𐤔𐤄.𐤋𐤀𐤌𐤓|
ב 𐤆𐤀𐤕.𐤕𐤄𐤉𐤄.𐤕𐤅𐤓𐤕.𐤄𐤌𐤑𐤓𐤏.𐤁𐤉𐤅𐤌.𐤈𐤄𐤓𐤕𐤅.𐤅𐤄
𐤅𐤁𐤀.𐤀𐤋.𐤄𐤊𐤄𐤍|
ג 𐤅𐤉𐤑𐤀.𐤄𐤊𐤄𐤍.𐤀𐤋.𐤌𐤇𐤅𐤑.𐤋𐤌𐤇𐤍𐤄.𐤅𐤓𐤀𐤄.𐤄𐤊𐤄𐤍
.𐤅𐤄𐤍𐤄.𐤍𐤓𐤐𐤀.𐤍𐤂𐤏.𐤄𐤑𐤓𐤏𐤕.𐤌𐤍.𐤄𐤑𐤓𐤅𐤏|
ד 𐤅𐤑𐤅𐤄.𐤄𐤊𐤄𐤍.𐤅𐤋𐤒𐤇.𐤋𐤌𐤈𐤄𐤓.𐤔𐤕𐤉.𐤑𐤐𐤓𐤉𐤌.𐤇
𐤉𐤅𐤕.𐤈𐤄𐤓𐤅𐤕.𐤅𐤏𐤑.𐤀𐤓𐤆.𐤅𐤔𐤍𐤉.𐤕𐤅𐤋𐤏𐤕.𐤅𐤀𐤆𐤁|
ה 𐤅𐤑𐤅𐤄.𐤄𐤊𐤄𐤍.𐤅𐤔𐤇𐤈.𐤀𐤕.𐤄𐤑𐤐𐤅𐤓.𐤄𐤀𐤇𐤕.𐤀𐤋.𐤊
𐤋𐤉.𐤇𐤓𐤔.𐤏𐤋.𐤌𐤉𐤌.𐤇𐤉𐤉𐤌|
ו 𐤀𐤕.𐤄𐤑𐤐𐤓.𐤄𐤇𐤉𐤄.𐤉𐤒𐤇.𐤀𐤕𐤄.𐤅𐤀𐤕.𐤏𐤑.𐤄𐤀𐤓
𐤆.𐤅𐤀𐤕.𐤔𐤍𐤉.𐤄𐤕𐤅𐤋𐤏𐤕.𐤅𐤀𐤕.𐤄𐤀𐤆𐤁.𐤅𐤈𐤁𐤋.𐤀𐤅𐤕𐤌.𐤅
𐤀𐤕.𐤄𐤑𐤐𐤓.𐤄𐤇𐤉𐤄.𐤁𐤃𐤌.𐤄𐤑𐤐𐤓.𐤄𐤔𐤇𐤈𐤄.𐤏𐤋.𐤄𐤌
𐤉𐤌.𐤄𐤇𐤉𐤉𐤌|
ז 𐤅𐤄𐤆𐤄.𐤏𐤋.𐤄𐤌𐤈𐤄𐤓.𐤌𐤍.𐤄𐤑𐤓𐤏𐤕.𐤔𐤁𐤏.𐤐𐤏𐤌𐤉
𐤌.𐤅𐤈𐤄𐤓𐤅.𐤅𐤔𐤋𐤇.𐤀𐤕.𐤄𐤑𐤐𐤓.𐤄𐤇𐤉𐤄.𐤏𐤋.𐤐𐤍𐤉.𐤄𐤔𐤃
𐤄|
ח 𐤅𐤊𐤁𐤎.𐤄𐤌𐤈𐤄𐤓.𐤀𐤕.𐤁𐤂𐤃𐤉𐤅.𐤅𐤂𐤋𐤇.𐤀𐤕.𐤊𐤋.𐤔
𐤏𐤓𐤅.𐤅𐤓𐤇𐤑.𐤁𐤌𐤉𐤌.𐤅𐤈𐤄𐤓.𐤅𐤀𐤇𐤓.𐤉𐤁𐤅𐤀.𐤀𐤋.𐤄𐤌𐤇𐤍𐤄
.𐤅𐤉𐤔𐤁.𐤌𐤇𐤅𐤑.𐤋𐤀𐤄𐤋𐤅.𐤔𐤁𐤏𐤕.𐤉𐤌𐤉𐤌|
ט 𐤅𐤄𐤉𐤄.𐤁𐤉𐤅𐤌.𐤄𐤔𐤁𐤉𐤏𐤉.𐤉𐤂𐤋𐤇.𐤀𐤕.𐤊𐤋.𐤔𐤏𐤓𐤅.
𐤀𐤕.𐤓𐤀𐤔𐤅.𐤅𐤀𐤕.𐤆𐤒𐤍𐤅.𐤅𐤀𐤕.𐤂𐤁𐤕.𐤏𐤉𐤍𐤉𐤅.𐤅𐤀𐤕.𐤊𐤋.

𐤔𐤏𐤓𐤅.𐤉𐤂𐤋𐤇.𐤅𐤊𐤁𐤎.𐤀𐤕.𐤁𐤂𐤃𐤉𐤅.𐤅𐤓𐤇𐤑.𐤀𐤕.𐤁𐤔𐤓𐤅
.𐤁𐤌𐤉𐤌.𐤅𐤈𐤄𐤓|
𐤉 𐤅𐤁𐤉𐤅𐤌.𐤄𐤔𐤌𐤉𐤍𐤉.𐤉𐤒𐤇.𐤔𐤍𐤉.𐤊𐤁𐤔𐤉𐤌.𐤕𐤌𐤉𐤌
𐤉𐤌.𐤅𐤊𐤁𐤔𐤄.𐤀𐤇𐤕.𐤁𐤕.𐤔𐤍𐤕𐤄.𐤕𐤌𐤉𐤌𐤄.𐤅𐤔𐤋𐤔𐤄.𐤏𐤔
𐤓𐤍𐤉𐤌.𐤎𐤋𐤕.𐤌𐤍𐤇𐤄.𐤁𐤋𐤅𐤋𐤄.𐤁𐤔𐤌𐤍.𐤅𐤋𐤂.𐤀𐤇𐤃.𐤔𐤌𐤍|
𐤉𐤀 𐤅𐤄𐤏𐤌𐤉𐤃.𐤄𐤊𐤄𐤍.𐤄𐤌𐤈𐤄𐤓.𐤀𐤕.𐤄𐤀𐤉𐤔.𐤄𐤌𐤈𐤄
𐤓.𐤅𐤀𐤕𐤌.𐤋𐤐𐤍𐤉.𐤉𐤄𐤅𐤄.𐤐𐤕𐤇.𐤀𐤄𐤋.𐤌𐤅𐤏𐤃|
𐤉𐤁 𐤅𐤋𐤒𐤇.𐤄𐤊𐤄𐤍.𐤀𐤕.𐤄𐤊𐤁𐤔.𐤄𐤀𐤇𐤃.𐤅𐤄𐤒𐤓𐤉𐤁.𐤀
𐤕𐤅.𐤋𐤀𐤔𐤌.𐤅𐤀𐤕.𐤋𐤂.𐤄𐤔𐤌𐤍.𐤅𐤄𐤍𐤉𐤐.𐤀𐤕𐤌.𐤕𐤍𐤅𐤐𐤄.𐤋𐤐
𐤍𐤉.𐤉𐤄𐤅𐤄|
𐤉𐤂 𐤅𐤔𐤇𐤈.𐤀𐤕.𐤄𐤊𐤁𐤔.𐤁𐤌𐤒𐤅𐤌.𐤀𐤔𐤓.𐤉𐤔𐤇𐤈.𐤀𐤕.
𐤄𐤇𐤈𐤀𐤕.𐤅𐤀𐤕.𐤄𐤏𐤋𐤄.𐤁𐤌𐤒𐤅𐤌.𐤄𐤒𐤃𐤔.𐤊𐤉.𐤊𐤇𐤈𐤀
𐤕.𐤄𐤀𐤔𐤌.𐤋𐤊𐤄𐤍.𐤒𐤃𐤔.𐤒𐤃𐤔𐤉𐤌.𐤄𐤅𐤀|
𐤉𐤃 𐤅𐤋𐤒𐤇.𐤄𐤊𐤄𐤍.𐤌𐤃𐤌.𐤄𐤀𐤔𐤌.𐤅𐤍𐤕𐤍.𐤄𐤊𐤄𐤍.𐤏𐤋.
𐤕𐤍𐤅𐤊.𐤀𐤆𐤍.𐤄𐤌𐤈𐤄𐤓.𐤄𐤉𐤌𐤍𐤉𐤕.𐤅𐤏𐤋.𐤁𐤄𐤍.𐤉𐤃𐤅.𐤄𐤉𐤌
𐤍𐤉𐤕.𐤅𐤏𐤋.𐤁𐤄𐤍.𐤓𐤂𐤋𐤅.𐤄𐤉𐤌𐤍𐤉𐤕|
𐤉𐤄 𐤅𐤋𐤒𐤇.𐤄𐤊𐤄𐤍.𐤌𐤋𐤂.𐤄𐤔𐤌𐤍.𐤅𐤉𐤑𐤒.𐤏𐤋.𐤊𐤐.𐤄𐤊
𐤄𐤍.𐤄𐤔𐤌𐤀𐤋𐤉𐤕|
𐤉𐤅 𐤅𐤈𐤁𐤋.𐤄𐤊𐤄𐤍.𐤀𐤕.𐤀𐤑𐤁𐤏𐤅.𐤄𐤉𐤌𐤍𐤉𐤕.𐤌𐤍.𐤄𐤔𐤌
𐤍.𐤀𐤔𐤓.𐤏𐤋.𐤊𐤐𐤅.𐤄𐤔𐤌𐤀𐤋𐤉𐤕.𐤅𐤄𐤆𐤄.𐤌𐤍.𐤄𐤔𐤌𐤍.𐤁𐤀
𐤑𐤁𐤏𐤅.𐤔𐤁𐤏.𐤐𐤏𐤌𐤉𐤌.𐤋𐤐𐤍𐤉.𐤉𐤄𐤅𐤄|
𐤉𐤆 𐤅𐤌𐤉𐤕𐤓.𐤄𐤔𐤌𐤍.𐤀𐤔𐤓.𐤏𐤋.𐤊𐤐𐤅.𐤉𐤕𐤍.𐤄𐤊𐤄𐤍.𐤏𐤋.
𐤕𐤍𐤅𐤊.𐤀𐤆𐤍.𐤄𐤌𐤈𐤄𐤓.𐤄𐤉𐤌𐤍𐤉𐤕.𐤅𐤏𐤋.𐤁𐤄𐤍.𐤉𐤃𐤅.𐤄𐤉𐤌
𐤍𐤉𐤕.𐤅𐤏𐤋.𐤁𐤄𐤍.𐤓𐤂𐤋𐤅.𐤄𐤉𐤌𐤍𐤉𐤕.𐤏𐤋.𐤃𐤌.𐤄𐤀𐤔𐤌|
𐤉𐤇 𐤅𐤄𐤍𐤅𐤕𐤓.𐤁𐤔𐤌𐤍.𐤀𐤔𐤓.𐤏𐤋.𐤊𐤐.𐤄𐤊𐤄𐤍.𐤉𐤕𐤍.𐤏𐤋.𐤓
𐤀𐤔.𐤄𐤌𐤈𐤄𐤓.𐤅𐤊𐤐𐤓.𐤏𐤋𐤉𐤅.𐤄𐤊𐤄𐤍.𐤋𐤐𐤍𐤉.𐤉𐤄𐤅𐤄|
𐤉𐤈 𐤅𐤏𐤔𐤄.𐤄𐤊𐤄𐤍.𐤀𐤕.𐤄𐤇𐤈𐤀𐤕.𐤅𐤊𐤐𐤓.𐤏𐤋.𐤄𐤌𐤈𐤄
𐤓.𐤌𐤈𐤌𐤀𐤕𐤅.𐤅𐤀𐤇𐤓.𐤉𐤔𐤇𐤈.𐤀𐤕.𐤄𐤏𐤋𐤄|
𐤊 𐤅𐤄𐤏𐤋𐤄.𐤄𐤊𐤄𐤍.𐤀𐤕.𐤄𐤏𐤋𐤄.𐤅𐤀𐤕.𐤄𐤌𐤍𐤇𐤄.𐤄𐤌
𐤆𐤁𐤇𐤄.𐤅𐤊𐤐𐤓.𐤏𐤋𐤉𐤅.𐤄𐤊𐤄𐤍.𐤅𐤈𐤄𐤓|

𐤊𐤀 𐤅𐤀𐤌.𐤃𐤋.𐤄𐤅𐤀.𐤅𐤀𐤉𐤍.𐤉𐤃𐤅.𐤌𐤔𐤂𐤕.𐤅𐤋𐤒𐤇.𐤊𐤁𐤔
.𐤀𐤇𐤃.𐤀𐤔𐤌.𐤋𐤕𐤍𐤅𐤐𐤄.𐤋𐤊𐤐𐤓.𐤏𐤋𐤉𐤅.𐤅𐤏𐤔𐤓𐤅𐤍.𐤎𐤋𐤕.𐤀
𐤇𐤃.𐤁𐤋𐤅𐤋.𐤁𐤔𐤌𐤍.𐤋𐤌𐤍𐤇𐤄.𐤅𐤋𐤂.𐤔𐤌𐤍|

𐤊𐤁 𐤅𐤔𐤕𐤉.𐤕𐤓𐤉𐤌.𐤀𐤅.𐤔𐤍𐤉.𐤁𐤍𐤉.𐤉𐤅𐤍𐤄.𐤀𐤔𐤓.𐤕𐤔𐤉𐤂
.𐤉𐤃𐤅.𐤅𐤄𐤉𐤄.𐤀𐤇𐤃.𐤇𐤈𐤀𐤕.𐤅𐤄𐤀𐤇𐤃.𐤏𐤋𐤄|

𐤊𐤂 𐤅𐤄𐤁𐤉𐤀.𐤀𐤕𐤌.𐤁𐤉𐤅𐤌.𐤄𐤔𐤌𐤉𐤍𐤉.𐤋𐤈𐤄𐤓𐤕𐤅.𐤀𐤋.
𐤄𐤊𐤄𐤍.𐤀𐤋.𐤐𐤕𐤇.𐤀𐤄𐤋.𐤌𐤅𐤏𐤃.𐤋𐤐𐤍𐤉.𐤉𐤄𐤅𐤄|

𐤊𐤃 𐤅𐤋𐤒𐤇.𐤄𐤊𐤄𐤍.𐤀𐤕.𐤊𐤁𐤔.𐤄𐤀𐤔𐤌.𐤅𐤀𐤕.𐤋𐤂.𐤄𐤔
𐤌𐤍.𐤅𐤄𐤍𐤉𐤐.𐤀𐤕𐤌.𐤄𐤊𐤄𐤍.𐤕𐤍𐤅𐤐𐤄.𐤋𐤐𐤍𐤉.𐤉𐤄𐤅𐤄|

𐤊𐤄 𐤅𐤔𐤇𐤈.𐤀𐤕.𐤊𐤁𐤔.𐤄𐤀𐤔𐤌.𐤅𐤋𐤒𐤇.𐤄𐤊𐤄𐤍.𐤌𐤃𐤌.
𐤄𐤀𐤔𐤌.𐤅𐤍𐤕𐤍.𐤏𐤋.𐤕𐤍𐤅𐤊.𐤀𐤆𐤍.𐤄𐤌𐤈𐤄𐤓.𐤄𐤉𐤌𐤍𐤉𐤕.𐤅𐤏
𐤋.𐤁𐤄𐤍.𐤉𐤃𐤅.𐤄𐤉𐤌𐤍𐤉𐤕.𐤅𐤏𐤋.𐤁𐤄𐤍.𐤓𐤂𐤋𐤅.𐤄𐤉𐤌𐤍𐤉𐤕|

𐤊𐤅 𐤅𐤌𐤍.𐤄𐤔𐤌𐤍.𐤉𐤑𐤒.𐤄𐤊𐤄𐤍.𐤏𐤋.𐤊𐤐.𐤄𐤊𐤄𐤍.𐤄𐤔𐤌𐤀
𐤋𐤉𐤕|

𐤊𐤆 𐤅𐤄𐤆𐤄.𐤄𐤊𐤄𐤍.𐤁𐤀𐤑𐤁𐤏𐤅.𐤄𐤉𐤌𐤍𐤉𐤕.𐤌𐤍.𐤄𐤔𐤌𐤍.
𐤀𐤔𐤓.𐤏𐤋.𐤊𐤐𐤅.𐤄𐤔𐤌𐤀𐤋𐤉𐤕.𐤔𐤁𐤏.𐤐𐤏𐤌𐤉𐤌.𐤋𐤐𐤍𐤉.𐤉𐤄𐤅
𐤄|

𐤊𐤇 𐤅𐤍𐤕𐤍.𐤄𐤊𐤄𐤍.𐤌𐤍.𐤄𐤔𐤌𐤍.𐤀𐤔𐤓.𐤏𐤋.𐤊𐤐𐤅.𐤏𐤋.𐤕𐤍𐤅𐤊
.𐤀𐤆𐤍.𐤄𐤌𐤈𐤄𐤓.𐤄𐤉𐤌𐤍𐤉𐤕.𐤅𐤏𐤋.𐤁𐤄𐤍.𐤉𐤃𐤅.𐤄𐤉𐤌𐤍𐤉𐤕.
𐤅𐤏𐤋.𐤁𐤄𐤍.𐤓𐤂𐤋𐤅.𐤄𐤉𐤌𐤍𐤉𐤕.𐤏𐤋.𐤌𐤒𐤅𐤌.𐤃𐤌.𐤄𐤀𐤔𐤌|

𐤊𐤈 𐤅𐤄𐤍𐤅𐤕𐤓.𐤌𐤍.𐤄𐤔𐤌𐤍.𐤀𐤔𐤓.𐤏𐤋.𐤊𐤐.𐤄𐤊𐤄𐤍.𐤉𐤕𐤍.
𐤏𐤋.𐤓𐤀𐤔.𐤄𐤌𐤈𐤄𐤓.𐤋𐤊𐤐𐤓.𐤏𐤋𐤉𐤅.𐤋𐤐𐤍𐤉.𐤉𐤄𐤅𐤄|

𐤋 𐤅𐤏𐤔𐤄.𐤀𐤕.𐤄𐤀𐤇𐤃.𐤌𐤍.𐤄𐤕𐤓𐤉𐤌.𐤀𐤅.𐤌𐤍.𐤁𐤍𐤉.𐤄
𐤉𐤅𐤍𐤄.𐤌𐤀𐤔𐤓.𐤕𐤔𐤉𐤂.𐤉𐤃𐤅|

𐤋𐤀 𐤀𐤕.𐤀𐤔𐤓.𐤕𐤔𐤉𐤂.𐤉𐤃𐤅.𐤀𐤕.𐤄𐤀𐤇𐤃.𐤇𐤈𐤀𐤕.𐤅
𐤀𐤕.𐤄𐤀𐤇𐤃.𐤏𐤋𐤄.𐤏𐤋.𐤄𐤌𐤍𐤇𐤄.𐤅𐤊𐤐𐤓.𐤄𐤊𐤄𐤍.𐤏𐤋.𐤄
𐤌𐤈𐤄𐤓.𐤋𐤐𐤍𐤉.𐤉𐤄𐤅𐤄|

𐤋𐤁 𐤆𐤀𐤕.𐤕𐤅𐤓𐤕.𐤀𐤔𐤓.𐤁𐤅.𐤍𐤂𐤏.𐤑𐤓𐤏𐤕.𐤀𐤔𐤓.𐤋𐤀.
𐤕𐤔𐤉𐤂.𐤉𐤃𐤅.𐤁𐤈𐤄𐤓𐤕𐤅|

𐤋𐤂 𐤅𐤉𐤃𐤁𐤓.𐤉𐤄𐤅𐤄.𐤀𐤋.𐤌𐤔𐤄.𐤅𐤀𐤋.𐤀𐤄𐤓𐤍.𐤋𐤀𐤌𐤓|

𐤋𐤃 𐤊𐤉.𐤕𐤁𐤀𐤅.𐤀𐤋.𐤀𐤓𐤑.𐤊𐤍𐤏𐤍.𐤀𐤔𐤓.𐤀𐤍𐤉.𐤍𐤕𐤍.𐤋𐤊
𐤌.𐤋𐤀𐤇𐤆𐤄.𐤅𐤍𐤕𐤕𐤉.𐤍𐤂𐤏.𐤑𐤓𐤏𐤕.𐤁𐤁𐤉𐤕.𐤀𐤓𐤑.𐤀𐤇
𐤆𐤕𐤊𐤌|

𐤋𐤄 𐤅𐤁𐤀.𐤀𐤔𐤓.𐤋𐤅.𐤄𐤁𐤉𐤕.𐤅𐤄𐤂𐤉𐤃.𐤋𐤊𐤄𐤍.𐤋𐤀𐤌𐤓.𐤊𐤍
𐤂𐤏.𐤍𐤓𐤀𐤄.𐤋𐤉.𐤁𐤁𐤉𐤕|

𐤋𐤅 𐤅𐤑𐤅𐤄.𐤄𐤊𐤄𐤍.𐤅𐤐𐤍𐤅.𐤀𐤕.𐤄𐤁𐤉𐤕.𐤁𐤈𐤓𐤌.𐤉𐤁𐤀.𐤄𐤊
𐤄𐤍.𐤋𐤓𐤀𐤅𐤕.𐤀𐤕.𐤄𐤍𐤂𐤏.𐤅𐤋𐤀.𐤉𐤈𐤌𐤀.𐤊𐤋.𐤀𐤔𐤓.𐤁𐤁𐤉𐤕
.𐤅𐤀𐤇𐤓.𐤊𐤍.𐤉𐤁𐤀.𐤄𐤊𐤄𐤍.𐤋𐤓𐤀𐤅𐤕.𐤀𐤕.𐤄𐤁𐤉𐤕|

𐤋𐤆 𐤅𐤓𐤀𐤄.𐤀𐤕.𐤄𐤍𐤂𐤏.𐤅𐤄𐤍𐤄.𐤄𐤍𐤂𐤏.𐤁𐤒𐤉𐤓𐤕.𐤄𐤁
𐤉𐤕.𐤔𐤒𐤏𐤓𐤅𐤓𐤕.𐤉𐤓𐤒𐤓𐤒𐤕.𐤀𐤅.𐤀𐤃𐤌𐤃𐤌𐤕.𐤅𐤌𐤓𐤀𐤉𐤄
𐤍.𐤔𐤐𐤋.𐤌𐤍.𐤄𐤒𐤉𐤓|

𐤋𐤇 𐤅𐤉𐤑𐤀.𐤄𐤊𐤄𐤍.𐤌𐤍.𐤄𐤁𐤉𐤕.𐤀𐤋.𐤐𐤕𐤇.𐤄𐤁𐤉𐤕.𐤅𐤄
𐤎𐤂𐤉𐤓.𐤀𐤕.𐤄𐤁𐤉𐤕.𐤔𐤁𐤏𐤕.𐤉𐤌𐤉𐤌|

𐤋𐤈 𐤅𐤔𐤁.𐤄𐤊𐤄𐤍.𐤁𐤉𐤅𐤌.𐤄𐤔𐤁𐤉𐤏𐤉.𐤅𐤓𐤀𐤄.𐤅𐤄𐤍𐤄.𐤐𐤔
𐤄.𐤄𐤍𐤂𐤏.𐤁𐤒𐤉𐤓𐤕.𐤄𐤁𐤉𐤕|

𐤌 𐤅𐤑𐤅𐤄.𐤄𐤊𐤄𐤍.𐤅𐤇𐤋𐤑𐤅.𐤀𐤕.𐤄𐤀𐤁𐤍𐤉𐤌.𐤀𐤔𐤓.𐤁𐤄
𐤍.𐤄𐤍𐤂𐤏.𐤅𐤄𐤔𐤋𐤉𐤊𐤅.𐤀𐤕𐤄𐤍.𐤀𐤋.𐤌𐤇𐤅𐤑.𐤋𐤏𐤉𐤓.𐤀𐤋.𐤌
𐤒𐤅𐤌.𐤈𐤌𐤀|

𐤌𐤀 𐤅𐤀𐤕.𐤄𐤁𐤉𐤕.𐤉𐤒𐤑𐤏.𐤌𐤁𐤉𐤕.𐤎𐤁𐤉𐤁.𐤅𐤔𐤐𐤊𐤅.𐤀
𐤕.𐤄𐤏𐤐𐤓.𐤀𐤔𐤓.𐤄𐤒𐤑𐤅.𐤀𐤋.𐤌𐤇𐤅𐤑.𐤋𐤏𐤉𐤓.𐤀𐤋.𐤌𐤒𐤅𐤌.
𐤈𐤌𐤀|

𐤌𐤁 𐤅𐤋𐤒𐤇𐤅.𐤀𐤁𐤍𐤉𐤌.𐤀𐤇𐤓𐤅𐤕.𐤅𐤄𐤁𐤉𐤀𐤅.𐤀𐤋.𐤕𐤇𐤕.
𐤄𐤀𐤁𐤍𐤉𐤌.𐤅𐤏𐤐𐤓.𐤀𐤇𐤓.𐤉𐤒𐤇.𐤅𐤈𐤇.𐤀𐤕.𐤄𐤁𐤉𐤕|

𐤌𐤂 𐤅𐤀𐤌.𐤉𐤔𐤅𐤁.𐤄𐤍𐤂𐤏.𐤅𐤐𐤓𐤇.𐤁𐤁𐤉𐤕.𐤀𐤇𐤓.𐤇𐤋𐤑.
𐤀𐤕.𐤄𐤀𐤁𐤍𐤉𐤌.𐤅𐤀𐤇𐤓𐤉.𐤄𐤒𐤑𐤅𐤕.𐤀𐤕.𐤄𐤁𐤉𐤕.𐤅𐤀𐤇𐤓
𐤉.𐤄𐤈𐤅𐤇|

𐤌𐤃 𐤅𐤁𐤀.𐤄𐤊𐤄𐤍.𐤅𐤓𐤀𐤄.𐤅𐤄𐤍𐤄.𐤐𐤔𐤄.𐤄𐤍𐤂𐤏.𐤁𐤁𐤉𐤕.
𐤑𐤓𐤏𐤕.𐤌𐤌𐤀𐤓𐤕.𐤄𐤅𐤀.𐤁𐤁𐤉𐤕.𐤈𐤌𐤀.𐤄𐤅𐤀|

𐤌𐤄 𐤅𐤍𐤕𐤑.𐤀𐤕.𐤄𐤁𐤉𐤕.𐤀𐤕.𐤀𐤁𐤍𐤉𐤅.𐤅𐤀𐤕.𐤏𐤑𐤉𐤅.𐤅𐤀
𐤕.𐤊𐤋.𐤏𐤐𐤓.𐤄𐤁𐤉𐤕.𐤅𐤄𐤅𐤑𐤉𐤀.𐤀𐤋.𐤌𐤇𐤅𐤑.𐤋𐤏𐤉𐤓.𐤀𐤋.
𐤌𐤒𐤅𐤌.𐤈𐤌𐤀|

46 𐤅𐤄𐤁𐤀.𐤀𐤋.𐤄𐤁𐤉𐤕.𐤊𐤋.𐤉𐤌𐤉.𐤄𐤎𐤂𐤉𐤓.𐤀𐤕𐤅.𐤉𐤈𐤌𐤀.𐤏𐤃.𐤄𐤏𐤓𐤁|

47 𐤅𐤄𐤔𐤊𐤁.𐤁𐤁𐤉𐤕.𐤉𐤊𐤁𐤎.𐤀𐤕.𐤁𐤂𐤃𐤉𐤅.𐤅𐤄𐤀𐤊𐤋.𐤁𐤁𐤉𐤕.𐤉𐤊𐤁𐤎.𐤀𐤕.𐤁𐤂𐤃𐤉𐤅|

48 𐤅𐤀𐤌.𐤁𐤀.𐤉𐤁𐤀.𐤄𐤊𐤄𐤍.𐤅𐤓𐤀𐤄.𐤅𐤄𐤍𐤄.𐤋𐤀.𐤐𐤔𐤄.𐤄𐤍𐤂𐤏.𐤁𐤁𐤉𐤕.𐤀𐤇𐤓𐤉.𐤄𐤈𐤇.𐤀𐤕.𐤄𐤁𐤉𐤕.𐤅𐤈𐤄𐤓.𐤄𐤊𐤄𐤍.𐤀𐤕.𐤄𐤁𐤉𐤕.𐤊𐤉.𐤍𐤓𐤐𐤀.𐤄𐤍𐤂𐤏|

49 𐤅𐤋𐤒𐤇.𐤋𐤇𐤈𐤀.𐤀𐤕.𐤄𐤁𐤉𐤕.𐤔𐤕𐤉.𐤑𐤐𐤓𐤉𐤌.𐤅𐤏𐤑.𐤀𐤓𐤆.𐤅𐤔𐤍𐤉.𐤕𐤅𐤋𐤏𐤕.𐤅𐤀𐤆𐤁|

50 𐤅𐤔𐤇𐤈.𐤀𐤕.𐤄𐤑𐤐𐤓.𐤄𐤀𐤇𐤕.𐤀𐤋.𐤊𐤋𐤉.𐤇𐤓𐤔.𐤏𐤋.𐤌𐤉𐤌.𐤇𐤉𐤉𐤌|

51 𐤅𐤋𐤒𐤇.𐤀𐤕.𐤏𐤑.𐤄𐤀𐤓𐤆.𐤅𐤀𐤕.𐤄𐤀𐤆𐤁.𐤅𐤀𐤕.𐤔𐤍𐤉.𐤄𐤕𐤅𐤋𐤏𐤕.𐤅𐤀𐤕.𐤄𐤑𐤐𐤓.𐤄𐤇𐤉𐤄.𐤅𐤈𐤁𐤋.𐤀𐤕𐤌.𐤁𐤃𐤌.𐤄𐤑𐤐𐤓.𐤄𐤔𐤇𐤅𐤈𐤄.𐤅𐤁𐤌𐤉𐤌.𐤄𐤇𐤉𐤉𐤌.𐤅𐤄𐤆𐤄.𐤀𐤋.𐤄𐤁𐤉𐤕.𐤔𐤁𐤏.𐤐𐤏𐤌𐤉𐤌|

52 𐤅𐤇𐤈𐤀.𐤀𐤕.𐤄𐤁𐤉𐤕.𐤁𐤃𐤌.𐤄𐤑𐤐𐤅𐤓.𐤅𐤁𐤌𐤉𐤌.𐤄𐤇𐤉𐤉𐤌.𐤅𐤁𐤑𐤐𐤅𐤓.𐤄𐤇𐤉𐤄.𐤅𐤁𐤏𐤑.𐤄𐤀𐤓𐤆.𐤅𐤁𐤀𐤆𐤁.𐤅𐤁𐤔𐤍𐤉.𐤄𐤕𐤅𐤋𐤏𐤕|

53 𐤅𐤔𐤋𐤇.𐤀𐤕.𐤄𐤑𐤐𐤓.𐤄𐤇𐤉𐤄.𐤀𐤋.𐤌𐤇𐤅𐤑.𐤋𐤏𐤉𐤓.𐤀𐤋.𐤐𐤍𐤉.𐤄𐤔𐤃𐤄.𐤅𐤊𐤐𐤓.𐤏𐤋.𐤄𐤁𐤉𐤕.𐤅𐤈𐤄𐤓|

54 𐤆𐤀𐤕.𐤄𐤕𐤅𐤓𐤄.𐤋𐤊𐤋.𐤍𐤂𐤏.𐤄𐤑𐤓𐤏𐤕.𐤅𐤋𐤍𐤕𐤒|

55 𐤅𐤋𐤑𐤓𐤏𐤕.𐤄𐤁𐤂𐤃.𐤅𐤋𐤁𐤉𐤕|

56 𐤅𐤋𐤔𐤀𐤕.𐤅𐤋𐤎𐤐𐤇𐤕.𐤅𐤋𐤁𐤄𐤓𐤕|

57 𐤋𐤄𐤅𐤓𐤕.𐤁𐤉𐤅𐤌.𐤄𐤈𐤌𐤀.𐤅𐤁𐤉𐤅𐤌.𐤄𐤈𐤄𐤓.𐤆𐤀𐤕.𐤕𐤅𐤓𐤕.𐤄𐤑𐤓𐤏𐤕||

𐤋𐤋𐤅𐤉𐤌.𐤇𐤋𐤒 15

1 𐤅𐤉𐤃𐤁𐤓.𐤉𐤄𐤅𐤄.𐤀𐤋.𐤌𐤔𐤄.𐤅𐤀𐤋.𐤀𐤄𐤓𐤍.𐤋𐤀𐤌𐤓|

2 𐤃𐤁𐤓𐤅.𐤀𐤋.𐤁𐤍𐤉.𐤉𐤔𐤓𐤀𐤋.𐤅𐤀𐤌𐤓𐤕𐤌.𐤀𐤋𐤄𐤌.𐤀𐤉𐤔.𐤀𐤉𐤔.𐤊𐤉.𐤉𐤄𐤉𐤄.𐤆𐤁.𐤌𐤁𐤔𐤓𐤅.𐤆𐤅𐤁𐤅.𐤈𐤌𐤀.𐤄𐤅𐤀|

𐤂 𐤅𐤆𐤀𐤕.𐤕𐤄𐤉𐤄.𐤈𐤌𐤀𐤕𐤅.𐤁𐤆𐤅𐤁𐤅.𐤓𐤓.𐤁𐤔𐤓𐤅.𐤀𐤕.
𐤆𐤅𐤁𐤅.𐤀𐤅.𐤄𐤇𐤕𐤉𐤌.𐤁𐤔𐤓𐤅.𐤌𐤆𐤅𐤁𐤅.𐤈𐤌𐤀𐤕𐤅.𐤄𐤅𐤀|
𐤃 𐤊𐤋.𐤄𐤌𐤔𐤊𐤁.𐤀𐤔𐤓.𐤉𐤔𐤊𐤁.𐤏𐤋𐤉𐤅.𐤄𐤆𐤁.𐤉𐤈𐤌𐤀.𐤅
𐤊𐤋.𐤄𐤊𐤋𐤉.𐤀𐤔𐤓.𐤉𐤔𐤁.𐤏𐤋𐤉𐤅.𐤉𐤈𐤌𐤀|
𐤄 𐤅𐤀𐤉𐤔.𐤀𐤔𐤓.𐤉𐤂𐤏.𐤁𐤌𐤔𐤊𐤁𐤅.𐤉𐤊𐤁𐤎.𐤁𐤂𐤃𐤉𐤅.𐤅𐤓
𐤇𐤑.𐤁𐤌𐤉𐤌.𐤅𐤈𐤌𐤀.𐤏𐤃.𐤄𐤏𐤓𐤁|
𐤅 𐤅𐤄𐤉𐤔𐤁.𐤏𐤋.𐤄𐤊𐤋𐤉.𐤀𐤔𐤓.𐤉𐤔𐤁.𐤏𐤋𐤉𐤅.𐤄𐤆𐤁.𐤉𐤊𐤁
𐤎.𐤁𐤂𐤃𐤉𐤅.𐤅𐤓𐤇𐤑.𐤁𐤌𐤉𐤌.𐤅𐤈𐤌𐤀.𐤏𐤃.𐤄𐤏𐤓𐤁|
𐤆 𐤅𐤄𐤍𐤂𐤏.𐤁𐤁𐤔𐤓.𐤄𐤆𐤁.𐤉𐤊𐤁𐤎.𐤁𐤂𐤃𐤉𐤅.𐤅𐤓𐤇𐤑.𐤁
𐤌𐤉𐤌.𐤅𐤈𐤌𐤀.𐤏𐤃.𐤄𐤏𐤓𐤁|
𐤇 𐤅𐤊𐤉.𐤉𐤓𐤒.𐤄𐤆𐤁.𐤁𐤈𐤄𐤅𐤓.𐤅𐤊𐤁𐤎.𐤁𐤂𐤃𐤉𐤅.𐤅𐤓𐤇𐤑.
𐤁𐤌𐤉𐤌.𐤅𐤈𐤌𐤀.𐤏𐤃.𐤄𐤏𐤓𐤁|
𐤈 𐤅𐤊𐤋.𐤄𐤌𐤓𐤊𐤁.𐤀𐤔𐤓.𐤉𐤓𐤊𐤁.𐤏𐤋𐤉𐤅.𐤄𐤆𐤁.𐤉𐤈𐤌𐤀|
𐤉 𐤅𐤊𐤋.𐤄𐤍𐤂𐤏.𐤁𐤊𐤋.𐤀𐤔𐤓.𐤉𐤄𐤉𐤄.𐤕𐤇𐤕𐤉𐤅.𐤉𐤈𐤌
𐤀.𐤏𐤃.𐤄𐤏𐤓𐤁.𐤅𐤄𐤍𐤔𐤀.𐤀𐤅𐤕𐤌.𐤉𐤊𐤁𐤎.𐤁𐤂𐤃𐤉𐤅.𐤅𐤓𐤇
𐤑.𐤁𐤌𐤉𐤌.𐤅𐤈𐤌𐤀.𐤏𐤃.𐤄𐤏𐤓𐤁|
𐤉𐤀 𐤅𐤊𐤋.𐤀𐤔𐤓.𐤉𐤂𐤏.𐤁𐤅.𐤄𐤆𐤁.𐤅𐤉𐤃𐤉𐤅.𐤋𐤀.𐤔𐤈𐤐.𐤁𐤌
𐤉𐤌.𐤅𐤊𐤁𐤎.𐤁𐤂𐤃𐤉𐤅.𐤅𐤓𐤇𐤑.𐤁𐤌𐤉𐤌.𐤅𐤈𐤌𐤀.𐤏𐤃.𐤄𐤏𐤓
𐤁|
𐤉𐤁 𐤅𐤊𐤋𐤉.𐤇𐤓𐤔.𐤀𐤔𐤓.𐤉𐤂𐤏.𐤁𐤅.𐤄𐤆𐤁.𐤉𐤔𐤁𐤓.𐤅𐤊𐤋.𐤊
𐤋𐤉.𐤏𐤑.𐤉𐤔𐤈𐤐.𐤁𐤌𐤉𐤌|
𐤉𐤂 𐤅𐤊𐤉.𐤉𐤈𐤄𐤓.𐤄𐤆𐤁.𐤌𐤆𐤅𐤁𐤅.𐤅𐤎𐤐𐤓.𐤋𐤅.𐤔𐤁𐤏𐤕.𐤉𐤌
𐤉𐤌.𐤋𐤈𐤄𐤓𐤕𐤅.𐤅𐤊𐤁𐤎.𐤁𐤂𐤃𐤉𐤅.𐤅𐤓𐤇𐤑.𐤁𐤔𐤓𐤅.𐤁𐤌𐤉𐤌.
𐤇𐤉𐤉𐤌.𐤅𐤈𐤄𐤓|
𐤉𐤃 𐤅𐤁𐤉𐤅𐤌.𐤄𐤔𐤌𐤉𐤍𐤉.𐤉𐤒𐤇.𐤋𐤅.𐤔𐤕𐤉.𐤕𐤓𐤉𐤌.𐤀𐤅.𐤔𐤍
𐤉.𐤁𐤍𐤉.𐤉𐤅𐤍𐤄.𐤅𐤁𐤀.𐤋𐤐𐤍𐤉.𐤉𐤄𐤅𐤄.𐤀𐤋.𐤐𐤕𐤇.𐤀𐤄𐤋.𐤌𐤅𐤏
𐤃.𐤅𐤍𐤕𐤍𐤌.𐤀𐤋.𐤄𐤊𐤄𐤍|
𐤈𐤅 𐤅𐤏𐤔𐤄.𐤀𐤕𐤌.𐤄𐤊𐤄𐤍.𐤀𐤇𐤃.𐤇𐤈𐤀𐤕.𐤅𐤄𐤀𐤇𐤃.
𐤏𐤋𐤄.𐤅𐤊𐤐𐤓.𐤏𐤋𐤉𐤅.𐤄𐤊𐤄𐤍.𐤋𐤐𐤍𐤉.𐤉𐤄𐤅𐤄.𐤌𐤆𐤅𐤁𐤅|
𐤈𐤆 𐤅𐤀𐤉𐤔.𐤊𐤉.𐤕𐤑𐤀.𐤌𐤌𐤍𐤅.𐤔𐤊𐤁𐤕.𐤆𐤓𐤏.𐤅𐤓𐤇𐤑.𐤁
𐤌𐤉𐤌.𐤀𐤕.𐤊𐤋.𐤁𐤔𐤓𐤅.𐤅𐤈𐤌𐤀.𐤏𐤃.𐤄𐤏𐤓𐤁|

יז 𐤅𐤊𐤋.𐤁𐤂𐤃.𐤅𐤊𐤋.𐤏𐤅𐤓.𐤀𐤔𐤓.𐤉𐤄𐤉𐤄.𐤏𐤋𐤉𐤅.𐤔𐤊𐤁
𐤕.𐤆𐤓𐤏.𐤅𐤊𐤁𐤎.𐤁𐤌𐤉𐤌.𐤅𐤈𐤌𐤀.𐤏𐤃.𐤄𐤏𐤓𐤁|
יח 𐤅𐤀𐤔𐤄.𐤀𐤔𐤓.𐤉𐤔𐤊𐤁.𐤀𐤉𐤔.𐤀𐤕𐤄.𐤔𐤊𐤁𐤕.𐤆𐤓𐤏.𐤅
𐤓𐤇𐤑𐤅.𐤁𐤌𐤉𐤌.𐤅𐤈𐤌𐤀𐤅.𐤏𐤃.𐤄𐤏𐤓𐤁|
יט 𐤅𐤀𐤔𐤄.𐤊𐤉.𐤕𐤄𐤉𐤄.𐤆𐤁𐤄.𐤃𐤌.𐤉𐤄𐤉𐤄.𐤆𐤁𐤄.𐤁
𐤁𐤔𐤓𐤄.𐤔𐤁𐤏𐤕.𐤉𐤌𐤉𐤌.𐤕𐤄𐤉𐤄.𐤁𐤍𐤃𐤕𐤄.𐤅𐤊𐤋.𐤄𐤍𐤂𐤏.
𐤁𐤄.𐤉𐤈𐤌𐤀.𐤏𐤃.𐤄𐤏𐤓𐤁|
כ 𐤅𐤊𐤋.𐤀𐤔𐤓.𐤕𐤔𐤊𐤁.𐤏𐤋𐤉𐤄.𐤁𐤍𐤃𐤕𐤄.𐤉𐤈𐤌𐤀.𐤅𐤊𐤋.
𐤀𐤔𐤓.𐤕𐤔𐤁.𐤏𐤋𐤉𐤅.𐤉𐤈𐤌𐤀|
כא 𐤅𐤊𐤋.𐤄𐤍𐤂𐤏.𐤁𐤌𐤔𐤊𐤁𐤄.𐤉𐤊𐤁𐤎.𐤁𐤂𐤃𐤉𐤅.𐤅𐤓𐤇𐤑.
𐤁𐤌𐤉𐤌.𐤅𐤈𐤌𐤀.𐤏𐤃.𐤄𐤏𐤓𐤁|
כב 𐤅𐤊𐤋.𐤄𐤍𐤂𐤏.𐤁𐤊𐤋.𐤊𐤋𐤉.𐤀𐤔𐤓.𐤕𐤔𐤁.𐤏𐤋𐤉𐤅.𐤉𐤊𐤁
𐤎.𐤁𐤂𐤃𐤉𐤅.𐤅𐤓𐤇𐤑.𐤁𐤌𐤉𐤌.𐤅𐤈𐤌𐤀.𐤏𐤃.𐤄𐤏𐤓𐤁|
כג 𐤅𐤀𐤌.𐤏𐤋.𐤄𐤌𐤔𐤊𐤁.𐤄𐤅𐤀.𐤀𐤅.𐤏𐤋.𐤄𐤊𐤋𐤉.𐤀𐤔𐤓.𐤄𐤅
𐤀.𐤉𐤔𐤁𐤕.𐤏𐤋𐤉𐤅.𐤁𐤍𐤂𐤏𐤅.𐤁𐤅.𐤉𐤈𐤌𐤀.𐤏𐤃.𐤄𐤏𐤓𐤁|
כד 𐤅𐤀𐤌.𐤔𐤊𐤁.𐤉𐤔𐤊𐤁.𐤀𐤉𐤔.𐤀𐤕𐤄.𐤅𐤕𐤄𐤉.𐤍𐤃𐤕𐤄.
𐤏𐤋𐤉𐤄.𐤅𐤈𐤌𐤀.𐤔𐤁𐤏𐤕.𐤉𐤌𐤉𐤌.𐤅𐤊𐤋.𐤄𐤌𐤔𐤊𐤁.𐤀𐤔𐤓.𐤉𐤔
𐤊𐤁.𐤏𐤋𐤉𐤅.𐤉𐤈𐤌𐤀|
כה 𐤅𐤀𐤔𐤄.𐤊𐤉.𐤉𐤆𐤅𐤁.𐤆𐤅𐤁.𐤃𐤌𐤄.𐤉𐤌𐤉𐤌.𐤓𐤁𐤉𐤌.𐤁𐤋
𐤀.𐤏𐤕.𐤍𐤃𐤕𐤄.𐤀𐤅.𐤊𐤉.𐤕𐤆𐤅𐤁.𐤏𐤋.𐤍𐤃𐤕𐤄.𐤊𐤋.𐤉𐤌𐤉.𐤆
𐤅𐤁.𐤈𐤌𐤀𐤕𐤄.𐤊𐤉𐤌𐤉.𐤍𐤃𐤕𐤄.𐤕𐤄𐤉𐤄.𐤈𐤌𐤀𐤄.𐤄𐤅𐤀|
כו 𐤊𐤋.𐤄𐤌𐤔𐤊𐤁.𐤀𐤔𐤓.𐤕𐤔𐤊𐤁.𐤏𐤋𐤉𐤅.𐤊𐤋.𐤉𐤌𐤉.𐤆𐤅𐤁
𐤄.𐤊𐤌𐤔𐤊𐤁.𐤍𐤃𐤕𐤄.𐤉𐤄𐤉𐤄.𐤋𐤄.𐤅𐤊𐤋.𐤄𐤊𐤋𐤉.𐤀𐤔𐤓.𐤕𐤔
𐤁.𐤏𐤋𐤉𐤅.𐤈𐤌𐤀.𐤉𐤄𐤉𐤄.𐤊𐤈𐤌𐤀𐤕.𐤍𐤃𐤕𐤄|
כז 𐤅𐤊𐤋.𐤄𐤍𐤅𐤂𐤏.𐤁𐤌.𐤉𐤈𐤌𐤀.𐤅𐤊𐤁𐤎.𐤁𐤂𐤃𐤉𐤅.𐤅𐤓𐤇
𐤑.𐤁𐤌𐤉𐤌.𐤅𐤈𐤌𐤀.𐤏𐤃.𐤄𐤏𐤓𐤁|
כח 𐤅𐤀𐤌.𐤈𐤄𐤓𐤄.𐤌𐤆𐤅𐤁𐤄.𐤅𐤎𐤐𐤓𐤄.𐤋𐤄.𐤔𐤁𐤏𐤕.𐤉𐤌𐤉
𐤌.𐤅𐤀𐤇𐤓.𐤕𐤈𐤄𐤓|
כט 𐤅𐤁𐤉𐤅𐤌.𐤄𐤔𐤌𐤉𐤍𐤉.𐤕𐤒𐤇.𐤋𐤄.𐤔𐤕𐤉.𐤕𐤓𐤉𐤌.𐤀𐤅.
𐤔𐤍𐤉.𐤁𐤍𐤉.𐤉𐤅𐤍𐤄.𐤅𐤄𐤁𐤉𐤀𐤄.𐤀𐤅𐤕𐤌.𐤀𐤋.𐤄𐤊𐤄𐤍.𐤀𐤋.𐤐𐤕
𐤇.𐤀𐤄𐤋.𐤌𐤅𐤏𐤃|

30 𐤅𐤏𐤔𐤄.𐤄𐤊𐤄𐤍.𐤀𐤕.𐤄𐤀𐤇𐤃.𐤇𐤈𐤀𐤕.𐤅𐤀𐤕.𐤄𐤀
𐤇𐤃.𐤏𐤋𐤄.𐤅𐤊𐤐𐤓.𐤏𐤋𐤉𐤄.𐤄𐤊𐤄𐤍.𐤋𐤐𐤍𐤉.𐤉𐤄𐤅𐤄.𐤌𐤆𐤅𐤁.
𐤈𐤌𐤀𐤕𐤄|

31 𐤅𐤄𐤆𐤓𐤕𐤌.𐤀𐤕.𐤁𐤍𐤉.𐤉𐤔𐤓𐤀𐤋.𐤌𐤈𐤌𐤀𐤕𐤌.𐤅𐤋𐤀.𐤉
𐤌𐤕𐤅.𐤁𐤈𐤌𐤀𐤕𐤌.𐤁𐤈𐤌𐤀𐤌.𐤀𐤕.𐤌𐤔𐤊𐤍𐤉.𐤀𐤔𐤓.𐤁𐤕𐤅𐤊
𐤌|

32 𐤆𐤀𐤕.𐤕𐤅𐤓𐤕.𐤄𐤆𐤁.𐤅𐤀𐤔𐤓.𐤕𐤑𐤀.𐤌𐤌𐤍𐤅.𐤔𐤊𐤁𐤕.
𐤆𐤓𐤏.𐤋𐤈𐤌𐤀𐤄.𐤁𐤄|

33 𐤅𐤄𐤃𐤅𐤄.𐤁𐤍𐤃𐤕𐤄.𐤅𐤄𐤆𐤁.𐤀𐤕.𐤆𐤅𐤁𐤅.𐤋𐤆𐤊𐤓.𐤅𐤋𐤍
𐤒𐤁𐤄.𐤅𐤋𐤀𐤉𐤔.𐤀𐤔𐤓.𐤉𐤔𐤊𐤁.𐤏𐤌.𐤈𐤌𐤀𐤄||

𐤋𐤋𐤅𐤉𐤌.𐤇𐤋𐤒 16

1 𐤅𐤉𐤃𐤁𐤓.𐤉𐤄𐤅𐤄.𐤀𐤋.𐤌𐤔𐤄.𐤀𐤇𐤓𐤉.𐤌𐤅𐤕.𐤔𐤍𐤉.𐤁𐤍𐤉.
𐤀𐤄𐤓𐤍.𐤁𐤒𐤓𐤁𐤕𐤌.𐤋𐤐𐤍𐤉.𐤉𐤄𐤅𐤄.𐤅𐤉𐤌𐤕𐤅|

2 𐤅𐤉𐤀𐤌𐤓.𐤉𐤄𐤅𐤄.𐤀𐤋.𐤌𐤔𐤄.𐤃𐤁𐤓.𐤀𐤋.𐤀𐤄𐤓𐤍.𐤀𐤇𐤉𐤊
.𐤅𐤀𐤋.𐤉𐤁𐤀.𐤁𐤊𐤋.𐤏𐤕.𐤀𐤋.𐤄𐤒𐤃𐤔.𐤌𐤁𐤉𐤕.𐤋𐤐𐤓𐤊𐤕.𐤀𐤋
.𐤐𐤍𐤉.𐤄𐤊𐤐𐤓𐤕.𐤀𐤔𐤓.𐤏𐤋.𐤄𐤀𐤓𐤍.𐤅𐤋𐤀.𐤉𐤌𐤅𐤕.𐤊𐤉.𐤁𐤏𐤍𐤍.
𐤀𐤓𐤀𐤄.𐤏𐤋.𐤄𐤊𐤐𐤓𐤕|

3 𐤁𐤆𐤀𐤕.𐤉𐤁𐤀.𐤀𐤄𐤓𐤍.𐤀𐤋.𐤄𐤒𐤃𐤔.𐤁𐤐𐤓.𐤁𐤍.𐤁𐤒𐤓.𐤋
𐤇𐤈𐤀𐤕.𐤅𐤀𐤉𐤋.𐤋𐤏𐤋𐤄|

4 𐤊𐤕𐤍𐤕.𐤁𐤃.𐤒𐤃𐤔.𐤉𐤋𐤁𐤔.𐤅𐤌𐤊𐤍𐤎𐤉.𐤁𐤃.𐤉𐤄𐤉𐤅.
𐤏𐤋.𐤁𐤔𐤓𐤅.𐤅𐤁𐤀𐤁𐤍𐤈.𐤁𐤃.𐤉𐤇𐤂𐤓.𐤅𐤁𐤌𐤑𐤍𐤐𐤕.𐤁𐤃.𐤉𐤑
𐤍𐤐.𐤁𐤂𐤃𐤉.𐤒𐤃𐤔.𐤄𐤌.𐤅𐤓𐤇𐤑.𐤁𐤌𐤉𐤌.𐤀𐤕.𐤁𐤔𐤓𐤅.𐤅𐤋𐤁
𐤔𐤌|

5 𐤅𐤌𐤀𐤕.𐤏𐤃𐤕.𐤁𐤍𐤉.𐤉𐤔𐤓𐤀𐤋.𐤉𐤒𐤇.𐤔𐤍𐤉.𐤔𐤏𐤉𐤓𐤉.
𐤏𐤆𐤉𐤌.𐤋𐤇𐤈𐤀𐤕.𐤅𐤀𐤉𐤋.𐤀𐤇𐤃.𐤋𐤏𐤋𐤄|

6 𐤅𐤄𐤒𐤓𐤉𐤁.𐤀𐤄𐤓𐤍.𐤀𐤕.𐤐𐤓.𐤄𐤇𐤈𐤀𐤕.𐤀𐤔𐤓.𐤋𐤅.𐤅𐤊𐤐𐤓
.𐤁𐤏𐤃𐤅.𐤅𐤁𐤏𐤃.𐤁𐤉𐤕𐤅|

7 𐤅𐤋𐤒𐤇.𐤀𐤕.𐤔𐤍𐤉.𐤄𐤔𐤏𐤉𐤓𐤌.𐤅𐤄𐤏𐤌𐤉𐤃.𐤀𐤕𐤌.𐤋𐤐
𐤍𐤉.𐤉𐤄𐤅𐤄.𐤐𐤕𐤇.𐤀𐤄𐤋.𐤌𐤅𐤏𐤃|

ח ונתן.אהרן.על.שני.השעירם.גרלות.גורל.אחד.ליהוה.וגורל.אחד.לעזאזל׃

ט והקריב.אהרן.את.השעיר.אשר.עלה.עליו.הגורל.ליהוה.ועשהו.חטאת׃

י והשעיר.אשר.עלה.עליו.הגורל.לעזאזל.יעמד.חי.לפני.יהוה.לכפר.עליו.לשלח.אתו.לעזאזל.המדברה׃

יא והקריב.אהרן.את.פר.החטאת.אשר.לו.וכפר.בעדו.ובעד.ביתו.ושחט.את.פר.החטאת.אשר.לו׃

יב ולקח.מלא.המחתה.גחלי.אש.מעל.המזבח.מלפני.יהוה.ומלא.חפניו.קטרת.סמים.דקה.והביא.מבית.לפרכת׃

יג ונתן.את.הקטרת.על.האש.לפני.יהוה.וכסה.ענן.הקטרת.את.הכפרת.אשר.על.העדות.ולא.ימות׃

יד ולקח.מדם.הפר.והזה.באצבעו.על.פני.הכפרת.קדמה.ולפני.הכפרת.יזה.שבע.פעמים.מן.הדם.באצבעו׃

טו ושחט.את.שעיר.החטאת.אשר.לעם.והביא.את.דמו.אל.מבית.לפרכת.ועשה.את.דמו.כאשר.עשה.לדם.הפר.והזה.אתו.על.הכפרת.ולפני.הכפרת׃

טז וכפר.על.הקדש.מטמאת.בני.ישראל.ומפשעיהם.לכל.חטאתם.וכן.יעשה.לאהל.מועד.השכן.אתם.בתוך.טמאתם׃

יז וכל.אדם.לא.יהיה.באהל.מועד.בבאו.לכפר.בקדש.עד.צאתו.וכפר.בעדו.ובעד.ביתו.ובעד.כל.קהל.ישראל׃

18 𐤅𐤉𐤑𐤀.𐤀𐤋.𐤄𐤌𐤆𐤁𐤇.𐤀𐤔𐤓.𐤋𐤐𐤍𐤉.𐤉𐤄𐤅𐤄.𐤅𐤊𐤐𐤓.
𐤏𐤋𐤉𐤅.𐤅𐤋𐤒𐤇.𐤌𐤃𐤌.𐤄𐤐𐤓.𐤅𐤌𐤃𐤌.𐤄𐤔𐤏𐤉𐤓.𐤅𐤍𐤕𐤍.𐤏𐤋.
𐤒𐤓𐤍𐤅𐤕.𐤄𐤌𐤆𐤁𐤇.𐤎𐤁𐤉𐤁|
19 𐤅𐤄𐤆𐤄.𐤏𐤋𐤉𐤅.𐤌𐤍.𐤄𐤃𐤌.𐤁𐤀𐤑𐤁𐤏𐤅.𐤔𐤁𐤏.𐤐𐤏𐤌
𐤉𐤌.𐤅𐤈𐤄𐤓𐤅.𐤅𐤒𐤃𐤔𐤅.𐤌𐤈𐤌𐤀𐤕.𐤁𐤍𐤉.𐤉𐤔𐤓𐤀𐤋|
20 𐤅𐤊𐤋𐤄.𐤌𐤊𐤐𐤓.𐤀𐤕.𐤄𐤒𐤃𐤔.𐤅𐤀𐤕.𐤀𐤄𐤋.𐤌𐤅𐤏𐤃.𐤅
𐤀𐤕.𐤄𐤌𐤆𐤁𐤇.𐤅𐤄𐤒𐤓𐤉𐤁.𐤀𐤕.𐤄𐤔𐤏𐤉𐤓.𐤄𐤇𐤉|
21 𐤅𐤎𐤌𐤊.𐤀𐤄𐤓𐤍.𐤀𐤕.𐤔𐤕𐤉.𐤉𐤃𐤅.‖𐤉𐤃𐤉𐤅.𐤒𐤓𐤉‖.𐤏𐤋.
𐤓𐤀𐤔.𐤄𐤔𐤏𐤉𐤓.𐤄𐤇𐤉.𐤅𐤄𐤕𐤅𐤃𐤄.𐤏𐤋𐤉𐤅.𐤀𐤕.𐤊𐤋.𐤏𐤅𐤍𐤕.
𐤁𐤍𐤉.𐤉𐤔𐤓𐤀𐤋.𐤅𐤀𐤕.𐤊𐤋.𐤐𐤔𐤏𐤉𐤄𐤌.𐤋𐤊𐤋.𐤇𐤈𐤀𐤕𐤌.𐤅𐤍
𐤕𐤍.𐤀𐤕𐤌.𐤏𐤋.𐤓𐤀𐤔.𐤄𐤔𐤏𐤉𐤓.𐤅𐤔𐤋𐤇.𐤁𐤉𐤃.𐤀𐤉𐤔.𐤏𐤕
𐤉.𐤄𐤌𐤃𐤁𐤓𐤄|
22 𐤅𐤍𐤔𐤀.𐤄𐤔𐤏𐤉𐤓.𐤏𐤋𐤉𐤅.𐤀𐤕.𐤊𐤋.𐤏𐤅𐤍𐤕𐤌.𐤀𐤋.𐤀𐤓
𐤑.𐤂𐤆𐤓𐤄.𐤅𐤔𐤋𐤇.𐤀𐤕.𐤄𐤔𐤏𐤉𐤓.𐤁𐤌𐤃𐤁𐤓|
23 𐤅𐤁𐤀.𐤀𐤄𐤓𐤍.𐤀𐤋.𐤀𐤄𐤋.𐤌𐤅𐤏𐤃.𐤅𐤐𐤔𐤈.𐤀𐤕.𐤁𐤂𐤃
𐤉.𐤄𐤁𐤃.𐤀𐤔𐤓.𐤋𐤁𐤔.𐤁𐤁𐤀𐤅.𐤀𐤋.𐤄𐤒𐤃𐤔.𐤅𐤄𐤍𐤉𐤇𐤌.𐤔
𐤌|
24 𐤅𐤓𐤇𐤑.𐤀𐤕.𐤁𐤔𐤓𐤅.𐤁𐤌𐤉𐤌.𐤁𐤌𐤒𐤅𐤌.𐤒𐤃𐤅𐤔.𐤅𐤋𐤁
𐤔.𐤀𐤕.𐤁𐤂𐤃𐤉𐤅.𐤅𐤉𐤑𐤀.𐤅𐤏𐤔𐤄.𐤀𐤕.𐤏𐤋𐤕𐤅.𐤅𐤀𐤕.𐤏𐤋𐤕
.𐤄𐤏𐤌.𐤅𐤊𐤐𐤓.𐤁𐤏𐤃𐤅.𐤅𐤁𐤏𐤃.𐤄𐤏𐤌|
25 𐤅𐤀𐤕.𐤇𐤋𐤁.𐤄𐤇𐤈𐤀𐤕.𐤉𐤒𐤈𐤉𐤓.𐤄𐤌𐤆𐤁𐤇𐤄|
26 𐤅𐤄𐤌𐤔𐤋𐤇.𐤀𐤕.𐤄𐤔𐤏𐤉𐤓.𐤋𐤏𐤆𐤀𐤆𐤋.𐤉𐤊𐤁𐤎.𐤁𐤂
𐤃𐤉𐤅.𐤅𐤓𐤇𐤑.𐤀𐤕.𐤁𐤔𐤓𐤅.𐤁𐤌𐤉𐤌.𐤅𐤀𐤇𐤓𐤉.𐤊𐤍.𐤉𐤁𐤅𐤀.𐤀𐤋
.𐤄𐤌𐤇𐤍𐤄|
27 𐤅𐤀𐤕.𐤐𐤓.𐤄𐤇𐤈𐤀𐤕.𐤅𐤀𐤕.𐤔𐤏𐤉𐤓.𐤄𐤇𐤈𐤀𐤕.𐤀𐤔
𐤓.𐤄𐤅𐤁𐤀.𐤀𐤕.𐤃𐤌𐤌.𐤋𐤊𐤐𐤓.𐤁𐤒𐤃𐤔.𐤉𐤅𐤑𐤉𐤀.𐤀𐤋.𐤌𐤇𐤅
𐤑.𐤋𐤌𐤇𐤍𐤄.𐤅𐤔𐤓𐤐𐤅.𐤁𐤀𐤔.𐤀𐤕.𐤏𐤓𐤕𐤌.𐤅𐤀𐤕.𐤁𐤔𐤓𐤌.𐤅𐤀
𐤕.𐤐𐤓𐤔𐤌|
28 𐤅𐤄𐤔𐤓𐤐.𐤀𐤕𐤌.𐤉𐤊𐤁𐤎.𐤁𐤂𐤃𐤉𐤅.𐤅𐤓𐤇𐤑.𐤀𐤕.𐤁𐤔𐤓
𐤅.𐤁𐤌𐤉𐤌.𐤅𐤀𐤇𐤓𐤉.𐤊𐤍.𐤉𐤁𐤅𐤀.𐤀𐤋.𐤄𐤌𐤇𐤍𐤄|

29 𐤅𐤄𐤉𐤕𐤄.𐤋𐤊𐤌.𐤋𐤇𐤒𐤕.𐤏𐤅𐤋𐤌.𐤁𐤇𐤃𐤔.𐤄𐤔𐤁𐤉
𐤏𐤉.𐤁𐤏𐤔𐤅𐤓.𐤋𐤇𐤃𐤔.𐤕𐤏𐤍𐤅.𐤀𐤕.𐤍𐤐𐤔𐤕𐤉𐤊𐤌.𐤅𐤊𐤋.𐤌𐤋
𐤀𐤊𐤄.𐤋𐤀.𐤕𐤏𐤔𐤅.𐤄𐤀𐤆𐤓𐤇.𐤅𐤄𐤂𐤓.𐤄𐤂𐤓.𐤁𐤕𐤅𐤊𐤊𐤌|

30 𐤊𐤉.𐤁𐤉𐤅𐤌.𐤄𐤆𐤄.𐤉𐤊𐤐𐤓.𐤏𐤋𐤉𐤊𐤌.𐤋𐤈𐤄𐤓.𐤀𐤕𐤊
𐤌.𐤌𐤊𐤋.𐤇𐤈𐤀𐤕𐤉𐤊𐤌.𐤋𐤐𐤍𐤉.𐤉𐤄𐤅𐤄.𐤕𐤈𐤄𐤓𐤅|

31 𐤔𐤁𐤕.𐤔𐤁𐤕𐤅𐤍.𐤄𐤉𐤀.𐤋𐤊𐤌.𐤅𐤏𐤍𐤉𐤕𐤌.𐤀𐤕.𐤍𐤐𐤔𐤕
𐤉𐤊𐤌.𐤇𐤒𐤕.𐤏𐤅𐤋𐤌|

32 𐤅𐤊𐤐𐤓.𐤄𐤊𐤄𐤍.𐤀𐤔𐤓.𐤉𐤌𐤔𐤇.𐤀𐤕𐤅.𐤅𐤀𐤔𐤓.𐤉𐤌𐤋𐤀.
𐤀𐤕.𐤉𐤃𐤅.𐤋𐤊𐤄𐤍.𐤕𐤇𐤕.𐤀𐤁𐤉𐤅.𐤅𐤋𐤁𐤔.𐤀𐤕.𐤁𐤂𐤃𐤉.𐤄𐤁
𐤃.𐤁𐤂𐤃𐤉.𐤄𐤒𐤃𐤔|

33 𐤅𐤊𐤐𐤓.𐤀𐤕.𐤌𐤒𐤃𐤔.𐤄𐤒𐤃𐤔.𐤅𐤀𐤕.𐤀𐤄𐤋.𐤌𐤅𐤏𐤃.
𐤅𐤀𐤕.𐤄𐤌𐤆𐤁𐤇.𐤉𐤊𐤐𐤓.𐤅𐤏𐤋.𐤄𐤊𐤄𐤍𐤉𐤌.𐤅𐤏𐤋.𐤊𐤋.𐤏𐤌.𐤄
𐤒𐤄𐤋.𐤉𐤊𐤐𐤓|

34 𐤅𐤄𐤉𐤕𐤄.𐤆𐤀𐤕.𐤋𐤊𐤌.𐤋𐤇𐤒𐤕.𐤏𐤅𐤋𐤌.𐤋𐤊𐤐𐤓.𐤏𐤋.
𐤁𐤍𐤉.𐤉𐤔𐤓𐤀𐤋.𐤌𐤊𐤋.𐤇𐤈𐤀𐤕𐤌.𐤀𐤇𐤕.𐤁𐤔𐤍𐤄.𐤅𐤉𐤏𐤔.𐤊
𐤀𐤔𐤓.𐤑𐤅𐤄.𐤉𐤄𐤅𐤄.𐤀𐤕.𐤌𐤔𐤄||

𐤋𐤋𐤅𐤉𐤌.𐤇𐤋𐤒 17

1 𐤅𐤉𐤃𐤁𐤓.𐤉𐤄𐤅𐤄.𐤀𐤋.𐤌𐤔𐤄.𐤋𐤀𐤌𐤓|

2 𐤃𐤁𐤓.𐤀𐤋.𐤀𐤄𐤓𐤍.𐤅𐤀𐤋.𐤁𐤍𐤉𐤅.𐤅𐤀𐤋.𐤊𐤋.𐤁𐤍𐤉.𐤉𐤔𐤓𐤀𐤋
.𐤅𐤀𐤌𐤓𐤕.𐤀𐤋𐤉𐤄𐤌.𐤆𐤄.𐤄𐤃𐤁𐤓.𐤀𐤔𐤓.𐤑𐤅𐤄.𐤉𐤄𐤅𐤄.𐤋𐤀
𐤌𐤓|

3 𐤀𐤉𐤔.𐤀𐤉𐤔.𐤌𐤁𐤉𐤕.𐤉𐤔𐤓𐤀𐤋.𐤀𐤔𐤓.𐤉𐤔𐤇𐤈.𐤔𐤅𐤓.
𐤀𐤅.𐤊𐤔𐤁.𐤀𐤅.𐤏𐤆.𐤁𐤌𐤇𐤍𐤄.𐤀𐤅.𐤀𐤔𐤓.𐤉𐤔𐤇𐤈.𐤌𐤇𐤅𐤑.
𐤋𐤌𐤇𐤍𐤄|

4 𐤅𐤀𐤋.𐤐𐤕𐤇.𐤀𐤄𐤋.𐤌𐤅𐤏𐤃.𐤋𐤀.𐤄𐤁𐤉𐤀𐤅.𐤋𐤄𐤒𐤓𐤉𐤁.
𐤒𐤓𐤁𐤍.𐤋𐤉𐤄𐤅𐤄.𐤋𐤐𐤍𐤉.𐤌𐤔𐤊𐤍.𐤉𐤄𐤅𐤄.𐤃𐤌.𐤉𐤇𐤔𐤁.𐤋𐤀𐤉
𐤔.𐤄𐤄𐤅𐤀.𐤃𐤌.𐤔𐤐𐤊.𐤅𐤍𐤊𐤓𐤕.𐤄𐤀𐤉𐤔.𐤄𐤄𐤅𐤀.𐤌𐤒𐤓𐤁.𐤏
𐤌𐤅|

5 𐤋𐤌𐤏𐤍.𐤀𐤔𐤓.𐤉𐤁𐤉𐤀𐤅.𐤁𐤍𐤉.𐤉𐤔𐤓𐤀𐤋.𐤀𐤕.𐤆𐤁𐤇𐤉𐤄
𐤌.𐤀𐤔𐤓.𐤄𐤌.𐤆𐤁𐤇𐤉𐤌.𐤏𐤋.𐤐𐤍𐤉.𐤄𐤔𐤃𐤄.𐤅𐤄𐤁𐤉𐤀𐤌.𐤋
𐤉𐤄𐤅𐤄.𐤀𐤋.𐤐𐤕𐤇.𐤀𐤄𐤋.𐤌𐤅𐤏𐤃.𐤀𐤋.𐤄𐤊𐤄𐤍.𐤅𐤆𐤁𐤇𐤅.𐤆
𐤁𐤇𐤉.𐤔𐤋𐤌𐤉𐤌.𐤋𐤉𐤄𐤅𐤄.𐤀𐤅𐤕𐤌|

6 𐤅𐤆𐤓𐤒.𐤄𐤊𐤄𐤍.𐤀𐤕.𐤄𐤃𐤌.𐤏𐤋.𐤌𐤆𐤁𐤇.𐤉𐤄𐤅𐤄.𐤐𐤕
𐤇.𐤀𐤄𐤋.𐤌𐤅𐤏𐤃.𐤅𐤄𐤒𐤈𐤉𐤓.𐤄𐤇𐤋𐤁.𐤋𐤓𐤉𐤇.𐤍𐤉𐤇𐤇.𐤋𐤉
𐤄𐤅𐤄|

7 𐤅𐤋𐤀.𐤉𐤆𐤁𐤇𐤅.𐤏𐤅𐤃.𐤀𐤕.𐤆𐤁𐤇𐤉𐤄𐤌.𐤋𐤔𐤏𐤉𐤓𐤌.
𐤀𐤔𐤓.𐤄𐤌.𐤆𐤍𐤉𐤌.𐤀𐤇𐤓𐤉𐤄𐤌.𐤇𐤒𐤕.𐤏𐤅𐤋𐤌.𐤕𐤄𐤉𐤄.𐤆
𐤀𐤕.𐤋𐤄𐤌.𐤋𐤃𐤓𐤕𐤌|

8 𐤅𐤀𐤋𐤄𐤌.𐤕𐤀𐤌𐤓.𐤀𐤉𐤔.𐤀𐤉𐤔.𐤌𐤁𐤉𐤕.𐤉𐤔𐤓𐤀𐤋.𐤅𐤌𐤍.
𐤄𐤂𐤓.𐤀𐤔𐤓.𐤉𐤂𐤅𐤓.𐤁𐤕𐤅𐤊𐤌.𐤀𐤔𐤓.𐤉𐤏𐤋𐤄.𐤏𐤋𐤄.𐤀𐤅.𐤆
𐤁𐤇|

9 𐤅𐤀𐤋.𐤐𐤕𐤇.𐤀𐤄𐤋.𐤌𐤅𐤏𐤃.𐤋𐤀.𐤉𐤁𐤉𐤀𐤍𐤅.𐤋𐤏𐤔𐤅𐤕.𐤀
𐤕𐤅.𐤋𐤉𐤄𐤅𐤄.𐤅𐤍𐤊𐤓𐤕.𐤄𐤀𐤉𐤔.𐤄𐤄𐤅𐤀.𐤌𐤏𐤌𐤉𐤅|

10 𐤅𐤀𐤉𐤔.𐤀𐤉𐤔.𐤌𐤁𐤉𐤕.𐤉𐤔𐤓𐤀𐤋.𐤅𐤌𐤍.𐤄𐤂𐤓.𐤄𐤂𐤓.𐤁
𐤕𐤅𐤊𐤌.𐤀𐤔𐤓.𐤉𐤀𐤊𐤋.𐤊𐤋.𐤃𐤌.𐤅𐤍𐤕𐤕𐤉.𐤐𐤍𐤉.𐤁𐤍𐤐𐤔.𐤄𐤀
𐤊𐤋𐤕.𐤀𐤕.𐤄𐤃𐤌.𐤅𐤄𐤊𐤓𐤕𐤉.𐤀𐤕𐤄.𐤌𐤒𐤓𐤁.𐤏𐤌𐤄|

11 𐤊𐤉.𐤍𐤐𐤔.𐤄𐤁𐤔𐤓.𐤁𐤃𐤌.𐤄𐤅𐤀.𐤅𐤀𐤍𐤉.𐤍𐤕𐤕𐤉𐤅.𐤋𐤊𐤌.
𐤏𐤋.𐤄𐤌𐤆𐤁𐤇.𐤋𐤊𐤐𐤓.𐤏𐤋.𐤍𐤐𐤔𐤕𐤉𐤊𐤌.𐤊𐤉.𐤄𐤃𐤌.𐤄𐤅𐤀.
𐤁𐤍𐤐𐤔.𐤉𐤊𐤐𐤓|

12 𐤏𐤋.𐤊𐤍.𐤀𐤌𐤓𐤕𐤉.𐤋𐤁𐤍𐤉.𐤉𐤔𐤓𐤀𐤋.𐤊𐤋.𐤍𐤐𐤔.𐤌𐤊𐤌.𐤋
𐤀.𐤕𐤀𐤊𐤋.𐤃𐤌.𐤅𐤄𐤂𐤓.𐤄𐤂𐤓.𐤁𐤕𐤅𐤊𐤊𐤌.𐤋𐤀.𐤉𐤀𐤊𐤋.𐤃
𐤌|

13 𐤅𐤀𐤉𐤔.𐤀𐤉𐤔.𐤌𐤁𐤍𐤉.𐤉𐤔𐤓𐤀𐤋.𐤅𐤌𐤍.𐤄𐤂𐤓.𐤄𐤂𐤓.𐤁
𐤕𐤅𐤊𐤌.𐤀𐤔𐤓.𐤉𐤑𐤅𐤃.𐤑𐤉𐤃.𐤇𐤉𐤄.𐤀𐤅.𐤏𐤅𐤐.𐤀𐤔𐤓.𐤉𐤀𐤊
𐤋.𐤅𐤔𐤐𐤊.𐤀𐤕.𐤃𐤌𐤅.𐤅𐤊𐤎𐤄𐤅.𐤁𐤏𐤐𐤓|

14 𐤊𐤉.𐤍𐤐𐤔.𐤊𐤋.𐤁𐤔𐤓.𐤃𐤌𐤅.𐤁𐤍𐤐𐤔𐤅.𐤄𐤅𐤀.𐤅𐤀𐤌𐤓.𐤋𐤁𐤍
𐤉.𐤉𐤔𐤓𐤀𐤋.𐤃𐤌.𐤊𐤋.𐤁𐤔𐤓.𐤋𐤀.𐤕𐤀𐤊𐤋𐤅.𐤊𐤉.𐤍𐤐𐤔.𐤊𐤋.𐤁
𐤔𐤓.𐤃𐤌𐤅.𐤄𐤅𐤀.𐤊𐤋.𐤀𐤊𐤋𐤉𐤅.𐤉𐤊𐤓𐤕|

..טו.. 𐤅𐤊𐤋.𐤍𐤐𐤔.𐤀𐤔𐤓.𐤕𐤀𐤊𐤋.𐤍𐤁𐤋𐤄.𐤅𐤈𐤓𐤐𐤄.𐤁𐤀𐤆𐤓𐤇.
𐤅𐤁𐤂𐤓.𐤅𐤊𐤁𐤎.𐤁𐤂𐤃𐤉𐤅.𐤅𐤓𐤇𐤑.𐤁𐤌𐤉𐤌.𐤅𐤈𐤌𐤀.𐤏𐤃.𐤄
𐤏𐤓𐤁.𐤅𐤈𐤄𐤓|

..טז.. 𐤅𐤀𐤌.𐤋𐤀.𐤉𐤊𐤁𐤎.𐤅𐤁𐤔𐤓𐤅.𐤋𐤀.𐤉𐤓𐤇𐤑.𐤅𐤍𐤔𐤀.𐤏𐤅𐤍𐤅||

..יח.. 𐤋𐤋𐤅𐤉𐤌.𐤇𐤋𐤒

..א.. 𐤅𐤉𐤃𐤁𐤓.𐤉𐤄𐤅𐤄.𐤀𐤋.𐤌𐤔𐤄.𐤋𐤀𐤌𐤓|

..ב.. 𐤃𐤁𐤓.𐤀𐤋.𐤁𐤍𐤉.𐤉𐤔𐤓𐤀𐤋.𐤅𐤀𐤌𐤓𐤕.𐤀𐤋𐤄𐤌.𐤀𐤍𐤉.𐤉𐤄𐤅
𐤄.𐤀𐤋𐤄𐤉𐤊𐤌|

..ג.. 𐤊𐤌𐤏𐤔𐤄.𐤀𐤓𐤑.𐤌𐤑𐤓𐤉𐤌.𐤀𐤔𐤓.𐤉𐤔𐤁𐤕𐤌.𐤁𐤄.𐤋𐤀.
𐤕𐤏𐤔𐤅.𐤅𐤊𐤌𐤏𐤔𐤄.𐤀𐤓𐤑.𐤊𐤍𐤏𐤍.𐤀𐤔𐤓.𐤀𐤍𐤉.𐤌𐤁𐤉𐤀.𐤀
𐤕𐤊𐤌.𐤔𐤌𐤄.𐤋𐤀.𐤕𐤏𐤔𐤅.𐤅𐤁𐤇𐤒𐤕𐤉𐤄𐤌.𐤋𐤀.𐤕𐤋𐤊𐤅|

..ד.. 𐤀𐤕.𐤌𐤔𐤐𐤈𐤉.𐤕𐤏𐤔𐤅.𐤅𐤀𐤕.𐤇𐤒𐤕𐤉.𐤕𐤔𐤌𐤓𐤅.𐤋𐤋𐤊
𐤕.𐤁𐤄𐤌.𐤀𐤍𐤉.𐤉𐤄𐤅𐤄.𐤀𐤋𐤄𐤉𐤊𐤌|

..ה.. 𐤅𐤔𐤌𐤓𐤕𐤌.𐤀𐤕.𐤇𐤒𐤕𐤉.𐤅𐤀𐤕.𐤌𐤔𐤐𐤈𐤉.𐤀𐤔𐤓.𐤉𐤏𐤔
𐤄.𐤀𐤕𐤌.𐤄𐤀𐤃𐤌.𐤅𐤇𐤉.𐤁𐤄𐤌.𐤀𐤍𐤉.𐤉𐤄𐤅𐤄|

..ו.. 𐤀𐤉𐤔.𐤀𐤉𐤔.𐤀𐤋.𐤊𐤋.𐤔𐤀𐤓.𐤁𐤔𐤓𐤅.𐤋𐤀.𐤕𐤒𐤓𐤁𐤅.𐤋𐤂𐤋
𐤅𐤕.𐤏𐤓𐤅𐤄.𐤀𐤍𐤉.𐤉𐤄𐤅𐤄|

..ז.. 𐤏𐤓𐤅𐤕.𐤀𐤁𐤉𐤊.𐤅𐤏𐤓𐤅𐤕.𐤀𐤌𐤊.𐤋𐤀.𐤕𐤂𐤋𐤄.𐤀𐤌𐤊.𐤄𐤅
𐤀.𐤋𐤀.𐤕𐤂𐤋𐤄.𐤏𐤓𐤅𐤕𐤄|

..ח.. 𐤏𐤓𐤅𐤕.𐤀𐤔𐤕.𐤀𐤁𐤉𐤊.𐤋𐤀.𐤕𐤂𐤋𐤄.𐤏𐤓𐤅𐤕.𐤀𐤁𐤉𐤊.𐤄𐤅
𐤀|

..ט.. 𐤏𐤓𐤅𐤕.𐤀𐤇𐤅𐤕𐤊.𐤁𐤕.𐤀𐤁𐤉𐤊.𐤀𐤅.𐤁𐤕.𐤀𐤌𐤊.𐤌𐤅𐤋𐤃
𐤕.𐤁𐤉𐤕.𐤀𐤅.𐤌𐤅𐤋𐤃𐤕.𐤇𐤅𐤑.𐤋𐤀.𐤕𐤂𐤋𐤄.𐤏𐤓𐤅𐤕𐤍|

..י.. 𐤏𐤓𐤅𐤕.𐤁𐤕.𐤁𐤍𐤊.𐤀𐤅.𐤁𐤕.𐤁𐤕𐤊.𐤋𐤀.𐤕𐤂𐤋𐤄.𐤏𐤓𐤅𐤕
𐤍.𐤊𐤉.𐤏𐤓𐤅𐤕𐤊.𐤄𐤍𐤄|

..יא.. 𐤏𐤓𐤅𐤕.𐤁𐤕.𐤀𐤔𐤕.𐤀𐤁𐤉𐤊.𐤌𐤅𐤋𐤃𐤕.𐤀𐤁𐤉𐤊.𐤀𐤇𐤅𐤕
𐤊.𐤄𐤅𐤀.𐤋𐤀.𐤕𐤂𐤋𐤄.𐤏𐤓𐤅𐤕𐤄|

..יב.. 𐤏𐤓𐤅𐤕.𐤀𐤇𐤅𐤕.𐤀𐤁𐤉𐤊.𐤋𐤀.𐤕𐤂𐤋𐤄.𐤔𐤀𐤓.𐤀𐤁𐤉𐤊.
𐤄𐤅𐤀|

𐤉𐤂 𐤏𐤓𐤅𐤕.𐤀𐤇𐤅𐤕.𐤀𐤌𐤊.𐤋𐤀.𐤕𐤂𐤋𐤄.𐤊𐤉.𐤔𐤀𐤓.𐤀𐤌𐤊.
𐤄𐤅𐤀|
𐤉𐤃 𐤏𐤓𐤅𐤕.𐤀𐤇𐤉.𐤀𐤁𐤉𐤊.𐤋𐤀.𐤕𐤂𐤋𐤄.𐤀𐤋.𐤀𐤔𐤕𐤅.𐤋𐤀
.𐤕𐤒𐤓𐤁.𐤃𐤃𐤕𐤊.𐤄𐤅𐤀|
𐤈𐤅 𐤏𐤓𐤅𐤕.𐤊𐤋𐤕𐤊.𐤋𐤀.𐤕𐤂𐤋𐤄.𐤀𐤔𐤕.𐤁𐤍𐤊.𐤄𐤅𐤀.𐤋𐤀.
𐤕𐤂𐤋𐤄.𐤏𐤓𐤅𐤕𐤄|
𐤈𐤆 𐤏𐤓𐤅𐤕.𐤀𐤔𐤕.𐤀𐤇𐤉𐤊.𐤋𐤀.𐤕𐤂𐤋𐤄.𐤏𐤓𐤅𐤕.𐤀𐤇𐤉𐤊.
𐤄𐤅𐤀|
𐤉𐤆 𐤏𐤓𐤅𐤕.𐤀𐤔𐤄.𐤅𐤁𐤕𐤄.𐤋𐤀.𐤕𐤂𐤋𐤄.𐤀𐤕.𐤁𐤕.𐤁𐤍𐤄.𐤅
𐤀𐤕.𐤁𐤕.𐤁𐤕𐤄.𐤋𐤀.𐤕𐤒𐤇.𐤋𐤂𐤋𐤅𐤕.𐤏𐤓𐤅𐤕𐤄.𐤔𐤀𐤓𐤄.𐤄𐤍
𐤄.𐤆𐤌𐤄.𐤄𐤅𐤀|
𐤉𐤇 𐤅𐤀𐤔𐤄.𐤀𐤋.𐤀𐤇𐤕𐤄.𐤋𐤀.𐤕𐤒𐤇.𐤋𐤑𐤓𐤓.𐤋𐤂𐤋𐤅𐤕.𐤏
𐤓𐤅𐤕𐤄.𐤏𐤋𐤉𐤄.𐤁𐤇𐤉𐤉𐤄|
𐤉𐤈 𐤅𐤀𐤋.𐤀𐤔𐤄.𐤁𐤍𐤃𐤕.𐤈𐤌𐤀𐤕𐤄.𐤋𐤀.𐤕𐤒𐤓𐤁.𐤋𐤂𐤋𐤅
𐤕.𐤏𐤓𐤅𐤕𐤄|
𐤊 𐤅𐤀𐤋.𐤀𐤔𐤕.𐤏𐤌𐤉𐤕𐤊.𐤋𐤀.𐤕𐤕𐤍.𐤔𐤊𐤁𐤕𐤊.𐤋𐤆𐤓𐤏.
𐤋𐤈𐤌𐤀𐤄.𐤁𐤄|
𐤊𐤀 𐤅𐤌𐤆𐤓𐤏𐤊.𐤋𐤀.𐤕𐤕𐤍.𐤋𐤄𐤏𐤁𐤉𐤓.𐤋𐤌𐤋𐤊.𐤅𐤋𐤀.𐤕𐤇𐤋
𐤋.𐤀𐤕.𐤔𐤌.𐤀𐤋𐤄𐤉𐤊.𐤀𐤍𐤉.𐤉𐤄𐤅𐤄|
𐤊𐤁 𐤅𐤀𐤕.𐤆𐤊𐤓.𐤋𐤀.𐤕𐤔𐤊𐤁.𐤌𐤔𐤊𐤁𐤉.𐤀𐤔𐤄.𐤕𐤅𐤏𐤁𐤄.
𐤄𐤅𐤀|
𐤊𐤂 𐤅𐤁𐤊𐤋.𐤁𐤄𐤌𐤄.𐤋𐤀.𐤕𐤕𐤍.𐤔𐤊𐤁𐤕𐤊.𐤋𐤈𐤌𐤀𐤄.𐤁𐤄.𐤅
𐤀𐤔𐤄.𐤋𐤀.𐤕𐤏𐤌𐤃.𐤋𐤐𐤍𐤉.𐤁𐤄𐤌𐤄.𐤋𐤓𐤁𐤏𐤄.𐤕𐤁𐤋.𐤄𐤅𐤀|
𐤊𐤃 𐤀𐤋.𐤕𐤈𐤌𐤀𐤅.𐤁𐤊𐤋.𐤀𐤋𐤄.𐤊𐤉.𐤁𐤊𐤋.𐤀𐤋𐤄.𐤍𐤈𐤌𐤀𐤅
.𐤄𐤂𐤅𐤉𐤌.𐤀𐤔𐤓.𐤀𐤍𐤉.𐤌𐤔𐤋𐤇.𐤌𐤐𐤍𐤉𐤊𐤌|
𐤊𐤄 𐤅𐤕𐤈𐤌𐤀.𐤄𐤀𐤓𐤑.𐤅𐤀𐤐𐤒𐤃.𐤏𐤅𐤍𐤄.𐤏𐤋𐤉𐤄.𐤅𐤕𐤒𐤀.
𐤄𐤀𐤓𐤑.𐤀𐤕.𐤉𐤔𐤁𐤉𐤄|
𐤊𐤅 𐤅𐤔𐤌𐤓𐤕𐤌.𐤀𐤕𐤌.𐤀𐤕.𐤇𐤒𐤕𐤉.𐤅𐤀𐤕.𐤌𐤔𐤐𐤈𐤉.𐤅𐤋
𐤀.𐤕𐤏𐤔𐤅.𐤌𐤊𐤋.𐤄𐤕𐤅𐤏𐤁𐤕.𐤄𐤀𐤋𐤄.𐤄𐤀𐤆𐤓𐤇.𐤅𐤄𐤂𐤓.𐤄
𐤂𐤓.𐤁𐤕𐤅𐤊𐤊𐤌|

27 𐤊𐤉.𐤀𐤕.𐤊𐤋.𐤄𐤕𐤅𐤏𐤁𐤕.𐤄𐤀𐤋.𐤏𐤔𐤅.𐤀𐤍𐤔𐤉.𐤄𐤀𐤓
𐤑.𐤀𐤔𐤓.𐤋𐤐𐤍𐤉𐤊𐤌.𐤅𐤕𐤈𐤌𐤀.𐤄𐤀𐤓𐤑|
28 𐤅𐤋𐤀.𐤕𐤒𐤉𐤀.𐤄𐤀𐤓𐤑.𐤀𐤕𐤊𐤌.𐤁𐤈𐤌𐤀𐤊𐤌.𐤀𐤕𐤄.
𐤊𐤀𐤔𐤓.𐤒𐤀𐤄.𐤀𐤕.𐤄𐤂𐤅𐤉.𐤀𐤔𐤓.𐤋𐤐𐤍𐤉𐤊𐤌|
29 𐤊𐤉.𐤊𐤋.𐤀𐤔𐤓.𐤉𐤏𐤔𐤄.𐤌𐤊𐤋.𐤄𐤕𐤅𐤏𐤁𐤅𐤕.𐤄𐤀𐤋𐤄.
𐤅𐤍𐤊𐤓𐤕𐤅.𐤄𐤍𐤐𐤔𐤅𐤕.𐤄𐤏𐤔𐤕.𐤌𐤒𐤓𐤁.𐤏𐤌𐤌|
30 𐤅𐤔𐤌𐤓𐤕𐤌.𐤀𐤕.𐤌𐤔𐤌𐤓𐤕𐤉.𐤋𐤁𐤋𐤕𐤉.𐤏𐤔𐤅𐤕.𐤌𐤇
𐤒𐤅𐤕.𐤄𐤕𐤅𐤏𐤁𐤕.𐤀𐤔𐤓.𐤍𐤏𐤔𐤅.𐤋𐤐𐤍𐤉𐤊𐤌.𐤅𐤋𐤀.𐤕𐤈𐤌𐤀𐤅.
𐤁𐤄𐤌.𐤀𐤍𐤉.𐤉𐤄𐤅𐤄.𐤀𐤋𐤄𐤉𐤊𐤌||

𐤋𐤋𐤅𐤉𐤌.𐤇𐤋𐤒 19

1 𐤅𐤉𐤃𐤁𐤓.𐤉𐤄𐤅𐤄.𐤀𐤋.𐤌𐤔𐤄.𐤋𐤀𐤌𐤓|
2 𐤃𐤁𐤓.𐤀𐤋.𐤊𐤋.𐤏𐤃𐤕.𐤁𐤍𐤉.𐤉𐤔𐤓𐤀𐤋.𐤅𐤀𐤌𐤓𐤕.𐤀𐤋𐤄
𐤌.𐤒𐤃𐤔𐤉𐤌.𐤕𐤄𐤉𐤅.𐤊𐤉.𐤒𐤃𐤅𐤔.𐤀𐤍𐤉.𐤉𐤄𐤅𐤄.𐤀𐤋𐤄𐤉𐤊
𐤌|
3 𐤀𐤉𐤔.𐤀𐤌𐤅.𐤅𐤀𐤁𐤉𐤅.𐤕𐤉𐤓𐤀𐤅.𐤅𐤀𐤕.𐤔𐤁𐤕𐤕𐤉.𐤕𐤔𐤌𐤓
𐤅.𐤀𐤍𐤉.𐤉𐤄𐤅𐤄.𐤀𐤋𐤄𐤉𐤊𐤌|
4 𐤀𐤋.𐤕𐤐𐤍𐤅.𐤀𐤋.𐤄𐤀𐤋𐤉𐤋𐤉𐤌.𐤅𐤀𐤋𐤄𐤉.𐤌𐤎𐤊𐤄.𐤋𐤀.𐤕
𐤏𐤔𐤅.𐤋𐤊𐤌.𐤀𐤍𐤉.𐤉𐤄𐤅𐤄.𐤀𐤋𐤄𐤉𐤊𐤌|
5 𐤅𐤊𐤉.𐤕𐤆𐤁𐤇𐤅.𐤆𐤁𐤇.𐤔𐤋𐤌𐤉𐤌.𐤋𐤉𐤄𐤅𐤄.𐤋𐤓𐤑𐤍𐤊𐤌.
𐤕𐤆𐤁𐤇𐤄𐤅|
6 𐤁𐤉𐤅𐤌.𐤆𐤁𐤇𐤊𐤌.𐤉𐤀𐤊𐤋.𐤅𐤌𐤌𐤇𐤓𐤕.𐤅𐤄𐤍𐤅𐤕𐤓.𐤏𐤃.
𐤉𐤅𐤌.𐤄𐤔𐤋𐤉𐤔𐤉.𐤁𐤀𐤔.𐤉𐤔𐤓𐤐|
7 𐤅𐤀𐤌.𐤄𐤀𐤊𐤋.𐤉𐤀𐤊𐤋.𐤁𐤉𐤅𐤌.𐤄𐤔𐤋𐤉𐤔𐤉.𐤐𐤂𐤅𐤋.𐤄𐤅𐤀
.𐤋𐤀.𐤉𐤓𐤑𐤄|
8 𐤅𐤀𐤊𐤋𐤉𐤅.𐤏𐤅𐤍𐤅.𐤉𐤔𐤀.𐤊𐤉.𐤀𐤕.𐤒𐤃𐤔.𐤉𐤄𐤅𐤄.𐤇𐤋𐤋.
𐤅𐤍𐤊𐤓𐤕𐤄.𐤄𐤍𐤐𐤔.𐤄𐤄𐤅𐤀.𐤌𐤏𐤌𐤉𐤄|
9 𐤅𐤁𐤒𐤑𐤓𐤊𐤌.𐤀𐤕.𐤒𐤑𐤉𐤓.𐤀𐤓𐤑𐤊𐤌.𐤋𐤀.𐤕𐤊𐤋𐤄.𐤐
𐤀𐤕.𐤔𐤃𐤊.𐤋𐤒𐤑𐤓.𐤅𐤋𐤒𐤈.𐤒𐤑𐤉𐤓𐤊.𐤋𐤀.𐤕𐤋𐤒𐤈|

10 𐤅𐤊𐤓𐤌𐤊.𐤋𐤀.𐤕𐤏𐤅𐤋𐤋.𐤅𐤐𐤓𐤈.𐤊𐤓𐤌𐤊.𐤋𐤀.𐤕𐤋𐤒𐤈.𐤋
𐤏𐤍𐤉.𐤅𐤋𐤂𐤓.𐤕𐤏𐤆𐤁.𐤀𐤕𐤌.𐤀𐤍𐤉.𐤉𐤄𐤅𐤄.𐤀𐤋𐤄𐤉𐤊𐤌|
11 𐤋𐤀.𐤕𐤂𐤍𐤁𐤅.𐤅𐤋𐤀.𐤕𐤊𐤇𐤔𐤅.𐤅𐤋𐤀.𐤕𐤔𐤒𐤓𐤅.𐤀𐤉𐤔.𐤁
𐤏𐤌𐤉𐤕𐤅|
12 𐤅𐤋𐤀.𐤕𐤔𐤁𐤏𐤅.𐤁𐤔𐤌𐤉.𐤋𐤔𐤒𐤓.𐤅𐤇𐤋𐤋𐤕.𐤀𐤕.𐤔𐤌.𐤀
𐤋𐤄𐤉𐤊.𐤀𐤍𐤉.𐤉𐤄𐤅𐤄|
13 𐤋𐤀.𐤕𐤏𐤔𐤒.𐤀𐤕.𐤓𐤏𐤊.𐤅𐤋𐤀.𐤕𐤂𐤆𐤋.𐤋𐤀.𐤕𐤋𐤉𐤍.𐤐
𐤏𐤋𐤕.𐤔𐤊𐤉𐤓.𐤀𐤕𐤊.𐤏𐤃.𐤁𐤒𐤓|
14 𐤋𐤀.𐤕𐤒𐤋𐤋.𐤇𐤓𐤔.𐤅𐤋𐤐𐤍𐤉.𐤏𐤅𐤓.𐤋𐤀.𐤕𐤕𐤍.𐤌𐤊𐤔𐤋.𐤅
𐤉𐤓𐤀𐤕.𐤌𐤀𐤋𐤄𐤉𐤊.𐤀𐤍𐤉.𐤉𐤄𐤅𐤄|
15 𐤋𐤀.𐤕𐤏𐤔𐤅.𐤏𐤅𐤋.𐤁𐤌𐤔𐤐𐤈.𐤋𐤀.𐤕𐤔𐤀.𐤐𐤍𐤉.𐤃𐤋.𐤅𐤋
𐤀.𐤕𐤄𐤃𐤓.𐤐𐤍𐤉.𐤂𐤃𐤅𐤋.𐤁𐤑𐤃𐤒.𐤕𐤔𐤐𐤈.𐤏𐤌𐤉𐤕𐤊|
16 𐤋𐤀.𐤕𐤋𐤊.𐤓𐤊𐤉𐤋.𐤁𐤏𐤌𐤉𐤊.𐤋𐤀.𐤕𐤏𐤌𐤃.𐤏𐤋.𐤃𐤌.𐤓
𐤏𐤊.𐤀𐤍𐤉.𐤉𐤄𐤅𐤄|
17 𐤋𐤀.𐤕𐤔𐤍𐤀.𐤀𐤕.𐤀𐤇𐤉𐤊.𐤁𐤋𐤁𐤁𐤊.𐤄𐤅𐤊𐤇.𐤕𐤅𐤊𐤉
𐤇.𐤀𐤕.𐤏𐤌𐤉𐤕𐤊.𐤅𐤋𐤀.𐤕𐤔𐤀.𐤏𐤋𐤉𐤅.𐤇𐤈𐤀|
18 𐤋𐤀.𐤕𐤒𐤌.𐤅𐤋𐤀.𐤕𐤈𐤓.𐤀𐤕.𐤁𐤍𐤉.𐤏𐤌𐤊.𐤅𐤀𐤄𐤁𐤕.𐤋
𐤓𐤏𐤊.𐤊𐤌𐤅𐤊.𐤀𐤍𐤉.𐤉𐤄𐤅𐤄|
19 𐤀𐤕.𐤇𐤒𐤕𐤉.𐤕𐤔𐤌𐤓𐤅.𐤁𐤄𐤌𐤕𐤊.𐤋𐤀.𐤕𐤓𐤁𐤉𐤏.𐤊𐤋
𐤀𐤉𐤌.𐤔𐤃𐤊.𐤋𐤀.𐤕𐤆𐤓𐤏.𐤊𐤋𐤀𐤉𐤌.𐤅𐤁𐤂𐤃.𐤊𐤋𐤀𐤉𐤌.𐤔
𐤏𐤈𐤍𐤆.𐤋𐤀.𐤉𐤏𐤋𐤄.𐤏𐤋𐤉𐤊|
20 𐤅𐤀𐤉𐤔.𐤊𐤉.𐤉𐤔𐤊𐤁.𐤀𐤕.𐤀𐤔𐤄.𐤔𐤊𐤁𐤕.𐤆𐤓𐤏.𐤅𐤄𐤅
𐤀.𐤔𐤐𐤇𐤄.𐤍𐤇𐤓𐤐𐤕.𐤋𐤀𐤉𐤔.𐤅𐤄𐤐𐤃𐤄.𐤋𐤀.𐤍𐤐𐤃𐤕𐤄.𐤀𐤅.
𐤇𐤐𐤔𐤄.𐤋𐤀.𐤍𐤕𐤍.𐤋𐤄.𐤁𐤒𐤓𐤕.𐤕𐤄𐤉𐤄.𐤋𐤀.𐤉𐤅𐤌𐤕𐤅.𐤊𐤉.𐤋
𐤀.𐤇𐤐𐤔𐤄|
21 𐤅𐤄𐤁𐤉𐤀.𐤀𐤕.𐤀𐤔𐤌𐤅.𐤋𐤉𐤄𐤅𐤄.𐤀𐤋.𐤐𐤕𐤇.𐤀𐤄𐤋.𐤌𐤅
𐤏𐤃.𐤀𐤉𐤋.𐤀𐤔𐤌|
22 𐤅𐤊𐤐𐤓.𐤏𐤋𐤉𐤅.𐤄𐤊𐤄𐤍.𐤁𐤀𐤉𐤋.𐤄𐤀𐤔𐤌.𐤋𐤐𐤍𐤉.𐤉𐤄𐤅𐤄
.𐤏𐤋.𐤇𐤈𐤀𐤕𐤅.𐤀𐤔𐤓.𐤇𐤈𐤀.𐤅𐤍𐤎𐤋𐤇.𐤋𐤅.𐤌𐤇𐤈𐤀𐤕𐤅.𐤀
𐤔𐤓.𐤇𐤈𐤀|

..𐤊𐤂.. 𐤅𐤊𐤉.𐤕𐤁𐤀𐤅.𐤀𐤋.𐤄𐤀𐤓𐤑.𐤅𐤍𐤈𐤏𐤕𐤌.𐤊𐤋.𐤏𐤑.𐤌𐤀
𐤊𐤋.𐤅𐤏𐤓𐤋𐤕𐤌.𐤏𐤓𐤋𐤕𐤅.𐤀𐤕.𐤐𐤓𐤉𐤅.𐤔𐤋𐤔.𐤔𐤍𐤉𐤌.𐤉𐤄𐤉𐤄.
𐤋𐤊𐤌.𐤏𐤓𐤋𐤉𐤌.𐤋𐤀.𐤉𐤀𐤊𐤋|
..𐤊𐤃.. 𐤅𐤁𐤔𐤍𐤄.𐤄𐤓𐤁𐤉𐤏𐤕.𐤉𐤄𐤉𐤄.𐤊𐤋.𐤐𐤓𐤉𐤅.𐤒𐤃𐤔.𐤄𐤋
𐤅𐤋𐤉𐤌.𐤋𐤉𐤄𐤅𐤄|
..𐤊𐤄.. 𐤅𐤁𐤔𐤍𐤄.𐤄𐤇𐤌𐤉𐤔𐤕.𐤕𐤀𐤊𐤋𐤅.𐤀𐤕.𐤐𐤓𐤉𐤅.𐤋𐤄𐤅𐤎𐤉𐤐
.𐤋𐤊𐤌.𐤕𐤁𐤅𐤀𐤕𐤅.𐤀𐤍𐤉.𐤉𐤄𐤅𐤄.𐤀𐤋𐤄𐤉𐤊𐤌|
..𐤊𐤅.. 𐤋𐤀.𐤕𐤀𐤊𐤋𐤅.𐤏𐤋.𐤄𐤃𐤌.𐤋𐤀.𐤕𐤍𐤇𐤔𐤅.𐤅𐤋𐤀.𐤕𐤏𐤅𐤍𐤍
𐤅|
..𐤊𐤆.. 𐤋𐤀.𐤕𐤒𐤐𐤅.𐤐𐤀𐤕.𐤓𐤀𐤔𐤊𐤌.𐤅𐤋𐤀.𐤕𐤔𐤇𐤉𐤕.𐤀𐤕.𐤐
𐤀𐤕.𐤆𐤒𐤍𐤊|
..𐤊𐤇.. 𐤅𐤔𐤓𐤈.𐤋𐤍𐤐𐤔.𐤋𐤀.𐤕𐤕𐤍𐤅.𐤁𐤁𐤔𐤓𐤊𐤌.𐤅𐤊𐤕𐤁𐤕.𐤒𐤏
𐤒𐤏.𐤋𐤀.𐤕𐤕𐤍𐤅.𐤁𐤊𐤌.𐤀𐤍𐤉.𐤉𐤄𐤅𐤄|
..𐤊𐤈.. 𐤀𐤋.𐤕𐤇𐤋𐤋.𐤀𐤕.𐤁𐤕𐤊.𐤋𐤄𐤆𐤍𐤅𐤕𐤄.𐤅𐤋𐤀.𐤕𐤆𐤍𐤄.
𐤄𐤀𐤓𐤑.𐤅𐤌𐤋𐤀𐤄.𐤄𐤀𐤓𐤑.𐤆𐤌𐤄|
..𐤋.. 𐤀𐤕.𐤔𐤁𐤕𐤕𐤉.𐤕𐤔𐤌𐤓𐤅.𐤅𐤌𐤒𐤃𐤔𐤉.𐤕𐤉𐤓𐤀𐤅.𐤀𐤍𐤉
.𐤉𐤄𐤅𐤄|
..𐤋𐤀.. 𐤀𐤋.𐤕𐤐𐤍𐤅.𐤀𐤋.𐤄𐤀𐤁𐤕.𐤅𐤀𐤋.𐤄𐤉𐤃𐤏𐤍𐤉𐤌.𐤀𐤋.𐤕𐤁
𐤒𐤔𐤅.𐤋𐤈𐤌𐤀𐤄.𐤁𐤄𐤌.𐤀𐤍𐤉.𐤉𐤄𐤅𐤄.𐤀𐤋𐤄𐤉𐤊𐤌|
..𐤋𐤁.. 𐤌𐤐𐤍𐤉.𐤔𐤉𐤁𐤄.𐤕𐤒𐤅𐤌.𐤅𐤄𐤃𐤓𐤕.𐤐𐤍𐤉.𐤆𐤒𐤍.𐤅𐤉𐤓𐤀
𐤕.𐤌𐤀𐤋𐤄𐤉𐤊.𐤀𐤍𐤉.𐤉𐤄𐤅𐤄|
..𐤋𐤂.. 𐤅𐤊𐤉.𐤉𐤂𐤅𐤓.𐤀𐤕𐤊.𐤂𐤓.𐤁𐤀𐤓𐤑𐤊𐤌.𐤋𐤀.𐤕𐤅𐤍𐤅.𐤀𐤕𐤅
|
..𐤋𐤃.. 𐤊𐤀𐤆𐤓𐤇.𐤌𐤊𐤌.𐤉𐤄𐤉𐤄.𐤋𐤊𐤌.𐤄𐤂𐤓.𐤄𐤂𐤓.𐤀𐤕𐤊
𐤌.𐤅𐤀𐤄𐤁𐤕.𐤋𐤅.𐤊𐤌𐤅𐤊.𐤊𐤉.𐤂𐤓𐤉𐤌.𐤄𐤉𐤉𐤕𐤌.𐤁𐤀𐤓𐤑.𐤌𐤑
𐤓𐤉𐤌.𐤀𐤍𐤉.𐤉𐤄𐤅𐤄.𐤀𐤋𐤄𐤉𐤊𐤌|
..𐤋𐤄.. 𐤋𐤀.𐤕𐤏𐤔𐤅.𐤏𐤅𐤋.𐤁𐤌𐤔𐤐𐤈.𐤁𐤌𐤃𐤄.𐤁𐤌𐤔𐤒𐤋.𐤅𐤁𐤌
𐤔𐤅𐤓𐤄|
..𐤋𐤅.. 𐤌𐤀𐤆𐤍𐤉.𐤑𐤃𐤒.𐤀𐤁𐤍𐤉.𐤑𐤃𐤒.𐤀𐤉𐤐𐤕.𐤑𐤃𐤒.𐤅
𐤄𐤉𐤍.𐤑𐤃𐤒.𐤉𐤄𐤉𐤄.𐤋𐤊𐤌.𐤀𐤍𐤉.𐤉𐤄𐤅𐤄.𐤀𐤋𐤄𐤉𐤊𐤌.𐤀𐤔
𐤓.𐤄𐤅𐤑𐤀𐤕𐤉.𐤀𐤕𐤊𐤌.𐤌𐤀𐤓𐤑.𐤌𐤑𐤓𐤉𐤌|

37 ושמרתם.את.כל.חקתי.ואת.כל.משפטי.ו
עשיתם.אתם.אני.יהוה||

ללוים.חלק 20

1 וידבר.יהוה.אל.משה.לאמר|
2 ואל.בני.ישראל.תאמר.איש.איש.מבני.יש
ראל.ומן.הגר.הגר.בישראל.אשר.יתן.מזרעו.
למלך.מות.יומת.עם.הארץ.ירגמהו.באבן|
3 ואני.אתן.את.פני.באיש.ההוא.והכרתי.א
תו.מקרב.עמו.כי.מזרעו.נתן.למלך.למען.טמא
.את.מקדשי.ולחלל.את.שם.קדשי|
4 ואם.העלם.יעלימו.עם.הארץ.את.עיניה
ם.מן.האיש.ההוא.בתתו.מזרעו.למלך.לבלתי.
המית.אתו|
5 ושמתי.אני.את.פני.באיש.ההוא.ובמשפח
תו.והכרתי.אתו.ואת.כל.הזנים.אחריו.לזנו
ת.אחרי.המלך.מקרב.עמם|
6 והנפש.אשר.תפנה.אל.האבת.ואל.הידענים
.לזנות.אחריהם.ונתתי.את.פני.בנפש.ההוא.ו
הכרתי.אתו.מקרב.עמו|
7 והתקדשתם.והייתם.קדשים.כי.אני.יה
וה.אלהיכם|
8 ושמרתם.את.חקתי.ועשיתם.אתם.אני.יה
וה.מקדשכם|
9 כי.איש.איש.אשר.יקלל.את.אביו.ואת.א
מו.מות.יומת.אביו.ואמו.קלל.דמיו.בו|
10 ואיש.אשר.ינאף.את.אשת.איש.אשר.ינא
ף.את.אשת.רעהו.מות.יומת.הנאף.והנאפת|
11 ואיש.אשר.ישכב.את.אשת.אביו.ערות.אב
יו.גלה.מות.יומתו.שניהם.דמיהם.בם|

..𐤉𐤁.. 𐤅𐤀𐤉𐤔.𐤀𐤔𐤓.𐤉𐤔𐤊𐤁.𐤀𐤕.𐤊𐤋𐤕𐤅.𐤌𐤅𐤕.𐤉𐤅𐤌𐤕𐤅.𐤔𐤍
𐤉𐤄𐤌.𐤕𐤁𐤋.𐤏𐤔𐤅.𐤃𐤌𐤉𐤄𐤌.𐤁𐤌|
..𐤉𐤂.. 𐤅𐤀𐤉𐤔.𐤀𐤔𐤓.𐤉𐤔𐤊𐤁.𐤀𐤕.𐤆𐤊𐤓.𐤌𐤔𐤊𐤁𐤉.𐤀𐤔𐤄.
𐤕𐤅𐤏𐤁𐤄.𐤏𐤔𐤅.𐤔𐤍𐤉𐤄𐤌.𐤌𐤅𐤕.𐤉𐤅𐤌𐤕𐤅.𐤃𐤌𐤉𐤄𐤌.𐤁𐤌|
..𐤉𐤃.. 𐤅𐤀𐤉𐤔.𐤀𐤔𐤓.𐤉𐤒𐤇.𐤀𐤕.𐤀𐤔𐤄.𐤅𐤀𐤕.𐤀𐤌𐤄.𐤆𐤌
𐤄.𐤄𐤅𐤀.𐤁𐤀𐤔.𐤉𐤔𐤓𐤐𐤅.𐤀𐤕𐤅.𐤅𐤀𐤕𐤄𐤍.𐤅𐤋𐤀.𐤕𐤄𐤉𐤄.𐤆𐤌
𐤄.𐤁𐤕𐤅𐤊𐤊𐤌|
..𐤉𐤄.. 𐤅𐤀𐤉𐤔.𐤀𐤔𐤓.𐤉𐤕𐤍.𐤔𐤊𐤁𐤕𐤅.𐤁𐤁𐤄𐤌𐤄.𐤌𐤅𐤕.𐤉𐤅𐤌𐤕.
𐤅𐤀𐤕.𐤄𐤁𐤄𐤌𐤄.𐤕𐤄𐤓𐤂𐤅|
..𐤉𐤅.. 𐤅𐤀𐤔𐤄.𐤀𐤔𐤓.𐤕𐤒𐤓𐤁.𐤀𐤋.𐤊𐤋.𐤁𐤄𐤌𐤄.𐤋𐤓𐤁𐤏𐤄.𐤀
𐤕𐤄.𐤅𐤄𐤓𐤂𐤕.𐤀𐤕.𐤄𐤀𐤔𐤄.𐤅𐤀𐤕.𐤄𐤁𐤄𐤌𐤄.𐤌𐤅𐤕.𐤉𐤅𐤌𐤕𐤅
.𐤃𐤌𐤉𐤄𐤌.𐤁𐤌|
..𐤉𐤆.. 𐤅𐤀𐤉𐤔.𐤀𐤔𐤓.𐤉𐤒𐤇.𐤀𐤕.𐤀𐤇𐤕𐤅.𐤁𐤕.𐤀𐤁𐤉𐤅.𐤀𐤅.𐤁
𐤕.𐤀𐤌𐤅.𐤅𐤓𐤀𐤄.𐤀𐤕.𐤏𐤓𐤅𐤕𐤄.𐤅𐤄𐤉𐤀.𐤕𐤓𐤀𐤄.𐤀𐤕.𐤏𐤓𐤅𐤕
𐤅.𐤇𐤎𐤃.𐤄𐤅𐤀.𐤅𐤍𐤊𐤓𐤕𐤅.𐤋𐤏𐤉𐤍𐤉.𐤁𐤍𐤉.𐤏𐤌𐤌.𐤏𐤓𐤅𐤕.𐤀𐤇
𐤕𐤅.𐤂𐤋𐤄.𐤏𐤅𐤍𐤅.𐤉𐤔𐤀|
..𐤉𐤇.. 𐤅𐤀𐤉𐤔.𐤀𐤔𐤓.𐤉𐤔𐤊𐤁.𐤀𐤕.𐤀𐤔𐤄.𐤃𐤅𐤄.𐤅𐤂𐤋𐤄.𐤀𐤕
.𐤏𐤓𐤅𐤕𐤄.𐤀𐤕.𐤌𐤒𐤓𐤄.𐤄𐤏𐤓𐤄.𐤅𐤄𐤉𐤀.𐤂𐤋𐤕𐤄.𐤀𐤕.𐤌𐤒𐤅
𐤓.𐤃𐤌𐤉𐤄.𐤅𐤍𐤊𐤓𐤕𐤅.𐤔𐤍𐤉𐤄𐤌.𐤌𐤒𐤓𐤁.𐤏𐤌𐤌|
..𐤉𐤈.. 𐤅𐤏𐤓𐤅𐤕.𐤀𐤇𐤅𐤕.𐤀𐤌𐤊.𐤅𐤀𐤇𐤅𐤕.𐤀𐤁𐤉𐤊.𐤋𐤀.𐤕𐤂𐤋
𐤄.𐤊𐤉.𐤀𐤕.𐤔𐤀𐤓𐤅.𐤄𐤏𐤓𐤄.𐤏𐤅𐤍𐤌.𐤉𐤔𐤀𐤅|
..𐤊.. 𐤅𐤀𐤉𐤔.𐤀𐤔𐤓.𐤉𐤔𐤊𐤁.𐤀𐤕.𐤃𐤃𐤕𐤅.𐤏𐤓𐤅𐤕.𐤃𐤃𐤅.
𐤂𐤋𐤄.𐤇𐤈𐤀𐤌.𐤉𐤔𐤀𐤅.𐤏𐤓𐤉𐤓𐤉𐤌.𐤉𐤌𐤕𐤅|
..𐤊𐤀.. 𐤅𐤀𐤉𐤔.𐤀𐤔𐤓.𐤉𐤒𐤇.𐤀𐤕.𐤀𐤔𐤕.𐤀𐤇𐤉𐤅.𐤍𐤃𐤄.𐤄𐤅
𐤀.𐤏𐤓𐤅𐤕.𐤀𐤇𐤉𐤅.𐤂𐤋𐤄.𐤏𐤓𐤉𐤓𐤉𐤌.𐤉𐤄𐤉𐤅|
..𐤊𐤁.. 𐤅𐤔𐤌𐤓𐤕𐤌.𐤀𐤕.𐤊𐤋.𐤇𐤒𐤕𐤉.𐤅𐤀𐤕.𐤊𐤋.𐤌𐤔𐤐𐤈𐤉.𐤅
𐤏𐤔𐤉𐤕𐤌.𐤀𐤕𐤌.𐤅𐤋𐤀.𐤕𐤒𐤉𐤀.𐤀𐤕𐤊𐤌.𐤄𐤀𐤓𐤑.𐤀𐤔𐤓.𐤀
𐤍𐤉.𐤌𐤁𐤉𐤀.𐤀𐤕𐤊𐤌.𐤔𐤌𐤄.𐤋𐤔𐤁𐤕.𐤁𐤄|
..𐤊𐤂.. 𐤅𐤋𐤀.𐤕𐤋𐤊𐤅.𐤁𐤇𐤒𐤕.𐤄𐤂𐤅𐤉.𐤀𐤔𐤓.𐤀𐤍𐤉.𐤌𐤔𐤋𐤇.
𐤌𐤐𐤍𐤉𐤊𐤌.𐤊𐤉.𐤀𐤕.𐤊𐤋.𐤀𐤋𐤄.𐤏𐤔𐤅.𐤅𐤀𐤒𐤑.𐤁𐤌|

24 ואמר.לכם.אתם.תירשו.את.אדמתם.ואני
.אתננה.לכם.לרשת.אתה.ארץ.זבת.חלב.ודב
ש.אני.יהוה.אלהיכם.אשר.הבדלתי.אתכם.מ
ן.העמים|
25 והבדלתם.בין.הבהמה.הטהרה.לטמאה.ו
בין.העוף.הטמא.לטהר.ולא.תשקצו.את.נפשת
יכם.בבהמה.ובעוף.ובכל.אשר.תרמש.האדמה.
אשר.הבדלתי.לכם.לטמא|
26 והייתם.לי.קדשים.כי.קדוש.אני.יהוה
.ואבדל.אתכם.מן.העמים.להיות.לי|
27 ואיש.או.אשה.כי.יהיה.בהם.אוב.או.יד
עני.מות.יומתו.באבן.ירגמו.אתם.דמיהם.בם
||

ללוים.חלק 21

1 ויאמר.יהוה.אל.משה.אמר.אל.הכהנים.בני
.אהרן.ואמרת.אלהם.לנפש.לא.יטמא.בעמיו|
2 כי.אם.לשארו.הקרב.אליו.לאמו.ולאביו.ול
בנו.ולבתו.ולאחיו|
3 ולאחתו.הבתולה.הקרובה.אליו.אשר.לא.ה
יתה.לאיש.לה.יטמא|
4 לא.יטמא.בעל.בעמיו.להחלו|
5 לא.יקרחה.||יקרחו.קרי||.קרחה.בראשם.ופ
את.זקנם.לא.יגלחו.ובבשרם.לא.ישרטו.שרט
ת|
6 קדשים.יהיו.לאלהיהם.ולא.יחללו.שם.א
להיהם.כי.את.אשי.יהוה.לחם.אלהיהם.הם.
מקריבם.והיו.קדש|
7 אשה.זנה.וחללה.לא.יקחו.ואשה.גרושה.
מאישה.לא.יקחו.כי.קדש.הוא.לאלהיו|

𐤇 𐤅𐤒𐤃𐤔𐤕𐤅.𐤊𐤉.𐤀𐤕.𐤋𐤇𐤌.𐤀𐤋𐤄𐤉𐤊.𐤄𐤅𐤀.𐤌𐤒𐤓𐤉𐤁.
𐤒𐤃𐤔.𐤉𐤄𐤉𐤄.𐤋𐤊.𐤊𐤉.𐤒𐤃𐤅𐤔.𐤀𐤍𐤉.𐤉𐤄𐤅𐤄.𐤌𐤒𐤃𐤔𐤊
𐤌|

𐤈 𐤅𐤁𐤕.𐤀𐤉𐤔.𐤊𐤄𐤍.𐤊𐤉.𐤕𐤇𐤋.𐤋𐤆𐤍𐤅𐤕.𐤀𐤕.𐤀𐤁𐤉𐤄.
𐤄𐤉𐤀.𐤌𐤇𐤋𐤋𐤕.𐤁𐤀𐤔.𐤕𐤔𐤓𐤐|

𐤉 𐤅𐤄𐤊𐤄𐤍.𐤄𐤂𐤃𐤅𐤋.𐤌𐤀𐤇𐤉𐤅.𐤀𐤔𐤓.𐤉𐤅𐤑𐤒.𐤏𐤋.𐤓𐤀
𐤔𐤅.𐤔𐤌𐤍.𐤄𐤌𐤔𐤇𐤄.𐤅𐤌𐤋𐤀.𐤀𐤕.𐤉𐤃𐤅.𐤋𐤋𐤁𐤔.𐤀𐤕.𐤄𐤁𐤂
𐤃𐤉𐤌.𐤀𐤕.𐤓𐤀𐤔𐤅.𐤋𐤀.𐤉𐤐𐤓𐤏.𐤅𐤁𐤂𐤃𐤉𐤅.𐤋𐤀.𐤉𐤐𐤓𐤌|

𐤉𐤀 𐤅𐤏𐤋.𐤊𐤋.𐤍𐤐𐤔𐤕.𐤌𐤕.𐤋𐤀.𐤉𐤁𐤀.𐤋𐤀𐤁𐤉𐤅.𐤅𐤋𐤀𐤌𐤅.𐤋
𐤀.𐤉𐤈𐤌𐤀|

𐤉𐤁 𐤅𐤌𐤍.𐤄𐤌𐤒𐤃𐤔.𐤋𐤀.𐤉𐤑𐤀.𐤅𐤋𐤀.𐤉𐤇𐤋𐤋.𐤀𐤕.𐤌𐤒
𐤃𐤔.𐤀𐤋𐤄𐤉𐤅.𐤊𐤉.𐤍𐤆𐤓.𐤔𐤌𐤍.𐤌𐤔𐤇𐤕.𐤀𐤋𐤄𐤉𐤅.𐤏𐤋𐤉𐤅.
𐤀𐤍𐤉.𐤉𐤄𐤅𐤄|

𐤉𐤂 𐤅𐤄𐤅𐤀.𐤀𐤔𐤄.𐤁𐤁𐤕𐤅𐤋𐤉𐤄.𐤉𐤒𐤇|

𐤉𐤃 𐤀𐤋𐤌𐤍𐤄.𐤅𐤂𐤓𐤅𐤔𐤄.𐤅𐤇𐤋𐤋𐤄.𐤆𐤍𐤄.𐤀𐤕.𐤀𐤋𐤄.𐤋𐤀.
𐤉𐤒𐤇.𐤊𐤉.𐤀𐤌.𐤁𐤕𐤅𐤋𐤄.𐤌𐤏𐤌𐤉𐤅.𐤉𐤒𐤇.𐤀𐤔𐤄|

𐤈𐤅 𐤅𐤋𐤀.𐤉𐤇𐤋𐤋.𐤆𐤓𐤏𐤅.𐤁𐤏𐤌𐤉𐤅.𐤊𐤉.𐤀𐤍𐤉.𐤉𐤄𐤅𐤄.𐤌𐤒
𐤃𐤔𐤅|

𐤈𐤆 𐤅𐤉𐤃𐤁𐤓.𐤉𐤄𐤅𐤄.𐤀𐤋.𐤌𐤔𐤄.𐤋𐤀𐤌𐤓|

𐤉𐤆 𐤃𐤁𐤓.𐤀𐤋.𐤀𐤄𐤓𐤍.𐤋𐤀𐤌𐤓.𐤀𐤉𐤔.𐤌𐤆𐤓𐤏𐤊.𐤋𐤃𐤓𐤕
𐤌.𐤀𐤔𐤓.𐤉𐤄𐤉𐤄.𐤁𐤅.𐤌𐤅𐤌.𐤋𐤀.𐤉𐤒𐤓𐤁.𐤋𐤄𐤒𐤓𐤉𐤁.𐤋𐤇𐤌.
𐤀𐤋𐤄𐤉𐤅|

𐤉𐤇 𐤊𐤉.𐤊𐤋.𐤀𐤉𐤔.𐤀𐤔𐤓.𐤁𐤅.𐤌𐤅𐤌.𐤋𐤀.𐤉𐤒𐤓𐤁.𐤀𐤉𐤔.𐤏𐤅
𐤓.𐤀𐤅.𐤐𐤎𐤇.𐤀𐤅.𐤇𐤓𐤌.𐤀𐤅.𐤔𐤓𐤅𐤏|

𐤉𐤈 𐤀𐤅.𐤀𐤉𐤔.𐤀𐤔𐤓.𐤉𐤄𐤉𐤄.𐤁𐤅.𐤔𐤁𐤓.𐤓𐤂𐤋.𐤀𐤅.𐤔𐤁𐤓.
𐤉𐤃|

𐤊 𐤀𐤅.𐤂𐤁𐤍.𐤀𐤅.𐤃𐤒.𐤀𐤅.𐤕𐤁𐤋𐤋.𐤁𐤏𐤉𐤍𐤅.𐤀𐤅.𐤂𐤓𐤁.𐤀
𐤅.𐤉𐤋𐤐𐤕.𐤀𐤅.𐤌𐤓𐤅𐤇.𐤀𐤔𐤊|

𐤊𐤀 𐤊𐤋.𐤀𐤉𐤔.𐤀𐤔𐤓.𐤁𐤅.𐤌𐤅𐤌.𐤌𐤆𐤓𐤏.𐤀𐤄𐤓𐤍.𐤄𐤊𐤄𐤍.𐤋
𐤀.𐤉𐤂𐤔.𐤋𐤄𐤒𐤓𐤉𐤁.𐤀𐤕.𐤀𐤔𐤉.𐤉𐤄𐤅𐤄.𐤌𐤅𐤌.𐤁𐤅.𐤀𐤕.𐤋𐤇
𐤌.𐤀𐤋𐤄𐤉𐤅.𐤋𐤀.𐤉𐤂𐤔.𐤋𐤄𐤒𐤓𐤉𐤁|

22 𐤋𐤇𐤌.𐤀𐤋𐤄𐤉𐤅.𐤌𐤒𐤃𐤔𐤉.𐤄𐤒𐤃𐤔𐤉𐤌.𐤅𐤌𐤍.𐤄𐤒𐤃
𐤔𐤉𐤌.𐤉𐤀𐤊𐤋|

23 𐤀𐤊.𐤀𐤋.𐤄𐤐𐤓𐤊𐤕.𐤋𐤀.𐤉𐤁𐤀.𐤅𐤀𐤋.𐤄𐤌𐤆𐤁𐤇.𐤋𐤀.𐤉
𐤂𐤔.𐤊𐤉.𐤌𐤅𐤌.𐤁𐤅.𐤅𐤋𐤀.𐤉𐤇𐤋𐤋.𐤀𐤕.𐤌𐤒𐤃𐤔𐤉.𐤊𐤉.𐤀𐤍𐤉.
𐤉𐤄𐤅𐤄.𐤌𐤒𐤃𐤔𐤌|

24 𐤅𐤉𐤃𐤁𐤓.𐤌𐤔𐤄.𐤀𐤋.𐤀𐤄𐤓𐤍.𐤅𐤀𐤋.𐤁𐤍𐤉𐤅.𐤅𐤀𐤋.𐤊𐤋.𐤁
𐤍𐤉.𐤉𐤔𐤓𐤀𐤋||

22 𐤋𐤋𐤅𐤉𐤌.𐤇𐤋𐤒

1 𐤅𐤉𐤃𐤁𐤓.𐤉𐤄𐤅𐤄.𐤀𐤋.𐤌𐤔𐤄.𐤋𐤀𐤌𐤓|

2 𐤃𐤁𐤓.𐤀𐤋.𐤀𐤄𐤓𐤍.𐤅𐤀𐤋.𐤁𐤍𐤉𐤅.𐤅𐤉𐤍𐤆𐤓𐤅.𐤌𐤒𐤃𐤔𐤉.𐤁
𐤍𐤉.𐤉𐤔𐤓𐤀𐤋.𐤅𐤋𐤀.𐤉𐤇𐤋𐤋𐤅.𐤀𐤕.𐤔𐤌.𐤒𐤃𐤔𐤉.𐤀𐤔𐤓.𐤄𐤌.
𐤌𐤒𐤃𐤔𐤉𐤌.𐤋𐤉.𐤀𐤍𐤉.𐤉𐤄𐤅𐤄|

3 𐤀𐤌𐤓.𐤀𐤋𐤄𐤌.𐤋𐤃𐤓𐤕𐤉𐤊𐤌.𐤊𐤋.𐤀𐤉𐤔.𐤀𐤔𐤓.𐤉𐤒𐤓𐤁.
𐤌𐤊𐤋.𐤆𐤓𐤏𐤊𐤌.𐤀𐤋.𐤄𐤒𐤃𐤔𐤉𐤌.𐤀𐤔𐤓.𐤉𐤒𐤃𐤉𐤔𐤅.𐤁𐤍𐤉
.𐤉𐤔𐤓𐤀𐤋.𐤋𐤉𐤄𐤅𐤄.𐤅𐤈𐤌𐤀𐤕𐤅.𐤏𐤋𐤉𐤅.𐤅𐤍𐤊𐤓𐤕𐤄.𐤄𐤍𐤐𐤔.𐤄
𐤄𐤅𐤀.𐤌𐤋𐤐𐤍𐤉.𐤀𐤍𐤉.𐤉𐤄𐤅𐤄|

4 𐤀𐤉𐤔.𐤀𐤉𐤔.𐤌𐤆𐤓𐤏.𐤀𐤄𐤓𐤍.𐤅𐤄𐤅𐤀.𐤑𐤓𐤅𐤏.𐤀𐤅.𐤆𐤁.
𐤁𐤒𐤃𐤔𐤉𐤌.𐤋𐤀.𐤉𐤀𐤊𐤋.𐤏𐤃.𐤀𐤔𐤓.𐤉𐤈𐤄𐤓.𐤅𐤄𐤍𐤂𐤏.𐤁
𐤊𐤋.𐤈𐤌𐤀.𐤍𐤐𐤔.𐤀𐤅.𐤀𐤉𐤔.𐤀𐤔𐤓.𐤕𐤑𐤀.𐤌𐤌𐤍𐤅.𐤔𐤊𐤁𐤕.
𐤆𐤓𐤏|

5 𐤀𐤅.𐤀𐤉𐤔.𐤀𐤔𐤓.𐤉𐤂𐤏.𐤁𐤊𐤋.𐤔𐤓𐤑.𐤀𐤔𐤓.𐤉𐤈𐤌𐤀.𐤋𐤅
.𐤀𐤅.𐤁𐤀𐤃𐤌.𐤀𐤔𐤓.𐤉𐤈𐤌𐤀.𐤋𐤅.𐤋𐤊𐤋.𐤈𐤌𐤀𐤕𐤅|

6 𐤍𐤐𐤔.𐤀𐤔𐤓.𐤕𐤂𐤏.𐤁𐤅.𐤅𐤈𐤌𐤀𐤄.𐤏𐤃.𐤄𐤏𐤓𐤁.𐤅𐤋𐤀.𐤉
𐤀𐤊𐤋.𐤌𐤍.𐤄𐤒𐤃𐤔𐤉𐤌.𐤊𐤉.𐤀𐤌.𐤓𐤇𐤑.𐤁𐤔𐤓𐤅.𐤁𐤌𐤉𐤌|

7 𐤅𐤁𐤀.𐤄𐤔𐤌𐤔.𐤅𐤈𐤄𐤓.𐤅𐤀𐤇𐤓.𐤉𐤀𐤊𐤋.𐤌𐤍.𐤄𐤒𐤃𐤔𐤉
𐤌.𐤊𐤉.𐤋𐤇𐤌𐤅.𐤄𐤅𐤀|

8 𐤍𐤁𐤋𐤄.𐤅𐤈𐤓𐤐𐤄.𐤋𐤀.𐤉𐤀𐤊𐤋.𐤋𐤈𐤌𐤀𐤄.𐤁𐤄.𐤀𐤍𐤉.𐤉𐤄𐤅
𐤄|

9 𐤅𐤔𐤌𐤓𐤅.𐤀𐤕.𐤌𐤔𐤌𐤓𐤕𐤉.𐤅𐤋𐤀.𐤉𐤔𐤀𐤅.𐤏𐤋𐤉𐤅.𐤇𐤈𐤀.
𐤅𐤌𐤕𐤅.𐤁𐤅.𐤊𐤉.𐤉𐤇𐤋𐤋𐤄𐤅.𐤀𐤍𐤉.𐤉𐤄𐤅𐤄.𐤌𐤒𐤃𐤔𐤌|
10 𐤅𐤊𐤋.𐤆𐤓.𐤋𐤀.𐤉𐤀𐤊𐤋.𐤒𐤃𐤔.𐤕𐤅𐤔𐤁.𐤊𐤄𐤍.𐤅𐤔𐤊𐤉𐤓.
𐤋𐤀.𐤉𐤀𐤊𐤋.𐤒𐤃𐤔|
11 𐤅𐤊𐤄𐤍.𐤊𐤉.𐤉𐤒𐤍𐤄.𐤍𐤐𐤔.𐤒𐤍𐤉𐤍.𐤊𐤎𐤐𐤅.𐤄𐤅𐤀.𐤉𐤀𐤊𐤋.
𐤁𐤅.𐤅𐤄𐤉𐤋𐤉𐤃.𐤁𐤉𐤕𐤅.𐤄𐤌.𐤉𐤀𐤊𐤋𐤅.𐤁𐤋𐤇𐤌𐤅|
12 𐤅𐤁𐤕.𐤊𐤄𐤍.𐤊𐤉.𐤕𐤄𐤉𐤄.𐤋𐤀𐤉𐤔.𐤆𐤓.𐤄𐤅𐤀.𐤁𐤕𐤓𐤅𐤌
𐤕.𐤄𐤒𐤃𐤔𐤉𐤌.𐤋𐤀.𐤕𐤀𐤊𐤋|
13 𐤅𐤁𐤕.𐤊𐤄𐤍.𐤊𐤉.𐤕𐤄𐤉𐤄.𐤀𐤋𐤌𐤍𐤄.𐤅𐤂𐤓𐤅𐤔𐤄.𐤅𐤆𐤓𐤏
.𐤀𐤉𐤍.𐤋𐤄.𐤅𐤔𐤁𐤄.𐤀𐤋.𐤁𐤉𐤕.𐤀𐤁𐤉𐤄.𐤊𐤍𐤏𐤅𐤓𐤉𐤄.𐤌𐤋𐤇𐤌.
𐤀𐤁𐤉𐤄.𐤕𐤀𐤊𐤋.𐤅𐤊𐤋.𐤆𐤓.𐤋𐤀.𐤉𐤀𐤊𐤋.𐤁𐤅|
14 𐤅𐤀𐤉𐤔.𐤊𐤉.𐤉𐤀𐤊𐤋.𐤒𐤃𐤔.𐤁𐤔𐤂𐤂𐤄.𐤅𐤉𐤎𐤐.𐤇𐤌
𐤔𐤉𐤕𐤅.𐤏𐤋𐤉𐤅.𐤅𐤍𐤕𐤍.𐤋𐤊𐤄𐤍.𐤀𐤕.𐤄𐤒𐤃𐤔|
15 𐤅𐤋𐤀.𐤉𐤇𐤋𐤋𐤅.𐤀𐤕.𐤒𐤃𐤔𐤉.𐤁𐤍𐤉.𐤉𐤔𐤓𐤀𐤋.𐤀𐤕.𐤀𐤔
𐤓.𐤉𐤓𐤉𐤌𐤅.𐤋𐤉𐤄𐤅𐤄|
16 𐤅𐤄𐤔𐤉𐤀𐤅.𐤀𐤅𐤕𐤌.𐤏𐤅𐤍.𐤀𐤔𐤌𐤄.𐤁𐤀𐤊𐤋𐤌.𐤀𐤕.𐤒𐤃
𐤔𐤉𐤄𐤌.𐤊𐤉.𐤀𐤍𐤉.𐤉𐤄𐤅𐤄.𐤌𐤒𐤃𐤔𐤌|
17 𐤅𐤉𐤃𐤁𐤓.𐤉𐤄𐤅𐤄.𐤀𐤋.𐤌𐤔𐤄.𐤋𐤀𐤌𐤓|
18 𐤃𐤁𐤓.𐤀𐤋.𐤀𐤄𐤓𐤍.𐤅𐤀𐤋.𐤁𐤍𐤉𐤅.𐤅𐤀𐤋.𐤊𐤋.𐤁𐤍𐤉.𐤉𐤔𐤓𐤀
𐤋.𐤅𐤀𐤌𐤓𐤕.𐤀𐤋𐤄𐤌.𐤀𐤉𐤔.𐤀𐤉𐤔.𐤌𐤁𐤉𐤕.𐤉𐤔𐤓𐤀𐤋.𐤅𐤌𐤍.𐤄
𐤂𐤓.𐤁𐤉𐤔𐤓𐤀𐤋.𐤀𐤔𐤓.𐤉𐤒𐤓𐤉𐤁.𐤒𐤓𐤁𐤍𐤅.𐤋𐤊𐤋.𐤍𐤃𐤓𐤉𐤄𐤌.
𐤅𐤋𐤊𐤋.𐤍𐤃𐤁𐤅𐤕𐤌.𐤀𐤔𐤓.𐤉𐤒𐤓𐤉𐤁𐤅.𐤋𐤉𐤄𐤅𐤄.𐤋𐤏𐤋𐤄|
19 𐤋𐤓𐤑𐤍𐤊𐤌.𐤕𐤌𐤉𐤌.𐤆𐤊𐤓.𐤁𐤁𐤒𐤓.𐤁𐤊𐤔𐤁𐤉𐤌.𐤅𐤁𐤏
𐤆𐤉𐤌|
20 𐤊𐤋.𐤀𐤔𐤓.𐤁𐤅.𐤌𐤅𐤌.𐤋𐤀.𐤕𐤒𐤓𐤉𐤁𐤅.𐤊𐤉.𐤋𐤀.𐤋𐤓𐤑𐤅𐤍.
𐤉𐤄𐤉𐤄.𐤋𐤊𐤌|
21 𐤅𐤀𐤉𐤔.𐤊𐤉.𐤉𐤒𐤓𐤉𐤁.𐤆𐤁𐤇.𐤔𐤋𐤌𐤉𐤌.𐤋𐤉𐤄𐤅𐤄.𐤋𐤐
𐤋𐤀.𐤍𐤃𐤓.𐤀𐤅.𐤋𐤍𐤃𐤁𐤄.𐤁𐤁𐤒𐤓.𐤀𐤅.𐤁𐤑𐤀𐤍.𐤕𐤌𐤉𐤌.𐤉𐤄𐤉
𐤄.𐤋𐤓𐤑𐤅𐤍.𐤊𐤋.𐤌𐤅𐤌.𐤋𐤀.𐤉𐤄𐤉𐤄.𐤁𐤅|

22 ࠏࠅࠓࠕ.ࠀࠅ.ࠔࠁࠅࠓ.ࠀࠅ.ࠇࠓࠅࠑ.ࠀࠅ.ࠉࠁࠋࠕ.ࠀࠅ.ࠂࠓࠁ.
ࠀࠅ.ࠉࠋࠐࠕ.ࠋࠀ.ࠕࠒࠓࠉࠁࠅ.ࠀࠋࠄ.ࠋࠉࠄࠅࠄ.ࠅࠀࠔࠄ.ࠋࠀ.ࠕ
ࠕࠍࠅ.ࠌࠄࠌ.ࠏࠋ.ࠄࠌࠆࠁࠇ.ࠋࠉࠄࠅࠄ|

23 ࠅࠔࠅࠓ.ࠅࠔࠄ.ࠔࠓࠅࠏ.ࠅࠒࠋࠅࠈ.ࠍࠃࠁࠄ.ࠕࠏࠔࠄ.ࠀࠕࠅ.
ࠅࠋࠍࠃࠓ.ࠋࠀ.ࠉࠓࠑࠄ|

24 ࠅࠌࠏࠅࠊ.ࠅࠊࠕࠅࠕ.ࠅࠍࠕࠅࠒ.ࠅࠊࠓࠅࠕ.ࠋࠀ.ࠕࠒࠓࠉࠁࠅ.ࠋ
ࠉࠄࠅࠄ.ࠅࠁࠀࠓࠑࠊࠌ.ࠋࠀ.ࠕࠏࠔࠅ|

25 ࠅࠌࠉࠃ.ࠁࠍ.ࠍࠊࠓ.ࠋࠀ.ࠕࠒࠓࠉࠁࠅ.ࠀࠕ.ࠋࠇࠌ.ࠀࠋࠄࠉ
ࠊࠌ.ࠌࠊࠋ.ࠀࠋࠄ.ࠊࠉ.ࠌࠔࠇࠕࠌ.ࠁࠄࠌ.ࠌࠅࠌ.ࠁࠌ.ࠋࠀ.ࠉࠓ
ࠑࠅ.ࠋࠊࠌ|

26 ࠅࠉࠃࠁࠓ.ࠉࠄࠅࠄ.ࠀࠋ.ࠌࠔࠄ.ࠋࠀࠌࠓ|

27 ࠔࠅࠓ.ࠀࠅ.ࠊࠔࠁ.ࠀࠅ.ࠏࠆ.ࠊࠉ.ࠉࠅࠋࠃ.ࠅࠄࠉࠄ.ࠔࠁࠏ
ࠕ.ࠉࠌࠉࠌ.ࠕࠇࠕ.ࠀࠌࠅ.ࠅࠌࠉࠅࠌ.ࠄࠔࠌࠉࠍࠉ.ࠅࠄࠋࠀࠄ.ࠉࠓ
ࠑࠄ.ࠋࠒࠓࠁࠍ.ࠀࠔࠄ.ࠋࠉࠄࠅࠄ|

28 ࠅࠔࠅࠓ.ࠀࠅ.ࠔࠄ.ࠀࠕࠅ.ࠅࠀࠕ.ࠁࠍࠅ.ࠋࠀ.ࠕࠔࠇࠈࠅ.ࠁࠉࠅ
ࠌ.ࠀࠇࠃ|

29 ࠅࠊࠉ.ࠕࠆࠁࠇࠅ.ࠆࠁࠇ.ࠕࠅࠃࠄ.ࠋࠉࠄࠅࠄ.ࠋࠓࠑࠍࠊ
ࠌ.ࠕࠆࠁࠇࠅ|

30 ࠁࠉࠅࠌ.ࠄࠄࠅࠀ.ࠉࠀࠊࠋ.ࠋࠀ.ࠕࠅࠕࠉࠓࠅ.ࠌࠌࠍࠅ.ࠏࠃ.ࠁ
ࠒࠓ.ࠀࠍࠉ.ࠉࠄࠅࠄ|

31 ࠅࠔࠌࠓࠕࠌ.ࠌࠑࠅࠕࠉ.ࠅࠏࠔࠉࠕࠌ.ࠀࠕࠌ.ࠀࠍࠉ.ࠉࠄࠅࠄ
|

32 ࠅࠋࠀ.ࠕࠇࠋࠋࠅ.ࠀࠕ.ࠔࠌ.ࠒࠃࠔࠉ.ࠅࠍࠒࠃࠔࠕࠉ.ࠁࠕ
ࠅࠊ.ࠁࠍࠉ.ࠉࠔࠓࠀࠋ.ࠀࠍࠉ.ࠉࠄࠅࠄ.ࠌࠒࠃࠔࠊࠌ|

33 ࠄࠌࠅࠑࠉࠀ.ࠀࠕࠊࠌ.ࠌࠀࠓࠑ.ࠌࠑࠓࠉࠌ.ࠋࠄࠉࠅࠕ.ࠋ
ࠊࠌ.ࠋࠀࠋࠄࠉࠌ.ࠀࠍࠉ.ࠉࠄࠅࠄ‖

23 ࠋࠋࠅࠉࠌ.ࠇࠋࠒ

1 ࠅࠉࠃࠁࠓ.ࠉࠄࠅࠄ.ࠀࠋ.ࠌࠔࠄ.ࠋࠀࠌࠓ|

2 𐤃𐤁𐤓.𐤀𐤋.𐤁𐤍𐤉.𐤉𐤔𐤓𐤀𐤋.𐤅𐤀𐤌𐤓𐤕.𐤀𐤋𐤄𐤌.𐤌𐤅𐤏𐤃𐤉.
𐤉𐤄𐤅𐤄.𐤀𐤔𐤓.𐤕𐤒𐤓𐤀𐤅.𐤀𐤕𐤌.𐤌𐤒𐤓𐤀𐤉.𐤒𐤃𐤔.𐤀𐤋𐤄.𐤄
𐤌.𐤌𐤅𐤏𐤃𐤉|
3 𐤔𐤔𐤕.𐤉𐤌𐤉𐤌.𐤕𐤏𐤔𐤄.𐤌𐤋𐤀𐤊𐤄.𐤅𐤁𐤉𐤅𐤌.𐤄𐤔𐤁𐤉𐤏
𐤉.𐤔𐤁𐤕.𐤔𐤁𐤕𐤅𐤍.𐤌𐤒𐤓𐤀.𐤒𐤃𐤔.𐤊𐤋.𐤌𐤋𐤀𐤊𐤄.𐤋𐤀.𐤕𐤏
𐤔𐤅.𐤔𐤁𐤕.𐤄𐤅𐤀.𐤋𐤉𐤄𐤅𐤄.𐤁𐤊𐤋.𐤌𐤅𐤔𐤁𐤕𐤉𐤊𐤌|
4 𐤀𐤋𐤄.𐤌𐤅𐤏𐤃𐤉.𐤉𐤄𐤅𐤄.𐤌𐤒𐤓𐤀𐤉.𐤒𐤃𐤔.𐤀𐤔𐤓.𐤕𐤒
𐤓𐤀𐤅.𐤀𐤕𐤌.𐤁𐤌𐤅𐤏𐤃𐤌|
5 𐤁𐤇𐤃𐤔.𐤄𐤓𐤀𐤔𐤅𐤍.𐤁𐤀𐤓𐤁𐤏𐤄.𐤏𐤔𐤓.𐤋𐤇𐤃𐤔.𐤁𐤉𐤍.
𐤄𐤏𐤓𐤁𐤉𐤌.𐤐𐤎𐤇.𐤋𐤉𐤄𐤅𐤄|
6 𐤅𐤁𐤇𐤌𐤔𐤄.𐤏𐤔𐤓.𐤉𐤅𐤌.𐤋𐤇𐤃𐤔.𐤄𐤆𐤄.𐤇𐤂.𐤄𐤌𐤑𐤅
𐤕.𐤋𐤉𐤄𐤅𐤄.𐤔𐤁𐤏𐤕.𐤉𐤌𐤉𐤌.𐤌𐤑𐤅𐤕.𐤕𐤀𐤊𐤋𐤅|
7 𐤁𐤉𐤅𐤌.𐤄𐤓𐤀𐤔𐤅𐤍.𐤌𐤒𐤓𐤀.𐤒𐤃𐤔.𐤉𐤄𐤉𐤄.𐤋𐤊𐤌.𐤊𐤋.
𐤌𐤋𐤀𐤊𐤕.𐤏𐤁𐤃𐤄.𐤋𐤀.𐤕𐤏𐤔𐤅|
8 𐤅𐤄𐤒𐤓𐤁𐤕𐤌.𐤀𐤔𐤄.𐤋𐤉𐤄𐤅𐤄.𐤔𐤁𐤏𐤕.𐤉𐤌𐤉𐤌.𐤁𐤉𐤅𐤌.
𐤄𐤔𐤁𐤉𐤏𐤉.𐤌𐤒𐤓𐤀.𐤒𐤃𐤔.𐤊𐤋.𐤌𐤋𐤀𐤊𐤕.𐤏𐤁𐤃𐤄.𐤋𐤀.𐤕
𐤏𐤔𐤅|
9 𐤅𐤉𐤃𐤁𐤓.𐤉𐤄𐤅𐤄.𐤀𐤋.𐤌𐤔𐤄.𐤋𐤀𐤌𐤓|
10 𐤃𐤁𐤓.𐤀𐤋.𐤁𐤍𐤉.𐤉𐤔𐤓𐤀𐤋.𐤅𐤀𐤌𐤓𐤕.𐤀𐤋𐤄𐤌.𐤊𐤉.𐤕𐤁
𐤀𐤅.𐤀𐤋.𐤄𐤀𐤓𐤑.𐤀𐤔𐤓.𐤀𐤍𐤉.𐤍𐤕𐤍.𐤋𐤊𐤌.𐤅𐤒𐤑𐤓𐤕𐤌.𐤀𐤕.
𐤒𐤑𐤉𐤓𐤄.𐤅𐤄𐤁𐤀𐤕𐤌.𐤀𐤕.𐤏𐤌𐤓.𐤓𐤀𐤔𐤉𐤕.𐤒𐤑𐤉𐤓𐤊𐤌.𐤀
𐤋.𐤄𐤊𐤄𐤍|
11 𐤅𐤄𐤍𐤉𐤐.𐤀𐤕.𐤄𐤏𐤌𐤓.𐤋𐤐𐤍𐤉.𐤉𐤄𐤅𐤄.𐤋𐤓𐤑𐤍𐤊𐤌.𐤌𐤌
𐤇𐤓𐤕.𐤄𐤔𐤁𐤕.𐤉𐤍𐤉𐤐𐤍𐤅.𐤄𐤊𐤄𐤍|
12 𐤅𐤏𐤔𐤉𐤕𐤌.𐤁𐤉𐤅𐤌.𐤄𐤍𐤉𐤐𐤊𐤌.𐤀𐤕.𐤄𐤏𐤌𐤓.𐤊𐤁𐤔.𐤕
𐤌𐤉𐤌.𐤁𐤍.𐤔𐤍𐤕𐤅.𐤋𐤏𐤋𐤄.𐤋𐤉𐤄𐤅𐤄|
13 𐤅𐤌𐤍𐤇𐤕𐤅.𐤔𐤍𐤉.𐤏𐤔𐤓𐤍𐤉𐤌.𐤎𐤋𐤕.𐤁𐤋𐤅𐤋𐤄.𐤁𐤔𐤌𐤍.
𐤀𐤔𐤄.𐤋𐤉𐤄𐤅𐤄.𐤓𐤉𐤇.𐤍𐤉𐤇𐤇.𐤅𐤍𐤎𐤊𐤄.𐤉𐤉𐤍.𐤓𐤁𐤉𐤏𐤕.𐤄
𐤄𐤉𐤍|

..יד.. 𐤅𐤋𐤇𐤌.𐤅𐤒𐤋𐤉.𐤅𐤊𐤓𐤌𐤋.𐤋𐤀.𐤕𐤀𐤊𐤋𐤅.𐤏𐤃.𐤏𐤑𐤌.𐤄
𐤉𐤅𐤌.𐤄𐤆𐤄.𐤏𐤃.𐤄𐤁𐤉𐤀𐤊𐤌.𐤀𐤕.𐤒𐤓𐤁𐤍.𐤀𐤋𐤄𐤉𐤊𐤌.𐤇
𐤒𐤕.𐤏𐤅𐤋𐤌.𐤋𐤃𐤓𐤕𐤉𐤊𐤌.𐤁𐤊𐤋.𐤌𐤔𐤁𐤕𐤉𐤊𐤌|

..טו.. 𐤅𐤎𐤐𐤓𐤕𐤌.𐤋𐤊𐤌.𐤌𐤌𐤇𐤓𐤕.𐤄𐤔𐤁𐤕.𐤌𐤉𐤅𐤌.𐤄𐤁𐤉𐤀𐤊
𐤌.𐤀𐤕.𐤏𐤌𐤓.𐤄𐤕𐤍𐤅𐤐𐤄.𐤔𐤁𐤏.𐤔𐤁𐤕𐤅𐤕.𐤕𐤌𐤉𐤌𐤕.𐤕𐤄𐤉
𐤉𐤍𐤄|

..טז.. 𐤏𐤃.𐤌𐤌𐤇𐤓𐤕.𐤄𐤔𐤁𐤕.𐤄𐤔𐤁𐤉𐤏𐤕.𐤕𐤎𐤐𐤓𐤅.𐤇𐤌𐤔
𐤉𐤌.𐤉𐤅𐤌.𐤅𐤄𐤒𐤓𐤁𐤕𐤌.𐤌𐤍𐤇𐤄.𐤇𐤃𐤔𐤄.𐤋𐤉𐤄𐤅𐤄|

..יז.. 𐤌𐤌𐤅𐤔𐤁𐤕𐤉𐤊𐤌.𐤕𐤁𐤉𐤀𐤅.𐤋𐤇𐤌.𐤕𐤍𐤅𐤐𐤄.𐤔𐤕𐤉𐤌.
𐤔𐤍𐤉.𐤏𐤔𐤓𐤍𐤉𐤌.𐤎𐤋𐤕.𐤕𐤄𐤉𐤉𐤍𐤄.𐤇𐤌𐤑.𐤕𐤀𐤐𐤉𐤍𐤄.𐤁𐤊
𐤅𐤓𐤉𐤌.𐤋𐤉𐤄𐤅𐤄|

..יח.. 𐤅𐤄𐤒𐤓𐤁𐤕𐤌.𐤏𐤋.𐤄𐤋𐤇𐤌.𐤔𐤁𐤏𐤕.𐤊𐤁𐤔𐤉𐤌.𐤕𐤌𐤉
𐤌𐤌.𐤁𐤍𐤉.𐤔𐤍𐤄.𐤅𐤐𐤓.𐤁𐤍.𐤁𐤒𐤓.𐤀𐤇𐤃.𐤅𐤀𐤉𐤋𐤌.𐤔𐤍𐤉𐤌.𐤉
𐤄𐤉𐤅.𐤏𐤋𐤄.𐤋𐤉𐤄𐤅𐤄.𐤅𐤌𐤍𐤇𐤕𐤌.𐤅𐤍𐤎𐤊𐤉𐤄𐤌.𐤀𐤔𐤄.𐤓𐤉𐤇.
𐤍𐤉𐤇𐤇.𐤋𐤉𐤄𐤅𐤄|

..יט.. 𐤅𐤏𐤔𐤉𐤕𐤌.𐤔𐤏𐤉𐤓.𐤏𐤆𐤉𐤌.𐤀𐤇𐤃.𐤋𐤇𐤈𐤀𐤕.𐤅𐤔
𐤍𐤉.𐤊𐤁𐤔𐤉𐤌.𐤁𐤍𐤉.𐤔𐤍𐤄.𐤋𐤆𐤁𐤇.𐤔𐤋𐤌𐤉𐤌|

..כ.. 𐤅𐤄𐤍𐤉𐤐.𐤄𐤊𐤄𐤍.𐤀𐤕𐤌.𐤏𐤋.𐤋𐤇𐤌.𐤄𐤁𐤊𐤅𐤓𐤉𐤌.𐤕𐤍𐤅
𐤐𐤄.𐤋𐤐𐤍𐤉.𐤉𐤄𐤅𐤄.𐤏𐤋.𐤔𐤍𐤉.𐤊𐤁𐤔𐤉𐤌.𐤒𐤃𐤔.𐤉𐤄𐤉𐤅.𐤋𐤉
𐤄𐤅𐤄.𐤋𐤊𐤄𐤍|

..כא.. 𐤅𐤒𐤓𐤀𐤕𐤌.𐤁𐤏𐤑𐤌.𐤄𐤉𐤅𐤌.𐤄𐤆𐤄.𐤌𐤒𐤓𐤀.𐤒𐤃𐤔.
𐤉𐤄𐤉𐤄.𐤋𐤊𐤌.𐤊𐤋.𐤌𐤋𐤀𐤊𐤕.𐤏𐤁𐤃𐤄.𐤋𐤀.𐤕𐤏𐤔𐤅.𐤇𐤒𐤕.
𐤏𐤅𐤋𐤌.𐤁𐤊𐤋.𐤌𐤅𐤔𐤁𐤕𐤉𐤊𐤌.𐤋𐤃𐤓𐤕𐤉𐤊𐤌|

..כב.. 𐤅𐤁𐤒𐤑𐤓𐤊𐤌.𐤀𐤕.𐤒𐤑𐤉𐤓.𐤀𐤓𐤑𐤊𐤌.𐤋𐤀.𐤕𐤊𐤋𐤄.𐤐
𐤀𐤕.𐤔𐤃𐤊.𐤁𐤒𐤑𐤓𐤊.𐤅𐤋𐤒𐤈.𐤒𐤑𐤉𐤓𐤊.𐤋𐤀.𐤕𐤋𐤒𐤈.𐤋𐤏
𐤍𐤉.𐤅𐤋𐤂𐤓.𐤕𐤏𐤆𐤁.𐤀𐤕𐤌.𐤀𐤍𐤉.𐤉𐤄𐤅𐤄.𐤀𐤋𐤄𐤉𐤊𐤌|

..כג.. 𐤅𐤉𐤃𐤁𐤓.𐤉𐤄𐤅𐤄.𐤀𐤋.𐤌𐤔𐤄.𐤋𐤀𐤌𐤓|

..כד.. 𐤃𐤁𐤓.𐤀𐤋.𐤁𐤍𐤉.𐤉𐤔𐤓𐤀𐤋.𐤋𐤀𐤌𐤓.𐤁𐤇𐤃𐤔.𐤄𐤔𐤁𐤉
𐤏𐤉.𐤁𐤀𐤇𐤃.𐤋𐤇𐤃𐤔.𐤉𐤄𐤉𐤄.𐤋𐤊𐤌.𐤔𐤁𐤕𐤅𐤍.𐤆𐤊𐤓𐤅𐤍.𐤕
𐤓𐤅𐤏𐤄.𐤌𐤒𐤓𐤀.𐤒𐤃𐤔|

כה 𐤊𐤋.𐤌𐤋𐤀𐤊𐤕.𐤏𐤁𐤃𐤄.𐤋𐤀.𐤕𐤏𐤔𐤅.𐤅𐤄𐤒𐤓𐤁𐤕𐤌.𐤀
𐤔𐤄.𐤋𐤉𐤄𐤅𐤄|
כו 𐤅𐤉𐤃𐤁𐤓.𐤉𐤄𐤅𐤄.𐤀𐤋.𐤌𐤔𐤄.𐤋𐤀𐤌𐤓|
כז 𐤀𐤊.𐤁𐤏𐤔𐤅𐤓.𐤋𐤇𐤃𐤔.𐤄𐤔𐤁𐤉𐤏𐤉.𐤄𐤆𐤄.𐤉𐤅𐤌.𐤄
𐤊𐤐𐤓𐤉𐤌.𐤄𐤅𐤀.𐤌𐤒𐤓𐤀.𐤒𐤃𐤔.𐤉𐤄𐤉𐤄.𐤋𐤊𐤌.𐤅𐤏𐤍𐤉𐤕𐤌.𐤀
𐤕.𐤍𐤐𐤔𐤕𐤉𐤊𐤌.𐤅𐤄𐤒𐤓𐤁𐤕𐤌.𐤀𐤔𐤄.𐤋𐤉𐤄𐤅𐤄|
כח 𐤅𐤊𐤋.𐤌𐤋𐤀𐤊𐤄.𐤋𐤀.𐤕𐤏𐤔𐤅.𐤁𐤏𐤑𐤌.𐤄𐤉𐤅𐤌.𐤄𐤆𐤄.
𐤊𐤉.𐤉𐤅𐤌.𐤊𐤐𐤓𐤉𐤌.𐤄𐤅𐤀.𐤋𐤊𐤐𐤓.𐤏𐤋𐤉𐤊𐤌.𐤋𐤐𐤍𐤉.𐤉𐤄𐤅𐤄.𐤀
𐤋𐤄𐤉𐤊𐤌|
כט 𐤊𐤉.𐤊𐤋.𐤄𐤍𐤐𐤔.𐤀𐤔𐤓.𐤋𐤀.𐤕𐤏𐤍𐤄.𐤁𐤏𐤑𐤌.𐤄𐤉𐤅𐤌.
𐤄𐤆𐤄.𐤅𐤍𐤊𐤓𐤕𐤄.𐤌𐤏𐤌𐤉𐤄|
ל 𐤅𐤊𐤋.𐤄𐤍𐤐𐤔.𐤀𐤔𐤓.𐤕𐤏𐤔𐤄.𐤊𐤋.𐤌𐤋𐤀𐤊𐤄.𐤁𐤏𐤑𐤌.
𐤄𐤉𐤅𐤌.𐤄𐤆𐤄.𐤅𐤄𐤀𐤁𐤃𐤕𐤉.𐤀𐤕.𐤄𐤍𐤐𐤔.𐤄𐤄𐤅𐤀.𐤌𐤒𐤓𐤁.
𐤏𐤌𐤄|
לא 𐤊𐤋.𐤌𐤋𐤀𐤊𐤄.𐤋𐤀.𐤕𐤏𐤔𐤅.𐤇𐤒𐤕.𐤏𐤅𐤋𐤌.𐤋𐤃𐤓𐤕𐤉
𐤊𐤌.𐤁𐤊𐤋.𐤌𐤔𐤁𐤕𐤉𐤊𐤌|
לב 𐤔𐤁𐤕.𐤔𐤁𐤕𐤅𐤍.𐤄𐤅𐤀.𐤋𐤊𐤌.𐤅𐤏𐤍𐤉𐤕𐤌.𐤀𐤕.𐤍𐤐𐤔𐤕𐤉
𐤊𐤌.𐤁𐤕𐤔𐤏𐤄.𐤋𐤇𐤃𐤔.𐤁𐤏𐤓𐤁.𐤌𐤏𐤓𐤁.𐤏𐤃.𐤏𐤓𐤁.𐤕𐤔𐤁
𐤕𐤅.𐤔𐤁𐤕𐤊𐤌|
לג 𐤅𐤉𐤃𐤁𐤓.𐤉𐤄𐤅𐤄.𐤀𐤋.𐤌𐤔𐤄.𐤋𐤀𐤌𐤓|
לד 𐤃𐤁𐤓.𐤀𐤋.𐤁𐤍𐤉.𐤉𐤔𐤓𐤀𐤋.𐤋𐤀𐤌𐤓.𐤁𐤇𐤌𐤔𐤄.𐤏𐤔𐤓.
𐤉𐤅𐤌.𐤋𐤇𐤃𐤔.𐤄𐤔𐤁𐤉𐤏𐤉.𐤄𐤆𐤄.𐤇𐤂.𐤄𐤎𐤊𐤅𐤕.𐤔𐤁𐤏𐤕
.𐤉𐤌𐤉𐤌.𐤋𐤉𐤄𐤅𐤄|
לה 𐤁𐤉𐤅𐤌.𐤄𐤓𐤀𐤔𐤅𐤍.𐤌𐤒𐤓𐤀.𐤒𐤃𐤔.𐤊𐤋.𐤌𐤋𐤀𐤊𐤕.𐤏𐤁
𐤃𐤄.𐤋𐤀.𐤕𐤏𐤔𐤅|
לו 𐤔𐤁𐤏𐤕.𐤉𐤌𐤉𐤌.𐤕𐤒𐤓𐤉𐤁𐤅.𐤀𐤔𐤄.𐤋𐤉𐤄𐤅𐤄.𐤁𐤉𐤅𐤌.
𐤄𐤔𐤌𐤉𐤍𐤉.𐤌𐤒𐤓𐤀.𐤒𐤃𐤔.𐤉𐤄𐤉𐤄.𐤋𐤊𐤌.𐤅𐤄𐤒𐤓𐤁𐤕𐤌.𐤀
𐤔𐤄.𐤋𐤉𐤄𐤅𐤄.𐤏𐤑𐤓𐤕.𐤄𐤅𐤀.𐤊𐤋.𐤌𐤋𐤀𐤊𐤕.𐤏𐤁𐤃𐤄.𐤋𐤀.
𐤕𐤏𐤔𐤅|

37 אלה מועדי יהוה אשר תקראו אתם מק
ראי קדש להקריב אשה ליהוה עלה ומנחה
זבח ונסכים דבר יום ביומו׃

38 מלבד שבתת יהוה ומלבד מתנותיכם ומ
לבד כל נדריכם ומלבד כל נדבותיכם אשר
תתנו ליהוה׃

39 אך בחמשה עשר יום לחדש השביעי ב
אספכם את תבואת הארץ תחגו את חג יהו
ה שבעת ימים ביום הראשון שבתון וביום ה
שמיני שבתון׃

40 ולקחתם לכם ביום הראשון פרי עץ הד
ר כפת תמרים וענף עץ עבת וערבי נחל ושמ
חתם לפני יהוה אלהיכם שבעת ימים׃

41 וחגתם אתו חג ליהוה שבעת ימים ב
שנה חקת עולם לדרתיכם בחדש השביעי
תחגו אתו׃

42 בסכת תשבו שבעת ימים כל האזרח ב
ישראל ישבו בסכת׃

43 למען ידעו דרתיכם כי בסכות הושבת
י את בני ישראל בהוציאי אותם מארץ מצר
ים אני יהוה אלהיכם׃

44 וידבר משה את מעדי יהוה אל בני י
שראל׃׃

ללוים חלק 24

1 וידבר יהוה אל משה לאמר׃

2 צו את בני ישראל ויקחו אליך שמן זית
זך כתית למאור להעלת נר תמיד׃

𐤂 𐤌𐤇𐤅𐤑.𐤋𐤐𐤓𐤊𐤕.𐤄𐤏𐤃𐤕.𐤁𐤀𐤄𐤋.𐤌𐤅𐤏𐤃.𐤉𐤏𐤓𐤊.𐤀
𐤕𐤅.𐤀𐤄𐤓𐤍.𐤌𐤏𐤓𐤁.𐤏𐤃.𐤁𐤒𐤓.𐤋𐤐𐤍𐤉.𐤉𐤄𐤅𐤄.𐤕𐤌𐤉𐤃.𐤇
𐤒𐤕.𐤏𐤅𐤋𐤌.𐤋𐤃𐤓𐤕𐤉𐤊𐤌|

𐤃 𐤏𐤋.𐤄𐤌𐤍𐤓𐤄.𐤄𐤈𐤄𐤓𐤄.𐤉𐤏𐤓𐤊.𐤀𐤕.𐤄𐤍𐤓𐤅𐤕.𐤋𐤐𐤍𐤉.
𐤉𐤄𐤅𐤄.𐤕𐤌𐤉𐤃|

𐤄 𐤅𐤋𐤒𐤇𐤕.𐤎𐤋𐤕.𐤅𐤀𐤐𐤉𐤕.𐤀𐤕𐤄.𐤔𐤕𐤉𐤌.𐤏𐤔𐤓𐤄.𐤇𐤋
𐤅𐤕.𐤔𐤍𐤉.𐤏𐤔𐤓𐤍𐤉𐤌.𐤉𐤄𐤉𐤄.𐤄𐤇𐤋𐤄.𐤄𐤀𐤇𐤕|

𐤅 𐤅𐤔𐤌𐤕.𐤀𐤅𐤕𐤌.𐤔𐤕𐤉𐤌.𐤌𐤏𐤓𐤊𐤅𐤕.𐤔𐤔.𐤄𐤌𐤏𐤓𐤊𐤕.
𐤏𐤋.𐤄𐤔𐤋𐤇𐤍.𐤄𐤈𐤄𐤓.𐤋𐤐𐤍𐤉.𐤉𐤄𐤅𐤄|

𐤆 𐤅𐤍𐤕𐤕.𐤏𐤋.𐤄𐤌𐤏𐤓𐤊𐤕.𐤋𐤁𐤍𐤄.𐤆𐤊𐤄.𐤅𐤄𐤉𐤕𐤄.𐤋𐤋𐤇
𐤌.𐤋𐤀𐤆𐤊𐤓𐤄.𐤀𐤔𐤄.𐤋𐤉𐤄𐤅𐤄|

𐤇 𐤁𐤉𐤅𐤌.𐤄𐤔𐤁𐤕.𐤁𐤉𐤅𐤌.𐤄𐤔𐤁𐤕.𐤉𐤏𐤓𐤊𐤍𐤅.𐤋𐤐𐤍𐤉.𐤉𐤄𐤅
𐤄.𐤕𐤌𐤉𐤃.𐤌𐤀𐤕.𐤁𐤍𐤉.𐤉𐤔𐤓𐤀𐤋.𐤁𐤓𐤉𐤕.𐤏𐤅𐤋𐤌|

𐤈 𐤅𐤄𐤉𐤕𐤄.𐤋𐤀𐤄𐤓𐤍.𐤅𐤋𐤁𐤍𐤉𐤅.𐤅𐤀𐤊𐤋𐤄𐤅.𐤁𐤌𐤒𐤅𐤌.𐤒𐤃
𐤔.𐤊𐤉.𐤒𐤃𐤔.𐤒𐤃𐤔𐤉𐤌.𐤄𐤅𐤀.𐤋𐤅.𐤌𐤀𐤔𐤉.𐤉𐤄𐤅𐤄.𐤇𐤒.
𐤏𐤅𐤋𐤌|

𐤉 𐤅𐤉𐤑𐤀.𐤁𐤍.𐤀𐤔𐤄.𐤉𐤔𐤓𐤀𐤋𐤉𐤕.𐤅𐤄𐤅𐤀.𐤁𐤍.𐤀𐤉𐤔.𐤌
𐤑𐤓𐤉.𐤁𐤕𐤅𐤊.𐤁𐤍𐤉.𐤉𐤔𐤓𐤀𐤋.𐤅𐤉𐤍𐤑𐤅.𐤁𐤌𐤇𐤍𐤄.𐤁𐤍.𐤄𐤉𐤔𐤓
𐤀𐤋𐤉𐤕.𐤅𐤀𐤉𐤔.𐤄𐤉𐤔𐤓𐤀𐤋𐤉|

𐤉𐤀 𐤅𐤉𐤒𐤁.𐤁𐤍.𐤄𐤀𐤔𐤄.𐤄𐤉𐤔𐤓𐤀𐤋𐤉𐤕.𐤀𐤕.𐤄𐤔𐤌.𐤅𐤉𐤒
𐤋𐤋.𐤅𐤉𐤁𐤉𐤀𐤅.𐤀𐤕𐤅.𐤀𐤋.𐤌𐤔𐤄.𐤅𐤔𐤌.𐤀𐤌𐤅.𐤔𐤋𐤌𐤉𐤕.𐤁𐤕.
𐤃𐤁𐤓𐤉.𐤋𐤌𐤈𐤄.𐤃𐤍|

𐤉𐤁 𐤅𐤉𐤍𐤉𐤇𐤄𐤅.𐤁𐤌𐤔𐤌𐤓.𐤋𐤐𐤓𐤔.𐤋𐤄𐤌.𐤏𐤋.𐤐𐤉.𐤉𐤄𐤅𐤄|

𐤉𐤂 𐤅𐤉𐤃𐤁𐤓.𐤉𐤄𐤅𐤄.𐤀𐤋.𐤌𐤔𐤄.𐤋𐤀𐤌𐤓|

𐤉𐤃 𐤄𐤅𐤑𐤀.𐤀𐤕.𐤄𐤌𐤒𐤋𐤋.𐤀𐤋.𐤌𐤇𐤅𐤑.𐤋𐤌𐤇𐤍𐤄.𐤅𐤎𐤌
𐤊𐤅.𐤊𐤋.𐤄𐤔𐤌𐤏𐤉𐤌.𐤀𐤕.𐤉𐤃𐤉𐤄𐤌.𐤏𐤋.𐤓𐤀𐤔𐤅.𐤅𐤓𐤂𐤌𐤅.𐤀
𐤕𐤅.𐤊𐤋.𐤄𐤏𐤃𐤄|

𐤉𐤄 𐤅𐤀𐤋.𐤁𐤍𐤉.𐤉𐤔𐤓𐤀𐤋.𐤕𐤃𐤁𐤓.𐤋𐤀𐤌𐤓.𐤀𐤉𐤔.𐤀𐤉𐤔.𐤊
𐤉.𐤉𐤒𐤋𐤋.𐤀𐤋𐤄𐤉𐤅.𐤅𐤍𐤔𐤀.𐤇𐤈𐤀𐤅|

𐤉𐤅 𐤅𐤍𐤒𐤁.𐤔𐤌.𐤉𐤄𐤅𐤄.𐤌𐤅𐤕.𐤉𐤅𐤌𐤕.𐤓𐤂𐤅𐤌.𐤉𐤓𐤂𐤌𐤅.𐤁𐤅.
𐤊𐤋.𐤄𐤏𐤃𐤄.𐤊𐤂𐤓.𐤊𐤀𐤆𐤓𐤇.𐤁𐤍𐤒𐤁𐤅.𐤔𐤌.𐤉𐤅𐤌𐤕|

..𐤉𐤆.. 𐤅𐤀𐤉𐤔.𐤊𐤉.𐤉𐤊𐤄.𐤊𐤋.𐤍𐤐𐤔.𐤀𐤃𐤌.𐤌𐤅𐤕.𐤉𐤅𐤌𐤕|
..𐤉𐤇.. 𐤅𐤌𐤊𐤄.𐤍𐤐𐤔.𐤁𐤄𐤌𐤄.𐤉𐤔𐤋𐤌𐤍𐤄.𐤍𐤐𐤔.𐤕𐤇𐤕.𐤍𐤐𐤔|
..𐤉𐤈.. 𐤅𐤀𐤉𐤔.𐤊𐤉.𐤉𐤕𐤍.𐤌𐤅𐤌.𐤁𐤏𐤌𐤉𐤕𐤅.𐤊𐤀𐤔𐤓.𐤏𐤔𐤄.
𐤊𐤍.𐤉𐤏𐤔𐤄.𐤋𐤅|
..𐤊.. 𐤔𐤁𐤓.𐤕𐤇𐤕.𐤔𐤁𐤓.𐤏𐤉𐤍.𐤕𐤇𐤕.𐤏𐤉𐤍.𐤔𐤍.𐤕𐤇𐤕.
𐤔𐤍.𐤊𐤀𐤔𐤓.𐤉𐤕𐤍.𐤌𐤅𐤌.𐤁𐤀𐤃𐤌.𐤊𐤍.𐤉𐤍𐤕𐤍.𐤁𐤅|
..𐤊𐤀.. 𐤅𐤌𐤊𐤄.𐤁𐤄𐤌𐤄.𐤉𐤔𐤋𐤌𐤍𐤄.𐤅𐤌𐤊𐤄.𐤀𐤃𐤌.𐤉𐤅𐤌𐤕|
..𐤊𐤁.. 𐤌𐤔𐤐𐤈.𐤀𐤇𐤃.𐤉𐤄𐤉𐤄.𐤋𐤊𐤌.𐤊𐤂𐤓.𐤊𐤀𐤆𐤓𐤇.𐤉𐤄
𐤉𐤄.𐤊𐤉.𐤀𐤍𐤉.𐤉𐤄𐤅𐤄.𐤀𐤋𐤄𐤉𐤊𐤌|
..𐤊𐤂.. 𐤅𐤉𐤃𐤁𐤓.𐤌𐤔𐤄.𐤀𐤋.𐤁𐤍𐤉.𐤉𐤔𐤓𐤀𐤋.𐤅𐤉𐤅𐤑𐤉𐤀𐤅.𐤀𐤕.
𐤄𐤌𐤒𐤋𐤋.𐤀𐤋.𐤌𐤇𐤅𐤑.𐤋𐤌𐤇𐤍𐤄.𐤅𐤉𐤓𐤂𐤌𐤅.𐤀𐤕𐤅.𐤀𐤁𐤍.𐤅𐤁
𐤍𐤉.𐤉𐤔𐤓𐤀𐤋.𐤏𐤔𐤅.𐤊𐤀𐤔𐤓.𐤑𐤅𐤄.𐤉𐤄𐤅𐤄.𐤀𐤕.𐤌𐤔𐤄||

𐤋𐤋𐤅𐤉𐤌.𐤇𐤋𐤒 ..𐤊𐤄..

..𐤀.. 𐤅𐤉𐤃𐤁𐤓.𐤉𐤄𐤅𐤄.𐤀𐤋.𐤌𐤔𐤄.𐤁𐤄𐤓.𐤎𐤉𐤍𐤉.𐤋𐤀𐤌𐤓|
..𐤁.. 𐤃𐤁𐤓.𐤀𐤋.𐤁𐤍𐤉.𐤉𐤔𐤓𐤀𐤋.𐤅𐤀𐤌𐤓𐤕.𐤀𐤋𐤄𐤌.𐤊𐤉.𐤕𐤁𐤀
𐤅.𐤀𐤋.𐤄𐤀𐤓𐤑.𐤀𐤔𐤓.𐤀𐤍𐤉.𐤍𐤕𐤍.𐤋𐤊𐤌.𐤅𐤔𐤁𐤕𐤄.𐤄𐤀𐤓𐤑.
𐤔𐤁𐤕.𐤋𐤉𐤄𐤅𐤄|
..𐤂.. 𐤔𐤔.𐤔𐤍𐤉𐤌.𐤕𐤆𐤓𐤏.𐤔𐤃𐤊.𐤅𐤔𐤔.𐤔𐤍𐤉𐤌.𐤕𐤆𐤌𐤓.𐤊
𐤓𐤌𐤊.𐤅𐤀𐤎𐤐𐤕.𐤀𐤕.𐤕𐤁𐤅𐤀𐤕𐤄|
..𐤃.. 𐤅𐤁𐤔𐤍𐤄.𐤄𐤔𐤁𐤉𐤏𐤕.𐤔𐤁𐤕.𐤔𐤁𐤕𐤅𐤍.𐤉𐤄𐤉𐤄.𐤋𐤀𐤓𐤑
.𐤔𐤁𐤕.𐤋𐤉𐤄𐤅𐤄.𐤔𐤃𐤊.𐤋𐤀.𐤕𐤆𐤓𐤏.𐤅𐤊𐤓𐤌𐤊.𐤋𐤀.𐤕𐤆𐤌𐤓
|
..𐤄.. 𐤀𐤕.𐤎𐤐𐤉𐤇.𐤒𐤑𐤉𐤓𐤊.𐤋𐤀.𐤕𐤒𐤑𐤅𐤓.𐤅𐤀𐤕.𐤏𐤍𐤁𐤉.𐤍
𐤆𐤉𐤓𐤊.𐤋𐤀.𐤕𐤁𐤑𐤓.𐤔𐤍𐤕.𐤔𐤁𐤕𐤅𐤍.𐤉𐤄𐤉𐤄.𐤋𐤀𐤓𐤑|
..𐤅.. 𐤅𐤄𐤉𐤕𐤄.𐤔𐤁𐤕.𐤄𐤀𐤓𐤑.𐤋𐤊𐤌.𐤋𐤀𐤊𐤋𐤄.𐤋𐤊.𐤅𐤋𐤏𐤁𐤃
𐤊.𐤅𐤋𐤀𐤌𐤕𐤊.𐤅𐤋𐤔𐤊𐤉𐤓𐤊.𐤅𐤋𐤕𐤅𐤔𐤁𐤊.𐤄𐤂𐤓𐤉𐤌.𐤏𐤌𐤊|
..𐤆.. 𐤅𐤋𐤁𐤄𐤌𐤕𐤊.𐤅𐤋𐤇𐤉𐤄.𐤀𐤔𐤓.𐤁𐤀𐤓𐤑𐤊.𐤕𐤄𐤉𐤄.𐤊𐤋.
𐤕𐤁𐤅𐤀𐤕𐤄.𐤋𐤀𐤊𐤋|

ח 𐤅𐤎𐤐𐤓𐤕.𐤋𐤊.𐤔𐤁𐤏.𐤔𐤁𐤕𐤕.𐤔𐤍𐤉𐤌.𐤔𐤁𐤏.𐤔𐤍𐤉𐤌.𐤔
𐤁𐤏.𐤐𐤏𐤌𐤉𐤌.𐤅𐤄𐤉𐤅.𐤋𐤊.𐤉𐤌𐤉.𐤔𐤁𐤏.𐤔𐤁𐤕𐤕.𐤄𐤔𐤍𐤉𐤌.
𐤕𐤔𐤏.𐤅𐤀𐤓𐤁𐤏𐤉𐤌.𐤔𐤍𐤄|
ט 𐤅𐤄𐤏𐤁𐤓𐤕.𐤔𐤅𐤐𐤓.𐤕𐤓𐤅𐤏𐤄.𐤁𐤇𐤃𐤔.𐤄𐤔𐤁𐤏𐤉.𐤁𐤏
𐤔𐤅𐤓.𐤋𐤇𐤃𐤔.𐤁𐤉𐤅𐤌.𐤄𐤊𐤐𐤓𐤉𐤌.𐤕𐤏𐤁𐤉𐤓𐤅.𐤔𐤅𐤐𐤓.𐤁𐤊𐤋.
𐤀𐤓𐤑𐤊𐤌|
י 𐤅𐤒𐤃𐤔𐤕𐤌.𐤀𐤕.𐤔𐤍𐤕.𐤄𐤇𐤌𐤔𐤉𐤌.𐤔𐤍𐤄.𐤅𐤒𐤓𐤀𐤕
𐤌.𐤃𐤓𐤅𐤓.𐤁𐤀𐤓𐤑.𐤋𐤊𐤋.𐤉𐤔𐤁𐤉𐤄.𐤉𐤅𐤁𐤋.𐤄𐤅𐤀.𐤕𐤄𐤉𐤄.𐤋
𐤊𐤌.𐤅𐤔𐤁𐤕𐤌.𐤀𐤉𐤔.𐤀𐤋.𐤀𐤇𐤆𐤕𐤅.𐤅𐤀𐤉𐤔.𐤀𐤋.𐤌𐤔𐤐𐤇𐤕
𐤅.𐤕𐤔𐤁𐤅|
יא 𐤉𐤅𐤁𐤋.𐤄𐤅𐤀.𐤔𐤍𐤕.𐤄𐤇𐤌𐤔𐤉𐤌.𐤔𐤍𐤄.𐤕𐤄𐤉𐤄.𐤋𐤊𐤌.
𐤋𐤀.𐤕𐤆𐤓𐤏𐤅.𐤅𐤋𐤀.𐤕𐤒𐤑𐤓𐤅.𐤀𐤕.𐤎𐤐𐤉𐤇𐤉𐤄.𐤅𐤋𐤀.𐤕𐤁𐤑
𐤓𐤅.𐤀𐤕.𐤍𐤆𐤓𐤉𐤄|
יב 𐤊𐤉.𐤉𐤅𐤁𐤋.𐤄𐤅𐤀.𐤒𐤃𐤔.𐤕𐤄𐤉𐤄.𐤋𐤊𐤌.𐤌𐤍.𐤄𐤔𐤃𐤄.
𐤕𐤀𐤊𐤋𐤅.𐤀𐤕.𐤕𐤁𐤅𐤀𐤕𐤄|
יג 𐤁𐤔𐤍𐤕.𐤄𐤉𐤅𐤁𐤋.𐤄𐤆𐤀𐤕.𐤕𐤔𐤁𐤅.𐤀𐤉𐤔.𐤀𐤋.𐤀𐤇𐤆
𐤕𐤅|
יד 𐤅𐤊𐤉.𐤕𐤌𐤊𐤓𐤅.𐤌𐤌𐤊𐤓.𐤋𐤏𐤌𐤉𐤕𐤊.𐤀𐤅.𐤒𐤍𐤄.𐤌𐤉𐤃.
𐤏𐤌𐤉𐤕𐤊.𐤀𐤋.𐤕𐤅𐤍𐤅.𐤀𐤉𐤔.𐤀𐤕.𐤀𐤇𐤉𐤅|
טו 𐤁𐤌𐤎𐤐𐤓.𐤔𐤍𐤉𐤌.𐤀𐤇𐤓.𐤄𐤉𐤅𐤁𐤋.𐤕𐤒𐤍𐤄.𐤌𐤀𐤕.𐤏𐤌
𐤉𐤕𐤊.𐤁𐤌𐤎𐤐𐤓.𐤔𐤍𐤉.𐤕𐤁𐤅𐤀𐤕.𐤉𐤌𐤊𐤓.𐤋𐤊|
טז 𐤋𐤐𐤉.𐤓𐤁.𐤄𐤔𐤍𐤉𐤌.𐤕𐤓𐤁𐤄.𐤌𐤒𐤍𐤕𐤅.𐤅𐤋𐤐𐤉.𐤌𐤏𐤈.𐤄
𐤔𐤍𐤉𐤌.𐤕𐤌𐤏𐤉𐤈.𐤌𐤒𐤍𐤕𐤅.𐤊𐤉.𐤌𐤎𐤐𐤓.𐤕𐤁𐤅𐤀𐤕.𐤄𐤅𐤀.𐤌
𐤊𐤓.𐤋𐤊|
יז 𐤅𐤋𐤀.𐤕𐤅𐤍𐤅.𐤀𐤉𐤔.𐤀𐤕.𐤏𐤌𐤉𐤕𐤅.𐤅𐤉𐤓𐤀𐤕.𐤌𐤀𐤋𐤄𐤉
𐤊.𐤊𐤉.𐤀𐤍𐤉.𐤉𐤄𐤅𐤄.𐤀𐤋𐤄𐤉𐤊𐤌|
יח 𐤅𐤏𐤔𐤉𐤕𐤌.𐤀𐤕.𐤇𐤒𐤕𐤉.𐤅𐤀𐤕.𐤌𐤔𐤐𐤈𐤉.𐤕𐤔𐤌𐤓𐤅.𐤅
𐤏𐤔𐤉𐤕𐤌.𐤀𐤕𐤌.𐤅𐤉𐤔𐤁𐤕𐤌.𐤏𐤋.𐤄𐤀𐤓𐤑.𐤋𐤁𐤈𐤇|
יט 𐤅𐤍𐤕𐤍𐤄.𐤄𐤀𐤓𐤑.𐤐𐤓𐤉𐤄.𐤅𐤀𐤊𐤋𐤕𐤌.𐤋𐤔𐤁𐤏.𐤅𐤉𐤔𐤁
𐤕𐤌.𐤋𐤁𐤈𐤇.𐤏𐤋𐤉𐤄|

20 𐤅𐤊𐤉.𐤕𐤀𐤌𐤓𐤅.𐤌𐤄.𐤍𐤀𐤊𐤋.𐤁𐤔𐤍𐤄.𐤄𐤔𐤁𐤉𐤏𐤕.𐤄𐤍.
𐤋𐤀.𐤍𐤆𐤓𐤏.𐤅𐤋𐤀.𐤍𐤀𐤎𐤐.𐤀𐤕.𐤕𐤁𐤅𐤀𐤕𐤍𐤅|
21 𐤅𐤑𐤅𐤉𐤕𐤉.𐤀𐤕.𐤁𐤓𐤊𐤕𐤉.𐤋𐤊𐤌.𐤁𐤔𐤍𐤄.𐤄𐤔𐤔𐤉𐤕.𐤅
𐤏𐤔𐤕.𐤀𐤕.𐤄𐤕𐤁𐤅𐤀𐤄.𐤋𐤔𐤋𐤔.𐤄𐤔𐤍𐤉𐤌|
22 𐤅𐤆𐤓𐤏𐤕𐤌.𐤀𐤕.𐤄𐤔𐤍𐤄.𐤄𐤔𐤌𐤉𐤍𐤕.𐤅𐤀𐤊𐤋𐤕𐤌.𐤌𐤍.
𐤄𐤕𐤁𐤅𐤀𐤄.𐤉𐤔𐤍.𐤏𐤃.𐤄𐤔𐤍𐤄.𐤄𐤕𐤔𐤉𐤏𐤕.𐤏𐤃.𐤁𐤅𐤀.𐤕
𐤁𐤅𐤀𐤕𐤄.𐤕𐤀𐤊𐤋𐤅.𐤉𐤔𐤍|
23 𐤅𐤄𐤀𐤓𐤑.𐤋𐤀.𐤕𐤌𐤊𐤓.𐤋𐤑𐤌𐤕𐤕.𐤊𐤉.𐤋𐤉.𐤄𐤀𐤓𐤑.𐤊
𐤉.𐤂𐤓𐤉𐤌.𐤅𐤕𐤅𐤔𐤁𐤉𐤌.𐤀𐤕𐤌.𐤏𐤌𐤃𐤉|
24 𐤅𐤁𐤊𐤋.𐤀𐤓𐤑.𐤀𐤇𐤆𐤕𐤊𐤌.𐤂𐤀𐤋𐤄.𐤕𐤕𐤍𐤅.𐤋𐤀𐤓𐤑|
25 𐤊𐤉.𐤉𐤌𐤅𐤊.𐤀𐤇𐤉𐤊.𐤅𐤌𐤊𐤓.𐤌𐤀𐤇𐤆𐤕𐤅.𐤅𐤁𐤀.𐤂𐤀𐤋
𐤅.𐤄𐤒𐤓𐤁.𐤀𐤋𐤉𐤅.𐤅𐤂𐤀𐤋.𐤀𐤕.𐤌𐤌𐤊𐤓.𐤀𐤇𐤉𐤅|
26 𐤅𐤀𐤉𐤔.𐤊𐤉.𐤋𐤀.𐤉𐤄𐤉𐤄.𐤋𐤅.𐤂𐤀𐤋.𐤅𐤄𐤔𐤉𐤂𐤄.𐤉𐤃𐤅
.𐤅𐤌𐤑𐤀.𐤊𐤃𐤉.𐤂𐤀𐤋𐤕𐤅|
27 𐤅𐤇𐤔𐤁.𐤀𐤕.𐤔𐤍𐤉.𐤌𐤌𐤊𐤓𐤅.𐤅𐤄𐤔𐤉𐤁.𐤀𐤕.𐤄𐤏𐤃𐤐.
𐤋𐤀𐤉𐤔.𐤀𐤔𐤓.𐤌𐤊𐤓.𐤋𐤅.𐤅𐤔𐤁.𐤋𐤀𐤇𐤆𐤕𐤅|
28 𐤅𐤀𐤌.𐤋𐤀.𐤌𐤑𐤀𐤄.𐤉𐤃𐤅.𐤃𐤉.𐤄𐤔𐤉𐤁.𐤋𐤅.𐤅𐤄𐤉𐤄.𐤌
𐤌𐤊𐤓𐤅.𐤁𐤉𐤃.𐤄𐤒𐤍𐤄.𐤀𐤕𐤅.𐤏𐤃.𐤔𐤍𐤕.𐤄𐤉𐤅𐤁𐤋.𐤅𐤉𐤑𐤀.𐤁
𐤉𐤁𐤋.𐤅𐤔𐤁.𐤋𐤀𐤇𐤆𐤕𐤅|
29 𐤅𐤀𐤉𐤔.𐤊𐤉.𐤉𐤌𐤊𐤓.𐤁𐤉𐤕.𐤌𐤅𐤔𐤁.𐤏𐤉𐤓.𐤇𐤅𐤌𐤄.𐤅𐤄
𐤉𐤕𐤄.𐤂𐤀𐤋𐤕𐤅.𐤏𐤃.𐤕𐤌.𐤔𐤍𐤕.𐤌𐤌𐤊𐤓𐤅.𐤉𐤌𐤉𐤌.𐤕𐤄𐤉𐤄.
𐤂𐤀𐤋𐤕𐤅|
30 𐤅𐤀𐤌.𐤋𐤀.𐤉𐤂𐤀𐤋.𐤏𐤃.𐤌𐤋𐤀𐤕.𐤋𐤅.𐤔𐤍𐤄.𐤕𐤌𐤉𐤌𐤄
.𐤅𐤒𐤌.𐤄𐤁𐤉𐤕.𐤀𐤔𐤓.𐤁𐤏𐤉𐤓.𐤀𐤔𐤓.𐤋𐤀.‖𐤋𐤅.𐤒𐤓𐤉‖.𐤇𐤌𐤄.
𐤋𐤑𐤌𐤉𐤕𐤕.𐤋𐤒𐤍𐤄.𐤀𐤕𐤅.𐤋𐤃𐤓𐤕𐤉𐤅.𐤋𐤀.𐤉𐤑𐤀.𐤁𐤉𐤁𐤋|
31 𐤅𐤁𐤕𐤉.𐤄𐤇𐤑𐤓𐤉𐤌.𐤀𐤔𐤓.𐤀𐤉𐤍.𐤋𐤄𐤌.𐤇𐤌𐤄.𐤎𐤁𐤉
𐤁.𐤏𐤋.𐤔𐤃𐤄.𐤄𐤀𐤓𐤑.𐤉𐤇𐤔𐤁.𐤂𐤀𐤋𐤄.𐤕𐤄𐤉𐤄.𐤋𐤅.𐤅𐤁𐤉
𐤁𐤋.𐤉𐤑𐤀|
32 𐤅𐤏𐤓𐤉.𐤄𐤋𐤅𐤉𐤌.𐤁𐤕𐤉.𐤏𐤓𐤉.𐤀𐤇𐤆𐤕𐤌.𐤂𐤀𐤋𐤕.𐤏
𐤅𐤋𐤌.𐤕𐤄𐤉𐤄.𐤋𐤋𐤅𐤉𐤌|

𐤋𐤂 𐤅𐤀𐤔𐤓.𐤉𐤂𐤀𐤋.𐤌𐤍.𐤄𐤋𐤅𐤉𐤌.𐤅𐤉𐤑𐤀.𐤌𐤌𐤊𐤓.𐤁𐤉𐤕.𐤅
𐤏𐤉𐤓.𐤀𐤇𐤆𐤕𐤅.𐤁𐤉𐤁𐤋.𐤊𐤉.𐤁𐤕𐤉.𐤏𐤓𐤉.𐤄𐤋𐤅𐤉𐤌.𐤄𐤅𐤀.𐤀
𐤇𐤆𐤕𐤌.𐤁𐤕𐤅𐤊.𐤁𐤍𐤉.𐤉𐤔𐤓𐤀𐤋|

𐤋𐤃 𐤅𐤔𐤃𐤄.𐤌𐤂𐤓𐤔.𐤏𐤓𐤉𐤄𐤌.𐤋𐤀.𐤉𐤌𐤊𐤓.𐤊𐤉.𐤀𐤇𐤆
𐤕.𐤏𐤅𐤋𐤌.𐤄𐤅𐤀.𐤋𐤄𐤌|

𐤋𐤄 𐤅𐤊𐤉.𐤉𐤌𐤅𐤊.𐤀𐤇𐤉𐤊.𐤅𐤌𐤈𐤄.𐤉𐤃𐤅.𐤏𐤌𐤊.𐤅𐤄𐤇𐤆𐤒
𐤕.𐤁𐤅.𐤂𐤓.𐤅𐤕𐤅𐤔𐤁.𐤅𐤇𐤉.𐤏𐤌𐤊|

𐤋𐤅 𐤀𐤋.𐤕𐤒𐤇.𐤌𐤀𐤕𐤅.𐤍𐤔𐤊.𐤅𐤕𐤓𐤁𐤉𐤕.𐤅𐤉𐤓𐤀𐤕.𐤌𐤀𐤋
𐤄𐤉𐤊.𐤅𐤇𐤉.𐤀𐤇𐤉𐤊.𐤏𐤌𐤊|

𐤋𐤆 𐤀𐤕.𐤊𐤎𐤐𐤊.𐤋𐤀.𐤕𐤕𐤍.𐤋𐤅.𐤁𐤍𐤔𐤊.𐤅𐤁𐤌𐤓𐤁𐤉𐤕.𐤋𐤀.
𐤕𐤕𐤍.𐤀𐤊𐤋𐤊|

𐤋𐤇 𐤀𐤍𐤉.𐤉𐤄𐤅𐤄.𐤀𐤋𐤄𐤉𐤊𐤌.𐤀𐤔𐤓.𐤄𐤅𐤑𐤀𐤕𐤉.𐤀𐤕𐤊𐤌
.𐤌𐤀𐤓𐤑.𐤌𐤑𐤓𐤉𐤌.𐤋𐤕𐤕.𐤋𐤊𐤌.𐤀𐤕.𐤀𐤓𐤑.𐤊𐤍𐤏𐤍.𐤋𐤄𐤉𐤅
𐤕.𐤋𐤊𐤌.𐤋𐤀𐤋𐤄𐤉𐤌|

𐤋𐤈 𐤅𐤊𐤉.𐤉𐤌𐤅𐤊.𐤀𐤇𐤉𐤊.𐤏𐤌𐤊.𐤅𐤍𐤌𐤊𐤓.𐤋𐤊.𐤋𐤀.𐤕𐤏𐤁
𐤃.𐤁𐤅.𐤏𐤁𐤃𐤕.𐤏𐤁𐤃|

𐤌 𐤊𐤔𐤊𐤉𐤓.𐤊𐤕𐤅𐤔𐤁.𐤉𐤄𐤉𐤄.𐤏𐤌𐤊.𐤏𐤃.𐤔𐤍𐤕.𐤄𐤉
𐤁𐤋.𐤉𐤏𐤁𐤃.𐤏𐤌𐤊|

𐤌𐤀 𐤅𐤉𐤑𐤀.𐤌𐤏𐤌𐤊.𐤄𐤅𐤀.𐤅𐤁𐤍𐤉𐤅.𐤏𐤌𐤅.𐤅𐤔𐤁.𐤀𐤋.𐤌𐤔𐤐
𐤇𐤕𐤅.𐤅𐤀𐤋.𐤀𐤇𐤆𐤕.𐤀𐤁𐤕𐤉𐤅.𐤉𐤔𐤅𐤁|

𐤌𐤁 𐤊𐤉.𐤏𐤁𐤃𐤉.𐤄𐤌.𐤀𐤔𐤓.𐤄𐤅𐤑𐤀𐤕𐤉.𐤀𐤕𐤌.𐤌𐤀𐤓𐤑
.𐤌𐤑𐤓𐤉𐤌.𐤋𐤀.𐤉𐤌𐤊𐤓𐤅.𐤌𐤌𐤊𐤓𐤕.𐤏𐤁𐤃|

𐤌𐤂 𐤋𐤀.𐤕𐤓𐤃𐤄.𐤁𐤅.𐤁𐤐𐤓𐤊.𐤅𐤉𐤓𐤀𐤕.𐤌𐤀𐤋𐤄𐤉𐤊|

𐤌𐤃 𐤅𐤏𐤁𐤃𐤊.𐤅𐤀𐤌𐤕𐤊.𐤀𐤔𐤓.𐤉𐤄𐤉𐤅.𐤋𐤊.𐤌𐤀𐤕.𐤄𐤂𐤅
𐤉𐤌.𐤀𐤔𐤓.𐤎𐤁𐤉𐤁𐤕𐤉𐤊𐤌.𐤌𐤄𐤌.𐤕𐤒𐤍𐤅.𐤏𐤁𐤃.𐤅𐤀𐤌𐤄|

𐤌𐤄 𐤅𐤂𐤌.𐤌𐤁𐤍𐤉.𐤄𐤕𐤅𐤔𐤁𐤉𐤌.𐤄𐤂𐤓𐤉𐤌.𐤏𐤌𐤊𐤌.𐤌𐤄𐤌
.𐤕𐤒𐤍𐤅.𐤅𐤌𐤌𐤔𐤐𐤇𐤕𐤌.𐤀𐤔𐤓.𐤏𐤌𐤊𐤌.𐤀𐤔𐤓.𐤄𐤅𐤋𐤉𐤃𐤅.𐤁
𐤀𐤓𐤑𐤊𐤌.𐤅𐤄𐤉𐤅.𐤋𐤊𐤌.𐤋𐤀𐤇𐤆𐤄|

𐤌𐤅 𐤅𐤄𐤕𐤍𐤇𐤋𐤕𐤌.𐤀𐤕𐤌.𐤋𐤁𐤍𐤉𐤊𐤌.𐤀𐤇𐤓𐤉𐤊𐤌.𐤋𐤓𐤔
𐤕.𐤀𐤇𐤆𐤄.𐤋𐤏𐤋𐤌.𐤁𐤄𐤌.𐤕𐤏𐤁𐤃𐤅.𐤅𐤁𐤀𐤇𐤉𐤊𐤌.𐤁𐤍𐤉.𐤉
𐤔𐤓𐤀𐤋.𐤀𐤉𐤔.𐤁𐤀𐤇𐤉𐤅.𐤋𐤀.𐤕𐤓𐤃𐤄.𐤁𐤅.𐤁𐤐𐤓𐤊|

מז וכי.תשיג.יד.גר.ותושב.עמך.ומך.אחיך.עמו.ונמכר.לגר.תושב.עמך.או.לעקר.משפחת.גר|

מח אחרי.נמכר.גאלה.תהיה.לו.אחד.מאחיו.יגאלנו|

מט או.דדו.או.בן.דדו.יגאלנו.או.משאר.בשרו.ממשפחתו.יגאלנו.או.השיגה.ידו.ונגאל|

נ וחשב.עם.קנהו.משנת.המכרו.לו.עד.שנת.היבל.והיה.כסף.ממכרו.במספר.שנים.כימי.שכיר.יהיה.עמו|

נא אם.עוד.רבות.בשנים.לפיהן.ישיב.גאלתו.מכסף.מקנתו|

נב ואם.מעט.נשאר.בשנים.עד.שנת.היבל.וחשב.לו.כפי.שניו.ישיב.את.גאלתו|

נג כשכיר.שנה.בשנה.יהיה.עמו.לא.ירדנו.בפרך.לעיניך|

נד ואם.לא.יגאל.באלה.ויצא.בשנת.היבל.הוא.ובניו.עמו|

נה כי.לי.בני.ישראל.עבדים.עבדי.הם.אשר.הוצאתי.אותם.מארץ.מצרים.אני.יהוה.אלהיכם||

כו ללוים.חלק

א לא.תעשו.לכם.אלילם.ופסל.ומצבה.לא.תקימו.לכם.ואבן.משכית.לא.תתנו.בארצכם.להשתחות.עליה.כי.אני.יהוה.אלהיכם|

ב את.שבתתי.תשמרו.ומקדשי.תיראו.אני.יהוה|

ࠂ ࠀࠌ.ࠁࠇࠒࠕࠉ.ࠕࠋࠊࠅ.ࠅࠀࠕ.ࠌࠑࠅࠕࠉ.ࠕࠔࠌࠓࠅ.ࠅࠏࠔ
ࠉࠕࠌ.ࠀࠕࠌ
ࠃ ࠅࠍࠕࠕࠉ.ࠂࠔࠌࠉࠊࠌ.ࠁࠏࠕࠌ.ࠅࠍࠕࠍࠄ.ࠄࠀࠓࠑ.ࠉࠁࠅࠋ
ࠄ.ࠅࠏࠑ.ࠄࠔࠃࠄ.ࠉࠕࠍ.ࠐࠓࠉࠅ
ࠄ ࠅࠄࠔࠉࠂ.ࠋࠊࠌ.ࠃࠉࠔ.ࠀࠕ.ࠁࠑࠉࠓ.ࠅࠁࠑࠉࠓ.ࠉࠔࠉࠂ.
ࠀࠕ.ࠆࠓࠏ.ࠅࠀࠊࠋࠕࠌ.ࠋࠇࠌࠊࠌ.ࠋࠔࠁࠏ.ࠅࠉࠔࠁࠕࠌ.ࠋࠁ
ࠈࠇ.ࠁࠀࠓࠑࠊࠌ
ࠅ ࠅࠍࠕࠕࠉ.ࠔࠋࠅࠌ.ࠁࠀࠓࠑ.ࠅࠔࠊࠁࠕࠌ.ࠅࠀࠉࠍ.ࠌࠇࠓࠉࠃ.
ࠅࠄࠔࠁࠕࠉ.ࠇࠉࠄ.ࠓࠏࠄ.ࠌࠍ.ࠄࠀࠓࠑ.ࠅࠇࠓࠁ.ࠋࠀ.ࠕࠏࠁࠓ.
ࠁࠀࠓࠑࠊࠌ
ࠆ ࠅࠓࠃࠐࠕࠌ.ࠀࠕ.ࠀࠉࠁࠉࠊࠌ.ࠅࠍࠐࠋࠅ.ࠋࠐࠍࠉࠊࠌ.ࠋࠇࠓࠁ
ࠇ ࠅࠓࠃࠐࠅ.ࠌࠊࠌ.ࠇࠌࠔࠄ.ࠌࠀࠄ.ࠅࠌࠀࠄ.ࠌࠊࠌ.ࠓࠁࠁࠄ.ࠉ
ࠓࠃࠐࠅ.ࠅࠍࠐࠋࠅ.ࠀࠉࠁࠉࠊࠌ.ࠋࠐࠍࠉࠊࠌ.ࠋࠇࠓࠁ
ࠈ ࠅࠐࠍࠉࠕࠉ.ࠀࠋࠉࠊࠌ.ࠅࠄࠐࠓࠉࠕࠉ.ࠀࠕࠊࠌ.ࠅࠄࠓࠁࠉࠕࠉ
.ࠀࠕࠊࠌ.ࠅࠄࠒࠉࠌࠕࠉ.ࠀࠕ.ࠁࠓࠉࠕࠉ.ࠀࠕࠊࠌ
ࠉ ࠅࠀࠊࠋࠕࠌ.ࠉࠔࠍ.ࠍࠅࠔࠍ.ࠅࠉࠔࠍ.ࠌࠐࠍࠉ.ࠇࠃࠔ.ࠕࠅࠑ
ࠉࠀࠅ
ࠉࠀ ࠅࠍࠕࠕࠉ.ࠌࠔࠊࠍࠉ.ࠁࠕࠅࠊࠊࠌ.ࠅࠋࠀ.ࠕࠂࠏࠋ.ࠍࠐࠔࠉ.
ࠀࠕࠊࠌ
ࠉࠁ ࠅࠄࠕࠄࠋࠊࠕࠉ.ࠁࠕࠅࠊࠊࠌ.ࠅࠄࠉࠉࠕࠉ.ࠋࠊࠌ.ࠋࠀࠋࠄࠉ
ࠌ.ࠅࠀࠕࠌ.ࠕࠄࠉࠅ.ࠋࠉ.ࠋࠏࠌ
ࠉࠂ ࠀࠍࠉ.ࠉࠄࠅࠄ.ࠀࠋࠄࠉࠊࠌ.ࠀࠔࠓ.ࠄࠅࠑࠀࠕࠉ.ࠀࠕࠊࠌ
.ࠌࠀࠓࠑ.ࠌࠑࠓࠉࠌ.ࠌࠄࠉࠅࠕ.ࠋࠄࠌ.ࠏࠁࠃࠉࠌ.ࠅࠀࠔࠁࠓ.ࠌࠈ
ࠕ.ࠏࠋࠊࠌ.ࠅࠀࠅࠋࠊ.ࠀࠕࠊࠌ.ࠒࠅࠌࠌࠉࠅࠕ
ࠉࠃ ࠅࠀࠌ.ࠋࠀ.ࠕࠔࠌࠏࠅ.ࠋࠉ.ࠅࠋࠀ.ࠕࠏࠔࠅ.ࠀࠕ.ࠊࠋ.ࠄࠌ
ࠑࠅࠕ.ࠄࠀࠋࠄ
ࠉࠄ ࠅࠀࠌ.ࠁࠇࠒࠕࠉ.ࠕࠌࠀࠎࠅ.ࠅࠀࠌ.ࠀࠕ.ࠌࠔࠐࠈࠉ.ࠕࠂ
ࠏࠋ.ࠍࠐࠔࠊࠌ.ࠋࠁࠋࠕࠉ.ࠏࠔࠅࠕ.ࠀࠕ.ࠊࠋ.ࠌࠑࠅࠕࠉ.ࠋࠄࠐࠓ
ࠊࠌ.ࠀࠕ.ࠁࠓࠉࠕࠉ
ࠉࠅ ࠀࠐ.ࠀࠍࠉ.ࠀࠏࠔࠄ.ࠆࠀࠕ.ࠋࠊࠌ.ࠅࠄࠐࠒࠃࠕࠉ.ࠏࠋࠉ
ࠊࠌ.ࠁࠄࠋࠄ.ࠀࠕ.ࠄࠔࠇࠐࠕ.ࠅࠀࠕ.ࠄࠒࠃࠇࠕ.ࠌࠊࠋࠅࠕ.ࠏ

𐤉𐤍𐤉𐤌.𐤅𐤌𐤃𐤉𐤁𐤕.𐤍𐤐𐤔.𐤅𐤆𐤓𐤏𐤕𐤌.𐤋𐤓𐤉𐤒.𐤆𐤓𐤏𐤊𐤌.𐤅𐤀
𐤊𐤋𐤄𐤅.𐤀𐤉𐤁𐤉𐤊𐤌|
..𐤉𐤆..𐤅𐤍𐤕𐤕𐤉.𐤐𐤍𐤉.𐤁𐤊𐤌.𐤅𐤍𐤂𐤐𐤕𐤌.𐤋𐤐𐤍𐤉.𐤀𐤉𐤁𐤉𐤊𐤌.𐤅
𐤓𐤃𐤅.𐤁𐤊𐤌.𐤔𐤍𐤀𐤉𐤊𐤌.𐤅𐤍𐤎𐤕𐤌.𐤅𐤀𐤉𐤍.𐤓𐤃𐤐.𐤀𐤕𐤊𐤌|
..𐤉𐤇..𐤅𐤀𐤌.𐤏𐤃.𐤀𐤋𐤄.𐤋𐤀.𐤕𐤔𐤌𐤏𐤅.𐤋𐤉.𐤅𐤉𐤎𐤐𐤕𐤉.𐤋𐤉𐤎
𐤓𐤄.𐤀𐤕𐤊𐤌.𐤔𐤁𐤏.𐤏𐤋.𐤇𐤈𐤀𐤕𐤉𐤊𐤌|
..𐤉𐤈..𐤅𐤔𐤁𐤓𐤕𐤉.𐤀𐤕.𐤂𐤀𐤅𐤍.𐤏𐤆𐤊𐤌.𐤅𐤍𐤕𐤕𐤉.𐤀𐤕.𐤔𐤌
𐤉𐤊𐤌.𐤊𐤁𐤓𐤆𐤋.𐤅𐤀𐤕.𐤀𐤓𐤑𐤊𐤌.𐤊𐤍𐤇𐤔𐤄|
..𐤊..𐤅𐤕𐤌.𐤋𐤓𐤉𐤒.𐤊𐤇𐤊𐤌.𐤅𐤋𐤀.𐤕𐤕𐤍.𐤀𐤓𐤑𐤊𐤌.𐤀𐤕.𐤉
𐤁𐤅𐤋𐤄.𐤅𐤏𐤑.𐤄𐤀𐤓𐤑.𐤋𐤀.𐤉𐤕𐤍.𐤐𐤓𐤉𐤅|
..𐤊𐤀..𐤅𐤀𐤌.𐤕𐤋𐤊𐤅.𐤏𐤌𐤉.𐤒𐤓𐤉.𐤅𐤋𐤀.𐤕𐤀𐤁𐤅.𐤋𐤔𐤌𐤏.𐤋𐤉.𐤅
𐤉𐤎𐤐𐤕𐤉.𐤏𐤋𐤉𐤊𐤌.𐤌𐤊𐤄.𐤔𐤁𐤏.𐤊𐤇𐤈𐤀𐤕𐤉𐤊𐤌|
..𐤊𐤁..𐤅𐤄𐤔𐤋𐤇𐤕𐤉.𐤁𐤊𐤌.𐤀𐤕.𐤇𐤉𐤕.𐤄𐤔𐤃𐤄.𐤅𐤔𐤊𐤋𐤄.
𐤀𐤕𐤊𐤌.𐤅𐤄𐤊𐤓𐤉𐤕𐤄.𐤀𐤕.𐤁𐤄𐤌𐤕𐤊𐤌.𐤅𐤄𐤌𐤏𐤉𐤈𐤄.𐤀𐤕
𐤊𐤌.𐤅𐤍𐤔𐤌𐤅.𐤃𐤓𐤊𐤉𐤊𐤌|
..𐤊𐤂..𐤅𐤀𐤌.𐤁𐤀𐤋𐤄.𐤋𐤀.𐤕𐤅𐤎𐤓𐤅.𐤋𐤉.𐤅𐤄𐤋𐤊𐤕𐤌.𐤏𐤌𐤉.𐤒𐤓
𐤉|
..𐤊𐤃..𐤅𐤄𐤋𐤊𐤕𐤉.𐤀𐤐.𐤀𐤍𐤉.𐤏𐤌𐤊𐤌.𐤁𐤒𐤓𐤉.𐤅𐤄𐤊𐤉𐤕𐤉.𐤀
𐤕𐤊𐤌.𐤂𐤌.𐤀𐤍𐤉.𐤔𐤁𐤏.𐤏𐤋.𐤇𐤈𐤀𐤕𐤉𐤊𐤌|
..𐤊𐤄..𐤅𐤄𐤁𐤀𐤕𐤉.𐤏𐤋𐤉𐤊𐤌.𐤇𐤓𐤁.𐤍𐤒𐤌𐤕.𐤍𐤒𐤌.𐤁𐤓𐤉𐤕.𐤅𐤍
𐤀𐤎𐤐𐤕𐤌.𐤀𐤋.𐤏𐤓𐤉𐤊𐤌.𐤅𐤔𐤋𐤇𐤕𐤉.𐤃𐤁𐤓.𐤁𐤕𐤅𐤊𐤊𐤌.𐤅𐤍𐤕
𐤕𐤌.𐤁𐤉𐤃.𐤀𐤅𐤉𐤁|
..𐤊𐤅..𐤁𐤔𐤁𐤓𐤉.𐤋𐤊𐤌.𐤌𐤈𐤄.𐤋𐤇𐤌.𐤅𐤀𐤐𐤅.𐤏𐤔𐤓.𐤍𐤔𐤉𐤌.𐤋
𐤇𐤌𐤊𐤌.𐤁𐤕𐤍𐤅𐤓.𐤀𐤇𐤃.𐤅𐤄𐤔𐤉𐤁𐤅.𐤋𐤇𐤌𐤊𐤌.𐤁𐤌𐤔𐤒𐤋.𐤅
𐤀𐤊𐤋𐤕𐤌.𐤅𐤋𐤀.𐤕𐤔𐤁𐤏𐤅|
..𐤊𐤆..𐤅𐤀𐤌.𐤁𐤆𐤀𐤕.𐤋𐤀.𐤕𐤔𐤌𐤏𐤅.𐤋𐤉.𐤅𐤄𐤋𐤊𐤕𐤌.𐤏𐤌𐤉.
𐤁𐤒𐤓𐤉|
..𐤊𐤇..𐤅𐤄𐤋𐤊𐤕𐤉.𐤏𐤌𐤊𐤌.𐤁𐤇𐤌𐤕.𐤒𐤓𐤉.𐤅𐤉𐤎𐤓𐤕𐤉.𐤀𐤕𐤊
𐤌.𐤀𐤐.𐤀𐤍𐤉.𐤔𐤁𐤏.𐤏𐤋.𐤇𐤈𐤀𐤕𐤉𐤊𐤌|
..𐤊𐤈..𐤅𐤀𐤊𐤋𐤕𐤌.𐤁𐤔𐤓.𐤁𐤍𐤉𐤊𐤌.𐤅𐤁𐤔𐤓.𐤁𐤍𐤕𐤉𐤊𐤌.𐤕𐤀𐤊
𐤋𐤅|

ל והשמדתי. את. במתיכם. והכרתי. את. חמ
ניכם. ונתתי. את. פגריכם. על. פגרי. גלוליכם.
וגעלה. נפשי. אתכם׃
לא ונתתי. את. עריכם. חרבה. והשמותי. את. מ
קדשיכם. ולא. אריח. בריח. ניחחכם׃
לב והשמתי. אני. את. הארץ. ושממו. עליה. אי
ביכם. הישבים. בה׃
לג ואתכם. אזרה. בגוים. והריקתי. אחריכ
ם. חרב. והיתה. ארצכם. שממה. ועריכם. יהיו.
חרבה׃
לד אז. תרצה. הארץ. את. שבתתיה. כל. ימי.
השמה. ואתם. בארץ. איביכם. אז. תשבת. האר
ץ. והרצת. את. שבתתיה׃
לה כל. ימי. השמה. תשבת. את. אשר. לא. שבתה.
בשבתתיכם. בשבתכם. עליה׃
לו והנשארים. בכם. והבאתי. מרך. בלבבם. בא
רצת. איביהם. ורדף. אתם. קול. עלה. נדף. ונסו. מ
נסת. חרב. ונפלו. ואין. רדף׃
לז וכשלו. איש. באחיו. כמפני. חרב. ורדף. אי
ן. ולא. תהיה. לכם. תקומה. לפני. איביכם׃
לח ואבדתם. בגוים. ואכלה. אתכם. ארץ. איב
יכם׃
לט והנשארים. בכם. ימקו. בעונם. בארצת. א
יביכם. ואף. בעונת. אבתם. אתם. ימקו׃
מ והתודו. את. עונם. ואת. עון. אבתם. במעלם
.אשר. מעלו. בי. ואף. אשר. הלכו. עמי. בקרי׃
מא אף. אני. אלך. עמם. בקרי. והבאתי. אתם. ב
ארץ. איביהם. או. אז. יכנע. לבבם. הערל. ואז.
ירצו. את. עונם׃

42 𐤅𐤆𐤊𐤓𐤕𐤉.𐤀𐤕.𐤁𐤓𐤉𐤕𐤉.𐤉𐤏𐤒𐤅𐤁.𐤅𐤀𐤐.𐤀𐤕.𐤁𐤓𐤉
𐤕𐤉.𐤉𐤑𐤇𐤒.𐤅𐤀𐤐.𐤀𐤕.𐤁𐤓𐤉𐤕𐤉.𐤀𐤁𐤓𐤄𐤌.𐤀𐤆𐤊𐤓.𐤅𐤄𐤀
𐤓𐤑.𐤀𐤆𐤊𐤓|
43 𐤅𐤄𐤀𐤓𐤑.𐤕𐤏𐤆𐤁.𐤌𐤄𐤌.𐤅𐤕𐤓𐤑.𐤀𐤕.𐤔𐤁𐤕𐤕𐤉𐤄.
𐤁𐤄𐤔𐤌𐤄.𐤌𐤄𐤌.𐤅𐤄𐤌.𐤉𐤓𐤑𐤅.𐤀𐤕.𐤏𐤅𐤍𐤌.𐤉𐤏𐤍.𐤅𐤁𐤉𐤏𐤍.𐤁
𐤌𐤔𐤐𐤈𐤉.𐤌𐤀𐤎𐤅.𐤅𐤀𐤕.𐤇𐤒𐤕𐤉.𐤂𐤏𐤋𐤄.𐤍𐤐𐤔𐤌|
44 𐤅𐤀𐤐.𐤂𐤌.𐤆𐤀𐤕.𐤁𐤄𐤉𐤅𐤕𐤌.𐤁𐤀𐤓𐤑.𐤀𐤉𐤁𐤉𐤄𐤌.𐤋
𐤀.𐤌𐤀𐤎𐤕𐤉𐤌.𐤅𐤋𐤀.𐤂𐤏𐤋𐤕𐤉𐤌.𐤋𐤊𐤋𐤕𐤌.𐤋𐤄𐤐𐤓.𐤁𐤓𐤉𐤕
𐤉.𐤀𐤕𐤌.𐤊𐤉.𐤀𐤍𐤉.𐤉𐤄𐤅𐤄.𐤀𐤋𐤄𐤉𐤄𐤌|
45 𐤅𐤆𐤊𐤓𐤕𐤉.𐤋𐤄𐤌.𐤁𐤓𐤉𐤕.𐤓𐤀𐤔𐤍𐤉𐤌.𐤀𐤔𐤓.𐤄𐤅𐤑𐤀
𐤕𐤉.𐤀𐤕𐤌.𐤌𐤀𐤓𐤑.𐤌𐤑𐤓𐤉𐤌.𐤋𐤏𐤉𐤍𐤉.𐤄𐤂𐤅𐤉𐤌.𐤋𐤄𐤉𐤕.
𐤋𐤄𐤌.𐤋𐤀𐤋𐤄𐤉𐤌.𐤀𐤍𐤉.𐤉𐤄𐤅𐤄|
46 𐤀𐤋𐤄.𐤄𐤇𐤒𐤉𐤌.𐤅𐤄𐤌𐤔𐤐𐤈𐤉𐤌.𐤅𐤄𐤕𐤅𐤓𐤕.𐤀𐤔𐤓.𐤍
𐤕𐤍.𐤉𐤄𐤅𐤄.𐤁𐤉𐤍𐤅.𐤅𐤁𐤉𐤍.𐤁𐤍𐤉.𐤉𐤔𐤓𐤀𐤋.𐤁𐤄𐤓.𐤎𐤉𐤍𐤉.𐤁𐤉
𐤃.𐤌𐤔𐤄||

𐤋𐤋𐤅𐤉𐤌.𐤇𐤋𐤒 27

1 𐤅𐤉𐤃𐤁𐤓.𐤉𐤄𐤅𐤄.𐤀𐤋.𐤌𐤔𐤄.𐤋𐤀𐤌𐤓|
2 𐤃𐤁𐤓.𐤀𐤋.𐤁𐤍𐤉.𐤉𐤔𐤓𐤀𐤋.𐤅𐤀𐤌𐤓𐤕.𐤀𐤋𐤄𐤌.𐤀𐤉𐤔.𐤊𐤉
.𐤉𐤐𐤋𐤀.𐤍𐤃𐤓.𐤁𐤏𐤓𐤊𐤊.𐤍𐤐𐤔𐤕.𐤋𐤉𐤄𐤅𐤄|
3 𐤅𐤄𐤉𐤄.𐤏𐤓𐤊𐤊.𐤄𐤆𐤊𐤓.𐤌𐤁𐤍.𐤏𐤔𐤓𐤉𐤌.𐤔𐤍𐤄.𐤅𐤏𐤃.
𐤁𐤍.𐤔𐤔𐤉𐤌.𐤔𐤍𐤄.𐤅𐤄𐤉𐤄.𐤏𐤓𐤊𐤊.𐤇𐤌𐤔𐤉𐤌.𐤔𐤒𐤋.𐤊𐤎𐤐.
𐤁𐤔𐤒𐤋.𐤄𐤒𐤃𐤔|
4 𐤅𐤀𐤌.𐤍𐤒𐤁𐤄.𐤄𐤅𐤀.𐤅𐤄𐤉𐤄.𐤏𐤓𐤊𐤊.𐤔𐤋𐤔𐤉𐤌.𐤔𐤒𐤋|
5 𐤅𐤀𐤌.𐤌𐤁𐤍.𐤇𐤌𐤔.𐤔𐤍𐤉𐤌.𐤅𐤏𐤃.𐤁𐤍.𐤏𐤔𐤓𐤉𐤌.𐤔𐤍𐤄.𐤅
𐤄𐤉𐤄.𐤏𐤓𐤊𐤊.𐤄𐤆𐤊𐤓.𐤏𐤔𐤓𐤉𐤌.𐤔𐤒𐤋𐤉𐤌.𐤅𐤋𐤍𐤒𐤁𐤄.𐤏
𐤔𐤓𐤕.𐤔𐤒𐤋𐤉𐤌|
6 𐤅𐤀𐤌.𐤌𐤁𐤍.𐤇𐤃𐤔.𐤅𐤏𐤃.𐤁𐤍.𐤇𐤌𐤔.𐤔𐤍𐤉𐤌.𐤅𐤄𐤉𐤄.𐤏
𐤓𐤊𐤊.𐤄𐤆𐤊𐤓.𐤇𐤌𐤔𐤄.𐤔𐤒𐤋𐤉𐤌.𐤊𐤎𐤐.𐤅𐤋𐤍𐤒𐤁𐤄.𐤏𐤓𐤊𐤊
.𐤔𐤋𐤔𐤕.𐤔𐤒𐤋𐤉𐤌.𐤊𐤎𐤐|

ז 𐤅𐤀𐤌.𐤌𐤁𐤍.𐤔𐤔𐤉𐤌.𐤔𐤍𐤄.𐤅𐤌𐤏𐤋𐤄.𐤀𐤌.𐤆𐤊𐤓.𐤅𐤄𐤉
𐤄.𐤏𐤓𐤊𐤊.𐤇𐤌𐤔𐤄.𐤏𐤔𐤓.𐤔𐤒𐤋.𐤅𐤋𐤍𐤒𐤁𐤄.𐤏𐤔𐤓𐤄.𐤔𐤒𐤋
𐤉𐤌|
ח 𐤅𐤀𐤌.𐤌𐤊.𐤄𐤅𐤀.𐤌𐤏𐤓𐤊𐤊.𐤅𐤄𐤏𐤌𐤉𐤃𐤅.𐤋𐤐𐤍𐤉.𐤄𐤊𐤄𐤍.
𐤅𐤄𐤏𐤓𐤉𐤊.𐤀𐤕𐤅.𐤄𐤊𐤄𐤍.𐤏𐤋.𐤐𐤉.𐤀𐤔𐤓.𐤕𐤔𐤉𐤂.𐤉𐤃.𐤄𐤍
𐤃𐤓.𐤉𐤏𐤓𐤉𐤊𐤍𐤅.𐤄𐤊𐤄𐤍|
ט 𐤅𐤀𐤌.𐤁𐤄𐤌𐤄.𐤀𐤔𐤓.𐤉𐤒𐤓𐤉𐤁𐤅.𐤌𐤌𐤍𐤄.𐤒𐤓𐤁𐤍.𐤋𐤉𐤄𐤅
𐤄.𐤊𐤋.𐤀𐤔𐤓.𐤉𐤕𐤍.𐤌𐤌𐤍𐤅.𐤋𐤉𐤄𐤅𐤄.𐤉𐤄𐤉𐤄.𐤒𐤃𐤔|
י 𐤋𐤀.𐤉𐤇𐤋𐤉𐤐𐤍𐤅.𐤅𐤋𐤀.𐤉𐤌𐤉𐤓.𐤀𐤕𐤅.𐤈𐤅𐤁.𐤁𐤓𐤏.𐤀𐤅.𐤓
𐤏.𐤁𐤈𐤅𐤁.𐤅𐤀𐤌.𐤄𐤌𐤓.𐤉𐤌𐤉𐤓.𐤁𐤄𐤌𐤄.𐤁𐤁𐤄𐤌𐤄.𐤅𐤄𐤉𐤄.𐤄
𐤅𐤀.𐤅𐤕𐤌𐤅𐤓𐤕𐤅.𐤉𐤄𐤉𐤄.𐤒𐤃𐤔|
יא 𐤅𐤀𐤌.𐤊𐤋.𐤁𐤄𐤌𐤄.𐤈𐤌𐤀𐤄.𐤀𐤔𐤓.𐤋𐤀.𐤉𐤒𐤓𐤉𐤁𐤅.𐤌𐤌
𐤍𐤄.𐤒𐤓𐤁𐤍.𐤋𐤉𐤄𐤅𐤄.𐤅𐤄𐤏𐤌𐤉𐤃.𐤀𐤕.𐤄𐤁𐤄𐤌𐤄.𐤋𐤐𐤍𐤉.𐤄
𐤊𐤄𐤍|
יב 𐤅𐤄𐤏𐤓𐤉𐤊.𐤄𐤊𐤄𐤍.𐤀𐤕𐤄.𐤁𐤉𐤍.𐤈𐤅𐤁.𐤅𐤁𐤉𐤍.𐤓𐤏.𐤊𐤏
𐤓𐤊𐤊.𐤄𐤊𐤄𐤍.𐤊𐤍.𐤉𐤄𐤉𐤄|
יג 𐤅𐤀𐤌.𐤂𐤀𐤋.𐤉𐤂𐤀𐤋𐤍𐤄.𐤅𐤉𐤎𐤐.𐤇𐤌𐤉𐤔𐤕𐤅.𐤏𐤋.𐤏𐤓
𐤊𐤊|
יד 𐤅𐤀𐤉𐤔.𐤊𐤉.𐤉𐤒𐤃𐤔.𐤀𐤕.𐤁𐤉𐤕𐤅.𐤒𐤃𐤔.𐤋𐤉𐤄𐤅𐤄.𐤅
𐤄𐤏𐤓𐤉𐤊𐤅.𐤄𐤊𐤄𐤍.𐤁𐤉𐤍.𐤈𐤅𐤁.𐤅𐤁𐤉𐤍.𐤓𐤏.𐤊𐤀𐤔𐤓.𐤉𐤏𐤓𐤉𐤊
.𐤀𐤕𐤅.𐤄𐤊𐤄𐤍.𐤊𐤍.𐤉𐤒𐤅𐤌|
טו 𐤅𐤀𐤌.𐤄𐤌𐤒𐤃𐤉𐤔.𐤉𐤂𐤀𐤋.𐤀𐤕.𐤁𐤉𐤕𐤅.𐤅𐤉𐤎𐤐.𐤇𐤌
𐤉𐤔𐤉𐤕.𐤊𐤎𐤐.𐤏𐤓𐤊𐤊.𐤏𐤋𐤉𐤅.𐤅𐤄𐤉𐤄.𐤋𐤅|
טז 𐤅𐤀𐤌.𐤌𐤔𐤃𐤄.𐤀𐤇𐤆𐤕𐤅.𐤉𐤒𐤃𐤉𐤔.𐤀𐤉𐤔.𐤋𐤉𐤄𐤅𐤄
.𐤅𐤄𐤉𐤄.𐤏𐤓𐤊𐤊.𐤋𐤐𐤉.𐤆𐤓𐤏𐤅.𐤆𐤓𐤏.𐤇𐤌𐤓.𐤔𐤏𐤓𐤉𐤌.𐤁𐤇
𐤌𐤔𐤉𐤌.𐤔𐤒𐤋.𐤊𐤎𐤐|
יז 𐤀𐤌.𐤌𐤔𐤍𐤕.𐤄𐤉𐤁𐤋.𐤉𐤒𐤃𐤉𐤔.𐤔𐤃𐤄𐤅.𐤊𐤏𐤓𐤊𐤊.𐤉
𐤒𐤅𐤌|
יח 𐤅𐤀𐤌.𐤀𐤇𐤓.𐤄𐤉𐤁𐤋.𐤉𐤒𐤃𐤉𐤔.𐤔𐤃𐤄𐤅.𐤅𐤇𐤔𐤁.𐤋𐤅.
𐤄𐤊𐤄𐤍.𐤀𐤕.𐤄𐤊𐤎𐤐.𐤏𐤋.𐤐𐤉.𐤄𐤔𐤍𐤉𐤌.𐤄𐤍𐤅𐤕𐤓𐤕.𐤏𐤃.𐤔
𐤍𐤕.𐤄𐤉𐤁𐤋.𐤅𐤍𐤂𐤓𐤏.𐤌𐤏𐤓𐤊𐤊|

𐤉𐤈 𐤅𐤀𐤌.𐤂𐤀𐤋.𐤉𐤂𐤀𐤋.𐤀𐤕.𐤄𐤔𐤃𐤄.𐤄𐤌𐤒𐤃𐤉𐤔.𐤀
𐤕𐤅.𐤅𐤉𐤎𐤐.𐤇𐤌𐤔𐤉𐤕.𐤊𐤎𐤐.𐤏𐤓𐤊𐤊.𐤏𐤋𐤉𐤅.𐤅𐤒𐤌.𐤋𐤅|
𐤊 𐤅𐤀𐤌.𐤋𐤀.𐤉𐤂𐤀𐤋.𐤀𐤕.𐤄𐤔𐤃𐤄.𐤅𐤀𐤌.𐤌𐤊𐤓.𐤀𐤕.𐤄
𐤔𐤃𐤄.𐤋𐤀𐤉𐤔.𐤀𐤇𐤓.𐤋𐤀.𐤉𐤂𐤀𐤋.𐤏𐤅𐤃|
𐤊𐤀 𐤅𐤄𐤉𐤄.𐤄𐤔𐤃𐤄.𐤁𐤑𐤀𐤕𐤅.𐤁𐤉𐤁𐤋.𐤒𐤃𐤔.𐤋𐤉𐤄𐤅𐤄.
𐤊𐤔𐤃𐤄.𐤄𐤇𐤓𐤌.𐤋𐤊𐤄𐤍.𐤕𐤄𐤉𐤄.𐤀𐤇𐤆𐤕𐤅|
𐤊𐤁 𐤅𐤀𐤌.𐤀𐤕.𐤔𐤃𐤄.𐤌𐤒𐤍𐤕𐤅.𐤀𐤔𐤓.𐤋𐤀.𐤌𐤔𐤃𐤄.𐤀𐤇
𐤆𐤕𐤅.𐤉𐤒𐤃𐤉𐤔.𐤋𐤉𐤄𐤅𐤄|
𐤊𐤂 𐤅𐤇𐤔𐤁.𐤋𐤅.𐤄𐤊𐤄𐤍.𐤀𐤕.𐤌𐤊𐤎𐤕.𐤄𐤏𐤓𐤊𐤊.𐤏𐤃.𐤔𐤍
𐤕.𐤄𐤉𐤁𐤋.𐤅𐤍𐤕𐤍.𐤀𐤕.𐤄𐤏𐤓𐤊𐤊.𐤁𐤉𐤅𐤌.𐤄𐤄𐤅𐤀.𐤒𐤃𐤔.𐤋𐤉
𐤄𐤅𐤄|
𐤊𐤃 𐤁𐤔𐤍𐤕.𐤄𐤉𐤅𐤁𐤋.𐤉𐤔𐤅𐤁.𐤄𐤔𐤃𐤄.𐤋𐤀𐤔𐤓.𐤒𐤍𐤄𐤅.𐤌
𐤀𐤕𐤅.𐤋𐤀𐤔𐤓.𐤋𐤅.𐤀𐤇𐤆𐤕.𐤄𐤀𐤓𐤑|
𐤊𐤄 𐤅𐤊𐤋.𐤏𐤓𐤊𐤊.𐤉𐤄𐤉𐤄.𐤁𐤔𐤒𐤋.𐤄𐤒𐤃𐤔.𐤏𐤔𐤓𐤉𐤌.𐤂
𐤓𐤄.𐤉𐤄𐤉𐤄.𐤄𐤔𐤒𐤋|
𐤊𐤅 𐤀𐤊.𐤁𐤊𐤅𐤓.𐤀𐤔𐤓.𐤉𐤁𐤊𐤓.𐤋𐤉𐤄𐤅𐤄.𐤁𐤁𐤄𐤌𐤄.𐤋𐤀.𐤉
𐤒𐤃𐤉𐤔.𐤀𐤉𐤔.𐤀𐤕𐤅.𐤀𐤌.𐤔𐤅𐤓.𐤀𐤌.𐤔𐤄.𐤋𐤉𐤄𐤅𐤄.𐤄𐤅𐤀|
𐤊𐤆 𐤅𐤀𐤌.𐤁𐤁𐤄𐤌𐤄.𐤄𐤈𐤌𐤀𐤄.𐤅𐤐𐤃𐤄.𐤁𐤏𐤓𐤊𐤊.𐤅𐤉𐤎𐤐.
𐤇𐤌𐤔𐤕𐤅.𐤏𐤋𐤉𐤅.𐤅𐤀𐤌.𐤋𐤀.𐤉𐤂𐤀𐤋.𐤅𐤍𐤌𐤊𐤓.𐤁𐤏𐤓𐤊𐤊|
𐤊𐤇 𐤀𐤊.𐤊𐤋.𐤇𐤓𐤌.𐤀𐤔𐤓.𐤉𐤇𐤓𐤌.𐤀𐤉𐤔.𐤋𐤉𐤄𐤅𐤄.𐤌𐤊𐤋.
𐤀𐤔𐤓.𐤋𐤅.𐤌𐤀𐤃𐤌.𐤅𐤁𐤄𐤌𐤄.𐤅𐤌𐤔𐤃𐤄.𐤀𐤇𐤆𐤕𐤅.𐤋𐤀.𐤉𐤌
𐤊𐤓.𐤅𐤋𐤀.𐤉𐤂𐤀𐤋.𐤊𐤋.𐤇𐤓𐤌.𐤒𐤃𐤔.𐤒𐤃𐤔𐤉𐤌.𐤄𐤅𐤀.𐤋𐤉
𐤄𐤅𐤄|
𐤊𐤈 𐤊𐤋.𐤇𐤓𐤌.𐤀𐤔𐤓.𐤉𐤇𐤓𐤌.𐤌𐤍.𐤄𐤀𐤃𐤌.𐤋𐤀.𐤉𐤐𐤃𐤄.
𐤌𐤅𐤕.𐤉𐤅𐤌𐤕|
𐤋 𐤅𐤊𐤋.𐤌𐤏𐤔𐤓.𐤄𐤀𐤓𐤑.𐤌𐤆𐤓𐤏.𐤄𐤀𐤓𐤑.𐤌𐤐𐤓𐤉.𐤄𐤏
𐤑.𐤋𐤉𐤄𐤅𐤄.𐤄𐤅𐤀.𐤒𐤃𐤔.𐤋𐤉𐤄𐤅𐤄|
𐤋𐤀 𐤅𐤀𐤌.𐤂𐤀𐤋.𐤉𐤂𐤀𐤋.𐤀𐤉𐤔.𐤌𐤌𐤏𐤔𐤓𐤅.𐤇𐤌𐤔𐤉𐤕𐤅.
𐤉𐤎𐤐.𐤏𐤋𐤉𐤅|
𐤋𐤁 𐤅𐤊𐤋.𐤌𐤏𐤔𐤓.𐤁𐤒𐤓.𐤅𐤑𐤀𐤍.𐤊𐤋.𐤀𐤔𐤓.𐤉𐤏𐤁𐤓.𐤕𐤇𐤕
.𐤄𐤔𐤁𐤈.𐤄𐤏𐤔𐤉𐤓𐤉.𐤉𐤄𐤉𐤄.𐤒𐤃𐤔.𐤋𐤉𐤄𐤅𐤄|

..לג..לא.יבקר.בין.טוב.לרע.ולא.ימירנו.ואם.
המר.ימירנו.והיה.הוא.ותמורתו.יהיה.קדש.ל
א.יגאל|
..לד..אלה.המצות.אשר.צוה.יהוה.את.משה.א
ל.בני.ישראל.בהר.סיני||

≥Y≥ǂ.99△ᗰ9.9ᒉǂ
.|99△ᗰ9|.

..1.. ΦᏟH.99△ᗰ9

.Ꮯ∃ᛋ9.≥Y≥ǂ.99△ᗰ9.∃Wᗰ.Ꮯᛋ.∃ᛋ∃≥.99△≥ᛋ ..1..
ヤᏟ.X≥YW∃.∃YW9.≥YW∃.W△HᏟ.△Hᛋ9.△Oᛋᗰ
|9ᗰᛋᏟ.ᗰ≥9ヤᗰ.ヤ9ᛋᗰ.ᗰXᛋ
HᒉWᗰᏟ.Ꮯᛋ9W≥.≥Y9.X△O.Ꮯᛋ.Wᛋ9.Xᛋ.ᛋᛋW ..2..
^Ꮯ^Ꮯ.9ᛋ⌐.Ꮯᛋ.XᛋᗰW.9ᒉǂᗰ9.ᗰX9ᛋ.X≥9Ꮯ.ᗰX
|ᗰXᏟ
≥9.ᛋ9ヤ.ᛋヤ≥.Ꮯᛋ.∃ᏟOᗰᛋ.∃YW.ᗰ≥9WO.Y9ᗰ ..3..
|Y9∃ᛋᛋ.∃Xᛋ.ᗰXᛋ9ヤᏟ.ᗰXᛋ.ᛋ△ΦᒉX.Ꮯᛋ9W
Ꮯ.Wᛋ9.W≥ᛋ.∃⊗ᗰᏟ.W≥ᛋ.W≥ᛋ.ᛋ≥∃≥.ᗰᛋXᛋᛋ ..4..
|ᛋᛋ∃.ᛋ≥X9ᛋ.X≥9
Ꮯ.ᗰᛋXᛋ.ᛋ△ᗰO≥.9Wᛋ.ᗰ≥WYᛋ∃.XᛋᗰW.∃Ꮯᛋᛋ ..5..
|9ᛋᛋ≥△W.Y9.9ᛋヤ≥Ꮯᛋ.Y9ᛋᛋ9
|≥△W≥9ᛋヤ.Y9.Ꮯᛋ≥ᗰᏟW.YᛋOᗰWᏟ ..6..
|9△Y≥ᗰO.Y9.YᛋWHY.∃△ᛋ∃≥Ꮯ ..7..
|9OᛋヤY9.Y9.ᏟᛋYXY.9ᛋWW≥Ꮯ ..8..
|YᏟH.Y9.9ᛋ≥Ꮯᛋ.YᏟᛋ9⌐Ꮯ ..9..
ᛋ∃≥ᗰO.Y9.OᗰW≥Ꮯᛋ.ᗰ≥9ᒉᛋᏟ.ᒉǂᛋ≥.≥Y9Ꮯ ..10..
|9ᛋヤ∃△ᒉ.Y9.Ꮯᛋ≥Ꮯᗰ^.∃WYᗰᏟ.△
|≥YO△^.Y9.Y△≥9ᛋ.Yᗰ≥Y9Ꮯ ..11..
|≥△W≥ᗰO.Y9.9⌐O≥Hᛋ.Y△Ꮯ ..12..
|Y9ᛋO.Y9.Ꮯᛋ≥O^ᒉ.9WᛋᏟ ..13..
|ᏟᛋᛋO△.Y9.ᒉǂ≥Ꮯᛋ.△^Ꮯ ..14..
|YY≥O.Y9.O9≥Hᛋ.≥ᏟXᒉYᏟ ..15..

16 𐤀𐤋𐤄.𐤒𐤓𐤉𐤀𐤉.||𐤒𐤓𐤅𐤀𐤉.𐤒𐤓𐤉||.𐤄𐤏𐤃𐤄.𐤍𐤔𐤉𐤀𐤉.
𐤌𐤈𐤅𐤕.𐤀𐤁𐤅𐤕𐤌.𐤓𐤀𐤔𐤉.𐤀𐤋𐤐𐤉.𐤉𐤔𐤓𐤀𐤋.𐤄𐤌|
17 𐤅𐤉𐤒𐤇.𐤌𐤔𐤄.𐤅𐤀𐤄𐤓𐤍.𐤀𐤕.𐤄𐤀𐤍𐤔𐤉𐤌.𐤄𐤀𐤋𐤄.𐤀
𐤔𐤓.𐤍𐤒𐤁𐤅.𐤁𐤔𐤌𐤅𐤕|
18 𐤅𐤀𐤕.𐤊𐤋.𐤄𐤏𐤃𐤄.𐤄𐤒𐤄𐤉𐤋𐤅.𐤁𐤀𐤇𐤃.𐤋𐤇𐤃𐤔.𐤄
𐤔𐤍𐤉.𐤅𐤉𐤕𐤉𐤋𐤃𐤅.𐤏𐤋.𐤌𐤔𐤐𐤇𐤕𐤌.𐤋𐤁𐤉𐤕.𐤀𐤁𐤕𐤌.𐤁𐤌𐤎
𐤐𐤓.𐤔𐤌𐤅𐤕.𐤌𐤁𐤍.𐤏𐤔𐤓𐤉𐤌.𐤔𐤍𐤄.𐤅𐤌𐤏𐤋𐤄.𐤋𐤂𐤋𐤂𐤋𐤕𐤌|
19 𐤊𐤀𐤔𐤓.𐤑𐤅𐤄.𐤉𐤄𐤅𐤄.𐤀𐤕.𐤌𐤔𐤄.𐤅𐤉𐤐𐤒𐤃𐤌.𐤁𐤌𐤃
𐤁𐤓.𐤎𐤉𐤍𐤉|
20 𐤅𐤉𐤄𐤉𐤅.𐤁𐤍𐤉.𐤓𐤀𐤅𐤁𐤍.𐤁𐤊𐤓.𐤉𐤔𐤓𐤀𐤋.𐤕𐤅𐤋𐤃𐤕𐤌.𐤋
𐤌𐤔𐤐𐤇𐤕𐤌.𐤋𐤁𐤉𐤕.𐤀𐤁𐤕𐤌.𐤁𐤌𐤎𐤐𐤓.𐤔𐤌𐤅𐤕.𐤋𐤂𐤋𐤂𐤋𐤕
𐤌.𐤊𐤋.𐤆𐤊𐤓.𐤌𐤁𐤍.𐤏𐤔𐤓𐤉𐤌.𐤔𐤍𐤄.𐤅𐤌𐤏𐤋𐤄.𐤊𐤋.𐤉𐤑𐤀.𐤑
𐤁𐤀|
21 𐤐𐤒𐤃𐤉𐤄𐤌.𐤋𐤌𐤈𐤄.𐤓𐤀𐤅𐤁𐤍.𐤔𐤔𐤄.𐤅𐤀𐤓𐤁𐤏𐤉𐤌.𐤀
𐤋𐤐.𐤅𐤇𐤌𐤔.𐤌𐤀𐤅𐤕|
22 𐤋𐤁𐤍𐤉.𐤔𐤌𐤏𐤅𐤍.𐤕𐤅𐤋𐤃𐤕𐤌.𐤋𐤌𐤔𐤐𐤇𐤕𐤌.𐤋𐤁𐤉𐤕.𐤀
𐤁𐤕𐤌.𐤐𐤒𐤃𐤉𐤅.𐤁𐤌𐤎𐤐𐤓.𐤔𐤌𐤅𐤕.𐤋𐤂𐤋𐤂𐤋𐤕𐤌.𐤊𐤋.𐤆𐤊𐤓.
𐤌𐤁𐤍.𐤏𐤔𐤓𐤉𐤌.𐤔𐤍𐤄.𐤅𐤌𐤏𐤋𐤄.𐤊𐤋.𐤉𐤑𐤀.𐤑𐤁𐤀|
23 𐤐𐤒𐤃𐤉𐤄𐤌.𐤋𐤌𐤈𐤄.𐤔𐤌𐤏𐤅𐤍.𐤕𐤔𐤏𐤄.𐤅𐤇𐤌𐤔𐤉𐤌.
𐤀𐤋𐤐.𐤅𐤔𐤋𐤔.𐤌𐤀𐤅𐤕|
24 𐤋𐤁𐤍𐤉.𐤂𐤃.𐤕𐤅𐤋𐤃𐤕𐤌.𐤋𐤌𐤔𐤐𐤇𐤕𐤌.𐤋𐤁𐤉𐤕.𐤀𐤁
𐤕𐤌.𐤁𐤌𐤎𐤐𐤓.𐤔𐤌𐤅𐤕.𐤌𐤁𐤍.𐤏𐤔𐤓𐤉𐤌.𐤔𐤍𐤄.𐤅𐤌𐤏𐤋𐤄.𐤊𐤋.
𐤉𐤑𐤀.𐤑𐤁𐤀|
25 𐤐𐤒𐤃𐤉𐤄𐤌.𐤋𐤌𐤈𐤄.𐤂𐤃.𐤇𐤌𐤔𐤄.𐤅𐤀𐤓𐤁𐤏𐤉𐤌.𐤀
𐤋𐤐.𐤅𐤔𐤔.𐤌𐤀𐤅𐤕.𐤅𐤇𐤌𐤔𐤉𐤌|
26 𐤋𐤁𐤍𐤉.𐤉𐤄𐤅𐤃𐤄.𐤕𐤅𐤋𐤃𐤕𐤌.𐤋𐤌𐤔𐤐𐤇𐤕𐤌.𐤋𐤁𐤉𐤕.
𐤀𐤁𐤕𐤌.𐤁𐤌𐤎𐤐𐤓.𐤔𐤌𐤕.𐤌𐤁𐤍.𐤏𐤔𐤓𐤉𐤌.𐤔𐤍𐤄.𐤅𐤌𐤏𐤋𐤄.𐤊
𐤋.𐤉𐤑𐤀.𐤑𐤁𐤀|
27 𐤐𐤒𐤃𐤉𐤄𐤌.𐤋𐤌𐤈𐤄.𐤉𐤄𐤅𐤃𐤄.𐤀𐤓𐤁𐤏𐤄.𐤅𐤔𐤁𐤏𐤉
𐤌.𐤀𐤋𐤐.𐤅𐤔𐤔.𐤌𐤀𐤅𐤕|

כח לבני.יששכר.תולדתם.למשפחתם.לבית.
אבתם.במספר.שמת.מבן.עשרים.שנה.ומעלה.כ
ל.יצא.צבא׃
כט פקדיהם.למטה.יששכר.ארבעה.וחמשי
ם.אלף.וארבע.מאות׃
ל לבני.זבולן.תולדתם.למשפחתם.לבית.
אבתם.במספר.שמת.מבן.עשרים.שנה.ומעלה.כ
ל.יצא.צבא׃
לא פקדיהם.למטה.זבולן.שבעה.וחמשים.
אלף.וארבע.מאות׃
לב לבני.יוסף.לבני.אפרים.תולדתם.למשפח
תם.לבית.אבתם.במספר.שמת.מבן.עשרים.שנ
ה.ומעלה.כל.יצא.צבא׃
לג פקדיהם.למטה.אפרים.ארבעים.אלף.וח
מש.מאות׃
לד לבני.מנשה.תולדתם.למשפחתם.לבית.א
בתם.במספר.שמות.מבן.עשרים.שנה.ומעלה.כל
.יצא.צבא׃
לה פקדיהם.למטה.מנשה.שנים.ושלשים.אל
ף.ומאתים׃
לו לבני.בנימן.תולדתם.למשפחתם.לבית.א
בתם.במספר.שמת.מבן.עשרים.שנה.ומעלה.כל.
יצא.צבא׃
לז פקדיהם.למטה.בנימן.חמשה.ושלשים.
אלף.וארבע.מאות׃
לח לבני.דן.תולדתם.למשפחתם.לבית.אבת
ם.במספר.שמת.מבן.עשרים.שנה.ומעלה.כל.יצ
א.צבא׃
לט פקדיהם.למטה.דן.שנים.וששים.אלף.ו
שבע.מאות׃

𐤌 𐤋𐤁𐤍𐤉.𐤀𐤔𐤓.𐤕𐤅𐤋𐤃𐤕𐤌.𐤋𐤌𐤔𐤐𐤇𐤕𐤌.𐤋𐤁𐤉𐤕.𐤀𐤁𐤕𐤌.𐤁𐤌𐤎𐤐𐤓.𐤔𐤌𐤕.𐤌𐤁𐤍.𐤏𐤔𐤓𐤉𐤌.𐤔𐤍𐤄.𐤅𐤌𐤏𐤋𐤄.𐤊𐤋.𐤉𐤑𐤀.𐤑𐤁𐤀|

𐤌𐤀 𐤐𐤒𐤃𐤉𐤄𐤌.𐤋𐤌𐤈𐤄.𐤀𐤔𐤓.𐤀𐤇𐤃.𐤅𐤀𐤓𐤁𐤏𐤉𐤌.𐤀𐤋𐤐.𐤅𐤇𐤌𐤔.𐤌𐤀𐤅𐤕|

𐤌𐤁 𐤁𐤍𐤉.𐤍𐤐𐤕𐤋𐤉.𐤕𐤅𐤋𐤃𐤕𐤌.𐤋𐤌𐤔𐤐𐤇𐤕𐤌.𐤋𐤁𐤉𐤕.𐤀𐤁𐤕𐤌.𐤁𐤌𐤎𐤐𐤓.𐤔𐤌𐤕.𐤌𐤁𐤍.𐤏𐤔𐤓𐤉𐤌.𐤔𐤍𐤄.𐤅𐤌𐤏𐤋𐤄.𐤊𐤋.𐤉𐤑𐤀.𐤑𐤁𐤀|

𐤌𐤂 𐤐𐤒𐤃𐤉𐤄𐤌.𐤋𐤌𐤈𐤄.𐤍𐤐𐤕𐤋𐤉.𐤔𐤋𐤔𐤄.𐤅𐤇𐤌𐤔𐤉𐤌.𐤀𐤋𐤐.𐤅𐤀𐤓𐤁𐤏.𐤌𐤀𐤅𐤕|

𐤌𐤃 𐤀𐤋𐤄.𐤄𐤐𐤒𐤃𐤉𐤌.𐤀𐤔𐤓.𐤐𐤒𐤃.𐤌𐤔𐤄.𐤅𐤀𐤄𐤓𐤍.𐤅𐤍𐤔𐤉𐤀𐤉.𐤉𐤔𐤓𐤀𐤋.𐤔𐤍𐤉𐤌.𐤏𐤔𐤓.𐤀𐤉𐤔.𐤀𐤉𐤔.𐤀𐤇𐤃.𐤋𐤁𐤉𐤕.𐤀𐤁𐤕𐤉𐤅.𐤄𐤉𐤅|

𐤌𐤄 𐤅𐤉𐤄𐤉𐤅.𐤊𐤋.𐤐𐤒𐤅𐤃𐤉.𐤁𐤍𐤉.𐤉𐤔𐤓𐤀𐤋.𐤋𐤁𐤉𐤕.𐤀𐤁𐤕𐤌.𐤌𐤁𐤍.𐤏𐤔𐤓𐤉𐤌.𐤔𐤍𐤄.𐤅𐤌𐤏𐤋𐤄.𐤊𐤋.𐤉𐤑𐤀.𐤑𐤁𐤀.𐤁𐤉𐤔𐤓𐤀𐤋|

𐤌𐤅 𐤅𐤉𐤄𐤉𐤅.𐤊𐤋.𐤄𐤐𐤒𐤃𐤉𐤌.𐤔𐤔.𐤌𐤀𐤅𐤕.𐤀𐤋𐤐.𐤅𐤔𐤋𐤔𐤕.𐤀𐤋𐤐𐤉𐤌.𐤅𐤇𐤌𐤔.𐤌𐤀𐤅𐤕.𐤅𐤇𐤌𐤔𐤉𐤌|

𐤌𐤆 𐤅𐤄𐤋𐤅𐤉𐤌.𐤋𐤌𐤈𐤄.𐤀𐤁𐤕𐤌.𐤋𐤀.𐤄𐤕𐤐𐤒𐤃𐤅.𐤁𐤕𐤅𐤊𐤌|

𐤌𐤇 𐤅𐤉𐤃𐤁𐤓.𐤉𐤄𐤅𐤄.𐤀𐤋.𐤌𐤔𐤄.𐤋𐤀𐤌𐤓|

𐤌𐤈 𐤀𐤊.𐤀𐤕.𐤌𐤈𐤄.𐤋𐤅𐤉.𐤋𐤀.𐤕𐤐𐤒𐤃.𐤅𐤀𐤕.𐤓𐤀𐤔𐤌.𐤋𐤀.𐤕𐤔𐤀.𐤁𐤕𐤅𐤊.𐤁𐤍𐤉.𐤉𐤔𐤓𐤀𐤋|

𐤍 𐤅𐤀𐤕𐤄.𐤄𐤐𐤒𐤃.𐤀𐤕.𐤄𐤋𐤅𐤉𐤌.𐤏𐤋.𐤌𐤔𐤊𐤍.𐤄𐤏𐤃𐤕.𐤅𐤏𐤋.𐤊𐤋.𐤊𐤋𐤉𐤅.𐤅𐤏𐤋.𐤊𐤋.𐤀𐤔𐤓.𐤋𐤅.𐤄𐤌𐤄.𐤉𐤔𐤀𐤅.𐤀𐤕.𐤄𐤌𐤔𐤊𐤍.𐤅𐤀𐤕.𐤊𐤋.𐤊𐤋𐤉𐤅.𐤅𐤄𐤌.𐤉𐤔𐤓𐤕𐤄𐤅.𐤅𐤎𐤁𐤉𐤁.𐤋𐤌𐤔𐤊𐤍.𐤉𐤇𐤍𐤅|

𐤍𐤀 𐤅𐤁𐤍𐤎𐤏.𐤄𐤌𐤔𐤊𐤍.𐤉𐤅𐤓𐤉𐤃𐤅.𐤀𐤕𐤅.𐤄𐤋𐤅𐤉𐤌.𐤅𐤁𐤇𐤍𐤕.𐤄𐤌𐤔𐤊𐤍.𐤉𐤒𐤉𐤌𐤅.𐤀𐤕𐤅.𐤄𐤋𐤅𐤉𐤌.𐤅𐤄𐤆𐤓.𐤄𐤒𐤓𐤁.𐤉𐤅𐤌𐤕|

𐤍𐤁 𐤅𐤇𐤍𐤅.𐤁𐤍𐤉.𐤉𐤔𐤓𐤀𐤋.𐤀𐤉𐤔.𐤏𐤋.𐤌𐤇𐤍𐤄𐤅.𐤅𐤀𐤉𐤔.𐤏𐤋.𐤃𐤂𐤋𐤅.𐤋𐤑𐤁𐤀𐤕𐤌|

53 𐤅𐤄𐤋𐤅𐤉𐤌.𐤉𐤇𐤍𐤅.𐤎𐤁𐤉𐤁.𐤋𐤌𐤔𐤊𐤍.𐤄𐤏𐤃𐤕.𐤅𐤋𐤀.𐤉
𐤄𐤉𐤄.𐤒𐤑𐤐.𐤏𐤋.𐤏𐤃𐤕.𐤁𐤍𐤉.𐤉𐤔𐤓𐤀𐤋.𐤅𐤔𐤌𐤓𐤅.𐤄𐤋𐤅𐤉𐤌.
𐤀𐤕.𐤌𐤔𐤌𐤓𐤕.𐤌𐤔𐤊𐤍.𐤄𐤏𐤃𐤅𐤕|
54 𐤅𐤉𐤏𐤔𐤅.𐤁𐤍𐤉.𐤉𐤔𐤓𐤀𐤋.𐤊𐤊𐤋.𐤀𐤔𐤓.𐤑𐤅𐤄.𐤉𐤄𐤅𐤄.
𐤀𐤕.𐤌𐤔𐤄.𐤊𐤍.𐤏𐤔𐤅||

𐤁𐤌𐤃𐤁𐤓.𐤇𐤋𐤒 2

1 𐤅𐤉𐤃𐤁𐤓.𐤉𐤄𐤅𐤄.𐤀𐤋.𐤌𐤔𐤄.𐤅𐤀𐤋.𐤀𐤄𐤓𐤍.𐤋𐤀𐤌𐤓|
2 𐤀𐤉𐤔.𐤏𐤋.𐤃𐤂𐤋𐤅.𐤁𐤀𐤕𐤕.𐤋𐤁𐤉𐤕.𐤀𐤁𐤕𐤌.𐤉𐤇𐤍𐤅.𐤁
𐤍𐤉.𐤉𐤔𐤓𐤀𐤋.𐤌𐤍𐤂𐤃.𐤎𐤁𐤉𐤁.𐤋𐤀𐤄𐤋.𐤌𐤅𐤏𐤃.𐤉𐤇𐤍𐤅|
3 𐤅𐤄𐤇𐤍𐤉𐤌.𐤒𐤃𐤌𐤄.𐤌𐤆𐤓𐤇𐤄.𐤃𐤂𐤋.𐤌𐤇𐤍𐤄.𐤉𐤄𐤅
𐤃𐤄.𐤋𐤑𐤁𐤀𐤕𐤌.𐤅𐤍𐤔𐤉𐤀.𐤋𐤁𐤍𐤉.𐤉𐤄𐤅𐤃𐤄.𐤍𐤇𐤔𐤅𐤍.𐤁𐤍.
𐤏𐤌𐤉𐤍𐤃𐤁|
4 𐤅𐤑𐤁𐤀𐤅.𐤅𐤐𐤒𐤃𐤉𐤄𐤌.𐤀𐤓𐤁𐤏𐤄.𐤅𐤔𐤁𐤏𐤉𐤌.𐤀𐤋𐤐.𐤅𐤔
𐤔.𐤌𐤀𐤅𐤕|
5 𐤅𐤄𐤇𐤍𐤉𐤌.𐤏𐤋𐤉𐤅.𐤌𐤈𐤄.𐤉𐤔𐤔𐤊𐤓.𐤅𐤍𐤔𐤉𐤀.𐤋𐤁𐤍𐤉.𐤉
𐤔𐤔𐤊𐤓.𐤍𐤕𐤍𐤀𐤋.𐤁𐤍.𐤑𐤅𐤏𐤓|
6 𐤅𐤑𐤁𐤀𐤅.𐤅𐤐𐤒𐤃𐤉𐤅.𐤀𐤓𐤁𐤏𐤄.𐤅𐤇𐤌𐤔𐤉𐤌.𐤀𐤋𐤐.𐤅𐤀𐤓𐤁
𐤏.𐤌𐤀𐤅𐤕|
7 𐤌𐤈𐤄.𐤆𐤁𐤅𐤋𐤍.𐤅𐤍𐤔𐤉𐤀.𐤋𐤁𐤍𐤉.𐤆𐤁𐤅𐤋𐤍.𐤀𐤋𐤉𐤀𐤁.𐤁𐤍
.𐤇𐤋𐤍|
8 𐤅𐤑𐤁𐤀𐤅.𐤅𐤐𐤒𐤃𐤉𐤅.𐤔𐤁𐤏𐤄.𐤅𐤇𐤌𐤔𐤉𐤌.𐤀𐤋𐤐.𐤅𐤀𐤓𐤁
𐤏.𐤌𐤀𐤅𐤕|
9 𐤊𐤋.𐤄𐤐𐤒𐤃𐤉𐤌.𐤋𐤌𐤇𐤍𐤄.𐤉𐤄𐤅𐤃𐤄.𐤌𐤀𐤕.𐤀𐤋𐤐.𐤅𐤔
𐤌𐤍𐤉𐤌.𐤀𐤋𐤐.𐤅𐤔𐤔𐤕.𐤀𐤋𐤐𐤉𐤌.𐤅𐤀𐤓𐤁𐤏.𐤌𐤀𐤅𐤕.𐤋𐤑𐤁𐤀𐤕
𐤌.𐤓𐤀𐤔𐤍𐤄.𐤉𐤎𐤏𐤅|
10 𐤃𐤂𐤋.𐤌𐤇𐤍𐤄.𐤓𐤀𐤅𐤁𐤍.𐤕𐤉𐤌𐤍𐤄.𐤋𐤑𐤁𐤀𐤕𐤌.𐤅𐤍𐤔
𐤉𐤀.𐤋𐤁𐤍𐤉.𐤓𐤀𐤅𐤁𐤍.𐤀𐤋𐤉𐤑𐤅𐤓.𐤁𐤍.𐤔𐤃𐤉𐤀𐤅𐤓|
11 𐤅𐤑𐤁𐤀𐤅.𐤅𐤐𐤒𐤃𐤉𐤅.𐤔𐤔𐤄.𐤅𐤀𐤓𐤁𐤏𐤉𐤌.𐤀𐤋𐤐.𐤅𐤇𐤌
𐤔.𐤌𐤀𐤅𐤕|

..𐤉𐤁.. 𐤅𐤄𐤇𐤅𐤍𐤌.𐤏𐤋𐤉𐤅.𐤌𐤈𐤄.𐤔𐤌𐤏𐤅𐤍.𐤅𐤍𐤔𐤉𐤀.𐤋𐤁𐤍𐤉.𐤔
𐤌𐤏𐤅𐤍.𐤔𐤋𐤌𐤉𐤀𐤋.𐤁𐤍.𐤑𐤅𐤓𐤉𐤔𐤃𐤉|
..𐤉𐤂.. 𐤅𐤑𐤁𐤀𐤅.𐤅𐤐𐤒𐤃𐤉𐤄𐤌.𐤕𐤔𐤏𐤄.𐤅𐤇𐤌𐤔𐤉𐤌.𐤀𐤋𐤐.𐤅
𐤔𐤋𐤔.𐤌𐤀𐤅𐤕|
..𐤉𐤃.. 𐤅𐤌𐤈𐤄.𐤂𐤃.𐤅𐤍𐤔𐤉𐤀.𐤋𐤁𐤍𐤉.𐤂𐤃.𐤀𐤋𐤉𐤎𐤐.𐤁𐤍.𐤓
𐤏𐤅𐤀𐤋|
..𐤈𐤅.. 𐤅𐤑𐤁𐤀𐤅.𐤅𐤐𐤒𐤃𐤉𐤄𐤌.𐤇𐤌𐤔𐤄.𐤅𐤀𐤓𐤁𐤏𐤉𐤌.𐤀𐤋𐤐.𐤅
𐤔𐤔.𐤌𐤀𐤅𐤕.𐤅𐤇𐤌𐤔𐤉𐤌|
..𐤈𐤆.. 𐤊𐤋.𐤄𐤐𐤒𐤃𐤉𐤌.𐤋𐤌𐤇𐤍𐤄.𐤓𐤀𐤅𐤁𐤍.𐤌𐤀𐤕.𐤀𐤋𐤐.𐤅𐤀
𐤇𐤃.𐤅𐤇𐤌𐤔𐤉𐤌.𐤀𐤋𐤐.𐤅𐤀𐤓𐤁𐤏.𐤌𐤀𐤅𐤕.𐤅𐤇𐤌𐤔𐤉𐤌.𐤋𐤑𐤁
𐤀𐤕𐤌.𐤅𐤔𐤍𐤉𐤌.𐤉𐤎𐤏𐤅|
..𐤉𐤆.. 𐤅𐤍𐤎𐤏.𐤀𐤄𐤋.𐤌𐤅𐤏𐤃.𐤌𐤇𐤍𐤄.𐤄𐤋𐤅𐤉𐤌.𐤁𐤕𐤅𐤊.𐤄𐤌
𐤇𐤍𐤕.𐤊𐤀𐤔𐤓.𐤉𐤇𐤍𐤅.𐤊𐤍.𐤉𐤎𐤏𐤅.𐤀𐤉𐤔.𐤏𐤋.𐤉𐤃𐤅.𐤋𐤃𐤂𐤋
𐤉𐤄𐤌|
..𐤉𐤇.. 𐤃𐤂𐤋.𐤌𐤇𐤍𐤄.𐤀𐤐𐤓𐤉𐤌.𐤉𐤌𐤄.𐤋𐤑𐤁𐤀𐤕𐤌.𐤅𐤍𐤔𐤉𐤀
.𐤋𐤁𐤍𐤉.𐤀𐤐𐤓𐤉𐤌.𐤀𐤋𐤉𐤔𐤌𐤏.𐤁𐤍.𐤏𐤌𐤉𐤄𐤅𐤃|
..𐤉𐤈.. 𐤅𐤑𐤁𐤀𐤅.𐤅𐤐𐤒𐤃𐤉𐤄𐤌.𐤀𐤓𐤁𐤏𐤉𐤌.𐤀𐤋𐤐.𐤅𐤇𐤌𐤔.𐤌
𐤀𐤅𐤕|
..𐤊.. 𐤅𐤏𐤋𐤉𐤅.𐤌𐤈𐤄.𐤌𐤍𐤔𐤄.𐤅𐤍𐤔𐤉𐤀.𐤋𐤁𐤍𐤉.𐤌𐤍𐤔𐤄.𐤂𐤌
𐤋𐤉𐤀𐤋.𐤁𐤍.𐤐𐤃𐤄𐤑𐤅𐤓|
..𐤊𐤀.. 𐤅𐤑𐤁𐤀𐤅.𐤅𐤐𐤒𐤃𐤉𐤄𐤌.𐤔𐤍𐤉𐤌.𐤅𐤔𐤋𐤔𐤉𐤌.𐤀𐤋𐤐.𐤅𐤌𐤀
𐤕𐤉𐤌|
..𐤊𐤁.. 𐤅𐤌𐤈𐤄.𐤁𐤍𐤉𐤌𐤍.𐤅𐤍𐤔𐤉𐤀.𐤋𐤁𐤍𐤉.𐤁𐤍𐤉𐤌𐤍.𐤀𐤁𐤉𐤃𐤍.
𐤁𐤍.𐤂𐤃𐤏𐤍𐤉|
..𐤊𐤂.. 𐤅𐤑𐤁𐤀𐤅.𐤅𐤐𐤒𐤃𐤉𐤄𐤌.𐤇𐤌𐤔𐤄.𐤅𐤔𐤋𐤔𐤉𐤌.𐤀𐤋𐤐.𐤅𐤀
𐤓𐤁𐤏.𐤌𐤀𐤅𐤕|
..𐤊𐤃.. 𐤊𐤋.𐤄𐤐𐤒𐤃𐤉𐤌.𐤋𐤌𐤇𐤍𐤄.𐤀𐤐𐤓𐤉𐤌.𐤌𐤀𐤕.𐤀𐤋𐤐.𐤅
𐤔𐤌𐤍𐤕.𐤀𐤋𐤐𐤉𐤌.𐤅𐤌𐤀𐤄.𐤋𐤑𐤁𐤀𐤕𐤌.𐤅𐤔𐤋𐤔𐤉𐤌.𐤉𐤎𐤏𐤅|
..𐤊𐤄.. 𐤃𐤂𐤋.𐤌𐤇𐤍𐤄.𐤃𐤍.𐤑𐤐𐤍𐤄.𐤋𐤑𐤁𐤀𐤕𐤌.𐤅𐤍𐤔𐤉𐤀.𐤋
𐤁𐤍𐤉.𐤃𐤍.𐤀𐤇𐤉𐤏𐤆𐤓.𐤁𐤍.𐤏𐤌𐤉𐤔𐤃𐤉|

ࠊࠅ ࠅࠑࠁࠀࠅ.ࠅࠐࠒࠃࠉࠄࠌ.ࠔࠍࠉࠌ.ࠅࠔࠔࠉࠌ.ࠀࠋࠐ.ࠅࠔࠁ
ࠏ.ࠌࠀࠅࠕ|

ࠊࠆ ࠅࠄࠇࠍࠉࠌ.ࠏࠋࠉࠅ.ࠌࠈࠄ.ࠀࠔࠓ.ࠅࠍࠔࠉࠀ.ࠋࠁࠍࠉ.ࠀࠔ
ࠓ.ࠐࠂࠏࠉࠀࠋ.ࠁࠍ.ࠏࠊࠓࠍ|

ࠊࠇ ࠅࠑࠁࠀࠅ.ࠅࠐࠒࠃࠉࠄࠌ.ࠀࠇࠃ.ࠅࠀࠓࠁࠏࠉࠌ.ࠀࠋࠐ.ࠅ
ࠇࠌࠔ.ࠌࠀࠅࠕ|

ࠊࠈ ࠅࠌࠈࠄ.ࠍࠐࠕࠋࠉ.ࠅࠍࠔࠉࠀ.ࠋࠁࠍࠉ.ࠍࠐࠕࠋࠉ.ࠀࠇࠉࠓࠏ
.ࠁࠍ.ࠏࠉࠍࠍ|

ࠋ ࠅࠑࠁࠀࠅ.ࠅࠐࠒࠃࠉࠄࠌ.ࠔࠋࠔࠄ.ࠅࠇࠌࠔࠉࠌ.ࠀࠋࠐ.ࠅ
ࠀࠓࠁࠏ.ࠌࠀࠅࠕ|

ࠋࠀ ࠊࠋ.ࠄࠐࠒࠃࠉࠌ.ࠋࠌࠇࠍࠄ.ࠃࠍ.ࠌࠀࠕ.ࠀࠋࠐ.ࠅࠔࠁࠏ
ࠄ.ࠅࠇࠌࠔࠉࠌ.ࠀࠋࠐ.ࠅࠔࠔ.ࠌࠀࠅࠕ.ࠋࠀࠇࠓࠍࠄ.ࠉࠎࠏࠅ.ࠋࠃ
ࠂࠋࠉࠄࠌ|

ࠋࠁ ࠀࠋࠄ.ࠐࠒࠅࠃࠉ.ࠁࠍࠉ.ࠉࠔࠓࠀࠋ.ࠋࠁࠉࠕ.ࠀࠁࠕࠌ.ࠊࠋ.
ࠐࠒࠅࠃࠉ.ࠄࠌࠇࠍࠕ.ࠋࠑࠁࠀࠕࠌ.ࠔࠔ.ࠌࠀࠅࠕ.ࠀࠋࠐ.ࠅࠔࠋࠔ
ࠕ.ࠀࠋࠐࠉࠌ.ࠅࠇࠌࠔ.ࠌࠀࠅࠕ.ࠅࠇࠌࠔࠉࠌ|

ࠋࠂ ࠅࠄࠋࠅࠉࠌ.ࠋࠀ.ࠄࠕࠐࠒࠃࠅ.ࠁࠕࠅࠊ.ࠁࠍࠉ.ࠉࠔࠓࠀࠋ.ࠊ
ࠀࠔࠓ.ࠑࠅࠄ.ࠉࠄࠅࠄ.ࠀࠕ.ࠌࠔࠄ|

ࠋࠃ ࠅࠉࠏࠔࠅ.ࠁࠍࠉ.ࠉࠔࠓࠀࠋ.ࠊࠊࠋ.ࠀࠔࠓ.ࠑࠅࠄ.ࠉࠄࠅࠄ.
ࠀࠕ.ࠌࠔࠄ.ࠊࠍ.ࠇࠍࠅ.ࠋࠃࠂࠋࠉࠄࠌ.ࠅࠊࠍ.ࠍࠎࠏࠅ.ࠀࠉࠔ.ࠋࠌ
ࠔࠐࠇࠕࠉࠅ.ࠏࠋ.ࠁࠉࠕ.ࠀࠁࠕࠉࠅ‖

ࠁࠌࠃࠁࠓ.ࠇࠋࠒ ࠂ

ࠀ ࠅࠀࠋࠄ.ࠕࠅࠋࠃࠕ.ࠀࠄࠓࠍ.ࠅࠌࠔࠄ.ࠁࠉࠅࠌ.ࠃࠁࠓ.ࠉࠄࠅࠄ.
ࠀࠕ.ࠌࠔࠄ.ࠁࠄࠓ.ࠎࠉࠍࠉ|

ࠁ ࠅࠀࠋࠄ.ࠔࠌࠅࠕ.ࠁࠍࠉ.ࠀࠄࠓࠍ.ࠄࠁࠊࠅࠓ.ࠍࠃࠁ.ࠅࠀࠁࠉࠄࠅ
ࠀ.ࠀࠋࠏࠆࠓ.ࠅࠀࠉࠕࠌࠓ|

ࠂ ࠀࠋࠄ.ࠔࠌࠅࠕ.ࠁࠍࠉ.ࠀࠄࠓࠍ.ࠄࠊࠄࠍࠉࠌ.ࠄࠌࠔࠇࠉࠌ.
ࠀࠔࠓ.ࠌࠋࠀ.ࠉࠃࠌ.ࠋࠊࠄࠍ|

4 𐤅𐤉𐤌𐤕.𐤍𐤃𐤁.𐤅𐤀𐤁𐤉𐤄𐤅𐤀.𐤋𐤐𐤍𐤉.𐤉𐤄𐤅𐤄.𐤁𐤄𐤒𐤓𐤁𐤌.
𐤀𐤔.𐤆𐤓𐤄.𐤋𐤐𐤍𐤉.𐤉𐤄𐤅𐤄.𐤁𐤌𐤃𐤁𐤓.𐤎𐤉𐤍𐤉.𐤅𐤁𐤍𐤉𐤌.𐤋𐤀.
𐤄𐤉𐤅.𐤋𐤄𐤌.𐤅𐤉𐤊𐤄𐤍.𐤀𐤋𐤏𐤆𐤓.𐤅𐤀𐤉𐤕𐤌𐤓.𐤏𐤋.𐤐𐤍𐤉.𐤀𐤄𐤓𐤍
.𐤀𐤁𐤉𐤄𐤌|

5 𐤅𐤉𐤃𐤁𐤓.𐤉𐤄𐤅𐤄.𐤀𐤋.𐤌𐤔𐤄.𐤋𐤀𐤌𐤓|

6 𐤄𐤒𐤓𐤁.𐤀𐤕.𐤌𐤈𐤄.𐤋𐤅𐤉.𐤅𐤄𐤏𐤌𐤃𐤕.𐤀𐤕𐤅.𐤋𐤐𐤍𐤉.𐤀𐤄
𐤓𐤍.𐤄𐤊𐤄𐤍.𐤅𐤔𐤓𐤕𐤅.𐤀𐤕𐤅|

7 𐤅𐤔𐤌𐤓𐤅.𐤀𐤕.𐤌𐤔𐤌𐤓𐤕𐤅.𐤅𐤀𐤕.𐤌𐤔𐤌𐤓𐤕.𐤊𐤋.𐤄𐤏𐤃𐤄
.𐤋𐤐𐤍𐤉.𐤀𐤄𐤋.𐤌𐤅𐤏𐤃.𐤋𐤏𐤁𐤃.𐤀𐤕.𐤏𐤁𐤃𐤕.𐤄𐤌𐤔𐤊𐤍|

8 𐤅𐤔𐤌𐤓𐤅.𐤀𐤕.𐤊𐤋.𐤊𐤋𐤉.𐤀𐤄𐤋.𐤌𐤅𐤏𐤃.𐤅𐤀𐤕.𐤌𐤔𐤌𐤓𐤕.
𐤁𐤍𐤉.𐤉𐤔𐤓𐤀𐤋.𐤋𐤏𐤁𐤃.𐤀𐤕.𐤏𐤁𐤃𐤕.𐤄𐤌𐤔𐤊𐤍|

9 𐤅𐤍𐤕𐤕𐤄.𐤀𐤕.𐤄𐤋𐤅𐤉𐤌.𐤋𐤀𐤄𐤓𐤍.𐤅𐤋𐤁𐤍𐤉𐤅.𐤍𐤕𐤅𐤍𐤌.𐤍𐤕
𐤅𐤍𐤌.𐤄𐤌𐤄.𐤋𐤅.𐤌𐤀𐤕.𐤁𐤍𐤉.𐤉𐤔𐤓𐤀𐤋|

10 𐤅𐤀𐤕.𐤀𐤄𐤓𐤍.𐤅𐤀𐤕.𐤁𐤍𐤉𐤅.𐤕𐤐𐤒𐤃.𐤅𐤔𐤌𐤓𐤅.𐤀𐤕.𐤊𐤄
𐤍𐤕𐤌.𐤅𐤄𐤆𐤓.𐤄𐤒𐤓𐤁.𐤉𐤅𐤌𐤕|

11 𐤅𐤉𐤃𐤁𐤓.𐤉𐤄𐤅𐤄.𐤀𐤋.𐤌𐤔𐤄.𐤋𐤀𐤌𐤓|

12 𐤅𐤀𐤍𐤉.𐤄𐤍𐤄.𐤋𐤒𐤇𐤕𐤉.𐤀𐤕.𐤄𐤋𐤅𐤉𐤌.𐤌𐤕𐤅𐤊.𐤁𐤍𐤉.𐤉
𐤔𐤓𐤀𐤋.𐤕𐤇𐤕.𐤊𐤋.𐤁𐤊𐤅𐤓.𐤐𐤈𐤓.𐤓𐤇𐤌.𐤌𐤁𐤍𐤉.𐤉𐤔𐤓𐤀𐤋.𐤅
𐤄𐤉𐤅.𐤋𐤉.𐤄𐤋𐤅𐤉𐤌|

13 𐤊𐤉.𐤋𐤉.𐤊𐤋.𐤁𐤊𐤅𐤓.𐤁𐤉𐤅𐤌.𐤄𐤊𐤕𐤉.𐤊𐤋.𐤁𐤊𐤅𐤓.𐤁𐤀𐤓
𐤑.𐤌𐤑𐤓𐤉𐤌.𐤄𐤒𐤃𐤔𐤕𐤉.𐤋𐤉.𐤊𐤋.𐤁𐤊𐤅𐤓.𐤁𐤉𐤔𐤓𐤀𐤋.𐤌𐤀
𐤃𐤌.𐤏𐤃.𐤁𐤄𐤌𐤄.𐤋𐤉.𐤉𐤄𐤉𐤅.𐤀𐤍𐤉.𐤉𐤄𐤅𐤄|

14 𐤅𐤉𐤃𐤁𐤓.𐤉𐤄𐤅𐤄.𐤀𐤋.𐤌𐤔𐤄.𐤁𐤌𐤃𐤁𐤓.𐤎𐤉𐤍𐤉.𐤋𐤀𐤌
𐤓|

15 𐤐𐤒𐤃.𐤀𐤕.𐤁𐤍𐤉.𐤋𐤅𐤉.𐤋𐤁𐤉𐤕.𐤀𐤁𐤕𐤌.𐤋𐤌𐤔𐤐𐤇𐤕𐤌.
𐤊𐤋.𐤆𐤊𐤓.𐤌𐤁𐤍.𐤇𐤃𐤔.𐤅𐤌𐤏𐤋𐤄.𐤕𐤐𐤒𐤃𐤌|

16 𐤅𐤉𐤐𐤒𐤃.𐤀𐤕𐤌.𐤌𐤔𐤄.𐤏𐤋.𐤐𐤉.𐤉𐤄𐤅𐤄.𐤊𐤀𐤔𐤓.𐤑𐤅𐤄
|

17 𐤅𐤉𐤄𐤉𐤅.𐤀𐤋𐤄.𐤁𐤍𐤉.𐤋𐤅𐤉.𐤁𐤔𐤌𐤕𐤌.𐤂𐤓𐤔𐤅𐤍.𐤅𐤒𐤄𐤕
.𐤅𐤌𐤓𐤓𐤉|

𐤉𐤇 𐤅𐤀𐤋𐤄.𐤔𐤌𐤅𐤕.𐤁𐤍𐤉.𐤂𐤓𐤔𐤅𐤍.𐤋𐤌𐤔𐤐𐤇𐤕𐤌.𐤋𐤁𐤍𐤉.𐤅
𐤔𐤌𐤏𐤉|

𐤉𐤈 𐤅𐤁𐤍𐤉.𐤒𐤄𐤕.𐤋𐤌𐤔𐤐𐤇𐤕𐤌.𐤏𐤌𐤓𐤌.𐤅𐤉𐤑𐤄𐤓.𐤇𐤁𐤓
𐤅𐤍.𐤅𐤏𐤆𐤉𐤀𐤋|

𐤊 𐤅𐤁𐤍𐤉.𐤌𐤓𐤓𐤉.𐤋𐤌𐤔𐤐𐤇𐤕𐤌.𐤌𐤇𐤋𐤉.𐤅𐤌𐤅𐤔𐤉.𐤀𐤋𐤄.
𐤄𐤌.𐤌𐤔𐤐𐤇𐤕.𐤄𐤋𐤅𐤉.𐤋𐤁𐤉𐤕.𐤀𐤁𐤕𐤌|

𐤊𐤀 𐤋𐤂𐤓𐤔𐤅𐤍.𐤌𐤔𐤐𐤇𐤕.𐤄𐤋𐤁𐤍𐤉.𐤅𐤌𐤔𐤐𐤇𐤕.𐤄𐤔𐤌𐤏𐤉
𐤀𐤋𐤄.𐤄𐤌.𐤌𐤔𐤐𐤇𐤕.𐤄𐤂𐤓𐤔𐤍𐤉|

𐤊𐤁 𐤐𐤒𐤃𐤉𐤄𐤌.𐤁𐤌𐤎𐤐𐤓.𐤊𐤋.𐤆𐤊𐤓.𐤌𐤁𐤍.𐤇𐤃𐤔.𐤅𐤌𐤏
𐤋𐤄.𐤐𐤒𐤃𐤉𐤄𐤌.𐤔𐤁𐤏𐤕.𐤀𐤋𐤐𐤉𐤌.𐤅𐤇𐤌𐤔.𐤌𐤀𐤅𐤕|

𐤊𐤂 𐤌𐤔𐤐𐤇𐤕.𐤄𐤂𐤓𐤔𐤍𐤉.𐤀𐤇𐤓𐤉.𐤄𐤌𐤔𐤊𐤍.𐤉𐤇𐤍𐤅.𐤉𐤌
𐤄|

𐤊𐤃 𐤅𐤍𐤔𐤉𐤀.𐤁𐤉𐤕.𐤀𐤁.𐤋𐤂𐤓𐤔𐤍𐤉.𐤀𐤋𐤉𐤎𐤐.𐤁𐤍.𐤋𐤀𐤋|

𐤊𐤄 𐤅𐤌𐤔𐤌𐤓𐤕.𐤁𐤍𐤉.𐤂𐤓𐤔𐤅𐤍.𐤁𐤀𐤄𐤋.𐤌𐤅𐤏𐤃.𐤄𐤌𐤔𐤊𐤍.
𐤅𐤄𐤀𐤄𐤋.𐤌𐤊𐤎𐤄𐤅.𐤅𐤌𐤎𐤊.𐤐𐤕𐤇.𐤀𐤄𐤋.𐤌𐤅𐤏𐤃|

𐤊𐤅 𐤅𐤒𐤋𐤏𐤉.𐤄𐤇𐤑𐤓.𐤅𐤀𐤕.𐤌𐤎𐤊.𐤐𐤕𐤇.𐤄𐤇𐤑𐤓.𐤀𐤔𐤓
𐤏𐤋.𐤄𐤌𐤔𐤊𐤍.𐤅𐤏𐤋.𐤄𐤌𐤆𐤁𐤇.𐤎𐤁𐤉𐤁.𐤅𐤀𐤕.𐤌𐤉𐤕𐤓𐤉𐤅.𐤋
𐤊𐤋.𐤏𐤁𐤃𐤕𐤅|

𐤊𐤆 𐤅𐤋𐤒𐤄𐤕.𐤌𐤔𐤐𐤇𐤕.𐤄𐤏𐤌𐤓𐤌𐤉.𐤅𐤌𐤔𐤐𐤇𐤕.𐤄𐤉𐤑
𐤄𐤓𐤉.𐤅𐤌𐤔𐤐𐤇𐤕.𐤄𐤇𐤁𐤓𐤍𐤉.𐤅𐤌𐤔𐤐𐤇𐤕.𐤄𐤏𐤆𐤉𐤀𐤋𐤉.𐤀
𐤋𐤄.𐤄𐤌.𐤌𐤔𐤐𐤇𐤕.𐤄𐤒𐤄𐤕𐤉|

𐤊𐤇 𐤁𐤌𐤎𐤐𐤓.𐤊𐤋.𐤆𐤊𐤓.𐤌𐤁𐤍.𐤇𐤃𐤔.𐤅𐤌𐤏𐤋𐤄.𐤔𐤌𐤍𐤕.
𐤀𐤋𐤐𐤉𐤌.𐤅𐤔𐤔.𐤌𐤀𐤅𐤕.𐤔𐤌𐤓𐤉.𐤌𐤔𐤌𐤓𐤕.𐤄𐤒𐤃𐤔|

𐤊𐤈 𐤌𐤔𐤐𐤇𐤕.𐤁𐤍𐤉.𐤒𐤄𐤕.𐤉𐤇𐤍𐤅.𐤏𐤋.𐤉𐤓𐤊.𐤄𐤌𐤔𐤊𐤍.
𐤕𐤉𐤌𐤍𐤄|

𐤋 𐤅𐤍𐤔𐤉𐤀.𐤁𐤉𐤕.𐤀𐤁.𐤋𐤌𐤔𐤐𐤇𐤕.𐤄𐤒𐤄𐤕𐤉.𐤀𐤋𐤉𐤑
𐤐𐤍.𐤁𐤍.𐤏𐤆𐤉𐤀𐤋|

𐤋𐤀 𐤅𐤌𐤔𐤌𐤓𐤕𐤌.𐤄𐤀𐤓𐤍.𐤅𐤄𐤔𐤋𐤇𐤍.𐤅𐤄𐤌𐤍𐤓𐤄.𐤅𐤄𐤌𐤆𐤁
𐤇𐤕.𐤅𐤊𐤋𐤉.𐤄𐤒𐤃𐤔.𐤀𐤔𐤓.𐤉𐤔𐤓𐤕𐤅.𐤁𐤄𐤌.𐤅𐤄𐤌𐤎𐤊.𐤅𐤊𐤋.
𐤏𐤁𐤃𐤕𐤅|

𐤋𐤁 𐤅𐤍𐤔𐤉𐤀.𐤍𐤔𐤉𐤀𐤉.𐤄𐤋𐤅𐤉.𐤀𐤋𐤏𐤆𐤓.𐤁𐤍.𐤀𐤄𐤓𐤍.𐤄𐤊𐤄𐤍.𐤐𐤒𐤃𐤕.𐤔𐤌𐤓𐤉.𐤌𐤔𐤌𐤓𐤕.𐤄𐤒𐤃𐤔|

𐤋𐤂 𐤋𐤌𐤓𐤓𐤉.𐤌𐤔𐤐𐤇𐤕.𐤄𐤌𐤇𐤋𐤉.𐤅𐤌𐤔𐤐𐤇𐤕.𐤄𐤌𐤅𐤔𐤉.𐤀𐤋𐤄.𐤄𐤌.𐤌𐤔𐤐𐤇𐤕.𐤌𐤓𐤓𐤉|

𐤋𐤃 𐤅𐤐𐤒𐤃𐤉𐤄𐤌.𐤁𐤌𐤎𐤐𐤓.𐤊𐤋.𐤆𐤊𐤓.𐤌𐤁𐤍.𐤇𐤃𐤔.𐤅𐤌𐤏𐤋𐤄.𐤔𐤔𐤕.𐤀𐤋𐤐𐤉𐤌.𐤅𐤌𐤀𐤕𐤉𐤌|

𐤋𐤄 𐤅𐤍𐤔𐤉𐤀.𐤁𐤉𐤕.𐤀𐤁.𐤋𐤌𐤔𐤐𐤇𐤕.𐤌𐤓𐤓𐤉.𐤑𐤅𐤓𐤉𐤀𐤋.𐤁𐤍.𐤀𐤁𐤉𐤇𐤉𐤋.𐤏𐤋.𐤉𐤓𐤊.𐤄𐤌𐤔𐤊𐤍.𐤉𐤇𐤍𐤅.𐤑𐤐𐤍𐤄|

𐤋𐤅 𐤅𐤐𐤒𐤃𐤕.𐤌𐤔𐤌𐤓𐤕.𐤁𐤍𐤉.𐤌𐤓𐤓𐤉.𐤒𐤓𐤔𐤉.𐤄𐤌𐤔𐤊𐤍.𐤅𐤁𐤓𐤉𐤇𐤉𐤅.𐤅𐤏𐤌𐤃𐤉𐤅.𐤅𐤀𐤃𐤍𐤉𐤅.𐤅𐤊𐤋.𐤊𐤋𐤉𐤅.𐤅𐤊𐤋.𐤏𐤁𐤃𐤕𐤅|

𐤋𐤆 𐤅𐤏𐤌𐤃𐤉.𐤄𐤇𐤑𐤓.𐤎𐤁𐤉𐤁.𐤅𐤀𐤃𐤍𐤉𐤄𐤌.𐤅𐤉𐤕𐤃𐤕𐤌.𐤅𐤌𐤉𐤕𐤓𐤉𐤄𐤌|

𐤋𐤇 𐤅𐤄𐤇𐤍𐤉𐤌.𐤋𐤐𐤍𐤉.𐤄𐤌𐤔𐤊𐤍.𐤒𐤃𐤌𐤄.𐤋𐤐𐤍𐤉.𐤀𐤄𐤋.𐤌𐤅𐤏𐤃.𐤌𐤆𐤓𐤇𐤄.𐤌𐤔𐤄.𐤅𐤀𐤄𐤓𐤍.𐤅𐤁𐤍𐤉𐤅.𐤔𐤌𐤓𐤉𐤌.𐤌𐤔𐤌𐤓𐤕.𐤄𐤌𐤒𐤃𐤔.𐤋𐤌𐤔𐤌𐤓𐤕.𐤁𐤍𐤉.𐤉𐤔𐤓𐤀𐤋.𐤅𐤄𐤆𐤓.𐤄𐤒𐤓𐤁.𐤉𐤅𐤌𐤕|

𐤋𐤈 𐤊𐤋.𐤐𐤒𐤅𐤃𐤉.𐤄𐤋𐤅𐤉𐤌.𐤀𐤔𐤓.𐤐𐤒𐤃.𐤌𐤔𐤄.𐤅𐤀𐤄𐤓𐤍.𐤏𐤋.𐤐𐤉.𐤉𐤄𐤅𐤄.𐤋𐤌𐤔𐤐𐤇𐤕𐤌.𐤊𐤋.𐤆𐤊𐤓.𐤌𐤁𐤍.𐤇𐤃𐤔.𐤅𐤌𐤏𐤋𐤄.𐤔𐤍𐤉𐤌.𐤅𐤏𐤔𐤓𐤉𐤌.𐤀𐤋𐤐|

𐤌 𐤅𐤉𐤀𐤌𐤓.𐤉𐤄𐤅𐤄.𐤀𐤋.𐤌𐤔𐤄.𐤐𐤒𐤃.𐤊𐤋.𐤁𐤊𐤓.𐤆𐤊𐤓.𐤋𐤁𐤍𐤉.𐤉𐤔𐤓𐤀𐤋.𐤌𐤁𐤍.𐤇𐤃𐤔.𐤅𐤌𐤏𐤋𐤄.𐤅𐤔𐤀.𐤀𐤕.𐤌𐤎𐤐𐤓.𐤔𐤌𐤕𐤌|

𐤌𐤀 𐤅𐤋𐤒𐤇𐤕.𐤀𐤕.𐤄𐤋𐤅𐤉𐤌.𐤋𐤉.𐤀𐤍𐤉.𐤉𐤄𐤅𐤄.𐤕𐤇𐤕.𐤊𐤋.𐤁𐤊𐤓.𐤁𐤁𐤍𐤉.𐤉𐤔𐤓𐤀𐤋.𐤅𐤀𐤕.𐤁𐤄𐤌𐤕.𐤄𐤋𐤅𐤉𐤌.𐤕𐤇𐤕.𐤊𐤋.𐤁𐤊𐤅𐤓.𐤁𐤁𐤄𐤌𐤕.𐤁𐤍𐤉.𐤉𐤔𐤓𐤀𐤋|

𐤌𐤁 𐤅𐤉𐤐𐤒𐤃.𐤌𐤔𐤄.𐤊𐤀𐤔𐤓.𐤑𐤅𐤄.𐤉𐤄𐤅𐤄.𐤀𐤕𐤅.𐤀𐤕.𐤊𐤋.𐤁𐤊𐤓.𐤁𐤁𐤍𐤉.𐤉𐤔𐤓𐤀𐤋|

𐤌𐤂 𐤅𐤉𐤄𐤉.𐤊𐤋.𐤁𐤊𐤅𐤓.𐤆𐤊𐤓.𐤁𐤌𐤎𐤐𐤓.𐤔𐤌𐤅𐤕.𐤌𐤁𐤍.𐤇𐤃𐤔.𐤅𐤌𐤏𐤋𐤄.𐤋𐤐𐤒𐤃𐤉𐤄𐤌.𐤔𐤍𐤉𐤌.𐤅𐤏𐤔𐤓𐤉𐤌.𐤀𐤋𐤐.𐤔𐤋𐤔𐤄.𐤅𐤔𐤁𐤏𐤉𐤌.𐤅𐤌𐤀𐤕𐤉𐤌|

44 𐤅𐤉𐤃𐤁𐤓.𐤉𐤄𐤅𐤄.𐤀𐤋.𐤌𐤔𐤄.𐤋𐤀𐤌𐤓|
45 𐤒𐤇.𐤀𐤕.𐤄𐤋𐤅𐤉𐤌.𐤕𐤇𐤕.𐤊𐤋.𐤁𐤊𐤅𐤓.𐤁𐤁𐤍𐤉.𐤉𐤔𐤓
𐤀𐤋.𐤅𐤀𐤕.𐤁𐤄𐤌𐤕.𐤄𐤋𐤅𐤉𐤌.𐤕𐤇𐤕.𐤁𐤄𐤌𐤕𐤌.𐤅𐤄𐤉𐤅.𐤋𐤉.𐤄
𐤋𐤅𐤉𐤌.𐤀𐤍𐤉.𐤉𐤄𐤅𐤄|
46 𐤅𐤀𐤕.𐤐𐤃𐤅𐤉𐤉.𐤄𐤔𐤋𐤔𐤄.𐤅𐤄𐤔𐤁𐤏𐤉𐤌.𐤅𐤄𐤌𐤀𐤕𐤉
𐤌.𐤄𐤏𐤃𐤐𐤉𐤌.𐤏𐤋.𐤄𐤋𐤅𐤉𐤌.𐤌𐤁𐤊𐤅𐤓.𐤁𐤍𐤉.𐤉𐤔𐤓𐤀𐤋|
47 𐤅𐤋𐤒𐤇𐤕.𐤇𐤌𐤔𐤕.𐤇𐤌𐤔𐤕.𐤔𐤒𐤋𐤉𐤌.𐤋𐤂𐤋𐤂𐤋𐤕
.𐤁𐤔𐤒𐤋.𐤄𐤒𐤃𐤔.𐤕𐤒𐤇.𐤏𐤔𐤓𐤉𐤌.𐤂𐤓𐤄.𐤄𐤔𐤒𐤋|
48 𐤅𐤍𐤕𐤕𐤄.𐤄𐤊𐤎𐤐.𐤋𐤀𐤄𐤓𐤍.𐤅𐤋𐤁𐤍𐤉𐤅.𐤐𐤃𐤅𐤉𐤉.𐤄𐤏𐤃
𐤐𐤉𐤌.𐤁𐤄𐤌|
49 𐤅𐤉𐤒𐤇.𐤌𐤔𐤄.𐤀𐤕.𐤊𐤎𐤐.𐤄𐤐𐤃𐤉𐤅𐤌.𐤌𐤀𐤕.𐤄𐤏
𐤃𐤐𐤉𐤌.𐤏𐤋.𐤐𐤃𐤅𐤉𐤉.𐤄𐤋𐤅𐤉𐤌|
50 𐤌𐤀𐤕.𐤁𐤊𐤅𐤓.𐤁𐤍𐤉.𐤉𐤔𐤓𐤀𐤋.𐤋𐤒𐤇.𐤀𐤕.𐤄𐤊𐤎𐤐.𐤇
𐤌𐤔𐤄.𐤅𐤔𐤔𐤉𐤌.𐤅𐤔𐤋𐤔.𐤌𐤀𐤅𐤕.𐤅𐤀𐤋𐤐.𐤁𐤔𐤒𐤋.𐤄𐤒𐤃𐤔|
51 𐤅𐤉𐤕𐤍.𐤌𐤔𐤄.𐤀𐤕.𐤊𐤎𐤐.𐤄𐤐𐤃𐤉𐤌.𐤋𐤀𐤄𐤓𐤍.𐤅𐤋𐤁𐤍𐤉𐤅
.𐤏𐤋.𐤐𐤉.𐤉𐤄𐤅𐤄.𐤊𐤀𐤔𐤓.𐤑𐤅𐤄.𐤉𐤄𐤅𐤄.𐤀𐤕.𐤌𐤔𐤄||

𐤁𐤌𐤃𐤁𐤓.𐤇𐤋𐤒 4

1 𐤅𐤉𐤃𐤁𐤓.𐤉𐤄𐤅𐤄.𐤀𐤋.𐤌𐤔𐤄.𐤅𐤀𐤋.𐤀𐤄𐤓𐤍.𐤋𐤀𐤌𐤓|
2 𐤍𐤔𐤀.𐤀𐤕.𐤓𐤀𐤔.𐤁𐤍𐤉.𐤒𐤄𐤕.𐤌𐤕𐤅𐤊.𐤁𐤍𐤉.𐤋𐤅𐤉.𐤋𐤌𐤔
𐤐𐤇𐤕𐤌.𐤋𐤁𐤉𐤕.𐤀𐤁𐤕𐤌|
3 𐤌𐤁𐤍.𐤔𐤋𐤔𐤉𐤌.𐤔𐤍𐤄.𐤅𐤌𐤏𐤋𐤄.𐤅𐤏𐤃.𐤁𐤍.𐤇𐤌𐤔𐤉𐤌.
𐤔𐤍𐤄.𐤊𐤋.𐤁𐤀.𐤋𐤑𐤁𐤀.𐤋𐤏𐤔𐤅𐤕.𐤌𐤋𐤀𐤊𐤄.𐤁𐤀𐤄𐤋.𐤌𐤅𐤏
𐤃|
4 𐤆𐤀𐤕.𐤏𐤁𐤃𐤕.𐤁𐤍𐤉.𐤒𐤄𐤕.𐤁𐤀𐤄𐤋.𐤌𐤅𐤏𐤃.𐤒𐤃𐤔.
𐤄𐤒𐤃𐤔𐤉𐤌|
5 𐤅𐤁𐤀.𐤀𐤄𐤓𐤍.𐤅𐤁𐤍𐤉𐤅.𐤁𐤍𐤎𐤏.𐤄𐤌𐤇𐤍𐤄.𐤅𐤄𐤅𐤓𐤃𐤅.𐤀𐤕.
𐤐𐤓𐤊𐤕.𐤄𐤌𐤎𐤊.𐤅𐤊𐤎𐤅.𐤁𐤄.𐤀𐤕.𐤀𐤓𐤍.𐤄𐤏𐤃𐤕|
6 𐤅𐤍𐤕𐤍𐤅.𐤏𐤋𐤉𐤅.𐤊𐤎𐤅𐤉.𐤏𐤅𐤓.𐤕𐤇𐤔.𐤅𐤐𐤓𐤔𐤅.𐤁𐤂𐤃.𐤊𐤋
𐤉𐤋.𐤕𐤊𐤋𐤕.𐤌𐤋𐤌𐤏𐤋𐤄.𐤅𐤔𐤌𐤅.𐤁𐤃𐤉𐤅|

ז 𐤅𐤏𐤋.𐤔𐤋𐤇𐤍.𐤄𐤐𐤍𐤉𐤌.𐤉𐤐𐤓𐤔𐤅.𐤁𐤂𐤃.𐤕𐤊𐤋𐤕.𐤅𐤍𐤕𐤍
𐤅.𐤏𐤋𐤉𐤅.𐤀𐤕.𐤄𐤒𐤏𐤓𐤕.𐤅𐤀𐤕.𐤄𐤊𐤐𐤕.𐤅𐤀𐤕.𐤄𐤌𐤍𐤒𐤉𐤕.𐤅
𐤀𐤕.𐤒𐤔𐤅𐤕.𐤄𐤍𐤎𐤊.𐤅𐤋𐤇𐤌.𐤄𐤕𐤌𐤉𐤃.𐤏𐤋𐤉𐤅.𐤉𐤄𐤉𐤄|
ח 𐤅𐤐𐤓𐤔𐤅.𐤏𐤋𐤉𐤄𐤌.𐤁𐤂𐤃.𐤕𐤅𐤋𐤏𐤕.𐤔𐤍𐤉.𐤅𐤊𐤎𐤅.𐤀𐤕𐤅.
𐤁𐤌𐤊𐤎𐤄.𐤏𐤅𐤓.𐤕𐤇𐤔.𐤅𐤔𐤌𐤅.𐤀𐤕.𐤁𐤃𐤉𐤅|
ט 𐤅𐤋𐤒𐤇𐤅.𐤁𐤂𐤃.𐤕𐤊𐤋𐤕.𐤅𐤊𐤎𐤅.𐤀𐤕.𐤌𐤍𐤓𐤕.𐤄𐤌𐤀𐤅𐤓.
𐤅𐤀𐤕.𐤍𐤓𐤕𐤉𐤄.𐤅𐤀𐤕.𐤌𐤋𐤒𐤇𐤉𐤄.𐤅𐤀𐤕.𐤌𐤇𐤕𐤕𐤉𐤄.𐤅𐤀𐤕
.𐤊𐤋.𐤊𐤋𐤉.𐤔𐤌𐤍𐤄.𐤀𐤔𐤓.𐤉𐤔𐤓𐤕𐤅.𐤋𐤄.𐤁𐤄𐤌|
י 𐤅𐤍𐤕𐤍𐤅.𐤀𐤕𐤄.𐤅𐤀𐤕.𐤊𐤋.𐤊𐤋𐤉𐤄.𐤀𐤋.𐤌𐤊𐤎𐤄.𐤏𐤅𐤓.𐤕
𐤇𐤔.𐤅𐤍𐤕𐤍𐤅.𐤏𐤋.𐤄𐤌𐤅𐤈|
יא 𐤅𐤏𐤋.𐤌𐤆𐤁𐤇.𐤄𐤆𐤄𐤁.𐤉𐤐𐤓𐤔𐤅.𐤁𐤂𐤃.𐤕𐤊𐤋𐤕.𐤅𐤊
𐤎𐤅.𐤀𐤕𐤅.𐤁𐤌𐤊𐤎𐤄.𐤏𐤅𐤓.𐤕𐤇𐤔.𐤅𐤔𐤌𐤅.𐤀𐤕.𐤁𐤃𐤉𐤅|
יב 𐤅𐤋𐤒𐤇𐤅.𐤀𐤕.𐤊𐤋.𐤊𐤋𐤉.𐤄𐤔𐤓𐤕.𐤀𐤔𐤓.𐤉𐤔𐤓𐤕𐤅.𐤁𐤌.
𐤁𐤒𐤃𐤔.𐤅𐤍𐤕𐤍𐤅.𐤀𐤋.𐤁𐤂𐤃.𐤕𐤊𐤋𐤕.𐤅𐤊𐤎𐤅.𐤀𐤅𐤕𐤌.𐤁𐤌𐤊
𐤎𐤄.𐤏𐤅𐤓.𐤕𐤇𐤔.𐤅𐤍𐤕𐤍𐤅.𐤏𐤋.𐤄𐤌𐤅𐤈|
יג 𐤅𐤃𐤔𐤍𐤅.𐤀𐤕.𐤄𐤌𐤆𐤁𐤇.𐤅𐤐𐤓𐤔𐤅.𐤏𐤋𐤉𐤅.𐤁𐤂𐤃.𐤀𐤓
𐤂𐤌𐤍|
יד 𐤅𐤍𐤕𐤍𐤅.𐤏𐤋𐤉𐤅.𐤀𐤕.𐤊𐤋.𐤊𐤋𐤉𐤅.𐤀𐤔𐤓.𐤉𐤔𐤓𐤕𐤅.𐤏𐤋𐤉
𐤅.𐤁𐤄𐤌.𐤀𐤕.𐤄𐤌𐤇𐤕𐤕.𐤀𐤕.𐤄𐤌𐤆𐤋𐤂𐤕.𐤅𐤀𐤕.𐤄𐤉𐤏𐤉𐤌
.𐤅𐤀𐤕.𐤄𐤌𐤆𐤓𐤒𐤕.𐤊𐤋.𐤊𐤋𐤉.𐤄𐤌𐤆𐤁𐤇.𐤅𐤐𐤓𐤔𐤅.𐤏𐤋𐤉𐤅.𐤊
𐤎𐤅𐤉.𐤏𐤅𐤓.𐤕𐤇𐤔.𐤅𐤔𐤌𐤅.𐤁𐤃𐤉𐤅|
טו 𐤅𐤊𐤋𐤄.𐤀𐤄𐤓𐤍.𐤅𐤁𐤍𐤉𐤅.𐤋𐤊𐤎𐤕.𐤀𐤕.𐤄𐤒𐤃𐤔.𐤅𐤀𐤕.𐤊
𐤋.𐤊𐤋𐤉.𐤄𐤒𐤃𐤔.𐤁𐤍𐤎𐤏.𐤄𐤌𐤇𐤍𐤄.𐤅𐤀𐤇𐤓𐤉.𐤊𐤍.𐤉𐤁𐤀𐤅.
𐤁𐤍𐤉.𐤒𐤄𐤕.𐤋𐤔𐤀𐤕.𐤅𐤋𐤀.𐤉𐤂𐤏𐤅.𐤀𐤋.𐤄𐤒𐤃𐤔.𐤅𐤌𐤕𐤅.𐤀
𐤋𐤄.𐤌𐤔𐤀.𐤁𐤍𐤉.𐤒𐤄𐤕.𐤁𐤀𐤄𐤋.𐤌𐤅𐤏𐤃|
טז 𐤅𐤐𐤒𐤃𐤕.𐤀𐤋𐤏𐤆𐤓.𐤁𐤍.𐤀𐤄𐤓𐤍.𐤄𐤊𐤄𐤍.𐤔𐤌𐤍.𐤄𐤌𐤀𐤅
𐤓.𐤅𐤒𐤈𐤓𐤕.𐤄𐤎𐤌𐤉𐤌.𐤅𐤌𐤍𐤇𐤕.𐤄𐤕𐤌𐤉𐤃.𐤅𐤔𐤌𐤍.𐤄𐤌𐤔
𐤇𐤄.𐤐𐤒𐤃𐤕.𐤊𐤋.𐤄𐤌𐤔𐤊𐤍.𐤅𐤊𐤋.𐤀𐤔𐤓.𐤁𐤅.𐤁𐤒𐤃𐤔.𐤅𐤁𐤊
𐤋𐤉𐤅|
יז 𐤅𐤉𐤃𐤁𐤓.𐤉𐤄𐤅𐤄.𐤀𐤋.𐤌𐤔𐤄.𐤅𐤀𐤋.𐤀𐤄𐤓𐤍.𐤋𐤀𐤌𐤓|

𐤉𐤇 𐤀𐤋.𐤕𐤊𐤓𐤉𐤕𐤅.𐤀𐤕.𐤔𐤁𐤈.𐤌𐤔𐤐𐤇𐤕.𐤄𐤒𐤄𐤕𐤉.𐤌𐤕
𐤅𐤊.𐤄𐤋𐤅𐤉𐤌|
𐤉𐤈 𐤅𐤆𐤀𐤕.𐤏𐤔𐤅.𐤋𐤄𐤌.𐤅𐤇𐤉𐤅.𐤅𐤋𐤀.𐤉𐤌𐤕𐤅.𐤁𐤂𐤔𐤕𐤌.
𐤀𐤕.𐤒𐤃𐤔.𐤄𐤒𐤃𐤔𐤉𐤌.𐤀𐤄𐤓𐤍.𐤅𐤁𐤍𐤉𐤅.𐤉𐤁𐤀𐤅.𐤅𐤔𐤌𐤅.𐤀𐤅
𐤕𐤌.𐤀𐤉𐤔.𐤀𐤉𐤔.𐤏𐤋.𐤏𐤁𐤃𐤕𐤅.𐤅𐤀𐤋.𐤌𐤔𐤀𐤅|
𐤊 𐤅𐤋𐤀.𐤉𐤁𐤀𐤅.𐤋𐤓𐤀𐤅𐤕.𐤊𐤁𐤋𐤏.𐤀𐤕.𐤄𐤒𐤃𐤔.𐤅𐤌𐤕𐤅|
𐤊𐤀 𐤅𐤉𐤃𐤁𐤓.𐤉𐤄𐤅𐤄.𐤀𐤋.𐤌𐤔𐤄.𐤋𐤀𐤌𐤓|
𐤊𐤁 𐤍𐤔𐤀.𐤀𐤕.𐤓𐤀𐤔.𐤁𐤍𐤉.𐤂𐤓𐤔𐤅𐤍.𐤂𐤌.𐤄𐤌.𐤋𐤁𐤉𐤕.𐤀
𐤁𐤕𐤌.𐤋𐤌𐤔𐤐𐤇𐤕𐤌|
𐤊𐤂 𐤌𐤁𐤍.𐤔𐤋𐤔𐤉𐤌.𐤔𐤍𐤄.𐤅𐤌𐤏𐤋𐤄.𐤏𐤃.𐤁𐤍.𐤇𐤌𐤔𐤉𐤌.
𐤔𐤍𐤄.𐤕𐤐𐤒𐤃.𐤀𐤅𐤕𐤌.𐤊𐤋.𐤄𐤁𐤀.𐤋𐤑𐤁𐤀.𐤑𐤁𐤀.𐤋𐤏𐤁𐤃.
𐤏𐤁𐤃𐤄.𐤁𐤀𐤄𐤋.𐤌𐤅𐤏𐤃|
𐤊𐤃 𐤆𐤀𐤕.𐤏𐤁𐤃𐤕.𐤌𐤔𐤐𐤇𐤕.𐤄𐤂𐤓𐤔𐤍𐤉.𐤋𐤏𐤁𐤃.𐤅𐤋
𐤌𐤔𐤀|
𐤊𐤄 𐤅𐤍𐤔𐤀𐤅.𐤀𐤕.𐤉𐤓𐤉𐤏𐤕.𐤄𐤌𐤔𐤊𐤍.𐤅𐤀𐤕.𐤀𐤄𐤋.𐤌𐤅𐤏
𐤃.𐤌𐤊𐤎𐤄𐤅.𐤅𐤌𐤊𐤎𐤄.𐤄𐤕𐤇𐤔.𐤀𐤔𐤓.𐤏𐤋𐤉𐤅.𐤌𐤋𐤌𐤏𐤋𐤄.𐤅
𐤀𐤕.𐤌𐤎𐤊.𐤐𐤕𐤇.𐤀𐤄𐤋.𐤌𐤅𐤏𐤃|
𐤊𐤅 𐤅𐤀𐤕.𐤒𐤋𐤏𐤉.𐤄𐤇𐤑𐤓.𐤅𐤀𐤕.𐤌𐤎𐤊.𐤐𐤕𐤇.𐤔𐤏𐤓.𐤄
𐤇𐤑𐤓.𐤀𐤔𐤓.𐤏𐤋.𐤄𐤌𐤔𐤊𐤍.𐤅𐤏𐤋.𐤄𐤌𐤆𐤁𐤇.𐤎𐤁𐤉𐤁.𐤅𐤀𐤕
.𐤌𐤉𐤕𐤓𐤉𐤄𐤌.𐤅𐤀𐤕.𐤊𐤋.𐤊𐤋𐤉.𐤏𐤁𐤃𐤕𐤌.𐤅𐤀𐤕.𐤊𐤋.𐤀𐤔𐤓.
𐤉𐤏𐤔𐤄.𐤋𐤄𐤌.𐤅𐤏𐤁𐤃𐤅|
𐤊𐤆 𐤏𐤋.𐤐𐤉.𐤀𐤄𐤓𐤍.𐤅𐤁𐤍𐤉𐤅.𐤕𐤄𐤉𐤄.𐤊𐤋.𐤏𐤁𐤃𐤕.𐤁𐤍𐤉.
𐤄𐤂𐤓𐤔𐤍𐤉.𐤋𐤊𐤋.𐤌𐤔𐤀𐤌.𐤅𐤋𐤊𐤋.𐤏𐤁𐤃𐤕𐤌.𐤅𐤐𐤒𐤃𐤕𐤌.𐤏
𐤋𐤄𐤌.𐤁𐤌𐤔𐤌𐤓𐤕.𐤀𐤕.𐤊𐤋.𐤌𐤔𐤀𐤌|
𐤊𐤇 𐤆𐤀𐤕.𐤏𐤁𐤃𐤕.𐤌𐤔𐤐𐤇𐤕.𐤁𐤍𐤉.𐤄𐤂𐤓𐤔𐤍𐤉.𐤁𐤀𐤄𐤋
.𐤌𐤅𐤏𐤃.𐤅𐤌𐤔𐤌𐤓𐤕𐤌.𐤁𐤉𐤃.𐤀𐤉𐤕𐤌𐤓.𐤁𐤍.𐤀𐤄𐤓𐤍.𐤄𐤊𐤄𐤍|
𐤊𐤈 𐤁𐤍𐤉.𐤌𐤓𐤓𐤉.𐤋𐤌𐤔𐤐𐤇𐤕𐤌.𐤋𐤁𐤉𐤕.𐤀𐤁𐤕𐤌.𐤕𐤐𐤒
𐤃.𐤀𐤕𐤌|
𐤋 𐤌𐤁𐤍.𐤔𐤋𐤔𐤉𐤌.𐤔𐤍𐤄.𐤅𐤌𐤏𐤋𐤄.𐤅𐤏𐤃.𐤁𐤍.𐤇𐤌𐤔𐤉
𐤌.𐤔𐤍𐤄.𐤕𐤐𐤒𐤃𐤌.𐤊𐤋.𐤄𐤁𐤀.𐤋𐤑𐤁𐤀.𐤋𐤏𐤁𐤃.𐤀𐤕.𐤏𐤁
𐤃𐤕.𐤀𐤄𐤋.𐤌𐤅𐤏𐤃|

𐤋𐤀 𐤅𐤆𐤀𐤕.𐤌𐤔𐤌𐤓𐤕.𐤌𐤔𐤀𐤌.𐤋𐤊𐤋.𐤏𐤁𐤃𐤕𐤌.𐤁𐤀𐤄𐤋
.𐤌𐤅𐤏𐤃.𐤒𐤓𐤔𐤉.𐤄𐤌𐤔𐤊𐤍.𐤅𐤁𐤓𐤉𐤇𐤉𐤅.𐤅𐤏𐤌𐤅𐤃𐤉𐤅.𐤅𐤀𐤃𐤍
𐤉𐤅|

𐤋𐤁 𐤅𐤏𐤌𐤅𐤃𐤉.𐤄𐤇𐤑𐤓.𐤎𐤁𐤉𐤁.𐤅𐤀𐤃𐤍𐤉𐤄𐤌.𐤅𐤉𐤕𐤃𐤕
𐤌.𐤅𐤌𐤉𐤕𐤓𐤉𐤄𐤌.𐤋𐤊𐤋.𐤊𐤋𐤉𐤄𐤌.𐤅𐤋𐤊𐤋.𐤏𐤁𐤃𐤕𐤌.𐤅𐤁𐤔𐤌
𐤕.𐤕𐤐𐤒𐤃𐤅.𐤀𐤕.𐤊𐤋𐤉.𐤌𐤔𐤌𐤓𐤕.𐤌𐤔𐤀𐤌|

𐤋𐤂 𐤆𐤀𐤕.𐤏𐤁𐤃𐤕.𐤌𐤔𐤐𐤇𐤕.𐤁𐤍𐤉.𐤌𐤓𐤓𐤉.𐤋𐤊𐤋.𐤏𐤁
𐤃𐤕𐤌.𐤁𐤀𐤄𐤋.𐤌𐤅𐤏𐤃.𐤁𐤉𐤃.𐤀𐤉𐤕𐤌𐤓.𐤁𐤍.𐤀𐤄𐤓𐤍.𐤄𐤊𐤄
𐤍|

𐤋𐤃 𐤅𐤉𐤐𐤒𐤃.𐤌𐤔𐤄.𐤅𐤀𐤄𐤓𐤍.𐤅𐤍𐤔𐤉𐤀𐤉.𐤄𐤏𐤃𐤄.𐤀𐤕.
𐤁𐤍𐤉.𐤄𐤒𐤄𐤕𐤉.𐤋𐤌𐤔𐤐𐤇𐤕𐤌.𐤅𐤋𐤁𐤉𐤕.𐤀𐤁𐤕𐤌|

𐤋𐤄 𐤌𐤁𐤍.𐤔𐤋𐤔𐤉𐤌.𐤔𐤍𐤄.𐤅𐤌𐤏𐤋𐤄.𐤅𐤏𐤃.𐤁𐤍.𐤇𐤌𐤔𐤉𐤌
.𐤔𐤍𐤄.𐤊𐤋.𐤄𐤁𐤀.𐤋𐤑𐤁𐤀.𐤋𐤏𐤁𐤃𐤄.𐤁𐤀𐤄𐤋.𐤌𐤅𐤏𐤃|

𐤋𐤅 𐤅𐤉𐤄𐤉𐤅.𐤐𐤒𐤃𐤉𐤄𐤌.𐤋𐤌𐤔𐤐𐤇𐤕𐤌.𐤀𐤋𐤐𐤉𐤌.𐤔𐤁𐤏.
𐤌𐤀𐤅𐤕.𐤅𐤇𐤌𐤔𐤉𐤌|

𐤋𐤆 𐤀𐤋𐤄.𐤐𐤒𐤅𐤃𐤉.𐤌𐤔𐤐𐤇𐤕.𐤄𐤒𐤄𐤕𐤉.𐤊𐤋.𐤄𐤏𐤁𐤃.
𐤁𐤀𐤄𐤋.𐤌𐤅𐤏𐤃.𐤀𐤔𐤓.𐤐𐤒𐤃.𐤌𐤔𐤄.𐤅𐤀𐤄𐤓𐤍.𐤏𐤋.𐤐𐤉.𐤉𐤄𐤅
𐤄.𐤁𐤉𐤃.𐤌𐤔𐤄|

𐤋𐤇 𐤅𐤐𐤒𐤅𐤃𐤉.𐤁𐤍𐤉.𐤂𐤓𐤔𐤅𐤍.𐤋𐤌𐤔𐤐𐤇𐤅𐤕𐤌.𐤅𐤋𐤁𐤉𐤕.𐤀
𐤁𐤕𐤌|

𐤋𐤈 𐤌𐤁𐤍.𐤔𐤋𐤔𐤉𐤌.𐤔𐤍𐤄.𐤅𐤌𐤏𐤋𐤄.𐤅𐤏𐤃.𐤁𐤍.𐤇𐤌𐤔𐤉
𐤌.𐤔𐤍𐤄.𐤊𐤋.𐤄𐤁𐤀.𐤋𐤑𐤁𐤀.𐤋𐤏𐤁𐤃𐤄.𐤁𐤀𐤄𐤋.𐤌𐤅𐤏𐤃|

𐤌 𐤅𐤉𐤄𐤉𐤅.𐤐𐤒𐤃𐤉𐤄𐤌.𐤋𐤌𐤔𐤐𐤇𐤕𐤌.𐤋𐤁𐤉𐤕.𐤀𐤁𐤕𐤌
.𐤀𐤋𐤐𐤉𐤌.𐤅𐤔𐤔.𐤌𐤀𐤅𐤕.𐤅𐤔𐤋𐤔𐤉𐤌|

𐤌𐤀 𐤀𐤋𐤄.𐤐𐤒𐤅𐤃𐤉.𐤌𐤔𐤐𐤇𐤕.𐤁𐤍𐤉.𐤂𐤓𐤔𐤅𐤍.𐤊𐤋.𐤄𐤏𐤁
𐤃.𐤁𐤀𐤄𐤋.𐤌𐤅𐤏𐤃.𐤀𐤔𐤓.𐤐𐤒𐤃.𐤌𐤔𐤄.𐤅𐤀𐤄𐤓𐤍.𐤏𐤋.𐤐𐤉.
𐤉𐤄𐤅𐤄|

𐤌𐤁 𐤅𐤐𐤒𐤅𐤃𐤉.𐤌𐤔𐤐𐤇𐤕.𐤁𐤍𐤉.𐤌𐤓𐤓𐤉.𐤋𐤌𐤔𐤐𐤇𐤕𐤌.𐤋
𐤁𐤉𐤕.𐤀𐤁𐤕𐤌|

𐤌𐤂 𐤌𐤁𐤍.𐤔𐤋𐤔𐤉𐤌.𐤔𐤍𐤄.𐤅𐤌𐤏𐤋𐤄.𐤅𐤏𐤃.𐤁𐤍.𐤇𐤌𐤔𐤉
𐤌.𐤔𐤍𐤄.𐤊𐤋.𐤄𐤁𐤀.𐤋𐤑𐤁𐤀.𐤋𐤏𐤁𐤃𐤄.𐤁𐤀𐤄𐤋.𐤌𐤅𐤏𐤃|

מד ויהיו.פקדיהם.למשפחתם.שלשת.אלפי
ם.ומאתים׃
מה אלה.פקודי.משפחת.בני.מררי.אשר.פק
ד.משה.ואהרן.על.פי.יהוה.ביד.משה׃
מו כל.הפקדים.אשר.פקד.משה.ואהרן.ונשי
אי.ישראל.את.הלוים.למשפחתם.ולבית.אבת
ם׃
מז מבן.שלשים.שנה.ומעלה.ועד.בן.חמשי
ם.שנה.כל.הבא.לעבד.עבדת.עבדה.ועבדת.
משא.באהל.מועד׃
מח ויהיו.פקדיהם.שמנת.אלפים.וחמש.מאו
ת.ושמנים׃
מט על.פי.יהוה.פקד.אותם.ביד.משה.איש.
איש.על.עבדתו.ועל.משאו.ופקדיו.אשר.צוה.
יהוה.את.משה׃׃

במדבר.חלק ה

א וידבר.יהוה.אל.משה.לאמר׃
ב צו.את.בני.ישראל.וישלחו.מן.המחנה.כל.
צרוע.וכל.זב.וכל.טמא.לנפש׃
ג מזכר.עד.נקבה.תשלחו.אל.מחוץ.למחנ
ה.תשלחום.ולא.יטמאו.את.מחניהם.אשר.אני.
שכן.בתוכם׃
ד ויעשו.כן.בני.ישראל.וישלחו.אותם.אל.מ
חוץ.למחנה.כאשר.דבר.יהוה.אל.משה.כן.עש
ו.בני.ישראל׃
ה וידבר.יהוה.אל.משה.לאמר׃
ו דבר.אל.בני.ישראל.איש.או.אשה.כי.יעש
ו.מכל.חטאת.האדם.למעל.מעל.ביהוה.ואשמ
ה.הנפש.ההוא׃

7 𐤅𐤄𐤕𐤅𐤃𐤅.𐤀𐤕.𐤇𐤈𐤀𐤕𐤌.𐤀𐤔𐤓.𐤏𐤔𐤅.𐤅𐤄𐤔𐤉𐤁.𐤀𐤕.
𐤀𐤔𐤌𐤅.𐤁𐤓𐤀𐤔𐤅.𐤅𐤇𐤌𐤉𐤔𐤕𐤅.𐤉𐤎𐤐.𐤏𐤋𐤉𐤅.𐤅𐤍𐤕𐤍.𐤋𐤀𐤔𐤓.
𐤀𐤔𐤌.𐤋𐤅|
8 𐤅𐤀𐤌.𐤀𐤉𐤍.𐤋𐤀𐤉𐤔.𐤂𐤀𐤋.𐤋𐤄𐤔𐤉𐤁.𐤄𐤀𐤔𐤌.𐤀𐤋𐤉𐤅.
𐤄𐤀𐤔𐤌.𐤄𐤌𐤅𐤔𐤁.𐤋𐤉𐤄𐤅𐤄.𐤋𐤊𐤄𐤍.𐤌𐤋𐤁𐤃.𐤀𐤉𐤋.𐤄𐤊𐤐𐤓𐤉
𐤌.𐤀𐤔𐤓.𐤉𐤊𐤐𐤓.𐤁𐤅.𐤏𐤋𐤉𐤅|
9 𐤅𐤊𐤋.𐤕𐤓𐤅𐤌𐤄.𐤋𐤊𐤋.𐤒𐤃𐤔𐤉.𐤁𐤍𐤉.𐤉𐤔𐤓𐤀𐤋.𐤀𐤔𐤓.𐤉
𐤒𐤓𐤉𐤁𐤅.𐤋𐤊𐤄𐤍.𐤋𐤅.𐤉𐤄𐤉𐤄|
10 𐤅𐤀𐤉𐤔.𐤀𐤕.𐤒𐤃𐤔𐤉𐤅.𐤋𐤅.𐤉𐤄𐤉𐤅.𐤀𐤉𐤔.𐤀𐤔𐤓.𐤉𐤕𐤍
.𐤋𐤊𐤄𐤍.𐤋𐤅.𐤉𐤄𐤉𐤄|
11 𐤅𐤉𐤃𐤁𐤓.𐤉𐤄𐤅𐤄.𐤀𐤋.𐤌𐤔𐤄.𐤋𐤀𐤌𐤓|
12 𐤃𐤁𐤓.𐤀𐤋.𐤁𐤍𐤉.𐤉𐤔𐤓𐤀𐤋.𐤅𐤀𐤌𐤓𐤕.𐤀𐤋𐤄𐤌.𐤀𐤉𐤔.𐤀
𐤉𐤔.𐤊𐤉.𐤕𐤔𐤈𐤄.𐤀𐤔𐤕𐤅.𐤅𐤌𐤏𐤋𐤄.𐤁𐤅.𐤌𐤏𐤋|
13 𐤅𐤔𐤊𐤁.𐤀𐤉𐤔.𐤀𐤕𐤄.𐤔𐤊𐤁𐤕.𐤆𐤓𐤏.𐤅𐤍𐤏𐤋𐤌.𐤌𐤏𐤉𐤍
𐤉.𐤀𐤉𐤔𐤄.𐤅𐤍𐤎𐤕𐤓𐤄.𐤅𐤄𐤉𐤀.𐤍𐤈𐤌𐤀𐤄.𐤅𐤏𐤃.𐤀𐤉𐤍.𐤁𐤄.𐤅
𐤄𐤅𐤀.𐤋𐤀.𐤍𐤕𐤐𐤔𐤄|
14 𐤅𐤏𐤁𐤓.𐤏𐤋𐤉𐤅.𐤓𐤅𐤇.𐤒𐤍𐤀𐤄.𐤅𐤒𐤍𐤀.𐤀𐤕.𐤀𐤔𐤕𐤅.𐤅𐤄
𐤅𐤀.𐤍𐤈𐤌𐤀𐤄.𐤀𐤅.𐤏𐤁𐤓.𐤏𐤋𐤉𐤅.𐤓𐤅𐤇.𐤒𐤍𐤀𐤄.𐤅𐤒𐤍𐤀.𐤀𐤕.
𐤀𐤔𐤕𐤅.𐤅𐤄𐤉𐤀.𐤋𐤀.𐤍𐤈𐤌𐤀𐤄|
15 𐤅𐤄𐤁𐤉𐤀.𐤄𐤀𐤉𐤔.𐤀𐤕.𐤀𐤔𐤕𐤅.𐤀𐤋.𐤄𐤊𐤄𐤍.𐤅𐤄𐤁𐤉𐤀.
𐤀𐤕.𐤒𐤓𐤁𐤍𐤄.𐤏𐤋𐤉𐤄.𐤏𐤔𐤉𐤓𐤕.𐤄𐤀𐤉𐤐𐤄.𐤒𐤌𐤇.𐤔𐤏𐤓𐤉
𐤌.𐤋𐤀.𐤉𐤑𐤒.𐤏𐤋𐤉𐤅.𐤔𐤌𐤍.𐤅𐤋𐤀.𐤉𐤕𐤍.𐤏𐤋𐤉𐤅.𐤋𐤁𐤍𐤄.𐤊𐤉.
𐤌𐤍𐤇𐤕.𐤒𐤍𐤀𐤕.𐤄𐤅𐤀.𐤌𐤍𐤇𐤕.𐤆𐤊𐤓𐤅𐤍.𐤌𐤆𐤊𐤓𐤕.𐤏𐤅𐤍|
16 𐤅𐤄𐤒𐤓𐤉𐤁.𐤀𐤕𐤄.𐤄𐤊𐤄𐤍.𐤅𐤄𐤏𐤌𐤃𐤄.𐤋𐤐𐤍𐤉.𐤉𐤄𐤅𐤄|
17 𐤅𐤋𐤒𐤇.𐤄𐤊𐤄𐤍.𐤌𐤉𐤌.𐤒𐤃𐤔𐤉𐤌.𐤁𐤊𐤋𐤉.𐤇𐤓𐤔.𐤅𐤌
𐤍.𐤄𐤏𐤐𐤓.𐤀𐤔𐤓.𐤉𐤄𐤉𐤄.𐤁𐤒𐤓𐤒𐤏.𐤄𐤌𐤔𐤊𐤍.𐤉𐤒𐤇.𐤄𐤊𐤄
𐤍.𐤅𐤍𐤕𐤍.𐤀𐤋.𐤄𐤌𐤉𐤌|
18 𐤅𐤄𐤏𐤌𐤉𐤃.𐤄𐤊𐤄𐤍.𐤀𐤕.𐤄𐤀𐤔𐤄.𐤋𐤐𐤍𐤉.𐤉𐤄𐤅𐤄.𐤅𐤐𐤓
𐤏.𐤀𐤕.𐤓𐤀𐤔.𐤄𐤀𐤔𐤄.𐤅𐤍𐤕𐤍.𐤏𐤋.𐤊𐤐𐤉𐤄.𐤀𐤕.𐤌𐤍𐤇𐤕.𐤄
𐤆𐤊𐤓𐤅𐤍.𐤌𐤍𐤇𐤕.𐤒𐤍𐤀𐤕.𐤄𐤅𐤀.𐤅𐤁𐤉𐤃.𐤄𐤊𐤄𐤍.𐤉𐤄𐤉𐤅.𐤌𐤉
.𐤄𐤌𐤓𐤉𐤌.𐤄𐤌𐤀𐤓𐤓𐤉𐤌|

יט 𐤅𐤄𐤔𐤁𐤉𐤏.𐤀𐤕𐤄.𐤄𐤊𐤄𐤍.𐤅𐤀𐤌𐤓.𐤀𐤋.𐤄𐤀𐤔𐤄.𐤀𐤌.
𐤋𐤀.𐤔𐤊𐤁.𐤀𐤉𐤔.𐤀𐤕𐤊.𐤅𐤀𐤌.𐤋𐤀.𐤔𐤈𐤉𐤕.𐤈𐤌𐤀𐤄.𐤕𐤇
𐤕.𐤀𐤉𐤔𐤊.𐤄𐤍𐤒𐤉.𐤌𐤌𐤉.𐤄𐤌𐤓𐤉𐤌.𐤄𐤌𐤀𐤓𐤓𐤉𐤌.𐤄𐤀𐤋𐤄|
כ 𐤅𐤀𐤕.𐤊𐤉.𐤔𐤈𐤉𐤕.𐤕𐤇𐤕.𐤀𐤉𐤔𐤊.𐤅𐤊𐤉.𐤍𐤈𐤌𐤀𐤕.𐤅
𐤉𐤕𐤍.𐤀𐤉𐤔.𐤁𐤊.𐤀𐤕.𐤔𐤊𐤁𐤕𐤅.𐤌𐤁𐤋𐤏𐤃𐤉.𐤀𐤉𐤔𐤊|
כא 𐤅𐤄𐤔𐤁𐤉𐤏.𐤄𐤊𐤄𐤍.𐤀𐤕.𐤄𐤀𐤔𐤄.𐤁𐤔𐤁𐤏𐤕.𐤄𐤀𐤋𐤄.
𐤅𐤀𐤌𐤓.𐤄𐤊𐤄𐤍.𐤋𐤀𐤔𐤄.𐤉𐤕𐤍.𐤉𐤄𐤅𐤄.𐤀𐤅𐤕𐤊.𐤋𐤀𐤋𐤄.𐤅𐤋𐤔
𐤁𐤏𐤄.𐤁𐤕𐤅𐤊.𐤏𐤌𐤊.𐤁𐤕𐤕.𐤉𐤄𐤅𐤄.𐤀𐤕.𐤉𐤓𐤊𐤊.𐤍𐤐𐤋𐤕.𐤅𐤀
𐤕.𐤁𐤈𐤍𐤊.𐤑𐤁𐤄|
כב 𐤅𐤁𐤀𐤅.𐤄𐤌𐤉𐤌.𐤄𐤌𐤀𐤓𐤓𐤉𐤌.𐤄𐤀𐤋𐤄.𐤁𐤌𐤏𐤉𐤊.𐤋𐤑𐤁
𐤅𐤕.𐤁𐤈𐤍.𐤅𐤋𐤍𐤐𐤋.𐤉𐤓𐤊.𐤅𐤀𐤌𐤓𐤄.𐤄𐤀𐤔𐤄.𐤀𐤌𐤍.𐤀𐤌𐤍|
כג 𐤅𐤊𐤕𐤁.𐤀𐤕.𐤄𐤀𐤋𐤕.𐤄𐤀𐤋𐤄.𐤄𐤊𐤄𐤍.𐤁𐤎𐤐𐤓.𐤅𐤌𐤇𐤄
.𐤀𐤋.𐤌𐤉.𐤄𐤌𐤓𐤉𐤌|
כד 𐤅𐤄𐤔𐤒𐤄.𐤀𐤕.𐤄𐤀𐤔𐤄.𐤀𐤕.𐤌𐤉.𐤄𐤌𐤓𐤉𐤌.𐤄𐤌𐤀𐤓
𐤓𐤉𐤌.𐤅𐤁𐤀𐤅.𐤁𐤄.𐤄𐤌𐤉𐤌.𐤄𐤌𐤀𐤓𐤓𐤉𐤌.𐤋𐤌𐤓𐤉𐤌|
כה 𐤅𐤋𐤒𐤇.𐤄𐤊𐤄𐤍.𐤌𐤉𐤃.𐤄𐤀𐤔𐤄.𐤀𐤕.𐤌𐤍𐤇𐤕.𐤄𐤒𐤍
𐤀𐤕.𐤅𐤄𐤍𐤉𐤐.𐤀𐤕.𐤄𐤌𐤍𐤇𐤄.𐤋𐤐𐤍𐤉.𐤉𐤄𐤅𐤄.𐤅𐤄𐤒𐤓𐤉𐤁.𐤀𐤕
𐤄.𐤀𐤋.𐤄𐤌𐤆𐤁𐤇|
כו 𐤅𐤒𐤌𐤑.𐤄𐤊𐤄𐤍.𐤌𐤍.𐤄𐤌𐤍𐤇𐤄.𐤀𐤕.𐤀𐤆𐤊𐤓𐤕𐤄.𐤅𐤄
𐤒𐤈𐤉𐤓.𐤄𐤌𐤆𐤁𐤇𐤄.𐤅𐤀𐤇𐤓.𐤉𐤔𐤒𐤄.𐤀𐤕.𐤄𐤀𐤔𐤄.𐤀𐤕.
𐤄𐤌𐤉𐤌|
כז 𐤅𐤄𐤔𐤒𐤄.𐤀𐤕.𐤄𐤌𐤉𐤌.𐤅𐤄𐤉𐤕𐤄.𐤀𐤌.𐤍𐤈𐤌𐤀𐤄.𐤅𐤕
𐤌𐤏𐤋.𐤌𐤏𐤋.𐤁𐤀𐤉𐤔𐤄.𐤅𐤁𐤀𐤅.𐤁𐤄.𐤄𐤌𐤉𐤌.𐤄𐤌𐤀𐤓𐤓𐤉𐤌.𐤋
𐤌𐤓𐤉𐤌.𐤅𐤑𐤁𐤕𐤄.𐤁𐤈𐤍𐤄.𐤅𐤍𐤐𐤋𐤄.𐤉𐤓𐤊𐤄.𐤅𐤄𐤉𐤕𐤄.𐤄𐤀𐤔
𐤄.𐤋𐤀𐤋𐤄.𐤁𐤒𐤓𐤁.𐤏𐤌𐤄|
כח 𐤅𐤀𐤌.𐤋𐤀.𐤍𐤈𐤌𐤀𐤄.𐤄𐤀𐤔𐤄.𐤅𐤈𐤄𐤓𐤄.𐤄𐤅𐤀.𐤅𐤍𐤒𐤕
𐤄.𐤅𐤍𐤆𐤓𐤏𐤄.𐤆𐤓𐤏|
כט 𐤆𐤀𐤕.𐤕𐤅𐤓𐤕.𐤄𐤒𐤍𐤀𐤕.𐤀𐤔𐤓.𐤕𐤔𐤈𐤄.𐤀𐤔𐤄.𐤕
𐤇𐤕.𐤀𐤉𐤔𐤄.𐤅𐤍𐤈𐤌𐤀𐤄|

30 או.איש.אשר.תעבר.עליו.רוח.קנאה.וקנ
א.את.אשתו.והעמיד.את.האשה.לפני.יהוה.ו
עשה.לה.הכהן.את.כל.התורה.הזאת|
31 ונקה.האיש.מעון.והאשה.ההוא.תשא.את
.עונה||

במדבר.חלק 6

1 וידבר.יהוה.אל.משה.לאמר|
2 דבר.אל.בני.ישראל.ואמרת.אלהם.איש.או.
אשה.כי.יפלא.לנדר.נדר.נזיר.להזיר.ליהו
ה|
3 מיין.ושכר.יזיר.חמץ.יין.וחמץ.שכר.ל
א.ישתה.וכל.משרת.ענבים.לא.ישתה.וענבים.
לחים.ויבשים.לא.יאכל|
4 כל.ימי.נזרו.מכל.אשר.יעשה.מגפן.היין
.מחרצנים.ועד.זג.לא.יאכל|
5 כל.ימי.נדר.נזרו.תער.לא.יעבר.על.ראשו.
עד.מלאת.הימם.אשר.יזיר.ליהוה.קדש.יה
יה.גדל.פרע.שער.ראשו|
6 כל.ימי.הזירו.ליהוה.על.נפש.מת.לא.יבא|
7 לאביו.ולאמו.לאחיו.ולאחתו.לא.יטמא.ל
הם.במתם.כי.נזר.אלהיו.על.ראשו|
8 כל.ימי.נזרו.קדש.הוא.ליהוה|
9 וכי.ימות.מת.עליו.בפתע.פתאם.וטמא.רא
ש.נזרו.וגלח.ראשו.ביום.טהרתו.ביום.השבי
עי.יגלחנו|
10 וביום.השמיני.יבא.שתי.תרים.או.שני.ב
ני.יונה.אל.הכהן.אל.פתח.אהל.מועד|

יא 𐤅𐤏𐤔𐤄.𐤄𐤊𐤄𐤍.𐤀𐤇𐤃.𐤋𐤇𐤈𐤀𐤕.𐤅𐤀𐤇𐤃.𐤋𐤏𐤋𐤄.𐤅
𐤊𐤐𐤓.𐤏𐤋𐤉𐤅.𐤌𐤀𐤔𐤓.𐤇𐤈𐤀.𐤏𐤋.𐤄𐤍𐤐𐤔.𐤅𐤒𐤃𐤔.𐤀𐤕.𐤓𐤀
𐤔𐤅.𐤁𐤉𐤅𐤌.𐤄𐤄𐤅𐤀|
יב 𐤅𐤄𐤆𐤉𐤓.𐤋𐤉𐤄𐤅𐤄.𐤀𐤕.𐤉𐤌𐤉.𐤍𐤆𐤓𐤅.𐤅𐤄𐤁𐤉𐤀.𐤊𐤁𐤔.
𐤁𐤍.𐤔𐤍𐤕𐤅.𐤋𐤀𐤔𐤌.𐤅𐤄𐤉𐤌𐤉𐤌.𐤄𐤓𐤀𐤔𐤍𐤉𐤌.𐤉𐤐𐤋𐤅.𐤊𐤉.𐤈
𐤌𐤀.𐤍𐤆𐤓𐤅|
יג 𐤅𐤆𐤀𐤕.𐤕𐤅𐤓𐤕.𐤄𐤍𐤆𐤉𐤓.𐤁𐤉𐤅𐤌.𐤌𐤋𐤀𐤕.𐤉𐤌𐤉.𐤍𐤆
𐤓𐤅.𐤉𐤁𐤉𐤀.𐤀𐤕𐤅.𐤀𐤋.𐤐𐤕𐤇.𐤀𐤄𐤋.𐤌𐤅𐤏𐤃|
יד 𐤅𐤄𐤒𐤓𐤉𐤁.𐤀𐤕.𐤒𐤓𐤁𐤍𐤅.𐤋𐤉𐤄𐤅𐤄.𐤊𐤁𐤔.𐤁𐤍.𐤔𐤍𐤕𐤅.
𐤕𐤌𐤉𐤌.𐤀𐤇𐤃.𐤋𐤏𐤋𐤄.𐤅𐤊𐤁𐤔𐤄.𐤀𐤇𐤕.𐤁𐤕.𐤔𐤍𐤕𐤄.𐤕𐤌
𐤉𐤌𐤄.𐤋𐤇𐤈𐤀𐤕.𐤅𐤀𐤉𐤋.𐤀𐤇𐤃.𐤕𐤌𐤉𐤌.𐤋𐤔𐤋𐤌𐤉𐤌|
טו 𐤅𐤎𐤋.𐤌𐤑𐤅𐤕.𐤎𐤋𐤕.𐤇𐤋𐤕.𐤁𐤋𐤅𐤋𐤕.𐤁𐤔𐤌𐤍.𐤅𐤓𐤒𐤉𐤒
𐤉.𐤌𐤑𐤅𐤕.𐤌𐤔𐤇𐤉𐤌.𐤁𐤔𐤌𐤍.𐤅𐤌𐤍𐤇𐤕𐤌.𐤅𐤍𐤎𐤊𐤉𐤄𐤌|
טז 𐤅𐤄𐤒𐤓𐤉𐤁.𐤄𐤊𐤄𐤍.𐤋𐤐𐤍𐤉.𐤉𐤄𐤅𐤄.𐤅𐤏𐤔𐤄.𐤀𐤕.𐤇𐤈𐤀
𐤕𐤅.𐤅𐤀𐤕.𐤏𐤋𐤕𐤅|
יז 𐤅𐤀𐤕.𐤄𐤀𐤉𐤋.𐤉𐤏𐤔𐤄.𐤆𐤁𐤇.𐤔𐤋𐤌𐤉𐤌.𐤋𐤉𐤄𐤅𐤄.𐤏
𐤋.𐤎𐤋.𐤄𐤌𐤑𐤅𐤕.𐤅𐤏𐤔𐤄.𐤄𐤊𐤄𐤍.𐤀𐤕.𐤌𐤍𐤇𐤕𐤅.𐤅𐤀𐤕.𐤍𐤎𐤊
𐤅|
יח 𐤅𐤂𐤋𐤇.𐤄𐤍𐤆𐤉𐤓.𐤐𐤕𐤇.𐤀𐤄𐤋.𐤌𐤅𐤏𐤃.𐤀𐤕.𐤓𐤀𐤔.𐤍
𐤆𐤓𐤅.𐤅𐤋𐤒𐤇.𐤀𐤕.𐤔𐤏𐤓.𐤓𐤀𐤔.𐤍𐤆𐤓𐤅.𐤅𐤍𐤕𐤍.𐤏𐤋.𐤄𐤀𐤔.𐤀
𐤔𐤓.𐤕𐤇𐤕.𐤆𐤁𐤇.𐤄𐤔𐤋𐤌𐤉𐤌|
יט 𐤅𐤋𐤒𐤇.𐤄𐤊𐤄𐤍.𐤀𐤕.𐤄𐤆𐤓𐤏.𐤁𐤔𐤋𐤄.𐤌𐤍.𐤄𐤀𐤉𐤋.𐤅
𐤇𐤋𐤕.𐤌𐤑𐤄.𐤀𐤇𐤕.𐤌𐤍.𐤄𐤎𐤋.𐤅𐤓𐤒𐤉𐤒.𐤌𐤑𐤄.𐤀𐤇𐤃.𐤅𐤍
𐤕𐤍.𐤏𐤋.𐤊𐤐𐤉.𐤄𐤍𐤆𐤉𐤓.𐤀𐤇𐤓.𐤄𐤕𐤂𐤋𐤇𐤅.𐤀𐤕.𐤍𐤆𐤓𐤅|
כ 𐤅𐤄𐤍𐤉𐤐.𐤀𐤅𐤕𐤌.𐤄𐤊𐤄𐤍.𐤕𐤍𐤅𐤐𐤄.𐤋𐤐𐤍𐤉.𐤉𐤄𐤅𐤄.𐤒𐤃
𐤔.𐤄𐤅𐤀.𐤋𐤊𐤄𐤍.𐤏𐤋.𐤇𐤆𐤄.𐤄𐤕𐤍𐤅𐤐𐤄.𐤅𐤏𐤋.𐤔𐤅𐤒.𐤄𐤕𐤓𐤅
𐤌𐤄.𐤅𐤀𐤇𐤓.𐤉𐤔𐤕𐤄.𐤄𐤍𐤆𐤉𐤓.𐤉𐤉𐤍|
כא 𐤆𐤀𐤕.𐤕𐤅𐤓𐤕.𐤄𐤍𐤆𐤉𐤓.𐤀𐤔𐤓.𐤉𐤃𐤓.𐤒𐤓𐤁𐤍𐤅.𐤋𐤉𐤄𐤅
𐤄.𐤏𐤋.𐤍𐤆𐤓𐤅.𐤌𐤋𐤁𐤃.𐤀𐤔𐤓.𐤕𐤔𐤉𐤂.𐤉𐤃𐤅.𐤊𐤐𐤉.𐤍𐤃𐤓𐤅.
𐤀𐤔𐤓.𐤉𐤃𐤓.𐤊𐤍.𐤉𐤏𐤔𐤄.𐤏𐤋.𐤕𐤅𐤓𐤕.𐤍𐤆𐤓𐤅|
כב 𐤅𐤉𐤃𐤁𐤓.𐤉𐤄𐤅𐤄.𐤀𐤋.𐤌𐤔𐤄.𐤋𐤀𐤌𐤓|

𐤊𐤂 𐤃𐤁𐤓.𐤀𐤋.𐤀𐤄𐤓𐤍.𐤅𐤀𐤋.𐤁𐤍𐤉𐤅.𐤋𐤀𐤌𐤓.𐤊𐤄.𐤕𐤁𐤓𐤊𐤅.
𐤀𐤕.𐤁𐤍𐤉.𐤉𐤔𐤓𐤀𐤋.𐤀𐤌𐤅𐤓.𐤋𐤄𐤌|
𐤊𐤃 𐤉𐤁𐤓𐤊𐤊.𐤉𐤄𐤅𐤄.𐤅𐤉𐤔𐤌𐤓𐤊|
𐤊𐤄 𐤉𐤀𐤓.𐤉𐤄𐤅𐤄.𐤐𐤍𐤉𐤅.𐤀𐤋𐤉𐤊.𐤅𐤉𐤇𐤍𐤊|
𐤊𐤅 𐤉𐤔𐤀.𐤉𐤄𐤅𐤄.𐤐𐤍𐤉𐤅.𐤀𐤋𐤉𐤊.𐤅𐤉𐤔𐤌.𐤋𐤊.𐤔𐤋𐤅𐤌|
𐤊𐤆 𐤅𐤔𐤌𐤅.𐤀𐤕.𐤔𐤌𐤉.𐤏𐤋.𐤁𐤍𐤉.𐤉𐤔𐤓𐤀𐤋.𐤅𐤀𐤍𐤉.𐤀𐤁𐤓𐤊
𐤌‖

𐤁𐤌𐤃𐤁𐤓.𐤇𐤋𐤒 𐤆

𐤀 𐤅𐤉𐤄𐤉.𐤁𐤉𐤅𐤌.𐤊𐤋𐤅𐤕.𐤌𐤔𐤄.𐤋𐤄𐤒𐤉𐤌.𐤀𐤕.𐤄𐤌𐤔𐤊𐤍.𐤅
𐤉𐤌𐤔𐤇.𐤀𐤕𐤅.𐤅𐤉𐤒𐤃𐤔.𐤀𐤕𐤅.𐤅𐤀𐤕.𐤊𐤋.𐤊𐤋𐤉𐤅.𐤅𐤀𐤕.𐤄𐤌
𐤆𐤁𐤇.𐤅𐤀𐤕.𐤊𐤋.𐤊𐤋𐤉𐤅.𐤅𐤉𐤌𐤔𐤇𐤌.𐤅𐤉𐤒𐤃𐤔.𐤀𐤕𐤌|
𐤁 𐤅𐤉𐤒𐤓𐤉𐤁𐤅.𐤍𐤔𐤉𐤀𐤉.𐤉𐤔𐤓𐤀𐤋.𐤓𐤀𐤔𐤉.𐤁𐤉𐤕.𐤀𐤁𐤕𐤌.
𐤄𐤌.𐤍𐤔𐤉𐤀𐤉.𐤄𐤌𐤈𐤕.𐤄𐤌.𐤄𐤏𐤌𐤃𐤉𐤌.𐤏𐤋.𐤄𐤐𐤒𐤃𐤉𐤌|
𐤂 𐤅𐤉𐤁𐤉𐤀𐤅.𐤀𐤕.𐤒𐤓𐤁𐤍𐤌.𐤋𐤐𐤍𐤉.𐤉𐤄𐤅𐤄.𐤔𐤔.𐤏𐤂𐤋𐤕.
𐤑𐤁.𐤅𐤔𐤍𐤉.𐤏𐤔𐤓.𐤁𐤒𐤓.𐤏𐤂𐤋𐤄.𐤏𐤋.𐤔𐤍𐤉.𐤄𐤍𐤔𐤀𐤉𐤌.𐤅
𐤔𐤅𐤓.𐤋𐤀𐤇𐤃.𐤅𐤉𐤒𐤓𐤉𐤁𐤅.𐤀𐤅𐤕𐤌.𐤋𐤐𐤍𐤉.𐤄𐤌𐤔𐤊𐤍|
𐤃 𐤅𐤉𐤀𐤌𐤓.𐤉𐤄𐤅𐤄.𐤀𐤋.𐤌𐤔𐤄.𐤋𐤀𐤌𐤓|
𐤄 𐤒𐤇.𐤌𐤀𐤕𐤌.𐤅𐤄𐤉𐤅.𐤋𐤏𐤁𐤃.𐤀𐤕.𐤏𐤁𐤃𐤕.𐤀𐤄𐤋.𐤌𐤅
𐤏𐤃.𐤅𐤍𐤕𐤕𐤄.𐤀𐤅𐤕𐤌.𐤀𐤋.𐤄𐤋𐤅𐤉𐤌.𐤀𐤉𐤔.𐤊𐤐𐤉.𐤏𐤁𐤃𐤕𐤅|
𐤅 𐤅𐤉𐤒𐤇.𐤌𐤔𐤄.𐤀𐤕.𐤄𐤏𐤂𐤋𐤕.𐤅𐤀𐤕.𐤄𐤁𐤒𐤓.𐤅𐤉𐤕𐤍.𐤀
𐤅𐤕𐤌.𐤀𐤋.𐤄𐤋𐤅𐤉𐤌|
𐤆 𐤀𐤕.𐤔𐤕𐤉.𐤄𐤏𐤂𐤋𐤕.𐤅𐤀𐤕.𐤀𐤓𐤁𐤏𐤕.𐤄𐤁𐤒𐤓.𐤍𐤕𐤍.𐤋
𐤁𐤍𐤉.𐤂𐤓𐤔𐤅𐤍.𐤊𐤐𐤉.𐤏𐤁𐤃𐤕𐤌|
𐤇 𐤅𐤀𐤕.𐤀𐤓𐤁𐤏.𐤄𐤏𐤂𐤋𐤕.𐤅𐤀𐤕.𐤔𐤌𐤍𐤕.𐤄𐤁𐤒𐤓.𐤍𐤕𐤍.𐤋
𐤁𐤍𐤉.𐤌𐤓𐤓𐤉.𐤊𐤐𐤉.𐤏𐤁𐤃𐤕𐤌.𐤁𐤉𐤃.𐤀𐤉𐤕𐤌𐤓.𐤁𐤍.𐤀𐤄𐤓𐤍.
𐤄𐤊𐤄𐤍|
𐤈 𐤅𐤋𐤁𐤍𐤉.𐤒𐤄𐤕.𐤋𐤀.𐤍𐤕𐤍.𐤊𐤉.𐤏𐤁𐤃𐤕.𐤄𐤒𐤃𐤔.𐤏𐤋
𐤄𐤌.𐤁𐤊𐤕𐤐.𐤉𐤔𐤀𐤅|

10 𐤅𐤉𐤒𐤓𐤉𐤁𐤅.𐤄𐤍𐤔𐤀𐤉𐤌.𐤀𐤕.𐤇𐤍𐤊𐤕.𐤄𐤌𐤆𐤁𐤇.𐤁𐤉
𐤅𐤌.𐤄𐤌𐤔𐤇.𐤀𐤕𐤅.𐤅𐤉𐤒𐤓𐤉𐤁𐤅.𐤄𐤍𐤔𐤉𐤀𐤌.𐤀𐤕.𐤒𐤓𐤁𐤍𐤌.𐤋
𐤐𐤍𐤉.𐤄𐤌𐤆𐤁𐤇|

11 𐤅𐤉𐤀𐤌𐤓.𐤉𐤄𐤅𐤄.𐤀𐤋.𐤌𐤔𐤄.𐤍𐤔𐤉𐤀.𐤀𐤇𐤃.𐤋𐤉𐤅𐤌.𐤍
𐤔𐤉𐤀.𐤀𐤇𐤃.𐤋𐤉𐤅𐤌.𐤉𐤒𐤓𐤉𐤁𐤅.𐤀𐤕.𐤒𐤓𐤁𐤍𐤌.𐤋𐤇𐤍𐤊𐤕.𐤄
𐤌𐤆𐤁𐤇|

12 𐤅𐤉𐤄𐤉.𐤄𐤌𐤒𐤓𐤉𐤁.𐤁𐤉𐤅𐤌.𐤄𐤓𐤀𐤔𐤅𐤍.𐤀𐤕.𐤒𐤓𐤁𐤍𐤅.𐤍
𐤇𐤔𐤅𐤍.𐤁𐤍.𐤏𐤌𐤉𐤍𐤃𐤁.𐤋𐤌𐤈𐤄.𐤉𐤄𐤅𐤃𐤄|

13 𐤅𐤒𐤓𐤁𐤍𐤅.𐤒𐤏𐤓𐤕.𐤊𐤎𐤐.𐤀𐤇𐤕.𐤔𐤋𐤔𐤉𐤌.𐤅𐤌𐤀𐤄.𐤌
𐤔𐤒𐤋𐤄.𐤌𐤆𐤓𐤒.𐤀𐤇𐤃.𐤊𐤎𐤐.𐤔𐤁𐤏𐤉𐤌.𐤔𐤒𐤋.𐤁𐤔𐤒𐤋.
𐤄𐤒𐤃𐤔.𐤔𐤍𐤉𐤄𐤌.𐤌𐤋𐤀𐤉𐤌.𐤎𐤋𐤕.𐤁𐤋𐤅𐤋𐤄.𐤁𐤔𐤌𐤍.𐤋𐤌𐤍
𐤇𐤄|

14 𐤊𐤐.𐤀𐤇𐤕.𐤏𐤔𐤓𐤄.𐤆𐤄𐤁.𐤌𐤋𐤀𐤄.𐤒𐤈𐤓𐤕|

15 𐤐𐤓.𐤀𐤇𐤃.𐤁𐤍.𐤁𐤒𐤓.𐤀𐤉𐤋.𐤀𐤇𐤃.𐤊𐤁𐤔.𐤀𐤇𐤃.𐤁𐤍
.𐤔𐤍𐤕𐤅.𐤋𐤏𐤋𐤄|

16 𐤔𐤏𐤉𐤓.𐤏𐤆𐤉𐤌.𐤀𐤇𐤃.𐤋𐤇𐤈𐤀𐤕|

17 𐤅𐤋𐤆𐤁𐤇.𐤄𐤔𐤋𐤌𐤉𐤌.𐤁𐤒𐤓.𐤔𐤍𐤉𐤌.𐤀𐤉𐤋𐤌.𐤇𐤌𐤔
𐤄.𐤏𐤕𐤅𐤃𐤉𐤌.𐤇𐤌𐤔𐤄.𐤊𐤁𐤔𐤉𐤌.𐤁𐤍𐤉.𐤔𐤍𐤄.𐤇𐤌𐤔𐤄.𐤆
𐤄.𐤒𐤓𐤁𐤍.𐤍𐤇𐤔𐤅𐤍.𐤁𐤍.𐤏𐤌𐤉𐤍𐤃𐤁|

18 𐤁𐤉𐤅𐤌.𐤄𐤔𐤍𐤉.𐤄𐤒𐤓𐤉𐤁.𐤍𐤕𐤍𐤀𐤋.𐤁𐤍.𐤑𐤅𐤏𐤓.𐤍𐤔𐤉𐤀
.𐤉𐤔𐤔𐤊𐤓|

19 𐤄𐤒𐤓𐤁.𐤀𐤕.𐤒𐤓𐤁𐤍𐤅.𐤒𐤏𐤓𐤕.𐤊𐤎𐤐.𐤀𐤇𐤕.𐤔𐤋𐤔𐤉
𐤌.𐤅𐤌𐤀𐤄.𐤌𐤔𐤒𐤋𐤄.𐤌𐤆𐤓𐤒.𐤀𐤇𐤃.𐤊𐤎𐤐.𐤔𐤁𐤏𐤉𐤌.𐤔
𐤒𐤋.𐤁𐤔𐤒𐤋.𐤄𐤒𐤃𐤔.𐤔𐤍𐤉𐤄𐤌.𐤌𐤋𐤀𐤉𐤌.𐤎𐤋𐤕.𐤁𐤋𐤅𐤋𐤄.
𐤁𐤔𐤌𐤍.𐤋𐤌𐤍𐤇𐤄|

20 𐤊𐤐.𐤀𐤇𐤕.𐤏𐤔𐤓𐤄.𐤆𐤄𐤁.𐤌𐤋𐤀𐤄.𐤒𐤈𐤓𐤕|

21 𐤐𐤓.𐤀𐤇𐤃.𐤁𐤍.𐤁𐤒𐤓.𐤀𐤉𐤋.𐤀𐤇𐤃.𐤊𐤁𐤔.𐤀𐤇𐤃.𐤁𐤍
.𐤔𐤍𐤕𐤅.𐤋𐤏𐤋𐤄|

22 𐤔𐤏𐤉𐤓.𐤏𐤆𐤉𐤌.𐤀𐤇𐤃.𐤋𐤇𐤈𐤀𐤕|

23 𐤅𐤋𐤆𐤁𐤇.𐤄𐤔𐤋𐤌𐤉𐤌.𐤁𐤒𐤓.𐤔𐤍𐤉𐤌.𐤀𐤉𐤋𐤌.𐤇𐤌𐤔
𐤄.𐤏𐤕𐤅𐤃𐤉𐤌.𐤇𐤌𐤔𐤄.𐤊𐤁𐤔𐤉𐤌.𐤁𐤍𐤉.𐤔𐤍𐤄.𐤇𐤌𐤔𐤄.𐤆
𐤄.𐤒𐤓𐤁𐤍.𐤍𐤕𐤍𐤀𐤋.𐤁𐤍.𐤑𐤅𐤏𐤓|
24 𐤁𐤉𐤅𐤌.𐤄𐤔𐤋𐤉𐤔𐤉.𐤍𐤔𐤉𐤀.𐤋𐤁𐤍𐤉.𐤆𐤁𐤅𐤋𐤍.𐤀𐤋𐤉𐤀
𐤁.𐤁𐤍.𐤇𐤋𐤍|
25 𐤒𐤓𐤁𐤍𐤅.𐤒𐤏𐤓𐤕.𐤊𐤎𐤐.𐤀𐤇𐤕.𐤔𐤋𐤔𐤉𐤌.𐤅𐤌𐤀𐤄.𐤌𐤔
𐤒𐤋𐤄.𐤌𐤆𐤓𐤒.𐤀𐤇𐤃.𐤊𐤎𐤐.𐤔𐤁𐤏𐤉𐤌.𐤔𐤒𐤋.𐤁𐤔𐤒𐤋.𐤄
𐤒𐤃𐤔.𐤔𐤍𐤉𐤄𐤌.𐤌𐤋𐤀𐤉𐤌.𐤎𐤋𐤕.𐤁𐤋𐤅𐤋𐤄.𐤁𐤔𐤌𐤍.𐤋𐤌𐤍𐤇
𐤄|
26 𐤊𐤐.𐤀𐤇𐤕.𐤏𐤔𐤓𐤄.𐤆𐤄𐤁.𐤌𐤋𐤀𐤄.𐤒𐤈𐤓𐤕|
27 𐤐𐤓.𐤀𐤇𐤃.𐤁𐤍.𐤁𐤒𐤓.𐤀𐤉𐤋.𐤀𐤇𐤃.𐤊𐤁𐤔.𐤀𐤇𐤃.𐤁
𐤍.𐤔𐤍𐤕𐤅.𐤋𐤏𐤋𐤄|
28 𐤔𐤏𐤉𐤓.𐤏𐤆𐤉𐤌.𐤀𐤇𐤃.𐤋𐤇𐤈𐤀𐤕|
29 𐤅𐤋𐤆𐤁𐤇.𐤄𐤔𐤋𐤌𐤉𐤌.𐤁𐤒𐤓.𐤔𐤍𐤉𐤌.𐤀𐤉𐤋𐤌.𐤇𐤌𐤔
𐤄.𐤏𐤕𐤃𐤉𐤌.𐤇𐤌𐤔𐤄.𐤊𐤁𐤔𐤉𐤌.𐤁𐤍𐤉.𐤔𐤍𐤄.𐤇𐤌𐤔𐤄.𐤆
𐤄.𐤒𐤓𐤁𐤍.𐤀𐤋𐤉𐤀𐤁.𐤁𐤍.𐤇𐤋𐤍|
30 𐤁𐤉𐤅𐤌.𐤄𐤓𐤁𐤉𐤏𐤉.𐤍𐤔𐤉𐤀.𐤋𐤁𐤍𐤉.𐤓𐤀𐤅𐤁𐤍.𐤀𐤋𐤉𐤑𐤅
𐤓.𐤁𐤍.𐤔𐤃𐤉𐤀𐤅𐤓|
31 𐤒𐤓𐤁𐤍𐤅.𐤒𐤏𐤓𐤕.𐤊𐤎𐤐.𐤀𐤇𐤕.𐤔𐤋𐤔𐤉𐤌.𐤅𐤌𐤀𐤄.𐤌
𐤔𐤒𐤋𐤄.𐤌𐤆𐤓𐤒.𐤀𐤇𐤃.𐤊𐤎𐤐.𐤔𐤁𐤏𐤉𐤌.𐤔𐤒𐤋.𐤁𐤔𐤒𐤋.
𐤄𐤒𐤃𐤔.𐤔𐤍𐤉𐤄𐤌.𐤌𐤋𐤀𐤉𐤌.𐤎𐤋𐤕.𐤁𐤋𐤅𐤋𐤄.𐤁𐤔𐤌𐤍.𐤋𐤌𐤍
𐤇𐤄|
32 𐤊𐤐.𐤀𐤇𐤕.𐤏𐤔𐤓𐤄.𐤆𐤄𐤁.𐤌𐤋𐤀𐤄.𐤒𐤈𐤓𐤕|
33 𐤐𐤓.𐤀𐤇𐤃.𐤁𐤍.𐤁𐤒𐤓.𐤀𐤉𐤋.𐤀𐤇𐤃.𐤊𐤁𐤔.𐤀𐤇𐤃.𐤁
𐤍.𐤔𐤍𐤕𐤅.𐤋𐤏𐤋𐤄|
34 𐤔𐤏𐤉𐤓.𐤏𐤆𐤉𐤌.𐤀𐤇𐤃.𐤋𐤇𐤈𐤀𐤕|
35 𐤅𐤋𐤆𐤁𐤇.𐤄𐤔𐤋𐤌𐤉𐤌.𐤁𐤒𐤓.𐤔𐤍𐤉𐤌.𐤀𐤉𐤋𐤌.𐤇𐤌𐤔
𐤄.𐤏𐤕𐤃𐤉𐤌.𐤇𐤌𐤔𐤄.𐤊𐤁𐤔𐤉𐤌.𐤁𐤍𐤉.𐤔𐤍𐤄.𐤇𐤌𐤔𐤄.𐤆
𐤄.𐤒𐤓𐤁𐤍.𐤀𐤋𐤉𐤑𐤅𐤓.𐤁𐤍.𐤔𐤃𐤉𐤀𐤅𐤓|
36 𐤁𐤉𐤅𐤌.𐤄𐤇𐤌𐤉𐤔𐤉.𐤍𐤔𐤉𐤀.𐤋𐤁𐤍𐤉.𐤔𐤌𐤏𐤅𐤍.𐤔𐤋𐤌𐤉
𐤀𐤋.𐤁𐤍.𐤑𐤅𐤓𐤉𐤔𐤃𐤉|

𐤋𐤆 𐤒𐤓𐤁𐤍𐤅.𐤒𐤏𐤓𐤕.𐤊𐤎𐤐.𐤀𐤇𐤕.𐤔𐤋𐤔𐤉𐤌.𐤅𐤌𐤀𐤄.𐤌
𐤔𐤒𐤋𐤄.𐤌𐤆𐤓𐤒.𐤀𐤇𐤃.𐤊𐤎𐤐.𐤔𐤁𐤏𐤉𐤌.𐤔𐤒𐤋.𐤁𐤔𐤒𐤋.
𐤄𐤒𐤃𐤔.𐤔𐤍𐤉𐤄𐤌.𐤌𐤋𐤀𐤉𐤌.𐤎𐤋𐤕.𐤁𐤋𐤅𐤋𐤄.𐤁𐤔𐤌𐤍.𐤋𐤌𐤍
𐤇𐤄|
𐤋𐤇 𐤊𐤐.𐤀𐤇𐤕.𐤏𐤔𐤓𐤄.𐤆𐤄𐤁.𐤌𐤋𐤀𐤄.𐤒𐤈𐤓𐤕|
𐤋𐤈 𐤐𐤓.𐤀𐤇𐤃.𐤁𐤍.𐤁𐤒𐤓.𐤀𐤉𐤋.𐤀𐤇𐤃.𐤊𐤁𐤔.𐤀𐤇𐤃.
𐤁𐤍.𐤔𐤍𐤕𐤅.𐤋𐤏𐤋𐤄|
𐤌 𐤔𐤏𐤉𐤓.𐤏𐤆𐤉𐤌.𐤀𐤇𐤃.𐤋𐤇𐤈𐤀𐤕|
𐤌𐤀 𐤅𐤋𐤆𐤁𐤇.𐤄𐤔𐤋𐤌𐤉𐤌.𐤁𐤒𐤓.𐤔𐤍𐤉𐤌.𐤀𐤉𐤋𐤌.𐤇𐤌𐤔
𐤄.𐤏𐤕𐤃𐤉𐤌.𐤇𐤌𐤔𐤄.𐤊𐤁𐤔𐤉𐤌.𐤁𐤍𐤉.𐤔𐤍𐤄.𐤇𐤌𐤔𐤄.𐤆
𐤄.𐤒𐤓𐤁𐤍.𐤔𐤋𐤌𐤉𐤀𐤋.𐤁𐤍.𐤑𐤅𐤓𐤉𐤔𐤃𐤉|
𐤌𐤁 𐤁𐤉𐤅𐤌.𐤄𐤔𐤔𐤉.𐤍𐤔𐤉𐤀.𐤋𐤁𐤍𐤉.𐤂𐤃.𐤀𐤋𐤉𐤎𐤐.𐤁𐤍.
𐤃𐤏𐤅𐤀𐤋|
𐤌𐤂 𐤒𐤓𐤁𐤍𐤅.𐤒𐤏𐤓𐤕.𐤊𐤎𐤐.𐤀𐤇𐤕.𐤔𐤋𐤔𐤉𐤌.𐤅𐤌𐤀𐤄.𐤌
𐤔𐤒𐤋𐤄.𐤌𐤆𐤓𐤒.𐤀𐤇𐤃.𐤊𐤎𐤐.𐤔𐤁𐤏𐤉𐤌.𐤔𐤒𐤋.𐤁𐤔𐤒𐤋.
𐤄𐤒𐤃𐤔.𐤔𐤍𐤉𐤄𐤌.𐤌𐤋𐤀𐤉𐤌.𐤎𐤋𐤕.𐤁𐤋𐤅𐤋𐤄.𐤁𐤔𐤌𐤍.𐤋𐤌𐤍
𐤇𐤄|
𐤌𐤃 𐤊𐤐.𐤀𐤇𐤕.𐤏𐤔𐤓𐤄.𐤆𐤄𐤁.𐤌𐤋𐤀𐤄.𐤒𐤈𐤓𐤕|
𐤌𐤄 𐤐𐤓.𐤀𐤇𐤃.𐤁𐤍.𐤁𐤒𐤓.𐤀𐤉𐤋.𐤀𐤇𐤃.𐤊𐤁𐤔.𐤀𐤇𐤃.𐤁
𐤍.𐤔𐤍𐤕𐤅.𐤋𐤏𐤋𐤄|
𐤌𐤅 𐤔𐤏𐤉𐤓.𐤏𐤆𐤉𐤌.𐤀𐤇𐤃.𐤋𐤇𐤈𐤀𐤕|
𐤌𐤆 𐤅𐤋𐤆𐤁𐤇.𐤄𐤔𐤋𐤌𐤉𐤌.𐤁𐤒𐤓.𐤔𐤍𐤉𐤌.𐤀𐤉𐤋𐤌.𐤇𐤌𐤔
𐤄.𐤏𐤕𐤃𐤉𐤌.𐤇𐤌𐤔𐤄.𐤊𐤁𐤔𐤉𐤌.𐤁𐤍𐤉.𐤔𐤍𐤄.𐤇𐤌𐤔𐤄.𐤆
𐤄.𐤒𐤓𐤁𐤍.𐤀𐤋𐤉𐤎𐤐.𐤁𐤍.𐤃𐤏𐤅𐤀𐤋|
𐤌𐤇 𐤁𐤉𐤅𐤌.𐤄𐤔𐤁𐤉𐤏𐤉.𐤍𐤔𐤉𐤀.𐤋𐤁𐤍𐤉.𐤀𐤐𐤓𐤉𐤌.𐤀𐤋𐤉𐤔
𐤌𐤏.𐤁𐤍.𐤏𐤌𐤉𐤄𐤅𐤃|
𐤌𐤈 𐤒𐤓𐤁𐤍𐤅.𐤒𐤏𐤓𐤕.𐤊𐤎𐤐.𐤀𐤇𐤕.𐤔𐤋𐤔𐤉𐤌.𐤅𐤌𐤀𐤄.𐤌
𐤔𐤒𐤋𐤄.𐤌𐤆𐤓𐤒.𐤀𐤇𐤃.𐤊𐤎𐤐.𐤔𐤁𐤏𐤉𐤌.𐤔𐤒𐤋.𐤁𐤔𐤒𐤋.
𐤄𐤒𐤃𐤔.𐤔𐤍𐤉𐤄𐤌.𐤌𐤋𐤀𐤉𐤌.𐤎𐤋𐤕.𐤁𐤋𐤅𐤋𐤄.𐤁𐤔𐤌𐤍.𐤋𐤌𐤍
𐤇𐤄|
𐤍 𐤊𐤐.𐤀𐤇𐤕.𐤏𐤔𐤓𐤄.𐤆𐤄𐤁.𐤌𐤋𐤀𐤄.𐤒𐤈𐤓𐤕|

𐤍𐤀 𐤐𐤓.𐤀𐤇𐤃.𐤁𐤍.𐤁𐤒𐤓.𐤀𐤉𐤋.𐤀𐤇𐤃.𐤊𐤁𐤔.𐤀𐤇𐤃.𐤁𐤍
.𐤔𐤍𐤕𐤅.𐤋𐤏𐤋𐤄|
𐤍𐤁 𐤔𐤏𐤉𐤓.𐤏𐤆𐤉𐤌.𐤀𐤇𐤃.𐤋𐤇𐤈𐤀𐤕|
𐤍𐤂 𐤅𐤋𐤆𐤁𐤇.𐤄𐤔𐤋𐤌𐤉𐤌.𐤁𐤒𐤓.𐤔𐤍𐤉𐤌.𐤀𐤉𐤋𐤌.𐤇𐤌𐤔
𐤄.𐤏𐤕𐤃𐤉𐤌.𐤇𐤌𐤔𐤄.𐤊𐤁𐤔𐤉𐤌.𐤁𐤍𐤉.𐤔𐤍𐤄.𐤇𐤌𐤔𐤄.𐤆
𐤄.𐤒𐤓𐤁𐤍.𐤀𐤋𐤉𐤔𐤌𐤏.𐤁𐤍.𐤏𐤌𐤉𐤄𐤅𐤃|
𐤍𐤃 𐤁𐤉𐤅𐤌.𐤄𐤔𐤌𐤉𐤍𐤉.𐤍𐤔𐤉𐤀.𐤋𐤁𐤍𐤉.𐤌𐤍𐤔𐤄.𐤂𐤌𐤋𐤉𐤀
𐤋.𐤁𐤍.𐤐𐤃𐤄𐤑𐤅𐤓|
𐤍𐤄 𐤒𐤓𐤁𐤍𐤅.𐤒𐤏𐤓𐤕.𐤊𐤎𐤐.𐤀𐤇𐤕.𐤔𐤋𐤔𐤉𐤌.𐤅𐤌𐤀𐤄.𐤌𐤔
𐤒𐤋𐤄.𐤌𐤆𐤓𐤒.𐤀𐤇𐤃.𐤊𐤎𐤐.𐤔𐤁𐤏𐤉𐤌.𐤔𐤒𐤋.𐤁𐤔𐤒𐤋.𐤄
𐤒𐤃𐤔.𐤔𐤍𐤉𐤄𐤌.𐤌𐤋𐤀𐤉𐤌.𐤎𐤋𐤕.𐤁𐤋𐤅𐤋𐤄.𐤁𐤔𐤌𐤍.𐤋𐤌𐤍𐤇
𐤄|
𐤍𐤅 𐤊𐤐.𐤀𐤇𐤕.𐤏𐤔𐤓𐤄.𐤆𐤄𐤁.𐤌𐤋𐤀𐤄.𐤒𐤈𐤓𐤕|
𐤍𐤆 𐤐𐤓.𐤀𐤇𐤃.𐤁𐤍.𐤁𐤒𐤓.𐤀𐤉𐤋.𐤀𐤇𐤃.𐤊𐤁𐤔.𐤀𐤇𐤃.𐤁
𐤍.𐤔𐤍𐤕𐤅.𐤋𐤏𐤋𐤄|
𐤍𐤇 𐤔𐤏𐤉𐤓.𐤏𐤆𐤉𐤌.𐤀𐤇𐤃.𐤋𐤇𐤈𐤀𐤕|
𐤍𐤈 𐤅𐤋𐤆𐤁𐤇.𐤄𐤔𐤋𐤌𐤉𐤌.𐤁𐤒𐤓.𐤔𐤍𐤉𐤌.𐤀𐤉𐤋𐤌.𐤇𐤌𐤔
𐤄.𐤏𐤕𐤃𐤉𐤌.𐤇𐤌𐤔𐤄.𐤊𐤁𐤔𐤉𐤌.𐤁𐤍𐤉.𐤔𐤍𐤄.𐤇𐤌𐤔𐤄.𐤆
𐤄.𐤒𐤓𐤁𐤍.𐤂𐤌𐤋𐤉𐤀𐤋.𐤁𐤍.𐤐𐤃𐤄𐤑𐤅𐤓|
𐤎 𐤁𐤉𐤅𐤌.𐤄𐤕𐤔𐤉𐤏𐤉.𐤍𐤔𐤉𐤀.𐤋𐤁𐤍𐤉.𐤁𐤍𐤉𐤌𐤍.𐤀𐤁𐤉𐤃
𐤍.𐤁𐤍.𐤂𐤃𐤏𐤍𐤉|
𐤎𐤀 𐤒𐤓𐤁𐤍𐤅.𐤒𐤏𐤓𐤕.𐤊𐤎𐤐.𐤀𐤇𐤕.𐤔𐤋𐤔𐤉𐤌.𐤅𐤌𐤀𐤄.𐤌𐤔
𐤒𐤋𐤄.𐤌𐤆𐤓𐤒.𐤀𐤇𐤃.𐤊𐤎𐤐.𐤔𐤁𐤏𐤉𐤌.𐤔𐤒𐤋.𐤁𐤔𐤒𐤋.𐤄
𐤒𐤃𐤔.𐤔𐤍𐤉𐤄𐤌.𐤌𐤋𐤀𐤉𐤌.𐤎𐤋𐤕.𐤁𐤋𐤅𐤋𐤄.𐤁𐤔𐤌𐤍.𐤋𐤌𐤍𐤇
𐤄|
𐤎𐤁 𐤊𐤐.𐤀𐤇𐤕.𐤏𐤔𐤓𐤄.𐤆𐤄𐤁.𐤌𐤋𐤀𐤄.𐤒𐤈𐤓𐤕|
𐤎𐤂 𐤐𐤓.𐤀𐤇𐤃.𐤁𐤍.𐤁𐤒𐤓.𐤀𐤉𐤋.𐤀𐤇𐤃.𐤊𐤁𐤔.𐤀𐤇𐤃.𐤁
𐤍.𐤔𐤍𐤕𐤅.𐤋𐤏𐤋𐤄|
𐤎𐤃 𐤔𐤏𐤉𐤓.𐤏𐤆𐤉𐤌.𐤀𐤇𐤃.𐤋𐤇𐤈𐤀𐤕|

65 𐤅𐤋𐤆𐤁𐤇.𐤄𐤔𐤋𐤌𐤉𐤌.𐤁𐤒𐤓.𐤔𐤍𐤉𐤌.𐤀𐤉𐤋𐤌.𐤇𐤌𐤔𐤄
.𐤏𐤕𐤃𐤉𐤌.𐤇𐤌𐤔𐤄.𐤊𐤁𐤔𐤉𐤌.𐤁𐤍𐤉.𐤔𐤍𐤄.𐤇𐤌𐤔𐤄.𐤆𐤄.
𐤒𐤓𐤁𐤍.𐤀𐤁𐤉𐤃𐤍.𐤁𐤍.𐤂𐤃𐤏𐤍𐤉|
66 𐤁𐤉𐤅𐤌.𐤄𐤏𐤔𐤉𐤓𐤉.𐤍𐤔𐤉𐤀.𐤋𐤁𐤍𐤉.𐤃𐤍.𐤀𐤇𐤉𐤏𐤆𐤓.
𐤁𐤍.𐤏𐤌𐤉𐤔𐤃𐤉|
67 𐤒𐤓𐤁𐤍𐤅.𐤒𐤏𐤓𐤕.𐤊𐤎𐤐.𐤀𐤇𐤕.𐤔𐤋𐤔𐤉𐤌.𐤅𐤌𐤀𐤄.𐤌
𐤔𐤒𐤋𐤄.𐤌𐤆𐤓𐤒.𐤀𐤇𐤃.𐤊𐤎𐤐.𐤔𐤁𐤏𐤉𐤌.𐤔𐤒𐤋.𐤁𐤔𐤒𐤋.
𐤄𐤒𐤃𐤔.𐤔𐤍𐤉𐤄𐤌.𐤌𐤋𐤀𐤉𐤌.𐤎𐤋𐤕.𐤁𐤋𐤅𐤋𐤄.𐤁𐤔𐤌𐤍.𐤋𐤌𐤍
𐤇𐤄|
68 𐤊𐤐.𐤀𐤇𐤕.𐤏𐤔𐤓𐤄.𐤆𐤄𐤁.𐤌𐤋𐤀𐤄.𐤒𐤈𐤓𐤕|
69 𐤐𐤓.𐤀𐤇𐤃.𐤁𐤍.𐤁𐤒𐤓.𐤀𐤉𐤋.𐤀𐤇𐤃.𐤊𐤁𐤔.𐤀𐤇𐤃.𐤁
𐤍.𐤔𐤍𐤕𐤅.𐤋𐤏𐤋𐤄|
70 .𐤔𐤏𐤉𐤓.𐤏𐤆𐤉𐤌.𐤀𐤇𐤃.𐤋𐤇𐤈𐤀𐤕|
71 𐤅𐤋𐤆𐤁𐤇.𐤄𐤔𐤋𐤌𐤉𐤌.𐤁𐤒𐤓.𐤔𐤍𐤉𐤌.𐤀𐤉𐤋𐤌.𐤇𐤌𐤔
𐤄.𐤏𐤕𐤃𐤉𐤌.𐤇𐤌𐤔𐤄.𐤊𐤁𐤔𐤉𐤌.𐤁𐤍𐤉.𐤔𐤍𐤄.𐤇𐤌𐤔𐤄.𐤆
𐤄.𐤒𐤓𐤁𐤍.𐤀𐤇𐤉𐤏𐤆𐤓.𐤁𐤍.𐤏𐤌𐤉𐤔𐤃𐤉|
72 𐤁𐤉𐤅𐤌.𐤏𐤔𐤕𐤉.𐤏𐤔𐤓.𐤉𐤅𐤌.𐤍𐤔𐤉𐤀.𐤋𐤁𐤍𐤉.𐤀𐤔𐤓.𐤐
𐤂𐤏𐤉𐤀𐤋.𐤁𐤍.𐤏𐤊𐤓𐤍|
73 𐤒𐤓𐤁𐤍𐤅.𐤒𐤏𐤓𐤕.𐤊𐤎𐤐.𐤀𐤇𐤕.𐤔𐤋𐤔𐤉𐤌.𐤅𐤌𐤀𐤄.𐤌
𐤔𐤒𐤋𐤄.𐤌𐤆𐤓𐤒.𐤀𐤇𐤃.𐤊𐤎𐤐.𐤔𐤁𐤏𐤉𐤌.𐤔𐤒𐤋.𐤁𐤔𐤒𐤋.
𐤄𐤒𐤃𐤔.𐤔𐤍𐤉𐤄𐤌.𐤌𐤋𐤀𐤉𐤌.𐤎𐤋𐤕.𐤁𐤋𐤅𐤋𐤄.𐤁𐤔𐤌𐤍.𐤋𐤌𐤍
𐤇𐤄|
74 𐤊𐤐.𐤀𐤇𐤕.𐤏𐤔𐤓𐤄.𐤆𐤄𐤁.𐤌𐤋𐤀𐤄.𐤒𐤈𐤓𐤕|
75 𐤐𐤓.𐤀𐤇𐤃.𐤁𐤍.𐤁𐤒𐤓.𐤀𐤉𐤋.𐤀𐤇𐤃.𐤊𐤁𐤔.𐤀𐤇𐤃.𐤁
𐤍.𐤔𐤍𐤕𐤅.𐤋𐤏𐤋𐤄|
76 𐤔𐤏𐤉𐤓.𐤏𐤆𐤉𐤌.𐤀𐤇𐤃.𐤋𐤇𐤈𐤀𐤕|
77 𐤅𐤋𐤆𐤁𐤇.𐤄𐤔𐤋𐤌𐤉𐤌.𐤁𐤒𐤓.𐤔𐤍𐤉𐤌.𐤀𐤉𐤋𐤌.𐤇𐤌𐤔
𐤄.𐤏𐤕𐤃𐤉𐤌.𐤇𐤌𐤔𐤄.𐤊𐤁𐤔𐤉𐤌.𐤁𐤍𐤉.𐤔𐤍𐤄.𐤇𐤌𐤔𐤄.𐤆
𐤄.𐤒𐤓𐤁𐤍.𐤐𐤂𐤏𐤉𐤀𐤋.𐤁𐤍.𐤏𐤊𐤓𐤍|
78 𐤁𐤉𐤅𐤌.𐤔𐤍𐤉𐤌.𐤏𐤔𐤓.𐤉𐤅𐤌.𐤍𐤔𐤉𐤀.𐤋𐤁𐤍𐤉.𐤍𐤐𐤕𐤋𐤉.
𐤀𐤇𐤉𐤓𐤏.𐤁𐤍.𐤏𐤉𐤍𐤍|

..𐤏𐤈.. 𐤒𐤓𐤁𐤍𐤅.𐤒𐤏𐤓𐤕.𐤊𐤎𐤐.𐤀𐤇𐤕.𐤔𐤋𐤔𐤉𐤌.𐤅𐤌𐤀𐤄.𐤌𐤔𐤒𐤋𐤄.𐤌𐤆𐤓𐤒.𐤀𐤇𐤃.𐤊𐤎𐤐.𐤔𐤁𐤏𐤉𐤌.𐤔𐤒𐤋.𐤁𐤔𐤒𐤋.𐤄𐤒𐤃𐤔.𐤔𐤍𐤉𐤄𐤌.𐤌𐤋𐤀𐤉𐤌.𐤎𐤋𐤕.𐤁𐤋𐤅𐤋𐤄.𐤁𐤔𐤌𐤍.𐤋𐤌𐤍𐤇𐤄|

..𐤐.. 𐤊𐤐.𐤀𐤇𐤕.𐤏𐤔𐤓𐤄.𐤆𐤄𐤁.𐤌𐤋𐤀𐤄.𐤒𐤈𐤓𐤕|

..𐤐𐤀.. 𐤐𐤓.𐤀𐤇𐤃.𐤁𐤍.𐤁𐤒𐤓.𐤀𐤉𐤋.𐤀𐤇𐤃.𐤊𐤁𐤔.𐤀𐤇𐤃.𐤁𐤍.𐤔𐤍𐤕𐤅.𐤋𐤏𐤋𐤄|

..𐤐𐤁.. 𐤔𐤏𐤉𐤓.𐤏𐤆𐤉𐤌.𐤀𐤇𐤃.𐤋𐤇𐤈𐤀𐤕|

..𐤐𐤂.. 𐤅𐤋𐤆𐤁𐤇.𐤄𐤔𐤋𐤌𐤉𐤌.𐤁𐤒𐤓.𐤔𐤍𐤉𐤌.𐤀𐤉𐤋𐤌.𐤇𐤌𐤔𐤄.𐤏𐤕𐤃𐤉𐤌.𐤇𐤌𐤔𐤄.𐤊𐤁𐤔𐤉𐤌.𐤁𐤍𐤉.𐤔𐤍𐤄.𐤇𐤌𐤔𐤄.𐤆𐤄.𐤒𐤓𐤁𐤍.𐤀𐤇𐤉𐤓𐤏.𐤁𐤍.𐤏𐤉𐤍𐤍|

..𐤐𐤃.. 𐤆𐤀𐤕.𐤇𐤍𐤊𐤕.𐤄𐤌𐤆𐤁𐤇.𐤁𐤉𐤅𐤌.𐤄𐤌𐤔𐤇.𐤀𐤕𐤅.𐤌𐤀𐤕.𐤍𐤔𐤉𐤀𐤉.𐤉𐤔𐤓𐤀𐤋.𐤒𐤏𐤓𐤕.𐤊𐤎𐤐.𐤔𐤕𐤉𐤌.𐤏𐤔𐤓𐤄.𐤌𐤆𐤓𐤒𐤉.𐤊𐤎𐤐.𐤔𐤍𐤉𐤌.𐤏𐤔𐤓.𐤊𐤐𐤅𐤕.𐤆𐤄𐤁.𐤔𐤕𐤉𐤌.𐤏𐤔𐤓𐤄|

..𐤐𐤄.. 𐤔𐤋𐤔𐤉𐤌.𐤅𐤌𐤀𐤄.𐤄𐤒𐤏𐤓𐤄.𐤄𐤀𐤇𐤕.𐤊𐤎𐤐.𐤅𐤔𐤁𐤏𐤉𐤌.𐤄𐤌𐤆𐤓𐤒.𐤄𐤀𐤇𐤃.𐤊𐤋.𐤊𐤎𐤐.𐤄𐤊𐤋𐤉𐤌.𐤀𐤋𐤐𐤉𐤌.𐤅𐤀𐤓𐤁𐤏.𐤌𐤀𐤅𐤕.𐤁𐤔𐤒𐤋.𐤄𐤒𐤃𐤔|

..𐤐𐤅.. 𐤊𐤐𐤅𐤕.𐤆𐤄𐤁.𐤔𐤕𐤉𐤌.𐤏𐤔𐤓𐤄.𐤌𐤋𐤀𐤕.𐤒𐤈𐤓𐤕.𐤏𐤔𐤓𐤄.𐤏𐤔𐤓𐤄.𐤄𐤊𐤐.𐤁𐤔𐤒𐤋.𐤄𐤒𐤃𐤔.𐤊𐤋.𐤆𐤄𐤁.𐤄𐤊𐤐𐤅𐤕.𐤏𐤔𐤓𐤉𐤌.𐤅𐤌𐤀𐤄|

..𐤐𐤆.. 𐤊𐤋.𐤄𐤁𐤒𐤓.𐤋𐤏𐤋𐤄.𐤔𐤍𐤉𐤌.𐤏𐤔𐤓.𐤐𐤓𐤉𐤌.𐤀𐤉𐤋𐤌.𐤔𐤍𐤉𐤌.𐤏𐤔𐤓.𐤊𐤁𐤔𐤉𐤌.𐤁𐤍𐤉.𐤔𐤍𐤄.𐤔𐤍𐤉𐤌.𐤏𐤔𐤓.𐤅𐤌𐤍𐤇𐤕𐤌.𐤅𐤔𐤏𐤉𐤓𐤉.𐤏𐤆𐤉𐤌.𐤔𐤍𐤉𐤌.𐤏𐤔𐤓.𐤋𐤇𐤈𐤀𐤕|

..𐤐𐤇.. 𐤅𐤊𐤋.𐤁𐤒𐤓.𐤆𐤁𐤇.𐤄𐤔𐤋𐤌𐤉𐤌.𐤏𐤔𐤓𐤉𐤌.𐤅𐤀𐤓𐤁𐤏𐤄.𐤐𐤓𐤉𐤌.𐤀𐤉𐤋𐤌.𐤔𐤔𐤉𐤌.𐤏𐤕𐤃𐤉𐤌.𐤔𐤔𐤉𐤌.𐤊𐤁𐤔𐤉𐤌.𐤁𐤍𐤉.𐤔𐤍𐤄.𐤔𐤔𐤉𐤌.𐤆𐤀𐤕.𐤇𐤍𐤊𐤕.𐤄𐤌𐤆𐤁𐤇.𐤀𐤇𐤓𐤉.𐤄𐤌𐤔𐤇.𐤀𐤕𐤅|

..𐤐𐤈.. 𐤅𐤁𐤁𐤀.𐤌𐤔𐤄.𐤀𐤋.𐤀𐤄𐤋.𐤌𐤅𐤏𐤃.𐤋𐤃𐤁𐤓.𐤀𐤕𐤅.𐤅𐤉𐤔𐤌𐤏.𐤀𐤕.𐤄𐤒𐤅𐤋.𐤌𐤃𐤁𐤓.𐤀𐤋𐤉𐤅.𐤌𐤏𐤋.𐤄𐤊𐤐𐤓𐤕.𐤀𐤔𐤓.

𐤏𐤋.𐤀𐤓𐤍.𐤄𐤏𐤃𐤕.𐤌𐤁𐤉𐤍.𐤔𐤍𐤉.𐤄𐤊𐤓𐤁𐤉𐤌.𐤅𐤉𐤃𐤁𐤓.𐤀𐤋
𐤉𐤅||

𐤁𐤌𐤃𐤁𐤓.𐤇𐤋𐤒 ..𐤋..

..𐤀.. 𐤅𐤉𐤃𐤁𐤓.𐤉𐤄𐤅𐤄.𐤀𐤋.𐤌𐤔𐤄.𐤋𐤀𐤌𐤓|
..𐤁.. 𐤃𐤁𐤓.𐤀𐤋.𐤀𐤄𐤓𐤍.𐤅𐤀𐤌𐤓𐤕.𐤀𐤋𐤉𐤅.𐤁𐤄𐤏𐤋𐤕𐤊.𐤀𐤕.𐤄
𐤍𐤓𐤕.𐤀𐤋.𐤌𐤅𐤋.𐤐𐤍𐤉.𐤄𐤌𐤍𐤅𐤓𐤄.𐤉𐤀𐤉𐤓𐤅.𐤔𐤁𐤏𐤕.𐤄𐤍𐤓𐤅𐤕|
..𐤂.. 𐤅𐤉𐤏𐤔.𐤊𐤍.𐤀𐤄𐤓𐤍.𐤀𐤋.𐤌𐤅𐤋.𐤐𐤍𐤉.𐤄𐤌𐤍𐤅𐤓𐤄.𐤄𐤏𐤋𐤄.𐤍
𐤓𐤕𐤉𐤄.𐤊𐤀𐤔𐤓.𐤑𐤅𐤄.𐤉𐤄𐤅𐤄.𐤀𐤕.𐤌𐤔𐤄|
..𐤃.. 𐤅𐤆𐤄.𐤌𐤏𐤔𐤄.𐤄𐤌𐤍𐤓𐤄.𐤌𐤒𐤔𐤄.𐤆𐤄𐤁.𐤏𐤃.𐤉𐤓𐤊
𐤄.𐤏𐤃.𐤐𐤓𐤇𐤄.𐤌𐤒𐤔𐤄.𐤄𐤅𐤀.𐤊𐤌𐤓𐤀𐤄.𐤀𐤔𐤓.𐤄𐤓𐤀𐤄.𐤉
𐤄𐤅𐤄.𐤀𐤕.𐤌𐤔𐤄.𐤊𐤍.𐤏𐤔𐤄.𐤀𐤕.𐤄𐤌𐤍𐤓𐤄|
..𐤄.. 𐤅𐤉𐤃𐤁𐤓.𐤉𐤄𐤅𐤄.𐤀𐤋.𐤌𐤔𐤄.𐤋𐤀𐤌𐤓|
..𐤅.. 𐤒𐤇.𐤀𐤕.𐤄𐤋𐤅𐤉𐤌.𐤌𐤕𐤅𐤊.𐤁𐤍𐤉.𐤉𐤔𐤓𐤀𐤋.𐤅𐤈𐤄𐤓𐤕.𐤀
𐤕𐤌|
..𐤆.. 𐤅𐤊𐤄.𐤕𐤏𐤔𐤄.𐤋𐤄𐤌.𐤋𐤈𐤄𐤓𐤌.𐤄𐤆𐤄.𐤏𐤋𐤉𐤄𐤌.𐤌𐤉.
𐤇𐤈𐤀𐤕.𐤅𐤄𐤏𐤁𐤉𐤓𐤅.𐤕𐤏𐤓.𐤏𐤋.𐤊𐤋.𐤁𐤔𐤓𐤌.𐤅𐤊𐤁𐤎𐤅.𐤁𐤂
𐤃𐤉𐤄𐤌.𐤅𐤄𐤈𐤄𐤓𐤅|
..𐤇.. 𐤅𐤋𐤒𐤇𐤅.𐤐𐤓.𐤁𐤍.𐤁𐤒𐤓.𐤅𐤌𐤍𐤇𐤕𐤅.𐤎𐤋𐤕.𐤁𐤋𐤅𐤋𐤄.𐤁𐤔𐤌
𐤍.𐤅𐤐𐤓.𐤔𐤍𐤉.𐤁𐤍.𐤁𐤒𐤓.𐤕𐤒𐤇.𐤋𐤇𐤈𐤀𐤕|
..𐤈.. 𐤅𐤄𐤒𐤓𐤁𐤕.𐤀𐤕.𐤄𐤋𐤅𐤉𐤌.𐤋𐤐𐤍𐤉.𐤀𐤄𐤋.𐤌𐤅𐤏𐤃.𐤅𐤄𐤒
𐤄𐤋𐤕.𐤀𐤕.𐤊𐤋.𐤏𐤃𐤕.𐤁𐤍𐤉.𐤉𐤔𐤓𐤀𐤋|
..𐤉.. 𐤅𐤄𐤒𐤓𐤁𐤕.𐤀𐤕.𐤄𐤋𐤅𐤉𐤌.𐤋𐤐𐤍𐤉.𐤉𐤄𐤅𐤄.𐤅𐤎𐤌𐤊𐤅.𐤁𐤍
𐤉.𐤉𐤔𐤓𐤀𐤋.𐤀𐤕.𐤉𐤃𐤉𐤄𐤌.𐤏𐤋.𐤄𐤋𐤅𐤉𐤌|
..𐤉𐤀.. 𐤅𐤄𐤍𐤉𐤐.𐤀𐤄𐤓𐤍.𐤀𐤕.𐤄𐤋𐤅𐤉𐤌.𐤕𐤍𐤅𐤐𐤄.𐤋𐤐𐤍𐤉.𐤉𐤄𐤅𐤄.
𐤌𐤀𐤕.𐤁𐤍𐤉.𐤉𐤔𐤓𐤀𐤋.𐤅𐤄𐤉𐤅.𐤋𐤏𐤁𐤃.𐤀𐤕.𐤏𐤁𐤃𐤕.𐤉𐤄𐤅𐤄
|
..𐤉𐤁.. 𐤅𐤄𐤋𐤅𐤉𐤌.𐤉𐤎𐤌𐤊𐤅.𐤀𐤕.𐤉𐤃𐤉𐤄𐤌.𐤏𐤋.𐤓𐤀𐤔.𐤄𐤐𐤓𐤉
𐤌.𐤅𐤏𐤔𐤄.𐤀𐤕.𐤄𐤀𐤇𐤃.𐤇𐤈𐤀𐤕.𐤅𐤀𐤕.𐤄𐤀𐤇𐤃.𐤏𐤋𐤄.
𐤋𐤉𐤄𐤅𐤄.𐤋𐤊𐤐𐤓.𐤏𐤋.𐤄𐤋𐤅𐤉𐤌|

𐤉𐤂 𐤅𐤄𐤏𐤌𐤃𐤕.𐤀𐤕.𐤄𐤋𐤅𐤉𐤌.𐤋𐤐𐤍𐤉.𐤀𐤄𐤓𐤍.𐤅𐤋𐤐𐤍𐤉.𐤁𐤍
𐤉𐤅.𐤅𐤄𐤍𐤐𐤕.𐤀𐤕𐤌.𐤕𐤍𐤅𐤐𐤄.𐤋𐤉𐤄𐤅𐤄|
𐤉𐤃 𐤅𐤄𐤁𐤃𐤋𐤕.𐤀𐤕.𐤄𐤋𐤅𐤉𐤌.𐤌𐤕𐤅𐤊.𐤁𐤍𐤉.𐤉𐤔𐤓𐤀𐤋.𐤅𐤄
𐤉𐤅.𐤋𐤉.𐤄𐤋𐤅𐤉𐤌|
𐤈𐤅 𐤅𐤀𐤇𐤓𐤉.𐤊𐤍.𐤉𐤁𐤀𐤅.𐤄𐤋𐤅𐤉𐤌.𐤋𐤏𐤁𐤃.𐤀𐤕.𐤀𐤄𐤋.𐤌𐤅
𐤏𐤃.𐤅𐤈𐤄𐤓𐤕.𐤀𐤕𐤌.𐤅𐤄𐤍𐤐𐤕.𐤀𐤕𐤌.𐤕𐤍𐤅𐤐𐤄|
𐤈𐤆 𐤊𐤉.𐤍𐤕𐤍𐤉𐤌.𐤍𐤕𐤍𐤉𐤌.𐤄𐤌𐤄.𐤋𐤉.𐤌𐤕𐤅𐤊.𐤁𐤍𐤉.𐤉𐤔𐤓
𐤀𐤋.𐤕𐤇𐤕.𐤐𐤈𐤓𐤕.𐤊𐤋.𐤓𐤇𐤌.𐤁𐤊𐤅𐤓.𐤊𐤋.𐤌𐤁𐤍𐤉.𐤉𐤔𐤓𐤀𐤋.
𐤋𐤒𐤇𐤕𐤉.𐤀𐤕𐤌.𐤋𐤉|
𐤉𐤆 𐤊𐤉.𐤋𐤉.𐤊𐤋.𐤁𐤊𐤅𐤓.𐤁𐤁𐤍𐤉.𐤉𐤔𐤓𐤀𐤋.𐤁𐤀𐤃𐤌.𐤅𐤁𐤁𐤄
𐤌𐤄.𐤁𐤉𐤅𐤌.𐤄𐤊𐤕𐤉.𐤊𐤋.𐤁𐤊𐤅𐤓.𐤁𐤀𐤓𐤑.𐤌𐤑𐤓𐤉𐤌.𐤄𐤒𐤃
𐤔𐤕𐤉.𐤀𐤕𐤌.𐤋𐤉|
𐤉𐤇 𐤅𐤀𐤒𐤇.𐤀𐤕.𐤄𐤋𐤅𐤉𐤌.𐤕𐤇𐤕.𐤊𐤋.𐤁𐤊𐤅𐤓.𐤁𐤁𐤍𐤉.𐤉𐤔
𐤓𐤀𐤋|
𐤉𐤈 𐤅𐤀𐤕𐤍𐤄.𐤀𐤕.𐤄𐤋𐤅𐤉𐤌.𐤍𐤕𐤍𐤉𐤌.𐤋𐤀𐤄𐤓𐤍.𐤅𐤋𐤁𐤍𐤉𐤅.
𐤌𐤕𐤅𐤊.𐤁𐤍𐤉.𐤉𐤔𐤓𐤀𐤋.𐤋𐤏𐤁𐤃.𐤀𐤕.𐤏𐤁𐤃𐤕.𐤁𐤍𐤉.𐤉𐤔𐤓
𐤀𐤋.𐤁𐤀𐤄𐤋.𐤌𐤅𐤏𐤃.𐤅𐤋𐤊𐤐𐤓.𐤏𐤋.𐤁𐤍𐤉.𐤉𐤔𐤓𐤀𐤋.𐤅𐤋𐤀.𐤉𐤄
𐤉𐤄.𐤁𐤁𐤍𐤉.𐤉𐤔𐤓𐤀𐤋.𐤍𐤂𐤐.𐤁𐤂𐤔𐤕.𐤁𐤍𐤉.𐤉𐤔𐤓𐤀𐤋.𐤀𐤋.𐤄
𐤒𐤃𐤔|
𐤊 𐤅𐤉𐤏𐤔.𐤌𐤔𐤄.𐤅𐤀𐤄𐤓𐤍.𐤅𐤊𐤋.𐤏𐤃𐤕.𐤁𐤍𐤉.𐤉𐤔𐤓𐤀𐤋.
𐤋𐤋𐤅𐤉𐤌.𐤊𐤊𐤋.𐤀𐤔𐤓.𐤑𐤅𐤄.𐤉𐤄𐤅𐤄.𐤀𐤕.𐤌𐤔𐤄.𐤋𐤋𐤅𐤉𐤌.𐤊𐤍.
𐤏𐤔𐤅.𐤋𐤄𐤌.𐤁𐤍𐤉.𐤉𐤔𐤓𐤀𐤋|
𐤊𐤀 𐤅𐤉𐤕𐤇𐤈𐤀𐤅.𐤄𐤋𐤅𐤉𐤌.𐤅𐤉𐤊𐤁𐤎𐤅.𐤁𐤂𐤃𐤉𐤄𐤌.𐤅𐤉𐤍𐤐.
𐤀𐤄𐤓𐤍.𐤀𐤕𐤌.𐤕𐤍𐤅𐤐𐤄.𐤋𐤐𐤍𐤉.𐤉𐤄𐤅𐤄.𐤅𐤉𐤊𐤐𐤓.𐤏𐤋𐤉𐤄𐤌.𐤀
𐤄𐤓𐤍.𐤋𐤈𐤄𐤓𐤌|
𐤊𐤁 𐤅𐤀𐤇𐤓𐤉.𐤊𐤍.𐤁𐤀𐤅.𐤄𐤋𐤅𐤉𐤌.𐤋𐤏𐤁𐤃.𐤀𐤕.𐤏𐤁𐤃𐤕𐤌
.𐤁𐤀𐤄𐤋.𐤌𐤅𐤏𐤃.𐤋𐤐𐤍𐤉.𐤀𐤄𐤓𐤍.𐤅𐤋𐤐𐤍𐤉.𐤁𐤍𐤉𐤅.𐤊𐤀𐤔𐤓.𐤑𐤅
𐤄.𐤉𐤄𐤅𐤄.𐤀𐤕.𐤌𐤔𐤄.𐤏𐤋.𐤄𐤋𐤅𐤉𐤌.𐤊𐤍.𐤏𐤔𐤅.𐤋𐤄𐤌|
𐤊𐤂 𐤅𐤉𐤃𐤁𐤓.𐤉𐤄𐤅𐤄.𐤀𐤋.𐤌𐤔𐤄.𐤋𐤀𐤌𐤓|

כד 𐤆𐤀𐤕.𐤀𐤔𐤓.𐤋𐤋𐤅𐤉𐤌.𐤌𐤁𐤍.𐤇𐤌𐤔.𐤅𐤏𐤔𐤓𐤉𐤌.𐤔𐤍
𐤄.𐤅𐤌𐤏𐤋𐤄.𐤉𐤁𐤅𐤀.𐤋𐤑𐤁𐤀.𐤑𐤁𐤀.𐤁𐤏𐤁𐤃𐤕.𐤀𐤄𐤋.𐤌𐤅𐤏
𐤃|
כה 𐤅𐤌𐤁𐤍.𐤇𐤌𐤔𐤉𐤌.𐤔𐤍𐤄.𐤉𐤔𐤅𐤁.𐤌𐤑𐤁𐤀.𐤄𐤏𐤁𐤃𐤄.𐤅
𐤋𐤀.𐤉𐤏𐤁𐤃.𐤏𐤅𐤃|
כו 𐤅𐤔𐤓𐤕.𐤀𐤕.𐤀𐤇𐤉𐤅.𐤁𐤀𐤄𐤋.𐤌𐤅𐤏𐤃.𐤋𐤔𐤌𐤓.𐤌𐤔𐤌𐤓
𐤕.𐤅𐤏𐤁𐤃𐤄.𐤋𐤀.𐤉𐤏𐤁𐤃.𐤊𐤊𐤄.𐤕𐤏𐤔𐤄.𐤋𐤋𐤅𐤉𐤌.𐤁𐤌𐤔𐤌
𐤓𐤕𐤌||

𐤁𐤌𐤃𐤁𐤓.𐤇𐤋𐤒 ט

א 𐤅𐤉𐤃𐤁𐤓.𐤉𐤄𐤅𐤄.𐤀𐤋.𐤌𐤔𐤄.𐤁𐤌𐤃𐤁𐤓.𐤎𐤉𐤍𐤉.𐤁𐤔𐤍𐤄.
𐤄𐤔𐤍𐤉𐤕.𐤋𐤑𐤀𐤕𐤌.𐤌𐤀𐤓𐤑.𐤌𐤑𐤓𐤉𐤌.𐤁𐤇𐤃𐤔.𐤄𐤓𐤀𐤔𐤅
𐤍.𐤋𐤀𐤌𐤓|
ב 𐤅𐤉𐤏𐤔𐤅.𐤁𐤍𐤉.𐤉𐤔𐤓𐤀𐤋.𐤀𐤕.𐤄𐤐𐤎𐤇.𐤁𐤌𐤅𐤏𐤃𐤅|
ג 𐤁𐤀𐤓𐤁𐤏𐤄.𐤏𐤔𐤓.𐤉𐤅𐤌.𐤁𐤇𐤃𐤔.𐤄𐤆𐤄.𐤁𐤉𐤍.𐤄𐤏𐤓𐤁
𐤉𐤌.𐤕𐤏𐤔𐤅.𐤀𐤕𐤅.𐤁𐤌𐤅𐤏𐤃𐤅.𐤊𐤊𐤋.𐤇𐤒𐤕𐤉𐤅.𐤅𐤊𐤊𐤋.𐤌𐤔𐤐
𐤈𐤉𐤅.𐤕𐤏𐤔𐤅.𐤀𐤕𐤅|
ד 𐤅𐤉𐤃𐤁𐤓.𐤌𐤔𐤄.𐤀𐤋.𐤁𐤍𐤉.𐤉𐤔𐤓𐤀𐤋.𐤋𐤏𐤔𐤕.𐤄𐤐𐤎𐤇|
ה 𐤅𐤉𐤏𐤔𐤅.𐤀𐤕.𐤄𐤐𐤎𐤇.𐤁𐤓𐤀𐤔𐤅𐤍.𐤁𐤀𐤓𐤁𐤏𐤄.𐤏𐤔𐤓.𐤉𐤅
𐤌.𐤋𐤇𐤃𐤔.𐤁𐤉𐤍.𐤄𐤏𐤓𐤁𐤉𐤌.𐤁𐤌𐤃𐤁𐤓.𐤎𐤉𐤍𐤉.𐤊𐤊𐤋.𐤀𐤔
𐤓.𐤑𐤅𐤄.𐤉𐤄𐤅𐤄.𐤀𐤕.𐤌𐤔𐤄.𐤊𐤍.𐤏𐤔𐤅.𐤁𐤍𐤉.𐤉𐤔𐤓𐤀𐤋|
ו 𐤅𐤉𐤄𐤉.𐤀𐤍𐤔𐤉𐤌.𐤀𐤔𐤓.𐤄𐤉𐤅.𐤈𐤌𐤀𐤉𐤌.𐤋𐤍𐤐𐤔.𐤀𐤃𐤌.
𐤅𐤋𐤀.𐤉𐤊𐤋𐤅.𐤋𐤏𐤔𐤕.𐤄𐤐𐤎𐤇.𐤁𐤉𐤅𐤌.𐤄𐤄𐤅𐤀.𐤅𐤉𐤒𐤓𐤁𐤅.𐤋𐤐
𐤍𐤉.𐤌𐤔𐤄.𐤅𐤋𐤐𐤍𐤉.𐤀𐤄𐤓𐤍.𐤁𐤉𐤅𐤌.𐤄𐤄𐤅𐤀|
ז 𐤅𐤉𐤀𐤌𐤓𐤅.𐤄𐤀𐤍𐤔𐤉𐤌.𐤄𐤄𐤌𐤄.𐤀𐤋𐤉𐤅.𐤀𐤍𐤇𐤍𐤅.𐤈𐤌𐤀
𐤉𐤌.𐤋𐤍𐤐𐤔.𐤀𐤃𐤌.𐤋𐤌𐤄.𐤍𐤂𐤓𐤏.𐤋𐤁𐤋𐤕𐤉.𐤄𐤒𐤓𐤁.𐤀𐤕.𐤒
𐤓𐤁𐤍.𐤉𐤄𐤅𐤄.𐤁𐤌𐤏𐤃𐤅.𐤁𐤕𐤅𐤊.𐤁𐤍𐤉.𐤉𐤔𐤓𐤀𐤋|
ח 𐤅𐤉𐤀𐤌𐤓.𐤀𐤋𐤄𐤌.𐤌𐤔𐤄.𐤏𐤌𐤃𐤅.𐤅𐤀𐤔𐤌𐤏𐤄.𐤌𐤄.𐤉𐤑
𐤅𐤄.𐤉𐤄𐤅𐤄.𐤋𐤊𐤌|
ט 𐤅𐤉𐤃𐤁𐤓.𐤉𐤄𐤅𐤄.𐤀𐤋.𐤌𐤔𐤄.𐤋𐤀𐤌𐤓|

10 𐤃𐤁𐤓.𐤀𐤋.𐤁𐤍𐤉.𐤉𐤔𐤓𐤀𐤋.𐤋𐤀𐤌𐤓.𐤀𐤉𐤔.𐤀𐤉𐤔.𐤊𐤉.𐤉𐤄𐤉𐤄.𐤈𐤌𐤀.𐤋𐤍𐤐𐤔.𐤀𐤅.𐤁𐤃𐤓𐤊.𐤓𐤇𐤒𐤄.𐤋𐤊𐤌.𐤀𐤅.𐤋𐤃𐤓𐤕𐤉𐤊𐤌.𐤅𐤏𐤔𐤄.𐤐𐤎𐤇.𐤋𐤉𐤄𐤅𐤄|

11 𐤁𐤇𐤃𐤔.𐤄𐤔𐤍𐤉.𐤁𐤀𐤓𐤁𐤏𐤄.𐤏𐤔𐤓.𐤉𐤅𐤌.𐤁𐤉𐤍.𐤄𐤏𐤓𐤁𐤉𐤌.𐤉𐤏𐤔𐤅.𐤀𐤕𐤅.𐤏𐤋.𐤌𐤑𐤅𐤕.𐤅𐤌𐤓𐤓𐤉𐤌.𐤉𐤀𐤊𐤋𐤄𐤅|

12 𐤋𐤀.𐤉𐤔𐤀𐤉𐤓𐤅.𐤌𐤌𐤍𐤅.𐤏𐤃.𐤁𐤒𐤓.𐤅𐤏𐤑𐤌.𐤋𐤀.𐤉𐤔𐤁𐤓𐤅.𐤁𐤅.𐤊𐤊𐤋.𐤇𐤒𐤕.𐤄𐤐𐤎𐤇.𐤉𐤏𐤔𐤅.𐤀𐤕𐤅|

13 𐤅𐤄𐤀𐤉𐤔.𐤀𐤔𐤓.𐤄𐤅𐤀.𐤈𐤄𐤅𐤓.𐤅𐤁𐤃𐤓𐤊.𐤋𐤀.𐤄𐤉𐤄.𐤅𐤇𐤃𐤋.𐤋𐤏𐤔𐤅𐤕.𐤄𐤐𐤎𐤇.𐤅𐤍𐤊𐤓𐤕𐤄.𐤄𐤍𐤐𐤔.𐤄𐤄𐤅𐤀.𐤌𐤏𐤌𐤉𐤄.𐤊𐤉.𐤒𐤓𐤁𐤍.𐤉𐤄𐤅𐤄.𐤋𐤀.𐤄𐤒𐤓𐤉𐤁.𐤁𐤌𐤏𐤃𐤅.𐤇𐤈𐤀𐤅.𐤉𐤔𐤀.𐤄𐤀𐤉𐤔.𐤄𐤄𐤅𐤀|

14 𐤅𐤊𐤉.𐤉𐤂𐤅𐤓.𐤀𐤕𐤊𐤌.𐤂𐤓.𐤅𐤏𐤔𐤄.𐤐𐤎𐤇.𐤋𐤉𐤄𐤅𐤄.𐤊𐤇𐤒𐤕.𐤄𐤐𐤎𐤇.𐤅𐤊𐤌𐤔𐤐𐤈𐤅.𐤊𐤍.𐤉𐤏𐤔𐤄.𐤇𐤒𐤄.𐤀𐤇𐤕.𐤉𐤄𐤉𐤄.𐤋𐤊𐤌.𐤅𐤋𐤂𐤓.𐤅𐤋𐤀𐤆𐤓𐤇.𐤄𐤀𐤓𐤑|

15 𐤅𐤁𐤉𐤅𐤌.𐤄𐤒𐤉𐤌.𐤀𐤕.𐤄𐤌𐤔𐤊𐤍.𐤊𐤎𐤄.𐤄𐤏𐤍𐤍.𐤀𐤕.𐤄𐤌𐤔𐤊𐤍.𐤋𐤀𐤄𐤋.𐤄𐤏𐤃𐤕.𐤅𐤁𐤏𐤓𐤁.𐤉𐤄𐤉𐤄.𐤏𐤋.𐤄𐤌𐤔𐤊𐤍.𐤊𐤌𐤓𐤀𐤄.𐤀𐤔.𐤏𐤃.𐤁𐤒𐤓|

16 𐤊𐤍.𐤉𐤄𐤉𐤄.𐤕𐤌𐤉𐤃.𐤄𐤏𐤍𐤍.𐤉𐤊𐤎𐤍𐤅.𐤅𐤌𐤓𐤀𐤄.𐤀𐤔.𐤋𐤉𐤋𐤄|

17 𐤅𐤋𐤐𐤉.𐤄𐤏𐤋𐤕.𐤄𐤏𐤍𐤍.𐤌𐤏𐤋.𐤄𐤀𐤄𐤋.𐤅𐤀𐤇𐤓𐤉.𐤊𐤍.𐤉𐤎𐤏𐤅.𐤁𐤍𐤉.𐤉𐤔𐤓𐤀𐤋.𐤅𐤁𐤌𐤒𐤅𐤌.𐤀𐤔𐤓.𐤉𐤔𐤊𐤍.𐤔𐤌.𐤄𐤏𐤍𐤍.𐤔𐤌.𐤉𐤇𐤍𐤅.𐤁𐤍𐤉.𐤉𐤔𐤓𐤀𐤋|

18 𐤏𐤋.𐤐𐤉.𐤉𐤄𐤅𐤄.𐤉𐤎𐤏𐤅.𐤁𐤍𐤉.𐤉𐤔𐤓𐤀𐤋.𐤅𐤏𐤋.𐤐𐤉.𐤉𐤄𐤅𐤄.𐤉𐤇𐤍𐤅.𐤊𐤋.𐤉𐤌𐤉.𐤀𐤔𐤓.𐤉𐤔𐤊𐤍.𐤄𐤏𐤍𐤍.𐤏𐤋.𐤄𐤌𐤔𐤊𐤍.𐤉𐤇𐤍𐤅|

19 𐤅𐤁𐤄𐤀𐤓𐤉𐤊.𐤄𐤏𐤍𐤍.𐤏𐤋.𐤄𐤌𐤔𐤊𐤍.𐤉𐤌𐤉𐤌.𐤓𐤁𐤉𐤌.𐤅𐤔𐤌𐤓𐤅.𐤁𐤍𐤉.𐤉𐤔𐤓𐤀𐤋.𐤀𐤕.𐤌𐤔𐤌𐤓𐤕.𐤉𐤄𐤅𐤄.𐤅𐤋𐤀.𐤉𐤎𐤏𐤅|

20 𐤅𐤉𐤔.𐤀𐤔𐤓.𐤉𐤄𐤉𐤄.𐤄𐤏𐤍𐤍.𐤉𐤌𐤉𐤌.𐤌𐤎𐤐𐤓.𐤏𐤋.𐤄𐤌𐤔𐤊𐤍.𐤏𐤋.𐤐𐤉.𐤉𐤄𐤅𐤄.𐤉𐤇𐤍𐤅.𐤅𐤏𐤋.𐤐𐤉.𐤉𐤄𐤅𐤄.𐤉𐤎𐤏𐤅|

..כא.. 𐤅𐤉𐤔.𐤀𐤔𐤓.𐤉𐤄𐤉𐤄.𐤄𐤏𐤍𐤍.𐤌𐤏𐤓𐤁.𐤏𐤃.𐤁𐤒𐤓.𐤅𐤍𐤏
𐤋𐤄.𐤄𐤏𐤍𐤍.𐤁𐤁𐤒𐤓.𐤅𐤍𐤎𐤏𐤅.𐤀𐤅.𐤉𐤅𐤌𐤌.𐤅𐤋𐤉𐤋𐤄.𐤅𐤍𐤏𐤋𐤄.𐤄
𐤏𐤍𐤍.𐤅𐤍𐤎𐤏𐤅|

..כב.. 𐤀𐤅.𐤉𐤌𐤉𐤌.𐤀𐤅.𐤇𐤃𐤔.𐤀𐤅.𐤉𐤌𐤉𐤌.𐤁𐤄𐤀𐤓𐤉𐤊.𐤄𐤏𐤍
𐤍.𐤏𐤋.𐤄𐤌𐤔𐤊𐤍.𐤋𐤔𐤊𐤍.𐤏𐤋𐤉𐤅.𐤉𐤇𐤍𐤅.𐤁𐤍𐤉.𐤉𐤔𐤓𐤀𐤋.𐤅𐤋𐤀
.𐤉𐤎𐤏𐤅.𐤅𐤁𐤄𐤏𐤋𐤕𐤅.𐤉𐤎𐤏𐤅|

..כג.. 𐤏𐤋.𐤐𐤉.𐤉𐤄𐤅𐤄.𐤉𐤇𐤍𐤅.𐤅𐤏𐤋.𐤐𐤉.𐤉𐤄𐤅𐤄.𐤉𐤎𐤏𐤅.𐤀𐤕.
𐤌𐤔𐤌𐤓𐤕.𐤉𐤄𐤅𐤄.𐤔𐤌𐤓𐤅.𐤏𐤋.𐤐𐤉.𐤉𐤄𐤅𐤄.𐤁𐤉𐤃.𐤌𐤔𐤄||

𐤁𐤌𐤃𐤁𐤓.𐤇𐤋𐤒 ..י..

..א.. 𐤅𐤉𐤃𐤁𐤓.𐤉𐤄𐤅𐤄.𐤀𐤋.𐤌𐤔𐤄.𐤋𐤀𐤌𐤓|

..ב.. 𐤏𐤔𐤄.𐤋𐤊.𐤔𐤕𐤉.𐤇𐤑𐤅𐤑𐤓𐤕.𐤊𐤎𐤐.𐤌𐤒𐤔𐤄.𐤕𐤏𐤔𐤄
.𐤀𐤕𐤌.𐤅𐤄𐤉𐤅.𐤋𐤊.𐤋𐤌𐤒𐤓𐤀.𐤄𐤏𐤃𐤄.𐤅𐤋𐤌𐤎𐤏.𐤀𐤕.𐤄𐤌𐤇
𐤍𐤅𐤕|

..ג.. 𐤅𐤕𐤒𐤏𐤅.𐤁𐤄𐤍.𐤅𐤍𐤅𐤏𐤃𐤅.𐤀𐤋𐤉𐤊.𐤊𐤋.𐤄𐤏𐤃𐤄.𐤀𐤋.𐤐
𐤕𐤇.𐤀𐤄𐤋.𐤌𐤅𐤏𐤃|

..ד.. 𐤅𐤀𐤌.𐤁𐤀𐤇𐤕.𐤉𐤕𐤒𐤏𐤅.𐤅𐤍𐤅𐤏𐤃𐤅.𐤀𐤋𐤉𐤊.𐤄𐤍𐤔𐤉𐤀𐤉
𐤌.𐤓𐤀𐤔𐤉.𐤀𐤋𐤐𐤉.𐤉𐤔𐤓𐤀𐤋|

..ה.. 𐤅𐤕𐤒𐤏𐤕𐤌.𐤕𐤓𐤅𐤏𐤄.𐤅𐤍𐤎𐤏𐤅.𐤄𐤌𐤇𐤍𐤅𐤕.𐤄𐤇𐤍𐤉𐤌.𐤒
𐤃𐤌𐤄|

..ו.. 𐤅𐤕𐤒𐤏𐤕𐤌.𐤕𐤓𐤅𐤏𐤄.𐤔𐤍𐤉𐤕.𐤅𐤍𐤎𐤏𐤅.𐤄𐤌𐤇𐤍𐤅𐤕.𐤄𐤇
𐤍𐤉𐤌.𐤕𐤉𐤌𐤍𐤄.𐤕𐤓𐤅𐤏𐤄.𐤉𐤕𐤒𐤏𐤅.𐤋𐤌𐤎𐤏𐤉𐤄𐤌|

..ז.. 𐤅𐤁𐤄𐤒𐤄𐤉𐤋.𐤀𐤕.𐤄𐤒𐤄𐤋.𐤕𐤕𐤒𐤏𐤅.𐤅𐤋𐤀.𐤕𐤓𐤉𐤏𐤅|

..ח.. 𐤅𐤁𐤍𐤉.𐤀𐤄𐤓𐤍.𐤄𐤊𐤄𐤍𐤉𐤌.𐤉𐤕𐤒𐤏𐤅.𐤁𐤇𐤑𐤑𐤓𐤅𐤕.𐤅𐤄
𐤉𐤅.𐤋𐤊𐤌.𐤋𐤇𐤒𐤕.𐤏𐤅𐤋𐤌.𐤋𐤃𐤓𐤕𐤉𐤊𐤌|

..ט.. 𐤅𐤊𐤉.𐤕𐤁𐤀𐤅.𐤌𐤋𐤇𐤌𐤄.𐤁𐤀𐤓𐤑𐤊𐤌.𐤏𐤋.𐤄𐤑𐤓.𐤄𐤑𐤓
𐤓.𐤀𐤕𐤊𐤌.𐤅𐤄𐤓𐤏𐤕𐤌.𐤁𐤇𐤑𐤑𐤓𐤅𐤕.𐤅𐤍𐤆𐤊𐤓𐤕𐤌.𐤋𐤐𐤍𐤉.𐤉
𐤄𐤅𐤄.𐤀𐤋𐤄𐤉𐤊𐤌.𐤅𐤍𐤅𐤔𐤏𐤕𐤌.𐤌𐤀𐤉𐤁𐤉𐤊𐤌|

..י.. 𐤅𐤁𐤉𐤅𐤌.𐤔𐤌𐤇𐤕𐤊𐤌.𐤅𐤁𐤌𐤅𐤏𐤃𐤉𐤊𐤌.𐤅𐤁𐤓𐤀𐤔𐤉.𐤇
𐤃𐤔𐤉𐤊𐤌.𐤅𐤕𐤒𐤏𐤕𐤌.𐤁𐤇𐤑𐤑𐤓𐤕.𐤏𐤋.𐤏𐤋𐤕𐤉𐤊𐤌.𐤅𐤏𐤋

.𐤆𐤁𐤇𐤉.𐤔𐤋𐤌𐤉𐤊𐤌.𐤅𐤄𐤉𐤅.𐤋𐤊𐤌.𐤋𐤆𐤊𐤓𐤅𐤍.𐤋𐤐𐤍𐤉.𐤀𐤋𐤄
𐤉𐤊𐤌.𐤀𐤍𐤉.𐤉𐤄𐤅𐤄.𐤀𐤋𐤄𐤉𐤊𐤌|
11 𐤅𐤉𐤄𐤉.𐤁𐤔𐤍𐤄.𐤄𐤔𐤍𐤉𐤕.𐤁𐤇𐤃𐤔.𐤄𐤔𐤍𐤉.𐤁𐤏𐤔𐤓𐤉
𐤌.𐤁𐤇𐤃𐤔.𐤍𐤏𐤋𐤄.𐤄𐤏𐤍𐤍.𐤌𐤏𐤋.𐤌𐤔𐤊𐤍.𐤄𐤏𐤃𐤕|
12 𐤅𐤉𐤎𐤏𐤅.𐤁𐤍𐤉.𐤉𐤔𐤓𐤀𐤋.𐤋𐤌𐤎𐤏𐤉𐤄𐤌.𐤌𐤌𐤃𐤁𐤓.𐤎𐤉
𐤍𐤉.𐤅𐤉𐤔𐤊𐤍.𐤄𐤏𐤍𐤍.𐤁𐤌𐤃𐤁𐤓.𐤐𐤀𐤓𐤍|
13 𐤅𐤉𐤎𐤏𐤅.𐤁𐤓𐤀𐤔𐤍𐤄.𐤏𐤋.𐤐𐤉.𐤉𐤄𐤅𐤄.𐤁𐤉𐤃.𐤌𐤔𐤄|
14 𐤅𐤉𐤎𐤏.𐤃𐤂𐤋.𐤌𐤇𐤍𐤄.𐤁𐤍𐤉.𐤉𐤄𐤅𐤃𐤄.𐤁𐤓𐤀𐤔𐤍𐤄.
𐤋𐤑𐤁𐤀𐤕𐤌.𐤅𐤏𐤋.𐤑𐤁𐤀𐤅.𐤍𐤇𐤔𐤅𐤍.𐤁𐤍.𐤏𐤌𐤉𐤍𐤃𐤁|
15 𐤅𐤏𐤋.𐤑𐤁𐤀.𐤌𐤈𐤄.𐤁𐤍𐤉.𐤉𐤔𐤔𐤊𐤓.𐤍𐤕𐤍𐤀𐤋.𐤁𐤍.𐤑𐤅
𐤏𐤓|
16 𐤅𐤏𐤋.𐤑𐤁𐤀.𐤌𐤈𐤄.𐤁𐤍𐤉.𐤆𐤁𐤅𐤋𐤍.𐤀𐤋𐤉𐤀𐤁.𐤁𐤍.𐤇𐤋𐤅
𐤍|
17 𐤅𐤄𐤅𐤓𐤃.𐤄𐤌𐤔𐤊𐤍.𐤅𐤍𐤎𐤏𐤅.𐤁𐤍𐤉.𐤂𐤓𐤔𐤅𐤍.𐤅𐤁𐤍𐤉.𐤌𐤓
𐤓𐤉.𐤍𐤔𐤀𐤉.𐤄𐤌𐤔𐤊𐤍|
18 𐤅𐤍𐤎𐤏.𐤃𐤂𐤋.𐤌𐤇𐤍𐤄.𐤓𐤀𐤅𐤁𐤍.𐤋𐤑𐤁𐤀𐤕𐤌.𐤅𐤏𐤋.𐤑
𐤁𐤀𐤅.𐤀𐤋𐤉𐤑𐤅𐤓.𐤁𐤍.𐤔𐤃𐤉𐤀𐤅𐤓|
19 𐤅𐤏𐤋.𐤑𐤁𐤀.𐤌𐤈𐤄.𐤁𐤍𐤉.𐤔𐤌𐤏𐤅𐤍.𐤔𐤋𐤌𐤉𐤀𐤋.𐤁𐤍.𐤑
𐤅𐤓𐤉.𐤔𐤃𐤉|
20 𐤅𐤏𐤋.𐤑𐤁𐤀.𐤌𐤈𐤄.𐤁𐤍𐤉.𐤂𐤃.𐤀𐤋𐤉𐤎𐤐.𐤁𐤍.𐤃𐤏𐤅𐤀
𐤋|
21 𐤅𐤍𐤎𐤏𐤅.𐤄𐤒𐤄𐤕𐤉𐤌.𐤍𐤔𐤀𐤉.𐤄𐤌𐤒𐤃𐤔.𐤅𐤄𐤒𐤉𐤌𐤅.
𐤀𐤕.𐤄𐤌𐤔𐤊𐤍.𐤏𐤃.𐤁𐤀𐤌|
22 𐤅𐤍𐤎𐤏.𐤃𐤂𐤋.𐤌𐤇𐤍𐤄.𐤁𐤍𐤉.𐤀𐤐𐤓𐤉𐤌.𐤋𐤑𐤁𐤀𐤕𐤌.𐤅
𐤏𐤋.𐤑𐤁𐤀𐤅.𐤀𐤋𐤉𐤔𐤌𐤏.𐤁𐤍.𐤏𐤌𐤉𐤄𐤅𐤃|
23 𐤅𐤏𐤋.𐤑𐤁𐤀.𐤌𐤈𐤄.𐤁𐤍𐤉.𐤌𐤍𐤔𐤄.𐤂𐤌𐤋𐤉𐤀𐤋.𐤁𐤍.𐤐
𐤃𐤄.𐤑𐤅𐤓|
24 𐤅𐤏𐤋.𐤑𐤁𐤀.𐤌𐤈𐤄.𐤁𐤍𐤉.𐤁𐤍𐤉𐤌𐤍.𐤀𐤁𐤉𐤃𐤍.𐤁𐤍.𐤂
𐤃𐤏𐤅𐤍𐤉|

..𐤊𐤄.. 𐤅𐤍𐤎𐤏.𐤃𐤂𐤋.𐤌𐤇𐤍𐤄.𐤁𐤍𐤉.𐤃𐤍.𐤌𐤀𐤎𐤐.𐤋𐤊𐤋.𐤄𐤌
𐤇𐤍𐤕.𐤋𐤑𐤁𐤀𐤕𐤌.𐤅𐤏𐤋.𐤑𐤁𐤀𐤅.𐤀𐤇𐤉𐤏𐤆𐤓.𐤁𐤍.𐤏𐤌𐤉𐤔
𐤃𐤉|

..𐤊𐤅.. 𐤅𐤏𐤋.𐤑𐤁𐤀.𐤌𐤈𐤄.𐤁𐤍𐤉.𐤀𐤔𐤓.𐤐𐤂𐤏𐤉𐤀𐤋.𐤁𐤍.𐤏𐤊𐤓
𐤍|

..𐤊𐤆.. 𐤅𐤏𐤋.𐤑𐤁𐤀.𐤌𐤈𐤄.𐤁𐤍𐤉.𐤍𐤐𐤕𐤋𐤉.𐤀𐤇𐤉𐤓𐤏.𐤁𐤍.𐤏𐤉
𐤍𐤍|

..𐤊𐤇.. 𐤀𐤋𐤄.𐤌𐤎𐤏𐤉.𐤁𐤍𐤉.𐤉𐤔𐤓𐤀𐤋.𐤋𐤑𐤁𐤀𐤕𐤌.𐤅𐤉𐤎𐤏𐤅|

..𐤊𐤈.. 𐤅𐤉𐤀𐤌𐤓.𐤌𐤔𐤄.𐤋𐤇𐤁𐤁.𐤁𐤍.𐤓𐤏𐤅𐤀𐤋.𐤄𐤌𐤃𐤉𐤍𐤉.𐤇
𐤕𐤍.𐤌𐤔𐤄.𐤍𐤎𐤏𐤉𐤌.𐤀𐤍𐤇𐤍𐤅.𐤀𐤋.𐤄𐤌𐤒𐤅𐤌.𐤀𐤔𐤓.𐤀𐤌𐤓.𐤉
𐤄𐤅𐤄.𐤀𐤕𐤅.𐤀𐤕𐤍.𐤋𐤊𐤌.𐤋𐤊𐤄.𐤀𐤕𐤍𐤅.𐤅𐤄𐤈𐤁𐤍𐤅.𐤋𐤊.𐤊𐤉.𐤉
𐤄𐤅𐤄.𐤃𐤁𐤓.𐤈𐤅𐤁.𐤏𐤋.𐤉𐤔𐤓𐤀𐤋|

..𐤋.. 𐤅𐤉𐤀𐤌𐤓.𐤀𐤋𐤉𐤅.𐤋𐤀.𐤀𐤋𐤊.𐤊𐤉.𐤀𐤌.𐤀𐤋.𐤀𐤓𐤑𐤉.𐤅𐤀
𐤋.𐤌𐤅𐤋𐤃𐤕𐤉.𐤀𐤋𐤊|

..𐤋𐤀.. 𐤅𐤉𐤀𐤌𐤓.𐤀𐤋.𐤍𐤀.𐤕𐤏𐤆𐤁.𐤀𐤕𐤍𐤅.𐤊𐤉.𐤏𐤋.𐤊𐤍.𐤉𐤃
𐤏𐤕.𐤇𐤍𐤕𐤍𐤅.𐤁𐤌𐤃𐤁𐤓.𐤅𐤄𐤉𐤉𐤕.𐤋𐤍𐤅.𐤋𐤏𐤉𐤍𐤉𐤌|

..𐤋𐤁.. 𐤅𐤄𐤉𐤄.𐤊𐤉.𐤕𐤋𐤊.𐤏𐤌𐤍𐤅.𐤅𐤄𐤉𐤄.𐤄𐤈𐤅𐤁.𐤄𐤄𐤅𐤀.𐤀
𐤔𐤓.𐤉𐤉𐤈𐤉𐤁.𐤉𐤄𐤅𐤄.𐤏𐤌𐤍𐤅.𐤅𐤄𐤈𐤁𐤍𐤅.𐤋𐤊|

..𐤋𐤂.. 𐤅𐤉𐤎𐤏𐤅.𐤌𐤄𐤓.𐤉𐤄𐤅𐤄.𐤃𐤓𐤊.𐤔𐤋𐤔𐤕.𐤉𐤌𐤉𐤌.𐤅𐤀𐤓𐤅
𐤍.𐤁𐤓𐤉𐤕.𐤉𐤄𐤅𐤄.𐤍𐤎𐤏.𐤋𐤐𐤍𐤉𐤄𐤌.𐤃𐤓𐤊.𐤔𐤋𐤔𐤕.𐤉𐤌𐤉𐤌.
𐤋𐤕𐤅𐤓.𐤋𐤄𐤌.𐤌𐤍𐤅𐤇𐤄|

..𐤋𐤃.. 𐤅𐤏𐤍𐤍.𐤉𐤄𐤅𐤄.𐤏𐤋𐤉𐤄𐤌.𐤉𐤅𐤌𐤌.𐤁𐤍𐤎𐤏𐤌.𐤌𐤍.𐤄𐤌𐤇
𐤍𐤄|

..𐤋𐤄.. 𐤅𐤉𐤄𐤉.𐤁𐤍𐤎𐤏.𐤄𐤀𐤓𐤍.𐤅𐤉𐤀𐤌𐤓.𐤌𐤔𐤄.𐤒𐤅𐤌𐤄.𐤉𐤄𐤅
𐤄.𐤅𐤉𐤐𐤑𐤅.𐤀𐤉𐤁𐤉𐤊.𐤅𐤉𐤍𐤎𐤅.𐤌𐤔𐤍𐤀𐤉𐤊.𐤌𐤐𐤍𐤉𐤊|

..𐤋𐤅.. 𐤅𐤁𐤍𐤇𐤄.𐤉𐤀𐤌𐤓.𐤔𐤅𐤁𐤄.𐤉𐤄𐤅𐤄.𐤓𐤁𐤁𐤅𐤕.𐤀𐤋𐤐𐤉.𐤉
𐤔𐤓𐤀𐤋||

𐤁𐤌𐤃𐤁𐤓.𐤇𐤋𐤒 ..𐤉𐤀..

1 𐤅𐤉𐤄𐤉.𐤄𐤏𐤌.𐤊𐤌𐤕𐤀𐤍𐤍𐤉𐤌.𐤓𐤏.𐤁𐤀𐤆𐤍𐤉.𐤉𐤄𐤅𐤄.𐤅𐤉
𐤔𐤌𐤏.𐤉𐤄𐤅𐤄.𐤅𐤉𐤇𐤓.𐤀𐤐𐤅.𐤅𐤕𐤁𐤏𐤓.𐤁𐤌.𐤀𐤔.𐤉𐤄𐤅𐤄.𐤅𐤕𐤀
𐤊𐤋.𐤁𐤒𐤑𐤄.𐤄𐤌𐤇𐤍𐤄|
2 𐤅𐤉𐤑𐤏𐤒.𐤄𐤏𐤌.𐤀𐤋.𐤌𐤔𐤄.𐤅𐤉𐤕𐤐𐤋𐤋.𐤌𐤔𐤄.𐤀𐤋.𐤉𐤄𐤅
𐤄.𐤅𐤕𐤔𐤒𐤏.𐤄𐤀𐤔|
3 𐤅𐤉𐤒𐤓𐤀.𐤔𐤌.𐤄𐤌𐤒𐤅𐤌.𐤄𐤄𐤅𐤀.𐤕𐤁𐤏𐤓𐤄.𐤊𐤉.𐤁𐤏𐤓𐤄
𐤁𐤌.𐤀𐤔.𐤉𐤄𐤅𐤄|
4 𐤅𐤄𐤀𐤎𐤐𐤎𐤐.𐤀𐤔𐤓.𐤁𐤒𐤓𐤁𐤅.𐤄𐤕𐤀𐤅𐤅.𐤕𐤀𐤅𐤄.𐤅𐤉𐤔𐤁𐤅.
𐤅𐤉𐤁𐤊𐤅.𐤂𐤌.𐤁𐤍𐤉.𐤉𐤔𐤓𐤀𐤋.𐤅𐤉𐤀𐤌𐤓𐤅.𐤌𐤉.𐤉𐤀𐤊𐤋𐤍𐤅.𐤁𐤔𐤓
|
5 𐤆𐤊𐤓𐤍𐤅.𐤀𐤕.𐤄𐤃𐤂𐤄.𐤀𐤔𐤓.𐤍𐤀𐤊𐤋.𐤁𐤌𐤑𐤓𐤉𐤌.𐤇𐤍
𐤌.𐤀𐤕.𐤄𐤒𐤔𐤀𐤉𐤌.𐤅𐤀𐤕.𐤄𐤀𐤁𐤈𐤇𐤉𐤌.𐤅𐤀𐤕.𐤄𐤇𐤑𐤉𐤓.
𐤅𐤀𐤕.𐤄𐤁𐤑𐤋𐤉𐤌.𐤅𐤀𐤕.𐤄𐤔𐤅𐤌𐤉𐤌|
6 𐤅𐤏𐤕𐤄.𐤍𐤐𐤔𐤍𐤅.𐤉𐤁𐤔𐤄.𐤀𐤉𐤍.𐤊𐤋.𐤁𐤋𐤕𐤉.𐤀𐤋.𐤄𐤌𐤍.𐤏
𐤉𐤍𐤉𐤍𐤅|
7 𐤅𐤄𐤌𐤍.𐤊𐤆𐤓𐤏.𐤂𐤃.𐤄𐤅𐤀.𐤅𐤏𐤉𐤍𐤅.𐤊𐤏𐤉𐤍.𐤄𐤁𐤃𐤋𐤇
|
8 𐤔𐤈𐤅.𐤄𐤏𐤌.𐤅𐤋𐤒𐤈𐤅.𐤅𐤈𐤇𐤍𐤅.𐤁𐤓𐤇𐤉𐤌.𐤀𐤅.𐤃𐤊𐤅.𐤁𐤌
𐤃𐤊𐤄.𐤅𐤁𐤔𐤋𐤅.𐤁𐤐𐤓𐤅𐤓.𐤅𐤏𐤔𐤅.𐤀𐤕𐤅.𐤏𐤂𐤅𐤕.𐤅𐤄𐤉𐤄.𐤈𐤏𐤌
𐤅.𐤊𐤈𐤏𐤌.𐤋𐤔𐤃.𐤄𐤔𐤌𐤍|
9 𐤅𐤁𐤓𐤃𐤕.𐤄𐤈𐤋.𐤏𐤋.𐤄𐤌𐤇𐤍𐤄.𐤋𐤉𐤋𐤄.𐤉𐤓𐤃.𐤄𐤌𐤍.𐤏
𐤋𐤉𐤅|
10 𐤅𐤉𐤔𐤌𐤏.𐤌𐤔𐤄.𐤀𐤕.𐤄𐤏𐤌.𐤁𐤊𐤄.𐤋𐤌𐤔𐤐𐤇𐤕𐤉𐤅.𐤀
𐤉𐤔.𐤋𐤐𐤕𐤇.𐤀𐤄𐤋𐤅.𐤅𐤉𐤇𐤓.𐤀𐤐.𐤉𐤄𐤅𐤄.𐤌𐤀𐤃.𐤅𐤁𐤏𐤉𐤍𐤉.
𐤌𐤔𐤄.𐤓𐤏|
11 𐤅𐤉𐤀𐤌𐤓.𐤌𐤔𐤄.𐤀𐤋.𐤉𐤄𐤅𐤄.𐤋𐤌𐤄.𐤄𐤓𐤏𐤕.𐤋𐤏𐤁𐤃𐤊.
𐤅𐤋𐤌𐤄.𐤋𐤀.𐤌𐤑𐤕𐤉.𐤇𐤍.𐤁𐤏𐤉𐤍𐤉𐤊.𐤋𐤔𐤅𐤌.𐤀𐤕.𐤌𐤔𐤀.𐤊𐤋
.𐤄𐤏𐤌.𐤄𐤆𐤄.𐤏𐤋𐤉|
12 𐤄𐤀𐤍𐤊𐤉.𐤄𐤓𐤉𐤕𐤉.𐤀𐤕.𐤊𐤋.𐤄𐤏𐤌.𐤄𐤆𐤄.𐤀𐤌.𐤀𐤍𐤊
𐤉.𐤉𐤋𐤃𐤕𐤉𐤄𐤅.𐤊𐤉.𐤕𐤀𐤌𐤓.𐤀𐤋𐤉.𐤔𐤀𐤄𐤅.𐤁𐤇𐤉𐤒𐤊.𐤊𐤀

𐤔𐤓.𐤉𐤔𐤀.𐤄𐤀𐤌𐤍.𐤀𐤕.𐤄𐤉𐤍𐤒.𐤏𐤋.𐤄𐤀𐤃𐤌𐤄.𐤀𐤔𐤓.𐤍𐤔
𐤁𐤏𐤕.𐤋𐤀𐤁𐤕𐤉𐤅|
..𐤉𐤂.. 𐤌𐤀𐤉𐤍.𐤋𐤉.𐤁𐤔𐤓.𐤋𐤕𐤕.𐤋𐤊𐤋.𐤄𐤏𐤌.𐤄𐤆𐤄.𐤊𐤉.𐤉𐤁
𐤊𐤅.𐤏𐤋𐤉.𐤋𐤀𐤌𐤓.𐤕𐤍𐤄.𐤋𐤍𐤅.𐤁𐤔𐤓.𐤅𐤍𐤀𐤊𐤋𐤄|
..𐤉𐤃.. 𐤋𐤀.𐤀𐤅𐤊𐤋.𐤀𐤍𐤊𐤉.𐤋𐤁𐤃𐤉.𐤋𐤔𐤀𐤕.𐤀𐤕.𐤊𐤋.𐤄𐤏𐤌.
𐤄𐤆𐤄.𐤊𐤉.𐤊𐤁𐤃.𐤌𐤌𐤍𐤉|
..𐤉𐤄.. 𐤅𐤀𐤌.𐤊𐤊𐤄.𐤀𐤕.𐤏𐤔𐤄.𐤋𐤉.𐤄𐤓𐤂𐤍𐤉.𐤍𐤀.𐤄𐤓𐤂.𐤀𐤌
.𐤌𐤑𐤀𐤕𐤉.𐤇𐤍.𐤁𐤏𐤉𐤍𐤉𐤊.𐤅𐤀𐤋.𐤀𐤓𐤀𐤄.𐤁𐤓𐤏𐤕𐤉|
..𐤉𐤅.. 𐤅𐤉𐤀𐤌𐤓.𐤉𐤄𐤅𐤄.𐤀𐤋.𐤌𐤔𐤄.𐤀𐤎𐤐𐤄.𐤋𐤉.𐤔𐤁𐤏𐤉𐤌.𐤀
𐤉𐤔.𐤌𐤆𐤒𐤍𐤉.𐤉𐤔𐤓𐤀𐤋.𐤀𐤔𐤓.𐤉𐤃𐤏𐤕.𐤊𐤉.𐤄𐤌.𐤆𐤒𐤍𐤉.
𐤄𐤏𐤌.𐤅𐤔𐤈𐤓𐤉𐤅.𐤅𐤋𐤒𐤇𐤕.𐤀𐤕𐤌.𐤀𐤋.𐤀𐤄𐤋.𐤌𐤅𐤏𐤃.𐤅𐤄𐤕
𐤉𐤑𐤁𐤅.𐤔𐤌.𐤏𐤌𐤊|
..𐤉𐤆.. 𐤅𐤉𐤓𐤃𐤕𐤉.𐤅𐤃𐤁𐤓𐤕𐤉.𐤏𐤌𐤊.𐤔𐤌.𐤅𐤀𐤑𐤋𐤕𐤉.𐤌𐤍.𐤄
𐤓𐤅𐤇.𐤀𐤔𐤓.𐤏𐤋𐤉𐤊.𐤅𐤔𐤌𐤕𐤉.𐤏𐤋𐤉𐤄𐤌.𐤅𐤍𐤔𐤀𐤅.𐤀𐤕𐤊.𐤁𐤌
𐤔𐤀.𐤄𐤏𐤌.𐤅𐤋𐤀.𐤕𐤔𐤀.𐤀𐤕𐤄.𐤋𐤁𐤃𐤊|
..𐤉𐤇.. 𐤅𐤀𐤋.𐤄𐤏𐤌.𐤕𐤀𐤌𐤓.𐤄𐤕𐤒𐤃𐤔𐤅.𐤋𐤌𐤇𐤓.𐤅𐤀𐤊𐤋𐤕𐤌.
𐤁𐤔𐤓.𐤊𐤉.𐤁𐤊𐤉𐤕𐤌.𐤁𐤀𐤆𐤍𐤉.𐤉𐤄𐤅𐤄.𐤋𐤀𐤌𐤓.𐤌𐤉.𐤉𐤀𐤊𐤋
𐤍𐤅.𐤁𐤔𐤓.𐤊𐤉.𐤈𐤅𐤁.𐤋𐤍𐤅.𐤁𐤌𐤑𐤓𐤉𐤌.𐤅𐤍𐤕𐤍.𐤉𐤄𐤅𐤄.𐤋𐤊𐤌.𐤁
𐤔𐤓.𐤅𐤀𐤊𐤋𐤕𐤌|
..𐤉𐤈.. 𐤋𐤀.𐤉𐤅𐤌.𐤀𐤇𐤃.𐤕𐤀𐤊𐤋𐤅𐤍.𐤅𐤋𐤀.𐤉𐤅𐤌𐤉𐤌.𐤅𐤋𐤀.𐤇
𐤌𐤔𐤄.𐤉𐤌𐤉𐤌.𐤅𐤋𐤀.𐤏𐤔𐤓𐤄.𐤉𐤌𐤉𐤌.𐤅𐤋𐤀.𐤏𐤔𐤓𐤉𐤌.𐤉𐤅𐤌|
..𐤊.. 𐤏𐤃.𐤇𐤃𐤔.𐤉𐤌𐤉𐤌.𐤏𐤃.𐤀𐤔𐤓.𐤉𐤑𐤀.𐤌𐤀𐤐𐤊𐤌.𐤅
𐤄𐤉𐤄.𐤋𐤊𐤌.𐤋𐤆𐤓𐤀.𐤉𐤏𐤍.𐤊𐤉.𐤌𐤀𐤎𐤕𐤌.𐤀𐤕.𐤉𐤄𐤅𐤄.𐤀
𐤔𐤓.𐤁𐤒𐤓𐤁𐤊𐤌.𐤅𐤕𐤁𐤊𐤅.𐤋𐤐𐤍𐤉𐤅.𐤋𐤀𐤌𐤓.𐤋𐤌𐤄.𐤆𐤄.𐤉𐤑𐤀
𐤍𐤅.𐤌𐤌𐤑𐤓𐤉𐤌|
..𐤊𐤀.. 𐤅𐤉𐤀𐤌𐤓.𐤌𐤔𐤄.𐤔𐤔.𐤌𐤀𐤅𐤕.𐤀𐤋𐤐.𐤓𐤂𐤋𐤉.𐤄𐤏𐤌.𐤀
𐤔𐤓.𐤀𐤍𐤊𐤉.𐤁𐤒𐤓𐤁𐤅.𐤅𐤀𐤕𐤄.𐤀𐤌𐤓𐤕.𐤁𐤔𐤓.𐤀𐤕𐤍.𐤋𐤄𐤌.𐤅
𐤀𐤊𐤋𐤅.𐤇𐤃𐤔.𐤉𐤌𐤉𐤌|
..𐤊𐤁.. 𐤄𐤑𐤀𐤍.𐤅𐤁𐤒𐤓.𐤉𐤔𐤇𐤈.𐤋𐤄𐤌.𐤅𐤌𐤑𐤀.𐤋𐤄𐤌.𐤀𐤌.𐤀
𐤕.𐤊𐤋.𐤃𐤂𐤉.𐤄𐤉𐤌.𐤉𐤀𐤎𐤐.𐤋𐤄𐤌.𐤅𐤌𐤑𐤀.𐤋𐤄𐤌|

כג.. ויאמר.יהוה.אל.משה.היד.יהוה.תקצר.
עתה.תראה.היקרך.דברי.אם.לא׃
כד.. ויצא.משה.וידבר.אל.העם.את.דברי.י
הוה.ויאסף.שבעים.איש.מזקני.העם.ויעמ
ד.אתם.סביבת.האהל׃
כה.. וירד.יהוה.בענן.וידבר.אליו.ויאצל.מן.
הרוח.אשר.עליו.ויתן.על.שבעים.איש.הזקנ
ים.ויהי.כנוח.עליהם.הרוח.ויתנבאו.ולא.יס
פו׃
כו.. וישארו.שני.אנשים.במחנה.שם.האחד.
אלדד.ושם.השני.מידד.ותנח.עליהם.הרוח.
והמה.בכתבים.ולא.יצאו.האהלה.ויתנבאו.ב
מחנה׃
כז.. וירץ.הנער.ויגד.למשה.ויאמר.אלדד.ו
מידד.מתנבאים.במחנה׃
כח.. ויען.יהושע.בן.נון.משרת.משה.מבחריו.ו
יאמר.אדני.משה.כלאם׃
כט.. ויאמר.לו.משה.המקנא.אתה.לי.ומי.יתן.
כל.עם.יהוה.נביאים.כי.יתן.יהוה.את.רוחו.
עליהם׃
ל.. ויאסף.משה.אל.המחנה.הוא.וזקני.ישר
אל׃
לא.. ורוח.נסע.מאת.יהוה.ויגז.שלוים.מן.הי
ם.ויטש.על.המחנה.כדרך.יום.כה.וכדרך.יום.
כה.סביבות.המחנה.וכאמתים.על.פני.הארץ׃
לב.. ויקם.העם.כל.היום.ההוא.וכל.הלילה.וכ
ל.יום.המחרת.ויאספו.את.השלו.הממעיט.אס
ף.עשרה.חמרים.וישטחו.להם.שטוח.סביבות.
המחנה׃

לג הבשר.עודנו.בין.שניהם.טרם.יכרת.ואף.
יהוה.חרה.בעם.ויך.יהוה.בעם.מכה.רבה.מא
ד|
לד ויקרא.את.שם.המקום.ההוא.קברות.הת
אוה.כי.שם.קברו.את.העם.המתאוים|
לה מקברות.התאוה.נסעו.העם.חצרות.ויהי
ו.בחצרות||

במדבר.חלק יב

א ותדבר.מרים.ואהרן.במשה.על.אדות.האש
ה.הכשית.אשר.לקח.כי.אשה.כשית.לקח|
ב ויאמרו.הרק.אך.במשה.דבר.יהוה.הלא.ג
ם.בנו.דבר.וישמע.יהוה|
ג והאיש.משה.ענו.||עניו.קרי||.מאד.מכל.ה
אדם.אשר.על.פני.האדמה|
ד ויאמר.יהוה.פתאם.אל.משה.ואל.אהרן.ואל
.מרים.צאו.שלשתכם.אל.אהל.מועד.ויצאו.ש
לשתם|
ה וירד.יהוה.בעמוד.ענן.ויעמד.פתח.האה
ל.ויקרא.אהרן.ומרים.ויצאו.שניהם|
ו ויאמר.שמעו.נא.דברי.אם.יהיה.נביאכם.
יהוה.במראה.אליו.אתודע.בחלום.אדבר.בו|
ז לא.כן.עבדי.משה.בכל.ביתי.נאמן.הוא|
ח פה.אל.פה.אדבר.בו.ומראה.ולא.בחידת.ות
מנת.יהוה.יביט.ומדוע.לא.יראתם.לדבר.בע
בדי.במשה|
ט ויחר.אף.יהוה.בם.וילך|
י והענן.סר.מעל.האהל.והנה.מרים.מצרעת
.כשלג.ויפן.אהרן.אל.מרים.והנה.מצרעת|

11 𐤅𐤉𐤀𐤌𐤓.𐤀𐤄𐤓𐤍.𐤀𐤋.𐤌𐤔𐤄.𐤁𐤉.𐤀𐤃𐤍𐤉.𐤀𐤋.𐤍𐤀.𐤕𐤔
𐤕.𐤏𐤋𐤉𐤍𐤅.𐤇𐤈𐤀𐤕.𐤀𐤔𐤓.𐤍𐤅𐤀𐤋𐤍𐤅.𐤅𐤀𐤔𐤓.𐤇𐤈𐤀𐤍𐤅|

12 𐤀𐤋.𐤍𐤀.𐤕𐤄𐤉.𐤊𐤌𐤕.𐤀𐤔𐤓.𐤁𐤑𐤀𐤕𐤅.𐤌𐤓𐤇𐤌.𐤀𐤌𐤅.
𐤅𐤉𐤀𐤊𐤋.𐤇𐤑𐤉.𐤁𐤔𐤓𐤅|

13 𐤅𐤉𐤑𐤏𐤒.𐤌𐤔𐤄.𐤀𐤋.𐤉𐤄𐤅𐤄.𐤋𐤀𐤌𐤓.𐤀𐤋.𐤍𐤀.𐤓𐤐𐤀.𐤍
𐤀.𐤋𐤄|

14 𐤅𐤉𐤀𐤌𐤓.𐤉𐤄𐤅𐤄.𐤀𐤋.𐤌𐤔𐤄.𐤅𐤀𐤁𐤉𐤄.𐤉𐤓𐤒.𐤉𐤓𐤒.𐤁
𐤐𐤍𐤉𐤄.𐤄𐤋𐤀.𐤕𐤊𐤋𐤌.𐤔𐤁𐤏𐤕.𐤉𐤌𐤉𐤌.𐤕𐤎𐤂𐤓.𐤔𐤁𐤏𐤕.𐤉
𐤌𐤉𐤌.𐤌𐤇𐤅𐤑.𐤋𐤌𐤇𐤍𐤄.𐤅𐤀𐤇𐤓.𐤕𐤀𐤎𐤐|

15 𐤅𐤕𐤎𐤂𐤓.𐤌𐤓𐤉𐤌.𐤌𐤇𐤅𐤑.𐤋𐤌𐤇𐤍𐤄.𐤔𐤁𐤏𐤕.𐤉𐤌𐤉𐤌.
𐤅𐤄𐤏𐤌.𐤋𐤀.𐤍𐤎𐤏.𐤏𐤃.𐤄𐤀𐤎𐤐.𐤌𐤓𐤉𐤌|

16 𐤅𐤀𐤇𐤓.𐤍𐤎𐤏𐤅.𐤄𐤏𐤌.𐤌𐤇𐤑𐤓𐤅𐤕.𐤅𐤉𐤇𐤍𐤅.𐤁𐤌𐤃𐤁𐤓.
𐤐𐤀𐤓𐤍||

𐤁𐤌𐤃𐤁𐤓.𐤇𐤋𐤒 13

1 𐤅𐤉𐤃𐤁𐤓.𐤉𐤄𐤅𐤄.𐤀𐤋.𐤌𐤔𐤄.𐤋𐤀𐤌𐤓|

2 𐤔𐤋𐤇.𐤋𐤊.𐤀𐤍𐤔𐤉𐤌.𐤅𐤉𐤕𐤓𐤅.𐤀𐤕.𐤀𐤓𐤑.𐤊𐤍𐤏𐤍.𐤀𐤔𐤓.
𐤀𐤍𐤉.𐤍𐤕𐤍.𐤋𐤁𐤍𐤉.𐤉𐤔𐤓𐤀𐤋.𐤀𐤉𐤔.𐤀𐤇𐤃.𐤀𐤉𐤔.𐤀𐤇𐤃.
𐤋𐤌𐤈𐤄.𐤀𐤁𐤕𐤉𐤅.𐤕𐤔𐤋𐤇𐤅.𐤊𐤋.𐤍𐤔𐤉𐤀.𐤁𐤄𐤌|

3 𐤅𐤉𐤔𐤋𐤇.𐤀𐤕𐤌.𐤌𐤔𐤄.𐤌𐤌𐤃𐤁𐤓.𐤐𐤀𐤓𐤍.𐤏𐤋.𐤐𐤉.𐤉𐤄𐤅
𐤄.𐤊𐤋𐤌.𐤀𐤍𐤔𐤉𐤌.𐤓𐤀𐤔𐤉.𐤁𐤍𐤉.𐤉𐤔𐤓𐤀𐤋.𐤄𐤌𐤄|

4 𐤅𐤀𐤋𐤄.𐤔𐤌𐤅𐤕𐤌.𐤋𐤌𐤈𐤄.𐤓𐤀𐤅𐤁𐤍.𐤔𐤌𐤅𐤏.𐤁𐤍.𐤆𐤊𐤅𐤓|

5 𐤋𐤌𐤈𐤄.𐤔𐤌𐤏𐤅𐤍.𐤔𐤐𐤈.𐤁𐤍.𐤇𐤅𐤓𐤉|

6 𐤋𐤌𐤈𐤄.𐤉𐤄𐤅𐤃𐤄.𐤊𐤋𐤁.𐤁𐤍.𐤉𐤐𐤍𐤄|

7 𐤋𐤌𐤈𐤄.𐤉𐤔𐤔𐤊𐤓.𐤉𐤂𐤀𐤋.𐤁𐤍.𐤉𐤅𐤎𐤐|

8 𐤋𐤌𐤈𐤄.𐤀𐤐𐤓𐤉𐤌.𐤄𐤅𐤔𐤏.𐤁𐤍.𐤍𐤅𐤍|

9 𐤋𐤌𐤈𐤄.𐤁𐤍𐤉𐤌𐤍.𐤐𐤋𐤈𐤉.𐤁𐤍.𐤓𐤐𐤅𐤀|

10 𐤋𐤌𐤈𐤄.𐤆𐤁𐤅𐤋𐤍.𐤂𐤃𐤉𐤀𐤋.𐤁𐤍.𐤎𐤅𐤃𐤉|

11 𐤋𐤌𐤈𐤄.𐤉𐤅𐤎𐤐.𐤋𐤌𐤈𐤄.𐤌𐤍𐤔𐤄.𐤂𐤃𐤉.𐤁𐤍.𐤎𐤅𐤎𐤉|

12 𐤋𐤌𐤈𐤄.𐤃𐤍.𐤏𐤌𐤉𐤀𐤋.𐤁𐤍.𐤂𐤌𐤋𐤉|

13 𐤋𐤌𐤈𐤄.𐤀𐤔𐤓.𐤎𐤕𐤅𐤓.𐤁𐤍.𐤌𐤉𐤊𐤀𐤋|
14 𐤋𐤌𐤈𐤄.𐤍𐤐𐤕𐤋𐤉.𐤍𐤇𐤁𐤉.𐤁𐤍.𐤅𐤐𐤎𐤉|
15 𐤋𐤌𐤈𐤄.𐤂𐤃.𐤂𐤀𐤅𐤀𐤋.𐤁𐤍.𐤌𐤊𐤉|
16 𐤀𐤋𐤄.𐤔𐤌𐤅𐤕.𐤄𐤀𐤍𐤔𐤉𐤌.𐤀𐤔𐤓.𐤔𐤋𐤇.𐤌𐤔𐤄.𐤋𐤕𐤅𐤓.
𐤀𐤕.𐤄𐤀𐤓𐤑.𐤅𐤉𐤒𐤓𐤀.𐤌𐤔𐤄.𐤋𐤄𐤅𐤔𐤏.𐤁𐤍.𐤍𐤅𐤍.𐤉𐤄𐤅𐤔𐤏|
17 𐤅𐤉𐤔𐤋𐤇.𐤀𐤕𐤌.𐤌𐤔𐤄.𐤋𐤕𐤅𐤓.𐤀𐤕.𐤀𐤓𐤑.𐤊𐤍𐤏𐤍.𐤅𐤉
𐤀𐤌𐤓.𐤀𐤋𐤄𐤌.𐤏𐤋𐤅.𐤆𐤄.𐤁𐤍𐤂𐤁.𐤅𐤏𐤋𐤉𐤕𐤌.𐤀𐤕.𐤄𐤄𐤓|
18 𐤅𐤓𐤀𐤉𐤕𐤌.𐤀𐤕.𐤄𐤀𐤓𐤑.𐤌𐤄.𐤄𐤅𐤀.𐤅𐤀𐤕.𐤄𐤏𐤌.𐤄𐤉
𐤔𐤁.𐤏𐤋𐤉𐤄.𐤄𐤇𐤆𐤒.𐤄𐤅𐤀.𐤄𐤓𐤐𐤄.𐤄𐤌𐤏𐤈.𐤄𐤅𐤀.𐤀𐤌.𐤓
𐤁|
19 𐤅𐤌𐤄.𐤄𐤀𐤓𐤑.𐤀𐤔𐤓.𐤄𐤅𐤀.𐤉𐤔𐤁.𐤁𐤄.𐤄𐤈𐤅𐤁𐤄.𐤄𐤅
𐤀.𐤀𐤌.𐤓𐤏𐤄.𐤅𐤌𐤄.𐤄𐤏𐤓𐤉𐤌.𐤀𐤔𐤓.𐤄𐤅𐤀.𐤉𐤅𐤔𐤁.𐤁𐤄𐤍𐤄.
𐤄𐤁𐤌𐤇𐤍𐤉𐤌.𐤀𐤌.𐤁𐤌𐤁𐤑𐤓𐤉𐤌|
20 𐤅𐤌𐤄.𐤄𐤀𐤓𐤑.𐤄𐤔𐤌𐤍𐤄.𐤄𐤅𐤀.𐤀𐤌.𐤓𐤆𐤄.𐤄𐤉𐤔.𐤁
𐤄.𐤏𐤑.𐤀𐤌.𐤀𐤉𐤍.𐤅𐤄𐤕𐤇𐤆𐤒𐤕𐤌.𐤅𐤋𐤒𐤇𐤕𐤌.𐤌𐤐𐤓𐤉.𐤄
𐤀𐤓𐤑.𐤅𐤄𐤉𐤌𐤉𐤌.𐤉𐤌𐤉.𐤁𐤊𐤅𐤓𐤉.𐤏𐤍𐤁𐤉𐤌|
21 𐤅𐤉𐤏𐤋𐤅.𐤅𐤉𐤕𐤓𐤅.𐤀𐤕.𐤄𐤀𐤓𐤑.𐤌𐤌𐤃𐤁𐤓.𐤑𐤍.𐤏𐤃.𐤓
𐤇𐤁.𐤋𐤁𐤀.𐤇𐤌𐤕|
22 𐤅𐤉𐤏𐤋𐤅.𐤁𐤍𐤂𐤁.𐤅𐤉𐤁𐤀.𐤏𐤃.𐤇𐤁𐤓𐤅𐤍.𐤅𐤔𐤌.𐤀𐤇𐤉𐤌
𐤍.𐤔𐤔𐤉.𐤅𐤕𐤋𐤌𐤉.𐤉𐤋𐤉𐤃𐤉.𐤄𐤏𐤍𐤒.𐤅𐤇𐤁𐤓𐤅𐤍.𐤔𐤁𐤏.𐤔𐤍𐤉
𐤌.𐤍𐤁𐤍𐤕𐤄.𐤋𐤐𐤍𐤉.𐤑𐤏𐤍.𐤌𐤑𐤓𐤉𐤌|
23 𐤅𐤉𐤁𐤀𐤅.𐤏𐤃.𐤍𐤇𐤋.𐤀𐤔𐤊𐤋.𐤅𐤉𐤊𐤓𐤕𐤅.𐤌𐤔𐤌.𐤆𐤌𐤅𐤓
𐤄.𐤅𐤀𐤔𐤊𐤅𐤋.𐤏𐤍𐤁𐤉𐤌.𐤀𐤇𐤃.𐤅𐤉𐤔𐤀𐤄𐤅.𐤁𐤌𐤅𐤈.𐤁𐤔𐤍𐤉𐤌
.𐤅𐤌𐤍.𐤄𐤓𐤌𐤍𐤉𐤌.𐤅𐤌𐤍.𐤄𐤕𐤀𐤍𐤉𐤌|
24 𐤋𐤌𐤒𐤅𐤌.𐤄𐤄𐤅𐤀.𐤒𐤓𐤀.𐤍𐤇𐤋.𐤀𐤔𐤊𐤅𐤋.𐤏𐤋.𐤀𐤃𐤅𐤕.
𐤄𐤀𐤔𐤊𐤅𐤋.𐤀𐤔𐤓.𐤊𐤓𐤕𐤅.𐤌𐤔𐤌.𐤁𐤍𐤉.𐤉𐤔𐤓𐤀𐤋|
25 𐤅𐤉𐤔𐤁𐤅.𐤌𐤕𐤅𐤓.𐤄𐤀𐤓𐤑.𐤌𐤒𐤑.𐤀𐤓𐤁𐤏𐤉𐤌.𐤉𐤅𐤌|
26 𐤅𐤉𐤋𐤊𐤅.𐤅𐤉𐤁𐤀𐤅.𐤀𐤋.𐤌𐤔𐤄.𐤅𐤀𐤋.𐤀𐤄𐤓𐤍.𐤅𐤀𐤋.𐤊𐤋.𐤏
𐤃𐤕.𐤁𐤍𐤉.𐤉𐤔𐤓𐤀𐤋.𐤀𐤋.𐤌𐤃𐤁𐤓.𐤐𐤀𐤓𐤍.𐤒𐤃𐤔𐤄.𐤅𐤉𐤔𐤉
𐤁𐤅.𐤀𐤕𐤌.𐤃𐤁𐤓.𐤅𐤀𐤕.𐤊𐤋.𐤄𐤏𐤃𐤄.𐤅𐤉𐤓𐤀𐤅𐤌.𐤀𐤕.𐤐𐤓𐤉.
𐤄𐤀𐤓𐤑|

27 𐤅𐤉𐤎𐤐𐤓𐤅.𐤋𐤅.𐤅𐤉𐤀𐤌𐤓𐤅.𐤁𐤀𐤍𐤅.𐤀𐤋.𐤄𐤀𐤓𐤑.𐤀𐤔𐤓.𐤔
𐤋𐤇𐤕𐤍𐤅.𐤅𐤂𐤌.𐤆𐤁𐤕.𐤇𐤋𐤁.𐤅𐤃𐤁𐤔.𐤄𐤅𐤀.𐤅𐤆𐤄.𐤐𐤓𐤉𐤄|
28 𐤀𐤐𐤎.𐤊𐤉.𐤏𐤆.𐤄𐤏𐤌.𐤄𐤉𐤔𐤁.𐤁𐤀𐤓𐤑.𐤅𐤄𐤏𐤓𐤉𐤌.𐤁
𐤑𐤓𐤅𐤕.𐤂𐤃𐤋𐤕.𐤌𐤀𐤃.𐤅𐤂𐤌.𐤉𐤋𐤃𐤉.𐤄𐤏𐤍𐤒.𐤓𐤀𐤉𐤍𐤅.𐤔
𐤌|
29 𐤏𐤌𐤋𐤒.𐤉𐤅𐤔𐤁.𐤁𐤀𐤓𐤑.𐤄𐤍𐤂𐤁.𐤅𐤄𐤇𐤕𐤉.𐤅𐤄𐤉𐤁𐤅
𐤎𐤉.𐤅𐤄𐤀𐤌𐤓𐤉.𐤉𐤅𐤔𐤁.𐤁𐤄𐤓.𐤅𐤄𐤊𐤍𐤏𐤍𐤉.𐤉𐤔𐤁.𐤏𐤋.𐤄𐤉𐤌.
𐤅𐤏𐤋.𐤉𐤃.𐤄𐤉𐤓𐤃𐤍|
30 𐤅𐤉𐤄𐤎.𐤊𐤋𐤁.𐤀𐤕.𐤄𐤏𐤌.𐤀𐤋.𐤌𐤔𐤄.𐤅𐤉𐤀𐤌𐤓.𐤏𐤋𐤄.
𐤍𐤏𐤋𐤄.𐤅𐤉𐤓𐤔𐤍𐤅.𐤀𐤕𐤄.𐤊𐤉.𐤉𐤊𐤅𐤋.𐤍𐤅𐤊𐤋.𐤋𐤄|
31 𐤅𐤄𐤀𐤍𐤔𐤉𐤌.𐤀𐤔𐤓.𐤏𐤋𐤅.𐤏𐤌𐤅.𐤀𐤌𐤓𐤅.𐤋𐤀.𐤍𐤅𐤊𐤋.𐤋𐤏
𐤋𐤅𐤕.𐤀𐤋.𐤄𐤏𐤌.𐤊𐤉.𐤇𐤆𐤒.𐤄𐤅𐤀.𐤌𐤌𐤍𐤅|
32 𐤅𐤉𐤅𐤑𐤉𐤀𐤅.𐤃𐤁𐤕.𐤄𐤀𐤓𐤑.𐤀𐤔𐤓.𐤕𐤓𐤅.𐤀𐤕𐤄.𐤀𐤋.𐤁
𐤍𐤉.𐤉𐤔𐤓𐤀𐤋.𐤋𐤀𐤌𐤓.𐤄𐤀𐤓𐤑.𐤀𐤔𐤓.𐤏𐤁𐤓𐤍𐤅.𐤁𐤄.𐤋𐤕𐤅𐤓.𐤀
𐤕𐤄.𐤀𐤓𐤑.𐤀𐤊𐤋𐤕.𐤉𐤅𐤔𐤁𐤉𐤄.𐤄𐤅𐤀.𐤅𐤊𐤋.𐤄𐤏𐤌.𐤀𐤔𐤓.𐤓
𐤀𐤉𐤍𐤅.𐤁𐤕𐤅𐤊𐤄.𐤀𐤍𐤔𐤉.𐤌𐤃𐤅𐤕|
33 𐤅𐤔𐤌.𐤓𐤀𐤉𐤍𐤅.𐤀𐤕.𐤄𐤍𐤐𐤉𐤋𐤉𐤌.𐤁𐤍𐤉.𐤏𐤍𐤒.𐤌𐤍.𐤄𐤍𐤐
𐤋𐤉𐤌.𐤅𐤍𐤄𐤉.𐤁𐤏𐤉𐤍𐤉𐤍𐤅.𐤊𐤇𐤂𐤁𐤉𐤌.𐤅𐤊𐤍.𐤄𐤉𐤉𐤍𐤅.𐤁𐤏𐤉𐤍
𐤉𐤄𐤌||

𐤁𐤌𐤃𐤁𐤓.𐤇𐤋𐤒 14

1 𐤅𐤕𐤔𐤀.𐤊𐤋.𐤄𐤏𐤃𐤄.𐤅𐤉𐤕𐤍𐤅.𐤀𐤕.𐤒𐤅𐤋𐤌.𐤅𐤉𐤁𐤊𐤅.𐤄𐤏
𐤌.𐤁𐤋𐤉𐤋𐤄.𐤄𐤄𐤅𐤀|
2 𐤅𐤉𐤋𐤍𐤅.𐤏𐤋.𐤌𐤔𐤄.𐤅𐤏𐤋.𐤀𐤄𐤓𐤍.𐤊𐤋.𐤁𐤍𐤉.𐤉𐤔𐤓𐤀𐤋.𐤅𐤉
𐤀𐤌𐤓𐤅.𐤀𐤋𐤄𐤌.𐤊𐤋.𐤄𐤏𐤃𐤄.𐤋𐤅.𐤌𐤕𐤍𐤅.𐤁𐤀𐤓𐤑.𐤌𐤑𐤓𐤉𐤌.
𐤀𐤅.𐤁𐤌𐤃𐤁𐤓.𐤄𐤆𐤄.𐤋𐤅.𐤌𐤕𐤍𐤅|
3 𐤅𐤋𐤌𐤄.𐤉𐤄𐤅𐤄.𐤌𐤁𐤉𐤀.𐤀𐤕𐤍𐤅.𐤀𐤋.𐤄𐤀𐤓𐤑.𐤄𐤆𐤀𐤕.
𐤋𐤍𐤐𐤋.𐤁𐤇𐤓𐤁.𐤍𐤔𐤉𐤍𐤅.𐤅𐤈𐤐𐤍𐤅.𐤉𐤄𐤉𐤅.𐤋𐤁𐤆.𐤄𐤋𐤅𐤀.𐤈𐤅𐤁.
𐤋𐤍𐤅.𐤔𐤅𐤁.𐤌𐤑𐤓𐤉𐤌𐤄|

ד 𐤅𐤉𐤀𐤌𐤓𐤅.𐤀𐤉𐤔.𐤀𐤋.𐤀𐤇𐤉𐤅.𐤍𐤕𐤍𐤄.𐤓𐤀𐤔.𐤅𐤍𐤔𐤅𐤁𐤄.
𐤌𐤑𐤓𐤉𐤌𐤄|
ה 𐤅𐤉𐤐𐤋.𐤌𐤔𐤄.𐤅𐤀𐤄𐤓𐤍.𐤏𐤋.𐤐𐤍𐤉𐤄𐤌.𐤋𐤐𐤍𐤉.𐤊𐤋.𐤒𐤄𐤋.
𐤏𐤃𐤕.𐤁𐤍𐤉.𐤉𐤔𐤓𐤀𐤋|
ו 𐤅𐤉𐤄𐤅𐤔𐤏.𐤁𐤍.𐤍𐤅𐤍.𐤅𐤊𐤋𐤁.𐤁𐤍.𐤉𐤐𐤍𐤄.𐤌𐤍.𐤄𐤕𐤓𐤉𐤌.𐤀𐤕
.𐤄𐤀𐤓𐤑.𐤒𐤓𐤏𐤅.𐤁𐤂𐤃𐤉𐤄𐤌|
ז 𐤅𐤉𐤀𐤌𐤓𐤅.𐤀𐤋.𐤊𐤋.𐤏𐤃𐤕.𐤁𐤍𐤉.𐤉𐤔𐤓𐤀𐤋.𐤋𐤀𐤌𐤓.𐤄𐤀
𐤓𐤑.𐤀𐤔𐤓.𐤏𐤁𐤓𐤍𐤅.𐤁𐤄.𐤋𐤕𐤅𐤓.𐤀𐤕𐤄.𐤈𐤅𐤁𐤄.𐤄𐤀𐤓𐤑.𐤌𐤀
𐤃.𐤌𐤀𐤃|
ח 𐤀𐤌.𐤇𐤐𐤑.𐤁𐤍𐤅.𐤉𐤄𐤅𐤄.𐤅𐤄𐤁𐤉𐤀.𐤀𐤕𐤍𐤅.𐤀𐤋.𐤄𐤀𐤓𐤑.
𐤄𐤆𐤀𐤕.𐤅𐤍𐤕𐤍𐤄.𐤋𐤍𐤅.𐤀𐤓𐤑.𐤀𐤔𐤓.𐤄𐤅𐤀.𐤆𐤁𐤕.𐤇𐤋𐤁.𐤅
𐤃𐤁𐤔|
ט 𐤀𐤊.𐤁𐤉𐤄𐤅𐤄.𐤀𐤋.𐤕𐤌𐤓𐤃𐤅.𐤅𐤀𐤕𐤌.𐤀𐤋.𐤕𐤉𐤓𐤀𐤅.𐤀𐤕
.𐤏𐤌.𐤄𐤀𐤓𐤑.𐤊𐤉.𐤋𐤇𐤌𐤍𐤅.𐤄𐤌.𐤎𐤓.𐤑𐤋𐤌.𐤌𐤏𐤋𐤉𐤄𐤌.𐤅𐤉
𐤄𐤅𐤄.𐤀𐤕𐤍𐤅.𐤀𐤋.𐤕𐤉𐤓𐤀𐤌|
י 𐤅𐤉𐤀𐤌𐤓𐤅.𐤊𐤋.𐤄𐤏𐤃𐤄.𐤋𐤓𐤂𐤅𐤌.𐤀𐤕𐤌.𐤁𐤀𐤁𐤍𐤉𐤌.𐤅
𐤊𐤁𐤅𐤃.𐤉𐤄𐤅𐤄.𐤍𐤓𐤀𐤄.𐤁𐤀𐤄𐤋.𐤌𐤅𐤏𐤃.𐤀𐤋.𐤊𐤋.𐤁𐤍𐤉.𐤉𐤔
𐤓𐤀𐤋|
יא 𐤅𐤉𐤀𐤌𐤓.𐤉𐤄𐤅𐤄.𐤀𐤋.𐤌𐤔𐤄.𐤏𐤃.𐤀𐤍𐤄.𐤉𐤍𐤀𐤑𐤍𐤉.𐤄
𐤏𐤌.𐤄𐤆𐤄.𐤅𐤏𐤃.𐤀𐤍𐤄.𐤋𐤀.𐤉𐤀𐤌𐤉𐤍𐤅.𐤁𐤉.𐤁𐤊𐤋.𐤄𐤀𐤕𐤅
𐤕.𐤀𐤔𐤓.𐤏𐤔𐤉𐤕𐤉.𐤁𐤒𐤓𐤁𐤅|
יב 𐤀𐤊𐤍𐤅.𐤁𐤃𐤁𐤓.𐤅𐤀𐤅𐤓𐤔𐤍𐤅.𐤅𐤀𐤏𐤔𐤄.𐤀𐤕𐤊.𐤋𐤂𐤅𐤉.𐤂
𐤃𐤅𐤋.𐤅𐤏𐤑𐤅𐤌.𐤌𐤌𐤍𐤅|
יג 𐤅𐤉𐤀𐤌𐤓.𐤌𐤔𐤄.𐤀𐤋.𐤉𐤄𐤅𐤄.𐤅𐤔𐤌𐤏𐤅.𐤌𐤑𐤓𐤉𐤌.𐤊𐤉.
𐤄𐤏𐤋𐤉𐤕.𐤁𐤊𐤇𐤊.𐤀𐤕.𐤄𐤏𐤌.𐤄𐤆𐤄.𐤌𐤒𐤓𐤁𐤅|
יד 𐤅𐤀𐤌𐤓𐤅.𐤀𐤋.𐤉𐤅𐤔𐤁.𐤄𐤀𐤓𐤑.𐤄𐤆𐤀𐤕.𐤔𐤌𐤏𐤅.𐤊𐤉.
𐤀𐤕𐤄.𐤉𐤄𐤅𐤄.𐤁𐤒𐤓𐤁.𐤄𐤏𐤌.𐤄𐤆𐤄.𐤀𐤔𐤓.𐤏𐤉𐤍.𐤁𐤏𐤉𐤍.𐤍
𐤓𐤀𐤄.𐤀𐤕𐤄.𐤉𐤄𐤅𐤄.𐤅𐤏𐤍𐤍𐤊.𐤏𐤌𐤃.𐤏𐤋𐤄𐤌.𐤅𐤁𐤏𐤌𐤃.𐤏𐤍
𐤍.𐤀𐤕𐤄.𐤄𐤋𐤊.𐤋𐤐𐤍𐤉𐤄𐤌.𐤉𐤅𐤌𐤌.𐤅𐤁𐤏𐤌𐤅𐤃.𐤀𐤔.𐤋𐤉𐤋𐤄|
טו 𐤅𐤄𐤌𐤕𐤄.𐤀𐤕.𐤄𐤏𐤌.𐤄𐤆𐤄.𐤊𐤀𐤉𐤔.𐤀𐤇𐤃.𐤅𐤀𐤌𐤓𐤅
.𐤄𐤂𐤅𐤉𐤌.𐤀𐤔𐤓.𐤔𐤌𐤏𐤅.𐤀𐤕.𐤔𐤌𐤏𐤊.𐤋𐤀𐤌𐤓|

16 𐤌𐤁𐤋𐤕𐤉.𐤉𐤊𐤋𐤕.𐤉𐤄𐤅𐤄.𐤋𐤄𐤁𐤉𐤀.𐤀𐤕.𐤄𐤏𐤌.𐤄𐤆
𐤄.𐤀𐤋.𐤄𐤀𐤓𐤑.𐤀𐤔𐤓.𐤍𐤔𐤁𐤏.𐤋𐤄𐤌.𐤅𐤉𐤔𐤇𐤈𐤌.𐤁𐤌𐤃𐤁𐤓
|
17 𐤅𐤏𐤕𐤄.𐤉𐤂𐤃𐤋.𐤍𐤀.𐤊𐤇.𐤀𐤃𐤍𐤉.𐤊𐤀𐤔𐤓.𐤃𐤁𐤓𐤕.
𐤋𐤀𐤌𐤓|
18 𐤉𐤄𐤅𐤄.𐤀𐤓𐤊.𐤀𐤐𐤉𐤌.𐤅𐤓𐤁.𐤇𐤎𐤃.𐤍𐤔𐤀.𐤏𐤅𐤍.𐤅𐤐𐤔𐤏
𐤅𐤍𐤒𐤄.𐤋𐤀.𐤉𐤍𐤒𐤄.𐤐𐤒𐤃.𐤏𐤅𐤍.𐤀𐤁𐤅𐤕.𐤏𐤋.𐤁𐤍𐤉𐤌.𐤏𐤋.𐤔
𐤋𐤔𐤉𐤌.𐤅𐤏𐤋.𐤓𐤁𐤏𐤉𐤌|
19 𐤎𐤋𐤇.𐤍𐤀.𐤋𐤏𐤅𐤍.𐤄𐤏𐤌.𐤄𐤆𐤄.𐤊𐤂𐤃𐤋.𐤇𐤎𐤃𐤊.𐤅
𐤊𐤀𐤔𐤓.𐤍𐤔𐤀𐤕𐤄.𐤋𐤏𐤌.𐤄𐤆𐤄.𐤌𐤌𐤑𐤓𐤉𐤌.𐤅𐤏𐤃.𐤄𐤍𐤄|
20 𐤅𐤉𐤀𐤌𐤓.𐤉𐤄𐤅𐤄.𐤎𐤋𐤇𐤕𐤉.𐤊𐤃𐤁𐤓𐤊|
21 𐤅𐤀𐤅𐤋𐤌.𐤇𐤉.𐤀𐤍𐤉.𐤅𐤉𐤌𐤋𐤀.𐤊𐤁𐤅𐤃.𐤉𐤄𐤅𐤄.𐤀𐤕.𐤊𐤋.
𐤄𐤀𐤓𐤑|
22 𐤊𐤉.𐤊𐤋.𐤄𐤀𐤍𐤔𐤉𐤌.𐤄𐤓𐤀𐤉𐤌.𐤀𐤕.𐤊𐤁𐤃𐤉.𐤅𐤀𐤕.𐤀
𐤕𐤕𐤉.𐤀𐤔𐤓.𐤏𐤔𐤉𐤕𐤉.𐤁𐤌𐤑𐤓𐤉𐤌.𐤅𐤁𐤌𐤃𐤁𐤓.𐤅𐤉𐤍𐤎𐤅.𐤀
𐤕𐤉.𐤆𐤄.𐤏𐤔𐤓.𐤐𐤏𐤌𐤉𐤌.𐤅𐤋𐤀.𐤔𐤌𐤏𐤅.𐤁𐤒𐤋𐤉|
23 𐤀𐤌.𐤉𐤓𐤀𐤅.𐤀𐤕.𐤄𐤀𐤓𐤑.𐤀𐤔𐤓.𐤍𐤔𐤁𐤏𐤕𐤉.𐤋𐤀𐤁𐤕
𐤌.𐤅𐤊𐤋.𐤌𐤍𐤀𐤑𐤉.𐤋𐤀.𐤉𐤓𐤀𐤅𐤄|
24 𐤅𐤏𐤁𐤃𐤉.𐤊𐤋𐤁.𐤏𐤒𐤁.𐤄𐤉𐤕𐤄.𐤓𐤅𐤇.𐤀𐤇𐤓𐤕.𐤏𐤌𐤅.
𐤅𐤉𐤌𐤋𐤀.𐤀𐤇𐤓𐤉.𐤅𐤄𐤁𐤀𐤕𐤉𐤅.𐤀𐤋.𐤄𐤀𐤓𐤑.𐤀𐤔𐤓.𐤁𐤀.𐤔
𐤌𐤄.𐤅𐤆𐤓𐤏𐤅.𐤉𐤅𐤓𐤔𐤍𐤄|
25 𐤅𐤄𐤏𐤌𐤋𐤒𐤉.𐤅𐤄𐤊𐤍𐤏𐤍𐤉.𐤉𐤅𐤔𐤁.𐤁𐤏𐤌𐤒.𐤌𐤇𐤓.𐤐𐤍𐤅.
𐤅𐤎𐤏𐤅.𐤋𐤊𐤌.𐤄𐤌𐤃𐤁𐤓.𐤃𐤓𐤊.𐤉𐤌.𐤎𐤅𐤐|
26 𐤅𐤉𐤃𐤁𐤓.𐤉𐤄𐤅𐤄.𐤀𐤋.𐤌𐤔𐤄.𐤅𐤀𐤋.𐤀𐤄𐤓𐤍.𐤋𐤀𐤌𐤓|
27 𐤏𐤃.𐤌𐤕𐤉.𐤋𐤏𐤃𐤄.𐤄𐤓𐤏𐤄.𐤄𐤆𐤀𐤕.𐤀𐤔𐤓.𐤄𐤌𐤄
𐤌𐤋𐤉𐤍𐤉𐤌.𐤏𐤋𐤉.𐤀𐤕.𐤕𐤋𐤍𐤕.𐤁𐤍𐤉.𐤉𐤔𐤓𐤀𐤋.𐤀𐤔𐤓.𐤄𐤌
𐤄.𐤌𐤋𐤉𐤍𐤉𐤌.𐤏𐤋𐤉.𐤔𐤌𐤏𐤕𐤉|
28 𐤀𐤌𐤓.𐤀𐤋𐤄𐤌.𐤇𐤉.𐤀𐤍𐤉.𐤍𐤀𐤌.𐤉𐤄𐤅𐤄.𐤀𐤌.𐤋𐤀.𐤊𐤀
𐤔𐤓.𐤃𐤁𐤓𐤕𐤌.𐤁𐤀𐤆𐤍𐤉.𐤊𐤍.𐤀𐤏𐤔𐤄.𐤋𐤊𐤌|

𐤊𐤈 𐤁𐤌𐤃𐤁𐤓.𐤄𐤆𐤄.𐤉𐤐𐤋𐤅.𐤐𐤂𐤓𐤉𐤊𐤌.𐤅𐤊𐤋.𐤐𐤒𐤃𐤉𐤊
𐤌.𐤋𐤊𐤋.𐤌𐤎𐤐𐤓𐤊𐤌.𐤌𐤁𐤍.𐤏𐤔𐤓𐤉𐤌.𐤔𐤍𐤄.𐤅𐤌𐤏𐤋𐤄.𐤀𐤔𐤓.
𐤄𐤋𐤉𐤍𐤕𐤌.𐤏𐤋𐤉|
𐤋 𐤀𐤌.𐤀𐤕𐤌.𐤕𐤁𐤀𐤅.𐤀𐤋.𐤄𐤀𐤓𐤑.𐤀𐤔𐤓.𐤍𐤔𐤀𐤕𐤉.𐤀
𐤕.𐤉𐤃𐤉.𐤋𐤔𐤊𐤍.𐤀𐤕𐤊𐤌.𐤁𐤄.𐤊𐤉.𐤀𐤌.𐤊𐤋𐤁.𐤁𐤍.𐤉𐤐𐤍𐤄.𐤅
𐤉𐤄𐤅𐤔𐤏.𐤁𐤍.𐤍𐤅𐤍|
𐤋𐤀 𐤅𐤈𐤐𐤊𐤌.𐤀𐤔𐤓.𐤀𐤌𐤓𐤕𐤌.𐤋𐤁𐤆.𐤉𐤄𐤉𐤄.𐤅𐤄𐤁𐤉𐤀𐤕
𐤉.𐤀𐤕𐤌.𐤅𐤉𐤃𐤏𐤅.𐤀𐤕.𐤄𐤀𐤓𐤑.𐤀𐤔𐤓.𐤌𐤀𐤎𐤕𐤌.𐤁𐤄|
𐤋𐤁 𐤅𐤐𐤂𐤓𐤉𐤊𐤌.𐤀𐤕𐤌.𐤉𐤐𐤋𐤅.𐤁𐤌𐤃𐤁𐤓.𐤄𐤆𐤄|
𐤋𐤂 𐤅𐤁𐤍𐤉𐤊𐤌.𐤉𐤄𐤉𐤅.𐤓𐤏𐤉𐤌.𐤁𐤌𐤃𐤁𐤓.𐤀𐤓𐤁𐤏𐤉𐤌.𐤔𐤍
𐤄.𐤅𐤍𐤔𐤀𐤅.𐤀𐤕.𐤆𐤍𐤅𐤕𐤉𐤊𐤌.𐤏𐤃.𐤕𐤌.𐤐𐤂𐤓𐤉𐤊𐤌.𐤁𐤌𐤃
𐤁𐤓|
𐤋𐤃 𐤁𐤌𐤎𐤐𐤓.𐤄𐤉𐤌𐤉𐤌.𐤀𐤔𐤓.𐤕𐤓𐤕𐤌.𐤀𐤕.𐤄𐤀𐤓𐤑.𐤀𐤓
𐤁𐤏𐤉𐤌.𐤉𐤅𐤌.𐤉𐤅𐤌.𐤋𐤔𐤍𐤄.𐤉𐤅𐤌.𐤋𐤔𐤍𐤄.𐤕𐤔𐤀𐤅.𐤀𐤕.𐤏𐤅𐤍
𐤕𐤉𐤊𐤌.𐤀𐤓𐤁𐤏𐤉𐤌.𐤔𐤍𐤄.𐤅𐤉𐤃𐤏𐤕𐤌.𐤀𐤕.𐤕𐤍𐤅𐤀𐤕𐤉|
𐤋𐤄 𐤀𐤍𐤉.𐤉𐤄𐤅𐤄.𐤃𐤁𐤓𐤕𐤉.𐤀𐤌.𐤋𐤀.𐤆𐤀𐤕.𐤀𐤏𐤔𐤄.𐤋
𐤊𐤋.𐤄𐤏𐤃𐤄.𐤄𐤓𐤏𐤄.𐤄𐤆𐤀𐤕.𐤄𐤍𐤅𐤏𐤃𐤉𐤌.𐤏𐤋𐤉.𐤁𐤌𐤃
𐤁𐤓.𐤄𐤆𐤄.𐤉𐤕𐤌𐤅.𐤅𐤔𐤌.𐤉𐤌𐤕𐤅|
𐤋𐤅 𐤅𐤄𐤀𐤍𐤔𐤉𐤌.𐤀𐤔𐤓.𐤔𐤋𐤇.𐤌𐤔𐤄.𐤋𐤕𐤅𐤓.𐤀𐤕.𐤄𐤀𐤓
𐤑.𐤅𐤉𐤔𐤁𐤅.𐤅𐤉𐤋𐤅𐤍𐤅.||𐤅𐤉𐤋𐤉𐤍𐤅.𐤒𐤓𐤉||.𐤏𐤋𐤉𐤅.𐤀𐤕.𐤊𐤋.𐤄𐤏
𐤃𐤄.𐤋𐤄𐤅𐤑𐤉𐤀.𐤃𐤁𐤄.𐤏𐤋.𐤄𐤀𐤓𐤑|
𐤋𐤆 𐤅𐤉𐤌𐤕𐤅.𐤄𐤀𐤍𐤔𐤉𐤌.𐤌𐤅𐤑𐤀𐤉.𐤃𐤁𐤕.𐤄𐤀𐤓𐤑.𐤓𐤏
𐤄.𐤁𐤌𐤂𐤐𐤄.𐤋𐤐𐤍𐤉.𐤉𐤄𐤅𐤄|
𐤋𐤇 𐤅𐤉𐤄𐤅𐤔𐤏.𐤁𐤍.𐤍𐤅𐤍.𐤅𐤊𐤋𐤁.𐤁𐤍.𐤉𐤐𐤍𐤄.𐤇𐤉𐤅.𐤌𐤍.𐤄𐤀𐤍
𐤔𐤉𐤌.𐤄𐤄𐤌.𐤄𐤄𐤋𐤊𐤉𐤌.𐤋𐤕𐤅𐤓.𐤀𐤕.𐤄𐤀𐤓𐤑|
𐤋𐤈 𐤅𐤉𐤃𐤁𐤓.𐤌𐤔𐤄.𐤀𐤕.𐤄𐤃𐤁𐤓𐤉𐤌.𐤄𐤀𐤋𐤄.𐤀𐤋.𐤊𐤋.
𐤁𐤍𐤉.𐤉𐤔𐤓𐤀𐤋.𐤅𐤉𐤕𐤀𐤁𐤋𐤅.𐤄𐤏𐤌.𐤌𐤀𐤃|
𐤌 𐤅𐤉𐤔𐤊𐤌𐤅.𐤁𐤁𐤒𐤓.𐤅𐤉𐤏𐤋𐤅.𐤀𐤋.𐤓𐤀𐤔.𐤄𐤄𐤓.𐤋𐤀𐤌𐤓.
𐤄𐤍𐤍𐤅.𐤅𐤏𐤋𐤉𐤍𐤅.𐤀𐤋.𐤄𐤌𐤒𐤅𐤌.𐤀𐤔𐤓.𐤀𐤌𐤓.𐤉𐤄𐤅𐤄.𐤊𐤉.𐤇
𐤈𐤀𐤍𐤅|

41 𐤅𐤉𐤀𐤌𐤓.𐤌𐤔𐤄.𐤋𐤌𐤄.𐤆𐤄.𐤀𐤕𐤌.𐤏𐤁𐤓𐤉𐤌.𐤀𐤕.𐤐𐤉
.𐤉𐤄𐤅𐤄.𐤅𐤄𐤅𐤀.𐤋𐤀.𐤕𐤑𐤋𐤇|
42 𐤀𐤋.𐤕𐤏𐤋𐤅.𐤊𐤉.𐤀𐤉𐤍.𐤉𐤄𐤅𐤄.𐤁𐤒𐤓𐤁𐤊𐤌.𐤅𐤋𐤀.𐤕𐤍
𐤂𐤐𐤅.𐤋𐤐𐤍𐤉.𐤀𐤉𐤁𐤉𐤊𐤌|
43 𐤊𐤉.𐤄𐤏𐤌𐤋𐤒𐤉.𐤅𐤄𐤊𐤍𐤏𐤍𐤉.𐤔𐤌.𐤋𐤐𐤍𐤉𐤊𐤌.𐤅𐤍𐤐𐤋𐤕
𐤌.𐤁𐤇𐤓𐤁.𐤊𐤉.𐤏𐤋.𐤊𐤍.𐤔𐤁𐤕𐤌.𐤌𐤀𐤇𐤓𐤉.𐤉𐤄𐤅𐤄.𐤅𐤋𐤀.𐤉
𐤄𐤉𐤄.𐤉𐤄𐤅𐤄.𐤏𐤌𐤊𐤌|
44 𐤅𐤉𐤏𐤐𐤋𐤅.𐤋𐤏𐤋𐤅𐤕.𐤀𐤋.𐤓𐤀𐤔.𐤄𐤄𐤓.𐤅𐤀𐤓𐤅𐤍.𐤁𐤓𐤉𐤕.
𐤉𐤄𐤅𐤄.𐤅𐤌𐤔𐤄.𐤋𐤀.𐤌𐤔𐤅.𐤌𐤒𐤓𐤁.𐤄𐤌𐤇𐤍𐤄|
45 𐤅𐤉𐤓𐤃.𐤄𐤏𐤌𐤋𐤒𐤉.𐤅𐤄𐤊𐤍𐤏𐤍𐤉.𐤄𐤉𐤔𐤁.𐤁𐤄𐤓.𐤄𐤄𐤅
𐤀.𐤅𐤉𐤊𐤅𐤌.𐤅𐤉𐤊𐤕𐤅𐤌.𐤏𐤃.𐤄𐤇𐤓𐤌𐤄||

𐤁𐤌𐤃𐤁𐤓.𐤇𐤋𐤒 17

1 𐤅𐤉𐤃𐤁𐤓.𐤉𐤄𐤅𐤄.𐤀𐤋.𐤌𐤔𐤄.𐤋𐤀𐤌𐤓|
2 𐤃𐤁𐤓.𐤀𐤋.𐤁𐤍𐤉.𐤉𐤔𐤓𐤀𐤋.𐤅𐤀𐤌𐤓𐤕.𐤀𐤋𐤄𐤌.𐤊𐤉.𐤕𐤁𐤀
𐤅.𐤀𐤋.𐤀𐤓𐤑.𐤌𐤅𐤔𐤁𐤕𐤉𐤊𐤌.𐤀𐤔𐤓.𐤀𐤍𐤉.𐤍𐤕𐤍.𐤋𐤊𐤌|
3 𐤅𐤏𐤔𐤉𐤕𐤌.𐤀𐤔𐤄.𐤋𐤉𐤄𐤅𐤄.𐤏𐤋𐤄.𐤀𐤅.𐤆𐤁𐤇.𐤋𐤐𐤋𐤀.
𐤍𐤃𐤓.𐤀𐤅.𐤁𐤍𐤃𐤁𐤄.𐤀𐤅.𐤁𐤌𐤏𐤃𐤉𐤊𐤌.𐤋𐤏𐤔𐤅𐤕.𐤓𐤉𐤇.𐤍𐤉
𐤇𐤇.𐤋𐤉𐤄𐤅𐤄.𐤌𐤍.𐤄𐤁𐤒𐤓.𐤀𐤅.𐤌𐤍.𐤄𐤑𐤀𐤍|
4 𐤅𐤄𐤒𐤓𐤉𐤁.𐤄𐤌𐤒𐤓𐤉𐤁.𐤒𐤓𐤁𐤍𐤅.𐤋𐤉𐤄𐤅𐤄.𐤌𐤍𐤇𐤄.𐤎𐤋
𐤕.𐤏𐤔𐤓𐤅𐤍.𐤁𐤋𐤅𐤋.𐤁𐤓𐤁𐤏𐤉𐤕.𐤄𐤄𐤉𐤍.𐤔𐤌𐤍|
5 𐤅𐤉𐤉𐤍.𐤋𐤍𐤎𐤊.𐤓𐤁𐤉𐤏𐤉𐤕.𐤄𐤄𐤉𐤍.𐤕𐤏𐤔𐤄.𐤏𐤋.𐤄𐤏𐤋
𐤄.𐤀𐤅.𐤋𐤆𐤁𐤇.𐤋𐤊𐤁𐤔.𐤄𐤀𐤇𐤃|
6 𐤀𐤅.𐤋𐤀𐤉𐤋.𐤕𐤏𐤔𐤄.𐤌𐤍𐤇𐤄.𐤎𐤋𐤕.𐤔𐤍𐤉.𐤏𐤔𐤓𐤍𐤉𐤌.𐤁
𐤋𐤅𐤋𐤄.𐤁𐤔𐤌𐤍.𐤔𐤋𐤔𐤉𐤕.𐤄𐤄𐤉𐤍|
7 𐤅𐤉𐤉𐤍.𐤋𐤍𐤎𐤊.𐤔𐤋𐤔𐤉𐤕.𐤄𐤄𐤉𐤍.𐤕𐤒𐤓𐤉𐤁.𐤓𐤉𐤇.𐤍𐤉
𐤇𐤇.𐤋𐤉𐤄𐤅𐤄|
8 𐤅𐤊𐤉.𐤕𐤏𐤔𐤄.𐤁𐤍.𐤁𐤒𐤓.𐤏𐤋𐤄.𐤀𐤅.𐤆𐤁𐤇.𐤋𐤐𐤋𐤀.𐤍𐤃
𐤓.𐤀𐤅.𐤔𐤋𐤌𐤉𐤌.𐤋𐤉𐤄𐤅𐤄|

𐤈 𐤅𐤄𐤒𐤓𐤉𐤁.𐤏𐤋.𐤁𐤍.𐤄𐤁𐤒𐤓.𐤌𐤍𐤇𐤄.𐤎𐤋𐤕.𐤔𐤋𐤔𐤄.𐤏
𐤔𐤓𐤍𐤉𐤌.𐤁𐤋𐤅𐤋.𐤁𐤔𐤌𐤍.𐤇𐤑𐤉.𐤄𐤄𐤉𐤍|
𐤉 𐤅𐤉𐤉𐤍.𐤕𐤒𐤓𐤉𐤁.𐤋𐤍𐤎𐤊.𐤇𐤑𐤉.𐤄𐤄𐤉𐤍.𐤀𐤔𐤄.𐤓𐤉𐤇
.𐤍𐤉𐤇𐤇.𐤋𐤉𐤄𐤅𐤄|
𐤉𐤀 𐤊𐤊𐤄.𐤉𐤏𐤔𐤄.𐤋𐤔𐤅𐤓.𐤄𐤀𐤇𐤃.𐤀𐤅.𐤋𐤀𐤉𐤋.𐤄𐤀𐤇𐤃
.𐤀𐤅.𐤋𐤔𐤄.𐤁𐤊𐤁𐤔𐤉𐤌.𐤀𐤅.𐤁𐤏𐤆𐤉𐤌|
𐤉𐤁 𐤊𐤌𐤎𐤐𐤓.𐤀𐤔𐤓.𐤕𐤏𐤔𐤅.𐤊𐤊𐤄.𐤕𐤏𐤔𐤅.𐤋𐤀𐤇𐤃.𐤊𐤌
𐤎𐤐𐤓𐤌|
𐤉𐤂 𐤊𐤋.𐤄𐤀𐤆𐤓𐤇.𐤉𐤏𐤔𐤄.𐤊𐤊𐤄.𐤀𐤕.𐤀𐤋𐤄.𐤋𐤄𐤒𐤓𐤉
𐤁.𐤀𐤔𐤄.𐤓𐤉𐤇.𐤍𐤉𐤇𐤇.𐤋𐤉𐤄𐤅𐤄|
𐤉𐤃 𐤅𐤊𐤉.𐤉𐤂𐤅𐤓.𐤀𐤕𐤊𐤌.𐤂𐤓.𐤀𐤅.𐤀𐤔𐤓.𐤁𐤕𐤅𐤊𐤊𐤌.𐤋𐤃
𐤓𐤕𐤉𐤊𐤌.𐤅𐤏𐤔𐤄.𐤀𐤔𐤄.𐤓𐤉𐤇.𐤍𐤉𐤇𐤇.𐤋𐤉𐤄𐤅𐤄.𐤊𐤀𐤔𐤓.
𐤕𐤏𐤔𐤅.𐤊𐤍.𐤉𐤏𐤔𐤄|
𐤈𐤅 𐤄𐤒𐤄𐤋.𐤇𐤒𐤄.𐤀𐤇𐤕.𐤋𐤊𐤌.𐤅𐤋𐤂𐤓.𐤄𐤂𐤓.𐤇𐤒𐤕.𐤏
𐤅𐤋𐤌.𐤋𐤃𐤓𐤕𐤉𐤊𐤌.𐤊𐤊𐤌.𐤊𐤂𐤓.𐤉𐤄𐤉𐤄.𐤋𐤐𐤍𐤉.𐤉𐤄𐤅𐤄|
𐤈𐤆 𐤕𐤅𐤓𐤄.𐤀𐤇𐤕.𐤅𐤌𐤔𐤐𐤈.𐤀𐤇𐤃.𐤉𐤄𐤉𐤄.𐤋𐤊𐤌.𐤅𐤋𐤂𐤓
.𐤄𐤂𐤓.𐤀𐤕𐤊𐤌|
𐤉𐤆 𐤅𐤉𐤃𐤁𐤓.𐤉𐤄𐤅𐤄.𐤀𐤋.𐤌𐤔𐤄.𐤋𐤀𐤌𐤓|
𐤉𐤇 𐤃𐤁𐤓.𐤀𐤋.𐤁𐤍𐤉.𐤉𐤔𐤓𐤀𐤋.𐤅𐤀𐤌𐤓𐤕.𐤀𐤋𐤄𐤌.𐤁𐤁𐤀𐤊
𐤌.𐤀𐤋.𐤄𐤀𐤓𐤑.𐤀𐤔𐤓.𐤀𐤍𐤉.𐤌𐤁𐤉𐤀.𐤀𐤕𐤊𐤌.𐤔𐤌𐤄|
𐤉𐤈 𐤅𐤄𐤉𐤄.𐤁𐤀𐤊𐤋𐤊𐤌.𐤌𐤋𐤇𐤌.𐤄𐤀𐤓𐤑.𐤕𐤓𐤉𐤌𐤅.𐤕𐤓𐤅
𐤌𐤄.𐤋𐤉𐤄𐤅𐤄|
𐤊 𐤓𐤀𐤔𐤉𐤕.𐤏𐤓𐤎𐤕𐤊𐤌.𐤇𐤋𐤄.𐤕𐤓𐤉𐤌𐤅.𐤕𐤓𐤅𐤌𐤄.𐤊𐤕
𐤓𐤅𐤌𐤕.𐤂𐤓𐤍.𐤊𐤍.𐤕𐤓𐤉𐤌𐤅.𐤀𐤕𐤄|
𐤊𐤀 𐤌𐤓𐤀𐤔𐤉𐤕.𐤏𐤓𐤎𐤕𐤉𐤊𐤌.𐤕𐤕𐤍𐤅.𐤋𐤉𐤄𐤅𐤄.𐤕𐤓𐤅𐤌𐤄.
𐤋𐤃𐤓𐤕𐤉𐤊𐤌|
𐤊𐤁 𐤅𐤊𐤉.𐤕𐤔𐤂𐤅.𐤅𐤋𐤀.𐤕𐤏𐤔𐤅.𐤀𐤕.𐤊𐤋.𐤄𐤌𐤑𐤅𐤕.𐤄𐤀𐤋
𐤄.𐤀𐤔𐤓.𐤃𐤁𐤓.𐤉𐤄𐤅𐤄.𐤀𐤋.𐤌𐤔𐤄|
𐤊𐤂 𐤀𐤕.𐤊𐤋.𐤀𐤔𐤓.𐤑𐤅𐤄.𐤉𐤄𐤅𐤄.𐤀𐤋𐤉𐤊𐤌.𐤁𐤉𐤃.𐤌𐤔𐤄
.𐤌𐤍.𐤄𐤉𐤅𐤌.𐤀𐤔𐤓.𐤑𐤅𐤄.𐤉𐤄𐤅𐤄.𐤅𐤄𐤋𐤀𐤄.𐤋𐤃𐤓𐤕𐤉𐤊𐤌|

..𐤊𐤃..𐤅𐤄𐤉𐤄.𐤀𐤌.𐤌𐤏𐤉𐤍𐤉.𐤄𐤏𐤃𐤄.𐤍𐤏𐤔𐤕𐤄.𐤋𐤔𐤂𐤂
𐤄.𐤅𐤏𐤔𐤅.𐤊𐤋.𐤄𐤏𐤃𐤄.𐤐𐤓.𐤁𐤍.𐤁𐤒𐤓.𐤀𐤇𐤃.𐤋𐤏𐤋𐤄.𐤋𐤓𐤉
𐤇.𐤍𐤉𐤇𐤇.𐤋𐤉𐤄𐤅𐤄.𐤅𐤌𐤍𐤇𐤕𐤅.𐤅𐤍𐤎𐤊𐤅.𐤊𐤌𐤔𐤐𐤈.𐤅𐤔𐤏𐤉𐤓
.𐤏𐤆𐤉𐤌.𐤀𐤇𐤃.𐤋𐤇𐤈𐤕|
..𐤊𐤄..𐤅𐤊𐤐𐤓.𐤄𐤊𐤄𐤍.𐤏𐤋.𐤊𐤋.𐤏𐤃𐤕.𐤁𐤍𐤉.𐤉𐤔𐤓𐤀𐤋.𐤅𐤍𐤎𐤋
𐤇.𐤋𐤄𐤌.𐤊𐤉.𐤔𐤂𐤂𐤄.𐤄𐤅𐤀.𐤅𐤄𐤌.𐤄𐤁𐤉𐤀𐤅.𐤀𐤕.𐤒𐤓𐤁𐤍𐤌
.𐤀𐤔𐤄.𐤋𐤉𐤄𐤅𐤄.𐤅𐤇𐤈𐤀𐤕𐤌.𐤋𐤐𐤍𐤉.𐤉𐤄𐤅𐤄.𐤏𐤋.𐤔𐤂𐤂𐤕
𐤌|
..𐤊𐤅..𐤅𐤍𐤎𐤋𐤇.𐤋𐤊𐤋.𐤏𐤃𐤕.𐤁𐤍𐤉.𐤉𐤔𐤓𐤀𐤋.𐤅𐤋𐤂𐤓.𐤄𐤂𐤓.
𐤁𐤕𐤅𐤊𐤌.𐤊𐤉.𐤋𐤊𐤋.𐤄𐤏𐤌.𐤁𐤔𐤂𐤂𐤄|
..𐤊𐤆..𐤅𐤀𐤌.𐤍𐤐𐤔.𐤀𐤇𐤕.𐤕𐤇𐤈𐤀.𐤁𐤔𐤂𐤂𐤄.𐤅𐤄𐤒𐤓𐤉𐤁
𐤄.𐤏𐤆.𐤁𐤕.𐤔𐤍𐤕𐤄.𐤋𐤇𐤈𐤀𐤕|
..𐤊𐤇..𐤅𐤊𐤐𐤓.𐤄𐤊𐤄𐤍.𐤏𐤋.𐤄𐤍𐤐𐤔.𐤄𐤔𐤂𐤂𐤕.𐤁𐤇𐤈𐤀𐤄.𐤁
𐤔𐤂𐤂𐤄.𐤋𐤐𐤍𐤉.𐤉𐤄𐤅𐤄.𐤋𐤊𐤐𐤓.𐤏𐤋𐤉𐤅.𐤅𐤍𐤎𐤋𐤇.𐤋𐤅|
..𐤊𐤈..𐤄𐤀𐤆𐤓𐤇.𐤁𐤁𐤍𐤉.𐤉𐤔𐤓𐤀𐤋.𐤅𐤋𐤂𐤓.𐤄𐤂𐤓.𐤁𐤕𐤅𐤊𐤌.
𐤕𐤅𐤓𐤄.𐤀𐤇𐤕.𐤉𐤄𐤉𐤄.𐤋𐤊𐤌.𐤋𐤏𐤔𐤄.𐤁𐤔𐤂𐤂𐤄|
..𐤋..𐤅𐤄𐤍𐤐𐤔.𐤀𐤔𐤓.𐤕𐤏𐤔𐤄.𐤁𐤉𐤃.𐤓𐤌𐤄.𐤌𐤍.𐤄𐤀𐤆𐤓𐤇
.𐤅𐤌𐤍.𐤄𐤂𐤓.𐤀𐤕.𐤉𐤄𐤅𐤄.𐤄𐤅𐤀.𐤌𐤂𐤃𐤐.𐤅𐤍𐤊𐤓𐤕𐤄.𐤄𐤍𐤐𐤔.
𐤄𐤄𐤅𐤀.𐤌𐤒𐤓𐤁.𐤏𐤌𐤄|
..𐤋𐤀..𐤊𐤉.𐤃𐤁𐤓.𐤉𐤄𐤅𐤄.𐤁𐤆𐤄.𐤅𐤀𐤕.𐤌𐤑𐤅𐤕𐤅.𐤄𐤐𐤓.𐤄𐤊𐤓
𐤕.𐤕𐤊𐤓𐤕.𐤄𐤍𐤐𐤔.𐤄𐤄𐤅𐤀.𐤏𐤅𐤍𐤄.𐤁𐤄|
..𐤋𐤁..𐤅𐤉𐤄𐤉𐤅.𐤁𐤍𐤉.𐤉𐤔𐤓𐤀𐤋.𐤁𐤌𐤃𐤁𐤓.𐤅𐤉𐤌𐤑𐤀𐤅.𐤀𐤉𐤔.
𐤌𐤒𐤔𐤔.𐤏𐤑𐤉𐤌.𐤁𐤉𐤅𐤌.𐤄𐤔𐤁𐤕|
..𐤋𐤂..𐤅𐤉𐤒𐤓𐤉𐤁𐤅.𐤀𐤕𐤅.𐤄𐤌𐤑𐤀𐤉𐤌.𐤀𐤕𐤅.𐤌𐤒𐤔𐤔.𐤏𐤑𐤉
𐤌.𐤀𐤋.𐤌𐤔𐤄.𐤅𐤀𐤋.𐤀𐤄𐤓𐤍.𐤅𐤀𐤋.𐤊𐤋.𐤄𐤏𐤃𐤄|
..𐤋𐤃..𐤅𐤉𐤍𐤉𐤇𐤅.𐤀𐤕𐤅.𐤁𐤌𐤔𐤌𐤓.𐤊𐤉.𐤋𐤀.𐤐𐤓𐤔.𐤌𐤄.𐤉𐤏𐤔
𐤄.𐤋𐤅|
..𐤋𐤄..𐤅𐤉𐤀𐤌𐤓.𐤉𐤄𐤅𐤄.𐤀𐤋.𐤌𐤔𐤄.𐤌𐤅𐤕.𐤉𐤅𐤌𐤕.𐤄𐤀𐤉𐤔.𐤓
𐤂𐤅𐤌.𐤀𐤕𐤅.𐤁𐤀𐤁𐤍𐤉𐤌.𐤊𐤋.𐤄𐤏𐤃𐤄.𐤌𐤇𐤅𐤑.𐤋𐤌𐤇𐤍𐤄|

..לו.. 𐤅𐤉𐤑𐤉𐤀𐤅.𐤀𐤕𐤅.𐤊𐤋.𐤄𐤏𐤃𐤄.𐤀𐤋.𐤌𐤇𐤅𐤑.𐤋𐤌𐤇𐤍𐤄
.𐤅𐤉𐤓𐤂𐤌𐤅.𐤀𐤕𐤅.𐤁𐤀𐤁𐤍𐤉𐤌.𐤅𐤉𐤌𐤕.𐤊𐤀𐤔𐤓.𐤑𐤅𐤄.𐤉𐤄𐤅𐤄.
𐤀𐤕.𐤌𐤔𐤄|
..לז.. 𐤅𐤉𐤀𐤌𐤓.𐤉𐤄𐤅𐤄.𐤀𐤋.𐤌𐤔𐤄.𐤋𐤀𐤌𐤓|
..לח.. 𐤃𐤁𐤓.𐤀𐤋.𐤁𐤍𐤉.𐤉𐤔𐤓𐤀𐤋.𐤅𐤀𐤌𐤓𐤕.𐤀𐤋𐤄𐤌.𐤅𐤏𐤔𐤅.𐤋
𐤄𐤌.𐤑𐤉𐤑𐤕.𐤏𐤋.𐤊𐤍𐤐𐤉.𐤁𐤂𐤃𐤉𐤄𐤌.𐤋𐤃𐤓𐤕𐤌.𐤅𐤍𐤕𐤍𐤅.
𐤏𐤋.𐤑𐤉𐤑𐤕.𐤄𐤊𐤍𐤐.𐤐𐤕𐤉𐤋.𐤕𐤊𐤋𐤕|
..לט.. 𐤅𐤄𐤉𐤄.𐤋𐤊𐤌.𐤋𐤑𐤉𐤑𐤕.𐤅𐤓𐤀𐤉𐤕𐤌.𐤀𐤕𐤅.𐤅𐤆𐤊𐤓𐤕
𐤌.𐤀𐤕.𐤊𐤋.𐤌𐤑𐤅𐤕.𐤉𐤄𐤅𐤄.𐤅𐤏𐤔𐤉𐤕𐤌.𐤀𐤕𐤌.𐤅𐤋𐤀.𐤕𐤕𐤓𐤅.
𐤀𐤇𐤓𐤉.𐤋𐤁𐤁𐤊𐤌.𐤅𐤀𐤇𐤓𐤉.𐤏𐤉𐤍𐤉𐤊𐤌.𐤀𐤔𐤓.𐤀𐤕𐤌.𐤆𐤍𐤉
𐤌.𐤀𐤇𐤓𐤉𐤄𐤌|
..מ.. 𐤋𐤌𐤏𐤍.𐤕𐤆𐤊𐤓𐤅.𐤅𐤏𐤔𐤉𐤕𐤌.𐤀𐤕.𐤊𐤋.𐤌𐤑𐤅𐤕𐤉.𐤅𐤄
𐤉𐤉𐤕𐤌.𐤒𐤃𐤔𐤉𐤌.𐤋𐤀𐤋𐤄𐤉𐤊𐤌|
..מא.. 𐤀𐤍𐤉.𐤉𐤄𐤅𐤄.𐤀𐤋𐤄𐤉𐤊𐤌.𐤀𐤔𐤓.𐤄𐤅𐤑𐤀𐤕𐤉.𐤀𐤕𐤊𐤌
𐤌𐤀𐤓𐤑.𐤌𐤑𐤓𐤉𐤌.𐤋𐤄𐤉𐤅𐤕.𐤋𐤊𐤌.𐤋𐤀𐤋𐤄𐤉𐤌.𐤀𐤍𐤉.𐤉𐤄𐤅
𐤄.𐤀𐤋𐤄𐤉𐤊𐤌‖

𐤁𐤌𐤃𐤁𐤓.𐤇𐤋𐤒 ..טז..

..א.. 𐤅𐤉𐤒𐤇.𐤒𐤓𐤇.𐤁𐤍.𐤉𐤑𐤄𐤓.𐤁𐤍.𐤒𐤄𐤕.𐤁𐤍.𐤋𐤅𐤉.𐤅𐤃𐤕𐤍.
𐤅𐤀𐤁𐤉𐤓𐤌.𐤁𐤍𐤉.𐤀𐤋𐤉𐤀𐤁.𐤅𐤀𐤅𐤍.𐤁𐤍.𐤐𐤋𐤕.𐤁𐤍𐤉.𐤓𐤀𐤅𐤁𐤍|
..ב.. 𐤅𐤉𐤒𐤌𐤅.𐤋𐤐𐤍𐤉.𐤌𐤔𐤄.𐤅𐤀𐤍𐤔𐤉𐤌.𐤌𐤁𐤍𐤉.𐤉𐤔𐤓𐤀𐤋.𐤇
𐤌𐤔𐤉𐤌.𐤅𐤌𐤀𐤕𐤉𐤌.𐤍𐤔𐤉𐤀𐤉.𐤏𐤃𐤄.𐤒𐤓𐤀𐤉.𐤌𐤅𐤏𐤃.𐤀𐤍
𐤔𐤉.𐤔𐤌|
..ג.. 𐤅𐤉𐤒𐤄𐤋𐤅.𐤏𐤋.𐤌𐤔𐤄.𐤅𐤏𐤋.𐤀𐤄𐤓𐤍.𐤅𐤉𐤀𐤌𐤓𐤅.𐤀𐤋𐤄𐤌.
𐤓𐤁.𐤋𐤊𐤌.𐤊𐤉.𐤊𐤋.𐤄𐤏𐤃𐤄.𐤊𐤋𐤌.𐤒𐤃𐤔𐤉𐤌.𐤅𐤁𐤕𐤅𐤊𐤌.𐤉
𐤄𐤅𐤄.𐤅𐤌𐤃𐤅𐤏.𐤕𐤕𐤍𐤔𐤀𐤅.𐤏𐤋.𐤒𐤄𐤋.𐤉𐤄𐤅𐤄|
..ד.. 𐤅𐤉𐤔𐤌𐤏.𐤌𐤔𐤄.𐤅𐤉𐤐𐤋.𐤏𐤋.𐤐𐤍𐤉𐤅|
..ה.. 𐤅𐤉𐤃𐤁𐤓.𐤀𐤋.𐤒𐤓𐤇.𐤅𐤀𐤋.𐤊𐤋.𐤏𐤃𐤕𐤅.𐤋𐤀𐤌𐤓.𐤁𐤒𐤓.𐤅
𐤉𐤃𐤏.𐤉𐤄𐤅𐤄.𐤀𐤕.𐤀𐤔𐤓.𐤋𐤅.𐤅𐤀𐤕.𐤄𐤒𐤃𐤅𐤔.𐤅𐤄𐤒𐤓𐤉𐤁.
𐤀𐤋𐤉𐤅.𐤅𐤀𐤕.𐤀𐤔𐤓.𐤉𐤁𐤇𐤓.𐤁𐤅.𐤉𐤒𐤓𐤉𐤁.𐤀𐤋𐤉𐤅|

ו 𐤆𐤀𐤕.𐤏𐤔𐤅.𐤒𐤇𐤅.𐤋𐤊𐤌.𐤌𐤇𐤕𐤅𐤕.𐤒𐤓𐤇.𐤅𐤊𐤋.𐤏𐤃
𐤕𐤅|

ז 𐤅𐤕𐤍𐤅.𐤁𐤄𐤍.𐤀𐤔.𐤅𐤔𐤉𐤌𐤅.𐤏𐤋𐤉𐤄𐤍.𐤒𐤈𐤓𐤕.𐤋𐤐𐤍𐤉.𐤉
𐤄𐤅𐤄.𐤌𐤇𐤓.𐤅𐤄𐤉𐤄.𐤄𐤀𐤉𐤔.𐤀𐤔𐤓.𐤉𐤁𐤇𐤓.𐤉𐤄𐤅𐤄.𐤄𐤅𐤀.
𐤄𐤒𐤃𐤅𐤔.𐤓𐤁.𐤋𐤊𐤌.𐤁𐤍𐤉.𐤋𐤅𐤉|

ח 𐤅𐤉𐤀𐤌𐤓.𐤌𐤔𐤄.𐤀𐤋.𐤒𐤓𐤇.𐤔𐤌𐤏𐤅.𐤍𐤀.𐤁𐤍𐤉.𐤋𐤅𐤉|

ט 𐤄𐤌𐤏𐤈.𐤌𐤊𐤌.𐤊𐤉.𐤄𐤁𐤃𐤉𐤋.𐤀𐤋𐤄𐤉.𐤉𐤔𐤓𐤀𐤋.𐤀𐤕
𐤊𐤌.𐤌𐤏𐤃𐤕.𐤉𐤔𐤓𐤀𐤋.𐤋𐤄𐤒𐤓𐤉𐤁.𐤀𐤕𐤊𐤌.𐤀𐤋𐤉𐤅.𐤋𐤏𐤁
𐤃.𐤀𐤕.𐤏𐤁𐤃𐤕.𐤌𐤔𐤊𐤍.𐤉𐤄𐤅𐤄.𐤅𐤋𐤏𐤌𐤃.𐤋𐤐𐤍𐤉.𐤄𐤏𐤃𐤄
.𐤋𐤔𐤓𐤕𐤌|

י 𐤅𐤉𐤒𐤓𐤁.𐤀𐤕𐤊.𐤅𐤀𐤕.𐤊𐤋.𐤀𐤇𐤉𐤊.𐤁𐤍𐤉.𐤋𐤅𐤉.𐤀𐤕𐤊.
𐤅𐤁𐤒𐤔𐤕𐤌.𐤂𐤌.𐤊𐤄𐤍𐤄|

יא 𐤋𐤊𐤍.𐤀𐤕𐤄.𐤅𐤊𐤋.𐤏𐤃𐤕𐤊.𐤄𐤍𐤏𐤃𐤉𐤌.𐤏𐤋.𐤉𐤄𐤅𐤄.𐤅
𐤀𐤄𐤓𐤍.𐤌𐤄.𐤄𐤅𐤀.𐤊𐤉.𐤕𐤋𐤅𐤍𐤅.||𐤕𐤋𐤉𐤍𐤅.𐤒𐤓𐤉||.𐤏𐤋𐤉𐤅|

יב 𐤅𐤉𐤔𐤋𐤇.𐤌𐤔𐤄.𐤋𐤒𐤓𐤀.𐤋𐤃𐤕𐤍.𐤅𐤋𐤀𐤁𐤉𐤓𐤌.𐤁𐤍𐤉.𐤀
𐤋𐤉𐤀𐤁.𐤅𐤉𐤀𐤌𐤓𐤅.𐤋𐤀.𐤍𐤏𐤋𐤄|

יג 𐤄𐤌𐤏𐤈.𐤊𐤉.𐤄𐤏𐤋𐤉𐤕𐤍𐤅.𐤌𐤀𐤓𐤑.𐤆𐤁𐤕.𐤇𐤋𐤁.𐤅𐤃
𐤁𐤔.𐤋𐤄𐤌𐤉𐤕𐤍𐤅.𐤁𐤌𐤃𐤁𐤓.𐤊𐤉.𐤕𐤔𐤕𐤓𐤓.𐤏𐤋𐤉𐤍𐤅.𐤂𐤌.𐤄
𐤔𐤕𐤓𐤓|

יד 𐤀𐤐.𐤋𐤀.𐤀𐤋.𐤀𐤓𐤑.𐤆𐤁𐤕.𐤇𐤋𐤁.𐤅𐤃𐤁𐤔.𐤄𐤁𐤉𐤀𐤕
𐤍𐤅.𐤅𐤕𐤕𐤍.𐤋𐤍𐤅.𐤍𐤇𐤋𐤕.𐤔𐤃𐤄.𐤅𐤊𐤓𐤌.𐤄𐤏𐤉𐤍𐤉.𐤄𐤀𐤍𐤔𐤉𐤌
.𐤄𐤄𐤌.𐤕𐤍𐤒𐤓.𐤋𐤀.𐤍𐤏𐤋𐤄|

טו 𐤅𐤉𐤇𐤓.𐤋𐤌𐤔𐤄.𐤌𐤀𐤃.𐤅𐤉𐤀𐤌𐤓.𐤀𐤋.𐤉𐤄𐤅𐤄.𐤀𐤋.𐤕𐤐𐤍
.𐤀𐤋.𐤌𐤍𐤇𐤕𐤌.𐤋𐤀.𐤇𐤌𐤅𐤓.𐤀𐤇𐤃.𐤌𐤄𐤌.𐤍𐤔𐤀𐤕𐤉.𐤅𐤋𐤀.
𐤄𐤓𐤏𐤕𐤉.𐤀𐤕.𐤀𐤇𐤃.𐤌𐤄𐤌|

טז 𐤅𐤉𐤀𐤌𐤓.𐤌𐤔𐤄.𐤀𐤋.𐤒𐤓𐤇.𐤀𐤕𐤄.𐤅𐤊𐤋.𐤏𐤃𐤕𐤊.𐤄𐤉
𐤅.𐤋𐤐𐤍𐤉.𐤉𐤄𐤅𐤄.𐤀𐤕𐤄.𐤅𐤄𐤌.𐤅𐤀𐤄𐤓𐤍.𐤌𐤇𐤓|

יז 𐤅𐤒𐤇𐤅.𐤀𐤉𐤔.𐤌𐤇𐤕𐤕𐤅.𐤅𐤍𐤕𐤕𐤌.𐤏𐤋𐤉𐤄𐤌.𐤒𐤈𐤓𐤕
.𐤅𐤄𐤒𐤓𐤁𐤕𐤌.𐤋𐤐𐤍𐤉.𐤉𐤄𐤅𐤄.𐤀𐤉𐤔.𐤌𐤇𐤕𐤕𐤅.𐤇𐤌𐤔𐤉𐤌.𐤅
𐤌𐤀𐤕𐤉𐤌.𐤌𐤇𐤕𐤕.𐤅𐤀𐤕𐤄.𐤅𐤀𐤄𐤓𐤍.𐤀𐤉𐤔.𐤌𐤇𐤕𐤕𐤅|

יח ויקחו.איש.מחתתו.ויתנו.עליהם.אש.וישימו.עליהם.קטרת.ויעמדו.פתח.אהל.מועד.ומשה.ואהרן׃

יט ויקהל.עליהם.קרח.את.כל.העדה.אל.פתח.אהל.מועד.וירא.כבוד.יהוה.אל.כל.העדה׃

כ וידבר.יהוה.אל.משה.ואל.אהרן.לאמר׃

כא הבדלו.מתוך.העדה.הזאת.ואכלה.אתם.כרגע׃

כב ויפלו.על.פניהם.ויאמרו.אל.אלהי.הרוחת.לכל.בשר.האיש.אחד.יחטא.ועל.כל.העדה.תקצף׃

כג וידבר.יהוה.אל.משה.לאמר׃

כד דבר.אל.העדה.לאמר.העלו.מסביב.למשכן.קרח.דתן.ואבירם׃

כה ויקם.משה.וילך.אל.דתן.ואבירם.וילכו.אחריו.זקני.ישראל׃

כו וידבר.אל.העדה.לאמר.סורו.נא.מעל.אהלי.האנשים.הרשעים.האלה.ואל.תגעו.בכל.אשר.להם.פן.תספו.בכל.חטאתם׃

כז ויעלו.מעל.משכן.קרח.דתן.ואבירם.מסביב.ודתן.ואבירם.יצאו.נצבים.פתח.אהליהם.ונשיהם.ובניהם.וטפם׃

כח ויאמר.משה.בזאת.תדעון.כי.יהוה.שלחני.לעשות.את.כל.המעשים.האלה.כי.לא.מלבי׃

כט אם.כמות.כל.האדם.ימתון.אלה.ופקדת.כל.האדם.יפקד.עליהם.לא.יהוה.שלחני׃

ל ואם.בריאה.יברא.יהוה.ופצתה.האדמה.את.פיה.ובלעה.אתם.ואת.כל.אשר.להם.וירדו.

𐤇𐤉𐤉𐤌.𐤔𐤀𐤋𐤄.𐤅𐤉𐤃𐤏𐤕𐤌.𐤊𐤉.𐤍𐤀𐤑𐤅.𐤄𐤀𐤍𐤔𐤉𐤌.𐤄𐤀
𐤋𐤄.𐤀𐤕.𐤉𐤄𐤅𐤄|
..𐤋𐤀.. 𐤅𐤉𐤄𐤉.𐤊𐤊𐤋𐤕𐤅.𐤋𐤃𐤁𐤓.𐤀𐤕.𐤊𐤋.𐤄𐤃𐤁𐤓𐤉𐤌.𐤄𐤀𐤋
𐤄.𐤅𐤕𐤁𐤒𐤏.𐤄𐤀𐤃𐤌𐤄.𐤀𐤔𐤓.𐤕𐤇𐤕𐤉𐤄𐤌|
..𐤋𐤁.. 𐤅𐤕𐤐𐤕𐤇.𐤄𐤀𐤓𐤑.𐤀𐤕.𐤐𐤉𐤄.𐤅𐤕𐤁𐤋𐤏.𐤀𐤕𐤌.𐤅𐤀𐤕.
𐤁𐤕𐤉𐤄𐤌.𐤅𐤀𐤕.𐤊𐤋.𐤄𐤀𐤃𐤌.𐤀𐤔𐤓.𐤋𐤒𐤓𐤇.𐤅𐤀𐤕.𐤊𐤋.𐤄𐤓
𐤊𐤅𐤔|
..𐤋𐤂.. 𐤅𐤉𐤓𐤃𐤅.𐤄𐤌.𐤅𐤊𐤋.𐤀𐤔𐤓.𐤋𐤄𐤌.𐤇𐤉𐤉𐤌.𐤔𐤀𐤋𐤄.𐤅𐤕
𐤊𐤎.𐤏𐤋𐤉𐤄𐤌.𐤄𐤀𐤓𐤑.𐤅𐤉𐤀𐤁𐤃𐤅.𐤌𐤕𐤅𐤊.𐤄𐤒𐤄𐤋|
..𐤋𐤃.. 𐤅𐤊𐤋.𐤉𐤔𐤓𐤀𐤋.𐤀𐤔𐤓.𐤎𐤁𐤉𐤁𐤕𐤉𐤄𐤌.𐤍𐤎𐤅.𐤋𐤒𐤋𐤌.
𐤊𐤉.𐤀𐤌𐤓𐤅.𐤐𐤍.𐤕𐤁𐤋𐤏𐤍𐤅.𐤄𐤀𐤓𐤑|
..𐤋𐤄.. 𐤅𐤀𐤔.𐤉𐤑𐤀𐤄.𐤌𐤀𐤕.𐤉𐤄𐤅𐤄.𐤅𐤕𐤀𐤊𐤋.𐤀𐤕.𐤄𐤇𐤌𐤔
𐤉𐤌.𐤅𐤌𐤀𐤕𐤉𐤌.𐤀𐤉𐤔.𐤌𐤒𐤓𐤉𐤁𐤉.𐤄𐤒𐤈𐤓𐤕||

𐤁𐤌𐤃𐤁𐤓.𐤇𐤋𐤒 ..𐤉𐤆..

..𐤀.. 𐤅𐤉𐤃𐤁𐤓.𐤉𐤄𐤅𐤄.𐤀𐤋.𐤌𐤔𐤄.𐤋𐤀𐤌𐤓|
..𐤁.. 𐤀𐤌𐤓.𐤀𐤋.𐤀𐤋𐤏𐤆𐤓.𐤁𐤍.𐤀𐤄𐤓𐤍.𐤄𐤊𐤄𐤍.𐤅𐤉𐤓𐤌.𐤀𐤕.𐤄
𐤌𐤇𐤕𐤕.𐤌𐤁𐤉𐤍.𐤄𐤔𐤓𐤐𐤄.𐤅𐤀𐤕.𐤄𐤀𐤔.𐤆𐤓𐤄.𐤄𐤋𐤀𐤄.𐤊𐤉
.𐤒𐤃𐤔𐤅|
..𐤂.. 𐤀𐤕.𐤌𐤇𐤕𐤅𐤕.𐤄𐤇𐤈𐤀𐤉𐤌.𐤄𐤀𐤋𐤄.𐤁𐤍𐤐𐤔𐤕𐤌.𐤅𐤏𐤔
𐤅.𐤀𐤕𐤌.𐤓𐤒𐤏𐤉.𐤐𐤇𐤉𐤌.𐤑𐤐𐤅𐤉.𐤋𐤌𐤆𐤁𐤇.𐤊𐤉.𐤄𐤒𐤓𐤉𐤁
𐤌.𐤋𐤐𐤍𐤉.𐤉𐤄𐤅𐤄.𐤅𐤉𐤒𐤃𐤔𐤅.𐤅𐤉𐤄𐤉𐤅.𐤋𐤀𐤅𐤕.𐤋𐤁𐤍𐤉.𐤉𐤔𐤓
𐤀𐤋|
..𐤃.. 𐤅𐤉𐤒𐤇.𐤀𐤋𐤏𐤆𐤓.𐤄𐤊𐤄𐤍.𐤀𐤕.𐤌𐤇𐤕𐤅𐤕.𐤄𐤍𐤇𐤔𐤕.
𐤀𐤔𐤓.𐤄𐤒𐤓𐤉𐤁𐤅.𐤄𐤔𐤓𐤐𐤉𐤌.𐤅𐤉𐤓𐤒𐤏𐤅𐤌.𐤑𐤐𐤅𐤉.𐤋𐤌𐤆𐤁
𐤇|
..𐤄.. 𐤆𐤊𐤓𐤅𐤍.𐤋𐤁𐤍𐤉.𐤉𐤔𐤓𐤀𐤋.𐤋𐤌𐤏𐤍.𐤀𐤔𐤓.𐤋𐤀.𐤉𐤒𐤓𐤁.𐤀
𐤉𐤔.𐤆𐤓.𐤀𐤔𐤓.𐤋𐤀.𐤌𐤆𐤓𐤏.𐤀𐤄𐤓𐤍.𐤄𐤅𐤀.𐤋𐤄𐤒𐤈𐤉𐤓.𐤒
𐤈𐤓𐤕.𐤋𐤐𐤍𐤉.𐤉𐤄𐤅𐤄.𐤅𐤋𐤀.𐤉𐤄𐤉𐤄.𐤊𐤒𐤓𐤇.𐤅𐤊𐤏𐤃𐤕𐤅.𐤊
𐤀𐤔𐤓.𐤃𐤁𐤓.𐤉𐤄𐤅𐤄.𐤁𐤉𐤃.𐤌𐤔𐤄.𐤋𐤅|

6 𐤅𐤉𐤋𐤍𐤅.𐤊𐤋.𐤏𐤃𐤕.𐤁𐤍𐤉.𐤉𐤔𐤓𐤀𐤋.𐤌𐤌𐤇𐤓𐤕.𐤏𐤋.𐤌𐤔
𐤄.𐤅𐤏𐤋.𐤀𐤄𐤓𐤍.𐤋𐤀𐤌𐤓.𐤀𐤕𐤌.𐤄𐤌𐤕𐤌.𐤀𐤕.𐤏𐤌.𐤉𐤄𐤅𐤄|
7 𐤅𐤉𐤄𐤉.𐤁𐤄𐤒𐤄𐤋.𐤄𐤏𐤃𐤄.𐤏𐤋.𐤌𐤔𐤄.𐤅𐤏𐤋.𐤀𐤄𐤓𐤍.𐤅
𐤉𐤐𐤍𐤅.𐤀𐤋.𐤀𐤄𐤋.𐤌𐤅𐤏𐤃.𐤅𐤄𐤍𐤄.𐤊𐤎𐤄𐤅.𐤄𐤏𐤍𐤍.𐤅𐤉𐤓𐤀.𐤊𐤁
𐤅𐤃.𐤉𐤄𐤅𐤄|
8 𐤅𐤉𐤁𐤀.𐤌𐤔𐤄.𐤅𐤀𐤄𐤓𐤍.𐤀𐤋.𐤐𐤍𐤉.𐤀𐤄𐤋.𐤌𐤅𐤏𐤃|
9 𐤅𐤉𐤃𐤁𐤓.𐤉𐤄𐤅𐤄.𐤀𐤋.𐤌𐤔𐤄.𐤋𐤀𐤌𐤓|
10 𐤄𐤓𐤌𐤅.𐤌𐤕𐤅𐤊.𐤄𐤏𐤃𐤄.𐤄𐤆𐤀𐤕.𐤅𐤀𐤊𐤋𐤄.𐤀𐤕𐤌.𐤊
𐤓𐤂𐤏.𐤅𐤉𐤐𐤋𐤅.𐤏𐤋.𐤐𐤍𐤉𐤄𐤌|
11 𐤅𐤉𐤀𐤌𐤓.𐤌𐤔𐤄.𐤀𐤋.𐤀𐤄𐤓𐤍.𐤒𐤇.𐤀𐤕.𐤄𐤌𐤇𐤕𐤄.𐤅𐤕
𐤍.𐤏𐤋𐤉𐤄.𐤀𐤔.𐤌𐤏𐤋.𐤄𐤌𐤆𐤁𐤇.𐤅𐤔𐤉𐤌.𐤒𐤈𐤓𐤕.𐤅𐤄𐤅𐤋𐤊.
𐤌𐤄𐤓𐤄.𐤀𐤋.𐤄𐤏𐤃𐤄.𐤅𐤊𐤐𐤓.𐤏𐤋𐤉𐤄𐤌.𐤊𐤉.𐤉𐤑𐤀.𐤄𐤒𐤑𐤐
.𐤌𐤋𐤐𐤍𐤉.𐤉𐤄𐤅𐤄.𐤄𐤇𐤋.𐤄𐤍𐤂𐤐|
12 𐤅𐤉𐤒𐤇.𐤀𐤄𐤓𐤍.𐤊𐤀𐤔𐤓.𐤃𐤁𐤓.𐤌𐤔𐤄.𐤅𐤉𐤓𐤑.𐤀𐤋.𐤕𐤅
𐤊.𐤄𐤒𐤄𐤋.𐤅𐤄𐤍𐤄.𐤄𐤇𐤋.𐤄𐤍𐤂𐤐.𐤁𐤏𐤌.𐤅𐤉𐤕𐤍.𐤀𐤕.𐤄𐤒𐤈
𐤓𐤕.𐤅𐤉𐤊𐤐𐤓.𐤏𐤋.𐤄𐤏𐤌|
13 𐤅𐤉𐤏𐤌𐤃.𐤁𐤉𐤍.𐤄𐤌𐤕𐤉𐤌.𐤅𐤁𐤉𐤍.𐤄𐤇𐤉𐤉𐤌.𐤅𐤕𐤏𐤑𐤓
.𐤄𐤌𐤂𐤐𐤄|
14 𐤅𐤉𐤄𐤉𐤅.𐤄𐤌𐤕𐤉𐤌.𐤁𐤌𐤂𐤐𐤄.𐤀𐤓𐤁𐤏𐤄.𐤏𐤔𐤓.𐤀𐤋𐤐.
𐤅𐤔𐤁𐤏.𐤌𐤀𐤅𐤕.𐤌𐤋𐤁𐤃.𐤄𐤌𐤕𐤉𐤌.𐤏𐤋.𐤃𐤁𐤓.𐤒𐤓𐤇|
15 𐤅𐤉𐤔𐤁.𐤀𐤄𐤓𐤍.𐤀𐤋.𐤌𐤔𐤄.𐤀𐤋.𐤐𐤕𐤇.𐤀𐤄𐤋.𐤌𐤅𐤏𐤃.𐤅
𐤄𐤌𐤂𐤐𐤄.𐤍𐤏𐤑𐤓𐤄|
16 𐤅𐤉𐤃𐤁𐤓.𐤉𐤄𐤅𐤄.𐤀𐤋.𐤌𐤔𐤄.𐤋𐤀𐤌𐤓|
17 𐤃𐤁𐤓.𐤀𐤋.𐤁𐤍𐤉.𐤉𐤔𐤓𐤀𐤋.𐤅𐤒𐤇.𐤌𐤀𐤕𐤌.𐤌𐤈𐤄.𐤌𐤈
𐤄.𐤋𐤁𐤉𐤕.𐤀𐤁.𐤌𐤀𐤕.𐤊𐤋.𐤍𐤔𐤉𐤀𐤄𐤌.𐤋𐤁𐤉𐤕.𐤀𐤁𐤕𐤌.𐤔𐤍
𐤉𐤌.𐤏𐤔𐤓.𐤌𐤈𐤅𐤕.𐤀𐤉𐤔.𐤀𐤕.𐤔𐤌𐤅.𐤕𐤊𐤕𐤁.𐤏𐤋.𐤌𐤈𐤄𐤅|
18 𐤅𐤀𐤕.𐤔𐤌.𐤀𐤄𐤓𐤍.𐤕𐤊𐤕𐤁.𐤏𐤋.𐤌𐤈𐤄.𐤋𐤅𐤉.𐤊𐤉.𐤌𐤈
𐤄.𐤀𐤇𐤃.𐤋𐤓𐤀𐤔.𐤁𐤉𐤕.𐤀𐤁𐤅𐤕𐤌|
19 𐤅𐤄𐤍𐤇𐤕𐤌.𐤁𐤀𐤄𐤋.𐤌𐤅𐤏𐤃.𐤋𐤐𐤍𐤉.𐤄𐤏𐤃𐤅𐤕.𐤀𐤔𐤓.
𐤀𐤅𐤏𐤃.𐤋𐤊𐤌.𐤔𐤌𐤄|

20 𐤅𐤄𐤉𐤄.𐤄𐤀𐤉𐤔.𐤀𐤔𐤓.𐤀𐤁𐤇𐤓.𐤁𐤅.𐤌𐤈𐤄𐤅.𐤉𐤐𐤓𐤇.𐤅
𐤄𐤔𐤊𐤕𐤉.𐤌𐤏𐤋𐤉.𐤀𐤕.𐤕𐤋𐤍𐤅𐤕.𐤁𐤍𐤉.𐤉𐤔𐤓𐤀𐤋.𐤀𐤔𐤓.𐤄𐤌.
𐤌𐤋𐤉𐤍𐤌.𐤏𐤋𐤉𐤊𐤌|

21 𐤅𐤉𐤃𐤁𐤓.𐤌𐤔𐤄.𐤀𐤋.𐤁𐤍𐤉.𐤉𐤔𐤓𐤀𐤋.𐤅𐤉𐤕𐤍𐤅.𐤀𐤋𐤉𐤅.𐤊
𐤋.𐤍𐤔𐤉𐤀𐤉𐤄𐤌.𐤌𐤈𐤄.𐤋𐤍𐤔𐤉𐤀.𐤀𐤇𐤃.𐤌𐤈𐤄.𐤋𐤍𐤔𐤉𐤀.
𐤀𐤇𐤃.𐤋𐤁𐤉𐤕.𐤀𐤁𐤕𐤌.𐤔𐤍𐤉𐤌.𐤏𐤔𐤓.𐤌𐤈𐤅𐤕.𐤅𐤌𐤈𐤄.𐤀
𐤄𐤓𐤍.𐤁𐤕𐤅𐤊.𐤌𐤈𐤅𐤕𐤌|

22 𐤅𐤉𐤍𐤇.𐤌𐤔𐤄.𐤀𐤕.𐤄𐤌𐤈𐤕.𐤋𐤐𐤍𐤉.𐤉𐤄𐤅𐤄.𐤁𐤀𐤄𐤋.𐤄
𐤏𐤃𐤕|

23 𐤅𐤉𐤄𐤉.𐤌𐤌𐤇𐤓𐤕.𐤅𐤉𐤁𐤀.𐤌𐤔𐤄.𐤀𐤋.𐤀𐤄𐤋.𐤄𐤏𐤃𐤅
𐤕.𐤅𐤄𐤍𐤄.𐤐𐤓𐤇.𐤌𐤈𐤄.𐤀𐤄𐤓𐤍.𐤋𐤁𐤉𐤕.𐤋𐤅𐤉.𐤅𐤉𐤑𐤀.𐤐𐤓𐤇.𐤅
𐤉𐤑𐤑.𐤑𐤉𐤑.𐤅𐤉𐤂𐤌𐤋.𐤔𐤒𐤃𐤉𐤌|

24 𐤅𐤉𐤑𐤀.𐤌𐤔𐤄.𐤀𐤕.𐤊𐤋.𐤄𐤌𐤈𐤕.𐤌𐤋𐤐𐤍𐤉.𐤉𐤄𐤅𐤄.𐤀
𐤋.𐤊𐤋.𐤁𐤍𐤉.𐤉𐤔𐤓𐤀𐤋.𐤅𐤉𐤓𐤀𐤅.𐤅𐤉𐤒𐤇𐤅.𐤀𐤉𐤔.𐤌𐤈𐤄𐤅|

25 𐤅𐤉𐤀𐤌𐤓.𐤉𐤄𐤅𐤄.𐤀𐤋.𐤌𐤔𐤄.𐤄𐤔𐤁.𐤀𐤕.𐤌𐤈𐤄.𐤀𐤄𐤓
𐤍.𐤋𐤐𐤍𐤉.𐤄𐤏𐤃𐤅𐤕.𐤋𐤌𐤔𐤌𐤓𐤕.𐤋𐤀𐤅𐤕.𐤋𐤁𐤍𐤉.𐤌𐤓𐤉.𐤅𐤕𐤊𐤋.
𐤕𐤋𐤅𐤍𐤕𐤌.𐤌𐤏𐤋𐤉.𐤅𐤋𐤀.𐤉𐤌𐤕𐤅|

26 𐤅𐤉𐤏𐤔.𐤌𐤔𐤄.𐤊𐤀𐤔𐤓.𐤑𐤅𐤄.𐤉𐤄𐤅𐤄.𐤀𐤕𐤅.𐤊𐤍.𐤏𐤔𐤄
|

27 𐤅𐤉𐤀𐤌𐤓𐤅.𐤁𐤍𐤉.𐤉𐤔𐤓𐤀𐤋.𐤀𐤋.𐤌𐤔𐤄.𐤋𐤀𐤌𐤓.𐤄𐤍.𐤂𐤅
𐤏𐤍𐤅.𐤀𐤁𐤃𐤍𐤅.𐤊𐤋𐤍𐤅.𐤀𐤁𐤃𐤍𐤅|

28 𐤊𐤋.𐤄𐤒𐤓𐤁.𐤄𐤒𐤓𐤁.𐤀𐤋.𐤌𐤔𐤊𐤍.𐤉𐤄𐤅𐤄.𐤉𐤌𐤅𐤕.𐤄𐤀
𐤌.𐤕𐤌𐤍𐤅.𐤋𐤂𐤅𐤏||

𐤁𐤌𐤃𐤁𐤓.𐤇𐤋𐤒 18

1 𐤅𐤉𐤀𐤌𐤓.𐤉𐤄𐤅𐤄.𐤀𐤋.𐤀𐤄𐤓𐤍.𐤀𐤕𐤄.𐤅𐤁𐤍𐤉𐤊.𐤅𐤁𐤉𐤕.𐤀
𐤁𐤉𐤊.𐤀𐤕𐤊.𐤕𐤔𐤀𐤅.𐤀𐤕.𐤏𐤅𐤍.𐤄𐤌𐤒𐤃𐤔.𐤅𐤀𐤕𐤄.𐤅𐤁𐤍𐤉𐤊.
𐤀𐤕𐤊.𐤕𐤔𐤀𐤅.𐤀𐤕.𐤏𐤅𐤍.𐤊𐤄𐤍𐤕𐤊𐤌|

ב 𐤅𐤂𐤌.𐤀𐤕.𐤀𐤇𐤉𐤊.𐤌𐤈𐤄.𐤋𐤅𐤉.𐤔𐤁𐤈.𐤀𐤁𐤉𐤊.𐤄𐤒𐤓𐤁
.𐤀𐤕𐤊.𐤅𐤉𐤋𐤅𐤅.𐤏𐤋𐤉𐤊.𐤅𐤉𐤔𐤓𐤕𐤅𐤊.𐤅𐤀𐤕𐤄.𐤅𐤁𐤍𐤉𐤊.𐤀𐤕𐤊.𐤋
𐤐𐤍𐤉.𐤀𐤄𐤋.𐤄𐤏𐤃𐤕|

ג 𐤅𐤔𐤌𐤓𐤅.𐤌𐤔𐤌𐤓𐤕𐤊.𐤅𐤌𐤔𐤌𐤓𐤕.𐤊𐤋.𐤄𐤀𐤄𐤋.𐤀𐤊.𐤀𐤋.
𐤊𐤋𐤉.𐤄𐤒𐤃𐤔.𐤅𐤀𐤋.𐤄𐤌𐤆𐤁𐤇.𐤋𐤀.𐤉𐤒𐤓𐤁𐤅.𐤅𐤋𐤀.𐤉𐤌𐤕𐤅.
𐤂𐤌.𐤄𐤌.𐤂𐤌.𐤀𐤕𐤌|

ד 𐤅𐤍𐤋𐤅𐤅.𐤏𐤋𐤉𐤊.𐤅𐤔𐤌𐤓𐤅.𐤀𐤕.𐤌𐤔𐤌𐤓𐤕.𐤀𐤄𐤋.𐤌𐤅𐤏𐤃.
𐤋𐤊𐤋.𐤏𐤁𐤃𐤕.𐤄𐤀𐤄𐤋.𐤅𐤆𐤓.𐤋𐤀.𐤉𐤒𐤓𐤁.𐤀𐤋𐤉𐤊𐤌|

ה 𐤅𐤔𐤌𐤓𐤕𐤌.𐤀𐤕.𐤌𐤔𐤌𐤓𐤕.𐤄𐤒𐤃𐤔.𐤅𐤀𐤕.𐤌𐤔𐤌𐤓𐤕.𐤄
𐤌𐤆𐤁𐤇.𐤅𐤋𐤀.𐤉𐤄𐤉𐤄.𐤏𐤅𐤃.𐤒𐤑𐤐.𐤏𐤋.𐤁𐤍𐤉.𐤉𐤔𐤓𐤀𐤋|

ו 𐤅𐤀𐤍𐤉.𐤄𐤍𐤄.𐤋𐤒𐤇𐤕𐤉.𐤀𐤕.𐤀𐤇𐤉𐤊𐤌.𐤄𐤋𐤅𐤉𐤌.𐤌𐤕𐤅
𐤊.𐤁𐤍𐤉.𐤉𐤔𐤓𐤀𐤋.𐤋𐤊𐤌.𐤌𐤕𐤍𐤄.𐤍𐤕𐤍𐤉𐤌.𐤋𐤉𐤄𐤅𐤄.𐤋𐤏𐤁𐤃
.𐤀𐤕.𐤏𐤁𐤃𐤕.𐤀𐤄𐤋.𐤌𐤅𐤏𐤃|

ז 𐤅𐤀𐤕𐤄.𐤅𐤁𐤍𐤉𐤊.𐤀𐤕𐤊.𐤕𐤔𐤌𐤓𐤅.𐤀𐤕.𐤊𐤄𐤍𐤕𐤊𐤌.𐤋𐤊
𐤋.𐤃𐤁𐤓.𐤄𐤌𐤆𐤁𐤇.𐤅𐤋𐤌𐤁𐤉𐤕.𐤋𐤐𐤓𐤊𐤕.𐤅𐤏𐤁𐤃𐤕𐤌.𐤏𐤁
𐤃𐤕.𐤌𐤕𐤍𐤄.𐤀𐤕𐤍.𐤀𐤕.𐤊𐤄𐤍𐤕𐤊𐤌.𐤅𐤄𐤆𐤓.𐤄𐤒𐤓𐤁.𐤉𐤅𐤌
𐤕|

ח 𐤅𐤉𐤃𐤁𐤓.𐤉𐤄𐤅𐤄.𐤀𐤋.𐤀𐤄𐤓𐤍.𐤅𐤀𐤍𐤉.𐤄𐤍𐤄.𐤍𐤕𐤕𐤉.𐤋𐤊.
𐤀𐤕.𐤌𐤔𐤌𐤓𐤕.𐤕𐤓𐤅𐤌𐤕𐤉.𐤋𐤊𐤋.𐤒𐤃𐤔𐤉.𐤁𐤍𐤉.𐤉𐤔𐤓𐤀𐤋.𐤋
𐤊.𐤍𐤕𐤕𐤉𐤌.𐤋𐤌𐤔𐤇𐤄.𐤅𐤋𐤁𐤍𐤉𐤊.𐤋𐤇𐤒.𐤏𐤅𐤋𐤌|

ט 𐤆𐤄.𐤉𐤄𐤉𐤄.𐤋𐤊.𐤌𐤒𐤃𐤔.𐤄𐤒𐤃𐤔𐤉𐤌.𐤌𐤍.𐤄𐤀𐤔.
𐤊𐤋.𐤒𐤓𐤁𐤍𐤌.𐤋𐤊𐤋.𐤌𐤍𐤇𐤕𐤌.𐤅𐤋𐤊𐤋.𐤇𐤈𐤀𐤕𐤌.𐤅𐤋𐤊𐤋.𐤀
𐤔𐤌𐤌.𐤀𐤔𐤓.𐤉𐤔𐤉𐤁𐤅.𐤋𐤉.𐤒𐤃𐤔.𐤒𐤃𐤔𐤉𐤌.𐤋𐤊.𐤄𐤅𐤀.𐤅𐤋
𐤁𐤍𐤉𐤊|

י 𐤁𐤒𐤃𐤔.𐤄𐤒𐤃𐤔𐤉𐤌.𐤕𐤀𐤊𐤋𐤍𐤅.𐤊𐤋.𐤆𐤊𐤓.𐤉𐤀𐤊𐤋.
𐤀𐤕𐤅.𐤒𐤃𐤔.𐤉𐤄𐤉𐤄.𐤋𐤊|

יא 𐤅𐤆𐤄.𐤋𐤊.𐤕𐤓𐤅𐤌𐤕.𐤌𐤕𐤍𐤌.𐤋𐤊𐤋.𐤕𐤍𐤅𐤐𐤕.𐤁𐤍𐤉.𐤉𐤔𐤓
𐤀𐤋.𐤋𐤊.𐤍𐤕𐤕𐤉𐤌.𐤅𐤋𐤁𐤍𐤉𐤊.𐤅𐤋𐤁𐤍𐤕𐤉𐤊.𐤀𐤕𐤊.𐤋𐤇𐤒.𐤏𐤅𐤋
𐤌.𐤊𐤋.𐤈𐤄𐤅𐤓.𐤁𐤁𐤉𐤕𐤊.𐤉𐤀𐤊𐤋.𐤀𐤕𐤅|

יב 𐤊𐤋.𐤇𐤋𐤁.𐤉𐤑𐤄𐤓.𐤅𐤊𐤋.𐤇𐤋𐤁.𐤕𐤉𐤓𐤅𐤔.𐤅𐤃𐤂𐤍.𐤓𐤀
𐤔𐤉𐤕𐤌.𐤀𐤔𐤓.𐤉𐤕𐤍𐤅.𐤋𐤉𐤄𐤅𐤄.𐤋𐤊.𐤍𐤕𐤕𐤉𐤌|

..𐤉𐤂.. 𐤁𐤊𐤅𐤓𐤉.𐤊𐤋.𐤀𐤔𐤓.𐤁𐤀𐤓𐤑𐤌.𐤀𐤔𐤓.𐤉𐤁𐤉𐤀𐤅.𐤋𐤉𐤄𐤅
𐤄.𐤋𐤊.𐤉𐤄𐤉𐤄.𐤊𐤋.𐤈𐤄𐤅𐤓.𐤁𐤁𐤉𐤕𐤊.𐤉𐤀𐤊𐤋𐤍𐤅|

..𐤉𐤃.. 𐤊𐤋.𐤇𐤓𐤌.𐤁𐤉𐤔𐤓𐤀𐤋.𐤋𐤊.𐤉𐤄𐤉𐤄|

..𐤈𐤅.. 𐤊𐤋.𐤐𐤈𐤓.𐤓𐤇𐤌.𐤋𐤊𐤋.𐤁𐤔𐤓.𐤀𐤔𐤓.𐤉𐤒𐤓𐤉𐤁𐤅.𐤋𐤉𐤄𐤅
𐤄.𐤁𐤀𐤃𐤌.𐤅𐤁𐤁𐤄𐤌𐤄.𐤉𐤄𐤉𐤄.𐤋𐤊.𐤀𐤊.𐤐𐤃𐤄.𐤕𐤐𐤃𐤄.𐤀
𐤕.𐤁𐤊𐤅𐤓.𐤄𐤀𐤃𐤌.𐤅𐤀𐤕.𐤁𐤊𐤅𐤓.𐤄𐤁𐤄𐤌𐤄.𐤄𐤈𐤌𐤀𐤄.𐤕𐤐
𐤃𐤄|

..𐤈𐤆.. 𐤅𐤐𐤃𐤅𐤉𐤅.𐤌𐤁𐤍.𐤇𐤃𐤔.𐤕𐤐𐤃𐤄.𐤁𐤏𐤓𐤊𐤊.𐤊𐤎𐤐.𐤇𐤌
𐤔𐤕.𐤔𐤒𐤋𐤉𐤌.𐤁𐤔𐤒𐤋.𐤄𐤒𐤃𐤔.𐤏𐤔𐤓𐤉𐤌.𐤂𐤓𐤄.𐤄𐤅𐤀|

..𐤉𐤆.. 𐤀𐤊.𐤁𐤊𐤅𐤓.𐤔𐤅𐤓.𐤀𐤅.𐤁𐤊𐤅𐤓.𐤊𐤔𐤁.𐤀𐤅.𐤁𐤊𐤅𐤓.𐤏𐤆.𐤋
𐤀.𐤕𐤐𐤃𐤄.𐤒𐤃𐤔.𐤄𐤌.𐤀𐤕.𐤃𐤌𐤌.𐤕𐤆𐤓𐤒.𐤏𐤋.𐤄𐤌𐤆𐤁
𐤇.𐤅𐤀𐤕.𐤇𐤋𐤁𐤌.𐤕𐤒𐤈𐤉𐤓.𐤀𐤔𐤄.𐤋𐤓𐤉𐤇.𐤍𐤉𐤇𐤇.𐤋𐤉𐤄𐤅
𐤄|

..𐤉𐤇.. 𐤅𐤁𐤔𐤓𐤌.𐤉𐤄𐤉𐤄.𐤋𐤊.𐤊𐤇𐤆𐤄.𐤄𐤕𐤍𐤅𐤐𐤄.𐤅𐤊𐤔𐤅𐤒.𐤄
𐤉𐤌𐤉𐤍.𐤋𐤊.𐤉𐤄𐤉𐤄|

..𐤉𐤈.. 𐤊𐤋.𐤕𐤓𐤅𐤌𐤕.𐤄𐤒𐤃𐤔𐤉𐤌.𐤀𐤔𐤓.𐤉𐤓𐤉𐤌𐤅.𐤁𐤍𐤉.𐤉𐤔
𐤓𐤀𐤋.𐤋𐤉𐤄𐤅𐤄.𐤍𐤕𐤕𐤉.𐤋𐤊.𐤅𐤋𐤁𐤍𐤉𐤊.𐤅𐤋𐤁𐤍𐤕𐤉𐤊.𐤀𐤕𐤊.𐤋
𐤇𐤒.𐤏𐤅𐤋𐤌.𐤁𐤓𐤉𐤕.𐤌𐤋𐤇.𐤏𐤅𐤋𐤌.𐤄𐤅𐤀.𐤋𐤐𐤍𐤉.𐤉𐤄𐤅𐤄.𐤋𐤊.
𐤅𐤋𐤆𐤓𐤏𐤊.𐤀𐤕𐤊|

..𐤊.. 𐤅𐤉𐤀𐤌𐤓.𐤉𐤄𐤅𐤄.𐤀𐤋.𐤀𐤄𐤓𐤍.𐤁𐤀𐤓𐤑𐤌.𐤋𐤀.𐤕𐤍𐤇𐤋.𐤅
𐤇𐤋𐤒.𐤋𐤀.𐤉𐤄𐤉𐤄.𐤋𐤊.𐤁𐤕𐤅𐤊𐤌.𐤀𐤍𐤉.𐤇𐤋𐤒𐤊.𐤅𐤍𐤇𐤋𐤕𐤊.
𐤁𐤕𐤅𐤊.𐤁𐤍𐤉.𐤉𐤔𐤓𐤀𐤋|

..𐤊𐤀.. 𐤅𐤋𐤁𐤍𐤉.𐤋𐤅𐤉.𐤄𐤍𐤄.𐤍𐤕𐤕𐤉.𐤊𐤋.𐤌𐤏𐤔𐤓.𐤁𐤉𐤔𐤓𐤀𐤋.𐤋
𐤍𐤇𐤋𐤄.𐤇𐤋𐤐.𐤏𐤁𐤃𐤕𐤌.𐤀𐤔𐤓.𐤄𐤌.𐤏𐤁𐤃𐤉𐤌.𐤀𐤕.𐤏𐤁
𐤃𐤕.𐤀𐤄𐤋.𐤌𐤅𐤏𐤃|

..𐤊𐤁.. 𐤅𐤋𐤀.𐤉𐤒𐤓𐤁𐤅.𐤏𐤅𐤃.𐤁𐤍𐤉.𐤉𐤔𐤓𐤀𐤋.𐤀𐤋.𐤀𐤄𐤋.𐤌𐤅𐤏
𐤃.𐤋𐤔𐤀𐤕.𐤇𐤈𐤀.𐤋𐤌𐤅𐤕|

..𐤊𐤂.. 𐤅𐤏𐤁𐤃.𐤄𐤋𐤅𐤉.𐤄𐤅𐤀.𐤀𐤕.𐤏𐤁𐤃𐤕.𐤀𐤄𐤋.𐤌𐤅𐤏𐤃.𐤅
𐤄𐤌.𐤉𐤔𐤀𐤅.𐤏𐤅𐤍𐤌.𐤇𐤒𐤕.𐤏𐤅𐤋𐤌.𐤋𐤃𐤓𐤕𐤉𐤊𐤌.𐤅𐤁𐤕𐤅𐤊.𐤁
𐤍𐤉.𐤉𐤔𐤓𐤀𐤋.𐤋𐤀.𐤉𐤍𐤇𐤋𐤅.𐤍𐤇𐤋𐤄|

..𐤊𐤃..𐤊𐤉.𐤀𐤕.𐤌𐤏𐤔𐤓.𐤁𐤍𐤉.𐤉𐤔𐤓𐤀𐤋.𐤀𐤔𐤓.𐤉𐤓𐤉𐤌𐤅.𐤋𐤉
𐤄𐤅𐤄.𐤕𐤓𐤅𐤌𐤄.𐤍𐤕𐤕𐤉.𐤋𐤋𐤅𐤉𐤌.𐤋𐤍𐤇𐤋𐤄.𐤏𐤋.𐤊𐤍.𐤀𐤌𐤓𐤕𐤉
.𐤋𐤄𐤌.𐤁𐤕𐤅𐤊.𐤁𐤍𐤉.𐤉𐤔𐤓𐤀𐤋.𐤋𐤀.𐤉𐤍𐤇𐤋𐤅.𐤍𐤇𐤋𐤄|

..𐤊𐤄..𐤅𐤉𐤃𐤁𐤓.𐤉𐤄𐤅𐤄.𐤀𐤋.𐤌𐤔𐤄.𐤋𐤀𐤌𐤓|

..𐤊𐤅..𐤅𐤀𐤋.𐤄𐤋𐤅𐤉𐤌.𐤕𐤃𐤁𐤓.𐤅𐤀𐤌𐤓𐤕.𐤀𐤋𐤄𐤌.𐤊𐤉.𐤕𐤒𐤇𐤅
.𐤌𐤀𐤕.𐤁𐤍𐤉.𐤉𐤔𐤓𐤀𐤋.𐤀𐤕.𐤄𐤌𐤏𐤔𐤓.𐤀𐤔𐤓.𐤍𐤕𐤕𐤉.𐤋𐤊𐤌.
𐤌𐤀𐤕𐤌.𐤁𐤍𐤇𐤋𐤕𐤊𐤌.𐤅𐤄𐤓𐤌𐤕𐤌.𐤌𐤌𐤍𐤅.𐤕𐤓𐤅𐤌𐤕.𐤉𐤄𐤅𐤄.
𐤌𐤏𐤔𐤓.𐤌𐤍.𐤄𐤌𐤏𐤔𐤓|

..𐤊𐤆..𐤅𐤍𐤇𐤔𐤁.𐤋𐤊𐤌.𐤕𐤓𐤅𐤌𐤕𐤊𐤌.𐤊𐤃𐤂𐤍.𐤌𐤍.𐤄𐤂𐤓𐤍.𐤅
𐤊𐤌𐤋𐤀𐤄.𐤌𐤍.𐤄𐤉𐤒𐤁|

..𐤊𐤇..𐤊𐤍.𐤕𐤓𐤉𐤌𐤅.𐤂𐤌.𐤀𐤕𐤌.𐤕𐤓𐤅𐤌𐤕.𐤉𐤄𐤅𐤄.𐤌𐤊𐤋.𐤌𐤏
𐤔𐤓𐤕𐤉𐤊𐤌.𐤀𐤔𐤓.𐤕𐤒𐤇𐤅.𐤌𐤀𐤕.𐤁𐤍𐤉.𐤉𐤔𐤓𐤀𐤋.𐤅𐤍𐤕𐤕𐤌.
𐤌𐤌𐤍𐤅.𐤀𐤕.𐤕𐤓𐤅𐤌𐤕.𐤉𐤄𐤅𐤄.𐤋𐤀𐤄𐤓𐤍.𐤄𐤊𐤄𐤍|

..𐤊𐤈..𐤌𐤊𐤋.𐤌𐤕𐤍𐤕𐤉𐤊𐤌.𐤕𐤓𐤉𐤌𐤅.𐤀𐤕.𐤊𐤋.𐤕𐤓𐤅𐤌𐤕.𐤉𐤄𐤅
𐤄.𐤌𐤊𐤋.𐤇𐤋𐤁𐤅.𐤀𐤕.𐤌𐤒𐤃𐤔𐤅.𐤌𐤌𐤍𐤅|

..𐤋..𐤅𐤀𐤌𐤓𐤕.𐤀𐤋𐤄𐤌.𐤁𐤄𐤓𐤉𐤌𐤊𐤌.𐤀𐤕.𐤇𐤋𐤁𐤅.𐤌𐤌𐤍𐤅.𐤅
𐤍𐤇𐤔𐤁.𐤋𐤋𐤅𐤉𐤌.𐤊𐤕𐤁𐤅𐤀𐤕.𐤂𐤓𐤍.𐤅𐤊𐤕𐤁𐤅𐤀𐤕.𐤉𐤒𐤁|

..𐤋𐤀..𐤅𐤀𐤊𐤋𐤕𐤌.𐤀𐤕𐤅.𐤁𐤊𐤋.𐤌𐤒𐤅𐤌.𐤀𐤕𐤌.𐤅𐤁𐤉𐤕𐤊𐤌.𐤊𐤉
.𐤔𐤊𐤓.𐤄𐤅𐤀.𐤋𐤊𐤌.𐤇𐤋𐤐.𐤏𐤁𐤃𐤕𐤊𐤌.𐤁𐤀𐤄𐤋.𐤌𐤅𐤏𐤃|

..𐤋𐤁..𐤅𐤋𐤀.𐤕𐤔𐤀𐤅.𐤏𐤋𐤉𐤅.𐤇𐤈𐤀.𐤁𐤄𐤓𐤉𐤌𐤊𐤌.𐤀𐤕.𐤇𐤋𐤁
𐤅.𐤌𐤌𐤍𐤅.𐤅𐤀𐤕.𐤒𐤃𐤔𐤉.𐤁𐤍𐤉.𐤉𐤔𐤓𐤀𐤋.𐤋𐤀.𐤕𐤇𐤋𐤋𐤅.𐤅𐤋𐤀.
𐤕𐤌𐤅𐤕𐤅|

𐤁𐤌𐤃𐤁𐤓.𐤇𐤋𐤒..𐤉𐤈..

..𐤀..𐤅𐤉𐤃𐤁𐤓.𐤉𐤄𐤅𐤄.𐤀𐤋.𐤌𐤔𐤄.𐤅𐤀𐤋.𐤀𐤄𐤓𐤍.𐤋𐤀𐤌𐤓|

..𐤁..𐤆𐤀𐤕.𐤇𐤒𐤕.𐤄𐤕𐤅𐤓𐤄.𐤀𐤔𐤓.𐤑𐤅𐤄.𐤉𐤄𐤅𐤄.𐤋𐤀𐤌𐤓.
𐤃𐤁𐤓.𐤀𐤋.𐤁𐤍𐤉.𐤉𐤔𐤓𐤀𐤋.𐤅𐤉𐤒𐤇𐤅.𐤀𐤋𐤉𐤊.𐤐𐤓𐤄.𐤀𐤃𐤌𐤄.
𐤕𐤌𐤉𐤌𐤄.𐤀𐤔𐤓.𐤀𐤉𐤍.𐤁𐤄.𐤌𐤅𐤌.𐤀𐤔𐤓.𐤋𐤀.𐤏𐤋𐤄.𐤏𐤋𐤉𐤄.
𐤏𐤋|

𐤂 𐤅𐤍𐤕𐤕𐤌.𐤀𐤕𐤄.𐤀𐤋.𐤀𐤋𐤏𐤆𐤓.𐤄𐤊𐤄𐤍.𐤅𐤄𐤅𐤑𐤉𐤀.𐤀
𐤕𐤄.𐤀𐤋.𐤌𐤇𐤅𐤑.𐤋𐤌𐤇𐤍𐤄.𐤅𐤔𐤇𐤈.𐤀𐤕𐤄.𐤋𐤐𐤍𐤉𐤅|
𐤃 𐤅𐤋𐤒𐤇.𐤀𐤋𐤏𐤆𐤓.𐤄𐤊𐤄𐤍.𐤌𐤃𐤌𐤄.𐤁𐤀𐤑𐤁𐤏𐤅.𐤅𐤄𐤆
𐤄.𐤀𐤋.𐤍𐤊𐤇.𐤐𐤍𐤉.𐤀𐤄𐤋.𐤌𐤅𐤏𐤃.𐤌𐤃𐤌𐤄.𐤔𐤁𐤏.𐤐𐤏𐤌𐤉𐤌
|
𐤄 𐤅𐤔𐤓𐤐.𐤀𐤕.𐤄𐤐𐤓𐤄.𐤋𐤏𐤉𐤍𐤉𐤅.𐤀𐤕.𐤏𐤓𐤄.𐤅𐤀𐤕.𐤁𐤔𐤓𐤄
.𐤅𐤀𐤕.𐤃𐤌𐤄.𐤏𐤋.𐤐𐤓𐤔𐤄.𐤉𐤔𐤓𐤐|
𐤅 𐤅𐤋𐤒𐤇.𐤄𐤊𐤄𐤍.𐤏𐤑.𐤀𐤓𐤆.𐤅𐤀𐤆𐤅𐤁.𐤅𐤔𐤍𐤉.𐤕𐤅𐤋𐤏𐤕.
𐤅𐤄𐤔𐤋𐤉𐤊.𐤀𐤋.𐤕𐤅𐤊.𐤔𐤓𐤐𐤕.𐤄𐤐𐤓𐤄|
𐤆 𐤅𐤊𐤁𐤎.𐤁𐤂𐤃𐤉𐤅.𐤄𐤊𐤄𐤍.𐤅𐤓𐤇𐤑.𐤁𐤔𐤓𐤅.𐤁𐤌𐤉𐤌.𐤅𐤀
𐤇𐤓.𐤉𐤁𐤅𐤀.𐤀𐤋.𐤄𐤌𐤇𐤍𐤄.𐤅𐤈𐤌𐤀.𐤄𐤊𐤄𐤍.𐤏𐤃.𐤄𐤏𐤓𐤁|
𐤇 𐤅𐤄𐤔𐤓𐤐.𐤀𐤕𐤄.𐤉𐤊𐤁𐤎.𐤁𐤂𐤃𐤉𐤅.𐤁𐤌𐤉𐤌.𐤅𐤓𐤇𐤑.𐤁𐤔
𐤓𐤅.𐤁𐤌𐤉𐤌.𐤅𐤈𐤌𐤀.𐤏𐤃.𐤄𐤏𐤓𐤁|
𐤈 𐤅𐤀𐤎𐤐.𐤀𐤉𐤔.𐤈𐤄𐤅𐤓.𐤀𐤕.𐤀𐤐𐤓.𐤄𐤐𐤓𐤄.𐤅𐤄𐤍𐤉𐤇.𐤌𐤇
𐤅𐤑.𐤋𐤌𐤇𐤍𐤄.𐤁𐤌𐤒𐤅𐤌.𐤈𐤄𐤅𐤓.𐤅𐤄𐤉𐤕𐤄.𐤋𐤏𐤃𐤕.𐤁𐤍𐤉.𐤉
𐤔𐤓𐤀𐤋.𐤋𐤌𐤔𐤌𐤓𐤕.𐤋𐤌𐤉.𐤍𐤃𐤄.𐤇𐤈𐤀𐤕.𐤄𐤅𐤀|
𐤉 𐤅𐤊𐤁𐤎.𐤄𐤀𐤎𐤐.𐤀𐤕.𐤀𐤐𐤓.𐤄𐤐𐤓𐤄.𐤀𐤕.𐤁𐤂𐤃𐤉𐤅.𐤅𐤈
𐤌𐤀.𐤏𐤃.𐤄𐤏𐤓𐤁.𐤅𐤄𐤉𐤕𐤄.𐤋𐤁𐤍𐤉.𐤉𐤔𐤓𐤀𐤋.𐤅𐤋𐤂𐤓.𐤄𐤂𐤓.
𐤁𐤕𐤅𐤊𐤌.𐤋𐤇𐤒𐤕.𐤏𐤅𐤋𐤌|
𐤉𐤀 𐤄𐤍𐤂𐤏.𐤁𐤌𐤕.𐤋𐤊𐤋.𐤍𐤐𐤔.𐤀𐤃𐤌.𐤅𐤈𐤌𐤀.𐤔𐤁𐤏𐤕.𐤉
𐤌𐤉𐤌|
𐤉𐤁 𐤄𐤅𐤀.𐤉𐤕𐤇𐤈𐤀.𐤁𐤅.𐤁𐤉𐤅𐤌.𐤄𐤔𐤋𐤉𐤔𐤉.𐤅𐤁𐤉𐤅𐤌.𐤄𐤔
𐤁𐤉𐤏𐤉.𐤉𐤈𐤄𐤓.𐤅𐤀𐤌.𐤋𐤀.𐤉𐤕𐤇𐤈𐤀.𐤁𐤉𐤅𐤌.𐤄𐤔𐤋𐤉𐤔𐤉.𐤅
𐤁𐤉𐤅𐤌.𐤄𐤔𐤁𐤉𐤏𐤉.𐤋𐤀.𐤉𐤈𐤄𐤓|
𐤉𐤂 𐤊𐤋.𐤄𐤍𐤂𐤏.𐤁𐤌𐤕.𐤁𐤍𐤐𐤔.𐤄𐤀𐤃𐤌.𐤀𐤔𐤓.𐤉𐤌𐤅𐤕.𐤅𐤋
𐤀.𐤉𐤕𐤇𐤈𐤀.𐤀𐤕.𐤌𐤔𐤊𐤍.𐤉𐤄𐤅𐤄.𐤈𐤌𐤀.𐤅𐤍𐤊𐤓𐤕𐤄.𐤄𐤍𐤐
𐤔.𐤄𐤄𐤅𐤀.𐤌𐤉𐤔𐤓𐤀𐤋.𐤊𐤉.𐤌𐤉.𐤍𐤃𐤄.𐤋𐤀.𐤆𐤓𐤒.𐤏𐤋𐤉𐤅.𐤈
𐤌𐤀.𐤉𐤄𐤉𐤄.𐤏𐤅𐤃.𐤈𐤌𐤀𐤕𐤅.𐤁𐤅|
𐤉𐤃 𐤆𐤀𐤕.𐤄𐤕𐤅𐤓𐤄.𐤀𐤃𐤌.𐤊𐤉.𐤉𐤌𐤅𐤕.𐤁𐤀𐤄𐤋.𐤊𐤋.𐤄𐤁
𐤀.𐤀𐤋.𐤄𐤀𐤄𐤋.𐤅𐤊𐤋.𐤀𐤔𐤓.𐤁𐤀𐤄𐤋.𐤉𐤈𐤌𐤀.𐤔𐤁𐤏𐤕.𐤉𐤌𐤉
𐤌|

15 𐤅𐤊𐤋.𐤊𐤋𐤉.𐤐𐤕𐤅𐤇.𐤀𐤔𐤓.𐤀𐤉𐤍.𐤑𐤌𐤉𐤃.𐤐𐤕𐤉𐤋.𐤏𐤋
𐤉𐤅.𐤈𐤌𐤀.𐤄𐤅𐤀|

16 𐤅𐤊𐤋.𐤀𐤔𐤓.𐤉𐤂𐤏.𐤏𐤋.𐤐𐤍𐤉.𐤄𐤔𐤃𐤄.𐤁𐤇𐤋𐤋.𐤇𐤓𐤁.
𐤀𐤅.𐤁𐤌𐤕.𐤀𐤅.𐤁𐤏𐤑𐤌.𐤀𐤃𐤌.𐤀𐤅.𐤁𐤒𐤁𐤓.𐤉𐤈𐤌𐤀.𐤔𐤁𐤏
𐤕.𐤉𐤌𐤉𐤌|

17 𐤅𐤋𐤒𐤇𐤅.𐤋𐤈𐤌𐤀.𐤌𐤏𐤐𐤓.𐤔𐤓𐤐𐤕.𐤄𐤇𐤈𐤀𐤕.𐤅𐤍𐤕𐤍.
𐤏𐤋𐤉𐤅.𐤌𐤉𐤌.𐤇𐤉𐤉𐤌.𐤀𐤋.𐤊𐤋𐤉|

18 𐤅𐤋𐤒𐤇.𐤀𐤆𐤅𐤁.𐤅𐤈𐤁𐤋.𐤁𐤌𐤉𐤌.𐤀𐤉𐤔.𐤈𐤄𐤅𐤓.𐤅𐤄𐤆
𐤄.𐤏𐤋.𐤄𐤀𐤄𐤋.𐤅𐤏𐤋.𐤊𐤋.𐤄𐤊𐤋𐤉𐤌.𐤅𐤏𐤋.𐤄𐤍𐤐𐤔𐤅𐤕.𐤀𐤔𐤓.
𐤄𐤉𐤅.𐤔𐤌.𐤅𐤏𐤋.𐤄𐤍𐤂𐤏.𐤁𐤏𐤑𐤌.𐤀𐤅.𐤁𐤇𐤋𐤋.𐤀𐤅.𐤁𐤌𐤕.𐤀𐤅
.𐤁𐤒𐤁𐤓|

19 𐤅𐤄𐤆𐤄.𐤄𐤈𐤄𐤓.𐤏𐤋.𐤄𐤈𐤌𐤀.𐤁𐤉𐤅𐤌.𐤄𐤔𐤋𐤉𐤔𐤉.𐤅
𐤁𐤉𐤅𐤌.𐤄𐤔𐤁𐤉𐤏𐤉.𐤅𐤇𐤈𐤀𐤅.𐤁𐤉𐤅𐤌.𐤄𐤔𐤁𐤉𐤏𐤉.𐤅𐤊𐤁𐤎.𐤁
𐤂𐤃𐤉𐤅.𐤅𐤓𐤇𐤑.𐤁𐤌𐤉𐤌.𐤅𐤈𐤄𐤓.𐤁𐤏𐤓𐤁|

20 𐤅𐤀𐤉𐤔.𐤀𐤔𐤓.𐤉𐤈𐤌𐤀.𐤅𐤋𐤀.𐤉𐤕𐤇𐤈𐤀.𐤅𐤍𐤊𐤓𐤕𐤄.𐤄
𐤍𐤐𐤔.𐤄𐤄𐤅𐤀.𐤌𐤕𐤅𐤊.𐤄𐤒𐤄𐤋.𐤊𐤉.𐤀𐤕.𐤌𐤒𐤃𐤔.𐤉𐤄𐤅𐤄.𐤈
𐤌𐤀.𐤌𐤉.𐤍𐤃𐤄.𐤋𐤀.𐤆𐤓𐤒.𐤏𐤋𐤉𐤅.𐤈𐤌𐤀.𐤄𐤅𐤀|

21 𐤅𐤄𐤉𐤕𐤄.𐤋𐤄𐤌.𐤋𐤇𐤒𐤕.𐤏𐤅𐤋𐤌.𐤅𐤌𐤆𐤄.𐤌𐤉.𐤄𐤍𐤃
𐤄.𐤉𐤊𐤁𐤎.𐤁𐤂𐤃𐤉𐤅.𐤅𐤄𐤍𐤂𐤏.𐤁𐤌𐤉.𐤄𐤍𐤃𐤄.𐤉𐤈𐤌𐤀.𐤏
𐤃.𐤄𐤏𐤓𐤁|

22 𐤅𐤊𐤋.𐤀𐤔𐤓.𐤉𐤂𐤏.𐤁𐤅.𐤄𐤈𐤌𐤀.𐤉𐤈𐤌𐤀.𐤅𐤄𐤍𐤐𐤔.𐤄𐤍
𐤂𐤏𐤕.𐤕𐤈𐤌𐤀.𐤏𐤃.𐤄𐤏𐤓𐤁‖

𐤁𐤌𐤃𐤁𐤓.𐤇𐤋𐤒 20

1 𐤅𐤉𐤁𐤀𐤅.𐤁𐤍𐤉.𐤉𐤔𐤓𐤀𐤋.𐤊𐤋.𐤄𐤏𐤃𐤄.𐤌𐤃𐤁𐤓.𐤑𐤍.𐤁𐤇
𐤃𐤔.𐤄𐤓𐤀𐤔𐤅𐤍.𐤅𐤉𐤔𐤁.𐤄𐤏𐤌.𐤁𐤒𐤃𐤔.𐤅𐤕𐤌𐤕.𐤔𐤌.𐤌𐤓𐤉
𐤌.𐤅𐤕𐤒𐤁𐤓.𐤔𐤌|

2 𐤅𐤋𐤀.𐤄𐤉𐤄.𐤌𐤉𐤌.𐤋𐤏𐤃𐤄.𐤅𐤉𐤒𐤄𐤋𐤅.𐤏𐤋.𐤌𐤔𐤄.𐤅𐤏𐤋.
𐤀𐤄𐤓𐤍|

𐤂 𐤅𐤉𐤓𐤁.𐤄𐤏𐤌.𐤏𐤌.𐤌𐤔𐤄.𐤅𐤉𐤀𐤌𐤓𐤅.𐤋𐤀𐤌𐤓.𐤅𐤋𐤅.𐤂𐤅𐤏𐤍
𐤅.𐤁𐤂𐤅𐤏.𐤀𐤇𐤉𐤍𐤅.𐤋𐤐𐤍𐤉.𐤉𐤄𐤅𐤄|
𐤃 𐤅𐤋𐤌𐤄.𐤄𐤁𐤀𐤕𐤌.𐤀𐤕.𐤒𐤄𐤋.𐤉𐤄𐤅𐤄.𐤀𐤋.𐤄𐤌𐤃𐤁𐤓.𐤄
𐤆𐤄.𐤋𐤌𐤅𐤕.𐤔𐤌.𐤀𐤍𐤇𐤍𐤅.𐤅𐤁𐤏𐤉𐤓𐤍𐤅|
𐤄 𐤅𐤋𐤌𐤄.𐤄𐤏𐤋𐤉𐤕𐤍𐤅.𐤌𐤌𐤑𐤓𐤉𐤌.𐤋𐤄𐤁𐤉𐤀.𐤀𐤕𐤍𐤅.𐤀𐤋.
𐤄𐤌𐤒𐤅𐤌.𐤄𐤓𐤏.𐤄𐤆𐤄.𐤋𐤀.𐤌𐤒𐤅𐤌.𐤆𐤓𐤏.𐤅𐤕𐤀𐤍𐤄.𐤅𐤂𐤐𐤍
.𐤅𐤓𐤌𐤅𐤍.𐤅𐤌𐤉𐤌.𐤀𐤉𐤍.𐤋𐤔𐤕𐤅𐤕|
𐤅 𐤅𐤉𐤁𐤀.𐤌𐤔𐤄.𐤅𐤀𐤄𐤓𐤍.𐤌𐤐𐤍𐤉.𐤄𐤒𐤄𐤋.𐤀𐤋.𐤐𐤕𐤇.𐤀𐤄
𐤋.𐤌𐤅𐤏𐤃.𐤅𐤉𐤐𐤋𐤅.𐤏𐤋.𐤐𐤍𐤉𐤄𐤌.𐤅𐤉𐤓𐤀.𐤊𐤁𐤅𐤃.𐤉𐤄𐤅𐤄.𐤀𐤋
𐤉𐤄𐤌|
𐤆 𐤅𐤉𐤃𐤁𐤓.𐤉𐤄𐤅𐤄.𐤀𐤋.𐤌𐤔𐤄.𐤋𐤀𐤌𐤓|
𐤇 𐤒𐤇.𐤀𐤕.𐤄𐤌𐤈𐤄.𐤅𐤄𐤒𐤄𐤋.𐤀𐤕.𐤄𐤏𐤃𐤄.𐤀𐤕𐤄.𐤅𐤀
𐤄𐤓𐤍.𐤀𐤇𐤉𐤊.𐤅𐤃𐤁𐤓𐤕𐤌.𐤀𐤋.𐤄𐤎𐤋𐤏.𐤋𐤏𐤉𐤍𐤉𐤄𐤌.𐤅𐤍𐤕𐤍.
𐤌𐤉𐤌𐤉𐤅.𐤅𐤄𐤅𐤑𐤀𐤕.𐤋𐤄𐤌.𐤌𐤉𐤌.𐤌𐤍.𐤄𐤎𐤋𐤏.𐤅𐤄𐤔𐤒𐤉𐤕.
𐤀𐤕.𐤄𐤏𐤃𐤄.𐤅𐤀𐤕.𐤁𐤏𐤉𐤓𐤌|
𐤈 𐤅𐤉𐤒𐤇.𐤌𐤔𐤄.𐤀𐤕.𐤄𐤌𐤈𐤄.𐤌𐤋𐤐𐤍𐤉.𐤉𐤄𐤅𐤄.𐤊𐤀𐤔𐤓.
𐤑𐤅𐤄𐤅|
𐤉 𐤅𐤉𐤒𐤄𐤋𐤅.𐤌𐤔𐤄.𐤅𐤀𐤄𐤓𐤍.𐤀𐤕.𐤄𐤒𐤄𐤋.𐤀𐤋.𐤐𐤍𐤉.𐤄
𐤎𐤋𐤏.𐤅𐤉𐤀𐤌𐤓.𐤋𐤄𐤌.𐤔𐤌𐤏𐤅.𐤍𐤀.𐤄𐤌𐤓𐤉𐤌.𐤄𐤌𐤍.𐤄𐤎𐤋𐤏.
𐤄𐤆𐤄.𐤍𐤅𐤑𐤉𐤀.𐤋𐤊𐤌.𐤌𐤉𐤌|
𐤉𐤀 𐤅𐤉𐤓𐤌.𐤌𐤔𐤄.𐤀𐤕.𐤉𐤃𐤅.𐤅𐤉𐤊.𐤀𐤕.𐤄𐤎𐤋𐤏.𐤁𐤌𐤈𐤄𐤅.
𐤐𐤏𐤌𐤉𐤌.𐤅𐤉𐤑𐤀𐤅.𐤌𐤉𐤌.𐤓𐤁𐤉𐤌.𐤅𐤕𐤔𐤕.𐤄𐤏𐤃𐤄.𐤅𐤁𐤏𐤉
𐤓𐤌|
𐤉𐤁 𐤅𐤉𐤀𐤌𐤓.𐤉𐤄𐤅𐤄.𐤀𐤋.𐤌𐤔𐤄.𐤅𐤀𐤋.𐤀𐤄𐤓𐤍.𐤉𐤏𐤍.𐤋𐤀.𐤄
𐤀𐤌𐤍𐤕𐤌.𐤁𐤉.𐤋𐤄𐤒𐤃𐤉𐤔𐤍𐤉.𐤋𐤏𐤉𐤍𐤉.𐤁𐤍𐤉.𐤉𐤔𐤓𐤀𐤋.𐤋𐤊
𐤍.𐤋𐤀.𐤕𐤁𐤉𐤀𐤅.𐤀𐤕.𐤄𐤒𐤄𐤋.𐤄𐤆𐤄.𐤀𐤋.𐤄𐤀𐤓𐤑.𐤀𐤔𐤓.𐤍
𐤕𐤕𐤉.𐤋𐤄𐤌|
𐤉𐤂 𐤄𐤌𐤄.𐤌𐤉.𐤌𐤓𐤉𐤁𐤄.𐤀𐤔𐤓.𐤓𐤁𐤅.𐤁𐤍𐤉.𐤉𐤔𐤓𐤀𐤋.𐤀𐤕.
𐤉𐤄𐤅𐤄.𐤅𐤉𐤒𐤃𐤔.𐤁𐤌|

14 𐤅𐤉𐤔𐤋𐤇.𐤌𐤔𐤄.𐤌𐤋𐤀𐤊𐤉𐤌.𐤌𐤒𐤃𐤔.𐤀𐤋.𐤌𐤋𐤊.𐤀
𐤃𐤅𐤌.𐤊𐤄.𐤀𐤌𐤓.𐤀𐤇𐤉𐤊.𐤉𐤔𐤓𐤀𐤋.𐤀𐤕𐤄.𐤉𐤃𐤏𐤕.𐤀𐤕.
𐤊𐤋.𐤄𐤕𐤋𐤀𐤄.𐤀𐤔𐤓.𐤌𐤑𐤀𐤕𐤍𐤅|
15 𐤅𐤉𐤓𐤃𐤅.𐤀𐤁𐤕𐤉𐤍𐤅.𐤌𐤑𐤓𐤉𐤌𐤄.𐤅𐤍𐤔𐤁.𐤁𐤌𐤑𐤓𐤉𐤌.𐤉
𐤌𐤉𐤌.𐤓𐤁𐤉𐤌.𐤅𐤉𐤓𐤏𐤅.𐤋𐤍𐤅.𐤌𐤑𐤓𐤉𐤌.𐤅𐤋𐤀𐤁𐤕𐤉𐤍𐤅|
16 𐤅𐤍𐤑𐤏𐤒.𐤀𐤋.𐤉𐤄𐤅𐤄.𐤅𐤉𐤔𐤌𐤏.𐤒𐤋𐤍𐤅.𐤅𐤉𐤔𐤋𐤇.𐤌𐤋
𐤀𐤊.𐤅𐤉𐤑𐤀𐤍𐤅.𐤌𐤌𐤑𐤓𐤉𐤌.𐤅𐤄𐤍𐤄.𐤀𐤍𐤇𐤍𐤅.𐤁𐤒𐤃𐤔.𐤏𐤉𐤓.
𐤒𐤑𐤄.𐤂𐤁𐤅𐤋𐤊|
17 𐤍𐤏𐤁𐤓𐤄.𐤍𐤀.𐤁𐤀𐤓𐤑𐤊.𐤋𐤀.𐤍𐤏𐤁𐤓.𐤁𐤔𐤃𐤄.𐤅𐤁𐤊𐤓
𐤌.𐤅𐤋𐤀.𐤍𐤔𐤕𐤄.𐤌𐤉.𐤁𐤀𐤓.𐤃𐤓𐤊.𐤄𐤌𐤋𐤊.𐤍𐤋𐤊.𐤋𐤀.𐤍𐤈𐤄.
𐤉𐤌𐤉𐤍.𐤅𐤔𐤌𐤀𐤅𐤋.𐤏𐤃.𐤀𐤔𐤓.𐤍𐤏𐤁𐤓.𐤂𐤁𐤋𐤊|
18 𐤅𐤉𐤀𐤌𐤓.𐤀𐤋𐤉𐤅.𐤀𐤃𐤅𐤌.𐤋𐤀.𐤕𐤏𐤁𐤓.𐤁𐤉.𐤐𐤍.𐤁𐤇𐤓𐤁.
𐤀𐤑𐤀.𐤋𐤒𐤓𐤀𐤕𐤊|
19 𐤅𐤉𐤀𐤌𐤓𐤅.𐤀𐤋𐤉𐤅.𐤁𐤍𐤉.𐤉𐤔𐤓𐤀𐤋.𐤁𐤌𐤎𐤋𐤄.𐤍𐤏𐤋𐤄.𐤅
𐤀𐤌.𐤌𐤉𐤌𐤉𐤊.𐤍𐤔𐤕𐤄.𐤀𐤍𐤉.𐤅𐤌𐤒𐤍𐤉.𐤅𐤍𐤕𐤕𐤉.𐤌𐤊𐤓𐤌.𐤓𐤒
.𐤀𐤉𐤍.𐤃𐤁𐤓.𐤁𐤓𐤂𐤋𐤉.𐤀𐤏𐤁𐤓𐤄|
20 𐤅𐤉𐤀𐤌𐤓.𐤋𐤀.𐤕𐤏𐤁𐤓.𐤅𐤉𐤑𐤀.𐤀𐤃𐤅𐤌.𐤋𐤒𐤓𐤀𐤕𐤅.𐤁
𐤏𐤌.𐤊𐤁𐤃.𐤅𐤁𐤉𐤃.𐤇𐤆𐤒𐤄|
21 𐤅𐤉𐤌𐤀𐤍.𐤀𐤃𐤅𐤌.𐤍𐤕𐤍.𐤀𐤕.𐤉𐤔𐤓𐤀𐤋.𐤏𐤁𐤓.𐤁𐤂𐤁𐤋𐤅.
𐤅𐤉𐤈.𐤉𐤔𐤓𐤀𐤋.𐤌𐤏𐤋𐤉𐤅|
22 𐤅𐤉𐤎𐤏𐤅.𐤌𐤒𐤃𐤔.𐤅𐤉𐤁𐤀𐤅.𐤁𐤍𐤉.𐤉𐤔𐤓𐤀𐤋.𐤊𐤋.𐤄𐤏
𐤃𐤄.𐤄𐤓.𐤄𐤄𐤓|
23 𐤅𐤉𐤀𐤌𐤓.𐤉𐤄𐤅𐤄.𐤀𐤋.𐤌𐤔𐤄.𐤅𐤀𐤋.𐤀𐤄𐤓𐤍.𐤁𐤄𐤓.𐤄𐤄𐤓
.𐤏𐤋.𐤂𐤁𐤅𐤋.𐤀𐤓𐤑.𐤀𐤃𐤅𐤌.𐤋𐤀𐤌𐤓|
24 𐤉𐤀𐤎𐤐.𐤀𐤄𐤓𐤍.𐤀𐤋.𐤏𐤌𐤉𐤅.𐤊𐤉.𐤋𐤀.𐤉𐤁𐤀.𐤀𐤋.𐤄𐤀
𐤓𐤑.𐤀𐤔𐤓.𐤍𐤕𐤕𐤉.𐤋𐤁𐤍𐤉.𐤉𐤔𐤓𐤀𐤋.𐤏𐤋.𐤀𐤔𐤓.𐤌𐤓𐤉𐤕𐤌.𐤀
𐤕.𐤐𐤉.𐤋𐤌𐤉.𐤌𐤓𐤉𐤁𐤄|
25 𐤒𐤇.𐤀𐤕.𐤀𐤄𐤓𐤍.𐤅𐤀𐤕.𐤀𐤋𐤏𐤆𐤓.𐤁𐤍𐤅.𐤅𐤄𐤏𐤋.𐤀𐤕𐤌
.𐤄𐤓.𐤄𐤄𐤓|
26 𐤅𐤄𐤐𐤔𐤈.𐤀𐤕.𐤀𐤄𐤓𐤍.𐤀𐤕.𐤁𐤂𐤃𐤉𐤅.𐤅𐤄𐤋𐤁𐤔𐤕𐤌.𐤀
𐤕.𐤀𐤋𐤏𐤆𐤓.𐤁𐤍𐤅.𐤅𐤀𐤄𐤓𐤍.𐤉𐤀𐤎𐤐.𐤅𐤌𐤕.𐤔𐤌|

27 𐤅𐤉𐤏𐤔.𐤌𐤔𐤄.𐤊𐤀𐤔𐤓.𐤑𐤅𐤄.𐤉𐤄𐤅𐤄.𐤅𐤉𐤏𐤋𐤅.𐤀𐤋.𐤄
𐤓.𐤄𐤄𐤓.𐤋𐤏𐤉𐤍𐤉.𐤊𐤋.𐤄𐤏𐤃𐤄|
28 𐤅𐤉𐤐𐤔𐤈.𐤌𐤔𐤄.𐤀𐤕.𐤀𐤄𐤓𐤍.𐤀𐤕.𐤁𐤂𐤃𐤉𐤅.𐤅𐤉𐤋𐤁𐤔.
𐤀𐤕𐤌.𐤀𐤕.𐤀𐤋𐤏𐤆𐤓.𐤁𐤍𐤅.𐤅𐤉𐤌𐤕.𐤀𐤄𐤓𐤍.𐤔𐤌.𐤁𐤓𐤀𐤔.𐤄
𐤄𐤓.𐤅𐤉𐤓𐤃.𐤌𐤔𐤄.𐤅𐤀𐤋𐤏𐤆𐤓.𐤌𐤍.𐤄𐤄𐤓|
29 𐤅𐤉𐤓𐤀𐤅.𐤊𐤋.𐤄𐤏𐤃𐤄.𐤊𐤉.𐤂𐤅𐤏.𐤀𐤄𐤓𐤍.𐤅𐤉𐤁𐤊𐤅.𐤀
𐤕.𐤀𐤄𐤓𐤍.𐤔𐤋𐤔𐤉𐤌.𐤉𐤅𐤌.𐤊𐤋.𐤁𐤉𐤕.𐤉𐤔𐤓𐤀𐤋||

𐤁𐤌𐤃𐤁𐤓.𐤇𐤋𐤒 21

1 𐤅𐤉𐤔𐤌𐤏.𐤄𐤊𐤍𐤏𐤍𐤉.𐤌𐤋𐤊.𐤏𐤓𐤃.𐤉𐤔𐤁.𐤄𐤍𐤂𐤁.𐤊𐤉.𐤁
𐤀.𐤉𐤔𐤓𐤀𐤋.𐤃𐤓𐤊.𐤄𐤀𐤕𐤓𐤉𐤌.𐤅𐤉𐤋𐤇𐤌.𐤁𐤉𐤔𐤓𐤀𐤋.𐤅𐤉𐤔
𐤁.𐤌𐤌𐤍𐤅.𐤔𐤁𐤉|
2 𐤅𐤉𐤃𐤓.𐤉𐤔𐤓𐤀𐤋.𐤍𐤃𐤓.𐤋𐤉𐤄𐤅𐤄.𐤅𐤉𐤀𐤌𐤓.𐤀𐤌.𐤍𐤕𐤍.𐤕
𐤕𐤍.𐤀𐤕.𐤄𐤏𐤌.𐤄𐤆𐤄.𐤁𐤉𐤃𐤉.𐤅𐤄𐤇𐤓𐤌𐤕𐤉.𐤀𐤕.𐤏𐤓𐤉𐤄
𐤌|
3 𐤅𐤉𐤔𐤌𐤏.𐤉𐤄𐤅𐤄.𐤁𐤒𐤅𐤋.𐤉𐤔𐤓𐤀𐤋.𐤅𐤉𐤕𐤍.𐤀𐤕.𐤄𐤊𐤍𐤏
𐤍𐤉.𐤅𐤉𐤇𐤓𐤌.𐤀𐤕𐤄𐤌.𐤅𐤀𐤕.𐤏𐤓𐤉𐤄𐤌.𐤅𐤉𐤒𐤓𐤀.𐤔𐤌.𐤄𐤌𐤒
𐤅𐤌.𐤇𐤓𐤌𐤄|
4 𐤅𐤉𐤎𐤏𐤅.𐤌𐤄𐤓.𐤄𐤄𐤓.𐤃𐤓𐤊.𐤉𐤌.𐤎𐤅𐤐.𐤋𐤎𐤁𐤁.𐤀𐤕.𐤀𐤓
𐤑.𐤀𐤃𐤅𐤌.𐤅𐤕𐤒𐤑𐤓.𐤍𐤐𐤔.𐤄𐤏𐤌.𐤁𐤃𐤓𐤊|
5 𐤅𐤉𐤃𐤁𐤓.𐤄𐤏𐤌.𐤁𐤀𐤋𐤄𐤉𐤌.𐤅𐤁𐤌𐤔𐤄.𐤋𐤌𐤄.𐤄𐤏𐤋𐤉𐤕
𐤍𐤅.𐤌𐤌𐤑𐤓𐤉𐤌.𐤋𐤌𐤅𐤕.𐤁𐤌𐤃𐤁𐤓.𐤊𐤉.𐤀𐤉𐤍.𐤋𐤇𐤌.𐤅𐤀𐤉𐤍.𐤌
𐤉𐤌.𐤅𐤍𐤐𐤔𐤍𐤅.𐤒𐤑𐤄.𐤁𐤋𐤇𐤌.𐤄𐤒𐤋𐤒𐤋|
6 𐤅𐤉𐤔𐤋𐤇.𐤉𐤄𐤅𐤄.𐤁𐤏𐤌.𐤀𐤕.𐤄𐤍𐤇𐤔𐤉𐤌.𐤄𐤔𐤓𐤐𐤉𐤌.𐤅
𐤉𐤍𐤔𐤊𐤅.𐤀𐤕.𐤄𐤏𐤌.𐤅𐤉𐤌𐤕.𐤏𐤌.𐤓𐤁.𐤌𐤉𐤔𐤓𐤀𐤋|
7 𐤅𐤉𐤁𐤀.𐤄𐤏𐤌.𐤀𐤋.𐤌𐤔𐤄.𐤅𐤉𐤀𐤌𐤓𐤅.𐤇𐤈𐤀𐤍𐤅.𐤊𐤉.𐤃𐤁
𐤓𐤍𐤅.𐤁𐤉𐤄𐤅𐤄.𐤅𐤁𐤊.𐤄𐤕𐤐𐤋𐤋.𐤀𐤋.𐤉𐤄𐤅𐤄.𐤅𐤉𐤎𐤓.𐤌𐤏𐤋𐤉𐤍𐤅.
𐤀𐤕.𐤄𐤍𐤇𐤔.𐤅𐤉𐤕𐤐𐤋𐤋.𐤌𐤔𐤄.𐤁𐤏𐤃.𐤄𐤏𐤌|
8 𐤅𐤉𐤀𐤌𐤓.𐤉𐤄𐤅𐤄.𐤀𐤋.𐤌𐤔𐤄.𐤏𐤔𐤄.𐤋𐤊.𐤔𐤓𐤐.𐤅𐤔𐤉𐤌.𐤀
𐤕𐤅.𐤏𐤋.𐤍𐤎.𐤅𐤄𐤉𐤄.𐤊𐤋.𐤄𐤍𐤔𐤅𐤊.𐤅𐤓𐤀𐤄.𐤀𐤕𐤅.𐤅𐤇𐤉|

𐤈 𐤅𐤉𐤏𐤔.𐤌𐤔𐤄.𐤍𐤇𐤔.𐤍𐤇𐤔𐤕.𐤅𐤉𐤔𐤌𐤄𐤅.𐤏𐤋.𐤄𐤍𐤎.𐤅
𐤄𐤉𐤄.𐤀𐤌.𐤍𐤔𐤊.𐤄𐤍𐤇𐤔.𐤀𐤕.𐤀𐤉𐤔.𐤅𐤄𐤁𐤉𐤈.𐤀𐤋.𐤍𐤇𐤔.
𐤄𐤍𐤇𐤔𐤕.𐤅𐤇𐤉|

𐤉 𐤅𐤉𐤎𐤏𐤅.𐤁𐤍𐤉.𐤉𐤔𐤓𐤀𐤋.𐤅𐤉𐤇𐤍𐤅.𐤁𐤀𐤁𐤕|

𐤉𐤀 𐤅𐤉𐤎𐤏𐤅.𐤌𐤀𐤁𐤕.𐤅𐤉𐤇𐤍𐤅.𐤁𐤏𐤉𐤉.𐤄𐤏𐤁𐤓𐤉𐤌.𐤁𐤌𐤃
𐤁𐤓.𐤀𐤔𐤓.𐤏𐤋.𐤐𐤍𐤉.𐤌𐤅𐤀𐤁.𐤌𐤌𐤆𐤓𐤇.𐤄𐤔𐤌𐤔|

𐤉𐤁 𐤌𐤔𐤌.𐤍𐤎𐤏𐤅.𐤅𐤉𐤇𐤍𐤅.𐤁𐤍𐤇𐤋.𐤆𐤓𐤃|

𐤉𐤂 𐤌𐤔𐤌.𐤍𐤎𐤏𐤅.𐤅𐤉𐤇𐤍𐤅.𐤌𐤏𐤁𐤓.𐤀𐤓𐤍𐤅𐤍.𐤀𐤔𐤓.𐤁𐤌𐤃𐤁
𐤓.𐤄𐤉𐤑𐤀.𐤌𐤂𐤁𐤅𐤋.𐤄𐤀𐤌𐤓𐤉.𐤊𐤉.𐤀𐤓𐤍𐤅𐤍.𐤂𐤁𐤅𐤋.𐤌𐤅𐤀𐤁.
𐤁𐤉𐤍.𐤌𐤅𐤀𐤁.𐤅𐤁𐤉𐤍.𐤄𐤀𐤌𐤓𐤉|

𐤉𐤃 𐤏𐤋.𐤊𐤍.𐤉𐤀𐤌𐤓.𐤁𐤎𐤐𐤓.𐤌𐤋𐤇𐤌𐤕.𐤉𐤄𐤅𐤄.𐤀𐤕.𐤅𐤄𐤁.
𐤁𐤎𐤅𐤐𐤄.𐤅𐤀𐤕.𐤄𐤍𐤇𐤋𐤉𐤌.𐤀𐤓𐤍𐤅𐤍|

𐤈𐤅 𐤅𐤀𐤔𐤃.𐤄𐤍𐤇𐤋𐤉𐤌.𐤀𐤔𐤓.𐤍𐤈𐤄.𐤋𐤔𐤁𐤕.𐤏𐤓.𐤅𐤍𐤔𐤏
𐤍.𐤋𐤂𐤁𐤅𐤋.𐤌𐤅𐤀𐤁|

𐤈𐤆 𐤅𐤌𐤔𐤌.𐤁𐤀𐤓𐤄.𐤄𐤅𐤀.𐤄𐤁𐤀𐤓.𐤀𐤔𐤓.𐤀𐤌𐤓.𐤉𐤄𐤅𐤄.𐤋
𐤌𐤔𐤄.𐤀𐤎𐤐.𐤀𐤕.𐤄𐤏𐤌.𐤅𐤀𐤕𐤍𐤄.𐤋𐤄𐤌.𐤌𐤉𐤌|

𐤉𐤆 𐤀𐤆.𐤉𐤔𐤉𐤓.𐤉𐤔𐤓𐤀𐤋.𐤀𐤕.𐤄𐤔𐤉𐤓𐤄.𐤄𐤆𐤀𐤕.𐤏𐤋
𐤉.𐤁𐤀𐤓.𐤏𐤍𐤅.𐤋𐤄|

𐤉𐤇 𐤁𐤀𐤓.𐤇𐤐𐤓𐤅𐤄.𐤔𐤓𐤉𐤌.𐤊𐤓𐤅𐤄.𐤍𐤃𐤉𐤁𐤉.𐤄𐤏𐤌.𐤁𐤌
𐤇𐤒𐤒.𐤁𐤌𐤔𐤏𐤍𐤕𐤌.𐤅𐤌𐤌𐤃𐤁𐤓.𐤌𐤕𐤍𐤄|

𐤉𐤈 𐤅𐤌𐤌𐤕𐤍𐤄.𐤍𐤇𐤋𐤉𐤀𐤋.𐤅𐤌𐤍𐤇𐤋𐤉𐤀𐤋.𐤁𐤌𐤅𐤕|

𐤊 𐤅𐤌𐤁𐤌𐤅𐤕.𐤄𐤂𐤉𐤀.𐤀𐤔𐤓.𐤁𐤔𐤃𐤄.𐤌𐤅𐤀𐤁.𐤓𐤀𐤔.𐤄
𐤐𐤎𐤂𐤄.𐤅𐤍𐤔𐤒𐤐𐤄.𐤏𐤋.𐤐𐤍𐤉.𐤄𐤉𐤔𐤉𐤌𐤍|

𐤊𐤀 𐤅𐤉𐤔𐤋𐤇.𐤉𐤔𐤓𐤀𐤋.𐤌𐤋𐤀𐤊𐤉𐤌.𐤀𐤋.𐤎𐤉𐤇𐤍.𐤌𐤋𐤊.𐤄
𐤀𐤌𐤓𐤉.𐤋𐤀𐤌𐤓|

𐤊𐤁 𐤀𐤏𐤁𐤓𐤄.𐤁𐤀𐤓𐤑𐤊.𐤋𐤀.𐤍𐤈𐤄.𐤁𐤔𐤃𐤄.𐤅𐤁𐤊𐤓𐤌.𐤋
𐤀.𐤍𐤔𐤕𐤄.𐤌𐤉.𐤁𐤀𐤓.𐤁𐤃𐤓𐤊.𐤄𐤌𐤋𐤊.𐤍𐤋𐤊.𐤏𐤃.𐤀𐤔𐤓.𐤍𐤏
𐤁𐤓.𐤂𐤁𐤋𐤊|

𐤊𐤂 𐤅𐤋𐤀.𐤍𐤕𐤍.𐤎𐤉𐤇𐤍.𐤀𐤕.𐤉𐤔𐤓𐤀𐤋.𐤏𐤁𐤓.𐤁𐤂𐤁𐤋𐤅.𐤅𐤉
𐤀𐤎𐤐.𐤎𐤉𐤇𐤍.𐤀𐤕.𐤊𐤋.𐤏𐤌𐤅.𐤅𐤉𐤑𐤀.𐤋𐤒𐤓𐤀𐤕.𐤉𐤔𐤓𐤀𐤋.
𐤄𐤌𐤃𐤁𐤓𐤄.𐤅𐤉𐤁𐤀.𐤉𐤄𐤑𐤄.𐤅𐤉𐤋𐤇𐤌.𐤁𐤉𐤔𐤓𐤀𐤋|

..𐤊𐤃.. 𐤅𐤉𐤊𐤄𐤅.𐤉𐤔𐤓𐤀𐤋.𐤋𐤐𐤉.𐤇𐤓𐤁.𐤅𐤉𐤉𐤓𐤔.𐤀𐤕.𐤀𐤓𐤑𐤅.
𐤌𐤀𐤓𐤍𐤍.𐤏𐤃.𐤉𐤁𐤒.𐤏𐤃.𐤁𐤍𐤉.𐤏𐤌𐤅𐤍.𐤊𐤉.𐤏𐤆.𐤂𐤁𐤅𐤋.𐤁
𐤍𐤉.𐤏𐤌𐤅𐤍|

..𐤊𐤄.. 𐤅𐤉𐤒𐤇.𐤉𐤔𐤓𐤀𐤋.𐤀𐤕.𐤊𐤋.𐤄𐤏𐤓𐤉𐤌.𐤄𐤀𐤋𐤄.𐤅𐤉𐤔𐤁.
𐤉𐤔𐤓𐤀𐤋.𐤁𐤊𐤋.𐤏𐤓𐤉.𐤄𐤀𐤌𐤓𐤉.𐤁𐤇𐤔𐤁𐤅𐤍.𐤅𐤁𐤊𐤋.𐤁𐤍𐤕𐤉
𐤄|

..𐤊𐤅.. 𐤊𐤉.𐤇𐤔𐤁𐤅𐤍.𐤏𐤉𐤓.𐤎𐤉𐤇𐤍.𐤌𐤋𐤊.𐤄𐤀𐤌𐤓𐤉.𐤄𐤅𐤀.𐤅
𐤄𐤅𐤀.𐤍𐤋𐤇𐤌.𐤁𐤌𐤋𐤊.𐤌𐤅𐤀𐤁.𐤄𐤓𐤀𐤔𐤅𐤍.𐤅𐤉𐤒𐤇.𐤀𐤕.𐤊𐤋.
𐤀𐤓𐤑𐤅.𐤌𐤉𐤃𐤅.𐤏𐤃.𐤀𐤓𐤍𐤍|

..𐤊𐤆.. 𐤏𐤋.𐤊𐤍.𐤉𐤀𐤌𐤓𐤅.𐤄𐤌𐤔𐤋𐤉𐤌.𐤁𐤀𐤅.𐤇𐤔𐤁𐤅𐤍.𐤕𐤁𐤍𐤄.
𐤅𐤕𐤊𐤅𐤍𐤍.𐤏𐤉𐤓.𐤎𐤉𐤇𐤅𐤍|

..𐤊𐤇.. 𐤊𐤉.𐤀𐤔.𐤉𐤑𐤀𐤄.𐤌𐤇𐤔𐤁𐤅𐤍.𐤋𐤄𐤁𐤄.𐤌𐤒𐤓𐤉𐤕.𐤎𐤉
𐤇𐤍.𐤀𐤊𐤋𐤄.𐤏𐤓.𐤌𐤅𐤀𐤁.𐤁𐤏𐤋𐤉.𐤁𐤌𐤅𐤕.𐤀𐤓𐤍𐤍|

..𐤊𐤈.. 𐤀𐤅𐤉.𐤋𐤊.𐤌𐤅𐤀𐤁.𐤀𐤁𐤃𐤕.𐤏𐤌.𐤊𐤌𐤅𐤔.𐤍𐤕𐤍.𐤁𐤍𐤉𐤅.
𐤐𐤋𐤉𐤈𐤌.𐤅𐤁𐤍𐤕𐤉𐤅.𐤁𐤔𐤁𐤉𐤕.𐤋𐤌𐤋𐤊.𐤀𐤌𐤓𐤉.𐤎𐤉𐤇𐤅𐤍|

..𐤋.. 𐤅𐤍𐤉𐤓𐤌.𐤀𐤁𐤃.𐤇𐤔𐤁𐤅𐤍.𐤏𐤃.𐤃𐤉𐤁𐤅𐤍.𐤅𐤍𐤔𐤉𐤌.𐤏
𐤃.𐤍𐤐𐤇.𐤀𐤔𐤓.𐤏𐤃.𐤌𐤉𐤃𐤁𐤀|

..𐤋𐤀.. 𐤅𐤉𐤔𐤁.𐤉𐤔𐤓𐤀𐤋.𐤁𐤀𐤓𐤑.𐤄𐤀𐤌𐤓𐤉|

..𐤋𐤁.. 𐤅𐤉𐤔𐤋𐤇.𐤌𐤔𐤄.𐤋𐤓𐤂𐤋.𐤀𐤕.𐤉𐤏𐤆𐤓.𐤅𐤉𐤋𐤊𐤃𐤅.𐤁𐤍
𐤕𐤉𐤄.𐤅𐤉𐤉𐤓𐤔.||𐤅𐤉𐤅𐤓𐤔.𐤒𐤓𐤉||.𐤀𐤕.𐤄𐤀𐤌𐤓𐤉.𐤀𐤔𐤓.𐤔𐤌|

..𐤋𐤂.. 𐤅𐤉𐤐𐤍𐤅.𐤅𐤉𐤏𐤋𐤅.𐤃𐤓𐤊.𐤄𐤁𐤔𐤍.𐤅𐤉𐤑𐤀.𐤏𐤅𐤂.𐤌𐤋𐤊.
𐤄𐤁𐤔𐤍.𐤋𐤒𐤓𐤀𐤕𐤌.𐤄𐤅𐤀.𐤅𐤊𐤋.𐤏𐤌𐤅.𐤋𐤌𐤋𐤇𐤌𐤄.𐤀𐤃𐤓𐤏
𐤉|

..𐤋𐤃.. 𐤅𐤉𐤀𐤌𐤓.𐤉𐤄𐤅𐤄.𐤀𐤋.𐤌𐤔𐤄.𐤀𐤋.𐤕𐤉𐤓𐤀.𐤀𐤕𐤅.𐤊𐤉.
𐤁𐤉𐤃𐤊.𐤍𐤕𐤕𐤉.𐤀𐤕𐤅.𐤅𐤀𐤕.𐤊𐤋.𐤏𐤌𐤅.𐤅𐤀𐤕.𐤀𐤓𐤑𐤅.𐤅𐤏𐤔
𐤉𐤕.𐤋𐤅.𐤊𐤀𐤔𐤓.𐤏𐤔𐤉𐤕.𐤋𐤎𐤉𐤇𐤍.𐤌𐤋𐤊.𐤄𐤀𐤌𐤓𐤉.𐤀𐤔𐤓.
𐤉𐤅𐤔𐤁.𐤁𐤇𐤔𐤁𐤅𐤍|

..𐤋𐤄.. 𐤅𐤉𐤊𐤅.𐤀𐤕𐤅.𐤅𐤀𐤕.𐤁𐤍𐤉𐤅.𐤅𐤀𐤕.𐤊𐤋.𐤏𐤌𐤅.𐤏𐤃.𐤁𐤋𐤕
𐤉.𐤄𐤔𐤀𐤉𐤓.𐤋𐤅.𐤔𐤓𐤉𐤃.𐤅𐤉𐤉𐤓𐤔𐤅.𐤀𐤕.𐤀𐤓𐤑𐤅||

𐤁𐤌𐤃𐤁𐤓.𐤇𐤋𐤒..𐤊𐤁..

1 𐤅𐤉𐤎𐤏𐤅.𐤁𐤍𐤉.𐤉𐤔𐤓𐤀𐤋.𐤅𐤉𐤇𐤍𐤅.𐤁𐤏𐤓𐤁𐤅𐤕.𐤌𐤅𐤀𐤁.𐤌𐤏
𐤁𐤓.𐤋𐤉𐤓𐤃𐤍.𐤉𐤓𐤇𐤅|
2 𐤅𐤉𐤓𐤀.𐤁𐤋𐤒.𐤁𐤍.𐤑𐤐𐤅𐤓.𐤀𐤕.𐤊𐤋.𐤀𐤔𐤓.𐤏𐤔𐤄.𐤉𐤔𐤓𐤀
𐤋.𐤋𐤀𐤌𐤓𐤉|
3 𐤅𐤉𐤂𐤓.𐤌𐤅𐤀𐤁.𐤌𐤐𐤍𐤉.𐤄𐤏𐤌.𐤌𐤀𐤃.𐤊𐤉.𐤓𐤁.𐤄𐤅𐤀.𐤅𐤉
𐤒𐤑.𐤌𐤅𐤀𐤁.𐤌𐤐𐤍𐤉.𐤁𐤍𐤉.𐤉𐤔𐤓𐤀𐤋|
4 𐤅𐤉𐤀𐤌𐤓.𐤌𐤅𐤀𐤁.𐤀𐤋.𐤆𐤒𐤍𐤉.𐤌𐤃𐤉𐤍.𐤏𐤕𐤄.𐤉𐤋𐤇𐤊𐤅
.𐤄𐤒𐤄𐤋.𐤀𐤕.𐤊𐤋.𐤎𐤁𐤉𐤁𐤕𐤉𐤍𐤅.𐤊𐤋𐤇𐤊.𐤄𐤔𐤅𐤓.𐤀𐤕.𐤉𐤓𐤒
.𐤄𐤔𐤃𐤄.𐤅𐤁𐤋𐤒.𐤁𐤍.𐤑𐤐𐤅𐤓.𐤌𐤋𐤊.𐤋𐤌𐤅𐤀𐤁.𐤁𐤏𐤕.𐤄𐤄𐤅𐤀|
5 𐤅𐤉𐤔𐤋𐤇.𐤌𐤋𐤀𐤊𐤉𐤌.𐤀𐤋.𐤁𐤋𐤏𐤌.𐤁𐤍.𐤁𐤏𐤅𐤓.𐤐𐤕𐤅𐤓𐤄.
𐤀𐤔𐤓.𐤏𐤋.𐤄𐤍𐤄𐤓.𐤀𐤓𐤑.𐤁𐤍𐤉.𐤏𐤌𐤅.𐤋𐤒𐤓𐤀.𐤋𐤅.𐤋𐤀𐤌𐤓.𐤄𐤍
𐤄.𐤏𐤌.𐤉𐤑𐤀.𐤌𐤌𐤑𐤓𐤉𐤌.𐤄𐤍𐤄.𐤊𐤎𐤄.𐤀𐤕.𐤏𐤉𐤍.𐤄𐤀𐤓𐤑
.𐤅𐤄𐤅𐤀.𐤉𐤔𐤁.𐤌𐤌𐤋𐤉|
6 𐤅𐤏𐤕𐤄.𐤋𐤊𐤄.𐤍𐤀.𐤀𐤓𐤄.𐤋𐤉.𐤀𐤕.𐤄𐤏𐤌.𐤄𐤆𐤄.𐤊𐤉.𐤏
𐤑𐤅𐤌.𐤄𐤅𐤀.𐤌𐤌𐤍𐤉.𐤀𐤅𐤋𐤉.𐤀𐤅𐤊𐤋.𐤍𐤊𐤄.𐤁𐤅.𐤅𐤀𐤂𐤓𐤔𐤍𐤅.𐤌𐤍
.𐤄𐤀𐤓𐤑.𐤊𐤉.𐤉𐤃𐤏𐤕𐤉.𐤀𐤕.𐤀𐤔𐤓.𐤕𐤁𐤓𐤊.𐤌𐤁𐤓𐤊.𐤅𐤀𐤔𐤓
.𐤕𐤀𐤓.𐤉𐤅𐤀𐤓|
7 𐤅𐤉𐤋𐤊𐤅.𐤆𐤒𐤍𐤉.𐤌𐤅𐤀𐤁.𐤅𐤆𐤒𐤍𐤉.𐤌𐤃𐤉𐤍.𐤅𐤒𐤎𐤌𐤉𐤌.
𐤁𐤉𐤃𐤌.𐤅𐤉𐤁𐤀𐤅.𐤀𐤋.𐤁𐤋𐤏𐤌.𐤅𐤉𐤃𐤁𐤓𐤅.𐤀𐤋𐤉𐤅.𐤃𐤁𐤓𐤉.𐤁𐤋
𐤒|
8 𐤅𐤉𐤀𐤌𐤓.𐤀𐤋𐤉𐤄𐤌.𐤋𐤉𐤍𐤅.𐤐𐤄.𐤄𐤋𐤉𐤋𐤄.𐤅𐤄𐤔𐤁𐤕𐤉.𐤀
𐤕𐤊𐤌.𐤃𐤁𐤓.𐤊𐤀𐤔𐤓.𐤉𐤃𐤁𐤓.𐤉𐤄𐤅𐤄.𐤀𐤋𐤉.𐤅𐤉𐤔𐤁𐤅.𐤔𐤓𐤉.
𐤌𐤅𐤀𐤁.𐤏𐤌.𐤁𐤋𐤏𐤌|
9 𐤅𐤉𐤁𐤀.𐤀𐤋𐤄𐤉𐤌.𐤀𐤋.𐤁𐤋𐤏𐤌.𐤅𐤉𐤀𐤌𐤓.𐤌𐤉.𐤄𐤀𐤍𐤔𐤉
𐤌.𐤄𐤀𐤋𐤄.𐤏𐤌𐤊|
10 𐤅𐤉𐤀𐤌𐤓.𐤁𐤋𐤏𐤌.𐤀𐤋.𐤄𐤀𐤋𐤄𐤉𐤌.𐤁𐤋𐤒.𐤁𐤍.𐤑𐤐𐤓.𐤌
𐤋𐤊.𐤌𐤅𐤀𐤁.𐤔𐤋𐤇.𐤀𐤋𐤉|
11 𐤄𐤍𐤄.𐤄𐤏𐤌.𐤄𐤉𐤑𐤀.𐤌𐤌𐤑𐤓𐤉𐤌.𐤅𐤉𐤊𐤎.𐤀𐤕.𐤏𐤉𐤍.
𐤄𐤀𐤓𐤑.𐤏𐤕𐤄.𐤋𐤊𐤄.𐤒𐤁𐤄.𐤋𐤉.𐤀𐤕𐤅.𐤀𐤅𐤋𐤉.𐤀𐤅𐤊𐤋.𐤋𐤄𐤋
𐤇𐤌.𐤁𐤅.𐤅𐤂𐤓𐤔𐤕𐤉𐤅|

12 𐤅𐤉𐤀𐤌𐤓.𐤀𐤋𐤄𐤉𐤌.𐤀𐤋.𐤁𐤋𐤏𐤌.𐤋𐤀.𐤕𐤋𐤊.𐤏𐤌𐤄𐤌.𐤋𐤀.𐤕𐤀𐤓.𐤀𐤕.𐤄𐤏𐤌.𐤊𐤉.𐤁𐤓𐤅𐤊.𐤄𐤅𐤀|

13 𐤅𐤉𐤒𐤌.𐤁𐤋𐤏𐤌.𐤁𐤁𐤒𐤓.𐤅𐤉𐤀𐤌𐤓.𐤀𐤋.𐤔𐤓𐤉.𐤁𐤋𐤒.𐤋𐤊𐤅.𐤀𐤋.𐤀𐤓𐤑𐤊𐤌.𐤊𐤉.𐤌𐤀𐤍.𐤉𐤄𐤅𐤄.𐤋𐤕𐤕𐤉.𐤋𐤄𐤋𐤊.𐤏𐤌𐤊𐤌|

14 𐤅𐤉𐤒𐤅𐤌𐤅.𐤔𐤓𐤉.𐤌𐤅𐤀𐤁.𐤅𐤉𐤁𐤀𐤅.𐤀𐤋.𐤁𐤋𐤒.𐤅𐤉𐤀𐤌𐤓𐤅.𐤌𐤀𐤍.𐤁𐤋𐤏𐤌.𐤄𐤋𐤊.𐤏𐤌𐤍𐤅|

15 𐤅𐤉𐤎𐤐.𐤏𐤅𐤃.𐤁𐤋𐤒.𐤔𐤋𐤇.𐤔𐤓𐤉𐤌.𐤓𐤁𐤉𐤌.𐤅𐤍𐤊𐤁𐤃𐤉𐤌.𐤌𐤀𐤋𐤄|

16 𐤅𐤉𐤁𐤀𐤅.𐤀𐤋.𐤁𐤋𐤏𐤌.𐤅𐤉𐤀𐤌𐤓𐤅.𐤋𐤅.𐤊𐤄.𐤀𐤌𐤓.𐤁𐤋𐤒.𐤁𐤍.𐤑𐤐𐤅𐤓.𐤀𐤋.𐤍𐤀.𐤕𐤌𐤍𐤏.𐤌𐤄𐤋𐤊.𐤀𐤋𐤉|

17 𐤊𐤉.𐤊𐤁𐤃.𐤀𐤊𐤁𐤃𐤊.𐤌𐤀𐤃.𐤅𐤊𐤋.𐤀𐤔𐤓.𐤕𐤀𐤌𐤓.𐤀𐤋𐤉.𐤀𐤏𐤔𐤄.𐤅𐤋𐤊𐤄.𐤍𐤀.𐤒𐤁𐤄.𐤋𐤉.𐤀𐤕.𐤄𐤏𐤌.𐤄𐤆𐤄|

18 𐤅𐤉𐤏𐤍.𐤁𐤋𐤏𐤌.𐤅𐤉𐤀𐤌𐤓.𐤀𐤋.𐤏𐤁𐤃𐤉.𐤁𐤋𐤒.𐤀𐤌.𐤉𐤕𐤍.𐤋𐤉.𐤁𐤋𐤒.𐤌𐤋𐤀.𐤁𐤉𐤕𐤅.𐤊𐤎𐤐.𐤅𐤆𐤄𐤁.𐤋𐤀.𐤀𐤅𐤊𐤋.𐤋𐤏𐤁𐤓.𐤀𐤕.𐤐𐤉.𐤉𐤄𐤅𐤄.𐤀𐤋𐤄𐤉.𐤋𐤏𐤔𐤅𐤕.𐤒𐤈𐤍𐤄.𐤀𐤅.𐤂𐤃𐤅𐤋𐤄|

19 𐤅𐤏𐤕𐤄.𐤔𐤁𐤅.𐤍𐤀.𐤁𐤆𐤄.𐤂𐤌.𐤀𐤕𐤌.𐤄𐤋𐤉𐤋𐤄.𐤅𐤀𐤃𐤏𐤄.𐤌𐤄.𐤉𐤎𐤐.𐤉𐤄𐤅𐤄.𐤃𐤁𐤓.𐤏𐤌𐤉|

20 𐤅𐤉𐤁𐤀.𐤀𐤋𐤄𐤉𐤌.𐤀𐤋.𐤁𐤋𐤏𐤌.𐤋𐤉𐤋𐤄.𐤅𐤉𐤀𐤌𐤓.𐤋𐤅.𐤀𐤌.𐤋𐤒𐤓𐤀.𐤋𐤊.𐤁𐤀𐤅.𐤄𐤀𐤍𐤔𐤉𐤌.𐤒𐤅𐤌.𐤋𐤊.𐤀𐤕𐤌.𐤅𐤀𐤊.𐤀𐤕.𐤄𐤃𐤁𐤓.𐤀𐤔𐤓.𐤀𐤃𐤁𐤓.𐤀𐤋𐤉𐤊.𐤀𐤕𐤅.𐤕𐤏𐤔𐤄|

21 𐤅𐤉𐤒𐤌.𐤁𐤋𐤏𐤌.𐤁𐤁𐤒𐤓.𐤅𐤉𐤇𐤁𐤔.𐤀𐤕.𐤀𐤕𐤍𐤅.𐤅𐤉𐤋𐤊.𐤏𐤌.𐤔𐤓𐤉.𐤌𐤅𐤀𐤁|

22 𐤅𐤉𐤇𐤓.𐤀𐤐.𐤀𐤋𐤄𐤉𐤌.𐤊𐤉.𐤄𐤅𐤋𐤊.𐤄𐤅𐤀.𐤅𐤉𐤕𐤉𐤑𐤁.𐤌𐤋𐤀𐤊.𐤉𐤄𐤅𐤄.𐤁𐤃𐤓𐤊.𐤋𐤔𐤈𐤍.𐤋𐤅.𐤅𐤄𐤅𐤀.𐤓𐤊𐤁.𐤏𐤋.𐤀𐤕𐤍𐤅.𐤅𐤔𐤍𐤉.𐤍𐤏𐤓𐤉𐤅.𐤏𐤌𐤅|

23 𐤅𐤕𐤓𐤀.𐤄𐤀𐤕𐤅𐤍.𐤀𐤕.𐤌𐤋𐤀𐤊.𐤉𐤄𐤅𐤄.𐤍𐤑𐤁.𐤁𐤃𐤓𐤊.𐤅𐤇𐤓𐤁𐤅.𐤔𐤋𐤅𐤐𐤄.𐤁𐤉𐤃𐤅.𐤅𐤕𐤈.𐤄𐤀𐤕𐤅𐤍.𐤌𐤍.𐤄𐤃𐤓𐤊.𐤅𐤕𐤋𐤊.𐤁𐤔𐤃𐤄.𐤅𐤉𐤊.𐤁𐤋𐤏𐤌.𐤀𐤕.𐤄𐤀𐤕𐤅𐤍.𐤋𐤄𐤈𐤕𐤄.𐤄𐤃𐤓𐤊|

24 𐤅𐤉𐤏𐤌𐤃.𐤌𐤋𐤀𐤊.𐤉𐤄𐤅𐤄.𐤁𐤌𐤔𐤏𐤅𐤋.𐤄𐤊𐤓𐤌𐤉𐤌.𐤂𐤃𐤓.𐤌𐤆𐤄.𐤅𐤂𐤃𐤓.𐤌𐤆𐤄|

..𐤊𐤄.. 𐤅𐤕𐤓𐤀.𐤄𐤀𐤕𐤅𐤍.𐤀𐤕.𐤌𐤋𐤀𐤊.𐤉𐤄𐤅𐤄.𐤅𐤕𐤋𐤇𐤑.𐤀𐤋.
𐤄𐤒𐤉𐤓.𐤅𐤕𐤋𐤇𐤑.𐤀𐤕.𐤓𐤂𐤋.𐤁𐤋𐤏𐤌.𐤀𐤋.𐤄𐤒𐤉𐤓.𐤅𐤉𐤎𐤐.
𐤋𐤄𐤊𐤕𐤄|
..𐤊𐤅.. 𐤅𐤉𐤅𐤎𐤐.𐤌𐤋𐤀𐤊.𐤉𐤄𐤅𐤄.𐤏𐤁𐤅𐤓.𐤅𐤉𐤏𐤌𐤃.𐤁𐤌𐤒𐤅𐤌.𐤑
𐤓.𐤀𐤔𐤓.𐤀𐤉𐤍.𐤃𐤓𐤊.𐤋𐤍𐤈𐤅𐤕.𐤉𐤌𐤉𐤍.𐤅𐤔𐤌𐤀𐤅𐤋|
..𐤊𐤆.. 𐤅𐤕𐤓𐤀.𐤄𐤀𐤕𐤅𐤍.𐤀𐤕.𐤌𐤋𐤀𐤊.𐤉𐤄𐤅𐤄.𐤅𐤕𐤓𐤁𐤑.𐤕𐤇
𐤕.𐤁𐤋𐤏𐤌.𐤅𐤉𐤇𐤓.𐤀𐤐.𐤁𐤋𐤏𐤌.𐤅𐤉𐤊.𐤀𐤕.𐤄𐤀𐤕𐤅𐤍.𐤁𐤌𐤒𐤋|
..𐤊𐤇.. 𐤅𐤉𐤐𐤕𐤇.𐤉𐤄𐤅𐤄.𐤀𐤕.𐤐𐤉.𐤄𐤀𐤕𐤅𐤍.𐤅𐤕𐤀𐤌𐤓.𐤋𐤁𐤋𐤏
𐤌.𐤌𐤄.𐤏𐤔𐤉𐤕𐤉.𐤋𐤊.𐤊𐤉.𐤄𐤊𐤉𐤕𐤍𐤉.𐤆𐤄.𐤔𐤋𐤔.𐤓𐤂𐤋𐤉
𐤌|
..𐤊𐤈.. 𐤅𐤉𐤀𐤌𐤓.𐤁𐤋𐤏𐤌.𐤋𐤀𐤕𐤅𐤍.𐤊𐤉.𐤄𐤕𐤏𐤋𐤋𐤕.𐤁𐤉.𐤋𐤅.𐤉
𐤔.𐤇𐤓𐤁.𐤁𐤉𐤃𐤉.𐤊𐤉.𐤏𐤕𐤄.𐤄𐤓𐤂𐤕𐤉𐤊|
..𐤋.. 𐤅𐤕𐤀𐤌𐤓.𐤄𐤀𐤕𐤅𐤍.𐤀𐤋.𐤁𐤋𐤏𐤌.𐤄𐤋𐤅𐤀.𐤀𐤍𐤊𐤉.𐤀𐤕𐤍
𐤊.𐤀𐤔𐤓.𐤓𐤊𐤁𐤕.𐤏𐤋𐤉.𐤌𐤏𐤅𐤃𐤊.𐤏𐤃.𐤄𐤉𐤅𐤌.𐤄𐤆𐤄.𐤄𐤄
𐤎𐤊𐤍.𐤄𐤎𐤊𐤍𐤕𐤉.𐤋𐤏𐤔𐤅𐤕.𐤋𐤊.𐤊𐤄.𐤅𐤉𐤀𐤌𐤓.𐤋𐤀|
..𐤋𐤀.. 𐤅𐤉𐤂𐤋.𐤉𐤄𐤅𐤄.𐤀𐤕.𐤏𐤉𐤍𐤉.𐤁𐤋𐤏𐤌.𐤅𐤉𐤓𐤀.𐤀𐤕.𐤌𐤋
𐤀𐤊.𐤉𐤄𐤅𐤄.𐤍𐤑𐤁.𐤁𐤃𐤓𐤊.𐤅𐤇𐤓𐤁𐤅.𐤔𐤋𐤐𐤄.𐤁𐤉𐤃𐤅.𐤅𐤉𐤒𐤃
.𐤅𐤉𐤔𐤕𐤇𐤅.𐤋𐤀𐤐𐤉𐤅|
..𐤋𐤁.. 𐤅𐤉𐤀𐤌𐤓.𐤀𐤋𐤉𐤅.𐤌𐤋𐤀𐤊.𐤉𐤄𐤅𐤄.𐤏𐤋.𐤌𐤄.𐤄𐤊𐤉𐤕.𐤀
𐤕.𐤀𐤕𐤍𐤊.𐤆𐤄.𐤔𐤋𐤅𐤔.𐤓𐤂𐤋𐤉𐤌.𐤄𐤍𐤄.𐤀𐤍𐤊𐤉.𐤉𐤑𐤀𐤕𐤉.
𐤋𐤔𐤈𐤍.𐤊𐤉.𐤉𐤓𐤈.𐤄𐤃𐤓𐤊.𐤋𐤍𐤂𐤃𐤉|
..𐤋𐤂.. 𐤅𐤕𐤓𐤀𐤍𐤉.𐤄𐤀𐤕𐤅𐤍.𐤅𐤕𐤈.𐤋𐤐𐤍𐤉.𐤆𐤄.𐤔𐤋𐤔.𐤓𐤂𐤋𐤉
𐤌.𐤀𐤅𐤋𐤉.𐤍𐤈𐤕𐤄.𐤌𐤐𐤍𐤉.𐤊𐤉.𐤏𐤕𐤄.𐤂𐤌.𐤀𐤕𐤊𐤄.𐤄𐤓𐤂𐤕
𐤉.𐤅𐤀𐤅𐤕𐤄.𐤄𐤇𐤉𐤉𐤕𐤉|
..𐤋𐤃.. 𐤅𐤉𐤀𐤌𐤓.𐤁𐤋𐤏𐤌.𐤀𐤋.𐤌𐤋𐤀𐤊.𐤉𐤄𐤅𐤄.𐤇𐤈𐤀𐤕𐤉.𐤊
𐤉.𐤋𐤀.𐤉𐤃𐤏𐤕𐤉.𐤊𐤉.𐤀𐤕𐤄.𐤍𐤑𐤁.𐤋𐤒𐤓𐤀𐤕𐤉.𐤁𐤃𐤓𐤊.𐤅
𐤏𐤕𐤄.𐤀𐤌.𐤓𐤏.𐤁𐤏𐤉𐤍𐤉𐤊.𐤀𐤔𐤅𐤁𐤄.𐤋𐤉|
..𐤋𐤄.. 𐤅𐤉𐤀𐤌𐤓.𐤌𐤋𐤀𐤊.𐤉𐤄𐤅𐤄.𐤀𐤋.𐤁𐤋𐤏𐤌.𐤋𐤊.𐤏𐤌.𐤄𐤀𐤍
𐤔𐤉𐤌.𐤅𐤀𐤐𐤎.𐤀𐤕.𐤄𐤃𐤁𐤓.𐤀𐤔𐤓.𐤀𐤃𐤁𐤓.𐤀𐤋𐤉𐤊.𐤀𐤕𐤅.𐤕
𐤃𐤁𐤓.𐤅𐤉𐤋𐤊.𐤁𐤋𐤏𐤌.𐤏𐤌.𐤔𐤓𐤉.𐤁𐤋𐤒|

..לו.. וישמע.בלק.כי.בא.בלעם.ויצא.לקראתו.
אל.עיר.מואב.אשר.על.גבל.ארנן.אשר.בקצה.
הגבול|

..לז.. ויאמר.בלק.אל.בלעם.הלא.שלח.שלחתי.
אליך.לקרא.לך.למה.לא.הלכת.אלי.האמנם.לא
אוכל.כבדך|

..לח.. ויאמר.בלעם.אל.בלק.הנה.באתי.אליך.ע
תה.היכול.אוכל.דבר.מאומה.הדבר.אשר.ישי
ם.אלהים.בפי.אתו.אדבר|

..לט.. וילך.בלעם.עם.בלק.ויבאו.קרית.חצות|

..מ.. ויזבח.בלק.בקר.וצאן.וישלח.לבלעם.ו
לשרים.אשר.אתו|

..מא.. ויהי.בבקר.ויקח.בלק.את.בלעם.ויעלהו
.במות.בעל.וירא.משם.קצה.העם||

..כג.. במדבר.חלק

..א.. ויאמר.בלעם.אל.בלק.בנה.לי.בזה.שבעה.
מזבחת.והכן.לי.בזה.שבעה.פרים.ושבעה.א
ילים|

..ב.. ויעש.בלק.כאשר.דבר.בלעם.ויעל.בלק.וב
לעם.פר.ואיל.במזבח|

..ג.. ויאמר.בלעם.לבלק.התיצב.על.עלתך.ואל
כה.אולי.יקרה.יהוה.לקראתי.ודבר.מה.יראנ
י.והגדתי.לך.וילך.שפי|

..ד.. ויקר.אלהים.אל.בלעם.ויאמר.אליו.את.ש
בעת.המזבחת.ערכתי.ואעל.פר.ואיל.במזב
ח|

..ה.. וישם.יהוה.דבר.בפי.בלעם.ויאמר.שוב.אל.
בלק.וכה.תדבר|

𐤅 𐤅𐤉𐤔𐤁.𐤀𐤋𐤉𐤅.𐤅𐤄𐤍𐤄.𐤍𐤑𐤁.𐤏𐤋.𐤏𐤋𐤕𐤅.𐤄𐤅𐤀.𐤅𐤊𐤋.𐤔𐤓
𐤉.𐤌𐤅𐤀𐤁|
𐤆 𐤅𐤉𐤔𐤀.𐤌𐤔𐤋𐤅.𐤅𐤉𐤀𐤌𐤓.𐤌𐤍.𐤀𐤓𐤌.𐤉𐤍𐤇𐤍𐤉.𐤁𐤋𐤒.𐤌𐤋
𐤊.𐤌𐤅𐤀𐤁.𐤌𐤄𐤓𐤓𐤉.𐤒𐤃𐤌.𐤋𐤊𐤄.𐤀𐤓𐤄.𐤋𐤉.𐤉𐤏𐤒𐤁.𐤅𐤋𐤊𐤄
.𐤆𐤏𐤌𐤄.𐤉𐤔𐤓𐤀𐤋|
𐤇 𐤌𐤄.𐤀𐤒𐤁.𐤋𐤀.𐤒𐤁𐤄.𐤀𐤋.𐤅𐤌𐤄.𐤀𐤆𐤏𐤌.𐤋𐤀.𐤆𐤏𐤌.
𐤉𐤄𐤅𐤄|
𐤈 𐤊𐤉.𐤌𐤓𐤀𐤔.𐤑𐤓𐤉𐤌.𐤀𐤓𐤀𐤍𐤅.𐤅𐤌𐤂𐤁𐤏𐤅𐤕.𐤀𐤔𐤅𐤓𐤍𐤅.
𐤄𐤍.𐤏𐤌.𐤋𐤁𐤃𐤃.𐤉𐤔𐤊𐤍.𐤅𐤁𐤂𐤅𐤉𐤌.𐤋𐤀.𐤉𐤕𐤇𐤔𐤁|
𐤉 𐤌𐤉.𐤌𐤍𐤄.𐤏𐤐𐤓.𐤉𐤏𐤒𐤁.𐤅𐤌𐤎𐤐𐤓.𐤀𐤕.𐤓𐤁𐤏.𐤉𐤔𐤓𐤀
𐤋.𐤕𐤌𐤕.𐤍𐤐𐤔𐤉.𐤌𐤅𐤕.𐤉𐤔𐤓𐤉𐤌.𐤅𐤕𐤄𐤉.𐤀𐤇𐤓𐤉𐤕𐤉.𐤊𐤌𐤄
𐤅|
𐤉𐤀 𐤅𐤉𐤀𐤌𐤓.𐤁𐤋𐤒.𐤀𐤋.𐤁𐤋𐤏𐤌.𐤌𐤄.𐤏𐤔𐤉𐤕.𐤋𐤉.𐤋𐤒𐤁.
𐤀𐤉𐤁𐤉.𐤋𐤒𐤇𐤕𐤉𐤊.𐤅𐤄𐤍𐤄.𐤁𐤓𐤊𐤕.𐤁𐤓𐤊|
𐤉𐤁 𐤅𐤉𐤏𐤍.𐤅𐤉𐤀𐤌𐤓.𐤄𐤋𐤀.𐤀𐤕.𐤀𐤔𐤓.𐤉𐤔𐤉𐤌.𐤉𐤄𐤅𐤄.𐤁𐤐
𐤉.𐤀𐤕𐤅.𐤀𐤔𐤌𐤓.𐤋𐤃𐤁𐤓|
𐤉𐤂 𐤅𐤉𐤀𐤌𐤓.𐤀𐤋𐤉𐤅.𐤁𐤋𐤒.𐤋𐤊.||𐤋𐤊𐤄.𐤒𐤓𐤉||.𐤍𐤀.𐤀𐤕𐤉.
𐤀𐤋.𐤌𐤒𐤅𐤌.𐤀𐤇𐤓.𐤀𐤔𐤓.𐤕𐤓𐤀𐤍𐤅.𐤌𐤔𐤌.𐤀𐤐𐤎.𐤒𐤑𐤄𐤅.𐤕
𐤓𐤀𐤄.𐤅𐤊𐤋𐤅.𐤋𐤀.𐤕𐤓𐤀𐤄.𐤅𐤒𐤁𐤍𐤅.𐤋𐤉.𐤌𐤔𐤌|
𐤉𐤃 𐤅𐤉𐤒𐤇𐤄𐤅.𐤔𐤃𐤄.𐤑𐤐𐤉𐤌.𐤀𐤋.𐤓𐤀𐤔.𐤄𐤐𐤎𐤂𐤄.𐤅𐤉
𐤁𐤍.𐤔𐤁𐤏𐤄.𐤌𐤆𐤁𐤇𐤕.𐤅𐤉𐤏𐤋.𐤐𐤓.𐤅𐤀𐤉𐤋.𐤁𐤌𐤆𐤁𐤇|
𐤈𐤅 𐤅𐤉𐤀𐤌𐤓.𐤀𐤋.𐤁𐤋𐤒.𐤄𐤕𐤉𐤑𐤁.𐤊𐤄.𐤏𐤋.𐤏𐤋𐤕𐤊.𐤅𐤀𐤍
𐤊𐤉.𐤀𐤒𐤓𐤄.𐤊𐤄|
𐤈𐤆 𐤅𐤉𐤒𐤓.𐤉𐤄𐤅𐤄.𐤀𐤋.𐤁𐤋𐤏𐤌.𐤅𐤉𐤔𐤌.𐤃𐤁𐤓.𐤁𐤐𐤉𐤅.𐤅𐤉𐤀
𐤌𐤓.𐤔𐤅𐤁.𐤀𐤋.𐤁𐤋𐤒.𐤅𐤊𐤄.𐤕𐤃𐤁𐤓|
𐤉𐤆 𐤅𐤉𐤁𐤀.𐤀𐤋𐤉𐤅.𐤅𐤄𐤍𐤅.𐤍𐤑𐤁.𐤏𐤋.𐤏𐤋𐤕𐤅.𐤅𐤔𐤓𐤉.𐤌𐤅𐤀𐤁
.𐤀𐤕𐤅.𐤅𐤉𐤀𐤌𐤓.𐤋𐤅.𐤁𐤋𐤒.𐤌𐤄.𐤃𐤁𐤓.𐤉𐤄𐤅𐤄|
𐤉𐤇 𐤅𐤉𐤔𐤀.𐤌𐤔𐤋𐤅.𐤅𐤉𐤀𐤌𐤓.𐤒𐤅𐤌.𐤁𐤋𐤒.𐤅𐤔𐤌𐤏.𐤄𐤀𐤆𐤉
𐤍𐤄.𐤏𐤃𐤉.𐤁𐤍𐤅.𐤑𐤐𐤓|
𐤉𐤈 𐤋𐤀.𐤀𐤉𐤔.𐤀𐤋.𐤅𐤉𐤊𐤆𐤁.𐤅𐤁𐤍.𐤀𐤃𐤌.𐤅𐤉𐤕𐤍𐤇𐤌.𐤄
𐤄𐤅𐤀.𐤀𐤌𐤓.𐤅𐤋𐤀.𐤉𐤏𐤔𐤄.𐤅𐤃𐤁𐤓.𐤅𐤋𐤀.𐤉𐤒𐤉𐤌𐤍𐤄|

20 𐤄𐤍𐤄.𐤁𐤓𐤊.𐤋𐤒𐤇𐤕𐤉.𐤅𐤁𐤓𐤊.𐤅𐤋𐤀.𐤀𐤔𐤉𐤁𐤍𐤄|
21 𐤋𐤀.𐤄𐤁𐤉𐤈.𐤀𐤅𐤍.𐤁𐤉𐤏𐤒𐤁.𐤅𐤋𐤀.𐤓𐤀𐤄.𐤏𐤌𐤋.𐤁𐤉𐤔
𐤓𐤀𐤋.𐤉𐤄𐤅𐤄.𐤀𐤋𐤄𐤉𐤅.𐤏𐤌𐤅.𐤅𐤕𐤓𐤅𐤏𐤕.𐤌𐤋𐤊.𐤁𐤅|
22 𐤀𐤋.𐤌𐤅𐤑𐤉𐤀𐤌.𐤌𐤌𐤑𐤓𐤉𐤌.𐤊𐤕𐤅𐤏𐤐𐤕.𐤓𐤀𐤌.𐤋𐤅|
23 𐤊𐤉.𐤋𐤀.𐤍𐤇𐤔.𐤁𐤉𐤏𐤒𐤁.𐤅𐤋𐤀.𐤒𐤎𐤌.𐤁𐤉𐤔𐤓𐤀𐤋.𐤊
𐤏𐤕.𐤉𐤀𐤌𐤓.𐤋𐤉𐤏𐤒𐤁.𐤅𐤋𐤉𐤔𐤓𐤀𐤋.𐤌𐤄.𐤐𐤏𐤋.𐤀𐤋|
24 𐤄𐤍.𐤏𐤌.𐤊𐤋𐤁𐤉𐤀.𐤉𐤒𐤅𐤌.𐤅𐤊𐤀𐤓𐤉.𐤉𐤕𐤍𐤔𐤀.𐤋𐤀.𐤉
𐤔𐤊𐤁.𐤏𐤃.𐤉𐤀𐤊𐤋.𐤈𐤓𐤐.𐤅𐤃𐤌.𐤇𐤋𐤋𐤉𐤌.𐤉𐤔𐤕𐤄|
25 𐤅𐤉𐤀𐤌𐤓.𐤁𐤋𐤒.𐤀𐤋.𐤁𐤋𐤏𐤌.𐤂𐤌.𐤒𐤁.𐤋𐤀.𐤕𐤒𐤁𐤍𐤅.
𐤂𐤌.𐤁𐤓𐤊.𐤋𐤀.𐤕𐤁𐤓𐤊𐤍𐤅|
26 𐤅𐤉𐤏𐤍.𐤁𐤋𐤏𐤌.𐤅𐤉𐤀𐤌𐤓.𐤀𐤋.𐤁𐤋𐤒.𐤄𐤋𐤀.𐤃𐤁𐤓𐤕𐤉.
𐤀𐤋𐤉𐤊.𐤋𐤀𐤌𐤓.𐤊𐤋.𐤀𐤔𐤓.𐤉𐤃𐤁𐤓.𐤉𐤄𐤅𐤄.𐤀𐤕𐤅.𐤀𐤏𐤔𐤄|
27 𐤅𐤉𐤀𐤌𐤓.𐤁𐤋𐤒.𐤀𐤋.𐤁𐤋𐤏𐤌.𐤋𐤊𐤄.𐤍𐤀.𐤀𐤒𐤇𐤊.𐤀𐤋.
𐤌𐤒𐤅𐤌.𐤀𐤇𐤓.𐤀𐤅𐤋𐤉.𐤉𐤉𐤔𐤓.𐤁𐤏𐤉𐤍𐤉.𐤄𐤀𐤋𐤄𐤉𐤌.𐤅𐤒𐤁𐤕
𐤅.𐤋𐤉.𐤌𐤔𐤌|
28 𐤅𐤉𐤒𐤇.𐤁𐤋𐤒.𐤀𐤕.𐤁𐤋𐤏𐤌.𐤓𐤀𐤔.𐤄𐤐𐤏𐤅𐤓.𐤄𐤍𐤔𐤒𐤐.
𐤏𐤋.𐤐𐤍𐤉.𐤄𐤉𐤔𐤉𐤌𐤍|
29 𐤅𐤉𐤀𐤌𐤓.𐤁𐤋𐤏𐤌.𐤀𐤋.𐤁𐤋𐤒.𐤁𐤍𐤄.𐤋𐤉.𐤁𐤆𐤄.𐤔𐤁𐤏
𐤄.𐤌𐤆𐤁𐤇𐤕.𐤅𐤄𐤊𐤍.𐤋𐤉.𐤁𐤆𐤄.𐤔𐤁𐤏𐤄.𐤐𐤓𐤉𐤌.𐤅𐤔𐤁𐤏𐤄.
𐤀𐤉𐤋𐤌|
30 𐤅𐤉𐤏𐤔.𐤁𐤋𐤒.𐤊𐤀𐤔𐤓.𐤀𐤌𐤓.𐤁𐤋𐤏𐤌.𐤅𐤉𐤏𐤋.𐤐𐤓.𐤅𐤀
𐤉𐤋.𐤁𐤌𐤆𐤁𐤇||

𐤁𐤌𐤃𐤁𐤓.𐤇𐤋𐤒 24

1 𐤅𐤉𐤓𐤀.𐤁𐤋𐤏𐤌.𐤊𐤉.𐤈𐤅𐤁.𐤁𐤏𐤉𐤍𐤉.𐤉𐤄𐤅𐤄.𐤋𐤁𐤓𐤊.𐤀𐤕.
𐤉𐤔𐤓𐤀𐤋.𐤅𐤋𐤀.𐤄𐤋𐤊.𐤊𐤐𐤏𐤌.𐤁𐤐𐤏𐤌.𐤋𐤒𐤓𐤀𐤕.𐤍𐤇𐤔𐤉𐤌.
𐤅𐤉𐤔𐤕.𐤀𐤋.𐤄𐤌𐤃𐤁𐤓.𐤐𐤍𐤉𐤅|
2 𐤅𐤉𐤔𐤀.𐤁𐤋𐤏𐤌.𐤀𐤕.𐤏𐤉𐤍𐤉𐤅.𐤅𐤉𐤓𐤀.𐤀𐤕.𐤉𐤔𐤓𐤀𐤋.𐤔
𐤊𐤍.𐤋𐤔𐤁𐤈𐤉𐤅.𐤅𐤕𐤄𐤉.𐤏𐤋𐤉𐤅.𐤓𐤅𐤇.𐤀𐤋𐤄𐤉𐤌|

𐤂 𐤅𐤉𐤔𐤀.𐤌𐤔𐤋𐤅.𐤅𐤉𐤀𐤌𐤓.𐤍𐤀𐤌.𐤁𐤋𐤏𐤌.𐤁𐤍𐤅.𐤁𐤏𐤓.𐤅𐤍𐤀
𐤌.𐤄𐤂𐤁𐤓.𐤔𐤕𐤌.𐤄𐤏𐤉𐤍|

𐤃 𐤍𐤀𐤌.𐤔𐤌𐤏.𐤀𐤌𐤓𐤉.𐤀𐤋.𐤀𐤔𐤓.𐤌𐤇𐤆𐤄.𐤔𐤃𐤉.𐤉𐤇
𐤆𐤄.𐤍𐤐𐤋.𐤅𐤂𐤋𐤅𐤉.𐤏𐤉𐤍𐤉𐤌|

𐤄 𐤌𐤄.𐤈𐤁𐤅.𐤀𐤄𐤋𐤉𐤊.𐤉𐤏𐤒𐤁.𐤌𐤔𐤊𐤍𐤕𐤉𐤊.𐤉𐤔𐤓𐤀𐤋|

𐤅 𐤊𐤍𐤇𐤋𐤉𐤌.𐤍𐤈𐤉𐤅.𐤊𐤂𐤍𐤕.𐤏𐤋𐤉.𐤍𐤄𐤓.𐤊𐤀𐤄𐤋𐤉𐤌.𐤍𐤈
𐤏.𐤉𐤄𐤅𐤄.𐤊𐤀𐤓𐤆𐤉𐤌.𐤏𐤋𐤉.𐤌𐤉𐤌|

𐤆 𐤉𐤆𐤋.𐤌𐤉𐤌.𐤌𐤃𐤋𐤉𐤅.𐤅𐤆𐤓𐤏𐤅.𐤁𐤌𐤉𐤌.𐤓𐤁𐤉𐤌.𐤅𐤉𐤓𐤌
.𐤌𐤀𐤂𐤂.𐤌𐤋𐤊𐤅.𐤅𐤕𐤍𐤔𐤀.𐤌𐤋𐤊𐤕𐤅|

𐤇 𐤀𐤋.𐤌𐤅𐤑𐤉𐤀𐤅.𐤌𐤌𐤑𐤓𐤉𐤌.𐤊𐤕𐤅𐤏𐤐𐤕.𐤓𐤀𐤌.𐤋𐤅.𐤉𐤀𐤊
𐤋.𐤂𐤅𐤉𐤌.𐤑𐤓𐤉𐤅.𐤅𐤏𐤑𐤌𐤕𐤉𐤄𐤌.𐤉𐤂𐤓𐤌.𐤅𐤇𐤑𐤉𐤅.𐤉𐤌𐤇
𐤑|

𐤈 𐤊𐤓𐤏.𐤔𐤊𐤁.𐤊𐤀𐤓𐤉.𐤅𐤊𐤋𐤁𐤉𐤀.𐤌𐤉.𐤉𐤒𐤉𐤌𐤍𐤅.𐤌𐤁𐤓𐤊
𐤉𐤊.𐤁𐤓𐤅𐤊.𐤅𐤀𐤓𐤓𐤊.𐤀𐤓𐤅𐤓|

𐤉 𐤅𐤉𐤇𐤓.𐤀𐤐.𐤁𐤋𐤒.𐤀𐤋.𐤁𐤋𐤏𐤌.𐤅𐤉𐤎𐤐𐤒.𐤀𐤕.𐤊𐤐𐤉𐤅.𐤅
𐤉𐤀𐤌𐤓.𐤁𐤋𐤒.𐤀𐤋.𐤁𐤋𐤏𐤌.𐤋𐤒𐤁.𐤀𐤉𐤁𐤉.𐤒𐤓𐤀𐤕𐤉𐤊.𐤅𐤄𐤍
𐤄.𐤁𐤓𐤊𐤕.𐤁𐤓𐤊.𐤆𐤄.𐤔𐤋𐤔.𐤐𐤏𐤌𐤉𐤌|

𐤉𐤀 𐤅𐤏𐤕𐤄.𐤁𐤓𐤇.𐤋𐤊.𐤀𐤋.𐤌𐤒𐤅𐤌𐤊.𐤀𐤌𐤓𐤕𐤉.𐤊𐤁𐤃.𐤀
𐤊𐤁𐤃𐤊.𐤅𐤄𐤍𐤄.𐤌𐤍𐤏𐤊.𐤉𐤄𐤅𐤄.𐤌𐤊𐤁𐤅𐤃|

𐤉𐤁 𐤅𐤉𐤀𐤌𐤓.𐤁𐤋𐤏𐤌.𐤀𐤋.𐤁𐤋𐤒.𐤄𐤋𐤀.𐤂𐤌.𐤀𐤋.𐤌𐤋𐤀𐤊𐤉
𐤊.𐤀𐤔𐤓.𐤔𐤋𐤇𐤕.𐤀𐤋𐤉.𐤃𐤁𐤓𐤕𐤉.𐤋𐤀𐤌𐤓|

𐤉𐤂 𐤀𐤌.𐤉𐤕𐤍.𐤋𐤉.𐤁𐤋𐤒.𐤌𐤋𐤀.𐤁𐤉𐤕𐤅.𐤊𐤎𐤐.𐤅𐤆𐤄𐤁.𐤋𐤀
.𐤀𐤅𐤊𐤋.𐤋𐤏𐤁𐤓.𐤀𐤕.𐤐𐤉.𐤉𐤄𐤅𐤄.𐤋𐤏𐤔𐤅𐤕.𐤈𐤅𐤁𐤄.𐤀𐤅.𐤓𐤏𐤄
.𐤌𐤋𐤁𐤉.𐤀𐤔𐤓.𐤉𐤃𐤁𐤓.𐤉𐤄𐤅𐤄.𐤀𐤕𐤅.𐤀𐤃𐤁𐤓|

𐤉𐤃 𐤅𐤏𐤕𐤄.𐤄𐤍𐤍𐤉.𐤄𐤅𐤋𐤊.𐤋𐤏𐤌𐤉.𐤋𐤊𐤄.𐤀𐤉𐤏𐤑𐤊.𐤀
𐤔𐤓.𐤉𐤏𐤔𐤄.𐤄𐤏𐤌.𐤄𐤆𐤄.𐤋𐤏𐤌𐤊.𐤁𐤀𐤇𐤓𐤉𐤕.𐤄𐤉𐤌𐤉𐤌|

𐤈𐤅 𐤅𐤉𐤔𐤀.𐤌𐤔𐤋𐤅.𐤅𐤉𐤀𐤌𐤓.𐤍𐤀𐤌.𐤁𐤋𐤏𐤌.𐤁𐤍𐤅.𐤁𐤏𐤓.𐤅𐤍
𐤀𐤌.𐤄𐤂𐤁𐤓.𐤔𐤕𐤌.𐤄𐤏𐤉𐤍|

𐤈𐤆 𐤍𐤀𐤌.𐤔𐤌𐤏.𐤀𐤌𐤓𐤉.𐤀𐤋.𐤅𐤉𐤃𐤏.𐤃𐤏𐤕.𐤏𐤋𐤉𐤅𐤍.𐤌
𐤇𐤆𐤄.𐤔𐤃𐤉.𐤉𐤇𐤆𐤄.𐤍𐤐𐤋.𐤅𐤂𐤋𐤅𐤉.𐤏𐤉𐤍𐤉𐤌|

..𐤉𐤆.. 𐤀𐤓𐤀𐤍𐤅.𐤅𐤋𐤀.𐤏𐤕𐤄.𐤀𐤔𐤅𐤓𐤍𐤅.𐤅𐤋𐤀.𐤒𐤓𐤅𐤁.𐤃𐤓𐤊.𐤊
𐤅𐤊𐤁.𐤌𐤉𐤏𐤒𐤁.𐤅𐤒𐤌.𐤔𐤁𐤈.𐤌𐤉𐤔𐤓𐤀𐤋.𐤅𐤌𐤇𐤑.𐤐𐤀𐤕𐤉.
𐤌𐤅𐤀𐤁.𐤅𐤒𐤓𐤒𐤓.𐤊𐤋.𐤁𐤍𐤉.𐤔𐤕|
..𐤉𐤇.. 𐤅𐤄𐤉𐤄.𐤀𐤃𐤅𐤌.𐤉𐤓𐤔𐤄.𐤅𐤄𐤉𐤄.𐤉𐤓𐤔𐤄.𐤔𐤏𐤉𐤓.𐤀𐤉
𐤁𐤉𐤅.𐤅𐤉𐤔𐤓𐤀𐤋.𐤏𐤔𐤄.𐤇𐤉𐤋|
..𐤉𐤈.. 𐤅𐤉𐤓𐤃.𐤌𐤉𐤏𐤒𐤁.𐤅𐤄𐤀𐤁𐤉𐤃.𐤔𐤓𐤉𐤃.𐤌𐤏𐤉𐤓|
..𐤊.. 𐤅𐤉𐤓𐤀.𐤀𐤕.𐤏𐤌𐤋𐤒.𐤅𐤉𐤔𐤀.𐤌𐤔𐤋𐤅.𐤅𐤉𐤀𐤌𐤓.𐤓𐤀𐤔𐤉
𐤕.𐤂𐤅𐤉𐤌.𐤏𐤌𐤋𐤒.𐤅𐤀𐤇𐤓𐤉𐤕𐤅.𐤏𐤃𐤉.𐤀𐤁𐤃|
..𐤊𐤀.. 𐤅𐤉𐤓𐤀.𐤀𐤕.𐤄𐤒𐤉𐤍𐤉.𐤅𐤉𐤔𐤀.𐤌𐤔𐤋𐤅.𐤅𐤉𐤀𐤌𐤓.𐤀𐤉𐤕
𐤍.𐤌𐤅𐤔𐤁𐤊.𐤅𐤔𐤉𐤌.𐤁𐤎𐤋𐤏.𐤒𐤍𐤊|
..𐤊𐤁.. 𐤊𐤉.𐤀𐤌.𐤉𐤄𐤉𐤄.𐤋𐤁𐤏𐤓.𐤒𐤉𐤍.𐤏𐤃.𐤌𐤄.𐤀𐤔𐤅𐤓.𐤕
𐤔𐤁𐤊|
..𐤊𐤂.. 𐤅𐤉𐤔𐤀.𐤌𐤔𐤋𐤅.𐤅𐤉𐤀𐤌𐤓.𐤀𐤅𐤉.𐤌𐤉.𐤉𐤇𐤉𐤄.𐤌𐤔𐤌𐤅.
𐤀𐤋|
..𐤊𐤃.. 𐤅𐤑𐤉𐤌.𐤌𐤉𐤃.𐤊𐤕𐤉𐤌.𐤅𐤏𐤍𐤅.𐤀𐤔𐤅𐤓.𐤅𐤏𐤍𐤅.𐤏𐤁𐤓.𐤅
𐤂𐤌.𐤄𐤅𐤀.𐤏𐤃𐤉.𐤀𐤁𐤃|
..𐤊𐤄.. 𐤅𐤉𐤒𐤌.𐤁𐤋𐤏𐤌.𐤅𐤉𐤋𐤊.𐤅𐤉𐤔𐤁.𐤋𐤌𐤒𐤌𐤅.𐤅𐤂𐤌.𐤁𐤋𐤒.
𐤄𐤋𐤊.𐤋𐤃𐤓𐤊𐤅||

𐤁𐤌𐤃𐤁𐤓.𐤇𐤋𐤒 ..𐤊𐤄..

..𐤀.. 𐤅𐤉𐤔𐤁.𐤉𐤔𐤓𐤀𐤋.𐤁𐤔𐤈𐤉𐤌.𐤅𐤉𐤇𐤋.𐤄𐤏𐤌.𐤋𐤆𐤍𐤅𐤕.𐤀
𐤋.𐤁𐤍𐤅𐤕.𐤌𐤅𐤀𐤁|
..𐤁.. 𐤅𐤕𐤒𐤓𐤀𐤍.𐤋𐤏𐤌.𐤋𐤆𐤁𐤇𐤉.𐤀𐤋𐤄𐤉𐤄𐤍.𐤅𐤉𐤀𐤊𐤋.𐤄𐤏
𐤌.𐤅𐤉𐤔𐤕𐤇𐤅𐤅.𐤋𐤀𐤋𐤄𐤉𐤄𐤍|
..𐤂.. 𐤅𐤉𐤑𐤌𐤃.𐤉𐤔𐤓𐤀𐤋.𐤋𐤁𐤏𐤋.𐤐𐤏𐤅𐤓.𐤅𐤉𐤇𐤓.𐤀𐤐.𐤉𐤄𐤅𐤄.
𐤁𐤉𐤔𐤓𐤀𐤋|
..𐤃.. 𐤅𐤉𐤀𐤌𐤓.𐤉𐤄𐤅𐤄.𐤀𐤋.𐤌𐤔𐤄.𐤒𐤇.𐤀𐤕.𐤊𐤋.𐤓𐤀𐤔𐤉.𐤄
𐤏𐤌.𐤅𐤄𐤅𐤒𐤏.𐤀𐤅𐤕𐤌.𐤋𐤉𐤄𐤅𐤄.𐤍𐤂𐤃.𐤄𐤔𐤌𐤔.𐤅𐤉𐤔𐤁.𐤇𐤓
𐤅𐤍.𐤀𐤐.𐤉𐤄𐤅𐤄.𐤌𐤉𐤔𐤓𐤀𐤋|

ה ויאמר.משה.אל.שפטי.ישראל.הרגו.איש.
אנשיו.הנצמדים.לבעל.פעור|
ו והנה.איש.מבני.ישראל.בא.ויקרב.אל.אח
יו.את.המדינית.לעיני.משה.ולעיני.כל.עד
ת.בני.ישראל.והמה.בכים.פתח.אהל.מועד|
ז וירא.פינחס.בן.אלעזר.בן.אהרן.הכהן.וי
קם.מתוך.העדה.ויקח.רמח.בידו|
ח ויבא.אחר.איש.ישראל.אל.הקבה.וידקר.
את.שניהם.את.איש.ישראל.ואת.האשה.אל.ק
בתה.ותעצר.המגפה.מעל.בני.ישראל|
ט ויהיו.המתים.במגפה.ארבעה.ועשרים.א
לף|
י וידבר.יהוה.אל.משה.לאמר|
יא פינחס.בן.אלעזר.בן.אהרן.הכהן.השיב.
את.חמתי.מעל.בני.ישראל.בקנאו.את.קנאת
י.בתוכם.ולא.כליתי.את.בני.ישראל.בקנאתי
|
יב לכן.אמר.הנני.נתן.לו.את.בריתי.שלום|
יג והיתה.לו.ולזרעו.אחריו.ברית.כהנת.עו
לם.תחת.אשר.קנא.לאלהיו.ויכפר.על.בני.ישר
אל|
יד ושם.איש.ישראל.המכה.אשר.הכה.את.ה
מדינית.זמרי.בן.סלוא.נשיא.בית.אב.לשמע
ני|
טו ושם.האשה.המכה.המדינית.כזבי.בת.
צור.ראש.אמות.בית.אב.במדין.הוא|
טז וידבר.יהוה.אל.משה.לאמר|
יז צרור.את.המדינים.והכיתם.אותם|
יח כי.צררים.הם.לכם.בנכליהם.אשר.נכלו.ל
כם.על.דבר.פעור.ועל.דבר.כזבי.בת.נשיא.מ

𐤃𐤉𐤍.𐤀𐤇𐤕𐤌.𐤄𐤌𐤊𐤄.𐤁𐤉𐤅𐤌.𐤄𐤌𐤂𐤐𐤄.𐤏𐤋.𐤃𐤁𐤓.𐤐𐤏𐤅
𐤓||

𐤁𐤌𐤃𐤁𐤓.𐤇𐤋𐤒 26

1 𐤅𐤉𐤄𐤉.𐤀𐤇𐤓𐤉.𐤄𐤌𐤂𐤐𐤄.𐤅𐤉𐤀𐤌𐤓.𐤉𐤄𐤅𐤄.𐤀𐤋.𐤌𐤔𐤄.
𐤅𐤀𐤋.𐤀𐤋𐤏𐤆𐤓.𐤁𐤍.𐤀𐤄𐤓𐤍.𐤄𐤊𐤄𐤍.𐤋𐤀𐤌𐤓|
2 𐤔𐤀𐤅.𐤀𐤕.𐤓𐤀𐤔.𐤊𐤋.𐤏𐤃𐤕.𐤁𐤍𐤉.𐤉𐤔𐤓𐤀𐤋.𐤌𐤁𐤍.𐤏𐤔
𐤓𐤉𐤌.𐤔𐤍𐤄.𐤅𐤌𐤏𐤋𐤄.𐤋𐤁𐤉𐤕.𐤀𐤁𐤕𐤌.𐤊𐤋.𐤉𐤑𐤀.𐤑𐤁𐤀.𐤁
𐤉𐤔𐤓𐤀𐤋|
3 𐤅𐤉𐤃𐤁𐤓.𐤌𐤔𐤄.𐤅𐤀𐤋𐤏𐤆𐤓.𐤄𐤊𐤄𐤍.𐤀𐤕𐤌.𐤁𐤏𐤓𐤁𐤕.
𐤌𐤅𐤀𐤁.𐤏𐤋.𐤉𐤓𐤃𐤍.𐤉𐤓𐤇𐤅.𐤋𐤀𐤌𐤓|
4 𐤌𐤁𐤍.𐤏𐤔𐤓𐤉𐤌.𐤔𐤍𐤄.𐤅𐤌𐤏𐤋𐤄.𐤊𐤀𐤔𐤓.𐤑𐤅𐤄.𐤉𐤄𐤅𐤄.
𐤀𐤕.𐤌𐤔𐤄.𐤅𐤁𐤍𐤉.𐤉𐤔𐤓𐤀𐤋.𐤄𐤉𐤑𐤀𐤉𐤌.𐤌𐤀𐤓𐤑.𐤌𐤑𐤓𐤉
𐤌|
5 𐤓𐤀𐤅𐤁𐤍.𐤁𐤊𐤅𐤓.𐤉𐤔𐤓𐤀𐤋.𐤁𐤍𐤉.𐤓𐤀𐤅𐤁𐤍.𐤇𐤍𐤅𐤊.𐤌𐤔𐤐𐤇
𐤕.𐤄𐤇𐤍𐤊𐤉.𐤋𐤐𐤋𐤅𐤀.𐤌𐤔𐤐𐤇𐤕.𐤄𐤐𐤋𐤀𐤉|
6 𐤋𐤇𐤑𐤓𐤍.𐤌𐤔𐤐𐤇𐤕.𐤄𐤇𐤑𐤓𐤅𐤍𐤉.𐤋𐤊𐤓𐤌𐤉.𐤌𐤔𐤐𐤇𐤕.
𐤄𐤊𐤓𐤌𐤉|
7 𐤀𐤋𐤄.𐤌𐤔𐤐𐤇𐤕.𐤄𐤓𐤀𐤅𐤁𐤍𐤉.𐤅𐤉𐤄𐤉𐤅.𐤐𐤒𐤃𐤉𐤄𐤌.𐤔
𐤋𐤔𐤄.𐤅𐤀𐤓𐤁𐤏𐤉𐤌.𐤀𐤋𐤐.𐤅𐤔𐤁𐤏.𐤌𐤀𐤅𐤕.𐤅𐤔𐤋𐤔𐤉𐤌|
8 𐤅𐤁𐤍𐤉.𐤐𐤋𐤅𐤀.𐤀𐤋𐤉𐤀𐤁|
9 𐤅𐤁𐤍𐤉.𐤀𐤋𐤉𐤀𐤁.𐤍𐤌𐤅𐤀𐤋.𐤅𐤃𐤕𐤍.𐤅𐤀𐤁𐤉𐤓𐤌.𐤄𐤅𐤀.𐤃
𐤕𐤍.𐤅𐤀𐤁𐤉𐤓𐤌.𐤒𐤓𐤅𐤀𐤉.||𐤒𐤓𐤉𐤀𐤉.𐤒𐤓𐤉||.𐤄𐤏𐤃𐤄.𐤀𐤔𐤓.
𐤄𐤑𐤅.𐤏𐤋.𐤌𐤔𐤄.𐤅𐤏𐤋.𐤀𐤄𐤓𐤍.𐤁𐤏𐤃𐤕.𐤒𐤓𐤇.𐤁𐤄𐤑𐤕𐤌.
𐤏𐤋.𐤉𐤄𐤅𐤄|
10 𐤅𐤕𐤐𐤕𐤇.𐤄𐤀𐤓𐤑.𐤀𐤕.𐤐𐤉𐤄.𐤅𐤕𐤁𐤋𐤏.𐤀𐤕𐤌.𐤅𐤀𐤕.
𐤒𐤓𐤇.𐤁𐤌𐤅𐤕.𐤄𐤏𐤃𐤄.𐤁𐤀𐤊𐤋.𐤄𐤀𐤔.𐤀𐤕.𐤇𐤌𐤔𐤉𐤌.𐤅𐤌
𐤀𐤕𐤉𐤌.𐤀𐤉𐤔.𐤅𐤉𐤄𐤉𐤅.𐤋𐤍𐤎|
11 𐤅𐤁𐤍𐤉.𐤒𐤓𐤇.𐤋𐤀.𐤌𐤕𐤅|

𐤉𐤁 𐤁𐤍𐤉.𐤔𐤌𐤏𐤅𐤍.𐤋𐤌𐤔𐤐𐤇𐤕𐤌.𐤋𐤍𐤌𐤅𐤀𐤋.𐤌𐤔𐤐𐤇𐤕.𐤄
𐤍𐤌𐤅𐤀𐤋𐤉.𐤋𐤉𐤌𐤉𐤍.𐤌𐤔𐤐𐤇𐤕.𐤄𐤉𐤌𐤉𐤍𐤉.𐤋𐤉𐤊𐤉𐤍.𐤌𐤔𐤐𐤇
𐤕.𐤄𐤉𐤊𐤉𐤍𐤉|
𐤉𐤂 𐤋𐤆𐤓𐤇.𐤌𐤔𐤐𐤇𐤕.𐤄𐤆𐤓𐤇𐤉.𐤋𐤔𐤀𐤅𐤋.𐤌𐤔𐤐𐤇𐤕.
𐤄𐤔𐤀𐤅𐤋𐤉|
𐤉𐤃 𐤀𐤋𐤄.𐤌𐤔𐤐𐤇𐤕.𐤄𐤔𐤌𐤏𐤍𐤉.𐤔𐤍𐤉𐤌.𐤅𐤏𐤔𐤓𐤉𐤌.𐤀𐤋
𐤐.𐤅𐤌𐤀𐤕𐤉𐤌|
𐤈𐤅 𐤁𐤍𐤉.𐤂𐤃.𐤋𐤌𐤔𐤐𐤇𐤕𐤌.𐤋𐤑𐤐𐤅𐤍.𐤌𐤔𐤐𐤇𐤕.𐤄𐤑𐤐𐤅
𐤍𐤉.𐤋𐤇𐤂𐤉.𐤌𐤔𐤐𐤇𐤕.𐤄𐤇𐤂𐤉.𐤋𐤔𐤅𐤍𐤉.𐤌𐤔𐤐𐤇𐤕.𐤄𐤔𐤅
𐤍𐤉|
𐤈𐤆 𐤋𐤀𐤆𐤍𐤉.𐤌𐤔𐤐𐤇𐤕.𐤄𐤀𐤆𐤍𐤉.𐤋𐤏𐤓𐤉.𐤌𐤔𐤐𐤇𐤕.𐤄
𐤏𐤓𐤉|
𐤉𐤆 𐤋𐤀𐤓𐤅𐤃.𐤌𐤔𐤐𐤇𐤕.𐤄𐤀𐤓𐤅𐤃𐤉.𐤋𐤀𐤓𐤀𐤋𐤉.𐤌𐤔𐤐𐤇
𐤕.𐤄𐤀𐤓𐤀𐤋𐤉|
𐤉𐤇 𐤀𐤋𐤄.𐤌𐤔𐤐𐤇𐤕.𐤁𐤍𐤉.𐤂𐤃.𐤋𐤐𐤒𐤃𐤉𐤄𐤌.𐤀𐤓𐤁𐤏𐤉
𐤌.𐤀𐤋𐤐.𐤅𐤇𐤌𐤔.𐤌𐤀𐤅𐤕|
𐤉𐤈 𐤁𐤍𐤉.𐤉𐤄𐤅𐤃𐤄.𐤏𐤓.𐤅𐤀𐤅𐤍𐤍.𐤅𐤉𐤌𐤕.𐤏𐤓.𐤅𐤀𐤅𐤍𐤍.𐤁𐤀𐤓
𐤑.𐤊𐤍𐤏𐤍|
𐤊 𐤅𐤉𐤄𐤉𐤅.𐤁𐤍𐤉.𐤉𐤄𐤅𐤃𐤄.𐤋𐤌𐤔𐤐𐤇𐤕𐤌.𐤋𐤔𐤋𐤄.𐤌𐤔𐤐
𐤇𐤕.𐤄𐤔𐤋𐤍𐤉.𐤋𐤐𐤓𐤑.𐤌𐤔𐤐𐤇𐤕.𐤄𐤐𐤓𐤑𐤉.𐤋𐤆𐤓𐤇.𐤌𐤔𐤐
𐤇𐤕.𐤄𐤆𐤓𐤇𐤉|
𐤊𐤀 𐤅𐤉𐤄𐤉𐤅.𐤁𐤍𐤉.𐤐𐤓𐤑.𐤋𐤇𐤑𐤓𐤍.𐤌𐤔𐤐𐤇𐤕.𐤄𐤇𐤑𐤓𐤍𐤉.
𐤋𐤇𐤌𐤅𐤋.𐤌𐤔𐤐𐤇𐤕.𐤄𐤇𐤌𐤅𐤋𐤉|
𐤊𐤁 𐤀𐤋𐤄.𐤌𐤔𐤐𐤇𐤕.𐤉𐤄𐤅𐤃𐤄.𐤋𐤐𐤒𐤃𐤉𐤄𐤌.𐤔𐤔𐤄.𐤅𐤔
𐤁𐤏𐤉𐤌.𐤀𐤋𐤐.𐤅𐤇𐤌𐤔.𐤌𐤀𐤅𐤕|
𐤊𐤂 𐤁𐤍𐤉.𐤉𐤔𐤔𐤊𐤓.𐤋𐤌𐤔𐤐𐤇𐤕𐤌.𐤕𐤅𐤋𐤏.𐤌𐤔𐤐𐤇𐤕.𐤄
𐤕𐤅𐤋𐤏𐤉.𐤋𐤐𐤅𐤄.𐤌𐤔𐤐𐤇𐤕.𐤄𐤐𐤅𐤍𐤉|
𐤊𐤃 𐤋𐤉𐤔𐤅𐤁.𐤌𐤔𐤐𐤇𐤕.𐤄𐤉𐤔𐤅𐤁𐤉.𐤋𐤔𐤌𐤓𐤍.𐤌𐤔𐤐𐤇𐤕.
𐤄𐤔𐤌𐤓𐤍𐤉|
𐤊𐤄 𐤀𐤋𐤄.𐤌𐤔𐤐𐤇𐤕.𐤉𐤔𐤔𐤊𐤓.𐤋𐤐𐤒𐤃𐤉𐤄𐤌.𐤀𐤓𐤁𐤏𐤄.
𐤅𐤔𐤔𐤉𐤌.𐤀𐤋𐤐.𐤅𐤔𐤋𐤔.𐤌𐤀𐤅𐤕|

כו בני.זבולן.למשפחתם.לסרד.משפחת.הס
רדי.לאלון.משפחת.האלני.ליחלאל.משפחת.
היחלאלי׃
כז אלה.משפחת.הזבולני.לפקדיהם.ששי
ם.אלף.וחמש.מאות׃
כח בני.יוסף.למשפחתם.מנשה.ואפרים׃
כט בני.מנשה.למכיר.משפחת.המכירי.ומכ
יר.הוליד.את.גלעד.לגלעד.משפחת.הגלע
די׃
ל אלה.בני.גלעד.איעזר.משפחת.האיע
זרי.לחלק.משפחת.החלקי׃
לא ואשריאל.משפחת.האשראלי.ושכם.משפ
חת.השכמי׃
לב ושמידע.משפחת.השמידעי.וחפר.משפ
חת.החפרי׃
לג וצלפחד.בן.חפר.לא.היו.לו.בנים.כי.אם.
בנות.ושם.בנות.צלפחד.מחלה.ונעה.חגלה.מ
לכה.ותרצה׃
לד אלה.משפחת.מנשה.ופקדיהם.שנים.וח
משים.אלף.ושבע.מאות׃
לה אלה.בני.אפרים.למשפחתם.לשותלח.מש
פחת.השתלחי.לבכר.משפחת.הבכרי.לתחן.מ
שפחת.התחני׃
לו ואלה.בני.שותלח.לערן.משפחת.הערני׃
לז אלה.משפחת.בני.אפרים.לפקדיהם.שני
ם.ושלשים.אלף.וחמש.מאות.אלה.בני.יוסף.ל
משפחתם׃
לח בני.בנימן.למשפחתם.לבלע.משפחת.הב
לעי.לאשבל.משפחת.האשבלי.לאחירם.משפח
ת.האחירמי׃

לט 𐤋𐤔𐤐𐤅𐤐𐤌.𐤌𐤔𐤐𐤇𐤕.𐤄𐤔𐤅𐤐𐤌𐤉.𐤋𐤇𐤅𐤐𐤌.𐤌𐤔𐤐𐤇𐤕
.𐤄𐤇𐤅𐤐𐤌𐤉|

מ 𐤅𐤉𐤄𐤉𐤅.𐤁𐤍𐤉.𐤁𐤋𐤏.𐤀𐤓𐤃.𐤅𐤍𐤏𐤌𐤍.𐤌𐤔𐤐𐤇𐤕.𐤄𐤀
𐤓𐤃𐤉.𐤋𐤍𐤏𐤌𐤍.𐤌𐤔𐤐𐤇𐤕.𐤄𐤍𐤏𐤌𐤉|

מא 𐤀𐤋𐤄.𐤁𐤍𐤉.𐤁𐤍𐤉𐤌𐤍.𐤋𐤌𐤔𐤐𐤇𐤕𐤌.𐤅𐤐𐤒𐤃𐤉𐤄𐤌.𐤇
𐤌𐤔𐤄.𐤅𐤀𐤓𐤁𐤏𐤉𐤌.𐤀𐤋𐤐.𐤅𐤔𐤔.𐤌𐤀𐤅𐤕|

מב 𐤀𐤋𐤄.𐤁𐤍𐤉.𐤃𐤍.𐤋𐤌𐤔𐤐𐤇𐤕𐤌.𐤋𐤔𐤅𐤇𐤌.𐤌𐤔𐤐𐤇𐤕.
𐤄𐤔𐤅𐤇𐤌𐤉.𐤀𐤋𐤄.𐤌𐤔𐤐𐤇𐤕.𐤃𐤍.𐤋𐤌𐤔𐤐𐤇𐤕𐤌|

מג 𐤊𐤋.𐤌𐤔𐤐𐤇𐤕.𐤄𐤔𐤅𐤇𐤌𐤉.𐤋𐤐𐤒𐤃𐤉𐤄𐤌.𐤀𐤓𐤁𐤏𐤄.
𐤅𐤔𐤔𐤉𐤌.𐤀𐤋𐤐.𐤅𐤀𐤓𐤁𐤏.𐤌𐤀𐤅𐤕|

מד 𐤁𐤍𐤉.𐤀𐤔𐤓.𐤋𐤌𐤔𐤐𐤇𐤕𐤌.𐤋𐤉𐤌𐤍𐤄.𐤌𐤔𐤐𐤇𐤕.𐤄𐤉
𐤌𐤍𐤄.𐤋𐤉𐤔𐤅𐤉.𐤌𐤔𐤐𐤇𐤕.𐤄𐤉𐤔𐤅𐤉.𐤋𐤁𐤓𐤉𐤏𐤄.𐤌𐤔𐤐𐤇𐤕.
𐤄𐤁𐤓𐤉𐤏𐤉|

מה 𐤋𐤁𐤍𐤉.𐤁𐤓𐤉𐤏𐤄.𐤋𐤇𐤁𐤓.𐤌𐤔𐤐𐤇𐤕.𐤄𐤇𐤁𐤓𐤉.𐤋𐤌𐤋
𐤊𐤉𐤀𐤋.𐤌𐤔𐤐𐤇𐤕.𐤄𐤌𐤋𐤊𐤉𐤀𐤋𐤉|

מו 𐤅𐤔𐤌.𐤁𐤕.𐤀𐤔𐤓.𐤔𐤓𐤇|

מז 𐤀𐤋𐤄.𐤌𐤔𐤐𐤇𐤕.𐤁𐤍𐤉.𐤀𐤔𐤓.𐤋𐤐𐤒𐤃𐤉𐤄𐤌.𐤔𐤋𐤔
𐤄.𐤅𐤇𐤌𐤔𐤉𐤌.𐤀𐤋𐤐.𐤅𐤀𐤓𐤁𐤏.𐤌𐤀𐤅𐤕|

מח 𐤁𐤍𐤉.𐤍𐤐𐤕𐤋𐤉.𐤋𐤌𐤔𐤐𐤇𐤕𐤌.𐤋𐤉𐤇𐤑𐤀𐤋.𐤌𐤔𐤐𐤇𐤕
.𐤄𐤉𐤇𐤑𐤀𐤋𐤉.𐤋𐤂𐤅𐤍𐤉.𐤌𐤔𐤐𐤇𐤕.𐤄𐤂𐤅𐤍𐤉|

מט 𐤋𐤉𐤑𐤓.𐤌𐤔𐤐𐤇𐤕.𐤄𐤉𐤑𐤓𐤉.𐤋𐤔𐤋𐤌.𐤌𐤔𐤐𐤇𐤕.𐤄
𐤔𐤋𐤌𐤉|

נ 𐤀𐤋𐤄.𐤌𐤔𐤐𐤇𐤕.𐤍𐤐𐤕𐤋𐤉.𐤋𐤌𐤔𐤐𐤇𐤕𐤌.𐤅𐤐𐤒𐤃𐤉𐤄
𐤌.𐤇𐤌𐤔𐤄.𐤅𐤀𐤓𐤁𐤏𐤉𐤌.𐤀𐤋𐤐.𐤅𐤀𐤓𐤁𐤏.𐤌𐤀𐤅𐤕|

נא 𐤀𐤋𐤄.𐤐𐤒𐤅𐤃𐤉.𐤁𐤍𐤉.𐤉𐤔𐤓𐤀𐤋.𐤔𐤔.𐤌𐤀𐤅𐤕.𐤀𐤋𐤐.𐤅𐤀
𐤋𐤐.𐤔𐤁𐤏.𐤌𐤀𐤅𐤕.𐤅𐤔𐤋𐤔𐤉𐤌|

נב 𐤅𐤉𐤃𐤁𐤓.𐤉𐤄𐤅𐤄.𐤀𐤋.𐤌𐤔𐤄.𐤋𐤀𐤌𐤓|

נג 𐤋𐤀𐤋𐤄.𐤕𐤇𐤋𐤒.𐤄𐤀𐤓𐤑.𐤁𐤍𐤇𐤋𐤄.𐤁𐤌𐤎𐤐𐤓.𐤔𐤌𐤅𐤕
|

נד 𐤋𐤓𐤁.𐤕𐤓𐤁𐤄.𐤍𐤇𐤋𐤕𐤅.𐤅𐤋𐤌𐤏𐤈.𐤕𐤌𐤏𐤉𐤈.𐤍𐤇𐤋𐤕𐤅.
𐤀𐤉𐤔.𐤋𐤐𐤉.𐤐𐤒𐤃𐤉𐤅.𐤉𐤕𐤍.𐤍𐤇𐤋𐤕𐤅|

נה 𐤀𐤊.𐤁𐤂𐤅𐤓𐤋.𐤉𐤇𐤋𐤒.𐤀𐤕.𐤄𐤀𐤓𐤑.𐤋𐤔𐤌𐤅𐤕.𐤌𐤈𐤅𐤕
.𐤀𐤁𐤕𐤌.𐤉𐤍𐤇𐤋𐤅|
נו 𐤏𐤋.𐤐𐤉.𐤄𐤂𐤅𐤓𐤋.𐤕𐤇𐤋𐤒.𐤍𐤇𐤋𐤕𐤅.𐤁𐤉𐤍.𐤓𐤁.𐤋𐤌𐤏𐤈
|
נז 𐤅𐤀𐤋𐤄.𐤐𐤒𐤅𐤃𐤉.𐤄𐤋𐤅𐤉.𐤋𐤌𐤔𐤐𐤇𐤕𐤌.𐤋𐤂𐤓𐤔𐤅𐤍.𐤌
𐤔𐤐𐤇𐤕.𐤄𐤂𐤓𐤔𐤍𐤉.𐤋𐤒𐤄𐤕.𐤌𐤔𐤐𐤇𐤕.𐤄𐤒𐤄𐤕𐤉.𐤋𐤌𐤓𐤓
𐤉.𐤌𐤔𐤐𐤇𐤕.𐤄𐤌𐤓𐤓𐤉|
נח 𐤀𐤋𐤄.𐤌𐤔𐤐𐤇𐤕.𐤋𐤅𐤉.𐤌𐤔𐤐𐤇𐤕.𐤄𐤋𐤁𐤍𐤉.𐤌𐤔𐤐𐤇𐤕
.𐤄𐤇𐤁𐤓𐤍𐤉.𐤌𐤔𐤐𐤇𐤕.𐤄𐤌𐤇𐤋𐤉.𐤌𐤔𐤐𐤇𐤕.𐤄𐤌𐤅𐤔𐤉.𐤌𐤔
𐤐𐤇𐤕.𐤄𐤒𐤓𐤇𐤉.𐤅𐤒𐤄𐤕.𐤄𐤅𐤋𐤃.𐤀𐤕.𐤏𐤌𐤓𐤌|
נט 𐤅𐤔𐤌.𐤀𐤔𐤕.𐤏𐤌𐤓𐤌.𐤉𐤅𐤊𐤁𐤃.𐤁𐤕.𐤋𐤅𐤉.𐤀𐤔𐤓.𐤉𐤋
𐤃𐤄.𐤀𐤕𐤄.𐤋𐤋𐤅𐤉.𐤁𐤌𐤑𐤓𐤉𐤌.𐤅𐤕𐤋𐤃.𐤋𐤏𐤌𐤓𐤌.𐤀𐤕.𐤀𐤄
𐤓𐤍.𐤅𐤀𐤕.𐤌𐤔𐤄.𐤅𐤀𐤕.𐤌𐤓𐤉𐤌.𐤀𐤇𐤕𐤌|
ס 𐤅𐤉𐤅𐤋𐤃.𐤋𐤀𐤄𐤓𐤍.𐤀𐤕.𐤍𐤃𐤁.𐤅𐤀𐤕.𐤀𐤁𐤉𐤄𐤅𐤀.𐤀𐤕.
𐤀𐤋𐤏𐤆𐤓.𐤅𐤀𐤕.𐤀𐤉𐤕𐤌𐤓|
סא 𐤅𐤉𐤌𐤕.𐤍𐤃𐤁.𐤅𐤀𐤁𐤉𐤄𐤅𐤀.𐤁𐤄𐤒𐤓𐤉𐤁𐤌.𐤀𐤔.𐤆𐤓𐤄.
𐤋𐤐𐤍𐤉.𐤉𐤄𐤅𐤄|
סב 𐤅𐤉𐤄𐤉𐤅.𐤐𐤒𐤃𐤉𐤄𐤌.𐤔𐤋𐤔𐤄.𐤅𐤏𐤔𐤓𐤉𐤌.𐤀𐤋𐤐.𐤊𐤋.
𐤆𐤊𐤓.𐤌𐤁𐤍.𐤇𐤃𐤔.𐤅𐤌𐤏𐤋𐤄.𐤊𐤉.𐤋𐤀.𐤄𐤕𐤐𐤒𐤃𐤅.𐤁𐤕𐤅𐤊.
𐤁𐤍𐤉.𐤉𐤔𐤓𐤀𐤋.𐤊𐤉.𐤋𐤀.𐤍𐤕𐤍.𐤋𐤄𐤌.𐤍𐤇𐤋𐤄.𐤁𐤕𐤅𐤊.𐤁𐤍𐤉.𐤉
𐤔𐤓𐤀𐤋|
סג 𐤀𐤋𐤄.𐤐𐤒𐤅𐤃𐤉.𐤌𐤔𐤄.𐤅𐤀𐤋𐤏𐤆𐤓.𐤄𐤊𐤄𐤍.𐤀𐤔𐤓.𐤐
𐤒𐤃𐤅.𐤀𐤕.𐤁𐤍𐤉.𐤉𐤔𐤓𐤀𐤋.𐤁𐤏𐤓𐤁𐤕.𐤌𐤅𐤀𐤁.𐤏𐤋.𐤉𐤓𐤃𐤍.𐤉
𐤓𐤇𐤅|
סד 𐤅𐤁𐤀𐤋𐤄.𐤋𐤀.𐤄𐤉𐤄.𐤀𐤉𐤔.𐤌𐤐𐤒𐤅𐤃𐤉.𐤌𐤔𐤄.𐤅𐤀𐤄𐤓
𐤍.𐤄𐤊𐤄𐤍.𐤀𐤔𐤓.𐤐𐤒𐤃𐤅.𐤀𐤕.𐤁𐤍𐤉.𐤉𐤔𐤓𐤀𐤋.𐤁𐤌𐤃𐤁𐤓.𐤎𐤉
𐤍𐤉|
סה 𐤊𐤉.𐤀𐤌𐤓.𐤉𐤄𐤅𐤄.𐤋𐤄𐤌.𐤌𐤅𐤕.𐤉𐤌𐤕𐤅.𐤁𐤌𐤃𐤁𐤓.𐤅𐤋𐤀.
𐤍𐤅𐤕𐤓.𐤌𐤄𐤌.𐤀𐤉𐤔.𐤊𐤉.𐤀𐤌.𐤊𐤋𐤁.𐤁𐤍.𐤉𐤐𐤍𐤄.𐤅𐤉𐤄𐤅𐤔𐤏.𐤁
𐤍.𐤍𐤅𐤍| ||

𐤁𐤌𐤃𐤁𐤓.𐤇𐤋𐤒 כז

א 𐤅𐤕𐤒𐤓𐤁𐤍𐤄.𐤁𐤍𐤅𐤕.𐤑𐤋𐤐𐤇𐤃.𐤁𐤍.𐤇𐤐𐤓.𐤁𐤍.𐤂𐤋𐤏𐤃.
𐤁𐤍.𐤌𐤊𐤉𐤓.𐤁𐤍.𐤌𐤍𐤔𐤄.𐤋𐤌𐤔𐤐𐤇𐤕.𐤌𐤍𐤔𐤄.𐤁𐤍.𐤉𐤅𐤎𐤐.𐤅𐤀
𐤋𐤄.𐤔𐤌𐤅𐤕.𐤁𐤍𐤕𐤉𐤅.𐤌𐤇𐤋𐤄.𐤍𐤏𐤄.𐤅𐤇𐤂𐤋𐤄.𐤅𐤌𐤋𐤊𐤄.𐤅𐤕
𐤓𐤑𐤄|

ב 𐤅𐤕𐤏𐤌𐤃𐤍𐤄.𐤋𐤐𐤍𐤉.𐤌𐤔𐤄.𐤅𐤋𐤐𐤍𐤉.𐤀𐤋𐤏𐤆𐤓.𐤄𐤊𐤄𐤍.
𐤅𐤋𐤐𐤍𐤉.𐤄𐤍𐤔𐤉𐤀𐤌.𐤅𐤊𐤋.𐤄𐤏𐤃𐤄.𐤐𐤕𐤇.𐤀𐤄𐤋.𐤌𐤅𐤏𐤃.𐤋
𐤀𐤌𐤓|

ג 𐤀𐤁𐤉𐤍𐤅.𐤌𐤕.𐤁𐤌𐤃𐤁𐤓.𐤅𐤄𐤅𐤀.𐤋𐤀.𐤄𐤉𐤄.𐤁𐤕𐤅𐤊.𐤄𐤏
𐤃𐤄.𐤄𐤍𐤅𐤏𐤃𐤉𐤌.𐤏𐤋.𐤉𐤄𐤅𐤄.𐤁𐤏𐤃𐤕.𐤒𐤓𐤇.𐤊𐤉.𐤁𐤇𐤈
𐤀𐤅.𐤌𐤕.𐤅𐤁𐤍𐤉𐤌.𐤋𐤀.𐤄𐤉𐤅.𐤋𐤅|

ד 𐤋𐤌𐤄.𐤉𐤂𐤓𐤏.𐤔𐤌.𐤀𐤁𐤉𐤍𐤅.𐤌𐤕𐤅𐤊.𐤌𐤔𐤐𐤇𐤕𐤅.𐤊𐤉.
𐤀𐤉𐤍.𐤋𐤅.𐤁𐤍.𐤕𐤍𐤄.𐤋𐤍𐤅.𐤀𐤇𐤆𐤄.𐤁𐤕𐤅𐤊.𐤀𐤇𐤉.𐤀𐤁𐤉𐤍𐤅|

ה 𐤅𐤉𐤒𐤓𐤁.𐤌𐤔𐤄.𐤀𐤕.𐤌𐤔𐤐𐤈𐤍.𐤋𐤐𐤍𐤉.𐤉𐤄𐤅𐤄|

ו 𐤅𐤉𐤀𐤌𐤓.𐤉𐤄𐤅𐤄.𐤀𐤋.𐤌𐤔𐤄.𐤋𐤀𐤌𐤓|

ז 𐤊𐤍.𐤁𐤍𐤅𐤕.𐤑𐤋𐤐𐤇𐤃.𐤃𐤁𐤓𐤕.𐤍𐤕𐤍.𐤕𐤕𐤍.𐤋𐤄𐤌.𐤀𐤇
𐤆𐤕.𐤍𐤇𐤋𐤄.𐤁𐤕𐤅𐤊.𐤀𐤇𐤉.𐤀𐤁𐤉𐤄𐤌.𐤅𐤄𐤏𐤁𐤓𐤕.𐤀𐤕.𐤍𐤇
𐤋𐤕.𐤀𐤁𐤉𐤄𐤍.𐤋𐤄𐤍|

ח 𐤅𐤀𐤋.𐤁𐤍𐤉.𐤉𐤔𐤓𐤀𐤋.𐤕𐤃𐤁𐤓.𐤋𐤀𐤌𐤓.𐤀𐤉𐤔.𐤊𐤉.𐤉𐤌𐤅
𐤕.𐤅𐤁𐤍.𐤀𐤉𐤍.𐤋𐤅.𐤅𐤄𐤏𐤁𐤓𐤕𐤌.𐤀𐤕.𐤍𐤇𐤋𐤕𐤅.𐤋𐤁𐤕𐤅|

ט 𐤅𐤀𐤌.𐤀𐤉𐤍.𐤋𐤅.𐤁𐤕.𐤅𐤍𐤕𐤕𐤌.𐤀𐤕.𐤍𐤇𐤋𐤕𐤅.𐤋𐤀𐤇𐤉𐤅|

י 𐤅𐤀𐤌.𐤀𐤉𐤍.𐤋𐤅.𐤀𐤇𐤉𐤌.𐤅𐤍𐤕𐤕𐤌.𐤀𐤕.𐤍𐤇𐤋𐤕𐤅.𐤋𐤀
𐤇𐤉.𐤀𐤁𐤉𐤅|

יא 𐤅𐤀𐤌.𐤀𐤉𐤍.𐤀𐤇𐤉𐤌.𐤋𐤀𐤁𐤉𐤅.𐤅𐤍𐤕𐤕𐤌.𐤀𐤕.𐤍𐤇𐤋𐤕𐤅.
𐤋𐤔𐤀𐤓𐤅.𐤄𐤒𐤓𐤁.𐤀𐤋𐤉𐤅.𐤌𐤌𐤔𐤐𐤇𐤕𐤅.𐤅𐤉𐤓𐤔.𐤀𐤕𐤄.𐤅𐤄𐤉
𐤕𐤄.𐤋𐤁𐤍𐤉.𐤉𐤔𐤓𐤀𐤋.𐤋𐤇𐤒𐤕.𐤌𐤔𐤐𐤈.𐤊𐤀𐤔𐤓.𐤑𐤅𐤄.𐤉𐤄𐤅
𐤄.𐤀𐤕.𐤌𐤔𐤄|

יב 𐤅𐤉𐤀𐤌𐤓.𐤉𐤄𐤅𐤄.𐤀𐤋.𐤌𐤔𐤄.𐤏𐤋𐤄.𐤀𐤋.𐤄𐤓.𐤄𐤏𐤁𐤓𐤉
𐤌.𐤄𐤆𐤄.𐤅𐤓𐤀𐤄.𐤀𐤕.𐤄𐤀𐤓𐤑.𐤀𐤔𐤓.𐤍𐤕𐤕𐤉.𐤋𐤁𐤍𐤉.𐤉𐤔𐤓
𐤀𐤋|

יג וראיתה.אתה.ונאספת.אל.עמיך.גם.את
ה.כאשר.נאסף.אהרן.אחיך׃
יד כאשר.מריתם.פי.במדבר.צן.במריבת.ה
עדה.להקדישני.במים.לעיניהם.הם.מי.מר
יבת.קדש.מדבר.צן׃
טו וידבר.משה.אל.יהוה.לאמר׃
טז יפקד.יהוה.אלהי.הרוחת.לכל.בשר.איש.
על.העדה׃
יז אשר.יצא.לפניהם.ואשר.יבא.לפניהם.וא
שר.יוציאם.ואשר.יביאם.ולא.תהיה.עדת.י
הוה.כצאן.אשר.אין.להם.רעה׃
יח ויאמר.יהוה.אל.משה.קח.לך.את.יהושע.
בן.נון.איש.אשר.רוח.בו.וסמכת.את.ידך.עליו׃
יט והעמדת.אתו.לפני.אלעזר.הכהן.ולפני.
כל.העדה.וצויתה.אתו.לעיניהם׃
כ ונתתה.מהודך.עליו.למען.ישמעו.כל.ע
דת.בני.ישראל׃
כא ולפני.אלעזר.הכהן.יעמד.ושאל.לו.במש
פט.האורים.לפני.יהוה.על.פיו.יצאו.ועל.פיו.
יבאו.הוא.וכל.בני.ישראל.אתו.וכל.העדה׃
כב ויעש.משה.כאשר.צוה.יהוה.אתו.ויקח.
את.יהושע.ויעמדהו.לפני.אלעזר.הכהן.ולפנ
י.כל.העדה׃
כג ויסמך.את.ידיו.עליו.ויצוהו.כאשר.דב
ר.יהוה.ביד.משה׃׃

במדבר.חלק כח

א וידבר.יהוה.אל.משה.לאמר׃

ב צו.את.בני.ישראל.ואמרת.אלהם.את.קרבנ
י.לחמי.לאשי.ריח.ניחחי.תשמרו.להקריב.ל
י.במועדו|
ג ואמרת.להם.זה.האשה.אשר.תקריבו.ליהו
ה.כבשים.בני.שנה.תמימם.שנים.ליום.עלה.ת
מיד|
ד את.הכבש.אחד.תעשה.בבקר.ואת.הכבש.
השני.תעשה.בין.הערבים|
ה ועשירית.האיפה.סלת.למנחה.בלולה.בשמ
ן.כתית.רביעת.ההין|
ו עלת.תמיד.העשיה.בהר.סיני.לריח.ניח
ח.אשה.ליהוה|
ז ונסכו.רביעת.ההין.לכבש.האחד.בקדש.
הסך.נסך.שכר.ליהוה|
ח ואת.הכבש.השני.תעשה.בין.הערבים.כמנ
חת.הבקר.וכנסכו.תעשה.אשה.ריח.ניחח.לי
הוה|
ט וביום.השבת.שני.כבשים.בני.שנה.תמימ
ם.ושני.עשרנים.סלת.מנחה.בלולה.בשמן.ונסכ
ו|
י עלת.שבת.בשבתו.על.עלת.התמיד.ונסכ
ה|
יא ובראשי.חדשיכם.תקריבו.עלה.ליהוה.פ
רים.בני.בקר.שנים.ואיל.אחד.כבשים.בני.ש
נה.שבעה.תמימם|
יב ושלשה.עשרנים.סלת.מנחה.בלולה.בשמן.
לפר.האחד.ושני.עשרנים.סלת.מנחה.בלולה.
בשמן.לאיל.האחד|
יג ועשרן.עשרון.סלת.מנחה.בלולה.בשמן.לכ
בש.האחד.עלה.ריח.ניחח.אשה.ליהוה|

14 𐤅𐤍𐤎𐤊𐤉𐤄𐤌.𐤇𐤑𐤉.𐤄𐤄𐤉𐤍.𐤉𐤄𐤉𐤄.𐤋𐤐𐤓.𐤅𐤔𐤋𐤉𐤔
𐤕.𐤄𐤄𐤉𐤍.𐤋𐤀𐤉𐤋.𐤅𐤓𐤁𐤉𐤏𐤕.𐤄𐤄𐤉𐤍.𐤋𐤊𐤁𐤔.𐤉𐤉𐤍.𐤆𐤀𐤕.
𐤏𐤋𐤕.𐤇𐤃𐤔.𐤁𐤇𐤃𐤔𐤅.𐤋𐤇𐤃𐤔𐤉.𐤄𐤔𐤍𐤄|
15 𐤅𐤔𐤏𐤉𐤓.𐤏𐤆𐤉𐤌.𐤀𐤇𐤃.𐤋𐤇𐤈𐤀𐤕.𐤋𐤉𐤄𐤅𐤄.𐤏𐤋.
𐤏𐤋𐤕.𐤄𐤕𐤌𐤉𐤃.𐤉𐤏𐤔𐤄.𐤅𐤍𐤎𐤊𐤅|
16 𐤅𐤁𐤇𐤃𐤔.𐤄𐤓𐤀𐤔𐤅𐤍.𐤁𐤀𐤓𐤁𐤏𐤄.𐤏𐤔𐤓.𐤉𐤅𐤌.𐤋𐤇𐤃
𐤔.𐤐𐤎𐤇.𐤋𐤉𐤄𐤅𐤄|
17 𐤅𐤁𐤇𐤌𐤔𐤄.𐤏𐤔𐤓.𐤉𐤅𐤌.𐤋𐤇𐤃𐤔.𐤄𐤆𐤄.𐤇𐤂.𐤔𐤁
𐤏𐤕.𐤉𐤌𐤉𐤌.𐤌𐤑𐤅𐤕.𐤉𐤀𐤊𐤋|
18 𐤁𐤉𐤅𐤌.𐤄𐤓𐤀𐤔𐤅𐤍.𐤌𐤒𐤓𐤀.𐤒𐤃𐤔.𐤊𐤋.𐤌𐤋𐤀𐤊𐤕.𐤏𐤁
𐤃𐤄.𐤋𐤀.𐤕𐤏𐤔𐤅|
19 𐤅𐤄𐤒𐤓𐤁𐤕𐤌.𐤀𐤔𐤄.𐤏𐤋𐤄.𐤋𐤉𐤄𐤅𐤄.𐤐𐤓𐤉𐤌.𐤁𐤍𐤉.𐤁
𐤒𐤓.𐤔𐤍𐤉𐤌.𐤅𐤀𐤉𐤋.𐤀𐤇𐤃.𐤅𐤔𐤁𐤏𐤄.𐤊𐤁𐤔𐤉𐤌.𐤁𐤍𐤉.𐤔𐤍𐤄
.𐤕𐤌𐤉𐤌𐤌.𐤉𐤄𐤉𐤅.𐤋𐤊𐤌|
20 𐤅𐤌𐤍𐤇𐤕𐤌.𐤎𐤋𐤕.𐤁𐤋𐤅𐤋𐤄.𐤁𐤔𐤌𐤍.𐤔𐤋𐤔𐤄.𐤏𐤔𐤓𐤍𐤉
𐤌.𐤋𐤐𐤓.𐤅𐤔𐤍𐤉.𐤏𐤔𐤓𐤍𐤉𐤌.𐤋𐤀𐤉𐤋.𐤕𐤏𐤔𐤅|
21 𐤏𐤔𐤓𐤅𐤍.𐤏𐤔𐤓𐤅𐤍.𐤕𐤏𐤔𐤄.𐤋𐤊𐤁𐤔.𐤄𐤀𐤇𐤃.𐤋𐤔𐤁𐤏
𐤕.𐤄𐤊𐤁𐤔𐤉𐤌|
22 𐤅𐤔𐤏𐤉𐤓.𐤇𐤈𐤀𐤕.𐤀𐤇𐤃.𐤋𐤊𐤐𐤓.𐤏𐤋𐤉𐤊𐤌|
23 𐤌𐤋𐤁𐤃.𐤏𐤋𐤕.𐤄𐤁𐤒𐤓.𐤀𐤔𐤓.𐤋𐤏𐤋𐤕.𐤄𐤕𐤌𐤉𐤃.𐤕
𐤏𐤔𐤅.𐤀𐤕.𐤀𐤋𐤄|
24 𐤊𐤀𐤋𐤄.𐤕𐤏𐤔𐤅.𐤋𐤉𐤅𐤌.𐤔𐤁𐤏𐤕.𐤉𐤌𐤉𐤌.𐤋𐤇𐤌.𐤀𐤔
𐤄.𐤓𐤉𐤇.𐤍𐤉𐤇𐤇.𐤋𐤉𐤄𐤅𐤄.𐤏𐤋.𐤏𐤅𐤋𐤕.𐤄𐤕𐤌𐤉𐤃.𐤉𐤏𐤔𐤄
.𐤅𐤍𐤎𐤊𐤅|
25 𐤅𐤁𐤉𐤅𐤌.𐤄𐤔𐤁𐤉𐤏𐤉.𐤌𐤒𐤓𐤀.𐤒𐤃𐤔.𐤉𐤄𐤉𐤄.𐤋𐤊𐤌.
𐤊𐤋.𐤌𐤋𐤀𐤊𐤕.𐤏𐤁𐤃𐤄.𐤋𐤀.𐤕𐤏𐤔𐤅|
26 𐤅𐤁𐤉𐤅𐤌.𐤄𐤁𐤊𐤅𐤓𐤉𐤌.𐤁𐤄𐤒𐤓𐤉𐤁𐤊𐤌.𐤌𐤍𐤇𐤄.𐤇𐤃𐤔
𐤄.𐤋𐤉𐤄𐤅𐤄.𐤁𐤔𐤁𐤏𐤕𐤉𐤊𐤌.𐤌𐤒𐤓𐤀.𐤒𐤃𐤔.𐤉𐤄𐤉𐤄.𐤋𐤊𐤌
.𐤊𐤋.𐤌𐤋𐤀𐤊𐤕.𐤏𐤁𐤃𐤄.𐤋𐤀.𐤕𐤏𐤔𐤅|

𐤊𐤆 𐤅𐤄𐤒𐤓𐤁𐤕𐤌 . 𐤏𐤅𐤋𐤄 . 𐤋𐤓𐤉𐤇 . 𐤍𐤉𐤇𐤇 . 𐤋𐤉𐤄𐤅𐤄 . 𐤐𐤓𐤉
𐤌 . 𐤁𐤍𐤉 . 𐤁𐤒𐤓 . 𐤔𐤍𐤉𐤌 . 𐤀𐤉𐤋 . 𐤀𐤇𐤃 . 𐤔𐤁𐤏𐤄 . 𐤊𐤁𐤔𐤉𐤌 . 𐤁𐤍
𐤉 . 𐤔𐤍𐤄 |

𐤊𐤇 𐤅𐤌𐤍𐤇𐤕𐤌 . 𐤎𐤋𐤕 . 𐤁𐤋𐤅𐤋𐤄 . 𐤁𐤔𐤌𐤍 . 𐤔𐤋𐤔𐤄 . 𐤏𐤔𐤓𐤍𐤉
𐤌 . 𐤋𐤐𐤓 . 𐤄𐤀𐤇𐤃 . 𐤔𐤍𐤉 . 𐤏𐤔𐤓𐤍𐤉𐤌 . 𐤋𐤀𐤉𐤋 . 𐤄𐤀𐤇𐤃 |

𐤊𐤈 𐤏𐤔𐤓𐤅𐤍 . 𐤏𐤔𐤓𐤅𐤍 . 𐤋𐤊𐤁𐤔 . 𐤄𐤀𐤇𐤃 . 𐤋𐤔𐤁𐤏𐤕 . 𐤄𐤊𐤁
𐤔𐤉𐤌 |

𐤋 𐤔𐤏𐤉𐤓 . 𐤏𐤆𐤉𐤌 . 𐤀𐤇𐤃 . 𐤋𐤊𐤐𐤓 . 𐤏𐤋𐤉𐤊𐤌 |

𐤋𐤀 𐤌𐤋𐤁𐤃 . 𐤏𐤋𐤕 . 𐤄𐤕𐤌𐤉𐤃 . 𐤅𐤌𐤍𐤇𐤕𐤅 . 𐤕𐤏𐤔𐤅 . 𐤕𐤌𐤉𐤌
𐤌 . 𐤉𐤄𐤉𐤅 . 𐤋𐤊𐤌 . 𐤅𐤍𐤎𐤊𐤉𐤄𐤌 ||

𐤁𐤌𐤃𐤁𐤓 . 𐤇𐤋𐤒 𐤊𐤈

𐤀 𐤅𐤁𐤇𐤃𐤔 . 𐤄𐤔𐤁𐤉𐤏𐤉 . 𐤁𐤀𐤇𐤃 . 𐤋𐤇𐤃𐤔 . 𐤌𐤒𐤓𐤀 . 𐤒
𐤃𐤔 . 𐤉𐤄𐤉𐤄 . 𐤋𐤊𐤌 . 𐤊𐤋 . 𐤌𐤋𐤀𐤊𐤕 . 𐤏𐤁𐤃𐤄 . 𐤋𐤀 . 𐤕𐤏𐤔𐤅 . 𐤉
𐤅𐤌 . 𐤕𐤓𐤅𐤏𐤄 . 𐤉𐤄𐤉𐤄 . 𐤋𐤊𐤌 |

𐤁 𐤅𐤏𐤔𐤉𐤕𐤌 . 𐤏𐤋𐤄 . 𐤋𐤓𐤉𐤇 . 𐤍𐤉𐤇𐤇 . 𐤋𐤉𐤄𐤅𐤄 . 𐤐𐤓 . 𐤁𐤍 . 𐤁
𐤒𐤓 . 𐤀𐤇𐤃 . 𐤀𐤉𐤋 . 𐤀𐤇𐤃 . 𐤊𐤁𐤔𐤉𐤌 . 𐤁𐤍𐤉 . 𐤔𐤍𐤄 . 𐤔𐤁𐤏𐤄 .
𐤕𐤌𐤉𐤌𐤌 |

𐤂 𐤅𐤌𐤍𐤇𐤕𐤌 . 𐤎𐤋𐤕 . 𐤁𐤋𐤅𐤋𐤄 . 𐤁𐤔𐤌𐤍 . 𐤔𐤋𐤔𐤄 . 𐤏𐤔𐤓𐤍𐤉𐤌
. 𐤋𐤐𐤓 . 𐤔𐤍𐤉 . 𐤏𐤔𐤓𐤍𐤉𐤌 . 𐤋𐤀𐤉𐤋 |

𐤃 𐤅𐤏𐤔𐤓𐤅𐤍 . 𐤀𐤇𐤃 . 𐤋𐤊𐤁𐤔 . 𐤄𐤀𐤇𐤃 . 𐤋𐤔𐤁𐤏𐤕 . 𐤄𐤊𐤁
𐤔𐤉𐤌 |

𐤄 𐤅𐤔𐤏𐤉𐤓 . 𐤏𐤆𐤉𐤌 . 𐤀𐤇𐤃 . 𐤇𐤈𐤀𐤕 . 𐤋𐤊𐤐𐤓 . 𐤏𐤋𐤉𐤊𐤌 |

𐤅 𐤌𐤋𐤁𐤃 . 𐤏𐤋𐤕 . 𐤄𐤇𐤃𐤔 . 𐤅𐤌𐤍𐤇𐤕𐤄 . 𐤅𐤏𐤋𐤕 . 𐤄𐤕𐤌𐤉𐤃
. 𐤅𐤌𐤍𐤇𐤕𐤄 . 𐤅𐤍𐤎𐤊𐤉𐤄𐤌 . 𐤊𐤌𐤔𐤐𐤈𐤌 . 𐤋𐤓𐤉𐤇 . 𐤍𐤉𐤇𐤇 . 𐤀𐤔
𐤄 . 𐤋𐤉𐤄𐤅𐤄 |

𐤆 𐤅𐤁𐤏𐤔𐤅𐤓 . 𐤋𐤇𐤃𐤔 . 𐤄𐤔𐤁𐤉𐤏𐤉 . 𐤄𐤆𐤄 . 𐤌𐤒𐤓𐤀 . 𐤒𐤃
𐤔 . 𐤉𐤄𐤉𐤄 . 𐤋𐤊𐤌 . 𐤅𐤏𐤍𐤉𐤕𐤌 . 𐤀𐤕 . 𐤍𐤐𐤔𐤕𐤉𐤊𐤌 . 𐤊𐤋 . 𐤌𐤋𐤀𐤊
𐤄 . 𐤋𐤀 . 𐤕𐤏𐤔𐤅 |

8 𐤅𐤄𐤒𐤓𐤁𐤕𐤌.𐤏𐤋𐤄.𐤋𐤉𐤄𐤅𐤄.𐤓𐤉𐤇.𐤍𐤉𐤇𐤇.𐤐𐤓.𐤁𐤍.𐤁
𐤒𐤓.𐤀𐤇𐤃.𐤀𐤉𐤋.𐤀𐤇𐤃.𐤊𐤁𐤔𐤉𐤌.𐤁𐤍𐤉.𐤔𐤍𐤄.𐤔𐤁𐤏𐤄.
𐤕𐤌𐤉𐤌𐤌.𐤉𐤄𐤉𐤅.𐤋𐤊𐤌|

9 𐤅𐤌𐤍𐤇𐤕𐤌.𐤎𐤋𐤕.𐤁𐤋𐤅𐤋𐤄.𐤁𐤔𐤌𐤍.𐤔𐤋𐤔𐤄.𐤏𐤔𐤓𐤍𐤉
𐤌.𐤋𐤐𐤓.𐤔𐤍𐤉.𐤏𐤔𐤓𐤍𐤉𐤌.𐤋𐤀𐤉𐤋.𐤄𐤀𐤇𐤃|

10 𐤏𐤔𐤓𐤅𐤍.𐤏𐤔𐤓𐤅𐤍.𐤋𐤊𐤁𐤔.𐤄𐤀𐤇𐤃.𐤋𐤔𐤁𐤏𐤕.𐤄𐤊𐤁
𐤔𐤉𐤌|

11 𐤔𐤏𐤉𐤓.𐤏𐤆𐤉𐤌.𐤀𐤇𐤃.𐤇𐤈𐤀𐤕.𐤌𐤋𐤁𐤃.𐤇𐤈𐤀𐤕
.𐤄𐤊𐤐𐤓𐤉𐤌.𐤅𐤏𐤋𐤕.𐤄𐤕𐤌𐤉𐤃.𐤅𐤌𐤍𐤇𐤕𐤄.𐤅𐤍𐤎𐤊𐤉𐤄𐤌|

12 𐤅𐤁𐤇𐤌𐤔𐤄.𐤏𐤔𐤓.𐤉𐤅𐤌.𐤋𐤇𐤃𐤔.𐤄𐤔𐤁𐤉𐤏𐤉.𐤌𐤒𐤓
𐤀.𐤒𐤃𐤔.𐤉𐤄𐤉𐤄.𐤋𐤊𐤌.𐤊𐤋.𐤌𐤋𐤀𐤊𐤕.𐤏𐤁𐤃𐤄.𐤋𐤀.𐤕𐤏
𐤔𐤅.𐤅𐤇𐤂𐤕𐤌.𐤇𐤂.𐤋𐤉𐤄𐤅𐤄.𐤔𐤁𐤏𐤕.𐤉𐤌𐤉𐤌|

13 𐤅𐤄𐤒𐤓𐤁𐤕𐤌.𐤏𐤋𐤄.𐤀𐤔𐤄.𐤓𐤉𐤇.𐤍𐤉𐤇𐤇.𐤋𐤉𐤄𐤅𐤄.𐤐
𐤓𐤉𐤌.𐤁𐤍𐤉.𐤁𐤒𐤓.𐤔𐤋𐤔𐤄.𐤏𐤔𐤓.𐤀𐤉𐤋𐤌.𐤔𐤍𐤉𐤌.𐤊𐤁𐤔𐤉𐤌.
𐤁𐤍𐤉.𐤔𐤍𐤄.𐤀𐤓𐤁𐤏𐤄.𐤏𐤔𐤓.𐤕𐤌𐤉𐤌𐤌.𐤉𐤄𐤉𐤅|

14 𐤅𐤌𐤍𐤇𐤕𐤌.𐤎𐤋𐤕.𐤁𐤋𐤅𐤋𐤄.𐤁𐤔𐤌𐤍.𐤔𐤋𐤔𐤄.𐤏𐤔𐤓𐤍𐤉
𐤌.𐤋𐤐𐤓.𐤄𐤀𐤇𐤃.𐤋𐤔𐤋𐤔𐤄.𐤏𐤔𐤓.𐤐𐤓𐤉𐤌.𐤔𐤍𐤉.𐤏𐤔𐤓𐤍𐤉𐤌
.𐤋𐤀𐤉𐤋.𐤄𐤀𐤇𐤃.𐤋𐤔𐤍𐤉.𐤄𐤀𐤉𐤋𐤌|

15 𐤅𐤏𐤔𐤓𐤅𐤍.𐤏𐤔𐤓𐤅𐤍.𐤋𐤊𐤁𐤔.𐤄𐤀𐤇𐤃.𐤋𐤀𐤓𐤁𐤏𐤄.𐤏𐤔
𐤓.𐤊𐤁𐤔𐤉𐤌|

16 𐤅𐤔𐤏𐤉𐤓.𐤏𐤆𐤉𐤌.𐤀𐤇𐤃.𐤇𐤈𐤀𐤕.𐤌𐤋𐤁𐤃.𐤏𐤋𐤕.𐤄
𐤕𐤌𐤉𐤃.𐤌𐤍𐤇𐤕𐤄.𐤅𐤍𐤎𐤊𐤄|

17 𐤅𐤁𐤉𐤅𐤌.𐤄𐤔𐤍𐤉.𐤐𐤓𐤉𐤌.𐤁𐤍𐤉.𐤁𐤒𐤓.𐤔𐤍𐤉𐤌.𐤏𐤔𐤓.𐤀
𐤉𐤋𐤌.𐤔𐤍𐤉𐤌.𐤊𐤁𐤔𐤉𐤌.𐤁𐤍𐤉.𐤔𐤍𐤄.𐤀𐤓𐤁𐤏𐤄.𐤏𐤔𐤓.𐤕𐤌𐤉
𐤌𐤌|

18 𐤅𐤌𐤍𐤇𐤕𐤌.𐤅𐤍𐤎𐤊𐤉𐤄𐤌.𐤋𐤐𐤓𐤉𐤌.𐤋𐤀𐤉𐤋𐤌.𐤅𐤋𐤊𐤁𐤔𐤉
𐤌.𐤁𐤌𐤎𐤐𐤓𐤌.𐤊𐤌𐤔𐤐𐤈|

19 𐤅𐤔𐤏𐤉𐤓.𐤏𐤆𐤉𐤌.𐤀𐤇𐤃.𐤇𐤈𐤀𐤕.𐤌𐤋𐤁𐤃.𐤏𐤋𐤕.
𐤄𐤕𐤌𐤉𐤃.𐤅𐤌𐤍𐤇𐤕𐤄.𐤅𐤍𐤎𐤊𐤉𐤄𐤌|

20 𐤅𐤁𐤉𐤅𐤌.𐤄𐤔𐤋𐤉𐤔𐤉.𐤐𐤓𐤉𐤌.𐤏𐤔𐤕𐤉.𐤏𐤔𐤓.𐤀𐤉𐤋𐤌.
𐤔𐤍𐤉𐤌.𐤊𐤁𐤔𐤉𐤌.𐤁𐤍𐤉.𐤔𐤍𐤄.𐤀𐤓𐤁𐤏𐤄.𐤏𐤔𐤓.𐤕𐤌𐤉𐤌𐤌|

𐤊𐤀 𐤅𐤌𐤍𐤇𐤕𐤌.𐤅𐤍𐤎𐤊𐤉𐤄𐤌.𐤋𐤐𐤓𐤉𐤌.𐤋𐤀𐤉𐤋𐤌.𐤅𐤋𐤊𐤁𐤔𐤉
𐤌.𐤁𐤌𐤎𐤐𐤓𐤌.𐤊𐤌𐤔𐤐𐤈|

𐤊𐤁 𐤅𐤔𐤏𐤉𐤓.𐤇𐤈𐤀𐤕.𐤀𐤇𐤃.𐤌𐤋𐤁𐤃.𐤏𐤋𐤕.𐤄𐤕𐤌𐤉𐤃
.𐤅𐤌𐤍𐤇𐤕𐤄.𐤅𐤍𐤎𐤊𐤄|

𐤊𐤂 𐤅𐤁𐤉𐤅𐤌.𐤄𐤓𐤁𐤉𐤏𐤉.𐤐𐤓𐤉𐤌.𐤏𐤔𐤓𐤄.𐤀𐤉𐤋𐤌.𐤔𐤍𐤉𐤌.
𐤊𐤁𐤔𐤉𐤌.𐤁𐤍𐤉.𐤔𐤍𐤄.𐤀𐤓𐤁𐤏𐤄.𐤏𐤔𐤓.𐤕𐤌𐤉𐤌𐤌|

𐤊𐤃 𐤌𐤍𐤇𐤕𐤌.𐤅𐤍𐤎𐤊𐤉𐤄𐤌.𐤋𐤐𐤓𐤉𐤌.𐤋𐤀𐤉𐤋𐤌.𐤅𐤋𐤊𐤁𐤔𐤉
𐤌.𐤁𐤌𐤎𐤐𐤓𐤌.𐤊𐤌𐤔𐤐𐤈|

𐤊𐤄 𐤅𐤔𐤏𐤉𐤓.𐤏𐤆𐤉𐤌.𐤀𐤇𐤃.𐤇𐤈𐤀𐤕.𐤌𐤋𐤁𐤃.𐤏𐤋𐤕.
𐤄𐤕𐤌𐤉𐤃.𐤌𐤍𐤇𐤕𐤄.𐤅𐤍𐤎𐤊𐤄|

𐤊𐤅 𐤅𐤁𐤉𐤅𐤌.𐤄𐤇𐤌𐤉𐤔𐤉.𐤐𐤓𐤉𐤌.𐤕𐤔𐤏𐤄.𐤀𐤉𐤋𐤌.𐤔𐤍𐤉𐤌
.𐤊𐤁𐤔𐤉𐤌.𐤁𐤍𐤉.𐤔𐤍𐤄.𐤀𐤓𐤁𐤏𐤄.𐤏𐤔𐤓.𐤕𐤌𐤉𐤌𐤌|

𐤊𐤆 𐤅𐤌𐤍𐤇𐤕𐤌.𐤅𐤍𐤎𐤊𐤉𐤄𐤌.𐤋𐤐𐤓𐤉𐤌.𐤋𐤀𐤉𐤋𐤌.𐤅𐤋𐤊𐤁𐤔
𐤉𐤌.𐤁𐤌𐤎𐤐𐤓𐤌.𐤊𐤌𐤔𐤐𐤈|

𐤊𐤇 𐤅𐤔𐤏𐤉𐤓.𐤇𐤈𐤀𐤕.𐤀𐤇𐤃.𐤌𐤋𐤁𐤃.𐤏𐤋𐤕.𐤄𐤕𐤌𐤉𐤃
.𐤅𐤌𐤍𐤇𐤕𐤄.𐤅𐤍𐤎𐤊𐤄|

𐤊𐤈 𐤅𐤁𐤉𐤅𐤌.𐤄𐤔𐤔𐤉.𐤐𐤓𐤉𐤌.𐤔𐤌𐤍𐤄.𐤀𐤉𐤋𐤌.𐤔𐤍𐤉𐤌.𐤊
𐤁𐤔𐤉𐤌.𐤁𐤍𐤉.𐤔𐤍𐤄.𐤀𐤓𐤁𐤏𐤄.𐤏𐤔𐤓.𐤕𐤌𐤉𐤌𐤌|

𐤋 𐤅𐤌𐤍𐤇𐤕𐤌.𐤅𐤍𐤎𐤊𐤉𐤄𐤌.𐤋𐤐𐤓𐤉𐤌.𐤋𐤀𐤉𐤋𐤌.𐤅𐤋𐤊𐤁𐤔
𐤉𐤌.𐤁𐤌𐤎𐤐𐤓𐤌.𐤊𐤌𐤔𐤐𐤈|

𐤋𐤀 𐤅𐤔𐤏𐤉𐤓.𐤇𐤈𐤀𐤕.𐤀𐤇𐤃.𐤌𐤋𐤁𐤃.𐤏𐤋𐤕.𐤄𐤕𐤌𐤉𐤃
.𐤌𐤍𐤇𐤕𐤄.𐤅𐤍𐤎𐤊𐤉𐤄|

𐤋𐤁 𐤅𐤁𐤉𐤅𐤌.𐤄𐤔𐤁𐤉𐤏𐤉.𐤐𐤓𐤉𐤌.𐤔𐤁𐤏𐤄.𐤀𐤉𐤋𐤌.𐤔𐤍𐤉𐤌
.𐤊𐤁𐤔𐤉𐤌.𐤁𐤍𐤉.𐤔𐤍𐤄.𐤀𐤓𐤁𐤏𐤄.𐤏𐤔𐤓.𐤕𐤌𐤉𐤌𐤌|

𐤋𐤂 𐤅𐤌𐤍𐤇𐤕𐤌.𐤅𐤍𐤎𐤊𐤄𐤌.𐤋𐤐𐤓𐤉𐤌.𐤋𐤀𐤉𐤋𐤌.𐤅𐤋𐤊𐤁𐤔𐤉
𐤌.𐤁𐤌𐤎𐤐𐤓𐤌.𐤊𐤌𐤔𐤐𐤈𐤌|

𐤋𐤃 𐤅𐤔𐤏𐤉𐤓.𐤇𐤈𐤀𐤕.𐤀𐤇𐤃.𐤌𐤋𐤁𐤃.𐤏𐤋𐤕.𐤄𐤕𐤌𐤉
𐤃.𐤌𐤍𐤇𐤕𐤄.𐤅𐤍𐤎𐤊𐤄|

𐤋𐤄 𐤁𐤉𐤅𐤌.𐤄𐤔𐤌𐤉𐤍𐤉.𐤏𐤑𐤓𐤕.𐤕𐤄𐤉𐤄.𐤋𐤊𐤌.𐤊𐤋.𐤌𐤋𐤀
𐤊𐤕.𐤏𐤁𐤃𐤄.𐤋𐤀.𐤕𐤏𐤔𐤅|

36 והקרבתם.עלה.אשה.ריח.ניחח.ליהוה.פר.אחד.איל.אחד.כבשים.בני.שנה.שבעה.תמימם׃

37 מנחתם.ונסכיהם.לפר.לאיל.ולכבשים.במספרם.כמשפט׃

38 ושעיר.חטאת.אחד.מלבד.עלת.התמיד.ומנחתה.ונסכה׃

39 אלה.תעשו.ליהוה.במועדיכם.לבד.מנדריכם.ונדבתיכם.לעלתיכם.ולמנחתיכם.ולנסכיכם.ולשלמיכם׃׃

במדבר.חלק 30

1 ויאמר.משה.אל.בני.ישראל.ככל.אשר.צוה.יהוה.את.משה׃

2 וידבר.משה.אל.ראשי.המטות.לבני.ישראל.לאמר.זה.הדבר.אשר.צוה.יהוה׃

3 איש.כי.ידר.נדר.ליהוה.או.השבע.שבעה.לאסר.אסר.על.נפשו.לא.יחל.דברו.ככל.היצא.מפיו.יעשה׃

4 ואשה.כי.תדר.נדר.ליהוה.ואסרה.אסר.בבית.אביה.בנעריה׃

5 ושמע.אביה.את.נדרה.ואסרה.אשר.אסרה.על.נפשה.והחריש.לה.אביה.וקמו.כל.נדריה.וכל.אסר.אשר.אסרה.על.נפשה.יקום׃

6 ואם.הניא.אביה.אתה.ביום.שמעו.כל.נדריה.ואסריה.אשר.אסרה.על.נפשה.לא.יקום.ויהוה.יסלח.לה.כי.הניא.אביה.אתה׃

7 ואם.היו.תהיה.לאיש.ונדריה.עליה.או.מבטא.שפתיה.אשר.אסרה.על.נפשה׃

ח 𐤅𐤔𐤌𐤏.𐤀𐤉𐤔𐤄.𐤁𐤉𐤅𐤌.𐤔𐤌𐤏𐤅.𐤅𐤄𐤇𐤓𐤉𐤔.𐤋𐤄.𐤅𐤒𐤌𐤅
.𐤍𐤃𐤓𐤉𐤄.𐤅𐤀𐤎𐤓𐤄.𐤀𐤔𐤓.𐤀𐤎𐤓𐤄.𐤏𐤋.𐤍𐤐𐤔𐤄.𐤉𐤒𐤌𐤅|

ט 𐤅𐤀𐤌.𐤁𐤉𐤅𐤌.𐤔𐤌𐤏.𐤀𐤉𐤔𐤄.𐤉𐤍𐤉𐤀.𐤀𐤅𐤕𐤄.𐤅𐤄𐤐𐤓.𐤀
𐤕.𐤍𐤃𐤓𐤄.𐤀𐤔𐤓.𐤏𐤋𐤉𐤄.𐤅𐤀𐤕.𐤌𐤁𐤈𐤀.𐤔𐤐𐤕𐤉𐤄.𐤀𐤔𐤓.
𐤀𐤎𐤓𐤄.𐤏𐤋.𐤍𐤐𐤔𐤄.𐤅𐤉𐤄𐤅𐤄.𐤉𐤎𐤋𐤇.𐤋𐤄|

י 𐤅𐤍𐤃𐤓.𐤀𐤋𐤌𐤍𐤄.𐤅𐤂𐤓𐤅𐤔𐤄.𐤊𐤋.𐤀𐤔𐤓.𐤀𐤎𐤓𐤄.𐤏𐤋.𐤍
𐤐𐤔𐤄.𐤉𐤒𐤅𐤌.𐤏𐤋𐤉𐤄|

יא 𐤅𐤀𐤌.𐤁𐤉𐤕.𐤀𐤉𐤔𐤄.𐤍𐤃𐤓𐤄.𐤀𐤅.𐤀𐤎𐤓𐤄.𐤀𐤎𐤓.𐤏𐤋.𐤍
𐤐𐤔𐤄.𐤁𐤔𐤁𐤏𐤄|

יב 𐤅𐤔𐤌𐤏.𐤀𐤉𐤔𐤄.𐤅𐤄𐤇𐤓𐤔.𐤋𐤄.𐤋𐤀.𐤄𐤍𐤉𐤀.𐤀𐤕𐤄.𐤅
𐤒𐤌𐤅.𐤊𐤋.𐤍𐤃𐤓𐤉𐤄.𐤅𐤊𐤋.𐤀𐤎𐤓.𐤀𐤔𐤓.𐤀𐤎𐤓𐤄.𐤏𐤋.𐤍𐤐𐤔𐤄.
𐤉𐤒𐤅𐤌|

יג 𐤅𐤀𐤌.𐤄𐤐𐤓.𐤉𐤐𐤓.𐤀𐤕𐤌.𐤀𐤉𐤔𐤄.𐤁𐤉𐤅𐤌.𐤔𐤌𐤏𐤅.𐤊𐤋.
𐤌𐤅𐤑𐤀.𐤔𐤐𐤕𐤉𐤄.𐤋𐤍𐤃𐤓𐤉𐤄.𐤅𐤋𐤀𐤎𐤓.𐤍𐤐𐤔𐤄.𐤋𐤀.𐤉𐤒𐤅𐤌.
𐤀𐤉𐤔𐤄.𐤄𐤐𐤓𐤌.𐤅𐤉𐤄𐤅𐤄.𐤉𐤎𐤋𐤇.𐤋𐤄|

יד 𐤊𐤋.𐤍𐤃𐤓.𐤅𐤊𐤋.𐤔𐤁𐤏𐤕.𐤀𐤎𐤓.𐤋𐤏𐤍𐤕.𐤍𐤐𐤔.𐤀𐤉𐤔𐤄
.𐤉𐤒𐤉𐤌𐤍𐤅.𐤅𐤀𐤉𐤔𐤄.𐤉𐤐𐤓𐤍𐤅|

טו 𐤅𐤀𐤌.𐤄𐤇𐤓𐤔.𐤉𐤇𐤓𐤉𐤔.𐤋𐤄.𐤀𐤉𐤔𐤄.𐤌𐤉𐤅𐤌.𐤀𐤋.𐤉𐤅
𐤌.𐤅𐤄𐤒𐤉𐤌.𐤀𐤕.𐤊𐤋.𐤍𐤃𐤓𐤉𐤄.𐤀𐤅.𐤀𐤕.𐤊𐤋.𐤀𐤎𐤓𐤉𐤄.𐤀𐤔
𐤓.𐤏𐤋𐤉𐤄.𐤄𐤒𐤉𐤌.𐤀𐤕𐤌.𐤊𐤉.𐤄𐤇𐤓𐤔.𐤋𐤄.𐤁𐤉𐤅𐤌.𐤔𐤌𐤏𐤅|

טז 𐤅𐤀𐤌.𐤄𐤐𐤓.𐤉𐤐𐤓.𐤀𐤕𐤌.𐤀𐤇𐤓𐤉.𐤔𐤌𐤏𐤅.𐤅𐤍𐤔𐤀.𐤀𐤕.
𐤏𐤅𐤍𐤄|

יז 𐤀𐤋𐤄.𐤄𐤇𐤒𐤉𐤌.𐤀𐤔𐤓.𐤑𐤅𐤄.𐤉𐤄𐤅𐤄.𐤀𐤕.𐤌𐤔𐤄.𐤁
𐤉𐤍.𐤀𐤉𐤔.𐤋𐤀𐤔𐤕𐤅.𐤁𐤉𐤍.𐤀𐤁.𐤋𐤁𐤕𐤅.𐤁𐤍𐤏𐤓𐤉𐤄.𐤁𐤉𐤕.𐤀𐤁
𐤉𐤄||

𐤁𐤌𐤃𐤁𐤓.𐤇𐤋𐤒 לא

א 𐤅𐤉𐤃𐤁𐤓.𐤉𐤄𐤅𐤄.𐤀𐤋.𐤌𐤔𐤄.𐤋𐤀𐤌𐤓|

ב 𐤍𐤒𐤌.𐤍𐤒𐤌𐤕.𐤁𐤍𐤉.𐤉𐤔𐤓𐤀𐤋.𐤌𐤀𐤕.𐤄𐤌𐤃𐤉𐤍𐤉𐤌.𐤀
𐤇𐤓.𐤕𐤀𐤎𐤐.𐤀𐤋.𐤏𐤌𐤉𐤊|

3 𐤅𐤉𐤃𐤁𐤓.𐤌𐤔𐤄.𐤀𐤋.𐤄𐤏𐤌.𐤋𐤀𐤌𐤓.𐤄𐤇𐤋𐤑𐤅.𐤌𐤀𐤕𐤊
𐤌.𐤀𐤍𐤔𐤉𐤌.𐤋𐤑𐤁𐤀.𐤅𐤉𐤄𐤉𐤅.𐤏𐤋.𐤌𐤃𐤉𐤍.𐤋𐤕𐤕.𐤍𐤒𐤌𐤕.𐤉
𐤄𐤅𐤄.𐤁𐤌𐤃𐤉𐤍|

4 𐤀𐤋𐤐.𐤋𐤌𐤈𐤄.𐤀𐤋𐤐.𐤋𐤌𐤈𐤄.𐤋𐤊𐤋.𐤌𐤈𐤅𐤕.𐤉𐤔𐤓𐤀𐤋.
𐤕𐤔𐤋𐤇𐤅.𐤋𐤑𐤁𐤀|

5 𐤅𐤉𐤌𐤎𐤓𐤅.𐤌𐤀𐤋𐤐𐤉.𐤉𐤔𐤓𐤀𐤋.𐤀𐤋𐤐.𐤋𐤌𐤈𐤄.𐤔𐤍𐤉𐤌.𐤏
𐤔𐤓.𐤀𐤋𐤐.𐤇𐤋𐤅𐤑𐤉.𐤑𐤁𐤀|

6 𐤅𐤉𐤔𐤋𐤇𐤌.𐤌𐤔𐤄.𐤀𐤋𐤐.𐤋𐤌𐤈𐤄.𐤋𐤑𐤁𐤀.𐤀𐤕𐤌.𐤅
𐤀𐤕.𐤐𐤉𐤍𐤇𐤎.𐤁𐤍.𐤀𐤋𐤏𐤆𐤓.𐤄𐤊𐤄𐤍.𐤋𐤑𐤁𐤀.𐤅𐤊𐤋𐤉.𐤄𐤒
𐤃𐤔.𐤅𐤇𐤑𐤑𐤓𐤅𐤕.𐤄𐤕𐤓𐤅𐤏𐤄.𐤁𐤉𐤃𐤅|

7 𐤅𐤉𐤑𐤁𐤀𐤅.𐤏𐤋.𐤌𐤃𐤉𐤍.𐤊𐤀𐤔𐤓.𐤑𐤅𐤄.𐤉𐤄𐤅𐤄.𐤀𐤕.𐤌
𐤔𐤄.𐤅𐤉𐤄𐤓𐤂𐤅.𐤊𐤋.𐤆𐤊𐤓|

8 𐤅𐤀𐤕.𐤌𐤋𐤊𐤉.𐤌𐤃𐤉𐤍.𐤄𐤓𐤂𐤅.𐤏𐤋.𐤇𐤋𐤋𐤉𐤄𐤌.𐤀𐤕.𐤀𐤅
𐤉.𐤅𐤀𐤕.𐤓𐤒𐤌.𐤅𐤀𐤕.𐤑𐤅𐤓.𐤅𐤀𐤕.𐤇𐤅𐤓.𐤅𐤀𐤕.𐤓𐤁𐤏.𐤇𐤌𐤔𐤕
.𐤌𐤋𐤊𐤉.𐤌𐤃𐤉𐤍.𐤅𐤀𐤕.𐤁𐤋𐤏𐤌.𐤁𐤍.𐤁𐤏𐤅𐤓.𐤄𐤓𐤂𐤅.𐤁𐤇𐤓𐤁|

9 𐤅𐤉𐤔𐤁𐤅.𐤁𐤍𐤉.𐤉𐤔𐤓𐤀𐤋.𐤀𐤕.𐤍𐤔𐤉.𐤌𐤃𐤉𐤍.𐤅𐤀𐤕.𐤈𐤐
𐤌.𐤅𐤀𐤕.𐤊𐤋.𐤁𐤄𐤌𐤕𐤌.𐤅𐤀𐤕.𐤊𐤋.𐤌𐤒𐤍𐤄𐤌.𐤅𐤀𐤕.𐤊𐤋.𐤇𐤉
𐤋𐤌.𐤁𐤆𐤆𐤅|

10 𐤅𐤀𐤕.𐤊𐤋.𐤏𐤓𐤉𐤄𐤌.𐤁𐤌𐤅𐤔𐤁𐤕𐤌.𐤅𐤀𐤕.𐤊𐤋.𐤈𐤉𐤓𐤕
𐤌.𐤔𐤓𐤐𐤅.𐤁𐤀𐤔|

11 𐤅𐤉𐤒𐤇𐤅.𐤀𐤕.𐤊𐤋.𐤄𐤔𐤋𐤋.𐤅𐤀𐤕.𐤊𐤋.𐤄𐤌𐤋𐤒𐤅𐤇.𐤁𐤀
𐤃𐤌.𐤅𐤁𐤁𐤄𐤌𐤄|

12 𐤅𐤉𐤁𐤀𐤅.𐤀𐤋.𐤌𐤔𐤄.𐤅𐤀𐤋.𐤀𐤋𐤏𐤆𐤓.𐤄𐤊𐤄𐤍.𐤅𐤀𐤋.𐤏
𐤃𐤕.𐤁𐤍𐤉.𐤉𐤔𐤓𐤀𐤋.𐤀𐤕.𐤄𐤔𐤁𐤉.𐤅𐤀𐤕.𐤄𐤌𐤋𐤒𐤅𐤇.𐤅𐤀𐤕.
𐤄𐤔𐤋𐤋.𐤀𐤋.𐤄𐤌𐤇𐤍𐤄.𐤀𐤋.𐤏𐤓𐤁𐤕.𐤌𐤅𐤀𐤁.𐤀𐤔𐤓.𐤏𐤋.𐤉𐤓
𐤃𐤍.𐤉𐤓𐤇𐤅|

13 𐤅𐤉𐤑𐤀𐤅.𐤌𐤔𐤄.𐤅𐤀𐤋𐤏𐤆𐤓.𐤄𐤊𐤄𐤍.𐤅𐤊𐤋.𐤍𐤔𐤉𐤀𐤉.𐤄
𐤏𐤃𐤄.𐤋𐤒𐤓𐤀𐤕𐤌.𐤀𐤋.𐤌𐤇𐤅𐤑.𐤋𐤌𐤇𐤍𐤄|

14 𐤅𐤉𐤒𐤑𐤐.𐤌𐤔𐤄.𐤏𐤋.𐤐𐤒𐤅𐤃𐤉.𐤄𐤇𐤉𐤋.𐤔𐤓𐤉.𐤄𐤀𐤋
𐤐𐤉𐤌.𐤅𐤔𐤓𐤉.𐤄𐤌𐤀𐤅𐤕.𐤄𐤁𐤀𐤉𐤌.𐤌𐤑𐤁𐤀.𐤄𐤌𐤋𐤇𐤌𐤄|

15 𐤅𐤉𐤀𐤌𐤓.𐤀𐤋𐤉𐤄𐤌.𐤌𐤔𐤄.𐤄𐤇𐤉𐤉𐤕𐤌.𐤊𐤋.𐤍𐤒𐤁𐤄|

16 𐤄𐤍.𐤄𐤍𐤄.𐤄𐤉𐤅.𐤋𐤁𐤍𐤉.𐤉𐤔𐤓𐤀𐤋.𐤁𐤃𐤁𐤓.𐤁𐤋𐤏𐤌.𐤋𐤌
𐤎𐤓.𐤌𐤏𐤋.𐤁𐤉𐤄𐤅𐤄.𐤏𐤋.𐤃𐤁𐤓.𐤐𐤏𐤅𐤓.𐤅𐤕𐤄𐤉.𐤄𐤌𐤂𐤐𐤄.𐤁
𐤏𐤃𐤕.𐤉𐤄𐤅𐤄|

17 𐤅𐤏𐤕𐤄.𐤄𐤓𐤂𐤅.𐤊𐤋.𐤆𐤊𐤓.𐤁𐤈𐤐.𐤅𐤊𐤋.𐤀𐤔𐤄.𐤉𐤃𐤏
𐤕.𐤀𐤉𐤔.𐤋𐤌𐤔𐤊𐤁.𐤆𐤊𐤓.𐤄𐤓𐤂𐤅|

18 𐤅𐤊𐤋.𐤄𐤈𐤐.𐤁𐤍𐤔𐤉𐤌.𐤀𐤔𐤓.𐤋𐤀.𐤉𐤃𐤏𐤅.𐤌𐤔𐤊𐤁.𐤆
𐤊𐤓.𐤄𐤇𐤉𐤅.𐤋𐤊𐤌|

19 𐤅𐤀𐤕𐤌.𐤇𐤍𐤅.𐤌𐤇𐤅𐤑.𐤋𐤌𐤇𐤍𐤄.𐤔𐤁𐤏𐤕.𐤉𐤌𐤉𐤌.𐤊
𐤋.𐤄𐤓𐤂.𐤍𐤐𐤔.𐤅𐤊𐤋.𐤍𐤂𐤏.𐤁𐤇𐤋𐤋.𐤕𐤕𐤇𐤈𐤀𐤅.𐤁𐤉𐤅𐤌.𐤄𐤔
𐤋𐤉𐤔𐤉.𐤅𐤁𐤉𐤅𐤌.𐤄𐤔𐤁𐤉𐤏𐤉.𐤀𐤕𐤌.𐤅𐤔𐤁𐤉𐤊𐤌|

20 𐤅𐤊𐤋.𐤁𐤂𐤃.𐤅𐤊𐤋.𐤊𐤋𐤉.𐤏𐤅𐤓.𐤅𐤊𐤋.𐤌𐤏𐤔𐤄.𐤏𐤆𐤉𐤌.
𐤅𐤊𐤋.𐤊𐤋𐤉.𐤏𐤑.𐤕𐤕𐤇𐤈𐤀𐤅|

21 𐤅𐤉𐤀𐤌𐤓.𐤀𐤋𐤏𐤆𐤓.𐤄𐤊𐤄𐤍.𐤀𐤋.𐤀𐤍𐤔𐤉.𐤄𐤑𐤁𐤀.𐤄𐤁
𐤀𐤉𐤌.𐤋𐤌𐤋𐤇𐤌𐤄.𐤆𐤀𐤕.𐤇𐤒𐤕.𐤄𐤕𐤅𐤓𐤄.𐤀𐤔𐤓.𐤑𐤅𐤄.𐤉
𐤄𐤅𐤄.𐤀𐤕.𐤌𐤔𐤄|

22 𐤀𐤊.𐤀𐤕.𐤄𐤆𐤄𐤁.𐤅𐤀𐤕.𐤄𐤊𐤎𐤐.𐤀𐤕.𐤄𐤍𐤇𐤔𐤕.𐤀𐤕
.𐤄𐤁𐤓𐤆𐤋.𐤀𐤕.𐤄𐤁𐤃𐤉𐤋.𐤅𐤀𐤕.𐤄𐤏𐤐𐤓𐤕|

23 𐤊𐤋.𐤃𐤁𐤓.𐤀𐤔𐤓.𐤉𐤁𐤀.𐤁𐤀𐤔.𐤕𐤏𐤁𐤉𐤓𐤅.𐤁𐤀𐤔.𐤅𐤈
𐤄𐤓.𐤀𐤊.𐤁𐤌𐤉.𐤍𐤃𐤄.𐤉𐤕𐤇𐤈𐤀.𐤅𐤊𐤋.𐤀𐤔𐤓.𐤋𐤀.𐤉𐤁𐤀.𐤁
𐤀𐤔.𐤕𐤏𐤁𐤉𐤓𐤅.𐤁𐤌𐤉𐤌|

24 𐤅𐤊𐤁𐤎𐤕𐤌.𐤁𐤂𐤃𐤉𐤊𐤌.𐤁𐤉𐤅𐤌.𐤄𐤔𐤁𐤉𐤏𐤉.𐤅𐤈𐤄𐤓
𐤕𐤌.𐤅𐤀𐤇𐤓.𐤕𐤁𐤀𐤅.𐤀𐤋.𐤄𐤌𐤇𐤍𐤄|

25 𐤅𐤉𐤀𐤌𐤓.𐤉𐤄𐤅𐤄.𐤀𐤋.𐤌𐤔𐤄.𐤋𐤀𐤌𐤓|

26 𐤔𐤀.𐤀𐤕.𐤓𐤀𐤔.𐤌𐤋𐤒𐤅𐤇.𐤄𐤔𐤁𐤉.𐤁𐤀𐤃𐤌.𐤅𐤁𐤁𐤄𐤌
𐤄.𐤀𐤕𐤄.𐤅𐤀𐤋𐤏𐤆𐤓.𐤄𐤊𐤄𐤍.𐤅𐤓𐤀𐤔𐤉.𐤀𐤁𐤅𐤕.𐤄𐤏𐤃𐤄|

27 𐤅𐤇𐤑𐤉𐤕.𐤀𐤕.𐤄𐤌𐤋𐤒𐤅𐤇.𐤁𐤉𐤍.𐤕𐤐𐤔𐤉.𐤄𐤌𐤋𐤇𐤌
𐤄.𐤄𐤉𐤑𐤀𐤉𐤌.𐤋𐤑𐤁𐤀.𐤅𐤁𐤉𐤍.𐤊𐤋.𐤄𐤏𐤃𐤄|

28 𐤅𐤄𐤓𐤌𐤕.𐤌𐤊𐤎.𐤋𐤉𐤄𐤅𐤄.𐤌𐤀𐤕.𐤀𐤍𐤔𐤉.𐤄𐤌𐤋𐤇𐤌𐤄.
𐤄𐤉𐤑𐤀𐤉𐤌.𐤋𐤑𐤁𐤀.𐤀𐤇𐤃.𐤍𐤐𐤔.𐤌𐤇𐤌𐤔.𐤄𐤌𐤀𐤅𐤕.𐤌𐤍.
𐤄𐤀𐤃𐤌.𐤅𐤌𐤍.𐤄𐤁𐤒𐤓.𐤅𐤌𐤍.𐤄𐤇𐤌𐤓𐤉𐤌.𐤅𐤌𐤍.𐤄𐤑𐤀𐤍|

כט ממחציתם. תקחו. ונתתה. לאלעזר. הכהן. תרומת. יהוה|

ל וממחצית. בני. ישראל. תקח. אחד. אחז. מן. החמשים. מן. האדם. מן. הבקר. מן. החמרים. ומן. הצאן. מכל. הבהמה. ונתתה. אתם. ללוים. שמרי. משמרת. משכן. יהוה|

לא ויעש. משה. ואלעזר. הכהן. כאשר. צוה. יהוה. את. משה|

לב ויהי. המלקוח. יתר. הבז. אשר. בזזו. עם. הצבא. צאן. שש. מאות. אלף. ושבעים. אלף. וחמשת. אלפים|

לג ובקר. שנים. ושבעים. אלף|

לד וחמרים. אחד. וששים. אלף|

לה ונפש. אדם. מן. הנשים. אשר. לא. ידעו. משכב. זכר. כל. נפש. שנים. ושלשים. אלף|

לו ותהי. המחצה. חלק. היצאים. בצבא. מספר. הצאן. שלש. מאות. אלף. ושלשים. אלף. ושבעת. אלפים. וחמש. מאות|

לז ויהי. המכס. ליהוה. מן. הצאן. שש. מאות. חמש. ושבעים|

לח והבקר. ששה. ושלשים. אלף. ומכסם. ליהוה. שנים. ושבעים|

לט וחמרים. שלשים. אלף. וחמש. מאות. ומכסם. ליהוה. אחד. וששים|

מ ונפש. אדם. ששה. עשר. אלף. ומכסם. ליהוה. שנים. ושלשים. נפש|

מא ויתן. משה. את. מכס. תרומת. יהוה. לאלעזר. הכהן. כאשר. צוה. יהוה. את. משה|

מב וממחצית. בני. ישראל. אשר. חצה. משה. מן. האנשים. הצבאים|

..𐤌𐤂.. 𐤅𐤕𐤄𐤉.𐤌𐤇𐤑𐤕.𐤄𐤏𐤃𐤄.𐤌𐤍.𐤄𐤑𐤀𐤍.𐤔𐤋𐤔.𐤌𐤀𐤅
𐤕.𐤀𐤋𐤐.𐤅𐤔𐤋𐤔𐤉𐤌.𐤀𐤋𐤐.𐤔𐤁𐤏𐤕.𐤀𐤋𐤐𐤉𐤌.𐤅𐤇𐤌𐤔.𐤌𐤀𐤅
𐤕|

..𐤌𐤃.. 𐤅𐤁𐤒𐤓.𐤔𐤔𐤄.𐤅𐤔𐤋𐤔𐤉𐤌.𐤀𐤋𐤐|

..𐤌𐤄.. 𐤅𐤇𐤌𐤓𐤉𐤌.𐤔𐤋𐤔𐤉𐤌.𐤀𐤋𐤐.𐤅𐤇𐤌𐤔.𐤌𐤀𐤅𐤕|

..𐤌𐤅.. 𐤅𐤍𐤐𐤔.𐤀𐤃𐤌.𐤔𐤔𐤄.𐤏𐤔𐤓.𐤀𐤋𐤐|

..𐤌𐤆.. 𐤅𐤉𐤒𐤇.𐤌𐤔𐤄.𐤌𐤌𐤇𐤑𐤕.𐤁𐤍𐤉.𐤉𐤔𐤓𐤀𐤋.𐤀𐤕.𐤄𐤀
𐤇𐤆.𐤀𐤇𐤃.𐤌𐤍.𐤄𐤇𐤌𐤔𐤉𐤌.𐤌𐤍.𐤄𐤀𐤃𐤌.𐤅𐤌𐤍.𐤄𐤁𐤄𐤌
𐤄.𐤅𐤉𐤕𐤍.𐤀𐤕𐤌.𐤋𐤋𐤅𐤉𐤌.𐤔𐤌𐤓𐤉.𐤌𐤔𐤌𐤓𐤕.𐤌𐤔𐤊𐤍.𐤉𐤄𐤅𐤄.
𐤊𐤀𐤔𐤓.𐤑𐤅𐤄.𐤉𐤄𐤅𐤄.𐤀𐤕.𐤌𐤔𐤄|

..𐤌𐤇.. 𐤅𐤉𐤒𐤓𐤁𐤅.𐤀𐤋.𐤌𐤔𐤄.𐤄𐤐𐤒𐤃𐤉𐤌.𐤀𐤔𐤓.𐤋𐤀𐤋𐤐𐤉.𐤄
𐤑𐤁𐤀.𐤔𐤓𐤉.𐤄𐤀𐤋𐤐𐤉𐤌.𐤅𐤔𐤓𐤉.𐤄𐤌𐤀𐤅𐤕|

..𐤌𐤈.. 𐤅𐤉𐤀𐤌𐤓𐤅.𐤀𐤋.𐤌𐤔𐤄.𐤏𐤁𐤃𐤉𐤊.𐤍𐤔𐤀𐤅.𐤀𐤕.𐤓𐤀𐤔.
𐤀𐤍𐤔𐤉.𐤄𐤌𐤋𐤇𐤌𐤄.𐤀𐤔𐤓.𐤁𐤉𐤃𐤍𐤅.𐤅𐤋𐤀.𐤍𐤐𐤒𐤃.𐤌𐤌𐤍𐤅.
𐤀𐤉𐤔|

..𐤍.. 𐤅𐤍𐤒𐤓𐤁.𐤀𐤕.𐤒𐤓𐤁𐤍.𐤉𐤄𐤅𐤄.𐤀𐤉𐤔.𐤀𐤔𐤓.𐤌𐤑𐤀.𐤊𐤋
𐤉.𐤆𐤄𐤁.𐤀𐤑𐤏𐤃𐤄.𐤅𐤑𐤌𐤉𐤃.𐤈𐤁𐤏𐤕.𐤏𐤂𐤉𐤋.𐤅𐤊𐤅𐤌𐤆
.𐤋𐤊𐤐𐤓.𐤏𐤋.𐤍𐤐𐤔𐤕𐤉𐤍𐤅.𐤋𐤐𐤍𐤉.𐤉𐤄𐤅𐤄|

..𐤍𐤀.. 𐤅𐤉𐤒𐤇.𐤌𐤔𐤄.𐤅𐤀𐤋𐤏𐤆𐤓.𐤄𐤊𐤄𐤍.𐤀𐤕.𐤄𐤆𐤄𐤁.𐤌𐤀
𐤕𐤌.𐤊𐤋.𐤊𐤋𐤉.𐤌𐤏𐤔𐤄|

..𐤍𐤁.. 𐤅𐤉𐤄𐤉.𐤊𐤋.𐤆𐤄𐤁.𐤄𐤕𐤓𐤅𐤌𐤄.𐤀𐤔𐤓.𐤄𐤓𐤉𐤌𐤅.𐤋𐤉𐤄𐤅
𐤄.𐤔𐤔𐤄.𐤏𐤔𐤓.𐤀𐤋𐤐.𐤔𐤁𐤏.𐤌𐤀𐤅𐤕.𐤅𐤇𐤌𐤔𐤉𐤌.𐤔𐤒𐤋.𐤌
𐤀𐤕.𐤔𐤓𐤉.𐤄𐤀𐤋𐤐𐤉𐤌.𐤅𐤌𐤀𐤕.𐤔𐤓𐤉.𐤄𐤌𐤀𐤅𐤕|

..𐤍𐤂.. 𐤀𐤍𐤔𐤉.𐤄𐤑𐤁𐤀.𐤁𐤆𐤆𐤅.𐤀𐤉𐤔.𐤋𐤅|

..𐤍𐤃.. 𐤅𐤉𐤒𐤇.𐤌𐤔𐤄.𐤅𐤀𐤋𐤏𐤆𐤓.𐤄𐤊𐤄𐤍.𐤀𐤕.𐤄𐤆𐤄𐤁.𐤌
𐤀𐤕.𐤔𐤓𐤉.𐤄𐤀𐤋𐤐𐤉𐤌.𐤅𐤄𐤌𐤀𐤅𐤕.𐤅𐤉𐤁𐤀𐤅.𐤀𐤕𐤅.𐤀𐤋.𐤀𐤄𐤋.
𐤌𐤅𐤏𐤃.𐤆𐤊𐤓𐤅𐤍.𐤋𐤁𐤍𐤉.𐤉𐤔𐤓𐤀𐤋.𐤋𐤐𐤍𐤉.𐤉𐤄𐤅𐤄||

..𐤋𐤁.. 𐤁𐤌𐤃𐤁𐤓.𐤇𐤋𐤒

א 𐤅𐤌𐤒𐤍𐤄.𐤓𐤁.𐤄𐤉𐤄.𐤋𐤁𐤍𐤉.𐤓𐤀𐤅𐤁𐤍.𐤅𐤋𐤁𐤍𐤉.𐤂𐤃.𐤏𐤑𐤅
𐤌.𐤌𐤀𐤃.𐤅𐤉𐤓𐤀𐤅.𐤀𐤕.𐤀𐤓𐤑.𐤉𐤏𐤆𐤓.𐤅𐤀𐤕.𐤀𐤓𐤑.𐤂𐤋𐤏
𐤃.𐤅𐤄𐤍𐤄.𐤄𐤌𐤒𐤅𐤌.𐤌𐤒𐤅𐤌.𐤌𐤒𐤍𐤄|
ב 𐤅𐤉𐤁𐤀𐤅.𐤁𐤍𐤉.𐤂𐤃.𐤅𐤁𐤍𐤉.𐤓𐤀𐤅𐤁𐤍.𐤅𐤉𐤀𐤌𐤓𐤅.𐤀𐤋.𐤌𐤔
𐤄.𐤅𐤀𐤋.𐤀𐤋𐤏𐤆𐤓.𐤄𐤊𐤄𐤍.𐤅𐤀𐤋.𐤍𐤔𐤉𐤀𐤉.𐤄𐤏𐤃𐤄.𐤋𐤀𐤌𐤓
|
ג 𐤏𐤈𐤓𐤅𐤕.𐤅𐤃𐤉𐤁𐤍.𐤅𐤉𐤏𐤆𐤓.𐤅𐤍𐤌𐤓𐤄.𐤅𐤇𐤔𐤁𐤅𐤍.𐤅𐤀𐤋
𐤏𐤋𐤄.𐤅𐤔𐤁𐤌.𐤅𐤍𐤁𐤅.𐤅𐤁𐤏𐤍|
ד 𐤄𐤀𐤓𐤑.𐤀𐤔𐤓.𐤄𐤊𐤄.𐤉𐤄𐤅𐤄.𐤋𐤐𐤍𐤉.𐤏𐤃𐤕.𐤉𐤔𐤓𐤀𐤋.
𐤀𐤓𐤑.𐤌𐤒𐤍𐤄.𐤄𐤅𐤀.𐤅𐤋𐤏𐤁𐤃𐤉𐤊.𐤌𐤒𐤍𐤄|
ה 𐤅𐤉𐤀𐤌𐤓𐤅.𐤀𐤌.𐤌𐤑𐤀𐤍𐤅.𐤇𐤍.𐤁𐤏𐤉𐤍𐤉𐤊.𐤉𐤕𐤍.𐤀𐤕.𐤄
𐤀𐤓𐤑.𐤄𐤆𐤀𐤕.𐤋𐤏𐤁𐤃𐤉𐤊.𐤋𐤀𐤇𐤆𐤄.𐤀𐤋.𐤕𐤏𐤁𐤓𐤍𐤅.𐤀
𐤕.𐤄𐤉𐤓𐤃𐤍|
ו 𐤅𐤉𐤀𐤌𐤓.𐤌𐤔𐤄.𐤋𐤁𐤍𐤉.𐤂𐤃.𐤅𐤋𐤁𐤍𐤉.𐤓𐤀𐤅𐤁𐤍.𐤄𐤀𐤇𐤉
𐤊𐤌.𐤉𐤁𐤀𐤅.𐤋𐤌𐤋𐤇𐤌𐤄.𐤅𐤀𐤕𐤌.𐤕𐤔𐤁𐤅.𐤐𐤄|
ז 𐤅𐤋𐤌𐤄.𐤕𐤍𐤅𐤀𐤅𐤍.||𐤕𐤍𐤉𐤀𐤅𐤍.𐤒𐤓𐤉||.𐤀𐤕.𐤋𐤁.𐤁𐤍𐤉.𐤉𐤔
𐤓𐤀𐤋.𐤌𐤏𐤁𐤓.𐤀𐤋.𐤄𐤀𐤓𐤑.𐤀𐤔𐤓.𐤍𐤕𐤍.𐤋𐤄𐤌.𐤉𐤄𐤅𐤄|
ח 𐤊𐤄.𐤏𐤔𐤅.𐤀𐤁𐤕𐤉𐤊𐤌.𐤁𐤔𐤋𐤇𐤉.𐤀𐤕𐤌.𐤌𐤒𐤃𐤔.𐤁𐤓𐤍
𐤏.𐤋𐤓𐤀𐤅𐤕.𐤀𐤕.𐤄𐤀𐤓𐤑|
ט 𐤅𐤉𐤏𐤋𐤅.𐤏𐤃.𐤍𐤇𐤋.𐤀𐤔𐤊𐤅𐤋.𐤅𐤉𐤓𐤀𐤅.𐤀𐤕.𐤄𐤀𐤓𐤑.𐤅𐤉
𐤍𐤉𐤀𐤅.𐤀𐤕.𐤋𐤁.𐤁𐤍𐤉.𐤉𐤔𐤓𐤀𐤋.𐤋𐤁𐤋𐤕𐤉.𐤁𐤀.𐤀𐤋.𐤄𐤀𐤓𐤑.
𐤀𐤔𐤓.𐤍𐤕𐤍.𐤋𐤄𐤌.𐤉𐤄𐤅𐤄|
י 𐤅𐤉𐤇𐤓.𐤀𐤐.𐤉𐤄𐤅𐤄.𐤁𐤉𐤅𐤌.𐤄𐤄𐤅𐤀.𐤅𐤉𐤔𐤁𐤏.𐤋𐤀𐤌𐤓|
יא 𐤀𐤌.𐤉𐤓𐤀𐤅.𐤄𐤀𐤍𐤔𐤉𐤌.𐤄𐤏𐤋𐤉𐤌.𐤌𐤌𐤑𐤓𐤉𐤌.𐤌𐤁𐤍.
𐤏𐤔𐤓𐤉𐤌.𐤔𐤍𐤄.𐤅𐤌𐤏𐤋𐤄.𐤀𐤕.𐤄𐤀𐤃𐤌𐤄.𐤀𐤔𐤓.𐤍𐤔𐤁𐤏𐤕
𐤉.𐤋𐤀𐤁𐤓𐤄𐤌.𐤋𐤉𐤑𐤇𐤒.𐤅𐤋𐤉𐤏𐤒𐤁.𐤊𐤉.𐤋𐤀.𐤌𐤋𐤀𐤅.𐤀𐤇𐤓
𐤉|
יב 𐤁𐤋𐤕𐤉.𐤊𐤋𐤁.𐤁𐤍.𐤉𐤐𐤍𐤄.𐤄𐤒𐤍𐤆𐤉.𐤅𐤉𐤄𐤅𐤔𐤏.𐤁𐤍.𐤍𐤅
𐤍.𐤊𐤉.𐤌𐤋𐤀𐤅.𐤀𐤇𐤓𐤉.𐤉𐤄𐤅𐤄|

יג 𐤅𐤉𐤇𐤓.𐤀𐤐.𐤉𐤄𐤅𐤄.𐤁𐤉𐤔𐤓𐤀𐤋.𐤅𐤉𐤍𐤏𐤌.𐤁𐤌𐤃𐤁𐤓.𐤀
𐤓𐤁𐤏𐤉𐤌.𐤔𐤍𐤄.𐤏𐤃.𐤕𐤌.𐤊𐤋.𐤄𐤃𐤅𐤓.𐤄𐤏𐤔𐤄.𐤄𐤓𐤏.𐤁𐤏
𐤉𐤍𐤉.𐤉𐤄𐤅𐤄|

יד 𐤅𐤄𐤍𐤄.𐤒𐤌𐤕𐤌.𐤕𐤇𐤕.𐤀𐤁𐤕𐤉𐤊𐤌.𐤕𐤓𐤁𐤅𐤕.𐤀𐤍𐤔𐤉
𐤌.𐤇𐤈𐤀𐤉𐤌.𐤋𐤎𐤐𐤅𐤕.𐤏𐤅𐤃.𐤏𐤋.𐤇𐤓𐤅𐤍.𐤀𐤐.𐤉𐤄𐤅𐤄.𐤀𐤋.𐤉
𐤔𐤓𐤀𐤋|

טו 𐤊𐤉.𐤕𐤔𐤅𐤁𐤍.𐤌𐤀𐤇𐤓𐤉𐤅.𐤅𐤉𐤎𐤐.𐤏𐤅𐤃.𐤋𐤄𐤍𐤉𐤇𐤅.𐤁𐤌
𐤃𐤁𐤓.𐤅𐤔𐤇𐤕𐤌.𐤋𐤊𐤋.𐤄𐤏𐤌.𐤄𐤆𐤄|

טז 𐤅𐤉𐤂𐤔𐤅.𐤀𐤋𐤉𐤅.𐤅𐤉𐤀𐤌𐤓𐤅.𐤂𐤃𐤓𐤕.𐤑𐤀𐤍.𐤍𐤁𐤍𐤄.𐤋𐤌
𐤒𐤍𐤍𐤅.𐤐𐤄.𐤅𐤏𐤓𐤉𐤌.𐤋𐤈𐤐𐤍𐤅|

יז 𐤅𐤀𐤍𐤇𐤍𐤅.𐤍𐤇𐤋𐤑.𐤇𐤔𐤉𐤌.𐤋𐤐𐤍𐤉.𐤁𐤍𐤉.𐤉𐤔𐤓𐤀𐤋.𐤏
𐤃.𐤀𐤔𐤓.𐤀𐤌.𐤄𐤁𐤉𐤀𐤍𐤌.𐤀𐤋.𐤌𐤒𐤅𐤌𐤌.𐤅𐤉𐤔𐤁.𐤈𐤐𐤍𐤅.𐤁𐤏
𐤓𐤉.𐤄𐤌𐤁𐤑𐤓.𐤌𐤐𐤍𐤉.𐤉𐤔𐤁𐤉.𐤄𐤀𐤓𐤑|

יח 𐤋𐤀.𐤍𐤔𐤅𐤁.𐤀𐤋.𐤁𐤕𐤉𐤍𐤅.𐤏𐤃.𐤄𐤕𐤍𐤇𐤋.𐤁𐤍𐤉.𐤉𐤔𐤓𐤀
𐤋.𐤀𐤉𐤔.𐤍𐤇𐤋𐤕𐤅|

יט 𐤊𐤉.𐤋𐤀.𐤍𐤍𐤇𐤋.𐤀𐤕𐤌.𐤌𐤏𐤁𐤓.𐤋𐤉𐤓𐤃𐤍.𐤅𐤄𐤋𐤀𐤄.𐤊
𐤉.𐤁𐤀𐤄.𐤍𐤇𐤋𐤕𐤍𐤅.𐤀𐤋𐤉𐤍𐤅.𐤌𐤏𐤁𐤓.𐤄𐤉𐤓𐤃𐤍.𐤌𐤆𐤓𐤇𐤄|

כ 𐤅𐤉𐤀𐤌𐤓.𐤀𐤋𐤉𐤄𐤌.𐤌𐤔𐤄.𐤀𐤌.𐤕𐤏𐤔𐤅𐤍.𐤀𐤕.𐤄𐤃𐤁
𐤓.𐤄𐤆𐤄.𐤀𐤌.𐤕𐤇𐤋𐤑𐤅.𐤋𐤐𐤍𐤉.𐤉𐤄𐤅𐤄.𐤋𐤌𐤋𐤇𐤌𐤄|

כא 𐤅𐤏𐤁𐤓.𐤋𐤊𐤌.𐤊𐤋.𐤇𐤋𐤅𐤑.𐤀𐤕.𐤄𐤉𐤓𐤃𐤍.𐤋𐤐𐤍𐤉.𐤉𐤄𐤅
𐤄.𐤏𐤃.𐤄𐤅𐤓𐤉𐤔𐤅.𐤀𐤕.𐤀𐤉𐤁𐤉𐤅.𐤌𐤐𐤍𐤉𐤅|

כב 𐤅𐤍𐤊𐤁𐤔𐤄.𐤄𐤀𐤓𐤑.𐤋𐤐𐤍𐤉.𐤉𐤄𐤅𐤄.𐤅𐤀𐤇𐤓.𐤕𐤔𐤁𐤅.𐤅𐤄
𐤉𐤉𐤕𐤌.𐤍𐤒𐤉𐤉𐤌.𐤌𐤉𐤄𐤅𐤄.𐤅𐤌𐤉𐤔𐤓𐤀𐤋.𐤅𐤄𐤉𐤕𐤄.𐤄𐤀𐤓𐤑.
𐤄𐤆𐤀𐤕.𐤋𐤊𐤌.𐤋𐤀𐤇𐤆𐤄.𐤋𐤐𐤍𐤉.𐤉𐤄𐤅𐤄|

כג 𐤅𐤀𐤌.𐤋𐤀.𐤕𐤏𐤔𐤅𐤍.𐤊𐤍.𐤄𐤍𐤄.𐤇𐤈𐤀𐤕𐤌.𐤋𐤉𐤄𐤅𐤄.𐤅
𐤃𐤏𐤅.𐤇𐤈𐤀𐤕𐤊𐤌.𐤀𐤔𐤓.𐤕𐤌𐤑𐤀.𐤀𐤕𐤊𐤌|

כד 𐤁𐤍𐤅.𐤋𐤊𐤌.𐤏𐤓𐤉𐤌.𐤋𐤈𐤐𐤊𐤌.𐤅𐤂𐤃𐤓𐤕.𐤋𐤑𐤍𐤀𐤊𐤌.𐤅
𐤄𐤉𐤑𐤀.𐤌𐤐𐤉𐤊𐤌.𐤕𐤏𐤔𐤅|

כה 𐤅𐤉𐤀𐤌𐤓.𐤁𐤍𐤉.𐤂𐤃.𐤅𐤁𐤍𐤉.𐤓𐤀𐤅𐤁𐤍.𐤀𐤋.𐤌𐤔𐤄.𐤋𐤀𐤌
𐤓.𐤏𐤁𐤃𐤉𐤊.𐤉𐤏𐤔𐤅.𐤊𐤀𐤔𐤓.𐤀𐤃𐤍𐤉.𐤌𐤑𐤅𐤄|

𐤊𐤅 𐤈𐤐𐤍𐤅.𐤍𐤔𐤉𐤍𐤅.𐤌𐤒𐤍𐤍𐤅.𐤅𐤊𐤋.𐤁𐤄𐤌𐤕𐤍𐤅.𐤉𐤄𐤉𐤅.𐤔𐤌.𐤁
𐤏𐤓𐤉.𐤄𐤂𐤋𐤏𐤃|

𐤊𐤆 𐤅𐤏𐤁𐤃𐤉𐤊.𐤉𐤏𐤁𐤓𐤅.𐤊𐤋.𐤇𐤋𐤅𐤑.𐤑𐤁𐤀.𐤋𐤐𐤍𐤉.𐤉𐤄𐤅
𐤄.𐤋𐤌𐤋𐤇𐤌𐤄.𐤊𐤀𐤔𐤓.𐤀𐤃𐤍𐤉.𐤃𐤁𐤓|

𐤊𐤇 𐤅𐤉𐤑𐤅.𐤋𐤄𐤌.𐤌𐤔𐤄.𐤀𐤕.𐤀𐤋𐤏𐤆𐤓.𐤄𐤊𐤄𐤍.𐤅𐤀𐤕.𐤉
𐤄𐤅𐤔𐤏.𐤁𐤍.𐤍𐤅𐤍.𐤅𐤀𐤕.𐤓𐤀𐤔𐤉.𐤀𐤁𐤅𐤕.𐤄𐤌𐤈𐤅𐤕.𐤋𐤁𐤍𐤉.𐤉
𐤔𐤓𐤀𐤋|

𐤊𐤈 𐤅𐤉𐤀𐤌𐤓.𐤌𐤔𐤄.𐤀𐤋𐤄𐤌.𐤀𐤌.𐤉𐤏𐤁𐤓𐤅.𐤁𐤍𐤉.𐤂𐤃.𐤅𐤁
𐤍𐤉.𐤓𐤀𐤅𐤁𐤍.𐤀𐤕𐤊𐤌.𐤀𐤕.𐤄𐤉𐤓𐤃𐤍.𐤊𐤋.𐤇𐤋𐤅𐤑.𐤋𐤌𐤋𐤇𐤌
𐤄.𐤋𐤐𐤍𐤉.𐤉𐤄𐤅𐤄.𐤅𐤍𐤊𐤁𐤔𐤄.𐤄𐤀𐤓𐤑.𐤋𐤐𐤍𐤉𐤊𐤌.𐤅𐤍𐤕𐤕𐤌.𐤋
𐤄𐤌.𐤀𐤕.𐤀𐤓𐤑.𐤄𐤂𐤋𐤏𐤃.𐤋𐤀𐤇𐤆𐤄|

𐤋 𐤅𐤀𐤌.𐤋𐤀.𐤉𐤏𐤁𐤓𐤅.𐤇𐤋𐤅𐤑𐤉𐤌.𐤀𐤕𐤊𐤌.𐤅𐤍𐤀𐤇𐤆𐤅.
𐤁𐤕𐤊𐤊𐤌.𐤁𐤀𐤓𐤑.𐤊𐤍𐤏𐤍|

𐤋𐤀 𐤅𐤉𐤏𐤍𐤅.𐤁𐤍𐤉.𐤂𐤃.𐤅𐤁𐤍𐤉.𐤓𐤀𐤅𐤁𐤍.𐤋𐤀𐤌𐤓.𐤀𐤕.𐤀𐤔𐤓
.𐤃𐤁𐤓.𐤉𐤄𐤅𐤄.𐤀𐤋.𐤏𐤁𐤃𐤉𐤊.𐤊𐤍.𐤍𐤏𐤔𐤄|

𐤋𐤁 𐤍𐤇𐤍𐤅.𐤍𐤏𐤁𐤓.𐤇𐤋𐤅𐤑𐤉𐤌.𐤋𐤐𐤍𐤉.𐤉𐤄𐤅𐤄.𐤀𐤓𐤑.𐤊𐤍𐤏
𐤍.𐤅𐤀𐤕𐤍𐤅.𐤀𐤇𐤆𐤕.𐤍𐤇𐤋𐤕𐤍𐤅.𐤌𐤏𐤁𐤓.𐤋𐤉𐤓𐤃𐤍|

𐤋𐤂 𐤅𐤉𐤕𐤍.𐤋𐤄𐤌.𐤌𐤔𐤄.𐤋𐤁𐤍𐤉.𐤂𐤃.𐤅𐤋𐤁𐤍𐤉.𐤓𐤀𐤅𐤁𐤍.𐤅𐤋
𐤇𐤑𐤉.𐤔𐤁𐤈.𐤌𐤍𐤔𐤄.𐤁𐤍.𐤉𐤅𐤎𐤐.𐤀𐤕.𐤌𐤌𐤋𐤊𐤕.𐤎𐤉𐤇𐤍.𐤌
𐤋𐤊.𐤄𐤀𐤌𐤓𐤉.𐤅𐤀𐤕.𐤌𐤌𐤋𐤊𐤕.𐤏𐤅𐤂.𐤌𐤋𐤊.𐤄𐤁𐤔𐤍.𐤄𐤀𐤓𐤑
.𐤋𐤏𐤓𐤉𐤄.𐤁𐤂𐤁𐤋𐤕.𐤏𐤓𐤉.𐤄𐤀𐤓𐤑.𐤎𐤁𐤉𐤁|

𐤋𐤃 𐤅𐤉𐤁𐤍𐤅.𐤁𐤍𐤉.𐤂𐤃.𐤀𐤕.𐤃𐤉𐤁𐤍.𐤅𐤀𐤕.𐤏𐤈𐤓𐤕.𐤅𐤀𐤕
.𐤏𐤓𐤏𐤓|

𐤋𐤄 𐤅𐤀𐤕.𐤏𐤈𐤓𐤕.𐤔𐤅𐤐𐤍.𐤅𐤀𐤕.𐤉𐤏𐤆𐤓.𐤅𐤉𐤂𐤁𐤄𐤄|

𐤋𐤅 𐤅𐤀𐤕.𐤁𐤉𐤕.𐤍𐤌𐤓𐤄.𐤅𐤀𐤕.𐤁𐤉𐤕.𐤄𐤓𐤍.𐤏𐤓𐤉.𐤌𐤁𐤑𐤓.𐤅
𐤂𐤃𐤓𐤕.𐤑𐤀𐤍|

𐤋𐤆 𐤅𐤁𐤍𐤉.𐤓𐤀𐤅𐤁𐤍.𐤁𐤍𐤅.𐤀𐤕.𐤇𐤔𐤁𐤅𐤍.𐤅𐤀𐤕.𐤀𐤋𐤏𐤋𐤀.𐤅
𐤀𐤕.𐤒𐤓𐤉𐤕𐤉𐤌|

𐤋𐤇 𐤅𐤀𐤕.𐤍𐤁𐤅.𐤅𐤀𐤕.𐤁𐤏𐤋.𐤌𐤏𐤅𐤍.𐤌𐤅𐤎𐤁𐤕.𐤔𐤌.𐤅𐤀𐤕.𐤔
𐤁𐤌𐤄.𐤅𐤉𐤒𐤓𐤀𐤅.𐤁𐤔𐤌𐤕.𐤀𐤕.𐤔𐤌𐤅𐤕.𐤄𐤏𐤓𐤉𐤌.𐤀𐤔𐤓.𐤁𐤍𐤅

|

39 וילכו.בני.מכיר.בן.מנשה.גלעדה.וילכ
דה.ויורש.את.האמרי.אשר.בה|
40 ויתן.משה.את.הגלעד.למכיר.בן.מנשה.
וישב.בה|
41 ויאיר.בן.מנשה.הלך.וילכד.את.חותיה
ם.ויקרא.אתהן.חות.יאיר|
42 ונבח.הלך.וילכד.את.קנת.ואת.בנתיה.ו
יקרא.לה.נבח.בשמו||

במדבר.חלק ..33..

1 אלה.מסעי.בני.ישראל.אשר.יצאו.מארץ.
מצרים.לצבאתם.ביד.משה.ואהרן|
2 ויכתב.משה.את.מוצאיהם.למסעיהם.על.
פי.יהוה.ואלה.מסעיהם.למוצאיהם|
3 ויסעו.מרעמסס.בחדש.הראשון.בחמשה.
עשר.יום.לחדש.הראשון.ממחרת.הפסח.יצא
ו.בני.ישראל.ביד.רמה.לעיני.כל.מצרים|
4 ומצרים.מקברים.את.אשר.הכה.יהוה.בה
ם.כל.בכור.ובאלהיהם.עשה.יהוה.שפטים|
5 ויסעו.בני.ישראל.מרעמסס.ויחנו.בסכת|
6 ויסעו.מסכת.ויחנו.באתם.אשר.בקצה.המ
דבר|
7 ויסעו.מאתם.וישב.על.פי.החירת.אשר.על
.פני.בעל.צפון.ויחנו.לפני.מגדל|
8 ויסעו.מפני.החירת.ויעברו.בתוך.הים.המ
דברה.וילכו.דרך.שלשת.ימים.במדבר.אתם.ו
יחנו.במרה|
9 ויסעו.ממרה.ויבאו.אילמה.ובאילם.שתי
ם.עשרה.עינת.מים.ושבעים.תמרים.ויחנו.ש
ם|

10 𐤅𐤉𐤎𐤏𐤅.𐤌𐤀𐤉𐤋𐤌.𐤅𐤉𐤇𐤍𐤅.𐤏𐤋.𐤉𐤌.𐤎𐤅𐤐|
11 𐤅𐤉𐤎𐤏𐤅.𐤌𐤉𐤌.𐤎𐤅𐤐.𐤅𐤉𐤇𐤍𐤅.𐤁𐤌𐤃𐤁𐤓.𐤎𐤉𐤍|
12 𐤅𐤉𐤎𐤏𐤅.𐤌𐤌𐤃𐤁𐤓.𐤎𐤉𐤍.𐤅𐤉𐤇𐤍𐤅.𐤁𐤃𐤐𐤒𐤄|
13 𐤅𐤉𐤎𐤏𐤅.𐤌𐤃𐤐𐤒𐤄.𐤅𐤉𐤇𐤍𐤅.𐤁𐤀𐤋𐤅𐤔|
14 𐤅𐤉𐤎𐤏𐤅.𐤌𐤀𐤋𐤅𐤔.𐤅𐤉𐤇𐤍𐤅.𐤁𐤓𐤐𐤉𐤃𐤌.𐤅𐤋𐤀.𐤄𐤉𐤄.𐤔
𐤌.𐤌𐤉𐤌.𐤋𐤏𐤌.𐤋𐤔𐤕𐤅𐤕|
15 𐤅𐤉𐤎𐤏𐤅.𐤌𐤓𐤐𐤉𐤃𐤌.𐤅𐤉𐤇𐤍𐤅.𐤁𐤌𐤃𐤁𐤓.𐤎𐤉𐤍𐤉|
16 𐤅𐤉𐤎𐤏𐤅.𐤌𐤌𐤃𐤁𐤓.𐤎𐤉𐤍𐤉.𐤅𐤉𐤇𐤍𐤅.𐤁𐤒𐤁𐤓𐤕.𐤄𐤕𐤀𐤅
𐤄|
17 𐤅𐤉𐤎𐤏𐤅.𐤌𐤒𐤁𐤓𐤕.𐤄𐤕𐤀𐤅𐤄.𐤅𐤉𐤇𐤍𐤅.𐤁𐤇𐤑𐤓𐤕|
18 𐤅𐤉𐤎𐤏𐤅.𐤌𐤇𐤑𐤓𐤕.𐤅𐤉𐤇𐤍𐤅.𐤁𐤓𐤕𐤌𐤄|
19 𐤅𐤉𐤎𐤏𐤅.𐤌𐤓𐤕𐤌𐤄.𐤅𐤉𐤇𐤍𐤅.𐤁𐤓𐤌𐤍.𐤐𐤓𐤑|
20 𐤅𐤉𐤎𐤏𐤅.𐤌𐤓𐤌𐤍.𐤐𐤓𐤑.𐤅𐤉𐤇𐤍𐤅.𐤁𐤋𐤁𐤍𐤄|
21 𐤅𐤉𐤎𐤏𐤅.𐤌𐤋𐤁𐤍𐤄.𐤅𐤉𐤇𐤍𐤅.𐤁𐤓𐤎𐤄|
22 𐤅𐤉𐤎𐤏𐤅.𐤌𐤓𐤎𐤄.𐤅𐤉𐤇𐤍𐤅.𐤁𐤒𐤄𐤋𐤕𐤄|
23 𐤅𐤉𐤎𐤏𐤅.𐤌𐤒𐤄𐤋𐤕𐤄.𐤅𐤉𐤇𐤍𐤅.𐤁𐤄𐤓.𐤔𐤐𐤓|
24 𐤅𐤉𐤎𐤏𐤅.𐤌𐤄𐤓.𐤔𐤐𐤓.𐤅𐤉𐤇𐤍𐤅.𐤁𐤇𐤓𐤃𐤄|
25 𐤅𐤉𐤎𐤏𐤅.𐤌𐤇𐤓𐤃𐤄.𐤅𐤉𐤇𐤍𐤅.𐤁𐤌𐤒𐤄𐤋𐤕|
26 𐤅𐤉𐤎𐤏𐤅.𐤌𐤌𐤒𐤄𐤋𐤕.𐤅𐤉𐤇𐤍𐤅.𐤁𐤕𐤇𐤕|
27 𐤅𐤉𐤎𐤏𐤅.𐤌𐤕𐤇𐤕.𐤅𐤉𐤇𐤍𐤅.𐤁𐤕𐤓𐤇|
28 𐤅𐤉𐤎𐤏𐤅.𐤌𐤕𐤓𐤇.𐤅𐤉𐤇𐤍𐤅.𐤁𐤌𐤕𐤒𐤄|
29 𐤅𐤉𐤎𐤏𐤅.𐤌𐤌𐤕𐤒𐤄.𐤅𐤉𐤇𐤍𐤅.𐤁𐤇𐤔𐤌𐤍𐤄|
30 𐤅𐤉𐤎𐤏𐤅.𐤌𐤇𐤔𐤌𐤍𐤄.𐤅𐤉𐤇𐤍𐤅.𐤁𐤌𐤎𐤓𐤅𐤕|
31 𐤅𐤉𐤎𐤏𐤅.𐤌𐤌𐤎𐤓𐤅𐤕.𐤅𐤉𐤇𐤍𐤅.𐤁𐤁𐤍𐤉.𐤉𐤏𐤒𐤍|
32 𐤅𐤉𐤎𐤏𐤅.𐤌𐤁𐤍𐤉.𐤉𐤏𐤒𐤍.𐤅𐤉𐤇𐤍𐤅.𐤁𐤇𐤓.𐤄𐤂𐤃𐤂𐤃|
33 𐤅𐤉𐤎𐤏𐤅.𐤌𐤇𐤓.𐤄𐤂𐤃𐤂𐤃.𐤅𐤉𐤇𐤍𐤅.𐤁𐤉𐤈𐤁𐤕𐤄|
34 𐤅𐤉𐤎𐤏𐤅.𐤌𐤉𐤈𐤁𐤕𐤄.𐤅𐤉𐤇𐤍𐤅.𐤁𐤏𐤁𐤓𐤍𐤄|
35 𐤅𐤉𐤎𐤏𐤅.𐤌𐤏𐤁𐤓𐤍𐤄.𐤅𐤉𐤇𐤍𐤅.𐤁𐤏𐤑𐤉𐤍.𐤂𐤁𐤓|
36 𐤅𐤉𐤎𐤏𐤅.𐤌𐤏𐤑𐤉𐤍.𐤂𐤁𐤓.𐤅𐤉𐤇𐤍𐤅.𐤁𐤌𐤃𐤁𐤓.𐤑𐤍.𐤄𐤅
𐤀.𐤒𐤃𐤔|

𐤋𐤆 𐤅𐤉𐤎𐤏𐤅.𐤌𐤒𐤃𐤔.𐤅𐤉𐤇𐤍𐤅.𐤁𐤄𐤓.𐤄𐤄𐤓.𐤁𐤒𐤑𐤄.𐤀𐤓
𐤑.𐤀𐤃𐤅𐤌|
𐤋𐤇 𐤅𐤉𐤏𐤋.𐤀𐤄𐤓𐤍.𐤄𐤊𐤄𐤍.𐤀𐤋.𐤄𐤓.𐤄𐤄𐤓.𐤏𐤋.𐤐𐤉.𐤉𐤄𐤅
𐤄.𐤅𐤉𐤌𐤕.𐤔𐤌.𐤁𐤔𐤍𐤕.𐤄𐤀𐤓𐤁𐤏𐤉𐤌.𐤋𐤑𐤀𐤕.𐤁𐤍𐤉.𐤉𐤔𐤓
𐤀𐤋.𐤌𐤀𐤓𐤑.𐤌𐤑𐤓𐤉𐤌.𐤁𐤇𐤃𐤔.𐤄𐤇𐤌𐤉𐤔𐤉.𐤁𐤀𐤇𐤃.𐤋
𐤇𐤃𐤔|
𐤋𐤈 𐤅𐤀𐤄𐤓𐤍.𐤁𐤍.𐤔𐤋𐤔.𐤅𐤏𐤔𐤓𐤉𐤌.𐤅𐤌𐤀𐤕.𐤔𐤍𐤄.𐤁𐤌𐤕𐤅.
𐤁𐤄𐤓.𐤄𐤄𐤓|
𐤌 𐤅𐤉𐤔𐤌𐤏.𐤄𐤊𐤍𐤏𐤍𐤉.𐤌𐤋𐤊.𐤏𐤓𐤃.𐤅𐤄𐤅𐤀.𐤉𐤔𐤁.𐤁𐤍
𐤂𐤁.𐤁𐤀𐤓𐤑.𐤊𐤍𐤏𐤍.𐤁𐤁𐤀.𐤁𐤍𐤉.𐤉𐤔𐤓𐤀𐤋|
𐤌𐤀 𐤅𐤉𐤎𐤏𐤅.𐤌𐤄𐤓.𐤄𐤄𐤓.𐤅𐤉𐤇𐤍𐤅.𐤁𐤑𐤋𐤌𐤍𐤄|
𐤌𐤁 𐤅𐤉𐤎𐤏𐤅.𐤌𐤑𐤋𐤌𐤍𐤄.𐤅𐤉𐤇𐤍𐤅.𐤁𐤐𐤅𐤍𐤍|
𐤌𐤂 𐤅𐤉𐤎𐤏𐤅.𐤌𐤐𐤅𐤍𐤍.𐤅𐤉𐤇𐤍𐤅.𐤁𐤀𐤁𐤕|
𐤌𐤃 𐤅𐤉𐤎𐤏𐤅.𐤌𐤀𐤁𐤕.𐤅𐤉𐤇𐤍𐤅.𐤁𐤏𐤉𐤉.𐤄𐤏𐤁𐤓𐤉𐤌.𐤁𐤂
𐤁𐤅𐤋.𐤌𐤅𐤀𐤁|
𐤌𐤄 𐤅𐤉𐤎𐤏𐤅.𐤌𐤏𐤉𐤉𐤌.𐤅𐤉𐤇𐤍𐤅.𐤁𐤃𐤉𐤁𐤍.𐤂𐤃|
𐤌𐤅 𐤅𐤉𐤎𐤏𐤅.𐤌𐤃𐤉𐤁𐤍.𐤂𐤃.𐤅𐤉𐤇𐤍𐤅.𐤁𐤏𐤋𐤌𐤍.𐤃𐤁𐤋𐤕𐤉
𐤌𐤄|
𐤌𐤆 𐤅𐤉𐤎𐤏𐤅.𐤌𐤏𐤋𐤌𐤍.𐤃𐤁𐤋𐤕𐤉𐤌𐤄.𐤅𐤉𐤇𐤍𐤅.𐤁𐤄𐤓𐤉.𐤄
𐤏𐤁𐤓𐤉𐤌.𐤋𐤐𐤍𐤉.𐤍𐤁𐤅|
𐤌𐤇 𐤅𐤉𐤎𐤏𐤅.𐤌𐤄𐤓𐤉.𐤄𐤏𐤁𐤓𐤉𐤌.𐤅𐤉𐤇𐤍𐤅.𐤁𐤏𐤓𐤁𐤕.𐤌𐤅𐤀
𐤁.𐤏𐤋.𐤉𐤓𐤃𐤍.𐤉𐤓𐤇𐤅|
𐤌𐤈 𐤅𐤉𐤇𐤍𐤅.𐤏𐤋.𐤄𐤉𐤓𐤃𐤍.𐤌𐤁𐤉𐤕.𐤄𐤉𐤔𐤌𐤕.𐤏𐤃.𐤀𐤁
𐤋.𐤄𐤔𐤈𐤉𐤌.𐤁𐤏𐤓𐤁𐤕.𐤌𐤅𐤀𐤁|
𐤍 𐤅𐤉𐤃𐤁𐤓.𐤉𐤄𐤅𐤄.𐤀𐤋.𐤌𐤔𐤄.𐤁𐤏𐤓𐤁𐤕.𐤌𐤅𐤀𐤁.𐤏𐤋.𐤉
𐤓𐤃𐤍.𐤉𐤓𐤇𐤅.𐤋𐤀𐤌𐤓|
𐤍𐤀 𐤃𐤁𐤓.𐤀𐤋.𐤁𐤍𐤉.𐤉𐤔𐤓𐤀𐤋.𐤅𐤀𐤌𐤓𐤕.𐤀𐤋𐤄𐤌.𐤊𐤉.𐤀𐤕
𐤌.𐤏𐤁𐤓𐤉𐤌.𐤀𐤕.𐤄𐤉𐤓𐤃𐤍.𐤀𐤋.𐤀𐤓𐤑.𐤊𐤍𐤏𐤍|
𐤍𐤁 𐤅𐤄𐤅𐤓𐤔𐤕𐤌.𐤀𐤕.𐤊𐤋.𐤉𐤔𐤁𐤉.𐤄𐤀𐤓𐤑.𐤌𐤐𐤍𐤉𐤊𐤌.𐤅𐤀
𐤁𐤃𐤕𐤌.𐤀𐤕.𐤊𐤋.𐤌𐤔𐤊𐤉𐤕𐤌.𐤅𐤀𐤕.𐤊𐤋.𐤑𐤋𐤌𐤉.𐤌𐤎𐤊𐤕
𐤌.𐤕𐤀𐤁𐤃𐤅.𐤅𐤀𐤕.𐤊𐤋.𐤁𐤌𐤕𐤌.𐤕𐤔𐤌𐤉𐤃𐤅|

53 𐤅𐤄𐤅𐤓𐤔𐤕𐤌.𐤀𐤕.𐤄𐤀𐤓𐤑.𐤅𐤉𐤔𐤁𐤕𐤌.𐤁𐤄.𐤊𐤉.𐤋𐤊𐤌.
𐤍𐤕𐤕𐤉.𐤀𐤕.𐤄𐤀𐤓𐤑.𐤋𐤓𐤔𐤕.𐤀𐤕𐤄|
54 𐤅𐤄𐤕𐤍𐤇𐤋𐤕𐤌.𐤀𐤕.𐤄𐤀𐤓𐤑.𐤁𐤂𐤅𐤓𐤋.𐤋𐤌𐤔𐤐𐤇𐤕𐤉
𐤊𐤌.𐤋𐤓𐤁.𐤕𐤓𐤁𐤅.𐤀𐤕.𐤍𐤇𐤋𐤕𐤅.𐤅𐤋𐤌𐤏𐤈.𐤕𐤌𐤏𐤉𐤈.𐤀𐤕.𐤍
𐤇𐤋𐤕𐤅.𐤀𐤋.𐤀𐤔𐤓.𐤉𐤑𐤀.𐤋𐤅.𐤔𐤌𐤄.𐤄𐤂𐤅𐤓𐤋.𐤋𐤅.𐤉𐤄𐤉𐤄.𐤋
𐤌𐤈𐤅𐤕.𐤀𐤁𐤕𐤉𐤊𐤌.𐤕𐤕𐤍𐤇𐤋𐤅|
55 𐤅𐤀𐤌.𐤋𐤀.𐤕𐤅𐤓𐤉𐤔𐤅.𐤀𐤕.𐤉𐤔𐤁𐤉.𐤄𐤀𐤓𐤑.𐤌𐤐𐤍𐤉𐤊𐤌.
𐤅𐤄𐤉𐤄.𐤀𐤔𐤓.𐤕𐤅𐤕𐤉𐤓𐤅.𐤌𐤄𐤌.𐤋𐤔𐤊𐤉𐤌.𐤁𐤏𐤉𐤍𐤉𐤊𐤌.𐤅𐤋
𐤑𐤍𐤉𐤍𐤌.𐤁𐤑𐤃𐤉𐤊𐤌.𐤅𐤑𐤓𐤓𐤅.𐤀𐤕𐤊𐤌.𐤏𐤋.𐤄𐤀𐤓𐤑.𐤀𐤔𐤓
.𐤀𐤕𐤌.𐤉𐤔𐤁𐤉𐤌.𐤁𐤄|
56 𐤅𐤄𐤉𐤄.𐤊𐤀𐤔𐤓.𐤃𐤌𐤉𐤕𐤉.𐤋𐤏𐤔𐤅𐤕.𐤋𐤄𐤌.𐤀𐤏𐤔𐤄.
𐤋𐤊𐤌||

𐤁𐤌𐤃𐤁𐤓.𐤇𐤋𐤒 34

1 𐤅𐤉𐤃𐤁𐤓.𐤉𐤄𐤅𐤄.𐤀𐤋.𐤌𐤔𐤄.𐤋𐤀𐤌𐤓|
2 𐤑𐤅.𐤀𐤕.𐤁𐤍𐤉.𐤉𐤔𐤓𐤀𐤋.𐤅𐤀𐤌𐤓𐤕.𐤀𐤋𐤄𐤌.𐤊𐤉.𐤀𐤕𐤌.
𐤁𐤀𐤉𐤌.𐤀𐤋.𐤄𐤀𐤓𐤑.𐤊𐤍𐤏𐤍.𐤆𐤀𐤕.𐤄𐤀𐤓𐤑.𐤀𐤔𐤓.𐤕𐤐𐤋.𐤋
𐤊𐤌.𐤁𐤍𐤇𐤋𐤄.𐤀𐤓𐤑.𐤊𐤍𐤏𐤍.𐤋𐤂𐤁𐤋𐤕𐤉𐤄|
3 𐤅𐤄𐤉𐤄.𐤋𐤊𐤌.𐤐𐤀𐤕.𐤍𐤂𐤁.𐤌𐤌𐤃𐤁𐤓.𐤑𐤍.𐤏𐤋.𐤉𐤃𐤉.
𐤀𐤃𐤅𐤌.𐤅𐤄𐤉𐤄.𐤋𐤊𐤌.𐤂𐤁𐤅𐤋.𐤍𐤂𐤁.𐤌𐤒𐤑𐤄.𐤉𐤌.𐤄𐤌𐤋𐤇.
𐤒𐤃𐤌𐤄|
4 𐤅𐤍𐤎𐤁.𐤋𐤊𐤌.𐤄𐤂𐤁𐤅𐤋.𐤌𐤍𐤂𐤁.𐤋𐤌𐤏𐤋𐤄.𐤏𐤒𐤓𐤁𐤉𐤌.𐤅
𐤏𐤁𐤓.𐤑𐤍𐤄.𐤅𐤄𐤉𐤄.||𐤅𐤄𐤉𐤅.𐤒𐤓𐤉||.𐤕𐤅𐤑𐤀𐤕𐤉𐤅.𐤌𐤍𐤂𐤁.𐤋
𐤒𐤃𐤔.𐤁𐤓𐤍𐤏.𐤅𐤉𐤑𐤀.𐤇𐤑𐤓.𐤀𐤃𐤓.𐤅𐤏𐤁𐤓.𐤏𐤑𐤌𐤍𐤄|
5 𐤅𐤍𐤎𐤁.𐤄𐤂𐤁𐤅𐤋.𐤌𐤏𐤑𐤌𐤅𐤍.𐤍𐤇𐤋𐤄.𐤌𐤑𐤓𐤉𐤌.𐤅𐤄𐤉𐤅.
𐤕𐤅𐤑𐤀𐤕𐤉𐤅.𐤄𐤉𐤌𐤄|
6 𐤅𐤂𐤁𐤅𐤋.𐤉𐤌.𐤅𐤄𐤉𐤄.𐤋𐤊𐤌.𐤄𐤉𐤌.𐤄𐤂𐤃𐤅𐤋.𐤅𐤂𐤁𐤅𐤋.𐤆
𐤄.𐤉𐤄𐤉𐤄.𐤋𐤊𐤌.𐤂𐤁𐤅𐤋.𐤉𐤌|
7 𐤅𐤆𐤄.𐤉𐤄𐤉𐤄.𐤋𐤊𐤌.𐤂𐤁𐤅𐤋.𐤑𐤐𐤅𐤍.𐤌𐤍.𐤄𐤉𐤌.𐤄𐤂𐤃
𐤋.𐤕𐤕𐤀𐤅.𐤋𐤊𐤌.𐤄𐤓.𐤄𐤄𐤓|

8 𐤌𐤄𐤓.𐤄𐤄𐤓.𐤕𐤕𐤀𐤅.𐤋𐤁𐤀.𐤇𐤌𐤕.𐤅𐤄𐤉𐤅.𐤕𐤅𐤑𐤀𐤕.𐤄
𐤂𐤁𐤋.𐤑𐤃𐤃𐤄|
9 𐤅𐤉𐤑𐤀.𐤄𐤂𐤁𐤋.𐤆𐤐𐤓𐤍𐤄.𐤅𐤄𐤉𐤅.𐤕𐤅𐤑𐤀𐤕𐤉𐤅.𐤇𐤑𐤓.
𐤏𐤉𐤍𐤍.𐤆𐤄.𐤉𐤄𐤉𐤄.𐤋𐤊𐤌.𐤂𐤁𐤅𐤋.𐤑𐤐𐤅𐤍|
10 𐤅𐤄𐤕𐤀𐤅𐤉𐤕𐤌.𐤋𐤊𐤌.𐤋𐤂𐤁𐤅𐤋.𐤒𐤃𐤌𐤄.𐤌𐤇𐤑𐤓.𐤏𐤉
𐤍𐤍.𐤔𐤐𐤌𐤄|
11 𐤅𐤉𐤓𐤃.𐤄𐤂𐤁𐤋.𐤌𐤔𐤐𐤌.𐤄𐤓𐤁𐤋𐤄.𐤌𐤒𐤃𐤌.𐤋𐤏𐤉𐤍.𐤅
𐤉𐤓𐤃.𐤄𐤂𐤁𐤅𐤋.𐤅𐤌𐤇𐤄.𐤏𐤋.𐤊𐤕𐤐.𐤉𐤌.𐤊𐤍𐤓𐤕.𐤒𐤃𐤌𐤄|
12 𐤅𐤉𐤓𐤃.𐤄𐤂𐤁𐤅𐤋.𐤄𐤉𐤓𐤃𐤍𐤄.𐤅𐤄𐤉𐤅.𐤕𐤅𐤑𐤀𐤕𐤉𐤅.𐤉𐤌
.𐤄𐤌𐤋𐤇.𐤆𐤀𐤕.𐤕𐤄𐤉𐤄.𐤋𐤊𐤌.𐤄𐤀𐤓𐤑.𐤋𐤂𐤁𐤋𐤕𐤉𐤄.𐤎𐤁
𐤉𐤁|
13 𐤅𐤉𐤑𐤅.𐤌𐤔𐤄.𐤀𐤕.𐤁𐤍𐤉.𐤉𐤔𐤓𐤀𐤋.𐤋𐤀𐤌𐤓.𐤆𐤀𐤕.𐤄
𐤀𐤓𐤑.𐤀𐤔𐤓.𐤕𐤕𐤍𐤇𐤋𐤅.𐤀𐤕𐤄.𐤁𐤂𐤅𐤓𐤋.𐤀𐤔𐤓.𐤑𐤅𐤄.𐤉𐤄𐤅
𐤄.𐤋𐤕𐤕.𐤋𐤕𐤔𐤏𐤕.𐤄𐤌𐤈𐤅𐤕.𐤅𐤇𐤑𐤉.𐤄𐤌𐤈𐤄|
14 𐤊𐤉.𐤋𐤒𐤇𐤅.𐤌𐤈𐤄.𐤁𐤍𐤉.𐤄𐤓𐤀𐤅𐤁𐤍𐤉.𐤋𐤁𐤉𐤕.𐤀𐤁𐤕
𐤌.𐤅𐤌𐤈𐤄.𐤁𐤍𐤉.𐤄𐤂𐤃𐤉.𐤋𐤁𐤉𐤕.𐤀𐤁𐤕𐤌.𐤅𐤇𐤑𐤉.𐤌𐤈𐤄.
𐤌𐤍𐤔𐤄.𐤋𐤒𐤇𐤅.𐤍𐤇𐤋𐤕𐤌|
15 𐤔𐤍𐤉.𐤄𐤌𐤈𐤅𐤕.𐤅𐤇𐤑𐤉.𐤄𐤌𐤈𐤄.𐤋𐤒𐤇𐤅.𐤍𐤇𐤋𐤕𐤌.
𐤌𐤏𐤁𐤓.𐤋𐤉𐤓𐤃𐤍.𐤉𐤓𐤇𐤅.𐤒𐤃𐤌𐤄.𐤌𐤆𐤓𐤇𐤄|
16 𐤅𐤉𐤃𐤁𐤓.𐤉𐤄𐤅𐤄.𐤀𐤋.𐤌𐤔𐤄.𐤋𐤀𐤌𐤓|
17 𐤀𐤋𐤄.𐤔𐤌𐤅𐤕.𐤄𐤀𐤍𐤔𐤉𐤌.𐤀𐤔𐤓.𐤉𐤍𐤇𐤋𐤅.𐤋𐤊𐤌.𐤀𐤕
.𐤄𐤀𐤓𐤑.𐤀𐤋𐤏𐤆𐤓.𐤄𐤊𐤄𐤍.𐤅𐤉𐤄𐤅𐤔𐤏.𐤁𐤍.𐤍𐤅𐤍|
18 𐤅𐤍𐤔𐤉𐤀.𐤀𐤇𐤃.𐤍𐤔𐤉𐤀.𐤀𐤇𐤃.𐤌𐤌𐤈𐤄.𐤕𐤒𐤇𐤅.𐤋
𐤍𐤇𐤋.𐤀𐤕.𐤄𐤀𐤓𐤑|
19 𐤅𐤀𐤋𐤄.𐤔𐤌𐤅𐤕.𐤄𐤀𐤍𐤔𐤉𐤌.𐤋𐤌𐤈𐤄.𐤉𐤄𐤅𐤃𐤄.𐤊𐤋𐤁.
𐤁𐤍.𐤉𐤐𐤍𐤄|
20 𐤅𐤋𐤌𐤈𐤄.𐤁𐤍𐤉.𐤔𐤌𐤏𐤅𐤍.𐤔𐤌𐤅𐤀𐤋.𐤁𐤍.𐤏𐤌𐤉𐤄𐤅𐤃|
21 𐤋𐤌𐤈𐤄.𐤁𐤍𐤉𐤌𐤍.𐤀𐤋𐤉𐤃𐤃.𐤁𐤍.𐤊𐤎𐤋𐤅𐤍|
22 𐤅𐤋𐤌𐤈𐤄.𐤁𐤍𐤉.𐤃𐤍.𐤍𐤔𐤉𐤀.𐤁𐤒𐤉.𐤁𐤍.𐤉𐤂𐤋𐤉|
23 𐤋𐤁𐤍𐤉.𐤉𐤅𐤎𐤐.𐤋𐤌𐤈𐤄.𐤁𐤍𐤉.𐤌𐤍𐤔𐤄.𐤍𐤔𐤉𐤀.𐤇𐤍𐤉𐤀
𐤋.𐤁𐤍.𐤀𐤐𐤃|

כד ולמטה בני אפרים נשיא קמואל בן שפט
ן|
כה ולמטה בני זבולן נשיא אליצפן בן פרנך
|
כו ולמטה בני יששכר נשיא פלטיאל בן עז
ן|
כז ולמטה בני אשר נשיא אחיהוד בן של
מי|
כח ולמטה בני נפתלי נשיא פדהאל בן עמי
הוד|
כט אלה אשר צוה יהוה לנחל את בני ישראל
בארץ כנען||

במדבר חלק לה

א וידבר יהוה אל משה בערבת מואב על יר
דן ירחו לאמר|
ב צו את בני ישראל ונתנו ללוים מנחלת א
חזתם ערים לשבת ומגרש לערים סביבתי
הם תתנו ללוים|
ג והיו הערים להם לשבת ומגרשיהם יהיו.
לבהמתם ולרכשם ולכל חיתם|
ד ומגרשי הערים אשר תתנו ללוים מקיר.
העיר וחוצה אלף אמה סביב|
ה ומדתם מחוץ לעיר את פאת קדמה אלפי
ם באמה ואת פאת נגב אלפים באמה ואת פא
ת ים אלפים באמה ואת פאת צפון אלפים בא
מה והעיר בתוך זה יהיה להם מגרשי הער
ים|

𐤅 𐤅𐤀𐤕.𐤄𐤏𐤓𐤉𐤌.𐤀𐤔𐤓.𐤕𐤕𐤍𐤅.𐤋𐤋𐤅𐤉𐤌.𐤀𐤕.𐤔𐤔.𐤏𐤓𐤉.
𐤄𐤌𐤒𐤋𐤈.𐤀𐤔𐤓.𐤕𐤕𐤍𐤅.𐤋𐤍𐤎.𐤔𐤌𐤄.𐤄𐤓𐤑𐤇.𐤅𐤏𐤋𐤉𐤄𐤌.
𐤕𐤕𐤍𐤅.𐤀𐤓𐤁𐤏𐤉𐤌.𐤅𐤔𐤕𐤉𐤌.𐤏𐤉𐤓|

𐤆 𐤊𐤋.𐤄𐤏𐤓𐤉𐤌.𐤀𐤔𐤓.𐤕𐤕𐤍𐤅.𐤋𐤋𐤅𐤉𐤌.𐤀𐤓𐤁𐤏𐤉𐤌.𐤅𐤔𐤌
𐤍𐤄.𐤏𐤉𐤓.𐤀𐤕𐤄𐤍.𐤅𐤀𐤕.𐤌𐤂𐤓𐤔𐤉𐤄𐤍|

𐤇 𐤅𐤄𐤏𐤓𐤉𐤌.𐤀𐤔𐤓.𐤕𐤕𐤍𐤅.𐤌𐤀𐤇𐤆𐤕.𐤁𐤍𐤉.𐤉𐤔𐤓𐤀𐤋.𐤌
𐤀𐤕.𐤄𐤓𐤁.𐤕𐤓𐤁𐤅.𐤅𐤌𐤀𐤕.𐤄𐤌𐤏𐤈.𐤕𐤌𐤏𐤉𐤈𐤅.𐤀𐤉𐤔.𐤊𐤐𐤉
.𐤍𐤇𐤋𐤕𐤅.𐤀𐤔𐤓.𐤉𐤍𐤇𐤋𐤅.𐤉𐤕𐤍.𐤌𐤏𐤓𐤉𐤅.𐤋𐤋𐤅𐤉𐤌|

𐤈 𐤅𐤉𐤃𐤁𐤓.𐤉𐤄𐤅𐤄.𐤀𐤋.𐤌𐤔𐤄.𐤋𐤀𐤌𐤓|

𐤉 𐤃𐤁𐤓.𐤀𐤋.𐤁𐤍𐤉.𐤉𐤔𐤓𐤀𐤋.𐤅𐤀𐤌𐤓𐤕.𐤀𐤋𐤄𐤌.𐤊𐤉.𐤀𐤕
𐤌.𐤏𐤁𐤓𐤉𐤌.𐤀𐤕.𐤄𐤉𐤓𐤃𐤍.𐤀𐤓𐤑𐤄.𐤊𐤍𐤏𐤍|

𐤉𐤀 𐤅𐤄𐤒𐤓𐤉𐤕𐤌.𐤋𐤊𐤌.𐤏𐤓𐤉𐤌.𐤏𐤓𐤉.𐤌𐤒𐤋𐤈.𐤕𐤄𐤉𐤉𐤍𐤄
.𐤋𐤊𐤌.𐤅𐤍𐤎.𐤔𐤌𐤄.𐤓𐤑𐤇.𐤌𐤊𐤄.𐤍𐤐𐤔.𐤁𐤔𐤂𐤂𐤄|

𐤉𐤁 𐤅𐤄𐤉𐤅.𐤋𐤊𐤌.𐤄𐤏𐤓𐤉𐤌.𐤋𐤌𐤒𐤋𐤈.𐤌𐤂𐤀𐤋.𐤅𐤋𐤀.𐤉𐤌𐤅
𐤕.𐤄𐤓𐤑𐤇.𐤏𐤃.𐤏𐤌𐤃𐤅.𐤋𐤐𐤍𐤉.𐤄𐤏𐤃𐤄.𐤋𐤌𐤔𐤐𐤈|

𐤉𐤂 𐤅𐤄𐤏𐤓𐤉𐤌.𐤀𐤔𐤓.𐤕𐤕𐤍𐤅.𐤔𐤔.𐤏𐤓𐤉.𐤌𐤒𐤋𐤈.𐤕𐤄𐤉𐤉
𐤍𐤄.𐤋𐤊𐤌|

𐤉𐤃 𐤀𐤕.𐤔𐤋𐤔.𐤄𐤏𐤓𐤉𐤌.𐤕𐤕𐤍𐤅.𐤌𐤏𐤁𐤓.𐤋𐤉𐤓𐤃𐤍.𐤅𐤀𐤕.
𐤔𐤋𐤔.𐤄𐤏𐤓𐤉𐤌.𐤕𐤕𐤍𐤅.𐤁𐤀𐤓𐤑.𐤊𐤍𐤏𐤍.𐤏𐤓𐤉.𐤌𐤒𐤋𐤈.𐤕𐤄
𐤉𐤉𐤍𐤄|

𐤉𐤄 𐤋𐤁𐤍𐤉.𐤉𐤔𐤓𐤀𐤋.𐤅𐤋𐤂𐤓.𐤅𐤋𐤕𐤅𐤔𐤁.𐤁𐤕𐤅𐤊𐤌.𐤕𐤄𐤉𐤉𐤍
𐤄.𐤔𐤔.𐤄𐤏𐤓𐤉𐤌.𐤄𐤀𐤋𐤄.𐤋𐤌𐤒𐤋𐤈.𐤋𐤍𐤅𐤎.𐤔𐤌𐤄.𐤊𐤋.𐤌𐤊
𐤄.𐤍𐤐𐤔.𐤁𐤔𐤂𐤂𐤄|

𐤉𐤅 𐤅𐤀𐤌.𐤁𐤊𐤋𐤉.𐤁𐤓𐤆𐤋.𐤄𐤊𐤄𐤅.𐤅𐤉𐤌𐤕.𐤓𐤑𐤇.𐤄𐤅𐤀.𐤌𐤅
𐤕.𐤉𐤅𐤌𐤕.𐤄𐤓𐤑𐤇|

𐤉𐤆 𐤅𐤀𐤌.𐤁𐤀𐤁𐤍.𐤉𐤃.𐤀𐤔𐤓.𐤉𐤌𐤅𐤕.𐤁𐤄.𐤄𐤊𐤄𐤅.𐤅𐤉𐤌𐤕.
𐤓𐤑𐤇.𐤄𐤅𐤀.𐤌𐤅𐤕.𐤉𐤅𐤌𐤕.𐤄𐤓𐤑𐤇|

𐤉𐤇 𐤀𐤅.𐤁𐤊𐤋𐤉.𐤏𐤑.𐤉𐤃.𐤀𐤔𐤓.𐤉𐤌𐤅𐤕.𐤁𐤅.𐤄𐤊𐤄𐤅.𐤅𐤉𐤌
𐤕.𐤓𐤑𐤇.𐤄𐤅𐤀.𐤌𐤅𐤕.𐤉𐤅𐤌𐤕.𐤄𐤓𐤑𐤇|

𐤉𐤈 𐤂𐤀𐤋.𐤄𐤃𐤌.𐤄𐤅𐤀.𐤉𐤌𐤉𐤕.𐤀𐤕.𐤄𐤓𐤑𐤇.𐤁𐤐𐤂𐤏𐤅.
𐤁𐤅.𐤄𐤅𐤀.𐤉𐤌𐤉𐤕𐤍𐤅|

20 ࠅࠀࠌ.ࠁࠔࠍࠀࠄ.ࠉࠄࠃࠐࠍࠅ.ࠀࠅ.ࠄࠔࠋࠉࠊ.ࠏࠋࠉࠅ.ࠁࠑ
ࠃࠉࠄ.ࠅࠉࠌࠕ|
21 ࠀࠅ.ࠁࠀࠉࠁࠄ.ࠄࠊࠄࠅ.ࠁࠉࠃࠅ.ࠅࠉࠌࠕ.ࠌࠅࠕ.ࠉࠅࠌࠕ.ࠄ
ࠌࠊࠄ.ࠓࠑࠇ.ࠄࠅࠀ.ࠂࠀࠋ.ࠄࠃࠌ.ࠉࠌࠉࠕ.ࠀࠕ.ࠄࠓࠑࠇ.ࠁ
ࠐࠂࠏࠅ.ࠁࠅ|
22 ࠅࠀࠌ.ࠁࠐࠕࠏ.ࠁࠋࠀ.ࠀࠉࠁࠄ.ࠄࠃࠐࠅ.ࠀࠅ.ࠄࠔࠋࠉࠊ.ࠏ
ࠋࠉࠅ.ࠊࠋ.ࠊࠋࠉ.ࠁࠋࠀ.ࠑࠃࠉࠄ|
23 ࠀࠅ.ࠁࠊࠋ.ࠀࠁࠍ.ࠀࠔࠓ.ࠉࠌࠅࠕ.ࠁࠄ.ࠁࠋࠀ.ࠓࠀࠅࠕ.ࠅࠉࠐ
ࠋ.ࠏࠋࠉࠅ.ࠅࠉࠌࠕ.ࠅࠄࠅࠀ.ࠋࠀ.ࠀࠅࠉࠁ.ࠋࠅ.ࠅࠋࠀ.ࠌࠁࠒࠔ.ࠓࠏࠕ
ࠅ|
24 ࠅࠔࠐࠈࠅ.ࠄࠏࠃࠄ.ࠁࠉࠍ.ࠄࠌࠊࠄ.ࠅࠁࠉࠍ.ࠂࠀࠋ.ࠄࠃ
ࠌ.ࠏࠋ.ࠄࠌࠔࠐࠈࠉࠌ.ࠄࠀࠋࠄ|
25 ࠅࠄࠑࠉࠋࠅ.ࠄࠏࠃࠄ.ࠀࠕ.ࠄࠓࠑࠇ.ࠌࠉࠃ.ࠂࠀࠋ.ࠄࠃ
ࠌ.ࠅࠄࠔࠉࠁࠅ.ࠀࠕࠅ.ࠄࠏࠃࠄ.ࠀࠋ.ࠏࠉࠓ.ࠌࠒࠋࠈࠅ.ࠀࠔࠓ.ࠍࠎ
.ࠔࠌࠄ.ࠅࠉࠔࠁ.ࠁࠄ.ࠏࠃ.ࠌࠅࠕ.ࠄࠊࠄࠍ.ࠄࠂࠃࠋ.ࠀࠔࠓ.ࠌࠔ
ࠇ.ࠀࠕࠅ.ࠁࠔࠌࠍ.ࠄࠒࠃࠔ|
26 ࠅࠀࠌ.ࠉࠑࠀ.ࠉࠑࠀ.ࠄࠓࠑࠇ.ࠀࠕ.ࠂࠁࠅࠋ.ࠏࠉࠓ.ࠌࠒ
ࠋࠈࠅ.ࠀࠔࠓ.ࠉࠍࠅࠎ.ࠔࠌࠄ|
27 ࠅࠌࠑࠀ.ࠀࠕࠅ.ࠂࠀࠋ.ࠄࠃࠌ.ࠌࠇࠅࠑ.ࠋࠂࠁࠅࠋ.ࠏࠉࠓ.
ࠌࠒࠋࠈࠅ.ࠅࠓࠑࠇ.ࠂࠀࠋ.ࠄࠃࠌ.ࠀࠕ.ࠄࠓࠑࠇ.ࠀࠉࠍ.ࠋࠅ.ࠃ
ࠌ|
28 ࠊࠉ.ࠁࠏࠉࠓ.ࠌࠒࠋࠈࠅ.ࠉࠔࠁ.ࠏࠃ.ࠌࠅࠕ.ࠄࠊࠄࠍ.ࠄࠂ
ࠃࠋ.ࠅࠀࠇࠓࠉ.ࠌࠅࠕ.ࠄࠊࠄࠍ.ࠄࠂࠃࠋ.ࠉࠔࠅࠁ.ࠄࠓࠑࠇ.ࠀࠋ.
ࠀࠓࠑ.ࠀࠇࠆࠕࠅ|
29 ࠅࠄࠉࠅ.ࠀࠋࠄ.ࠋࠊࠌ.ࠋࠇࠒࠕ.ࠌࠔࠐࠈ.ࠋࠃࠓࠕࠉࠊࠌ.
ࠁࠊࠋ.ࠌࠅࠔࠁࠕࠉࠊࠌ|
30 ࠊࠋ.ࠌࠊࠄ.ࠍࠐࠔ.ࠋࠐࠉ.ࠏࠃࠉࠌ.ࠉࠓࠑࠇ.ࠀࠕ.ࠄࠓࠑ
ࠇ.ࠅࠏࠃ.ࠀࠇࠃ.ࠋࠀ.ࠉࠏࠍࠄ.ࠁࠍࠐࠔ.ࠋࠌࠅࠕ|
31 ࠅࠋࠀ.ࠕࠒࠇࠅ.ࠊࠐࠓ.ࠋࠍࠐࠔ.ࠓࠑࠇ.ࠀࠔࠓ.ࠄࠅࠀ.ࠓࠔࠏ.
ࠋࠌࠅࠕ.ࠊࠉ.ࠌࠅࠕ.ࠉࠅࠌࠕ|

..32.. ࠅࠋࠀ.ࠕࠒࠇࠅ.ࠊࠐࠓ.ࠋࠍࠅࠎ.ࠀࠋ.ࠏࠉࠓ.ࠌࠒࠋࠈࠅ.ࠋࠔࠅࠁ
.ࠋࠔࠁࠕ.ࠁࠀࠓࠑ.ࠏࠃ.ࠌࠅࠕ.ࠄࠊࠄࠍ|

..33.. ࠅࠋࠀ.ࠕࠇࠍࠉࠐࠅ.ࠀࠕ.ࠄࠀࠓࠑ.ࠀࠔࠓ.ࠀࠕࠌ.ࠁࠄ.ࠊࠉ.
ࠄࠃࠌ.ࠄࠅࠀ.ࠉࠇࠍࠉࠐ.ࠀࠕ.ࠄࠀࠓࠑ.ࠅࠋࠀࠓࠑ.ࠋࠀ.ࠉࠊࠐࠓ.ࠋ
ࠃࠌ.ࠀࠔࠓ.ࠔࠐࠊ.ࠁࠄ.ࠊࠉ.ࠀࠌ.ࠁࠃࠌ.ࠔࠐࠊࠅ|

..34.. ࠅࠋࠀ.ࠕࠈࠌࠀ.ࠀࠕ.ࠄࠀࠓࠑ.ࠀࠔࠓ.ࠀࠕࠌ.ࠉࠔࠁࠉࠌ.
ࠁࠄ.ࠀࠔࠓ.ࠀࠍࠉ.ࠔࠊࠍ.ࠁࠕࠅࠊࠄ.ࠊࠉ.ࠀࠍࠉ.ࠉࠄࠅࠄ.ࠔࠊࠍ.ࠁ
ࠕࠅࠊ.ࠁࠍࠉ.ࠉࠔࠓࠀࠋ||

ࠁࠌࠃࠁࠓ.ࠇࠋࠒ ..36..

..1.. ࠅࠉࠒࠓࠁࠅ.ࠓࠀࠔࠉ.ࠄࠀࠁࠅࠕ.ࠋࠌࠔࠐࠇࠕ.ࠁࠍࠉ.ࠂࠋࠏࠃ
.ࠁࠍ.ࠌࠊࠉࠓ.ࠁࠍ.ࠌࠍࠔࠄ.ࠌࠌࠔࠐࠇࠕ.ࠁࠍࠉ.ࠉࠅࠎࠐ.ࠅࠉࠃࠁࠓ
ࠅ.ࠋࠐࠍࠉ.ࠌࠔࠄ.ࠅࠋࠐࠍࠉ.ࠄࠍࠔࠉࠀࠉࠌ.ࠓࠀࠔࠉ.ࠀࠁࠅࠕ.ࠋࠁࠍࠉ.
ࠉࠔࠓࠀࠋ|

..2.. ࠅࠉࠀࠌࠓࠅ.ࠀࠕ.ࠀࠃࠍࠉ.ࠑࠅࠄ.ࠉࠄࠅࠄ.ࠋࠕࠕ.ࠀࠕ.ࠄࠀࠓ
ࠑ.ࠁࠍࠇࠋࠄ.ࠁࠂࠅࠓࠋ.ࠋࠁࠍࠉ.ࠉࠔࠓࠀࠋ.ࠅࠀࠃࠍࠉ.ࠑࠅࠄ.ࠁࠉ
ࠄࠅࠄ.ࠋࠕࠕ.ࠀࠕ.ࠍࠇࠋࠕ.ࠑࠋࠐࠇࠃ.ࠀࠇࠉࠍࠅ.ࠋࠁࠍࠕࠉࠅ|

..3.. ࠅࠄࠉࠅ.ࠋࠀࠇࠃ.ࠌࠁࠍࠉ.ࠔࠁࠈࠉ.ࠁࠍࠉ.ࠉࠔࠓࠀࠋ.ࠋࠍࠔࠉ
ࠌ.ࠅࠍࠂࠓࠏࠄ.ࠍࠇࠋࠕࠍ.ࠌࠍࠇࠋࠕ.ࠀࠁࠕࠉࠍࠅ.ࠅࠍࠅࠎࠐ.ࠏࠋ.ࠍ
ࠇࠋࠕ.ࠄࠌࠈࠄ.ࠀࠔࠓ.ࠕࠄࠉࠉࠍࠄ.ࠋࠄࠌ.ࠅࠌࠂࠓࠋ.ࠍࠇࠋࠕࠍ
ࠅ.ࠉࠂࠓࠏ|

..4.. ࠅࠀࠌ.ࠉࠄࠉࠄ.ࠄࠉࠁࠋ.ࠋࠁࠍࠉ.ࠉࠔࠓࠀࠋ.ࠅࠍࠅࠎࠐࠄ.ࠍࠇࠋ
ࠕࠍ.ࠏࠋ.ࠍࠇࠋࠕ.ࠄࠌࠈࠄ.ࠀࠔࠓ.ࠕࠄࠉࠉࠍࠄ.ࠋࠄࠌ.ࠅࠌࠍࠇࠋ
ࠕ.ࠌࠈࠄ.ࠀࠁࠕࠉࠍࠅ.ࠉࠂࠓࠏ.ࠍࠇࠋࠕࠍ|

..5.. ࠅࠉࠑࠅ.ࠌࠔࠄ.ࠀࠕ.ࠁࠍࠉ.ࠉࠔࠓࠀࠋ.ࠏࠋ.ࠐࠉ.ࠉࠄࠅࠄ.ࠋࠀ
ࠌࠓ.ࠊࠍ.ࠌࠈࠄ.ࠁࠍࠉ.ࠉࠅࠎࠐ.ࠃࠁࠓࠉࠌ|

..6.. ࠆࠄ.ࠄࠃࠁࠓ.ࠀࠔࠓ.ࠑࠅࠄ.ࠉࠄࠅࠄ.ࠋࠁࠍࠅࠕ.ࠑࠋࠐࠇࠃ.
ࠋࠀࠌࠓ.ࠋࠈࠅࠁ.ࠁࠏࠉࠍࠉࠄࠌ.ࠕࠄࠉࠉࠍࠄ.ࠋࠍࠔࠉࠌ.ࠀࠊ.ࠋࠌ
ࠔࠐࠇࠕ.ࠌࠈࠄ.ࠀࠁࠉࠄࠌ.ࠕࠄࠉࠉࠍࠄ.ࠋࠍࠔࠉࠌ|

ז 𐤅𐤋𐤀.𐤕𐤎𐤁.𐤍𐤇𐤋𐤄.𐤋𐤁𐤍𐤉.𐤉𐤔𐤓𐤀𐤋.𐤌𐤌𐤈𐤄.𐤀𐤋.𐤌
𐤈𐤄.𐤊𐤉.𐤀𐤉𐤔.𐤁𐤍𐤇𐤋𐤕.𐤌𐤈𐤄.𐤀𐤁𐤕𐤉𐤅.𐤉𐤃𐤁𐤒𐤅.𐤁𐤍𐤉.
𐤉𐤔𐤓𐤀𐤋|
ח 𐤅𐤊𐤋.𐤁𐤕.𐤉𐤓𐤔𐤕.𐤍𐤇𐤋𐤄.𐤌𐤌𐤈𐤅𐤕.𐤁𐤍𐤉.𐤉𐤔𐤓𐤀𐤋.𐤋
𐤀𐤇𐤃.𐤌𐤌𐤔𐤐𐤇𐤕.𐤌𐤈𐤄.𐤀𐤁𐤉𐤄.𐤕𐤄𐤉𐤄.𐤋𐤀𐤔𐤄.𐤋𐤌
𐤏𐤍.𐤉𐤉𐤓𐤔𐤅.𐤁𐤍𐤉.𐤉𐤔𐤓𐤀𐤋.𐤀𐤉𐤔.𐤍𐤇𐤋𐤕.𐤀𐤁𐤕𐤉𐤅|
ט 𐤅𐤋𐤀.𐤕𐤎𐤁.𐤍𐤇𐤋𐤄.𐤌𐤌𐤈𐤄.𐤋𐤌𐤈𐤄.𐤀𐤇𐤓.𐤊𐤉.𐤀𐤉
𐤔.𐤁𐤍𐤇𐤋𐤕𐤅.𐤉𐤃𐤁𐤒𐤅.𐤌𐤈𐤅𐤕.𐤁𐤍𐤉.𐤉𐤔𐤓𐤀𐤋|
י 𐤊𐤀𐤔𐤓.𐤑𐤅𐤄.𐤉𐤄𐤅𐤄.𐤀𐤕.𐤌𐤔𐤄.𐤊𐤍.𐤏𐤔𐤅.𐤁𐤍𐤅𐤕.
𐤑𐤋𐤐𐤇𐤃|
יא 𐤅𐤕𐤄𐤉𐤉𐤍𐤄.𐤌𐤇𐤋𐤄.𐤕𐤓𐤑𐤄.𐤅𐤇𐤂𐤋𐤄.𐤅𐤌𐤋𐤊𐤄.𐤅𐤍
𐤏𐤄.𐤁𐤍𐤅𐤕.𐤑𐤋𐤐𐤇𐤃.𐤋𐤁𐤍𐤉.𐤃𐤃𐤉𐤄𐤍.𐤋𐤍𐤔𐤉𐤌|
יב 𐤌𐤌𐤔𐤐𐤇𐤕.𐤁𐤍𐤉.𐤌𐤍𐤔𐤄.𐤁𐤍.𐤉𐤅𐤎𐤐.𐤄𐤉𐤅.𐤋𐤍𐤔𐤉𐤌.𐤅
𐤕𐤄𐤉.𐤍𐤇𐤋𐤕𐤍.𐤏𐤋.𐤌𐤈𐤄.𐤌𐤔𐤐𐤇𐤕.𐤀𐤁𐤉𐤄𐤍|
יג 𐤀𐤋𐤄.𐤄𐤌𐤑𐤅𐤕.𐤅𐤄𐤌𐤔𐤐𐤈𐤉𐤌.𐤀𐤔𐤓.𐤑𐤅𐤄.𐤉𐤄𐤅𐤄.
𐤁𐤉𐤃.𐤌𐤔𐤄.𐤀𐤋.𐤁𐤍𐤉.𐤉𐤔𐤓𐤀𐤋.𐤁𐤏𐤓𐤁𐤕.𐤌𐤅𐤀𐤁.𐤏𐤋.𐤉𐤓
𐤃𐤍.𐤉𐤓𐤇𐤅||

ספר.
הדברים.אשר.דבר.משה
.|ספר.דברים|.

דברים.חלק 1

1 אלה.הדברים.אשר.דבר.משה.אל.כל.ישראל.בעבר.הירדן.במדבר.בערבה.מול.סוף.בין.פארן.ובין.תפל.ולבן.וחצרת.ודי.זהב|

2 אחד.עשר.יום.מחרב.דרך.הר.שעיר.עד.קדש.ברנע|

3 ויהי.בארבעים.שנה.בעשתי.עשר.חדש.באחד.לחדש.דבר.משה.אל.בני.ישראל.ככל.אשר.צוה.יהוה.אתו.אלהם|

4 אחרי.הכתו.את.סיחן.מלך.האמרי.אשר.יושב.בחשבון.ואת.עוג.מלך.הבשן.אשר.יושב.בעשתרת.באדרעי|

5 בעבר.הירדן.בארץ.מואב.הואיל.משה.באר.את.התורה.הזאת.לאמר|

6 יהוה.אלהינו.דבר.אלינו.בחרב.לאמר.רב.לכם.שבת.בהר.הזה|

7 פנו.וסעו.לכם.ובאו.הר.האמרי.ואל.כל.שכניו.בערבה.בהר.ובשפלה.ובנגב.ובחוף.הים.ארץ.הכנעני.והלבנון.עד.הנהר.הגדל.נהר.פרת|

ח 𐤓𐤀𐤄.𐤍𐤕𐤕𐤉.𐤋𐤐𐤍𐤉𐤊𐤌.𐤀𐤕.𐤄𐤀𐤓𐤑.𐤁𐤀𐤅.𐤅𐤓𐤔𐤅.𐤀𐤕
.𐤄𐤀𐤓𐤑.𐤀𐤔𐤓.𐤍𐤔𐤁𐤏.𐤉𐤄𐤅𐤄.𐤋𐤀𐤁𐤕𐤉𐤊𐤌.𐤋𐤀𐤁𐤓𐤄𐤌.𐤋
𐤉𐤑𐤇𐤒.𐤅𐤋𐤉𐤏𐤒𐤁.𐤋𐤕𐤕.𐤋𐤄𐤌.𐤅𐤋𐤆𐤓𐤏𐤌.𐤀𐤇𐤓𐤉𐤄𐤌|
ט 𐤅𐤀𐤌𐤓.𐤀𐤋𐤊𐤌.𐤁𐤏𐤕.𐤄𐤄𐤅𐤀.𐤋𐤀𐤌𐤓.𐤋𐤀.𐤀𐤅𐤊𐤋.𐤋𐤁
𐤃𐤉.𐤔𐤀𐤕.𐤀𐤕𐤊𐤌|
י 𐤉𐤄𐤅𐤄.𐤀𐤋𐤄𐤉𐤊𐤌.𐤄𐤓𐤁𐤄.𐤀𐤕𐤊𐤌.𐤅𐤄𐤍𐤊𐤌.𐤄𐤉𐤅𐤌
.𐤊𐤊𐤅𐤊𐤁𐤉.𐤄𐤔𐤌𐤉𐤌.𐤋𐤓𐤁|
יא 𐤉𐤄𐤅𐤄.𐤀𐤋𐤄𐤉.𐤀𐤁𐤅𐤕𐤊𐤌.𐤉𐤎𐤐.𐤏𐤋𐤉𐤊𐤌.𐤊𐤊𐤌.𐤀
𐤋𐤐.𐤐𐤏𐤌𐤉𐤌.𐤅𐤉𐤁𐤓𐤊.𐤀𐤕𐤊𐤌.𐤊𐤀𐤔𐤓.𐤃𐤁𐤓.𐤋𐤊𐤌|
יב 𐤀𐤉𐤊𐤄.𐤀𐤔𐤀.𐤋𐤁𐤃𐤉.𐤈𐤓𐤇𐤊𐤌.𐤅𐤌𐤔𐤀𐤊𐤌.𐤅𐤓𐤉𐤁
𐤊𐤌|
יג 𐤄𐤁𐤅.𐤋𐤊𐤌.𐤀𐤍𐤔𐤉𐤌.𐤇𐤊𐤌𐤉𐤌.𐤅𐤍𐤁𐤍𐤉𐤌.𐤅𐤉𐤃𐤏𐤉
𐤌.𐤋𐤔𐤁𐤈𐤉𐤊𐤌.𐤅𐤀𐤔𐤉𐤌𐤌.𐤁𐤓𐤀𐤔𐤉𐤊𐤌|
יד 𐤅𐤕𐤏𐤍𐤅.𐤀𐤕𐤉.𐤅𐤕𐤀𐤌𐤓𐤅.𐤈𐤅𐤁.𐤄𐤃𐤁𐤓.𐤀𐤔𐤓.𐤃𐤁𐤓
𐤕.𐤋𐤏𐤔𐤅𐤕|
טו 𐤅𐤀𐤒𐤇.𐤀𐤕.𐤓𐤀𐤔𐤉.𐤔𐤁𐤈𐤉𐤊𐤌.𐤀𐤍𐤔𐤉𐤌.𐤇𐤊𐤌𐤉
𐤌.𐤅𐤉𐤃𐤏𐤉𐤌.𐤅𐤀𐤕𐤍.𐤀𐤕𐤌.𐤓𐤀𐤔𐤉𐤌.𐤏𐤋𐤉𐤊𐤌.𐤔𐤓𐤉.𐤀𐤋
𐤐𐤉𐤌.𐤅𐤔𐤓𐤉.𐤌𐤀𐤅𐤕.𐤅𐤔𐤓𐤉.𐤇𐤌𐤔𐤉𐤌.𐤅𐤔𐤓𐤉.𐤏𐤔𐤓𐤕.𐤅𐤔
𐤈𐤓𐤉𐤌.𐤋𐤔𐤁𐤈𐤉𐤊𐤌|
טז 𐤅𐤀𐤑𐤅𐤄.𐤀𐤕.𐤔𐤐𐤈𐤉𐤊𐤌.𐤁𐤏𐤕.𐤄𐤄𐤅𐤀.𐤋𐤀𐤌𐤓.𐤔𐤌
𐤏.𐤁𐤉𐤍.𐤀𐤇𐤉𐤊𐤌.𐤅𐤔𐤐𐤈𐤕𐤌.𐤑𐤃𐤒.𐤁𐤉𐤍.𐤀𐤉𐤔.𐤅𐤁𐤉𐤍.
𐤀𐤇𐤉𐤅.𐤅𐤁𐤉𐤍.𐤂𐤓𐤅|
יז 𐤋𐤀.𐤕𐤊𐤉𐤓𐤅.𐤐𐤍𐤉𐤌.𐤁𐤌𐤔𐤐𐤈.𐤊𐤒𐤈𐤍.𐤊𐤂𐤃𐤋.𐤕
𐤔𐤌𐤏𐤅𐤍.𐤋𐤀.𐤕𐤂𐤅𐤓𐤅.𐤌𐤐𐤍𐤉.𐤀𐤉𐤔.𐤊𐤉.𐤄𐤌𐤔𐤐𐤈.𐤋𐤀𐤋𐤄
𐤉𐤌.𐤄𐤅𐤀.𐤅𐤄𐤃𐤁𐤓.𐤀𐤔𐤓.𐤉𐤒𐤔𐤄.𐤌𐤊𐤌.𐤕𐤒𐤓𐤁𐤅𐤍.𐤀𐤋𐤉.
𐤅𐤔𐤌𐤏𐤕𐤉𐤅|
יח 𐤅𐤀𐤑𐤅𐤄.𐤀𐤕𐤊𐤌.𐤁𐤏𐤕.𐤄𐤄𐤅𐤀.𐤀𐤕.𐤊𐤋.𐤄𐤃𐤁𐤓𐤉
𐤌.𐤀𐤔𐤓.𐤕𐤏𐤔𐤅𐤍|
יט 𐤅𐤍𐤎𐤏.𐤌𐤇𐤓𐤁.𐤅𐤍𐤋𐤊.𐤀𐤕.𐤊𐤋.𐤄𐤌𐤃𐤁𐤓.𐤄𐤂𐤃𐤅𐤋.
𐤅𐤄𐤍𐤅𐤓𐤀.𐤄𐤄𐤅𐤀.𐤀𐤔𐤓.𐤓𐤀𐤉𐤕𐤌.𐤃𐤓𐤊.𐤄𐤓.𐤄𐤀𐤌𐤓𐤉.𐤊

𐤀𐤔𐤓.𐤑𐤅𐤄.𐤉𐤄𐤅𐤄.𐤀𐤋𐤄𐤉𐤍𐤅.𐤀𐤕𐤍𐤅.𐤅𐤍𐤁𐤀.𐤏𐤃.𐤒𐤃𐤔.
𐤁𐤓𐤍𐤏|
20 𐤅𐤀𐤌𐤓.𐤀𐤋𐤊𐤌.𐤁𐤀𐤕𐤌.𐤏𐤃.𐤄𐤓.𐤄𐤀𐤌𐤓𐤉.𐤀𐤔𐤓.𐤉
𐤄𐤅𐤄.𐤀𐤋𐤄𐤉𐤍𐤅.𐤍𐤕𐤍.𐤋𐤍𐤅|
21 𐤓𐤀𐤄.𐤍𐤕𐤍.𐤉𐤄𐤅𐤄.𐤀𐤋𐤄𐤉𐤊.𐤋𐤐𐤍𐤉𐤊.𐤀𐤕.𐤄𐤀𐤓𐤑.
𐤏𐤋𐤄.𐤓𐤔.𐤊𐤀𐤔𐤓.𐤃𐤁𐤓.𐤉𐤄𐤅𐤄.𐤀𐤋𐤄𐤉.𐤀𐤁𐤕𐤉𐤊.𐤋𐤊.𐤀
𐤋.𐤕𐤉𐤓𐤀.𐤅𐤀𐤋.𐤕𐤇𐤕|
22 𐤅𐤕𐤒𐤓𐤁𐤅𐤍.𐤀𐤋𐤉.𐤊𐤋𐤊𐤌.𐤅𐤕𐤀𐤌𐤓𐤅.𐤍𐤔𐤋𐤇𐤄.𐤀𐤍𐤔
𐤉𐤌.𐤋𐤐𐤍𐤉𐤍𐤅.𐤅𐤉𐤇𐤐𐤓𐤅.𐤋𐤍𐤅.𐤀𐤕.𐤄𐤀𐤓𐤑.𐤅𐤉𐤔𐤁𐤅.𐤀𐤕𐤍𐤅.
𐤃𐤁𐤓.𐤀𐤕.𐤄𐤃𐤓𐤊.𐤀𐤔𐤓.𐤍𐤏𐤋𐤄.𐤁𐤄.𐤅𐤀𐤕.𐤄𐤏𐤓𐤉𐤌.𐤀
𐤔𐤓.𐤍𐤁𐤀.𐤀𐤋𐤉𐤄𐤍|
23 𐤅𐤉𐤉𐤈𐤁.𐤁𐤏𐤉𐤍𐤉.𐤄𐤃𐤁𐤓.𐤅𐤀𐤒𐤇.𐤌𐤊𐤌.𐤔𐤍𐤉𐤌.𐤏
𐤔𐤓.𐤀𐤍𐤔𐤉𐤌.𐤀𐤉𐤔.𐤀𐤇𐤃.𐤋𐤔𐤁𐤈|
24 𐤅𐤉𐤐𐤍𐤅.𐤅𐤉𐤏𐤋𐤅.𐤄𐤄𐤓𐤄.𐤅𐤉𐤁𐤀𐤅.𐤏𐤃.𐤍𐤇𐤋.𐤀𐤔𐤊𐤋.
𐤅𐤉𐤓𐤂𐤋𐤅.𐤀𐤕𐤄|
25 𐤅𐤉𐤒𐤇𐤅.𐤁𐤉𐤃𐤌.𐤌𐤐𐤓𐤉.𐤄𐤀𐤓𐤑.𐤅𐤉𐤓𐤃𐤅.𐤀𐤋𐤉𐤍𐤅.
𐤅𐤉𐤔𐤁𐤅.𐤀𐤕𐤍𐤅.𐤃𐤁𐤓.𐤅𐤉𐤀𐤌𐤓𐤅.𐤈𐤅𐤁𐤄.𐤄𐤀𐤓𐤑.𐤀𐤔𐤓.𐤉
𐤄𐤅𐤄.𐤀𐤋𐤄𐤉𐤍𐤅.𐤍𐤕𐤍.𐤋𐤍𐤅|
26 𐤅𐤋𐤀.𐤀𐤁𐤉𐤕𐤌.𐤋𐤏𐤋𐤕.𐤅𐤕𐤌𐤓𐤅.𐤀𐤕.𐤐𐤉.𐤉𐤄𐤅𐤄.𐤀𐤋
𐤄𐤉𐤊𐤌|
27 𐤅𐤕𐤓𐤂𐤍𐤅.𐤁𐤀𐤄𐤋𐤉𐤊𐤌.𐤅𐤕𐤀𐤌𐤓𐤅.𐤁𐤔𐤍𐤀𐤕.𐤉𐤄𐤅𐤄.
𐤀𐤕𐤍𐤅.𐤄𐤅𐤑𐤉𐤀𐤍𐤅.𐤌𐤀𐤓𐤑.𐤌𐤑𐤓𐤉𐤌.𐤋𐤕𐤕.𐤀𐤕𐤍𐤅.𐤁𐤉𐤃
.𐤄𐤀𐤌𐤓𐤉.𐤋𐤄𐤔𐤌𐤉𐤃𐤍𐤅|
28 𐤀𐤍𐤄.𐤀𐤍𐤇𐤍𐤅.𐤏𐤋𐤉𐤌.𐤀𐤇𐤉𐤍𐤅.𐤄𐤌𐤎𐤅.𐤀𐤕.𐤋𐤁𐤁𐤍𐤅
.𐤋𐤀𐤌𐤓.𐤏𐤌.𐤂𐤃𐤅𐤋.𐤅𐤓𐤌.𐤌𐤌𐤍𐤅.𐤏𐤓𐤉𐤌.𐤂𐤃𐤋𐤕.𐤅𐤁𐤑𐤅𐤓
𐤕.𐤁𐤔𐤌𐤉𐤌.𐤅𐤂𐤌.𐤁𐤍𐤉.𐤏𐤍𐤒𐤉𐤌.𐤓𐤀𐤉𐤍𐤅.𐤔𐤌|
29 𐤅𐤀𐤌𐤓.𐤀𐤋𐤊𐤌.𐤋𐤀.𐤕𐤏𐤓𐤑𐤅𐤍.𐤅𐤋𐤀.𐤕𐤉𐤓𐤀𐤅𐤍.𐤌𐤄
𐤌|
30 𐤉𐤄𐤅𐤄.𐤀𐤋𐤄𐤉𐤊𐤌.𐤄𐤄𐤋𐤊.𐤋𐤐𐤍𐤉𐤊𐤌.𐤄𐤅𐤀.𐤉𐤋𐤇𐤌
.𐤋𐤊𐤌.𐤊𐤊𐤋.𐤀𐤔𐤓.𐤏𐤔𐤄.𐤀𐤕𐤊𐤌.𐤁𐤌𐤑𐤓𐤉𐤌.𐤋𐤏𐤉𐤍𐤉𐤊
𐤌|

𐤋𐤀 𐤅𐤁𐤌𐤃𐤁𐤓.𐤀𐤔𐤓.𐤓𐤀𐤉𐤕.𐤀𐤔𐤓.𐤍𐤔𐤀𐤊.𐤉𐤄𐤅𐤄.𐤀𐤋
𐤄𐤉𐤊.𐤊𐤀𐤔𐤓.𐤉𐤔𐤀.𐤀𐤉𐤔.𐤀𐤕.𐤁𐤍𐤅.𐤁𐤊𐤋.𐤄𐤃𐤓𐤊.𐤀𐤔𐤓.
𐤄𐤋𐤊𐤕𐤌.𐤏𐤃.𐤁𐤀𐤊𐤌.𐤏𐤃.𐤄𐤌𐤒𐤅𐤌.𐤄𐤆𐤄|
𐤋𐤁 𐤅𐤁𐤃𐤁𐤓.𐤄𐤆𐤄.𐤀𐤉𐤍𐤊𐤌.𐤌𐤀𐤌𐤉𐤍𐤌.𐤁𐤉𐤄𐤅𐤄.𐤀𐤋
𐤄𐤉𐤊𐤌|
𐤋𐤂 𐤄𐤄𐤋𐤊.𐤋𐤐𐤍𐤉𐤊𐤌.𐤁𐤃𐤓𐤊.𐤋𐤕𐤅𐤓.𐤋𐤊𐤌.𐤌𐤒𐤅𐤌.𐤋𐤇
𐤍𐤕𐤊𐤌.𐤁𐤀𐤔.𐤋𐤉𐤋𐤄.𐤋𐤓𐤀𐤕𐤊𐤌.𐤁𐤃𐤓𐤊.𐤀𐤔𐤓.𐤕𐤋𐤊𐤅.𐤁
𐤄.𐤅𐤁𐤏𐤍𐤍.𐤉𐤅𐤌𐤌|
𐤋𐤃 𐤅𐤉𐤔𐤌𐤏.𐤉𐤄𐤅𐤄.𐤀𐤕.𐤒𐤅𐤋.𐤃𐤁𐤓𐤉𐤊𐤌.𐤅𐤉𐤒𐤑𐤐.𐤅
𐤉𐤔𐤁𐤏.𐤋𐤀𐤌𐤓|
𐤋𐤄 𐤀𐤌.𐤉𐤓𐤀𐤄.𐤀𐤉𐤔.𐤁𐤀𐤍𐤔𐤉𐤌.𐤄𐤀𐤋𐤄.𐤄𐤃𐤅𐤓.𐤄𐤓
𐤏.𐤄𐤆𐤄.𐤀𐤕.𐤄𐤀𐤓𐤑.𐤄𐤈𐤅𐤁𐤄.𐤀𐤔𐤓.𐤍𐤔𐤁𐤏𐤕𐤉.𐤋𐤕𐤕.
𐤋𐤀𐤁𐤕𐤉𐤊𐤌|
𐤋𐤅 𐤆𐤅𐤋𐤕𐤉.𐤊𐤋𐤁.𐤁𐤍.𐤉𐤐𐤍𐤄.𐤄𐤅𐤀.𐤉𐤓𐤀𐤍𐤄.𐤅𐤋𐤅.𐤀𐤕𐤍.
𐤀𐤕.𐤄𐤀𐤓𐤑.𐤀𐤔𐤓.𐤃𐤓𐤊.𐤁𐤄.𐤅𐤋𐤁𐤍𐤉𐤅.𐤉𐤏𐤍.𐤀𐤔𐤓.𐤌𐤋𐤀.
𐤀𐤇𐤓𐤉.𐤉𐤄𐤅𐤄|
𐤋𐤆 𐤂𐤌.𐤁𐤉.𐤄𐤕𐤀𐤍𐤐.𐤉𐤄𐤅𐤄.𐤁𐤂𐤋𐤋𐤊𐤌.𐤋𐤀𐤌𐤓.𐤂𐤌.
𐤀𐤕𐤄.𐤋𐤀.𐤕𐤁𐤀.𐤔𐤌|
𐤋𐤇 𐤉𐤄𐤅𐤔𐤏.𐤁𐤍.𐤍𐤅𐤍.𐤄𐤏𐤌𐤃.𐤋𐤐𐤍𐤉𐤊.𐤄𐤅𐤀.𐤉𐤁𐤀.𐤔𐤌
𐤄.𐤀𐤕𐤅.𐤇𐤆𐤒.𐤊𐤉.𐤄𐤅𐤀.𐤉𐤍𐤇𐤋𐤍𐤄.𐤀𐤕.𐤉𐤔𐤓𐤀𐤋|
𐤋𐤈 𐤅𐤈𐤐𐤊𐤌.𐤀𐤔𐤓.𐤀𐤌𐤓𐤕𐤌.𐤋𐤁𐤆.𐤉𐤄𐤉𐤄.𐤅𐤁𐤍𐤉𐤊𐤌.
𐤀𐤔𐤓.𐤋𐤀.𐤉𐤃𐤏𐤅.𐤄𐤉𐤅𐤌.𐤈𐤅𐤁.𐤅𐤓𐤏.𐤄𐤌𐤄.𐤉𐤁𐤀𐤅.𐤔𐤌𐤄.
𐤅𐤋𐤄𐤌.𐤀𐤕𐤍𐤍𐤄.𐤅𐤄𐤌.𐤉𐤉𐤓𐤔𐤅𐤄|
𐤌 𐤅𐤀𐤕𐤌.𐤐𐤍𐤅.𐤋𐤊𐤌.𐤅𐤎𐤏𐤅.𐤄𐤌𐤃𐤁𐤓𐤄.𐤃𐤓𐤊.𐤉𐤌.𐤎
𐤅𐤐|
𐤌𐤀 𐤅𐤕𐤏𐤍𐤅.𐤅𐤕𐤀𐤌𐤓𐤅.𐤀𐤋𐤉.𐤇𐤈𐤀𐤍𐤅.𐤋𐤉𐤄𐤅𐤄.𐤀𐤍𐤇𐤍𐤅
.𐤍𐤏𐤋𐤄.𐤅𐤍𐤋𐤇𐤌𐤍𐤅.𐤊𐤊𐤋.𐤀𐤔𐤓.𐤑𐤅𐤍𐤅.𐤉𐤄𐤅𐤄.𐤀𐤋𐤄𐤉𐤍𐤅.𐤅
𐤕𐤇𐤂𐤓𐤅.𐤀𐤉𐤔.𐤀𐤕.𐤊𐤋𐤉.𐤌𐤋𐤇𐤌𐤕𐤅.𐤅𐤕𐤄𐤉𐤍𐤅.𐤋𐤏𐤋𐤕.
𐤄𐤄𐤓𐤄|

42 𐤅𐤉𐤀𐤌𐤓.𐤉𐤄𐤅𐤄.𐤀𐤋𐤉.𐤀𐤌𐤓.𐤋𐤄𐤌.𐤋𐤀.𐤕𐤏𐤋𐤅.𐤅𐤋𐤀
.𐤕𐤋𐤇𐤌𐤅.𐤊𐤉.𐤀𐤉𐤍𐤍𐤉.𐤁𐤒𐤓𐤁𐤊𐤌.𐤅𐤋𐤀.𐤕𐤍𐤂𐤐𐤅.𐤋𐤐𐤍𐤉.𐤀
𐤉𐤁𐤉𐤊𐤌|

43 𐤅𐤀𐤃𐤁𐤓.𐤀𐤋𐤉𐤊𐤌.𐤅𐤋𐤀.𐤔𐤌𐤏𐤕𐤌.𐤅𐤕𐤌𐤓𐤅.𐤀𐤕.𐤐
𐤉.𐤉𐤄𐤅𐤄.𐤅𐤕𐤆𐤃𐤅.𐤅𐤕𐤏𐤋𐤅.𐤄𐤄𐤓𐤄|

44 𐤅𐤉𐤑𐤀.𐤄𐤀𐤌𐤓𐤉.𐤄𐤉𐤔𐤁.𐤁𐤄𐤓.𐤄𐤄𐤅𐤀.𐤋𐤒𐤓𐤀𐤕
𐤊𐤌.𐤅𐤉𐤓𐤃𐤐𐤅.𐤀𐤕𐤊𐤌.𐤊𐤀𐤔𐤓.𐤕𐤏𐤔𐤉𐤍𐤄.𐤄𐤃𐤁𐤓𐤉𐤌.𐤅
𐤉𐤊𐤕𐤅.𐤀𐤕𐤊𐤌.𐤁𐤔𐤏𐤉𐤓.𐤏𐤃.𐤇𐤓𐤌𐤄|

45 𐤅𐤕𐤔𐤁𐤅.𐤅𐤕𐤁𐤊𐤅.𐤋𐤐𐤍𐤉.𐤉𐤄𐤅𐤄.𐤅𐤋𐤀.𐤔𐤌𐤏.𐤉𐤄𐤅𐤄.
𐤁𐤒𐤋𐤊𐤌.𐤅𐤋𐤀.𐤄𐤀𐤆𐤉𐤍.𐤀𐤋𐤉𐤊𐤌|

46 𐤅𐤕𐤔𐤁𐤅.𐤁𐤒𐤃𐤔.𐤉𐤌𐤉𐤌.𐤓𐤁𐤉𐤌.𐤊𐤉𐤌𐤉𐤌.𐤀𐤔𐤓.𐤉
𐤔𐤁𐤕𐤌||

𐤃𐤁𐤓𐤉𐤌.𐤇𐤋𐤒 2

1 𐤅𐤍𐤐𐤍.𐤅𐤍𐤎𐤏.𐤄𐤌𐤃𐤁𐤓𐤄.𐤃𐤓𐤊.𐤉𐤌.𐤎𐤅𐤐.𐤊𐤀𐤔𐤓.𐤃𐤁
𐤓.𐤉𐤄𐤅𐤄.𐤀𐤋𐤉.𐤅𐤍𐤎𐤁.𐤀𐤕.𐤄𐤓.𐤔𐤏𐤉𐤓.𐤉𐤌𐤉𐤌.𐤓𐤁𐤉𐤌|

2 𐤅𐤉𐤀𐤌𐤓.𐤉𐤄𐤅𐤄.𐤀𐤋𐤉.𐤋𐤀𐤌𐤓|

3 𐤓𐤁.𐤋𐤊𐤌.𐤎𐤁.𐤀𐤕.𐤄𐤄𐤓.𐤄𐤆𐤄.𐤐𐤍𐤅.𐤋𐤊𐤌.𐤑𐤐𐤍𐤄|

4 𐤅𐤀𐤕.𐤄𐤏𐤌.𐤑𐤅.𐤋𐤀𐤌𐤓.𐤀𐤕𐤌.𐤏𐤁𐤓𐤉𐤌.𐤁𐤂𐤁𐤅𐤋.𐤀
𐤇𐤉𐤊𐤌.𐤁𐤍𐤉.𐤏𐤔𐤅.𐤄𐤉𐤔𐤁𐤉𐤌.𐤁𐤔𐤏𐤉𐤓.𐤅𐤉𐤉𐤓𐤀𐤅.𐤌𐤊𐤌
.𐤅𐤍𐤔𐤌𐤓𐤕𐤌.𐤌𐤀𐤃|

5 𐤀𐤋.𐤕𐤕𐤂𐤓𐤅.𐤁𐤌.𐤊𐤉.𐤋𐤀.𐤀𐤕𐤍.𐤋𐤊𐤌.𐤌𐤀𐤓𐤑𐤌.𐤏
𐤃.𐤌𐤃𐤓𐤊.𐤊𐤐.𐤓𐤂𐤋.𐤊𐤉.𐤉𐤓𐤔𐤄.𐤋𐤏𐤔𐤅.𐤍𐤕𐤕𐤉.𐤀𐤕.𐤄𐤓
.𐤔𐤏𐤉𐤓|

6 𐤀𐤊𐤋.𐤕𐤔𐤁𐤓𐤅.𐤌𐤀𐤕𐤌.𐤁𐤊𐤎𐤐.𐤅𐤀𐤊𐤋𐤕𐤌.𐤅𐤂𐤌.𐤌𐤉
𐤌.𐤕𐤊𐤓𐤅.𐤌𐤀𐤕𐤌.𐤁𐤊𐤎𐤐.𐤅𐤔𐤕𐤉𐤕𐤌|

7 𐤊𐤉.𐤉𐤄𐤅𐤄.𐤀𐤋𐤄𐤉𐤊.𐤁𐤓𐤊𐤊.𐤁𐤊𐤋.𐤌𐤏𐤔𐤄.𐤉𐤃𐤊.𐤉
𐤃𐤏.𐤋𐤊𐤕𐤊.𐤀𐤕.𐤄𐤌𐤃𐤁𐤓.𐤄𐤂𐤃𐤋.𐤄𐤆𐤄.𐤆𐤄.𐤀𐤓𐤁𐤏
𐤉𐤌.𐤔𐤍𐤄.𐤉𐤄𐤅𐤄.𐤀𐤋𐤄𐤉𐤊.𐤏𐤌𐤊.𐤋𐤀.𐤇𐤎𐤓𐤕.𐤃𐤁𐤓|

ח 𐤅𐤍𐤏𐤁𐤓.𐤌𐤀𐤕.𐤀𐤇𐤉𐤍𐤅.𐤁𐤍𐤉.𐤏𐤔𐤅.𐤄𐤉𐤔𐤁𐤉𐤌.𐤁𐤔𐤏
𐤉𐤓.𐤌𐤃𐤓𐤊.𐤄𐤏𐤓𐤁𐤄.𐤌𐤀𐤉𐤋𐤕.𐤅𐤌𐤏𐤑𐤉𐤍.𐤂𐤁𐤓.𐤅𐤍𐤐𐤍.𐤅𐤍
𐤏𐤁𐤓.𐤃𐤓𐤊.𐤌𐤃𐤁𐤓.𐤌𐤅𐤀𐤁|
ט 𐤅𐤉𐤀𐤌𐤓.𐤉𐤄𐤅𐤄.𐤀𐤋𐤉.𐤀𐤋.𐤕𐤑𐤓.𐤀𐤕.𐤌𐤅𐤀𐤁.𐤅𐤀𐤋.𐤕
𐤕𐤂𐤓.𐤁𐤌.𐤌𐤋𐤇𐤌𐤄.𐤊𐤉.𐤋𐤀.𐤀𐤕𐤍.𐤋𐤊.𐤌𐤀𐤓𐤑𐤅.𐤉𐤓𐤔𐤄.
𐤊𐤉.𐤋𐤁𐤍𐤉.𐤋𐤅𐤈.𐤍𐤕𐤕𐤉.𐤀𐤕.𐤏𐤓.𐤉𐤓𐤔𐤄|
י 𐤄𐤀𐤌𐤉𐤌.𐤋𐤐𐤍𐤉𐤌.𐤉𐤔𐤁𐤅.𐤁𐤄.𐤏𐤌.𐤂𐤃𐤅𐤋.𐤅𐤓𐤁.𐤅𐤓
𐤌.𐤊𐤏𐤍𐤒𐤉𐤌|
יא 𐤓𐤐𐤀𐤉𐤌.𐤉𐤇𐤔𐤁𐤅.𐤀𐤐.𐤄𐤌.𐤊𐤏𐤍𐤒𐤉𐤌.𐤅𐤄𐤌𐤀𐤁𐤉𐤌
.𐤉𐤒𐤓𐤀𐤅.𐤋𐤄𐤌.𐤀𐤌𐤉𐤌|
יב 𐤅𐤁𐤔𐤏𐤉𐤓.𐤉𐤔𐤁𐤅.𐤄𐤇𐤓𐤉𐤌.𐤋𐤐𐤍𐤉𐤌.𐤅𐤁𐤍𐤉.𐤏𐤔𐤅.𐤉
𐤉𐤓𐤔𐤅𐤌.𐤅𐤉𐤔𐤌𐤉𐤃𐤅𐤌.𐤌𐤐𐤍𐤉𐤄𐤌.𐤅𐤉𐤔𐤁𐤅.𐤕𐤇𐤕𐤌.𐤊𐤀
𐤔𐤓.𐤏𐤔𐤄.𐤉𐤔𐤓𐤀𐤋.𐤋𐤀𐤓𐤑.𐤉𐤓𐤔𐤕𐤅.𐤀𐤔𐤓.𐤍𐤕𐤍.𐤉𐤄𐤅𐤄.
𐤋𐤄𐤌|
יג 𐤏𐤕𐤄.𐤒𐤌𐤅.𐤅𐤏𐤁𐤓𐤅.𐤋𐤊𐤌.𐤀𐤕.𐤍𐤇𐤋.𐤆𐤓𐤃.𐤅𐤍𐤏𐤁
𐤓.𐤀𐤕.𐤍𐤇𐤋.𐤆𐤓𐤃|
יד 𐤅𐤄𐤉𐤌𐤉𐤌.𐤀𐤔𐤓.𐤄𐤋𐤊𐤍𐤅.𐤌𐤒𐤃𐤔.𐤁𐤓𐤍𐤏.𐤏𐤃.𐤀
𐤔𐤓.𐤏𐤁𐤓𐤍𐤅.𐤀𐤕.𐤍𐤇𐤋.𐤆𐤓𐤃.𐤔𐤋𐤔𐤉𐤌.𐤅𐤔𐤌𐤍𐤄.𐤔𐤍𐤄.𐤏
𐤃.𐤕𐤌.𐤊𐤋.𐤄𐤃𐤅𐤓.𐤀𐤍𐤔𐤉.𐤄𐤌𐤋𐤇𐤌𐤄.𐤌𐤒𐤓𐤁.𐤄𐤌𐤇𐤍𐤄
.𐤊𐤀𐤔𐤓.𐤍𐤔𐤁𐤏.𐤉𐤄𐤅𐤄.𐤋𐤄𐤌|
טו 𐤅𐤂𐤌.𐤉𐤃.𐤉𐤄𐤅𐤄.𐤄𐤉𐤕𐤄.𐤁𐤌.𐤋𐤄𐤌𐤌.𐤌𐤒𐤓𐤁.𐤄𐤌
𐤇𐤍𐤄.𐤏𐤃.𐤕𐤌𐤌|
טז 𐤅𐤉𐤄𐤉.𐤊𐤀𐤔𐤓.𐤕𐤌𐤅.𐤊𐤋.𐤀𐤍𐤔𐤉.𐤄𐤌𐤋𐤇𐤌𐤄.𐤋𐤌𐤅𐤕
.𐤌𐤒𐤓𐤁.𐤄𐤏𐤌|
יז 𐤅𐤉𐤃𐤁𐤓.𐤉𐤄𐤅𐤄.𐤀𐤋𐤉.𐤋𐤀𐤌𐤓|
יח 𐤀𐤕𐤄.𐤏𐤁𐤓.𐤄𐤉𐤅𐤌.𐤀𐤕.𐤂𐤁𐤅𐤋.𐤌𐤅𐤀𐤁.𐤀𐤕.𐤏𐤓|
יט 𐤅𐤒𐤓𐤁𐤕.𐤌𐤅𐤋.𐤁𐤍𐤉.𐤏𐤌𐤅𐤍.𐤀𐤋.𐤕𐤑𐤓𐤌.𐤅𐤀𐤋.𐤕𐤕𐤂
𐤓.𐤁𐤌.𐤊𐤉.𐤋𐤀.𐤀𐤕𐤍.𐤌𐤀𐤓𐤑.𐤁𐤍𐤉.𐤏𐤌𐤅𐤍.𐤋𐤊.𐤉𐤓𐤔𐤄.𐤊𐤉
.𐤋𐤁𐤍𐤉.𐤋𐤅𐤈.𐤍𐤕𐤕𐤉𐤄.𐤉𐤓𐤔𐤄|
כ 𐤀𐤓𐤑.𐤓𐤐𐤀𐤉𐤌.𐤕𐤇𐤔𐤁.𐤀𐤐.𐤄𐤅𐤀.𐤓𐤐𐤀𐤉𐤌.𐤉𐤔𐤁𐤅.
𐤁𐤄.𐤋𐤐𐤍𐤉𐤌.𐤅𐤄𐤏𐤌𐤍𐤉𐤌.𐤉𐤒𐤓𐤀𐤅.𐤋𐤄𐤌.𐤆𐤌𐤆𐤌𐤉𐤌|

..𐤊𐤀.. 𐤏𐤌.𐤂𐤃𐤅𐤋.𐤅𐤓𐤁.𐤅𐤓𐤌.𐤊𐤏𐤍𐤒𐤉𐤌.𐤅𐤉𐤔𐤌𐤉𐤃𐤌.𐤉𐤄𐤅𐤄.𐤌𐤐𐤍𐤉𐤄𐤌.𐤅𐤉𐤉𐤓𐤔𐤌.𐤅𐤉𐤔𐤁𐤅.𐤕𐤇𐤕𐤌|

..𐤊𐤁.. 𐤊𐤀𐤔𐤓.𐤏𐤔𐤄.𐤋𐤁𐤍𐤉.𐤏𐤔𐤅.𐤄𐤉𐤔𐤁𐤉𐤌.𐤁𐤔𐤏𐤉𐤓.𐤀𐤔𐤓.𐤄𐤔𐤌𐤉𐤃.𐤀𐤕.𐤄𐤇𐤓𐤉.𐤌𐤐𐤍𐤉𐤄𐤌.𐤅𐤉𐤉𐤓𐤔𐤌.𐤅𐤉𐤔𐤁𐤅.𐤕𐤇𐤕𐤌.𐤏𐤃.𐤄𐤉𐤅𐤌.𐤄𐤆𐤄|

..𐤊𐤂.. 𐤅𐤄𐤏𐤅𐤉𐤌.𐤄𐤉𐤔𐤁𐤉𐤌.𐤁𐤇𐤑𐤓𐤉𐤌.𐤏𐤃.𐤏𐤆𐤄.𐤊𐤐𐤕𐤓𐤉𐤌.𐤄𐤉𐤑𐤀𐤉𐤌.𐤌𐤊𐤐𐤕𐤅𐤓.𐤄𐤔𐤌𐤉𐤃𐤌.𐤅𐤉𐤔𐤁𐤅.𐤕𐤇𐤕𐤌|

..𐤊𐤃.. 𐤒𐤅𐤌𐤅.𐤎𐤏𐤅.𐤅𐤏𐤁𐤓𐤅.𐤀𐤕.𐤍𐤇𐤋.𐤀𐤓𐤍𐤍.𐤓𐤀𐤄.𐤍𐤕𐤕𐤉.𐤁𐤉𐤃𐤊.𐤀𐤕.𐤎𐤉𐤇𐤍.𐤌𐤋𐤊.𐤇𐤔𐤁𐤅𐤍.𐤄𐤀𐤌𐤓𐤉.𐤅𐤀𐤕.𐤀𐤓𐤑𐤅.𐤄𐤇𐤋.𐤓𐤔.𐤅𐤄𐤕𐤂𐤓.𐤁𐤅.𐤌𐤋𐤇𐤌𐤄|

..𐤊𐤄.. 𐤄𐤉𐤅𐤌.𐤄𐤆𐤄.𐤀𐤇𐤋.𐤕𐤕.𐤐𐤇𐤃𐤊.𐤅𐤉𐤓𐤀𐤕𐤊.𐤏𐤋.𐤐𐤍𐤉.𐤄𐤏𐤌𐤉𐤌.𐤕𐤇𐤕.𐤊𐤋.𐤄𐤔𐤌𐤉𐤌.𐤀𐤔𐤓.𐤉𐤔𐤌𐤏𐤅𐤍.𐤔𐤌𐤏𐤊.𐤅𐤓𐤂𐤆𐤅.𐤅𐤇𐤋𐤅.𐤌𐤐𐤍𐤉𐤊|

..𐤊𐤅.. 𐤅𐤀𐤔𐤋𐤇.𐤌𐤋𐤀𐤊𐤉𐤌.𐤌𐤌𐤃𐤁𐤓.𐤒𐤃𐤌𐤅𐤕.𐤀𐤋.𐤎𐤉𐤇𐤅𐤍.𐤌𐤋𐤊.𐤇𐤔𐤁𐤅𐤍.𐤃𐤁𐤓𐤉.𐤔𐤋𐤅𐤌.𐤋𐤀𐤌𐤓|

..𐤊𐤆.. 𐤀𐤏𐤁𐤓𐤄.𐤁𐤀𐤓𐤑𐤊.𐤁𐤃𐤓𐤊.𐤁𐤃𐤓𐤊.𐤀𐤋𐤊.𐤋𐤀.𐤀𐤎𐤅𐤓.𐤉𐤌𐤉𐤍.𐤅𐤔𐤌𐤀𐤅𐤋|

..𐤊𐤇.. 𐤀𐤊𐤋.𐤁𐤊𐤎𐤐.𐤕𐤔𐤁𐤓𐤍𐤉.𐤅𐤀𐤊𐤋𐤕𐤉.𐤅𐤌𐤉𐤌.𐤁𐤊𐤎𐤐.𐤕𐤕𐤍.𐤋𐤉.𐤅𐤔𐤕𐤉𐤕𐤉.𐤓𐤒.𐤀𐤏𐤁𐤓𐤄.𐤁𐤓𐤂𐤋𐤉|

..𐤊𐤈.. 𐤊𐤀𐤔𐤓.𐤏𐤔𐤅.𐤋𐤉.𐤁𐤍𐤉.𐤏𐤔𐤅.𐤄𐤉𐤔𐤁𐤉𐤌.𐤁𐤔𐤏𐤉𐤓.𐤅𐤄𐤌𐤅𐤀𐤁𐤉𐤌.𐤄𐤉𐤔𐤁𐤉𐤌.𐤁𐤏𐤓.𐤏𐤃.𐤀𐤔𐤓.𐤀𐤏𐤁𐤓.𐤀𐤕.𐤄𐤉𐤓𐤃𐤍.𐤀𐤋.𐤄𐤀𐤓𐤑.𐤀𐤔𐤓.𐤉𐤄𐤅𐤄.𐤀𐤋𐤄𐤉𐤍𐤅.𐤍𐤕𐤍.𐤋𐤍𐤅|

..𐤋.. 𐤅𐤋𐤀.𐤀𐤁𐤄.𐤎𐤉𐤇𐤍.𐤌𐤋𐤊.𐤇𐤔𐤁𐤅𐤍.𐤄𐤏𐤁𐤓𐤍𐤅.𐤁𐤅.𐤊𐤉.𐤄𐤒𐤔𐤄.𐤉𐤄𐤅𐤄.𐤀𐤋𐤄𐤉𐤊.𐤀𐤕.𐤓𐤅𐤇𐤅.𐤅𐤀𐤌𐤑.𐤀𐤕.𐤋𐤁𐤁𐤅.𐤋𐤌𐤏𐤍.𐤕𐤕𐤅.𐤁𐤉𐤃𐤊.𐤊𐤉𐤅𐤌.𐤄𐤆𐤄|

..𐤋𐤀.. 𐤅𐤉𐤀𐤌𐤓.𐤉𐤄𐤅𐤄.𐤀𐤋𐤉.𐤓𐤀𐤄.𐤄𐤇𐤋𐤕𐤉.𐤕𐤕.𐤋𐤐𐤍𐤉𐤊.𐤀𐤕.𐤎𐤉𐤇𐤍.𐤅𐤀𐤕.𐤀𐤓𐤑𐤅.𐤄𐤇𐤋.𐤓𐤔.𐤋𐤓𐤔𐤕.𐤀𐤕.𐤀𐤓𐤑𐤅
|

..𐤋𐤁.. 𐤅𐤉𐤑𐤀.𐤎𐤉𐤇𐤍.𐤋𐤒𐤓𐤀𐤕𐤍𐤅.𐤄𐤅𐤀.𐤅𐤊𐤋.𐤏𐤌𐤅.𐤋𐤌𐤋𐤇𐤌𐤄.𐤉𐤄𐤑𐤄|

לג ויתנהו יהוה אלהינו לפנינו ונך אתו ואת בנו ‖בניו קרי‖ ואת כל עמו׃

לד ונלכד את כל עריו בעת ההוא ונחרם את כל עיר מתם והנשים והטף לא השארנו שריד׃

לה רק הבהמה בזזנו לנו ושלל הערים אשר לכדנו׃

לו מערער אשר על שפת נחל ארנן והעיר אשר בנחל ועד הגלעד לא היתה קריה אשר שגבה ממנו את הכל נתן יהוה אלהינו לפנינו׃

לז רק אל ארץ בני עמון לא קרבת כל יד נחל יבק וערי ההר וכל אשר צוה יהוה אלהינו‖

דברים חלק ג

א ונפן ונעל דרך הבשן ויצא עוג מלך הבשן לקראתנו הוא וכל עמו למלחמה אדרעי׃

ב ויאמר יהוה אלי אל תירא אתו כי בידך נתתי אתו ואת כל עמו ואת ארצו ועשית לו כאשר עשית לסיחן מלך האמרי אשר יושב בחשבון׃

ג ויתן יהוה אלהינו בידנו גם את עוג מלך הבשן ואת כל עמו ונכהו עד בלתי השאיר לו שריד׃

ד ונלכד את כל עריו בעת ההוא לא היתה קריה אשר לא לקחנו מאתם ששים עיר כל חבל ארגב ממלכת עוג בבשן׃

ה כל אלה ערים בצרות חומה גבהה דלתים ובריח לבד מערי הפרזי הרבה מאד׃

6 𐤅𐤍𐤇𐤓𐤌.𐤀𐤅𐤕𐤌.𐤊𐤀𐤔𐤓.𐤏𐤔𐤉𐤍𐤅.𐤋𐤎𐤉𐤇𐤍.𐤌𐤋𐤊.𐤇𐤔
𐤁𐤅𐤍.𐤄𐤇𐤓𐤌.𐤊𐤋.𐤏𐤉𐤓.𐤌𐤕𐤌.𐤄𐤍𐤔𐤉𐤌.𐤅𐤄𐤈𐤐|

7 𐤅𐤊𐤋.𐤄𐤁𐤄𐤌𐤄.𐤅𐤔𐤋𐤋.𐤄𐤏𐤓𐤉𐤌.𐤁𐤆𐤅𐤍𐤅.𐤋𐤍𐤅|

8 𐤅𐤍𐤒𐤇.𐤁𐤏𐤕.𐤄𐤄𐤅𐤀.𐤀𐤕.𐤄𐤀𐤓𐤑.𐤌𐤉𐤃.𐤔𐤍𐤉.𐤌𐤋𐤊
𐤉.𐤄𐤀𐤌𐤓𐤉.𐤀𐤔𐤓.𐤁𐤏𐤁𐤓.𐤄𐤉𐤓𐤃𐤍.𐤌𐤍𐤇𐤋.𐤀𐤓𐤍𐤍.𐤏𐤃.
𐤄𐤓.𐤇𐤓𐤌𐤅𐤍|

9 𐤑𐤉𐤃𐤍𐤉𐤌.𐤉𐤒𐤓𐤀𐤅.𐤋𐤇𐤓𐤌𐤅𐤍.𐤔𐤓𐤉𐤍.𐤅𐤄𐤀𐤌𐤓𐤉.𐤉
𐤒𐤓𐤀𐤅.𐤋𐤅.𐤔𐤍𐤉𐤓|

10 𐤊𐤋.𐤏𐤓𐤉.𐤄𐤌𐤉𐤔𐤓.𐤅𐤊𐤋.𐤄𐤂𐤋𐤏𐤃.𐤅𐤊𐤋.𐤄𐤁𐤔𐤍.𐤏
𐤃.𐤎𐤋𐤊𐤄.𐤅𐤀𐤃𐤓𐤏𐤉.𐤏𐤓𐤉.𐤌𐤌𐤋𐤊𐤕.𐤏𐤅𐤂.𐤁𐤁𐤔𐤍|

11 𐤊𐤉.𐤓𐤒.𐤏𐤅𐤂.𐤌𐤋𐤊.𐤄𐤁𐤔𐤍.𐤍𐤔𐤀𐤓.𐤌𐤉𐤕𐤓.𐤄𐤓𐤐𐤀
𐤉𐤌.𐤄𐤍𐤄.𐤏𐤓𐤔𐤅.𐤏𐤓𐤔.𐤁𐤓𐤆𐤋.𐤄𐤋𐤄.𐤄𐤅𐤀.𐤁𐤓𐤁𐤕.𐤁𐤍𐤉.
𐤏𐤌𐤅𐤍.𐤕𐤔𐤏.𐤀𐤌𐤅𐤕.𐤀𐤓𐤊𐤄.𐤅𐤀𐤓𐤁𐤏.𐤀𐤌𐤅𐤕.𐤓𐤇𐤁𐤄.𐤁
𐤀𐤌𐤕.𐤀𐤉𐤔|

12 𐤅𐤀𐤕.𐤄𐤀𐤓𐤑.𐤄𐤆𐤀𐤕.𐤉𐤓𐤔𐤍𐤅.𐤁𐤏𐤕.𐤄𐤄𐤅𐤀.𐤌𐤏𐤓
𐤏𐤓.𐤀𐤔𐤓.𐤏𐤋.𐤍𐤇𐤋.𐤀𐤓𐤍𐤍.𐤅𐤇𐤑𐤉.𐤄𐤓.𐤄𐤂𐤋𐤏𐤃.𐤅𐤏𐤓𐤉
𐤅.𐤍𐤕𐤕𐤉.𐤋𐤓𐤀𐤅𐤁𐤍𐤉.𐤅𐤋𐤂𐤃𐤉|

13 𐤅𐤉𐤕𐤓.𐤄𐤂𐤋𐤏𐤃.𐤅𐤊𐤋.𐤄𐤁𐤔𐤍.𐤌𐤌𐤋𐤊𐤕.𐤏𐤅𐤂.𐤍𐤕
𐤕𐤉.𐤋𐤇𐤑𐤉.𐤔𐤁𐤈.𐤄𐤌𐤍𐤔𐤄.𐤊𐤋.𐤇𐤁𐤋.𐤄𐤀𐤓𐤂𐤁.𐤋𐤊𐤋.
𐤄𐤁𐤔𐤍.𐤄𐤄𐤅𐤀.𐤉𐤒𐤓𐤀.𐤀𐤓𐤑.𐤓𐤐𐤀𐤉𐤌|

14 𐤉𐤀𐤉𐤓.𐤁𐤍.𐤌𐤍𐤔𐤄.𐤋𐤒𐤇.𐤀𐤕.𐤊𐤋.𐤇𐤁𐤋.𐤀𐤓𐤂𐤁.
𐤏𐤃.𐤂𐤁𐤅𐤋.𐤄𐤂𐤔𐤅𐤓𐤉.𐤅𐤄𐤌𐤏𐤊𐤕𐤉.𐤅𐤉𐤒𐤓𐤀.𐤀𐤕𐤌.𐤏𐤋.
𐤔𐤌𐤅.𐤀𐤕.𐤄𐤁𐤔𐤍.𐤇𐤅𐤕.𐤉𐤀𐤉𐤓.𐤏𐤃.𐤄𐤉𐤅𐤌.𐤄𐤆𐤄|

15 𐤅𐤋𐤌𐤊𐤉𐤓.𐤍𐤕𐤕𐤉.𐤀𐤕.𐤄𐤂𐤋𐤏𐤃|

16 𐤅𐤋𐤓𐤀𐤅𐤁𐤍𐤉.𐤅𐤋𐤂𐤃𐤉.𐤍𐤕𐤕𐤉.𐤌𐤍.𐤄𐤂𐤋𐤏𐤃.𐤅𐤏𐤃.
𐤍𐤇𐤋.𐤀𐤓𐤍𐤍.𐤕𐤅𐤊.𐤄𐤍𐤇𐤋.𐤅𐤂𐤁𐤋.𐤅𐤏𐤃.𐤉𐤁𐤒.𐤄𐤍𐤇𐤋.𐤂
𐤁𐤅𐤋.𐤁𐤍𐤉.𐤏𐤌𐤅𐤍|

17 𐤅𐤄𐤏𐤓𐤁𐤄.𐤅𐤄𐤉𐤓𐤃𐤍.𐤅𐤂𐤁𐤋.𐤌𐤊𐤍𐤓𐤕.𐤅𐤏𐤃.𐤉𐤌.𐤄
𐤏𐤓𐤁𐤄.𐤉𐤌.𐤄𐤌𐤋𐤇.𐤕𐤇𐤕.𐤀𐤔𐤃𐤕.𐤄𐤐𐤎𐤂𐤄.𐤌𐤆𐤓𐤇
𐤄|

𐤉𐤇 𐤅𐤀𐤑𐤅.𐤀𐤕𐤊𐤌.𐤁𐤏𐤕.𐤄𐤄𐤅𐤀.𐤋𐤀𐤌𐤓.𐤉𐤄𐤅𐤄.𐤀𐤋𐤄
𐤉𐤊𐤌.𐤍𐤕𐤍.𐤋𐤊𐤌.𐤀𐤕.𐤄𐤀𐤓𐤑.𐤄𐤆𐤀𐤕.𐤋𐤓𐤔𐤕𐤄.𐤇𐤋𐤅𐤑
𐤉𐤌.𐤕𐤏𐤁𐤓𐤅.𐤋𐤐𐤍𐤉.𐤀𐤇𐤉𐤊𐤌.𐤁𐤍𐤉.𐤉𐤔𐤓𐤀𐤋.𐤊𐤋.𐤁𐤍𐤉.𐤇
𐤉𐤋|
𐤉𐤈 𐤓𐤒.𐤍𐤔𐤉𐤊𐤌.𐤅𐤈𐤐𐤊𐤌.𐤅𐤌𐤒𐤍𐤊𐤌.𐤉𐤃𐤏𐤕𐤉.𐤊𐤉.𐤌
𐤒𐤍𐤄.𐤓𐤁.𐤋𐤊𐤌.𐤉𐤔𐤁𐤅.𐤁𐤏𐤓𐤉𐤊𐤌.𐤀𐤔𐤓.𐤍𐤕𐤕𐤉.𐤋𐤊𐤌|
𐤊 𐤏𐤃.𐤀𐤔𐤓.𐤉𐤍𐤉𐤇.𐤉𐤄𐤅𐤄.𐤋𐤀𐤇𐤉𐤊𐤌.𐤊𐤊𐤌.𐤅𐤉𐤓
𐤔𐤅.𐤂𐤌.𐤄𐤌.𐤀𐤕.𐤄𐤀𐤓𐤑.𐤀𐤔𐤓.𐤉𐤄𐤅𐤄.𐤀𐤋𐤄𐤉𐤊𐤌.𐤍𐤕𐤍.
𐤋𐤄𐤌.𐤁𐤏𐤁𐤓.𐤄𐤉𐤓𐤃𐤍.𐤅𐤔𐤁𐤕𐤌.𐤀𐤉𐤔.𐤋𐤉𐤓𐤔𐤕𐤅.𐤀𐤔𐤓.
𐤍𐤕𐤕𐤉.𐤋𐤊𐤌|
𐤊𐤀 𐤅𐤀𐤕.𐤉𐤄𐤅𐤔𐤅𐤏.𐤑𐤅𐤉𐤕𐤉.𐤁𐤏𐤕.𐤄𐤄𐤅𐤀.𐤋𐤀𐤌𐤓.𐤏𐤉
𐤍𐤉𐤊.𐤄𐤓𐤀𐤕.𐤀𐤕.𐤊𐤋.𐤀𐤔𐤓.𐤏𐤔𐤄.𐤉𐤄𐤅𐤄.𐤀𐤋𐤄𐤉𐤊𐤌.𐤋
𐤔𐤍𐤉.𐤄𐤌𐤋𐤊𐤉𐤌.𐤄𐤀𐤋𐤄.𐤊𐤍.𐤉𐤏𐤔𐤄.𐤉𐤄𐤅𐤄.𐤋𐤊𐤋.𐤄𐤌𐤌
𐤋𐤊𐤅𐤕.𐤀𐤔𐤓.𐤀𐤕𐤄.𐤏𐤁𐤓.𐤔𐤌𐤄|
𐤊𐤁 𐤋𐤀.𐤕𐤉𐤓𐤀𐤅𐤌.𐤊𐤉.𐤉𐤄𐤅𐤄.𐤀𐤋𐤄𐤉𐤊𐤌.𐤄𐤅𐤀.𐤄𐤍𐤋𐤇
𐤌.𐤋𐤊𐤌|
𐤊𐤂 𐤅𐤀𐤕𐤇𐤍𐤍.𐤀𐤋.𐤉𐤄𐤅𐤄.𐤁𐤏𐤕.𐤄𐤄𐤅𐤀.𐤋𐤀𐤌𐤓|
𐤊𐤃 𐤀𐤃𐤍𐤉.𐤉𐤄𐤅𐤄.𐤀𐤕𐤄.𐤄𐤇𐤋𐤅𐤕.𐤋𐤄𐤓𐤀𐤅𐤕.𐤀𐤕.𐤏
𐤁𐤃𐤊.𐤀𐤕.𐤂𐤃𐤋𐤊.𐤅𐤀𐤕.𐤉𐤃𐤊.𐤄𐤇𐤆𐤒𐤄.𐤀𐤔𐤓.𐤌𐤉.
𐤀𐤋.𐤁𐤔𐤌𐤉𐤌.𐤅𐤁𐤀𐤓𐤑.𐤀𐤔𐤓.𐤉𐤏𐤔𐤄.𐤊𐤌𐤏𐤔𐤉𐤊.𐤅𐤊𐤂
𐤁𐤅𐤓𐤕𐤊|
𐤊𐤄 𐤀𐤏𐤁𐤓𐤄.𐤍𐤀.𐤅𐤀𐤓𐤀𐤄.𐤀𐤕.𐤄𐤀𐤓𐤑.𐤄𐤈𐤅𐤁𐤄.𐤀𐤔
𐤓.𐤁𐤏𐤁𐤓.𐤄𐤉𐤓𐤃𐤍.𐤄𐤄𐤓.𐤄𐤈𐤅𐤁.𐤄𐤆𐤄.𐤅𐤄𐤋𐤁𐤍𐤅𐤍|
𐤊𐤅 𐤅𐤉𐤕𐤏𐤁𐤓.𐤉𐤄𐤅𐤄.𐤁𐤉.𐤋𐤌𐤏𐤍𐤊𐤌.𐤅𐤋𐤀.𐤔𐤌𐤏.𐤀𐤋𐤉.
𐤅𐤉𐤀𐤌𐤓.𐤉𐤄𐤅𐤄.𐤀𐤋𐤉.𐤓𐤁.𐤋𐤊.𐤀𐤋.𐤕𐤅𐤎𐤐.𐤃𐤁𐤓.𐤀𐤋𐤉.𐤏𐤅
𐤃.𐤁𐤃𐤁𐤓.𐤄𐤆𐤄|
𐤊𐤆 𐤏𐤋𐤄.𐤓𐤀𐤔.𐤄𐤐𐤎𐤂𐤄.𐤅𐤔𐤀.𐤏𐤉𐤍𐤉𐤊.𐤉𐤌𐤄.𐤅𐤑𐤐𐤍
𐤄.𐤅𐤕𐤉𐤌𐤍𐤄.𐤅𐤌𐤆𐤓𐤇𐤄.𐤅𐤓𐤀𐤄.𐤁𐤏𐤉𐤍𐤉𐤊.𐤊𐤉.𐤋𐤀.𐤕𐤏
𐤁𐤓.𐤀𐤕.𐤄𐤉𐤓𐤃𐤍.𐤄𐤆𐤄|

𐤊𐤇 𐤅𐤑𐤅.𐤀𐤕.𐤉𐤄𐤅𐤔𐤏.𐤅𐤇𐤆𐤒𐤄𐤅.𐤅𐤀𐤌𐤑𐤄𐤅.𐤊𐤉.𐤄𐤅𐤀
.𐤉𐤏𐤁𐤓.𐤋𐤐𐤍𐤉.𐤄𐤏𐤌.𐤄𐤆𐤄.𐤅𐤄𐤅𐤀.𐤉𐤍𐤇𐤉𐤋.𐤀𐤅𐤕𐤌.𐤀𐤕.
𐤄𐤀𐤓𐤑.𐤀𐤔𐤓.𐤕𐤓𐤀𐤄|

𐤊𐤈 𐤅𐤍𐤔𐤁.𐤁𐤂𐤉𐤀.𐤌𐤅𐤋.𐤁𐤉𐤕.𐤐𐤏𐤅𐤓‖

𐤃𐤁𐤓𐤉𐤌.𐤇𐤋𐤒 𐤃

𐤀 𐤅𐤏𐤕𐤄.𐤉𐤔𐤓𐤀𐤋.𐤔𐤌𐤏.𐤀𐤋.𐤄𐤇𐤒𐤉𐤌.𐤅𐤀𐤋.𐤄𐤌𐤔𐤐
𐤈𐤉𐤌.𐤀𐤔𐤓.𐤀𐤍𐤊𐤉.𐤌𐤋𐤌𐤃.𐤀𐤕𐤊𐤌.𐤋𐤏𐤔𐤅𐤕.𐤋𐤌𐤏𐤍.𐤕
𐤇𐤉𐤅.𐤅𐤁𐤀𐤕𐤌.𐤅𐤉𐤓𐤔𐤕𐤌.𐤀𐤕.𐤄𐤀𐤓𐤑.𐤀𐤔𐤓.𐤉𐤄𐤅𐤄.𐤀𐤋
𐤄𐤉.𐤀𐤁𐤕𐤉𐤊𐤌.𐤍𐤕𐤍.𐤋𐤊𐤌|

𐤁 𐤋𐤀.𐤕𐤎𐤐𐤅.𐤏𐤋.𐤄𐤃𐤁𐤓.𐤀𐤔𐤓.𐤀𐤍𐤊𐤉.𐤌𐤑𐤅𐤄.𐤀𐤕𐤊
𐤌.𐤅𐤋𐤀.𐤕𐤂𐤓𐤏𐤅.𐤌𐤌𐤍𐤅.𐤋𐤔𐤌𐤓.𐤀𐤕.𐤌𐤑𐤅𐤕.𐤉𐤄𐤅𐤄.𐤀𐤋
𐤄𐤉𐤊𐤌.𐤀𐤔𐤓.𐤀𐤍𐤊𐤉.𐤌𐤑𐤅𐤄.𐤀𐤕𐤊𐤌|

𐤂 𐤏𐤉𐤍𐤉𐤊𐤌.𐤄𐤓𐤀𐤕.𐤀𐤕.𐤀𐤔𐤓.𐤏𐤔𐤄.𐤉𐤄𐤅𐤄.𐤁𐤁𐤏𐤋.
𐤐𐤏𐤅𐤓.𐤊𐤉.𐤊𐤋.𐤄𐤀𐤉𐤔.𐤀𐤔𐤓.𐤄𐤋𐤊.𐤀𐤇𐤓𐤉.𐤁𐤏𐤋.𐤐𐤏𐤅𐤓.
𐤄𐤔𐤌𐤉𐤃𐤅.𐤉𐤄𐤅𐤄.𐤀𐤋𐤄𐤉𐤊.𐤌𐤒𐤓𐤁𐤊|

𐤃 𐤅𐤀𐤕𐤌.𐤄𐤃𐤁𐤒𐤉𐤌.𐤁𐤉𐤄𐤅𐤄.𐤀𐤋𐤄𐤉𐤊𐤌.𐤇𐤉𐤉𐤌.𐤊
𐤋𐤊𐤌.𐤄𐤉𐤅𐤌|

𐤄 𐤓𐤀𐤄.𐤋𐤌𐤃𐤕𐤉.𐤀𐤕𐤊𐤌.𐤇𐤒𐤉𐤌.𐤅𐤌𐤔𐤐𐤈𐤉𐤌.𐤊𐤀𐤔
𐤓.𐤑𐤅𐤍𐤉.𐤉𐤄𐤅𐤄.𐤀𐤋𐤄𐤉.𐤋𐤏𐤔𐤅𐤕.𐤊𐤍.𐤁𐤒𐤓𐤁.𐤄𐤀𐤓𐤑.𐤀
𐤔𐤓.𐤀𐤕𐤌.𐤁𐤀𐤉𐤌.𐤔𐤌𐤄.𐤋𐤓𐤔𐤕𐤄|

𐤅 𐤅𐤔𐤌𐤓𐤕𐤌.𐤅𐤏𐤔𐤉𐤕𐤌.𐤊𐤉.𐤄𐤅𐤀.𐤇𐤊𐤌𐤕𐤊𐤌.𐤅𐤁𐤉𐤍𐤕
𐤊𐤌.𐤋𐤏𐤉𐤍𐤉.𐤄𐤏𐤌𐤉𐤌.𐤀𐤔𐤓.𐤉𐤔𐤌𐤏𐤅𐤍.𐤀𐤕.𐤊𐤋.𐤄𐤇𐤒
𐤉𐤌.𐤄𐤀𐤋𐤄.𐤅𐤀𐤌𐤓𐤅.𐤓𐤒.𐤏𐤌.𐤇𐤊𐤌.𐤅𐤍𐤁𐤅𐤍.𐤄𐤂𐤅𐤉.𐤄𐤂
𐤃𐤅𐤋.𐤄𐤆𐤄|

𐤆 𐤊𐤉.𐤌𐤉.𐤂𐤅𐤉.𐤂𐤃𐤅𐤋.𐤀𐤔𐤓.𐤋𐤅.𐤀𐤋𐤄𐤉𐤌.𐤒𐤓𐤁𐤉𐤌.
𐤀𐤋𐤉𐤅.𐤊𐤉𐤄𐤅𐤄.𐤀𐤋𐤄𐤉𐤍𐤅.𐤁𐤊𐤋.𐤒𐤓𐤀𐤍𐤅.𐤀𐤋𐤉𐤅|

𐤈 𐤓𐤒.𐤄𐤔𐤌𐤓.𐤋𐤊.𐤅𐤔𐤌𐤓.𐤍𐤐𐤔𐤊.𐤌𐤀𐤃.𐤐𐤍.𐤕𐤔𐤊𐤇.𐤀
𐤕.𐤄𐤃𐤁𐤓𐤉𐤌.𐤀𐤔𐤓.𐤓𐤀𐤅.𐤏𐤉𐤍𐤉𐤊.𐤅𐤐𐤍.𐤉𐤎𐤅𐤓𐤅.𐤌𐤋𐤁𐤁𐤊.
𐤊𐤋.𐤉𐤌𐤉.𐤇𐤉𐤉𐤊.𐤅𐤄𐤅𐤃𐤏𐤕𐤌.𐤋𐤁𐤍𐤉𐤊.𐤅𐤋𐤁𐤍𐤉.𐤁𐤍𐤉𐤊|
𐤉 𐤉𐤅𐤌.𐤀𐤔𐤓.𐤏𐤌𐤃𐤕.𐤋𐤐𐤍𐤉.𐤉𐤄𐤅𐤄.𐤀𐤋𐤄𐤉𐤊.𐤁𐤇𐤓
𐤁.𐤁𐤀𐤌𐤓.𐤉𐤄𐤅𐤄.𐤀𐤋𐤉.𐤄𐤒𐤄𐤋.𐤋𐤉.𐤀𐤕.𐤄𐤏𐤌.𐤅𐤀𐤔𐤌𐤏
𐤌.𐤀𐤕.𐤃𐤁𐤓𐤉.𐤀𐤔𐤓.𐤉𐤋𐤌𐤃𐤅𐤍.𐤋𐤉𐤓𐤀𐤄.𐤀𐤕𐤉.𐤊𐤋.𐤄𐤉
𐤌𐤉𐤌.𐤀𐤔𐤓.𐤄𐤌.𐤇𐤉𐤉𐤌.𐤏𐤋.𐤄𐤀𐤃𐤌𐤄.𐤅𐤀𐤕.𐤁𐤍𐤉𐤄𐤌.
𐤉𐤋𐤌𐤃𐤅𐤍|
𐤉𐤀 𐤅𐤕𐤒𐤓𐤁𐤅𐤍.𐤅𐤕𐤏𐤌𐤃𐤅𐤍.𐤕𐤇𐤕.𐤄𐤄𐤓.𐤅𐤄𐤄𐤓.𐤁𐤏𐤓.𐤁
𐤀𐤔.𐤏𐤃.𐤋𐤁.𐤄𐤔𐤌𐤉𐤌.𐤇𐤔𐤊.𐤏𐤍𐤍.𐤅𐤏𐤓𐤐𐤋|
𐤉𐤁 𐤅𐤉𐤃𐤁𐤓.𐤉𐤄𐤅𐤄.𐤀𐤋𐤉𐤊𐤌.𐤌𐤕𐤅𐤊.𐤄𐤀𐤔.𐤒𐤅𐤋.𐤃𐤁𐤓
𐤉𐤌.𐤀𐤕𐤌.𐤔𐤌𐤏𐤉𐤌.𐤅𐤕𐤌𐤅𐤍𐤄.𐤀𐤉𐤍𐤊𐤌.𐤓𐤀𐤉𐤌.𐤆𐤅𐤋𐤕𐤉
.𐤒𐤅𐤋|
𐤉𐤂 𐤅𐤉𐤂𐤃.𐤋𐤊𐤌.𐤀𐤕.𐤁𐤓𐤉𐤕𐤅.𐤀𐤔𐤓.𐤑𐤅𐤄.𐤀𐤕𐤊𐤌.𐤋
𐤏𐤔𐤅𐤕.𐤏𐤔𐤓𐤕.𐤄𐤃𐤁𐤓𐤉𐤌.𐤅𐤉𐤊𐤕𐤁𐤌.𐤏𐤋.𐤔𐤍𐤉.𐤋𐤇𐤅𐤕.
𐤀𐤁𐤍𐤉𐤌|
𐤉𐤃 𐤅𐤀𐤕𐤉.𐤑𐤅𐤄.𐤉𐤄𐤅𐤄.𐤁𐤏𐤕.𐤄𐤄𐤅𐤀.𐤋𐤋𐤌𐤃.𐤀𐤕𐤊
𐤌.𐤇𐤒𐤉𐤌.𐤅𐤌𐤔𐤐𐤈𐤉𐤌.𐤋𐤏𐤔𐤕𐤊𐤌.𐤀𐤕𐤌.𐤁𐤀𐤓𐤑.𐤀𐤔𐤓
.𐤀𐤕𐤌.𐤏𐤁𐤓𐤉𐤌.𐤔𐤌𐤄.𐤋𐤓𐤔𐤕𐤄|
𐤉𐤄 𐤅𐤍𐤔𐤌𐤓𐤕𐤌.𐤌𐤀𐤃.𐤋𐤍𐤐𐤔𐤕𐤉𐤊𐤌.𐤊𐤉.𐤋𐤀.𐤓𐤀𐤉𐤕𐤌
.𐤊𐤋.𐤕𐤌𐤅𐤍𐤄.𐤁𐤉𐤅𐤌.𐤃𐤁𐤓.𐤉𐤄𐤅𐤄.𐤀𐤋𐤉𐤊𐤌.𐤁𐤇𐤓𐤁.𐤌𐤕𐤅
𐤊.𐤄𐤀𐤔|
𐤉𐤅 𐤐𐤍.𐤕𐤔𐤇𐤕𐤅𐤍.𐤅𐤏𐤔𐤉𐤕𐤌.𐤋𐤊𐤌.𐤐𐤎𐤋.𐤕𐤌𐤅𐤍𐤕.𐤊𐤋.
𐤎𐤌𐤋.𐤕𐤁𐤍𐤉𐤕.𐤆𐤊𐤓.𐤀𐤅.𐤍𐤒𐤁𐤄|
𐤉𐤆 𐤕𐤁𐤍𐤉𐤕.𐤊𐤋.𐤁𐤄𐤌𐤄.𐤀𐤔𐤓.𐤁𐤀𐤓𐤑.𐤕𐤁𐤍𐤉𐤕.𐤊𐤋.
𐤑𐤐𐤅𐤓.𐤊𐤍𐤐.𐤀𐤔𐤓.𐤕𐤏𐤅𐤐.𐤁𐤔𐤌𐤉𐤌|
𐤉𐤇 𐤕𐤁𐤍𐤉𐤕.𐤊𐤋.𐤓𐤌𐤔.𐤁𐤀𐤃𐤌𐤄.𐤕𐤁𐤍𐤉𐤕.𐤃𐤂𐤄.
𐤀𐤔𐤓.𐤁𐤌𐤉𐤌.𐤌𐤕𐤇𐤕.𐤋𐤀𐤓𐤑|
𐤉𐤈 𐤅𐤐𐤍.𐤕𐤔𐤀.𐤏𐤉𐤍𐤉𐤊.𐤄𐤔𐤌𐤉𐤌𐤄.𐤅𐤓𐤀𐤉𐤕.𐤀𐤕.𐤄𐤔
𐤌𐤔.𐤅𐤀𐤕.𐤄𐤉𐤓𐤇.𐤅𐤀𐤕.𐤄𐤊𐤅𐤊𐤁𐤉𐤌.𐤊𐤋.𐤑𐤁𐤀.𐤄𐤔𐤌𐤉
𐤌.𐤅𐤍𐤃𐤇𐤕.𐤅𐤄𐤔𐤕𐤇𐤅𐤉𐤕.𐤋𐤄𐤌.𐤅𐤏𐤁𐤃𐤕𐤌.𐤀𐤔𐤓.𐤇𐤋

𐤒.𐤉𐤄𐤅𐤄.𐤀𐤋𐤄𐤉𐤊.𐤀𐤕𐤌.𐤋𐤊𐤋.𐤄𐤏𐤌𐤉𐤌.𐤕𐤇𐤕.𐤊𐤋.𐤄
𐤔𐤌𐤉𐤌|
..𐤊.. 𐤅𐤀𐤕𐤊𐤌.𐤋𐤒𐤇.𐤉𐤄𐤅𐤄.𐤅𐤉𐤑𐤀.𐤀𐤕𐤊𐤌.𐤌𐤊𐤅𐤓.𐤄
𐤁𐤓𐤆𐤋.𐤌𐤌𐤑𐤓𐤉𐤌.𐤋𐤄𐤉𐤅𐤕.𐤋𐤅.𐤋𐤏𐤌.𐤍𐤇𐤋𐤄.𐤊𐤉𐤅𐤌.𐤄
𐤆𐤄|
..𐤊𐤀.. 𐤅𐤉𐤄𐤅𐤄.𐤄𐤕𐤀𐤍𐤐.𐤁𐤉.𐤏𐤋.𐤃𐤁𐤓𐤉𐤊𐤌.𐤅𐤉𐤔𐤁𐤏.𐤋𐤁
𐤋𐤕𐤉.𐤏𐤁𐤓𐤉.𐤀𐤕.𐤄𐤉𐤓𐤃𐤍.𐤅𐤋𐤁𐤋𐤕𐤉.𐤁𐤀.𐤀𐤋.𐤄𐤀𐤓𐤑.
𐤄𐤈𐤅𐤁𐤄.𐤀𐤔𐤓.𐤉𐤄𐤅𐤄.𐤀𐤋𐤄𐤉𐤊.𐤍𐤕𐤍.𐤋𐤊.𐤍𐤇𐤋𐤄|
..𐤊𐤁.. 𐤊𐤉.𐤀𐤍𐤊𐤉.𐤌𐤕.𐤁𐤀𐤓𐤑.𐤄𐤆𐤀𐤕.𐤀𐤉𐤍𐤍𐤉.𐤏𐤁𐤓.𐤀
𐤕.𐤄𐤉𐤓𐤃𐤍.𐤅𐤀𐤕𐤌.𐤏𐤁𐤓𐤉𐤌.𐤅𐤉𐤓𐤔𐤕𐤌.𐤀𐤕.𐤄𐤀𐤓𐤑.𐤄
𐤈𐤅𐤁𐤄.𐤄𐤆𐤀𐤕|
..𐤊𐤂.. 𐤄𐤔𐤌𐤓𐤅.𐤋𐤊𐤌.𐤐𐤍.𐤕𐤔𐤊𐤇𐤅.𐤀𐤕.𐤁𐤓𐤉𐤕.𐤉𐤄𐤅𐤄.𐤀
𐤋𐤄𐤉𐤊𐤌.𐤀𐤔𐤓.𐤊𐤓𐤕.𐤏𐤌𐤊𐤌.𐤅𐤏𐤔𐤉𐤕𐤌.𐤋𐤊𐤌.𐤐𐤎𐤋.𐤕
𐤌𐤅𐤍𐤕.𐤊𐤋.𐤀𐤔𐤓.𐤑𐤅𐤊.𐤉𐤄𐤅𐤄.𐤀𐤋𐤄𐤉𐤊|
..𐤊𐤃.. 𐤊𐤉.𐤉𐤄𐤅𐤄.𐤀𐤋𐤄𐤉𐤊.𐤀𐤔.𐤀𐤊𐤋𐤄.𐤄𐤅𐤀.𐤀𐤋.𐤒𐤍𐤀|
..𐤊𐤄.. 𐤊𐤉.𐤕𐤅𐤋𐤉𐤃.𐤁𐤍𐤉𐤌.𐤅𐤁𐤍𐤉.𐤁𐤍𐤉𐤌.𐤅𐤍𐤅𐤔𐤍𐤕𐤌.𐤁𐤀𐤓
𐤑.𐤅𐤄𐤔𐤇𐤕𐤌.𐤅𐤏𐤔𐤉𐤕𐤌.𐤐𐤎𐤋.𐤕𐤌𐤅𐤍𐤕.𐤊𐤋.𐤅𐤏𐤔𐤉𐤕𐤌.
𐤄𐤓𐤏.𐤁𐤏𐤉𐤍𐤉.𐤉𐤄𐤅𐤄.𐤀𐤋𐤄𐤉𐤊.𐤋𐤄𐤊𐤏𐤉𐤎𐤅|
..𐤊𐤅.. 𐤄𐤏𐤉𐤃𐤕𐤉.𐤁𐤊𐤌.𐤄𐤉𐤅𐤌.𐤀𐤕.𐤄𐤔𐤌𐤉𐤌.𐤅𐤀𐤕.𐤄𐤀
𐤓𐤑.𐤊𐤉.𐤀𐤁𐤃.𐤕𐤀𐤁𐤃𐤅𐤍.𐤌𐤄𐤓.𐤌𐤏𐤋.𐤄𐤀𐤓𐤑.𐤀𐤔𐤓.𐤀
𐤕𐤌.𐤏𐤁𐤓𐤉𐤌.𐤀𐤕.𐤄𐤉𐤓𐤃𐤍.𐤔𐤌𐤄.𐤋𐤓𐤔𐤕𐤄.𐤋𐤀.𐤕𐤀𐤓𐤉
𐤊𐤍.𐤉𐤌𐤉𐤌.𐤏𐤋𐤉𐤄.𐤊𐤉.𐤄𐤔𐤌𐤃.𐤕𐤔𐤌𐤃𐤅𐤍|
..𐤊𐤆.. 𐤅𐤄𐤐𐤉𐤑.𐤉𐤄𐤅𐤄.𐤀𐤕𐤊𐤌.𐤁𐤏𐤌𐤉𐤌.𐤅𐤍𐤔𐤀𐤓𐤕𐤌.𐤌
𐤕𐤉.𐤌𐤎𐤐𐤓.𐤁𐤂𐤅𐤉𐤌.𐤀𐤔𐤓.𐤉𐤍𐤄𐤂.𐤉𐤄𐤅𐤄.𐤀𐤕𐤊𐤌.𐤔𐤌
𐤄|
..𐤊𐤇.. 𐤅𐤏𐤁𐤃𐤕𐤌.𐤔𐤌.𐤀𐤋𐤄𐤉𐤌.𐤌𐤏𐤔𐤄.𐤉𐤃𐤉.𐤀𐤃𐤌.𐤏
𐤑.𐤅𐤀𐤁𐤍.𐤀𐤔𐤓.𐤋𐤀.𐤉𐤓𐤀𐤅𐤍.𐤅𐤋𐤀.𐤉𐤔𐤌𐤏𐤅𐤍.𐤅𐤋𐤀.𐤉𐤀𐤊𐤋
𐤅𐤍.𐤅𐤋𐤀.𐤉𐤓𐤉𐤇𐤍|
..𐤊𐤈.. 𐤅𐤁𐤒𐤔𐤕𐤌.𐤌𐤔𐤌.𐤀𐤕.𐤉𐤄𐤅𐤄.𐤀𐤋𐤄𐤉𐤊.𐤅𐤌𐤑𐤀𐤕.
𐤊𐤉.𐤕𐤃𐤓𐤔𐤍𐤅.𐤁𐤊𐤋.𐤋𐤁𐤁𐤊.𐤅𐤁𐤊𐤋.𐤍𐤐𐤔𐤊|

..𐤋.. 𐤁𐤑𐤓.𐤋𐤊.𐤅𐤌𐤑𐤀𐤅𐤊.𐤊𐤋.𐤄𐤃𐤁𐤓𐤉𐤌.𐤄𐤀𐤋𐤄.𐤁𐤀
𐤇𐤓𐤉𐤕.𐤄𐤉𐤌𐤉𐤌.𐤅𐤔𐤁𐤕.𐤏𐤃.𐤉𐤄𐤅𐤄.𐤀𐤋𐤄𐤉𐤊.𐤅𐤔𐤌𐤏
𐤕.𐤁𐤒𐤋𐤅|

..𐤋𐤀.. 𐤊𐤉.𐤀𐤋.𐤓𐤇𐤅𐤌.𐤉𐤄𐤅𐤄.𐤀𐤋𐤄𐤉𐤊.𐤋𐤀.𐤉𐤓𐤐𐤊.𐤅𐤋𐤀.𐤉
𐤔𐤇𐤉𐤕𐤊.𐤅𐤋𐤀.𐤉𐤔𐤊𐤇.𐤀𐤕.𐤁𐤓𐤉𐤕.𐤀𐤁𐤕𐤉𐤊.𐤀𐤔𐤓.𐤍𐤔
𐤁𐤏.𐤋𐤄𐤌|

..𐤋𐤁.. 𐤊𐤉.𐤔𐤀𐤋.𐤍𐤀.𐤋𐤉𐤌𐤉𐤌.𐤓𐤀𐤔𐤍𐤉𐤌.𐤀𐤔𐤓.𐤄𐤉𐤅.𐤋𐤐𐤍
𐤉𐤊.𐤋𐤌𐤍.𐤄𐤉𐤅𐤌.𐤀𐤔𐤓.𐤁𐤓𐤀.𐤀𐤋𐤄𐤉𐤌.𐤀𐤃𐤌.𐤏𐤋.𐤄𐤀𐤓
𐤑.𐤅𐤋𐤌𐤒𐤑𐤄.𐤄𐤔𐤌𐤉𐤌.𐤅𐤏𐤃.𐤒𐤑𐤄.𐤄𐤔𐤌𐤉𐤌.𐤄𐤍𐤄𐤉
𐤄.𐤊𐤃𐤁𐤓.𐤄𐤂𐤃𐤅𐤋.𐤄𐤆𐤄.𐤀𐤅.𐤄𐤍𐤔𐤌𐤏.𐤊𐤌𐤄𐤅|

..𐤋𐤂.. 𐤄𐤔𐤌𐤏.𐤏𐤌.𐤒𐤅𐤋.𐤀𐤋𐤄𐤉𐤌.𐤌𐤃𐤁𐤓.𐤌𐤕𐤅𐤊.𐤄𐤀𐤔
.𐤊𐤀𐤔𐤓.𐤔𐤌𐤏𐤕.𐤀𐤕𐤄.𐤅𐤉𐤇𐤉|

..𐤋𐤃.. 𐤀𐤅.𐤄𐤍𐤎𐤄.𐤀𐤋𐤄𐤉𐤌.𐤋𐤁𐤅𐤀.𐤋𐤒𐤇𐤕.𐤋𐤅.𐤂𐤅𐤉.𐤌𐤒
𐤓𐤁.𐤂𐤅𐤉.𐤁𐤌𐤎𐤕.𐤁𐤀𐤕𐤕.𐤅𐤁𐤌𐤅𐤐𐤕𐤉𐤌.𐤅𐤁𐤌𐤋𐤇𐤌𐤄.𐤅𐤁
𐤉𐤃.𐤇𐤆𐤒𐤄.𐤅𐤁𐤆𐤓𐤅𐤏.𐤍𐤈𐤅𐤉𐤄.𐤅𐤁𐤌𐤅𐤓𐤀𐤉𐤌.𐤂𐤃𐤋𐤉
𐤌.𐤊𐤊𐤋.𐤀𐤔𐤓.𐤏𐤔𐤄.𐤋𐤊𐤌.𐤉𐤄𐤅𐤄.𐤀𐤋𐤄𐤉𐤊𐤌.𐤁𐤌𐤑𐤓𐤉
𐤌.𐤋𐤏𐤉𐤍𐤉𐤊|

..𐤋𐤄.. 𐤀𐤕𐤄.𐤄𐤓𐤀𐤕.𐤋𐤃𐤏𐤕.𐤊𐤉.𐤉𐤄𐤅𐤄.𐤄𐤅𐤀.𐤄𐤀𐤋𐤄𐤉
𐤌.𐤀𐤉𐤍.𐤏𐤅𐤃.𐤌𐤋𐤁𐤃𐤅|

..𐤋𐤅.. 𐤌𐤍.𐤄𐤔𐤌𐤉𐤌.𐤄𐤔𐤌𐤉𐤏𐤊.𐤀𐤕.𐤒𐤋𐤅.𐤋𐤉𐤎𐤓𐤊.𐤅𐤏𐤋.
𐤄𐤀𐤓𐤑.𐤄𐤓𐤀𐤊.𐤀𐤕.𐤀𐤔𐤅.𐤄𐤂𐤃𐤅𐤋𐤄.𐤅𐤃𐤁𐤓𐤉𐤅.𐤔𐤌𐤏
𐤕.𐤌𐤕𐤅𐤊.𐤄𐤀𐤔|

..𐤋𐤆.. 𐤅𐤕𐤇𐤕.𐤊𐤉.𐤀𐤄𐤁.𐤀𐤕.𐤀𐤁𐤕𐤉𐤊.𐤅𐤉𐤁𐤇𐤓.𐤁𐤆𐤓𐤏
𐤅.𐤀𐤇𐤓𐤉𐤅.𐤅𐤉𐤅𐤑𐤀𐤊.𐤁𐤐𐤍𐤉𐤅.𐤁𐤊𐤇𐤅.𐤄𐤂𐤃𐤋.𐤌𐤌𐤑𐤓𐤉
𐤌|

..𐤋𐤇.. 𐤋𐤄𐤅𐤓𐤉𐤔.𐤂𐤅𐤉𐤌.𐤂𐤃𐤋𐤉𐤌.𐤅𐤏𐤑𐤌𐤉𐤌.𐤌𐤌𐤊.𐤌𐤐
𐤍𐤉𐤊.𐤋𐤄𐤁𐤉𐤀𐤊.𐤋𐤕𐤕.𐤋𐤊.𐤀𐤕.𐤀𐤓𐤑𐤌.𐤍𐤇𐤋𐤄.𐤊𐤉𐤅𐤌.𐤄
𐤆𐤄|

..𐤋𐤈.. 𐤅𐤉𐤃𐤏𐤕.𐤄𐤉𐤅𐤌.𐤅𐤄𐤔𐤁𐤕.𐤀𐤋.𐤋𐤁𐤁𐤊.𐤊𐤉.𐤉𐤄𐤅𐤄.
𐤄𐤅𐤀.𐤄𐤀𐤋𐤄𐤉𐤌.𐤁𐤔𐤌𐤉𐤌.𐤌𐤌𐤏𐤋.𐤅𐤏𐤋.𐤄𐤀𐤓𐤑.𐤌𐤕𐤇
𐤕.𐤀𐤉𐤍.𐤏𐤅𐤃|

..𐤌.. 𐤅𐤔𐤌𐤓𐤕.𐤀𐤕.𐤇𐤒𐤉𐤅.𐤅𐤀𐤕.𐤌𐤑𐤅𐤕𐤉𐤅.𐤀𐤔𐤓.𐤀𐤍𐤊
𐤉.𐤌𐤑𐤅𐤊.𐤄𐤉𐤅𐤌.𐤀𐤔𐤓.𐤉𐤉𐤈𐤁.𐤋𐤊.𐤅𐤋𐤁𐤍𐤉𐤊.𐤀𐤇𐤓𐤉𐤊.𐤅
𐤋𐤌𐤏𐤍.𐤕𐤀𐤓𐤉𐤊.𐤉𐤌𐤉𐤌.𐤏𐤋.𐤄𐤀𐤃𐤌𐤄.𐤀𐤔𐤓.𐤉𐤄𐤅𐤄.𐤀
𐤋𐤄𐤉𐤊.𐤍𐤕𐤍.𐤋𐤊.𐤊𐤋.𐤄𐤉𐤌𐤉𐤌|

..𐤌𐤀.. 𐤀𐤆.𐤉𐤁𐤃𐤉𐤋.𐤌𐤔𐤄.𐤔𐤋𐤔.𐤏𐤓𐤉𐤌.𐤁𐤏𐤁𐤓.𐤄𐤉𐤓
𐤃𐤍.𐤌𐤆𐤓𐤇𐤄.𐤔𐤌𐤔|

..𐤌𐤁.. 𐤋𐤍𐤎.𐤔𐤌𐤄.𐤓𐤅𐤑𐤇.𐤀𐤔𐤓.𐤉𐤓𐤑𐤇.𐤀𐤕.𐤓𐤏𐤄𐤅.𐤁𐤁
𐤋𐤉.𐤃𐤏𐤕.𐤅𐤄𐤅𐤀.𐤋𐤀.𐤔𐤍𐤀.𐤋𐤅.𐤌𐤕𐤌𐤅𐤋.𐤔𐤋𐤔𐤅𐤌.𐤅𐤍𐤎.𐤀
𐤋.𐤀𐤇𐤕.𐤌𐤍.𐤄𐤏𐤓𐤉𐤌.𐤄𐤀𐤋.𐤅𐤇𐤉|

..𐤌𐤂.. 𐤀𐤕.𐤁𐤑𐤓.𐤁𐤌𐤃𐤁𐤓.𐤁𐤀𐤓𐤑.𐤄𐤌𐤉𐤔𐤓.𐤋𐤓𐤀𐤅𐤁𐤍𐤉.
𐤅𐤀𐤕.𐤓𐤀𐤌𐤕.𐤁𐤂𐤋𐤏𐤃.𐤋𐤂𐤃𐤉.𐤅𐤀𐤕.𐤂𐤅𐤋𐤍.𐤁𐤁𐤔𐤍.𐤋𐤌
𐤍𐤔𐤉|

..𐤌𐤃.. 𐤅𐤆𐤀𐤕.𐤄𐤕𐤅𐤓𐤄.𐤀𐤔𐤓.𐤔𐤌.𐤌𐤔𐤄.𐤋𐤐𐤍𐤉.𐤁𐤍𐤉.𐤉
𐤔𐤓𐤀𐤋|

..𐤌𐤄.. 𐤀𐤋𐤄.𐤄𐤏𐤃𐤕.𐤅𐤄𐤇𐤒𐤉𐤌.𐤅𐤄𐤌𐤔𐤐𐤈𐤉𐤌.𐤀𐤔𐤓.
𐤃𐤁𐤓.𐤌𐤔𐤄.𐤀𐤋.𐤁𐤍𐤉.𐤉𐤔𐤓𐤀𐤋.𐤁𐤑𐤀𐤕𐤌.𐤌𐤌𐤑𐤓𐤉𐤌|

..𐤌𐤅.. 𐤁𐤏𐤁𐤓.𐤄𐤉𐤓𐤃𐤍.𐤁𐤂𐤉𐤀.𐤌𐤅𐤋.𐤁𐤉𐤕.𐤐𐤏𐤅𐤓.𐤁𐤀𐤓
𐤑.𐤎𐤉𐤇𐤍.𐤌𐤋𐤊.𐤄𐤀𐤌𐤓𐤉.𐤀𐤔𐤓.𐤉𐤅𐤔𐤁.𐤁𐤇𐤔𐤁𐤅𐤍.𐤀𐤔𐤓
.𐤄𐤊𐤄.𐤌𐤔𐤄.𐤅𐤁𐤍𐤉.𐤉𐤔𐤓𐤀𐤋.𐤁𐤑𐤀𐤕𐤌.𐤌𐤌𐤑𐤓𐤉𐤌|

..𐤌𐤆.. 𐤅𐤉𐤉𐤓𐤔𐤅.𐤀𐤕.𐤀𐤓𐤑𐤅.𐤅𐤀𐤕.𐤀𐤓𐤑.𐤏𐤅𐤂.𐤌𐤋𐤊.𐤄𐤁
𐤔𐤍.𐤔𐤍𐤉.𐤌𐤋𐤊𐤉.𐤄𐤀𐤌𐤓𐤉.𐤀𐤔𐤓.𐤁𐤏𐤁𐤓.𐤄𐤉𐤓𐤃𐤍.𐤌𐤆𐤓
𐤇.𐤔𐤌𐤔|

..𐤌𐤇.. 𐤌𐤏𐤓𐤏𐤓.𐤀𐤔𐤓.𐤏𐤋.𐤔𐤐𐤕.𐤍𐤇𐤋.𐤀𐤓𐤍𐤍.𐤅𐤏𐤃.𐤄𐤓.
𐤔𐤉𐤀𐤍.𐤄𐤅𐤀.𐤇𐤓𐤌𐤅𐤍|

..𐤌𐤈.. 𐤅𐤊𐤋.𐤄𐤏𐤓𐤁𐤄.𐤏𐤁𐤓.𐤄𐤉𐤓𐤃𐤍.𐤌𐤆𐤓𐤇𐤄.𐤅𐤏𐤃.𐤉
𐤌.𐤄𐤏𐤓𐤁𐤄.𐤕𐤇𐤕.𐤀𐤔𐤃𐤕.𐤄𐤐𐤎𐤂𐤄||

𐤃𐤁𐤓𐤉𐤌.𐤇𐤋𐤒 ..𐤄..

..𐤀.. 𐤅𐤉𐤒𐤓𐤀.𐤌𐤔𐤄.𐤀𐤋.𐤊𐤋.𐤉𐤔𐤓𐤀𐤋.𐤅𐤉𐤀𐤌𐤓.𐤀𐤋𐤄𐤌.𐤔
𐤌𐤏.𐤉𐤔𐤓𐤀𐤋.𐤀𐤕.𐤄𐤇𐤒𐤉𐤌.𐤅𐤀𐤕.𐤄𐤌𐤔𐤐𐤈𐤉𐤌.𐤀𐤔𐤓.

אנכי.דבר.באזניכם.היום.ולמדתם.אתם.וש
מרתם.לעשתם|
ב יהוה.אלהינו.כרת.עמנו.ברית.בחרב|
ג לא.את.אבתינו.כרת.יהוה.את.הברית.הז
את.כי.אתנו.אנחנו.אלה.פה.היום.כלנו.חיים|
ד פנים.בפנים.דבר.יהוה.עמכם.בהר.מתוך.
האש|
ה אנכי.עמד.בין.יהוה.וביניכם.בעת.ההוא
להגיד.לכם.את.דבר.יהוה.כי.יראתם.מפני.
האש.ולא.עליתם.בהר.לאמר|
ו אנכי.יהוה.אלהיך.אשר.הוצאתיך.מארץ.
מצרים.מבית.עבדים|
ז לא.יהיה.לך.אלהים.אחרים.על.פני|
ח לא.תעשה.לך.פסל.כל.תמונה.אשר.בשמים.
ממעל.ואשר.בארץ.מתחת.ואשר.במים.מתחת.
לארץ|
ט לא.תשתחוה.להם.ולא.תעבדם.כי.אנכי.
יהוה.אלהיך.אל.קנא.פקד.עון.אבות.על.בני
ם.ועל.שלשים.ועל.רבעים.לשנאי|
י ועשה.חסד.לאלפים.לאהבי.ולשמרי.מצ
ותו||מצותי.קרי|||
יא לא.תשא.את.שם.יהוה.אלהיך.לשוא.כי.ל
א.ינקה.יהוה.את.אשר.ישא.את.שמו.לשוא|
יב שמור.את.יום.השבת.לקדשו.כאשר.צוך.י
הוה.אלהיך|
יג ששת.ימים.תעבד.ועשית.כל.מלאכתך|
יד ויום.השביעי.שבת.ליהוה.אלהיך.לא.ת
עשה.כל.מלאכה.אתה.ובנך.ובתך.ועבדך.ואמ
תך.ושורך.וחמרך.וכל.בהמתך.וגרך.אשר.בשע
ריך.למען.ינוח.עבדך.ואמתך.כמוך|

טו וזכרת.כי.עבד.היית.בארץ.מצרים.וי
צאך.יהוה.אלהיך.משם.ביד.חזקה.ובזרע.
נטויה.על.כן.צוך.יהוה.אלהיך.לעשות.את.יו
ם.השבת|

טז כבד.את.אביך.ואת.אמך.כאשר.צוך.יהו
ה.אלהיך.למען.יאריכן.ימיך.ולמען.ייטב.ל
ך.על.האדמה.אשר.יהוה.אלהיך.נתן.לך|

יז לא.תרצח|

יח ולא.תנאף|

יט ולא.תגנב|

כ ולא.תענה.ברעך.עד.שוא|

כא ולא.תחמד.אשת.רעך.
ולא.תתאוה.בית.רעך.שדהו.ועבדו.ואמ
תו.שורו.וחמרו.וכל.אשר.לרעך|

כב את.הדברים.האלה.דבר.יהוה.אל.כל.קה
לכם.בהר.מתוך.האש.הענן.והערפל.קול.גדול.
ולא.יסף.ויכתבם.על.שני.לחת.אבנים.ויתנם.
אלי|

כג ויהי.כשמעכם.את.הקול.מתוך.החשך.וה
הר.בער.באש.ותקרבון.אלי.כל.ראשי.שבטיכ
ם.וזקניכם|

כד ותאמרו.הן.הראנו.יהוה.אלהינו.את.כב
דו.ואת.גדלו.ואת.קלו.שמענו.מתוך.האש.היו
ם.הזה.ראינו.כי.ידבר.אלהים.את.האדם.ו
חי|

כה ועתה.למה.נמות.כי.תאכלנו.האש.הגדל
ה.הזאת.אם.יספים.אנחנו.לשמע.את.קול.יה
וה.אלהינו.עוד.ומתנו|

כו כי.מי.כל.בשר.אשר.שמע.קול.אלהים.חי
ים.מדבר.מתוך.האש.כמנו.ויחי|

27 𐤒𐤓𐤁.𐤀𐤕𐤄.𐤅𐤔𐤌𐤏.𐤀𐤕.𐤊𐤋.𐤀𐤔𐤓.𐤉𐤀𐤌𐤓.𐤉𐤄𐤅𐤄.
𐤀𐤋𐤄𐤉𐤍𐤅.𐤅𐤀𐤕.𐤕𐤃𐤁𐤓.𐤀𐤋𐤉𐤍𐤅.𐤀𐤕.𐤊𐤋.𐤀𐤔𐤓.𐤉𐤃𐤁𐤓.
𐤉𐤄𐤅𐤄.𐤀𐤋𐤄𐤉𐤍𐤅.𐤀𐤋𐤉𐤊.𐤅𐤔𐤌𐤏𐤍𐤅.𐤅𐤏𐤔𐤉𐤍𐤅|
28 𐤅𐤉𐤔𐤌𐤏.𐤉𐤄𐤅𐤄.𐤀𐤕.𐤒𐤅𐤋.𐤃𐤁𐤓𐤉𐤊𐤌.𐤁𐤃𐤁𐤓𐤊𐤌.
𐤀𐤋𐤉.𐤅𐤉𐤀𐤌𐤓.𐤉𐤄𐤅𐤄.𐤀𐤋𐤉.𐤔𐤌𐤏𐤕𐤉.𐤀𐤕.𐤒𐤅𐤋.𐤃𐤁𐤓𐤉.
𐤄𐤏𐤌.𐤄𐤆𐤄.𐤀𐤔𐤓.𐤃𐤁𐤓𐤅.𐤀𐤋𐤉𐤊.𐤄𐤉𐤈𐤉𐤁𐤅.𐤊𐤋.𐤀𐤔𐤓.
𐤃𐤁𐤓𐤅|
29 𐤌𐤉.𐤉𐤕𐤍.𐤅𐤄𐤉𐤄.𐤋𐤁𐤁𐤌.𐤆𐤄.𐤋𐤄𐤌.𐤋𐤉𐤓𐤀𐤄.𐤀𐤕
𐤉.𐤅𐤋𐤔𐤌𐤓.𐤀𐤕.𐤊𐤋.𐤌𐤑𐤅𐤕𐤉.𐤊𐤋.𐤄𐤉𐤌𐤉𐤌.𐤋𐤌𐤏𐤍.𐤉𐤉𐤈
𐤁.𐤋𐤄𐤌.𐤅𐤋𐤁𐤍𐤉𐤄𐤌.𐤋𐤏𐤋𐤌|
30 𐤋𐤊.𐤀𐤌𐤓.𐤋𐤄𐤌.𐤔𐤅𐤁𐤅.𐤋𐤊𐤌.𐤋𐤀𐤄𐤋𐤉𐤊𐤌|
31 𐤅𐤀𐤕𐤄.𐤐𐤄.𐤏𐤌𐤃.𐤏𐤌𐤃𐤉.𐤅𐤀𐤃𐤁𐤓𐤄.𐤀𐤋𐤉𐤊.𐤀𐤕
.𐤊𐤋.𐤄𐤌𐤑𐤅𐤄.𐤅𐤄𐤇𐤒𐤉𐤌.𐤅𐤄𐤌𐤔𐤐𐤈𐤉𐤌.𐤀𐤔𐤓.𐤕𐤋𐤌𐤃
𐤌.𐤅𐤏𐤔𐤅.𐤁𐤀𐤓𐤑.𐤀𐤔𐤓.𐤀𐤍𐤊𐤉.𐤍𐤕𐤍.𐤋𐤄𐤌.𐤋𐤓𐤔𐤕𐤄|
32 𐤅𐤔𐤌𐤓𐤕𐤌.𐤋𐤏𐤔𐤅𐤕.𐤊𐤀𐤔𐤓.𐤑𐤅𐤄.𐤉𐤄𐤅𐤄.𐤀𐤋𐤄𐤉
𐤊𐤌.𐤀𐤕𐤊𐤌.𐤋𐤀.𐤕𐤎𐤓𐤅.𐤉𐤌𐤉𐤍.𐤅𐤔𐤌𐤀𐤋|
33 𐤁𐤊𐤋.𐤄𐤃𐤓𐤊.𐤀𐤔𐤓.𐤑𐤅𐤄.𐤉𐤄𐤅𐤄.𐤀𐤋𐤄𐤉𐤊𐤌.𐤀𐤕
𐤊𐤌.𐤕𐤋𐤊𐤅.𐤋𐤌𐤏𐤍.𐤕𐤇𐤉𐤅𐤍.𐤅𐤈𐤅𐤁.𐤋𐤊𐤌.𐤅𐤄𐤀𐤓𐤊𐤕𐤌.𐤉𐤌
𐤉𐤌.𐤁𐤀𐤓𐤑.𐤀𐤔𐤓.𐤕𐤉𐤓𐤔𐤅𐤍||

𐤃𐤁𐤓𐤉𐤌.𐤇𐤋𐤒 6

1 𐤅𐤆𐤀𐤕.𐤄𐤌𐤑𐤅𐤄.𐤄𐤇𐤒𐤉𐤌.𐤅𐤄𐤌𐤔𐤐𐤈𐤉𐤌.𐤀𐤔𐤓.𐤑
𐤅𐤄.𐤉𐤄𐤅𐤄.𐤀𐤋𐤄𐤉𐤊𐤌.𐤋𐤋𐤌𐤃.𐤀𐤕𐤊𐤌.𐤋𐤏𐤔𐤅𐤕.𐤁𐤀𐤓𐤑.
𐤀𐤔𐤓.𐤀𐤕𐤌.𐤏𐤁𐤓𐤉𐤌.𐤔𐤌𐤄.𐤋𐤓𐤔𐤕𐤄|
2 𐤋𐤌𐤏𐤍.𐤕𐤉𐤓𐤀.𐤀𐤕.𐤉𐤄𐤅𐤄.𐤀𐤋𐤄𐤉𐤊.𐤋𐤔𐤌𐤓.𐤀𐤕.𐤊𐤋
.𐤇𐤒𐤕𐤉𐤅.𐤅𐤌𐤑𐤅𐤕𐤉𐤅.𐤀𐤔𐤓.𐤀𐤍𐤊𐤉.𐤌𐤑𐤅𐤊.𐤀𐤕𐤄.𐤅𐤁𐤍𐤊.
𐤅𐤁𐤍.𐤁𐤍𐤊.𐤊𐤋.𐤉𐤌𐤉.𐤇𐤉𐤉𐤊.𐤅𐤋𐤌𐤏𐤍.𐤉𐤀𐤓𐤊𐤍.𐤉𐤌𐤉𐤊|
3 𐤅𐤔𐤌𐤏𐤕.𐤉𐤔𐤓𐤀𐤋.𐤅𐤔𐤌𐤓𐤕.𐤋𐤏𐤔𐤅𐤕.𐤀𐤔𐤓.𐤉𐤉𐤈𐤁.
𐤋𐤊.𐤅𐤀𐤔𐤓.𐤕𐤓𐤁𐤅𐤍.𐤌𐤀𐤃.𐤊𐤀𐤔𐤓.𐤃𐤁𐤓.𐤉𐤄𐤅𐤄.𐤀𐤋𐤄𐤉.
𐤀𐤁𐤕𐤉𐤊.𐤋𐤊.𐤀𐤓𐤑.𐤆𐤁𐤕.𐤇𐤋𐤁.𐤅𐤃𐤁𐤔|

ד 𐤔𐤌𐤏.𐤉𐤔𐤓𐤀𐤋.𐤉𐤄𐤅𐤄.𐤀𐤋𐤄𐤉𐤍𐤅.𐤉𐤄𐤅𐤄.𐤀𐤇𐤃|
ה 𐤅𐤀𐤄𐤁𐤕.𐤀𐤕.𐤉𐤄𐤅𐤄.𐤀𐤋𐤄𐤉𐤊.𐤁𐤊𐤋.𐤋𐤁𐤁𐤊.𐤅𐤁𐤊𐤋.𐤍
𐤐𐤔𐤊.𐤅𐤁𐤊𐤋.𐤌𐤀𐤃𐤊|
ו 𐤅𐤄𐤉𐤅.𐤄𐤃𐤁𐤓𐤉𐤌.𐤄𐤀𐤋𐤄.𐤀𐤔𐤓.𐤀𐤍𐤊𐤉.𐤌𐤑𐤅𐤊.𐤄𐤉𐤅
𐤌.𐤏𐤋.𐤋𐤁𐤁𐤊|
ז 𐤅𐤔𐤍𐤍𐤕𐤌.𐤋𐤁𐤍𐤉𐤊.𐤅𐤃𐤁𐤓𐤕.𐤁𐤌.𐤁𐤔𐤁𐤕𐤊.𐤁𐤁𐤉𐤕𐤊.
𐤅𐤁𐤋𐤊𐤕𐤊.𐤁𐤃𐤓𐤊.𐤅𐤁𐤔𐤊𐤁𐤊.𐤅𐤁𐤒𐤅𐤌𐤊|
ח 𐤅𐤒𐤔𐤓𐤕𐤌.𐤋𐤀𐤅𐤕.𐤏𐤋.𐤉𐤃𐤊.𐤅𐤄𐤉𐤅.𐤋𐤈𐤈𐤐𐤕.𐤁𐤉𐤍.
𐤏𐤉𐤍𐤉𐤊|
ט 𐤅𐤊𐤕𐤁𐤕𐤌.𐤏𐤋.𐤌𐤆𐤆𐤅𐤕.𐤁𐤉𐤕𐤊.𐤅𐤁𐤔𐤏𐤓𐤉𐤊|
י 𐤅𐤄𐤉𐤄.𐤊𐤉.𐤉𐤁𐤉𐤀𐤊.𐤉𐤄𐤅𐤄.𐤀𐤋𐤄𐤉𐤊.𐤀𐤋.𐤄𐤀𐤓𐤑.
𐤀𐤔𐤓.𐤍𐤔𐤁𐤏.𐤋𐤀𐤁𐤕𐤉𐤊.𐤋𐤀𐤁𐤓𐤄𐤌.𐤋𐤉𐤑𐤇𐤒.𐤅𐤋𐤉𐤏𐤒
𐤁.𐤋𐤕𐤕.𐤋𐤊.𐤏𐤓𐤉𐤌.𐤂𐤃𐤋𐤕.𐤅𐤈𐤁𐤕.𐤀𐤔𐤓.𐤋𐤀.𐤁𐤍𐤉𐤕|
יא 𐤅𐤁𐤕𐤉𐤌.𐤌𐤋𐤀𐤉𐤌.𐤊𐤋.𐤈𐤅𐤁.𐤀𐤔𐤓.𐤋𐤀.𐤌𐤋𐤀𐤕.𐤅𐤁𐤓
𐤕.𐤇𐤑𐤅𐤁𐤉𐤌.𐤀𐤔𐤓.𐤋𐤀.𐤇𐤑𐤁𐤕.𐤊𐤓𐤌𐤉𐤌.𐤅𐤆𐤉𐤕𐤉𐤌.
𐤀𐤔𐤓.𐤋𐤀.𐤍𐤈𐤏𐤕.𐤅𐤀𐤊𐤋𐤕.𐤅𐤔𐤁𐤏𐤕|
יב 𐤄𐤔𐤌𐤓.𐤋𐤊.𐤐𐤍.𐤕𐤔𐤊𐤇.𐤀𐤕.𐤉𐤄𐤅𐤄.𐤀𐤔𐤓.𐤄𐤅𐤑𐤉
𐤀𐤊.𐤌𐤀𐤓𐤑.𐤌𐤑𐤓𐤉𐤌.𐤌𐤁𐤉𐤕.𐤏𐤁𐤃𐤉𐤌|
יג 𐤀𐤕.𐤉𐤄𐤅𐤄.𐤀𐤋𐤄𐤉𐤊.𐤕𐤉𐤓𐤀.𐤅𐤀𐤕𐤅.𐤕𐤏𐤁𐤃.𐤅𐤁𐤔
𐤌𐤅.𐤕𐤔𐤁𐤏|
יד 𐤋𐤀.𐤕𐤋𐤊𐤅𐤍.𐤀𐤇𐤓𐤉.𐤀𐤋𐤄𐤉𐤌.𐤀𐤇𐤓𐤉𐤌.𐤌𐤀𐤋𐤄𐤉.
𐤄𐤏𐤌𐤉𐤌.𐤀𐤔𐤓.𐤎𐤁𐤉𐤁𐤅𐤕𐤉𐤊𐤌|
טו 𐤊𐤉.𐤀𐤋.𐤒𐤍𐤀.𐤉𐤄𐤅𐤄.𐤀𐤋𐤄𐤉𐤊.𐤁𐤒𐤓𐤁𐤊.𐤐𐤍.𐤉𐤇𐤓
𐤄.𐤀𐤐.𐤉𐤄𐤅𐤄.𐤀𐤋𐤄𐤉𐤊.𐤁𐤊.𐤅𐤄𐤔𐤌𐤉𐤃𐤊.𐤌𐤏𐤋.𐤐𐤍𐤉.𐤄𐤀
𐤃𐤌𐤄|
טז 𐤋𐤀.𐤕𐤍𐤎𐤅.𐤀𐤕.𐤉𐤄𐤅𐤄.𐤀𐤋𐤄𐤉𐤊𐤌.𐤊𐤀𐤔𐤓.𐤍𐤎𐤉𐤕
𐤌.𐤁𐤌𐤎𐤄|
יז 𐤔𐤌𐤅𐤓.𐤕𐤔𐤌𐤓𐤅𐤍.𐤀𐤕.𐤌𐤑𐤅𐤕.𐤉𐤄𐤅𐤄.𐤀𐤋𐤄𐤉𐤊𐤌.𐤅
𐤏𐤃𐤕𐤉𐤅.𐤅𐤇𐤒𐤉𐤅.𐤀𐤔𐤓.𐤑𐤅𐤊|

יח 𐤅𐤏𐤔𐤉𐤕.𐤄𐤉𐤔𐤓.𐤅𐤄𐤈𐤅𐤁.𐤁𐤏𐤉𐤍𐤉.𐤉𐤄𐤅𐤄.𐤋𐤌𐤏𐤍.
𐤉𐤉𐤈𐤁.𐤋𐤊.𐤅𐤁𐤀𐤕.𐤅𐤉𐤓𐤔𐤕.𐤀𐤕.𐤄𐤀𐤓𐤑.𐤄𐤈𐤁𐤄.𐤀𐤔𐤓.
𐤍𐤔𐤁𐤏.𐤉𐤄𐤅𐤄.𐤋𐤀𐤁𐤕𐤉𐤊|

יט 𐤋𐤄𐤃𐤐.𐤀𐤕.𐤊𐤋.𐤀𐤉𐤁𐤉𐤊.𐤌𐤐𐤍𐤉𐤊.𐤊𐤀𐤔𐤓.𐤃𐤁𐤓.
𐤉𐤄𐤅𐤄|

כ 𐤊𐤉.𐤉𐤔𐤀𐤋𐤊.𐤁𐤍𐤊.𐤌𐤇𐤓.𐤋𐤀𐤌𐤓.𐤌𐤄.𐤄𐤏𐤃𐤕.𐤅𐤄
𐤇𐤒𐤉𐤌.𐤅𐤄𐤌𐤔𐤐𐤈𐤉𐤌.𐤀𐤔𐤓.𐤑𐤅𐤄.𐤉𐤄𐤅𐤄.𐤀𐤋𐤄𐤉𐤍𐤅.𐤀
𐤕𐤊𐤌|

כא 𐤅𐤀𐤌𐤓𐤕.𐤋𐤁𐤍𐤊.𐤏𐤁𐤃𐤉𐤌.𐤄𐤉𐤉𐤍𐤅.𐤋𐤐𐤓𐤏𐤄.𐤁𐤌𐤑𐤓
𐤉𐤌.𐤅𐤉𐤅𐤑𐤉𐤀𐤍𐤅.𐤉𐤄𐤅𐤄.𐤌𐤌𐤑𐤓𐤉𐤌.𐤁𐤉𐤃.𐤇𐤆𐤒𐤄|

כב 𐤅𐤉𐤕𐤍.𐤉𐤄𐤅𐤄.𐤀𐤅𐤕𐤕.𐤅𐤌𐤐𐤕𐤉𐤌.𐤂𐤃𐤋𐤉𐤌.𐤅𐤓𐤏𐤉𐤌
.𐤁𐤌𐤑𐤓𐤉𐤌.𐤁𐤐𐤓𐤏𐤄.𐤅𐤁𐤊𐤋.𐤁𐤉𐤕𐤅.𐤋𐤏𐤉𐤍𐤉𐤍𐤅|

כג 𐤅𐤀𐤅𐤕𐤍𐤅.𐤄𐤅𐤑𐤉𐤀.𐤌𐤔𐤌.𐤋𐤌𐤏𐤍.𐤄𐤁𐤉𐤀.𐤀𐤕𐤍𐤅.𐤋
𐤕𐤕.𐤋𐤍𐤅.𐤀𐤕.𐤄𐤀𐤓𐤑.𐤀𐤔𐤓.𐤍𐤔𐤁𐤏.𐤋𐤀𐤁𐤕𐤉𐤍𐤅|

כד 𐤅𐤉𐤑𐤅𐤍𐤅.𐤉𐤄𐤅𐤄.𐤋𐤏𐤔𐤅𐤕.𐤀𐤕.𐤊𐤋.𐤄𐤇𐤒𐤉𐤌.𐤄𐤀
𐤋𐤄.𐤋𐤉𐤓𐤀𐤄.𐤀𐤕.𐤉𐤄𐤅𐤄.𐤀𐤋𐤄𐤉𐤍𐤅.𐤋𐤈𐤅𐤁.𐤋𐤍𐤅.𐤊𐤋.𐤄𐤉𐤌
𐤉𐤌.𐤋𐤇𐤉𐤕𐤍𐤅.𐤊𐤄𐤉𐤅𐤌.𐤄𐤆𐤄|

כה 𐤅𐤑𐤃𐤒𐤄.𐤕𐤄𐤉𐤄.𐤋𐤍𐤅.𐤊𐤉.𐤍𐤔𐤌𐤓.𐤋𐤏𐤔𐤅𐤕.𐤀𐤕.𐤊
𐤋.𐤄𐤌𐤑𐤅𐤄.𐤄𐤆𐤀𐤕.𐤋𐤐𐤍𐤉.𐤉𐤄𐤅𐤄.𐤀𐤋𐤄𐤉𐤍𐤅.𐤊𐤀𐤔𐤓.𐤑𐤅
𐤍𐤅||

𐤃𐤁𐤓𐤉𐤌.𐤇𐤋𐤒 ז

א 𐤊𐤉.𐤉𐤁𐤉𐤀𐤊.𐤉𐤄𐤅𐤄.𐤀𐤋𐤄𐤉𐤊.𐤀𐤋.𐤄𐤀𐤓𐤑.𐤀𐤔𐤓.𐤀
𐤕𐤄.𐤁𐤀.𐤔𐤌𐤄.𐤋𐤓𐤔𐤕𐤄.𐤅𐤍𐤔𐤋.𐤂𐤅𐤉𐤌.𐤓𐤁𐤉𐤌.𐤌𐤐𐤍𐤉𐤊.
𐤄𐤇𐤕𐤉.𐤅𐤄𐤂𐤓𐤂𐤔𐤉.𐤅𐤄𐤀𐤌𐤓𐤉.𐤅𐤄𐤊𐤍𐤏𐤍𐤉.𐤅𐤄𐤐𐤓𐤆𐤉.𐤅
𐤄𐤇𐤅𐤉.𐤅𐤄𐤉𐤁𐤅𐤎𐤉.𐤔𐤁𐤏𐤄.𐤂𐤅𐤉𐤌.𐤓𐤁𐤉𐤌.𐤅𐤏𐤑𐤅𐤌𐤉𐤌.
𐤌𐤌𐤊|

ב 𐤅𐤍𐤕𐤍𐤌.𐤉𐤄𐤅𐤄.𐤀𐤋𐤄𐤉𐤊.𐤋𐤐𐤍𐤉𐤊.𐤅𐤄𐤊𐤉𐤕𐤌.𐤄𐤇𐤓𐤌.
𐤕𐤇𐤓𐤉𐤌.𐤀𐤕𐤌.𐤋𐤀.𐤕𐤊𐤓𐤕.𐤋𐤄𐤌.𐤁𐤓𐤉𐤕.𐤅𐤋𐤀.𐤕𐤇𐤍𐤌|

3 ולא תתחתן בם בתך לא תתן לבנו ובתו לא תקח לבנך׃

4 כי יסיר את בנך מאחרי ועבדו אלהים אחרים וחרה אף יהוה בכם והשמידך מהר׃

5 כי אם כה תעשו להם מזבחתיהם תתצו ומצבתם תשברו ואשירהם תגדעון ופסיליהם תשרפון באש׃

6 כי עם קדוש אתה ליהוה אלהיך בך בחר יהוה אלהיך להיות לו לעם סגלה מכל העמים אשר על פני האדמה׃

7 לא מרבכם מכל העמים חשק יהוה בכם ויבחר בכם כי אתם המעט מכל העמים׃

8 כי מאהבת יהוה אתכם ומשמרו את השבעה אשר נשבע לאבתיכם הוציא יהוה אתכם ביד חזקה ויפדך מבית עבדים מיד פרעה מלך מצרים׃

9 וידעת כי יהוה אלהיך הוא האלהים האל הנאמן שמר הברית והחסד לאהביו ולשמרי מצותו לאלף דור׃

10 ומשלם לשנאיו אל פניו להאבידו לא יאחר לשנאו אל פניו ישלם לו׃

11 ושמרת את המצוה ואת החקים ואת המשפטים אשר אנכי מצוך היום לעשותם׃

12 והיה עקב תשמעון את המשפטים האלה ושמרתם ועשיתם אתם ושמר יהוה אלהיך לך את הברית ואת החסד אשר נשבע לאבתיך׃

13 ואהבך וברכך והרבך וברך פרי בטנך ופרי אדמתך דגנך ותירשך ויצהרך שגר אלפיך ועשתרת צאנך על האדמה אשר נשבע לאבתיך לתת לך׃

𐤉𐤃 𐤁𐤓𐤅𐤊.𐤕𐤄𐤉𐤄.𐤌𐤊𐤋.𐤄𐤏𐤌𐤉𐤌.𐤋𐤀.𐤉𐤄𐤉𐤄.𐤁𐤊.𐤏
𐤒𐤓.𐤅𐤏𐤒𐤓𐤄.𐤅𐤁𐤁𐤄𐤌𐤕𐤊|
𐤈𐤅 𐤅𐤄𐤎𐤉𐤓.𐤉𐤄𐤅𐤄.𐤌𐤌𐤊.𐤊𐤋.𐤇𐤋𐤉.𐤅𐤊𐤋.𐤌𐤃𐤅𐤉.𐤌𐤑𐤓
𐤉𐤌.𐤄𐤓𐤏𐤉𐤌.𐤀𐤔𐤓.𐤉𐤃𐤏𐤕.𐤋𐤀.𐤉𐤔𐤉𐤌𐤌.𐤁𐤊.𐤅𐤍𐤕𐤍𐤌.
𐤁𐤊𐤋.𐤔𐤍𐤀𐤉𐤊|
𐤈𐤆 𐤅𐤀𐤊𐤋𐤕.𐤀𐤕.𐤊𐤋.𐤄𐤏𐤌𐤉𐤌.𐤀𐤔𐤓.𐤉𐤄𐤅𐤄.𐤀𐤋𐤄𐤉𐤊.
𐤍𐤕𐤍.𐤋𐤊.𐤋𐤀.𐤕𐤇𐤎.𐤏𐤉𐤍𐤊.𐤏𐤋𐤉𐤄𐤌.𐤅𐤋𐤀.𐤕𐤏𐤁𐤃.𐤀𐤕.
𐤀𐤋𐤄𐤉𐤄𐤌.𐤊𐤉.𐤌𐤅𐤒𐤔.𐤄𐤅𐤀.𐤋𐤊|
𐤉𐤆 𐤊𐤉.𐤕𐤀𐤌𐤓.𐤁𐤋𐤁𐤁𐤊.𐤓𐤁𐤉𐤌.𐤄𐤂𐤅𐤉𐤌.𐤄𐤀𐤋𐤄.𐤌𐤌
𐤍𐤉.𐤀𐤉𐤊𐤄.𐤀𐤅𐤊𐤋.𐤋𐤄𐤅𐤓𐤉𐤔𐤌|
𐤉𐤇 𐤋𐤀.𐤕𐤉𐤓𐤀.𐤌𐤄𐤌.𐤆𐤊𐤓.𐤕𐤆𐤊𐤓.𐤀𐤕.𐤀𐤔𐤓.𐤏𐤔𐤄.
𐤉𐤄𐤅𐤄.𐤀𐤋𐤄𐤉𐤊.𐤋𐤐𐤓𐤏𐤄.𐤅𐤋𐤊𐤋.𐤌𐤑𐤓𐤉𐤌|
𐤉𐤈 𐤄𐤌𐤎𐤕.𐤄𐤂𐤃𐤋𐤕.𐤀𐤔𐤓.𐤓𐤀𐤅.𐤏𐤉𐤍𐤉𐤊.𐤅𐤄𐤀𐤕𐤕.
𐤅𐤄𐤌𐤐𐤕𐤉𐤌.𐤅𐤄𐤉𐤃.𐤄𐤇𐤆𐤒𐤄.𐤅𐤄𐤆𐤓𐤏.𐤄𐤍𐤈𐤅𐤉𐤄.𐤀
𐤔𐤓.𐤄𐤅𐤑𐤀𐤊.𐤉𐤄𐤅𐤄.𐤀𐤋𐤄𐤉𐤊.𐤊𐤍.𐤉𐤏𐤔𐤄.𐤉𐤄𐤅𐤄.𐤀𐤋𐤄
𐤉𐤊.𐤋𐤊𐤋.𐤄𐤏𐤌𐤉𐤌.𐤀𐤔𐤓.𐤀𐤕𐤄.𐤉𐤓𐤀.𐤌𐤐𐤍𐤉𐤄𐤌|
𐤊 𐤅𐤂𐤌.𐤀𐤕.𐤄𐤑𐤓𐤏𐤄.𐤉𐤔𐤋𐤇.𐤉𐤄𐤅𐤄.𐤀𐤋𐤄𐤉𐤊.𐤁𐤌
.𐤏𐤃.𐤀𐤁𐤃.𐤄𐤍𐤔𐤀𐤓𐤉𐤌.𐤅𐤄𐤍𐤎𐤕𐤓𐤉𐤌.𐤌𐤐𐤍𐤉𐤊|
𐤊𐤀 𐤋𐤀.𐤕𐤏𐤓𐤑.𐤌𐤐𐤍𐤉𐤄𐤌.𐤊𐤉.𐤉𐤄𐤅𐤄.𐤀𐤋𐤄𐤉𐤊.𐤁𐤒𐤓
𐤁𐤊.𐤀𐤋.𐤂𐤃𐤅𐤋.𐤅𐤍𐤅𐤓𐤀|
𐤊𐤁 𐤅𐤍𐤔𐤋.𐤉𐤄𐤅𐤄.𐤀𐤋𐤄𐤉𐤊.𐤀𐤕.𐤄𐤂𐤅𐤉𐤌.𐤄𐤀𐤋.𐤌𐤐𐤍𐤉
𐤊.𐤌𐤏𐤈.𐤌𐤏𐤈.𐤋𐤀.𐤕𐤅𐤊𐤋.𐤊𐤋𐤕𐤌.𐤌𐤄𐤓.𐤐𐤍.𐤕𐤓𐤁𐤄.𐤏𐤋
𐤉𐤊.𐤇𐤉𐤕.𐤄𐤔𐤃𐤄|
𐤊𐤂 𐤅𐤍𐤕𐤍𐤌.𐤉𐤄𐤅𐤄.𐤀𐤋𐤄𐤉𐤊.𐤋𐤐𐤍𐤉𐤊.𐤅𐤄𐤌𐤌.𐤌𐤄𐤅𐤌𐤄.
𐤂𐤃𐤋𐤄.𐤏𐤃.𐤄𐤔𐤌𐤃𐤌|
𐤊𐤃 𐤅𐤍𐤕𐤍.𐤌𐤋𐤊𐤉𐤄𐤌.𐤁𐤉𐤃𐤊.𐤅𐤄𐤀𐤁𐤃𐤕.𐤀𐤕.𐤔𐤌𐤌.
𐤌𐤕𐤇𐤕.𐤄𐤔𐤌𐤉𐤌.𐤋𐤀.𐤉𐤕𐤉𐤑𐤁.𐤀𐤉𐤔.𐤁𐤐𐤍𐤉𐤊.𐤏𐤃.𐤄
𐤔𐤌𐤃𐤊.𐤀𐤕𐤌|
𐤊𐤄 𐤐𐤎𐤉𐤋𐤉.𐤀𐤋𐤄𐤉𐤄𐤌.𐤕𐤔𐤓𐤐𐤅𐤍.𐤁𐤀𐤔.𐤋𐤀.𐤕𐤇𐤌𐤃.
𐤊𐤎𐤐.𐤅𐤆𐤄𐤁.𐤏𐤋𐤉𐤄𐤌.𐤅𐤋𐤒𐤇𐤕.𐤋𐤊.𐤐𐤍.𐤕𐤅𐤒𐤔.𐤁𐤅.𐤊𐤉.
𐤕𐤅𐤏𐤁𐤕.𐤉𐤄𐤅𐤄.𐤀𐤋𐤄𐤉𐤊.𐤄𐤅𐤀|

כו 𐤅𐤋𐤀.𐤕𐤁𐤉𐤀.𐤕𐤅𐤏𐤁𐤄.𐤀𐤋.𐤁𐤉𐤕𐤊.𐤅𐤄𐤉𐤉𐤕.𐤇𐤓𐤌.
𐤊𐤌𐤄𐤅.𐤔𐤒𐤑.𐤕𐤔𐤒𐤑𐤍𐤅.𐤅𐤕𐤏𐤁.𐤕𐤕𐤏𐤁𐤍𐤅.𐤊𐤉.𐤇𐤓𐤌.
𐤄𐤅𐤀‖

𐤃𐤁𐤓𐤉𐤌.𐤇𐤋𐤒 ח

א 𐤊𐤋.𐤄𐤌𐤑𐤅𐤄.𐤀𐤔𐤓.𐤀𐤍𐤊𐤉.𐤌𐤑𐤅𐤊.𐤄𐤉𐤅𐤌.𐤕𐤔𐤌𐤓𐤅𐤍.
𐤋𐤏𐤔𐤅𐤕.𐤋𐤌𐤏𐤍.𐤕𐤇𐤉𐤅𐤍.𐤅𐤓𐤁𐤉𐤕𐤌.𐤅𐤁𐤀𐤕𐤌.𐤅𐤉𐤓𐤔𐤕𐤌.
𐤀𐤕.𐤄𐤀𐤓𐤑.𐤀𐤔𐤓.𐤍𐤔𐤁𐤏.𐤉𐤄𐤅𐤄.𐤋𐤀𐤁𐤕𐤉𐤊𐤌|
ב 𐤅𐤆𐤊𐤓𐤕.𐤀𐤕.𐤊𐤋.𐤄𐤃𐤓𐤊.𐤀𐤔𐤓.𐤄𐤋𐤉𐤊𐤊.𐤉𐤄𐤅𐤄.𐤀
𐤋𐤄𐤉𐤊.𐤆𐤄.𐤀𐤓𐤁𐤏𐤉𐤌.𐤔𐤍𐤄.𐤁𐤌𐤃𐤁𐤓.𐤋𐤌𐤏𐤍.𐤏𐤍𐤕𐤊.
𐤋𐤍𐤎𐤕𐤊.𐤋𐤃𐤏𐤕.𐤀𐤕.𐤀𐤔𐤓.𐤁𐤋𐤁𐤁𐤊.𐤄𐤕𐤔𐤌𐤓.𐤌𐤑𐤅𐤕𐤅
.‖𐤌𐤑𐤅𐤕𐤉𐤅.𐤒𐤓𐤉‖.𐤀𐤌.𐤋𐤀|
ג 𐤅𐤉𐤏𐤍𐤊.𐤅𐤉𐤓𐤏𐤁𐤊.𐤅𐤉𐤀𐤊𐤋𐤊.𐤀𐤕.𐤄𐤌𐤍.𐤀𐤔𐤓.𐤋𐤀.𐤉
𐤃𐤏𐤕.𐤅𐤋𐤀.𐤉𐤃𐤏𐤅𐤍.𐤀𐤁𐤕𐤉𐤊.𐤋𐤌𐤏𐤍.𐤄𐤅𐤃𐤏𐤊.𐤊𐤉.𐤋𐤀
.𐤏𐤋.𐤄𐤋𐤇𐤌.𐤋𐤁𐤃𐤅.𐤉𐤇𐤉𐤄.𐤄𐤀𐤃𐤌.𐤊𐤉.𐤏𐤋.𐤊𐤋.𐤌𐤅𐤑
𐤀.𐤐𐤉.𐤉𐤄𐤅𐤄.𐤉𐤇𐤉𐤄.𐤄𐤀𐤃𐤌|
ד 𐤔𐤌𐤋𐤕𐤊.𐤋𐤀.𐤁𐤋𐤕𐤄.𐤌𐤏𐤋𐤉𐤊.𐤅𐤓𐤂𐤋𐤊.𐤋𐤀.𐤁𐤑𐤒
𐤄.𐤆𐤄.𐤀𐤓𐤁𐤏𐤉𐤌.𐤔𐤍𐤄|
ה 𐤅𐤉𐤃𐤏𐤕.𐤏𐤌.𐤋𐤁𐤁𐤊.𐤊𐤉.𐤊𐤀𐤔𐤓.𐤉𐤉𐤎𐤓.𐤀𐤉𐤔.𐤀𐤕.
𐤁𐤍𐤅.𐤉𐤄𐤅𐤄.𐤀𐤋𐤄𐤉𐤊.𐤌𐤉𐤎𐤓𐤊|
ו 𐤅𐤔𐤌𐤓𐤕.𐤀𐤕.𐤌𐤑𐤅𐤕.𐤉𐤄𐤅𐤄.𐤀𐤋𐤄𐤉𐤊.𐤋𐤋𐤊𐤕.𐤁𐤃𐤓
𐤊𐤉𐤅.𐤅𐤋𐤉𐤓𐤀𐤄.𐤀𐤕𐤅|
ז 𐤊𐤉.𐤉𐤄𐤅𐤄.𐤀𐤋𐤄𐤉𐤊.𐤌𐤁𐤉𐤀𐤊.𐤀𐤋.𐤀𐤓𐤑.𐤈𐤅𐤁𐤄.𐤀
𐤓𐤑.𐤍𐤇𐤋𐤉.𐤌𐤉𐤌.𐤏𐤉𐤍𐤕.𐤅𐤕𐤄𐤌𐤕.𐤉𐤑𐤀𐤉𐤌.𐤁𐤁𐤒𐤏𐤄.
𐤅𐤁𐤄𐤓|
ח 𐤀𐤓𐤑.𐤇𐤈𐤄.𐤅𐤔𐤏𐤓𐤄.𐤅𐤂𐤐𐤍.𐤅𐤕𐤀𐤍𐤄.𐤅𐤓𐤌𐤅𐤍.𐤀𐤓𐤑.
𐤆𐤉𐤕.𐤔𐤌𐤍.𐤅𐤃𐤁𐤔|
ט 𐤀𐤓𐤑.𐤀𐤔𐤓.𐤋𐤀.𐤁𐤌𐤎𐤊𐤍𐤕.𐤕𐤀𐤊𐤋.𐤁𐤄.𐤋𐤇𐤌.𐤋𐤀.
𐤕𐤇𐤎𐤓.𐤊𐤋.𐤁𐤄.𐤀𐤓𐤑.𐤀𐤔𐤓.𐤀𐤁𐤍𐤉𐤄.𐤁𐤓𐤆𐤋.𐤅𐤌𐤄𐤓𐤓𐤉
𐤄.𐤕𐤇𐤑𐤁.𐤍𐤇𐤔𐤕|

י 𐤅𐤀𐤊𐤋𐤕.𐤅𐤔𐤁𐤏𐤕.𐤅𐤁𐤓𐤊𐤕.𐤀𐤕.𐤉𐤄𐤅𐤄.𐤀𐤋𐤄𐤉𐤊.
𐤏𐤋.𐤄𐤀𐤓𐤑.𐤄𐤈𐤁𐤄.𐤀𐤔𐤓.𐤍𐤕𐤍.𐤋𐤊|
יא 𐤄𐤔𐤌𐤓.𐤋𐤊.𐤐𐤍.𐤕𐤔𐤊𐤇.𐤀𐤕.𐤉𐤄𐤅𐤄.𐤀𐤋𐤄𐤉𐤊.𐤋𐤁𐤋
𐤕𐤉.𐤔𐤌𐤓.𐤌𐤑𐤅𐤕𐤉𐤅.𐤅𐤌𐤔𐤐𐤈𐤉𐤅.𐤅𐤇𐤒𐤕𐤉𐤅.𐤀𐤔𐤓.𐤀𐤍𐤊
𐤉.𐤌𐤑𐤅𐤊.𐤄𐤉𐤅𐤌|
יב 𐤐𐤍.𐤕𐤀𐤊𐤋.𐤅𐤔𐤁𐤏𐤕.𐤅𐤁𐤕𐤉𐤌.𐤈𐤅𐤁𐤉𐤌.𐤕𐤁𐤍𐤄.𐤅𐤉
𐤔𐤁𐤕|
יג 𐤅𐤁𐤒𐤓𐤊.𐤅𐤑𐤀𐤍𐤊.𐤉𐤓𐤁𐤉𐤍.𐤅𐤊𐤎𐤐.𐤅𐤆𐤄𐤁.𐤉𐤓𐤁𐤄.𐤋
𐤊.𐤅𐤊𐤋.𐤀𐤔𐤓.𐤋𐤊.𐤉𐤓𐤁𐤄|
יד 𐤅𐤓𐤌.𐤋𐤁𐤁𐤊.𐤅𐤔𐤊𐤇𐤕.𐤀𐤕.𐤉𐤄𐤅𐤄.𐤀𐤋𐤄𐤉𐤊.𐤄𐤌𐤅
𐤑𐤉𐤀𐤊.𐤌𐤀𐤓𐤑.𐤌𐤑𐤓𐤉𐤌.𐤌𐤁𐤉𐤕.𐤏𐤁𐤃𐤉𐤌|
טו 𐤄𐤌𐤅𐤋𐤉𐤊𐤊.𐤁𐤌𐤃𐤁𐤓.𐤄𐤂𐤃𐤋.𐤅𐤄𐤍𐤅𐤓𐤀.𐤍𐤇𐤔.𐤔𐤓
𐤐.𐤅𐤏𐤒𐤓𐤁.𐤅𐤑𐤌𐤀𐤅𐤍.𐤀𐤔𐤓.𐤀𐤉𐤍.𐤌𐤉𐤌.𐤄𐤌𐤅𐤑𐤉𐤀.𐤋𐤊.𐤌
𐤉𐤌.𐤌𐤑𐤅𐤓.𐤄𐤇𐤋𐤌𐤉𐤔|
טז 𐤄𐤌𐤀𐤊𐤋𐤊.𐤌𐤍.𐤁𐤌𐤃𐤁𐤓.𐤀𐤔𐤓.𐤋𐤀.𐤉𐤃𐤏𐤅𐤍.𐤀𐤁𐤕
𐤉𐤊.𐤋𐤌𐤏𐤍.𐤏𐤍𐤕𐤊.𐤅𐤋𐤌𐤏𐤍.𐤍𐤎𐤕𐤊.𐤋𐤄𐤉𐤈𐤁𐤊.𐤁𐤀𐤇𐤓𐤉
𐤕𐤊|
יז 𐤅𐤀𐤌𐤓𐤕.𐤁𐤋𐤁𐤁𐤊.𐤊𐤇𐤉.𐤅𐤏𐤑𐤌.𐤉𐤃𐤉.𐤏𐤔𐤄.𐤋𐤉.
𐤀𐤕.𐤄𐤇𐤉𐤋.𐤄𐤆𐤄|
יח 𐤅𐤆𐤊𐤓𐤕.𐤀𐤕.𐤉𐤄𐤅𐤄.𐤀𐤋𐤄𐤉𐤊.𐤊𐤉.𐤄𐤅𐤀.𐤄𐤍𐤕𐤍.𐤋
𐤊.𐤊𐤇.𐤋𐤏𐤔𐤅𐤕.𐤇𐤉𐤋.𐤋𐤌𐤏𐤍.𐤄𐤒𐤉𐤌.𐤀𐤕.𐤁𐤓𐤉𐤕𐤅.𐤀𐤔
𐤓.𐤍𐤔𐤁𐤏.𐤋𐤀𐤁𐤕𐤉𐤊.𐤊𐤉𐤅𐤌.𐤄𐤆𐤄|
יט 𐤅𐤄𐤉𐤄.𐤀𐤌.𐤔𐤊𐤇.𐤕𐤔𐤊𐤇.𐤀𐤕.𐤉𐤄𐤅𐤄.𐤀𐤋𐤄𐤉𐤊.
𐤅𐤄𐤋𐤊𐤕.𐤀𐤇𐤓𐤉.𐤀𐤋𐤄𐤉𐤌.𐤀𐤇𐤓𐤉𐤌.𐤅𐤏𐤁𐤃𐤕𐤌.𐤅𐤄𐤔𐤕
𐤇𐤅𐤉𐤕.𐤋𐤄𐤌.𐤄𐤏𐤃𐤕𐤉.𐤁𐤊𐤌.𐤄𐤉𐤅𐤌.𐤊𐤉.𐤀𐤁𐤃.𐤕𐤀𐤁
𐤃𐤅𐤍|
כ 𐤊𐤂𐤅𐤉𐤌.𐤀𐤔𐤓.𐤉𐤄𐤅𐤄.𐤌𐤀𐤁𐤉𐤃.𐤌𐤐𐤍𐤉𐤊𐤌.𐤊𐤍.𐤕
𐤀𐤁𐤃𐤅𐤍.𐤏𐤒𐤁.𐤋𐤀.𐤕𐤔𐤌𐤏𐤅𐤍.𐤁𐤒𐤅𐤋.𐤉𐤄𐤅𐤄.𐤀𐤋𐤄𐤉𐤊𐤌|

|

ט 𐤃𐤁𐤓𐤉𐤌.𐤇𐤋𐤒

א שמע ישראל אתה עבר היום את הירדן לבא לרשת גוים גדלים ועצמים ממך ערים גדלת ובצרת בשמים׃

ב עם גדול ורם בני ענקים אשר אתה ידעת ואתה שמעת מי יתיצב לפני בני ענק׃

ג וידעת היום כי יהוה אלהיך הוא העבר לפניך אש אכלה הוא ישמידם והוא יכניעם לפניך והורשתם והאבדתם מהר כאשר דבר יהוה לך׃

ד אל תאמר בלבבך בהדף יהוה אלהיך אתם מלפניך לאמר בצדקתי הביאני יהוה לרשת את הארץ הזאת וברשעת הגוים האלה יהוה מורישם מפניך׃

ה לא בצדקתך ובישר לבבך אתה בא לרשת את ארצם כי ברשעת הגוים האלה יהוה אלהיך מורישם מפניך ולמען הקים את הדבר אשר נשבע יהוה לאבתיך לאברהם ליצחק וליעקב׃

ו וידעת כי לא בצדקתך יהוה אלהיך נתן לך את הארץ הטובה הזאת לרשתה כי עם קשה ערף אתה׃

ז זכר אל תשכח את אשר הקצפת את יהוה אלהיך במדבר למן היום אשר יצאת מארץ מצרים עד באכם עד המקום הזה ממרים הייתם עם יהוה׃

ח ובחרב הקצפתם את יהוה ויתאנף יהוה בכם להשמיד אתכם׃

ט בעלתי ההרה לקחת לוחת האבנים לוחת הברית אשר כרת יהוה עמכם ואשב בהר אר

𐤁𐤏𐤉𐤌.𐤉𐤅𐤌.𐤅𐤀𐤓𐤁𐤏𐤉𐤌.𐤋𐤉𐤋𐤄.𐤋𐤇𐤌.𐤋𐤀.𐤀𐤊𐤋𐤕𐤉.𐤅𐤌
𐤉𐤌.𐤋𐤀.𐤔𐤕𐤉𐤕𐤉|

10 𐤅𐤉𐤕𐤍.𐤉𐤄𐤅𐤄.𐤀𐤋𐤉.𐤀𐤕.𐤔𐤍𐤉.𐤋𐤅𐤇𐤕.𐤄𐤀𐤁𐤍𐤉𐤌.
𐤊𐤕𐤁𐤉𐤌.𐤁𐤀𐤑𐤁𐤏.𐤀𐤋𐤄𐤉𐤌.𐤅𐤏𐤋𐤉𐤄𐤌.𐤊𐤊𐤋.𐤄𐤃𐤁𐤓𐤉
𐤌.𐤀𐤔𐤓.𐤃𐤁𐤓.𐤉𐤄𐤅𐤄.𐤏𐤌𐤊𐤌.𐤁𐤄𐤓.𐤌𐤕𐤅𐤊.𐤄𐤀𐤔.𐤁𐤉𐤅𐤌
.𐤄𐤒𐤄𐤋|

11 𐤅𐤉𐤄𐤉.𐤌𐤒𐤑.𐤀𐤓𐤁𐤏𐤉𐤌.𐤉𐤅𐤌.𐤅𐤀𐤓𐤁𐤏𐤉𐤌.𐤋𐤉𐤋𐤄.
𐤍𐤕𐤍.𐤉𐤄𐤅𐤄.𐤀𐤋𐤉.𐤀𐤕.𐤔𐤍𐤉.𐤋𐤇𐤕.𐤄𐤀𐤁𐤍𐤉𐤌.𐤋𐤅𐤇𐤕.𐤄
𐤁𐤓𐤉𐤕|

12 𐤅𐤉𐤀𐤌𐤓.𐤉𐤄𐤅𐤄.𐤀𐤋𐤉.𐤒𐤅𐤌.𐤓𐤃.𐤌𐤄𐤓.𐤌𐤆𐤄.𐤊𐤉.
𐤔𐤇𐤕.𐤏𐤌𐤊.𐤀𐤔𐤓.𐤄𐤅𐤑𐤀𐤕.𐤌𐤌𐤑𐤓𐤉𐤌.𐤎𐤓𐤅.𐤌𐤄𐤓.𐤌𐤍.
𐤄𐤃𐤓𐤊.𐤀𐤔𐤓.𐤑𐤅𐤉𐤕𐤌.𐤏𐤔𐤅.𐤋𐤄𐤌.𐤌𐤎𐤊𐤄|

13 𐤅𐤉𐤀𐤌𐤓.𐤉𐤄𐤅𐤄.𐤀𐤋𐤉.𐤋𐤀𐤌𐤓.𐤓𐤀𐤉𐤕𐤉.𐤀𐤕.𐤄𐤏𐤌.
𐤄𐤆𐤄.𐤅𐤄𐤍𐤄.𐤏𐤌.𐤒𐤔𐤄.𐤏𐤓𐤐.𐤄𐤅𐤀|

14 𐤄𐤓𐤐.𐤌𐤌𐤍𐤉.𐤅𐤀𐤔𐤌𐤉𐤃𐤌.𐤅𐤀𐤌𐤇𐤄.𐤀𐤕.𐤔𐤌𐤌.𐤌
𐤕𐤇𐤕.𐤄𐤔𐤌𐤉𐤌.𐤅𐤀𐤏𐤔𐤄.𐤀𐤅𐤕𐤊.𐤋𐤂𐤅𐤉.𐤏𐤑𐤅𐤌.𐤅𐤓𐤁.𐤌
𐤌𐤍𐤅|

15 𐤅𐤀𐤐𐤍.𐤅𐤀𐤓𐤃.𐤌𐤍.𐤄𐤄𐤓.𐤅𐤄𐤄𐤓.𐤁𐤏𐤓.𐤁𐤀𐤔.𐤅𐤔𐤍𐤉.𐤋
𐤇𐤕.𐤄𐤁𐤓𐤉𐤕.𐤏𐤋.𐤔𐤕𐤉.𐤉𐤃𐤉|

16 𐤅𐤀𐤓𐤀.𐤅𐤄𐤍𐤄.𐤇𐤈𐤀𐤕𐤌.𐤋𐤉𐤄𐤅𐤄.𐤀𐤋𐤄𐤉𐤊𐤌.𐤏𐤔
𐤉𐤕𐤌.𐤋𐤊𐤌.𐤏𐤂𐤋.𐤌𐤎𐤊𐤄.𐤎𐤓𐤕𐤌.𐤌𐤄𐤓.𐤌𐤍.𐤄𐤃𐤓𐤊.𐤀
𐤔𐤓.𐤑𐤅𐤄.𐤉𐤄𐤅𐤄.𐤀𐤕𐤊𐤌|

17 𐤅𐤀𐤕𐤐𐤔.𐤁𐤔𐤍𐤉.𐤄𐤋𐤇𐤕.𐤅𐤀𐤔𐤋𐤊𐤌.𐤌𐤏𐤋.𐤔𐤕𐤉.𐤉
𐤃𐤉.𐤅𐤀𐤔𐤁𐤓𐤌.𐤋𐤏𐤉𐤍𐤉𐤊𐤌|

18 𐤅𐤀𐤕𐤍𐤐𐤋.𐤋𐤐𐤍𐤉.𐤉𐤄𐤅𐤄.𐤊𐤓𐤀𐤔𐤍𐤄.𐤀𐤓𐤁𐤏𐤉𐤌.𐤉𐤅𐤌.
𐤅𐤀𐤓𐤁𐤏𐤉𐤌.𐤋𐤉𐤋𐤄.𐤋𐤇𐤌.𐤋𐤀.𐤀𐤊𐤋𐤕𐤉.𐤅𐤌𐤉𐤌.𐤋𐤀.𐤔𐤕
𐤉𐤕𐤉.𐤏𐤋.𐤊𐤋.𐤇𐤈𐤀𐤕𐤊𐤌.𐤀𐤔𐤓.𐤇𐤈𐤀𐤕𐤌.𐤋𐤏𐤔𐤅𐤕.𐤄
𐤓𐤏.𐤁𐤏𐤉𐤍𐤉.𐤉𐤄𐤅𐤄.𐤋𐤄𐤊𐤏𐤉𐤎𐤅|

19 𐤊𐤉.𐤉𐤂𐤓𐤕𐤉.𐤌𐤐𐤍𐤉.𐤄𐤀𐤐.𐤅𐤄𐤇𐤌𐤄.𐤀𐤔𐤓.𐤒𐤑𐤐.
𐤉𐤄𐤅𐤄.𐤏𐤋𐤉𐤊𐤌.𐤋𐤄𐤔𐤌𐤉𐤃.𐤀𐤕𐤊𐤌.𐤅𐤉𐤔𐤌𐤏.𐤉𐤄𐤅𐤄.𐤀
𐤋𐤉.𐤂𐤌.𐤁𐤐𐤏𐤌.𐤄𐤄𐤅𐤀|

20 𐤅𐤁𐤀𐤄𐤓𐤍.𐤄𐤕𐤀𐤍𐤐.𐤉𐤄𐤅𐤄.𐤌𐤀𐤃.𐤋𐤄𐤔𐤌𐤉𐤃𐤅.𐤅𐤀
𐤕𐤐𐤋𐤋.𐤂𐤌.𐤁𐤏𐤃.𐤀𐤄𐤓𐤍.𐤁𐤏𐤕.𐤄𐤄𐤅𐤀|
21 𐤅𐤀𐤕.𐤇𐤈𐤀𐤕𐤊𐤌.𐤀𐤔𐤓.𐤏𐤔𐤉𐤕𐤌.𐤀𐤕.𐤄𐤏𐤂𐤋.𐤋
𐤒𐤇𐤕𐤉.𐤅𐤀𐤔𐤓𐤐.𐤀𐤕𐤅.𐤁𐤀𐤔.𐤅𐤀𐤊𐤕.𐤀𐤕𐤅.𐤈𐤇𐤅𐤍.𐤄𐤉𐤈
𐤁.𐤏𐤃.𐤀𐤔𐤓.𐤃𐤒.𐤋𐤏𐤐𐤓.𐤅𐤀𐤔𐤋𐤊.𐤀𐤕.𐤏𐤐𐤓𐤅.𐤀𐤋.𐤄𐤍𐤇
𐤋.𐤄𐤉𐤓𐤃.𐤌𐤍.𐤄𐤄𐤓|
22 𐤅𐤁𐤕𐤁𐤏𐤓𐤄.𐤅𐤁𐤌𐤎𐤄.𐤅𐤁𐤒𐤁𐤓𐤕.𐤄𐤕𐤀𐤅𐤄.𐤌𐤒𐤑𐤐
𐤉𐤌.𐤄𐤉𐤉𐤕𐤌.𐤀𐤕.𐤉𐤄𐤅𐤄|
23 𐤅𐤁𐤔𐤋𐤇.𐤉𐤄𐤅𐤄.𐤀𐤕𐤊𐤌.𐤌𐤒𐤃𐤔.𐤁𐤓𐤍𐤏.𐤋𐤀𐤌𐤓.
𐤏𐤋𐤅.𐤅𐤓𐤔𐤅.𐤀𐤕.𐤄𐤀𐤓𐤑.𐤀𐤔𐤓.𐤍𐤕𐤕𐤉.𐤋𐤊𐤌.𐤅𐤕𐤌𐤓𐤅.𐤀𐤕.
𐤐𐤉.𐤉𐤄𐤅𐤄.𐤀𐤋𐤄𐤉𐤊𐤌.𐤅𐤋𐤀.𐤄𐤀𐤌𐤍𐤕𐤌.𐤋𐤅.𐤅𐤋𐤀.𐤔𐤌𐤏𐤕
𐤌.𐤁𐤒𐤋𐤅|
24 𐤌𐤌𐤓𐤉𐤌.𐤄𐤉𐤉𐤕𐤌.𐤏𐤌.𐤉𐤄𐤅𐤄.𐤌𐤉𐤅𐤌.𐤃𐤏𐤕𐤉.𐤀
𐤕𐤊𐤌|
25 𐤅𐤀𐤕𐤍𐤐𐤋.𐤋𐤐𐤍𐤉.𐤉𐤄𐤅𐤄.𐤀𐤕.𐤀𐤓𐤁𐤏𐤉𐤌.𐤄𐤉𐤅𐤌.𐤅𐤀
𐤕.𐤀𐤓𐤁𐤏𐤉𐤌.𐤄𐤋𐤉𐤋𐤄.𐤀𐤔𐤓.𐤄𐤕𐤍𐤐𐤋𐤕𐤉.𐤊𐤉.𐤀𐤌𐤓.𐤉𐤄
𐤅𐤄.𐤋𐤄𐤔𐤌𐤉𐤃.𐤀𐤕𐤊𐤌|
26 𐤅𐤀𐤕𐤐𐤋𐤋.𐤀𐤋.𐤉𐤄𐤅𐤄.𐤅𐤀𐤌𐤓.𐤀𐤃𐤍𐤉.𐤉𐤄𐤅𐤄.𐤀𐤋.𐤕
𐤔𐤇𐤕.𐤏𐤌𐤊.𐤅𐤍𐤇𐤋𐤕𐤊.𐤀𐤔𐤓.𐤐𐤃𐤉𐤕.𐤁𐤂𐤃𐤋𐤊.𐤀𐤔𐤓.
𐤄𐤅𐤑𐤀𐤕.𐤌𐤌𐤑𐤓𐤉𐤌.𐤁𐤉𐤃.𐤇𐤆𐤒𐤄|
27 𐤆𐤊𐤓.𐤋𐤏𐤁𐤃𐤉𐤊.𐤋𐤀𐤁𐤓𐤄𐤌.𐤋𐤉𐤑𐤇𐤒.𐤅𐤋𐤉𐤏𐤒
𐤁.𐤀𐤋.𐤕𐤐𐤍.𐤀𐤋.𐤒𐤔𐤉.𐤄𐤏𐤌.𐤄𐤆𐤄.𐤅𐤀𐤋.𐤓𐤔𐤏𐤅.𐤅𐤀𐤋.𐤇
𐤈𐤀𐤕𐤅|
28 𐤐𐤍.𐤉𐤀𐤌𐤓𐤅.𐤄𐤀𐤓𐤑.𐤀𐤔𐤓.𐤄𐤅𐤑𐤀𐤕𐤍𐤅.𐤌𐤔𐤌.𐤌𐤁𐤋
𐤉.𐤉𐤊𐤋𐤕.𐤉𐤄𐤅𐤄.𐤋𐤄𐤁𐤉𐤀𐤌.𐤀𐤋.𐤄𐤀𐤓𐤑.𐤀𐤔𐤓.𐤃𐤁𐤓.𐤋
𐤄𐤌.𐤅𐤌𐤔𐤍𐤀𐤕𐤅.𐤀𐤅𐤕𐤌.𐤄𐤅𐤑𐤉𐤀𐤌.𐤋𐤄𐤌𐤕𐤌.𐤁𐤌𐤃𐤁𐤓|
29 𐤅𐤄𐤌.𐤏𐤌𐤊.𐤅𐤍𐤇𐤋𐤕𐤊.𐤀𐤔𐤓.𐤄𐤅𐤑𐤀𐤕.𐤁𐤊𐤇𐤊.𐤄
𐤂𐤃𐤋.𐤅𐤁𐤆𐤓𐤏𐤊.𐤄𐤍𐤈𐤅𐤉𐤄||

𐤃𐤁𐤓𐤉𐤌.𐤇𐤋𐤒 10

1 𐤁𐤏𐤕.𐤄𐤄𐤅𐤀.𐤀𐤌𐤓.𐤉𐤄𐤅𐤄.𐤀𐤋𐤉.𐤐𐤎𐤋.𐤋𐤊.𐤔𐤍𐤉.𐤋𐤅
𐤇𐤕.𐤀𐤁𐤍𐤉𐤌.𐤊𐤓𐤀𐤔𐤍𐤉𐤌.𐤅𐤏𐤋𐤄.𐤀𐤋𐤉.𐤄𐤄𐤓𐤄.𐤅𐤏𐤔𐤉
𐤕.𐤋𐤊.𐤀𐤓𐤅𐤍.𐤏𐤑|
2 𐤅𐤀𐤊𐤕𐤁.𐤏𐤋.𐤄𐤋𐤇𐤕.𐤀𐤕.𐤄𐤃𐤁𐤓𐤉𐤌.𐤀𐤔𐤓.𐤄𐤉𐤅.𐤏
𐤋.𐤄𐤋𐤇𐤕.𐤄𐤓𐤀𐤔𐤍𐤉𐤌.𐤀𐤔𐤓.𐤔𐤁𐤓𐤕.𐤅𐤔𐤌𐤕𐤌.𐤁𐤀𐤓𐤅𐤍|
3 𐤅𐤀𐤏𐤔.𐤀𐤓𐤅𐤍.𐤏𐤑𐤉.𐤔𐤈𐤉𐤌.𐤅𐤀𐤐𐤎𐤋.𐤔𐤍𐤉.𐤋𐤇𐤕.
𐤀𐤁𐤍𐤉𐤌.𐤊𐤓𐤀𐤔𐤍𐤉𐤌.𐤅𐤀𐤏𐤋.𐤄𐤄𐤓𐤄.𐤅𐤔𐤍𐤉.𐤄𐤋𐤇𐤕.𐤁𐤉
𐤃𐤉|
4 𐤅𐤉𐤊𐤕𐤁.𐤏𐤋.𐤄𐤋𐤇𐤕.𐤊𐤌𐤊𐤕𐤁.𐤄𐤓𐤀𐤔𐤅𐤍.𐤀𐤕.𐤏𐤔
𐤓𐤕.𐤄𐤃𐤁𐤓𐤉𐤌.𐤀𐤔𐤓.𐤃𐤁𐤓.𐤉𐤄𐤅𐤄.𐤀𐤋𐤉𐤊𐤌.𐤁𐤄𐤓.𐤌𐤕𐤅
𐤊.𐤄𐤀𐤔.𐤁𐤉𐤅𐤌.𐤄𐤒𐤄𐤋.𐤅𐤉𐤕𐤍𐤌.𐤉𐤄𐤅𐤄.𐤀𐤋𐤉|
5 𐤅𐤀𐤐𐤍.𐤅𐤀𐤓𐤃.𐤌𐤍.𐤄𐤄𐤓.𐤅𐤀𐤔𐤌.𐤀𐤕.𐤄𐤋𐤇𐤕.𐤁𐤀𐤓𐤅𐤍.
𐤀𐤔𐤓.𐤏𐤔𐤉𐤕𐤉.𐤅𐤉𐤄𐤉𐤅.𐤔𐤌.𐤊𐤀𐤔𐤓.𐤑𐤅𐤍𐤉.𐤉𐤄𐤅𐤄|
6 𐤅𐤁𐤍𐤉.𐤉𐤔𐤓𐤀𐤋.𐤍𐤎𐤏𐤅.𐤌𐤁𐤀𐤓𐤕.𐤁𐤍𐤉.𐤉𐤏𐤒𐤍.𐤌𐤅𐤎𐤓
𐤄.𐤔𐤌.𐤌𐤕.𐤀𐤄𐤓𐤍.𐤅𐤉𐤒𐤁𐤓.𐤔𐤌.𐤅𐤉𐤊𐤄𐤍.𐤀𐤋𐤏𐤆𐤓.𐤁𐤍𐤅.
𐤕𐤇𐤕𐤉𐤅|
7 𐤌𐤔𐤌.𐤍𐤎𐤏𐤅.𐤄𐤂𐤃𐤂𐤃𐤄.𐤅𐤌𐤍.𐤄𐤂𐤃𐤂𐤃𐤄.𐤉𐤈
𐤁𐤕𐤄.𐤀𐤓𐤑.𐤍𐤇𐤋𐤉.𐤌𐤉𐤌|
8 𐤁𐤏𐤕.𐤄𐤄𐤅𐤀.𐤄𐤁𐤃𐤉𐤋.𐤉𐤄𐤅𐤄.𐤀𐤕.𐤔𐤁𐤈.𐤄𐤋𐤅𐤉.𐤋
𐤔𐤀𐤕.𐤀𐤕.𐤀𐤓𐤅𐤍.𐤁𐤓𐤉𐤕.𐤉𐤄𐤅𐤄.𐤋𐤏𐤌𐤃.𐤋𐤐𐤍𐤉.𐤉𐤄𐤅𐤄.𐤋
𐤔𐤓𐤕𐤅.𐤅𐤋𐤁𐤓𐤊.𐤁𐤔𐤌𐤅.𐤏𐤃.𐤄𐤉𐤅𐤌.𐤄𐤆𐤄|
9 𐤏𐤋.𐤊𐤍.𐤋𐤀.𐤄𐤉𐤄.𐤋𐤋𐤅𐤉.𐤇𐤋𐤒.𐤅𐤍𐤇𐤋𐤄.𐤏𐤌.𐤀𐤇𐤉
𐤅.𐤉𐤄𐤅𐤄.𐤄𐤅𐤀.𐤍𐤇𐤋𐤕𐤅.𐤊𐤀𐤔𐤓.𐤃𐤁𐤓.𐤉𐤄𐤅𐤄.𐤀𐤋𐤄𐤉𐤊.𐤋
𐤅|
10 𐤅𐤀𐤍𐤊𐤉.𐤏𐤌𐤃𐤕𐤉.𐤁𐤄𐤓.𐤊𐤉𐤌𐤉𐤌.𐤄𐤓𐤀𐤔𐤍𐤉𐤌.𐤀
𐤓𐤁𐤏𐤉𐤌.𐤉𐤅𐤌.𐤅𐤀𐤓𐤁𐤏𐤉𐤌.𐤋𐤉𐤋𐤄.𐤅𐤉𐤔𐤌𐤏.𐤉𐤄𐤅𐤄.𐤀𐤋𐤉
.𐤂𐤌.𐤁𐤐𐤏𐤌.𐤄𐤄𐤅𐤀.𐤋𐤀.𐤀𐤁𐤄.𐤉𐤄𐤅𐤄.𐤄𐤔𐤇𐤉𐤕𐤊|
11 𐤅𐤉𐤀𐤌𐤓.𐤉𐤄𐤅𐤄.𐤀𐤋𐤉.𐤒𐤅𐤌.𐤋𐤊.𐤋𐤌𐤎𐤏.𐤋𐤐𐤍𐤉.𐤄𐤏
𐤌.𐤅𐤉𐤁𐤀𐤅.𐤅𐤉𐤓𐤔𐤅.𐤀𐤕.𐤄𐤀𐤓𐤑.𐤀𐤔𐤓.𐤍𐤔𐤁𐤏𐤕𐤉.𐤋𐤀𐤁𐤕
𐤌.𐤋𐤕𐤕.𐤋𐤄𐤌|

12 𐤅𐤏𐤕𐤄.𐤉𐤔𐤓𐤀𐤋.𐤌𐤄.𐤉𐤄𐤅𐤄.𐤀𐤋𐤄𐤉𐤊.𐤔𐤀𐤋.𐤌𐤏𐤌𐤊.𐤊𐤉.𐤀𐤌.𐤋𐤉𐤓𐤀𐤄.𐤀𐤕.𐤉𐤄𐤅𐤄.𐤀𐤋𐤄𐤉𐤊.𐤋𐤋𐤊𐤕.𐤁𐤊𐤋.𐤃𐤓𐤊𐤉𐤅.𐤅𐤋𐤀𐤄𐤁𐤄.𐤀𐤕𐤅.𐤅𐤋𐤏𐤁𐤃.𐤀𐤕.𐤉𐤄𐤅𐤄.𐤀𐤋𐤄𐤉𐤊.𐤁𐤊𐤋.𐤋𐤁𐤁𐤊.𐤅𐤁𐤊𐤋.𐤍𐤐𐤔𐤊|

13 𐤋𐤔𐤌𐤓.𐤀𐤕.𐤌𐤑𐤅𐤕.𐤉𐤄𐤅𐤄.𐤅𐤀𐤕.𐤇𐤒𐤕𐤉𐤅.𐤀𐤔𐤓.𐤀𐤍𐤊𐤉.𐤌𐤑𐤅𐤊.𐤄𐤉𐤅𐤌.𐤋𐤈𐤅𐤁.𐤋𐤊|

14 𐤄𐤍.𐤋𐤉𐤄𐤅𐤄.𐤀𐤋𐤄𐤉𐤊.𐤄𐤔𐤌𐤉𐤌.𐤅𐤔𐤌𐤉.𐤄𐤔𐤌𐤉𐤌.𐤄𐤀𐤓𐤑.𐤅𐤊𐤋.𐤀𐤔𐤓.𐤁𐤄|

15 𐤓𐤒.𐤁𐤀𐤁𐤕𐤉𐤊.𐤇𐤔𐤒.𐤉𐤄𐤅𐤄.𐤋𐤀𐤄𐤁𐤄.𐤀𐤅𐤕𐤌.𐤅𐤉𐤁𐤇𐤓.𐤁𐤆𐤓𐤏𐤌.𐤀𐤇𐤓𐤉𐤄𐤌.𐤁𐤊𐤌.𐤌𐤊𐤋.𐤄𐤏𐤌𐤉𐤌.𐤊𐤉𐤅𐤌.𐤄𐤆𐤄|

16 𐤅𐤌𐤋𐤕𐤌.𐤀𐤕.𐤏𐤓𐤋𐤕.𐤋𐤁𐤁𐤊𐤌.𐤅𐤏𐤓𐤐𐤊𐤌.𐤋𐤀.𐤕𐤒𐤔𐤅.𐤏𐤅𐤃|

17 𐤊𐤉.𐤉𐤄𐤅𐤄.𐤀𐤋𐤄𐤉𐤊𐤌.𐤄𐤅𐤀.𐤀𐤋𐤄𐤉.𐤄𐤀𐤋𐤄𐤉𐤌.𐤅𐤀𐤃𐤍𐤉.𐤄𐤀𐤃𐤍𐤉𐤌.𐤄𐤀𐤋.𐤄𐤂𐤃𐤋.𐤄𐤂𐤁𐤓.𐤅𐤄𐤍𐤅𐤓𐤀.𐤀𐤔𐤓.𐤋𐤀.𐤉𐤔𐤀.𐤐𐤍𐤉𐤌.𐤅𐤋𐤀.𐤉𐤒𐤇.𐤔𐤇𐤃|

18 𐤏𐤔𐤄.𐤌𐤔𐤐𐤈.𐤉𐤕𐤅𐤌.𐤅𐤀𐤋𐤌𐤍𐤄.𐤅𐤀𐤄𐤁.𐤂𐤓.𐤋𐤕𐤕.𐤋𐤅.𐤋𐤇𐤌.𐤅𐤔𐤌𐤋𐤄|

19 𐤅𐤀𐤄𐤁𐤕𐤌.𐤀𐤕.𐤄𐤂𐤓.𐤊𐤉.𐤂𐤓𐤉𐤌.𐤄𐤉𐤉𐤕𐤌.𐤁𐤀𐤓𐤑.𐤌𐤑𐤓𐤉𐤌|

20 𐤀𐤕.𐤉𐤄𐤅𐤄.𐤀𐤋𐤄𐤉𐤊.𐤕𐤉𐤓𐤀.𐤀𐤕𐤅.𐤕𐤏𐤁𐤃.𐤅𐤁𐤅.𐤕𐤃𐤁𐤒.𐤅𐤁𐤔𐤌𐤅.𐤕𐤔𐤁𐤏|

21 𐤄𐤅𐤀.𐤕𐤄𐤋𐤕𐤊.𐤅𐤄𐤅𐤀.𐤀𐤋𐤄𐤉𐤊.𐤀𐤔𐤓.𐤏𐤔𐤄.𐤀𐤕𐤊.𐤀𐤕.𐤄𐤂𐤃𐤋𐤕.𐤅𐤀𐤕.𐤄𐤍𐤅𐤓𐤀𐤕.𐤄𐤀𐤋𐤄.𐤀𐤔𐤓.𐤓𐤀𐤅.𐤏𐤉𐤍𐤉𐤊|

22 𐤁𐤔𐤁𐤏𐤉𐤌.𐤍𐤐𐤔.𐤉𐤓𐤃𐤅.𐤀𐤁𐤕𐤉𐤊.𐤌𐤑𐤓𐤉𐤌𐤄.𐤅𐤏𐤕𐤄.𐤔𐤌𐤊.𐤉𐤄𐤅𐤄.𐤀𐤋𐤄𐤉𐤊.𐤊𐤊𐤅𐤊𐤁𐤉.𐤄𐤔𐤌𐤉𐤌.𐤋𐤓𐤁||

𐤃𐤁𐤓𐤉𐤌.𐤇𐤋𐤒 11

1 𐤅𐤀𐤄𐤁𐤕.𐤀𐤕.𐤉𐤄𐤅𐤄.𐤀𐤋𐤄𐤉𐤊.𐤅𐤔𐤌𐤓𐤕.𐤌𐤔𐤌𐤓𐤕𐤅.𐤅
𐤇𐤒𐤕𐤉𐤅.𐤅𐤌𐤔𐤐𐤈𐤉𐤅.𐤅𐤌𐤑𐤅𐤕𐤉𐤅.𐤊𐤋.𐤄𐤉𐤌𐤉𐤌|
2 𐤅𐤉𐤃𐤏𐤕𐤌.𐤄𐤉𐤅𐤌.𐤊𐤉.𐤋𐤀.𐤀𐤕.𐤁𐤍𐤉𐤊𐤌.𐤀𐤔𐤓.𐤋𐤀.
𐤉𐤃𐤏𐤅.𐤅𐤀𐤔𐤓.𐤋𐤀.𐤓𐤀𐤅.𐤀𐤕.𐤌𐤅𐤎𐤓.𐤉𐤄𐤅𐤄.𐤀𐤋𐤄𐤉𐤊𐤌.
𐤀𐤕.𐤂𐤃𐤋𐤅.𐤀𐤕.𐤉𐤃𐤅.𐤄𐤇𐤆𐤒𐤄.𐤅𐤆𐤓𐤏𐤅.𐤄𐤍𐤈𐤅𐤉𐤄|
3 𐤅𐤀𐤕.𐤀𐤕𐤕𐤉𐤅.𐤅𐤀𐤕.𐤌𐤏𐤔𐤉𐤅.𐤀𐤔𐤓.𐤏𐤔𐤄.𐤁𐤕𐤅𐤊.𐤌
𐤑𐤓𐤉𐤌.𐤋𐤐𐤓𐤏𐤄.𐤌𐤋𐤊.𐤌𐤑𐤓𐤉𐤌.𐤅𐤋𐤊𐤋.𐤀𐤓𐤑𐤅|
4 𐤅𐤀𐤔𐤓.𐤏𐤔𐤄.𐤋𐤇𐤉𐤋.𐤌𐤑𐤓𐤉𐤌.𐤋𐤎𐤅𐤎𐤉𐤅.𐤅𐤋𐤓𐤊𐤁𐤅.
𐤀𐤔𐤓.𐤄𐤑𐤉𐤐.𐤀𐤕.𐤌𐤉.𐤉𐤌.𐤎𐤅𐤐.𐤏𐤋.𐤐𐤍𐤉𐤄𐤌.𐤁𐤓𐤃𐤐𐤌.
𐤀𐤇𐤓𐤉𐤄𐤌.𐤅𐤉𐤀𐤁𐤃𐤌.𐤉𐤄𐤅𐤄.𐤏𐤃.𐤄𐤉𐤅𐤌.𐤄𐤆𐤄|
5 𐤅𐤀𐤔𐤓.𐤏𐤔𐤄.𐤋𐤊𐤌.𐤁𐤌𐤃𐤁𐤓.𐤏𐤃.𐤁𐤀𐤊𐤌.𐤏𐤃.𐤄𐤌
𐤒𐤅𐤌.𐤄𐤆𐤄|
6 𐤅𐤀𐤔𐤓.𐤏𐤔𐤄.𐤋𐤃𐤕𐤍.𐤅𐤋𐤀𐤁𐤉𐤓𐤌.𐤁𐤍𐤉.𐤀𐤋𐤉𐤀𐤁.𐤁𐤍.
𐤓𐤀𐤅𐤁𐤍.𐤀𐤔𐤓.𐤐𐤑𐤕𐤄.𐤄𐤀𐤓𐤑.𐤀𐤕.𐤐𐤉𐤄.𐤅𐤕𐤁𐤋𐤏𐤌.𐤅𐤀
𐤕.𐤁𐤕𐤉𐤄𐤌.𐤅𐤀𐤕.𐤀𐤄𐤋𐤉𐤄𐤌.𐤅𐤀𐤕.𐤊𐤋.𐤄𐤉𐤒𐤅𐤌.𐤀𐤔𐤓.
𐤁𐤓𐤂𐤋𐤉𐤄𐤌.𐤁𐤒𐤓𐤁.𐤊𐤋.𐤉𐤔𐤓𐤀𐤋|
7 𐤊𐤉.𐤏𐤉𐤍𐤉𐤊𐤌.𐤄𐤓𐤀𐤕.𐤀𐤕.𐤊𐤋.𐤌𐤏𐤔𐤄.𐤉𐤄𐤅𐤄.𐤄
𐤂𐤃𐤋.𐤀𐤔𐤓.𐤏𐤔𐤄|
8 𐤅𐤔𐤌𐤓𐤕𐤌.𐤀𐤕.𐤊𐤋.𐤄𐤌𐤑𐤅𐤄.𐤀𐤔𐤓.𐤀𐤍𐤊𐤉.𐤌𐤑𐤅𐤊.𐤄
𐤉𐤅𐤌.𐤋𐤌𐤏𐤍.𐤕𐤇𐤆𐤒𐤅.𐤅𐤁𐤀𐤕𐤌.𐤅𐤉𐤓𐤔𐤕𐤌.𐤀𐤕.𐤄𐤀𐤓𐤑.
𐤀𐤔𐤓.𐤀𐤕𐤌.𐤏𐤁𐤓𐤉𐤌.𐤔𐤌𐤄.𐤋𐤓𐤔𐤕𐤄|
9 𐤅𐤋𐤌𐤏𐤍.𐤕𐤀𐤓𐤉𐤊𐤅.𐤉𐤌𐤉𐤌.𐤏𐤋.𐤄𐤀𐤃𐤌𐤄.𐤀𐤔𐤓.𐤍𐤔
𐤁𐤏.𐤉𐤄𐤅𐤄.𐤋𐤀𐤁𐤕𐤉𐤊𐤌.𐤋𐤕𐤕.𐤋𐤄𐤌.𐤅𐤋𐤆𐤓𐤏𐤌.𐤀𐤓𐤑.
𐤆𐤁𐤕.𐤇𐤋𐤁.𐤅𐤃𐤁𐤔|
10 𐤊𐤉.𐤄𐤀𐤓𐤑.𐤀𐤔𐤓.𐤀𐤕𐤄.𐤁𐤀.𐤔𐤌𐤄.𐤋𐤓𐤔𐤕𐤄.𐤋𐤀.
𐤊𐤀𐤓𐤑.𐤌𐤑𐤓𐤉𐤌.𐤄𐤅𐤀.𐤀𐤔𐤓.𐤉𐤑𐤀𐤕𐤌.𐤌𐤔𐤌.𐤀𐤔𐤓.𐤕
𐤆𐤓𐤏.𐤀𐤕.𐤆𐤓𐤏𐤊.𐤅𐤄𐤔𐤒𐤉𐤕.𐤁𐤓𐤂𐤋𐤊.𐤊𐤂𐤍.𐤄𐤉𐤓𐤒|
11 𐤅𐤄𐤀𐤓𐤑.𐤀𐤔𐤓.𐤀𐤕𐤌.𐤏𐤁𐤓𐤉𐤌.𐤔𐤌𐤄.𐤋𐤓𐤔𐤕𐤄.𐤀
𐤓𐤑.𐤄𐤓𐤉𐤌.𐤅𐤁𐤒𐤏𐤕.𐤋𐤌𐤈𐤓.𐤄𐤔𐤌𐤉𐤌.𐤕𐤔𐤕𐤄.𐤌𐤉𐤌|

יב ארץ.אשר.יהוה.אלהיך.דרש.אתה.תמי
ד.עיני.יהוה.אלהיך.בה.מרשית.השנה.ועד.
אחרית.שנה׃
יג והיה.אם.שמע.תשמעו.אל.מצותי.אשר.א
נכי.מצוה.אתכם.היום.לאהבה.את.יהוה.אלה
יכם.ולעבדו.בכל.לבבכם.ובכל.נפשכם׃
יד ונתתי.מטר.ארצכם.בעתו.יורה.ומלקוש.ו
אספת.דגנך.ותירשך.ויצהרך׃
טו ונתתי.עשב.בשדך.לבהמתך.ואכלת.ושבע
ת׃
טז השמרו.לכם.פן.יפתה.לבבכם.וסרתם.ועב
דתם.אלהים.אחרים.והשתחויתם.להם׃
יז וחרה.אף.יהוה.בכם.ועצר.את.השמים.ול
א.יהיה.מטר.והאדמה.לא.תתן.את.יבולה.וא
בדתם.מהרה.מעל.הארץ.הטבה.אשר.יהוה.נת
ן.לכם׃
יח ושמתם.את.דברי.אלה.על.לבבכם.ועל.נפ
שכם.וקשרתם.אתם.לאות.על.ידכם.והיו.לט
טפת.בין.עיניכם׃
יט ולמדתם.אתם.את.בניכם.לדבר.בם.בשב
תך.בביתך.ובלכתך.בדרך.ובשכבך.ובקומך׃
כ וכתבתם.על.מזוזות.ביתך.ובשעריך׃
כא למען.ירבו.ימיכם.וימי.בניכם.על.האד
מה.אשר.נשבע.יהוה.לאבתיכם.לתת.להם.כי
מי.השמים.על.הארץ׃
כב כי.אם.שמר.תשמרון.את.כל.המצוה.הזא
ת.אשר.אנכי.מצוה.אתכם.לעשתה.לאהבה.א
ת.יהוה.אלהיכם.ללכת.בכל.דרכיו.ולדבקה.
בו׃
כג והוריש.יהוה.את.כל.הגוים.האלה.מלפניכם
וירשתם.גוים.גדלים.ועצמים.מכם׃

..24.. 𐤊𐤋.𐤄𐤌𐤒𐤅𐤌.𐤀𐤔𐤓.𐤕𐤃𐤓𐤊.𐤊𐤐.𐤓𐤂𐤋𐤊𐤌.𐤁𐤅.𐤋𐤊𐤌
.𐤉𐤄𐤉𐤄.𐤌𐤍.𐤄𐤌𐤃𐤁𐤓.𐤅𐤄𐤋𐤁𐤍𐤅𐤍.𐤌𐤍.𐤄𐤍𐤄𐤓.𐤍𐤄𐤓.𐤐𐤓𐤕.𐤅
𐤏𐤃.𐤄𐤉𐤌.𐤄𐤀𐤇𐤓𐤅𐤍.𐤉𐤄𐤉𐤄.𐤂𐤁𐤋𐤊𐤌|

..25.. 𐤋𐤀.𐤉𐤕𐤉𐤑𐤁.𐤀𐤉𐤔.𐤁𐤐𐤍𐤉𐤊𐤌.𐤐𐤇𐤃𐤊𐤌.𐤅𐤌𐤅𐤓𐤀
𐤊𐤌.𐤉𐤕𐤍.𐤉𐤄𐤅𐤄.𐤀𐤋𐤄𐤉𐤊𐤌.𐤏𐤋.𐤐𐤍𐤉.𐤊𐤋.𐤄𐤀𐤓𐤑.𐤀𐤔𐤓
.𐤕𐤃𐤓𐤊𐤅.𐤁𐤄.𐤊𐤀𐤔𐤓.𐤃𐤁𐤓.𐤋𐤊𐤌|

..26.. 𐤓𐤀𐤄.𐤀𐤍𐤊𐤉.𐤍𐤕𐤍.𐤋𐤐𐤍𐤉𐤊𐤌.𐤄𐤉𐤅𐤌.𐤁𐤓𐤊𐤄.𐤅𐤒𐤋𐤋
𐤄|

..27.. 𐤀𐤕.𐤄𐤁𐤓𐤊𐤄.𐤀𐤔𐤓.𐤕𐤔𐤌𐤏𐤅.𐤀𐤋.𐤌𐤑𐤅𐤕.𐤉𐤄𐤅𐤄.
𐤀𐤋𐤄𐤉𐤊𐤌.𐤀𐤔𐤓.𐤀𐤍𐤊𐤉.𐤌𐤑𐤅𐤄.𐤀𐤕𐤊𐤌.𐤄𐤉𐤅𐤌|

..28.. 𐤅𐤄𐤒𐤋𐤋𐤄.𐤀𐤌.𐤋𐤀.𐤕𐤔𐤌𐤏𐤅.𐤀𐤋.𐤌𐤑𐤅𐤕.𐤉𐤄𐤅𐤄.𐤀
𐤋𐤄𐤉𐤊𐤌.𐤅𐤎𐤓𐤕𐤌.𐤌𐤍.𐤄𐤃𐤓𐤊.𐤀𐤔𐤓.𐤀𐤍𐤊𐤉.𐤌𐤑𐤅𐤄.𐤀𐤕
𐤊𐤌.𐤄𐤉𐤅𐤌.𐤋𐤋𐤊𐤕.𐤀𐤇𐤓𐤉.𐤀𐤋𐤄𐤉𐤌.𐤀𐤇𐤓𐤉𐤌.𐤀𐤔𐤓.𐤋
𐤀.𐤉𐤃𐤏𐤕𐤌|

..29.. 𐤅𐤄𐤉𐤄.𐤊𐤉.𐤉𐤁𐤉𐤀𐤊.𐤉𐤄𐤅𐤄.𐤀𐤋𐤄𐤉𐤊.𐤀𐤋.𐤄𐤀𐤓𐤑
.𐤀𐤔𐤓.𐤀𐤕𐤄.𐤁𐤀.𐤔𐤌𐤄.𐤋𐤓𐤔𐤕𐤄.𐤅𐤍𐤕𐤕𐤄.𐤀𐤕.𐤄𐤁𐤓𐤊
𐤄.𐤏𐤋.𐤄𐤓.𐤂𐤓𐤆𐤉𐤌.𐤅𐤀𐤕.𐤄𐤒𐤋𐤋𐤄.𐤏𐤋.𐤄𐤓.𐤏𐤉𐤁𐤋|

..30.. 𐤄𐤋𐤀.𐤄𐤌𐤄.𐤁𐤏𐤁𐤓.𐤄𐤉𐤓𐤃𐤍.𐤀𐤇𐤓𐤉.𐤃𐤓𐤊.𐤌𐤁𐤅
𐤀.𐤄𐤔𐤌𐤔.𐤁𐤀𐤓𐤑.𐤄𐤊𐤍𐤏𐤍𐤉.𐤄𐤉𐤔𐤁.𐤁𐤏𐤓𐤁𐤄.𐤌𐤅𐤋.𐤄
𐤂𐤋𐤂𐤋.𐤀𐤑𐤋.𐤀𐤋𐤅𐤍𐤉.𐤌𐤓𐤄|

..31.. 𐤊𐤉.𐤀𐤕𐤌.𐤏𐤁𐤓𐤉𐤌.𐤀𐤕.𐤄𐤉𐤓𐤃𐤍.𐤋𐤁𐤀.𐤋𐤓𐤔𐤕.𐤀
𐤕.𐤄𐤀𐤓𐤑.𐤀𐤔𐤓.𐤉𐤄𐤅𐤄.𐤀𐤋𐤄𐤉𐤊𐤌.𐤍𐤕𐤍.𐤋𐤊𐤌.𐤅𐤉𐤓𐤔𐤕
𐤌.𐤅𐤉𐤔𐤁𐤕𐤌.𐤁𐤄|

..32.. 𐤅𐤔𐤌𐤓𐤕𐤌.𐤋𐤏𐤔𐤅𐤕.𐤀𐤕.𐤊𐤋.𐤄𐤇𐤒𐤉𐤌.𐤅𐤀𐤕.𐤄𐤌
𐤔𐤐𐤈𐤉𐤌.𐤀𐤔𐤓.𐤀𐤍𐤊𐤉.𐤍𐤕𐤍.𐤋𐤐𐤍𐤉𐤊𐤌.𐤄𐤉𐤅𐤌||

𐤃𐤁𐤓𐤉𐤌.𐤇𐤋𐤒 ..12..

..1.. 𐤀𐤋𐤄.𐤄𐤇𐤒𐤉𐤌.𐤅𐤄𐤌𐤔𐤐𐤈𐤉𐤌.𐤀𐤔𐤓.𐤕𐤔𐤌𐤓𐤅𐤍.𐤋𐤏
𐤔𐤅𐤕.𐤁𐤀𐤓𐤑.𐤀𐤔𐤓.𐤍𐤕𐤍.𐤉𐤄𐤅𐤄.𐤀𐤋𐤄𐤉.𐤀𐤁𐤕𐤉𐤊.𐤋𐤊.𐤋

𐤓𐤔𐤕𐤄.𐤊𐤋.𐤄𐤉𐤌𐤉𐤌.𐤀𐤔𐤓.𐤀𐤕𐤌.𐤇𐤉𐤉𐤌.𐤏𐤋.𐤄𐤀𐤃𐤌𐤄|

ב 𐤀𐤁𐤃.𐤕𐤀𐤁𐤃𐤅𐤍.𐤀𐤕.𐤊𐤋.𐤄𐤌𐤒𐤌𐤅𐤕.𐤀𐤔𐤓.𐤏𐤁𐤃𐤅.𐤔𐤌.𐤄𐤂𐤅𐤉𐤌.𐤀𐤔𐤓.𐤀𐤕𐤌.𐤉𐤓𐤔𐤉𐤌.𐤀𐤕𐤌.𐤀𐤕.𐤀𐤋𐤄𐤉𐤄𐤌.𐤏𐤋.𐤄𐤄𐤓𐤉𐤌.𐤄𐤓𐤌𐤉𐤌.𐤅𐤏𐤋.𐤄𐤂𐤁𐤏𐤅𐤕.𐤅𐤕𐤇𐤕.𐤊𐤋.𐤏𐤑.𐤓𐤏𐤍𐤍|

ג 𐤅𐤍𐤕𐤑𐤕𐤌.𐤀𐤕.𐤌𐤆𐤁𐤇𐤕𐤌.𐤅𐤔𐤁𐤓𐤕𐤌.𐤀𐤕.𐤌𐤑𐤁𐤕𐤌.𐤅𐤀𐤔𐤓𐤉𐤄𐤌.𐤕𐤔𐤓𐤐𐤅𐤍.𐤁𐤀𐤔.𐤅𐤐𐤎𐤉𐤋𐤉.𐤀𐤋𐤄𐤉𐤄𐤌.𐤕𐤂𐤃𐤏𐤅𐤍.𐤅𐤀𐤁𐤃𐤕𐤌.𐤀𐤕.𐤔𐤌𐤌.𐤌𐤍.𐤄𐤌𐤒𐤅𐤌.𐤄𐤄𐤅𐤀|

ד 𐤋𐤀.𐤕𐤏𐤔𐤅𐤍.𐤊𐤍.𐤋𐤉𐤄𐤅𐤄.𐤀𐤋𐤄𐤉𐤊𐤌|

ה 𐤊𐤉.𐤀𐤌.𐤀𐤋.𐤄𐤌𐤒𐤅𐤌.𐤀𐤔𐤓.𐤉𐤁𐤇𐤓.𐤉𐤄𐤅𐤄.𐤀𐤋𐤄𐤉𐤊𐤌.𐤌𐤊𐤋.𐤔𐤁𐤈𐤉𐤊𐤌.𐤋𐤔𐤅𐤌.𐤀𐤕.𐤔𐤌𐤅.𐤔𐤌.𐤋𐤔𐤊𐤍𐤅.𐤕𐤃𐤓𐤔𐤅.𐤅𐤁𐤀𐤕.𐤔𐤌𐤄|

ו 𐤅𐤄𐤁𐤀𐤕𐤌.𐤔𐤌𐤄.𐤏𐤋𐤕𐤉𐤊𐤌.𐤅𐤆𐤁𐤇𐤉𐤊𐤌.𐤅𐤀𐤕.𐤌𐤏𐤔𐤓𐤕𐤉𐤊𐤌.𐤅𐤀𐤕.𐤕𐤓𐤅𐤌𐤕.𐤉𐤃𐤊𐤌.𐤅𐤍𐤃𐤓𐤉𐤊𐤌.𐤅𐤍𐤃𐤁𐤕𐤉𐤊𐤌.𐤅𐤁𐤊𐤓𐤕.𐤁𐤒𐤓𐤊𐤌.𐤅𐤑𐤀𐤍𐤊𐤌|

ז 𐤅𐤀𐤊𐤋𐤕𐤌.𐤔𐤌.𐤋𐤐𐤍𐤉.𐤉𐤄𐤅𐤄.𐤀𐤋𐤄𐤉𐤊𐤌.𐤅𐤔𐤌𐤇𐤕𐤌.𐤁𐤊𐤋.𐤌𐤔𐤋𐤇.𐤉𐤃𐤊𐤌.𐤀𐤕𐤌.𐤅𐤁𐤕𐤉𐤊𐤌.𐤀𐤔𐤓.𐤁𐤓𐤊𐤊.𐤉𐤄𐤅𐤄.𐤀𐤋𐤄𐤉𐤊|

ח 𐤋𐤀.𐤕𐤏𐤔𐤅𐤍.𐤊𐤊𐤋.𐤀𐤔𐤓.𐤀𐤍𐤇𐤍𐤅.𐤏𐤔𐤉𐤌.𐤐𐤄.𐤄𐤉𐤅𐤌.𐤀𐤉𐤔.𐤊𐤋.𐤄𐤉𐤔𐤓.𐤁𐤏𐤉𐤍𐤉𐤅|

ט 𐤊𐤉.𐤋𐤀.𐤁𐤀𐤕𐤌.𐤏𐤃.𐤏𐤕𐤄.𐤀𐤋.𐤄𐤌𐤍𐤅𐤇𐤄.𐤅𐤀𐤋.𐤄𐤍𐤇𐤋𐤄.𐤀𐤔𐤓.𐤉𐤄𐤅𐤄.𐤀𐤋𐤄𐤉𐤊.𐤍𐤕𐤍.𐤋𐤊|

י 𐤅𐤏𐤁𐤓𐤕𐤌.𐤀𐤕.𐤄𐤉𐤓𐤃𐤍.𐤅𐤉𐤔𐤁𐤕𐤌.𐤁𐤀𐤓𐤑.𐤀𐤔𐤓.𐤉𐤄𐤅𐤄.𐤀𐤋𐤄𐤉𐤊𐤌.𐤌𐤍𐤇𐤉𐤋.𐤀𐤕𐤊𐤌.𐤅𐤄𐤍𐤉𐤇.𐤋𐤊𐤌.𐤌𐤊𐤋.𐤀𐤉𐤁𐤉𐤊𐤌.𐤌𐤎𐤁𐤉𐤁.𐤅𐤉𐤔𐤁𐤕𐤌.𐤁𐤈𐤇|

יא 𐤅𐤄𐤉𐤄.𐤄𐤌𐤒𐤅𐤌.𐤀𐤔𐤓.𐤉𐤁𐤇𐤓.𐤉𐤄𐤅𐤄.𐤀𐤋𐤄𐤉𐤊𐤌.𐤁𐤅.𐤋𐤔𐤊𐤍.𐤔𐤌𐤅.𐤔𐤌.𐤔𐤌𐤄.𐤕𐤁𐤉𐤀𐤅.𐤀𐤕.𐤊𐤋.𐤀𐤔𐤓.𐤀𐤍𐤊𐤉.𐤌𐤑𐤅𐤄.𐤀𐤕𐤊𐤌.𐤏𐤅𐤋𐤕𐤉𐤊𐤌.𐤅𐤆𐤁𐤇𐤉𐤊𐤌.𐤌𐤏𐤔𐤓𐤕𐤉𐤊𐤌.𐤅𐤕𐤓𐤌𐤕.𐤉𐤃𐤊𐤌.𐤅𐤊𐤋.𐤌𐤁𐤇𐤓.𐤍𐤃𐤓𐤉𐤊𐤌.𐤀𐤔𐤓.𐤕𐤃𐤓𐤅.𐤋𐤉𐤄𐤅𐤄|

..𐤉𐤁.. 𐤅𐤔𐤌𐤇𐤕𐤌.𐤋𐤐𐤍𐤉.𐤉𐤄𐤅𐤄.𐤀𐤋𐤄𐤉𐤊𐤌.𐤀𐤕𐤌.𐤅𐤁𐤍𐤉
𐤊𐤌.𐤅𐤁𐤍𐤕𐤉𐤊𐤌.𐤅𐤏𐤁𐤃𐤉𐤊𐤌.𐤅𐤀𐤌𐤄𐤕𐤉𐤊𐤌.𐤅𐤄𐤋𐤅𐤉.𐤀
𐤔𐤓.𐤁𐤔𐤏𐤓𐤉𐤊𐤌.𐤊𐤉.𐤀𐤉𐤍.𐤋𐤅.𐤇𐤋𐤒.𐤅𐤍𐤇𐤋𐤄.𐤀𐤕𐤊𐤌|
..𐤉𐤂.. 𐤄𐤔𐤌𐤓.𐤋𐤊.𐤐𐤍.𐤕𐤏𐤋𐤄.𐤏𐤋𐤕𐤉𐤊.𐤁𐤊𐤋.𐤌𐤒𐤅𐤌.𐤀𐤔
𐤓.𐤕𐤓𐤀𐤄|
..𐤉𐤃.. 𐤊𐤉.𐤀𐤌.𐤁𐤌𐤒𐤅𐤌.𐤀𐤔𐤓.𐤉𐤁𐤇𐤓.𐤉𐤄𐤅𐤄.𐤁𐤀𐤇𐤃.
𐤔𐤁𐤈𐤉𐤊.𐤔𐤌.𐤕𐤏𐤋𐤄.𐤏𐤋𐤕𐤉𐤊.𐤅𐤔𐤌.𐤕𐤏𐤔𐤄.𐤊𐤋.𐤀𐤔𐤓
𐤀𐤍𐤊𐤉.𐤌𐤑𐤅𐤊|
..𐤈𐤅.. 𐤓𐤒.𐤁𐤊𐤋.𐤀𐤅𐤕.𐤍𐤐𐤔𐤊.𐤕𐤆𐤁𐤇.𐤅𐤀𐤊𐤋𐤕.𐤁𐤔𐤓.𐤊𐤁
𐤓𐤊𐤕.𐤉𐤄𐤅𐤄.𐤀𐤋𐤄𐤉𐤊.𐤀𐤔𐤓.𐤍𐤕𐤍.𐤋𐤊.𐤁𐤊𐤋.𐤔𐤏𐤓𐤉𐤊.𐤄
𐤈𐤌𐤀.𐤅𐤄𐤈𐤄𐤅𐤓.𐤉𐤀𐤊𐤋𐤍𐤅.𐤊𐤑𐤁𐤉.𐤅𐤊𐤀𐤉𐤋|
..𐤈𐤆.. 𐤓𐤒.𐤄𐤃𐤌.𐤋𐤀.𐤕𐤀𐤊𐤋𐤅.𐤏𐤋.𐤄𐤀𐤓𐤑.𐤕𐤔𐤐𐤊𐤍𐤅.𐤊𐤌
𐤉𐤌|
..𐤉𐤆.. 𐤋𐤀.𐤕𐤅𐤊𐤋.𐤋𐤀𐤊𐤋.𐤁𐤔𐤏𐤓𐤉𐤊.𐤌𐤏𐤔𐤓.𐤃𐤂𐤍𐤊.𐤅𐤕
𐤉𐤓𐤔𐤊.𐤅𐤉𐤑𐤄𐤓𐤊.𐤅𐤁𐤊𐤓𐤕.𐤁𐤒𐤓𐤊.𐤅𐤑𐤀𐤍𐤊.𐤅𐤊𐤋.𐤍𐤃𐤓𐤉
𐤊.𐤀𐤔𐤓.𐤕𐤃𐤓.𐤅𐤍𐤃𐤁𐤕𐤉𐤊.𐤅𐤕𐤓𐤅𐤌𐤕.𐤉𐤃𐤊|
..𐤉𐤇.. 𐤊𐤉.𐤀𐤌.𐤋𐤐𐤍𐤉.𐤉𐤄𐤅𐤄.𐤀𐤋𐤄𐤉𐤊.𐤕𐤀𐤊𐤋𐤍𐤅.𐤁𐤌𐤒𐤅𐤌
.𐤀𐤔𐤓.𐤉𐤁𐤇𐤓.𐤉𐤄𐤅𐤄.𐤀𐤋𐤄𐤉𐤊.𐤁𐤅.𐤀𐤕𐤄.𐤅𐤁𐤍𐤊.𐤅𐤁𐤕𐤊.𐤅
𐤏𐤁𐤃𐤊.𐤅𐤀𐤌𐤕𐤊.𐤅𐤄𐤋𐤅𐤉.𐤀𐤔𐤓.𐤁𐤔𐤏𐤓𐤉𐤊.𐤅𐤔𐤌𐤇𐤕.𐤋𐤐
𐤍𐤉.𐤉𐤄𐤅𐤄.𐤀𐤋𐤄𐤉𐤊.𐤁𐤊𐤋.𐤌𐤔𐤋𐤇.𐤉𐤃𐤊|
..𐤉𐤈.. 𐤄𐤔𐤌𐤓.𐤋𐤊.𐤐𐤍.𐤕𐤏𐤆𐤁.𐤀𐤕.𐤄𐤋𐤅𐤉.𐤊𐤋.𐤉𐤌𐤉𐤊.𐤏
𐤋.𐤀𐤃𐤌𐤕𐤊|
..𐤊.. 𐤊𐤉.𐤉𐤓𐤇𐤉𐤁.𐤉𐤄𐤅𐤄.𐤀𐤋𐤄𐤉𐤊.𐤀𐤕.𐤂𐤁𐤅𐤋𐤊.𐤊𐤀𐤔
𐤓.𐤃𐤁𐤓.𐤋𐤊.𐤅𐤀𐤌𐤓𐤕.𐤀𐤊𐤋𐤄.𐤁𐤔𐤓.𐤊𐤉.𐤕𐤀𐤅𐤄.𐤍𐤐𐤔𐤊.𐤋
𐤀𐤊𐤋.𐤁𐤔𐤓.𐤁𐤊𐤋.𐤀𐤅𐤕.𐤍𐤐𐤔𐤊.𐤕𐤀𐤊𐤋.𐤁𐤔𐤓|
..𐤊𐤀.. 𐤊𐤉.𐤉𐤓𐤇𐤒.𐤌𐤌𐤊.𐤄𐤌𐤒𐤅𐤌.𐤀𐤔𐤓.𐤉𐤁𐤇𐤓.𐤉𐤄𐤅𐤄.
𐤀𐤋𐤄𐤉𐤊.𐤋𐤔𐤅𐤌.𐤔𐤌𐤅.𐤔𐤌.𐤅𐤆𐤁𐤇𐤕.𐤌𐤁𐤒𐤓𐤊.𐤅𐤌𐤑𐤀𐤍
𐤊.𐤀𐤔𐤓.𐤍𐤕𐤍.𐤉𐤄𐤅𐤄.𐤋𐤊.𐤊𐤀𐤔𐤓.𐤑𐤅𐤉𐤕𐤊.𐤅𐤀𐤊𐤋𐤕.𐤁𐤔
𐤏𐤓𐤉𐤊.𐤁𐤊𐤋.𐤀𐤅𐤕.𐤍𐤐𐤔𐤊|
..𐤊𐤁.. 𐤀𐤊.𐤊𐤀𐤔𐤓.𐤉𐤀𐤊𐤋.𐤀𐤕.𐤄𐤑𐤁𐤉.𐤅𐤀𐤕.𐤄𐤀𐤉𐤋.𐤊𐤍.
𐤕𐤀𐤊𐤋𐤍𐤅.𐤄𐤈𐤌𐤀.𐤅𐤄𐤈𐤄𐤅𐤓.𐤉𐤇𐤃𐤅.𐤉𐤀𐤊𐤋𐤍𐤅|

𐤊𐤂 𐤓𐤒.𐤇𐤆𐤒.𐤋𐤁𐤋𐤕𐤉.𐤀𐤊𐤋.𐤄𐤃𐤌.𐤊𐤉.𐤄𐤃𐤌.𐤄𐤅𐤀
𐤄𐤍𐤐𐤔.𐤅𐤋𐤀.𐤕𐤀𐤊𐤋.𐤄𐤍𐤐𐤔.𐤏𐤌.𐤄𐤁𐤔𐤓|

𐤊𐤃 𐤋𐤀.𐤕𐤀𐤊𐤋𐤍𐤅.𐤏𐤋.𐤄𐤀𐤓𐤑.𐤕𐤔𐤐𐤊𐤍𐤅.𐤊𐤌𐤉𐤌|

𐤊𐤄 𐤋𐤀.𐤕𐤀𐤊𐤋𐤍𐤅.𐤋𐤌𐤏𐤍.𐤉𐤉𐤈𐤁.𐤋𐤊.𐤅𐤋𐤁𐤍𐤉𐤊.𐤀𐤇𐤓𐤉
𐤊.𐤊𐤉.𐤕𐤏𐤔𐤄.𐤄𐤉𐤔𐤓.𐤁𐤏𐤉𐤍𐤉.𐤉𐤄𐤅𐤄|

𐤊𐤅 𐤓𐤒.𐤒𐤃𐤔𐤉𐤊.𐤀𐤔𐤓.𐤉𐤄𐤉𐤅.𐤋𐤊.𐤅𐤍𐤃𐤓𐤉𐤊.𐤕𐤔𐤀.𐤅
𐤁𐤀𐤕.𐤀𐤋.𐤄𐤌𐤒𐤅𐤌.𐤀𐤔𐤓.𐤉𐤁𐤇𐤓.𐤉𐤄𐤅𐤄|

𐤊𐤆 𐤅𐤏𐤔𐤉𐤕.𐤏𐤋𐤕𐤉𐤊.𐤄𐤁𐤔𐤓.𐤅𐤄𐤃𐤌.𐤏𐤋.𐤌𐤆𐤁𐤇.𐤉
𐤄𐤅𐤄.𐤀𐤋𐤄𐤉𐤊.𐤅𐤃𐤌.𐤆𐤁𐤇𐤉𐤊.𐤉𐤔𐤐𐤊.𐤏𐤋.𐤌𐤆𐤁𐤇.𐤉
𐤄𐤅𐤄.𐤀𐤋𐤄𐤉𐤊.𐤅𐤄𐤁𐤔𐤓.𐤕𐤀𐤊𐤋|

𐤊𐤇 𐤔𐤌𐤓.𐤅𐤔𐤌𐤏𐤕.𐤀𐤕.𐤊𐤋.𐤄𐤃𐤁𐤓𐤉𐤌.𐤄𐤀𐤋𐤄.𐤀𐤔𐤓.
𐤀𐤍𐤊𐤉.𐤌𐤑𐤅𐤊.𐤋𐤌𐤏𐤍.𐤉𐤉𐤈𐤁.𐤋𐤊.𐤅𐤋𐤁𐤍𐤉𐤊.𐤀𐤇𐤓𐤉𐤊.𐤏
𐤃.𐤏𐤅𐤋𐤌.𐤊𐤉.𐤕𐤏𐤔𐤄.𐤄𐤈𐤅𐤁.𐤅𐤄𐤉𐤔𐤓.𐤁𐤏𐤉𐤍𐤉.𐤉𐤄𐤅𐤄.
𐤀𐤋𐤄𐤉𐤊|

𐤊𐤈 𐤊𐤉.𐤉𐤊𐤓𐤉𐤕.𐤉𐤄𐤅𐤄.𐤀𐤋𐤄𐤉𐤊.𐤀𐤕.𐤄𐤂𐤅𐤉𐤌.𐤀𐤔
𐤓.𐤀𐤕𐤄.𐤁𐤀.𐤔𐤌𐤄.𐤋𐤓𐤔𐤕.𐤀𐤅𐤕𐤌.𐤌𐤐𐤍𐤉𐤊.𐤅𐤉𐤓𐤔𐤕.𐤀𐤕
𐤌.𐤅𐤉𐤔𐤁𐤕.𐤁𐤀𐤓𐤑𐤌|

𐤋 𐤄𐤔𐤌𐤓.𐤋𐤊.𐤐𐤍.𐤕𐤍𐤒𐤔.𐤀𐤇𐤓𐤉𐤄𐤌.𐤀𐤇𐤓𐤉.𐤄𐤔𐤌
𐤃𐤌.𐤌𐤐𐤍𐤉𐤊.𐤅𐤐𐤍.𐤕𐤃𐤓𐤔.𐤋𐤀𐤋𐤄𐤉𐤄𐤌.𐤋𐤀𐤌𐤓.𐤀𐤉𐤊𐤄.
𐤉𐤏𐤁𐤃𐤅.𐤄𐤂𐤅𐤉𐤌.𐤄𐤀𐤋𐤄.𐤀𐤕.𐤀𐤋𐤄𐤉𐤄𐤌.𐤅𐤀𐤏𐤔𐤄.𐤊
𐤍.𐤂𐤌.𐤀𐤍𐤉|

𐤋𐤀 𐤋𐤀.𐤕𐤏𐤔𐤄.𐤊𐤍.𐤋𐤉𐤄𐤅𐤄.𐤀𐤋𐤄𐤉𐤊.𐤊𐤉.𐤊𐤋.𐤕𐤅𐤏𐤁
𐤕.𐤉𐤄𐤅𐤄.𐤀𐤔𐤓.𐤔𐤍𐤀.𐤏𐤔𐤅.𐤋𐤀𐤋𐤄𐤉𐤄𐤌.𐤊𐤉.𐤂𐤌.𐤀𐤕.
𐤁𐤍𐤉𐤄𐤌.𐤅𐤀𐤕.𐤁𐤍𐤕𐤉𐤄𐤌.𐤉𐤔𐤓𐤐𐤅.𐤁𐤀𐤔.𐤋𐤀𐤋𐤄𐤉𐤄𐤌||

𐤃𐤁𐤓𐤉𐤌.𐤇𐤋𐤒 𐤉𐤂

𐤀 𐤀𐤕.𐤊𐤋.𐤄𐤃𐤁𐤓.𐤀𐤔𐤓.𐤀𐤍𐤊𐤉.𐤌𐤑𐤅𐤄.𐤀𐤕𐤊𐤌.𐤀𐤕𐤅.
𐤕𐤔𐤌𐤓𐤅.𐤋𐤏𐤔𐤅𐤕.𐤋𐤀.𐤕𐤎𐤐.𐤏𐤋𐤉𐤅.𐤅𐤋𐤀.𐤕𐤂𐤓𐤏.𐤌𐤌𐤍𐤅|

𐤁 𐤊𐤉.𐤉𐤒𐤅𐤌.𐤁𐤒𐤓𐤁𐤊.𐤍𐤁𐤉𐤀.𐤀𐤅.𐤇𐤋𐤌.𐤇𐤋𐤅𐤌.𐤅𐤍𐤕𐤍.
𐤀𐤋𐤉𐤊.𐤀𐤅𐤕.𐤀𐤅.𐤌𐤅𐤐𐤕|

𐤂 𐤅𐤁𐤀.𐤄𐤀𐤅𐤕.𐤅𐤄𐤌𐤅𐤐𐤕.𐤀𐤔𐤓.𐤃𐤁𐤓.𐤀𐤋𐤉𐤊.𐤋𐤀𐤌𐤓.𐤍
𐤋𐤊𐤄.𐤀𐤇𐤓𐤉.𐤀𐤋𐤄𐤉𐤌.𐤀𐤇𐤓𐤉𐤌.𐤀𐤔𐤓.𐤋𐤀.𐤉𐤃𐤏𐤕𐤌.𐤅
𐤍𐤏𐤁𐤃𐤌|

𐤃 𐤋𐤀.𐤕𐤔𐤌𐤏.𐤀𐤋.𐤃𐤁𐤓𐤉.𐤄𐤍𐤁𐤉𐤀.𐤄𐤄𐤅𐤀.𐤀𐤅.𐤀𐤋.
𐤇𐤅𐤋𐤌.𐤄𐤇𐤋𐤅𐤌.𐤄𐤄𐤅𐤀.𐤊𐤉.𐤌𐤍𐤎𐤄.𐤉𐤄𐤅𐤄.𐤀𐤋𐤄𐤉𐤊𐤌.
𐤀𐤕𐤊𐤌.𐤋𐤃𐤏𐤕.𐤄𐤉𐤔𐤊𐤌.𐤀𐤄𐤁𐤉𐤌.𐤀𐤕.𐤉𐤄𐤅𐤄.𐤀𐤋𐤄
𐤉𐤊𐤌.𐤁𐤊𐤋.𐤋𐤁𐤁𐤊𐤌.𐤅𐤁𐤊𐤋.𐤍𐤐𐤔𐤊𐤌|

𐤄 𐤀𐤇𐤓𐤉.𐤉𐤄𐤅𐤄.𐤀𐤋𐤄𐤉𐤊𐤌.𐤕𐤋𐤊𐤅.𐤅𐤀𐤕𐤅.𐤕𐤉𐤓𐤀𐤅.𐤅𐤀
𐤕.𐤌𐤑𐤅𐤕𐤉𐤅.𐤕𐤔𐤌𐤓𐤅.𐤅𐤁𐤒𐤋𐤅.𐤕𐤔𐤌𐤏𐤅.𐤅𐤀𐤕𐤅.𐤕𐤏𐤁𐤃𐤅.
𐤅𐤁𐤅.𐤕𐤃𐤁𐤒𐤅𐤍|

𐤅 𐤅𐤄𐤍𐤁𐤉𐤀.𐤄𐤄𐤅𐤀.𐤀𐤅.𐤇𐤋𐤌.𐤄𐤇𐤋𐤅𐤌.𐤄𐤄𐤅𐤀.𐤉𐤅𐤌𐤕.
𐤊𐤉.𐤃𐤁𐤓.𐤎𐤓𐤄.𐤏𐤋.𐤉𐤄𐤅𐤄.𐤀𐤋𐤄𐤉𐤊𐤌.𐤄𐤌𐤅𐤑𐤉𐤀.𐤀𐤕
𐤊𐤌.𐤌𐤀𐤓𐤑.𐤌𐤑𐤓𐤉𐤌.𐤅𐤄𐤐𐤃𐤊.𐤌𐤁𐤉𐤕.𐤏𐤁𐤃𐤉𐤌.𐤋𐤄𐤃
𐤉𐤇𐤊.𐤌𐤍.𐤄𐤃𐤓𐤊.𐤀𐤔𐤓.𐤑𐤅𐤊.𐤉𐤄𐤅𐤄.𐤀𐤋𐤄𐤉𐤊.𐤋𐤋𐤊𐤕.𐤁
𐤄.𐤅𐤁𐤏𐤓𐤕.𐤄𐤓𐤏.𐤌𐤒𐤓𐤁𐤊|

𐤆 𐤊𐤉.𐤉𐤎𐤉𐤕𐤊.𐤀𐤇𐤉𐤊.𐤁𐤍.𐤀𐤌𐤊.𐤀𐤅.𐤁𐤍𐤊.𐤀𐤅.𐤁𐤕𐤊.
𐤀𐤅.𐤀𐤔𐤕.𐤇𐤉𐤒𐤊.𐤀𐤅.𐤓𐤏𐤊.𐤀𐤔𐤓.𐤊𐤍𐤐𐤔𐤊.𐤁𐤎𐤕𐤓.𐤋𐤀
𐤌𐤓.𐤍𐤋𐤊𐤄.𐤅𐤍𐤏𐤁𐤃𐤄.𐤀𐤋𐤄𐤉𐤌.𐤀𐤇𐤓𐤉𐤌.𐤀𐤔𐤓.𐤋𐤀.𐤉
𐤃𐤏𐤕.𐤀𐤕𐤄.𐤅𐤀𐤁𐤕𐤉𐤊|

𐤇 𐤌𐤀𐤋𐤄𐤉.𐤄𐤏𐤌𐤉𐤌.𐤀𐤔𐤓.𐤎𐤁𐤉𐤁𐤕𐤉𐤊𐤌.𐤄𐤒𐤓𐤁𐤉𐤌
.𐤀𐤋𐤉𐤊.𐤀𐤅.𐤄𐤓𐤇𐤒𐤉𐤌.𐤌𐤌𐤊.𐤌𐤒𐤑𐤄.𐤄𐤀𐤓𐤑.𐤅𐤏𐤃.𐤒
𐤑𐤄.𐤄𐤀𐤓𐤑|

𐤈 𐤋𐤀.𐤕𐤀𐤁𐤄.𐤋𐤅.𐤅𐤋𐤀.𐤕𐤔𐤌𐤏.𐤀𐤋𐤉𐤅.𐤅𐤋𐤀.𐤕𐤇𐤅𐤎.𐤏
𐤉𐤍𐤊.𐤏𐤋𐤉𐤅.𐤅𐤋𐤀.𐤕𐤇𐤌𐤋.𐤅𐤋𐤀.𐤕𐤊𐤎𐤄.𐤏𐤋𐤉𐤅|

𐤉 𐤊𐤉.𐤄𐤓𐤂.𐤕𐤄𐤓𐤂𐤍𐤅.𐤉𐤃𐤊.𐤕𐤄𐤉𐤄.𐤁𐤅.𐤁𐤓𐤀𐤔𐤅𐤍
𐤄.𐤋𐤄𐤌𐤉𐤕𐤅.𐤅𐤉𐤃.𐤊𐤋.𐤄𐤏𐤌.𐤁𐤀𐤇𐤓𐤍𐤄|

𐤉𐤀 𐤅𐤎𐤒𐤋𐤕𐤅.𐤁𐤀𐤁𐤍𐤉𐤌.𐤅𐤌𐤕.𐤊𐤉.𐤁𐤒𐤔.𐤋𐤄𐤃𐤉𐤇𐤊.
𐤌𐤏𐤋.𐤉𐤄𐤅𐤄.𐤀𐤋𐤄𐤉𐤊.𐤄𐤌𐤅𐤑𐤉𐤀𐤊.𐤌𐤀𐤓𐤑.𐤌𐤑𐤓𐤉𐤌.𐤌
𐤁𐤉𐤕.𐤏𐤁𐤃𐤉𐤌|

𐤉𐤁 𐤅𐤊𐤋.𐤉𐤔𐤓𐤀𐤋.𐤉𐤔𐤌𐤏𐤅.𐤅𐤉𐤓𐤀𐤅𐤍.𐤅𐤋𐤀.𐤉𐤅𐤎𐤐𐤅.𐤋𐤏
𐤔𐤅𐤕.𐤊𐤃𐤁𐤓.𐤄𐤓𐤏.𐤄𐤆𐤄.𐤁𐤒𐤓𐤁𐤊|

13 𐤊𐤉.𐤕𐤔𐤌𐤏.𐤁𐤀𐤇𐤕.𐤏𐤓𐤉𐤊.𐤀𐤔𐤓.𐤉𐤄𐤅𐤄.𐤀𐤋𐤄𐤉𐤊.𐤍𐤕𐤍.𐤋𐤊.𐤋𐤔𐤁𐤕.𐤔𐤌.𐤋𐤀𐤌𐤓|

14 𐤉𐤑𐤀𐤅.𐤀𐤍𐤔𐤉𐤌.𐤁𐤍𐤉.𐤁𐤋𐤉𐤏𐤋.𐤌𐤒𐤓𐤁𐤊.𐤅𐤉𐤃𐤉𐤇𐤅.𐤀𐤕.𐤉𐤔𐤁𐤉.𐤏𐤉𐤓𐤌.𐤋𐤀𐤌𐤓.𐤍𐤋𐤊𐤄.𐤅𐤍𐤏𐤁𐤃𐤄.𐤀𐤋𐤄𐤉𐤌.𐤀𐤇𐤓𐤉𐤌.𐤀𐤔𐤓.𐤋𐤀.𐤉𐤃𐤏𐤕𐤌|

15 𐤅𐤃𐤓𐤔𐤕.𐤅𐤇𐤒𐤓𐤕.𐤅𐤔𐤀𐤋𐤕.𐤄𐤉𐤈𐤁.𐤅𐤄𐤍𐤄.𐤀𐤌𐤕.𐤍𐤊𐤅𐤍.𐤄𐤃𐤁𐤓.𐤍𐤏𐤔𐤕𐤄.𐤄𐤕𐤅𐤏𐤁𐤄.𐤄𐤆𐤀𐤕.𐤁𐤒𐤓𐤁𐤊|

16 𐤄𐤊𐤄.𐤕𐤊𐤄.𐤀𐤕.𐤉𐤔𐤁𐤉.𐤄𐤏𐤉𐤓.𐤄𐤄𐤅𐤀.||𐤄𐤄𐤉𐤀.𐤒𐤓𐤉||.𐤋𐤐𐤉.𐤇𐤓𐤁.𐤄𐤇𐤓𐤌.𐤀𐤕𐤄.𐤅𐤀𐤕.𐤊𐤋.𐤀𐤔𐤓.𐤁𐤄.𐤅𐤀𐤕.𐤁𐤄𐤌𐤕𐤄.𐤋𐤐𐤉.𐤇𐤓𐤁|

17 𐤅𐤀𐤕.𐤊𐤋.𐤔𐤋𐤋𐤄.𐤕𐤒𐤁𐤑.𐤀𐤋.𐤕𐤅𐤊.𐤓𐤇𐤁𐤄.𐤅𐤔𐤓𐤐𐤕.𐤁𐤀𐤔.𐤀𐤕.𐤄𐤏𐤉𐤓.𐤅𐤀𐤕.𐤊𐤋.𐤔𐤋𐤋𐤄.𐤊𐤋𐤉𐤋.𐤋𐤉𐤄𐤅𐤄.𐤀𐤋𐤄𐤉𐤊.𐤅𐤄𐤉𐤕𐤄.𐤕𐤋.𐤏𐤅𐤋𐤌.𐤋𐤀.𐤕𐤁𐤍𐤄.𐤏𐤅𐤃|

18 𐤅𐤋𐤀.𐤉𐤃𐤁𐤒.𐤁𐤉𐤃𐤊.𐤌𐤀𐤅𐤌𐤄.𐤌𐤍.𐤄𐤇𐤓𐤌.𐤋𐤌𐤏𐤍.𐤉𐤔𐤅𐤁.𐤉𐤄𐤅𐤄.𐤌𐤇𐤓𐤅𐤍.𐤀𐤐𐤅.𐤅𐤍𐤕𐤍.𐤋𐤊.𐤓𐤇𐤌𐤉𐤌.𐤅𐤓𐤇𐤌𐤊.𐤅𐤄𐤓𐤁𐤊.𐤊𐤀𐤔𐤓.𐤍𐤔𐤁𐤏.𐤋𐤀𐤁𐤕𐤉𐤊|

19 𐤊𐤉.𐤕𐤔𐤌𐤏.𐤁𐤒𐤅𐤋.𐤉𐤄𐤅𐤄.𐤀𐤋𐤄𐤉𐤊.𐤋𐤔𐤌𐤓.𐤀𐤕.𐤊𐤋.𐤌𐤑𐤅𐤕𐤉𐤅.𐤀𐤔𐤓.𐤀𐤍𐤊𐤉.𐤌𐤑𐤅𐤊.𐤄𐤉𐤅𐤌.𐤋𐤏𐤔𐤅𐤕.𐤄𐤉𐤔𐤓.𐤁𐤏𐤉𐤍𐤉.𐤉𐤄𐤅𐤄.𐤀𐤋𐤄𐤉𐤊||

𐤃𐤁𐤓𐤉𐤌.𐤇𐤋𐤒 14

1 𐤁𐤍𐤉𐤌.𐤀𐤕𐤌.𐤋𐤉𐤄𐤅𐤄.𐤀𐤋𐤄𐤉𐤊𐤌.𐤋𐤀.𐤕𐤕𐤂𐤃𐤃𐤅.𐤅𐤋𐤀.𐤕𐤔𐤉𐤌𐤅.𐤒𐤓𐤇𐤄.𐤁𐤉𐤍.𐤏𐤉𐤍𐤉𐤊𐤌.𐤋𐤌𐤕|

2 𐤊𐤉.𐤏𐤌.𐤒𐤃𐤅𐤔.𐤀𐤕𐤄.𐤋𐤉𐤄𐤅𐤄.𐤀𐤋𐤄𐤉𐤊.𐤅𐤁𐤊.𐤁𐤇𐤓.𐤉𐤄𐤅𐤄.𐤋𐤄𐤉𐤅𐤕.𐤋𐤅.𐤋𐤏𐤌.𐤎𐤂𐤋𐤄.𐤌𐤊𐤋.𐤄𐤏𐤌𐤉𐤌.𐤀𐤔𐤓.𐤏𐤋.𐤐𐤍𐤉.𐤄𐤀𐤃𐤌𐤄|

3 𐤋𐤀.𐤕𐤀𐤊𐤋.𐤊𐤋.𐤕𐤅𐤏𐤁𐤄|

4 𐤆𐤀𐤕.𐤄𐤁𐤄𐤌𐤄.𐤀𐤔𐤓.𐤕𐤀𐤊𐤋𐤅.𐤔𐤅𐤓.𐤔𐤄.𐤊𐤔𐤁𐤉𐤌.𐤅𐤔𐤄.𐤏𐤆𐤉𐤌|

ה 𐤀𐤉𐤋.𐤅𐤑𐤁𐤉.𐤅𐤉𐤇𐤌𐤅𐤓.𐤅𐤀𐤒𐤅.𐤅𐤃𐤉𐤔𐤍.𐤅𐤕𐤀𐤅.𐤅𐤆𐤌𐤓
|
ו 𐤅𐤊𐤋.𐤁𐤄𐤌𐤄.𐤌𐤐𐤓𐤎𐤕.𐤐𐤓𐤎𐤄.𐤅𐤔𐤎𐤏𐤕.𐤔𐤎𐤏.𐤔𐤕𐤉
.𐤐𐤓𐤎𐤅𐤕.𐤌𐤏𐤋𐤕.𐤂𐤓𐤄.𐤁𐤁𐤄𐤌𐤄.𐤀𐤕𐤄.𐤕𐤀𐤊𐤋𐤅|
ז 𐤀𐤊.𐤀𐤕.𐤆𐤄.𐤋𐤀.𐤕𐤀𐤊𐤋𐤅.𐤌𐤌𐤏𐤋𐤉.𐤄𐤂𐤓𐤄.𐤅𐤌𐤌𐤐
𐤓𐤉𐤎𐤉.𐤄𐤐𐤓𐤎𐤄.𐤄𐤔𐤎𐤅𐤏𐤄.𐤀𐤕.𐤄𐤂𐤌𐤋.𐤅𐤀𐤕.𐤄𐤀𐤓𐤍𐤁
𐤕.𐤅𐤀𐤕.𐤄𐤔𐤐𐤍.𐤊𐤉.𐤌𐤏𐤋𐤄.𐤂𐤓𐤄.𐤄𐤌𐤄.𐤅𐤐𐤓𐤎𐤄.𐤋𐤀.𐤄
𐤐𐤓𐤉𐤎𐤅.𐤈𐤌𐤀𐤉𐤌.𐤄𐤌.𐤋𐤊𐤌|
ח 𐤅𐤀𐤕.𐤄𐤇𐤆𐤉𐤓.𐤊𐤉.𐤌𐤐𐤓𐤉𐤎.𐤐𐤓𐤎𐤄.𐤄𐤅𐤀.𐤅𐤋𐤀.𐤂𐤓
𐤄.𐤈𐤌𐤀.𐤄𐤅𐤀.𐤋𐤊𐤌.𐤌𐤁𐤔𐤓𐤌.𐤋𐤀.𐤕𐤀𐤊𐤋𐤅.𐤅𐤁𐤍𐤁𐤋𐤕𐤌.
𐤋𐤀.𐤕𐤂𐤏𐤅|
ט 𐤀𐤕.𐤆𐤄.𐤕𐤀𐤊𐤋𐤅.𐤌𐤊𐤋.𐤀𐤔𐤓.𐤁𐤌𐤉𐤌.𐤊𐤋.𐤀𐤔𐤓.𐤋𐤅
.𐤎𐤍𐤐𐤉𐤓.𐤅𐤒𐤔𐤒𐤔𐤕.𐤕𐤀𐤊𐤋𐤅|
י 𐤅𐤊𐤋.𐤀𐤔𐤓.𐤀𐤉𐤍.𐤋𐤅.𐤎𐤍𐤐𐤉𐤓.𐤅𐤒𐤔𐤒𐤔𐤕.𐤋𐤀.𐤕𐤀𐤊
𐤋𐤅.𐤈𐤌𐤀.𐤄𐤅𐤀.𐤋𐤊𐤌|
יא 𐤊𐤋.𐤑𐤐𐤅𐤓.𐤈𐤄𐤓𐤄.𐤕𐤀𐤊𐤋𐤅|
יב 𐤅𐤆𐤄.𐤀𐤔𐤓.𐤋𐤀.𐤕𐤀𐤊𐤋𐤅.𐤌𐤄𐤌.𐤄𐤍𐤔𐤓.𐤅𐤄𐤐𐤓𐤎.𐤅𐤄
𐤏𐤆𐤍𐤉𐤄|
יג 𐤅𐤄𐤓𐤀𐤄.𐤅𐤀𐤕.𐤄𐤀𐤉𐤄.𐤅𐤄𐤃𐤉𐤄.𐤋𐤌𐤉𐤍𐤄|
יד 𐤅𐤀𐤕.𐤊𐤋.𐤏𐤓𐤁.𐤋𐤌𐤉𐤍𐤅|
טו 𐤅𐤀𐤕.𐤁𐤕.𐤄𐤉𐤏𐤍𐤄.𐤅𐤀𐤕.𐤄𐤕𐤇𐤌𐤎.𐤅𐤀𐤕.𐤄𐤔𐤇𐤐.
𐤅𐤀𐤕.𐤄𐤍𐤑.𐤋𐤌𐤉𐤍𐤄𐤅|
טז 𐤀𐤕.𐤄𐤊𐤅𐤎.𐤅𐤀𐤕.𐤄𐤉𐤍𐤔𐤅𐤐.𐤅𐤄𐤕𐤍𐤔𐤌𐤕|
יז 𐤅𐤄𐤒𐤀𐤕.𐤅𐤀𐤕.𐤄𐤓𐤇𐤌𐤄.𐤅𐤀𐤕.𐤄𐤔𐤋𐤊|
יח 𐤅𐤄𐤇𐤎𐤉𐤃𐤄.𐤅𐤄𐤀𐤍𐤐𐤄.𐤋𐤌𐤉𐤍𐤄.𐤅𐤄𐤃𐤅𐤊𐤉𐤐𐤕.𐤅𐤄
𐤏𐤈𐤋𐤐|
יט 𐤅𐤊𐤋.𐤔𐤓𐤑.𐤄𐤏𐤅𐤐.𐤈𐤌𐤀.𐤄𐤅𐤀.𐤋𐤊𐤌.𐤋𐤀.𐤉𐤀𐤊𐤋𐤅|
כ 𐤊𐤋.𐤏𐤅𐤐.𐤈𐤄𐤅𐤓.𐤕𐤀𐤊𐤋𐤅|
כא 𐤋𐤀.𐤕𐤀𐤊𐤋𐤅.𐤊𐤋.𐤍𐤁𐤋𐤄.𐤋𐤂𐤓.𐤀𐤔𐤓.𐤁𐤔𐤏𐤓𐤉𐤊.𐤕
𐤕𐤍𐤍𐤄.𐤅𐤀𐤊𐤋𐤄.𐤀𐤅.𐤌𐤊𐤓.𐤋𐤍𐤊𐤓𐤉.𐤊𐤉.𐤏𐤌.𐤒𐤃𐤅𐤔.𐤀𐤕
𐤄.𐤋𐤉𐤄𐤅𐤄.𐤀𐤋𐤄𐤉𐤊.𐤋𐤀.𐤕𐤁𐤔𐤋.𐤂𐤃𐤉.𐤁𐤇𐤋𐤁.𐤀𐤌𐤅|

..כב..עשר.תעשר.את.כל.תבואת.זרעך.היצא.
השדה.שנה.שנה|
..כג..ואכלת.לפני.יהוה.אלהיך.במקום.אשר.י
בחר.לשכן.שמו.שם.מעשר.דגנך.תירשך.ויצ
הרך.ובכרת.בקרך.וצאנך.למען.תלמד.ליראה.
את.יהוה.אלהיך.כל.הימים|
..כד..וכי.ירבה.ממך.הדרך.כי.לא.תוכל.שאתו.
כי.ירחק.ממך.המקום.אשר.יבחר.יהוה.אלה
יך.לשום.שמו.שם.כי.יברכך.יהוה.אלהיך|
..כה..ונתתה.בכסף.וצרת.הכסף.בידך.והלכת.א
ל.המקום.אשר.יבחר.יהוה.אלהיך.בו|
..כו..ונתתה.הכסף.בכל.אשר.תאוה.נפשך.בבקר.
ובצאן.וביין.ובשכר.ובכל.אשר.תשאלך.נפשך.ו
אכלת.שם.לפני.יהוה.אלהיך.ושמחת.אתה.וב
יתך|
..כז..והלוי.אשר.בשעריך.לא.תעזבנו.כי.אין
לו.חלק.ונחלה.עמך|
..כח..מקצה.שלש.שנים.תוציא.את.כל.מעשר.
תבואתך.בשנה.ההוא.והנחת.בשעריך|
..כט..ובא.הלוי.כי.אין.לו.חלק.ונחלה.עמך.וה
גר.והיתום.והאלמנה.אשר.בשעריך.ואכלו.וש
בעו.למען.יברכך.יהוה.אלהיך.בכל.מעשה.י
דך.אשר.תעשה||

דברים.חלק..טו..

..א..מקץ.שבע.שנים.תעשה.שמטה|
..ב..וזה.דבר.השמטה.שמוט.כל.בעל.משה.יד
ו.אשר.ישה.ברעהו.לא.יגש.את.רעהו.ואת.אח
יו.כי.קרא.שמטה.ליהוה|

𐤂 𐤀𐤕.𐤄𐤍𐤊𐤓𐤉.𐤕𐤂𐤔.𐤅𐤀𐤔𐤓.𐤉𐤄𐤉𐤄.𐤋𐤊.𐤀𐤕.𐤀𐤇𐤉
𐤊.𐤕𐤔𐤌𐤈.𐤉𐤃𐤊|
𐤃 𐤀𐤐𐤎.𐤊𐤉.𐤋𐤀.𐤉𐤄𐤉𐤄.𐤁𐤊.𐤀𐤁𐤉𐤅𐤍.𐤊𐤉.𐤁𐤓𐤊.𐤉𐤁𐤓𐤊
𐤊.𐤉𐤄𐤅𐤄.𐤁𐤀𐤓𐤑.𐤀𐤔𐤓.𐤉𐤄𐤅𐤄.𐤀𐤋𐤄𐤉𐤊.𐤍𐤕𐤍.𐤋𐤊.𐤍𐤇𐤋
𐤄.𐤋𐤓𐤔𐤕𐤄|
𐤄 𐤓𐤒.𐤀𐤌.𐤔𐤌𐤅𐤏.𐤕𐤔𐤌𐤏.𐤁𐤒𐤅𐤋.𐤉𐤄𐤅𐤄.𐤀𐤋𐤄𐤉𐤊.𐤋𐤔
𐤌𐤓.𐤋𐤏𐤔𐤅𐤕.𐤀𐤕.𐤊𐤋.𐤄𐤌𐤑𐤅𐤄.𐤄𐤆𐤀𐤕.𐤀𐤔𐤓.𐤀𐤍𐤊𐤉.𐤌
𐤑𐤅𐤊.𐤄𐤉𐤅𐤌|
𐤅 𐤊𐤉.𐤉𐤄𐤅𐤄.𐤀𐤋𐤄𐤉𐤊.𐤁𐤓𐤊𐤊.𐤊𐤀𐤔𐤓.𐤃𐤁𐤓.𐤋𐤊.𐤅𐤄𐤏
𐤁𐤈𐤕.𐤂𐤅𐤉𐤌.𐤓𐤁𐤉𐤌.𐤅𐤀𐤕𐤄.𐤋𐤀.𐤕𐤏𐤁𐤈.𐤅𐤌𐤔𐤋𐤕.𐤁𐤂𐤅
𐤉𐤌.𐤓𐤁𐤉𐤌.𐤅𐤁𐤊.𐤋𐤀.𐤉𐤌𐤔𐤋𐤅|
𐤆 𐤊𐤉.𐤉𐤄𐤉𐤄.𐤁𐤊.𐤀𐤁𐤉𐤅𐤍.𐤌𐤀𐤇𐤃.𐤀𐤇𐤉𐤊.𐤁𐤀𐤇𐤃
.𐤔𐤏𐤓𐤉𐤊.𐤁𐤀𐤓𐤑𐤊.𐤀𐤔𐤓.𐤉𐤄𐤅𐤄.𐤀𐤋𐤄𐤉𐤊.𐤍𐤕𐤍.𐤋𐤊.𐤋𐤀.
𐤕𐤀𐤌𐤑.𐤀𐤕.𐤋𐤁𐤁𐤊.𐤅𐤋𐤀.𐤕𐤒𐤐𐤑.𐤀𐤕.𐤉𐤃𐤊.𐤌𐤀𐤇𐤉𐤊.
𐤄𐤀𐤁𐤉𐤅𐤍|
𐤇 𐤊𐤉.𐤐𐤕𐤇.𐤕𐤐𐤕𐤇.𐤀𐤕.𐤉𐤃𐤊.𐤋𐤅.𐤅𐤄𐤏𐤁𐤈.𐤕𐤏𐤁𐤉
𐤈𐤍𐤅.𐤃𐤉.𐤌𐤇𐤎𐤓𐤅.𐤀𐤔𐤓.𐤉𐤇𐤎𐤓.𐤋𐤅|
𐤈 𐤄𐤔𐤌𐤓.𐤋𐤊.𐤐𐤍.𐤉𐤄𐤉𐤄.𐤃𐤁𐤓.𐤏𐤌.𐤋𐤁𐤁𐤊.𐤁𐤋𐤉𐤏𐤋.
𐤋𐤀𐤌𐤓.𐤒𐤓𐤁𐤄.𐤔𐤍𐤕.𐤄𐤔𐤁𐤏.𐤔𐤍𐤕.𐤄𐤔𐤌𐤈𐤄.𐤅𐤓𐤏𐤄.𐤏
𐤉𐤍𐤊.𐤁𐤀𐤇𐤉𐤊.𐤄𐤀𐤁𐤉𐤅𐤍.𐤅𐤋𐤀.𐤕𐤕𐤍.𐤋𐤅.𐤅𐤒𐤓𐤀.𐤏𐤋𐤉𐤊.
𐤀𐤋.𐤉𐤄𐤅𐤄.𐤅𐤄𐤉𐤄.𐤁𐤊.𐤇𐤈𐤀|
𐤉 𐤍𐤕𐤅𐤍.𐤕𐤕𐤍.𐤋𐤅.𐤅𐤋𐤀.𐤉𐤓𐤏.𐤋𐤁𐤁𐤊.𐤁𐤕𐤕𐤊.𐤋𐤅.𐤊𐤉.𐤁
𐤂𐤋𐤋.𐤄𐤃𐤁𐤓.𐤄𐤆𐤄.𐤉𐤁𐤓𐤊𐤊.𐤉𐤄𐤅𐤄.𐤀𐤋𐤄𐤉𐤊.𐤁𐤊𐤋.𐤌
𐤏𐤔𐤊.𐤅𐤁𐤊𐤋.𐤌𐤔𐤋𐤇.𐤉𐤃𐤊|
𐤉𐤀 𐤊𐤉.𐤋𐤀.𐤉𐤇𐤃𐤋.𐤀𐤁𐤉𐤅𐤍.𐤌𐤒𐤓𐤁.𐤄𐤀𐤓𐤑.𐤏𐤋.𐤊𐤍.
𐤀𐤍𐤊𐤉.𐤌𐤑𐤅𐤊.𐤋𐤀𐤌𐤓.𐤐𐤕𐤇.𐤕𐤐𐤕𐤇.𐤀𐤕.𐤉𐤃𐤊.𐤋𐤀𐤇𐤉
𐤊.𐤋𐤏𐤍𐤉𐤊.𐤅𐤋𐤀𐤁𐤉𐤍𐤊.𐤁𐤀𐤓𐤑𐤊|
𐤉𐤁 𐤊𐤉.𐤉𐤌𐤊𐤓.𐤋𐤊.𐤀𐤇𐤉𐤊.𐤄𐤏𐤁𐤓𐤉.𐤀𐤅.𐤄𐤏𐤁𐤓𐤉𐤄.𐤅
𐤏𐤁𐤃𐤊.𐤔𐤔.𐤔𐤍𐤉𐤌.𐤅𐤁𐤔𐤍𐤄.𐤄𐤔𐤁𐤉𐤏𐤕.𐤕𐤔𐤋𐤇𐤍𐤅.𐤇
𐤐𐤔𐤉.𐤌𐤏𐤌𐤊|

13 𐤅𐤊𐤉.𐤕𐤔𐤋𐤇𐤍𐤅.𐤇𐤐𐤔𐤉.𐤌𐤏𐤌𐤊.𐤋𐤀.𐤕𐤔𐤋𐤇𐤍𐤅.𐤓𐤉𐤒𐤌|

14 𐤄𐤏𐤍𐤉𐤒.𐤕𐤏𐤍𐤉𐤒.𐤋𐤅.𐤌𐤑𐤀𐤍𐤊.𐤅𐤌𐤂𐤓𐤍𐤊.𐤅𐤌𐤉𐤒𐤁𐤊.𐤀𐤔𐤓.𐤁𐤓𐤊𐤊.𐤉𐤄𐤅𐤄.𐤀𐤋𐤄𐤉𐤊.𐤕𐤕𐤍.𐤋𐤅|

15 𐤅𐤆𐤊𐤓𐤕.𐤊𐤉.𐤏𐤁𐤃.𐤄𐤉𐤉𐤕.𐤁𐤀𐤓𐤑.𐤌𐤑𐤓𐤉𐤌.𐤅𐤉𐤐𐤃𐤊.𐤉𐤄𐤅𐤄.𐤀𐤋𐤄𐤉𐤊.𐤏𐤋.𐤊𐤍.𐤀𐤍𐤊𐤉.𐤌𐤑𐤅𐤊.𐤀𐤕.𐤄𐤃𐤁𐤓.𐤄𐤆𐤄.𐤄𐤉𐤅𐤌|

16 𐤅𐤄𐤉𐤄.𐤊𐤉.𐤉𐤀𐤌𐤓.𐤀𐤋𐤉𐤊.𐤋𐤀.𐤀𐤑𐤀.𐤌𐤏𐤌𐤊.𐤊𐤉.𐤀𐤄𐤁𐤊.𐤅𐤀𐤕.𐤁𐤉𐤕𐤊.𐤊𐤉.𐤈𐤅𐤁.𐤋𐤅.𐤏𐤌𐤊|

17 𐤅𐤋𐤒𐤇𐤕.𐤀𐤕.𐤄𐤌𐤓𐤑𐤏.𐤅𐤍𐤕𐤕𐤄.𐤁𐤀𐤆𐤍𐤅.𐤅𐤁𐤃𐤋𐤕.𐤅𐤄𐤉𐤄.𐤋𐤊.𐤏𐤁𐤃.𐤏𐤅𐤋𐤌.𐤅𐤀𐤐.𐤋𐤀𐤌𐤕𐤊.𐤕𐤏𐤔𐤄.𐤊𐤍|

18 𐤋𐤀.𐤉𐤒𐤔𐤄.𐤁𐤏𐤉𐤍𐤊.𐤁𐤔𐤋𐤇𐤊.𐤀𐤕𐤅.𐤇𐤐𐤔𐤉.𐤌𐤏𐤌𐤊.𐤊𐤉.𐤌𐤔𐤍𐤄.𐤔𐤊𐤓.𐤔𐤊𐤉𐤓.𐤏𐤁𐤃𐤊.𐤔𐤔.𐤔𐤍𐤉𐤌.𐤅𐤁𐤓𐤊𐤊.𐤉𐤄𐤅𐤄.𐤀𐤋𐤄𐤉𐤊.𐤁𐤊𐤋.𐤀𐤔𐤓.𐤕𐤏𐤔𐤄|

19 𐤊𐤋.𐤄𐤁𐤊𐤅𐤓.𐤀𐤔𐤓.𐤉𐤅𐤋𐤃.𐤁𐤁𐤒𐤓𐤊.𐤅𐤁𐤑𐤀𐤍𐤊.𐤄𐤆𐤊𐤓.𐤕𐤒𐤃𐤉𐤔.𐤋𐤉𐤄𐤅𐤄.𐤀𐤋𐤄𐤉𐤊.𐤋𐤀.𐤕𐤏𐤁𐤃.𐤁𐤁𐤊𐤓.𐤔𐤅𐤓𐤊.𐤅𐤋𐤀.𐤕𐤂𐤆.𐤁𐤊𐤅𐤓.𐤑𐤀𐤍𐤊|

20 𐤋𐤐𐤍𐤉.𐤉𐤄𐤅𐤄.𐤀𐤋𐤄𐤉𐤊.𐤕𐤀𐤊𐤋𐤍𐤅.𐤔𐤍𐤄.𐤁𐤔𐤍𐤄.𐤁𐤌𐤒𐤅𐤌.𐤀𐤔𐤓.𐤉𐤁𐤇𐤓.𐤉𐤄𐤅𐤄.𐤀𐤕𐤄.𐤅𐤁𐤉𐤕𐤊|

21 𐤅𐤊𐤉.𐤉𐤄𐤉𐤄.𐤁𐤅.𐤌𐤅𐤌.𐤐𐤎𐤇.𐤀𐤅.𐤏𐤅𐤓.𐤊𐤋.𐤌𐤅𐤌.𐤓𐤏.𐤋𐤀.𐤕𐤆𐤁𐤇𐤍𐤅.𐤋𐤉𐤄𐤅𐤄.𐤀𐤋𐤄𐤉𐤊|

22 𐤁𐤔𐤏𐤓𐤉𐤊.𐤕𐤀𐤊𐤋𐤍𐤅.𐤄𐤈𐤌𐤀.𐤅𐤄𐤈𐤄𐤅𐤓.𐤉𐤇𐤃𐤅.𐤊𐤑𐤁𐤉.𐤅𐤊𐤀𐤉𐤋|

23 𐤓𐤒.𐤀𐤕.𐤃𐤌𐤅.𐤋𐤀.𐤕𐤀𐤊𐤋.𐤏𐤋.𐤄𐤀𐤓𐤑.𐤕𐤔𐤐𐤊𐤍𐤅.𐤊𐤌𐤉𐤌‖

𐤃𐤁𐤓𐤉𐤌.𐤇𐤋𐤒 16

1 𐤔𐤌𐤅𐤓.𐤀𐤕.𐤇𐤃𐤔.𐤄𐤀𐤁𐤉𐤁.𐤅𐤏𐤔𐤉𐤕.𐤐𐤎𐤇.𐤋𐤉𐤄𐤅𐤄.𐤀𐤋𐤄𐤉𐤊.𐤊𐤉.𐤁𐤇𐤃𐤔.𐤄𐤀𐤁𐤉𐤁.𐤄𐤅𐤑𐤉𐤀𐤊.𐤉𐤄𐤅𐤄.𐤀𐤋𐤄𐤉𐤊.𐤌𐤌𐤑𐤓𐤉𐤌.𐤋𐤉𐤋𐤄|

ב 𐤅𐤆𐤁𐤇𐤕.𐤐𐤎𐤇.𐤋𐤉𐤄𐤅𐤄.𐤀𐤋𐤄𐤉𐤊.𐤑𐤀𐤍.𐤅𐤁𐤒𐤓.𐤁𐤌
𐤒𐤅𐤌.𐤀𐤔𐤓.𐤉𐤁𐤇𐤓.𐤉𐤄𐤅𐤄.𐤋𐤔𐤊𐤍.𐤔𐤌𐤅.𐤔𐤌|
ג 𐤋𐤀.𐤕𐤀𐤊𐤋.𐤏𐤋𐤉𐤅.𐤇𐤌𐤑.𐤔𐤁𐤏𐤕.𐤉𐤌𐤉𐤌.𐤕𐤀𐤊𐤋.
𐤏𐤋𐤉𐤅.𐤌𐤑𐤅𐤕.𐤋𐤇𐤌.𐤏𐤍𐤉.𐤊𐤉.𐤁𐤇𐤐𐤆𐤅𐤍.𐤉𐤑𐤀𐤕.𐤌𐤀𐤓
𐤑.𐤌𐤑𐤓𐤉𐤌.𐤋𐤌𐤏𐤍.𐤕𐤆𐤊𐤓.𐤀𐤕.𐤉𐤅𐤌.𐤑𐤀𐤕𐤊.𐤌𐤀𐤓𐤑.
𐤌𐤑𐤓𐤉𐤌.𐤊𐤋.𐤉𐤌𐤉.𐤇𐤉𐤉𐤊|
ד 𐤅𐤋𐤀.𐤉𐤓𐤀𐤄.𐤋𐤊.𐤔𐤀𐤓.𐤁𐤊𐤋.𐤂𐤁𐤋𐤊.𐤔𐤁𐤏𐤕.𐤉𐤌𐤉
𐤌.𐤅𐤋𐤀.𐤉𐤋𐤉𐤍.𐤌𐤍.𐤄𐤁𐤔𐤓.𐤀𐤔𐤓.𐤕𐤆𐤁𐤇.𐤁𐤏𐤓𐤁.𐤁𐤉𐤅𐤌.
𐤄𐤓𐤀𐤔𐤅𐤍.𐤋𐤁𐤒𐤓|
ה 𐤋𐤀.𐤕𐤅𐤊𐤋.𐤋𐤆𐤁𐤇.𐤀𐤕.𐤄𐤐𐤎𐤇.𐤁𐤀𐤇𐤃.𐤔𐤏𐤓𐤉𐤊.
𐤀𐤔𐤓.𐤉𐤄𐤅𐤄.𐤀𐤋𐤄𐤉𐤊.𐤍𐤕𐤍.𐤋𐤊|
ו 𐤊𐤉.𐤀𐤌.𐤀𐤋.𐤄𐤌𐤒𐤅𐤌.𐤀𐤔𐤓.𐤉𐤁𐤇𐤓.𐤉𐤄𐤅𐤄.𐤀𐤋𐤄𐤉
𐤊.𐤋𐤔𐤊𐤍.𐤔𐤌𐤅.𐤔𐤌.𐤕𐤆𐤁𐤇.𐤀𐤕.𐤄𐤐𐤎𐤇.𐤁𐤏𐤓𐤁.𐤊𐤁𐤅𐤀
.𐤄𐤔𐤌𐤔.𐤌𐤅𐤏𐤃.𐤑𐤀𐤕𐤊.𐤌𐤌𐤑𐤓𐤉𐤌|
ז 𐤅𐤁𐤔𐤋𐤕.𐤅𐤀𐤊𐤋𐤕.𐤁𐤌𐤒𐤅𐤌.𐤀𐤔𐤓.𐤉𐤁𐤇𐤓.𐤉𐤄𐤅𐤄.𐤀
𐤋𐤄𐤉𐤊.𐤁𐤅.𐤅𐤐𐤍𐤉𐤕.𐤁𐤁𐤒𐤓.𐤅𐤄𐤋𐤊𐤕.𐤋𐤀𐤄𐤋𐤉𐤊|
ח 𐤔𐤔𐤕.𐤉𐤌𐤉𐤌.𐤕𐤀𐤊𐤋.𐤌𐤑𐤅𐤕.𐤅𐤁𐤉𐤅𐤌.𐤄𐤔𐤁𐤉𐤏𐤉.𐤏
𐤑𐤓𐤕.𐤋𐤉𐤄𐤅𐤄.𐤀𐤋𐤄𐤉𐤊.𐤋𐤀.𐤕𐤏𐤔𐤄.𐤌𐤋𐤀𐤊𐤄|
ט 𐤔𐤁𐤏𐤄.𐤔𐤁𐤏𐤕.𐤕𐤎𐤐𐤓.𐤋𐤊.𐤌𐤄𐤇𐤋.𐤇𐤓𐤌𐤔.𐤁𐤒𐤌
𐤄.𐤕𐤇𐤋.𐤋𐤎𐤐𐤓.𐤔𐤁𐤏𐤄.𐤔𐤁𐤏𐤅𐤕|
י 𐤅𐤏𐤔𐤉𐤕.𐤇𐤂.𐤔𐤁𐤏𐤅𐤕.𐤋𐤉𐤄𐤅𐤄.𐤀𐤋𐤄𐤉𐤊.𐤌𐤎𐤕.
𐤍𐤃𐤁𐤕.𐤉𐤃𐤊.𐤀𐤔𐤓.𐤕𐤕𐤍.𐤊𐤀𐤔𐤓.𐤉𐤁𐤓𐤊𐤊.𐤉𐤄𐤅𐤄.𐤀𐤋
𐤄𐤉𐤊|
יא 𐤅𐤔𐤌𐤇𐤕.𐤋𐤐𐤍𐤉.𐤉𐤄𐤅𐤄.𐤀𐤋𐤄𐤉𐤊.𐤀𐤕𐤄.𐤅𐤁𐤍𐤊.𐤅𐤁𐤕
𐤊.𐤅𐤏𐤁𐤃𐤊.𐤅𐤀𐤌𐤕𐤊.𐤅𐤄𐤋𐤅𐤉.𐤀𐤔𐤓.𐤁𐤔𐤏𐤓𐤉𐤊.𐤅𐤄𐤂𐤓.𐤅
𐤄𐤉𐤕𐤅𐤌.𐤅𐤄𐤀𐤋𐤌𐤍𐤄.𐤀𐤔𐤓.𐤁𐤒𐤓𐤁𐤊.𐤁𐤌𐤒𐤅𐤌.𐤀𐤔𐤓.𐤉𐤁
𐤇𐤓.𐤉𐤄𐤅𐤄.𐤀𐤋𐤄𐤉𐤊.𐤋𐤔𐤊𐤍.𐤔𐤌𐤅.𐤔𐤌|
יב 𐤅𐤆𐤊𐤓𐤕.𐤊𐤉.𐤏𐤁𐤃.𐤄𐤉𐤉𐤕.𐤁𐤌𐤑𐤓𐤉𐤌.𐤅𐤔𐤌𐤓𐤕.𐤅
𐤏𐤔𐤉𐤕.𐤀𐤕.𐤄𐤇𐤒𐤉𐤌.𐤄𐤀𐤋𐤄|
יג 𐤇𐤂.𐤄𐤎𐤊𐤕.𐤕𐤏𐤔𐤄.𐤋𐤊.𐤔𐤁𐤏𐤕.𐤉𐤌𐤉𐤌.𐤁𐤀𐤎𐤐
𐤊.𐤌𐤂𐤓𐤍𐤊.𐤅𐤌𐤉𐤒𐤁𐤊|

14 𐤅𐤔𐤌𐤇𐤕.𐤁𐤇𐤂𐤊.𐤀𐤕𐤄.𐤅𐤁𐤍𐤊.𐤅𐤁𐤕𐤊.𐤅𐤏𐤁𐤃𐤊.𐤅
𐤀𐤌𐤕𐤊.𐤅𐤄𐤋𐤅𐤉.𐤅𐤄𐤂𐤓.𐤅𐤄𐤉𐤕𐤅𐤌.𐤅𐤄𐤀𐤋𐤌𐤍𐤄.𐤀𐤔𐤓.𐤁𐤔
𐤏𐤓𐤉𐤊|

15 𐤔𐤁𐤏𐤕.𐤉𐤌𐤉𐤌.𐤕𐤇𐤂.𐤋𐤉𐤄𐤅𐤄.𐤀𐤋𐤄𐤉𐤊.𐤁𐤌𐤒𐤅𐤌
.𐤀𐤔𐤓.𐤉𐤁𐤇𐤓.𐤉𐤄𐤅𐤄.𐤊𐤉.𐤉𐤁𐤓𐤊𐤊.𐤉𐤄𐤅𐤄.𐤀𐤋𐤄𐤉𐤊.𐤁𐤊
𐤋.𐤕𐤁𐤅𐤀𐤕𐤊.𐤅𐤁𐤊𐤋.𐤌𐤏𐤔𐤄.𐤉𐤃𐤉𐤊.𐤅𐤄𐤉𐤉𐤕.𐤀𐤊.𐤔𐤌
𐤇|

16 𐤔𐤋𐤅𐤔.𐤐𐤏𐤌𐤉𐤌.𐤁𐤔𐤍𐤄.𐤉𐤓𐤀𐤄.𐤊𐤋.𐤆𐤊𐤅𐤓𐤊.𐤀𐤕.
𐤐𐤍𐤉.𐤉𐤄𐤅𐤄.𐤀𐤋𐤄𐤉𐤊.𐤁𐤌𐤒𐤅𐤌.𐤀𐤔𐤓.𐤉𐤁𐤇𐤓.𐤁𐤇𐤂.𐤄𐤌
𐤑𐤅𐤕.𐤅𐤁𐤇𐤂.𐤄𐤔𐤁𐤏𐤅𐤕.𐤅𐤁𐤇𐤂.𐤄𐤎𐤊𐤅𐤕.𐤅𐤋𐤀.𐤉𐤓𐤀𐤄.
𐤀𐤕.𐤐𐤍𐤉.𐤉𐤄𐤅𐤄.𐤓𐤉𐤒𐤌|

17 𐤀𐤉𐤔.𐤊𐤌𐤕𐤍𐤕.𐤉𐤃𐤅.𐤊𐤁𐤓𐤊𐤕.𐤉𐤄𐤅𐤄.𐤀𐤋𐤄𐤉𐤊.𐤀
𐤔𐤓.𐤍𐤕𐤍.𐤋𐤊|

18 𐤔𐤐𐤈𐤉𐤌.𐤅𐤔𐤈𐤓𐤉𐤌.𐤕𐤕𐤍.𐤋𐤊.𐤁𐤊𐤋.𐤔𐤏𐤓𐤉𐤊.𐤀𐤔
𐤓.𐤉𐤄𐤅𐤄.𐤀𐤋𐤄𐤉𐤊.𐤍𐤕𐤍.𐤋𐤊.𐤋𐤔𐤁𐤈𐤉𐤊.𐤅𐤔𐤐𐤈𐤅.𐤀𐤕.𐤄𐤏
𐤌.𐤌𐤔𐤐𐤈.𐤑𐤃𐤒|

19 𐤋𐤀.𐤕𐤈𐤄.𐤌𐤔𐤐𐤈.𐤋𐤀.𐤕𐤊𐤉𐤓.𐤐𐤍𐤉𐤌.𐤅𐤋𐤀.𐤕𐤒𐤇.
𐤔𐤇𐤃.𐤊𐤉.𐤄𐤔𐤇𐤃.𐤉𐤏𐤅𐤓.𐤏𐤉𐤍𐤉.𐤇𐤊𐤌𐤉𐤌.𐤅𐤉𐤎𐤋𐤐.
𐤃𐤁𐤓𐤉.𐤑𐤃𐤉𐤒𐤌|

20 𐤑𐤃𐤒.𐤑𐤃𐤒.𐤕𐤓𐤃𐤐.𐤋𐤌𐤏𐤍.𐤕𐤇𐤉𐤄.𐤅𐤉𐤓𐤔𐤕.
𐤀𐤕.𐤄𐤀𐤓𐤑.𐤀𐤔𐤓.𐤉𐤄𐤅𐤄.𐤀𐤋𐤄𐤉𐤊.𐤍𐤕𐤍.𐤋𐤊|

21 𐤋𐤀.𐤕𐤈𐤏.𐤋𐤊.𐤀𐤔𐤓𐤄.𐤊𐤋.𐤏𐤑.𐤀𐤑𐤋.𐤌𐤆𐤁𐤇.𐤉
𐤄𐤅𐤄.𐤀𐤋𐤄𐤉𐤊.𐤀𐤔𐤓.𐤕𐤏𐤔𐤄.𐤋𐤊|

22 𐤅𐤋𐤀.𐤕𐤒𐤉𐤌.𐤋𐤊.𐤌𐤑𐤁𐤄.𐤀𐤔𐤓.𐤔𐤍𐤀.𐤉𐤄𐤅𐤄.𐤀𐤋
𐤄𐤉𐤊‖

𐤃𐤁𐤓𐤉𐤌.𐤇𐤋𐤒 17

1 𐤋𐤀.𐤕𐤆𐤁𐤇.𐤋𐤉𐤄𐤅𐤄.𐤀𐤋𐤄𐤉𐤊.𐤔𐤅𐤓.𐤅𐤔𐤄.𐤀𐤔𐤓.𐤉𐤄
𐤉𐤄.𐤁𐤅.𐤌𐤅𐤌.𐤊𐤋.𐤃𐤁𐤓.𐤓𐤏.𐤊𐤉.𐤕𐤅𐤏𐤁𐤕.𐤉𐤄𐤅𐤄.𐤀𐤋𐤄𐤉
𐤊.𐤄𐤅𐤀|

ב כי.ימצא.בקרבך.באחד.שעריך.אשר.יהו
ה.אלהיך.נתן.לך.איש.או.אשה.אשר.יעשה.א
ת.הרע.בעיני.יהוה.אלהיך.לעבר.בריתו|
ג וילך.ויעבד.אלהים.אחרים.וישתחו.לה
ם.ולשמש.או.לירח.או.לכל.צבא.השמים.אשר.
לא.צויתי|
ד והגד.לך.ושמעת.ודרשת.היטב.והנה.אמ
ת.נכון.הדבר.נעשתה.התועבה.הזאת.בישר
אל|
ה והוצאת.את.האיש.ההוא.או.את.האשה.ה
הוא.אשר.עשו.את.הדבר.הרע.הזה.אל.שערי
ך.את.האיש.או.את.האשה.וסקלתם.באבנים.ו
מתו|
ו על.פי.שנים.עדים.או.שלשה.עדים.יומת.
המת.לא.יומת.על.פי.עד.אחד|
ז יד.העדים.תהיה.בו.בראשנה.להמיתו.וי
ד.כל.העם.באחרנה.ובערת.הרע.מקרבך|
ח כי.יפלא.ממך.דבר.למשפט.בין.דם.לדם.ב
ין.דין.לדין.ובין.נגע.לנגע.דברי.ריבת.ב
שעריך.וקמת.ועלית.אל.המקום.אשר.יבחר.י
הוה.אלהיך.בו|
ט ובאת.אל.הכהנים.הלוים.ואל.השפט.אשר.
יהיה.בימים.ההם.ודרשת.והגידו.לך.את.ד
בר.המשפט|
י ועשית.על.פי.הדבר.אשר.יגידו.לך.מן.
המקום.ההוא.אשר.יבחר.יהוה.ושמרת.לעשות
.ככל.אשר.יורוך|
יא על.פי.התורה.אשר.יורוך.ועל.המשפט.אש
ר.יאמרו.לך.תעשה.לא.תסור.מן.הדבר.אשר.י
גידו.לך.ימין.ושמאל|

יב והאיש.אשר.יעשה.בזדון.לבלתי.שמע.אל.הכהן.העמד.לשרת.שם.את.יהוה.אלהיך.או.אל.השפט.ומת.האיש.ההוא.ובערת.הרע.מישראל|

יג וכל.העם.ישמעו.ויראו.ולא.יזידון.עוד|

יד כי.תבא.אל.הארץ.אשר.יהוה.אלהיך.נתן.לך.וירשתה.וישבתה.בה.ואמרת.אשימה.עלי.מלך.ככל.הגוים.אשר.סביבתי|

טו שום.תשים.עליך.מלך.אשר.יבחר.יהוה.אלהיך.בו.מקרב.אחיך.תשים.עליך.מלך.לא.תוכל.לתת.עליך.איש.נכרי.אשר.לא.אחיך.הוא|

טז רק.לא.ירבה.לו.סוסים.ולא.ישיב.את.העם.מצרימה.למען.הרבות.סוס.ויהוה.אמר.לכם.לא.תספון.לשוב.בדרך.הזה.עוד|

יז ולא.ירבה.לו.נשים.ולא.יסור.לבבו.וכסף.וזהב.לא.ירבה.לו.מאד|

יח והיה.כשבתו.על.כסא.ממלכתו.וכתב.לו.את.משנה.התורה.הזאת.על.ספר.מלפני.הכהנים.הלוים|

יט והיתה.עמו.וקרא.בו.כל.ימי.חייו.למען.ילמד.ליראה.את.יהוה.אלהיו.לשמר.את.כל.דברי.התורה.הזאת.ואת.החקים.האלה.לעשתם|

כ לבלתי.רום.לבבו.מאחיו.ולבלתי.סור.מן.המצוה.ימין.ושמאול.למען.יאריך.ימים.על.ממלכתו.הוא.ובניו.בקרב.ישראל||

דברים.חלק יח

א 𐤋𐤀.𐤉𐤄𐤉𐤄.𐤋𐤊𐤄𐤍𐤉𐤌.𐤄𐤋𐤅𐤉𐤌.𐤊𐤋.𐤔𐤁𐤈.𐤋𐤅𐤉.𐤇𐤋
𐤒.𐤅𐤍𐤇𐤋𐤄.𐤏𐤌.𐤉𐤔𐤓𐤀𐤋.𐤀𐤔𐤉.𐤉𐤄𐤅𐤄.𐤅𐤍𐤇𐤋𐤕𐤅.𐤉𐤀𐤊𐤋
𐤅𐤍|

ב 𐤅𐤍𐤇𐤋𐤄.𐤋𐤀.𐤉𐤄𐤉𐤄.𐤋𐤅.𐤁𐤒𐤓𐤁.𐤀𐤇𐤉𐤅.𐤉𐤄𐤅𐤄.𐤄𐤅𐤀.
𐤍𐤇𐤋𐤕𐤅.𐤊𐤀𐤔𐤓.𐤃𐤁𐤓.𐤋𐤅|

ג 𐤅𐤆𐤄.𐤉𐤄𐤉𐤄.𐤌𐤔𐤐𐤈.𐤄𐤊𐤄𐤍𐤉𐤌.𐤌𐤀𐤕.𐤄𐤏𐤌.𐤌𐤀
𐤕.𐤆𐤁𐤇𐤉.𐤄𐤆𐤁𐤇.𐤀𐤌.𐤔𐤅𐤓.𐤀𐤌.𐤔𐤄.𐤅𐤍𐤕𐤍.𐤋𐤊𐤄𐤍.𐤄
𐤆𐤓𐤏.𐤅𐤄𐤋𐤇𐤉𐤉𐤌.𐤅𐤄𐤒𐤁𐤄|

ד 𐤓𐤀𐤔𐤉𐤕.𐤃𐤂𐤍𐤊.𐤕𐤉𐤓𐤔𐤊.𐤅𐤉𐤑𐤄𐤓𐤊.𐤅𐤓𐤀𐤔𐤉𐤕.
𐤂𐤆.𐤑𐤀𐤍𐤊.𐤕𐤕𐤍.𐤋𐤅|

ה 𐤊𐤉.𐤁𐤅.𐤁𐤇𐤓.𐤉𐤄𐤅𐤄.𐤀𐤋𐤄𐤉𐤊.𐤌𐤊𐤋.𐤔𐤁𐤈𐤉𐤊.𐤋𐤏𐤌
𐤃.𐤋𐤔𐤓𐤕.𐤁𐤔𐤌.𐤉𐤄𐤅𐤄.𐤄𐤅𐤀.𐤅𐤁𐤍𐤉𐤅.𐤊𐤋.𐤄𐤉𐤌𐤉𐤌|

ו 𐤅𐤊𐤉.𐤉𐤁𐤀.𐤄𐤋𐤅𐤉.𐤌𐤀𐤇𐤃.𐤔𐤏𐤓𐤉𐤊.𐤌𐤊𐤋.𐤉𐤔𐤓𐤀𐤋.
𐤀𐤔𐤓.𐤄𐤅𐤀.𐤂𐤓.𐤔𐤌.𐤅𐤁𐤀.𐤁𐤊𐤋.𐤀𐤅𐤕.𐤍𐤐𐤔𐤅.𐤀𐤋.𐤄𐤌𐤒𐤅
𐤌.𐤀𐤔𐤓.𐤉𐤁𐤇𐤓.𐤉𐤄𐤅𐤄|

ז 𐤅𐤔𐤓𐤕.𐤁𐤔𐤌.𐤉𐤄𐤅𐤄.𐤀𐤋𐤄𐤉𐤅.𐤊𐤊𐤋.𐤀𐤇𐤉𐤅.𐤄𐤋𐤅𐤉𐤌.
𐤄𐤏𐤌𐤃𐤉𐤌.𐤔𐤌.𐤋𐤐𐤍𐤉.𐤉𐤄𐤅𐤄|

ח 𐤇𐤋𐤒.𐤊𐤇𐤋𐤒.𐤉𐤀𐤊𐤋𐤅.𐤋𐤁𐤃.𐤌𐤌𐤊𐤓𐤉𐤅.𐤏𐤋.𐤄𐤀𐤁𐤅
𐤕|

ט 𐤊𐤉.𐤀𐤕𐤄.𐤁𐤀.𐤀𐤋.𐤄𐤀𐤓𐤑.𐤀𐤔𐤓.𐤉𐤄𐤅𐤄.𐤀𐤋𐤄𐤉𐤊.
𐤍𐤕𐤍.𐤋𐤊.𐤋𐤀.𐤕𐤋𐤌𐤃.𐤋𐤏𐤔𐤅𐤕.𐤊𐤕𐤅𐤏𐤁𐤕.𐤄𐤂𐤅𐤉𐤌.𐤄𐤄
𐤌|

י 𐤋𐤀.𐤉𐤌𐤑𐤀.𐤁𐤊.𐤌𐤏𐤁𐤉𐤓.𐤁𐤍𐤅.𐤅𐤁𐤕𐤅.𐤁𐤀𐤔.𐤒𐤎𐤌.
𐤒𐤎𐤌𐤉𐤌.𐤌𐤏𐤅𐤍𐤍.𐤅𐤌𐤍𐤇𐤔.𐤅𐤌𐤊𐤔𐤐|

יא 𐤅𐤇𐤁𐤓.𐤇𐤁𐤓.𐤅𐤔𐤀𐤋.𐤀𐤅𐤁.𐤅𐤉𐤃𐤏𐤍𐤉.𐤅𐤃𐤓𐤔.𐤀𐤋.𐤄
𐤌𐤕𐤉𐤌|

יב 𐤊𐤉.𐤕𐤅𐤏𐤁𐤕.𐤉𐤄𐤅𐤄.𐤊𐤋.𐤏𐤔𐤄.𐤀𐤋𐤄.𐤅𐤁𐤂𐤋𐤋.𐤄𐤕
𐤅𐤏𐤁𐤕.𐤄𐤀𐤋𐤄.𐤉𐤄𐤅𐤄.𐤀𐤋𐤄𐤉𐤊.𐤌𐤅𐤓𐤉𐤔.𐤀𐤅𐤕𐤌.𐤌𐤐𐤍𐤉
𐤊|

יג 𐤕𐤌𐤉𐤌.𐤕𐤄𐤉𐤄.𐤏𐤌.𐤉𐤄𐤅𐤄.𐤀𐤋𐤄𐤉𐤊|

יד כי.הגוים.האלה.אשר.אתה.יורש.אותם.
אל.מעננים.ואל.קסמים.ישמעו.ואתה.לא.כן.נ
תן.לך.יהוה.אלהיך|
טו נביא.מקרבך.מאחיך.כמני.יקים.לך.יהו
ה.אלהיך.אליו.תשמעון|
טז ככל.אשר.שאלת.מעם.יהוה.אלהיך.בחרב
.ביום.הקהל.לאמר.לא.אסף.לשמע.את.קול.יהו
ה.אלהי.ואת.האש.הגדלה.הזאת.לא.אראה.
עוד.ולא.אמות|
יז ויאמר.יהוה.אלי.היטיבו.אשר.דברו|
יח נביא.אקים.להם.מקרב.אחיהם.כמוך.ונ
תתי.דברי.בפיו.ודבר.אליהם.את.כל.אשר.א
צונו|
יט והיה.האיש.אשר.לא.ישמע.אל.דברי.א
שר.ידבר.בשמי.אנכי.אדרש.מעמו|
כ אך.הנביא.אשר.יזיד.לדבר.דבר.בשמ
י.את.אשר.לא.צויתיו.לדבר.ואשר.ידבר.בשם
.אלהים.אחרים.ומת.הנביא.ההוא|
כא וכי.תאמר.בלבבך.איכה.נדע.את.הדבר.
אשר.לא.דברו.יהוה|
כב אשר.ידבר.הנביא.בשם.יהוה.ולא.יהיה.
הדבר.ולא.יבוא.הוא.הדבר.אשר.לא.דברו.יה
וה.בזדון.דברו.הנביא.לא.תגור.ממנו||

דברים.חלק יט

א כי.יכרית.יהוה.אלהיך.את.הגוים.אשר.י
הוה.אלהיך.נתן.לך.את.ארצם.וירשתם.וישבת
.בעריהם.ובבתיהם|
ב שלוש.ערים.תבדיל.לך.בתוך.ארצך.אשר.י
הוה.אלהיך.נתן.לך.לרשתה|

ג 𐤕𐤊𐤉𐤍.𐤋𐤊.𐤄𐤃𐤓𐤊.𐤅𐤔𐤋𐤔𐤕.𐤀𐤕.𐤂𐤁𐤅𐤋.𐤀𐤓𐤑𐤊.𐤀
𐤔𐤓.𐤉𐤍𐤇𐤉𐤋𐤊.𐤉𐤄𐤅𐤄.𐤀𐤋𐤄𐤉𐤊.𐤅𐤄𐤉𐤄.𐤋𐤍𐤅𐤎.𐤔𐤌𐤄.𐤊𐤋.
𐤓𐤑𐤇|

ד 𐤅𐤆𐤄.𐤃𐤁𐤓.𐤄𐤓𐤑𐤇.𐤀𐤔𐤓.𐤉𐤍𐤅𐤎.𐤔𐤌𐤄.𐤅𐤇𐤉.𐤀𐤔
𐤓.𐤉𐤊𐤄.𐤀𐤕.𐤓𐤏𐤄𐤅.𐤁𐤁𐤋𐤉.𐤃𐤏𐤕.𐤅𐤄𐤅𐤀.𐤋𐤀.𐤔𐤍𐤀.𐤋𐤅.𐤌
𐤕𐤌𐤋.𐤔𐤋𐤔𐤌|

ה 𐤅𐤀𐤔𐤓.𐤉𐤁𐤀.𐤀𐤕.𐤓𐤏𐤄𐤅.𐤁𐤉𐤏𐤓.𐤋𐤇𐤈𐤁.𐤏𐤑𐤉𐤌.𐤅𐤍
𐤃𐤇𐤄.𐤉𐤃𐤅.𐤁𐤂𐤓𐤆𐤍.𐤋𐤊𐤓𐤕.𐤄𐤏𐤑.𐤅𐤍𐤔𐤋.𐤄𐤁𐤓𐤆𐤋.𐤌
𐤍.𐤄𐤏𐤑.𐤅𐤌𐤑𐤀.𐤀𐤕.𐤓𐤏𐤄𐤅.𐤅𐤌𐤕.𐤄𐤅𐤀.𐤉𐤍𐤅𐤎.𐤀𐤋.𐤀𐤇
𐤕.𐤄𐤏𐤓𐤉𐤌.𐤄𐤀𐤋𐤄.𐤅𐤇𐤉|

ו 𐤐𐤍.𐤉𐤓𐤃𐤐.𐤂𐤀𐤋.𐤄𐤃𐤌.𐤀𐤇𐤓𐤉.𐤄𐤓𐤑𐤇.𐤊𐤉.𐤉𐤇𐤌.
𐤋𐤁𐤁𐤅.𐤅𐤄𐤔𐤉𐤂𐤅.𐤊𐤉.𐤉𐤓𐤁𐤄.𐤄𐤃𐤓𐤊.𐤅𐤄𐤊𐤄𐤅.𐤍𐤐𐤔.𐤅𐤋𐤅.
𐤀𐤉𐤍.𐤌𐤔𐤐𐤈.𐤌𐤅𐤕.𐤊𐤉.𐤋𐤀.𐤔𐤍𐤀.𐤄𐤅𐤀.𐤋𐤅.𐤌𐤕𐤌𐤅𐤋.𐤔𐤋
𐤔𐤅𐤌|

ז 𐤏𐤋.𐤊𐤍.𐤀𐤍𐤊𐤉.𐤌𐤑𐤅𐤊.𐤋𐤀𐤌𐤓.𐤔𐤋𐤔.𐤏𐤓𐤉𐤌.𐤕𐤁𐤃
𐤉𐤋.𐤋𐤊|

ח 𐤅𐤀𐤌.𐤉𐤓𐤇𐤉𐤁.𐤉𐤄𐤅𐤄.𐤀𐤋𐤄𐤉𐤊.𐤀𐤕.𐤂𐤁𐤋𐤊.𐤊𐤀𐤔𐤓
.𐤍𐤔𐤁𐤏.𐤋𐤀𐤁𐤕𐤉𐤊.𐤅𐤍𐤕𐤍.𐤋𐤊.𐤀𐤕.𐤊𐤋.𐤄𐤀𐤓𐤑.𐤀𐤔𐤓.𐤃
𐤁𐤓.𐤋𐤕𐤕.𐤋𐤀𐤁𐤕𐤉𐤊|

ט 𐤊𐤉.𐤕𐤔𐤌𐤓.𐤀𐤕.𐤊𐤋.𐤄𐤌𐤑𐤅𐤄.𐤄𐤆𐤀𐤕.𐤋𐤏𐤔𐤕𐤄.
𐤀𐤔𐤓.𐤀𐤍𐤊𐤉.𐤌𐤑𐤅𐤊.𐤄𐤉𐤅𐤌.𐤋𐤀𐤄𐤁𐤄.𐤀𐤕.𐤉𐤄𐤅𐤄.𐤀𐤋𐤄
𐤉𐤊.𐤅𐤋𐤋𐤊𐤕.𐤁𐤃𐤓𐤊𐤉𐤅.𐤊𐤋.𐤄𐤉𐤌𐤉𐤌.𐤅𐤉𐤎𐤐𐤕.𐤋𐤊.𐤏𐤅𐤃.
𐤔𐤋𐤔.𐤏𐤓𐤉𐤌.𐤏𐤋.𐤄𐤔𐤋𐤔.𐤄𐤀𐤋𐤄|

י 𐤅𐤋𐤀.𐤉𐤔𐤐𐤊.𐤃𐤌.𐤍𐤒𐤉.𐤁𐤒𐤓𐤁.𐤀𐤓𐤑𐤊.𐤀𐤔𐤓.𐤉𐤄
𐤅𐤄.𐤀𐤋𐤄𐤉𐤊.𐤍𐤕𐤍.𐤋𐤊.𐤍𐤇𐤋𐤄.𐤅𐤄𐤉𐤄.𐤏𐤋𐤉𐤊.𐤃𐤌𐤉𐤌|

יא 𐤅𐤊𐤉.𐤉𐤄𐤉𐤄.𐤀𐤉𐤔.𐤔𐤍𐤀.𐤋𐤓𐤏𐤄𐤅.𐤅𐤀𐤓𐤁.𐤋𐤅.𐤅𐤒𐤌.
𐤏𐤋𐤉𐤅.𐤅𐤄𐤊𐤄𐤅.𐤍𐤐𐤔.𐤅𐤌𐤕.𐤅𐤍𐤎.𐤀𐤋.𐤀𐤇𐤕.𐤄𐤏𐤓𐤉𐤌.𐤄𐤀
𐤋|

יב 𐤅𐤔𐤋𐤇𐤅.𐤆𐤒𐤍𐤉.𐤏𐤉𐤓𐤅.𐤅𐤋𐤒𐤇𐤅.𐤀𐤕𐤅.𐤌𐤔𐤌.𐤅𐤍𐤕𐤍𐤅
.𐤀𐤕𐤅.𐤁𐤉𐤃.𐤂𐤀𐤋.𐤄𐤃𐤌.𐤅𐤌𐤕|

יג לא תחוס עינך עליו ובערת דם הנקי מישראל וטוב לך|

יד לא תסיג גבול רעך אשר גבלו ראשנים בנחלתך אשר תנחל בארץ אשר יהוה אלהיך נתן לך לרשתה|

טו לא יקום עד אחד באיש לכל עון ולכל חטאת בכל חטא אשר יחטא על פי שני עדים או על פי שלשה עדים יקום דבר|

טז כי יקום עד חמס באיש לענות בו סרה|

יז ועמדו שני האנשים אשר להם הריב לפני יהוה לפני הכהנים והשפטים אשר יהיו בימים ההם|

יח ודרשו השפטים היטב והנה עד שקר העד שקר ענה באחיו|

יט ועשיתם לו כאשר זמם לעשות לאחיו ובערת הרע מקרבך|

כ והנשארים ישמעו ויראו ולא יספו לעשות עוד כדבר הרע הזה בקרבך|

כא ולא תחוס עינך נפש בנפש עין בעין שן בשן יד ביד רגל ברגל||

דברים חלק כ

א כי תצא למלחמה על איבך וראית סוס ורכב עם רב ממך לא תירא מהם כי יהוה אלהיך עמך המעלך מארץ מצרים|

ב והיה כקרבכם אל המלחמה ונגש הכהן ודבר אל העם|

ג ואמר אלהם שמע ישראל אתם קרבים היום למלחמה על איביכם אל ירך לבבכם אל תיראו ואל תחפזו ואל תערצו מפניהם|

𐤃 𐤊𐤉.𐤉𐤄𐤅𐤄.𐤀𐤋𐤄𐤉𐤊𐤌.𐤄𐤄𐤋𐤊.𐤏𐤌𐤊𐤌.𐤋𐤄𐤋𐤇𐤌.𐤋
𐤊𐤌.𐤏𐤌.𐤀𐤉𐤁𐤉𐤊𐤌.𐤋𐤄𐤅𐤔𐤉𐤏.𐤀𐤕𐤊𐤌|
𐤄 𐤅𐤃𐤁𐤓𐤅.𐤄𐤔𐤈𐤓𐤉𐤌.𐤀𐤋.𐤄𐤏𐤌.𐤋𐤀𐤌𐤓.𐤌𐤉.𐤄𐤀𐤉𐤔.
𐤀𐤔𐤓.𐤁𐤍𐤄.𐤁𐤉𐤕.𐤇𐤃𐤔.𐤅𐤋𐤀.𐤇𐤍𐤊𐤅.𐤉𐤋𐤊.𐤅𐤉𐤔𐤁.𐤋𐤁𐤉
𐤕𐤅.𐤐𐤍.𐤉𐤌𐤅𐤕.𐤁𐤌𐤋𐤇𐤌𐤄.𐤅𐤀𐤉𐤔.𐤀𐤇𐤓.𐤉𐤇𐤍𐤊𐤍𐤅|
𐤅 𐤅𐤌𐤉.𐤄𐤀𐤉𐤔.𐤀𐤔𐤓.𐤍𐤈𐤏.𐤊𐤓𐤌.𐤅𐤋𐤀.𐤇𐤋𐤋𐤅.𐤉𐤋𐤊.𐤅𐤉
𐤔𐤁.𐤋𐤁𐤉𐤕𐤅.𐤐𐤍.𐤉𐤌𐤅𐤕.𐤁𐤌𐤋𐤇𐤌𐤄.𐤅𐤀𐤉𐤔.𐤀𐤇𐤓.𐤉𐤇𐤋𐤋
𐤍𐤅|
𐤆 𐤅𐤌𐤉.𐤄𐤀𐤉𐤔.𐤀𐤔𐤓.𐤀𐤓𐤔.𐤀𐤔𐤄.𐤅𐤋𐤀.𐤋𐤒𐤇𐤄.𐤉𐤋𐤊
.𐤅𐤉𐤔𐤁.𐤋𐤁𐤉𐤕𐤅.𐤐𐤍.𐤉𐤌𐤅𐤕.𐤁𐤌𐤋𐤇𐤌𐤄.𐤅𐤀𐤉𐤔.𐤀𐤇𐤓.𐤉
𐤒𐤇𐤍𐤄|
𐤇 𐤅𐤉𐤎𐤐𐤅.𐤄𐤔𐤈𐤓𐤉𐤌.𐤋𐤃𐤁𐤓.𐤀𐤋.𐤄𐤏𐤌.𐤅𐤀𐤌𐤓𐤅.𐤌𐤉.𐤄
𐤀𐤉𐤔.𐤄𐤉𐤓𐤀.𐤅𐤓𐤊.𐤄𐤋𐤁𐤁.𐤉𐤋𐤊.𐤅𐤉𐤔𐤁.𐤋𐤁𐤉𐤕𐤅.𐤅𐤋𐤀.𐤉𐤌
𐤎.𐤀𐤕.𐤋𐤁𐤁.𐤀𐤇𐤉𐤅.𐤊𐤋𐤁𐤁𐤅|
𐤈 𐤅𐤄𐤉𐤄.𐤊𐤊𐤋𐤕.𐤄𐤔𐤈𐤓𐤉𐤌.𐤋𐤃𐤁𐤓.𐤀𐤋.𐤄𐤏𐤌.𐤅𐤐𐤒
𐤃𐤅.𐤔𐤓𐤉.𐤑𐤁𐤀𐤅𐤕.𐤁𐤓𐤀𐤔.𐤄𐤏𐤌|
𐤉 𐤊𐤉.𐤕𐤒𐤓𐤁.𐤀𐤋.𐤏𐤉𐤓.𐤋𐤄𐤋𐤇𐤌.𐤏𐤋𐤉𐤄.𐤅𐤒𐤓𐤀𐤕.
𐤀𐤋𐤉𐤄.𐤋𐤔𐤋𐤅𐤌|
𐤉𐤀 𐤅𐤄𐤉𐤄.𐤀𐤌.𐤔𐤋𐤅𐤌.𐤕𐤏𐤍𐤊.𐤅𐤐𐤕𐤇𐤄.𐤋𐤊.𐤅𐤄𐤉𐤄.𐤊𐤋.
𐤄𐤏𐤌.𐤄𐤍𐤌𐤑𐤀.𐤁𐤄.𐤉𐤄𐤉𐤅.𐤋𐤊.𐤋𐤌𐤎.𐤅𐤏𐤁𐤃𐤅𐤊|
𐤉𐤁 𐤅𐤀𐤌.𐤋𐤀.𐤕𐤔𐤋𐤉𐤌.𐤏𐤌𐤊.𐤅𐤏𐤔𐤕𐤄.𐤏𐤌𐤊.𐤌𐤋𐤇𐤌
𐤄.𐤅𐤑𐤓𐤕.𐤏𐤋𐤉𐤄|
𐤉𐤂 𐤅𐤍𐤕𐤍𐤄.𐤉𐤄𐤅𐤄.𐤀𐤋𐤄𐤉𐤊.𐤁𐤉𐤃𐤊.𐤅𐤄𐤊𐤉𐤕.𐤀𐤕.𐤊𐤋
.𐤆𐤊𐤅𐤓𐤄.𐤋𐤐𐤉.𐤇𐤓𐤁|
𐤉𐤃 𐤓𐤒.𐤄𐤍𐤔𐤉𐤌.𐤅𐤄𐤈𐤐.𐤅𐤄𐤁𐤄𐤌𐤄.𐤅𐤊𐤋.𐤀𐤔𐤓.𐤉𐤄𐤉
𐤄.𐤁𐤏𐤉𐤓.𐤊𐤋.𐤔𐤋𐤋𐤄.𐤕𐤁𐤆.𐤋𐤊.𐤅𐤀𐤊𐤋𐤕.𐤀𐤕.𐤔𐤋𐤋.𐤀𐤉
𐤁𐤉𐤊.𐤀𐤔𐤓.𐤍𐤕𐤍.𐤉𐤄𐤅𐤄.𐤀𐤋𐤄𐤉𐤊.𐤋𐤊|
𐤈𐤅 𐤊𐤍.𐤕𐤏𐤔𐤄.𐤋𐤊𐤋.𐤄𐤏𐤓𐤉𐤌.𐤄𐤓𐤇𐤒𐤕.𐤌𐤌𐤊.𐤌𐤀𐤃
.𐤀𐤔𐤓.𐤋𐤀.𐤌𐤏𐤓𐤉.𐤄𐤂𐤅𐤉𐤌.𐤄𐤀𐤋𐤄.𐤄𐤍𐤄|
𐤈𐤆 𐤓𐤒.𐤌𐤏𐤓𐤉.𐤄𐤏𐤌𐤉𐤌.𐤄𐤀𐤋𐤄.𐤀𐤔𐤓.𐤉𐤄𐤅𐤄.𐤀𐤋𐤄𐤉
𐤊.𐤍𐤕𐤍.𐤋𐤊.𐤍𐤇𐤋𐤄.𐤋𐤀.𐤕𐤇𐤉𐤄.𐤊𐤋.𐤍𐤔𐤌𐤄|

יז כי.החרם.תחרימם.החתי.והאמרי.הכנעני.והפרזי.החוי.והיבוסי.כאשר.צוך.יהוה.אלהיך|

יח למען.אשר.לא.ילמדו.אתכם.לעשות.ככל.תועבתם.אשר.עשו.לאלהיהם.וחטאתם.ליהוה.אלהיכם|

יט כי.תצור.אל.עיר.ימים.רבים.להלחם.עליה.לתפשה.לא.תשחית.את.עצה.לנדח.עליו.גרזן.כי.ממנו.תאכל.ואתו.לא.תכרת.כי.האדם.עץ.השדה.לבא.מפניך.במצור|

כ רק.עץ.אשר.תדע.כי.לא.עץ.מאכל.הוא.אתו.תשחית.וכרת.ובנית.מצור.על.העיר.אשר.הוא.עשה.עמך.מלחמה.עד.רדתה||

דברים.חלק כא

א כי.ימצא.חלל.באדמה.אשר.יהוה.אלהיך.נתן.לך.לרשתה.נפל.בשדה.לא.נודע.מי.הכהו|

ב ויצאו.זקניך.ושפטיך.ומדדו.אל.הערים.אשר.סביבת.החלל|

ג והיה.העיר.הקרבה.אל.החלל.ולקחו.זקני.העיר.ההוא.עגלת.בקר.אשר.לא.עבד.בה.אשר.לא.משכה.בעל|

ד והורדו.זקני.העיר.ההוא.את.העגלה.אל.נחל.איתן.אשר.לא.יעבד.בו.ולא.יזרע.וערפו.שם.את.העגלה.בנחל|

ה ונגשו.הכהנים.בני.לוי.כי.בם.בחר.יהוה.אלהיך.לשרתו.ולברך.בשם.יהוה.ועל.פיהם.יהיה.כל.ריב.וכל.נגע|

ו וכל.זקני.העיר.ההוא.הקרבים.אל.החלל.
ירחצו.את.ידיהם.על.העגלה.הערופה.בנח
ל|
ז וענו.ואמרו.ידינו.לא.שפכה.||שפכו.קרי||.א
ת.הדם.הזה.ועינינו.לא.ראו|
ח כפר.לעמך.ישראל.אשר.פדית.יהוה.ואל.ת
תן.דם.נקי.בקרב.עמך.ישראל.ונכפר.להם.הד
ם|
ט ואתה.תבער.הדם.הנקי.מקרבך.כי.תעש
ה.הישר.בעיני.יהוה|
י כי.תצא.למלחמה.על.איביך.ונתנו.יהוה
.אלהיך.בידך.ושבית.שביו|
יא וראית.בשביה.אשת.יפת.תאר.וחשקת.ב
ה.ולקחת.לך.לאשה|
יב והבאתה.אל.תוך.ביתך.וגלחה.את.ראשה
.ועשתה.את.צפרניה|
יג והסירה.את.שמלת.שביה.מעליה.וישבה.
בביתך.ובכתה.את.אביה.ואת.אמה.ירח.ימי
ם.ואחר.כן.תבוא.אליה.ובעלתה.והיתה.לך.לא
שה|
יד והיה.אם.לא.חפצת.בה.ושלחתה.לנפשה.
ומכר.לא.תמכרנה.בכסף.לא.תתעמר.בה.תחת.
אשר.עניתה|
טו כי.תהיין.לאיש.שתי.נשים.האחת.אהו
בה.והאחת.שנואה.וילדו.לו.בנים.האהובה.וה
שנואה.והיה.הבן.הבכור.לשניאה|
טז והיה.ביום.הנחילו.את.בניו.את.אשר.יה
יה.לו.לא.יוכל.לבכר.את.בן.האהובה.על.פני.ב
ן.השנואה.הבכר|

17 כי.את.הבכר.בן.השנואה.יכיר.לתת.לו.פ
י.שנים.בכל.אשר.ימצא.לו.כי.הוא.ראשית.אנ
ו.לו.משפט.הבכרה|

18 כי.יהיה.לאיש.בן.סורר.ומורה.איננו.שמ
ע.בקול.אביו.ובקול.אמו.ויסרו.אתו.ולא.ישמע
.אליהם|

19 ותפשו.בו.אביו.ואמו.והוציאו.אתו.אל.ז
קני.עירו.ואל.שער.מקמו|

20 ואמרו.אל.זקני.עירו.בננו.זה.סורר.ומר
ה.איננו.שמע.בקלנו.זולל.וסבא|

21 ורגמהו.כל.אנשי.עירו.באבנים.ומת.ובע
רת.הרע.מקרבך.וכל.ישראל.ישמעו.ויראו|

22 וכי.יהיה.באיש.חטא.משפט.מות.והומת.
ותלית.אתו.על.עץ|

23 לא.תלין.נבלתו.על.העץ.כי.קבור.תקברנ
ו.ביום.ההוא.כי.קללת.אלהים.תלוי.ולא.תטמ
א.את.אדמתך.אשר.יהוה.אלהיך.נתן.לך.נחל
ה||

דברים.חלק 22

1 לא.תראה.את.שור.אחיך.או.את.שיו.נדחי
ם.והתעלמת.מהם.השב.תשיבם.לאחיך|

2 ואם.לא.קרוב.אחיך.אליך.ולא.ידעתו.וא
ספתו.אל.תוך.ביתך.והיה.עמך.עד.דרש.אחי
ך.אתו.והשבתו.לו|

3 וכן.תעשה.לחמרו.וכן.תעשה.לשמלתו.וכן.
תעשה.לכל.אבדת.אחיך.אשר.תאבד.ממנו.ומ
צאתה.לא.תוכל.להתעלם|

4 לא.תראה.את.חמור.אחיך.או.שורו.נפלים.
בדרך.והתעלמת.מהם.הקם.תקים.עמו|

5 𐤋𐤀.𐤉𐤄𐤉𐤄.𐤊𐤋𐤉.𐤂𐤁𐤓.𐤏𐤋.𐤀𐤔𐤄.𐤅𐤋𐤀.𐤉𐤋𐤁𐤔.𐤂𐤁
𐤓.𐤔𐤌𐤋𐤕.𐤀𐤔𐤄.𐤊𐤉.𐤕𐤅𐤏𐤁𐤕.𐤉𐤄𐤅𐤄.𐤀𐤋𐤄𐤉𐤊.𐤊𐤋.𐤏𐤔
𐤄.𐤀𐤋𐤄|
6 𐤊𐤉.𐤉𐤒𐤓𐤀.𐤒𐤍.𐤑𐤐𐤅𐤓.𐤋𐤐𐤍𐤉𐤊.𐤁𐤃𐤓𐤊.𐤁𐤊𐤋.𐤏𐤑.𐤀
𐤅.𐤏𐤋.𐤄𐤀𐤓𐤑.𐤀𐤐𐤓𐤇𐤉𐤌.𐤀𐤅.𐤁𐤉𐤑𐤉𐤌.𐤅𐤄𐤀𐤌.𐤓𐤁𐤑𐤕.
𐤏𐤋.𐤄𐤀𐤐𐤓𐤇𐤉𐤌.𐤀𐤅.𐤏𐤋.𐤄𐤁𐤉𐤑𐤉𐤌.𐤋𐤀.𐤕𐤒𐤇.𐤄𐤀𐤌.
𐤏𐤋.𐤄𐤁𐤍𐤉𐤌|
7 𐤔𐤋𐤇.𐤕𐤔𐤋𐤇.𐤀𐤕.𐤄𐤀𐤌.𐤅𐤀𐤕.𐤄𐤁𐤍𐤉𐤌.𐤕𐤒𐤇.𐤋𐤊
.𐤋𐤌𐤏𐤍.𐤉𐤉𐤈𐤁.𐤋𐤊.𐤅𐤄𐤀𐤓𐤊𐤕.𐤉𐤌𐤉𐤌|
8 𐤊𐤉.𐤕𐤁𐤍𐤄.𐤁𐤉𐤕.𐤇𐤃𐤔.𐤅𐤏𐤔𐤉𐤕.𐤌𐤏𐤒𐤄.𐤋𐤂𐤂𐤊.
𐤅𐤋𐤀.𐤕𐤔𐤉𐤌.𐤃𐤌𐤉𐤌.𐤁𐤁𐤉𐤕𐤊.𐤊𐤉.𐤉𐤐𐤋.𐤄𐤍𐤐𐤋.𐤌𐤌𐤍𐤅|
9 𐤋𐤀.𐤕𐤆𐤓𐤏.𐤊𐤓𐤌𐤊.𐤊𐤋𐤀𐤉𐤌.𐤐𐤍.𐤕𐤒𐤃𐤔.𐤄𐤌𐤋𐤀
𐤄.𐤄𐤆𐤓𐤏.𐤀𐤔𐤓.𐤕𐤆𐤓𐤏.𐤅𐤕𐤁𐤅𐤀𐤕.𐤄𐤊𐤓𐤌|
10 𐤋𐤀.𐤕𐤇𐤓𐤔.𐤁𐤔𐤅𐤓.𐤅𐤁𐤇𐤌𐤓.𐤉𐤇𐤃𐤅|
11 𐤋𐤀.𐤕𐤋𐤁𐤔.𐤔𐤏𐤈𐤍𐤆.𐤑𐤌𐤓.𐤅𐤐𐤔𐤕𐤉𐤌.𐤉𐤇𐤃𐤅|
12 𐤂𐤃𐤋𐤉𐤌.𐤕𐤏𐤔𐤄.𐤋𐤊.𐤏𐤋.𐤀𐤓𐤁𐤏.𐤊𐤍𐤐𐤅𐤕.𐤊𐤎𐤅𐤕
𐤊.𐤀𐤔𐤓.𐤕𐤊𐤎𐤄.𐤁𐤄|
13 𐤊𐤉.𐤉𐤒𐤇.𐤀𐤉𐤔.𐤀𐤔𐤄.𐤅𐤁𐤀.𐤀𐤋𐤉𐤄.𐤅𐤔𐤍𐤀𐤄|
14 𐤅𐤔𐤌.𐤋𐤄.𐤏𐤋𐤉𐤋𐤕.𐤃𐤁𐤓𐤉𐤌.𐤅𐤄𐤅𐤑𐤀.𐤏𐤋𐤉𐤄.𐤔
𐤌.𐤓𐤏.𐤅𐤀𐤌𐤓.𐤀𐤕.𐤄𐤀𐤔𐤄.𐤄𐤆𐤀𐤕.𐤋𐤒𐤇𐤕𐤉.𐤅𐤀𐤒𐤓𐤁.
𐤀𐤋𐤉𐤄.𐤅𐤋𐤀.𐤌𐤑𐤀𐤕𐤉.𐤋𐤄.𐤁𐤕𐤅𐤋𐤉𐤌|
15 𐤅𐤋𐤒𐤇.𐤀𐤁𐤉.𐤄𐤍𐤏𐤓.‖𐤄𐤍𐤏𐤓𐤄.𐤒𐤓𐤉‖.𐤅𐤀𐤌𐤄.𐤅𐤄𐤅
𐤑𐤉𐤀𐤅.𐤀𐤕.𐤁𐤕𐤅𐤋𐤉.𐤄𐤍𐤏𐤓.‖𐤄𐤍𐤏𐤓𐤄.𐤒𐤓𐤉‖.𐤀𐤋.𐤆𐤒𐤍
𐤉.𐤄𐤏𐤉𐤓.𐤄𐤔𐤏𐤓𐤄|
16 𐤅𐤀𐤌𐤓.𐤀𐤁𐤉.𐤄𐤍𐤏𐤓.‖𐤄𐤍𐤏𐤓𐤄.𐤒𐤓𐤉‖.𐤀𐤋.𐤄𐤆𐤒𐤍𐤉
𐤌.𐤀𐤕.𐤁𐤕𐤉.𐤍𐤕𐤕𐤉.𐤋𐤀𐤉𐤔.𐤄𐤆𐤄.𐤋𐤀𐤔𐤄.𐤅𐤉𐤔𐤍𐤀𐤄|
17 𐤅𐤄𐤍𐤄.𐤄𐤅𐤀.𐤔𐤌.𐤏𐤋𐤉𐤋𐤕.𐤃𐤁𐤓𐤉𐤌.𐤋𐤀𐤌𐤓.𐤋𐤀.𐤌
𐤑𐤀𐤕𐤉.𐤋𐤁𐤕𐤊.𐤁𐤕𐤅𐤋𐤉𐤌.𐤅𐤀𐤋𐤄.𐤁𐤕𐤅𐤋𐤉.𐤁𐤕𐤉.𐤅𐤉𐤐𐤓𐤔𐤅.
𐤄𐤔𐤌𐤋𐤄.𐤋𐤐𐤍𐤉.𐤆𐤒𐤍𐤉.𐤄𐤏𐤉𐤓|
18 𐤅𐤋𐤒𐤇𐤅.𐤆𐤒𐤍𐤉.𐤄𐤏𐤉𐤓.𐤄𐤄𐤅𐤀.𐤀𐤕.𐤄𐤀𐤉𐤔.𐤅𐤉𐤎
𐤓𐤅.𐤀𐤕𐤅|

יט וענשו.אתו.מאה.כסף.ונתנו.לאבי.הנערה.
כי.הוציא.שם.רע.על.בתולת.ישראל.ולו.תהי
ה.לאשה.לא.יוכל.לשלחה.כל.ימיו|
כ ואם.אמת.היה.הדבר.הזה.לא.נמצאו.ב
תולים.לנער.||לנערה.קרי|||
כא והוציאו.את.הנער.||הנערה.קרי||.אל.פתח
.בית.אביה.וסקלוה.אנשי.עירה.באבנים.ומת
ה.כי.עשתה.נבלה.בישראל.לזנות.בית.אביה
.ובערת.הרע.מקרבך|
כב כי.ימצא.איש.שכב.עם.אשה.בעלת.בעל.
ומתו.גם.שניהם.האיש.השכב.עם.האשה.והא
שה.ובערת.הרע.מישראל|
כג כי.יהיה.נער.||נערה.קרי||.בתולה.מארש
ה.לאיש.ומצאה.איש.בעיר.ושכב.עמה|
כד והוצאתם.את.שניהם.אל.שער.העיר.הה
וא.וסקלתם.אתם.באבנים.ומתו.את.הנער.||הנ
ערה.קרי||.על.דבר.אשר.לא.צעקה.בעיר.ואת.
האיש.על.דבר.אשר.ענה.את.אשת.רעהו.ובער
ת.הרע.מקרבך|
כה ואם.בשדה.ימצא.האיש.את.הנער.||הנע
רה.קרי||.המארשה.והחזיק.בה.האיש.ושכב.
עמה.ומת.האיש.אשר.שכב.עמה.לבדו|
כו ולנער.||ולנערה.קרי||.לא.תעשה.דבר.אין.
לנער.||לנערה.קרי||.חטא.מות.כי.כאשר.יקום.
איש.על.רעהו.ורצחו.נפש.כן.הדבר.הזה|
כז כי.בשדה.מצאה.צעקה.הנער.||הנערה.
קרי||.המארשה.ואין.מושיע.לה|
כח כי.ימצא.איש.נער.||נערה.קרי||.בתולה.א
שר.לא.ארשה.ותפשה.ושכב.עמה.ונמצאו|

29 𐤅𐤍𐤕𐤍.𐤄𐤀𐤉𐤔.𐤄𐤔𐤊𐤁.𐤏𐤌𐤄.𐤋𐤀𐤁𐤉.𐤄𐤍𐤏𐤓.||𐤄𐤍
𐤏𐤓𐤄.𐤒𐤓𐤉||.𐤇𐤌𐤔𐤉𐤌.𐤊𐤎𐤐.𐤅𐤋𐤅.𐤕𐤄𐤉𐤄.𐤋𐤀𐤔𐤄.𐤕𐤇
𐤕.𐤀𐤔𐤓.𐤏𐤍𐤄.𐤋𐤀.𐤉𐤅𐤊𐤋.𐤔𐤋𐤇𐤄.𐤊𐤋.𐤉𐤌𐤉𐤅||

𐤃𐤁𐤓𐤉𐤌.𐤇𐤋𐤒 23

1 𐤋𐤀.𐤉𐤒𐤇.𐤀𐤉𐤔.𐤀𐤕.𐤀𐤔𐤕.𐤀𐤁𐤉𐤅.𐤅𐤋𐤀.𐤉𐤂𐤋𐤄.𐤊𐤍
𐤐.𐤀𐤁𐤉𐤅|
2 𐤋𐤀.𐤉𐤁𐤀.𐤐𐤑𐤅𐤏.𐤃𐤊𐤀.𐤅𐤊𐤓𐤅𐤕.𐤔𐤐𐤊𐤄.𐤁𐤒𐤄𐤋.𐤉𐤄
𐤅𐤄|
3 𐤋𐤀.𐤉𐤁𐤀.𐤌𐤌𐤆𐤓.𐤁𐤒𐤄𐤋.𐤉𐤄𐤅𐤄.𐤂𐤌.𐤃𐤅𐤓.𐤏𐤔𐤉𐤓
𐤉.𐤋𐤀.𐤉𐤁𐤀.𐤋𐤅.𐤁𐤒𐤄𐤋.𐤉𐤄𐤅𐤄|
4 𐤋𐤀.𐤉𐤁𐤀.𐤏𐤌𐤅𐤍𐤉.𐤅𐤌𐤅𐤀𐤁𐤉.𐤁𐤒𐤄𐤋.𐤉𐤄𐤅𐤄.𐤂𐤌.𐤃
𐤅𐤓.𐤏𐤔𐤉𐤓𐤉.𐤋𐤀.𐤉𐤁𐤀.𐤋𐤄𐤌.𐤁𐤒𐤄𐤋.𐤉𐤄𐤅𐤄.𐤏𐤃.𐤏𐤅𐤋𐤌|
5 𐤏𐤋.𐤃𐤁𐤓.𐤀𐤔𐤓.𐤋𐤀.𐤒𐤃𐤌𐤅.𐤀𐤕𐤊𐤌.𐤁𐤋𐤇𐤌.𐤅𐤁𐤌𐤉
𐤌.𐤁𐤃𐤓𐤊.𐤁𐤑𐤀𐤕𐤊𐤌.𐤌𐤌𐤑𐤓𐤉𐤌.𐤅𐤀𐤔𐤓.𐤔𐤊𐤓.𐤏𐤋𐤉𐤊.
𐤀𐤕.𐤁𐤋𐤏𐤌.𐤁𐤍.𐤁𐤏𐤅𐤓.𐤌𐤐𐤕𐤅𐤓.𐤀𐤓𐤌.𐤍𐤄𐤓𐤉𐤌.𐤋𐤒𐤋𐤋𐤊|
6 𐤅𐤋𐤀.𐤀𐤁𐤄.𐤉𐤄𐤅𐤄.𐤀𐤋𐤄𐤉𐤊.𐤋𐤔𐤌𐤏.𐤀𐤋.𐤁𐤋𐤏𐤌.𐤅𐤉
𐤄𐤐𐤊.𐤉𐤄𐤅𐤄.𐤀𐤋𐤄𐤉𐤊.𐤋𐤊.𐤀𐤕.𐤄𐤒𐤋𐤋𐤄.𐤋𐤁𐤓𐤊𐤄.𐤊𐤉.𐤀
𐤄𐤁𐤊.𐤉𐤄𐤅𐤄.𐤀𐤋𐤄𐤉𐤊|
7 𐤋𐤀.𐤕𐤃𐤓𐤔.𐤔𐤋𐤌𐤌.𐤅𐤈𐤁𐤕𐤌.𐤊𐤋.𐤉𐤌𐤉𐤊.𐤋𐤏𐤅𐤋𐤌|
8 𐤋𐤀.𐤕𐤕𐤏𐤁.𐤀𐤃𐤌𐤉.𐤊𐤉.𐤀𐤇𐤉𐤊.𐤄𐤅𐤀.
𐤋𐤀.𐤕𐤕𐤏𐤁.𐤌𐤑𐤓𐤉.𐤊𐤉.𐤂𐤓.𐤄𐤉𐤉𐤕.𐤁𐤀𐤓𐤑𐤅|
9 𐤁𐤍𐤉𐤌.𐤀𐤔𐤓.𐤉𐤅𐤋𐤃𐤅.𐤋𐤄𐤌.𐤃𐤅𐤓.𐤔𐤋𐤉𐤔𐤉.𐤉𐤁𐤀.𐤋
𐤄𐤌.𐤁𐤒𐤄𐤋.𐤉𐤄𐤅𐤄|
10 𐤊𐤉.𐤕𐤑𐤀.𐤌𐤇𐤍𐤄.𐤏𐤋.𐤀𐤉𐤁𐤉𐤊.𐤅𐤍𐤔𐤌𐤓𐤕.𐤌𐤊𐤋.
𐤃𐤁𐤓.𐤓𐤏|
11 𐤊𐤉.𐤉𐤄𐤉𐤄.𐤁𐤊.𐤀𐤉𐤔.𐤀𐤔𐤓.𐤋𐤀.𐤉𐤄𐤉𐤄.𐤈𐤄𐤅𐤓.𐤌
𐤒𐤓𐤄.𐤋𐤉𐤋𐤄.𐤅𐤉𐤑𐤀.𐤀𐤋.𐤌𐤇𐤅𐤑.𐤋𐤌𐤇𐤍𐤄.𐤋𐤀.𐤉𐤁𐤀.𐤀
𐤋.𐤕𐤅𐤊.𐤄𐤌𐤇𐤍𐤄|

יב והיה.לפנות.ערב.ירחץ.במים.וכבא.השמ
ש.יבא.אל.תוך.המחנה׃
יג ויד.תהיה.לך.מחוץ.למחנה.ויצאת.שמ
ה.חוץ׃
יד ויתד.תהיה.לך.על.אזנך.והיה.בשבתך.
חוץ.וחפרתה.בה.ושבת.וכסית.את.צאתך׃
טו כי.יהוה.אלהיך.מתהלך.בקרב.מחנך.לה
צילך.ולתת.איביך.לפניך.והיה.מחניך.קדו
ש.ולא.יראה.בך.ערות.דבר.ושב.מאחריך׃
טז לא.תסגיר.עבד.אל.אדניו.אשר.ינצל.א
ליך.מעם.אדניו׃
יז עמך.ישב.בקרבך.במקום.אשר.יבחר.בא
חד.שעריך.בטוב.לו.לא.תוננו׃
יח לא.תהיה.קדשה.מבנות.ישראל.ולא.יהי
ה.קדש.מבני.ישראל׃
יט לא.תביא.אתנן.זונה.ומחיר.כלב.בית.י
הוה.אלהיך.לכל.נדר.כי.תועבת.יהוה.אלהיך
.גם.שניהם׃
כ לא.תשיך.לאחיך.נשך.כסף.נשך.אכל.נש
ך.כל.דבר.אשר.ישך׃
כא לנכרי.תשיך.ולאחיך.לא.תשיך.למען.יב
רכך.יהוה.אלהיך.בכל.משלח.ידך.על.הארץ.
אשר.אתה.בא.שמה.לרשתה׃
כב כי.תדר.נדר.ליהוה.אלהיך.לא.תאחר.ל
שלמו.כי.דרש.ידרשנו.יהוה.אלהיך.מעמך.ו
היה.בך.חטא׃
כג וכי.תחדל.לנדר.לא.יהיה.בך.חטא׃
כד מוצא.שפתיך.תשמר.ועשית.כאשר.נדר
ת.ליהוה.אלהיך.נדבה.אשר.דברת.בפיך׃
כה כי.תבא.בכרם.רעך.ואכלת.ענבים.כנפשך
.שבעך.ואל.כליך.לא.תתן׃

26 𐤊𐤉.𐤕𐤁𐤀.𐤁𐤒𐤌𐤕.𐤓𐤏𐤊.𐤅𐤒𐤈𐤐𐤕.𐤌𐤋𐤉𐤋𐤕.𐤁𐤉𐤃𐤊.𐤅𐤇𐤓𐤌𐤔.𐤋𐤀.𐤕𐤍𐤉𐤐.𐤏𐤋.𐤒𐤌𐤕.𐤓𐤏𐤊|

𐤃𐤁𐤓𐤉𐤌.𐤇𐤋𐤒 24

1 𐤊𐤉.𐤉𐤒𐤇.𐤀𐤉𐤔.𐤀𐤔𐤄.𐤅𐤁𐤏𐤋𐤄.𐤅𐤄𐤉𐤄.𐤀𐤌.𐤋𐤀.𐤕𐤌𐤑𐤀.𐤇𐤍.𐤁𐤏𐤉𐤍𐤉𐤅.𐤊𐤉.𐤌𐤑𐤀.𐤁𐤄.𐤏𐤓𐤅𐤕.𐤃𐤁𐤓.𐤅𐤊𐤕𐤁.𐤋𐤄.𐤎𐤐𐤓.𐤊𐤓𐤉𐤕𐤕.𐤅𐤍𐤕𐤍.𐤁𐤉𐤃𐤄.𐤅𐤔𐤋𐤇𐤄.𐤌𐤁𐤉𐤕𐤅|

2 𐤅𐤉𐤑𐤀𐤄.𐤌𐤁𐤉𐤕𐤅.𐤅𐤄𐤋𐤊𐤄.𐤅𐤄𐤉𐤕𐤄.𐤋𐤀𐤉𐤔.𐤀𐤇𐤓|

3 𐤅𐤔𐤍𐤀𐤄.𐤄𐤀𐤉𐤔.𐤄𐤀𐤇𐤓𐤅𐤍.𐤅𐤊𐤕𐤁.𐤋𐤄.𐤎𐤐𐤓.𐤊𐤓𐤉𐤕𐤕.𐤅𐤍𐤕𐤍.𐤁𐤉𐤃𐤄.𐤅𐤔𐤋𐤇𐤄.𐤌𐤁𐤉𐤕𐤅.𐤀𐤅.𐤊𐤉.𐤉𐤌𐤅𐤕.𐤄𐤀𐤉𐤔.𐤄𐤀𐤇𐤓𐤅𐤍.𐤀𐤔𐤓.𐤋𐤒𐤇𐤄.𐤋𐤅.𐤋𐤀𐤔𐤄|

4 𐤋𐤀.𐤉𐤅𐤊𐤋.𐤁𐤏𐤋𐤄.𐤄𐤓𐤀𐤔𐤅𐤍.𐤀𐤔𐤓.𐤔𐤋𐤇𐤄.𐤋𐤔𐤅𐤁.𐤋𐤒𐤇𐤕𐤄.𐤋𐤄𐤉𐤅𐤕.𐤋𐤅.𐤋𐤀𐤔𐤄.𐤀𐤇𐤓𐤉.𐤀𐤔𐤓.𐤄𐤈𐤌𐤀𐤄.𐤊𐤉.𐤕𐤅𐤏𐤁𐤄.𐤄𐤅𐤀.𐤋𐤐𐤍𐤉.𐤉𐤄𐤅𐤄.𐤅𐤋𐤀.𐤕𐤇𐤈𐤉𐤀.𐤀𐤕.𐤄𐤀𐤓𐤑.𐤀𐤔𐤓.𐤉𐤄𐤅𐤄.𐤀𐤋𐤄𐤉𐤊.𐤍𐤕𐤍.𐤋𐤊.𐤍𐤇𐤋𐤄|

5 𐤊𐤉.𐤉𐤒𐤇.𐤀𐤉𐤔.𐤀𐤔𐤄.𐤇𐤃𐤔𐤄.𐤋𐤀.𐤉𐤑𐤀.𐤁𐤑𐤁𐤀.𐤅𐤋𐤀.𐤉𐤏𐤁𐤓.𐤏𐤋𐤉𐤅.𐤋𐤊𐤋.𐤃𐤁𐤓.𐤍𐤒𐤉.𐤉𐤄𐤉𐤄.𐤋𐤁𐤉𐤕𐤅.𐤔𐤍𐤄.𐤀𐤇𐤕.𐤅𐤔𐤌𐤇.𐤀𐤕.𐤀𐤔𐤕𐤅.𐤀𐤔𐤓.𐤋𐤒𐤇|

6 𐤋𐤀.𐤉𐤇𐤁𐤋.𐤓𐤇𐤉𐤌.𐤅𐤓𐤊𐤁.𐤊𐤉.𐤍𐤐𐤔.𐤄𐤅𐤀.𐤇𐤁𐤋|

7 𐤊𐤉.𐤉𐤌𐤑𐤀.𐤀𐤉𐤔.𐤂𐤍𐤁.𐤍𐤐𐤔.𐤌𐤀𐤇𐤉𐤅.𐤌𐤁𐤍𐤉.𐤉𐤔𐤓𐤀𐤋.𐤅𐤄𐤕𐤏𐤌𐤓.𐤁𐤅.𐤅𐤌𐤊𐤓𐤅.𐤅𐤌𐤕.𐤄𐤂𐤍𐤁.𐤄𐤄𐤅𐤀.𐤅𐤁𐤏𐤓𐤕.𐤄𐤓𐤏.𐤌𐤒𐤓𐤁𐤊|

8 𐤄𐤔𐤌𐤓.𐤁𐤍𐤂𐤏.𐤄𐤑𐤓𐤏𐤕.𐤋𐤔𐤌𐤓.𐤌𐤀𐤃.𐤅𐤋𐤏𐤔𐤅𐤕.𐤊𐤊𐤋.𐤀𐤔𐤓.𐤉𐤅𐤓𐤅.𐤀𐤕𐤊𐤌.𐤄𐤊𐤄𐤍𐤉𐤌.𐤄𐤋𐤅𐤉𐤌.𐤊𐤀𐤔𐤓.𐤑𐤅𐤉𐤕𐤌.𐤕𐤔𐤌𐤓𐤅.𐤋𐤏𐤔𐤅𐤕|

9 𐤆𐤊𐤅𐤓.𐤀𐤕.𐤀𐤔𐤓.𐤏𐤔𐤄.𐤉𐤄𐤅𐤄.𐤀𐤋𐤄𐤉𐤊.𐤋𐤌𐤓𐤉𐤌.𐤁𐤃𐤓𐤊.𐤁𐤑𐤀𐤕𐤊𐤌.𐤌𐤌𐤑𐤓𐤉𐤌|

10 𐤊𐤉.𐤕𐤔𐤄.𐤁𐤓𐤏𐤊.𐤌𐤔𐤀𐤕.𐤌𐤀𐤅𐤌𐤄.𐤋𐤀.𐤕𐤁𐤀.𐤀𐤋.𐤁𐤉𐤕𐤅.𐤋𐤏𐤁𐤈.𐤏𐤁𐤈𐤅|

11 𐤁𐤇𐤅𐤑.𐤕𐤏𐤌𐤃.𐤅𐤄𐤀𐤉𐤔.𐤀𐤔𐤓.𐤀𐤕𐤄.𐤍𐤔𐤄.𐤁𐤅.𐤉
𐤅𐤑𐤉𐤀.𐤀𐤋𐤉𐤊.𐤀𐤕.𐤄𐤏𐤁𐤅𐤈.𐤄𐤇𐤅𐤑𐤄|
12 𐤅𐤀𐤌.𐤀𐤉𐤔.𐤏𐤍𐤉.𐤄𐤅𐤀.𐤋𐤀.𐤕𐤔𐤊𐤁.𐤁𐤏𐤁𐤈𐤅|
13 𐤄𐤔𐤁.𐤕𐤔𐤉𐤁.𐤋𐤅.𐤀𐤕.𐤄𐤏𐤁𐤅𐤈.𐤊𐤁𐤀.𐤄𐤔𐤌𐤔.𐤅𐤔
𐤊𐤁.𐤁𐤔𐤋𐤌𐤕𐤅.𐤅𐤁𐤓𐤊𐤊.𐤅𐤋𐤊.𐤕𐤄𐤉𐤄.𐤑𐤃𐤒𐤄.𐤋𐤐𐤍𐤉.𐤉𐤄
𐤅𐤄.𐤀𐤋𐤄𐤉𐤊|
14 𐤋𐤀.𐤕𐤏𐤔𐤒.𐤔𐤊𐤉𐤓.𐤏𐤍𐤉.𐤅𐤀𐤁𐤉𐤅𐤍.𐤌𐤀𐤇𐤉𐤊.𐤀𐤅.
𐤌𐤂𐤓𐤊.𐤀𐤔𐤓.𐤁𐤀𐤓𐤑𐤊.𐤁𐤔𐤏𐤓𐤉𐤊|
15 𐤁𐤉𐤅𐤌𐤅.𐤕𐤕𐤍.𐤔𐤊𐤓𐤅.𐤅𐤋𐤀.𐤕𐤁𐤅𐤀.𐤏𐤋𐤉𐤅.𐤄𐤔𐤌𐤔.𐤊
𐤉.𐤏𐤍𐤉.𐤄𐤅𐤀.𐤅𐤀𐤋𐤉𐤅.𐤄𐤅𐤀.𐤍𐤔𐤀.𐤀𐤕.𐤍𐤐𐤔𐤅.𐤅𐤋𐤀.𐤉𐤒𐤓𐤀
.𐤏𐤋𐤉𐤊.𐤀𐤋.𐤉𐤄𐤅𐤄.𐤅𐤄𐤉𐤄.𐤁𐤊.𐤇𐤈𐤀|
16 𐤋𐤀.𐤉𐤅𐤌𐤕𐤅.𐤀𐤁𐤅𐤕.𐤏𐤋.𐤁𐤍𐤉𐤌.𐤅𐤁𐤍𐤉𐤌.𐤋𐤀.𐤉𐤅𐤌𐤕𐤅
.𐤏𐤋.𐤀𐤁𐤅𐤕.𐤀𐤉𐤔.𐤁𐤇𐤈𐤀𐤅.𐤉𐤅𐤌𐤕𐤅|
17 𐤋𐤀.𐤕𐤈𐤄.𐤌𐤔𐤐𐤈.𐤂𐤓.𐤉𐤕𐤅𐤌.𐤅𐤋𐤀.𐤕𐤇𐤁𐤋.𐤁𐤂
𐤃.𐤀𐤋𐤌𐤍𐤄|
18 𐤅𐤆𐤊𐤓𐤕.𐤊𐤉.𐤏𐤁𐤃.𐤄𐤉𐤉𐤕.𐤁𐤌𐤑𐤓𐤉𐤌.𐤅𐤉𐤐𐤃𐤊.𐤉
𐤄𐤅𐤄.𐤀𐤋𐤄𐤉𐤊.𐤌𐤔𐤌.𐤏𐤋.𐤊𐤍.𐤀𐤍𐤊𐤉.𐤌𐤑𐤅𐤊.𐤋𐤏𐤔𐤅𐤕.𐤀
𐤕.𐤄𐤃𐤁𐤓.𐤄𐤆𐤄|
19 𐤊𐤉.𐤕𐤒𐤑𐤓.𐤒𐤑𐤉𐤓𐤊.𐤁𐤔𐤃𐤊.𐤅𐤔𐤊𐤇𐤕.𐤏𐤌𐤓.𐤁
𐤔𐤃𐤄.𐤋𐤀.𐤕𐤔𐤅𐤁.𐤋𐤒𐤇𐤕𐤅.𐤋𐤂𐤓.𐤋𐤉𐤕𐤅𐤌.𐤅𐤋𐤀𐤋𐤌𐤍𐤄.
𐤉𐤄𐤉𐤄.𐤋𐤌𐤏𐤍.𐤉𐤁𐤓𐤊𐤊.𐤉𐤄𐤅𐤄.𐤀𐤋𐤄𐤉𐤊.𐤁𐤊𐤋.𐤌𐤏𐤔𐤄.
𐤉𐤃𐤉𐤊|
20 𐤊𐤉.𐤕𐤇𐤁𐤈.𐤆𐤉𐤕𐤊.𐤋𐤀.𐤕𐤐𐤀𐤓.𐤀𐤇𐤓𐤉𐤊.𐤋𐤂𐤓.
𐤋𐤉𐤕𐤅𐤌.𐤅𐤋𐤀𐤋𐤌𐤍𐤄.𐤉𐤄𐤉𐤄|
21 𐤊𐤉.𐤕𐤁𐤑𐤓.𐤊𐤓𐤌𐤊.𐤋𐤀.𐤕𐤏𐤅𐤋𐤋.𐤀𐤇𐤓𐤉𐤊.𐤋𐤂𐤓.𐤋
𐤉𐤕𐤅𐤌.𐤅𐤋𐤀𐤋𐤌𐤍𐤄.𐤉𐤄𐤉𐤄|
22 𐤅𐤆𐤊𐤓𐤕.𐤊𐤉.𐤏𐤁𐤃.𐤄𐤉𐤉𐤕.𐤁𐤀𐤓𐤑.𐤌𐤑𐤓𐤉𐤌.𐤏𐤋
.𐤊𐤍.𐤀𐤍𐤊𐤉.𐤌𐤑𐤅𐤊.𐤋𐤏𐤔𐤅𐤕.𐤀𐤕.𐤄𐤃𐤁𐤓.𐤄𐤆𐤄‖

𐤃𐤁𐤓𐤉𐤌.𐤇𐤋𐤒 25

𐤀 𐤊𐤉.𐤉𐤄𐤉𐤄.𐤓𐤉𐤁.𐤁𐤉𐤍.𐤀𐤍𐤔𐤉𐤌.𐤅𐤍𐤂𐤔𐤅.𐤀𐤋.𐤄𐤌𐤔𐤐
𐤈.𐤅𐤔𐤐𐤈𐤅𐤌.𐤅𐤄𐤑𐤃𐤉𐤒𐤅.𐤀𐤕.𐤄𐤑𐤃𐤉𐤒.𐤅𐤄𐤓𐤔𐤉𐤏𐤅.𐤀
𐤕.𐤄𐤓𐤔𐤏|
𐤁 𐤅𐤄𐤉𐤄.𐤀𐤌.𐤁𐤍.𐤄𐤊𐤅𐤕.𐤄𐤓𐤔𐤏.𐤅𐤄𐤐𐤉𐤋𐤅.𐤄𐤔𐤐𐤈.𐤅𐤄
𐤊𐤄𐤅.𐤋𐤐𐤍𐤉𐤅.𐤊𐤃𐤉.𐤓𐤔𐤏𐤕𐤅.𐤁𐤌𐤎𐤐𐤓|
𐤂 𐤀𐤓𐤁𐤏𐤉𐤌.𐤉𐤊𐤍𐤅.𐤋𐤀.𐤉𐤎𐤉𐤐.𐤐𐤍.𐤉𐤎𐤉𐤐.𐤋𐤄𐤊𐤕𐤅.𐤏
𐤋.𐤀𐤋𐤄.𐤌𐤊𐤄.𐤓𐤁𐤄.𐤅𐤍𐤒𐤋𐤄.𐤀𐤇𐤉𐤊.𐤋𐤏𐤉𐤍𐤉𐤊|
𐤃 𐤋𐤀.𐤕𐤇𐤎𐤌.𐤔𐤅𐤓.𐤁𐤃𐤉𐤔𐤅|
𐤄 𐤊𐤉.𐤉𐤔𐤁𐤅.𐤀𐤇𐤉𐤌.𐤉𐤇𐤃𐤅.𐤅𐤌𐤕.𐤀𐤇𐤃.𐤌𐤄𐤌.𐤅𐤁𐤍.
𐤀𐤉𐤍.𐤋𐤅.𐤋𐤀.𐤕𐤄𐤉𐤄.𐤀𐤔𐤕.𐤄𐤌𐤕.𐤄𐤇𐤅𐤑𐤄.𐤋𐤀𐤉𐤔.𐤆
𐤓.𐤉𐤁𐤌𐤄.𐤉𐤁𐤀.𐤏𐤋𐤉𐤄.𐤅𐤋𐤒𐤇𐤄.𐤋𐤅.𐤋𐤀𐤔𐤄.𐤅𐤉𐤁𐤌𐤄|
𐤅 𐤅𐤄𐤉𐤄.𐤄𐤁𐤊𐤅𐤓.𐤀𐤔𐤓.𐤕𐤋𐤃.𐤉𐤒𐤅𐤌.𐤏𐤋.𐤔𐤌.𐤀𐤇𐤉𐤅.
𐤄𐤌𐤕.𐤅𐤋𐤀.𐤉𐤌𐤇𐤄.𐤔𐤌𐤅.𐤌𐤉𐤔𐤓𐤀𐤋|
𐤆 𐤅𐤀𐤌.𐤋𐤀.𐤉𐤇𐤐𐤑.𐤄𐤀𐤉𐤔.𐤋𐤒𐤇𐤕.𐤀𐤕.𐤉𐤁𐤌𐤕𐤅.𐤅
𐤏𐤋𐤕𐤄.𐤉𐤁𐤌𐤕𐤅.𐤄𐤔𐤏𐤓𐤄.𐤀𐤋.𐤄𐤆𐤒𐤍𐤉𐤌.𐤅𐤀𐤌𐤓𐤄.𐤌𐤀
𐤉𐤍.𐤉𐤁𐤌𐤉.𐤋𐤄𐤒𐤉𐤌.𐤋𐤀𐤇𐤉𐤅.𐤔𐤌.𐤁𐤉𐤔𐤓𐤀𐤋.𐤋𐤀.𐤀𐤁𐤄
.𐤉𐤁𐤌𐤉|
𐤇 𐤅𐤒𐤓𐤀𐤅.𐤋𐤅.𐤆𐤒𐤍𐤉.𐤏𐤉𐤓𐤅.𐤅𐤃𐤁𐤓𐤅.𐤀𐤋𐤉𐤅.𐤅𐤏𐤌𐤃.𐤅
𐤀𐤌𐤓.𐤋𐤀.𐤇𐤐𐤑𐤕𐤉.𐤋𐤒𐤇𐤕𐤄|
𐤈 𐤅𐤍𐤂𐤔𐤄.𐤉𐤁𐤌𐤕𐤅.𐤀𐤋𐤉𐤅.𐤋𐤏𐤉𐤍𐤉.𐤄𐤆𐤒𐤍𐤉𐤌.𐤅𐤇𐤋
𐤑𐤄.𐤍𐤏𐤋𐤅.𐤌𐤏𐤋.𐤓𐤂𐤋𐤅.𐤅𐤉𐤓𐤒𐤄.𐤁𐤐𐤍𐤉𐤅.𐤅𐤏𐤍𐤕𐤄.𐤅𐤀𐤌𐤓
𐤄.𐤊𐤊𐤄.𐤉𐤏𐤔𐤄.𐤋𐤀𐤉𐤔.𐤀𐤔𐤓.𐤋𐤀.𐤉𐤁𐤍𐤄.𐤀𐤕.𐤁𐤉𐤕.𐤀
𐤇𐤉𐤅|
𐤉 𐤅𐤍𐤒𐤓𐤀.𐤔𐤌𐤅.𐤁𐤉𐤔𐤓𐤀𐤋.𐤁𐤉𐤕.𐤇𐤋𐤅𐤑.𐤄𐤍𐤏𐤋|
𐤉𐤀 𐤊𐤉.𐤉𐤍𐤑𐤅.𐤀𐤍𐤔𐤉𐤌.𐤉𐤇𐤃𐤅.𐤀𐤉𐤔.𐤅𐤀𐤇𐤉𐤅.𐤅𐤒𐤓𐤁
𐤄.𐤀𐤔𐤕.𐤄𐤀𐤇𐤃.𐤋𐤄𐤑𐤉𐤋.𐤀𐤕.𐤀𐤉𐤔𐤄.𐤌𐤉𐤃.𐤌𐤊𐤄𐤅.
𐤅𐤔𐤋𐤇𐤄.𐤉𐤃𐤄.𐤅𐤄𐤇𐤆𐤉𐤒𐤄.𐤁𐤌𐤁𐤔𐤉𐤅|
𐤉𐤁 𐤅𐤒𐤑𐤕𐤄.𐤀𐤕.𐤊𐤐𐤄.𐤋𐤀.𐤕𐤇𐤅𐤎.𐤏𐤉𐤍𐤊|
𐤉𐤂 𐤋𐤀.𐤉𐤄𐤉𐤄.𐤋𐤊.𐤁𐤊𐤉𐤎𐤊.𐤀𐤁𐤍.𐤅𐤀𐤁𐤍.𐤂𐤃𐤅𐤋𐤄.𐤅
𐤒𐤈𐤍𐤄|

𐤉𐤃 𐤋𐤀.𐤉𐤄𐤉𐤄.𐤋𐤊.𐤁𐤁𐤉𐤕𐤊.𐤀𐤉𐤐𐤄.𐤅𐤀𐤉𐤐𐤄.𐤂𐤃𐤅𐤋
𐤄.𐤅𐤒𐤈𐤍𐤄|

𐤈𐤅 𐤀𐤁𐤍.𐤔𐤋𐤌𐤄.𐤅𐤑𐤃𐤒.𐤉𐤄𐤉𐤄.𐤋𐤊.𐤀𐤉𐤐𐤄.𐤔𐤋𐤌𐤄.𐤅
𐤑𐤃𐤒.𐤉𐤄𐤉𐤄.𐤋𐤊.𐤋𐤌𐤏𐤍.𐤉𐤀𐤓𐤉𐤊𐤅.𐤉𐤌𐤉𐤊.𐤏𐤋.𐤄𐤀𐤃
𐤌𐤄.𐤀𐤔𐤓.𐤉𐤄𐤅𐤄.𐤀𐤋𐤄𐤉𐤊.𐤍𐤕𐤍.𐤋𐤊|

𐤈𐤆 𐤊𐤉.𐤕𐤅𐤏𐤁𐤕.𐤉𐤄𐤅𐤄.𐤀𐤋𐤄𐤉𐤊.𐤊𐤋.𐤏𐤔𐤄.𐤀𐤋𐤄.𐤊𐤋
𐤏𐤔𐤄.𐤏𐤅𐤋|

𐤉𐤆 𐤆𐤊𐤅𐤓.𐤀𐤕.𐤀𐤔𐤓.𐤏𐤔𐤄.𐤋𐤊.𐤏𐤌𐤋𐤒.𐤁𐤃𐤓𐤊.𐤁𐤑
𐤀𐤕𐤊𐤌.𐤌𐤌𐤑𐤓𐤉𐤌|

𐤉𐤇 𐤀𐤔𐤓.𐤒𐤓𐤊.𐤁𐤃𐤓𐤊.𐤅𐤉𐤆𐤍𐤁.𐤁𐤊.𐤊𐤋.𐤄𐤍𐤇𐤔𐤋𐤉𐤌.
𐤀𐤇𐤓𐤉𐤊.𐤅𐤀𐤕𐤄.𐤏𐤉𐤐.𐤅𐤉𐤂𐤏.𐤅𐤋𐤀.𐤉𐤓𐤀.𐤀𐤋𐤄𐤉𐤌|

𐤉𐤈 𐤅𐤄𐤉𐤄.𐤁𐤄𐤍𐤉𐤇.𐤉𐤄𐤅𐤄.𐤀𐤋𐤄𐤉𐤊.𐤋𐤊.𐤌𐤊𐤋.𐤀𐤉𐤁
𐤉𐤊.𐤌𐤎𐤁𐤉𐤁.𐤁𐤀𐤓𐤑.𐤀𐤔𐤓.𐤉𐤄𐤅𐤄.𐤀𐤋𐤄𐤉𐤊.𐤍𐤕𐤍.𐤋𐤊.𐤍
𐤇𐤋𐤄.𐤋𐤓𐤔𐤕𐤄.𐤕𐤌𐤇𐤄.𐤀𐤕.𐤆𐤊𐤓.𐤏𐤌𐤋𐤒.𐤌𐤕𐤇𐤕.𐤄
𐤔𐤌𐤉𐤌.𐤋𐤀.𐤕𐤔𐤊𐤇||

𐤃𐤁𐤓𐤉𐤌.𐤇𐤋𐤒 𐤊𐤅

𐤀 𐤅𐤄𐤉𐤄.𐤊𐤉.𐤕𐤁𐤅𐤀.𐤀𐤋.𐤄𐤀𐤓𐤑.𐤀𐤔𐤓.𐤉𐤄𐤅𐤄.𐤀𐤋𐤄𐤉
𐤊.𐤍𐤕𐤍.𐤋𐤊.𐤍𐤇𐤋𐤄.𐤅𐤉𐤓𐤔𐤕𐤄.𐤅𐤉𐤔𐤁𐤕.𐤁𐤄|

𐤁 𐤅𐤋𐤒𐤇𐤕.𐤌𐤓𐤀𐤔𐤉𐤕.𐤊𐤋.𐤐𐤓𐤉.𐤄𐤀𐤃𐤌𐤄.𐤀𐤔𐤓.𐤕𐤁
𐤉𐤀.𐤌𐤀𐤓𐤑𐤊.𐤀𐤔𐤓.𐤉𐤄𐤅𐤄.𐤀𐤋𐤄𐤉𐤊.𐤍𐤕𐤍.𐤋𐤊.𐤅𐤔𐤌𐤕.𐤁
𐤈𐤍𐤀.𐤅𐤄𐤋𐤊𐤕.𐤀𐤋.𐤄𐤌𐤒𐤅𐤌.𐤀𐤔𐤓.𐤉𐤁𐤇𐤓.𐤉𐤄𐤅𐤄.𐤀𐤋𐤄
𐤉𐤊.𐤋𐤔𐤊𐤍.𐤔𐤌𐤅.𐤔𐤌|

𐤂 𐤅𐤁𐤀𐤕.𐤀𐤋.𐤄𐤊𐤄𐤍.𐤀𐤔𐤓.𐤉𐤄𐤉𐤄.𐤁𐤉𐤌𐤉𐤌.𐤄𐤄𐤌.𐤅
𐤀𐤌𐤓𐤕.𐤀𐤋𐤉𐤅.𐤄𐤂𐤃𐤕𐤉.𐤄𐤉𐤅𐤌.𐤋𐤉𐤄𐤅𐤄.𐤀𐤋𐤄𐤉𐤊.𐤊𐤉.
𐤁𐤀𐤕𐤉.𐤀𐤋.𐤄𐤀𐤓𐤑.𐤀𐤔𐤓.𐤍𐤔𐤁𐤏.𐤉𐤄𐤅𐤄.𐤋𐤀𐤁𐤕𐤉𐤍𐤅.𐤋
𐤕𐤕.𐤋𐤍𐤅|

𐤃 𐤅𐤋𐤒𐤇.𐤄𐤊𐤄𐤍.𐤄𐤈𐤍𐤀.𐤌𐤉𐤃𐤊.𐤅𐤄𐤍𐤉𐤇𐤅.𐤋𐤐𐤍𐤉.𐤌
𐤆𐤁𐤇.𐤉𐤄𐤅𐤄.𐤀𐤋𐤄𐤉𐤊|

ו 𐤅𐤏𐤍𐤉𐤕.𐤅𐤀𐤌𐤓𐤕.𐤋𐤐𐤍𐤉.𐤉𐤄𐤅𐤄.𐤀𐤋𐤄𐤉𐤊.𐤀𐤓𐤌𐤉.𐤀𐤁
𐤃.𐤀𐤁𐤉.𐤅𐤉𐤓𐤃.𐤌𐤑𐤓𐤉𐤌𐤄.𐤅𐤉𐤂𐤓.𐤔𐤌.𐤁𐤌𐤕𐤉.𐤌𐤏𐤈.𐤅
𐤉𐤄𐤉.𐤔𐤌.𐤋𐤂𐤅𐤉.𐤂𐤃𐤅𐤋.𐤏𐤑𐤅𐤌.𐤅𐤓𐤁|

ז 𐤅𐤉𐤓𐤏𐤅.𐤀𐤕𐤍𐤅.𐤄𐤌𐤑𐤓𐤉𐤌.𐤅𐤉𐤏𐤍𐤅𐤍𐤅.𐤅𐤉𐤕𐤍𐤅.𐤏𐤋𐤉𐤍𐤅.
𐤏𐤁𐤃𐤄.𐤒𐤔𐤄|

ח 𐤅𐤍𐤑𐤏𐤒.𐤀𐤋.𐤉𐤄𐤅𐤄.𐤀𐤋𐤄𐤉.𐤀𐤁𐤕𐤉𐤍𐤅.𐤅𐤉𐤔𐤌𐤏.𐤉
𐤄𐤅𐤄.𐤀𐤕.𐤒𐤋𐤍𐤅.𐤅𐤉𐤓𐤀.𐤀𐤕.𐤏𐤍𐤉𐤍𐤅.𐤅𐤀𐤕.𐤏𐤌𐤋𐤍𐤅.𐤅𐤀𐤕.
𐤋𐤇𐤑𐤍𐤅|

ט 𐤅𐤉𐤅𐤑𐤀𐤍𐤅.𐤉𐤄𐤅𐤄.𐤌𐤌𐤑𐤓𐤉𐤌.𐤁𐤉𐤃.𐤇𐤆𐤒𐤄.𐤅𐤁𐤆
𐤓𐤏.𐤍𐤈𐤅𐤉𐤄.𐤅𐤁𐤌𐤓𐤀.𐤂𐤃𐤋.𐤅𐤁𐤀𐤕𐤅𐤕.𐤅𐤁𐤌𐤐𐤕𐤉𐤌|

י 𐤅𐤉𐤁𐤀𐤍𐤅.𐤀𐤋.𐤄𐤌𐤒𐤅𐤌.𐤄𐤆𐤄.𐤅𐤉𐤕𐤍.𐤋𐤍𐤅.𐤀𐤕.𐤄𐤀𐤓
𐤑.𐤄𐤆𐤀𐤕.𐤀𐤓𐤑.𐤆𐤁𐤕.𐤇𐤋𐤁.𐤅𐤃𐤁𐤔|

יא 𐤅𐤏𐤕𐤄.𐤄𐤍𐤄.𐤄𐤁𐤀𐤕𐤉.𐤀𐤕.𐤓𐤀𐤔𐤉𐤕.𐤐𐤓𐤉.𐤄𐤀𐤃
𐤌𐤄.𐤀𐤔𐤓.𐤍𐤕𐤕𐤄.𐤋𐤉.𐤉𐤄𐤅𐤄.𐤅𐤄𐤍𐤇𐤕𐤅.𐤋𐤐𐤍𐤉.𐤉𐤄𐤅𐤄.𐤀
𐤋𐤄𐤉𐤊.𐤅𐤄𐤔𐤕𐤇𐤅𐤉𐤕.𐤋𐤐𐤍𐤉.𐤉𐤄𐤅𐤄.𐤀𐤋𐤄𐤉𐤊|

יב 𐤅𐤔𐤌𐤇𐤕.𐤁𐤊𐤋.𐤄𐤈𐤅𐤁.𐤀𐤔𐤓.𐤍𐤕𐤍.𐤋𐤊.𐤉𐤄𐤅𐤄.𐤀𐤋𐤄
𐤉𐤊.𐤅𐤋𐤁𐤉𐤕𐤊.𐤀𐤕𐤄.𐤅𐤄𐤋𐤅𐤉.𐤅𐤄𐤂𐤓.𐤀𐤔𐤓.𐤁𐤒𐤓𐤁𐤊|

יג 𐤊𐤉.𐤕𐤊𐤋𐤄.𐤋𐤏𐤔𐤓.𐤀𐤕.𐤊𐤋.𐤌𐤏𐤔𐤓.𐤕𐤁𐤅𐤀𐤕𐤊.𐤁
𐤔𐤍𐤄.𐤄𐤔𐤋𐤉𐤔𐤕.𐤔𐤍𐤕.𐤄𐤌𐤏𐤔𐤓.𐤅𐤍𐤕𐤕𐤄.𐤋𐤋𐤅𐤉.𐤋𐤂𐤓.
𐤋𐤉𐤕𐤅𐤌.𐤅𐤋𐤀𐤋𐤌𐤍𐤄.𐤅𐤀𐤊𐤋𐤅.𐤁𐤔𐤏𐤓𐤉𐤊.𐤅𐤔𐤁𐤏𐤅|

יד 𐤅𐤀𐤌𐤓𐤕.𐤋𐤐𐤍𐤉.𐤉𐤄𐤅𐤄.𐤀𐤋𐤄𐤉𐤊.𐤁𐤏𐤓𐤕𐤉.𐤄𐤒𐤃𐤔
.𐤌𐤍.𐤄𐤁𐤉𐤕.𐤅𐤂𐤌.𐤍𐤕𐤕𐤉𐤅.𐤋𐤋𐤅𐤉.𐤅𐤋𐤂𐤓.𐤋𐤉𐤕𐤅𐤌.𐤅𐤋𐤀𐤋
𐤌𐤍𐤄.𐤊𐤊𐤋.𐤌𐤑𐤅𐤕𐤊.𐤀𐤔𐤓.𐤑𐤅𐤉𐤕𐤍𐤉.𐤋𐤀.𐤏𐤁𐤓𐤕𐤉.𐤌𐤌
𐤑𐤅𐤕𐤉𐤊.𐤅𐤋𐤀.𐤔𐤊𐤇𐤕𐤉|

יה 𐤋𐤀.𐤀𐤊𐤋𐤕𐤉.𐤁𐤀𐤍𐤉.𐤌𐤌𐤍𐤅.𐤅𐤋𐤀.𐤁𐤏𐤓𐤕𐤉.𐤌𐤌𐤍𐤅.
𐤁𐤈𐤌𐤀.𐤅𐤋𐤀.𐤍𐤕𐤕𐤉.𐤌𐤌𐤍𐤅.𐤋𐤌𐤕.𐤔𐤌𐤏𐤕𐤉.𐤁𐤒𐤅𐤋.𐤉𐤄𐤅
𐤄.𐤀𐤋𐤄𐤉.𐤏𐤔𐤉𐤕𐤉.𐤊𐤊𐤋.𐤀𐤔𐤓.𐤑𐤅𐤉𐤕𐤍𐤉|

יו 𐤄𐤔𐤒𐤉𐤐𐤄.𐤌𐤌𐤏𐤅𐤍.𐤒𐤃𐤔𐤊.𐤌𐤍.𐤄𐤔𐤌𐤉𐤌.𐤅𐤁𐤓𐤊.
𐤀𐤕.𐤏𐤌𐤊.𐤀𐤕.𐤉𐤔𐤓𐤀𐤋.𐤅𐤀𐤕.𐤄𐤀𐤃𐤌𐤄.𐤀𐤔𐤓.𐤍𐤕𐤕𐤄.
𐤋𐤍𐤅.𐤊𐤀𐤔𐤓.𐤍𐤔𐤁𐤏𐤕.𐤋𐤀𐤁𐤕𐤉𐤍𐤅.𐤀𐤓𐤑.𐤆𐤁𐤕.𐤇𐤋𐤁.𐤅
𐤃𐤁𐤔|

16 𐤄𐤉𐤅𐤌.𐤄𐤆𐤄.𐤉𐤄𐤅𐤄.𐤀𐤋𐤄𐤉𐤊.𐤌𐤑𐤅𐤊.𐤋𐤏𐤔𐤅𐤕.𐤀
𐤕.𐤄𐤇𐤒𐤉𐤌.𐤄𐤀𐤋𐤄.𐤅𐤀𐤕.𐤄𐤌𐤔𐤐𐤈𐤉𐤌.𐤅𐤔𐤌𐤓𐤕.𐤅𐤏𐤔
𐤉𐤕.𐤀𐤅𐤕𐤌.𐤁𐤊𐤋.𐤋𐤁𐤁𐤊.𐤅𐤁𐤊𐤋.𐤍𐤐𐤔𐤊|

17 𐤀𐤕.𐤉𐤄𐤅𐤄.𐤄𐤀𐤌𐤓𐤕.𐤄𐤉𐤅𐤌.𐤋𐤄𐤉𐤅𐤕.𐤋𐤊.𐤋𐤀𐤋𐤄
𐤉𐤌.𐤅𐤋𐤋𐤊𐤕.𐤁𐤃𐤓𐤊𐤉𐤅.𐤅𐤋𐤔𐤌𐤓.𐤇𐤒𐤉𐤅.𐤅𐤌𐤑𐤅𐤕𐤉𐤅.𐤅𐤌𐤔
𐤐𐤈𐤉𐤅.𐤅𐤋𐤔𐤌𐤏.𐤁𐤒𐤋𐤅|

18 𐤅𐤉𐤄𐤅𐤄.𐤄𐤀𐤌𐤉𐤓𐤊.𐤄𐤉𐤅𐤌.𐤋𐤄𐤉𐤅𐤕.𐤋𐤅.𐤋𐤏𐤌.𐤎𐤂𐤋
𐤄.𐤊𐤀𐤔𐤓.𐤃𐤁𐤓.𐤋𐤊.𐤅𐤋𐤔𐤌𐤓.𐤊𐤋.𐤌𐤑𐤅𐤕𐤉𐤅|

19 𐤅𐤋𐤕𐤕𐤊.𐤏𐤋𐤉𐤅𐤍.𐤏𐤋.𐤊𐤋.𐤄𐤂𐤅𐤉𐤌.𐤀𐤔𐤓.𐤏𐤔𐤄.𐤋
𐤕𐤄𐤋𐤄.𐤅𐤋𐤔𐤌.𐤅𐤋𐤕𐤐𐤀𐤓𐤕.𐤅𐤋𐤄𐤉𐤕𐤊.𐤏𐤌.𐤒𐤃𐤔.𐤋𐤉𐤄𐤅
𐤄.𐤀𐤋𐤄𐤉𐤊.𐤊𐤀𐤔𐤓.𐤃𐤁𐤓||

𐤃𐤁𐤓𐤉𐤌.𐤇𐤋𐤒 27

1 𐤅𐤉𐤑𐤅.𐤌𐤔𐤄.𐤅𐤆𐤒𐤍𐤉.𐤉𐤔𐤓𐤀𐤋.𐤀𐤕.𐤄𐤏𐤌.𐤋𐤀𐤌𐤓.
𐤔𐤌𐤓.𐤀𐤕.𐤊𐤋.𐤄𐤌𐤑𐤅𐤄.𐤀𐤔𐤓.𐤀𐤍𐤊𐤉.𐤌𐤑𐤅𐤄.𐤀𐤕𐤊𐤌.𐤄
𐤉𐤅𐤌|

2 𐤅𐤄𐤉𐤄.𐤁𐤉𐤅𐤌.𐤀𐤔𐤓.𐤕𐤏𐤁𐤓𐤅.𐤀𐤕.𐤄𐤉𐤓𐤃𐤍.𐤀𐤋.𐤄𐤀
𐤓𐤑.𐤀𐤔𐤓.𐤉𐤄𐤅𐤄.𐤀𐤋𐤄𐤉𐤊.𐤍𐤕𐤍.𐤋𐤊.𐤅𐤄𐤒𐤌𐤕.𐤋𐤊.𐤀𐤁𐤍
𐤉𐤌.𐤂𐤃𐤋𐤅𐤕.𐤅𐤔𐤃𐤕.𐤀𐤕𐤌.𐤁𐤔𐤉𐤃|

3 𐤅𐤊𐤕𐤁𐤕.𐤏𐤋𐤉𐤄𐤍.𐤀𐤕.𐤊𐤋.𐤃𐤁𐤓𐤉.𐤄𐤕𐤅𐤓𐤄.𐤄𐤆𐤀
𐤕.𐤁𐤏𐤁𐤓𐤊.𐤋𐤌𐤏𐤍.𐤀𐤔𐤓.𐤕𐤁𐤀.𐤀𐤋.𐤄𐤀𐤓𐤑.𐤀𐤔𐤓.𐤉𐤄𐤅
𐤄.𐤀𐤋𐤄𐤉𐤊.𐤍𐤕𐤍.𐤋𐤊.𐤀𐤓𐤑.𐤆𐤁𐤕.𐤇𐤋𐤁.𐤅𐤃𐤁𐤔.𐤊𐤀𐤔𐤓
.𐤃𐤁𐤓.𐤉𐤄𐤅𐤄.𐤀𐤋𐤄𐤉.𐤀𐤁𐤕𐤉𐤊.𐤋𐤊|

4 𐤅𐤄𐤉𐤄.𐤁𐤏𐤁𐤓𐤊𐤌.𐤀𐤕.𐤄𐤉𐤓𐤃𐤍.𐤕𐤒𐤉𐤌𐤅.𐤀𐤕.𐤄𐤀
𐤁𐤍𐤉𐤌.𐤄𐤀𐤋𐤄.𐤀𐤔𐤓.𐤀𐤍𐤊𐤉.𐤌𐤑𐤅𐤄.𐤀𐤕𐤊𐤌.𐤄𐤉𐤅𐤌.𐤁𐤄
𐤓.𐤏𐤉𐤁𐤋.𐤅𐤔𐤃𐤕.𐤀𐤅𐤕𐤌.𐤁𐤔𐤉𐤃|

5 𐤅𐤁𐤍𐤉𐤕.𐤔𐤌.𐤌𐤆𐤁𐤇.𐤋𐤉𐤄𐤅𐤄.𐤀𐤋𐤄𐤉𐤊.𐤌𐤆𐤁𐤇.𐤀
𐤁𐤍𐤉𐤌.𐤋𐤀.𐤕𐤍𐤉𐤐.𐤏𐤋𐤉𐤄𐤌.𐤁𐤓𐤆𐤋|

6 𐤀𐤁𐤍𐤉𐤌.𐤔𐤋𐤌𐤅𐤕.𐤕𐤁𐤍𐤄.𐤀𐤕.𐤌𐤆𐤁𐤇.𐤉𐤄𐤅𐤄.𐤀𐤋𐤄
𐤉𐤊.𐤅𐤄𐤏𐤋𐤉𐤕.𐤏𐤋𐤉𐤅.𐤏𐤅𐤋𐤕.𐤋𐤉𐤄𐤅𐤄.𐤀𐤋𐤄𐤉𐤊|

ז 𐤅𐤆𐤁𐤇𐤕.𐤔𐤋𐤌𐤉𐤌.𐤅𐤀𐤊𐤋𐤕.𐤔𐤌.𐤅𐤔𐤌𐤇𐤕.𐤋𐤐𐤍𐤉.𐤉
𐤄𐤅𐤄.𐤀𐤋𐤄𐤉𐤊|
ח 𐤅𐤊𐤕𐤁𐤕.𐤏𐤋.𐤄𐤀𐤁𐤍𐤉𐤌.𐤀𐤕.𐤊𐤋.𐤃𐤁𐤓𐤉.𐤄𐤕𐤅𐤓𐤄.𐤄
𐤆𐤀𐤕.𐤁𐤀𐤓.𐤄𐤉𐤈𐤁|
ט 𐤅𐤉𐤃𐤁𐤓.𐤌𐤔𐤄.𐤅𐤄𐤊𐤄𐤍𐤉𐤌.𐤄𐤋𐤅𐤉𐤌.𐤀𐤋.𐤊𐤋.𐤉𐤔𐤓
𐤀𐤋.𐤋𐤀𐤌𐤓.𐤄𐤎𐤊𐤕.𐤅𐤔𐤌𐤏.𐤉𐤔𐤓𐤀𐤋.𐤄𐤉𐤅𐤌.𐤄𐤆𐤄.𐤍𐤄𐤉
𐤉𐤕.𐤋𐤏𐤌.𐤋𐤉𐤄𐤅𐤄.𐤀𐤋𐤄𐤉𐤊|
י 𐤅𐤔𐤌𐤏𐤕.𐤁𐤒𐤅𐤋.𐤉𐤄𐤅𐤄.𐤀𐤋𐤄𐤉𐤊.𐤅𐤏𐤔𐤉𐤕.𐤀𐤕.𐤌
𐤑𐤅𐤕𐤅.𐤅𐤀𐤕.𐤇𐤒𐤉𐤅.𐤀𐤔𐤓.𐤀𐤍𐤊𐤉.𐤌𐤑𐤅𐤊.𐤄𐤉𐤅𐤌|
יא 𐤅𐤉𐤑𐤅.𐤌𐤔𐤄.𐤀𐤕.𐤄𐤏𐤌.𐤁𐤉𐤅𐤌.𐤄𐤄𐤅𐤀.𐤋𐤀𐤌𐤓|
יב 𐤀𐤋𐤄.𐤉𐤏𐤌𐤃𐤅.𐤋𐤁𐤓𐤊.𐤀𐤕.𐤄𐤏𐤌.𐤏𐤋.𐤄𐤓.𐤂𐤓𐤆𐤉
𐤌.𐤁𐤏𐤁𐤓𐤊𐤌.𐤀𐤕.𐤄𐤉𐤓𐤃𐤍.𐤔𐤌𐤏𐤅𐤍.𐤅𐤋𐤅𐤉.𐤅𐤉𐤄𐤅𐤃𐤄.𐤅𐤉
𐤔𐤔𐤊𐤓.𐤅𐤉𐤅𐤎𐤐.𐤅𐤁𐤍𐤉𐤌𐤍|
יג 𐤅𐤀𐤋𐤄.𐤉𐤏𐤌𐤃𐤅.𐤏𐤋.𐤄𐤒𐤋𐤋𐤄.𐤁𐤄𐤓.𐤏𐤉𐤁𐤋.𐤓𐤀𐤅𐤁
𐤍.𐤂𐤃.𐤅𐤀𐤔𐤓.𐤅𐤆𐤁𐤅𐤋𐤍.𐤃𐤍.𐤅𐤍𐤐𐤕𐤋𐤉|
יד 𐤅𐤏𐤍𐤅.𐤄𐤋𐤅𐤉𐤌.𐤅𐤀𐤌𐤓𐤅.𐤀𐤋.𐤊𐤋.𐤀𐤉𐤔.𐤉𐤔𐤓𐤀𐤋.𐤒𐤅
𐤋.𐤓𐤌|
טו 𐤀𐤓𐤅𐤓.𐤄𐤀𐤉𐤔.𐤀𐤔𐤓.𐤉𐤏𐤔𐤄.𐤐𐤎𐤋.𐤅𐤌𐤎𐤊𐤄.𐤕𐤅𐤏
𐤁𐤕.𐤉𐤄𐤅𐤄.𐤌𐤏𐤔𐤄.𐤉𐤃𐤉.𐤇𐤓𐤔.𐤅𐤔𐤌.𐤁𐤎𐤕𐤓.𐤅𐤏𐤍𐤅.𐤊𐤋
𐤄𐤏𐤌.𐤅𐤀𐤌𐤓𐤅.𐤀𐤌𐤍|
טז 𐤀𐤓𐤅𐤓.𐤌𐤒𐤋𐤄.𐤀𐤁𐤉𐤅.𐤅𐤀𐤌𐤅.𐤅𐤀𐤌𐤓.𐤊𐤋.𐤄𐤏𐤌.𐤀𐤌𐤍|
יז 𐤀𐤓𐤅𐤓.𐤌𐤎𐤉𐤂.𐤂𐤁𐤅𐤋.𐤓𐤏𐤄𐤅.𐤅𐤀𐤌𐤓.𐤊𐤋.𐤄𐤏𐤌.𐤀
𐤌𐤍|
יח 𐤀𐤓𐤅𐤓.𐤌𐤔𐤂𐤄.𐤏𐤅𐤓.𐤁𐤃𐤓𐤊.𐤅𐤀𐤌𐤓.𐤊𐤋.𐤄𐤏𐤌.𐤀𐤌
𐤍|
יט 𐤀𐤓𐤅𐤓.𐤌𐤈𐤄.𐤌𐤔𐤐𐤈.𐤂𐤓.𐤉𐤕𐤅𐤌.𐤅𐤀𐤋𐤌𐤍𐤄.𐤅𐤀𐤌𐤓.
𐤊𐤋.𐤄𐤏𐤌.𐤀𐤌𐤍|
כ 𐤀𐤓𐤅𐤓.𐤔𐤊𐤁.𐤏𐤌.𐤀𐤔𐤕.𐤀𐤁𐤉𐤅.𐤊𐤉.𐤂𐤋𐤄.𐤊𐤍𐤐.𐤀
𐤁𐤉𐤅.𐤅𐤀𐤌𐤓.𐤊𐤋.𐤄𐤏𐤌.𐤀𐤌𐤍|
כא 𐤀𐤓𐤅𐤓.𐤔𐤊𐤁.𐤏𐤌.𐤊𐤋.𐤁𐤄𐤌𐤄.𐤅𐤀𐤌𐤓.𐤊𐤋.𐤄𐤏𐤌.𐤀𐤌
𐤍|

22 𐤀𐤓𐤅𐤓.𐤔𐤊𐤁.𐤏𐤌.𐤀𐤇𐤕𐤅.𐤁𐤕.𐤀𐤁𐤉𐤅.𐤀𐤅.𐤁𐤕.𐤀𐤌𐤅.
𐤅𐤀𐤌𐤓.𐤊𐤋.𐤄𐤏𐤌.𐤀𐤌𐤍|
23 𐤀𐤓𐤅𐤓.𐤔𐤊𐤁.𐤏𐤌.𐤇𐤕𐤍𐤕𐤅.𐤅𐤀𐤌𐤓.𐤊𐤋.𐤄𐤏𐤌.𐤀𐤌𐤍|
24 𐤀𐤓𐤅𐤓.𐤌𐤊𐤄.𐤓𐤏𐤄𐤅.𐤁𐤎𐤕𐤓.𐤅𐤀𐤌𐤓.𐤊𐤋.𐤄𐤏𐤌.𐤀𐤌
𐤍|
25 𐤀𐤓𐤅𐤓.𐤋𐤒𐤇.𐤔𐤇𐤃.𐤋𐤄𐤊𐤅𐤕.𐤍𐤐𐤔.𐤃𐤌.𐤍𐤒𐤉.𐤅𐤀𐤌
𐤓.𐤊𐤋.𐤄𐤏𐤌.𐤀𐤌𐤍|
26 𐤀𐤓𐤅𐤓.𐤀𐤔𐤓.𐤋𐤀.𐤉𐤒𐤉𐤌.𐤀𐤕.𐤃𐤁𐤓𐤉.𐤄𐤕𐤅𐤓𐤄.𐤄
𐤆𐤀𐤕.𐤋𐤏𐤔𐤅𐤕.𐤀𐤅𐤕𐤌.𐤅𐤀𐤌𐤓.𐤊𐤋.𐤄𐤏𐤌.𐤀𐤌𐤍||

𐤃𐤁𐤓𐤉𐤌.𐤇𐤋𐤒 28

1 𐤅𐤄𐤉𐤄.𐤀𐤌.𐤔𐤌𐤅𐤏.𐤕𐤔𐤌𐤏.𐤁𐤒𐤅𐤋.𐤉𐤄𐤅𐤄.𐤀𐤋𐤄𐤉𐤊.
𐤋𐤔𐤌𐤓.𐤋𐤏𐤔𐤅𐤕.𐤀𐤕.𐤊𐤋.𐤌𐤑𐤅𐤕𐤉𐤅.𐤀𐤔𐤓.𐤀𐤍𐤊𐤉.𐤌𐤑𐤅
𐤊.𐤄𐤉𐤅𐤌.𐤅𐤍𐤕𐤍𐤊.𐤉𐤄𐤅𐤄.𐤀𐤋𐤄𐤉𐤊.𐤏𐤋𐤉𐤅𐤍.𐤏𐤋.𐤊𐤋.𐤂𐤅𐤉
𐤉.𐤄𐤀𐤓𐤑|
2 𐤅𐤁𐤀𐤅.𐤏𐤋𐤉𐤊.𐤊𐤋.𐤄𐤁𐤓𐤊𐤅𐤕.𐤄𐤀𐤋𐤄.𐤅𐤄𐤔𐤉𐤂𐤊.𐤊𐤉.
𐤕𐤔𐤌𐤏.𐤁𐤒𐤅𐤋.𐤉𐤄𐤅𐤄.𐤀𐤋𐤄𐤉𐤊|
3 𐤁𐤓𐤅𐤊.𐤀𐤕𐤄.𐤁𐤏𐤉𐤓.𐤅𐤁𐤓𐤅𐤊.𐤀𐤕𐤄.𐤁𐤔𐤃𐤄|
4 𐤁𐤓𐤅𐤊.𐤐𐤓𐤉.𐤁𐤈𐤍𐤊.𐤅𐤐𐤓𐤉.𐤀𐤃𐤌𐤕𐤊.𐤅𐤐𐤓𐤉.𐤁𐤄𐤌𐤕𐤊
.𐤔𐤂𐤓.𐤀𐤋𐤐𐤉𐤊.𐤅𐤏𐤔𐤕𐤓𐤅𐤕.𐤑𐤀𐤍𐤊|
5 𐤁𐤓𐤅𐤊.𐤈𐤍𐤀𐤊.𐤅𐤌𐤔𐤀𐤓𐤕𐤊|
6 𐤁𐤓𐤅𐤊.𐤀𐤕𐤄.𐤁𐤁𐤀𐤊.𐤅𐤁𐤓𐤅𐤊.𐤀𐤕𐤄.𐤁𐤑𐤀𐤕𐤊|
7 𐤉𐤕𐤍.𐤉𐤄𐤅𐤄.𐤀𐤕.𐤀𐤉𐤁𐤉𐤊.𐤄𐤒𐤌𐤉𐤌.𐤏𐤋𐤉𐤊.𐤍𐤂𐤐𐤉
𐤌.𐤋𐤐𐤍𐤉𐤊.𐤁𐤃𐤓𐤊.𐤀𐤇𐤃.𐤉𐤑𐤀𐤅.𐤀𐤋𐤉𐤊.𐤅𐤁𐤔𐤁𐤏𐤄.𐤃
𐤓𐤊𐤉𐤌.𐤉𐤍𐤅𐤎𐤅.𐤋𐤐𐤍𐤉𐤊|
8 𐤉𐤑𐤅.𐤉𐤄𐤅𐤄.𐤀𐤕𐤊.𐤀𐤕.𐤄𐤁𐤓𐤊𐤄.𐤁𐤀𐤎𐤌𐤉𐤊.𐤅𐤁𐤊𐤋.
𐤌𐤔𐤋𐤇.𐤉𐤃𐤊.𐤅𐤁𐤓𐤊𐤊.𐤁𐤀𐤓𐤑.𐤀𐤔𐤓.𐤉𐤄𐤅𐤄.𐤀𐤋𐤄𐤉𐤊.𐤍
𐤕𐤍.𐤋𐤊|

𐤈 𐤉𐤒𐤉𐤌𐤊.𐤉𐤄𐤅𐤄.𐤋𐤅.𐤋𐤏𐤌.𐤒𐤃𐤅𐤔.𐤊𐤀𐤔𐤓.𐤍𐤔𐤁𐤏.
𐤋𐤊.𐤊𐤉.𐤕𐤔𐤌𐤓.𐤀𐤕.𐤌𐤑𐤅𐤕.𐤉𐤄𐤅𐤄.𐤀𐤋𐤄𐤉𐤊.𐤅𐤄𐤋𐤊𐤕.𐤁
𐤃𐤓𐤊𐤉𐤅|

𐤉 𐤅𐤓𐤀𐤅.𐤊𐤋.𐤏𐤌𐤉.𐤄𐤀𐤓𐤑.𐤊𐤉.𐤔𐤌.𐤉𐤄𐤅𐤄.𐤍𐤒𐤓𐤀.𐤏
𐤋𐤉𐤊.𐤅𐤉𐤓𐤀𐤅.𐤌𐤌𐤊|

𐤉𐤀 𐤅𐤄𐤅𐤕𐤓𐤊.𐤉𐤄𐤅𐤄.𐤋𐤈𐤅𐤁𐤄.𐤁𐤐𐤓𐤉.𐤁𐤈𐤍𐤊.𐤅𐤁𐤐𐤓𐤉.𐤁
𐤄𐤌𐤕𐤊.𐤅𐤁𐤐𐤓𐤉.𐤀𐤃𐤌𐤕𐤊.𐤏𐤋.𐤄𐤀𐤃𐤌𐤄.𐤀𐤔𐤓.𐤍𐤔𐤁𐤏.
𐤉𐤄𐤅𐤄.𐤋𐤀𐤁𐤕𐤉𐤊.𐤋𐤕𐤕.𐤋𐤊|

𐤉𐤁 𐤉𐤐𐤕𐤇.𐤉𐤄𐤅𐤄.𐤋𐤊.𐤀𐤕.𐤀𐤅𐤑𐤓𐤅.𐤄𐤈𐤅𐤁.𐤀𐤕.𐤄𐤔𐤌
𐤉𐤌.𐤋𐤕𐤕.𐤌𐤈𐤓.𐤀𐤓𐤑𐤊.𐤁𐤏𐤕𐤅.𐤅𐤋𐤁𐤓𐤊.𐤀𐤕.𐤊𐤋.𐤌𐤏𐤔
𐤄.𐤉𐤃𐤊.𐤅𐤄𐤋𐤅𐤉𐤕.𐤂𐤅𐤉𐤌.𐤓𐤁𐤉𐤌.𐤅𐤀𐤕𐤄.𐤋𐤀.𐤕𐤋𐤅𐤄|

𐤉𐤂 𐤅𐤍𐤕𐤍𐤊.𐤉𐤄𐤅𐤄.𐤋𐤓𐤀𐤔.𐤅𐤋𐤀.𐤋𐤆𐤍𐤁.𐤅𐤄𐤉𐤉𐤕.𐤓𐤒.𐤋
𐤌𐤏𐤋𐤄.𐤅𐤋𐤀.𐤕𐤄𐤉𐤄.𐤋𐤌𐤈𐤄.𐤊𐤉.𐤕𐤔𐤌𐤏.𐤀𐤋.𐤌𐤑𐤅𐤕.𐤉
𐤄𐤅𐤄.𐤀𐤋𐤄𐤉𐤊.𐤀𐤔𐤓.𐤀𐤍𐤊𐤉.𐤌𐤑𐤅𐤊.𐤄𐤉𐤅𐤌.𐤋𐤔𐤌𐤓.𐤅𐤋𐤏
𐤔𐤅𐤕|

𐤉𐤃 𐤅𐤋𐤀.𐤕𐤎𐤅𐤓.𐤌𐤊𐤋.𐤄𐤃𐤁𐤓𐤉𐤌.𐤀𐤔𐤓.𐤀𐤍𐤊𐤉.𐤌𐤑𐤅
𐤄.𐤀𐤕𐤊𐤌.𐤄𐤉𐤅𐤌.𐤉𐤌𐤉𐤍.𐤅𐤔𐤌𐤀𐤅𐤋.𐤋𐤋𐤊𐤕.𐤀𐤇𐤓𐤉.𐤀𐤋
𐤄𐤉𐤌.𐤀𐤇𐤓𐤉𐤌.𐤋𐤏𐤁𐤃𐤌|

𐤉𐤄 𐤅𐤄𐤉𐤄.𐤀𐤌.𐤋𐤀.𐤕𐤔𐤌𐤏.𐤁𐤒𐤅𐤋.𐤉𐤄𐤅𐤄.𐤀𐤋𐤄𐤉𐤊.𐤋
𐤔𐤌𐤓.𐤋𐤏𐤔𐤅𐤕.𐤀𐤕.𐤊𐤋.𐤌𐤑𐤅𐤕𐤉𐤅.𐤅𐤇𐤒𐤕𐤉𐤅.𐤀𐤔𐤓.𐤀𐤍
𐤊𐤉.𐤌𐤑𐤅𐤊.𐤄𐤉𐤅𐤌.𐤅𐤁𐤀𐤅.𐤏𐤋𐤉𐤊.𐤊𐤋.𐤄𐤒𐤋𐤋𐤅𐤕.𐤄𐤀𐤋𐤄.
𐤅𐤄𐤔𐤉𐤂𐤅𐤊|

𐤉𐤅 𐤀𐤓𐤅𐤓.𐤀𐤕𐤄.𐤁𐤏𐤉𐤓.𐤅𐤀𐤓𐤅𐤓.𐤀𐤕𐤄.𐤁𐤔𐤃𐤄|

𐤉𐤆 𐤀𐤓𐤅𐤓.𐤈𐤍𐤀𐤊.𐤅𐤌𐤔𐤀𐤓𐤕𐤊|

𐤉𐤇 𐤀𐤓𐤅𐤓.𐤐𐤓𐤉.𐤁𐤈𐤍𐤊.𐤅𐤐𐤓𐤉.𐤀𐤃𐤌𐤕𐤊.𐤔𐤂𐤓.𐤀𐤋𐤐𐤉𐤊
.𐤅𐤏𐤔𐤕𐤓𐤕.𐤑𐤀𐤍𐤊|

𐤉𐤈 𐤀𐤓𐤅𐤓.𐤀𐤕𐤄.𐤁𐤁𐤀𐤊.𐤅𐤀𐤓𐤅𐤓.𐤀𐤕𐤄.𐤁𐤑𐤀𐤕𐤊|

𐤊 𐤉𐤔𐤋𐤇.𐤉𐤄𐤅𐤄.𐤁𐤊.𐤀𐤕.𐤄𐤌𐤀𐤓𐤄.𐤀𐤕.𐤄𐤌𐤄𐤅𐤌𐤄.
𐤅𐤀𐤕.𐤄𐤌𐤂𐤏𐤓𐤕.𐤁𐤊𐤋.𐤌𐤔𐤋𐤇.𐤉𐤃𐤊.𐤀𐤔𐤓.𐤕𐤏𐤔𐤄.𐤏
𐤃.𐤄𐤔𐤌𐤃𐤊.𐤅𐤏𐤃.𐤀𐤁𐤃𐤊.𐤌𐤄𐤓.𐤌𐤐𐤍𐤉.𐤓𐤏.𐤌𐤏𐤋𐤋𐤉𐤊
.𐤀𐤔𐤓.𐤏𐤆𐤁𐤕𐤍𐤉|

..ࠊࠀ.. ࠉࠃࠁࠒ.ࠉࠄࠅࠄ.ࠁࠊ.ࠀࠕ.ࠄࠃࠁࠓ.ࠏࠃ.ࠊࠋࠕࠅ.ࠀࠕ
ࠊ.ࠌࠏࠋ.ࠄࠀࠃࠌࠄ.ࠀࠔࠓ.ࠀࠕࠄ.ࠁࠀ.ࠔࠌࠄ.ࠋࠓࠔࠕࠄ|
..ࠊࠁ.. ࠉࠊࠊࠄ.ࠉࠄࠅࠄ.ࠁࠔࠇࠐࠕ.ࠅࠁࠒࠃࠇࠕ.ࠅࠁࠃࠋࠒࠕ.ࠅ
ࠁࠇࠓࠇࠓ.ࠅࠁࠇࠓࠁ.ࠅࠁࠔࠃࠐࠅࠍ.ࠅࠁࠉࠓࠒࠅࠍ.ࠅࠓࠃࠐࠅࠊ.ࠏࠃ.
ࠀࠁࠃࠊ|
..ࠊࠂ.. ࠅࠄࠉࠅ.ࠔࠌࠉࠊ.ࠀࠔࠓ.ࠏࠋ.ࠓࠀࠔࠊ.ࠍࠇࠔࠕ.ࠅࠄࠀࠓࠑ.
ࠀࠔࠓ.ࠕࠇࠕࠉࠊ.ࠁࠓࠆࠋ|
..ࠊࠃ.. ࠉࠕࠍ.ࠉࠄࠅࠄ.ࠀࠕ.ࠌࠈࠓ.ࠀࠓࠑࠊ.ࠀࠁࠒ.ࠅࠏࠐࠓ.ࠌࠍ.
ࠄࠔࠌࠉࠌ.ࠉࠓࠃ.ࠏࠋࠉࠊ.ࠏࠃ.ࠄࠔࠌࠃࠊ|
..ࠊࠄ.. ࠉࠕࠍࠊ.ࠉࠄࠅࠄ.ࠍࠂࠐ.ࠋࠐࠍࠉ.ࠀࠉࠁࠉࠊ.ࠁࠃࠓࠊ.ࠀࠇ
ࠃ.ࠕࠑࠀ.ࠀࠋࠉࠅ.ࠅࠁࠔࠁࠏࠄ.ࠃࠓࠊࠉࠌ.ࠕࠍࠅࠎ.ࠋࠐࠍࠉࠅ.ࠅࠄ
ࠉࠉࠕ.ࠋࠆࠏࠅࠄ.ࠋࠊࠋ.ࠌࠌࠋࠊࠅࠕ.ࠄࠀࠓࠑ|
..ࠊࠅ.. ࠅࠄࠉࠕࠄ.ࠍࠁࠋࠕࠊ.ࠋࠌࠀࠊࠋ.ࠋࠊࠋ.ࠏࠅࠐ.ࠄࠔࠌࠉࠌ.ࠅࠋ
ࠁࠄࠌࠕ.ࠄࠀࠓࠑ.ࠅࠀࠉࠍ.ࠌࠇࠓࠉࠃ|
..ࠊࠆ.. ࠉࠊࠊࠄ.ࠉࠄࠅࠄ.ࠁࠔࠇࠉࠍ.ࠌࠑࠓࠉࠌ.ࠅࠁࠏࠐࠋࠉࠌ.ࠅ||
ࠁࠈࠇࠓࠉࠌ.ࠒࠓࠉ||.ࠅࠁࠂࠓࠁ.ࠅࠁࠇࠓࠎ.ࠀࠔࠓ.ࠋࠀ.ࠕࠅࠊࠋ.ࠋ
ࠄࠓࠐࠀ|
..ࠊࠇ.. ࠉࠊࠊࠄ.ࠉࠄࠅࠄ.ࠁࠔࠂࠏࠅࠍ.ࠅࠁࠏࠅࠓࠅࠍ.ࠅࠁࠕࠌࠄࠅࠍ.ࠋ
ࠁࠁ|
..ࠊࠈ.. ࠅࠄࠉࠉࠕ.ࠌࠌࠔࠔ.ࠁࠑࠄࠓࠉࠌ.ࠊࠀࠔࠓ.ࠉࠌࠔࠔ.ࠄࠏ
ࠅࠓ.ࠁࠀࠐࠋࠄ.ࠅࠋࠀ.ࠕࠑࠋࠉࠇ.ࠀࠕ.ࠃࠓࠊࠉࠊ.ࠅࠄࠉࠉࠕ.ࠀࠊ.
ࠏࠔࠅࠒ.ࠅࠂࠆࠅࠋ.ࠊࠋ.ࠄࠉࠌࠉࠌ.ࠅࠀࠉࠍ.ࠌࠅࠔࠉࠏ|
..ࠋ.. ࠀࠔࠄ.ࠕࠀࠓࠔ.ࠅࠀࠉࠔ.ࠀࠇࠓ.ࠉࠔࠂࠋࠍࠄ.||ࠉࠔࠊࠁࠍ
ࠄ.ࠒࠓࠉ||.ࠁࠉࠕ.ࠕࠁࠍࠄ.ࠅࠋࠀ.ࠕࠔࠁ.ࠁࠅ.ࠊࠓࠌ.ࠕࠈࠏ.ࠅࠋࠀ.
ࠕࠇࠋࠋࠍࠅ|
..ࠋࠀ.. ࠔࠅࠓࠊ.ࠈࠁࠅࠇ.ࠋࠏࠉࠍࠉࠊ.ࠅࠋࠀ.ࠕࠀࠊࠋ.ࠌࠌࠍࠅ.ࠇࠌࠓ
ࠊ.ࠂࠆࠅࠋ.ࠌࠋࠐࠍࠉࠊ.ࠅࠋࠀ.ࠉࠔࠅࠁ.ࠋࠊ.ࠑࠀࠍࠊ.ࠍࠕࠍࠅࠕ.ࠋࠀ
ࠉࠁࠉࠊ.ࠅࠀࠉࠍ.ࠋࠊ.ࠌࠅࠔࠉࠏ|
..ࠋࠁ.. ࠁࠍࠉࠊ.ࠅࠁࠍࠕࠉࠊ.ࠍࠕࠍࠉࠌ.ࠋࠏࠌ.ࠀࠇࠓ.ࠅࠏࠉࠍࠉࠊ.ࠓ
ࠀࠅࠕ.ࠅࠊࠋࠅࠕ.ࠀࠋࠉࠄࠌ.ࠊࠋ.ࠄࠉࠅࠌ.ࠅࠀࠉࠍ.ࠋࠀࠋ.ࠉࠃࠊ|

𐤋𐤂 𐤐𐤓𐤉.𐤀𐤃𐤌𐤕𐤊.𐤅𐤊𐤋.𐤉𐤂𐤉𐤏𐤊.𐤉𐤀𐤊𐤋.𐤏𐤌.𐤀𐤔𐤓.
𐤋𐤀.𐤉𐤃𐤏𐤕.𐤅𐤄𐤉𐤉𐤕.𐤓𐤒.𐤏𐤔𐤅𐤒.𐤅𐤓𐤑𐤅𐤑.𐤊𐤋.𐤄𐤉𐤌𐤉𐤌
|
𐤋𐤃 𐤅𐤄𐤉𐤉𐤕.𐤌𐤔𐤂𐤏.𐤌𐤌𐤓𐤀𐤄.𐤏𐤉𐤍𐤉𐤊.𐤀𐤔𐤓.𐤕𐤓𐤀
𐤄|
𐤋𐤄 𐤉𐤊𐤊𐤄.𐤉𐤄𐤅𐤄.𐤁𐤔𐤇𐤉𐤍.𐤓𐤏.𐤏𐤋.𐤄𐤁𐤓𐤊𐤉𐤌.𐤅𐤏𐤋.
𐤄𐤔𐤒𐤉𐤌.𐤀𐤔𐤓.𐤋𐤀.𐤕𐤅𐤊𐤋.𐤋𐤄𐤓𐤐𐤀.𐤌𐤊𐤐.𐤓𐤂𐤋𐤊.𐤅𐤏𐤃.
𐤒𐤃𐤒𐤃𐤊|
𐤋𐤅 𐤉𐤅𐤋𐤊.𐤉𐤄𐤅𐤄.𐤀𐤕𐤊.𐤅𐤀𐤕.𐤌𐤋𐤊𐤊.𐤀𐤔𐤓.𐤕𐤒𐤉𐤌.𐤏
𐤋𐤉𐤊.𐤀𐤋.𐤂𐤅𐤉.𐤀𐤔𐤓.𐤋𐤀.𐤉𐤃𐤏𐤕.𐤀𐤕𐤄.𐤅𐤀𐤁𐤕𐤉𐤊.𐤅𐤏
𐤁𐤃𐤕.𐤔𐤌.𐤀𐤋𐤄𐤉𐤌.𐤀𐤇𐤓𐤉𐤌.𐤏𐤑.𐤅𐤀𐤁𐤍|
𐤋𐤆 𐤅𐤄𐤉𐤉𐤕.𐤋𐤔𐤌𐤄.𐤋𐤌𐤔𐤋.𐤅𐤋𐤔𐤍𐤉𐤍𐤄.𐤁𐤊𐤋.𐤄𐤏𐤌𐤉
𐤌.𐤀𐤔𐤓.𐤉𐤍𐤄𐤂𐤊.𐤉𐤄𐤅𐤄.𐤔𐤌𐤄|
𐤋𐤇 𐤆𐤓𐤏.𐤓𐤁.𐤕𐤅𐤑𐤉𐤀.𐤄𐤔𐤃𐤄.𐤅𐤌𐤏𐤈.𐤕𐤀𐤎𐤐.𐤊𐤉.
𐤉𐤇𐤎𐤋𐤍𐤅.𐤄𐤀𐤓𐤁𐤄|
𐤋𐤈 𐤊𐤓𐤌𐤉𐤌.𐤕𐤈𐤏.𐤅𐤏𐤁𐤃𐤕.𐤅𐤉𐤉𐤍.𐤋𐤀.𐤕𐤔𐤕𐤄.𐤅𐤋
𐤀.𐤕𐤀𐤂𐤓.𐤊𐤉.𐤕𐤀𐤊𐤋𐤍𐤅.𐤄𐤕𐤋𐤏𐤕|
𐤌 𐤆𐤉𐤕𐤉𐤌.𐤉𐤄𐤉𐤅.𐤋𐤊.𐤁𐤊𐤋.𐤂𐤁𐤅𐤋𐤊.𐤅𐤔𐤌𐤍.𐤋𐤀.𐤕
𐤎𐤅𐤊.𐤊𐤉.𐤉𐤔𐤋.𐤆𐤉𐤕𐤊|
𐤌𐤀 𐤁𐤍𐤉𐤌.𐤅𐤁𐤍𐤅𐤕.𐤕𐤅𐤋𐤉𐤃.𐤅𐤋𐤀.𐤉𐤄𐤉𐤅.𐤋𐤊.𐤊𐤉.𐤉𐤋𐤊𐤅
.𐤁𐤔𐤁𐤉|
𐤌𐤁 𐤊𐤋.𐤏𐤑𐤊.𐤅𐤐𐤓𐤉.𐤀𐤃𐤌𐤕𐤊.𐤉𐤉𐤓𐤔.𐤄𐤑𐤋𐤑𐤋|
𐤌𐤂 𐤄𐤂𐤓.𐤀𐤔𐤓.𐤁𐤒𐤓𐤁𐤊.𐤉𐤏𐤋𐤄.𐤏𐤋𐤉𐤊.𐤌𐤏𐤋𐤄.𐤌𐤏
𐤋𐤄.𐤅𐤀𐤕𐤄.𐤕𐤓𐤃.𐤌𐤈𐤄.𐤌𐤈𐤄|
𐤌𐤃 𐤄𐤅𐤀.𐤉𐤋𐤅𐤊.𐤅𐤀𐤕𐤄.𐤋𐤀.𐤕𐤋𐤅𐤍𐤅.𐤄𐤅𐤀.𐤉𐤄𐤉𐤄.𐤋𐤓
𐤀𐤔.𐤅𐤀𐤕𐤄.𐤕𐤄𐤉𐤄.𐤋𐤆𐤍𐤁|
𐤌𐤄 𐤅𐤁𐤀𐤅.𐤏𐤋𐤉𐤊.𐤊𐤋.𐤄𐤒𐤋𐤋𐤅𐤕.𐤄𐤀𐤋𐤄.𐤅𐤓𐤃𐤐𐤅𐤊.𐤅𐤄
𐤔𐤉𐤂𐤅𐤊.𐤏𐤃.𐤄𐤔𐤌𐤃𐤊.𐤊𐤉.𐤋𐤀.𐤔𐤌𐤏𐤕.𐤁𐤒𐤅𐤋.𐤉𐤄𐤅𐤄
.𐤀𐤋𐤄𐤉𐤊.𐤋𐤔𐤌𐤓.𐤌𐤑𐤅𐤕𐤉𐤅.𐤅𐤇𐤒𐤕𐤉𐤅.𐤀𐤔𐤓.𐤑𐤅𐤊|
𐤌𐤅 𐤅𐤄𐤉𐤅.𐤁𐤊.𐤋𐤀𐤅𐤕.𐤅𐤋𐤌𐤅𐤐𐤕.𐤅𐤁𐤆𐤓𐤏𐤊.𐤏𐤃.𐤏𐤅𐤋𐤌|

47 𐤕𐤇𐤕.𐤀𐤔𐤓.𐤋𐤀.𐤏𐤁𐤃𐤕.𐤀𐤕.𐤉𐤄𐤅𐤄.𐤀𐤋𐤄𐤉𐤊.
𐤁𐤔𐤌𐤇𐤄.𐤅𐤁𐤈𐤅𐤁.𐤋𐤁𐤁.𐤌𐤓𐤁.𐤊𐤋|

48 𐤅𐤏𐤁𐤃𐤕.𐤀𐤕.𐤀𐤉𐤁𐤉𐤊.𐤀𐤔𐤓.𐤉𐤔𐤋𐤇𐤍𐤅.𐤉𐤄𐤅𐤄.𐤁
𐤊.𐤁𐤓𐤏𐤁.𐤅𐤁𐤑𐤌𐤀.𐤅𐤁𐤏𐤉𐤓𐤌.𐤅𐤁𐤇𐤎𐤓.𐤊𐤋.𐤅𐤍𐤕𐤍.𐤏𐤋.𐤁𐤓
𐤆𐤋.𐤏𐤋.𐤑𐤅𐤀𐤓𐤊.𐤏𐤃.𐤄𐤔𐤌𐤉𐤃𐤅.𐤀𐤕𐤊|

49 𐤉𐤔𐤀.𐤉𐤄𐤅𐤄.𐤏𐤋𐤉𐤊.𐤂𐤅𐤉.𐤌𐤓𐤇𐤅𐤒.𐤌𐤒𐤑𐤄.𐤄
𐤀𐤓𐤑.𐤊𐤀𐤔𐤓.𐤉𐤃𐤀𐤄.𐤄𐤍𐤔𐤓.𐤂𐤅𐤉.𐤀𐤔𐤓.𐤋𐤀.𐤕𐤔𐤌𐤏.
𐤋𐤔𐤍𐤅|

50 𐤂𐤅𐤉.𐤏𐤆.𐤐𐤍𐤉𐤌.𐤀𐤔𐤓.𐤋𐤀.𐤉𐤔𐤀.𐤐𐤍𐤉𐤌.𐤋𐤆𐤒𐤍.𐤅
𐤍𐤏𐤓.𐤋𐤀.𐤉𐤇𐤍|

51 𐤅𐤀𐤊𐤋.𐤐𐤓𐤉.𐤁𐤄𐤌𐤕𐤊.𐤅𐤐𐤓𐤉.𐤀𐤃𐤌𐤕𐤊.𐤏𐤃.𐤄𐤔𐤌
𐤃𐤊.𐤀𐤔𐤓.𐤋𐤀.𐤉𐤔𐤀𐤉𐤓.𐤋𐤊.𐤃𐤂𐤍.𐤕𐤉𐤓𐤅𐤔.𐤅𐤉𐤑𐤄𐤓.𐤔
𐤂𐤓.𐤀𐤋𐤐𐤉𐤊.𐤅𐤏𐤔𐤕𐤓𐤕.𐤑𐤀𐤍𐤊.𐤏𐤃.𐤄𐤀𐤁𐤉𐤃𐤅.𐤀𐤕𐤊|

52 𐤅𐤄𐤑𐤓.𐤋𐤊.𐤁𐤊𐤋.𐤔𐤏𐤓𐤉𐤊.𐤏𐤃.𐤓𐤃𐤕.𐤇𐤌𐤕𐤉𐤊.𐤄
𐤂𐤁𐤄𐤅𐤕.𐤅𐤄𐤁𐤑𐤓𐤅𐤕.𐤀𐤔𐤓.𐤀𐤕𐤄.𐤁𐤈𐤇.𐤁𐤄𐤍.𐤁𐤊𐤋.𐤀𐤓
𐤑𐤊.𐤅𐤄𐤑𐤓.𐤋𐤊.𐤁𐤊𐤋.𐤔𐤏𐤓𐤉𐤊.𐤁𐤊𐤋.𐤀𐤓𐤑𐤊.𐤀𐤔𐤓.𐤍𐤕𐤍.
𐤉𐤄𐤅𐤄.𐤀𐤋𐤄𐤉𐤊.𐤋𐤊|

53 𐤅𐤀𐤊𐤋𐤕.𐤐𐤓𐤉.𐤁𐤈𐤍𐤊.𐤁𐤔𐤓.𐤁𐤍𐤉𐤊.𐤅𐤁𐤍𐤕𐤉𐤊.𐤀𐤔𐤓.
𐤍𐤕𐤍.𐤋𐤊.𐤉𐤄𐤅𐤄.𐤀𐤋𐤄𐤉𐤊.𐤁𐤌𐤑𐤅𐤓.𐤅𐤁𐤌𐤑𐤅𐤒.𐤀𐤔𐤓.𐤉𐤑
𐤉𐤒.𐤋𐤊.𐤀𐤉𐤁𐤊|

54 𐤄𐤀𐤉𐤔.𐤄𐤓𐤊.𐤁𐤊.𐤅𐤄𐤏𐤍𐤂.𐤌𐤀𐤃.𐤕𐤓𐤏.𐤏𐤉𐤍𐤅.𐤁
𐤀𐤇𐤉𐤅.𐤅𐤁𐤀𐤔𐤕.𐤇𐤉𐤒𐤅.𐤅𐤁𐤉𐤕𐤓.𐤁𐤍𐤉𐤅.𐤀𐤔𐤓.𐤉𐤅𐤕𐤉𐤓|

55 𐤌𐤕𐤕.𐤋𐤀𐤇𐤃.𐤌𐤄𐤌.𐤌𐤁𐤔𐤓.𐤁𐤍𐤉𐤅.𐤀𐤔𐤓.𐤉𐤀𐤊𐤋.
𐤌𐤁𐤋𐤉.𐤄𐤔𐤀𐤉𐤓.𐤋𐤅.𐤊𐤋.𐤁𐤌𐤑𐤅𐤓.𐤅𐤁𐤌𐤑𐤅𐤒.𐤀𐤔𐤓.𐤉𐤑𐤉
𐤒.𐤋𐤊.𐤀𐤉𐤁𐤊.𐤁𐤊𐤋.𐤔𐤏𐤓𐤉𐤊|

56 𐤄𐤓𐤊𐤄.𐤁𐤊.𐤅𐤄𐤏𐤍𐤂𐤄.𐤀𐤔𐤓.𐤋𐤀.𐤍𐤎𐤕𐤄.𐤊𐤐.𐤓𐤂𐤋
𐤄.𐤄𐤑𐤂.𐤏𐤋.𐤄𐤀𐤓𐤑.𐤌𐤄𐤕𐤏𐤍𐤂.𐤅𐤌𐤓𐤊.𐤕𐤓𐤏.𐤏𐤉𐤍𐤄.
𐤁𐤀𐤉𐤔.𐤇𐤉𐤒𐤄.𐤅𐤁𐤁𐤍𐤄.𐤅𐤁𐤁𐤕𐤄|

57 𐤅𐤁𐤔𐤋𐤉𐤕𐤄.𐤄𐤉𐤅𐤑𐤕.𐤌𐤁𐤉𐤍.𐤓𐤂𐤋𐤉𐤄.𐤅𐤁𐤁𐤍𐤉𐤄.
𐤀𐤔𐤓.𐤕𐤋𐤃.𐤊𐤉.𐤕𐤀𐤊𐤋𐤌.𐤁𐤇𐤎𐤓.𐤊𐤋.𐤁𐤎𐤕𐤓.𐤁𐤌𐤑𐤅𐤓.
𐤅𐤁𐤌𐤑𐤅𐤒.𐤀𐤔𐤓.𐤉𐤑𐤉𐤒.𐤋𐤊.𐤀𐤉𐤁𐤊.𐤁𐤔𐤏𐤓𐤉𐤊|

נח 𐤀𐤌.𐤋𐤀.𐤕𐤔𐤌𐤓.𐤋𐤏𐤔𐤅𐤕.𐤀𐤕.𐤊𐤋.𐤃𐤁𐤓𐤉.𐤄𐤕𐤅𐤓𐤄
.𐤄𐤆𐤀𐤕.𐤄𐤊𐤕𐤅𐤁𐤉𐤌.𐤁𐤎𐤐𐤓.𐤄𐤆𐤄.𐤋𐤉𐤓𐤀𐤄.𐤀𐤕.𐤄𐤔
𐤌.𐤄𐤍𐤊𐤁𐤃.𐤅𐤄𐤍𐤅𐤓𐤀.𐤄𐤆𐤄.𐤀𐤕.𐤉𐤄𐤅𐤄.𐤀𐤋𐤄𐤉𐤊|

נט 𐤅𐤄𐤐𐤋𐤀.𐤉𐤄𐤅𐤄.𐤀𐤕.𐤌𐤊𐤕𐤊.𐤅𐤀𐤕.𐤌𐤊𐤅𐤕.𐤆𐤓𐤏𐤊.
𐤌𐤊𐤅𐤕.𐤂𐤃𐤋𐤅𐤕.𐤅𐤍𐤀𐤌𐤍𐤅𐤕.𐤅𐤇𐤋𐤉𐤌.𐤓𐤏𐤉𐤌.𐤅𐤍𐤀𐤌𐤍𐤉𐤌
|

ס 𐤅𐤄𐤔𐤉𐤁.𐤁𐤊.𐤀𐤕.𐤊𐤋.𐤌𐤃𐤅𐤄.𐤌𐤑𐤓𐤉𐤌.𐤀𐤔𐤓.𐤉𐤂
𐤓𐤕.𐤌𐤐𐤍𐤉𐤄𐤌.𐤅𐤃𐤁𐤒𐤅.𐤁𐤊|

סא 𐤂𐤌.𐤊𐤋.𐤇𐤋𐤉.𐤅𐤊𐤋.𐤌𐤊𐤄.𐤀𐤔𐤓.𐤋𐤀.𐤊𐤕𐤅𐤁.𐤁𐤎𐤐𐤓.
𐤄𐤕𐤅𐤓𐤄.𐤄𐤆𐤀𐤕.𐤉𐤏𐤋𐤌.𐤉𐤄𐤅𐤄.𐤏𐤋𐤉𐤊.𐤏𐤃.𐤄𐤔𐤌𐤃
𐤊|

סב 𐤅𐤍𐤔𐤀𐤓𐤕𐤌.𐤁𐤌𐤕𐤉.𐤌𐤏𐤈.𐤕𐤇𐤕.𐤀𐤔𐤓.𐤄𐤉𐤉𐤕𐤌.
𐤊𐤊𐤅𐤊𐤁𐤉.𐤄𐤔𐤌𐤉𐤌.𐤋𐤓𐤁.𐤊𐤉.𐤋𐤀.𐤔𐤌𐤏𐤕.𐤁𐤒𐤅𐤋.𐤉𐤄𐤅
𐤄.𐤀𐤋𐤄𐤉𐤊|

סג 𐤅𐤄𐤉𐤄.𐤊𐤀𐤔𐤓.𐤔𐤔.𐤉𐤄𐤅𐤄.𐤏𐤋𐤉𐤊𐤌.𐤋𐤄𐤉𐤈𐤉𐤁.𐤀
𐤕𐤊𐤌.𐤅𐤋𐤄𐤓𐤁𐤅𐤕.𐤀𐤕𐤊𐤌.𐤊𐤍.𐤉𐤔𐤉𐤔.𐤉𐤄𐤅𐤄.𐤏𐤋𐤉𐤊𐤌.𐤋
𐤄𐤀𐤁𐤉𐤃.𐤀𐤕𐤊𐤌.𐤅𐤋𐤄𐤔𐤌𐤉𐤃.𐤀𐤕𐤊𐤌.𐤅𐤍𐤎𐤇𐤕𐤌.𐤌𐤏
𐤋.𐤄𐤀𐤃𐤌𐤄.𐤀𐤔𐤓.𐤀𐤕𐤄.𐤁𐤀.𐤔𐤌𐤄.𐤋𐤓𐤔𐤕𐤄|

סד 𐤅𐤄𐤐𐤉𐤑𐤊.𐤉𐤄𐤅𐤄.𐤁𐤊𐤋.𐤄𐤏𐤌𐤉𐤌.𐤌𐤒𐤑𐤄.𐤄𐤀𐤓
𐤑.𐤅𐤏𐤃.𐤒𐤑𐤄.𐤄𐤀𐤓𐤑.𐤅𐤏𐤁𐤃𐤕.𐤔𐤌.𐤀𐤋𐤄𐤉𐤌.𐤀𐤇𐤓
𐤉𐤌.𐤀𐤔𐤓.𐤋𐤀.𐤉𐤃𐤏𐤕.𐤀𐤕𐤄.𐤅𐤀𐤁𐤕𐤉𐤊.𐤏𐤑.𐤅𐤀𐤁𐤍|

סה 𐤅𐤁𐤂𐤅𐤉𐤌.𐤄𐤄𐤌.𐤋𐤀.𐤕𐤓𐤂𐤉𐤏.𐤅𐤋𐤀.𐤉𐤄𐤉𐤄.𐤌𐤍𐤅𐤇
𐤋𐤊𐤐.𐤓𐤂𐤋𐤊.𐤅𐤍𐤕𐤍.𐤉𐤄𐤅𐤄.𐤋𐤊.𐤔𐤌.𐤋𐤁.𐤓𐤂𐤆.𐤅𐤊𐤋𐤉𐤅𐤍.
𐤏𐤉𐤍𐤉𐤌.𐤅𐤃𐤀𐤁𐤅𐤍.𐤍𐤐𐤔|

סו 𐤅𐤄𐤉𐤅.𐤇𐤉𐤉𐤊.𐤕𐤋𐤀𐤉𐤌.𐤋𐤊.𐤌𐤍𐤂𐤃.𐤅𐤐𐤇𐤃𐤕.𐤋𐤉
𐤋𐤄.𐤅𐤉𐤅𐤌𐤌.𐤅𐤋𐤀.𐤕𐤀𐤌𐤉𐤍.𐤁𐤇𐤉𐤉𐤊|

סז 𐤁𐤁𐤒𐤓.𐤕𐤀𐤌𐤓.𐤌𐤉.𐤉𐤕𐤍.𐤏𐤓𐤁.𐤅𐤁𐤏𐤓𐤁.𐤕𐤀𐤌𐤓.𐤌
𐤉.𐤉𐤕𐤍.𐤁𐤒𐤓.𐤌𐤐𐤇𐤃.𐤋𐤁𐤁𐤊.𐤀𐤔𐤓.𐤕𐤐𐤇𐤃.𐤅𐤌𐤌𐤓𐤀𐤄.
𐤏𐤉𐤍𐤉𐤊.𐤀𐤔𐤓.𐤕𐤓𐤀𐤄|

68 והשיבך.יהוה.מצרים.באניות.בדרך.אש
ר.אמרתי.לך.לא.תסיף.עוד.לראתה.והתמכרת
ם.שם.לאיביך.לעבדים.ולשפחות.ואין.קנה ||

29 דברים.חלק

1 אלה.דברי.הברית.אשר.צוה.יהוה.את.מש
ה.לכרת.את.בני.ישראל.בארץ.מואב.מלבד.ה
ברית.אשר.כרת.אתם.בחרב |
2 ויקרא.משה.אל.כל.ישראל.ויאמר.אלהם.א
תם.ראיתם.את.כל.אשר.עשה.יהוה.לעיניכם.
בארץ.מצרים.לפרעה.ולכל.עבדיו.ולכל.ארצו
|
3 המסות.הגדלת.אשר.ראו.עיניך.האתת.ו
המפתים.הגדלים.ההם |
4 ולא.נתן.יהוה.לכם.לב.לדעת.ועינים.לרא
ות.ואזנים.לשמע.עד.היום.הזה |
5 ואולך.אתכם.ארבעים.שנה.במדבר.לא.בלו.
שלמתיכם.מעליכם.ונעלך.לא.בלתה.מעל.רג
לך |
6 לחם.לא.אכלתם.ויין.ושכר.לא.שתיתם.למ
ען.תדעו.כי.אני.יהוה.אלהיכם |
7 ותבאו.אל.המקום.הזה.ויצא.סיחן.מלך.
חשבון.ועוג.מלך.הבשן.לקראתנו.למלחמה.ונ
כם |
8 ונקח.את.ארצם.ונתנה.לנחלה.לראובני.ול
גדי.ולחצי.שבט.המנשי |
9 ושמרתם.את.דברי.הברית.הזאת.ועשית
ם.אתם.למען.תשכילו.את.כל.אשר.תעשון |

10 𐤀𐤕𐤌.𐤍𐤑𐤁𐤉𐤌.𐤄𐤉𐤅𐤌.𐤊𐤋𐤊𐤌.𐤋𐤐𐤍𐤉.𐤉𐤄𐤅𐤄.𐤀𐤋𐤄
𐤉𐤊𐤌.𐤓𐤀𐤔𐤉𐤊𐤌.𐤔𐤁𐤈𐤉𐤊𐤌.𐤆𐤒𐤍𐤉𐤊𐤌.𐤅𐤔𐤈𐤓𐤉𐤊𐤌.𐤊
𐤋.𐤀𐤉𐤔.𐤉𐤔𐤓𐤀𐤋|
11 𐤈𐤐𐤊𐤌.𐤍𐤔𐤉𐤊𐤌.𐤅𐤂𐤓𐤊.𐤀𐤔𐤓.𐤁𐤒𐤓𐤁.𐤌𐤇𐤍𐤉𐤊.𐤌
𐤇𐤈𐤁.𐤏𐤑𐤉𐤊.𐤏𐤃.𐤔𐤀𐤁.𐤌𐤉𐤌𐤉𐤊|
12 𐤋𐤏𐤁𐤓𐤊.𐤁𐤁𐤓𐤉𐤕.𐤉𐤄𐤅𐤄.𐤀𐤋𐤄𐤉𐤊.𐤅𐤁𐤀𐤋𐤕𐤅.𐤀𐤔𐤓
.𐤉𐤄𐤅𐤄.𐤀𐤋𐤄𐤉𐤊.𐤊𐤓𐤕.𐤏𐤌𐤊.𐤄𐤉𐤅𐤌|
13 𐤋𐤌𐤏𐤍.𐤄𐤒𐤉𐤌.𐤀𐤕𐤊.𐤄𐤉𐤅𐤌.𐤋𐤅.𐤋𐤏𐤌.𐤅𐤄𐤅𐤀.𐤉𐤄𐤉
𐤄.𐤋𐤊.𐤋𐤀𐤋𐤄𐤉𐤌.𐤊𐤀𐤔𐤓.𐤃𐤁𐤓.𐤋𐤊.𐤅𐤊𐤀𐤔𐤓.𐤍𐤔𐤁𐤏.𐤋𐤀
𐤁𐤕𐤉𐤊.𐤋𐤀𐤁𐤓𐤄𐤌.𐤋𐤉𐤑𐤇𐤒.𐤅𐤋𐤉𐤏𐤒𐤁|
14 𐤅𐤋𐤀.𐤀𐤕𐤊𐤌.𐤋𐤁𐤃𐤊𐤌.𐤀𐤍𐤊𐤉.𐤊𐤓𐤕.𐤀𐤕.𐤄𐤁𐤓𐤉
𐤕.𐤄𐤆𐤀𐤕.𐤅𐤀𐤕.𐤄𐤀𐤋𐤄.𐤄𐤆𐤀𐤕|
15 𐤊𐤉.𐤀𐤕.𐤀𐤔𐤓.𐤉𐤔𐤍𐤅.𐤐𐤄.𐤏𐤌𐤍𐤅.𐤏𐤌𐤃.𐤄𐤉𐤅𐤌.𐤋𐤐𐤍
𐤉.𐤉𐤄𐤅𐤄.𐤀𐤋𐤄𐤉𐤍𐤅.𐤅𐤀𐤕.𐤀𐤔𐤓.𐤀𐤉𐤍𐤍𐤅.𐤐𐤄.𐤏𐤌𐤍𐤅.𐤄𐤉𐤅
𐤌|
16 𐤊𐤉.𐤀𐤕𐤌.𐤉𐤃𐤏𐤕𐤌.𐤀𐤕.𐤀𐤔𐤓.𐤉𐤔𐤁𐤍𐤅.𐤁𐤀𐤓𐤑.𐤌
𐤑𐤓𐤉𐤌.𐤅𐤀𐤕.𐤀𐤔𐤓.𐤏𐤁𐤓𐤍𐤅.𐤁𐤒𐤓𐤁.𐤄𐤂𐤅𐤉𐤌.𐤀𐤔𐤓.𐤏𐤁𐤓
𐤕𐤌|
17 𐤅𐤕𐤓𐤀𐤅.𐤀𐤕.𐤔𐤒𐤅𐤑𐤉𐤄𐤌.𐤅𐤀𐤕.𐤂𐤋𐤋𐤉𐤄𐤌.𐤏𐤑.𐤅
𐤀𐤁𐤍.𐤊𐤎𐤐.𐤅𐤆𐤄𐤁.𐤀𐤔𐤓.𐤏𐤌𐤄𐤌|
18 𐤐𐤍.𐤉𐤔.𐤁𐤊𐤌.𐤀𐤉𐤔.𐤀𐤅.𐤀𐤔𐤄.𐤀𐤅.𐤌𐤔𐤐𐤇𐤄.𐤀𐤅.𐤔
𐤁𐤈.𐤀𐤔𐤓.𐤋𐤁𐤁𐤅.𐤐𐤍𐤄.𐤄𐤉𐤅𐤌.𐤌𐤏𐤌.𐤉𐤄𐤅𐤄.𐤀𐤋𐤄𐤉𐤍𐤅.𐤋𐤋
𐤊𐤕.𐤋𐤏𐤁𐤃.𐤀𐤕.𐤀𐤋𐤄𐤉.𐤄𐤂𐤅𐤉𐤌.𐤄𐤄𐤌.𐤐𐤍.𐤉𐤔.𐤁𐤊𐤌.
𐤔𐤓𐤔.𐤐𐤓𐤄.𐤓𐤀𐤔.𐤅𐤋𐤏𐤍𐤄|
19 𐤅𐤄𐤉𐤄.𐤁𐤔𐤌𐤏𐤅.𐤀𐤕.𐤃𐤁𐤓𐤉.𐤄𐤀𐤋𐤄.𐤄𐤆𐤀𐤕.𐤅𐤄
𐤕𐤁𐤓𐤊.𐤁𐤋𐤁𐤁𐤅.𐤋𐤀𐤌𐤓.𐤔𐤋𐤅𐤌.𐤉𐤄𐤉𐤄.𐤋𐤉.𐤊𐤉.𐤁𐤔𐤓𐤓𐤅𐤕.
𐤋𐤁𐤉.𐤀𐤋𐤊.𐤋𐤌𐤏𐤍.𐤎𐤐𐤅𐤕.𐤄𐤓𐤅𐤄.𐤀𐤕.𐤄𐤑𐤌𐤀𐤄|
20 𐤋𐤀.𐤉𐤀𐤁𐤄.𐤉𐤄𐤅𐤄.𐤎𐤋𐤇.𐤋𐤅.𐤊𐤉.𐤀𐤆.𐤉𐤏𐤔𐤍.𐤀𐤐.
𐤉𐤄𐤅𐤄.𐤅𐤒𐤍𐤀𐤕𐤅.𐤁𐤀𐤉𐤔.𐤄𐤄𐤅𐤀.𐤅𐤓𐤁𐤑𐤄.𐤁𐤅.𐤊𐤋.𐤄𐤀𐤋
𐤄.𐤄𐤊𐤕𐤅𐤁𐤄.𐤁𐤎𐤐𐤓.𐤄𐤆𐤄.𐤅𐤌𐤇𐤄.𐤉𐤄𐤅𐤄.𐤀𐤕.𐤔𐤌𐤅.𐤌
𐤕𐤇𐤕.𐤄𐤔𐤌𐤉𐤌|

21 𐤅𐤄𐤁𐤃𐤉𐤋𐤅.𐤉𐤄𐤅𐤄.𐤋𐤓𐤏𐤄.𐤌𐤊𐤋.𐤔𐤁𐤈𐤉.𐤉𐤔𐤓𐤀𐤋.𐤊𐤊𐤋.𐤀𐤋𐤅𐤕.𐤄𐤁𐤓𐤉𐤕.𐤄𐤊𐤕𐤅𐤁𐤄.𐤁𐤎𐤐𐤓.𐤄𐤕𐤅𐤓𐤄.𐤄𐤆𐤄|

22 𐤅𐤀𐤌𐤓.𐤄𐤃𐤅𐤓.𐤄𐤀𐤇𐤓𐤅𐤍.𐤁𐤍𐤉𐤊𐤌.𐤀𐤔𐤓.𐤉𐤒𐤅𐤌𐤅.𐤌𐤀𐤇𐤓𐤉𐤊𐤌.𐤅𐤄𐤍𐤊𐤓𐤉.𐤀𐤔𐤓.𐤉𐤁𐤀.𐤌𐤀𐤓𐤑.𐤓𐤇𐤅𐤒𐤄.𐤅𐤓𐤀𐤅.𐤀𐤕.𐤌𐤊𐤅𐤕.𐤄𐤀𐤓𐤑.𐤄𐤄𐤅𐤀.𐤅𐤀𐤕.𐤕𐤇𐤋𐤀𐤉𐤄.𐤀𐤔𐤓.𐤇𐤋𐤄.𐤉𐤄𐤅𐤄.𐤁𐤄|

23 𐤂𐤐𐤓𐤉𐤕.𐤅𐤌𐤋𐤇.𐤔𐤓𐤐𐤄.𐤊𐤋.𐤀𐤓𐤑𐤄.𐤋𐤀.𐤕𐤆𐤓𐤏.𐤅𐤋𐤀.𐤕𐤑𐤌𐤇.𐤅𐤋𐤀.𐤉𐤏𐤋𐤄.𐤁𐤄.𐤊𐤋.𐤏𐤔𐤁.𐤊𐤌𐤄𐤐𐤊𐤕.𐤎𐤃𐤌.𐤅𐤏𐤌𐤓𐤄.𐤀𐤃𐤌𐤄.𐤅𐤑𐤁𐤉𐤉𐤌.‖𐤅𐤑𐤁𐤅𐤉𐤌.𐤒𐤓𐤉‖.𐤀𐤔𐤓.𐤄𐤐𐤊.𐤉𐤄𐤅𐤄.𐤁𐤀𐤐𐤅.𐤅𐤁𐤇𐤌𐤕𐤅|

24 𐤅𐤀𐤌𐤓𐤅.𐤊𐤋.𐤄𐤂𐤅𐤉𐤌.𐤏𐤋.𐤌𐤄.𐤏𐤔𐤄.𐤉𐤄𐤅𐤄.𐤊𐤊𐤄.𐤋𐤀𐤓𐤑.𐤄𐤆𐤀𐤕.𐤌𐤄.𐤇𐤓𐤉.𐤄𐤀𐤐.𐤄𐤂𐤃𐤅𐤋.𐤄𐤆𐤄|

25 𐤅𐤀𐤌𐤓𐤅.𐤏𐤋.𐤀𐤔𐤓.𐤏𐤆𐤁𐤅.𐤀𐤕.𐤁𐤓𐤉𐤕.𐤉𐤄𐤅𐤄.𐤀𐤋𐤄𐤉.𐤀𐤁𐤕𐤌.𐤀𐤔𐤓.𐤊𐤓𐤕.𐤏𐤌𐤌.𐤁𐤄𐤅𐤑𐤉𐤀𐤅.𐤀𐤕𐤌.𐤌𐤀𐤓𐤑.𐤌𐤑𐤓𐤉𐤌|

26 𐤅𐤉𐤋𐤊𐤅.𐤅𐤉𐤏𐤁𐤃𐤅.𐤀𐤋𐤄𐤉𐤌.𐤀𐤇𐤓𐤉𐤌.𐤅𐤉𐤔𐤕𐤇𐤅𐤅.𐤋𐤄𐤌.𐤀𐤋𐤄𐤉𐤌.𐤀𐤔𐤓.𐤋𐤀.𐤉𐤃𐤏𐤅𐤌.𐤅𐤋𐤀.𐤇𐤋𐤒.𐤋𐤄𐤌|

27 𐤅𐤉𐤇𐤓.𐤀𐤐.𐤉𐤄𐤅𐤄.𐤁𐤀𐤓𐤑.𐤄𐤄𐤅𐤀.𐤋𐤄𐤁𐤉𐤀.𐤏𐤋𐤉𐤄.𐤀𐤕.𐤊𐤋.𐤄𐤒𐤋𐤋𐤄.𐤄𐤊𐤕𐤅𐤁𐤄.𐤁𐤎𐤐𐤓.𐤄𐤆𐤄|

28 𐤅𐤉𐤕𐤔𐤌.𐤉𐤄𐤅𐤄.𐤌𐤏𐤋.𐤀𐤃𐤌𐤕𐤌.𐤁𐤀𐤐.𐤅𐤁𐤇𐤌𐤄.𐤅𐤁𐤒𐤑𐤐.𐤂𐤃𐤅𐤋.𐤅𐤉𐤔𐤋𐤊𐤌.𐤀𐤋.𐤀𐤓𐤑.𐤀𐤇𐤓𐤕.𐤊𐤉𐤅𐤌.𐤄𐤆𐤄|

29 𐤄𐤍𐤎𐤕𐤓𐤕.𐤋𐤉𐤄𐤅𐤄.𐤀𐤋𐤄𐤉𐤍𐤅.𐤅𐤄𐤍𐤂𐤋𐤕.𐤋𐤍𐤅.𐤅𐤋𐤁𐤍𐤉𐤍𐤅.𐤏𐤃.𐤏𐤅𐤋𐤌.𐤋𐤏𐤔𐤅𐤕.𐤀𐤕.𐤊𐤋.𐤃𐤁𐤓𐤉.𐤄𐤕𐤅𐤓𐤄.𐤄𐤆𐤀𐤕‖

𐤃𐤁𐤓𐤉𐤌.𐤇𐤋𐤒 30

1 𐤅𐤄𐤉𐤄.𐤊𐤉.𐤉𐤁𐤀𐤅.𐤏𐤋𐤉𐤊.𐤊𐤋.𐤄𐤃𐤁𐤓𐤉𐤌.𐤄𐤀𐤋𐤄.𐤄𐤁𐤓𐤊𐤄.𐤅𐤄𐤒𐤋𐤋𐤄.𐤀𐤔𐤓.𐤍𐤕𐤕𐤉.𐤋𐤐𐤍𐤉𐤊.𐤅𐤄𐤔𐤁𐤕.𐤀𐤋.𐤋

𐤁𐤁𐤊.𐤁𐤊𐤋.𐤄𐤂𐤅𐤉𐤌.𐤀𐤔𐤓.𐤄𐤃𐤉𐤇𐤊.𐤉𐤄𐤅𐤄.𐤀𐤋𐤄𐤉𐤊.
𐤔𐤌𐤄|
ב 𐤅𐤔𐤁𐤕.𐤏𐤃.𐤉𐤄𐤅𐤄.𐤀𐤋𐤄𐤉𐤊.𐤅𐤔𐤌𐤏𐤕.𐤁𐤒𐤋𐤅.𐤊𐤊𐤋.
𐤀𐤔𐤓.𐤀𐤍𐤊𐤉.𐤌𐤑𐤅𐤊.𐤄𐤉𐤅𐤌.𐤀𐤕𐤄.𐤅𐤁𐤍𐤉𐤊.𐤁𐤊𐤋.𐤋𐤁𐤁𐤊.
𐤅𐤁𐤊𐤋.𐤍𐤐𐤔𐤊|
ג 𐤅𐤔𐤁.𐤉𐤄𐤅𐤄.𐤀𐤋𐤄𐤉𐤊.𐤀𐤕.𐤔𐤁𐤅𐤕𐤊.𐤅𐤓𐤇𐤌𐤊.𐤅𐤔𐤁.𐤅
𐤒𐤁𐤑𐤊.𐤌𐤊𐤋.𐤄𐤏𐤌𐤉𐤌.𐤀𐤔𐤓.𐤄𐤐𐤉𐤑𐤊.𐤉𐤄𐤅𐤄.𐤀𐤋𐤄𐤉
𐤊.𐤔𐤌𐤄|
ד 𐤀𐤌.𐤉𐤄𐤉𐤄.𐤍𐤃𐤇𐤊.𐤁𐤒𐤑𐤄.𐤄𐤔𐤌𐤉𐤌.𐤌𐤔𐤌.𐤉𐤒
𐤁𐤑𐤊.𐤉𐤄𐤅𐤄.𐤀𐤋𐤄𐤉𐤊.𐤅𐤌𐤔𐤌.𐤉𐤒𐤇𐤊|
ה 𐤅𐤄𐤁𐤉𐤀𐤊.𐤉𐤄𐤅𐤄.𐤀𐤋𐤄𐤉𐤊.𐤀𐤋.𐤄𐤀𐤓𐤑.𐤀𐤔𐤓.𐤉𐤓𐤔
𐤅.𐤀𐤁𐤕𐤉𐤊.𐤅𐤉𐤓𐤔𐤕𐤄.𐤅𐤄𐤉𐤈𐤁𐤊.𐤅𐤄𐤓𐤁𐤊.𐤌𐤀𐤁𐤕𐤉𐤊|
ו 𐤅𐤌𐤋.𐤉𐤄𐤅𐤄.𐤀𐤋𐤄𐤉𐤊.𐤀𐤕.𐤋𐤁𐤁𐤊.𐤅𐤀𐤕.𐤋𐤁𐤁.𐤆𐤓𐤏
𐤊.𐤋𐤀𐤄𐤁𐤄.𐤀𐤕.𐤉𐤄𐤅𐤄.𐤀𐤋𐤄𐤉𐤊.𐤁𐤊𐤋.𐤋𐤁𐤁𐤊.𐤅𐤁𐤊𐤋.𐤍𐤐
𐤔𐤊.𐤋𐤌𐤏𐤍.𐤇𐤉𐤉𐤊|
ז 𐤅𐤍𐤕𐤍.𐤉𐤄𐤅𐤄.𐤀𐤋𐤄𐤉𐤊.𐤀𐤕.𐤊𐤋.𐤄𐤀𐤋𐤅𐤕.𐤄𐤀𐤋𐤄.𐤏
𐤋.𐤀𐤉𐤁𐤉𐤊.𐤅𐤏𐤋.𐤔𐤍𐤀𐤉𐤊.𐤀𐤔𐤓.𐤓𐤃𐤐𐤅𐤊|
ח 𐤅𐤀𐤕𐤄.𐤕𐤔𐤅𐤁.𐤅𐤔𐤌𐤏𐤕.𐤁𐤒𐤅𐤋.𐤉𐤄𐤅𐤄.𐤅𐤏𐤔𐤉𐤕.𐤀
𐤕.𐤊𐤋.𐤌𐤑𐤅𐤕𐤉𐤅.𐤀𐤔𐤓.𐤀𐤍𐤊𐤉.𐤌𐤑𐤅𐤊.𐤄𐤉𐤅𐤌|
ט 𐤅𐤄𐤅𐤕𐤉𐤓𐤊.𐤉𐤄𐤅𐤄.𐤀𐤋𐤄𐤉𐤊.𐤁𐤊𐤋.𐤌𐤏𐤔𐤄.𐤉𐤃𐤊.𐤁
𐤐𐤓𐤉.𐤁𐤈𐤍𐤊.𐤅𐤁𐤐𐤓𐤉.𐤁𐤄𐤌𐤕𐤊.𐤅𐤁𐤐𐤓𐤉.𐤀𐤃𐤌𐤕𐤊.𐤋𐤈𐤁
𐤄.𐤊𐤉.𐤉𐤔𐤅𐤁.𐤉𐤄𐤅𐤄.𐤋𐤔𐤅𐤔.𐤏𐤋𐤉𐤊.𐤋𐤈𐤅𐤁.𐤊𐤀𐤔𐤓.𐤔𐤔.
𐤏𐤋.𐤀𐤁𐤕𐤉𐤊|
י 𐤊𐤉.𐤕𐤔𐤌𐤏.𐤁𐤒𐤅𐤋.𐤉𐤄𐤅𐤄.𐤀𐤋𐤄𐤉𐤊.𐤋𐤔𐤌𐤓.𐤌𐤑𐤅
𐤕𐤉𐤅.𐤅𐤇𐤒𐤕𐤉𐤅.𐤄𐤊𐤕𐤅𐤁𐤄.𐤁𐤎𐤐𐤓.𐤄𐤕𐤅𐤓𐤄.𐤄𐤆𐤄.𐤊𐤉.
𐤕𐤔𐤅𐤁.𐤀𐤋.𐤉𐤄𐤅𐤄.𐤀𐤋𐤄𐤉𐤊.𐤁𐤊𐤋.𐤋𐤁𐤁𐤊.𐤅𐤁𐤊𐤋.𐤍𐤐𐤔𐤊|
יא 𐤊𐤉.𐤄𐤌𐤑𐤅𐤄.𐤄𐤆𐤀𐤕.𐤀𐤔𐤓.𐤀𐤍𐤊𐤉.𐤌𐤑𐤅𐤊.𐤄𐤉𐤅𐤌.
𐤋𐤀.𐤍𐤐𐤋𐤀𐤕.𐤄𐤅𐤀.𐤌𐤌𐤊.𐤅𐤋𐤀.𐤓𐤇𐤒𐤄.𐤄𐤅𐤀|
יב 𐤋𐤀.𐤁𐤔𐤌𐤉𐤌.𐤄𐤅𐤀.𐤋𐤀𐤌𐤓.𐤌𐤉.𐤉𐤏𐤋𐤄.𐤋𐤍𐤅.𐤄𐤔𐤌
𐤉𐤌𐤄.𐤅𐤉𐤒𐤇𐤄.𐤋𐤍𐤅.𐤅𐤉𐤔𐤌𐤏𐤍𐤅.𐤀𐤕𐤄.𐤅𐤍𐤏𐤔𐤍𐤄|

יג . ולא . מעבר . לים . הוא . לאמר . מי . יעבר . לנו . א
ל . עבר . הים . ויקחה . לנו . וישמענו . אתה . ונעשנה
|
יד . כי . קרוב . אליך . הדבר . מאד . בפיך . ובלבב
ך . לעשתו|
טו . ראה . נתתי . לפניך . היום . את . החיים . ואת .
הטוב . ואת . המות . ואת . הרע|
טז . אשר . אנכי . מצוך . היום . לאהבה . את . יהוה .
אלהיך . ללכת . בדרכיו . ולשמר . מצותיו . וחקתי
ו . ומשפטיו . וחיית . ורבית . וברכך . יהוה . אלהיך .
בארץ . אשר . אתה . בא . שמה . לרשתה|
יז . ואם . יפנה . לבבך . ולא . תשמע . ונדחת . והש
תחוית . לאלהים . אחרים . ועבדתם|
יח . הגדתי . לכם . היום . כי . אבד . תאבדון . לא .
תאריכן . ימים . על . האדמה . אשר . אתה . עבר . א
ת . הירדן . לבא . שמה . לרשתה|
יט . העידתי . בכם . היום . את . השמים . ואת . ה
ארץ . החיים . והמות . נתתי . לפניך . הברכה . והק
ללה . ובחרת . בחיים . למען . תחיה . אתה . וזרעך
|
כ . לאהבה . את . יהוה . אלהיך . לשמע . בקלו . ול
דבקה . בו . כי . הוא . חייך . וארך . ימיך . לשבת . על
. האדמה . אשר . נשבע . יהוה . לאבתיך . לאברהם .
ליצחק . וליעקב . לתת . להם||

דברים . חלק . גי

א . וילך . משה . וידבר . את . הדברים . האלה . אל .
כל . ישראל|

2 𐤅𐤉𐤀𐤌𐤓.𐤀𐤋𐤄𐤌.𐤁𐤍.𐤌𐤀𐤄.𐤅𐤏𐤔𐤓𐤉𐤌.𐤔𐤍𐤄.𐤀𐤍𐤊𐤉.
𐤄𐤉𐤅𐤌.𐤋𐤀.𐤀𐤅𐤊𐤋.𐤏𐤅𐤃.𐤋𐤑𐤀𐤕.𐤅𐤋𐤁𐤅𐤀.𐤅𐤉𐤄𐤅𐤄.𐤀𐤌𐤓.
𐤀𐤋𐤉.𐤋𐤀.𐤕𐤏𐤁𐤓.𐤀𐤕.𐤄𐤉𐤓𐤃𐤍.𐤄𐤆𐤄|

3 𐤉𐤄𐤅𐤄.𐤀𐤋𐤄𐤉𐤊.𐤄𐤅𐤀.𐤏𐤁𐤓.𐤋𐤐𐤍𐤉𐤊.𐤄𐤅𐤀.𐤉𐤔𐤌𐤉𐤃
.𐤀𐤕.𐤄𐤂𐤅𐤉𐤌.𐤄𐤀𐤋𐤄.𐤌𐤋𐤐𐤍𐤉𐤊.𐤅𐤉𐤓𐤔𐤕𐤌.𐤉𐤄𐤅𐤔𐤏.𐤄𐤅
𐤀.𐤏𐤁𐤓.𐤋𐤐𐤍𐤉𐤊.𐤊𐤀𐤔𐤓.𐤃𐤁𐤓.𐤉𐤄𐤅𐤄|

4 𐤅𐤏𐤔𐤄.𐤉𐤄𐤅𐤄.𐤋𐤄𐤌.𐤊𐤀𐤔𐤓.𐤏𐤔𐤄.𐤋𐤎𐤉𐤇𐤅𐤍.𐤅𐤋𐤏
𐤅𐤂.𐤌𐤋𐤊𐤉.𐤄𐤀𐤌𐤓𐤉.𐤅𐤋𐤀𐤓𐤑𐤌.𐤀𐤔𐤓.𐤄𐤔𐤌𐤉𐤃.𐤀𐤕𐤌|

5 𐤅𐤍𐤕𐤍𐤌.𐤉𐤄𐤅𐤄.𐤋𐤐𐤍𐤉𐤊𐤌.𐤅𐤏𐤔𐤉𐤕𐤌.𐤋𐤄𐤌.𐤊𐤊𐤋.𐤄𐤌
𐤑𐤅𐤄.𐤀𐤔𐤓.𐤑𐤅𐤉𐤕𐤉.𐤀𐤕𐤊𐤌|

6 𐤇𐤆𐤒𐤅.𐤅𐤀𐤌𐤑𐤅.𐤀𐤋.𐤕𐤉𐤓𐤀𐤅.𐤅𐤀𐤋.𐤕𐤏𐤓𐤑𐤅.𐤌𐤐𐤍𐤉
𐤄𐤌.𐤊𐤉.𐤉𐤄𐤅𐤄.𐤀𐤋𐤄𐤉𐤊.𐤄𐤅𐤀.𐤄𐤄𐤋𐤊.𐤏𐤌𐤊.𐤋𐤀.𐤉𐤓𐤐𐤊.
𐤅𐤋𐤀.𐤉𐤏𐤆𐤁𐤊|

7 𐤅𐤉𐤒𐤓𐤀.𐤌𐤔𐤄.𐤋𐤉𐤄𐤅𐤔𐤏.𐤅𐤉𐤀𐤌𐤓.𐤀𐤋𐤉𐤅.𐤋𐤏𐤉𐤍𐤉.
𐤊𐤋.𐤉𐤔𐤓𐤀𐤋.𐤇𐤆𐤒.𐤅𐤀𐤌𐤑.𐤊𐤉.𐤀𐤕𐤄.𐤕𐤁𐤅𐤀.𐤀𐤕.𐤄𐤏
𐤌.𐤄𐤆𐤄.𐤀𐤋.𐤄𐤀𐤓𐤑.𐤀𐤔𐤓.𐤍𐤔𐤁𐤏.𐤉𐤄𐤅𐤄.𐤋𐤀𐤁𐤕𐤌.𐤋
𐤕𐤕.𐤋𐤄𐤌.𐤅𐤀𐤕𐤄.𐤕𐤍𐤇𐤉𐤋𐤍𐤄.𐤀𐤅𐤕𐤌|

8 𐤅𐤉𐤄𐤅𐤄.𐤄𐤅𐤀.𐤄𐤄𐤋𐤊.𐤋𐤐𐤍𐤉𐤊.𐤄𐤅𐤀.𐤉𐤄𐤉𐤄.𐤏𐤌𐤊.𐤋
𐤀.𐤉𐤓𐤐𐤊.𐤅𐤋𐤀.𐤉𐤏𐤆𐤁𐤊.𐤋𐤀.𐤕𐤉𐤓𐤀.𐤅𐤋𐤀.𐤕𐤇𐤕|

9 𐤅𐤉𐤊𐤕𐤁.𐤌𐤔𐤄.𐤀𐤕.𐤄𐤕𐤅𐤓𐤄.𐤄𐤆𐤀𐤕.𐤅𐤉𐤕𐤍𐤄.𐤀𐤋.
𐤄𐤊𐤄𐤍𐤉𐤌.𐤁𐤍𐤉.𐤋𐤅𐤉.𐤄𐤍𐤔𐤀𐤉𐤌.𐤀𐤕.𐤀𐤓𐤅𐤍.𐤁𐤓𐤉𐤕.𐤉𐤄𐤅
𐤄.𐤅𐤀𐤋.𐤊𐤋.𐤆𐤒𐤍𐤉.𐤉𐤔𐤓𐤀𐤋|

10 𐤅𐤉𐤑𐤅.𐤌𐤔𐤄.𐤀𐤅𐤕𐤌.𐤋𐤀𐤌𐤓.𐤌𐤒𐤑.𐤔𐤁𐤏.𐤔𐤍𐤉𐤌.
𐤁𐤌𐤏𐤃.𐤔𐤍𐤕.𐤄𐤔𐤌𐤈𐤄.𐤁𐤇𐤂.𐤄𐤎𐤊𐤅𐤕|

11 𐤁𐤁𐤅𐤀.𐤊𐤋.𐤉𐤔𐤓𐤀𐤋.𐤋𐤓𐤀𐤅𐤕.𐤀𐤕.𐤐𐤍𐤉.𐤉𐤄𐤅𐤄.𐤀𐤋
𐤄𐤉𐤊.𐤁𐤌𐤒𐤅𐤌.𐤀𐤔𐤓.𐤉𐤁𐤇𐤓.𐤕𐤒𐤓𐤀.𐤀𐤕.𐤄𐤕𐤅𐤓𐤄.𐤄𐤆
𐤀𐤕.𐤍𐤂𐤃.𐤊𐤋.𐤉𐤔𐤓𐤀𐤋.𐤁𐤀𐤆𐤍𐤉𐤄𐤌|

12 𐤄𐤒𐤄𐤋.𐤀𐤕.𐤄𐤏𐤌.𐤄𐤀𐤍𐤔𐤉𐤌.𐤅𐤄𐤍𐤔𐤉𐤌.𐤅𐤄𐤈𐤐.𐤅
𐤂𐤓𐤊.𐤀𐤔𐤓.𐤁𐤔𐤏𐤓𐤉𐤊.𐤋𐤌𐤏𐤍.𐤉𐤔𐤌𐤏𐤍.𐤅𐤋𐤌𐤏𐤍.𐤉𐤋𐤌𐤃
𐤅.𐤅𐤉𐤓𐤀𐤅.𐤀𐤕.𐤉𐤄𐤅𐤄.𐤀𐤋𐤄𐤉𐤊𐤌.𐤅𐤔𐤌𐤓𐤅.𐤋𐤏𐤔𐤅𐤕.𐤀𐤕.
𐤊𐤋.𐤃𐤁𐤓𐤉.𐤄𐤕𐤅𐤓𐤄.𐤄𐤆𐤀𐤕|

יג 𐤅𐤁𐤍𐤉𐤄𐤌 . 𐤀𐤔𐤓 . 𐤋𐤀 . 𐤉𐤃𐤏𐤅 . 𐤉𐤔𐤌𐤏𐤅 . 𐤅𐤋𐤌𐤃𐤅 . 𐤋𐤉
𐤓𐤀𐤄 . 𐤀𐤕 . 𐤉𐤄𐤅𐤄 . 𐤀𐤋𐤄𐤉𐤊𐤌 . 𐤊𐤋 . 𐤄𐤉𐤌𐤉𐤌 . 𐤀𐤔𐤓 . 𐤀𐤕𐤌 .
𐤇𐤉𐤉𐤌 . 𐤏𐤋 . 𐤄𐤀𐤃𐤌𐤄 . 𐤀𐤔𐤓 . 𐤀𐤕𐤌 . 𐤏𐤁𐤓𐤉𐤌 . 𐤀𐤕 . 𐤄𐤉𐤓
𐤃𐤍 . 𐤔𐤌𐤄 . 𐤋𐤓𐤔𐤕𐤄|

יד 𐤅𐤉𐤀𐤌𐤓 . 𐤉𐤄𐤅𐤄 . 𐤀𐤋 . 𐤌𐤔𐤄 . 𐤄𐤍 . 𐤒𐤓𐤁𐤅 . 𐤉𐤌𐤉𐤊 . 𐤋𐤌𐤅
𐤕 . 𐤒𐤓𐤀 . 𐤀𐤕 . 𐤉𐤄𐤅𐤔𐤏 . 𐤅𐤄𐤕𐤉𐤑𐤁𐤅 . 𐤁𐤀𐤄𐤋 . 𐤌𐤅𐤏𐤃 . 𐤅𐤀
𐤑𐤅𐤍𐤅 . 𐤅𐤉𐤋𐤊 . 𐤌𐤔𐤄 . 𐤅𐤉𐤄𐤅𐤔𐤏 . 𐤅𐤉𐤕𐤉𐤑𐤁𐤅 . 𐤁𐤀𐤄𐤋 . 𐤌𐤅𐤏
𐤃|

טו 𐤅𐤉𐤓𐤀 . 𐤉𐤄𐤅𐤄 . 𐤁𐤀𐤄𐤋 . 𐤁𐤏𐤌𐤅𐤃 . 𐤏𐤍𐤍 . 𐤅𐤉𐤏𐤌𐤃 . 𐤏𐤌
𐤅𐤃 . 𐤄𐤏𐤍𐤍 . 𐤏𐤋 . 𐤐𐤕𐤇 . 𐤄𐤀𐤄𐤋|

טז 𐤅𐤉𐤀𐤌𐤓 . 𐤉𐤄𐤅𐤄 . 𐤀𐤋 . 𐤌𐤔𐤄 . 𐤄𐤍𐤊 . 𐤔𐤊𐤁 . 𐤏𐤌 . 𐤀𐤁𐤕𐤉
𐤊 . 𐤅𐤒𐤌 . 𐤄𐤏𐤌 . 𐤄𐤆𐤄 . 𐤅𐤆𐤍𐤄 . 𐤀𐤇𐤓𐤉 . 𐤀𐤋𐤄𐤉 . 𐤍𐤊𐤓 . 𐤄𐤀𐤓
𐤑 . 𐤀𐤔𐤓 . 𐤄𐤅𐤀 . 𐤁𐤀 . 𐤔𐤌𐤄 . 𐤁𐤒𐤓𐤁𐤅 . 𐤅𐤏𐤆𐤁𐤍𐤉 . 𐤅𐤄𐤐𐤓 . 𐤀𐤕 .
𐤁𐤓𐤉𐤕𐤉 . 𐤀𐤔𐤓 . 𐤊𐤓𐤕𐤉 . 𐤀𐤕𐤅|

יז 𐤅𐤇𐤓𐤄 . 𐤀𐤐𐤉 . 𐤁𐤅 . 𐤁𐤉𐤅𐤌 . 𐤄𐤄𐤅𐤀 . 𐤅𐤏𐤆𐤁𐤕𐤉𐤌 . 𐤅𐤄𐤎
𐤕𐤓𐤕𐤉 . 𐤐𐤍𐤉 . 𐤌𐤄𐤌 . 𐤅𐤄𐤉𐤄 . 𐤋𐤀𐤊𐤋 . 𐤅𐤌𐤑𐤀𐤄𐤅 . 𐤓𐤏𐤅𐤕 . 𐤓𐤁𐤅
𐤕 . 𐤅𐤑𐤓𐤅𐤕 . 𐤅𐤀𐤌𐤓 . 𐤁𐤉𐤅𐤌 . 𐤄𐤄𐤅𐤀 . 𐤄𐤋𐤀 . 𐤏𐤋 . 𐤊𐤉 . 𐤀𐤉𐤍 . 𐤀𐤋
𐤄𐤉 . 𐤁𐤒𐤓𐤁𐤉 . 𐤌𐤑𐤀𐤅𐤍𐤉 . 𐤄𐤓𐤏𐤅𐤕 . 𐤄𐤀𐤋𐤄|

יח 𐤅𐤀𐤍𐤊𐤉 . 𐤄𐤎𐤕𐤓 . 𐤀𐤎𐤕𐤉𐤓 . 𐤐𐤍𐤉 . 𐤁𐤉𐤅𐤌 . 𐤄𐤄𐤅𐤀 . 𐤏𐤋 .
𐤊𐤋 . 𐤄𐤓𐤏𐤄 . 𐤀𐤔𐤓 . 𐤏𐤔𐤄 . 𐤊𐤉 . 𐤐𐤍𐤄 . 𐤀𐤋 . 𐤀𐤋𐤄𐤉𐤌 . 𐤀𐤇𐤓𐤉
𐤌|

יט 𐤅𐤏𐤕𐤄 . 𐤊𐤕𐤁𐤅 . 𐤋𐤊𐤌 . 𐤀𐤕 . 𐤄𐤔𐤉𐤓𐤄 . 𐤄𐤆𐤀𐤕 . 𐤅𐤋𐤌
𐤃𐤄 . 𐤀𐤕 . 𐤁𐤍𐤉 . 𐤉𐤔𐤓𐤀𐤋 . 𐤔𐤉𐤌𐤄 . 𐤁𐤐𐤉𐤄𐤌 . 𐤋𐤌𐤏𐤍 . 𐤕𐤄𐤉
𐤄 . 𐤋𐤉 . 𐤄𐤔𐤉𐤓𐤄 . 𐤄𐤆𐤀𐤕 . 𐤋𐤏𐤃 . 𐤁𐤁𐤍𐤉 . 𐤉𐤔𐤓𐤀𐤋|

כ 𐤊𐤉 . 𐤀𐤁𐤉𐤀𐤍𐤅 . 𐤀𐤋 . 𐤄𐤀𐤃𐤌𐤄 . 𐤀𐤔𐤓 . 𐤍𐤔𐤁𐤏𐤕𐤉 . 𐤋
𐤀𐤁𐤕𐤉𐤅 . 𐤆𐤁𐤕 . 𐤇𐤋𐤁 . 𐤅𐤃𐤁𐤔 . 𐤅𐤀𐤊𐤋 . 𐤅𐤔𐤁𐤏 . 𐤅𐤃𐤔𐤍 . 𐤅𐤐𐤍
𐤄 . 𐤀𐤋 . 𐤀𐤋𐤄𐤉𐤌 . 𐤀𐤇𐤓𐤉𐤌 . 𐤅𐤏𐤁𐤃𐤅𐤌 . 𐤅𐤍𐤀𐤑𐤅𐤍𐤉 . 𐤅𐤄𐤐𐤓 .
𐤀𐤕 . 𐤁𐤓𐤉𐤕𐤉|

כא 𐤅𐤄𐤉𐤄 . 𐤊𐤉 . 𐤕𐤌𐤑𐤀𐤍 . 𐤀𐤕𐤅 . 𐤓𐤏𐤅𐤕 . 𐤓𐤁𐤅𐤕 . 𐤅𐤑𐤓𐤅𐤕 . 𐤅
𐤏𐤍𐤕𐤄 . 𐤄𐤔𐤉𐤓𐤄 . 𐤄𐤆𐤀𐤕 . 𐤋𐤐𐤍𐤉𐤅 . 𐤋𐤏𐤃 . 𐤊𐤉 . 𐤋𐤀 . 𐤕𐤔𐤊
𐤇 . 𐤌𐤐𐤉 . 𐤆𐤓𐤏𐤅 . 𐤊𐤉 . 𐤉𐤃𐤏𐤕𐤉 . 𐤀𐤕 . 𐤉𐤑𐤓𐤅 . 𐤀𐤔𐤓 . 𐤄𐤅𐤀 .

𐤏𐤔𐤄.𐤄𐤉𐤅𐤌.𐤁𐤈𐤓𐤌.𐤀𐤁𐤉𐤀𐤍𐤅.𐤀𐤋.𐤄𐤀𐤓𐤑.𐤀𐤔𐤓.𐤍𐤔𐤁
𐤏𐤕𐤉|
..כב..𐤅𐤉𐤊𐤕𐤁.𐤌𐤔𐤄.𐤀𐤕.𐤄𐤔𐤉𐤓𐤄.𐤄𐤆𐤀𐤕.𐤁𐤉𐤅𐤌.𐤄𐤄
𐤅𐤀.𐤅𐤉𐤋𐤌𐤃𐤄.𐤀𐤕.𐤁𐤍𐤉.𐤉𐤔𐤓𐤀𐤋|
..כג..𐤅𐤉𐤑𐤅.𐤀𐤕.𐤉𐤄𐤅𐤔𐤏.𐤁𐤍.𐤍𐤅𐤍.𐤅𐤉𐤀𐤌𐤓.𐤇𐤆𐤒.𐤅𐤀𐤌
𐤑.𐤊𐤉.𐤀𐤕𐤄.𐤕𐤁𐤉𐤀.𐤀𐤕.𐤁𐤍𐤉.𐤉𐤔𐤓𐤀𐤋.𐤀𐤋.𐤄𐤀𐤓𐤑.𐤀
𐤔𐤓.𐤍𐤔𐤁𐤏𐤕𐤉.𐤋𐤄𐤌.𐤅𐤀𐤍𐤊𐤉.𐤀𐤄𐤉𐤄.𐤏𐤌𐤊|
..כד..𐤅𐤉𐤄𐤉.𐤊𐤊𐤋𐤅𐤕.𐤌𐤔𐤄.𐤋𐤊𐤕𐤁.𐤀𐤕.𐤃𐤁𐤓𐤉.𐤄𐤕𐤅𐤓
𐤄.𐤄𐤆𐤀𐤕.𐤏𐤋.𐤎𐤐𐤓.𐤏𐤃.𐤕𐤌𐤌|
..כה..𐤅𐤉𐤑𐤅.𐤌𐤔𐤄.𐤀𐤕.𐤄𐤋𐤅𐤉𐤌.𐤍𐤔𐤀𐤉.𐤀𐤓𐤅𐤍.𐤁𐤓𐤉𐤕.𐤉
𐤄𐤅𐤄.𐤋𐤀𐤌𐤓|
..כו..𐤋𐤒𐤇.𐤀𐤕.𐤎𐤐𐤓.𐤄𐤕𐤅𐤓𐤄.𐤄𐤆𐤄.𐤅𐤔𐤌𐤕𐤌.𐤀𐤕𐤅.𐤌
𐤑𐤃.𐤀𐤓𐤅𐤍.𐤁𐤓𐤉𐤕.𐤉𐤄𐤅𐤄.𐤀𐤋𐤄𐤉𐤊𐤌.𐤅𐤄𐤉𐤄.𐤔𐤌.𐤁𐤊.𐤋
𐤏𐤃|
..כז..𐤊𐤉.𐤀𐤍𐤊𐤉.𐤉𐤃𐤏𐤕𐤉.𐤀𐤕.𐤌𐤓𐤉𐤊.𐤅𐤀𐤕.𐤏𐤓𐤐𐤊.𐤄
𐤒𐤔𐤄.𐤄𐤍.𐤁𐤏𐤅𐤃𐤍𐤉.𐤇𐤉.𐤏𐤌𐤊𐤌.𐤄𐤉𐤅𐤌.𐤌𐤌𐤓𐤉𐤌.𐤄𐤉
𐤕𐤌.𐤏𐤌.𐤉𐤄𐤅𐤄.𐤅𐤀𐤐.𐤊𐤉.𐤀𐤇𐤓𐤉.𐤌𐤅𐤕𐤉|
..כח..𐤄𐤒𐤄𐤉𐤋𐤅.𐤀𐤋𐤉.𐤀𐤕.𐤊𐤋.𐤆𐤒𐤍𐤉.𐤔𐤁𐤈𐤉𐤊𐤌.𐤅𐤔
𐤈𐤓𐤉𐤊𐤌.𐤅𐤀𐤃𐤁𐤓𐤄.𐤁𐤀𐤆𐤍𐤉𐤄𐤌.𐤀𐤕.𐤄𐤃𐤁𐤓𐤉𐤌.𐤄𐤀
𐤋𐤄.𐤅𐤀𐤏𐤉𐤃𐤄.𐤁𐤌.𐤀𐤕.𐤄𐤔𐤌𐤉𐤌.𐤅𐤀𐤕.𐤄𐤀𐤓𐤑|
..כט..𐤊𐤉.𐤉𐤃𐤏𐤕𐤉.𐤀𐤇𐤓𐤉.𐤌𐤅𐤕𐤉.𐤊𐤉.𐤄𐤔𐤇𐤕.𐤕𐤔
𐤇𐤕𐤅𐤍.𐤅𐤎𐤓𐤕𐤌.𐤌𐤍.𐤄𐤃𐤓𐤊.𐤀𐤔𐤓.𐤑𐤅𐤉𐤕𐤉.𐤀𐤕𐤊𐤌.𐤅𐤒
𐤓𐤀𐤕.𐤀𐤕𐤊𐤌.𐤄𐤓𐤏𐤄.𐤁𐤀𐤇𐤓𐤉𐤕.𐤄𐤉𐤌𐤉𐤌.𐤊𐤉.𐤕𐤏𐤔𐤅.
𐤀𐤕.𐤄𐤓𐤏.𐤁𐤏𐤉𐤍𐤉.𐤉𐤄𐤅𐤄.𐤋𐤄𐤊𐤏𐤉𐤎𐤅.𐤁𐤌𐤏𐤔𐤄.𐤉𐤃𐤉
𐤊𐤌|
..ל..𐤅𐤉𐤃𐤁𐤓.𐤌𐤔𐤄.𐤁𐤀𐤆𐤍𐤉.𐤊𐤋.𐤒𐤄𐤋.𐤉𐤔𐤓𐤀𐤋.𐤀𐤕.
𐤃𐤁𐤓𐤉.𐤄𐤔𐤉𐤓𐤄.𐤄𐤆𐤀𐤕.𐤏𐤃.𐤕𐤌𐤌||

𐤃𐤁𐤓𐤉𐤌.𐤇𐤋𐤒..לב..

1 𐤄𐤀𐤆𐤉𐤍𐤅.𐤄𐤔𐤌𐤉𐤌.𐤅𐤀𐤃𐤁𐤓𐤄.𐤅𐤕𐤔𐤌𐤏.𐤄𐤀𐤓𐤑.
𐤀𐤌𐤓𐤉.𐤐𐤉|
2 𐤉𐤏𐤓𐤐.𐤊𐤌𐤈𐤓.𐤋𐤒𐤇𐤉.𐤕𐤆𐤋.𐤊𐤈𐤋.𐤀𐤌𐤓𐤕𐤉.𐤊𐤔𐤏
𐤉𐤓𐤌.𐤏𐤋𐤉.𐤃𐤔𐤀.𐤅𐤊𐤓𐤁𐤉𐤁𐤉𐤌.𐤏𐤋𐤉.𐤏𐤔𐤁|
3 𐤊𐤉.𐤔𐤌.𐤉𐤄𐤅𐤄.𐤀𐤒𐤓𐤀.𐤄𐤁𐤅.𐤂𐤃𐤋.𐤋𐤀𐤋𐤄𐤉𐤍𐤅|
4 𐤄𐤑𐤅𐤓.𐤕𐤌𐤉𐤌.𐤐𐤏𐤋𐤅.𐤊𐤉.𐤊𐤋.𐤃𐤓𐤊𐤉𐤅.𐤌𐤔𐤐𐤈.𐤀𐤋.
𐤀𐤌𐤅𐤍𐤄.𐤅𐤀𐤉𐤍.𐤏𐤅𐤋.𐤑𐤃𐤉𐤒.𐤅𐤉𐤔𐤓.𐤄𐤅𐤀|
5 𐤔𐤇𐤕.𐤋𐤅.𐤋𐤀.𐤁𐤍𐤉𐤅.𐤌𐤅𐤌𐤌.𐤃𐤅𐤓.𐤏𐤒𐤔.𐤅𐤐𐤕𐤋𐤕𐤋|
6 𐤄.𐤋𐤉𐤄𐤅𐤄.𐤕𐤂𐤌𐤋𐤅.𐤆𐤀𐤕.𐤏𐤌.𐤍𐤁𐤋.𐤅𐤋𐤀.𐤇𐤊𐤌.𐤄
𐤋𐤅𐤀.𐤄𐤅𐤀.𐤀𐤁𐤉𐤊.𐤒𐤍𐤊.𐤄𐤅𐤀.𐤏𐤔𐤊.𐤅𐤉𐤊𐤍𐤍𐤊|
7 𐤆𐤊𐤓.𐤉𐤌𐤅𐤕.𐤏𐤅𐤋𐤌.𐤁𐤉𐤍𐤅.𐤔𐤍𐤅𐤕.𐤃𐤅𐤓.𐤅𐤃𐤅𐤓.𐤔𐤀𐤋
.𐤀𐤁𐤉𐤊.𐤅𐤉𐤂𐤃𐤊.𐤆𐤒𐤍𐤉𐤊.𐤅𐤉𐤀𐤌𐤓𐤅.𐤋𐤊|
8 𐤁𐤄𐤍𐤇𐤋.𐤏𐤋𐤉𐤅𐤍.𐤂𐤅𐤉𐤌.𐤁𐤄𐤐𐤓𐤉𐤃𐤅.𐤁𐤍𐤉.𐤀𐤃𐤌.𐤉
𐤑𐤁.𐤂𐤁𐤋𐤕.𐤏𐤌𐤉𐤌.𐤋𐤌𐤎𐤐𐤓.𐤁𐤍𐤉.𐤉𐤔𐤓𐤀𐤋|
9 𐤊𐤉.𐤇𐤋𐤒.𐤉𐤄𐤅𐤄.𐤏𐤌𐤅.𐤉𐤏𐤒𐤁.𐤇𐤁𐤋.𐤍𐤇𐤋𐤕𐤅|
10 𐤉𐤌𐤑𐤀𐤄𐤅.𐤁𐤀𐤓𐤑.𐤌𐤃𐤁𐤓.𐤅𐤁𐤕𐤄𐤅.𐤉𐤋𐤋.𐤉𐤔𐤌𐤍.
𐤉𐤎𐤁𐤁𐤍𐤄𐤅.𐤉𐤁𐤅𐤍𐤍𐤄𐤅.𐤉𐤑𐤓𐤍𐤄𐤅.𐤊𐤀𐤉𐤔𐤅𐤍.𐤏𐤉𐤍𐤅|
11 𐤊𐤍𐤔𐤓.𐤉𐤏𐤉𐤓.𐤒𐤍𐤅.𐤏𐤋.𐤂𐤅𐤆𐤋𐤉𐤅.𐤉𐤓𐤇𐤐.𐤐𐤓𐤔.
𐤊𐤍𐤐𐤉𐤅.𐤉𐤒𐤇𐤄𐤅.𐤉𐤔𐤀𐤄𐤅.𐤏𐤋.𐤀𐤁𐤓𐤕𐤅|
12 𐤉𐤄𐤅𐤄.𐤁𐤃𐤃.𐤉𐤍𐤇𐤍𐤅.𐤅𐤀𐤉𐤍.𐤏𐤌𐤅.𐤀𐤋.𐤍𐤊𐤓|
13 𐤉𐤓𐤊𐤁𐤄𐤅.𐤏𐤋.𐤁𐤌𐤅𐤕𐤉.||𐤁𐤌𐤕𐤉.𐤒𐤓𐤉||.𐤀𐤓𐤑.𐤅𐤉𐤀
𐤊𐤋.𐤕𐤍𐤅𐤁𐤕.𐤔𐤃𐤉.𐤅𐤉𐤍𐤒𐤄𐤅.𐤃𐤁𐤔.𐤌𐤎𐤋𐤏.𐤅𐤔𐤌𐤍.𐤌𐤇
𐤋𐤌𐤉𐤔.𐤑𐤅𐤓|
14 𐤇𐤌𐤀𐤕.𐤁𐤒𐤓.𐤅𐤇𐤋𐤁.𐤑𐤀𐤍.𐤏𐤌.𐤇𐤋𐤁.𐤊𐤓𐤉𐤌.𐤅𐤀
𐤉𐤋𐤉𐤌.𐤁𐤍𐤉.𐤁𐤔𐤍.𐤅𐤏𐤕𐤅𐤃𐤉𐤌.𐤏𐤌.𐤇𐤋𐤁.𐤊𐤋𐤉𐤅𐤕.𐤇𐤈
𐤄.𐤅𐤃𐤌.𐤏𐤍𐤁.𐤕𐤔𐤕𐤄.𐤇𐤌𐤓|
15 𐤅𐤉𐤔𐤌𐤍.𐤉𐤔𐤓𐤅𐤍.𐤅𐤉𐤁𐤏𐤈.𐤔𐤌𐤍𐤕.𐤏𐤁𐤉𐤕.𐤊𐤔𐤉𐤕.𐤅
𐤉𐤈𐤔.𐤀𐤋𐤅𐤄.𐤏𐤔𐤄𐤅.𐤅𐤉𐤍𐤁𐤋.𐤑𐤅𐤓.𐤉𐤔𐤏𐤕𐤅|
16 𐤉𐤒𐤍𐤀𐤄𐤅.𐤁𐤆𐤓𐤉𐤌.𐤁𐤕𐤅𐤏𐤁𐤕.𐤉𐤊𐤏𐤉𐤎𐤄𐤅|
17 𐤉𐤆𐤁𐤇𐤅.𐤋𐤔𐤃𐤉𐤌.𐤋𐤀.𐤀𐤋𐤄.𐤀𐤋𐤄𐤉𐤌.𐤋𐤀.𐤉𐤃
𐤏𐤅𐤌.𐤇𐤃𐤔𐤉𐤌.𐤌𐤒𐤓𐤁.𐤁𐤀𐤅.𐤋𐤀.𐤔𐤏𐤓𐤅𐤌.𐤀𐤁𐤕𐤉𐤊𐤌|

𐤉𐤇 𐤑𐤅𐤓.𐤉𐤋𐤃𐤊.𐤕𐤔𐤉.𐤅𐤕𐤔𐤊𐤇.𐤀𐤋.𐤌𐤇𐤋𐤋𐤊|
𐤉𐤈 𐤅𐤉𐤓𐤀.𐤉𐤄𐤅𐤄.𐤅𐤉𐤍𐤀𐤑.𐤌𐤊𐤏𐤎.𐤁𐤍𐤉𐤅.𐤅𐤁𐤍𐤕𐤉𐤅|
𐤊 𐤅𐤉𐤀𐤌𐤓.𐤀𐤎𐤕𐤉𐤓𐤄.𐤐𐤍𐤉.𐤌𐤄𐤌.𐤀𐤓𐤀𐤄.𐤌𐤄.𐤀𐤇𐤓
𐤉𐤕𐤌.𐤊𐤉.𐤃𐤅𐤓.𐤕𐤄𐤐𐤊𐤕.𐤄𐤌𐤄.𐤁𐤍𐤉𐤌.𐤋𐤀.𐤀𐤌𐤍.𐤁𐤌|
𐤊𐤀 𐤄𐤌.𐤒𐤍𐤀𐤅𐤍𐤉.𐤁𐤋𐤀.𐤀𐤋.𐤊𐤏𐤎𐤅𐤍𐤉.𐤁𐤄𐤁𐤋𐤉𐤄𐤌.𐤅
𐤀𐤍𐤉.𐤀𐤒𐤍𐤉𐤀𐤌.𐤁𐤋𐤀.𐤏𐤌.𐤁𐤂𐤅𐤉.𐤍𐤁𐤋.𐤀𐤊𐤏𐤉𐤎𐤌|
𐤊𐤁 𐤊𐤉.𐤀𐤔.𐤒𐤃𐤇𐤄.𐤁𐤀𐤐𐤉.𐤅𐤕𐤉𐤒𐤃.𐤏𐤃.𐤔𐤀𐤅𐤋.𐤕
𐤇𐤕𐤉𐤕.𐤅𐤕𐤀𐤊𐤋.𐤀𐤓𐤑.𐤅𐤉𐤁𐤋𐤄.𐤅𐤕𐤋𐤄𐤈.𐤌𐤅𐤎𐤃𐤉.𐤄𐤓
𐤉𐤌|
𐤊𐤂 𐤀𐤎𐤐𐤄.𐤏𐤋𐤉𐤌𐤅.𐤓𐤏𐤅𐤕.𐤇𐤑𐤉.𐤀𐤊𐤋𐤄.𐤁𐤌|
𐤊𐤃 𐤌𐤆𐤉.𐤓𐤏𐤁.𐤅𐤋𐤇𐤌𐤉.𐤓𐤔𐤐.𐤅𐤒𐤈𐤁.𐤌𐤓𐤉𐤓𐤉.𐤅𐤔𐤍.
𐤁𐤄𐤌𐤅𐤕.𐤀𐤔𐤋𐤇.𐤁𐤌.𐤏𐤌.𐤇𐤌𐤕.𐤆𐤇𐤋𐤉.𐤏𐤐𐤓|
𐤊𐤄 𐤌𐤇𐤅𐤑.𐤕𐤔𐤊𐤋.𐤇𐤓𐤁.𐤅𐤌𐤇𐤃𐤓𐤉𐤌.𐤀𐤉𐤌𐤄.𐤂𐤌.𐤁
𐤇𐤅𐤓.𐤂𐤌.𐤁𐤕𐤅𐤋𐤄.𐤉𐤅𐤍𐤒.𐤏𐤌.𐤀𐤉𐤔.𐤔𐤉𐤁𐤄|
𐤊𐤅 𐤀𐤌𐤓𐤕𐤉.𐤀𐤐𐤀𐤉𐤄𐤌.𐤀𐤔𐤁𐤉𐤕𐤄.𐤌𐤀𐤍𐤅𐤔.𐤆𐤊𐤓𐤌|
𐤊𐤆 𐤋𐤅𐤋𐤉.𐤊𐤏𐤎.𐤀𐤅𐤉𐤁.𐤀𐤂𐤅𐤓.𐤐𐤍.𐤉𐤍𐤊𐤓𐤅.𐤑𐤓𐤉𐤌𐤅.𐤐𐤍
.𐤉𐤀𐤌𐤓𐤅.𐤉𐤃𐤍𐤅.𐤓𐤌𐤄.𐤅𐤋𐤀.𐤉𐤄𐤅𐤄.𐤐𐤏𐤋.𐤊𐤋.𐤆𐤀𐤕|
𐤊𐤇 𐤊𐤉.𐤂𐤅𐤉.𐤀𐤁𐤃.𐤏𐤑𐤅𐤕.𐤄𐤌𐤄.𐤅𐤀𐤉𐤍.𐤁𐤄𐤌.𐤕𐤁𐤅𐤍
𐤄|
𐤊𐤈 𐤋𐤅.𐤇𐤊𐤌𐤅.𐤉𐤔𐤊𐤉𐤋𐤅.𐤆𐤀𐤕.𐤉𐤁𐤉𐤍𐤅.𐤋𐤀𐤇𐤓𐤉𐤕𐤌|
𐤋 𐤀𐤉𐤊𐤄.𐤉𐤓𐤃𐤐.𐤀𐤇𐤃.𐤀𐤋𐤐.𐤅𐤔𐤍𐤉𐤌.𐤉𐤍𐤉𐤎𐤅.𐤓𐤁
𐤁𐤄.𐤀𐤌.𐤋𐤀.𐤊𐤉.𐤑𐤅𐤓𐤌.𐤌𐤊𐤓𐤌.𐤅𐤉𐤄𐤅𐤄.𐤄𐤎𐤂𐤉𐤓𐤌|
𐤋𐤀 𐤊𐤉.𐤋𐤀.𐤊𐤑𐤅𐤓𐤍𐤅.𐤑𐤅𐤓𐤌.𐤅𐤀𐤉𐤁𐤉𐤍𐤅.𐤐𐤋𐤉𐤋𐤉𐤌|
𐤋𐤁 𐤊𐤉.𐤌𐤂𐤐𐤍.𐤎𐤃𐤌.𐤂𐤐𐤍𐤌.𐤅𐤌𐤔𐤃𐤌𐤕.𐤏𐤌𐤓𐤄.𐤏𐤍
𐤁𐤌𐤅.𐤏𐤍𐤁𐤉.𐤓𐤀𐤔.𐤀𐤔𐤊𐤋𐤕.𐤌𐤓𐤓𐤕.𐤋𐤌𐤅|
𐤋𐤂 𐤇𐤌𐤕.𐤕𐤍𐤉𐤍𐤌.𐤉𐤉𐤍𐤌.𐤅𐤓𐤀𐤔.𐤐𐤕𐤍𐤉𐤌.𐤀𐤊𐤆𐤓|
𐤋𐤃 𐤄𐤋𐤀.𐤄𐤅𐤀.𐤊𐤌𐤎.𐤏𐤌𐤃𐤉.𐤇𐤕𐤌.𐤁𐤀𐤅𐤑𐤓𐤕𐤉|
𐤋𐤄 𐤋𐤉.𐤍𐤒𐤌.𐤅𐤔𐤋𐤌.𐤋𐤏𐤕.𐤕𐤌𐤅𐤈.𐤓𐤂𐤋𐤌.𐤊𐤉.𐤒𐤓𐤅𐤁.
𐤉𐤅𐤌.𐤀𐤉𐤃𐤌.𐤅𐤇𐤔.𐤏𐤕𐤃𐤕.𐤋𐤌𐤅|
𐤋𐤅 𐤊𐤉.𐤉𐤃𐤉𐤍.𐤉𐤄𐤅𐤄.𐤏𐤌𐤅.𐤅𐤏𐤋.𐤏𐤁𐤃𐤉𐤅.𐤉𐤕𐤍𐤇𐤌.
𐤊𐤉.𐤉𐤓𐤀𐤄.𐤊𐤉.𐤀𐤆𐤋𐤕.𐤉𐤃.𐤅𐤀𐤐𐤎.𐤏𐤑𐤅𐤓.𐤅𐤏𐤆𐤅𐤁|

𐤋𐤆 𐤅𐤀𐤌𐤓.𐤀𐤉.𐤀𐤋𐤄𐤉𐤌𐤅.𐤑𐤅𐤓.𐤇𐤎𐤉𐤅.𐤁𐤅|
𐤋𐤇 𐤀𐤔𐤓.𐤇𐤋𐤁.𐤆𐤁𐤇𐤉𐤌𐤅.𐤉𐤀𐤊𐤋𐤅.𐤉𐤔𐤕𐤅.𐤉𐤉𐤍.𐤍𐤎
𐤉𐤊𐤌.𐤉𐤒𐤅𐤌𐤅.𐤅𐤉𐤏𐤆𐤓𐤊𐤌.𐤉𐤄𐤉.𐤏𐤋𐤉𐤊𐤌.𐤎𐤕𐤓𐤄|
𐤋𐤈 𐤓𐤀𐤅.𐤏𐤕𐤄.𐤊𐤉.𐤀𐤍𐤉.𐤀𐤍𐤉.𐤄𐤅𐤀.𐤅𐤀𐤉𐤍.𐤀𐤋𐤄𐤉𐤌.
𐤏𐤌𐤃𐤉.𐤀𐤍𐤉.𐤀𐤌𐤉𐤕.𐤅𐤀𐤇𐤉𐤄.𐤌𐤇𐤑𐤕𐤉.𐤅𐤀𐤍𐤉.𐤀𐤓𐤐
𐤀.𐤅𐤀𐤉𐤍.𐤌𐤉𐤃𐤉.𐤌𐤑𐤉𐤋|
𐤌 𐤊𐤉.𐤀𐤔𐤀.𐤀𐤋.𐤔𐤌𐤉𐤌.𐤉𐤃𐤉.𐤅𐤀𐤌𐤓𐤕𐤉.𐤇𐤉.𐤀𐤍
𐤊𐤉.𐤋𐤏𐤋𐤌|
𐤌𐤀 𐤀𐤌.𐤔𐤍𐤅𐤕𐤉.𐤁𐤓𐤒.𐤇𐤓𐤁𐤉.𐤅𐤕𐤀𐤇𐤆.𐤁𐤌𐤔𐤐𐤈.𐤉
𐤃𐤉.𐤀𐤔𐤉𐤁.𐤍𐤒𐤌.𐤋𐤑𐤓𐤉.𐤅𐤋𐤌𐤔𐤍𐤀𐤉.𐤀𐤔𐤋𐤌|
𐤌𐤁 𐤀𐤔𐤊𐤉𐤓.𐤇𐤑𐤉.𐤌𐤃𐤌.𐤅𐤇𐤓𐤁𐤉.𐤕𐤀𐤊𐤋.𐤁𐤔𐤓.𐤌
𐤃𐤌.𐤇𐤋𐤋.𐤅𐤔𐤁𐤉𐤄.𐤌𐤓𐤀𐤔.𐤐𐤓𐤏𐤅𐤕.𐤀𐤅𐤉𐤁|
𐤌𐤂 𐤄𐤓𐤍𐤉𐤍𐤅.𐤂𐤅𐤉𐤌.𐤏𐤌𐤅.𐤊𐤉.𐤃𐤌.𐤏𐤁𐤃𐤉𐤅.𐤉𐤒𐤅𐤌.𐤅
𐤍𐤒𐤌.𐤉𐤔𐤉𐤁.𐤋𐤑𐤓𐤉𐤅.𐤅𐤊𐤐𐤓.𐤀𐤃𐤌𐤕𐤅.𐤏𐤌𐤅|
𐤌𐤃 𐤅𐤉𐤁𐤀.𐤌𐤔𐤄.𐤅𐤉𐤃𐤁𐤓.𐤀𐤕.𐤊𐤋.𐤃𐤁𐤓𐤉.𐤄𐤔𐤉𐤓𐤄.
𐤄𐤆𐤀𐤕.𐤁𐤀𐤆𐤍𐤉.𐤄𐤏𐤌.𐤄𐤅𐤀.𐤅𐤄𐤅𐤔𐤏.𐤁𐤍.𐤍𐤅𐤍|
𐤌𐤄 𐤅𐤉𐤊𐤋.𐤌𐤔𐤄.𐤋𐤃𐤁𐤓.𐤀𐤕.𐤊𐤋.𐤄𐤃𐤁𐤓𐤉𐤌.𐤄𐤀𐤋𐤄.
𐤀𐤋.𐤊𐤋.𐤉𐤔𐤓𐤀𐤋|
𐤌𐤅 𐤅𐤉𐤀𐤌𐤓.𐤀𐤋𐤄𐤌.𐤔𐤉𐤌𐤅.𐤋𐤁𐤁𐤊𐤌.𐤋𐤊𐤋.𐤄𐤃𐤁𐤓𐤉𐤌
.𐤀𐤔𐤓.𐤀𐤍𐤊𐤉.𐤌𐤏𐤉𐤃.𐤁𐤊𐤌.𐤄𐤉𐤅𐤌.𐤀𐤔𐤓.𐤕𐤑𐤅𐤌.𐤀𐤕.
𐤁𐤍𐤉𐤊𐤌.𐤋𐤔𐤌𐤓.𐤋𐤏𐤔𐤅𐤕.𐤀𐤕.𐤊𐤋.𐤃𐤁𐤓𐤉.𐤄𐤕𐤅𐤓𐤄.𐤄𐤆
𐤀𐤕|
𐤌𐤆 𐤊𐤉.𐤋𐤀.𐤃𐤁𐤓.𐤓𐤒.𐤄𐤅𐤀.𐤌𐤊𐤌.𐤊𐤉.𐤄𐤅𐤀.𐤇𐤉𐤉𐤊
𐤌.𐤅𐤁𐤃𐤁𐤓.𐤄𐤆𐤄.𐤕𐤀𐤓𐤉𐤊𐤅.𐤉𐤌𐤉𐤌.𐤏𐤋.𐤄𐤀𐤃𐤌𐤄.𐤀𐤔
𐤓.𐤀𐤕𐤌.𐤏𐤁𐤓𐤉𐤌.𐤀𐤕.𐤄𐤉𐤓𐤃𐤍.𐤔𐤌𐤄.𐤋𐤓𐤔𐤕𐤄|
𐤌𐤇 𐤅𐤉𐤃𐤁𐤓.𐤉𐤄𐤅𐤄.𐤀𐤋.𐤌𐤔𐤄.𐤁𐤏𐤑𐤌.𐤄𐤉𐤅𐤌.𐤄𐤆𐤄.
𐤋𐤀𐤌𐤓|
𐤌𐤈 𐤏𐤋𐤄.𐤀𐤋.𐤄𐤓.𐤄𐤏𐤁𐤓𐤉𐤌.𐤄𐤆𐤄.𐤄𐤓.𐤍𐤁𐤅.𐤀𐤔𐤓.
𐤁𐤀𐤓𐤑.𐤌𐤅𐤀𐤁.𐤀𐤔𐤓.𐤏𐤋.𐤐𐤍𐤉.𐤉𐤓𐤇𐤅.𐤅𐤓𐤀𐤄.𐤀𐤕.𐤀𐤓𐤑.
𐤊𐤍𐤏𐤍.𐤀𐤔𐤓.𐤀𐤍𐤉.𐤍𐤕𐤍.𐤋𐤁𐤍𐤉.𐤉𐤔𐤓𐤀𐤋.𐤋𐤀𐤇𐤆𐤄|

50 ומת.בהר.אשר.אתה.עלה.שמה.והאסף.אל.
עמיך.כאשר.מת.אהרן.אחיך.בהר.ההר.ויאסף
.אל.עמיו|
51 על.אשר.מעלתם.בי.בתוך.בני.ישראל.במ
י.מריבת.קדש.מדבר.צן.על.אשר.לא.קדשת
ם.אותי.בתוך.בני.ישראל|
52 כי.מנגד.תראה.את.הארץ.ושמה.לא.תבו
א.אל.הארץ.אשר.אני.נתן.לבני.ישראל||

דברים.חלק 33

1 וזאת.הברכה.אשר.ברך.משה.איש.האלהי
ם.את.בני.ישראל.לפני.מותו|
2 ויאמר.יהוה.מסיני.בא.וזרח.משעיר.למו.
הופיע.מהר.פארן.ואתה.מרבבת.קדש.מימינו.
אשדת.||אש.דת.קרי||.למו|
3 אף.חבב.עמים.כל.קדשיו.בידך.והם.תכו.
לרגלך.ישא.מדברתיך|
4 תורה.צוה.לנו.משה.מורשה.קהלת.יעקב|
5 ויהי.בישרון.מלך.בהתאסף.ראשי.עם.יח
ד.שבטי.ישראל|
6 יחי.ראובן.ואל.ימת.ויהי.מתיו.מספר|
7 וזאת.ליהודה.ויאמר.שמע.יהוה.קול.יה
ודה.ואל.עמו.תביאנו.ידיו.רב.לו.ועזר.מצרי
ו.תהיה|
8 וללוי.אמר.תמיך.ואוריך.לאיש.חסידך.א
שר.נסיתו.במסה.תריבהו.על.מי.מריבה|
9 האמר.לאביו.ולאמו.לא.ראיתיו.ואת.אחי
ו.לא.הכיר.ואת.בנו.||בניו.קרי||.לא.ידע.כי.ש
מרו.אמרתך.ובריתך.ינצרו|

10 𐤉𐤅𐤓𐤅.𐤌𐤔𐤐𐤈𐤉𐤊.𐤋𐤉𐤏𐤒𐤁.𐤅𐤕𐤅𐤓𐤕𐤊.𐤋𐤉𐤔𐤓𐤀𐤋.𐤉
𐤔𐤉𐤌𐤅.𐤒𐤈𐤅𐤓𐤄.𐤁𐤀𐤐𐤊.𐤅𐤊𐤋𐤉𐤋.𐤏𐤋.𐤌𐤆𐤁𐤇𐤊|
11 𐤁𐤓𐤊.𐤉𐤄𐤅𐤄.𐤇𐤉𐤋𐤅.𐤅𐤐𐤏𐤋.𐤉𐤃𐤉𐤅.𐤕𐤓𐤑𐤄.𐤌𐤇𐤑.
𐤌𐤕𐤍𐤉𐤌.𐤒𐤌𐤉𐤅.𐤅𐤌𐤔𐤍𐤀𐤉𐤅.𐤌𐤍.𐤉𐤒𐤅𐤌𐤅𐤍|
12 𐤋𐤁𐤍𐤉𐤌𐤍.𐤀𐤌𐤓.𐤉𐤃𐤉𐤃.𐤉𐤄𐤅𐤄.𐤉𐤔𐤊𐤍.𐤋𐤁𐤈𐤇.𐤏
𐤋𐤉𐤅.𐤇𐤐𐤐.𐤏𐤋𐤉𐤅.𐤊𐤋.𐤄𐤉𐤅𐤌.𐤅𐤁𐤉𐤍.𐤊𐤕𐤐𐤉𐤅.𐤔𐤊𐤍|
13 𐤅𐤋𐤉𐤅𐤎𐤐.𐤀𐤌𐤓.𐤌𐤁𐤓𐤊𐤕.𐤉𐤄𐤅𐤄.𐤀𐤓𐤑𐤅.𐤌𐤌𐤂𐤃.𐤔
𐤌𐤉𐤌.𐤌𐤈𐤋.𐤅𐤌𐤕𐤄𐤅𐤌.𐤓𐤁𐤑𐤕.𐤕𐤇𐤕|
14 𐤅𐤌𐤌𐤂𐤃.𐤕𐤁𐤅𐤀𐤕.𐤔𐤌𐤔.𐤅𐤌𐤌𐤂𐤃.𐤂𐤓𐤔.𐤉𐤓𐤇
𐤉𐤌|
15 𐤅𐤌𐤓𐤀𐤔.𐤄𐤓𐤓𐤉.𐤒𐤃𐤌.𐤅𐤌𐤌𐤂𐤃.𐤂𐤁𐤏𐤅𐤕.𐤏𐤅𐤋𐤌|
16 𐤅𐤌𐤌𐤂𐤃.𐤀𐤓𐤑.𐤅𐤌𐤋𐤀𐤄.𐤅𐤓𐤑𐤅𐤍.𐤔𐤊𐤍𐤉.𐤎𐤍𐤄.𐤕𐤁
𐤅𐤀𐤕𐤄.𐤋𐤓𐤀𐤔.𐤉𐤅𐤎𐤐.𐤅𐤋𐤒𐤃𐤒𐤃.𐤍𐤆𐤉𐤓.𐤀𐤇𐤉𐤅|
17 𐤁𐤊𐤅𐤓.𐤔𐤅𐤓𐤅.𐤄𐤃𐤓.𐤋𐤅.𐤅𐤒𐤓𐤍𐤉.𐤓𐤀𐤌.𐤒𐤓𐤍𐤉𐤅.𐤁𐤄𐤌
.𐤏𐤌𐤉𐤌.𐤉𐤍𐤂𐤇.𐤉𐤇𐤃𐤅.𐤀𐤐𐤎𐤉.𐤀𐤓𐤑.𐤅𐤄𐤌.𐤓𐤁𐤁𐤅𐤕.𐤀
𐤐𐤓𐤉𐤌.𐤅𐤄𐤌.𐤀𐤋𐤐𐤉.𐤌𐤍𐤔𐤄|
18 𐤅𐤋𐤆𐤁𐤅𐤋𐤍.𐤀𐤌𐤓.𐤔𐤌𐤇.𐤆𐤁𐤅𐤋𐤍.𐤁𐤑𐤀𐤕𐤊.𐤅𐤉𐤔𐤔
𐤊𐤓.𐤁𐤀𐤄𐤋𐤉𐤊|
19 𐤏𐤌𐤉𐤌.𐤄𐤓.𐤉𐤒𐤓𐤀𐤅.𐤔𐤌.𐤉𐤆𐤁𐤇𐤅.𐤆𐤁𐤇𐤉.𐤑𐤃
𐤒.𐤊𐤉.𐤔𐤐𐤏.𐤉𐤌𐤉𐤌.𐤉𐤉𐤍𐤒𐤅.𐤅𐤔𐤐𐤅𐤍𐤉.𐤈𐤌𐤅𐤍𐤉.𐤇𐤅𐤋|
20 𐤅𐤋𐤂𐤃.𐤀𐤌𐤓.𐤁𐤓𐤅𐤊.𐤌𐤓𐤇𐤉𐤁.𐤂𐤃.𐤊𐤋𐤁𐤉𐤀.𐤔𐤊𐤍
.𐤅𐤈𐤓𐤐.𐤆𐤓𐤅𐤏.𐤀𐤐.𐤒𐤃𐤒𐤃|
21 𐤅𐤉𐤓𐤀.𐤓𐤀𐤔𐤉𐤕.𐤋𐤅.𐤊𐤉.𐤔𐤌.𐤇𐤋𐤒𐤕.𐤌𐤇𐤒𐤒.𐤎𐤐𐤅
𐤍.𐤅𐤉𐤕𐤀.𐤓𐤀𐤔𐤉.𐤏𐤌.𐤑𐤃𐤒𐤕.𐤉𐤄𐤅𐤄.𐤏𐤔𐤄.𐤅𐤌𐤔𐤐𐤈𐤉
𐤅.𐤏𐤌.𐤉𐤔𐤓𐤀𐤋|
22 𐤅𐤋𐤃𐤍.𐤀𐤌𐤓.𐤃𐤍.𐤂𐤅𐤓.𐤀𐤓𐤉𐤄.𐤉𐤆𐤍𐤒.𐤌𐤍.𐤄𐤁𐤔𐤍|
23 𐤅𐤋𐤍𐤐𐤕𐤋𐤉.𐤀𐤌𐤓.𐤍𐤐𐤕𐤋𐤉.𐤔𐤁𐤏.𐤓𐤑𐤅𐤍.𐤅𐤌𐤋𐤀.𐤁𐤓𐤊
𐤕.𐤉𐤄𐤅𐤄.𐤉𐤌.𐤅𐤃𐤓𐤅𐤌.𐤉𐤓𐤔𐤄|
24 𐤅𐤋𐤀𐤔𐤓.𐤀𐤌𐤓.𐤁𐤓𐤅𐤊.𐤌𐤁𐤍𐤉𐤌.𐤀𐤔𐤓.𐤉𐤄𐤉.𐤓𐤑𐤅𐤉.
𐤀𐤇𐤉𐤅.𐤅𐤈𐤁𐤋.𐤁𐤔𐤌𐤍.𐤓𐤂𐤋𐤅|
25 𐤁𐤓𐤆𐤋.𐤅𐤍𐤇𐤔𐤕.𐤌𐤍𐤏𐤋𐤉𐤊.𐤅𐤊𐤉𐤌𐤉𐤊.𐤃𐤁𐤀𐤊|

כו אין.כאל.ישרון.רכב.שמים.בעזרך.ובגא
ותו.שחקים׃
כז מענה.אלהי.קדם.ומתחת.זרעת.עולם.ו
יגרש.מפניך.אויב.ויאמר.השמד׃
כח וישכן.ישראל.בטח.בדד.עין.יעקב.אל.
ארץ.דגן.ותירוש.אף.שמיו.יערפו.טל׃
כט אשריך.ישראל.מי.כמוך.עם.נושע.ביהו
ה.מגן.עזרך.ואשר.חרב.גאותך.ויכחשו.איב
יך.לך.ואתה.על.במותימו.תדרך׃׃

דברים.חלק לד

א ויעל.משה.מערבת.מואב.אל.הר.נבו.ראש.הפ
סגה.אשר.על.פני.ירחו.ויראהו.יהוה.את.כל.
הארץ.את.הגלעד.עד.דן׃
ב ואת.כל.נפתלי.ואת.ארץ.אפרים.ומנשה.וא
ת.כל.ארץ.יהודה.עד.הים.האחרון׃
ג ואת.הנגב.ואת.הככר.בקעת.ירחו.עיר.ה
תמרים.עד.צער׃
ד ויאמר.יהוה.אליו.זאת.הארץ.אשר.נשבע
תי.לאברהם.ליצחק.וליעקב.לאמר.לזרעך.
אתננה.הראיתיך.בעיניך.ושמה.לא.תעבר׃
ה וימת.שם.משה.עבד.יהוה.בארץ.מואב.על.
פי.יהוה׃
ו ויקבר.אתו.בגי.בארץ.מואב.מול.בית.פעו
ר.ולא.ידע.איש.את.קברתו.עד.היום.הזה׃
ז ומשה.בן.מאה.ועשרים.שנה.במתו.לא.כהת
ה.עינו.ולא.נס.לחה׃
ח ויבכו.בני.ישראל.את.משה.בערבת.מואב.
שלשים.יום.ויתמו.ימי.בכי.אבל.משה׃

9 𐤅𐤉𐤄𐤅𐤔𐤏.𐤁𐤍.𐤍𐤅𐤍.𐤌𐤋𐤀.𐤓𐤅𐤇.𐤇𐤊𐤌𐤄.𐤊𐤉.𐤎𐤌𐤊.𐤌
𐤔𐤄.𐤀𐤕.𐤉𐤃𐤉𐤅.𐤏𐤋𐤉𐤅.𐤅𐤉𐤔𐤌𐤏𐤅.𐤀𐤋𐤉𐤅.𐤁𐤍𐤉.𐤉𐤔𐤓𐤀𐤋.
𐤅𐤉𐤏𐤔𐤅.𐤊𐤀𐤔𐤓.𐤑𐤅𐤄.𐤉𐤄𐤅𐤄.𐤀𐤕.𐤌𐤔𐤄|
10 𐤅𐤋𐤀.𐤒𐤌.𐤍𐤁𐤉𐤀.𐤏𐤅𐤃.𐤁𐤉𐤔𐤓𐤀𐤋.𐤊𐤌𐤔𐤄.𐤀𐤔𐤓.
𐤉𐤃𐤏𐤅.𐤉𐤄𐤅𐤄.𐤐𐤍𐤉𐤌.𐤀𐤋.𐤐𐤍𐤉𐤌|
11 𐤋𐤊𐤋.𐤄𐤀𐤕𐤕.𐤅𐤄𐤌𐤅𐤐𐤕𐤉𐤌.𐤀𐤔𐤓.𐤔𐤋𐤇𐤅.𐤉𐤄𐤅𐤄.𐤋
𐤏𐤔𐤅𐤕.𐤁𐤀𐤓𐤑.𐤌𐤑𐤓𐤉𐤌.𐤋𐤐𐤓𐤏𐤄.𐤅𐤋𐤊𐤋.𐤏𐤁𐤃𐤉𐤅.𐤅𐤋𐤊
𐤋.𐤀𐤓𐤑𐤅|
12 𐤅𐤋𐤊𐤋.𐤄𐤉𐤃.𐤄𐤇𐤆𐤒𐤄.𐤅𐤋𐤊𐤋.𐤄𐤌𐤅𐤓𐤀.𐤄𐤂𐤃𐤅𐤋.
𐤀𐤔𐤓.𐤏𐤔𐤄.𐤌𐤔𐤄.𐤋𐤏𐤉𐤍𐤉.𐤊𐤋.𐤉𐤔𐤓𐤀𐤋||

www.ingramcontent.com/pod-product-compliance
Lightning Source LLC
Chambersburg PA
CBHW071232160426
43196CB00009B/1035
* 9 7 8 0 6 9 2 2 7 5 5 3 5 *